# BUSINESS LAW

## TEXT AND CASES

# Commercial Law
# for Accountants

**Fourteenth Edition**

**Roger LeRoy Miller**
*Institute for University Studies*
*Arlington, Texas*

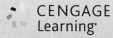

CENGAGE
Learning·

Australia · Brazil · Mexico · Singapore · United Kingdom · United States

# Business Law
TEXT AND CASES

# Commercial Law for Accountants

Fourteenth Edition

## Roger LeRoy Miller

**Vice President for Social Science and Qualitative Business:** *Erin Joyner*

**Product Director:** *Jason Fremder*

**Senior Product Manager:** *Vicky True-Baker*

**Managing Content Developer:** *Suzanne Wilder*

**Content Developer:** *Sarah Huber*

**Product Assistant:** *Christian Wood*

**Marketing Director:** *Kristen Hurd*

**Marketing Manager:** *Katie Jergens*

**Marketing Coordinator:** *Casey Binder*

**Production Director:** *Sharon Smith*

**Senior Content Project Manager:** *Ann Borman*

**Digital Content Specialist:** *Charles Nichols*

**Manufacturing Planner:** *Kevin Kluck*

**Senior Inventory Analyst:** *Terina Bradley*

**Senior IP Director:** *Julie Geagan-Chavez*

**IP Analyst:** *Jennifer Nonenmacher*

**IP Project Manager:** *Reba Frederics*

**Senior Art Director:** *Michelle Kunkler*

**Interior and Cover Designer:** *Harasymczuk Design*

**Design Elements:**
linen texture: Lisa-Blue/iStockphoto; justice scales: imagedb.com/Shutterstock; gavel: koosen/Shutterstock; media network: solarseven/Shutterstock; building windows: Nneirda/Shutterstock; puzzle icon: Shebeko/Shutterstock; spotlight: Ivan Lord/ Shutterstock; ethics scale: Lightspring/ Shutterstock; magnifying glass icon: sergign/ Shutterstock; globe: mj007/Shutterstock; compass: Taddeus/Shutterstock; Insight Global globe: evantravels/Shutterstock

P....
Prin... in the United States of America
...mber: 01   Print Year: 2016

For product information and technology assistance, contact us at
**Cengage Learning Customer & Sales Support,
1-800-354-9706**

For permission to use material from this text or product, submit all requests online at
**www.cengage.com/permissions.**

Further permissions questions can be emailed to
**permissionrequest@cengage.com.**

Library of Congress Control Number: 2016956305

**Student Edition ISBN:** 978-1-305-96728-1

**Cengage Learning**
20 Channel Center Street
Boston, MA 02210
USA

Cengage Learning is a leading provider of customized learning solutions with employees residing in nearly 40 different countries and sales in more than 125 countries around the world. Find your local representative at **www.cengage.com.**

Cengage Learning products are represented in Canada by Nelson Education, Ltd.

To learn more about Cengage Learning Solutions, visit **www.cengage.com.**

Purchase any of our products at your local college store or at our preferred online store **www.cengagebrain.com.**

# Brief Contents

## APPENDICES

# Contents

# Concept Summaries

# Exhibits

# Preface

The study of business law and the legal environment of business has universal applicability. A student entering any field of business must have at least a passing understanding of business law in order to function in the real world. *Business Law: Text and Cases: Commercial Law for Accountants,* Fourteenth Edition, provides the information that students need in an interesting and contemporary way.

This exciting text is tailor-made for those entering the field of accounting and includes topics from *Business Law* that accountants need to know. The text focuses on the basics of business law for accountants—including subjects on the revised 2017 CPA exam. It has a strong emphasis on business organizations, securities law and corporate governance, agency and employment, sales and lease contracts, creditors' rights and bankruptcy, professional liability, government regulation, and property.

For the Fourteenth Edition, I have spent a great deal of effort making this best-selling text more modern, exciting, and visually appealing than ever before. I have added twenty-seven new features, sixty new cases, and eleven new exhibits. The text also contains nearly one hundred and fifty new highlighted and numbered *Cases in Point* and *Examples,* and seventy-three new case problems. Special pedagogical elements within the text focus on legal, ethical, global, and corporate issues while addressing core curriculum requirements.

## Highlights of the Fourteenth Edition

Instructors have come to rely on the coverage, accuracy, and applicability of *Business Law: Commercial Law for Accountants.* To make sure that this text engages your students, solidifies their understanding of legal concepts, and provides the best teaching tools available, I now offer the following.

### New Coverage of Topics on the Revised 2017 CPA Exam

In 2016, the American Institute of CPAs (AICPA) issued its final report on "Maintaining the Relevance of the Uniform CPA Exam." In addition to more focus on critical thinking, authentic applications, and problem solving, the content of the exam will change to an extent.

The Fourteenth Edition of *Business Law: Commercial Law for Accountants* incorporates information on the new topics on the CPA exam, specifically addressing the following:

- Agency law (worker classification and duties of principals and agents)
- Employment law (Affordable Care Act)
- Business organizations (corporate governance issues, including Sarbanes-Oxley compliance and criminal liability for organizations and management)

In addition, the Fourteenth Edition continues to cover topics that are essential to new CPAs who are working with sophisticated business clients, regardless of whether the CPA exam covers these topics. I recognize that today's business leaders must often think "outside the box" when making business decisions. For this reason, I strongly emphasize business and critical thinking elements throughout the text. I have carefully chosen cases, features, and problems that are relevant to business operations. Almost all of the features and cases conclude with some type of critical thinking question. For those teaching future CPAs, this is consistent with the new CPA exam's focus on higher-order skills, such as critical thinking and problem solving.

### A Variety of New and Exciting Features

The Fourteenth Edition of *Business Law: Commercial Law for Accountants* is filled with many new features specifically designed to cover current legal topics of high interest. Each feature is related to a topic discussed in the text and ends with *Critical Thinking* or *Business Questions.* **Suggested answers to all the *Critical Thinking* and *Business Questions* are included in the *Solutions Manual* for this text.**

1. ***Ethics Today*** These features focus on the ethical aspects of a topic discussed in the text to emphasize that ethics is an integral part of a business law course. Examples include:

- Should an Innocent General Partner Be Jointly Liable for Fraud? (Chapter 3)
- Is It Fair to Classify Uber and Lyft Drivers as Independent Contractors? (Chapter 9)
- Is It Fair to Dock Employees' Pay for Bathroom Breaks? (Chapter 11)
- Should There Be More Relief for Student Loan Defaults? (Chapter 21)

2. *Global Insight* These features illustrate how other nations deal with specific legal concepts to give students a sense of the global legal environment. Subjects include:
   - Does Cloud Computing Have a Nationality? (Chapter 5)
   - Anti-Bribery Charges Take Their Toll on U.S. and Foreign Corporations (Chapter 6)
   - Islamic Law and *Respondeat Superior* (Chapter 10)

3. NEW *Digital Update* These features are designed to examine cutting-edge cyberlaw topics, such as the following:
   - Revenge Porn and Invasion of Privacy (Chapter 8)
   - Should Employees Have a "Right of Disconnecting"? (Chapter 11)
   - Hiring Discrimination Based on Social Media Posts (Chapter 12)
   - Pay with Your Smartphone (Chapter 15)
   - Google Faces an Antitrust Complaint from the European Union (Chapter 26)

4. *Managerial Strategy* These features emphasize the management aspects of business law and the legal environment. Topics include:
   - Can a Person Who Is Not a Member of a Protected Class Sue for Discrimination? (Chapter 4)
   - The SEC's New CEO Pay-Ratio Disclosure Rule (Chapter 7)
   - Union Organizing Using Your Company's E-Mail System (Chapter 11)

## Highlighted and Numbered *Examples* and *Case in Point* Illustrations

Many instructors use cases and examples to illustrate how the law applies to business. Students understand legal concepts better in the context of their real-world application. Therefore, for this edition of *Business Law: Commercial Law for Accountants,* I have expanded the number of highlighted numbered *Examples* and *Cases in Point* in every chapter. I have added 103 new *Cases in Point* and 43 new *Examples.*

*Examples* illustrate how the law applies in a specific situation. *Cases in Point* present the facts and issues of an actual case and then describe the court's decision and rationale. These two features are uniquely designed and consecutively numbered throughout each chapter for easy reference. The *Examples* and *Cases in Point* are integrated throughout the text to help students better understand how courts apply legal principles in the real world.

## New Unit-Ending *Application and Ethics* Features

For the Fourteenth Edition, I have created an entirely new feature that concludes each of the five units in the text. Each of these *Application and Ethics* features provides additional analysis on a topic related to that unit and explores its ethics ramifications. Each of the features ends with two questions—a *Critical Thinking* and an *Ethics Question.* Some topics covered by these features include the following:

- Business Start-Ups Online (Unit 1)
- Health Insurance and Small Business (Unit 2)
- Federal Student Loans—Default and Discharge (Unit 3)
- Business Planning for Divorce (Unit 5)

**Suggested answers to the questions in *Application and Ethics* features are included in the *Solutions Manual* for this text.**

## New Cases and Case Problems

For the Fourteenth Edition of *Business Law: Commercial Law for Accountants,* I have added sixty new cases and seventy-three new case problems, most from 2016 and 2015. The new cases and case problems have been carefully selected to illustrate important points of law and to be of high interest to students and instructors. I have made it a point to find recent cases that enhance learning and are relatively easy to understand.

1. *Spotlight Cases* and *Classic Cases.* Certain cases and case problems that are exceptionally good teaching cases are labeled as *Spotlight Cases* and *Spotlight Case Problems.* Examples include *Spotlight on Baseball Cards, Spotlight on Holiday Inns,* and *Spotlight on the Seattle Mariners.* Instructors will find these *Spotlight Cases* useful to illustrate the legal concepts under discussion, and students will enjoy studying the cases because they involve interesting and memorable facts. Other cases have been chosen as *Classic Cases* because they establish a legal precedent in a particular area of law.

2. *Critical Thinking* **Section.** Each case concludes with a *Critical Thinking* section, which normally includes two questions. The questions may address *Legal Environment, E-Commerce, Economic, Environmental, Ethical, Global, Political,* or *Technological* issues, or they may ask *What If the Facts Were Different?* Each *Classic Case* has a section titled *Impact of This Case on Today's Law* and one *Critical Thinking* question.

3. **Longer Excerpts for *Case Analysis*.** I have also included one longer case excerpt in every chapter—labeled *Case Analysis*—followed by three *Legal Reasoning Questions.* The questions are designed to guide students' analysis of the case and build their legal reasoning skills. These *Case Analysis* cases may be used for case-briefing assignments and are also tied to the *Special Case Analysis* questions found in every unit of the text.

**Suggested answers to all case-ending questions and case problems are included in the *Solutions Manual* for this text.**

## Business Case Problem with Sample Answer in Each Chapter

In response to those instructors who would like students to have sample answers available for some of the questions and case problems, I include a *Business Case Problem with Sample Answer* in each chapter. The *Business Case Problem with Sample Answer* is based on an actual case, and students can find a sample answer at the end of the text. **Suggested answers to the *Business Case Problems with Sample Answers* are provided in Appendix C at the end of the text and in the *Solutions Manual* for this text.**

## New Exhibits and Concept Summaries

For this edition, we have spent considerable effort reworking and redesigning all of the exhibits and *Concept Summaries* in the text to achieve better clarity and more visual appeal. In addition, we have added eleven new exhibits.

## Special Case Analysis Questions

For one chapter in every unit of the text, I provide a *Special Case Analysis* question that is based on the *Case Analysis* excerpt in that chapter. These special questions appear in the *Business Case Problems* section at the ends of selected chapters.

The *Special Case Analysis* questions are designed to build students' analytical skills. They test students' ability to perform IRAC (Issue, Rule, Application, and Conclusion) case analysis. Students must identify the legal issue presented in the chapter's *Case Analysis,* understand the rule of law, determine how the rule applies to the facts of the case, and describe the court's conclusion. Instructors can assign these questions as homework or use them in class to elicit student participation and teach case analysis. **Suggested answers to the *Special Case Analysis* questions can be found in the *Solutions Manual* for this text.**

## Reviewing Features in Every Chapter

In the Fourteenth Edition of *Business Law: Commercial Law for Accountants,* I continue to offer a *Reviewing* feature at the end of every chapter to help solidify students' understanding of the chapter materials. Each *Reviewing* feature presents a hypothetical scenario and then asks a series of questions that require students to identify the issues and apply the legal concepts discussed in the chapter.

These features are designed to help students review the chapter topics in a simple and interesting way and see how the legal principles discussed in the chapter affect the world in which they live. An instructor can use these features as the basis for in-class discussion or encourage students to use them for self-study prior to completing homework assignments. **Suggested answers to the questions posed in the *Reviewing* features can be found in the *Solutions Manual* for this text.**

## Two *Issue Spotters*

At the conclusion of each chapter, I have included a special section with two *Issue Spotters* related to the chapter's topics. These questions facilitate student learning and review of the chapter materials. **Suggested answers to the *Issue Spotters* in every chapter are provided in Appendix B at the end of the text and in the *Solutions Manual* for this text.**

## Legal Reasoning Group Activities

For instructors who want their students to engage in group projects, each chapter of the Fourteenth Edition includes a special *Legal Reasoning Group Activity.* Each activity begins by describing a business scenario and then poses several specific questions pertaining to the scenario. Each question is to be answered by a different group of students based on the information in the chapter. These projects may be used in class to spur discussion or as homework assignments. **Suggested answers to the *Legal Reasoning Group Activities* are included in the *Solutions Manual* for this text.**

# Supplements/Digital Learning Systems

*Business Law: Commercial Law for Accountants,* Fourteenth Edition, provides a comprehensive supplements package designed to make the tasks of teaching and learning more enjoyable and efficient. The following supplements and exciting new digital products are offered in conjunction with the text.

## MindTap

MindTap for *Business Law: Commercial Law for Accountants,* Fourteenth Edition, is a fully online, highly personalized learning experience built upon Cengage Learning content. MindTap combines student learning tools—such as readings, multimedia, activities, and assessments from CengageNOW—into a singular Learning Path that intuitively guides students through their course.

Instructors can personalize the experience by customizing authoritative Cengage Learning content and learning tools. MindTap offers instructors the ability to add their own content in the Learning Path with apps that integrate into the MindTap framework seamlessly with Learning Management Systems (LMS).

MindTap includes:

- **An Interactive Book with Whiteboard Videos and Interactive Cases.**
- **Automatically graded homework** with the following consistent question types:
  - **Worksheets**—Interactive Worksheets prepare students for class by ensuring reading and comprehension.
  - **Video Activities**—Real-world video exercises make business law engaging and relevant.
  - **Brief Hypotheticals**—These applications provide students practice in spotting the issue and applying the law in the context of a short, factual scenario.
  - **Case Problem Analyses**—These promote deeper critical thinking and legal reasoning by guiding students step-by-step through a case

problem and then adding in a critical thinking section based on "What If the Facts Were Different?" These now include a third section, a writing component, which requires students to demonstrate their ability to forecast the legal implications of real-world business scenarios.
- **Personalized Student Plan with multimedia study tools and videos.**
- **New Adaptive Test Prep** helps students study for exams.
- **Test Bank.**
- **Reporting and Assessment options.**

By using the MindTap system, students can complete the assignments online and can receive instant feedback on their answers. Instructors can utilize MindTap to upload their course syllabi, create and customize homework assignments, and keep track of their students' progress. By hiding, rearranging, or adding content, instructors control what students see and when they see it to match the Learning Path to their course syllabus exactly. Instructors can also communicate with their students about assignments and due dates, and create reports summarizing the data for an individual student or for the whole class.

## Cengage Learning Testing Powered by Cognero

*Cengage Learning Testing Powered by Cognero* is a flexible, online system that allows you to do the following:

- Author, edit, and manage *Test Bank* content from multiple Cengage Learning solutions.
- Create multiple test versions in an instant.
- Deliver tests from your LMS, your classroom, or wherever you want.

**Start Right Away!** *Cengage Learning Testing Powered by Cognero* works on any operating system or browser.

- No special installs or downloads are needed.
- Create tests from school, home, the coffee shop—anywhere with Internet access.

**What Will You Find?**

- *Simplicity at every step.* A desktop-inspired interface features drop-down menus and familiar intuitive tools that take you through content creation and management with ease.
- *Full-featured test generator.* Create ideal assessments with your choice of fifteen question

types—including true/false, multiple choice, opinion scale/Likert, and essay). Multi-language support, an equation editor, and unlimited meta-data help ensure your tests are complete and compliant.

- *Cross-compatible capability.* Import and export content to and from other systems.

## Instructor's Companion Web Site

The Web site for the Fourteenth Edition of *Business Law: Commercial Law for Accountants* can be found by going to www.cengagebrain.com and entering ISBN 9781305967281. The Instructor's Companion Web Site contains the following supplements:

- *Instructor's Manual.* Includes sections entitled "Additional Cases Addressing This Issue" at the end of selected case synopses.
- *Solutions Manual.* Provides answers to all questions presented in the text, including the questions in each case and feature, the *Issue Spotters,* the *Business Scenarios* and *Business Case Problems,* and the unit-ending features.
- *Test Bank.* A comprehensive test bank that contains multiple-choice, true/false, and short essay questions.
- *Case-Problem Cases.*
- *Case Printouts.*
- *PowerPoint Slides.*
- *Lecture Outlines.*

---

# For Users of the Thirteenth Edition

First of all, I want to thank you for helping make *Business Law* the best-selling business law text in America today. Second, I want to make you aware of the numerous additions and changes that have been made in this edition—many in response to comments from reviewers.

Every chapter of the Fourteenth Edition has been revised as necessary to incorporate new developments in the law or to streamline the presentations. Other major changes and additions for this edition include the following:

- Chapter 1 (Business Ethics)—This chapter contains two new cases, two new *Issue Spotters,* three new *Cases in Point* (including a case involving Tom Brady's suspension from the NFL as a result of "deflategate"), and three new case problems. The chapter includes a section on business ethics

and social media, and discusses stakeholders and corporate social responsibility. The chapter also provides step-by-step guidance on making ethical business decisions and includes materials on global business ethics. A new *Digital Update* feature examines whether employees should have the right to disconnect from their electronic devices after work hours.

- Chapters 2 through 7 (the remaining chapters of the Law and Business Management Unit)—This unit has been thoroughly revised and updated to improve flow and clarity and to provide more practical information and recent examples. I have included fifteen new cases and twenty new *Cases in Point* throughout the unit. After discussing ethics in the first chapter, I start off discussing small business forms, then move to partnerships, limited liability companies, and finally corporations. All of the chapters in the unit include new features. For instance, in Chapter 5, there is a *Global Insight* feature on whether cloud computing has a nationality and a *Digital Update* feature on software programs that can predict employee misconduct. I discuss crowdfunding and venture capital in that chapter as well. I have added new exhibits and key terms. In the chapter on securities law (Chapter 7), I have updated the materials on Regulation A offerings because the cap went from 5 million to 50 million in 2015. I also discuss how to deal with the SEC's new CEO pay-ratio disclosure rule in a *Managerial Strategy* feature.
- Chapter 9 (Agency Formation and Duties) and Chapter 10 (Agency Liability and Termination)—These two chapters have been updated to reflect the realities of the gig economy in which many people are working as independent contractors. A new *Ethics Today* feature continues that emphasis with a discussion of whether Uber and Lyft drivers should be considered employees rather than independent contractors. There is also a new *Global Insight* feature in Chapter 10 concerning Islamic law and *respondeat superior.* In addition, five new *Examples,* five new *Cases in Point,* and five new case problems have been added in these two chapters to help students comprehend the important issues and liability in agency relationships.
- Chapter 11 (Employment, Immigration, and Labor Law) and Chapter 12 (Employment Discrimination)—These two chapters covering employment law have been thoroughly updated to

include discussions of legal issues facing employers today. Chapter 11 has three new cases, three new *Cases in Point,* three new *Examples* (including one involving wage claims of the Oakland Raiders cheerleaders), and three new case problems. I have added two new features—an *Ethics Today* on whether employees should receive paid bathroom breaks and a *Managerial Strategy* on union organizing using company e-mail systems. Chapter 12 has a new section discussing discrimination based on military status and new coverage of same-sex discrimination and discrimination against transgender persons. All three cases are new. There are seven new *Cases in Point,* five new *Examples,* a new exhibit, and three new case problems. A *Digital Update* feature discusses hiring discrimination based on social media posts. I discuss relevant United States Supreme Court decisions affecting employment issues throughout both chapters.

- Chapter 13 (The Formation of Sales and Lease Contracts) and Chapter 14 (Performance and Breach of Sales and Lease Contracts)—The coverage of the Uniform Commercial Code has been streamlined and simplified. I have added four new cases and ten new *Cases in Point* to increase student comprehension, as well as new business scenarios and case problems.
- Chapters 15 through 17 (the negotiable instruments chapters)—The three negotiable instruments chapters have been revamped and simplified. I have added numerous new *Cases in Point* and *Examples* to clarify difficult topics for students. A *Digital Update* feature discusses paying with smartphones.
- Chapter 18 (Banking in the Digital Age)—I have updated this entire chapter to reflect the realities of banking in today's digital world. All three cases are new and recent. There are three new *Cases in Point,* a new *Issue Spotter,* and three new case problems. A new *Digital Update* feature explains how electronic payment systems are reducing the use of checks.
- Chapter 19 (Creditors' Rights and Remedies), Chapter 20 (Secured Transactions), and Chapter 21 (Bankruptcy Law)—These three chapters have been revised to be more up to date and comprehensible. Each chapter has two new cases and a new feature. We have also streamlined the materials to focus on those concepts that students need to know. I have added new exhibits, *Concept*

*Summaries,* key terms, *Examples,* and *Cases in Point* to better clarify concepts. Chapter 20 (Secured Transactions) was substantially reworked to clarify the general principles and exceptions. Chapter 21 (Bankruptcy Law) includes updated dollar amounts of various provisions of the Bankruptcy Code, six new *Cases in Point,* and an *Ethics Today* feature on whether there should be more relief for student loan debt.

- Chapter 22 (Professional Liability and Accountability)—The discussion of global accounting rules has been updated and I have included new subheads to discuss actual and constructive fraud. I have created a new exhibit to clarify the three basic rules of an accountant's liability to third parties, as well as three new *Cases in Point* and one new *Example.* There is also a new *Ethics Today* feature discussing a professional's responsibilities with respect to protecting data stored in the cloud.
- Chapter 24 (Consumer Law) and Chapter 26 (Antitrust Law)—These two chapters include all new cases, and both have been significantly updated with new coverage, *Examples,* and *Cases in Point.* A *Digital Update* in Chapter 24 deals with "native" ads on the Internet, and a *Digital Update* in Chapter 26 discusses the European Union's antitrust complaint against Google.
- Chapter 27 (Personal Property and Bailments) and Chapter 28 (Real Property and Landlord-Tenant Law)—I have rearranged the materials in the property chapters somewhat and now cover fixtures in the real property chapter. Each chapter includes two new cases as well as a *Classic Case* or *Spotlight Case.* There are six new *Examples,* seven new *Cases in Point,* two new exhibits, and seven new case problems in these two chapters. Both chapters also include new features (an *Ethics Today* and a *Digital Update*).
- Chapter 29 (Intellectual Property)—The materials on intellectual property rights have been thoroughly revised and updated to reflect the most current laws and trends. The 2016 case involves the Hustler Club and a trademark infringement claim between brothers. A *Digital Update* feature examines the problem of patent trolls. There are eleven new *Cases in Point,* including cases involving FedEx's color and logo, Google's digitalization of books, and how the Sherlock Holmes copyright fell into the public domain.

# Acknowledgments for Previous Editions

Since this project began many years ago, a sizable number of business law professors and others have helped us in revising the book, including the following:

**Jeffrey E. Allen**
*University of Miami*

**Judith Anshin**
*Sacramento City College*

**Thomas M. Apke**
*California State University, Fullerton*

**Raymond August**
*Washington State University*

**William Auslen**
*San Francisco City College*

**Mary B. Bader**
*Moorhead State University*

**Frank Bagan**
*County College of Morris*

**John J. Balek**
*Morton College, Illinois*

**Michael G. Barth**
*University of Phoenix*

**David L. Baumer**
*North Carolina State University*

**Barbara E. Behr**
*Bloomsburg University of Pennsylvania*

**Robert B. Bennett, Jr.**
*Butler University*

**Robert C. Bird**
*University of Connecticut*

**Heidi Boerstler**
*University of Colorado at Denver*

**Maria Kathleen Boss**
*California State University, Los Angeles*

**Lawrence J. Bradley**
*University of Notre Dame*

**Dean Bredeson**
*University of Texas at Austin*

**Kylar William Broadus, Esq.**
*Lincoln University in Missouri*

**Doug Brown**
*Montana State University*

**Kristi K. Brown**
*University of Texas at Austin*

**Elizabeth K. Brunn, Esq.**
*University of Baltimore; University of Maryland University College*

**William J. Burke**
*University of Massachusetts, Lowell*

**Kenneth Burns**
*University of Miami*

**Daniel R. Cahoy**
*Pennsylvania State University*

**Rita Cain**
*University of Missouri—Kansas City*

**Jeanne A. Calderon**
*New York University*

**Joseph E. Cantrell**
*DeAnza College, California*

**Donald Cantwell**
*University of Texas at Arlington*

**Arthur J. Casey**
*San Jose State University, College of Business, Organization and Management*

**Thomas D. Cavenagh**
*North Central College—Naperville, Illinois*

**Robert Chatov**
*State University of New York, Buffalo*

**Corey Ciocchetti**
*University of Denver*

**Nanette C. Clinch**
*San Jose State University, California*

**Robert J. Cox**
*Salt Lake Community College*

**Thomas Crane**
*University of Miami*

**Angela Crossin**
*Purdue University, Calumet*

**Kenneth S. Culott**
*University of Texas at Austin*

**Larry R. Curtis**
*Iowa State University*

**Richard Dalebout**
*Brigham Young University*

**William H. Daughtrey, Jr.**
*Virginia Commonwealth University*

**Michael DeAngelis**
*University of Rhode Island*

**James Doering**
*University of Wisconsin, Green Bay*

**John V. Dowdy**
*University of Texas at Arlington*

**Michele A. Dunkerley**
*University of Texas at Austin*

**Julia M. Dunlap, Esq.**
*University of California, San Diego*

**Paul Dusseault**
*Herkimer Community College (SUNY)*

**Maria Elena Ellison**
*Florida Atlantic University*

**Nena Ellison**
*Florida Atlantic University*

**O. E. Elmore**
*Texas A&M University*

**Robert J. Enders**
*California State Polytechnic University, Pomona*

**Michael Engber**
*Ball State University*

**David A. Escamilla**
*University of Texas at Austin*

**Denise M. Farag**
*Linfield College*

**James S. Fargason**
*Louisiana State University*

**Frank S. Forbes**
*University of Nebraska at Omaha*

**Joe W. Fowler**
*Oklahoma State University*

**Stanley G. Freeman**
*University of South Carolina*

**Joan Gabel**
*Florida State University*

Christ Gaetanos
*State University of New York, Fredonia*

Chester S. Galloway
*Auburn University*

Bob Garrett
*American River College, California*

Gary L. Giese
*University of Colorado at Denver*

Thomas Gossman
*Western Michigan University*

John D. Grigsby
*Pennsylvania College of Technology*

Dr. J. Keaton Grubbs
*Stephen F. Austin State University*

Patrick O. Gudridge
*University of Miami School of Law*

Paul Guymon
*William Rainey Harper College*

Jacqueline Hagerott
*Franklin University*

James M. Haine
*University of Wisconsin, Stevens Point*

Gerard Halpern
*University of Arkansas*

Christopher L. Hamilton
*Golden West College, California*

JoAnn W. Hammer
*University of Texas at Austin*

Charles Hartman
*Wright State University, Ohio*

Richard A. Hausler
*University of Miami School of Law*

Harry E. Hicks
*Butler University, Indianapolis*

Janine S. Hiller
*Virginia Polytechnic Institute and State University*

Rebecca L. Hillyer
*Chemeketa Community College*

E. Clayton Hipp, Jr.
*Clemson University*

Anthony H. Holliday, Jr.
*Howard University*

Telford Hollman
*University of Northern Iowa*

June A. Horrigan
*California State University, Sacramento*

John P. Huggard
*North Carolina State University*

Terry Hutchins
*Pembroke State University, North Carolina*

Robert Jesperson
*University of Houston*

Debra M. Johnson
*Montana State University—Billings*

Bryce J. Jones
*Northeast Missouri State University*

Margaret Jones
*Southwest Missouri State College*

Peter A. Karl III
*SUNY Institute of Technology at Utica*

Jack E. Karns
*East Carolina University*

Anne E. Kastle
*Edmonds Community College*

Tamra Kempf
*University of Miami*

Judith Kenney
*University of Miami*

Barbara Kincaid
*Southern Methodist University*

Carey Kirk
*University of Northern Iowa*

Nancy P. Klintworth
*University of Central Florida*

Kurtis P. Klumb
*University of Wisconsin at Milwaukee*

Kathleen M. Knutson
*College of St. Catherine, St. Paul, Minnesota*

Lisa Quinn Knych
*Syracuse University, Whitman School of Management*

Peter Kwiatkowski, Esq.
*Baldwin Wallace University*

Meg Costello Lambert
*Oakland Community College—Auburn Hills Campus*

Vonda M. Laughlin
*Carson-Newman College*

M. Alan Lawson
*Mt. San Antonio College*

Leslie E. Lenn
*St. Edwards University*

Susan Liebeler
*Loyola University*

Robert B. Long
*Oakland Community College*

Stuart MacDonald
*University of Central Oklahoma*

Thomas E. Maher
*California State University, Fullerton*

Sal Marchionna
*Triton College, Illinois*

Gene A. Marsh
*University of Alabama*

Michael Martin, J.D., M.B.A., LL.M.
*University of Northern Colorado, Monfort College of Business*

Karen Kay Matson
*University of Texas at Austin*

Woodrow J. Maxwell
*Hudson Valley Community College, New York*

Bruce E. May
*University of South Dakota*

Diane May
*Winona State University, Minnesota*

Gail McCracken
*University of Michigan, Dearborn*

John W. McGee
*Southwest Texas State University*

Cotton Meagher
*University of Nevada at Las Vegas*

Christopher Meakin
*University of Texas at Austin*

Roger E. Meiners
*University of Texas at Arlington*

Gerald S. Meisel
*Bergen Community College, New Jersey*

Jennifer Merton, J.D.
*University of Massachusetts at Amherst*

Richard Mills
*Cypress College*

David Minars
*City University of New York, Brooklyn*

Leo Moersen
*The George Washington University*

Alan Moggio
*Illinois Central College*

Violet E. Molnar
*Riverside City College*

James E. Moon
*Meyer, Johnson & Moon, Minneapolis*

Melinda Ann Mora
*University of Texas at Austin*

Bob Morgan
*Eastern Michigan University*

Barry S. Morinaka
*Baker College—Michigan*

Melanie Morris
*Raritan Valley Community College*

Joan Ann Mrava
*Los Angeles Southwest College*

Dwight D. Murphey
*Wichita State University*

Daniel E. Murray
*University of Miami School of Law*

Paula C. Murray
*University of Texas*

Gregory J. Naples
*Marquette University*

George A. Nation III
*Lehigh University*

Caleb L. Nichols
*Western Connecticut State University*

John M. Norwood
*University of Arkansas*

Jamie O'Brien
*University of Notre Dame*

Dr. Kelly E. O'Donnell, J.C.D
*California Lutheran University,
Thousand Oaks, California*

Michael J. O'Hara
*University of Nebraska at Omaha*

Rick F. Orsinger
*College of DuPage, Illinois*

Daniel J. O'Shea
*Hillsborough Community College*

Thomas L. Palmer
*Northern Arizona University*

Charles M. Patten
*University of Wisconsin, Oshkosh*

Patricia Pattison
*Texas State University, San Marcos*

Peyton J. Paxson
*University of Texas at Austin*

Carlton Perkins
*Texas Southern University*

Darren A. Prum
*The Florida State University*

Ralph L. Quinones
*University of Wisconsin, Oshkosh*

Carol D. Rasnic
*Virginia Commonwealth University*

Marvin H. Robertson
*Harding University*

Bert K. Robinson
*Kennesaw State University*

Norberto Ruiz
*Chabot College*

Gary K. Sambol
*Rutgers State University*

Rudy Sandoval
*University of Texas, San Antonio*

Sidney S. Sappington
*York College of Pennsylvania*

Martha Sartoris
*North Hennepin Community College*

Barbara P. Scheller
*Temple University*

S. Alan Schlact
*Kennesaw State University, Georgia*

Lorne H. Seidman
*University of Nevada at Las Vegas*

Ira Selkowitz
*University of Colorado at Denver*

Roscoe B. Shain
*Austin Peay University*

Bennett D. Shulman
*Lansing Community College, Michigan*

S. Jay Sklar
*Temple University*

Dana Blair Smith
*University of Texas at Austin*

Michael Smydra
*Oakland Community College—Royal Oak*

Arthur Southwick
*University of Michigan*

Sylvia A. Spade
*University of Texas at Austin*

John A. Sparks
*Grove City College, Pennsylvania*

Robert D. Sprague
*University of Wyoming*

Elisabeth Sperow
*California Polytechnic University, San
Luis Obispo*

Brenda Steuer
*North Harris College, Houston*

Craig Stilwell
*Michigan State University*

Irwin Stotsky
*University of Miami School of Law*

Larry Strate
*University of Nevada at Las Vegas*

Charles R. B. Stowe
*Sam Houston State University*

Raymond Mason Taylor
*North Carolina State University*

Thomas F. Taylor
*Campbell University*

Ray Teske
*University of Texas at San Antonio*

H. Allan Tolbert
*Central Texas College*

Jesse C. Trentadue
*University of North Dakota*

Edwin Tucker
*University of Connecticut*

Gary Victor
*Eastern Michigan University*

William H. Volz
*Wayne State University*

David Vyncke
*Scott Community College, Iowa*

William H. Walker,
*Indiana University–Purdue University,
Fort Wayne*

Diana Walsh
*County College of Morris*

Robert J. Walter
*University of Texas at El Paso*

Gary Watson
*California State University, Los Angeles*

Katherine Hannan Wears, J.D.
*Clarkson University School of Business*

John L. Weimer
*Nicholls State University, Louisiana*

Marshall Wilkerson
*University of Texas at Austin*

Melanie Stallings Williams
*California State University—
Northridge*

Arthur D. Wolfe
*Michigan State University*

Elizabeth A. Wolfe
*University of Texas at Austin*

Daniel R. Wrentmore
*Santa Barbara City College*

Eric D. Yordy
*Northern Arizona University*

Norman Gregory Young
*California State Polytechnic University,
Pomona*

Ronald C. Young
*Kalamazoo Valley Community College,
Michigan*

Bob Zaffram
*Erie Community College, Buffalo,
New York*

As in all past editions, I owe a debt of extreme gratitude to the numerous individuals who worked directly with me or at Cengage Learning. In particular, I wish to thank Vicky True-Baker, senior product manager; Suzanne Wilder, managing content developer; Sarah Huber, content developer; and Ann Borman, senior content project manager. I also thank Katie Jergens in marketing and Michelle Kunkler, art director. I am indebted as well to the staff at Lachina, the compositor, for accurately generating pages for this text and making it possible for me to meet an ambitious printing schedule.

I especially wish to thank Katherine Marie Silsbee for her management of the entire project, as well as for the application of her superb research and editorial skills. I also wish to thank William Eric Hollowell, who co-authored the *Instructor's Manual* and the *Test Bank,* for his excellent research efforts. I am grateful for the efforts of Vickie Reierson and Roxanna Lee for their proofreading and other assistance, which helped to ensure an error-free text. Finally, I thank Suzanne Jasin of K & M Consulting for her many special efforts on this project.

Through the years, I have enjoyed an ongoing correspondence with many of you who have found points on which you wish to comment. I continue to welcome all comments and promise to respond promptly. By incorporating your ideas, I can continue to write a business law text that is best for you and best for your students.

R.L.M.

*To Dan Benjamin,*

*I continue to marvel
at your ability to
improve my work.
Thanks.*

*R.L.M.*

# Law and Business Management

## CHAPTER 1

# Business Ethics

One of the most complex issues businesspersons and corporations face is ethics. It is not as well defined as the law, and yet it can have substantial impacts on a firm's finances and reputation, especially when the firm is involved in a well-publicized scandal. Some scandals arise from activities that are legal, but are ethically questionable. Other scandals arise from conduct that is both illegal and unethical.

Consider, for example, Volkswagen's corporate executives, who were accused of cheating on the pollution emissions tests of millions of vehicles that were sold in the United States. Volkswagen admitted in 2015 that it had installed "defeat device" software in its diesel models. The software detected when the car was being tested and changed its performance to improve the test outcome. As a result, the diesel cars showed low emissions—a feature that made the cars more attractive to today's consumers. Ultimately, millions of Volkswagen vehicles were recalled, and the company suffered its first quarterly loss in fifteen years.

## 1–1 Business Ethics

At the most basic level, the study of **ethics** is the study of what constitutes right or wrong behavior. It is a branch of philosophy focusing on morality and the way moral principles are derived and implemented. Ethics has to do with the fairness, justness, rightness, or wrongness of an action.

The study of **business ethics** typically looks at the decisions businesses make or have to make and whether those decisions are right or wrong. It has to do with how businesspersons apply moral and ethical principles in making their decisions. Those who study business ethics also evaluate what duties and responsibilities exist or should exist for businesses.

In this book, we include an *Application and Ethics* feature at the end of each unit to expand on the concepts of business ethics discussed in that unit. We also cover ethical issues in *Ethics Today* features that appear in a number of chapters.

### 1–1a Why Is Studying Business Ethics Important?

Over the last hundred years, the public perception of the corporation has changed from an entity that primarily generates revenues for its owners to an entity that participates in society as a corporate citizen. Originally, the only goal or duty of a corporation was to maximize profits. Although many people today may view this idea as greedy or inhumane, the rationale for the profit-maximization theory is still valid.

**Profit Maximization** In theory, if all firms strictly adhere to the goal of profit maximization, resources flow to where they are most highly valued by society. Corporations can focus on their strengths, and other entities that are better suited to deal with social problems and perform charitable acts can specialize in those activities. The government, through taxes and other financial allocations, can shift resources to those other entities to perform public services. Thus, in an ideal world, profit maximization leads to the most efficient allocation of scarce resources.

**The Rise of Corporate Citizenship** Over the years, as resources purportedly were not sufficiently reallocated to cover the costs of social needs, many people became dissatisfied with the profit-maximization theory. Investors and others began to look beyond profits and dividends and to consider the **triple bottom line**—a corporation's profits, its impact on people, and its impact on the planet. Magazines and Web sites began to rank companies based on their environmental impacts and their ethical decisions. The corporation came to be viewed as a "citizen" that was expected to participate in bettering communities and society.

Even so, many still believe that corporations are fundamentally profit-making entities that should have no responsibility other than profit maximization.

## 1–1b The Importance of Ethics in Making Business Decisions

Whether one believes in profit maximization or corporate citizenship, ethics is important in making business decisions. When making decisions, a business should evaluate:

1. The legal implications of each decision.
2. The public relations impact.
3. The safety risks for consumers and employees.
4. The financial implications.

This four-part analysis will assist the firm in making decisions that not only maximize profits but also reflect good corporate citizenship.

**Long-Run Profit Maximization** In attempting to maximize profits, corporate executives and employees have to distinguish between *short-run* and *long-run* profit maximization. In the short run, a company may increase its profits by continuing to sell a product even though it knows that the product is defective. In the long run, though, because of lawsuits, large settlements, and bad publicity, such unethical conduct will cause profits to suffer. Thus, business ethics is consistent only with long-run profit maximization. An overemphasis on short-term profit maximization is the most common reason that ethical problems occur in business.

■ **CASE IN POINT 1.1** When the powerful narcotic painkiller OxyContin was first marketed, its manufacturer, Purdue Pharma, claimed that it was unlikely to lead to drug addiction or abuse. Internal company documents later showed that the company's executives knew that OxyContin could be addictive, but kept this risk a secret to boost sales and maximize short-term profits.

Subsequently, Purdue Pharma and three former executives pleaded guilty to criminal charges that they had misled regulators, patients, and physicians about OxyContin's risks of addiction. Purdue Pharma agreed to pay $600 million in fines and other payments. The three former executives agreed to pay $34.5 million in fines and were barred from federal health programs for a period of fifteen years. Thus, the company's focus on maximizing profits in the short run led to unethical conduct that hurt profits in the long run.[1] ■

**The Internet Can Ruin Reputations** In the past, negative information or opinions about a company might remain hidden. Now, however, cyberspace provides a forum where disgruntled employees, unhappy consumers, or special interest groups can post derogatory remarks. Thus, the Internet has increased the potential for a major corporation (or other business) to suffer damage to its reputation or loss of profits through negative publicity.

Wal-Mart and Nike in particular have been frequent targets for advocacy groups that believe those corporations exploit their workers. Although some of these assertions may be unfounded or exaggerated, the courts generally have refused to consider them *defamatory* (a tort giving rise to a civil lawsuit). Most courts regard online attacks as expressions of opinion protected by the First Amendment. Even so, corporations often incur considerable expense in running marketing campaigns to thwart bad publicity and may even face legal costs if the allegations lead to litigation.

**Image Is Everything** The study of business ethics is concerned with the purposes of a business and how that business achieves those purposes. Thus, business ethics is concerned not only with the image of the business, but also with the impact that the business has on the environment, customers, suppliers, employees, and the global economy.

Unethical corporate decision making can negatively affect suppliers, consumers, the community, and society as a whole. It can also have a negative impact on the reputation of the company and the individuals who run that company. Hence, an in-depth understanding of business ethics is important to the long-run viability of any corporation today.

## 1–1c The Relationship of Law and Ethics

Because the law does not codify all ethical requirements, compliance with the law is not always sufficient to determine "right" behavior. Laws have to be general enough to apply in a variety of circumstances. Laws are broad in their purpose and their scope. They prohibit or require certain actions to avoid significant harm to society.

When two competing companies secretly agree to set prices on products, for instance, society suffers harm—typically, the companies will charge higher prices than they could if they continued to compete. This harm inflicted on consumers has negative consequences for the economy, and so colluding to set prices is an illegal activity. Similarly, when a company is preparing to issue stock, the law requires certain disclosures to potential investors. This requirement is meant to prevent harms that come

---

1. *United States v. Purdue Frederick Co.*, 495 F.Supp.2d 569 (W.D.Va. 2007).

with uninformed investing. Such harms occurred in the 1920s and may have contributed to the stock market crash and the Great Depression.

**Moral Minimum** Compliance with the law is sometimes called the **moral minimum.** If people and entities merely comply with the law, they are acting at the lowest ethical level society will tolerate. The study of ethics goes beyond those legal requirements to evaluate what is right for society. The following case illustrates some consequences of a businessperson's failure to meet the moral minimum.

**Case 1.1**

# Scott v. Carpanzano

United States Court of Appeals, Fifth Circuit, 556 Fed.Appx. 288 (2014).

**Background and Facts**   Rick Scott deposited $2 million into an escrow account maintained by a company owned by Salvatore Carpanzano. Immediately after the deposit was made, in violation of the escrow agreement, the funds were withdrawn. When Scott was unable to recover his money, he filed a suit against Salvatore Carpanzano and others, including Salvatore's daughter Carmela Carpanzano. In the complaint, Scott made no allegations of acts or knowledge on Carmela's part.

Salvatore failed to cooperate with discovery and did not respond to attempts to contact him by certified mail, regular mail, or e-mail. Salvatore also refused to make an appearance in the court and did not finalize a settlement negotiated between the parties' attorneys. Carmela denied that she was involved in her father's business or the Scott transaction. The court found that the defendants had intentionally failed to respond to the litigation and issued a judgment for more than $6 million in Scott's favor. The defendants appealed to the U.S. Court of Appeals for the Fifth Circuit.

## In the Language of the Court

*PER CURIAM* [By the Whole Court].

* * * *

A willful default is an *intentional failure to respond to litigation.* The district court found that [the] Defendants willfully defaulted based on evidence that the Defendants were aware of the proceedings against them and that [their] attorneys were specifically instructed not to enter an appearance [participate] in this case. [Emphasis added.]

The evidence substantially supports the district court's finding as to Mr. Carpanzano. First, Mr. Carpanzano's first attorney withdrew [from the case] because Mr. Carpanzano failed to cooperate with the discovery process and refused to appear as requested and ordered. Second, * * * Mr. Carpanzano instructed his second set of attorneys to negotiate settlement of this matter but not to enter an appearance in the district court. Significantly, Mr. Carpanzano never denies this allegation. Third, * * * Mr. Carpanzano and his attorneys were well aware that the case was proceeding toward default and * * * were in communication with each other during this time. Fourth, * * * once final execution of settlement papers was at hand, Mr. Carpanzano also ceased communication with his second set of attorneys and did not finalize the settlement. Finally, other than ambiguously suggesting that a health condition (unsupported by any evidence of what the condition was) and absence from the country (unsupported by any evidence that electronic communication was not possible from that country) prevented him from defending this action, Mr. Carpanzano offers no real reason why he did not answer the * * * complaint.

* * * *

By contrast, the record does not support the district court's finding that * * * Ms. [Carmela] Carpanzano also willfully defaulted.

* * * Ms. Carpanzano repeatedly indicated that [she was] relying on Mr. Carpanzano * * * to make sure [her] interests were protected. Nothing in the record contradicts this assertion. While [her] reliance on Mr. Carpanzano acting with the attorneys he retained may have been negligent, it does not amount to an intentional failure to respond to litigation.

* * * *

* * * [Furthermore] the * * * complaint * * * contains no factual allegations of acts or omissions on the part of Ms. Carpanzano. It does not allege that she ever was in contact with Scott, that she was in control of the * * * escrow account, or that she wrongfully transferred any funds out of the account. Nor does it allege any intent or knowledge on the part of Ms. Carpanzano * * *. Indeed, an examination of the complaint reveals that there is not a sufficient basis in the pleadings for the judgment * * * entered against Ms. Carpanzano.

The defenses presented by Ms. Carpanzano to the district court assert that she had no knowledge of the details of her father's business transactions, she did not personally enter into any contracts with Scott or seek to defraud him, and * * * she had limited involvement in the facts of this case.

* * * *

* * * Even if Scott were able to prove the entirety of the * * * complaint, we fail to see how it would justify a judgment * * * against Ms. Carpanzano.

**Decision and Remedy** *The U.S. Court of Appeals for the Fifth Circuit affirmed the judgment against Salvatore, but reversed the decision against Carmela. Scott had made no allegations of acts on Carmela's part.*

**Critical Thinking**

- **Ethical** *Are Salvatore's actions likely to affect his business's ability to profit in the long run? Discuss.*
- **Legal Environment** *Did Carmela Carpanzano meet the minimum acceptable standard for ethical business behavior? Explain.*

---

**Ethical Requirements** The study of ethics goes beyond legal requirements to evaluate what is right for society. Businesspersons thus must remember that an action that is legal is not necessarily ethical. For instance, a company's refusal to negotiate liability claims for alleged injuries because of a faulty product is legal. But it may not be ethical if the reason the business refuses to negotiate is to increase the injured party's legal costs and force the person to drop a legitimate claim.

**Private Company Codes of Ethics** Most companies attempt to link ethics and law through the creation of internal codes of ethics. Company codes are not law. Instead, they are rules that the company sets forth that it can also enforce (by terminating an employee who does not follow them, for instance). Codes of conduct typically outline the company's policies on particular issues and indicate how employees are expected to act.

■ **EXAMPLE 1.2** Google's code of conduct starts with the motto "Don't be evil." The code then makes general statements about how Google promotes integrity, mutual respect, and the highest standard of ethical business conduct. Google's code also provides specific rules on a number of issues, such as privacy, drugs and alcohol, conflicts of interest, co-worker relationships, and confidentiality.

It even has a dog policy. The company takes a stand against employment discrimination that goes further than the law requires—it prohibits discrimination based on sexual orientation, gender identity or expression, and veteran status. ■

**Industry Ethical Codes** Numerous industries have also developed their own codes of ethics. The American Institute of Certified Public Accountants (AICPA) has a comprehensive Code of Professional Conduct for the ethical practice of accounting. The American Bar Association has model rules of professional conduct for attorneys, and the American Nurses Association has a code of ethics that applies to nurses. These codes can give guidance to decision makers facing ethical questions.

Violation of an industry code may result in discipline of an employee or sanctions against a company from the industry organization. Remember, though, that these internal codes are not laws, so their effectiveness is determined by the commitment of the industry or company leadership to enforcing the codes.

■ **CASE IN POINT 1.3** National Football League (NFL) rules require footballs to be inflated to a minimum air pressure (pounds per square inch, or psi) as measured by the referees. This rule gained attention when the New

England Patriots played the Indianapolis Colts for the American Football Conference championship in early 2015. After Tom Brady, the Patriots quarterback, threw a pass that was intercepted, officials became suspicious that the football was underinflated. The game continued after NFL officials verified the psi in all the footballs, and the Patriots won.

Nevertheless, allegations continued that Brady and the Patriots had deflated balls during the game—a controversy popularly known as "deflategate." The NFL performed an investigation, and after arbitration, the league announced that Brady would be suspended for four games. Brady appealed, and a federal district court vacated the arbitrator's decision to suspend, but a federal appellate court reinstated Brady's suspension in 2016. The reviewing court held that the arbitrator had grounds to suspend Brady for being generally aware that the team had intentionally released air from the game balls.[2] ■

**"Gray Areas" in the Law** Because it is often highly subjective and subject to change over time without any sort of formal process, ethics is less certain than law. But the law can also be uncertain. Numerous "gray areas" in the law make it difficult to predict with certainty how a court will apply a given law to a particular action. In addition, laws frequently change.

---

# 1–2 Business Ethics and Social Media

Most young people may think of social media—Facebook, Flickr, Instagram, Tumblr, Twitter, Pinterest, Google+, LinkedIn, VR, and the like—as simply ways to communicate rapidly. Businesses, though, often face ethical issues with respect to these same social media platforms.

## 1–2a Hiring Procedures

In the past, to learn about a prospective employee, an employer would ask the candidate's former employers for references. Today, employers are likely to also conduct Internet searches to discover what job candidates have posted on their Facebook pages, blogs, and tweets.

On the one hand, job candidates may be judged by what they post on social media. On the other hand, though, they may be judged because they *do not*

participate in social media. Given that the vast majority of younger people do use social media, some employers have decided that the failure to do so raises a red flag. In either case, many people believe that judging a job candidate based on what she or he does outside the work environment is unethical.

## 1–2b The Use of Social Media to Discuss Work-Related Issues

Because so many Americans use social media daily, they often discuss work-related issues there. Numerous companies have strict guidelines about what is appropriate and inappropriate for employees to say when making posts on their own or others' social media accounts. A number of companies have fired employees for such activities as criticizing other employees or managers through social media outlets. Until recently, such disciplinary measures were considered ethical and legal.

**Responsibility of Employers** Today, in contrast, a ruling by the National Labor Relations Board (NLRB—the federal agency that investigates unfair labor practices) has changed the legality of such actions. ■ **EXAMPLE 1.4** At one time, Costco's social media policy specified that its employees should not make statements that would damage the company, harm another person's reputation, or violate the company's policies. Employees who violated these rules were subject to discipline and could be fired.

The NLRB ruled that Costco's social media policy violated federal labor law, which protects employees' right to engage in "concerted activities." Employees can freely associate with each other and have conversations about common workplace issues without employer interference. This right extends to social media posts. Therefore, an employer cannot broadly prohibit its employees from criticizing the company or co-workers, supervisors, or managers via social media. ■

**Responsibility of Employees** While most of the discussion in this chapter concerns the ethics of business management, employee ethics is also an important issue. For instance, is it ethical for employees to make negative posts in social media about other employees or, more commonly, about managers? After all, negative comments about managers reflect badly on those managers, who often are reluctant to respond via social media to such criticism. Disgruntled employees may exaggerate the negative qualities of managers whom they do not like.

---

2. *National Football League Management Council v. National Football League Players Association*, 820 F.3d 527 (2d Cir. 2016).

Some may consider the decision by the National Labor Relations Board outlined in *Example 1.4* to be too lenient toward employees and too stringent toward management. There is likely to be an ongoing debate about how to balance employees' right to free expression against employers' right to prevent the spreading of inaccurate negative statements across the Internet.

# 1–3 Ethical Principles and Philosophies

As Dean Krehmeyer, executive director of the Business Roundtable's Institute for Corporate Ethics, once said, "Evidence strongly suggests being ethical—doing the right thing—pays." Even if ethics "pays," though, instilling ethical business decision making into the fabric of a business organization is no small task.

How do business decision makers decide whether a given action is the "right" one for their firms? What ethical standards should be applied? Broadly speaking, **ethical reasoning**—the application of morals and ethics to a situation—applies to businesses just as it does to individuals. As businesses make decisions, they must analyze their alternatives in a variety of ways, one of which is the ethical implications of each alternative.

Generally, the study of ethics is divided into two major categories—duty-based ethics and outcome-based ethics. **Duty-based ethics** is rooted in the idea that every person has certain duties to others, including both humans and the planet. **Outcome-based ethics** focuses on the impacts of a decision on society or on key *stakeholders*.

## 1–3a Duty-Based Ethics

Duty-based ethics focuses on the obligations of the corporation. It deals with standards for behavior that traditionally were derived from revealed truths, religious authorities, or philosophical reasoning. These standards involve concepts of right and wrong, duties owed, and rights to be protected. Corporations today often describe these values or duties in their mission statements or strategic plans. Some companies base their statements on a nonreligious rationale, while others derive their values from religious doctrine.

**Religious Ethical Principles**  Nearly every religion has principles or beliefs about how one should treat others. In the Judeo-Christian tradition, which is the dominant religious tradition in the United States, the Ten Commandments of the Old Testament establish these fundamental rules for moral action. The principles of the Muslim faith are set out in the Qur'an, and Hindus find their principles in the four Vedas.

Religious rules generally are absolute with respect to the behavior of their adherents.  ■ **EXAMPLE 1.5**  The commandment "Thou shalt not steal" is an absolute mandate for a person who believes that the Ten Commandments reflect revealed truth. Even a benevolent motive for stealing (such as Robin Hood's) cannot justify the act because the act itself is inherently immoral and thus wrong. ■

For businesses, religious principles can be a unifying force for employees or a rallying point to increase employee motivation. They can also present problems, however, because different owners, suppliers, employees, and customers may have different religious backgrounds. Taking an action based on religious principles, especially when those principles address socially or politically controversial topics, can lead to negative publicity and even to protests or boycotts.

**Principles of Rights**  Another view of duty-based ethics focuses on basic rights. The principle that human beings have certain fundamental rights (to life, freedom, and the pursuit of happiness, for example) is deeply embedded in Western culture.

Those who adhere to this **principle of rights,** or "rights theory," believe that a key factor in determining whether a business decision is ethical is how that decision affects the rights of others. These others include the firm's owners, its employees, the consumers of its products or services, its suppliers, the community in which it does business, and society as a whole.

**Conflicting Rights.**  A potential dilemma for those who support rights theory is that they may disagree on which rights are most important. When considering all those affected by a business decision to downsize a firm, for example, how much weight should be given to employees relative to shareholders? Which employees should be laid off first—those with the highest salaries or those who have worked there for less time (and have less seniority)? How should the firm weigh the rights of customers relative to the community, or employees relative to society as a whole?

**Resolving Conflicts.**  In general, rights theorists believe that whichever right is stronger in a particular circumstance takes precedence.  ■ **EXAMPLE 1.6**  Murray

Chemical Corporation has to decide whether to keep a chemical plant in Utah open, thereby saving the jobs of a hundred and fifty workers, or shut it down. Closing the plant will avoid contaminating a river with pollutants that might endanger the health of tens of thousands of people. In this situation, a rights theorist can easily choose which group to favor because the value of the right to health and well-being is obviously stronger than the basic right to work. Not all choices are so clear-cut, however. ■

**Kantian Ethical Principles** Duty-based ethical standards may also be derived solely from philosophical reasoning. The German philosopher Immanuel Kant (1724–1804) identified some general guiding principles for moral behavior based on what he thought to be the fundamental nature of human beings. Kant believed that human beings are qualitatively different from other physical objects and are endowed with moral integrity and the capacity to reason and conduct their affairs rationally.

**People Are Not a Means to an End.** Based on this view of human beings, Kant said that when people are treated merely as a means to an end, they are being treated as the equivalent of objects and are being denied their basic humanity. For instance, a manager who treats subordinates as mere profit-making tools is less likely to retain motivated and loyal employees than a manager who respects employees. Management research has shown that, in fact, employees who feel empowered to share their thoughts, opinions, and solutions to problems are happier and more productive.

**Categorical Imperative.** When a business makes unethical decisions, it often rationalizes its action by saying that the company is "just one small part" of the problem or that its decision has had "only a small impact." A central theme in Kantian ethics is that individuals should evaluate their actions in light of the consequences that would follow if everyone in society acted in the same way. This **categorical imperative** can be applied to any action. ■ **EXAMPLE 1.7** CHS Fertilizer is deciding whether to invest in expensive equipment that will decrease profits but will also reduce pollution from its factories. If CHS has adopted Kant's categorical imperative, the decision makers will consider the consequences if every company invested in the equipment (or if no company did so). If the result would make the world a better place (less polluted), CHS's decision would be clear. ■

## 1–3b Outcome-Based Ethics: Utilitarianism

In contrast to duty-based ethics, outcome-based ethics focuses on the consequences of an action, not on the nature of the action itself or on any set of preestablished moral values or religious beliefs. Outcome-based ethics looks at the impacts of a decision in an attempt to maximize benefits and minimize harms.

The premier philosophical theory for outcome-based decision making is **utilitarianism,** a philosophical theory developed by Jeremy Bentham (1748–1832) and modified by John Stuart Mill (1806–1873)—both British philosophers. "The greatest good for the greatest number" is a paraphrase of the major premise of the utilitarian approach to ethics.

**Cost-Benefit Analysis** Under a utilitarian model of ethics, an action is morally correct, or "right," when, among the people it affects, it produces the greatest amount of good for the greatest number or creates the least amount of harm for the fewest people. When an action affects the majority adversely, it is morally wrong. Applying the utilitarian theory thus requires the following steps:

1.  A determination of which individuals will be affected by the action in question.
2.  A **cost-benefit analysis,** which involves an assessment of the negative and positive effects of alternative actions on these individuals.
3.  A choice among alternative actions that will produce maximum societal utility (the greatest positive net benefits for the greatest number of individuals).

Thus, if expanding a factory would provide hundreds of jobs but generate pollution that could endanger the lives of thousands of people, a utilitarian analysis would find that saving the lives of thousands creates greater good than providing jobs for hundreds.

**Problems with the Utilitarian Approach** There are problems with a strict utilitarian analysis. In some situations, an action that produces the greatest good for the most people may not seem to be the most ethical. ■ **EXAMPLE 1.8** Phazim Company is producing a drug that will cure a disease in 85 percent of patients, but the other 15 percent will experience agonizing side effects and a horrible, painful death. A quick utilitarian analysis would suggest that the drug should be produced and marketed because the majority of patients will benefit. Many people, however, have significant concerns about manufacturing a drug that will cause such harm to anyone. ■

## 1–3c Corporate Social Responsibility

In pairing duty-based concepts with outcome-based concepts, strategists and theorists developed the idea of the corporate citizen. **Corporate social responsibility (CSR)** combines a commitment to good citizenship with a commitment to making ethical decisions, improving society, and minimizing environmental impact.

CSR is a relatively new concept in the history of business, but a concept that becomes more important every year. Although CSR is not imposed on corporations by law, it does involve a commitment to self-regulation in a way that attends to the text and intent of the law as well as to ethical norms and global standards. A survey of U.S. executives undertaken by the Boston College Center for Corporate Citizenship found that more than 70 percent of those polled agreed that corporate citizenship must be treated as a priority. More than 60 percent said that good corporate citizenship added to their companies' profits.

CSR can be a successful strategy for companies, but corporate decision makers must not lose track of the two descriptors in the title: *corporate* and *social.* The company must link the responsibility of citizenship with the strategy and key principles of the business. Incorporating both the social and the corporate components of CSR and making ethical decisions can help companies grow and prosper. CSR is most successful when a company undertakes activities that are significant and related to its business operations.

**The Social Aspects of CSR** Because business controls so much of the wealth and power in this country, business has a responsibility to use that wealth and power in socially beneficial ways. Thus, the social aspect requires that corporations demonstrate that they are promoting goals that society deems worthwhile and are moving toward solutions to social problems. Companies may be judged on how much they donate to social causes, as well as how they conduct their operations with respect to employment discrimination, human rights, environmental concerns, and similar issues.

Some corporations publish annual social responsibility reports, which may also be called corporate sustainability (referring to the capacity to endure) or citizenship reports. ■ **EXAMPLE 1.9** The software company

Symantec Corporation issues corporate responsibility reports to demonstrate its focus on critical environmental, social, and governance issues. In its 2014 report, Symantec pointed out that 88 percent of facilities it owns or leases on a long-term basis are certified as environmentally friendly by the LEED program. LEED stands for Leadership in Energy and Environmental Design. Certification requires the achievement of high standards for energy efficiency, material usage in construction, and other environmental qualities. ■

**The Corporate Aspects of CSR** Arguably, any socially responsible activity will benefit a corporation. A corporation may see an increase in goodwill from the local community for creating a park, for instance. A corporation that is viewed as a good citizen may see an increase in sales.

At times, the benefit may not be immediate. Constructing a new plant that meets the high LEED standards may cost more initially. Nevertheless, over the life of the building, the savings in maintenance and utilities may more than make up for the extra cost of construction.

Surveys of college students about to enter the job market confirm that young people are looking for socially responsible employers. Socially responsible activities may thus cost a corporation now, but may lead to more impressive and more committed employees. Corporations that engage in meaningful social activities retain workers longer, particularly younger ones.

■ **EXAMPLE 1.10** Pacific Gas and Electric (PG&E) in California sends its employees out on Earth Day to help clean and restore state parks. PG&E also provides free solar panels for new Habitat for Humanity homes and donates food to the needy. LinkedIn employees participate in an "InDay" every month to donate time and resources to the community. Zappos donates large amounts of its goods to charities and pays its employees for time off if they are volunteering. ■

**Stakeholders** One view of CSR stresses that corporations have a duty not just to shareholders, but also to other groups affected by corporate decisions—called **stakeholders.** The rationale for this "stakeholder view" is that, in some circumstances, one or more of these other groups may have a greater stake in company decisions than the shareholders do.

Under this approach, a corporation considers the impact of its decisions on its employees, customers, creditors, suppliers, and the community in which it operates.

Stakeholders could also include advocacy groups such as environmental groups and animal rights groups. To avoid making a decision that may be perceived as unethical and result in negative publicity or protests, a corporation should consider the impact of its decision on the stakeholders.

The most difficult aspect of the stakeholder analysis is determining which group's interests should receive greater weight if the interests conflict. For instance, companies that are struggling financially sometimes lay off workers to reduce labor costs. But in recent years, some corporations have given greater weight to employees' interests and have found ways to avoid slashing their workforces. Companies finding alternatives to layoffs included Dell (extended unpaid holidays), Cisco Systems (four-day end-of-year shutdowns), Motorola (salary cuts), and Honda (voluntary unpaid vacation time).

# 1–4 Making Ethical Business Decisions

Even if officers, directors, and others in a company want to make ethical decisions, it is not always clear what is ethical in a given situation. Thinking beyond things that are easily measured, such as profits, can be challenging. Although profit projections are not always accurate, they are more objective than considering the personal impacts of decisions on employees, shareholders, customers, and the community. But this subjective component of decision making potentially has a great potential influence on a company's profits.

Companies once considered leaders in their industry, such as Enron and the worldwide accounting firm Arthur Andersen, were brought down by the unethical behavior of a few. A two-hundred-year-old British investment banking firm, Barings Bank, was destroyed by the actions of one employee and a few of his friends. Clearly, ensuring that all employees get on the ethical business decision-making "bandwagon" is crucial in today's fast-paced world.

Individuals entering the global corporate community, even in entry-level positions, must be prepared to make hard decisions. Sometimes, there is no "good" answer to the questions that arise. Therefore, it is important to have tools to help in the decision-making process and to create a framework for organizing those tools. Business decisions can be complex and may involve legal concerns, financial questions, possibly health and safety concerns, and ethical components.

## 1–4a A Systematic Approach

Organizing the ethical concerns and issues and approaching them systematically can help a businessperson eliminate various alternatives and identify the strengths and weaknesses of the remaining alternatives. Ethics consultant Leonard H. Bucklin of Corporate-Ethics.US™ has devised a procedure that he calls Business Process Pragmatism™. It involves five steps:

**Step 1: Inquiry.** First, the decision maker must understand the problem. This step involves identifying the parties involved (the stakeholders) and collecting the relevant facts. Once the ethical problem or problems are clarified, the decision maker lists any relevant legal and ethical principles that will guide the decision.

**Step 2: Discussion.** In this step, the decision maker lists possible actions. The ultimate goals for the decision are determined, and each option is evaluated using the laws and ethical principles listed in Step 1.

**Step 3: Decision.** In this step, those participating in the decision making work together to craft a consensus decision or consensus plan of action for the corporation.

**Step 4: Justification.** In this step, the decision maker articulates the reasons for the proposed action or series of actions. Generally, these reasons should come from the analysis done in Step 3. This step essentially results in documentation to be shared with stakeholders explaining why the proposal is an ethical solution to the problem.

**Step 5: Evaluation.** This final step occurs once the decision has been made and implemented. The solution should be analyzed to determine if it was effective. The results of this evaluation may be used in making future decisions.

## 1–4b The Importance of Ethical Leadership

Talking about ethical business decision making is meaningless if management does not set standards. Furthermore, managers must apply the same standards to themselves as they do to the company's employees. See this chapter's *Digital Update* feature for a discussion of an ethical dilemma that has arisen from the increased use of digital technology by employees after work hours.

**Attitude of Top Management**   One of the most important ways to create and maintain an ethical workplace is for top management to demonstrate its commitment to ethical decision making. A manager who is not totally committed to an ethical workplace rarely succeeds in creating one. Management's behavior, more than

## DIGITAL UPDATE — Should Employees Have a "Right of Disconnecting"?

Almost all jobs today involve digital technology, whether it be e-mail, Internet access, or smartphone use. Most employees, when interviewed, say that digital technology increases their productivity and flexibility.

The downside is what some call an "electronic leash"—meaning that employees are constantly connected and end up working when they are not "at work." Over one-third of full-time workers, for example, say that they frequently check e-mails outside normal working hours.

**Do Workers Have the Right to Disconnect?**

Because the boundaries between being "at work" and being "at leisure" can be so hazy, some labor unions in other countries have attempted to pass rules that allow employees to disconnect from e-mail and other work-related digital communication during nonworking hours. For instance, a French labor union representing high-tech workers signed an agreement with a large business association recognizing a "right of disconnecting." In Germany, Volkswagen and BMW no longer forward e-mail to staff from company servers after the end of the workday. Other German firms have declared that workers are not expected to check e-mail on weekends and holidays. The government is considering legislating such restrictions nationwide.

**The Thorny Issue of Overtime and the Fair Labor Standards Act**

Payment for overtime work is strictly regulated under the Fair Labor Standards Act (FLSA). According to the United States Supreme Court, in this context, *work* is "physical or mental exertion (whether burdensome or not) controlled or required by the employer and pursued necessarily for the benefit of the employer and his business."[a]

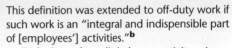

This definition was extended to off-duty work if such work is an "integral and indispensible part of [employees'] activities."[b]

Today's modern digital connectivity raises issues about the definition of *work*. Employees at several major companies, including Black & Decker, T-Mobile, and Verizon, have sued for unpaid overtime related to smartphone use. In another case, a police sergeant has sued the city of Chicago, claiming that he should have been paid overtime for hours spent using his personal digital assistant (PDA).[c] The police department issues PDAs to officers and requires them to respond to work-related text messages, e-mails, and voice mails not only while on duty, but also while off duty. Off-duty responses are not compensated by the city.

**Not All Employees Demand the "Right to Disconnect"**

According to a recent Gallup poll, 79 percent of full-time employees had either strongly positive or somewhat positive views of using computers, e-mail, tablets, and smartphones to work remotely outside of normal business hours. According to the same poll, 17 percent of them report "better overall lives" because of constant online connectivity with their work. Finally, working remotely after business hours apparently does not necessarily result in additional work-related stress.

**Critical Thinking** *From an ethical point of view, is there any difference between calling subordinates during off hours for work-related questions and sending them e-mails or text messages?*

a. *Tennessee Coal, Iron & R. Co. v. Muscoda Local No. 123*, 321 U.S. 590, 64 S.Ct. 698, 8 L.Ed. 949 (1944). Although Congress later passed a statute that superseded the holding in this case, the statute gave the courts broad authority to interpret the FLSA's definition of *work*. 29 U.S.C. Section 251(a). See *Integrity Staffing Solutions, Inc. v. Busk*, ___ U.S. ___, 135 S.Ct. 513, 190 L.Ed.2d 410 (2014).

b. *Steiner v. Mitchell*, 350 U.S. 247, 76 S.Ct. 330, 100 L.Ed. 267 (1956).
c. *Allen v. City of Chicago*, 2014 WL 5461856 (N.D.Ill. 2014).

---

anything else, sets the ethical tone of a firm. Employees take their cues from management.

Managers have found that discharging even one employee for ethical reasons has a tremendous impact as a deterrent to unethical behavior in the workplace. This is true even if the company has a written code of ethics.

If management does not enforce the company code, the code is essentially nonexistent.

The administration of a university may have had a similar concept in mind in the following case when it applied the school's professionalism standard to a student who had engaged in serious misconduct.

# Al-Dabagh v. Case Western Reserve University

United States Court of Appeals, Sixth Circuit, 777 F.3d 355 (2015).

**Background and Facts** The curriculum at Case Western Reserve University School of Medicine identifies nine "core competencies." At the top of the list is professionalism, which includes "ethical, honest, responsible and reliable behavior." The university's Committee on Students determines whether a student has met the professionalism requirements.

Amir Al-Dabagh enrolled at the school and did well academically. But he sexually harassed fellow students, often asked an instructor not to mark him late for class, received complaints from hospital staff about his demeanor, and was convicted of driving while intoxicated. The Committee on Students unanimously refused to certify him for graduation and dismissed him from the university.

He filed a suit in a federal district court against Case Western, alleging a breach of good faith and fair dealing. The court ordered the school to issue a diploma. Case Western appealed.

## In the Language of the Court

*SUTTON*, Circuit Judge.

\* \* \* \*

\* \* \* Case Western's student handbook \* \* \* makes clear that the only thing standing between Al-Dabagh and a diploma is the Committee on Students' finding that he lacks professionalism. Unhappily for Al-Dabagh, that is an academic judgment. And *we can no more substitute our personal views for the Committee's when it comes to an academic judgment than the Committee can substitute its views for ours when it comes to a judicial decision.* [Emphasis added.]

\* \* \* \*

\* \* \* *The Committee's professionalism determination is an academic judgment. That conclusion all but resolves this case. We may overturn the Committee only if it substantially departed from accepted academic norms when it refused to approve Al-Dabagh for graduation.* And given Al-Dabagh's track record—one member of the Committee does not recall encountering another student with Al-Dabagh's "repeated professionalism issues" in his quarter century of experience—we cannot see how it did. [Emphasis added.]

To the contrary, Al-Dabagh insists: The Committee's decision was a "punitive disciplinary measure" that had nothing to do with academics. \* \* \* His argument fails to wrestle with the prominent place of professionalism in the university's academic curriculum—which itself is an academic decision courts may not lightly disturb.

Even if professionalism is an academic criterion, Al-Dabagh persists that the university defined it too broadly. As he sees it, the only professional lapses that matter are the ones linked to academic performance. That is not how we see it or for that matter how the medical school sees it. That many professionalism-related cases involve classroom incidents does not establish that only classroom incidents are relevant to the professionalism inquiry \* \* \*. Our own standards indicate that professionalism does not end at the courtroom door. Why should hospitals operate any differently? As for the danger that an expansive view of professionalism might forgive, or provide a cloak for, arbitrary or discriminatory behavior, we see no such problem here. Nothing in the record suggests that the university had impermissible motives or acted in bad faith in this instance. And nothing in our deferential standard prevents us from invalidating genuinely objectionable actions when they occur.

**Decision and Remedy** *The U.S. Court of Appeals for the Sixth Circuit reversed the lower court's order to issue a diploma to Al-Dabagh. The federal appellate court found nothing to indicate that Case Western had "impermissible motives," acted in bad faith, or dealt unfairly with Al-Dabagh.*

## Critical Thinking

• **What If the Facts Were Different?** *Suppose that Case Western had tolerated Al-Dabagh's conduct and awarded him a diploma. What impact might that had on other students at the school? Why?*

**Behavior of Owners and Managers**   Certain types of behavior on the part of managers and owners contribute to unethical behavior among employees. Managers who set unrealistic production or sales goals increase the probability that employees will act unethically. If a sales quota can be met only through high-pressure, unethical sales tactics, employees will try to act "in the best interest of the company" and will continue to behave unethically. A manager who looks the other way when she or he knows about an employee's unethical behavior also sets an example—one indicating that ethical transgressions will be accepted.

Business owners and managers sometimes take more active roles in fostering unethical and illegal conduct. This sort of misbehavior can have negative consequences for the owners and managers and their business. Not only can a court sanction them, but it can also issue an injunction that prevents them from engaging in similar patterns of conduct in the future.

■ **CASE IN POINT 1.11**   John Robert Johnson, Jr., took a truck that needed repair along with its fifteen-ton trailer to Bubba Shaffer, doing business as Shaffer's Auto and Diesel Repair, LLC. The truck was supposedly fixed, and Johnson paid the bill, but the truck continued to leak oil and water. Johnson returned the truck to Shaffer, who again claimed to have fixed the problem. Johnson paid the second bill. The problems with the truck continued, however, so Johnson returned the truck and trailer to Shaffer a third time.

Johnson was given a verbal estimate of $1,000 for the repairs, but Shaffer ultimately sent an invoice for $5,863. Johnson offered to settle for $2,480, the amount of the initial estimate ($1,000), plus the costs of parts and shipping. Shaffer refused the offer and would not return Johnson's truck or trailer until full payment was made. Shaffer retained possession for almost four years and also charged Johnson a storage fee of $50 a day and 18 percent interest on the $5,863. Johnson sued for unfair trade practices and won. The court awarded him $3,500 in damages plus attorneys' fees and awarded Shaffer $1,000 (the amount of his estimate).[3] ■

The following case further demonstrates the types of situations that can occur when management demonstrates a lack of concern about ethics.

---

**3.** *Johnson Construction Co. v. Shaffer,* 87 So.3d 203 (La.App. 2012).

---

**Case Analysis 1.3**

# Moseley v. Pepco Energy Services, Inc.

United States District Court, District of New Jersey, 2011 WL 1584166 (2011).

### In the Language of the Court

Joseph H. *RODRIGUEZ*, District Judge.

* * * Plaintiff Moseley is an employee of Defendant Pepco Energy Services, Inc. ("PES"). He has been employed by PES or its corporate predecessors for over twenty-five years. PES, a subsidiary of Defendant Pepco Holdings, Inc. ("PHI"), provides deregulated energy and energy-related services for residential, small business, and large commercial customers.

* * * *

In 1998, Thomas Herzog held the position of Vice President of CTS. * * * In or around 2002, CTS merged with Potomic Electric Power Company, Inc., and each company became a subsidiary of PHI. Following the merger, according to Plaintiff, he continued to work for PHI, still as Maintenance Manager at Midtown Thermal, until December 31, 2009.

* * * *

Following the 2002 merger with PHI, employees were required to complete an annual ethics survey. By March of 2007, Plaintiff and two co-workers had discussed their respective observations of Herzog's conduct, which they deemed questionable and possibly unethical. Specifically, they felt that Herzog improperly used company assets and improperly hired immediate family members and friends who did not appear on the payroll. The three decided to disclose this information on PHI's annual "Ethics Survey."

The three planned to reveal that Herzog employed his daughter, Laurie, as his  secretary in the summer of 2005 and the beginning of 2006 without posting the position first and in violation of PHI's anti-nepotism policy.

* * * *

Next, Herzog hired his girlfriend's daughter as his secretary after his daughter had gone back to school. Plaintiff believed this was in violation of Company policy because the position again was not posted. Herzog also hired his son as a project manager, again through a third party independent contractor, Walter Ratai. Plaintiff thought this was wrong because (1) Herzog circumvented the Company's hiring process, (2) it violated Company policy, and (3) Herzog's son was being paid $75.00/hr, which was more than Plaintiff was making. * * *

Case 1.3 Continues

**Case 1.3 Continued**

In addition, Plaintiff had learned that Herzog was improperly using the Company's Eagles' tickets for personal use. Finally, Herzog had leased a new SUV with Company funds, but which was not approved by the Company.

\* \* \* \*

[After the surveys were completed, an] investigation ensued. Following the investigation, effective on or about May 10, 2007, Herzog was escorted out of the building. \* \* \* On March 8, 2008, Plaintiff received his annual performance evaluation \* \* \*; for the first time in twenty-three years, Plaintiff's performance review was negative. Plaintiff feels that this negative performance review was a further act of retaliation for his disclosure of Herzog's conduct.

\* \* \* \*

On or about June 11, 2008 the Plant/Operations Manager position was posted \* \* \*. Plaintiff applied for the position, but it was offered to [another person]. Plaintiff alleges that he "was not promoted to the position of Plant/Operations Manager despite his experience performing the job for the previous two and a half years, qualifications for same and seniority, as a direct and proximate result of his prior complaints and/or disclosures regarding the Herzog illegal conduct and activities."

\* \* \* \*

The New Jersey Legislature enacted the Conscientious Employee Protection Act (CEPA) to "protect and encourage employees to report illegal or unethical workplace activities." \* \* \* CEPA prohibits a New Jersey employer from taking "retaliatory action" against an employee who objects to "any activity, policy or practice which the employee reasonably believes" is in violation of applicable law. \* \* \* "To prevail on a claim under

this provision, a plaintiff must establish that: (1) he reasonably believed that [the complained-of] conduct was violating a law or rule or regulation promulgated pursuant to law; (2) he objected to the conduct; (3) an adverse employment action was taken against him; and (4) a causal connection exists between the whistleblowing activity and the adverse employment action.

\* \* \* \*

The first element of the *prima facie* case [a case sufficient to be sent to the jury] under CEPA is that the Plaintiff reasonably believed that the complained-of conduct (1) was violating a "law, rule, or regulation promulgated pursuant to law, including any violation involving deception of, or misrepresentation to, any shareholder, investor, client, patient, customer, employee, former employee, retiree or pensioner of the employer or any governmental entity"; or "(2) is fraudulent or criminal, including any activity, policy or practice of deception or misrepresentation which the employee reasonably believes may defraud any shareholder, investor, client, patient, customer, employee, former employee, retiree or pensioner of the employer or any governmental entity."

Although Defendants have argued that Plaintiff merely disclosed a violation of Company policy, Moseley has testified that in March 2007, he reported what he believed to be "unethical conduct, misappropriation of company funds, and theft" by his direct supervisor. \* \* \* *Moreover, a plaintiff need not demonstrate that there was a violation of the law or fraud, but instead that he "reasonably believed" that to be the case.* The facts in this case support an objectively reasonable belief that a violation of law or

fraudulent conduct was being committed by Plaintiff's supervisor. [Emphasis added.]

Regarding the causal connection between Plaintiff's whistleblowing activity and the negative adverse employment actions taken against him, Plaintiff stresses that he was employed by the Defendants for twenty-five years without a negative employment evaluation or any form of discipline until immediately after he disclosed the wrongful conduct of his supervisor. Not only did Plaintiff then receive a negative performance evaluation, but the posted position of Plant Manager was given to [another], despite [the other's] alleged past negative history and despite that Plaintiff asserts he had been acting in that job for over two years. Plaintiff contends that this is sufficient evidence of pretext.

*The Court is unable to find as a matter of law that Defendants' inferences prevail or that a jury could not reasonably adopt a contrary inference of retaliation.* There are questions of fact as to how much the individuals responsible for Plaintiff's negative performance evaluations knew about Plaintiff's complaints. "[A] finding of the required causal connection may be based solely on circumstantial evidence that the person ultimately responsible for an adverse employment action was aware of an employee's whistle-blowing activity." Because jurors may infer a causal connection from the surrounding circumstances, as well as temporal proximity, the Court will not grant summary judgment. [Emphasis added.]

\* \* \* \*

IT IS ORDERED on this 26th day of April, 2011 that Defendants' motion for summary judgment is hereby DENIED.

## Legal Reasoning Questions

1. Using duty-based ethical principles, what facts or circumstances in this case would lead Moseley to disclose Herzog's behavior?

2. Using outcome-based ethical principles, what issues would Moseley have to analyze in making the decision to report Herzog's behavior? What would be the risks to Moseley? The benefits?

3. Under the Business Process Pragmatism™ steps, what alternatives might Moseley have had in this situation?

**The Sarbanes-Oxley Act** Congress enacted the Sarbanes-Oxley Act[4] to help reduce corporate fraud and unethical management decisions. The act requires companies to set up confidential systems so that employees and others can "raise red flags" about suspected illegal or unethical auditing and accounting practices.

Some companies have implemented online reporting systems to accomplish this goal. In one such system, employees can click on an on-screen icon that anonymously links them with NAVEX Global, an organization based in Oregon. Through NAVEX Global, employees can report suspicious accounting practices, sexual harassment, and other possibly unethical behavior. NAVEX, in turn, alerts management personnel or the audit committee at the designated company to the possible problem.

# 1–5 Global Business Ethics

Just as different religions have different moral codes, different countries, regions, and even states have different ethical expectations and priorities. Some of these differences are based in religious values, whereas others are cultural in nature. Such differences make it even more difficult to determine what is ethical in a particular situation. For instance, in certain countries the consumption of alcohol is forbidden for religious reasons. It would be considered unethical for a U.S. business to produce alcohol in those countries and employ local workers to assist in alcohol production.

International transactions often involve issues related to employment and financing. Congress has addressed some of these issues, not eliminating the ethical components but clarifying some of the conflicts between the ethics of the United States and the ethics of other nations. For instance, the Civil Rights Act and the Foreign Corrupt Practices Act have clarified the U.S. ethical position on employment issues and bribery in foreign nations. (Other nations, including Mexico, have also enacted laws that prohibit bribery.)

## 1–5a Monitoring the Employment Practices of Foreign Suppliers

Many businesses contract with companies in developing nations to produce goods, such as shoes and clothing, because the wage rates in those nations are significantly lower than those in the United States. But what if one of those contractors hires women and children at below-minimum-wage rates or requires its employees to work long hours in a workplace full of health hazards? What if the company's supervisors routinely engage in workplace conduct that is offensive to women? What if plants located abroad routinely violate labor and environmental standards?

■ **EXAMPLE 1.12** Pegatron Corporation, a company based in China, manufactures and supplies parts to Apple, Inc., for iPads and other Apple products. After an explosion at a Pegatron factory in Shanghai, allegations surfaced that the conditions at the factory violated labor and environmental standards. Similar allegations were made about other Apple suppliers.

Apple started to evaluate practices at companies in its supply chain and to communicate its ethics policies to them. Its audits revealed numerous violations. Apple released a list of its suppliers for the first time and issued a lengthy "Supplier Responsibility Report" detailing supplier practices. Numerous facilities had withheld worker pay as a disciplinary measure. Some had falsified pay records and forced workers to use machines without safeguards. Others had engaged in unsafe environmental practices, such as dumping wastewater on neighboring farms. Apple terminated its relationship with one supplier and turned over its findings to the Fair Labor Association for further inquiry. ■

Given today's global communications network, few companies can assume that their actions in other nations will go unnoticed by "corporate watch" groups that discover and publicize unethical corporate behavior. As a result, U.S. businesses today usually take steps to avoid such adverse publicity—either by refusing to deal with certain suppliers or by arranging to monitor their suppliers' workplaces to make sure that the employees are not being mistreated.

## 1–5b The Foreign Corrupt Practices Act

Another ethical problem in international business dealings has to do with the legitimacy of certain side payments to government officials. In the United States, the majority of contracts are formed within the private sector. In many foreign countries, however, government officials make the decisions on most major construction and manufacturing contracts because of extensive government regulation and control over trade and industry.

Side payments to government officials in exchange for favorable business contracts are not unusual in such countries, nor have they been considered unethical. In the past, U.S. corporations doing business in these nations largely followed the dictum "When in Rome, do as the Romans do."

In the 1970s, however, the U.S. media uncovered a number of business scandals involving large side

---
**4.** 15 U.S.C. Sections 7201 *et seq.*

payments by U.S. corporations to foreign representatives for the purpose of securing advantageous international trade contracts. In response to this unethical behavior, Congress passed the Foreign Corrupt Practices Act[5] (FCPA), which prohibits U.S. businesspersons from bribing foreign officials to secure beneficial contracts.

**Prohibition against the Bribery of Foreign Officials** The first part of the FCPA applies to all U.S. companies and their directors, officers, shareholders, employees, and agents. This part prohibits the bribery of most officials of foreign governments if the purpose of the payment is to motivate the official to act in his or her official capacity to provide business opportunities.

The FCPA does not prohibit payments made to minor officials whose duties are ministerial. A ministerial action is a routine activity, such as the processing of paperwork, with little or no discretion involved in the action. These payments are often referred to as "grease," or facilitating payments. They are meant to accelerate the performance of administrative services that might otherwise be carried out at a slow pace. Thus, for instance, if a firm makes a payment to a minor official to speed up an import licensing process, the firm has not violated the FCPA.

Generally, the act, as amended, permits payments to foreign officials if such payments are lawful within the foreign country. Payments to private foreign companies or other third parties are permissible—unless the U.S. firm knows that the payments will be passed on to a foreign government in violation of the FCPA. The U.S. Department of Justice also uses the FCPA to prosecute foreign companies suspected of bribing officials outside the United States.

**Accounting Requirements** In the past, bribes were often concealed in corporate financial records. Thus, the second part of the FCPA is directed toward accountants.

All companies must keep detailed records that "accurately and fairly" reflect their financial activities. Their accounting systems must provide "reasonable assurance" that all transactions entered into by the companies are accounted for and legal. These requirements assist in detecting illegal bribes. The FCPA prohibits any person from making false statements to accountants or false entries in any record or account.

■ **CASE IN POINT 1.13** Noble Corporation, an international provider of offshore drilling services and equipment, was operating some drilling rigs offshore in Nigeria. Mark Jackson and James Ruehlen were officers at Noble. The U.S. government accused Noble of bribing Nigerian government officials and charged Jackson and Ruehlen individually with violating the FCPA's accounting provisions. Jackson and Ruehlen allegedly assisted in the bribery because they repeatedly allowed allegedly illegal payments to be posted on Noble's books as legitimate operating expenses.[6] ■

**Penalties for Violations** The FCPA provides that business firms that violate the act may be fined up to $2 million. Individual officers or directors who violate the FCPA may be fined up to $100,000 (the fine cannot be paid by the company) and may be imprisoned for up to five years. These statutory amounts can be significantly increased under the Alternative Fines Act[7] (up to twice the amount of any gain that the defendant obtained by making the corrupt payment).

Today, the U.S. government is actively seeking out violators and has around 150 FCPA investigations going on at any given time. In recent years, a high percentage of the total fines imposed by the Department of Justice have come from FCPA cases.

5. 15 U.S.C. Sections 78dd-1 *et seq.*

6. *S.E.C. v. Jackson*, 908 F.Supp.2d 834 (S.D.Tex—Houston Div. 2012).
7. 18 U.S.C. Section 3571.

## Reviewing: Business Ethics

James Stilton is the chief executive officer (CEO) of RightLiving, Inc., a company that buys life insurance policies at a discount from terminally ill persons and sells the policies to investors. RightLiving pays the terminally ill patients a percentage of the future death benefit (usually 65 percent) and then sells the policies to investors for 85 percent of the value of the future benefit. The patients receive the cash to use for medical and other expenses. The investors are "guaranteed" a positive return on their investment, and RightLiving profits on the difference between the purchase and sale prices. Stilton is aware that some sick patients might obtain insurance policies through fraud (by not revealing the illness on the insurance application). Insurance companies that discover this will cancel the policy and refuse to pay.

Stilton believes that most of the policies he has purchased are legitimate, but he knows that some probably are not. Using the information presented in this chapter, answer the following questions.

1. Would a person who adheres to the principle of rights consider it ethical for Stilton not to disclose the potential risk of cancellation to investors? Why or why not?
2. Using Immanuel Kant's categorical imperative, are the actions of RightLiving, Inc., ethical? Why or why not?
3. Under utilitarianism, are Stilton's actions ethical? Why or why not? What difference does it make if most of the policies are legitimate?
4. Using the Business Process Pragmatism™ steps discussed in this chapter, discuss the decision process Stilton should use in deciding whether to disclose the risk of fraudulent policies to potential investors.

**Debate This** . . . *Executives in large corporations are ultimately rewarded if their companies do well, particularly as evidenced by rising stock prices. Consequently, should we let those who run corporations decide what level of negative side effects of their goods or services is "acceptable"?*

## Terms and Concepts

business ethics 2
categorical imperative 8
corporate social responsibility (CSR) 9
cost-benefit analysis 8

duty-based ethics 7
ethical reasoning 7
ethics 2
moral minimum 4
outcome-based ethics 7

principle of rights 7
stakeholders 9
triple bottom line 2
utilitarianism 8

## Issue Spotters

1. Acme Corporation decides to respond to what it sees as a moral obligation to correct for past discrimination by adjusting pay differences among its employees. Does this raise an ethical conflict between Acme and its employees? Between Acme and its shareholders? Explain your answers. (See *Making Ethical Business Decisions.*)

2. Delta Tools, Inc., markets a product that under some circumstances is capable of seriously injuring consumers. Does Delta have an ethical duty to remove this product from the market, even if the injuries result only from misuse? Why or why not? (See *Making Ethical Business Decisions.*)

• **Check your answers to the Issue Spotters against the answers provided in Appendix B at the end of this text.**

## Business Scenarios

**1–1. Business Ethics.** Jason Trevor owns a commercial bakery in Blakely, Georgia, that produces a variety of goods sold in grocery stores. Trevor is required by law to perform internal tests on food produced at his plant to check for contamination. On three occasions, the tests of food products containing peanut butter were positive for salmonella contamination. Trevor was not required to report the results to U.S. Food and Drug Administration officials, however, so he did not. Instead, Trevor instructed his employees to simply repeat the tests until the results were negative. Meanwhile, the products that had originally tested positive for salmonella were eventually shipped out to retailers.

Five people who ate Trevor's baked goods that year became seriously ill, and one person died from a salmonella infection. Even though Trevor's conduct was legal, was it unethical for him to sell goods that had once tested positive for salmonella? Why or why not? (See *Business Ethics.*)

# Business Case Problems

## 1–2. Spotlight on Pfizer, Inc.—Corporate Social Responsibility.

Methamphetamine (meth) is an addictive drug made chiefly in small toxic labs (STLs) in homes, tents, barns, or hotel rooms. The manufacturing process is dangerous and often results in explosions, burns, and toxic fumes. Government entities spend time and resources to find and destroy STLs, imprison meth dealers and users, treat addicts, and provide services for affected families. Meth cannot be made without ingredients that are also used in cold and allergy medications. Arkansas has one of the highest numbers of STLs in the United States. To recoup the costs of fighting the meth epidemic, twenty counties in Arkansas filed a suit against Pfizer, Inc., which makes cold and allergy medications. What is Pfizer's ethical responsibility here, and to whom is it owed? Why? [*Ashley County, Arkansas v. Pfizer, Inc.,* 552 F.3d. 659 (8th Cir. 2009)] (See *Ethical Principles and Philosophies.*)

## 1–3. Business Case Problem with Sample Answer—Online Privacy.

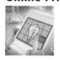

Facebook, Inc., launched a program called "Beacon" that automatically updated the profiles of users on Facebook's social networking site when those users had any activity on Beacon "partner" sites. For example, one partner site was Blockbuster.com. When a user rented or purchased a movie through Blockbuster.com, the user's Facebook profile would be updated to share the purchase. The Beacon program was set up as a default setting, so users never consented to the program, but they could opt out. What are the ethical implications of an opt-in program versus an opt-out program in social media? [*Lane v. Facebook, Inc.,* 696 F.3d 811 (9th Cir. 2011)] (See *Business Ethics and Social Media.*)

- **For a sample answer to Problem 1–3, go to Appendix C at the end of this text.**

## 1–4. Business Ethics on a Global Scale.

After the fall of the Soviet Union, the new government of Azerbaijan began converting certain state-controlled industries to private ownership. Ownership in these companies could be purchased through a voucher program. Frederic Bourke, Jr., and Viktor Kozeny wanted to purchase the Azerbaijani oil company, SOCAR, but it was unclear whether the Azerbaijani president would allow SOCAR to be put up for sale. Kozeny met with one of the vice presidents of SOCAR (who was also the son of the president of Azerbaijan) and other Azerbaijani leaders to discuss the sale of SOCAR. To obtain their cooperation, Kozeny set up a series of parent and subsidiary companies through which the Azerbaijani leaders would eventually receive two-thirds of the SOCAR profits without ever investing any of their own funds. In return, the Azerbaijani leaders would attempt to use their influence to convince the president to put SOCAR up for sale. Assume that Bourke and Kozeny are operating out of a U.S. company. Discuss the ethics of this scheme, both in terms of the Foreign Corrupt Practices Act (FCPA) and as a general ethical issue. What duties did Kozeny have under the FCPA? [*United States v. Kozeny,* 667 F.3d 122 (2d Cir. 2011)] (See *Making Ethical Business Decisions.*)

## 1–5. Business Ethics.

Mark Ramun worked as a manager for Allied Erecting and Dismantling Co., where he had a tense relationship with his father, who was Allied's president. After more than ten years, Mark left Allied, taking 15,000 pages of Allied's documents on DVDs and CDs, which constituted trade secrets. Later, he joined Genesis Equipment & Manufacturing, Inc., a competitor. Genesis soon developed a piece of equipment that incorporated elements of Allied equipment. How might business ethics have been violated in these circumstances? Discuss. [*Allied Erecting and Dismantling Co. v. Genesis Equipment & Manufacturing, Inc.,* 511 Fed.Appx. 398 (6th Cir. 2013)] (See *Business Ethics.*)

## 1–6. Business Ethics.

Stephen Glass made himself infamous as a dishonest journalist by fabricating material for more than forty articles for *The New Republic* magazine and other publications. He also fabricated supporting materials to delude *The New Republic*'s fact checkers. At the time, he was a law student at Georgetown University. Once suspicions were aroused, Glass tried to avoid detection. Later, Glass applied for admission to the California bar. The California Supreme Court denied his application, citing "numerous instances of dishonesty and disingenuousness" during his "rehabilitation" following the exposure of his misdeeds. How do these circumstances underscore the importance of ethics? Discuss. [*In re Glass,* 58 Cal.4th 500, 316 P.3d 1199 (2014)] (See *Business Ethics.*)

## 1–7. Business Ethics.

Operating out of an apartment in Secane, Pennsylvania, Hratch Ilanjian convinced Vicken Setrakian, the president of Kenset Corp., that he was an international businessman who could help Kenset turn around its business in the Middle East. At Ilanjian's insistence, Setrakian provided confidential business documents. Claiming that they had an agreement, Ilanjian demanded full, immediate payment and threatened to disclose the confidential information to a Kenset supplier if payment was not forthcoming. Kenset denied that they had a contract and filed a suit in a federal district court against Ilanjian, seeking return of the documents. During discovery, Ilanjian was uncooperative. Who behaved unethically in these circumstances? Explain. [*Kenset Corp. v. Ilanjian,* 600 Fed.Appx. 827 (3rd Cir. 2015)] (See *Business Ethics.*)

## 1–8. Business Ethics.

Priscilla Dickman worked as a medical technologist at the University of Connecticut Health Center. Dickman's supervisor received complaints that she was getting nonbusiness-related phone calls and was absent from her work area when she should have been working. Based on e-mails and other documents found on Dickman's work computer, the state investigated her for violations of state law. She was convicted of conducting "personal business for financial gain on state time utilizing state resources." Separate criminal investigations resulted in convictions for forgery and filing an unrelated fraudulent insurance claim. She "retired" from her job and filed a claim with the state of Connecticut against the health center, alleging that her former employer had initiated the investigations to harass her and force her to quit. For lack of "credible evidence or legal support," the claim was dismissed. Which of these acts, if any, were unethical? Why? *[Dickman v. University of Connecticut Health Center,* 162 Conn.App. 441, 132 A.3d 739 (2016)] (See *Business Ethics.*)

**1–9. A Question of Ethics—Consumer Rights.** *Best Buy, a national electronics retailer, offered a credit card that allowed users to earn "reward points" that could be redeemed for discounts on Best Buy goods. After reading a newspaper advertisement for the card, Gary Davis applied for, and was given, a credit card. As part of the application process, he visited a Web page containing Frequently Asked Questions as well as terms and conditions for the card. He clicked on a button affirming that he understood the terms and conditions. When Davis received his card, it came with seven brochures about the card and the reward point program. As he read the brochures, he discovered that a $59 annual fee would be charged for the card. Davis went back to the Web pages he had visited and found a statement that the card "may" have an annual fee. Davis sued, claiming that the company did not adequately disclose the fee. [Davis v. HSBC Bank Nevada, N.A., 691 F.3d 1152 (9th Cir. 2012)] (See Business Ethics.)*

**(a)** Online applications frequently have click-on buttons or check boxes for consumers to acknowledge that they have read and understand the terms and conditions of applications or purchases. Often, the terms and conditions are so long that they cannot all be seen on one screen and users must scroll to view the entire document. Is it unethical for companies to put terms and conditions, especially terms that may cost the consumer, in an electronic document that is too long to read on one screen? Why or why not? Does this differ from having a consumer sign a hard-copy document with terms and conditions printed on it? Why or why not?

**(b)** The Truth-in-Lending Act requires that credit terms be clearly and conspicuously disclosed in application materials. Assuming that the Best Buy credit-card materials had sufficient legal disclosures, discuss the ethical aspects of businesses strictly following the language of the law as opposed to following the intent of the law.

## Legal Reasoning Group Activity

**1–10. Global Business Ethics.** Pfizer, Inc., developed a new antibiotic called Trovan (trovafloxacinmesylate). Tests showed that in animals Trovan had life-threatening side effects, including joint disease, abnormal cartilage growth, liver damage, and a degenerative bone condition. Several years later, an epidemic of bacterial meningitis swept across Nigeria. Pfizer sent three U.S. physicians to test Trovan on children who were patients in Nigeria's Infectious Disease Hospital. Pfizer did not obtain the patients' consent, alert them to the risks, or tell them that Médecins Sans Frontières (Doctors without Borders) was providing an effective conventional treatment at the same site. Eleven children died in the experiment, and others were left blind, deaf, paralyzed, or brain damaged. Rabi Abdullahi and other Nigerian children filed a suit in a U.S. federal court against Pfizer, alleging a violation of a customary international law norm prohibiting involuntary medical experimentation on humans. (See *Global Business Ethics.*)

**(a)** One group should use the principles of ethical reasoning discussed in this chapter to develop three arguments that Pfizer's conduct was a violation of ethical standards.

**(b)** A second group should take a pro-Pfizer position and argue that the company did not violate any ethical standards (and counter the first group).

**(c)** A third group should come up with proposals for what Pfizer might have done differently to avert the consequences.

# CHAPTER 2

# Small Businesses and Franchises

A goal of many business students is to become an **entrepreneur,** one who initiates and assumes the financial risk of a new business enterprise and undertakes to provide or control its management. One of the first decisions an entrepreneur must make is which form of business organization will be most appropriate for the new endeavor.

In selecting an organizational form, the entrepreneur will consider a num-ber of factors. These include (1) ease of creation, (2) the liability of the own-ers, (3) tax considerations, and (4) the ability to raise capital. Keep these fac-tors in mind as you read this unit and learn about the various forms of busi-ness organization. Remember, too, in considering these business forms that the primary motive of an entrepreneur is to make profits.

Traditionally, entrepreneurs have used three major business forms—the sole proprietorship, the partnership, and the corporation. In this chapter, we examine sole proprietorships and also look at franchises. Although the franchise is not strictly speaking a business organizational form, it is widely used today by entrepreneurs.

## 2-1 General Considerations for Small Businesses

Most small businesses begin as sole proprietorships. Once the business is under way, the sole proprietorship form may become too limited. The owner and any additional investors may then want to establish a more formal orga-nization, such as a limited partnership (LP), a limited liability partnership (LLP), a limited liability company (LLC), or a corporation. These forms of business limit the owner's personal liability, or legal responsibility, for business debts and obligations. Each business form has its own advantages and disadvantages, but legal limited liability generally is necessary for those who wish to raise outside capital.

### 2-1a Requirements for All Business Forms

Any business, whatever its form, has to meet a vari-ety of legal requirements, which typically relate to the following:

1. Business name registration.
2. Occupational licensing.
3. State tax registration (for instance, to obtain permits for collecting and remitting sales taxes).
4. Health and environmental permits.
5. Zoning and building codes.
6. Import/export regulations.

If the business has employees, the owner must also comply with a host of laws governing the workplace.

### 2-1b Protecting Intellectual Property

Protecting rights in intellectual property is a central con-cern for many small businesses. For instance, software companies and app developers depend on their copy-rights and patents to protect their investments in the research and development required to create new pro-grams. Without copyright or patent protection, a com-petitor or a customer could simply copy the software or app.

**Trademarks** Choosing a trademark or service mark and making sure that it is protected under trademark law can be crucial to the success of a new business venture. Indeed, a factor to consider in choosing a name for a business entity is whether the business name will be used as a trademark. The general rule is that a trademark cannot be the same as another's mark or so similar that confusion might result.

For the most protection, trademarks should be registered with the U.S. Patent and Trademark Office (PTO). If the mark is federally registered, the owner may use the symbol ® with the mark. This well-known symbol puts others on notice of the registration and helps to prevent trademark infringement. An owner who has not registered can use the symbol ™. Registration with the PTO should be renewed five years after the initial registration and at ten-year intervals thereafter.

**Trade Secrets**  Much of the value of a small business may lie in its trade secrets, such as information about product development, production processes and techniques, and customer lists. Preserving the secrecy of the information is necessary for legal protection.

As a practical matter, trade secrets must be divulged to key employees. Thus, any business runs the risk that those employees might disclose the secrets to competitors—or even set up competing businesses themselves.

To protect their trade secrets, companies may require employees who have access to trade secrets to agree in their employment contracts never to divulge those secrets. A small business may also choose to include a covenant not to compete in an employment contract. A noncompete clause will help to protect against the possibility that a key employee will go to work for a competitor or set up a competing business.

### 2–1c  Obtaining Loans

Raising capital is critical to the growth of most small businesses. In the early days of a business, the sole proprietor may be able to contribute sufficient capital, but as the business becomes successful, more funds may be needed. The owner may want to raise capital from external sources to expand the business. One way to do this is to borrow funds.

Obtaining a bank loan is beneficial for small businesses because it allows the owner to retain full ownership and control of the business. Note, though, that the bank may place some restrictions on future business decisions as a condition of granting the loan. In addition, bank loans may not be available for some businesses. Banks are usually reluctant to lend significant sums to businesses that are not yet established. Even if a bank is willing to make

such a loan, the bank may require personal guaranty contracts from the owner, putting the owner's personal assets at risk.

Loans with desirable terms may be available from the U.S. Small Business Administration (SBA). One SBA program provides loans of up to $25,000 to businesspersons who are women, low-income individuals, or members of minority groups. Be aware that the SBA requires business owners to put some of their own funds at risk in the business. In addition, many states offer small-business grants to individuals starting a business.

## 2–2  Sole Proprietorships

In the earliest stages, as mentioned, a small business may operate as a **sole proprietorship,** which is the simplest form of business. In this form, the owner is the business. Thus, anyone who does business without creating a separate business organization has a sole proprietorship. The law considers all new, single-owner businesses to be sole proprietorships unless the owner affirmatively adopts some other form.

More than two-thirds of all U.S. businesses are sole proprietorships. Sole proprietors can own and manage any type of business from an informal, home-office or Web-based undertaking to a large restaurant or construction firm. About 99 percent of the sole proprietorships in the United States have revenues of less than $1 million per year.

### 2–2a  Advantages of the Sole Proprietorship

A major advantage of the sole proprietorship is that the proprietor owns the entire business and receives all of the profits (because she or he assumes all of the risk). In addition, starting a sole proprietorship is easier and less costly than starting any other kind of business because few legal formalities are required. Generally, no documents need to be filed with the government to start a sole proprietorship.[1]

---

1. Although starting a sole proprietorship involves fewer legal formalities than other business organizational forms, even a small sole proprietorship may need to comply with zoning requirements, obtain a state business license, and the like.

**Taxes** A sole proprietor pays only personal income taxes (including Social Security and Medicare taxes) on the business's profits. The profits are reported as personal income on the proprietor's personal income tax return. In other words, the business itself need not file an income tax return. Sole proprietors are allowed to establish retirement accounts that are tax-exempt until the funds are withdrawn.

Like any form of business enterprise, a sole proprietorship can be liable for other taxes, such as those collected and applied to the disbursement of unemployment compensation. Whether liability for the unpaid unemployment compensation taxes of a sole proprietorship remains with the seller or must be assumed by the buyer was at issue in the following case.

# A. Gadley Enterprises, Inc. v. Department of Labor and Industry Office of Unemployment Compensation Tax Services

Commonwealth Court of Pennsylvania, __ A.3d __, 2016 WL 55591 (2016).

## In the Language of the Court

*SIMPSON*, Judge.

* * * *

[Julianne Gresh (Predecessor)] operated [Romper Room Day Care (Romper Room)], a childcare center, as a sole proprietorship for 12 years. Predecessor owed the [Pennsylvania Department of Labor and Industry Office of Unemployment Compensation Tax Services (Department)] substantial unpaid UC [unemployment compensation] contributions, interest and penalties. She admitted liability and entered payment plans with the Department * * *. Pursuant to these payment plans, she made monthly payments in the minimal amount of $50. Predecessor was on the verge of losing her license to operate, and sought another entity to operate the location as a childcare facility.

[A. Gadley Enterprises, Inc. (Purchaser)] operated a childcare center, Young Environment Learning Center, in Erie, Pennsylvania. Purchaser decided to purchase assets from Predecessor in order to open a satellite location of Young Environmental Learning Center at the prior location of Romper Room. Purchaser and Predecessor executed an asset purchase agreement (Agreement).

Through the Agreement, Purchaser paid a total of $37,000 for Predecessor's tangible and intangible assets. This total was comprised of $10,000 for the use of the name "Romper Room," $10,790 for a covenant not to compete, and $17,210 for tangible assets listed on [an attached] Inventory List.

* * * The Inventory List did not include any of Predecessor's personal assets other than those used in the operation of Romper Room.

* * * Four days *after* executing the Agreement, * * * Predecessor notified the Department of the sale.

* * * The Department issued Purchaser a Notice of Assessment (Notice) in the amount of $43,370.49 for UC contributions, interest and penalties owed by Predecessor. The Notice stated Purchaser was liable because it purchased 51% or more of Predecessor's assets.

In response, Purchaser filed a petition [with the Department] for reassessment.

* * * *

Based on the evidence presented at the hearing [held on the petition], the Department issued its decision and order denying the petition for reassessment.

* * * *

Purchaser then filed a petition to review to this Court.

* * * *

[43 Pennsylvania Statutes Section 788.3(a), part of the state's Unemployment Compensation Law] provides:

(a) Every employer * * *, who shall sell in bulk fifty-one percent or more of his assets, including but not limited to, any stock of goods, wares or merchandise of any kind, fixtures, machinery, equipment, building or real estate, shall give the department ten (10) days' notice of the sale prior to completion of the transfer * * *. The employer shall present to the purchaser of such property, a certificate * * * showing that all reports have been filed and contributions, interest and penalties paid to the date of the proposed transfer. The failure of the

purchaser to require such certificate shall render such purchaser liable to the department for the unpaid contributions, interest and penalties.

* * * *

There is no dispute that Purchaser did not obtain a clearance certificate reflecting Predecessor's payment of UC liability. There is also no dispute that Predecessor owed the Department for outstanding UC contributions, interest and penalties in the amount of $43,370.49 at the time of the sale.

* * * *

Purchaser argues substantial evidence does not support the Department's finding that it purchased more than 51% of the [Predecessor's] assets.

* * * *

The Agreement establishes that the Inventory List sets forth all business assets of Predecessor. Gresh confirmed the Inventory List was a complete list of assets used in the operation of her business.

The Inventory List reflects a total value of assets equaling $19,210. * * * The parties reduced the purchase price by $2,000 to account for the reduced value of the assets when Purchaser removed certain assets from the complete Inventory List. Purchaser acquired all the assets included in the Inventory List, other than those removed, for $17,210. The amount constitutes approximately 90% of the value of the complete list of assets ($19,210 × .9 = $17,289).

The Agreement, supplemented by corroborating [supporting] testimony,

Case 2.1 Continued

constitutes substantial evidence to support the Department's finding that the sale qualified as a bulk sale of more than 51% of Predecessor's assets.

* * * *

Purchaser also argues the Department erred in construing the term "assets" in the bulk sales provision to include only business assets when determining whether a sale met the 51% threshold. Purchaser asserts the provision does not differentiate between business and personal assets of an employer and there is no legal distinction when the employer is a sole proprietor.

* * * *

* * * The definition of "employer" [in the UC Law] includes a sole proprietor like Predecessor.

The word "assets" is not defined in the [UC] Law.

[In Section 788.3(a)] the term "assets" precedes a list of examples, followed by the phrase "including but not limited to."

* * * *

* * * The examples * * * indicate that the term "assets" refers to business assets. This conclusion is buttressed [reinforced] by the context of the statute as a whole, which pertains to employers operating businesses and paying employees as part of their business operations.

*The factual circumstances surrounding the sale also indicate the term "assets" means "business assets." Here, the context is the sale of a business, in the childcare industry, to another business engaged in the same industry that intends to operate a childcare facility at the location of the former business. The Agreement reflects the intention of the parties that Purchaser would operate the childcare facility as a satellite location.* [Emphasis added.]

* * * *

* * * The provision does not treat sole proprietors differently than other employers. The provision contains no exemption of liability for a purchaser when an employer operates as a sole proprietorship. Nor does it contain an exemption from liability when the former employer entered a repayment plan with the Department.

Moreover, Purchaser's interpretation does not consider *the purpose of the bulk sales provision. That purpose is to ensure an employer does not divest itself of assets without satisfying outstanding liabilities, either itself or by the purchaser.* This Court agrees with the Department that Gresh's repayment agreement in the minimal amount of $50 per month does not satisfy the UC liability. [Emphasis added.]

* * * *

In sum, the Department's construction of assets as business assets is reasonable and consistent with the context and purpose of [the] bulk sales provision. Purchaser's failure to obtain a clearance certificate rendered it liable for Predecessor's unpaid UC contributions, interest and penalties, regardless of Predecessor's repayment agreement. Therefore, this Court upholds the Department's interpretation of the bulk sales provision.

* * * *

* * * For the foregoing reasons, we affirm the Department.

### Legal Reasoning Questions

**1.** As is clear from the law applied in this case, and the result, the liability of a business for unpaid taxes "follows the assets." Why?

**2.** What action can Gadley take now to avoid suffering the loss of the funds required to cover Gresh's unpaid taxes?

**3.** What action should a buyer take *before* purchasing the assets of a business to avoid liability for the seller's unpaid taxes?

---

**Flexibility** A sole proprietorship offers more flexibility than does a partnership or a corporation. The sole proprietor is free to make any decision she or he wishes concerning the business—including what kind of business to pursue, whom to hire, and when to take a vacation. The sole proprietor can sell or transfer all or part of the business to another party at any time without seeking approval from anyone else. In contrast, approval is typically required from partners in a partnership and from shareholders in a corporation.

## 2–2b Disadvantages of the Sole Proprietorship

The major disadvantage of the sole proprietorship is that the proprietor alone bears the burden of any losses or liabilities incurred by the business enterprise. In other words, the sole proprietor has unlimited liability for all obligations that arise in doing business. Any lawsuit against the business or its employees can lead to unlimited personal liability for the owner of a sole proprietorship.

■ **EXAMPLE 2.1** Aaron and Melissa Klein, owners of the Sweet Cakes by Melissa bakery, refused to bake a wedding cake for a same-sex couple's wedding. They claimed that their religious beliefs did not allow them to provide services for same-sex ceremonies. The Oregon State Bureau of Labor and Industries argued that their decision violated the law. In 2015, an administrative law judge ruled against the Kleins' motion to dismiss and ordered them to pay $135,000 in damages. As sole proprietors, the Kleins were personally responsible for paying the damages. ■

**Personal Assets at Risk** Creditors can pursue the owner's personal assets to satisfy any business debts. Although sole proprietors may obtain insurance to protect the business, liability can easily exceed policy limits. This unlimited liability is a major factor to be considered in choosing a business form.

■ **EXAMPLE 2.2** Sheila Fowler operates a golf shop near a world-class golf course as a sole proprietorship. One of Fowler's employees fails to secure a display of golf clubs. They fall on Dean Maheesh, a professional golfer, and seriously injure him. If Maheesh sues Fowler's shop and wins, Fowler's personal liability could easily exceed the limits of her insurance policy. Fowler could lose not only her business, but also her house, car, and any other personal assets that can be attached to pay the judgment. ■

**Lack of Continuity and Limited Ability to Raise Capital** The sole proprietorship also has the disadvantage of lacking continuity after the death of the proprietor. When the owner dies, so does the business—it is automatically dissolved.

Another disadvantage is that in raising capital, the proprietor is limited to his or her personal funds and any loans that he or she can obtain for the business. Lenders may be unwilling to make loans to sole proprietorships, particularly start-ups, because the sole proprietor risks unlimited personal liability and may not be able to pay. (See this chapter's *Digital Update* feature for a discussion of one court's refusal to discharge a loan made to a sole proprietor who had declared bankruptcy.)

---

## DIGITAL UPDATE    A Sole Proprietorship, Facebook Poker, and Bankruptcy

One major downside of a sole proprietorship is that it is more difficult for a sole proprietor to obtain funding for start-up and expansion. Moreover, if funding is obtained through loans, the sole proprietor is exposed to personal liability.

### Personal Liability Exposure for an Online Startup

A case in point went before the United States bankruptcy court in Massachusetts in 2015.[a] Michael Dewhurst, living in Raynham, Massachusetts, sometimes did computer work for Gerald Knappik. Dewhurst decided to start a new business venture—the commercial development of a Facebook poker–playing application. Dewhurst envisioned an application that would enable multiple individuals to play poker together over the Internet through Facebook. Dewhurst informed Knappik of his business plan and predicted that his Facebook poker application "was going to be something very big."

Knappik initially loaned $50,000 to Dewhurst for the project. The loan agreement stated, "The sole purpose of this loan agreement is to provide funds on a personal level for the startup of said business project, in conjunction with borrower's personal funds, not limited to startup costs, operating expenses, advertising costs."

That was the first of a series of personal loans that totaled $220,000.

Dewhurst had repaid only $9,000 on the total outstanding debt when he filed for bankruptcy. Ultimately, the bankruptcy court ascertained that at least $120,000 of the loans that were supposed to be used exclusively for the Facebook poker project had been used for other activities. Furthermore, Dewhurst kept "no contemporaneous records of his disbursements and uses of this cash, no cash journal, ledger, or disbursement slips of any kind."

### The Lender Objects to a Bankruptcy Discharge of Monies Owed

During bankruptcy proceedings, Knappik requested that the bankruptcy court deny discharge of Dewhurst's debts to him. Upon review, the court stated that "Dewhurst's failure to keep and preserve adequate records makes it impossible to reconstruct an accurate and complete account of financial affairs and business transactions." The bankruptcy judge ultimately denied discharge of $120,000 of the debt owed to Knappik. Thus, a sole proprietor's failed attempt to create an online poker-playing application led to personal liability even after he had filed for bankruptcy.

**Critical Thinking** *Sole proprietorships, as well as other businesses, routinely seek funding for online projects. How can the individuals involved avoid personal liability?*

---

a. *In re Dewhurst*, 528 Bankr. 211 (D.Mass. 2015).

# 2–3 Franchises

Instead of setting up a sole proprietorship to market their own products or services, many entrepreneurs opt to purchase a franchise. A **franchise** is an arrangement in which the owner of intellectual property—such as a trademark, a trade name, or a copyright—licenses others to use it in the selling of goods or services. A **franchisee** (a purchaser of a franchise) is generally legally independent of the **franchisor** (the seller of the franchise). At the same time, the franchisee is economically dependent on the franchisor's integrated business system. In other words, a franchisee can operate as an independent businessperson but still obtain the advantages of a regional or national organization.

Today, franchising companies and their franchisees account for a significant portion of all retail sales in this country. Well-known franchises include McDonald's, 7-Eleven, and Holiday Inn. Franchising has also become a popular way for businesses to expand their operations internationally without violating the legal restrictions that many nations impose on foreign ownership of businesses.

## 2–3a Types of Franchises

Many different kinds of businesses sell franchises, and numerous types of franchises are available. Generally, though, franchises fall into one of three classifications: distributorships, chain-style business operations, and manufacturing arrangements.

**Distributorship** In a *distributorship,* a manufacturer (the franchisor) licenses a dealer (the franchisee) to sell its product. Often, a distributorship covers an exclusive territory. Automobile dealerships and beer distributorships are common examples.

■ **EXAMPLE 2.3** Black Bear Beer Company distributes its brands of beer through a network of authorized wholesale distributors, each with an assigned territory. Marik signs a distributorship contract for the area from Gainesville to Ocala, Florida. If the contract states that Marik is the exclusive distributor in that area, then no other franchisee may distribute Black Bear beer in that region. ■

**Chain-Style Business Operation** In a *chain-style business operation,* a franchise operates under a franchisor's trade name and is identified as a member of a select group of dealers that engage in the franchisor's business. The franchisee is generally required to follow standardized or prescribed methods of operation. Often, the franchisor insists that the franchisee maintain certain standards of performance.

In addition, the franchisee may be required to obtain materials and supplies exclusively from the franchisor. Chipotle Mexican Grill and most other fast-food chains are examples of this type of franchise. Chain-style franchises are also common in service-related businesses, including real estate brokerage firms, such as Century 21, and tax-preparing services, such as H&R Block, Inc.

**Manufacturing Arrangement** In a *manufacturing,* or *processing-plant, arrangement,* the franchisor transmits to the franchisee the essential ingredients or formula to make a particular product. The franchisee then markets the product either at wholesale or at retail in accordance with the franchisor's standards. Examples of this type of franchise include Pepsi-Cola and other soft-drink bottling companies.

## 2–3b Laws Governing Franchising

Because a franchise relationship is primarily a contractual relationship, it is governed by contract law. If the franchise exists primarily for the sale of products manufactured by the franchisor, the law governing sales contracts as expressed in Article 2 of the Uniform Commercial Code applies.

Additionally, the federal government and most states have enacted laws governing certain aspects of franchising. Generally, these laws are designed to protect prospective franchisees from dishonest franchisors and to prevent franchisors from terminating franchises without good cause.

**Federal Regulation of Franchises** The federal government regulates franchising through laws that apply to specific industries and through the Franchise Rule, created by the Federal Trade Commission (FTC).

**Industry-Specific Standards.** Congress has enacted laws that protect franchisees in certain industries, such as automobile dealerships and service stations. These laws protect the franchisee from unreasonable demands and bad faith terminations of the franchise by the franchisor.

An automobile manufacturer–franchisor cannot make unreasonable demands of dealer-franchisees or set unrealistically high sales quotas. If an automobile manufacturer–franchisor terminates a franchise because of a dealer-franchisee's failure to comply with unreasonable demands, the manufacturer may be liable for damages.[2]

---

2. Automobile Dealers' Franchise Act, also known as the Automobile Dealers' Day in Court Act, 15 U.S.C. Sections 1221 *et seq.*

Similarly, federal law prescribes the conditions under which a franchisor of service stations can terminate the franchise.[3] In addition, federal antitrust laws sometimes apply in specified circumstances to prohibit certain types of anticompetitive agreements.

**The Franchise Rule.** The FTC's Franchise Rule requires franchisors to disclose certain material facts that a prospective franchisee needs in order to make an informed decision concerning the purchase of a franchise.[4] Those who violate the Franchise Rule are subject to substantial civil penalties, and the FTC can sue on behalf of injured parties to recover damages.

The rule requires the franchisor to make numerous written disclosures to prospective franchisees (see Exhibit 2–1). All representations made to a prospective franchisee must have a reasonable basis. For instance, if a franchisor provides projected earnings figures, the franchisor must indicate whether the figures are based on actual data or hypothetical examples. If a franchisor makes sales or earnings projections based on actual data for a specific franchise location, the franchisor must disclose the number and percentage of its existing franchises that have achieved this result.

**State Regulation of Franchising** State legislation varies but often is aimed at protecting franchisees from unfair practices and bad faith terminations by franchisors.

**State Disclosures.** A number of states have laws similar to the federal rules that require franchisors to provide presale disclosures to prospective franchisees.[5] Many state laws also require that a disclosure document (known as the Franchise Disclosure Document, or FDD) be registered or filed with a state official. State laws may also require that a franchisor submit advertising aimed at prospective franchisees to the state for approval.

To protect franchisees, a state law might require the disclosure of information such as the actual costs of operation, recurring expenses, and profits earned, along with facts substantiating these figures. State deceptive trade

---

**3.** Petroleum Marketing Practices Act (PMPA), 15 U.S.C. Sections 2801 *et seq.*
**4.** 16 C.F.R. Section 436.1.

**5.** These states include California, Florida, Hawaii, Illinois, Indiana, Maryland, Michigan, Minnesota, New York, North Dakota, Oregon, Rhode Island, South Dakota, Texas, Utah, Virginia, Washington, and Wisconsin.

**EXHIBIT 2–1**  The FTC's Franchise Rule Requirements

| REQUIREMENT | EXPLANATION |
| --- | --- |
| **Written (or Electronic) Disclosures** | The franchisor must make numerous disclosures, such as the range of goods and services included and the value and estimated profitability of the franchise. Disclosures can be delivered on paper or electronically. Prospective franchisees must be able to download or save any electronic disclosure documents. |
| **Reasonable Basis for Any Representations** | To prevent deception, all representations made to a prospective franchisee must have a reasonable basis at the time they are made. |
| **Projected Earnings Figures** | If a franchisor provides projected earnings figures, the franchisor must indicate whether the figures are based on actual data or hypothetical examples. The Franchise Rule does not require franchisors to provide potential earnings figures, however. |
| **Actual Data** | If a franchisor makes sales or earnings projections based on actual data for a specific franchise location, the franchisor must disclose the number and percentage of its existing franchises that have achieved this result. |
| **Explanation of Terms** | Franchisors are required to explain termination, cancellation, and renewal provisions of the franchise contract to potential franchisees before the agreement is signed. |

practices acts may also apply and prohibit certain types of actions by franchisors.

**May Require Good Cause to Terminate the Franchise.** To prevent arbitrary or bad faith terminations, a state law may prohibit termination without "good cause" or require that certain procedures be followed in terminating a franchise. ■ **CASE IN POINT 2.4** FMS, Inc., entered into a franchise agreement with Samsung Construction Equipment North America to become an authorized dealership selling Samsung construction equipment. Samsung then sold its equipment business to Volvo Construction Equipment North America, Inc., which was to continue selling Samsung brand equipment.

Later, Volvo rebranded the construction equipment under its own name and canceled FMS's franchise. FMS sued, claiming that Volvo had terminated the franchise without "good cause" in violation of state law. Because Volvo was no longer manufacturing the Samsung brand equipment, the court found that Volvo had good cause to terminate FMS's franchise. If Volvo had continued making the Samsung equipment, though, it could not have terminated the franchise.[6] ■

## 2–3c The Franchise Contract

The franchise relationship is defined by the contract between the franchisor and the franchisee. The franchise contract specifies the terms and conditions of the franchise and spells out the rights and duties of the franchisor and the franchisee. If either party fails to perform its contractual duties, that party may be subject to a lawsuit for breach of contract. Furthermore, if a franchisee is induced to enter into a franchise contract by the franchisor's fraudulent misrepresentation, the franchisor may be liable for damages. Generally, statutes and the case law governing franchising tend to emphasize the importance of good faith and fair dealing in franchise relationships.

Because each type of franchise relationship has its own characteristics, franchise contracts tend to differ. Nonetheless, certain major issues typically are addressed in a franchise contract. We look at some of them next.

**Payment for the Franchise** The franchisee ordinarily pays an initial fee or lump-sum price for the franchise license (the privilege of being granted a franchise). This fee is separate from the various products that the franchisee purchases from or through the franchisor. The franchise agreement may also require the franchisee to pay a

percentage of the franchisor's advertising costs and certain administrative expenses.

In some industries, the franchisor relies heavily on the initial sale of the franchise for realizing a profit. In other industries, the continued dealing between the parties brings profit to both. Generally, the franchisor receives a stated percentage of the annual (or monthly) sales or volume of business done by the franchisee.

**Business Premises** The franchise agreement may specify whether the premises for the business must be leased or purchased outright. Sometimes, a building must be constructed to meet the terms of the agreement. The agreement will specify whether the franchisor or the franchisee is responsible for supplying equipment and furnishings for the premises.

**Location of the Franchise** Typically, the franchisor determines the territory to be served. Some franchise contracts give the franchisee exclusive rights, or "territorial rights," to a certain geographic area. Other franchise contracts, while defining the territory allotted to a particular franchise, either specifically state that the franchise is nonexclusive or are silent on the issue of territorial rights.

Many franchise disputes arise over territorial rights, and the implied covenant of good faith and fair dealing often comes into play in this area of franchising. If the contract does not grant exclusive territorial rights to the franchisee and the franchisor allows a competing franchise to be established nearby, the franchisee may suffer significant lost profits. In this situation, a court may hold that the franchisor breached an implied covenant of good faith and fair dealing.

**Business Organization** The franchisor may require that the business use a particular organizational form and capital structure. The franchise agreement may also set out standards such as sales quotas and record-keeping requirements. Additionally, a franchisor may retain stringent control over the training of personnel involved in the operation and over administrative aspects of the business.

**Quality Control by the Franchisor** The day-to-day operation of the franchise business normally is left up to the franchisee. Nonetheless, the franchise agreement may specify that the franchisor will provide some degree of supervision and control so that it can protect the franchise's name and reputation.

**Means of Control.** When the franchise prepares a product, such as food, or provides a service, such as motel

---

6. *FMS, Inc. v. Volvo Construction Equipment North America, Inc.*, 557 F.3d 758 (7th Cir. 2009).

accommodations, the contract often states that the franchisor will establish certain standards for the facility. Typically, the contract will state that the franchisor is permitted to make periodic inspections to ensure that the standards are being maintained.

As a means of controlling quality, franchise agreements also typically limit the franchisee's ability to sell the franchise to another party. ■ **EXAMPLE 2.5**  Mark Keller, Inc., an authorized Jaguar franchise, contracts to sell its dealership to Henrique Autos West. A Jaguar franchise generally cannot be sold without Jaguar Cars' permission. Prospective franchisees must meet Jaguar's customer satisfaction standards. If Henrique Autos fails to meet those standards, Jaguar can refuse to allow the sale and can terminate the franchise. ■

**Degree of Control.**  As a general rule, the validity of a provision permitting the franchisor to establish and enforce certain quality standards is unquestioned. The franchisor has a legitimate interest in maintaining the quality of the product or service to protect its name and reputation.

If a franchisor exercises too much control over the operations of its franchisees, however, the franchisor risks potential liability. A franchisor may occasionally be held liable—under the doctrine of *respondeat superior*—for the tortious acts of the franchisees' employees.

■ **EXAMPLE 2.6**  The National Labor Relations Board (NLRB) received 180 employee complaints that certain McDonald's restaurants had engaged in unfair labor practices. Employees alleged that the restaurants had fired or penalized workers for participating in protests over wages and working conditions. Investigators found that at least some of the complaints had merit. The NLRB ruled that McDonald's USA, LLC, could be held jointly liable along with several of its franchisees for labor and wage violations. The NLRB reasoned that McDonald's exerts sufficient control over its franchisees to be found liable for the franchisees' employment law violations. ■

**Pricing Arrangements**  Franchises provide the franchisor with an outlet for the firm's goods and services. Depending on the nature of the business, the franchisor may require the franchisee to purchase certain supplies from the franchisor at an established price.[7] A franchisor cannot, however, set the prices at which the franchisee will resell the goods. Such price setting may be a violation of state or federal antitrust laws, or both. A franchisor can suggest retail prices but cannot mandate them.

## 2–4 Franchise Termination

The duration of the franchise is a matter to be determined between the parties. Sometimes, a franchise relationship starts with a short trial period, such as a year, so that the franchisee and the franchisor can determine whether they want to stay in business with one another. At other times, the duration of the franchise contract correlates with the term of the lease for the business premises, and both are renewable at the end of that period.

### 2–4a Grounds for Termination Set by Franchise Contract

Usually, the franchise agreement specifies that termination must be "for cause" and then defines the grounds for termination. Cause might include, for instance, the death or disability of the franchisee, insolvency of the franchisee, breach of the franchise agreement, or failure to meet specified sales quotas.

In the following case, franchise agreements provided that the franchisor could terminate a franchise for good cause.

---

7. Although a franchisor can require franchisees to purchase supplies from it, requiring a franchisee to purchase exclusively from the franchisor may violate federal antitrust laws.

**Case 2.2**

## Century 21 Real Estate, LLC v. All Professional Realty, Inc.
United States Court of Appeals, Ninth Circuit, 600 Fed.Appx. 502 (2015).

**Background and Facts**  Carol and Steve Wright owned All Professional Realty, Inc., and All Professional Hawaii Realty, Inc. The Wrights' companies signed four franchise agreements with Century 21 Real Estate, LLC, to operate offices in Sacramento and Folsom, California, and Honolulu, Hawaii, under the name "Century 21 All Professional." The agreements required All Professional to pay royalty and advertising fees. They also permitted Century 21 to terminate the agreements for good cause, including the franchisee's failure to operate at an approved location.

Case 2.2 Continued

All Professional signed a note for $75,000 payable to Century 21 and agreed to make annual payments on the note. Four years later, All Professional stopped remitting the fees and making payments on the note, and it closed the Folsom office. Century 21 terminated the franchise agreements. The Wrights and All Professional filed a suit against Century 21, alleging breach of contract. Century 21 filed a counterclaim for breach. A federal district court issued a summary judgment in the franchisor's favor. All Professional appealed.

### In the Language of the Court

*MEMORANDUM.*

\* \* \* \*

The district court did not err in granting summary judgment to Century 21 on the parties' cross-claims for breach of contract. *A \* \* \* breach of contract claim requires a contract, breach of that contract, damages and that Century 21 performed its obligations under the contract.* [Emphasis added.]

The Wrights' companies breached the franchise agreements by not paying required fees, not paying principal due on the note and by abandoning the Folsom office.

\* \* \* \*

\* \* \* It is undisputed that Century 21 provided the Wrights' companies with access to the Century 21 system defined in the franchise agreements [as "policies, procedures, and techniques designed to enable offices to compete more effectively in the real estate sales market" and "common use and promotion of certain Marks, copyrights, trade secrets, centralized advertising programs, recruiting programs, referral programs and sales management training programs."] Moreover, the franchise agreements specifically stated that the success of the franchise depended on the Wrights' efforts and that Century 21 made no guarantee or warranty that the Wrights would be successful. The Wrights have not created a triable issue [one necessitating a trial] that Century 21 failed to perform on the contract and that any such failure excused payment on the note.

Century 21 did not breach the agreements by preventing the Wrights from curing their defaults. Although the Wrights now claim they have the funds to pay Century 21, they testified repeatedly before the district court that they did not have the financial ability to cure their defaults.

Century 21 did not terminate the franchise agreements in bad faith. \* \* \* Century 21 had a legal right to terminate all four franchise agreements.

**Decision and Remedy** *The U.S. Court of Appeals for the Ninth Circuit affirmed the lower court's judgment in Century 21's favor. Century 21 did not breach the franchise agreements. All Professional did. The Wrights' nonpayment of the fees and the note, and the abandonment of one of the franchisee's offices, constituted a material breach of the contract. These actions provided Century 21 with legitimate grounds for termination of the franchise agreement.*

**Critical Thinking**
- **Economic** *What is the most likely reason that All Professional stopped paying the franchise fees and making note payments, in addition to closing one of its offices? Why is this an insufficient justification for breach of the franchisee's agreements with Century 21?*

---

**Notice Requirements** Most franchise contracts provide that notice of termination must be given. If no set time for termination is specified, then a reasonable time, with notice, is implied. A franchisee must be given reasonable time to wind up the business—that is, to do the accounting and return the copyright or trademark or any other property of the franchisor.

**Opportunity to Cure a Breach** A franchise agreement may allow the franchisee to attempt to cure an ordinary, curable breach within a certain time after notice so as to postpone, or even avoid, termination. Even when a contract contains a notice-and-cure provision, however, a franchisee's breach of the duty of honesty and fidelity may be enough to allow the franchisor to terminate the franchise.

■ **CASE IN POINT 2.7** Milind and Minaxi Upadhyaya entered into a franchise contract with 7-Eleven, Inc., to operate a store in Pennsylvania. The contract included a notice-and-cure provision. Under 7-Eleven's usual contract, franchisees lease the store and equipment, and receive a license to use 7-Eleven's trademarks and other intellectual property. 7-Eleven receives a percentage of the store's gross profit (net sales less the cost of goods sold).

A 7-Eleven manager noticed a high rate of certain questionable transactions at the Upadhyayas' store and began investigating. The investigation continued for nearly two years and revealed that the store had been misreporting its sales so as to conceal sales proceeds from 7-Eleven. Evidence indicated that nearly one-third of the store's sales transactions had not been properly recorded. 7-Eleven sent a "non-curable" notice of material breach and termination of the franchise to the Upadhyayas. The franchisees argued that they had not been given an opportunity to cure the breach. The court found there was sufficient evidence of fraud to warrant immediate termination without an opportunity to cure.[8] ∎

## 2–4b Wrongful Termination

Because a franchisor's termination of a franchise often has adverse consequences for the franchisee, much franchise litigation involves claims of wrongful termination. Generally, the termination provisions of contracts are more favorable to the franchisor than to the franchisee. This means that the franchisee, who normally invests substantial time and financial resources in making the franchise operation successful, may receive little or nothing for the business on termination. The franchisor owns the trademark and hence the business.

It is in this area that statutory and case law become important. The federal and state laws discussed earlier

---

8. *7-Eleven, Inc. v. Upadhyaya*, 926 F.Supp.2d 614 (E.D.Penn. 2013).

attempt, among other things, to protect franchisees from the arbitrary or unfair termination of their franchises by the franchisors.

## 2–4c The Importance of Good Faith and Fair Dealing

Generally, both statutory law and case law emphasize the importance of good faith and fair dealing in terminating a franchise relationship. In determining whether a franchisor has acted in good faith when terminating a franchise agreement, the courts usually try to balance the rights of both parties.

∎ **EXAMPLE 2.8**  A car dealership enters into lending agreements, commonly known as floor plan financing, to enable it to buy new vehicles from General Motors Corporation (GM). At first, the dealership obtains floor plan financing from GM, but then it switches to Main Street Bank. Later, the bank declines to provide further financing, and the dealership is unable to obtain the financing from any other lender, including GM. The franchise contract gives GM a right to terminate a dealership for failure to maintain a line of credit. Therefore, GM can terminate the franchise because of the dealership's inability to obtain floor plan financing. ∎

If a court perceives that a franchisor has arbitrarily or unfairly terminated a franchise, the franchisee will be provided with a remedy for wrongful termination. A court will be less likely to consider a termination wrongful if the franchisor's decision was made in the normal course of business and reasonable notice was given.

The importance of good faith and fair dealing in a franchise relationship is underscored by the consequences of the franchisor's acts in the following case.

## Spotlight on Holiday Inns

## Case 2.3 Holiday Inn Franchising, Inc. v. Hotel Associates, Inc.

Court of Appeals of Arkansas, 2011 Ark.App. 147, 382 S.W.3d 6 (2011).

**Background and Facts**  Buddy House was in the construction business in Arkansas and Texas. For decades, he collaborated on projects with Holiday Inn Franchising, Inc. Their relationship was characterized by good faith—many projects were undertaken without written contracts. At Holiday Inn's request, House inspected a hotel in Wichita Falls, Texas, to estimate the cost of getting it into shape. Holiday Inn wanted House to renovate the hotel and operate it as a Holiday Inn. House estimated that recovering the cost of renovation would take him more than ten years, so he asked for a franchise term longer than Holiday Inn's usual ten years. Holiday Inn refused, but said that if the hotel was run "appropriately," the term would be extended at the end of ten years. House bought the hotel, renovated it, and operated it as Hotel Associates, Inc. (HAI), generating substantial profits. He refused offers to sell it for as much as $15 million.

Case 2.3 Continued

Before the ten years had passed, Greg Aden, a Holiday Inn executive, developed a plan to license a different local hotel as a Holiday Inn instead of renewing House's franchise license. Aden stood to earn a commission from licensing the other hotel. No one informed House of Aden's plan. When the time came, HAI applied for an extension of its franchise, and Holiday Inn asked for major renovations. HAI spent $3 million to comply with this request. Holiday Inn did not renew HAI's license, however, but instead granted a franchise to the other hotel. HAI sold its hotel for $5 million and filed a suit in an Arkansas state court against Holiday Inn, asserting fraud. The court awarded HAI compensatory and punitive damages. Holiday Inn appealed.

## In the Language of the Court

Raymond R. *ABRAMSON*, Judge.

* * * *

Generally, a mere failure to volunteer information does not constitute fraud. But *silence can amount to actionable fraud in some circumstances where the parties have a relation of trust or confidence, where there is inequality of condition and knowledge, or where there are other attendant circumstances.* [Emphasis added.]

In this case, substantial evidence supports the existence of a duty on Holiday Inn's part to disclose the Aden [plan] to HAI. Buddy House had a long-term relationship with Holiday Inn characterized by honesty, trust, and the free flow of pertinent information. He testified that [Holiday Inn's] assurances at the onset of licensure [the granting of the license] led him to believe that he would be relicensed after ten years if the hotel was operated appropriately. Yet, despite Holiday Inn's having provided such an assurance to House, it failed to apprise House of an internal business plan * * * that advocated licensure of another facility instead of the renewal of his license. *A duty of disclosure may exist where information is peculiarly within the knowledge of one party and is of such a nature that the other party is justified in assuming its nonexistence.* Given House's history with Holiday Inn and the assurance he received, we are convinced he was justified in assuming that no obstacles had arisen that jeopardized his relicensure. [Emphasis added.]

Holiday Inn asserts that it would have provided Buddy House with the Aden [plan] if he had asked for it. But, Holiday Inn cannot satisfactorily explain why House should have been charged with the responsibility of inquiring about a plan that he did not know existed. Moreover, several Holiday Inn personnel testified that Buddy House in fact should have been provided with the Aden plan. Aden himself stated that * * * House should have been given the plan. * * * In light of these circumstances, we see no ground for reversal on this aspect of HAI's cause of action for fraud.

**Decision and Remedy** *The state intermediate appellate court affirmed the lower court's judgment and its award of compensatory damages. The appellate court increased the amount of punitive damages, however, citing Holiday Inn's "degree of reprehensibility."*

**Critical Thinking**
- **Legal Environment** *Why should House and HAI have been advised of Holiday Inn's plan to grant a franchise to a different hotel in their territory?*
- **Economic** *A jury awarded HAI $12 million in punitive damages. The court reduced this award to $1 million, but the appellate court reinstated the original award. What is the purpose of punitive damages? Did Holiday Inn's conduct warrant this award? Explain.*

## Reviewing: Small Businesses and Franchises

Carlos Del Rey decided to open a Mexican fast-food restaurant and signed a franchise contract with a national chain called La Grande Enchilada. The contract required the franchisee to strictly follow the franchisor's operating manual and stated that failure to do so would be grounds for terminating the franchise contract. The manual set forth detailed operating procedures and safety standards, and provided that a La Grande Enchilada representative would inspect the restaurant monthly to ensure compliance.

Nine months after Del Rey began operating his restaurant, a spark from the grill ignited an oily towel in the kitchen. No one was injured, but by the time firefighters were able to put out the fire, the kitchen had sustained extensive damage. The cook told the fire department that the towel was "about two feet from the grill" when it caught fire. This was in compliance with the franchisor's manual that required towels be placed at least one foot from the grills. Nevertheless, the next day La Grande Enchilada notified Del Rey that his franchise would terminate in thirty days for failure to follow the prescribed safety procedures. Using the information presented in the chapter, answer the following questions.

1. What type of franchise was Del Rey's La Grande Enchilada restaurant?
2. If Del Rey operates the restaurant as a sole proprietorship, who bears the loss for the damaged kitchen? Explain.
3. Assume that Del Rey files a lawsuit against La Grande Enchilada, claiming that his franchise was wrongfully terminated. What is the main factor that a court would consider in determining whether the franchise was wrongfully terminated?
4. Would a court be likely to rule that La Grande Enchilada had good cause to terminate Del Rey's franchise in this situation? Why or why not?

**Debate This** . . .   *All franchisors should be required by law to provide a comprehensive estimate of the profitability of a prospective franchise based on the experiences of their existing franchisees.*

## Terms and Concepts

| | | |
|---|---|---|
| entrepreneur 20 | franchisee 25 | sole proprietorship 21 |
| franchise 25 | franchisor 25 | |

## Issue Spotters

1. Frank plans to open a sporting goods store and to hire Gogi and Hap. Frank will invest only his own funds. He expects that he will not make a profit for at least eighteen months and will make only a small profit in the three years after that. He hopes to expand eventually. Would a sole proprietorship be an appropriate form for Frank's business? Why or why not? (See *Sole Proprietorships*.)

2. Anchor Bottling Company and U.S. Beverages, Inc. (USB), enter into a franchise agreement that states the franchise may be terminated at any time "for cause." Anchor fails to meet USB's specified sales quota. Does this constitute "cause" for termination? Why or why not? (See *Franchise Termination*.)

• **Check your answers to the Issue Spotters against the answers provided in Appendix B at the end of this text.**

## Business Scenarios

**2–1. Franchising.** Maria, Pablo, and Vicky are recent college graduates who would like to go into business for themselves. They are considering purchasing a franchise. If they enter into a franchising arrangement, they would have the support of a large company that could answer any questions they might have. Also, a firm that has been in business for many years would be experienced in dealing with some of the problems that novice businesspersons might encounter. These and other attributes of franchises can lessen some of the risks of the marketplace. What other aspects of franchising—positive and negative—should Maria, Pablo, and Vicky consider before committing themselves to a particular franchise? (See *Franchises*.)

**2–2. Control of a Franchise.** National Foods, Inc., sells franchises to its fast-food restaurants, known as Chicky-D's. Under the franchise agreement, franchisees agree to hire and train employees strictly according to Chicky-D's standards. Chicky-D's regional supervisors are required to approve all job candidates before they are hired and all general policies affecting those employees. Chicky-D's reserves the right to terminate a franchise for violating the franchisor's rules. In practice, however, Chicky-D's regional supervisors routinely approve new employees and individual franchisees' policies. After several incidents of racist comments and conduct by Tim, a recently hired assistant manager at a Chicky-D's, Sharon, a counterperson at the restaurant, resigns. Sharon files a suit in a federal district court against National. National files a motion for summary judgment, arguing that it is not liable for harassment by franchise employees. Will the court grant National's motion? Why or why not? (See *Franchises*.)

# Business Case Problems

**2–3. Spotlight on McDonald's—Franchise Termination.** J.C., Inc., had a franchise agreement with McDonald's Corp to operate McDonald's restaurants in Lancaster, Ohio. The agreement required J.C. to make monthly payments of certain percentages of gross sales to McDonald's. If any payment was more than thirty days late, McDonald's had the right to terminate the franchise. The agreement also stated that even if McDonald's accepted a late payment, that would not "constitute a waiver of any subsequent breach." McDonald's sometimes accepted J.C.'s late payments, but when J.C. defaulted on the payment for July 2010, McDonald's gave notice of thirty days to comply or surrender possession of the restaurants. J.C. missed the deadline. McDonald's demanded that J.C. vacate the restaurants, but J.C. refused. McDonald's alleged that J.C. had violated the franchise agreement. J.C. claimed that McDonald's had breached the implied covenant of good faith and fair dealing. Which party should prevail and why? [*McDonald's Corp. v. C.B. Management Co.,* 13 F.Supp.2d 705 (N.D.Ill. 1998)] (See *Franchise Termination*.)

**2–4. Franchise Disclosure.** Peaberry Coffee, Inc., owned and operated about twenty company stores in the Denver area. The company began a franchise program and prepared a disclosure document as required by the Federal Trade Commission (FTC). Peaberry sold ten franchises, and each franchisee received a disclosure document. Later, when the franchises did not do well, the franchisees sued Peaberry, claiming that its FTC disclosure document had been fraudulent. Specifically, the franchisees claimed that Peaberry had not disclosed that most of the company stores were unprofitable and that its parent company had suffered significant financial losses over the years. In addition, the franchisees stated that Peaberry had included in the franchisees' information packets an article from the *Denver Business Journal* in which an executive had said that Peaberry was profitable. That statement had proved to be false. The FTC disclosure document had also contained an exculpatory clause that said the buyers should not rely on any material that was not in the franchise contract itself. Can a franchisor disclaim the relevance of the information it provides to franchisees? Why or why not? [*Colorado Coffee Bean, LLC v. Peaberry Coffee, Inc.,* 251 P.3d 9 (Colo.App. 2010)] (See *Franchises*.)

**2–5. The Franchise Contract.** Kubota Tractor Corp. makes farm, industrial, and outdoor equipment. Its franchise contracts allow Kubota to enter into dealership agreements with "others at any location." Kejzar Motors, Inc., is a Kubota dealer in Nacogdoches and Jasper, Texas. These two Kejzar stores operate as one dealership with two locations. Kubota granted a dealership to Michael Hammer in Lufkin, Texas, which lies between Kejzar's two store locations. Kejzar filed a suit in a Texas state court against Kubota. Kejzar asked for an injunction to prevent Kubota from locating a dealership in the same market area. Kejzar argued that the new location would cause it to suffer a significant loss of profits. Which party in a franchise relationship typically determines the territory served by a franchisee? Which legal principles come into play in this area? How do these concepts most likely apply in this case? Discuss. [*Kejzar Motors, Inc. v. Kubota Tractor Corp.,* 334 S.W.3d 351 (Tex.App.—Tyler 2011)] (See *Franchises*.)

**2–6. Business Case Problem with Sample Answer— Franchise Termination.** George Oshana and GTO Investments, Inc., operated a Mobil gas station franchise in Itasca, Illinois. In 2010, Oshana and GTO became involved in a rental dispute with Buchanan Energy, to which Mobil had assigned the lease for the gas station facility. In November 2011, Buchanan terminated the franchise because Oshana and GTO had failed to pay the rent. Oshana and GTO, however, alleged that they had been "ready, willing, and able to pay the rent" but that Buchanan had failed to accept their electronic fund transfer. Have Oshana and GTO stated a claim for wrongful termination of their franchise? Why or why not? [*Oshana v. Buchanan Energy,* 2012 WL 426921 (N.D.Ill. 2012)] (See *Franchise Termination*.)

- **For a sample answer to Problem 2–6, go to Appendix C at the end of this text.**

**2–7. Quality Control.** JTH Tax, Inc., doing business as Liberty Tax Service, provides tax preparation and related loan services through company-owned and franchised stores. Liberty's agreement with its franchisees reserved the right to control their ads. In operations manuals, Liberty provided step-by-step instructions, directions, and limitations regarding the franchisees' ads and retained the right to unilaterally modify the steps at any time. The California attorney general filed a suit in a California state court against Liberty, alleging that its franchisees had used misleading or deceptive ads regarding refund anticipation loans and e-refund checks. Can Liberty be held liable? Discuss. [*People v. JTH Tax, Inc.,* 212 Cal.App.4th 1219, 151 Cal.Rptr.3d 728 (1 Dist. 2013)] (See *Franchises.*)

**2–8. Quality Control.** The franchise agreement of Domino's Pizza, L.L.C., sets out operational standards, including safety requirements, for a franchisee to follow but provides that the franchisee is an independent contractor. Each franchisee is free to use its own means and methods. For example, Domino's does not know whether a franchisee's delivery drivers are complying with vehicle safety requirements. MAC Pizza Management, Inc., operates a Domino's franchise. A vehicle driven by Joshua Balka, a MAC delivery driver, hydroplaned due to a bald tire and wet pavement. It struck the vehicle of Devavaram and Ruth Christopher, killing Ruth and injuring Devavaram. Is Domino's liable for negligence? Explain. [*Domino's Pizza, L.L.C. v. Reddy,* 2015 WL 1247349 (Tex.App.—Beaumont 2015)] (See *Franchises.*)

**2–9. Franchise Termination.** Executive Home Care Franchising, LLC, sells in-home health-care franchises. Clint, Massare, and Greer Marshall entered into a franchise agreement with Executive Home Care. The agreement provided that the franchisees' failure to comply with the agreement's terms would likely cause irreparable harm to the franchisor, entitling it to an injunction. About two years later, the Marshalls gave up their franchise. They returned thirteen boxes of documents, stationery, operating manuals, marketing materials, and other items—everything in their possession that featured Executive Home Care trademarks. They quit operating out of the franchised location. They transferred the phone number back to the franchisor and informed their clients that they were no longer associated with Executive Home Care. They continued to engage in the home health-care business, however, under the

name "Well-Being Home Care Corp." Is Exccutive Home Care entitled to an injunction against the Marshalls and their new company? Discuss. [*Executive Home Care Franchising, LLC v. Marshall Health Corp.,* __ F.3d __, 2016 WL 703801 (3d Cir. 2016)] (See *Franchise Termination.*)

**2–10. A Question of Ethics—Sole Proprietorship.** *In August 2004, Ralph Vilardo contacted Travel Center, Inc., in Cincinnati, Ohio, to buy a trip to Florida in December for his family to celebrate his fiftieth wedding anniversary. Vilardo paid $6,900 to David*  *Sheets, the sole proprietor of Travel Center. Vilardo also paid $195 to Sheets for a separate trip to Florida in February 2005. Sheets assured Vilardo that everything was set, but in fact no arrangements were made. Later, two unauthorized charges for travel services totaling $1,182.35 appeared on Vilardo's credit-card statement. Vilardo filed a suit in an Ohio state court against Sheets and his business, alleging, among other things, fraud and violations of the state consumer protection law. Vilardo served Sheets and Travel Center with copies of the complaint, the summons, a request for admissions, and other documents filed with the court, including a motion for summary judgment. Each of these filings asked for a response within a certain time period. Sheets responded once on his own behalf with a denial of all of Vilardo's claims. Travel Center did not respond. [Vilardo v. Sheets, 2006 -Ohio- 3473 (12 Dist. 2006)] (See Sole Proprietorships.)*

**(a)** Almost four months after Vilardo filed his complaint, Sheets decided that he was unable to adequately represent himself and retained an attorney, who asked the court for more time. Should the court grant this request? Why or why not? Ultimately, what should the court rule?

**(b)** Sheets admitted that Travel Center, Inc., was a sole proprietorship. He also argued that liability might be imposed on his business but not on himself. How would you rule with respect to this argument? Why? Would there be anything unethical about allowing Sheets to avoid liability on this basis? Explain.

# Legal Reasoning Group Activity

**2–11. Franchise Termination.** Walid Elkhatib, an Arab American, bought a Dunkin' Donuts franchise in Illinois. Ten years later, Dunkin' Donuts began offering breakfast sandwiches with bacon, ham, or sausage through its franchises. Elkhatib refused to sell these items at his store on the ground that his religion forbade the handling of pork. Elkhatib then opened a second franchise, at which he also refused to sell pork products.

The next year, at both locations, Elkhatib began selling meatless sandwiches. He also opened a third franchise. When he proposed to relocate this franchise, Dunkin' Donuts refused to approve the new location. The company also informed him that it would not renew any of his franchise

agreements because he did not carry the full sandwich line. Elkhatib filed a lawsuit against Dunkin' Donuts. (See *Franchise Termination.*)

**(a)** The first group will argue on behalf of Elkhatib that Dunkin' Donuts wrongfully terminated his franchises.

**(b)** The second group will take the side of Dunkin' Donuts and justify its decision to terminate the franchises.

**(c)** The third group will assess whether Dunkin' Donuts acted in good faith in its relationship with Elkhatib. Consider whether Dunkin' Donuts should be required to accommodate Elkhatib's religious beliefs and allow him not to serve pork in these three locations.

## CHAPTER 3

# All Forms of Partnerships

Historically, two or more persons entering into business together have most commonly organized their business as a partnership or a corporation. A *partnership* arises from an agreement, express or implied, between two or more persons to carry on a business for a profit. Partners are co-owners of the business and have joint control over its operation and the right to share in its profits.

In this chapter, we examine several forms of partnership. These include ordinary partnerships, or *general partnerships*, and special forms of partnerships known as *limited partnerships* and *limited liability partnerships*.

Although general partnerships are less common today than in the past, the limited liability forms of partnership are quite prevalent. Accountants, attorneys, and architects frequently organize as limited liability partnerships. DLA Piper, the second-largest U.S. law firm, for instance, is structured as two limited liability partnerships—DLA Piper U.S., LLP, and DLA Piper International, LLP.

## 3-1 Basic Partnership Concepts

Partnerships are governed both by common law concepts—in particular, those relating to agency—and by statutory law. As in so many other areas of business law, the National Conference of Commissioners on Uniform State Laws has drafted uniform laws for partnerships, and these have been widely adopted by the states.

### 3-1a Agency Concepts and Partnership Law

When two or more persons agree to do business as partners, they enter into a special relationship with one another. To an extent, their relationship is similar to an agency relationship because each partner is deemed to be the agent of the other partners and of the partnership. Thus, agency concepts apply—specifically, the imputation of knowledge of, and responsibility for, acts carried out within the scope of the partnership relationship. In their relationships with one another, partners, like agents, are bound by fiduciary ties.

In one important way, however, partnership law differs from agency law. The partners in a partnership agree to commit funds or other assets, labor, and skills to the business with the understanding that profits and losses will be shared. Thus, each partner has an *ownership interest* in the firm. In a nonpartnership agency relationship, the agent usually does not have an ownership interest in the business and is not obligated to bear a portion of ordinary business losses.

### 3-1b The Uniform Partnership Act

The Uniform Partnership Act (UPA) governs the operation of partnerships *in the absence of express agreement* and has done much to reduce controversies in the law relating to partnerships. A majority of the states have enacted the most recent version of the UPA (introduced in 1997 and last amended in 2013).

### 3-1c Definition of a Partnership

The UPA defines a **partnership** as "an association of two or more persons to carry on as co-owners a business for profit" [UPA 101(6)]. Note that the UPA's definition of *person* includes corporations, so a corporation can be a partner in a partnership [UPA 101(10)]. The *intent* to associate is a key element of a partnership, and one cannot join a partnership unless all other partners consent [UPA 401(i)].

## 3–1d Essential Elements of a Partnership

Conflicts sometimes arise over whether a business enterprise is a legal partnership, especially when there is no formal, written partnership agreement. To determine whether a partnership exists, courts usually look for the following three essential elements, which are implicit in the UPA's definition:

1. A sharing of profits or losses.
2. A joint ownership of the business.
3. An equal right to be involved in the management of the business.

If the evidence in a particular case is insufficient to establish all three factors, the UPA provides a set of guidelines to be used.

**The Sharing of Profits and Losses** The sharing of both profits and losses from a business creates a presumption that a partnership exists. ■ **EXAMPLE 3.1** Syd and Drake start a business that sells fruit smoothies near a college campus. They open a joint bank account, from which they pay for supplies and expenses, and they share the proceeds (and losses) that the smoothie stand generates. If a conflict arises as to their business relationship, a court will assume that a partnership exists unless the parties prove otherwise. ■

A court will not presume that a partnership exists, however, if shared profits were received as payment of any of the following [UPA 202(c)(3)]:

1. A debt by installments or interest on a loan.
2. Wages of an employee or for the services of an independent contractor.
3. Rent to a landlord.
4. An annuity to a surviving spouse or representative of a deceased partner.
5. A sale of the **goodwill** (the valuable reputation of a business viewed as an intangible asset) of a business or property.

■ **EXAMPLE 3.2** A debtor, Mason Snopel, owes a creditor, Alice Burns, $5,000 on an unsecured debt. They agree that Mason will pay 10 percent of his monthly business profits to Alice until the loan with interest has been repaid. Although Mason and Alice are sharing profits from the business, they are not presumed to be partners. ■

**Joint Property Ownership** Joint ownership of property does not in and of itself create a partnership [UPA 202(c)(1) and (2)]. The parties' intentions are key. ■ **EXAMPLE 3.3** Chiang and Burke jointly own farmland and lease it to a farmer for a share of the profits from the farming operation in lieu of fixed rental payments. This arrangement normally would not make Chiang, Burke, and the farmer partners. ■

## 3–1e Entity versus Aggregate

At common law, a partnership was treated only as an aggregate of individuals and never as a separate legal entity. Thus, at common law a lawsuit could never be brought by or against the firm in its own name. Each individual partner had to sue or be sued.

Today, in contrast, a majority of the states follow the UPA and treat a partnership as an entity for most purposes. For instance, a partnership usually can sue or be sued, collect judgments, and have all accounting performed in the name of the partnership entity [UPA 201, 307(a)].

As an entity, a partnership may hold the title to real or personal property in its name rather than in the names of the individual partners. Additionally, federal procedural laws permit the partnership to be treated as an entity in suits in federal courts and bankruptcy proceedings.

## 3–1f Tax Treatment of Partnerships

Modern law does treat a partnership as an aggregate of the individual partners rather than a separate legal entity in one situation—for federal income tax purposes. The partnership is a pass-through entity and not a taxpaying entity. A **pass-through entity** is a business entity that has no tax liability. The entity's income is passed through to the owners, who pay income taxes on it.

Thus, the income or losses the partnership incurs are "passed through" the entity framework and attributed to the partners on their individual tax returns. The partnership itself pays no taxes and is responsible only for filing an **information return** with the Internal Revenue Service.

A partner's profit from the partnership (whether distributed or not) is taxed as individual income to the individual partner. Similarly, partners can deduct a share of the partnership's losses on their individual tax returns (in proportion to their partnership interests).

## 3–2 Formation and Operation

A partnership is a voluntary association of individuals. As such, it is formed by the agreement of the partners.

## 3–2a The Partnership Agreement

As a general rule, agreements to form a partnership can be *oral, written,* or *implied by conduct.* Some partnership agreements, however, such as one authorizing partners to transfer interests in real property, must be in writing to be legally enforceable.

A partnership agreement, also known as **articles of partnership,** can include almost any terms that the parties wish, unless they are illegal or contrary to public policy or statute [UPA 103]. The provisions commonly included in a partnership agreement are listed in Exhibit 3–1.

The rights and duties of partners are governed largely by the specific terms of their partnership agreement. In the absence of provisions to the contrary in the partnership agreement, the law imposes certain rights and duties, as discussed in the following subsections. The character and nature of the partnership business generally influence the application of these rights and duties.

## 3–2b Duration of the Partnership

The partnership agreement can specify the duration of the partnership by stating that it will continue until a designated date or until the completion of a particular project. This is called a *partnership for a term.* Generally, withdrawing from a partnership for a term prematurely (before the expiration date) constitutes a breach of the agreement, and the responsible partner can be held liable for any resulting losses [UPA 602(b)(2)]. If no fixed duration is specified, the partnership is a *partnership at will.* A partnership at will can be dissolved at any time without liability.

## 3–2c Partnership by Estoppel

When a third person has reasonably and detrimentally relied on the representation that a nonpartner was part of a partnership, a court may conclude that a **partnership by estoppel** exists.

**EXHIBIT 3–1** Provisions Commonly Included in a Partnership Agreement

| | |
|---|---|
| **Basic Structure** | • Name of the partnership and the names of the partners.<br>• Location of the business and the state law under which the partnership is organized.<br>• Purpose and duration of the partnership. |
| **Capital Contributions** | • Amount of capital that each partner is contributing.<br>• The agreed-on value of any real or personal property that is contributed instead of cash.<br>• How losses and gains on contributed capital will be allocated, and whether contributions will earn interest. |
| **Sharing of Profits and Losses** | • Percentage of the profits and losses of the business that each partner will receive.<br>• When distributions of profit will be made and how net profit will be calculated. |
| **Management and Control** | • How management responsibilities will be divided among the partners.<br>• Name(s) of the managing partner or partners, and whether other partners have voting rights. |
| **Dissociation and Dissolution** | • Events that will cause the dissociation of a partner or dissolve the firm, such as the retirement, death, or incapacity of any partner.<br>• How partnership property will be valued and apportioned on dissociation and dissolution.<br>• Whether an arbitrator will determine the value of partnership property on dissociation and dissolution and whether that determination will be binding. |

**Liability Imposed** A partnership by estoppel may arise when a person who is not a partner holds himself or herself out as a partner and makes representations that third parties rely on. In this situation, a court may impose liability—but not partnership rights—on the alleged partner.

**Nonpartner as Agent** A partnership by estoppel may also be imposed when a partner represents, expressly or impliedly, that a nonpartner is a member of the firm. In this situation, the nonpartner may be regarded as an agent whose acts are binding on the partnership [UPA 308].

■ **CASE IN POINT 3.4** Jackson Paper Manufacturing Company made paper used by Stonewall Packaging, LLC. Jackson and Stonewall had officers and directors in common, and they shared employees, property, and equipment. In reliance on Jackson's business reputation, Best Cartage, Inc., agreed to provide transportation services for Stonewall and bought thirty-seven tractor-trailers to use in fulfilling the contract. Best provided the services until Stonewall terminated the agreement.

Best filed a suit for breach of contract against Stonewall and Jackson, seeking $500,678 in unpaid invoices and consequential damages of $1,315,336 for the tractor-trailers it had purchased. Best argued that Stonewall and Jackson had a partnership by estoppel. The court agreed, finding that "defendants combined labor, skills, and property to advance their alleged business partnership." Jackson had negotiated the agreement on Stonewall's behalf. Jackson also had bought real estate, equipment, and general supplies for Stonewall with no expectation that Stonewall would repay these expenditures. This was sufficient to prove a partnership by estoppel.[1] ■

## 3–2d Rights of Partners

The rights of partners in a partnership relate to the following areas: management, interest in the partnership, compensation, inspection of books, accounting, and property.

**Management Rights** In a general partnership, all partners have equal rights in managing the partnership [UPA 401(f)]. Unless the partners agree otherwise, each partner has one vote in management matters *regardless of the proportional size of his or her interest in the firm*. In a large partnership, partners often agree to delegate daily management responsibilities to a management committee made up of one or more of the partners.

The majority rule controls decisions on ordinary matters connected with partnership business, unless otherwise specified in the agreement. Decisions that significantly change the nature of the partnership or that are outside the ordinary course of the partnership business, however, require the *unanimous* consent of the partners [UPA 301(2), 401(i), 401(j)]. For instance, unanimous consent is likely required for a partnership to admit new partners, to amend the partnership agreement, or to enter a new line of business.

**Interest in the Partnership** Each partner is entitled to the proportion of business profits and losses that is specified in the partnership agreement. If the agreement does not apportion profits (indicate how the profits will be shared), the UPA provides that profits will be shared equally. If the agreement does not apportion losses, losses will be shared in the same ratio as profits [UPA 401(b)].

■ **EXAMPLE 3.5** The partnership agreement between Rick and Brett provides for capital contributions of $60,000 from Rick and $40,000 from Brett. If the agreement is silent as to how Rick and Brett will share profits or losses, they will share both profits and losses equally.

In contrast, if the agreement provides for profits to be shared in the same ratio as capital contributions, 60 percent of the profits will go to Rick, and 40 percent will go to Brett. Unless the agreement provides otherwise, losses will be shared in the same ratio as profits. ■

**Compensation** Devoting time, skill, and energy to partnership business is a partner's duty and generally is not a compensable service. Rather, as mentioned, a partner's income from the partnership takes the form of a distribution of profits according to the partner's share in the business.

Partners can, of course, agree otherwise. For instance, the managing partner of a law firm often receives a salary—in addition to her or his share of profits—for performing special administrative or managerial duties.

**Inspection of the Books** Partnership books and records must be kept accessible to all partners. Each partner has the right to receive full and complete information concerning the conduct of all aspects of partnership business [UPA 403]. Partners have a duty to provide the information to the firm, which has a duty to preserve it and to keep accurate records.

The partnership books must be kept at the firm's principal business office (unless the partners agree otherwise). Every partner is entitled to inspect all books and records on demand and can make copies of the materials. The

---

1. *Best Cartage, Inc. v. Stonewall Packaging, LLC*, 727 S.E.2d 291 (N.C.App. 2012).

personal representative of a deceased partner's estate has the same right of access to partnership books and records that the decedent would have had [UPA 403].

### Accounting of Partnership Assets or Profits

An accounting of partnership assets or profits is required to determine the value of each partner's share in the partnership. An accounting can be performed voluntarily, or it can be compelled by court order. Under UPA 405(b), a partner has the right to bring an action for an accounting during the term of the partnership, as well as on the partnership's dissolution.

### Property Rights

Property acquired *by* a partnership is the property of the partnership and not of the partners individually [UPA 203]. Partnership property includes all property that was originally contributed to the partnership and anything later purchased by the partnership or in the partnership's name (except in rare circumstances) [UPA 204].

A partner may use or possess partnership property only on behalf of the partnership [UPA 401(g)]. A partner is *not* a co-owner of partnership property and has no right to sell, mortgage, or transfer partnership property to another [UPA 501].[2]

Because partnership property is owned by the partnership and not by the individual partners, the property cannot be used to satisfy the personal debts of individual partners. A partner's creditor, however, can petition a court for a **charging order** to attach the partner's *interest* in the partnership to satisfy the partner's obligation [UPA 502]. A partner's interest in the partnership includes her or his proportionate share of any profits that are distributed. A partner can also assign her or his right to receive a share of the partnership profits to another to satisfy a debt.

## 3–2e  Duties and Liabilities of Partners

The duties and liabilities of partners are derived from agency law. Each partner is an agent of every other partner and acts as both a principal and an agent in any business transaction within the scope of the partnership agreement.

Each partner is also a general agent of the partnership in carrying out the usual business of the firm "or business of the kind carried on by the partnership" [UPA 301(1)]. Thus, every act of a partner concerning partnership business and "business of the kind" and every contract signed in the partnership's name bind the firm.

### Fiduciary Duties

The fiduciary duties that a partner owes to the partnership and to the other partners are the duty of care and the duty of loyalty [UPA 404(a)]. Under the UPA, a partner's *duty of care* is limited to refraining from "grossly negligent or reckless conduct, intentional misconduct, or a knowing violation of law" [UPA 404(c)].[3] A partner is not liable to the partnership for simple negligence or honest errors in judgment in conducting partnership business.

The *duty of loyalty* requires a partner to account to the partnership for "any property, profit, or benefit" derived by the partner in the conduct of the partnership's business or from the use of its property. A partner must also refrain from competing with the partnership in business or dealing with the firm as an adverse party [UPA 404(b)].

The duty of loyalty can be breached by self-dealing, misusing partnership property, disclosing trade secrets, or usurping a partnership business opportunity. The following case is a classic example.

---

2. Under the previous version of the UPA, partners were *tenants in partnership*. This meant that every partner was a co-owner with all other partners of the partnership property. The current UPA does not recognize this concept.

3. The previous version of the UPA touched only briefly on the duty of loyalty and left the details of the partners' fiduciary duties to be developed under the law of agency.

---

**Classic Case 3.1**

## Meinhard v. Salmon

Court of Appeals of New York, 249 N.Y. 458, 164 N.E. 545 (1928).

**Background and Facts**  Walter Salmon negotiated a twenty-year lease for the Hotel Bristol in New York City. To pay for the conversion of the building into shops and offices, Salmon entered into an agreement with Morton Meinhard to assume half of the cost. They agreed to share the profits and losses from the joint venture. (A *joint venture* is similar to a partnership but typically is created for a single project.) Salmon was to have the sole power to manage the building, however.

Less than four months before the end of the lease term, the building's owner, Elbridge Gerry, approached Salmon about a project to raze the converted structure, clear five adjacent lots, and

Case 3.1 Continues

**Case 3.1 Continued**

construct a single building across the whole property. Salmon agreed and signed a new lease in the name of his own business, Midpoint Realty Company, without telling Meinhard. When Meinhard learned of the deal, he filed a suit in a New York state court against Salmon. The court ruled in Meinhard's favor, and Salmon appealed.

### In the Language of the Court
*CARDOZO, C.J. [Chief Justice]*
* * * *

Joint adventurers, like copartners, owe to one another, while the enterprise continues, the duty of the finest loyalty. Many forms of conduct permissible in a work-a-day world for those acting at arm's length are forbidden to those bound by fiduciary ties. * * * Not honesty alone, but the punctilio [strictness in observance of details] of an honor the most sensitive, is then the standard of behavior. As to this there has developed a tradition that is unbending and inveterate [entrenched]. Uncompromising rigidity has been the attitude of courts * * * when petitioned to undermine the rule of undivided loyalty.

* * * The trouble about [Salmon's] conduct is that he excluded his coadventurer from any chance to compete, from any chance to enjoy the opportunity for benefit.

* * * The very fact that Salmon was in control with exclusive powers of direction charged him the more obviously with the duty of disclosure, [because] only through disclosure could opportunity be equalized.

* * * Authority is, of course, abundant that one partner may not appropriate to his own use a renewal of a lease, though its term is to begin at the expiration of the partnership. The lease at hand with its many changes is not strictly a renewal. Even so, the standard of loyalty for those in trust relations is without the fixed divisions of a graduated scale. * * * *A man obtaining [an] * * * opportunity * * * by the position he occupies as a partner is bound by his obligation to his copartners in such dealings not to separate his interest from theirs, but, if he acquires any benefit, to communicate it to them. Certain it is also that there may be no abuse of special opportunities growing out of a special trust as manager or agent.* [Emphasis added.]

* * * Very likely [Salmon] assumed in all good faith that with the approaching end of the venture he might ignore his coadventurer and take the extension for himself. He had given to the enterprise time and labor as well as money. He had made it a success. Meinhard, who had given money, but neither time nor labor, had already been richly paid. * * * [But] Salmon had put himself in a position in which thought of self was to be renounced, however hard the abnegation [self-denial]. He was much more than a coadventurer. He was a managing coadventurer. For him and for those like him the rule of undivided loyalty is relentless and supreme.

**Decision and Remedy**  *The Court of Appeals of New York held that Salmon had breached his fiduciary duty by failing to inform Meinhard of the business opportunity and secretly taking advantage of it himself. The court granted Meinhard an interest "measured by the value of half of the entire lease."*

**Impact of This Case on Today's Law**  *This classic case involved a joint venture, not a partnership. At the time, a member of a joint venture had only the duty to refrain from actively subverting the rights of the other members. The decision in this case imposed the highest standard of loyalty on joint-venture members. The duty is now the same in both joint ventures and partnerships. Courts today frequently quote the eloquent language used in this opinion when describing the standard of loyalty that applies to partnerships.*

**Critical Thinking**
- **What If the Facts Were Different?**  *Suppose that Salmon had disclosed Gerry's proposal to Meinhard, who had said that he was not interested. Would the result in this case have been different? Explain.*

**Waiver of Fiduciary Duties**  A partner's fiduciary duties may not be waived or eliminated in the partnership agreement. In fulfilling them, each partner must act consistently with the obligation of good faith and fair dealing [UPA 103(b), 404(d)]. The agreement can specify acts that the partners agree will violate a fiduciary duty.

Note that a partner may pursue his or her own interests without automatically violating these duties [UPA 404(e)]. The key is whether the partner has disclosed the interest to the other partners.  **■ EXAMPLE 3.6** Jayne Trell, a partner at Jacoby & Meyers, owns a shopping mall. Trell may vote against a partnership proposal to open a competing mall, provided that she has fully disclosed her interest in the existing shopping mall to the other partners at the firm. ■ A partner cannot make secret profits or put self-interest before his or her duty to the interest of the partnership, however.

**Authority of Partners** The UPA affirms general principles of agency law that pertain to a partner's authority to bind a partnership in contract. If a partner acts within the scope of her or his authority, the partnership is legally bound to honor the partner's commitments to third parties.

A partner may also subject the partnership to tort liability under agency principles. When a partner is carrying on partnership business with third parties in the usual way, apparent authority exists, and both the partner and the firm share liability. The partnership will not be liable, however, if the third parties *know* that the partner has no such authority.

**Limitations on Authority.** A partnership may limit a partner's capacity to act as the firm's agent or transfer property on its behalf by filing a "statement of partnership authority" in a designated state office [UPA 105, 303]. Such limits on a partner's authority normally are effective only with respect to third parties who are notified of the limitation. (An exception is made in real estate transactions when the statement of authority has been recorded with the appropriate state office.)

**The Scope of Implied Powers.** The agency concepts relating to apparent authority, actual authority, and ratification apply to partnerships. The extent of implied authority generally is broader for partners than for ordinary agents, however.

In an ordinary partnership, the partners can exercise all implied powers reasonably necessary and customary to carry on that particular business. Some customarily implied powers include the authority to make warranties on goods in the sales business and the power to enter into contracts consistent with the firm's regular course of business. ■ **EXAMPLE 3.7** Jamie Schwab is a partner in a firm that operates a retail tire store. He regularly promises that "each tire will be warranted for normal wear for 40,000 miles." Because Schwab has authority to make warranties, the partnership is bound to honor the warranty. Schwab would not, however, have the authority to sell the partnership's office equipment or other property without the consent of all of the other partners. ■

**Liability of Partners** One significant disadvantage associated with a traditional partnership is that the partners are *personally* liable for the debts of the partnership. In most states, the liability is essentially unlimited, because the acts of one partner in the ordinary course of business subject the other partners to personal liability [UPA 305]. Note that normally the partnership's assets must be exhausted before creditors can reach the partners' individual assets, however.

**Joint Liability.** Each partner in a partnership generally is jointly liable for the partnership's obligations. **Joint liability** means that a third party must sue all of the partners as a group, but each partner can be held liable for the full amount.[4] If, for instance, a third party sues one partner on a partnership contract, that partner has the right to demand that the other partners be sued with her or him. In fact, if the third party does not name all of the partners in the lawsuit, the assets of the partnership cannot be used to satisfy the judgment.

**Joint and Several Liability.** In the majority of the states, under UPA 306(a), partners are both jointly and severally (separately, or individually) liable for all partnership obligations. **Joint and several liability** means that a third party has the option of suing all of the partners together (jointly) or one or more of the partners separately (severally). All partners in a partnership can be held liable even if a particular partner did not participate in, know about, or ratify the conduct that gave rise to the lawsuit.

A judgment against one partner severally (separately) does not extinguish the others' liability. (Similarly, a release of one partner does not discharge the partners' several liability.) Those not sued in the first action normally may be sued subsequently, unless the court in the first action held that the partnership was in no way liable. If a plaintiff is successful in a suit against a partner or partners, he or she may collect on the judgment only against the assets of those partners named as defendants.

**Indemnification.** With joint and several liability, a partner who commits a tort can be required to indemnify (reimburse) the partnership for any damages it pays. Indemnification will typically be granted *unless* the tort was committed in the ordinary course of the partnership's business. ■ **EXAMPLE 3.8** Nicole Martin, a partner at Patti's Café, is working in the café's kitchen one day when her young son suffers serious injuries to his hands from a dough press. Her son, through his father, files a negligence

---

4. Under the prior version of the UPA, partners were subject to joint liability on partnership debts and contracts, but not on partnership debts arising from torts.

lawsuit against the partnership. Even if the suit is successful and the partnership pays damages to Martin's son, the firm is not entitled to indemnification. Martin would not be required to indemnify the partnership because her negligence occurred in the ordinary course of the partnership's business (making food for customers). ■

**Liability of Incoming Partners.** A partner newly admitted to an existing partnership is not personally liable for any partnership obligations incurred *before* the person became a partner [UPA 306(b)]. In other words, the new partner's liability to existing creditors of the partnership is limited to her or his capital contribution to the firm.

■ **EXAMPLE 3.9** Smartclub, an existing partnership with four members, admits a new partner, Alex Jaff. He contributes $100,000 to the partnership. Smartclub has debts amounting to $600,000 at the time Jaff joins the firm. Although Jaff's capital contribution of $100,000 can be used to satisfy Smartclub's obligations, Jaff is not personally liable for partnership debts incurred before he became a partner. If, however, the partnership incurs additional debts after Jaff becomes a partner, he will be personally liable for those amounts, along with all the other partners. ■

# 3–3 Dissociation and Termination

**Dissociation** occurs when a partner ceases to be associated in the carrying on of the partnership business. Dissociation normally entitles the partner to have his or her interest purchased by the partnership. It also terminates the partner's actual authority to act for the partnership and to participate in running its business.

Once dissociation occurs, the partnership may continue to do business without the dissociated partner.[5] If the partners no longer wish to (or are unable to) continue the business, the partnership may be terminated (dissolved).

## 3–3a Events That Cause Dissociation

Under UPA 601, a partner can be dissociated from a partnership in any of the following ways:

1. By the partner's voluntarily giving notice of an "express will to withdraw." (When a partner gives

notice of intent to withdraw, the remaining partners must decide whether to continue the partnership business. If they decide not to continue, the voluntary dissociation of a partner will dissolve the firm [UPA 801(1)].)

2. By the occurrence of an event specified in the partnership agreement.
3. By a unanimous vote of the other partners under certain circumstances, such as when a partner transfers substantially all of her or his interest in the partnership.
4. By order of a court or arbitrator if the partner has engaged in wrongful conduct that affects the partnership business. The court can order dissociation if a partner breached the partnership agreement or violated a duty owed to the partnership or to the other partners. Dissociation may also be ordered if the partner engaged in conduct that makes it "not reasonably practicable to carry on the business in partnership with the partner" [UPA 601(5)].
5. By the partner's declaring bankruptcy, assigning his or her interest in the partnership for the benefit of creditors, or becoming physically or mentally incapacitated, or by the partner's death.

## 3–3b Wrongful Dissociation

A partner has the *power* to dissociate from a partnership at any time, but she or he may not have the *right* to do so. If the partner lacks the right to dissociate, then the dissociation is considered wrongful under the law [UPA 602]. When a partner's dissociation breaches a partnership agreement, for instance, it is wrongful.

■ **EXAMPLE 3.10** Jenkins & Whalen's partnership agreement states that it is a breach of the agreement for any partner to assign partnership property to a creditor without the consent of the other partners. If Kenzie, a partner, makes such an assignment, she has not only breached the agreement but has also wrongfully dissociated from the partnership. ■

A partner who wrongfully dissociates is liable to the partnership and to the other partners for damages caused by the dissociation. This liability is in addition to any other obligation of the partner to the partnership or to the other partners.

## 3–3c Effects of Dissociation

Dissociation (rightful or wrongful) terminates some of the rights of the dissociated partner and requires that the partnership purchase his or her interest. It also alters the liability of the parties to third parties.

---

5. Under the previous version of the UPA, when a partner withdrew from a partnership, the partnership was considered dissolved, and the business had to end. The new UPA dramatically changed the law governing partnership breakups by no longer requiring that a partnership end if one partner dissociates.

**Rights and Duties**  On a partner's dissociation, his or her right to participate in the management and conduct of the partnership business terminates [UPA 603]. The partner's duty of loyalty also ends. A partner's duty of care continues only with respect to events that occurred before dissociation, unless the partner participates in winding up the partnership's business (discussed shortly).

■ **EXAMPLE 3.11**  Debbie Pearson is a partner at the accounting firm Bubb & Flint. If she leaves the partnership, she can immediately compete with the firm for new clients. She must exercise care in completing ongoing client transactions that involved the partnership, however. She must also account to Bubb & Flint for any fees received from the old clients based on those transactions. ■

**Buyouts**  After a partner's dissociation, his or her interest in the partnership must be purchased according to the rules in UPA 701. The **buyout price** is based on the amount that would have been distributed to the partner if the partnership had been wound up on the date of dissociation. Offset against the price are amounts owed by the partner to the partnership, including damages for wrongful dissociation.

**Liability to Third Parties**  For two years after a partner dissociates from a continuing partnership, the partnership may be bound by the acts of the dissociated partner based on apparent authority [UPA 702]. In other words, if a third party reasonably believed at the time of a transaction that the dissociated partner was still a partner, the partnership may be liable. Similarly, a dissociated partner may be liable for partnership obligations entered into during the two-year period following dissociation [UPA 703].

To avoid this possible liability, a partnership should notify its creditors, customers, and clients of a partner's dissociation. In addition, either the partnership or the dissociated partner can file a statement of dissociation in the appropriate state office to limit the dissociated partner's authority to ninety days after the filing [UPA 704]. Filing this statement helps to minimize the firm's potential liability for the former partner and vice versa.

### 3–3d Partnership Termination

The same events that cause dissociation can result in the end of the partnership if the remaining partners no longer wish to (or are unable to) continue the partnership business. A partner's departure will not necessarily end the partnership, though. Generally, the partnership can continue if the remaining partners consent [UPA 801].

The termination of a partnership is referred to as **dissolution,** which essentially means the commencement of the winding up process. **Winding up** is the actual process of collecting, liquidating, and distributing the partnership assets.

**Dissolution**  Dissolution of a partnership generally can be brought about by acts of the partners, by operation of law, or by judicial decree [UPA 801]. Any partnership (including one for a fixed term) can be dissolved by the partners' agreement. If the partnership agreement states that it will dissolve on a certain event, such as a partner's death or bankruptcy, then the occurrence of that event will dissolve the partnership. A partnership for a fixed term or a particular undertaking is dissolved by operation of law at the expiration of the term or on the completion of the undertaking.

■ **CASE IN POINT 3.12**  Clyde Webster, James Theis, and Larry Thomas formed T&T Agri-Partners Company to own and farm 180 acres in Christian County, Illinois. Under the partnership agreement, the firm was to continue until January 31, 2010, unless it was dissolved. The death of any partner would dissolve the partnership.

Webster died in 2002, but Theis and Thomas did not liquidate T&T and distribute its assets. Webster's estate, through its personal representative, Joseph Webster, filed a complaint in state court seeking to dissolve the partnership. The court ordered the partnership to be dissolved, but Theis and Thomas did not dissolve it.

In 2011, after a trial, the court found that the partnership had expired by its own terms on January 31, 2010, and again ordered the partnership dissolved. Theis and Thomas appealed, but the reviewing court affirmed. A partnership business cannot continue after one partner dies when the partnership agreement specified that the death of one partner would terminate the business.[6] ■

**Illegality or Impracticality.**  Any event that makes it unlawful for the partnership to continue its business will result in dissolution [UPA 801(4)]. Under the UPA, a court may order dissolution when it becomes obviously impractical for the firm to continue—for instance, if the business can only be operated at a loss [UPA 801(5)]

■ **CASE IN POINT 3.13**  Members of the Russell family began operating Russell Realty Associates (RRA) as a partnership. Eddie Russell had decision-making authority over the partnership's business, which involved buying, holding, leasing, and selling investment properties. After several years, Eddie and his sister, Nina Russell,

---

6. *Estate of Webster v. Thomas,* 2013 IL App (5th) 120121-U, 2013 WL 164041 (2013).

started having disputes, and Nina began to routinely question Eddie's business decisions. Because of their disagreements, RRA experienced two years of delays before it could sell one piece of property. Although the firm continued to profit, Eddie filed a complaint seeking a judicial dissolution of the partnership, which the court granted. Nina appealed.

The Virginia Supreme Court affirmed the lower court's decision that Russell Realty must be judicially dissolved. The partners' relationship had deteriorated to the point where the partnership was unable to function effectively. As a result, the firm had incurred substantial and unnecessary added costs, which frustrated the partnership's economic purpose and made it impracticable to continue.[7] ■

**Good Faith.** Each partner must exercise good faith when dissolving a partnership. Some state statutes allow partners injured by another partner's bad faith to file a tort claim for wrongful dissolution of a partnership.

■ **CASE IN POINT 3.14** Attorneys Randall Jordan and Mary Helen Moses formed a two-member partnership. Although the partnership was for an indefinite term, Jordan ended the partnership three years later and asked the court for declarations concerning the partners' financial obligations. Moses, who had objected to ending the partnership, filed a claim against Jordan for wrongful dissolution and for appropriating $180,000 in fees that should have gone to the partnership.

Ultimately, the court held in favor of Moses. A claim for wrongful dissolution of a partnership may be based on the excluded partner's loss of "an existing, or continuing, business opportunity" or of income and material assets. Because Jordan had attempted to appropriate partnership assets through dissolution, Moses could sue for wrongful dissolution.[8] ■

**Winding Up and Distribution of Assets** After dissolution, the partnership continues for the limited purpose of winding up the business. The partners cannot create new obligations on behalf of the partnership. They have authority only to complete transactions begun but not finished at the time of dissolution and to wind up the business of the partnership [UPA 803, 804(1)].

**Duties and Compensation.** Winding up includes collecting and preserving partnership assets, discharging liabilities (paying debts), and accounting to each partner for the value of his or her interest in the partnership. Partners continue to have fiduciary duties to one another and to the firm during this process.

UPA 401(h) provides that a partner is entitled to compensation for services in winding up partnership affairs above and apart from his or her share in the partnership profits. A partner may also receive reimbursement for expenses incurred in the process.

**Creditors' Claims.** Both creditors of the partnership and creditors of the individual partners can make claims on the partnership's assets. In general, partnership creditors share proportionately with the partners' individual creditors in the partners' assets, which include their interests in the partnership.

A partnership's assets are distributed according to the following priorities [UPA 807]:

1. Payment of debts, including those owed to partner and nonpartner creditors.
2. Return of capital contributions and distribution of profits to partners.[9]

If the partnership's liabilities are greater than its assets, the partners bear the losses in the same proportion in which they shared the profits unless they have agreed otherwise.

**Partnership Buy-Sell Agreements** Before entering into a partnership, partners may agree on how the assets will be valued and divided in the event that the partnership dissolves. Such an agreement may eliminate costly negotiations or litigation later.

The agreement may provide for one or more partners to buy out the other or others, should the situation warrant. This is called a **buy-sell agreement,** or simply a *buyout agreement.* Alternatively, the agreement may specify that one or more partners will determine the value of the interest being sold and that the other or others will decide whether to buy or sell.

Under UPA 701(a), if a partner's dissociation does not result in a dissolution of the partnership, a buyout of the partner's interest is mandatory. The UPA contains an extensive set of buyout rules that apply when the partners do not have a buyout agreement. Basically, a withdrawing partner receives the same amount through a buyout that he or she would receive if the business were winding up [UPA 701(b)].

---

7. *Russell Realty Associates v. Russell,* 724 S.E.2d 690 (Va.Sup.Ct. 2012).
8. *Jordan v. Moses,* 291 Ga. 39, 727 S.E.2d 469 (2012).

9. Under the previous version of the UPA, creditors of the partnership had priority over creditors of the individual partners. Also, in distributing partnership assets, third party creditors were paid before partner creditors, and capital contributions were returned before profits.

Which of two buyout provisions in five partnership agreements applied to the sale of one partner's interest was the dispute in the following case. Although this case involved limited liability partnerships (discussed shortly) rather than traditional partnerships, it illustrates how the courts interpret buyout provisions.

## Case Analysis 3.2

# Shamburger v. Shamburger

Court of Appeals of Arkansas, Division I, 2016 Ark.App. 57, 481 S.W.3d 448 (2016).

## In the Language of the Court

Cliff *HOOFMAN*, Judge
* * * *

There are five LLPs [limited liability partnerships] at issue in this case: (1) CMH Management, LLP; (2) S.E. Management, LLP; (3) Bryant Hospitality, LLP; (4) Winners Circle Hospitality, LLP; and (5) SJS Management, LLP. At the time these LLPs were created, they were each composed of six partners, or three married couples: Sarah Jane and Robert Shamburger, Karyn Ann and Ricky Alan Johnson, and Thresa Kay and James Shamburger, Jr. Each partner had a 16.667% interest in each of the five LLPs.

The partners executed partnership agreements in connection with each LLP, as well as separate buy-sell agreements setting forth the required procedure through which partners could transfer their interests. The buy-sell agreements * * * contained similar language regarding the transfer of a partner's interest. As an example, the relevant provisions of the buy-sell agreement for Bryant Hospitality, LLP, are set forth below:

1. * * * The parties agree that the only manner in which any of the partners may transfer a partnership interest * * * shall be in the manner set forth herein: (a) Any couple may give notice * * * of an intent to either buy the others' entire company interests or to sell their entire company interest. Such notice shall contain one price at which such transaction shall occur. The offeree couples, or any single partner, shall, for sixty (60) days, have the option to either buy the offerors' entire interests for such price, or to sell their entire interest for such price.

* * * *

(c) If neither option is timely accepted by both individuals of the offeree couples, the offer shall be deemed an offer to purchase only, and acceptance of such offer shall be presumed.

* * * *

3. In the event of the death or divorce of a partner, the purchase price of such partner's interest, and the spouse's interest, or the interest of both in the event of common disaster, shall be the higher of the figures achieved in paragraphs (a) and (b) below:

(a) The aggregate * * * revenue * * * for the preceding thirty-six months (or so long as the partnership has been in business, if less than that time), as reflected on the books of the partnership, multiplied by the partner's percentage ownership.

(b) The applicable percentage of partnership interest of the value of the real property * * * as determined by the average of two appraisals.

* * * *

Appellant [Thresa Kay Shamburger] and her husband, James, divorced. [Two and a half years later] Sarah Jane and Robert Shamburger mailed a letter to appellant and James, stating that their divorce proceeding had "adversely affected the operation of all the family partnerships" and that, "in an effort to avoid continued disagreements and acrimony harmful to the businesses we propose to purchase your collective interest in all the partnerships, for a total price of $400,000, or $200,000 to each of you." The letter further referred appellant and James to the buy-sell agreements associated with each partnership and stated that they had sixty days from their

receipt of the letter to make their election.

Appellant received the letter * * * but did not respond. Instead, she filed a complaint [in an Arkansas state court] against appellees [all of the partnerships and the other partners], alleging that her divorce from James had triggered the terms of the buy-sell agreements dealing with a divorced party's interest and that appellees were attempting to bypass that provision by attempting to invoke the transfer provision set forth in Paragraph 1 of the agreements. * * * Appellant requested an order from the * * * court * * * determining that the attempted buy-sell arrangement by Sarah Jane and Robert Shamburger was in violation of the buy-sell agreements.

* * * *

Separate appellees Sarah Jane and Robert Shamburger filed a counterclaim against appellant, alleging that appellant had failed to respond to their purchase offer within the sixty-day period required by the buy-sell agreements and that the offer should therefore be deemed an offer to purchase her interest for $200,000. Robert and Sarah Jane requested that the * * * court order specific performance of the terms of the buy-sell agreements.

* * * *

* * * The court granted appellees' motion for summary judgment * * * . In addition, the court granted the relief for specific performance requested in the counterclaim * * * . Appellant timely appealed.

* * * *

* * * *Where two provisions of a contract conflict, the specific provision controls over*

**Case 3.2 Continues**

**Case 3.2 Continued**

*a more general provision, as it is assumed that the specific provision expresses the parties' intent.* [Emphasis added.]

\* \* \* \*

\* \* \* We agree with appellant that the specific provision governing transfers in the event of a divorce or death of a partner controls over the more general provision found in Paragraph 1. Appellees argue that Sarah Jane and Robert Shamburger's offer to purchase appellant's and her ex-husband's interest was not necessarily due to the divorce. However, this argument is belied by Sarah Jane and Robert Shamburger's statements in their offer letter \* \* \* . Appellees also contend that the death-or-divorce provision is not more specific than the provision in Paragraph 1, and they compare the length and detail of the two provisions at issue. As appellant responds, however, it is the fact that the death-or-divorce provision applies only under specific and limited circumstances that renders it controlling over the more general provision in Paragraph 1, not the specificity of the language used to describe each method of purchase.

\* \* \* \*

In addition to the rule of construction discussed above, \* \* \* the use of the word "shall" in each buy-sell agreement's death-or-divorce provision further supports [appellant's] claim that application of this provision was mandatory under the circumstances in this case. \* \* \* *"Shall" is defined as "has a duty to" or "is required to."* \* \* \* *"Shall," when used in a contract provision, means that compliance with that provision is mandatory.* [Emphasis added.]

\* \* \* The combination of the specific nature of the death-or-divorce provision and its use of mandatory language such as "shall," indicates that compliance with this particular provision was required under the circumstances in this case. Appellees also contend that interpreting the death-or-divorce provision as mandatory supersedes the procedure set forth in Paragraph 1 of the agreements and "neutralizes" that provision in violation of our rule of construction that we will not adopt an interpretation neutralizing a provision if the various clauses of a contract can be reconciled. We disagree

because interpreting the application of the death-or-divorce provision as mandatory in this case does not mean that the procedure set forth in Paragraph 1 of the agreements does not apply in all other situations that do not involve the death or divorce of a partner. Furthermore, as appellant argues, it is also possible to reconcile the two provisions in such a way that the general procedures set forth in Paragraph 1 apply, even in the event of a divorce or death of a partner, but the value of the partner's or couple's interest is determined pursuant to the formula set forth in the death-or-divorce provision.

Based on our rules of construction, we agree with appellant that the [lower] court erred in interpreting the buy-sell agreements in such a manner as to find that the death-or-divorce provisions did not apply to the offer to purchase appellant's interest in the LLPs. Accordingly, we reverse the \* \* \* order granting summary judgment and remand for further proceedings.

**Legal Reasoning Questions**

1. Why would a partnership agreement contain one provision for a buyout on a partner's divorce or death and another for a partner's decision to quit the firm?

2. How did the court's interpretation of contract principles affect the result in this case?

3. The lower court awarded attorneys' fees to the defendants, who prevailed on their motion for summary judgment. By reversing the summary judgment, does the appellate court's decision also require a reversal of the award of attorneys' fees?

# 3–4 Limited Liability Partnerships

The **limited liability partnership (LLP)** is a hybrid form of business designed mostly for professionals who normally do business as partners in a partnership. Almost all of the states have enacted LLP statutes.

The major advantage of the LLP is that it allows a partnership to continue as a pass-through entity for tax purposes but limits the personal liability of the partners. The LLP is especially attractive for professional service firms and family businesses. All of the "Big Four" accounting firms—the four largest international accountancy and professional services firms—are organized as

LLPs, including Ernst & Young, LLP, and PricewaterhouseCoopers, LLP.

## 3–4a Formation of an LLP

LLPs must be formed and operated in compliance with state statutes, which may include provisions of the UPA. The appropriate form must be filed with a central state agency, usually the secretary of state's office, and the business's name must include either "Limited Liability Partnership" or "LLP" [UPA 1001, 1002]. An LLP must file an annual report with the state to remain qualified as an LLP in that state [UPA 1003].

In most states, it is relatively easy to convert a traditional partnership into an LLP because the firm's basic organizational structure remains the same. Additionally, all of the statutory and common law rules governing partnerships still apply, apart from those modified by the LLP statute. Normally, LLP statutes are simply amendments to a state's already existing partnership law.

### 3–4b  Liability in an LLP

An LLP allows professionals, such as attorneys and accountants, to avoid personal liability for the malpractice of other partners. Of course, a partner in an LLP is still liable for her or his own wrongful acts, such as negligence. Also liable is the partner who supervised the individual who committed a wrongful act. (This generally is true for all types of partners and partnerships, not just LLPs.)

■ **EXAMPLE 3.15** Five lawyers operate a law firm as an LLP. One of the attorneys, Dan Kolcher, is sued for malpractice and loses. The firm's malpractice insurance is insufficient to pay the judgment. If the firm had been organized as a traditional (general) partnership, the personal assets of the other attorneys could be used to satisfy the obligation. Because the firm is organized as an LLP, however, no other partner at the firm can be held *personally* liable for Kolcher's malpractice, unless she or he acted as Kolcher's supervisor. In the absence of a supervisor, only Kolcher's personal assets can be used to satisfy the judgment. ■

Although LLP statutes vary from state to state, generally each state statute limits the liability of partners in some way. For instance, Delaware law protects each innocent partner from the "debts and obligations of the partnership arising from negligence, wrongful acts, or misconduct." The UPA more broadly exempts partners in an LLP from personal liability for any partnership obligation, "whether arising in contract, tort, or otherwise" [UPA 306(c)].

**Liability outside the State of Formation**  When an LLP formed in one state wants to do business in another state, it may be required to file a statement of foreign qualification in the second state [UPA 1102]. Because state LLP statutes are not uniform, a question sometimes arises as to which law applies if the LLP statutes in the two states provide different liability protection. Most states apply the law of the state in which the LLP was formed, even when the firm does business in another state, which is also the rule under UPA 1101.

**Sharing Liability among Partners**  When more than one partner in an LLP commits malpractice, there

is a question as to how liability should be shared. Is each partner jointly and severally liable for the entire result, as a general partner would be in most states?

Some states provide instead for proportionate liability—that is, for separate determinations of the negligence of the partners. ■ **EXAMPLE 3.16** Accountants Zach and Lyla are partners in an LLP, with Zach supervising Lyla. Lyla negligently fails to file a tax return for a client, Centaur Tools. Centaur files a suit against Zach and Lyla. Under a proportionate liability statute, Zach will be liable for no more than his portion of the responsibility for the missed tax deadline. In a state that does not allow for proportionate liability, Zach can be held liable for the entire loss. ■

### 3–4c  Family Limited Liability Partnerships

A **family limited liability partnership (FLLP)** is a limited liability partnership in which the partners are related to each other—for example, as spouses, parents and children, siblings, or cousins. A person acting in a fiduciary capacity for persons so related can also be a partner. All of the partners must be natural persons or be acting in a fiduciary capacity for the benefit of natural persons.

Probably the most significant use of the FLLP form of business organization is in agriculture. Family-owned farms sometimes find this form to their benefit. The FLLP offers the same advantages as other LLPs with certain additional advantages. For instance, in Iowa, FLLPs are exempt from real estate transfer taxes when partnership real estate is transferred among partners.[10]

## 3–5  Limited Partnerships

We now look at a business organizational form that limits the liability of *some* of its owners—the **limited partnership (LP).** Limited partnerships originated in medieval Europe and have been in existence in the United States since the early 1800s. Today, most states and the District of Columbia have adopted laws based on the Revised Uniform Limited Partnership Act (RULPA).

Limited partnerships differ from traditional (general) partnerships in several ways. Exhibit 3–2 compares the characteristics of general and limited partnerships.[11]

---

10. Iowa Statutes Section 428A.2.
11. Under the UPA, a general partnership can be converted into a limited partnership and vice versa [UPA 902, 903]. The UPA also provides for the merger of a general partnership with one or more general or limited partnerships [UPA 905].

**EXHIBIT 3–2** A Comparison of General Partnerships and Limited Partnerships

| | GENERAL PARTNERSHIP (UPA) | LIMITED PARTNERSHIP (RULPA) |
|---|---|---|
| **Creation** | By agreement of two or more persons to carry on a business as co-owners for profit. | By agreement of two or more persons to carry on a business as co-owners for profit. Must include one or more general partners and one or more limited partners. Filing of a certificate with the secretary of state is required. |
| **Sharing of Profits and Losses** | By agreement. In the absence of agreement, profits are shared equally by the partners, and losses are shared in the same ratio as profits. | Profits are shared as required in the certificate agreement, and losses are shared likewise, up to the amount of the limited partners' capital contributions. In the absence of a provision in the certificate agreement, profits and losses are shared on the basis of percentages of capital contributions. |
| **Liability** | Unlimited personal liability of all partners. | Unlimited personal liability of all general partners; limited partners liable only to the extent of their capital contributions. |
| **Capital Contribution** | No minimum or mandatory amount; set by agreement. | Set by agreement. |
| **Management** | By agreement. In the absence of agreement, all partners have an equal voice. | Only the general partner (or the general partners). Limited partners have no voice or else are subject to liability as general partners (but only if a third party has reason to believe that the limited partner is a general partner). A limited partner may act as an agent or employee of the partnership and vote on amending the certificate or on the sale or dissolution of the partnership. |
| **Duration** | Terminated by agreement of the partners, but can continue to do business even when a partner dissociates from the partnership. | Terminated by agreement in the certificate or by retirement, death, or mental incompetence of a general partner in the absence of the right of the other general partners to continue the partnership. Death of a limited partner does not terminate the partnership, unless he or she is the only remaining limited partner. |
| **Distribution of Assets on Liquidation— Order of Priorities** | 1. Payment of debts, including those owed to partner and nonpartner creditors.<br>2. Return of capital contributions and distribution of profit to partners. | 1. Outside creditors and partner creditors.<br>2. Partners and former partners entitled to distributions of partnership assets.<br>3. Unless otherwise agreed, return of capital contributions and distribution of profit to partners. |

A limited partnership consists of at least one **general partner** and one or more **limited partners**. A general partner assumes management responsibility for the partnership and has full responsibility for the partnership and for all its debts. A limited partner contributes cash or other property and owns an interest in the firm but is not involved in management responsibilities. A limited partner is not personally liable for partnership debts beyond the amount of his or her investment. If a limited partner takes part in the management of the business, however, she or he may forfeit that limited liability.

In the following case, two firms—a corporation and a limited partnership—were involved in the construction of a residential development. One individual served as the president of the corporation and the sole general partner of the partnership. In addition, he took charge of the activities at the construction site. How did this individual's status affect his responsibility for those activities?

## Case 3.3

# DeWine v. Valley View Enterprises, Inc.

Court of Appeals of Ohio, Eleventh District, Trumbull County, 2015 –Ohio– 1222 (2015).

**Background and Facts** Valley View Enterprises, Inc., built Pine Lakes Golf Club and Estates in Trumbull County, Ohio, in two phases—Phase I and Phase II. Valley View Properties, Ltd., a limited partnership, cut out the roadways and constructed sewer, water, and storm-water lines with water inlets for the development. Joseph Ferrara was the owner and the president of Valley View Enterprises and the sole general partner of Valley View Properties. Ferrara failed to obtain the proper permits for the development work in a timely manner and failed to comply with their requirements once they had been obtained.

Michael DeWine, the state's attorney general, filed a lawsuit in an Ohio court against the Valley View entities and Ferrara, alleging violations of the state's water pollution control laws and seeking civil penalties. The court entered a judgment in the defendants' favor, holding with respect to Ferrara that "a corporate officer cannot be held liable merely by virtue of his status as a corporate officer." DeWine appealed.

## In the Language of the Court
Timothy J. *CANNON*, P.J. [Presiding Judge]
    * * * *

Here, the state sought civil penalties from three entities: the property owner and Phase II permit holder, Valley View Properties, Ltd.; the Phase I permit holder, Valley View Enterprises, Inc.; and the sole general partner of the property owner, Mr. Ferrara.

* * * The state alleges the trial court erred in its finding that "Valley View Properties is the only party against whom civil penalties can be assessed." The trial court also found Mr. Ferrara was not liable based on his "good faith" actions and Valley View Enterprises, Inc. was not liable because it had no relationship to Pine Lakes Estates; [and] the state failed to present evidence that Mr. Ferrara ordered activities that caused pollution.

* * * Although the trial court found that Valley View Enterprises, Inc. had no relationship to Pine Lake Estates, the evidence establishes that Valley View Enterprises, Inc. applied for and was granted the [Phase I] Permit and, as the permittee, was required to ensure compliance with the permit. The [Phase I] Permit explicitly states, "the permittee must comply with all conditions of this permit, any permit non-compliance constitutes a violation of [state law]." Additionally, * * * *the evidence demonstrates that Mr. Ferrara personally was in charge of the activities performed at the sites; authorized the construction activities at the sites; and failed to obtain necessary certifications and permits.* [Emphasis added.]

Moreover, the trial court's finding that "a corporate officer cannot be held liable merely by virtue of his status as a corporate officer" is erroneous and not supported by the evidence. Admittedly, Mr. Ferrara is the sole general partner of Valley View Properties, Ltd., an Ohio limited partnership. He is not, in relation to Valley View Properties, Ltd., a "corporate officer." Therefore, he is not, in the course of his conduct as the general partner of that limited partnership, entitled to the insulation from liability of a corporate officer.

**Case 3.3 Continues**

**Decision and Remedy**  *A state intermediate appellate court reversed the lower court's judgment in favor of the defendants. With respect to Ferrara's status in relation to Valley View Properties, he was the general partner and therefore not "entitled to the insulation from liability of a corporate officer." On remand, the trial court was to determine the number of violations established by the state and to issue and apportion penalties among the liable parties.*

**Critical Thinking**
- **Legal Environment**  *How are the penalties likely to be apportioned among the three defendants? Explain.*

## 3–5a Formation of an LP

In contrast to the private and informal agreement that usually suffices to form a general partnership, the formation of a limited partnership is a public and formal proceeding. The partners must strictly follow statutory requirements. Not only must a limited partnership have at least one general partner and one limited partner, but the partners must also sign a **certificate of limited partnership.**

The certificate of limited partnership must include certain information, including the name, mailing address, and capital contribution of each general and limited partner. The certificate must be filed with the designated state official—under the RULPA, the secretary of state. The certificate is usually open to public inspection.

## 3–5b Liabilities of Partners in an LP

General partners are personally liable to the partnership's creditors. Thus, at least one general partner is necessary in a limited partnership so that someone has personal liability. This policy can be circumvented in states that allow a corporation to be the general partner in a partnership. Because the corporation has limited liability by virtue of corporation statutes, if a corporation is the general partner, no one in the limited partnership has personal liability. (See this chapter's *Ethics Today* feature for a discussion of whether a general partner who is unaware of another general partner's wrongdoing should be held liable for it.)

The liability of a limited partner, as mentioned, is limited to the capital that she or he contributes or agrees to contribute to the partnership [RULPA 502]. Limited partners enjoy this limited liability only so long as they do not participate in management [RULPA 303].

A limited partner who participates in management will be just as liable as a general partner to any creditor who transacts business with the limited partnership.

Liability arises when the creditor believes, based on the limited partner's conduct, that the limited partner is a general partner [RULPA 303]. The extent to which a limited partner can engage in management before being exposed to liability is not always clear, however.

## 3–5c Rights and Duties in a Limited Partnership

With the exception of the right to participate in management, limited partners have essentially the same rights as general partners. Limited partners have a right of access to the partnership's books and to information regarding partnership business. On dissolution of the partnership, limited partners are entitled to a return of their contributions in accordance with the partnership certificate [RULPA 201(a)(10)]. They can also assign their interests subject to the certificate [RULPA 702, 704]. In addition, they can sue an outside party on behalf of the firm if the general partners with authority to do so have refused to file suit [RULPA 1001].

## 3–5d Dissociation and Dissolution

A general partner has the power to voluntarily dissociate, or withdraw, from a limited partnership unless the partnership agreement specifies otherwise. Under the RULPA, a limited partner can withdraw from the partnership by giving six months' notice, unless the partnership agreement specifies a term. In reality, though, most limited partnership agreements do specify a term, which eliminates the limited partner's right to withdraw. Also, some states have passed laws prohibiting the withdrawal of limited partners.

**Events That Cause Dissociation**  In a limited partnership, a general partner's voluntary dissociation from the firm normally will lead to dissolution *unless* all partners

## ETHICS TODAY — Should an Innocent General Partner Be Jointly Liable for Fraud?

When general partners in a limited partnership jointly engage in fraud, there is usually no question that they are jointly liable. But if one general partner engages in fraud and the other is unaware of the wrongdoing, is it fair to make the innocent partner share in the liability? Many states' limited partnership laws protect innocent general partners from suits for fraud brought by limited partners. The law is less clear, however, in some other situations.

### A Developer's Misconduct

Robert Bisno and James Coxeter formed two limited partnerships to redevelop certain property in downtown Berkeley, California. Without Coxeter's knowledge, Bisno took almost $500,000 from one of the partnerships to buy a personal home. He also made material misrepresentations to potential investors.

One of those investors, George Miske—after purchasing an interest in the limited partnership—discovered the fraud and brought a lawsuit. Coxeter argued that he was an innocent general partner and should not

be liable to Miske for Bisno's tortious conduct. Coxeter also claimed that Miske was a limited partner, not an innocent third party, and that the state's limited partnership law protected Coxeter from liability to a limited partner.

### A California Court Finds the Innocent Co-Developer Liable

The court disagreed with Coxeter, however. The fraud at issue had induced Miske to purchase the limited partnership interest. Therefore, the court reasoned, at the time the fraud was perpetrated by Bisno, Miske was an innocent third party. As a result, the court held that Coxeter—even though he was innocent of any wrongdoing—was jointly liable to Miske.[a]

**Critical Thinking** *Why might it be fair for the court to hold Coxeter liable for his partner's fraud?*

a. *Miske v. Bisno*, 204 Cal.App.4th 1249, 139 Cal.Rptr.3d 626 (2012). See also *In re Barlaam*, 2014 WL 3398381 (9th Cir. 2014).

agree to continue the business. Similarly, the bankruptcy, retirement, death, or mental incompetence of a general partner will cause the dissociation of that partner and the dissolution of the limited partnership unless the other members agree to continue the firm [RULPA 801].

Bankruptcy of a limited partner, however, does not dissolve the partnership unless it causes the bankruptcy of the firm. In addition, death or an assignment of the interest (right to receive distributions) of a limited partner does not dissolve a limited partnership [RULPA 702, 704, 705]. A limited partnership can be dissolved by court decree [RULPA 802].

**Distribution of Assets** On dissolution, creditors' claims, including those of partners who are creditors, take first priority. After that, partners and former partners receive unpaid distributions of partnership assets. Unless otherwise agreed, they are also entitled to a return of their contributions in the proportions in which they share in distributions [RULPA 804].

**Valuation of Assets** Disputes commonly arise about how the partnership's assets should be valued and distributed and whether the business should be sold. ■ CASE IN POINT 3.17 Actor Kevin Costner was a limited partner in

Midnight Star Enterprises, LP, which runs a casino, bar, and restaurant in South Dakota. There were two other limited partners, Carla and Francis Caneva, who owned a small percentage of the partnership (3.25 units each) and received salaries for managing its operations. Another company owned by Costner, Midnight Star Enterprises, Limited (MSEL), was the general partner. Costner thus controlled a majority of the partnership (93.5 units).

When communications broke down between the partners, MSEL asked a court to dissolve the partnership. MSEL's accountant determined that the firm's fair market value was $3.1 million. The Canevas presented evidence that a competitor would buy the business for $6.2 million. The Canevas wanted the court to force Costner to either buy the business for that price within ten days or sell it on the open market to the highest bidder. Ultimately, the state's highest court held in favor of Costner. A partner cannot force the sale of a limited partnership when the other partners want to continue the business. The court also accepted the $3.1 million buyout price of MSEL's accountant and ordered Costner to pay the Canevas the value of their 6.5 partnership units.[12] ■

12. *In re Dissolution of Midnight Star Enterprises, LP*, 2006 SD 98, 724 N.W.2d 334 (S.D.Sup.Ct. 2006).

**Buy-Sell Agreements**    As mentioned earlier, partners can agree ahead of time on how the partnership's assets will be valued and divided if the partnership dissolves. This is true for limited partnerships as well as for general partnerships. Buy-sell agreements can help the partners avoid disputes. Nonetheless, buy-sell agreements do not eliminate all potential for litigation, especially if the terms are subject to more than one interpretation.

■ **CASE IN POINT 3.18**    Natural Pork Production II, LLP (NPP), an Iowa limited liability partnership, raises hogs. Under a partnership buy-sell agreement, NPP was obligated to buy a dissociating partner's interests but could defer the purchase if it would adversely affect the firm's capital or cash flow. After these "impairment circumstances" changed, NPP was to make the purchase within thirty days. Two of NPP's limited partners, Craton Capital, LP, and Kruse Investment Company, notified NPP of their dissociation. A wave of similar notices from other limited partners followed.

NPP declared an impairment circumstance and refused to buy out the limited partners. Craton and Kruse filed a suit asking a state court to order NPP to buy their units. NPP claimed that it was not required to buy out the limited partners because of the impairment circumstance. The court ruled in the plaintiffs'

favor. The wording of the buyout provision stated the firm "shall" buy out the partners, which meant it was mandatory. The impairment circumstance only deferred the purchase, and thus NPP was required to buy out the limited partners.[13] ■

### 3–5e Limited Liability Limited Partnerships

A **limited liability limited partnership (LLLP)** is a type of limited partnership. An LLLP differs from a limited partnership in that a general partner in an LLLP has the same liability as a limited partner in a limited partnership. In other words, the liability of all partners is limited to the amount of their investments in the firm.

A few states provide expressly for LLLPs.[14] In states that do not provide for LLLPs but do allow for limited partnerships and limited liability partnerships, a limited partnership should probably still be able to register with the state as an LLLP.

---

13.  *Craton Capital, LP v. Natural Pork Production II, LLP,* 797 N.W.2d 623 (Iowa App. 2011).
14.  See, for example, Colorado Revised Statutes Annotated Section 7-62-109. Other states that provide for LLLPs include Delaware, Florida, Georgia, Kentucky, Maryland, Nevada, Texas, and Virginia.

---

## Reviewing: All Forms of Partnerships

Grace Tarnavsky and her sons, Manny and Jason, bought a ranch known as the Cowboy Palace in March 2014, and the three verbally agreed to share the business for five years. Grace contributed 50 percent of the investment, and each son contributed 25 percent. Manny agreed to handle the livestock, and Jason agreed to handle the bookkeeping. The Tarnavskys took out joint loans and opened a joint bank account into which they deposited the ranch's proceeds and from which they made payments for property, cattle, equipment, and supplies.

In September 2017, Manny severely injured his back while baling hay and became permanently unable to handle livestock. Manny therefore hired additional laborers to tend the livestock, causing the Cowboy Palace to incur significant debt. In September 2018, Al's Feed Barn filed a lawsuit against Jason to collect $32,400 in unpaid debts. Using the information presented in the chapter, answer the following questions.

1.  Was this relationship a partnership for a term or a partnership at will?
2.  Did Manny have the authority to hire additional laborers to work at the ranch after his injury? Why or why not?
3.  Under the current UPA, can Al's Feed Barn bring an action against Jason individually for the Cowboy Palace's debt? Why or why not?
4.  Suppose that after his back injury in 2017, Manny sent his mother and brother a notice indicating his intent to withdraw from the partnership. Can he still be held liable for the debt to Al's Feed Barn? Why or why not?

**Debate This** . . .    *A partnership should automatically end when one partner dissociates from the firm.*

## Terms and Concepts

articles of partnership 37
buyout price 43
buy-sell agreement 44
certificate of limited
   partnership 50
charging order 39
dissociation 42
dissolution 43
family limited liability partnership
   (FLLP) 47

general partner 49
goodwill 36
information return 36
joint and several liability 41
joint liability 41
limited liability limited partnership
   (LLLP) 52
limited liability partnership
   (LLP) 46
limited partner 49

limited partnership (LP) 47
partnership 35
partnership by estoppel 37
pass-through entity 36
winding up 43

## Issue Spotters

1. Darnell and Eliana are partners in D&E Designs, an architectural firm. When Darnell dies, his widow claims that as Darnell's heir, she is entitled to take his place as Eliana's partner or to receive a share of the firm's assets. Is she right? Why or why not? (See *Dissociation and Termination*.)

2. Finian and Gloria are partners in F&G Delivery Service. When business is slow, without Gloria's knowledge, Finian leases the delivery vehicles as moving vans. Because the vehicles would otherwise be sitting idle in a parking lot, can Finian keep the income resulting from the leasing of the delivery vehicles? Explain your answer. (See *Formation and Operation*.)

• Check your answers to the Issue Spotters against the answers provided in Appendix B at the end of this text.

## Business Scenarios

**3–1. Partnership Formation.** Daniel is the owner of a chain of shoe stores. He hires Rubya to be the manager of a new store, which is to open in Grand Rapids, Michigan. Daniel, by written contract, agrees to pay Rubya a monthly salary and 20 percent of the profits. Without Daniel's knowledge, Rubya represents himself to Classen as Daniel's partner and shows Classen the agreement to share profits. Classen extends credit to Rubya. Rubya defaults. Discuss whether Classen can hold Daniel liable as a partner. (See *Formation and Operation*.)

**3–2. Dissolution of a Limited Partnership.** Dorinda, Luis, and Elizabeth form a limited partnership. Dorinda is a general partner, and Luis and Elizabeth are limited partners. Consider the separate events below, and discuss fully whether each event constitutes a dissolution of the limited partnership. (See *Limited Partnerships*.)
**(a)** Luis assigns his partnership interest to Ashley.
**(b)** Elizabeth is petitioned into involuntary bankruptcy.
**(c)** Dorinda dies.

## Business Case Problems

**3–3. Fiduciary Duties of Partners.** Karl Horvath, Hein Rüsen, and Carl Thomas formed a partnership, HRT Enterprises, to buy a manufacturing plant. Rüsen and Thomas leased the plant to their own company, Merkur Steel. Merkur then sublet the premises to other companies owned by Rüsen and Thomas. The rent that these companies paid to Merkur was higher than the rent that Merkur paid to HRT. Rüsen and Thomas did not tell Horvath about the subleases. Did Rüsen and Thomas breach their fiduciary duties to HRT and Horvath? Discuss. [*Horvath v. HRT Enterprises,* 489 Mich.App. 992, 800 N.W.2d 595 (2011)] (See *Formation and Operation*.)

**3–4. Partnership Formation.** Patricia Garcia and Bernardo Lucero were in a romantic relationship. While they were seeing each other, Garcia and Lucero acquired an electronics service center, paying $30,000 apiece. Two years later, they purchased an apartment complex. The property was deeded to Lucero, but neither Garcia nor Lucero made a down payment. The couple considered both properties to be owned "50/50," and they agreed to share profits, losses, and management rights. When the couple's romantic relationship ended, Garcia asked a court to declare that she had a partnership with Lucero. In court, Lucero argued that the couple did not have a written partnership agreement. Did they have a partnership? Why or why not? [*Garcia v. Lucero,* 366 S.W.3d 275 (Tex. App. 2012)] (See *Formation and Operation*.)

**3–5. Winding Up.** Dan and Lori Cole operated a Curves franchise exercise facility in Angola, Indiana, as a partnership. The firm leased commercial space from Flying Cat, LLC, for a renewable three-year term and renewed the lease for a second three-year term. But two years after the renewal, the Coles divorced. By the end of the second term, Flying Cat was owed more than $21,000 on the lease. Without telling the landlord about the divorce, Lori signed another extension. More rent went unpaid. Flying Cat obtained a judgment in an Indiana state court against the partnership for almost $50,000. Can Dan be held liable? Why or why not? [*Curves for Women Angola v. Flying Cat, LLC,* 983 N.E.2d 629 (Ind.App. 2013)] (See *Dissociation and Termination.*)

### 3–6. Business Case Problem with Sample Answer—Partnerships.

 Karyl Paxton asked Christopher Sacco to work with her interior design business, Pierce Paxton Collections, in New Orleans. At the time, they were in a romantic relationship. Sacco was involved in every aspect of the business—bookkeeping, marketing, and design—but was not paid a salary. He was reimbursed, however, for expenses charged to his personal credit card, which Paxton also used. Sacco took no profits from the firm, saying that he wanted to "grow the business" and "build sweat equity." When Paxton and Sacco's personal relationship soured, she fired him. Sacco objected, claiming that they were partners. Is Sacco entitled to 50 percent of the profits of Pierce Paxton Collections? Explain. [*Sacco v. Paxton,* 133 So.3d 213 (La.App. 2014)] (See *Formation and Operation.*)

- For a sample answer to Problem 3–6, go to Appendix C at the end of this text.

### 3–7. Formation.

Leisa Reed and Randell Thurman lived together in Spring City, Tennessee. Randell and his father, Leroy, formed a cattle-raising operation and opened a bank account in the name of L&R Farm. Within a few years, Leroy quit the operation. Leisa and Randell each wrote a personal check for $5,000 to buy his cattle. Leisa picked up supplies, fed and administered medicine to cattle, collected hay, and participated in the bookkeeping for L&R. Later, checks drawn on her personal account for $12,000 to buy equipment and $35,000 to buy cattle were deposited into the L&R account. After several years, Leisa decided that she no longer wanted to associate with Randell, but they could not agree on a financial settlement. Was Leisa a partner in L&R? Is she entitled to half of the value of L&R's assets? Explain. [*Reed v. Thurman,* 2015 WL 1119449 (Tenn.App. 2015)] (See *Formation and Operation.*)

### 3–8. Formation and Operation.

FS Partners is a general partnership whose partners are Jerry Stahlman, a professional engineer, and Fitz & Smith, Inc., a corporation in the business of excavating and paving. Timothy Smith signed the partnership agreement on Fitz & Smith's behalf and deals with FS matters on Fitz & Smith's behalf. Stahlman handles the payment of FS's bills, including its tax bills, and is the designated partner on FS's federal tax return. FS was formed to buy and develop twenty acres of unoccupied, wooded land in York County, Pennsylvania. The deed to the property lists the owner as "FS Partners, a general partnership." When the taxes on the real estate were not paid, the York County Tax Claim Bureau published notice that the property would be sold at a tax sale. The bureau also mailed a notice to FS's address of record and posted a notice on the land. Is this sufficient notice of the tax sale? Discuss. [*FS Partners v. York County Tax Claim Bureau,* 132 A.3d 577 (Pa. 2016)] (See *Formation and Operation.*)

### 3–9. A Question of Ethics—Wrongful Dissociation.

 *Elliot Willensky and Beverly Moran formed a partnership to buy, renovate, and sell a house. Moran agreed to finance the effort, which was to cost no more than $60,000. Willensky agreed to oversee the work, which was to be done in six months. Willensky lived in the house during the renovation. As the project progressed, Willensky incurred excessive and unnecessary expenses, misappropriated funds for his personal use, did not pay bills on time, and did not keep Moran informed of the costs. More than a year later, the renovation was still not completed, and Willensky walked off the project. Moran completed the renovation, which ultimately cost $311,222, and sold the house. Moran then sued to dissolve the partnership and recover damages from Willensky for breach of contract and wrongful dissociation.* [Moran v. Willensky, *339 S.W.3d 651 (Tenn.App.Ct. 2010)*] (See *Dissociation and Termination.*)

**(a)** Moran alleged that Willensky had wrongfully dissociated from the partnership. When did this dissociation occur? Why was his dissociation wrongful?

**(b)** Which of Willensky's actions simply represent unethical behavior or bad management, and which constitute a breach of the agreement?

## Legal Reasoning Group Activity

### 3–10. Liability of Partners.

At least six months before the Summer Olympic Games in Atlanta, Georgia, Stafford Fontenot and four others agreed to sell Cajun food at the games and began making preparations. On May 19, the group (calling themselves "Prairie Cajun Seafood Catering of Louisiana") applied for a business license from the county health department. Later, Ted Norris sold a mobile kitchen to them for $40,000. They gave Norris an $8,000 check drawn on the "Prairie Cajun Seafood Catering of Louisiana" account and two promissory notes, one for $12,000 and the other for $20,000. The notes, which were dated June 12, listed only Fontenot "d/b/a Prairie Cajun Seafood" as the maker (*d/b/a* is an abbreviation for "doing business as").

On July 31, Fontenot and his friends signed a partnership agreement, which listed specific percentages of profits and losses. They drove the mobile kitchen to Atlanta, but business was "disastrous." When the notes were not paid, Norris filed a suit in a Louisiana state court against Fontenot, seeking payment. (See *Formation and Operation.*)

**(a)** The first group will discuss the elements of a partnership and determine whether a partnership exists among Fontenot and the others.

**(b)** The second group will determine who can be held liable on the notes and why.

## CHAPTER 4

# Limited Liability Companies and Special Business Forms

Our government allows entrepreneurs to choose from a variety of business organizational forms. In selecting among them, businesspersons are motivated to choose organizational forms that limit their liability. Limited liability may allow them to take more business risk, which is associated with the potential for higher profits.

A relatively new and increasingly common form of business organization is the *limited liability company (LLC)*. LLCs have become the organizational form of choice among many small businesses. Other special business forms include joint ventures, syndicates, joint stock companies, business trusts, and cooperatives.

## 4–1 The Limited Liability Company

A **limited liability company (LLC)** is a hybrid that combines the limited liability aspects of a corporation and the tax advantages of a partnership. The LLC has been available for only a few decades, but it has become the preferred structure for many small businesses.

LLCs are governed by state statutes, which vary from state to state. In an attempt to create more uniformity, the National Conference of Commissioners on Uniform State Laws issued the Uniform Limited Liability Company Act (ULLCA). Less than one-fifth of the states have adopted it, however. Thus, the law governing LLCs remains far from uniform.

Nevertheless, some provisions are common to most state statutes. We base our discussion of LLCs on these common elements.

### 4–1a The Nature of the LLC

LLCs share many characteristics with corporations. Like corporations, LLCs must be formed and operated in compliance with state law. Like the shareholders of a corporation, the owners of an LLC, who are called **members,** enjoy limited liability [ULLCA 303].[1]

**Limited Liability of Members** Members of LLCs are shielded from personal liability in most situations. In other words, the liability of members is normally limited to the amount of their investments.

An exception arises when a member has significantly contributed to the LLC's tortious conduct. ■ **CASE IN POINT 4.1** Randy Coley, the sole member and manager of East Coast Cablevision, LLC, installed cable television systems for many hotels and resorts. Coley established a DIRECTV Satellite Master Antenna Television (SMATV) account in the name of Massanutten Resort. The system provided programming to 168 timeshare units, as well as to the resort's bar, golf shop, lobbies, and waterpark. The bill for the resort's account was sent to (and paid by) East Coast Cablevision, which in turn billed the customers.

Over time, East Coast Cablevision began providing cable services to additional customers using the resort's SMATV account but did not pay DIRECTV for these other customers. Ultimately, another cable dealer affiliated with DIRECTV sued Coley for not paying for all of the DIRECTV programming transmissions that East Coast's customers had received. The court held that because Coley had played a direct role in the unauthorized transmissions, he could be held personally liable for them.[2] ■

**When Liability May Be Imposed** The members of an LLC, like the shareholders in a corporation, can lose their limited personal liability in certain circumstances. For instance, when an individual guarantees payment of

---

1. Members of an LLC can also bring derivative actions, which you will read about in regard to corporations, on behalf of the LLC [ULLCA 101]. As with a corporate shareholder's derivative suit, any damages recovered go to the LLC, not to the members personally.

2. *Sky Cable, LLC v. Coley,* ___ F.Supp.3d ___, 2013 WL 3517337 (W.D.Va. 2013).

a business loan to the LLC, that individual is personally liable for the business's obligation. In addition, if an LLC member fails to comply with certain formalities, such as by commingling personal and business funds, a court can impose personal liability.

Under various principles of corporate law, courts may hold the owners of a business liable for its debts. On rare occasions, for instance, courts ignore the corporate structure ("pierce the corporate veil") to expose the shareholders to personal liability when it is required to achieve justice.

Similarly, courts will sometimes pierce the veil of an LLC to hold its members personally liable. Note, however, that courts have reserved piercing the veil of an LLC for circumstances that are clearly extraordinary. There must normally be some flagrant disregard of the LLC formalities, as well as fraud or malfeasance on the part of the LLC member.

■ **CASE IN POINT 4.2** Tom and Shannon Brown purchased a new home in Hattiesburg, Mississippi, from Ray Richard and Nick Welch. Richard had hired Waldron Properties, LLC (WP), to build the home. Several years later, cracks began to develop in the walls of the Browns' home as a result of defects in the construction of the foundation. The Browns sued Murray Waldron, the sole member of WP, for breach of warranty under the state's New Home Warranty Act (NHWA). Because the required NHWA notice they had received when they bought the home was signed by Waldron personally, they claimed that Waldron was liable personally.

The trial court found that WP, not Waldron individually, was the builder of the Browns' home. The Browns appealed. They contended that even if WP was the builder, the court should pierce the veil of the LLC and hold Waldron personally liable. The state appellate court disagreed and affirmed the lower court's ruling. The Browns had not entered into a contract with either Waldron or WP. There was not sufficient evidence that Waldron had disregarded LLC formalities or had engaged in fraud or other misconduct to justify piercing the LLC's veil to hold him personally liable.[3] ■

### Other Similarities to Corporations

Another similarity between corporations and LLCs is that LLCs are legal entities apart from their owners. As a legal person, the LLC can sue or be sued, enter into contracts, and hold title to property [ULLCA 201]. The terminology used to describe LLCs formed in other states or nations is also similar to that used in corporate law. For instance, an LLC formed in one state but doing business in another state is referred to in the second state as a *foreign LLC.*

## 4-1b The Formation of the LLC

LLCs are creatures of statute and thus must follow state statutory requirements.

**Articles of Organization** To form an LLC, **articles of organization** must be filed with a central state agency—usually the secretary of state's office [ULLCA 202].[4] Typically, the articles must include the name of the business, its principal address, the name and address of a registered agent, the members' names, and how the LLC will be managed [ULLCA 203]. The business's name must include the words *Limited Liability Company* or the initials *LLC* [ULLCA 105(a)]. Although a majority of the states permit one-member LLCs, some states require at least two members.

**Preformation Contracts** Businesspersons sometimes enter into contracts on behalf of a business organization that is not yet formed. Persons who are forming a corporation, for instance, may enter into contracts during the process of incorporation but before the corporation becomes a legal entity. These contracts are referred to as *preincorporation contracts.* The individual promoters who sign the contracts are bound to their terms. Once the corporation is formed and adopts the preincorporation contracts (by means of a *novation,* which substitutes a new contract for the old contract), it can enforce the contract terms.

In dealing with the preorganization contracts of LLCs, courts may apply the well-established principles of corporate law relating to preincorporation contracts. That is to say, when the promoters of an LLC enter preformation contracts, the LLC, once formed, can adopt the contracts by a novation and then enforce them.

■ **CASE IN POINT 4.3** 607 South Park, LLC, entered into an agreement to sell a hotel to 607 Park View Associates, Ltd., which then assigned the rights to the purchase to another company, 02 Development, LLC. At the time, 02 Development did not yet exist—it was legally created several months later. 607 South Park subsequently refused to sell the hotel to 02 Development, and 02 Development sued for breach of the purchase agreement.

A California appellate court ruled that LLCs should be treated the same as corporations with respect to preorganization contracts. Although 02 Development did not exist when the agreement was executed, once it came into existence, it could enforce any preorganization contract made on its behalf.[5] ■

---

3. *Brown v. Waldron,* 186 So.3d 955 (Miss.App. 2016).

4. In addition to requiring articles of organization to be filed, a few states require that a notice of the intention to form an LLC be published in a local newspaper.

5. *02 Development, LLC v. 607 South Park, LLC,* 159 Cal.App.4th 609, 71 Cal.Rptr.3d 608 (2008). See also, *Davis Wine Co. v. Vina Y Bodega Estampa, S.A.,* 823 F.Supp.2d 1159 (D.Or. 2011).

## 4–1c Jurisdictional Requirements

As we have seen, LLCs and corporations share several characteristics, but a significant difference between these organizational forms involves federal jurisdictional requirements. Under the federal jurisdiction statute, a corporation is deemed to be a citizen of the state where it is incorporated and maintains its principal place of business. The statute does not mention the state citizenship of partnerships, LLCs, and other unincorporated associations. The courts, however, have tended to regard these entities as citizens of every state of which their members are citizens.

The state citizenship of an LLC may come into play when a party sues the LLC based on diversity of citizenship. Remember that when parties to a lawsuit are from different states and the amount in controversy exceeds $75,000, a federal court can exercise diversity jurisdiction. *Total* diversity of citizenship must exist, however.

■ **EXAMPLE 4.4** Jen Fong, a citizen of New York, wishes to bring a suit against Skycel, an LLC formed under the laws of Connecticut. One of Skycel's members also lives in New York. Fong will not be able to bring a suit against Skycel in federal court on the basis of diversity jurisdiction because the defendant LLC is also a citizen of New York. The same would be true if Fong was bringing a suit against multiple defendants and one of the defendants lived in New York. ■

## 4–1d Advantages of the LLC

The LLC offers many advantages to businesspersons, which is why this form of business organization has become increasingly popular.

**Limited Liability** A key advantage of the LLC is the limited liability of its members. The LLC as an entity can be held liable for any loss or injury caused by the wrongful acts or omissions of its members. As we have seen, however, members themselves generally are not personally liable.

In the following case, a consumer died as a result of using an allegedly defective product made and sold by an LLC. The consumer's children sought to hold the LLC's sole member and manager personally liable for the firm's actions.

**Case 4.1**

# Hodge v. Strong Built International, LLC

Court of Appeal of Louisiana, Third Circuit, 159 So.3d 1159 (2015).

**Background and Facts** Donald Hodge was hunting in a deer stand when its straps—which held Hodge high up in a tree—failed. When the straps failed, Hodge and the deer stand fell to the ground, killing Hodge. Louisiana-based Strong Built International, LLC, was the maker and seller of the deer stand, and Ken Killen was Strong Built's sole member and manager.

Hodge's children, Donald and Rachael Hodge, filed a lawsuit in a Louisiana state court against Strong Built and Killen. They sought damages on a theory of product liability for the injury and death of their father caused by the allegedly defective deer stand. Killen filed a motion for summary judgment, asserting that he was not personally liable to the Hodges. The court granted the motion and issued a summary judgment in Killen's favor, dismissing the claims against him. The Hodges appealed.

### In the Language of the Court

*AMY,* Judge.

* * * *

* * * An LLC member or manager's liability to third parties is delineated in [Louisiana Revised Statute (La.R.S.)] 12:1320, which states:

* * * *

* * * no member, manager, employee, or agent of a limited liability company is liable in such capacity for a debt, obligation, or liability of the limited liability company.

* * * *

* * * That protection is not unlimited. Pursuant to La.R.S. 12:1320(D), *a member or manager may be subjected to personal liability for claims involving * * * breach of a professional duty or other negligent or wrongful act.* [Emphasis added.]

* * * In an affidavit, Mr. Killen asserted that he is "not an engineer, nor a licensed professional in any profession in Louisiana or any other state." Mr. Killen also asserts that he:

Case 4.1 Continues

was a participant in the creation of the deer stand which * * * Strong Built International, L.L.C. manufactured and sold, but he never personally dictated or participated in the design, selection of materials used in the manufacture, or the manufacture of, or the selection of any warnings to any deer stand for the use or consumption by any consumer beyond my input and work as a manager * * * and member of * * * Strong Built International, L.L.C.

The plaintiffs offered no evidence to contradict Mr. Killen's affidavit in this regard. Accordingly, we find no basis for Mr. Killen's personal liability under the "breach of professional duty" exception.

Neither do we find sufficient evidence in the record to create a genuine issue of material fact with regard to the "other negligent or wrongful act" exception.

* * * With regard to [this exception], the member (or manager) must have a duty of care to the plaintiff. * * * That duty must be "something more" than the duties arising out of the LLC's contract with the plaintiff.

* * * *

* * * Mr. Killen states in his affidavit that not only was he not personally responsible for the design and manufacture of the deer stands while involved with Strong Built International * * * but that any involvement that he may have had was in his capacity as a member and manager. *The plaintiffs have submitted nothing to show that Mr. Killen's actions are "something more" than his duties as a member/manager of the LLC.* [Emphasis added.]

**Decision and Remedy**  *A state intermediate appellate court affirmed the judgment in Killen's favor. Under the applicable Louisiana state LLC statute, no member or manager of an LLC is liable in that capacity for the liability of the company. There are exceptions, but the Hodges failed to show that Killen's actions went beyond his duties as a member and manager of Strong Built.*

**Critical Thinking**

- **Economic**  *Why does the law allow—and even encourage—limits to the liability of a business organization's owners and managers for the firm's actions? Discuss.*

**Flexibility in Taxation**  Another advantage of the LLC is its flexibility in regard to taxation. An LLC that has *two or more members* can choose to be taxed as either a partnership or a corporation. A corporate entity normally must pay income taxes on its profits, and the shareholders must then pay personal income taxes on any of those profits that are distributed as dividends. An LLC that wants to distribute profits to its members almost always prefers to be taxed as a partnership to avoid the "double taxation" that is characteristic of the corporate entity.

Unless an LLC indicates that it wishes to be taxed as a corporation, the Internal Revenue Service (IRS) automatically taxes it as a partnership. This means that the LLC, as an entity, pays no taxes. Rather, as in a partnership, profits are "passed through" the LLC to the members, who then personally pay taxes on the profits. If an LLC's members want to reinvest profits in the business rather than distribute the profits to members, however, they may prefer to be taxed as a corporation. Corporate income tax rates may be lower than personal tax rates. Part of the attractiveness of the LLC is this flexibility with respect to taxation.

An LLC that has only *one member* cannot be taxed as a partnership. For federal income tax purposes, one-member LLCs are automatically taxed as sole proprietorships unless they indicate that they wish to be taxed as corporations. With respect to state taxes, most states follow the IRS rules.

**Management and Foreign Investors**  Another advantage of the LLC for businesspersons is the flexibility it offers in terms of business operations and management, as will be discussed shortly. Foreign investors are allowed to become LLC members, so organizing as an LLC can enable a business to attract investors from other countries. (Many nations—including France, Germany, Japan and places in Latin America—have particular business forms that provide for limited liability much like an LLC.)

## 4–1e Disadvantages of the LLC

The main disadvantage of the LLC is that state LLC statutes are not uniform. Therefore, businesses that operate in more than one state may not receive consistent treatment in these states.

Generally, most states apply to a foreign LLC (an LLC formed in another state) the law of the state where the LLC was formed. Difficulties can arise, though, when one state's court must interpret and apply another state's laws.

## 4–2 LLC Management and Operation

The members of an LLC have considerable flexibility in managing and operating the business. Here, we discuss management options, fiduciary duties owed, and the operating agreement and general operating procedures of LLCs.

### 4–2a Management of an LLC

Basically, LLC members have two options for managing the firm, as shown in Exhibit 4–1. The firm can be either a "member-managed" LLC or a "manager-managed" LLC. Most state LLC statutes and the ULLCA provide

that unless the articles of organization specify otherwise, an LLC is assumed to be member managed [ULLCA 203(a)(6)].

In a *member-managed* LLC, all of the members participate in management, and decisions are made by majority vote [ULLCA 404(a)]. In a *manager-managed* LLC, the members designate a group of persons to manage the firm. The management group may consist of only members, both members and nonmembers, or only nonmembers.

However an LLC is managed, its managers need to be aware of the firm's potential liability under employment-discrimination laws. Those laws may sometimes extend to individuals who are not members of a protected class, as discussed in this chapter's *Managerial Strategy* feature.

### 4–2b Fiduciary Duties

Under the ULLCA, managers in a manager-managed LLC owe fiduciary duties (the duty of loyalty and the duty of care) to the LLC and its members [ULLCA 409(a), 409(h)]. (This same rule applies in corporate law—corporate directors and officers owe fiduciary duties to the corporation and its shareholders.) Because not all states have adopted the ULLCA, though, some state statutes provide that managers owe fiduciary duties only to the LLC and not to the LLC's members.

To whom the fiduciary duties are owed can affect the outcome of litigation. ■ **CASE IN POINT 4.5** Leslie Polk and his children, Yurii and Dusty Polk and Lezanne Proctor, formed Polk Plumbing, LLC, in Alabama. Dusty and Lezanne were managers of the LLC. Eventually, Yurii quit the firm. A year and a half later, Leslie "fired" Dusty and Lezanne and denied them access to the LLC's books and offices, but continued to operate the business.

Dusty and Lezanne filed a suit in an Alabama state court against Leslie, claiming breach of fiduciary duty. The trial court instructed the jury that it could not consider the plaintiffs' "firing" as part of their claim. Thus, although the jury found in their favor, it awarded only one dollar to each in damages. The plaintiffs appealed, and a state intermediate appellate court reversed and remanded the case for a new trial. Leslie did not have the authority under the terms of the LLC's operating agreement to fire two managers. The trial court had erred in not allowing the jury to consider the circumstances of Dusty and Lezanne's "firing" as part of their breach-of-fiduciary-duty claim.[6] ■

**EXHIBIT 4–1 Management of an LLC**

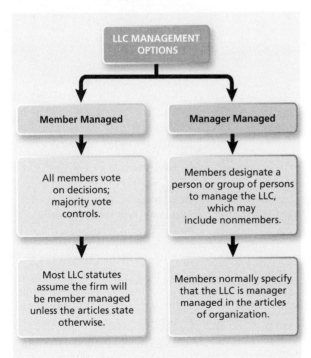

LLC MANAGEMENT OPTIONS

**Member Managed**

All members vote on decisions; majority vote controls.

Most LLC statutes assume the firm will be member managed unless the articles state otherwise.

**Manager Managed**

Members designate a person or group of persons to manage the LLC, which may include nonmembers.

Members normally specify that the LLC is manager managed in the articles of organization.

---

6. *Polk v. Polk*, 70 So.3d 363 (Ala.App. 2011).

## Can a Person Who Is Not a Member of a Protected Class Sue for Discrimination?

Under federal law and the laws of most states, discrimination in employment based on race, color, religion, national origin, gender, age, or disability is prohibited. Persons who are members of these protected classes can sue if they are subjected to discrimination. But can a person subjected to discrimination bring a lawsuit if he is not a member of a protected class, even though managers and other employees believe that he is? This somewhat unusual situation occurred in New Jersey.

### Courts in New Jersey

Myron Cowher worked at Carson & Roberts Site Construction & Engineering, Inc. For more than a year, at least two of his supervisors directed almost daily barrages of anti-Semitic remarks at him. They believed that he was Jewish, although his actual background was German-Irish and Lutheran.

Cowher brought a suit against the supervisors and the construction company, claiming a hostile work environment. The trial court, however, ruled that he did not have standing to sue under New Jersey law because he was not Jewish and, thus, was not a member of a protected class. Cowher appealed.

The appellate court disagreed with the trial court. The court ruled that if Cowher could prove that the discrimination "would not have occurred but for the perception that he was Jewish," his claim was covered by New Jersey's antidiscrimination law.[a] Thus, in the

appellate court's view, the nature of the discriminatory remarks—and not the actual characteristics of the plaintiff—determines whether the remarks are actionable.

Another New Jersey court followed the precedent set by the *Cowher* case to allow Shi-Juan Lin, a Chinese worker whose fiancé and child were black, to recover for racial discrimination. The employer created a hostile work environment by allowing Lin's supervisor to constantly use the "n" word at work. The employer knew that even though Lin was not black, she was hurt by the supervisor's remarks. Therefore, the court affirmed an administrative law judge's award of damages for pain and suffering, plus attorneys' fees.[b]

### Business Questions

1. *Should a manager for an LLC respond to employee complaints of discrimination any differently than a manager at a corporation, a partnership, or a sole proprietorship? Why or why not?*

2. *How can a company, whether an LLC or some other business form, reduce the chances of discrimination lawsuits?*

---

a. *Cowher v. Carson & Roberts*, 425 N.J.Super. 285, 40 A.3d 1171 (2012). See also, *Sheridan v. Egg Harbor Township Board of Education*, 2015 WL 9694404 (N.J.Sup.Ct. 2016), involving a plaintiff who alleged discrimination based on obesity.

b. *Lin v. Dane Construction Co.*, 2014 WL 8131876 (N.J.Super.A.D. 2015).

## 4–2c The LLC Operating Agreement

The members of an LLC can decide how to operate the various aspects of the business by forming an **operating agreement** [ULLCA 103(a)]. In many states, an operating agreement is not required for an LLC to exist, and if there is one, it need not be in writing. Generally, though, LLC members should protect their interests by creating a written operating agreement.

Operating agreements typically contain provisions relating to the following areas:

1. Management and how future managers will be chosen or removed. (Although most LLC statutes are silent on this issue, the ULLCA provides that members

may choose and remove managers by majority vote [ULLCA 404(b)(3)].)
2. How profits will be divided.
3. How membership interests may be transferred.
4. Whether the dissociation of a member, such as by death or departure, will trigger dissolution of the LLC.
5. Whether formal members' meetings will be held.
6. How voting rights will be apportioned. (If the agreement does not cover voting, LLC statutes in most states provide that voting rights are apportioned according to each member's capital contributions.[7]

---

7. In contrast, partners in a partnership generally have equal rights in management and equal voting rights unless they specify otherwise in their partnership agreement.

**EXHIBIT 4–2** Provisions Commonly Included in an LLC Operating Agreement

| | |
|---|---|
| **Management** | Sets forth who will manage the LLC and how future managers will be chosen or removed. (The ULLCA provides that members may choose and remove managers by majority vote.) |
| **Profits** | Establishes how profits will be divided among members. |
| **Membership** | Specifies how membership interests may be transferred. |
| **Dissociation and Dissolution** | Clarifies which events cause the dissociation of a member—such as by death or retirement—and trigger the LLC's dissolution. Provides a method of calculating a buyout price for a member's dissociation. |
| **Member Meetings** | Determines whether or not formal members' meetings will be held. |
| **Voting Rights** | Details how voting rights will be apportioned, such as according to each member's capital contribution or by allowing one vote for each member. |

Some states provide that, in the absence of an agreement to the contrary, each member has one vote.)

The provisions commonly included in operating agreements are also shown in Exhibit 4–2.

If a dispute arises and there is no agreement covering the topic under dispute, the state LLC statute will govern the outcome. For instance, most LLC statutes provide that if the members have not specified how profits will be divided, they will be divided equally among the members. When an issue is not covered by an operating agreement or by an LLC statute, the courts often apply principles of partnership law.

Of course, LLC members are bound by the operating agreement that they make, as the following case illustrates.

**Case 4.2**

# Mekonen v. Zewdu

Court of Appeals of Washington, 179 Wash.App. 1042 (2014).

**Background and Facts** Green Cab Taxi and Disabled Service Association LLC ("Green Cab") is a taxi service company in King County, Washington. The operating agreement requires the members to pay weekly fees. Members who do not pay are in default and must return their taxi licenses to the company. In addition, a member in default cannot hold a seat on the board or withdraw from the company without the consent of all of the members.

Case 4.2 Continues

**Case 4.2 Continued**

A disagreement arose among the members concerning the company's management, and several members, including Shumet Mekonen, withdrew from the company without the consent of the other members. Both sides continued to drive under the Green Cab name.

Mekonen's group filed a suit in a Washington state court against a group of members who had not withdrawn, including Dessie Zewdu. In part, the Mekonen group sought the right to operate as Green Cab. The court held that the plaintiffs could not represent themselves as Green Cab and ordered them to return their taxi licenses to the company. The plaintiffs appealed the order to return their licenses.

### In the Language of the Court

*LAU,* J. [Judge]

* * * *

* * * The [lower] court found in defendants' favor regarding * * * the right of management and control over Green Cab. It found plaintiffs had no right to represent themselves as part of Green Cab's management or to operate under Green Cab's name.

* * * *

* * * Plaintiffs seek to retain the taxicab licenses affixed to the cars they own. According to Paragraph 6.4 of the LLC Operating Agreement, "the Company shall hold all rights to any taxi and other licenses and permits necessary to operate its vehicles." *The Plaintiffs have no right to use the taxicab licenses unless they are members of Green Cab LLC in good standing and are making any contributions toward the company's operating expenses that the board of directors deems necessary.* Plaintiffs admit that they withdrew their membership from Green Cab LLC and that they have paid no weekly fees since [their withdrawal]. As a result, the Plaintiffs have no legal right to retain the King County taxicab licenses currently in their possession. [Emphasis added.]

* * * The [lower] court deemed the members "defaulting members."

* * * *

* * * Plaintiffs admitted to default both in failing to make weekly payments and in withdrawing from the company in violation of article 5.6 of the operating agreement. That article states, "A Member may not withdraw as a Member prior to dissolution and commencement of winding up of the Company * * * without the written consent of all the other Members." The trial court imposed relief that was reasonably calculated to install defendants as the proper group to manage Green Cab and to preserve their interests in operating the company * * *. Given the relative interests of the parties and the LLC, the trial court acted well within its discretion to order plaintiffs to return their taxi licenses.

**Decision and Remedy** *A state intermediate appellate court upheld the lower court's order to the plaintiffs to return their taxi licenses to Green Cab. Under the provisions of the company's operating agreement, the plaintiffs, as "defaulting members," had no right to retain and use the licenses.*

**Critical Thinking**
- **What If the Facts Were Different?** *Suppose that Green Cab had maintained a company Web site on which it posted its operating agreement, conducted all internal company business, and offered a forum where members could vent their complaints. How might the result have been different? Why?*
- **Legal Environment** *During discovery, the plaintiffs were asked to answer requests for admission, but they did not respond. Does it seem likely that their failure to answer affected the outcome? Why or why not?*

## 4–3 Dissociation and Dissolution of an LLC

Recall that in a partnership, *dissociation* occurs when a partner ceases to be associated in the carrying on of the partnership business. The same concept applies to LLCs. And like a partner in a partnership, a member of an LLC has the *power* to dissociate at any time but may not have the *right* to dissociate.

Under the ULLCA, the events that trigger a member's dissociation from an LLC are similar to the events causing a partner to be dissociated under the Uniform Partnership Act (UPA). These include voluntary withdrawal, expulsion by other members, court order, incompetence, bankruptcy, and death. Generally, if a member dies or otherwise dissociates from an LLC, the other members may continue to carry on the LLC business unless the operating agreement provides otherwise.

## 4–3a Effects of Dissociation

When a member dissociates from an LLC, he or she loses the right to participate in management and the right to act as an agent for the LLC. The member's duty of loyalty to the LLC also terminates, and the duty of care continues only with respect to events that occurred before dissociation.

Generally, the dissociated member also has a right to have his or her interest in the LLC bought out by the other members. The LLC's operating agreement may contain provisions establishing a buyout price. If it does not, the member's interest is usually purchased at fair value. In states that have adopted the ULLCA, the LLC must purchase the interest at fair value within 120 days after the dissociation.

If the member's dissociation violates the LLC's operating agreement, it is considered legally wrongful, and the dissociated member can be held liable for damages caused by the dissociation. ■ **EXAMPLE 4.6** Chadwick and Barrow are members in an LLC. Chadwick manages the accounts, and Barrow, who has many connections in the community and is a skilled investor, brings in the business. If Barrow wrongfully dissociates from the LLC, the LLC's business will suffer, and Chadwick can hold Barrow liable for the loss of business resulting from her withdrawal. ■

## 4–3b Dissolution

Regardless of whether a member's dissociation was wrongful or rightful, normally the dissociated member has no right to force the LLC to dissolve. The remaining members can opt either to continue or to dissolve the business.

Members can also stipulate in their operating agreement that certain events will cause dissolution, or they can agree that they have the power to dissolve the LLC by vote. As with partnerships, a court can order an LLC to be dissolved in certain circumstances. For instance, a court might order dissolution when the members have engaged in illegal or oppressive conduct, or when it is no longer feasible to carry on the business.

■ **CASE IN POINT 4.7** Three men—Walter Perkins, Gary Fordham, and David Thompson—formed Venture Sales, LLC, to develop a subdivision in Petal, Mississippi. Each of them contributed land and funds, resulting in total holdings of 466 acres of land and about $158,000 in cash.

Perkins, who was working as an assistant coach for the Cleveland Browns, trusted Fordham and Thompson to develop the property. More than ten years later, however, they still had not done so, although they had formed two other LLCs and developed two other subdivisions in the area.

Fordham and Thompson claimed that they did not know when they could develop Venture's property and suggested selling it at a discounted price, but Perkins disagreed. Perkins then sought a judicial dissolution of Venture Sales. The court ordered the dissolution. Because Venture Sales was not meeting the economic purpose for which it was established (developing a subdivision), continuing the business was impracticable.[8] ■

A judge's exercise of discretion to order the dissolution of an LLC was disputed in the following case.

---

**8.** *Venture Sales, LLC v. Perkins,* 86 So.3d 910 (Miss.Sup. 2012).

**Case Analysis 4.3**

# Reese v. Newman
District of Columbia Court of Appeals, 131 A.3d 880 (2016).

### In the Language of the Court
*KING,* Senior Judge:

* * * Allison Reese and * * * Nicole Newman were co-owners of ANR Construction Management, LLC * * *. Following disputes over management of the company, Newman notified Reese in writing that she intended to * * * dissolve and wind-up the LLC. Reese did not want to dissolve the LLC but preferred that Newman simply be dissociated so that Reese could continue the business herself. Newman filed an action

for judicial dissolution in [a District of Columbia court against Reese]. Reese filed a counterclaim for Newman's dissociation * * *. Following a jury trial, the jury * * * found grounds for both judicial dissolution and forced dissociation of Newman; the court, thereafter, ordered judicial dissolution of the LLC. * * * Reese appeals.

* * * *

Reese argues that the trial court erred when it purported to use discretion in choosing between dissolution of the

LLC, as proposed by Newman, and forcing dissociation of Newman from the LLC, as proposed by Reese. Reese argues that the [District of Columbia (D.C.)] statute [governing dissociation from an LLC] does not allow for any discretion by the court, and that, in fact, the statute mandates that the court order dissociation of Newman based on the jury's findings.

In matters of statutory interpretation, we review the trial court's decision

**Case 4.3 Continues**

**Case 4.3 Continued**

*de novo.* Our analysis starts with the plain language of the statute, as the general rule of statutory interpretation is that the intent of the lawmaker is to be found in the language that he has used. To that end, *the words of the statute should be construed according to their ordinary sense and with the meaning commonly attributed to them.* [Emphasis added.]

Reese argues that the court was required to dissociate Newman from the LLC under [D.C. Code] Section 29–806.02(5) which reads:

> A person *shall* be dissociated as a member from a limited liability company when:
> * * * *
> (5) On application by the company, the person is expelled as a member by judicial order because the person has:
> (A) Engaged, or is engaging, in wrongful conduct that has adversely and materially affected, or will adversely and materially affect, the company's activities and affairs;
> (B) Willfully or persistently committed, or is willfully and persistently committing, a material breach of the operating agreement or the person's duties or obligations under Section 29–804.09; or
> (C) Engaged in, or is engaging, in conduct relating to the company's activities which makes it not reasonably practicable to carry on the activities with the person as a member.

Reese's interpretation of the statute is that, upon application to the court by a company, a judge shall dissociate a member of an LLC, when that member commits any one of the actions described in subsections (5)(A)-(C).

* * * While the introductory language of Section 29–806.02 does use the word "shall"—that command is in no way directed at the trial judge. It reads, "a person shall be dissociated * * * when," and then goes on to recite fifteen separate circumstances describing different occasions when a person shall be dissociated from an LLC. That is to say, when one of the events described in subparagraphs (1) through (15) occurs, the member shall be dissociated. Subparagraph (5), however, is merely one instance for which a person shall be dissociated; that is, when and if a judge has ordered a member expelled because she finds that any conditions under (5)(A)-(C) have been established. In other words, the command in the introductory language is not directed at the trial judge, it is directed at all the circumstances set forth in subparagraphs (1) through (15) * * * . There is nothing in the language of Section 29–806.02(5) that strips a judge of her discretion because it does not require the judge to expel the member if any of the enumerated conditions are established. In short, Section 29–806.02(5) means: *when a judge has used her discretion to expel a member of an LLC by judicial order, under any of the enumerated circumstances in (5)(A)-(C), that member shall be dissociated.*

* * * Although Reese argues that the language of the "dissociation" section of the District's code should be read as forcing the hand of a trial judge who finds grounds for dissociation, Reese attempts to read the "dissolution" section differently.

Reese differentiates the sections by pointing to the dissolution section's express authorization to order a remedy other than dissolution in Section 29–807.01(b) which provides: "in a proceeding brought under subsection (a)(5) of this section, the * * * Court may order a remedy other than dissolution."

While we are satisfied that judicial dissolution of an LLC is discretionary under this statute, Reese's attempt to buttress [reinforce] her argument that Section 29–806.02(5) is compulsory by pointing to this express provision in the dissolution section and the absence of a similar express provision in the dissociation section is unavailing. First, * * * the only "shall" in the dissociation section is in the introductory language, and the same "shall" can be found in the same place, in the dissolution section: "a limited liability company is dissolved, and its activities and affairs *shall be wound up,* upon the occurrence of any of the following." If that language does not make the rest of the section mandatory in the dissolution section, and we are persuaded that it does not, it cannot be said that the "shall" in the introduction of the dissociation section does the opposite.
* * * *

In sum, we hold that Section 29–806.02(5) can only be interpreted to mean: when a judge finds that any of the events in (5)(A)-(C) have taken place, she may (*i.e.,* has discretion to) expel by judicial order a member of an LLC, and when a judge has done so the member shall be dissociated. *Moreover, when both grounds for dissociation of a member and dissolution of the LLC exist, the trial judge has discretion to choose either alternative.* [Emphasis added.]

Here, the jury * * * found that grounds were present for either outcome. The trial judge acknowledged that both options were on the table and then exercised her discretion in ordering that dissolution take place. We find no reason to disturb that order.
* * * *

Accordingly, the judgment in this appeal is therefore affirmed.

## Legal Reasoning Questions

**1.** What dispute gave rise to the action filed in the court in this case? How did that dispute lead to the issue on appeal?

**2.** What is the role of an appellate court when reviewing the exercise of discretion by a trial court?

**3.** Newman alleged that after she delivered her notice to dissolve ANR, Reese locked her out of the LLC's bank accounts, blocked her access to the LLC's files and e-mail, and ended her salary and health benefits. Did any of the jury's findings support these allegations? Explain.

## 4–3c Winding Up

When an LLC is dissolved, any members who did not wrongfully dissociate may participate in the winding up process. To wind up the business, members must collect, liquidate, and distribute the LLC's assets.

Members may preserve the assets for a reasonable time to optimize their return, and they continue to have the authority to perform reasonable acts in conjunction with winding up. In other words, the LLC will be bound by the reasonable acts of its members during the winding up process.

Once all of the LLC's assets have been sold, the proceeds are distributed. Debts to creditors are paid first (including debts owed to members who are creditors of the LLC). The members' capital contributions are returned next, and any remaining amounts are then distributed to members in equal shares or according to their operating agreement.

# 4–4 Special Business Forms

Besides the business forms already discussed in this unit, several other forms can be used to organize a business. For the most part, these special business forms are hybrid organizations—that is, they combine features of other organizational forms, such as partnerships and corporations. These forms include joint ventures, syndicates, joint stock companies, business trusts, and cooperatives.

## 4–4a Joint Venture

In a **joint venture,** two or more persons or business entities combine their efforts or their property for a single transaction or project or a related series of transactions or projects. For instance, when several contractors combine their resources to build and sell houses in a single development, their relationship is a joint venture. Unless otherwise agreed, joint venturers share profits and losses equally and have an equal voice in controlling the project.

Joint ventures range in size from very small activities to multimillion-dollar joint actions carried out by some of the world's largest corporations. Large organizations often form joint ventures with other enterprises to produce new products or services. ■ **EXAMPLE 4.8** Intel Corporation and Micron Technology, Inc., formed a joint venture to manufacture NAND flash memory. NAND is a data-storage chip widely used in digital cameras, cell phones, and portable music players. ■

**Similarities to Partnerships** A joint venture resembles a partnership and is taxed like a partnership. For this reason, most courts apply the same principles to joint ventures as they apply to partnerships. Joint venturers owe each other the same fiduciary duties, including the duty of loyalty, that partners owe each other. Thus, if one of the venturers secretly buys land that was to be acquired by the joint venture, the other joint venturers may be awarded damages for the breach of loyalty.

**Liability and Management Rights.** A joint venturer can be held personally liable for the venture's debts (because joint venturers share losses as well as profits). Like partners, joint venturers have equal rights to manage the activities of the enterprise, but they can agree to give control of the operation to one of the members.

**Authority to Enter Contracts.** Joint venturers have authority as agents to enter into contracts that will bind the joint venture. ■ **CASE IN POINT 4.9** Murdo Cameron developed components for replicas of vintage P-51 Mustang planes. Cameron and Douglas Anderson agreed in writing to collaborate on the design and manufacture of two P-51s, one for each of them.

Without Cameron's knowledge, Anderson borrowed funds from SPW Associates, LLP, to finance the construction, using the first plane as security for the loan. After Anderson built one plane, he defaulted on the loan. SPW filed a lawsuit to obtain possession of the aircraft.

The court ruled that Anderson and Cameron had entered into a joint venture and that the plane was the venture's property. Under partnership law, partners have the power as agents to bind the partnership. Because this principle applies to joint ventures, Anderson had the authority to grant SPW a security interest in the plane, and SPW was entitled to take possession of the plane.[9] ■

**Differences from Partnerships** Joint ventures differ from partnerships in several important ways. A joint venture is typically created for a single project or series of transactions, whereas a partnership usually (though not always) involves an ongoing business. Also, unlike most partnerships, a joint venture normally terminates when the project or the transaction for which it was formed has been completed.

Because the activities of a joint venture are more limited than the business of a partnership, the members of a joint venture are presumed to have less power to bind their co-venturers. Thus, the members of a joint venture have less implied and apparent authority than the

---

9. *SPW Associates, LLP v. Anderson,* 2006 ND 159, 718 N.W.2d 580 (N.D.Sup.Ct. 2006).

partners in a partnership (each of whom is treated as an agent of the other partners). In *Case in Point 4.9*, for instance, if Anderson's loan agreement with SPW had not been directly related to the business of building vintage planes, the court might have concluded that Anderson lacked the authority to bind the joint venture.

## 4–4b Syndicate

In a **syndicate,** or *investment group,* several individuals or firms join together to finance a particular project. Syndicates can finance projects such as the construction of a shopping center or the purchase of a professional basketball franchise. The form of such groups varies considerably.

A syndicate may be organized as a corporation or as a general or limited partnership. In some situations, the members do not have a legally recognized business arrangement but merely purchase and own property jointly.

## 4–4c Joint Stock Company

A **joint stock company** is a true hybrid of a partnership and a corporation. It has many characteristics of a corporation in that (1) its ownership is represented by transferable shares of stock, (2) it is managed by directors and officers of the company or association, and (3) it can have a perpetual existence.

Most of its other features, however, are more characteristic of a partnership, and it generally is treated as a partnership. Like a partnership, a joint stock company is formed by agreement (not statute). Property usually is held in the names of the owners, who are called shareholders, and they have personal liability. In a joint stock company, however, shareholders are not considered to be agents of each other, as they would be in a true partnership.

## 4–4d Business Trust

A **business trust** is created by a written trust agreement that sets forth the interests of the beneficiaries and the obligations and powers of the trustees. Legal ownership and management of the trust's property stay with one or more of the trustees, and the profits are distributed to the beneficiaries.

A business trust resembles a corporation in many respects. Beneficiaries of the trust, for instance, are not personally responsible for the trust's debts or obligations. In fact, in a number of states, business trusts must pay corporate taxes.

## 4–4e Cooperative

A **cooperative** is an association that is organized to provide an economic service to its members (or shareholders). It may or may not be incorporated. Most cooperatives are organized under state statutes for cooperatives, general business corporations, or LLCs. Co-ops range in size from small, local cooperatives to national businesses such as Ace Hardware and Land O'Lakes, a well-known producer of dairy products.

The cooperative form of business is generally adopted by groups of individuals who wish to pool their resources to gain some advantage in the marketplace. *Consumer purchasing co-ops,* for instance, are formed to obtain lower prices through quantity discounts. *Seller marketing co-ops* are formed to control the market and thereby enable members to sell their goods at higher prices.

**Incorporated Co-ops** Generally, an incorporated cooperative distributes dividends, or profits, to its owners on the basis of their transactions with the cooperative rather than on the basis of the amount of capital they contributed. Members of incorporated cooperatives have limited liability, as do shareholders of corporations and members of LLCs.

**Unincorporated Co-ops** Cooperatives that are not incorporated are often treated like partnerships. The members have joint liability for the cooperative's acts.

See Concept Summary 4.1 for a review of the types of special business forms discussed in this chapter.

## Concept Summary 4.1

### Special Business Forms

**Joint Venture**
An organization created by two or more persons in contemplation of a limited activity or a single transaction; similar to a partnership in many respects.

**Syndicate**
An investment group that undertakes to finance a particular project; may be organized as a corporation or as a general or limited partnership.

**Joint Stock Company**
A business form similar to a corporation in some respects (transferable shares of stock, management by directors and officers, perpetual existence) but otherwise resembling a partnership.

**Business Trust**
A business form created by a written trust agreement that sets forth the interests of the beneficiaries and the obligations and powers of the trustee(s). A business trust is similar to a corporation in many respects. Beneficiaries are not personally liable for the debts or obligations of the business trust.

**Cooperative**
An association organized to provide an economic service, without profit, to its members. A cooperative can take the form of a corporation or a partnership.

# Reviewing: Limited Liability Companies and Special Business Forms

The city of Papagos, Arizona, had a deteriorating bridge in need of repair on a prominent public roadway. The city posted notices seeking proposals for an artistic bridge design and reconstruction. Davidson Masonry, LLC, which was owned and managed by Carl Davidson and his wife, Marilyn Rowe, decided to submit a bid to create a decorative concrete structure that incorporated artistic metalwork. They contacted Shana Lafayette, a local sculptor who specialized in large-scale metal creations, to help them design the bridge. The city selected their bridge design and awarded them the contract for a commission of $184,000.

Davidson Masonry and Lafayette then entered into an agreement to work together on the bridge project. Davidson Masonry agreed to install and pay for concrete and structural work, and Lafayette agreed to install the metalwork at her expense. They agreed that overall profits would be split, with 25 percent going to Lafayette and 75 percent going to Davidson Masonry. Lafayette designed numerous metal sculptures of trout that were incorporated into colorful decorative concrete forms designed by Rowe. Davidson performed the structural engineering. The group worked together successfully until the completion of the project. Using the information presented in the chapter, answer the following questions.

1. Would Davidson Masonry automatically be taxed as a partnership or a corporation?
2. Is Davidson Masonry member managed or manager managed?

Continues

3. When Davidson Masonry and Lafayette entered an agreement to work together, what kind of special business form was created? Explain.

4. Suppose that during construction, Lafayette entered into an agreement to rent space in a warehouse that was close to the bridge so that she could work on her sculptures near the site where they would eventually be installed. She entered into the contract without the knowledge or consent of Davidson Masonry. In this situation, would a court be likely to hold that Davidson Masonry was bound by the contract that Lafayette entered? Why or why not?

**Debate This** . . . *Because LLCs are essentially just partnerships with limited liability for members, all partnership laws should apply.*

## Terms and Concepts

| | | |
|---|---|---|
| articles of organization 56 | joint stock company 66 | member 55 |
| business trust 66 | joint venture 65 | operating agreement 60 |
| cooperative 66 | limited liability company (LLC) 55 | syndicate 66 |

## Issue Spotters

1. Gabriel, Harris, and Ida are members of Jeweled Watches, LLC. What are their options with respect to the management of their firm? (See *LLC Management and Operation.*)

2. Greener Delivery Company and Hiway Trucking, Inc., form a business trust. Insta Equipment Company and Jiffy Supply Corporation form a joint stock company. Kwik Mart, Inc., and Luscious Produce, Inc., form an incorporated cooperative. What do these forms of business organization have in common? (See *Special Business Forms.*)

• Check your answers to the Issue Spotters against the answers provided in Appendix B at the end of this text.

## Business Scenarios

**4–1. Limited Liability Companies.** John, Lesa, and Tabir form a limited liability company. John contributes 60 percent of the capital, and Lesa and Tabir each contribute 20 percent. Nothing is decided about how profits will be divided. John assumes that he will be entitled to 60 percent of the profits, in accordance with his contribution. Lesa and Tabir, however, assume that the profits will be divided equally. A dispute over the profits arises, and ultimately a court has to decide the issue. What law will the court apply? In most states, what will result? How could this dispute have been avoided in the first place? Discuss fully. (See *The Limited Liability Company.*)

**4–2. Special Business Forms.** Bateson Corp. is considering entering into contracts with two organizations. One is a joint stock company that distributes home products east of the Mississippi River. The other is a business trust formed by a number of sole proprietors who are sellers of home products on the West Coast. Both contracts will require Bateson to make large capital outlays in order to supply the businesses with restaurant equipment. In both business organizations, at least two shareholders or beneficiaries are personally wealthy, but the organizations themselves have limited financial resources. The owner-managers of Bateson are not familiar with either form of business organization. Because each form resembles a corporation, they are concerned about potential limits on liability in the event that either organization breaches the contract by failing to pay for the equipment. Discuss fully Bateson's concern. (See *Special Business Forms.*)

## Business Case Problems

**4–3. Joint Venture.** Holiday Isle Resort & Marina, Inc., operated four restaurants, five bars, and various food kiosks at its resort in Islamorada, Florida. Holiday entered into a "joint-venture agreement" with Rip Tosun to operate a fifth restaurant, called "Rip's—A Place for Ribs." The agreement gave Tosun authority over the employees and "full authority as to the conduct of the business." It also prohibited Tosun from competing with Rip's without Holiday's approval but did not prevent Holiday from competing. Later, Tosun sold half of his interest in Rip's to Thomas Hallock. Soon, Tosun and Holiday opened the Olde Florida Steakhouse next to Rip's. Holiday stopped serving breakfast at Rip's and diverted employees and equipment from Rip's to the steakhouse, which then started offering breakfast. Hallock filed a suit in a Florida state court against Holiday. Did Holiday breach the joint-venture agreement? Did it breach the duties that joint venturers owe each other? Explain. [*Hallock v. Holiday Isle Resort & Marina, Inc.,* 4 So.3d 17 (Fla.App. 3 Dist. 2009)] (See *Special Business Forms.*)

**4–4. Limited Liability Companies.** Coco Investments, LLC, and other investors participated in a condominium conversion project to be managed by Zamir Manager River Terrace, LLC. The participants entered into a new LLC agreement for the project. The investors subsequently complained that Zamir had failed to disclose its plans for dramatic changes involving higher-than-expected construction costs and delays. They also claimed that Zamir had failed to provide financial information and had restructured loans in a manner that allowed Zamir representatives to avoid personal liability. The investors sued Zamir on various grounds, including breach of contract and breach of fiduciary duty. Zamir moved for summary judgment. How should the court rule? Explain. [*Coco Investments, LLC v. Zamir Manager River Terrace, LLC,* 26 Misc.3d 1231 (N.Y.Sup. 2010)] (See *The Limited Liability Company.*)

**4–5. LLC Dissolution.** Walter Van Houten and John King formed 1545 Ocean Avenue, LLC, with each managing 50 percent of the business. Its purpose was to renovate an existing building and construct a new commercial building. Van Houten and King quarreled over many aspects of the work on the properties. King claimed that Van Houten paid the contractors too much for the work performed. As the projects neared completion, King demanded that the LLC be dissolved and that Van Houten agree to a buyout. Because the parties could not agree on a buyout, King sued for dissolution. The trial court enjoined (prevented) further work on the projects until the dispute was settled. As the ground for dissolution, King cited the fights over management decisions. There was no claim of fraud or frustration of purpose. The trial court ordered that the LLC be dissolved, and Van Houten appealed. Should either of the owners be forced to dissolve the LLC before the completion of its purpose—that is, before the building projects are finished? Explain. [*In re 1545 Ocean Avenue, LLC,* 893 N.Y.S.2d 590 (N.Y.A.D. 2 Dept. 2010)] (See *Dissociation and Dissolution of an LLC.*)

**4–6. Business Case Problem with Sample Answer— LLC Operation.** After Hurricane Katrina struck the Gulf  Coast, James Williford, Patricia Mosser, Marquetta Smith, and Michael Floyd formed Bluewater Logistics, LLC, to bid on construction contracts. Under Mississippi law, every member of a member-managed LLC is entitled to participate in managing the business. The operating agreement provided for a "super majority" 75 percent vote to remove a member who

"has either committed a felony or under any other circumstances that would jeopardize the company status" as a contractor. After Bluewater had completed more than $5 million in contracts, Smith told Williford that she, Mosser, and Floyd were exercising their "super majority" vote to fire him. No reason was provided. Williford sued Bluewater and the other members. Did Smith, Mosser, and Floyd breach the state LLC statute, their fiduciary duties, or the Bluewater operating agreements? Discuss. [*Bluewater Logistics, LLC v. Williford,* 55 So.3d 148 (Miss. 2011)] (See *LLC Management and Operation.*)

• For a sample answer to Problem 4–6, go to Appendix C at the end of this text.

**4–7. Jurisdictional Requirements.** Fadal Machining Centers, LLC, and MAG Industrial Automation Centers, LLC, sued a New Jersey–based corporation, Mid-Atlantic CNC, Inc., in federal district court. Ten percent of MAG was owned by SP MAG Holdings, a Delaware LLC. SP MAG had six members, including a Delaware limited partnership called Silver Point Capital Fund and a Delaware LLC called SPCP Group III. In turn, Silver Point and SPCP Group had a common member, Robert O'Shea, who was a New Jersey citizen. Assuming that the amount in controversy exceeds $75,000, does the district court have diversity jurisdiction? Why or why not? [*Fadal Machining Centers, LLC v. Mid-Atlantic CNC, Inc.,* 2012 WL 8669 (9th Cir. 2012)] (See *The Limited Liability Company.*)

**4–8. Jurisdictional Requirements.** Siloam Springs Hotel, LLC, operates a Hampton Inn in Siloam Springs, Arkansas. Siloam bought insurance from Century Surety Co. to cover the hotel. When guests suffered injuries due to a leak of carbon monoxide from the heating element of an indoor swimming pool, Siloam filed a claim with Century. Century denied coverage, which Siloam disputed. Century asked a federal district court to resolve the dispute. In asserting that the federal court had jurisdiction, Century noted that the amount in controversy exceeded $75,000 and that the parties had complete diversity of citizenship. Century is "a corporation organized under the laws of Ohio, with its principal place of business in Michigan," and Siloam is "a corporation organized under the laws of Oklahoma, with its principal place of business in Arkansas." Can the court exercise diversity jurisdiction in this case? Discuss. [*Siloam Springs Hotel, L.L.C. v. Century Surety Co.,* 781 F.3d 1233 (10th Cir. 2015)] (See *The Limited Liability Company.*)

**4–9. Special Business Forms.** Randall and Peggy Norman operated a dairy farm in Pine River, Minnesota. About ten years after the operation was begun, the cows started to experience health issues. Over the next eighteen years, the herd suffered many serious health problems. Eventually, stray electrical voltage—which can use cow hooves as an unintended pathway, causing health issues—was detected. By then, milk production in the Normans' herd had declined from 27 percent above the state average to 20 percent below it. The Normans filed a suit in a Minnesota state court against Crow Wing

Cooperative Power & Light Company, a member-owned electrical cooperative that provided electricity to the Normans' farm. If Crow Wing is found to have acted negligently, can its members be held jointly liable for the cooperative's acts? Explain. [*Norman v. Crow Wing Co-operative Power & Light Co.,* __ N.W.2d __, 2016 WL 687472 (Minn.App. 2016)] (See *Special Business Forms.*)

### 4–10. A Question of Ethics—Limited Liability Companies.

 *Blushing Brides, LLC, a publisher of wedding planning magazines in Columbus, Ohio, opened an account with Gray Printing Co. in July 2000. On behalf of Blushing Brides, Louis Zacks, the firm's member-manager, signed a credit agreement that identified the firm as the "purchaser" and required payment within thirty days. Despite the agreement, Blushing Brides typically took up to six months to pay the full amount for its orders. Gray printed and shipped 10,000 copies of a fall/winter 2001 issue for Blushing Brides but had not been paid when the firm ordered 15,000 copies of a spring/summer 2002 issue. Gray refused to print the new order without an assurance of payment. On May 22, Zacks signed a promissory note payable to Gray within thirty days for $14,778, plus interest at 6 percent per year. Gray printed the new order but by October had been paid only $7,500. Gray filed a suit in an Ohio state court against Blushing Brides and Zacks to collect the balance.* [Gray Printing Co. v. Blushing Brides, LLC, *2006 WL 832587 (Ohio App. 2006)]* (See *The Limited Liability Company.*)

**(a)** Under what circumstances is a member of an LLC liable for the firm's debts? In this case, is Zacks personally liable under the credit agreement for the unpaid amount on Blushing Brides' account? Did Zacks's promissory note affect the parties' liability on the account? Explain.

**(b)** Should a member of an LLC assume an ethical responsibility to meet the obligations of the firm? Discuss.

**(c)** Gray shipped only 10,000 copies of the spring/summer 2002 issue of Blushing Brides' magazine, waiting for the publisher to identify a destination for the other 5,000 copies. The magazine had a retail price of $4.50 per copy. Did Gray have a legal or ethical duty to "mitigate the damages" by attempting to sell or otherwise distribute these copies itself? Why or why not?

### 4–11. Special Case Analysis—LLC Dissolution.

Go to Case Analysis 4.3, *Reese v. Newman.* Read the excerpt and answer the following questions.

**(a)** **Issue:** Which party's choice between two alternatives was at the heart of the issue on the appeal of the *Reese* case?

**(b)** **Rule of Law:** What rules of interpretation did the appellate court use to construe the language of the statutes that created those alternatives?

**(c)** **Applying the Rule of Law:** How did the court construe the language of those statutes?

**(d)** **Conclusion:** How did the court's construction of that language lead to the result?

## Legal Reasoning Group Activity

### 4–12. Fiduciary Duties in LLCs.

Newbury Properties Group owns, manages, and develops real property. Jerry Stoker and the Stoker Group, Inc. (the Stokers), also develop real property. Newbury entered into agreements with the Stokers concerning a large tract of property in Georgia. The parties formed Bellemare, LLC, to develop various parcels of the tract for residential purposes. The operating agreement of Bellemare indicated that "no Member shall be accountable to the LLC or to any other Member with respect to any other business or activity even if the business or activity competes with the LLC's business." Later, when the Newbury group contracted with other parties to develop parcels within the tract in competition with Bellemare, LLC, the Stokers sued, alleging breach of fiduciary duty. (See *LLC Management and Operation.*)

**(a)** The first group will discuss and outline the fiduciary duties that the members of an LLC owe to each other.

**(b)** The second group will determine whether the terms of an operating agreement can alter these fiduciary duties.

**(c)** The last group will decide in whose favor the court should rule in this situation.

# Corporate Formation and Financing

The corporation is a creature of statute. A corporation is an artificial being, existing only in law and being neither tangible nor visible. Its existence generally depends on state law, although some corporations, especially public organizations, are created under federal law. Each state has its own body of corporate law, and these laws are not entirely uniform.

The Model Business Corporation Act (MBCA) is a codification of modern corporation law that has been influential in shaping state corporation statutes. Today, the majority of state statutes are guided by the most recent version of the MBCA, often referred to as the Revised Model Business Corporation Act (RMBCA).

Keep in mind, however, that there is considerable variation among the laws of states that have used the MBCA or the RMBCA as a basis for their statutes. In addition, several states do not follow either act. Consequently, individual state corporation laws should be relied on to determine corporate law rather than the MBCA or RMBCA.

## 5–1 The Nature and Classification of Corporations

A corporation is a legal entity created and recognized by state law. This business entity can have one or more owners (called shareholders), and it operates under a name distinct from the names of its owners. Both individuals and other businesses can be shareholders. The corporation substitutes itself for its shareholders when conducting corporate business and incurring liability. Its authority to act and the liability for its actions, however, are separate and apart from the shareholders who own it.

A corporation is recognized under U.S. law as a person—an artificial *legal person,* as opposed to a *natural person.* As a "person," it enjoys many of the same rights and privileges under state and federal law that U.S. citizens enjoy. For instance, corporations possess the same right of access to the courts as citizens and can sue or be sued. The constitutional guarantees of due process, free speech, and freedom from unreasonable searches and seizures also apply to corporations.

### 5–1a Corporate Personnel

In a corporation, the responsibility for the overall management of the firm is entrusted to a *board of directors,* whose members are elected by the shareholders. The board of directors makes the policy decisions and hires *corporate officers* and other employees to run the daily business operations.

When an individual purchases a share of stock in a corporation, that person becomes a shareholder and an owner of the corporation. Unlike the partners in a partnership, the body of shareholders can change constantly without affecting the continued existence of the corporation. A shareholder can sue the corporation, and the corporation can sue a shareholder. Additionally, under certain circumstances, a shareholder can sue on behalf of a corporation.

### 5–1b The Limited Liability of Shareholders

One of the key advantages of the corporate form is the limited liability of its owners. Normally, corporate shareholders are not personally liable for the obligations of the corporation beyond the extent of their investments.

In certain limited situations, however, a court can *pierce the corporate veil* and impose liability on shareholders for the corporation's obligations. Additionally, creditors often will not extend credit to small companies unless the shareholders assume personal liability, as guarantors, for corporate obligations.

## 5–1c Corporate Earnings and Taxation

When a corporation earns profits, it can either pass them on to shareholders in the form of **dividends** or retain them as profits. These **retained earnings,** if invested properly, will yield higher corporate profits in the future. In theory, higher profits will cause the price of the company's stock to rise. Individual shareholders can then reap the benefits in the capital gains they receive when they sell their stock.

**Corporate Taxation** Whether a corporation retains its profits or passes them on to the shareholders as dividends, those profits are subject to income taxation by various levels of government. Failure to pay taxes can lead to severe consequences. The state can suspend the organization's corporate status until the taxes are paid and can even dissolve the corporation for failing to pay taxes.

Another important aspect of corporate taxation is that corporate profits can be subject to double taxation. The company pays tax on its profits. Then, if the profits are passed on to the shareholders as dividends, the shareholders must also pay income tax on them. (This is true unless the dividends represent distributions of capital, which are returns of holders' investments in the stock of the company.) The corporation normally does not receive a tax deduction for dividends it distributes. This double-taxation feature is one of the major disadvantages of the corporate form.

**Holding Companies** Some U.S. corporations use holding companies to reduce or defer their U.S. income taxes. At its simplest, a **holding company** (sometimes referred to as a *parent company*) is a company whose business activity consists of holding shares in another company. Typically, the holding company is established in a low-tax or no-tax offshore jurisdiction, such as the Cayman Islands, Dubai, Hong Kong, Luxembourg, Monaco, or Panama.

Sometimes, a U.S. corporation sets up a holding company in a low-tax offshore environment and then transfers its cash, bonds, stocks, and other investments to the holding company. In general, any profits received by the holding company on these investments are taxed at the rate of the offshore jurisdiction where the company is registered. Once the profits are brought "onshore," though, they are taxed at the federal corporate income tax rate. Any payments received by the shareholders are also taxable at the full U.S. rates.

## 5–1d Criminal Acts

Under modern criminal law, a corporation may be held liable for the criminal acts of its agents and employees.

Although corporations cannot be imprisoned, they can be fined. (Of course, corporate directors and officers can be imprisoned, and many have been in recent years.) In addition, under sentencing guidelines for crimes committed by corporate employees (white-collar crimes), corporations can face fines amounting to hundreds of millions of dollars.

## 5–1e Tort Liability

A corporation is liable for the torts committed by its agents or officers within the course and scope of their employment. The doctrine of *respondeat superior* applies to corporations in the same way as it does to other agency relationships.

■ **CASE IN POINT 5.1** Mark Bloom was an officer and a director of MB Investment Partners, Inc. (MB), at the time that he formed North Hills, LP, a stock investment fund. Bloom and other MB employees used MB's offices and equipment to administer investments in North Hills.

Later, investors in North Hills requested a full redemption of their investments. By that time, however, most of the funds that had been invested were gone. North Hills had, in fact, been a Ponzi scheme that Bloom had used to finance his lavish personal lifestyle, taking at least $20 million from North Hills for his personal use.

Barry Belmont and other North Hills investors filed a suit in a federal district court against MB, alleging fraud. The court held that MB was liable for Bloom's fraud. MB appealed, and the appellate court affirmed. Tort liability can be attributed to a corporation for the acts of its agent that were committed within the scope of the agent's employment.[1] ■

Because corporations can be liable for their employees' fraud and other misconduct, companies need to be careful about whom they hire and how much they monitor or supervise their employees. Some companies are using special software designed to predict employee misconduct before it occurs, as discussed in this chapter's *Digital Update* feature.

## 5–1f Classification of Corporations

Corporations can be classified in several ways. The classification of a corporation normally depends on its location, purpose, and ownership characteristics, as described in the following subsections.

**Domestic, Foreign, and Alien Corporations** A corporation is referred to as a **domestic corporation** by its

---

1. *Belmont v. MB Investment Partners, Inc.*, 708 F.3d 470 (3d Cir. 2013).

## DIGITAL UPDATE — Programs That Predict Employee Misconduct

Monitoring employees' e-mails and phone conversations at work is generally legal.[a] But what about using software to analyze employee behavior with the goal of predicting, rather than observing, wrongdoing? Now we are entering into the digital realm of *predictive analytics*.

Spy agencies around the world today use analytic software to predict who will engage in a terrorist act, where it will happen, and when. Software applied to data mining of employee behavior (usually just online) actually has been around for several years as well. For example, Amazon started using employee-monitoring programs to predict who might quit. But only recently have such programs been used to predict misconduct.

### JPMorgan Chase Attempts to Reduce Its Legal Bills

JPMorgan, the world's largest private financial institution, also is perhaps the world's largest purchaser of legal services in that sector. Its legal bills have exceeded $36 billion since the financial crisis of 2008. The company's management found that employees had

engaged in dubious mortgage bond sales and rigged foreign exchange and energy markets, among many other transgressions. The company hired an extra 2,500 compliance officers and spent almost $750 million on compliance operations during a recent three-year period.

Now JPMorgan is using new software to identify—in advance of any wrongdoing—"rogue" employees. The software analyzes a wide range of inputs on employees' behavior in an attempt to identify patterns that point to future misconduct. If successful, the program will certainly be copied by other financial institutions.

### An Ethical Problem?

A former Federal Reserve Bank examiner, Mark Williams, has raised an important issue with respect to predictive analytics: "Policing intentions can be a slippery slope. Do people get a scarlet letter for something they have yet to do?" In other words, will employees be labeled as wrongdoers before they have actually done anything wrong?

**Critical Thinking** *Is thinking about committing a crime illegal?*

a. Electronic Communications Privacy Act, 18 U.S.C.A. Sec. 2511(2)(d).

home state (the state in which it incorporates). A corporation formed in one state but doing business in another is referred to in the second state as a **foreign corporation.** A corporation formed in another country (say, Mexico) but doing business in the United States is referred to in the United States as an **alien corporation.**

A corporation does not have an automatic right to do business in a state other than its state of incorporation. In some instances, it must obtain a *certificate of authority* in any state in which it plans to do business. Once the certificate has been issued, the corporation generally can exercise in that state all of the powers conferred on it by

its home state. If a foreign corporation does business in a state without obtaining a certificate of authority, the state can impose substantial fines and sanctions on that corporation.

Note that most state statutes specify certain activities, such as soliciting orders via the Internet, that are not considered "doing business" within the state. For instance, a foreign corporation normally does not need a certificate of authority to sell goods or services via the Internet or by mail.

What constitutes doing business within a state? In the following case, the court answered that question.

**Case 5.1**

# Drake Manufacturing Co. v. Polyflow, Inc.
Superior Court of Pennsylvania, 2015 PA Super 16, 109 A.3d 250 (2015).

**Background and Facts** Drake Manufacturing Company, a Delaware corporation, entered into a contract to sell certain products to Polyflow, Inc., headquartered in Pennsylvania. Drake promised to ship the goods from Drake's plant in Sheffield, Pennsylvania, to Polyflow's place of business in Oaks, Pennsylvania, as well as to addresses in California, Canada, and Holland.

Case 5.1 Continues

Case 5.1 Continued

When Polyflow withheld payment of about $300,000 for some of the goods, Drake filed a breach of contract suit in a Pennsylvania state court against Polyflow seeking to collect the unpaid amount. But Drake had failed to obtain a certificate of authority to do business in Pennsylvania as a foreign corporation. Polyflow asserted that this failure to register with the state deprived Drake of the capacity to bring an action against Polyflow in the state's courts. The court issued a judgment in Drake's favor. Polyflow appealed.

## In the Language of the Court
Opinion by *JENKINS*, J. [Judge]:
* * * *

[15 Pennsylvania Consolidated Statutes (Pa.C.S.)] Section 4121 provides: "A foreign business corporation, before doing business in this Commonwealth, shall procure a certificate of authority to do so from the Department of State."

* * * Typical conduct requiring a certificate of authority includes maintaining an office to conduct local intrastate business [and] entering into contracts relating to local business or sales.

*A corporation is not "doing business" solely because it resorts to the courts of this Commonwealth to recover an indebtedness.* [Emphasis added.]
* * * *

[15 Pa.C.S.] Section 4141(a) provides in relevant part that "a nonqualified foreign business corporation doing business in this Commonwealth * * * shall not be permitted to maintain any action or proceeding in any court of this Commonwealth until the corporation has obtained a certificate of authority."
* * * *

* * * The evidence demonstrates that Drake failed to submit a certificate of authority into evidence prior to the verdict in violation of 15 Pa.C.S. Section 4121. Therefore, the trial court should not have permitted Drake to prosecute its action.

The trial court contends that Drake is exempt from the certificate of authority requirement because it merely commenced suit in Pennsylvania to collect a debt * * * . Drake did much more, however, than file suit or attempt to collect a debt. Drake maintains an office in Pennsylvania to conduct local business, conduct which typically requires a certificate of authority. Drake also entered into a contract with Polyflow, and * * * shipped couplings and portable swaging machines to Polyflow's place of business in Pennsylvania * * * . In short, *Drake's conduct was * * * regular, systematic, and extensive, * * * thus constituting the transaction of business and requiring Drake to obtain a certificate of authority.* [Emphasis added.]

We also hold that Drake needed a certificate of authority to sue Polyflow in Pennsylvania for Polyflow's failure to pay for out-of-state shipments in California, Canada and Holland. A foreign corporation that "does business" in Pennsylvania * * * must obtain a certificate in order to prosecute a lawsuit in this Commonwealth, regardless of whether the lawsuit itself concerns in-state conduct or out-of-state conduct.

**Decision and Remedy** *A state intermediate appellate court reversed the judgment in Drake's favor. Under Pennsylvania state statutes, Drake was required to obtain a certificate of authority to do business in that state. Drake failed to do so. The court should not have allowed Drake to prosecute its action against Polyflow.*

**Critical Thinking**
• **Legal Environment** *Why would the appellate court permit Polyflow to get away with not paying for delivered and presumably merchantable goods?*

---

**Public and Private Corporations** A **public corporation** is a corporation formed by the government to meet some political or governmental purpose. Cities and towns that incorporate are common examples. In addition, many federal government organizations, such as the U.S. Postal Service, the Tennessee Valley Authority, and AMTRAK, are public corporations.

Note that a public corporation is not the same as a **publicly held corporation**. A publicly held corporation (often called a *public company*) is any corporation whose shares are publicly traded in a securities market, such as the New York Stock Exchange or the NASDAQ.

Private corporations, in contrast, are created either wholly or in part for private benefit—that is, for profit. Most corporations are private. Although they may serve a public purpose, as a public electric or gas utility does, they are owned by private persons rather than by a government.[2]

---

**2.** The United States Supreme Court first recognized the property rights of private corporations and clarified the distinction between public and private corporations in the landmark case *Trustees of Dartmouth College v. Woodward*, 17 U.S. (4 Wheaton) 518, 4 L.Ed. 629 (1819).

**Nonprofit Corporations** Corporations formed for purposes other than making a profit are called *nonprofit* or *not-for-profit* corporations. Private hospitals, educational institutions, charities, and religious organizations, for instance, are frequently organized as nonprofit corporations. The nonprofit corporation is a convenient form of organization that allows various groups to own property and to form contracts without exposing the individual members to personal liability.

In some circumstances, a nonprofit corporation and its members may also be immune from liability for a personal injury caused by its negligence. Whether those circumstances were present in the following case was the question before the court.

## Case Analysis 5.2

# Pantano v. Newark Museum

Superior Court of New Jersey, Appellate Division, __ A.3d __, 2016 WL 528771 (2016).

### In the Language of the Court

*PER CURIAM.*

\* \* \* \*

\* \* \* Plaintiff [Loredana Pantano] slipped and fell on icy steps at an entrance to the [Newark] Museum, suffering injuries to her back. At the time, plaintiff was employed as an immigration attorney by La Casa de Don Pedro (La Casa), a nonprofit organization located in Newark [New Jersey]. Upon arrival at her office that day, plaintiff was told by La Casa's Director of Personal Development to go to the Museum for an educational panel discussion being held as part of La Casa's fortieth anniversary celebration.

\* \* \* The event was one of several organized to celebrate and commemorate the organization's history and role in the development of Newark. Staff members were not directly engaged in fundraising, but they were told to mingle with those attending the event, some of whom were contributors to La Casa. The Museum charged La Casa a fee for the use of the facility, specifically an auditorium to be used by the panel and those in attendance.

The Museum is a nonprofit association organized exclusively for charitable, artistic, scientific, educational, historical and cultural purposes \* \* \* . It does, on occasion, rent its facilities to the public in order to generate income.

Plaintiff filed suit [in a New Jersey state court against the Museum] alleging the Museum was negligent in its maintenance of the premises. \* \* \* The Museum moved for summary judgment, contending that plaintiff was a direct beneficiary of its charitable endeavors.

\* \* \* \*

\* \* \* The judge granted the Museum's motion, and this appeal followed.

Plaintiff contends that she was not a beneficiary of the Museum's charitable purposes at the time of her fall because she was on the premises at the direction of her employer. We agree that pursuant to the [New Jersey Supreme] Court's holding in *Mayer v. Fairlawn Jewish Center*, 38 N.J. 549, 186 A.2d 274 (1962), plaintiff was not a direct recipient of the Museum's good works.

\* \* \* \*

In pertinent part, the [state Charitable Immunity Act (CIA)] provides:

No nonprofit corporation \* \* \* shall \* \* \* be liable to respond in damages to any person who shall suffer damage from the negligence \* \* \* of such corporation \* \* \* where such person is a beneficiary, to whatever degree, of the works of such nonprofit corporation \* \* \* ; provided, however, that such immunity from liability shall not extend to any person \* \* \* where such person is one unconcerned in and unrelated to and outside of the benefactions of such corporation.

The CIA serves two primary purposes. *First, immunity preserves a charity's assets. Second, immunity recognizes that a beneficiary of the services of a charitable organization has entered into a relationship that exempts the benefactor from liability.* [Emphasis added.]

\* \* \* The established test for determining whether a party is a beneficiary of the works of a charity has two prongs. The first is that the institution pleading the immunity, at the time in question, was engaged in the performance of the charitable objectives it was organized to advance. The second is that the injured party must have been a direct recipient of those good works.

\* \* \* \*

As to the first prong, \* \* \* a qualifying organization does not lose its statutory immunity merely because it charges money for its services, unless it makes a profit or collects fees for services totally unrelated to its organizational pursuits. \* \* \* Hosting an educational panel

Case 5.2 Continues

**Case 5.2 Continued**

discussion in the auditorium was entirely consistent with the Museum's charitable endeavors.

The second prong of the test * * * distinguishes between persons benefiting from the charity, and persons who contribute to the charity by virtue of their attendance or participation.
* * * *

In *Mayer*, * * * an employee of the Development Corporation for Israel was promoting the sale of bonds at a dinner on the premises of [Fairlawn Jewish Center, the defendant, when he sustained an injury].

* * * *

* * * He was there in fulfillment of his function and obligation as an employee to engage in the employer's work at the direction of the employer, and not for the purpose of receiving personally the philanthropy of the Center. Under the circumstances present he was a stranger to the charity and the [CIA did] not stand in the way of recovery.
* * * *

* * * *[Thus, under the CIA,] to be a beneficiary under the second prong, the injured party must be a direct recipient of the Museum's good works. Only those*

*unconcerned in and unrelated to the benefactions of the organization are not beneficiaries.* [Emphasis added.]
* * * *

As an intermediate appellate court, we are bound to follow and enforce the decisions of the Supreme Court. Under [*Mayer*], plaintiff, as an employee of La Casa who was ordered on the day of her fall to attend the panel discussion at the Museum, was not a direct beneficiary of the Museum's charitable endeavors.

We therefore reverse the order granting summary judgment to the Museum and remand the matter.

**Legal Reasoning Questions**

**1.** How do the purposes of the CIA support each other?

**2.** Can a person be a direct beneficiary of a nonprofit's good works even though the person is on the nonprofit's premises under the direction of a third party? Explain.

**3.** Suppose that the museum had not been hosting an educational panel in its auditorium but instead had rented the facility to an organization for a sales conference. Would the result have been different? Discuss.

---

**Close Corporations** Most corporate enterprises in the United States fall into the category of close corporations. A **close corporation** is one whose shares are held by relatively few persons, often members of a family. Close corporations are also referred to as *closely held, family,* or *privately held* corporations.

Usually, the members of the small group constituting the shareholders of a close corporation are personally known to each other. Because the number of shareholders is so small, there is no trading market for the shares. In practice, a close corporation is often operated like a partnership.

The statutes in many states allow close corporations to depart significantly from certain formalities required by traditional corporation law.[3] Under the RMBCA, close corporations have considerable flexibility in determining their operating rules [RMBCA 7.32]. If all of a corporation's shareholders agree in writing, the corporation can operate without directors and bylaws. In addition, the corporation can operate without annual or special shareholders' or directors' meetings, stock certificates, or formal records of shareholders' or directors' decisions.[4]

**Management of Close Corporations.** Management of a close corporation resembles that of a sole proprietorship or a partnership, in that control is held by a single shareholder or a tightly knit group of shareholders. As a corporation, however, the firm must meet all specific legal requirements set forth in state statutes.

To prevent a majority shareholder from dominating the company, a close corporation may require that more than a simple majority of the directors approve any action taken by the board. In a larger corporation, such a requirement would typically apply only to extraordinary actions (such as selling all the corporate assets) and not to ordinary business decisions.

**Transfer of Shares in Close Corporations.** By definition, a close corporation has a small number of shareholders. Thus, the transfer of one shareholder's shares to someone else can cause serious management problems. The other

---

3. In some states, such as Maryland, a close corporation need not have a board of directors.

4. Shareholders cannot agree, however, to eliminate certain rights of shareholders, such as the right to inspect corporate records or the right to bring *derivative actions* (lawsuits on behalf of the corporation).

shareholders may find themselves required to share control with someone they do not know or like. ■ **EXAMPLE 5.2** Three siblings, Sherry, Karen, and Henry Johnson, are the only shareholders of Johnson's Car Wash, Inc. Henry wants to sell his shares, but Sherry and Karen do not want him to sell the shares to a third person unknown to them. ■

To avoid this situation, a close corporation can restrict the transferability of shares to outside persons. Shareholders can be required to offer their shares to the corporation or to the other shareholders before selling them to an outside purchaser. In fact, in a few states close corporations must transfer shares in this manner under state statutes.

One way the close corporation can effect restrictions on transferability is by spelling them out in a **shareholder agreement.** A shareholder agreement can also provide for proportional control when one of the original shareholders dies. The decedent's shares of stock in the corporation can be divided in such a way that the proportionate holdings of the survivors, and thus their proportionate control, will be maintained.

**Misappropriation of Close Corporation Funds.** Sometimes, a majority shareholder in a close corporation takes advantage of his or her position and misappropriates company funds. In such situations, the normal remedy for the injured minority shareholders is to have their shares appraised and to be paid the fair market value for them.

■ **CASE IN POINT 5.3** John Murray, Stephen Hopkins, and Paul Ryan were officers, directors, employees, and majority shareholders of Olympic Adhesives, Inc. Merek Rubin was a minority shareholder. Murray, Hopkins, and Ryan were paid salaries. Twice a year, they paid themselves additional compensation—between 75 and 98 percent of Olympic's net profits, allocated according to their stock ownership. Rubin filed a suit against the majority shareholders, alleging that their compensation deprived him of his share of Olympic's profits.

The court explained that a salary should reasonably relate to a corporate officer's ability and the quantity and quality of his or her services. The court found that a reasonable amount of compensation would have been 10 percent of Olympic's average annual net sales. Therefore, the additional compensation the majority shareholders paid themselves—based on stock ownership and not on performance—was excessive. The court ordered the defendants to repay Olympic nearly $6 million to be distributed among its shareholders. On appeal, the reviewing court affirmed this decision.[5] ■

---

5. *Rubin v. Murray,* 79 Mass.App.Ct. 64, 943 N.E.2d 949 (2011).

**S Corporations** A close corporation that meets the qualifying requirements specified in Subchapter S of the Internal Revenue Code can choose to operate as an **S corporation.** (A corporation will automatically be taxed under Subchapter C unless it elects S corporation status.) If a corporation has S corporation status, it can avoid the imposition of income taxes at the corporate level while retaining many of the advantages of a corporation, particularly limited liability.

**Important Requirements.**  Among the numerous requirements for S corporation status, the following are the most important:

1. The corporation must be a domestic corporation.
2. The corporation must not be a member of an affiliated group of corporations.
3. The shareholders must be individuals, estates, or certain trusts and tax-exempt organizations. Partnerships and nonqualifying trusts cannot be shareholders. Corporations can be shareholders under certain circumstances.
4. The corporation must have no more than one hundred shareholders.
5. The corporation must have only one class of stock, although it is not necessary that all shareholders have the same voting rights.
6. No shareholder of the corporation may be a nonresident alien.

**Effect of S Election.**  An S corporation is treated differently than a regular corporation for tax purposes. An S corporation is taxed like a partnership, so the corporate income passes through to the shareholders, who pay personal income tax on it. This treatment enables the S corporation to avoid the double taxation imposed on regular corporations.

In addition, the shareholders' tax brackets may be lower than the tax bracket that the corporation would have been in if the tax had been imposed at the corporate level. The resulting tax saving is particularly attractive when the corporation wants to accumulate earnings for some future business purpose. If the corporation has losses, the S election allows the shareholders to use the losses to offset other income.

In spite of these benefits, the S corporation has lost much of its appeal. The newer limited liability business forms (such as LLCs, LPs, and LLPs) offer similar tax advantages and greater flexibility.

**Professional Corporations** Professionals such as physicians, lawyers, dentists, and accountants can incorporate. A professional corporation is typically identified by the letters *P.C.* (professional corporation), *S.C.* (service corporation), or *P.A.* (professional association).

In general, the laws governing the formation and operation of professional corporations are similar to those governing ordinary business corporations. There are some differences in terms of liability, however, because the shareholder-owners are professionals who are held to a higher standard of conduct.

For liability purposes, some courts treat professional corporations somewhat like partnerships and hold each professional liable for malpractice committed within the scope of the business by others in the firm. A shareholder in a professional corporation generally cannot be held liable for torts committed by other professionals at the firm except those related to malpractice or breach of duty to clients.

**Benefit Corporations** A growing number of states have enacted legislation that creates a relatively new corporate form called a *benefit corporation*. A **benefit corporation** is a for-profit corporation that seeks to have a material positive impact on society and the environment. Benefit corporations differ from traditional corporations in the following ways:

1. *Purpose.* Although the corporation is designed to make a profit, its purpose is to benefit the public as a whole. (In contrast, the purpose of an ordinary business corporation is to provide long-term shareholder value.) The directors of a benefit corporation must, during the decision-making process, consider the impact of their decisions on society and the environment.
2. *Accountability.* Shareholders of a benefit corporation determine whether the company has achieved a material positive impact. Shareholders also have a right of private action, called a *benefit enforcement proceeding,* enabling them to sue the corporation if it fails to pursue or create public benefit.
3. *Transparency.* A benefit corporation must issue an annual benefit report on its overall social and environmental performance that uses a recognized third-party standard to assess its performance. The report must be delivered to the shareholders and posted on a public Web site.

See Concept Summary 5.1 for a review of the ways in which corporations are classified.

# 5–2 Corporate Formation and Powers

Many of today's largest companies started as sole proprietorships or partnerships. They converted to corporate entities as they grew because they needed to obtain additional capital by issuing shares of stock. Incorporating a business is much simpler today than it was twenty years ago, and many states allow businesses to incorporate via the Internet. Here, we examine the process by which a corporation comes into existence.

## 5–2a Promotional Activities

In the past, preliminary steps were taken to organize and promote a business prior to incorporating. Contracts were made with investors and others on behalf of the future corporation. Today, due to the relative ease of forming a corporation in most states, persons incorporating their business rarely, if ever, engage in preliminary promotional activities.

Nevertheless, businesspersons should understand that they are personally liable for any preincorporation contracts made with investors, accountants, or others on behalf of the future corporation. Personal liability continues until the newly formed corporation assumes liability for the preincorporation contracts through a novation.

## 5–2b Incorporation Procedures

Each state has its own set of incorporation procedures. Most often, they are listed on the secretary of state's Web site. Generally, however, all incorporators follow several basic steps, discussed next.

**Select the State of Incorporation** Because state corporate laws differ, individuals seeking to incorporate a business may look for the states that offer the most advantageous tax or other provisions. Many corporations, for instance, have chosen to incorporate in Delaware because it has historically had the least restrictive laws, along with provisions that favor corporate management. For reasons of convenience and cost, though, businesses often choose to incorporate in the state in which the corporation's business will primarily be conducted.

**Secure the Corporate Name** The choice of a corporate name is subject to state approval to ensure against duplication or deception. Most state statutes require a search to confirm that the chosen corporate name is available. A

# Concept Summary 5.1

## Classification of Corporations

**Domestic, Foreign, and Alien Corporations**
- A corporation is referred to as a *domestic corporation* in its home state (the state in which it incorporates).
- A corporation is referred to as a *foreign corporation* by any state that is not its home state.
- A corporation is referred to as an *alien corporation* if it originates in another country but does business in the United States.

**Public and Private Corporations**
- A *public corporation* is formed by a government (for instance, a city, town, or public project).
- A *private corporation* is formed wholly or in part for private benefit (profit). Most corporations are private corporations.

**Nonprofit Corporation**
- A *nonprofit corporation* is formed without a profit-making purpose (for example, charitable, educational, and religious organizations and hospitals).

**Close Corporation**
- A *close corporation* is owned by a family or a relatively small number of individuals. Because the number of shareholders is small and the transfer of shares is usually restricted, the shares are not traded in a public securities market.

**S Corporation**
- An *S corporation* is a small domestic corporation (must have no more than one hundred shareholders) that, under Subchapter S of the Internal Revenue Code, is given special tax treatment. An S corporation allows shareholders to enjoy the limited legal liability of the corporate form but avoid its double-taxation feature. (Shareholders pay taxes on the income at personal income tax rates, and the S corporation is not taxed separately.)

**Professional Corporation**
- A *professional corporation* is formed by professionals—such as physicians or lawyers—to obtain the advantages of incorporation. A professional corporation functions like an ordinary corporation but is treated differently in terms of liability. Courts may treat the shareholders like partners with regard to malpractice liability.

**Benefit Corporation**
- A *benefit corporation* is designed for businesses that want to consider society and the environment in addition to profit. Shareholders have a right to sue the corporation in enforcement proceedings if it fails to benefit the public.

new corporation's name cannot be the same as, or deceptively similar to, the name of an existing corporation doing business within the state. All states require the corporation's name to include the word *Corporation (Corp.), Incorporated (Inc.), Company (Co.), or Limited (Ltd.).*[6]

---

6. Failure to use one of these terms to disclose corporate status may be grounds for holding an individual incorporator liable for corporate contracts under agency law.

**Prepare the Articles of Incorporation** The primary document needed to incorporate a business is the **articles of incorporation** (for a sample, see Exhibit 5–1). The articles include basic information about the corporation and serve as a primary source of authority for its future organization and business functions. The person or persons who execute (sign) the articles are the *incorporators.*

**EXHIBIT 5–1** Sample Articles of Incorporation

**ARTICLE I.** The name of the corporation is _____ .

**ARTICLE II.** The period of its duration is _____ (may be a number of years or until a certain date).

**ARTICLE III.** The purpose (or purposes) for which the corporation is organized is (are) _____

**ARTICLE IV.** The aggregate number of shares that the corporation shall have the authority to issue is _____ with the par value of _____ dollar(s) each (or without par value).

**ARTICLE V.** The corporation will not commence business until it has received for the issuance of its shares consideration of the value of $1,000 (can be any sum not less than $1,000).

**ARTICLE VI.** The address of the corporation's registered office is _____ and the name of its registered agent at such address is _____ .

**ARTICLE VII.** The number of initial directors is _____ , and the names and addresses of the directors are

**ARTICLE VIII.** The names and addresses of the incorporators are

_____ (Name)    _____ (Address)    _____ (Signature)

_____ (Name)    _____ (Address)    _____ (Signature)

_____ (Name)    _____ (Address)    _____ (Signature)

Sworn to on _____ by the above-named incorporators.
(Date)

_____
Notary Public

(Notary Seal)

Articles of incorporation vary widely depending on the jurisdiction and the size and type of the corporation. Generally, though, the articles *must* include the following information [RMBCA 2.02]:

1. The name of the corporation.
2. The number of shares of stock the corporation is authorized to issue [RMBCA 2.02(a)]. (Large corporations often also state a par value for each share, such as $0.20 per share, and specify the various types or classes of stock authorized for issuance.)
3. The name and street address of the corporation's initial registered agent and registered office. The registered agent is the person who can receive legal documents (such as orders to appear in court) on behalf of the corporation. The registered office is usually the main corporate office.
4. The name and address of each incorporator.

In addition, the articles *may* set forth other information, such as the names and addresses of the initial members of the board of directors and the duration and purpose of the corporation. A corporation has perpetual existence unless the articles state otherwise. As to the corporation's purpose, a corporation can be formed for any lawful purpose, and the RMBCA does not require the articles to include a specific statement of purpose. Consequently, the articles often include only a general statement of purpose. By not mentioning specifics, the corporation avoids the need for future amendments to the corporate articles [RMBCA 2.02(b)(2)(i), 3.01]. Similarly, the articles do not provide much detail about the firm's operations, which are spelled out in the company's *bylaws* (discussed shortly).

**File the Articles with the State** Once the articles of incorporation have been prepared and signed, they are sent to the appropriate state official, usually the secretary of state, along with the required filing fee. In most states, the secretary of state then stamps the articles "Filed" and returns a copy of the articles to the incorporators. Once this occurs, the corporation officially exists.

## 5–2c First Organizational Meeting to Adopt Bylaws

After incorporation, the first organizational meeting must be held. If the articles of incorporation named the initial board of directors, then the directors, by majority vote, call the meeting. If the articles did not name the directors (as is typical), then the incorporators hold the meeting to elect the directors and complete any other business necessary.

Usually, the most important function of this meeting is the adoption of **bylaws,** which are the internal rules of management for the corporation. The bylaws cannot conflict with the state corporation statute or the articles of incorporation [RMBCA 2.06]. Under the RMBCA, the shareholders may amend or repeal the bylaws. The board of directors may also amend or repeal the bylaws, unless the articles of incorporation or provisions of the state corporation statute reserve this power to the shareholders [RMBCA 10.20].

The bylaws typically describe such matters as voting requirements for shareholders, the election of the board of directors, and the methods of replacing directors. Bylaws also frequently outline the manner and time of holding shareholders' and board meetings.

## 5–2d Improper Incorporation

The procedures for incorporation are very specific. If they are not followed precisely, others may be able to challenge the existence of the corporation. Errors in incorporation procedures can become important when, for instance, a third party who is attempting to enforce a contract or bring a suit for a tort injury learns of them.

***De Jure* Corporations** If a corporation has substantially complied with all conditions precedent to incorporation, the corporation is said to have *de jure* (rightful and lawful) existence. In most states and under RMBCA 2.03(b), the secretary of state's filing of the articles of incorporation is conclusive proof that all mandatory statutory provisions have been met [RMBCA 2.03(b)].

Sometimes, the incorporators fail to comply with all statutory mandates. If the defect is minor, such as an incorrect address listed on the articles of incorporation, most courts will overlook the defect and find that a *de jure* corporation exists.

***De Facto* Corporations** If the defect in formation is substantial, such as a corporation's failure to hold an organizational meeting to adopt bylaws, the outcome will vary depending on the jurisdiction. Some states, including Mississippi, New York, Ohio, and Oklahoma, recognize the common law doctrine of *de facto* corporation.[7] In those states, the courts will treat a corporation as a legal corporation despite a defect in its formation if the following three requirements are met:

1. A state statute exists under which the corporation can be validly incorporated.

---

7. See, for example, *In re Hausman,* 13 N.Y.3d 408, 921 N.E.2d 191, 893 N.Y.S.2d 499 (2009).

**2.** The parties have made a good faith attempt to comply with the statute.
**3.** The parties have already undertaken to do business as a corporation.

Many state courts, however, have interpreted their states' version of the RMBCA as abolishing the common law doctrine of *de facto* corporations. These states include Alaska, Arizona, Minnesota, New Mexico, Oregon, South Dakota, Tennessee, Utah, and Washington, as well as the District of Columbia. In those jurisdictions, if there is a substantial defect in complying with the incorporation statute, the corporation does not legally exist, and the incorporators are personally liable.

**Corporation by Estoppel** Sometimes, a business association holds itself out to others as being a corporation when it has made no attempt to incorporate. In those situations, the firm normally will be estopped (prevented) from denying corporate status in a lawsuit by a third party. The estoppel doctrine most commonly applies when a third party contracts with an entity that claims to be a corporation but has not filed articles of incorporation. It may also apply when a third party contracts with a person claiming to be an agent of a corporation that does not in fact exist.

When justice requires, courts in some states will treat an alleged corporation as if it were an actual corporation for the purpose of determining rights and liabilities in particular circumstances.[8] Recognition of corporate status does not extend beyond the resolution of the problem at hand.

■ **CASE IN POINT 5.4** W.P. Media, Inc., and Alabama MBA, Inc., agreed to form a wireless Internet services company. W.P. Media was to create a wireless network, and Alabama MBA was to contribute the capital. Hugh Brown signed the parties' contract on behalf of Alabama MBA as the chair of its board. At the time, however, Alabama MBA's articles of incorporation had not yet been filed. Brown filed the articles of incorporation the following year.

Later, Brown and Alabama MBA filed a suit alleging that W.P. Media had breached their contract by not building the wireless network. W.P. Media contended that Alabama MBA had not existed as a corporation when the agreement was signed and thus the agreement was void. The Supreme Court of Alabama held that because W.P. Media had treated Alabama MBA as a corporation,

W.P. Media was estopped from denying Alabama MBA's corporate existence.[9] ■

### 5–2e Corporate Powers

When a corporation is created, the express and implied powers necessary to achieve its purpose also come into existence.

**Express Powers** The express powers of a corporation are found in its articles of incorporation, in the law of the state of incorporation, and in the state and federal constitutions. Corporate bylaws and the resolutions of the corporation's board of directors also establish express powers.

The following order of priority is used if a conflict arises among the various documents involving a corporation:

**1.** The U.S. Constitution.
**2.** State constitutions.
**3.** State statutes.
**4.** The articles of incorporation.
**5.** Bylaws.
**6.** Resolutions of the board of directors.

It is important that the bylaws set forth the specific operating rules of the corporation. State corporation statutes frequently provide default rules that apply if the company's bylaws are silent on an issue.

On occasion, the U.S. government steps in to challenge what a corporation may consider one of its express powers. This chapter's *Global Insight* feature discusses a dispute between the government and Microsoft Corporation over a demand that the company provide the government with access to e-mail stored in servers on foreign soil.

**Implied Powers** When a corporation is created, it acquires certain implied powers. Barring express constitutional, statutory, or other prohibitions, the corporation has the implied power to perform all acts reasonably necessary to accomplish its corporate purposes. For this reason, a corporation has the implied power to borrow and lend funds within certain limits and to extend credit to parties with whom it has contracts.

Most often, the president or chief executive officer of the corporation signs the necessary documents on behalf of the corporation. Corporate officers such as these have the implied power to bind the corporation in matters directly connected with the *ordinary* business affairs of the enterprise.

---

**8.** Some states have expressly rejected the common law theory of corporation by estoppel, finding that it is inconsistent with their statutory law. Other states have abolished only the doctrines of *de facto* and *de jure* corporations. See, for example, *Stone v. Jetmar Properties, LLC,* 733 N.W.2d 480 (Minn.App. 2007).

**9.** *Brown v. W.P. Media, Inc.,* 17 So.3d 1167 (2009).

## GLOBAL INSIGHT — Does Cloud Computing Have a Nationality?

Everyone has heard of "the cloud," and most people use it for the storage of their digital data—photos, e-mails, music, documents, and just about anything else. Not surprisingly, major global digital players like Apple, Amazon, Google, and Microsoft have spent billions to create "clouds" of servers all over the world. In the clouds are stored confidential, organized, and secure data. The revenues generated by the U.S. cloud computing industry exceed $100 billion a year. But is the long-term picture for such revenues in doubt?

### Microsoft Battles and the Global Cloud Industry Waits

The U.S. government issued a warrant to Microsoft to produce e-mails related to a narcotics case from a Hotmail account. That account was hosted in a Microsoft cloud location in Ireland. Microsoft refused, but a magistrate judge in the Southern District of New York confirmed the government's right to the Ireland-located e-mails.[a] On appeal to a U.S. district court, Microsoft again lost.[b] Microsoft appealed to the United States Court of Appeals for the Second Circuit in 2015.[c]

Microsoft maintains that "the power to embark on unilateral law enforcement incursions into a foreign sovereign country—directly or indirectly—has profound policy consequences. Worse still, it threatens the privacy of U.S. citizens." According to Microsoft's deputy general counsel, David Howard, "The U.S. government doesn't have the power to search a home in another country, nor should it have the power search the content of e-mails stored overseas."

A number of organizations apparently agree with Microsoft. The ACLU, Apple, eBay, the Electronic Frontier Foundation, Fox News, the Irish government, and National Public Radio have filed "friend of the court" briefs in support of Microsoft's position.

### Impact on the Industry

More is at stake in this case than the issues Microsoft has identified. If Microsoft ultimately loses, some industry experts believe that U.S. technology companies may lose up to $35 billion a year from their cloud storage business. Foreign corporations and individuals will no longer trust U.S. companies to keep their data secret.

**Critical Thinking** *The law underlying the case against Microsoft is the Electronic Communications Privacy Act, which was enacted three years before the invention of the World Wide Web. Should that law still apply today? Why or why not?*

a. *In re Warrant to Search a Certain e-Mail Account Controlled and Maintained by Microsoft Corp.*, 15 F.Supp.3d 466 (S.D.N.Y. 2014).
b. *In re Warrant to Search a Certain e-Mail Account Controlled and Maintained by Microsoft Corp.*, 2014 WL 4629624 (S.D.N.Y. 2014).
c. *Microsoft Corporation v. United States of America*, ___ F.3d ___ (2d Cir. 2016).

There is a limit to what a corporate officer can do, though. A corporate officer does not have the authority to bind the corporation to an action that will greatly affect the corporate purpose or undertaking, such as the sale of substantial corporate assets.

***Ultra Vires* Doctrine** The term *ultra vires* means "beyond the power." In corporate law, acts of a corporation that are beyond its express or implied powers are *ultra vires* acts. In the past, most cases dealing with *ultra vires* acts involved contracts made for unauthorized purposes. Now, because the articles of incorporation of most private corporations do not state a specific purpose, the *ultra vires* doctrine has declined in importance.

Today, cases that allege *ultra vires* acts usually involve nonprofit corporations or municipal (public) corporations. ■ **CASE IN POINT 5.5** Four men formed a nonprofit corporation to create the Armenian Genocide Museum & Memorial (AGM&M). The bylaws appointed them as trustees (similar to corporate directors) for life. One of the trustees, Gerard L. Cafesjian, became the chair and president of AGM&M. Eventually, the relationship among the trustees deteriorated, and Cafesjian resigned.

The corporation then brought a suit claiming that Cafesjian had engaged in numerous *ultra vires* acts, self-dealing, and mismanagement. Although the bylaws required an 80 percent affirmative vote of the trustees to take action, Cafesjian had taken many actions without the board's approval. He had also entered into contracts for real estate transactions in which he had a personal interest. Because Cafesjian had taken actions that exceeded his authority and had failed to follow rules set forth in the bylaws, the court ruled that the corporation could go forward with its suit.[10] ■

10. *Armenian Assembly of America, Inc. v. Cafesjian*, 692 F.Supp.2d 20 (D.C. Cir. 2010).

**Remedies for *Ultra Vires* Acts**   Under Section 3.04 of the RMBCA, shareholders can seek an injunction from a court to prevent (or stop) the corporation from engaging in *ultra vires* acts. The attorney general in the state of incorporation can also bring an action to obtain an injunction against the *ultra vires* transactions or to seek dissolution of the corporation. The corporation or its shareholders (on behalf of the corporation) can seek damages from the officers and directors who were responsible for the *ultra vires* acts.

# 5–3 Piercing the Corporate Veil

Occasionally, the owners use a corporate entity to perpetrate a fraud, circumvent the law, or in some other way accomplish an illegitimate objective. In these situations, the courts will ignore the corporate structure by **piercing the corporate veil** and exposing the shareholders to personal liability [RMBCA 2.04].

Generally, courts pierce the veil when the corporate privilege is abused for personal benefit or when the corporate business is treated so carelessly that it is indistinguishable from that of a controlling shareholder. When the facts show that great injustice would result from a shareholder's use of a corporation to avoid individual responsibility, a court will look behind the corporate structure to the individual shareholders.

## 5–3a Factors That Lead Courts to Pierce the Corporate Veil

The following are some of the factors that frequently cause the courts to pierce the corporate veil:

1. A party is tricked or misled into dealing with the corporation rather than the individual.
2. The corporation is set up never to make a profit or always to be insolvent. Alternatively, it is too thinly capitalized—that is, it has insufficient capital at the time it is formed to meet its prospective debts or potential liabilities.
3. The corporation is formed to evade an existing legal obligation.
4. Statutory corporate formalities, such as holding required corporation meetings, are not followed.
5. Personal and corporate interests are mixed together, or **commingled,** to such an extent that the corporation has no separate identity.

State corporation codes usually do not prohibit a shareholder from lending funds to her or his corporation. Courts will scrutinize such a transaction closely if the loan comes from an officer, director, or majority shareholder, however. Loans from persons who control the corporation must be made in good faith and for fair value.

In the following case, the court looked at various factors in deciding whether to pierce the corporate veil.

**Case 5.3**

# Dog House Investments, LLC v. Teal Properties, Inc.

Court of Appeals of Tennessee, 448 S.W.3d 905 (2014).

**Background and Facts**   Dog House Investments, LLC, operated a dog "camp" in Nashville, Tennessee. Dog House leased the property from Teal Properties, Inc., which was owned by Jerry Teal, its sole shareholder. Under the lease, the landlord promised to repair damage from fire or other causes that rendered the property "untenantable" (unusable). Following a flood, Dog House notified Jerry that the property was untenantable. Jerry assured Dog House that the flood damage was covered by insurance but took no steps to restore the property. The parties then agreed that Dog House would undertake the repairs and be reimbursed by Teal Properties.

Dog House spent $39,000 to repair the damage and submitted invoices for reimbursement. Teal Properties recovered $40,000 from its insurance company but did not pay Dog House. Close to bankruptcy, Dog House filed a suit in a Tennessee state court against Teal Properties and Jerry. The court held Jerry personally liable for the repair costs. Jerry appealed.

## In the Language of the Court

David R. *FARMER,* J. [Judge]

\* \* \* \*

It is well-settled that courts may pierce the corporate veil and attribute the actions of a corporation to its shareholders when appropriate. *A party seeking to pierce the corporate veil bears the burden of*

Case 5.3 Continued

*demonstrating that the separate corporate entity is a sham or dummy or that disregarding the separate corporate entity is necessary to accomplish justice.* [Emphasis added.] When determining whether piercing the corporate veil is appropriate, the court must consider whether the corporate entity has been used to work a fraud or injustice in contravention of public policy and also:

(1) whether there was a failure to collect paid-in capital; (2) whether the corporation was grossly undercapitalized; (3) the nonissuance of stock certificates; (4) the sole ownership of stock by one individual; (5) the use of the same office or business location; (6) the employment of the same employees or attorneys; (7) the use of the corporation as an instrumentality or business conduit for an individual or another corporation; (8) the diversion of corporate assets by or to a stockholder or other entity to the detriment of creditors, or the manipulation of assets and liabilities in another; (9) the use of the corporation as a subterfuge in illegal transactions; (10) the formation and use of the corporation to transfer to it the existing liability of another person or entity; and (11) the failure to maintain arms length relationships among related entities.

*No single factor is conclusive and not every factor must exist to pierce the corporate veil. The question depends on the specific facts and circumstances of the case.* The equities, however, must substantially favor the party requesting the court to disregard the corporate status. The presumption of the corporation's separate identity should be set aside only with great caution and not precipitately [hastily]. [Emphasis added.]

In this case, Mr. Teal denied personal liability but admitted * * * that he owned the property leased by Dog House in Nashville. The trial court found that Teal Properties owns no property, has no assets, and has no cash except that which is deposited by Mr. Jerry Teal when he has the opportunity to do so; that Teal Properties receives rents and immediately pays it out to pay Mr. Teal's financial obligations; that Mr. Teal is the sole stockholder of Teal Properties and owns the corporation; and that Teal Properties has no purpose other than to collect the rent on properties owned by Mr. Teal. The trial court also found that Mr. Teal does not receive a salary from Teal Properties but utilizes its assets, including the flood insurance proceeds at issue in this case, to pay Mr. Teal's personal expenses and his personal obligations. The trial court found that Mr. Teal did not maintain an arms-length relationship with the corporation, and that it was, in fact, his alter ego. Mr. Teal does not dispute these findings * * * , but asserts that "there is no proof that Teal Properties is a sham or dummy corporation * * * ." We discern no error on the part of the trial court and affirm on this issue.

**Decision and Remedy**  *A state intermediate appellate court affirmed the lower court's decision. Teal Properties owned no property and had no assets. It received rent but paid it immediately to Jerry Teal. "Mr. Teal did not maintain an arms-length relationship with the corporation, and . . . it was, in fact, his alter ego."*

**Critical Thinking**
- **Ethical**  *The failure of Teal Properties and Jerry to reimburse the tenant, Dog House, for the repair costs placed Dog House in a dire financial situation. Does this consequence make the landlord's conduct unethical? Discuss.*
- **Legal Environment**  *The trial court also concluded, and the appellate court affirmed, that Teal Properties had breached its contract with Dog House. What was the contract? How was it breached?*

## 5–3b A Potential Problem for Close Corporations

The potential for corporate assets to be used for personal benefit is especially great in a close corporation. In such a corporation, the separate status of the corporate entity and the shareholders (often family members) must be carefully preserved. Practices that invite trouble for a close corporation include the commingling of corporate and personal funds and the shareholders' continuous personal use of corporate property (for instance, vehicles).

Typically, courts are reluctant to hold shareholders in close corporations personally liable for corporate obligations unless there is some evidence of fraud or wrongdoing. ■ **CASE IN POINT 5.6**  Pip, Jimmy, and Theodore Brennan are brothers and shareholders of Brennan's, Inc., which owns and operates New Orleans's famous Brennan's Restaurant. As a close corporation, Brennan's, Inc., did not hold formal corporate meetings with agendas and minutes, but it did maintain corporate books, hold corporate bank accounts, and file corporate tax returns.

The Brennan brothers retained attorney Edward Colbert to represent them in a family matter, and the attorney's bills were sent to the restaurant and paid from the corporate account. Later, when Brennan's, Inc., sued Colbert for malpractice, Colbert argued that the court should pierce the corporate veil because the Brennan brothers did not observe corporate formalities. The court refused to do so, however, because there was no evidence of fraud, malfeasance, or other wrongdoing by the Brennan brothers. There is no requirement for small, close corporations to operate with the formality usually expected of larger corporations.[11] ■

### 5–3c The Alter-Ego Theory

Sometimes, courts pierce the corporate veil under the theory that the corporation was not operated as a separate entity. Rather, it was just another side (the *alter ego*) of the individual or group that actually controlled the corporation. This is called the alter-ego theory.

The alter-ego theory is applied when a corporation is so dominated and controlled by an individual (or group) that the separate identities of the person (or group) and the corporation are no longer distinct. Courts use the alter-ego theory to avoid injustice or fraud that would result if wrongdoers were allowed to hide behind the protection of limited liability.

---

**11.** *Brennan's, Inc. v. Colbert*, 85 So.3d 787 (La.App.4th Cir. 2012).

■ **CASE IN POINT 5.7** Steiner Electric Company (Steiner) is an Illinois corporation that sells electrical products. Steiner sold goods to Delta Equipment Company and Sackett Systems, Inc., on credit. Both Delta and Sackett were owned and controlled by a single shareholder—Leonard J. Maniscalco. Steiner was not fully paid for the products it sold on credit to Delta and Sackett. Eventually, Steiner sued Delta and won a default judgment, but by that time, Delta had been dissolved. Steiner then asked a state court to pierce the corporate veil and hold Maniscalco liable for the debts of the two companies, claiming the companies were merely Maniscalco's alter egos.

The court agreed and held Maniscalco liable. Delta and Sackett were inadequately capitalized, transactions were not properly documented, funds were commingled, and corporate formalities were not observed. Maniscalco had consistently treated both companies in such a manner that they were, in practice, his alter egos.[12] ■

---

## 5–4 Corporate Financing

Part of the process of corporate formation involves financing. Corporations normally are financed by the issuance and sale of corporate securities. **Securities**—stocks and bonds—evidence an ownership interest in a corporation or a promise of repayment of debt by a corporation. The ways in which stocks and bonds differ are summarized in Exhibit 5–2.

---

**12.** *Steiner Electric Co. v. Maniscalco*, ___ N.E.3d ___, 2016 IL App (1st) 132023 (2016).

**EXHIBIT 5–2 How Do Stocks and Bonds Differ?**

| STOCKS | BONDS |
| --- | --- |
| 1. Stocks represent ownership. | 1. Bonds represent debt. |
| 2. Stocks (common) do not have a fixed dividend rate. | 2. Interest on bonds must always be paid, whether or not any profit is earned. |
| 3. Stockholders can elect the board of directors, which controls the corporation. | 3. Bondholders usually have no voice in or control over management of the corporation. |
| 4. Stocks do not have a maturity date. The corporation usually does not repay the stockholder. | 4. Bonds have a maturity date, when the corporation is to repay the bondholder the face value of the bond. |
| 5. All corporations issue or offer to sell stocks. This is the usual definition of a corporation. | 5. Corporations do not necessarily issue bonds. |
| 6. Stockholders have a claim against the property and income of the corporation after all creditors' claims have been met. | 6. Bondholders have a claim against the property and income of the corporation that must be met before the claims of stockholders. |

## 5–4a Bonds

**Bonds** are *debt securities*, which represent the borrowing of funds. Bonds are issued by business firms and by governments at all levels as evidence of funds they are borrowing from investors.

Bonds normally have a designated *maturity date*—the date when the principal, or face amount, of the bond is returned to the bondholder. Bondholders also receive fixed-dollar interest payments, usually semiannually, during the period of time prior to maturity. For that reason, they are sometimes referred to as *fixed-income securities*. Because debt financing represents a legal obligation of the corporation, various features and terms of a particular bond issue are specified in a lending agreement.

Of course, not all debt is in the form of bonds. For instance, some debt is in the form of accounts payable and notes payable, which typically are short-term debts. Bonds are simply a way for the corporation to split up its long-term debt so that it can be more easily marketed.

## 5–4b Stocks

Issuing stocks is another way for corporations to obtain financing [RMBCA 6.01]. **Stocks,** or *equity securities,* represent the purchase of ownership in the business firm. The two major types are *common stock* and *preferred stock.*

**Common Stock** The true ownership of a corporation is represented by **common stock.** Common stock provides an interest in the corporation with regard to (1) control, (2) earnings, and (3) net assets. A shareholder's interest is generally proportionate to the number of shares he or she owns out of the total number of shares issued. Any person who purchases common stock acquires voting rights—one vote per share held.

An issuing firm is not obligated to return a principal amount per share to each holder of its common stock, nor does the firm have to guarantee a dividend. Indeed, some corporations never pay dividends. Holders of common stock are investors who assume a *residual* position in the overall financial structure of a business. They benefit when the market price of the stock increases. In terms of receiving payment for their investments, they are last in line.

**Preferred Stock** **Preferred stock** is an equity security with *preferences.* Usually, this means that holders of preferred stock have priority over holders of common stock as to dividends and payment on dissolution of the

corporation. The preferences must be stated in the articles of incorporation. Holders of preferred stock may or may not have the right to vote.

Like other equity securities, preferred shares have no fixed maturity date on which the firm must pay them off. Although firms occasionally buy back preferred stock, they are not legally obligated to do so.

Holders of preferred stock have assumed a more cautious position than holders of common stock. They have a stronger position than common shareholders with respect to dividends and claims on assets, but they will not share in the full prosperity of the firm if it grows successfully over time. Preferred stockholders do receive fixed dividends periodically, however, and they may benefit to some extent from changes in the market price of the shares.

Exhibit 5–3 offers a summary of the types of stocks issued by corporations.

## 5–4c Venture Capital and Private Equity Capital

Corporations traditionally obtain financing by issuing and selling securities (stocks and bonds) in the capital market. Many investors do not want to purchase stock in a business that lacks a track record, however, and banks generally are reluctant to extend loans to high-risk enterprises. Therefore, to obtain funds, many entrepreneurs seek alternative financing.

**Venture Capital** Start-up businesses and high-risk enterprises often obtain venture capital financing. **Venture capital** is capital provided to new businesses by professional, outside investors (*venture capitalists,* usually groups of wealthy investors and securities firms). Venture capital investments are high risk—the investors must be willing to lose all of their invested funds—but offer the potential for well-above-average returns in the future.

To obtain venture capital financing, the start-up business typically gives up a share of its ownership to the venture capitalists. In addition to funding, venture capitalists may provide managerial and technical expertise, and they nearly always are given some control over the new company's decisions. Many Internet-based companies, such as Google and Amazon, were initially financed by venture capital.

**Private Equity Capital** Private equity firms pool funds from wealthy investors and use this **private equity capital** to invest in existing corporations. Usually, a

**EXHIBIT 5-3  Common and Preferred Stocks**

| COMMON STOCK | PREFERRED STOCK |
|---|---|
| Voting shares that represent ownership interest in a corporation.<br><br>Common stock has the lowest priority with respect to payment of dividends and distribution of assets on the corporation's dissolution. | Stock that has priority over common stock shares as to payment of dividends and distribution of assets on dissolution.<br><br>Dividend payments are usually a fixed percentage of the face value of the share. Preferred shares may or may not be voting shares. |

| CUMULATIVE PREFERRED STOCK | PARTICIPATING PREFERRED STOCK | CONVERTIBLE PREFERRED STOCK | REDEEMABLE PREFERRED STOCK |
|---|---|---|---|
| Preferred shares on which required dividends not paid in a given year must be paid in a subsequent year before any common-stock dividends can be paid. | Preferred shares entitling the owner to receive the preferred-stock dividend and additional dividends after the corporation has paid dividends on common stock. | Preferred shares that, under certain conditions, can be converted into a specified number of common shares either in the issuing corporation or, sometimes, in another corporation. | Preferred shares issued with the express condition that the issuing corporation has the right to repurchase the shares as specified. (Sometimes referred to as callable preferred stock.) |

private equity firm buys an entire corporation and then reorganizes it. Sometimes, divisions of the purchased company are sold off to pay down debt.

Ultimately, the private equity firm may sell shares in the reorganized (and perhaps more profitable) company to the public in an *initial public offering (IPO)*. Then the private equity firm can make profits by selling its shares in the company to the public.

## 5-4d Crowdfunding

Start-up businesses can also attempt to obtain financing through *crowdfunding*. **Crowdfunding** is a cooperative activity in which people network and pool funds and other resources via the Internet to assist a cause or invest in a venture. Sometimes, crowdfunding is used to raise funds for charitable purposes, such as disaster relief, but increasingly it is being used to finance budding entrepreneurs.

In 2016, new Securities and Exchange Commission (SEC) rules went into effect to allow companies to offer and sell securities through crowdfunding. The rules removed a decades-old ban on public solicitation for private investments, which means that companies can advertise investment opportunities to the general public. According to the SEC, the new rules are intended to help smaller companies raise capital while providing investors with additional protections. Companies are required to make specific disclosures and are limited to raising $1 million a year through crowdfunding.

# Reviewing: Corporate Formation and Financing

William Sharp was the sole shareholder and manager of Chickasaw Club, Inc., an S corporation that operated a popular nightclub of the same name in Columbus, Georgia. Sharp maintained a corporate checking account but paid the club's employees, suppliers, and entertainers in cash out of the club's proceeds. Sharp owned the property on which the club was located. He rented it to the club but made mortgage payments out of the club's proceeds and often paid other personal expenses with Chickasaw corporate funds.

At 12:45 A.M. on July 31, eighteen-year-old Aubrey Lynn Pursley, who was already intoxicated, entered the Chickasaw Club. A city ordinance prohibited individuals under the age of twenty-one from entering nightclubs, but Chickasaw employees did not check Pursley's identification to verify her age. Pursley drank more alcohol at Chickasaw and was visibly intoxicated when she left the club at 3:00 A.M. with a beer in her hand. Shortly afterward, Pursley lost control of her car, struck a tree, and was killed. Joseph Dancause, Pursley's stepfather, filed a tort lawsuit in a Georgia state court against Chickasaw Club, Inc., and William Sharp, seeking damages. Using the information presented in the chapter, answer the following questions.

1. Under what theory might the court in this case make an exception to the limited liability of shareholders and hold Sharp personally liable for the damages? What factors would be relevant to the court's decision?
2. Suppose that Chickasaw's articles of incorporation failed to describe the corporation's purpose or management structure, as required by state law. Would the court be likely to rule that Sharp is personally liable to Dancause on that basis? Why or why not?
3. Suppose that the club extended credit to its regular patrons, although neither the articles of incorporation nor the corporate bylaws authorized this practice. Would the corporation likely have the power to engage in this activity? Explain.
4. How would the court classify the Chickasaw Club corporation—domestic or foreign, public or private? Why?

**Debate This** . . . *The sole shareholder of an S corporation should not be able to avoid liability for the torts of her or his employees.*

## Terms and Concepts

alien corporation 73
articles of incorporation 80
benefit corporation 78
bond 87
bylaws 81
close corporation 76
commingle 84
common stock 87
crowdfunding 88

dividends 72
domestic corporation 72
foreign corporation 73
holding company 72
pierce the corporate veil 84
preferred stock 87
private equity capital 87
public corporation 74
publicly held corporation 75

retained earnings 72
S corporation 77
securities 86
shareholder agreement 77
stock 87
*ultra vires* 83
venture capital 87

## Issue Spotters

1. Northwest Brands, Inc., is a small business incorporated in Minnesota. Its one class of stock is owned by twelve members of a single family. Ordinarily, corporate income is taxed at the corporate and shareholder levels. Is there a way for Northwest Brands to avoid this double taxation? Explain your answer. (See *The Nature and Classification of Corporations*.)

2. The incorporators of Consumer Investments, Inc., want their new corporation to have the authority to transact nearly any conceivable type of business. Can they grant this authority to their firm? If so, how? If not, why not? (See *Piercing the Corporate Veil.*)

• **Check your answers to the Issue Spotters against the answers provided in Appendix B at the end of this text.**

## Business Scenarios

**5–1. Preincorporation.** Cummings, Okawa, and Taft are recent college graduates who want to form a corporation to manufacture and sell digital tablets. Peterson tells them he will set in motion the formation of their corporation. First, Peterson makes a contract with Owens for the purchase of a piece of land for $20,000. Owens does not know of the prospective corporate formation at the time the contract is signed. Second, Peterson makes a contract with Babcock to build a small plant on the property being purchased. Babcock's contract is conditional on the corporation's formation. Peterson secures all necessary subscription agreements and capitalization, and he files the articles of incorporation. (See *Corporate Formation.*)

**(a)** Discuss whether the newly formed corporation, Peterson, or both are liable on the contracts with Owens and Babcock.

**(b)** Discuss whether the corporation is automatically liable to Babcock on formation.

**5–2. *Ultra Vires* Doctrine.** Oya Paka and two business associates formed a corporation called Paka Corp. for the purpose of selling computer services. Oya, who owned 50 percent of the corporate shares, served as the corporation's president. Oya wished to obtain a personal loan from her bank for $250,000, but the bank required the note to be cosigned by a third party. Oya cosigned the note in the name of the corporation. Later, Oya defaulted on the note, and the bank sued the corporation for payment. The corporation asserted, as a defense, that Oya had exceeded her authority when she cosigned the note on behalf of the corporation. Had she? Explain. (See *Corporate Formation and Powers.*)

## Business Case Problems

**5–3. Spotlight on Smart Inventions—Piercing the Corporate Veil.**  Thomas Persson and Jon Nokes founded Smart Inventions, Inc., to market household consumer products. The success of their first product, the Smart Mop, continued with later products, which were sold through infomercials and other means. Persson and Nokes were the firm's officers and equal shareholders. Persson was responsible for product development, and Nokes was in charge of day-to-day operations. In time, they became dissatisfied with each other's efforts. Nokes represented the firm as financially "dying," "in a grim state, . . . worse than ever," and offered to buy all of Persson's shares for $1.6 million. Persson accepted.

On the day that they signed the agreement to transfer the shares, Smart Inventions began marketing a new product—the Tap Light. It was an instant success, generating millions of dollars in revenues. In negotiating with Persson, Nokes had intentionally kept the Tap Light a secret. Persson sued Smart Inventions, asserting fraud and other claims. Under what principle might Smart Inventions be liable for Nokes's fraud? Is Smart Inventions liable in this case? Explain. [*Persson v. Smart Inventions, Inc.,* 125 Cal.App.4th 1141, 23 Cal. Rptr.3d 335 (2 Dist. 2005)] (See *Piercing the Corporate Veil.*)

**5–4. Piercing the Corporate Veil.** Smith Services, Inc., a trucking business owned by Tony Smith, charged its fuel purchases to an account at Laker Express. When Smith Services was not paid on several contracts, it ceased doing business and was dissolved. Smith continued to provide trucking services, however, as a sole proprietor. Laker Express sought to recover

Smith Services' unpaid fuel charges, which amounted to about $35,000, from Smith. He argued that he was not personally liable for a corporate debt. Should the court pierce the corporate veil? Explain. [*Bear, Inc. v. Smith,* 303 S.W.3d 137 (Ky. App. 2010)] (See *Piercing the Corporate Veil.*)

**5–5. Close Corporations.** Mark Burnett and Kamran Pourgol were the only shareholders in a corporation that built and sold a house. When the buyers discovered that the house exceeded the amount of square footage allowed by the building permit, Pourgol agreed to renovate the house to conform to the permit. No work was done, however, and Burnett filed a suit against Pourgol. Burnett claimed that, without his knowledge, Pourgol had submitted incorrect plans to obtain the building permit, misrepresented the extent of the renovation, and failed to fix the house. Was Pourgol guilty of misconduct? If so, how might it have been avoided? Discuss. [*Burnett v. Pourgol,* 83 A.D.3d 756, 921 N.Y.S.2d 280 (2 Dept. 2011)] (See *Piercing the Corporate Veil.*)

**5–6. Piercing the Corporate Veil.** In 1997, Leon Greenblatt, Andrew Jahelka, and Richard Nichols incorporated Loop Corp. with only $1,000 of capital. Three years later, Banco Panamericano, Inc., which was run entirely by Greenblatt and owned by a Greenblatt family trust, extended a large line of credit to Loop. Loop's subsidiaries participated in the credit, giving $3 million to Loop while acquiring a security interest in Loop itself. Loop then opened an account with Wachovia Securities, LLC, to buy stock shares using credit provided by Wachovia. When the stock values plummeted, Loop owed Wachovia $1.89 million. Loop also defaulted on its loan from Banco, but Banco agreed to lend Loop millions of dollars more.

Rather than repay Wachovia with the influx of funds, Loop gave the funds to closely related entities and "compensated" Nichols and Jahelka without issuing any W-2 forms (forms reporting compensation to the Internal Revenue Service). Loop made loans to other related entities and shared office space, equipment, and telephone and fax numbers with related entities. Loop also moved employees among related entities, failed to file its tax returns on time (and sometimes did not file them at all), and failed to follow its own bylaws. In a lawsuit brought by Wachovia, can the court hold Greenblatt, Jahelka, and Nichols personally liable by piercing the corporate veil? Why or why not? [*Wachovia Securities, LLC v. Banco Panamericano, Inc.,* 674 F.3d 743 (9th Cir. 2012)] (See *Piercing the Corporate Veil.*)

**5–7. Business Case Problem with Sample Answer— Piercing the Corporate Veil.** Scott Snapp contracted with

Castlebrook Builders, Inc., which was owned by Stephen Kappeler, to remodel a house. Kappeler estimated that the remodeling would cost around $500,000. Eventually, however, Snapp paid Kappeler more than $1.3 million. Snapp filed a suit in an Ohio state court against Castlebrook, alleging breach of contract and fraud, among other things. During the trial, it was revealed that Castlebrook had issued no shares of stock and that personal and corporate funds had been commingled. The minutes of the corporate meetings all looked exactly the same. In addition, Kappeler could not provide an accounting for the Snapp project. In particular, he could not explain evidence of double and triple billing nor demonstrate that the amount Snapp paid had actually been spent on the remodeling project. Are these sufficient grounds to pierce the corporate veil? Explain. [*Snapp v. Castlebrook Builders, Inc.,* 2014 -Ohio- 163, 7 N.E.3d 574 (2014)] (See *Corporate Formation and Powers.*)

- For a sample answer to Problem 5–7, go to Appendix C at the end of this text.

**5–8. Torts.** Jennifer Hoffman took her cell phone to a store owned by R&K Trading, Inc., for repairs. Later, Hoffman filed a suit in a New York state court against R&K, Verizon Wireless, Inc., and others. Hoffman sought to recover damages for a variety of torts, including infliction of emotional distress and negligent hiring and supervision. She alleged that an R&K employee, Keith Press, had examined her phone in a back room, accessed private photos of her stored on her phone, and disseminated the photos to the public. Hoffman testified that "after the incident, she learned from another R&K employee that personal information and pictures had been removed from the phones of other customers." Can R&K be held liable for the torts of its employees? Explain. [*Hoffman v. Verizon Wireless, Inc.,* 5 N.Y.S.3d 123, 125 A.D.3d 806 (2015)] (See *The Nature and Classification of Corporations.*)

**5–9. A Question of Ethics—Piercing the Corporate Veil.** *In New York City, 2406-12 Amsterdam Associates LLC*

*brought an action in a New York state court against Alianza Dominicana and Alianza LLC to recover unpaid rent. The plaintiff asserted cause to pierce the corporate veil, alleging that Alianza Dominicana had made promises to pay its rent while discreetly forming Alianza LLC to avoid liability for it. According to 2406-12, Alianza LLC was 90 percent owned by Alianza Dominicana, had no employees, and had no function but to hold Alianza Dominicana's assets away from its creditors. The defendants filed a motion to dismiss the plaintiff's claim.* [*2406-12 Amsterdam Associates, LLC v. Alianza, LLC,* 136 A.D.3d 512, 25 N.Y.S.2d 167 (1 Dept. 2016)] (See *Piercing the Corporate Veil.*)

**(a)** Assuming that 2406-12's allegations are true, are there sufficient grounds to pierce Alianza LLC's corporate veil? Discuss.

**(b)** Suppose that the parties to this dispute were small, close corporations. How might that circumstance affect the result in this case?

# Legal Reasoning Group Activity

**5–10. Corporate versus LLC Form of Business.** The limited liability company (LLC) may be the best organizational form for most businesses. For a significant number of firms, however, the corporate form or some other form of organization may be better. (See *The Nature and Classification of Corporations.*)

**(a)** The first group will outline several reasons why a firm might be better off as a corporation than as an LLC.

**(b)** The second group will discuss the differences between corporations and LLCs in terms of their management structures.

# CHAPTER 6

# Corporate Directors, Officers, and Shareholders

A corporation joins together the efforts and resources of a large number of individuals for the purpose of producing greater returns than those persons could have obtained individually. Corporate directors, officers, and shareholders all play different roles within the corporate entity.

Sometimes, actions that may benefit the corporation as a whole do not coincide with the separate interests of the individuals making up the corporation. In such situations, it is important to know the rights and duties of all participants in the corporate enterprise. This chapter focuses on these rights and duties and the ways in which conflicts among corporate participants are resolved.

## 6–1 Role of Directors and Officers

The board of directors is the ultimate authority in every corporation. Directors have responsibility for all policy-making decisions necessary to the management of all corporate affairs. Additionally, the directors must act as a body in carrying out routine corporate business. The board selects and removes the corporate officers, determines the capital structure of the corporation, and declares dividends. Each director has one vote, and customarily the majority rules. The general areas of responsibility of the board of directors are shown in Exhibit 6–1.

Directors are sometimes inappropriately characterized as *agents* because they act on behalf of the corporation. No *individual* director, however, can act as an agent to bind the corporation. As a group, directors collectively control the corporation in a way that no agent is able to control a principal. In addition, although directors occupy positions of trust and control over the corporation, they are not *trustees,* because they do not hold title to property for the use and benefit of others.

Few qualifications are required for directors. Only a handful of states impose minimum age and residency requirements. A director may be a shareholder, but that is not necessary (unless the articles of incorporation or bylaws require ownership interest).

### 6–1a Election of Directors

Subject to statutory limitations, the number of directors is set forth in the corporation's articles or bylaws.

Historically, the minimum number of directors has been three, but today many states permit fewer. Normally, the incorporators appoint the first board of directors at the time the corporation is created, or the directors are named in the articles of incorporation. The initial board serves until the first annual shareholders' meeting. Subsequent directors are elected by a majority vote of the shareholders.

A director usually serves for a term of one year—from annual meeting to annual meeting. Most state statutes permit longer and staggered terms. A common practice is to elect one-third of the board members each year for a three-year term. In this way, there is greater management continuity.

**Removal of Directors** A director can be removed *for cause*—that is, for failing to perform a required duty—either as specified in the articles or bylaws or by shareholder action. The board of directors may also have the power to remove a director for cause, subject to shareholder review. In most states, a director cannot be removed without cause unless the shareholders reserved the right to do so at the time of election.

**Vacancies on the Board** Vacancies occur on the board if a director dies or resigns or when a new position is created through amendment of the articles or bylaws. In these situations, either the shareholders or the board itself can fill the vacant position, depending on state law or on the provisions of the bylaws. Often, for instance, an election is held and shareholders vote to fill the vacancy.

**EXHIBIT 6–1** Directors' Management Responsibilities

**Authorize Major Corporate Policy Decisions**

*Examples:*
- Oversee major contract negotiations and management-labor negotiations.
- Initiate negotiations on the sale or lease of corporate assets outside the regular course of business.
- Decide whether to pursue new product lines or business opportunities.

**Make Executive-Level Personnel Decisions**

*Examples:*
- Engage in selection of officers and determine their appropriate total compensation, which may include stock options.
- Supervise managerial employees and make decisions regarding their termination.

**Make Financial Decisions**

*Examples:*
- Make decisions regarding the issuance of authorized shares and bonds.
- Decide when to declare dividends to be paid to shareholders.

Note that even when an election is authorized, a court can invalidate the results if the directors have attempted to manipulate the election in order to reduce the shareholders' influence.

## 6–1b Compensation of Directors

In the past, corporate directors were rarely compensated. Today, directors are often paid at least nominal sums. In large corporations, they may receive more substantial compensation because of the time, work, effort, and especially risk involved.

Most states permit the corporate articles or bylaws to authorize compensation for directors. In fact, the Revised Model Business Corporation Act (RMBCA) states that unless the articles or bylaws provide otherwise, the board itself may set the directors' compensation [RMBCA 8.11]. Directors also receive indirect benefits, such as business contacts and prestige, and other rewards, such as stock options.

In many corporations, directors are also chief corporate officers (such as president or chief executive officer) and receive compensation in their managerial positions. A director who is also an officer of the corporation is referred to as an **inside director,** whereas a director who does not hold a management position is an **outside director.** Typically, a corporation's board of directors includes both inside and outside directors.

## 6–1c Board of Directors' Meetings

The board of directors conducts business by holding formal meetings with recorded minutes. The dates of regular meetings are usually established in the articles or bylaws or by board resolution, and ordinarily no further notice is required. Special meetings can be called as well, with notice sent to all directors.

Most states allow directors to participate in board of directors' meetings from remote locations. Directors can participate via telephone, Web conferencing, or Skype, provided that all the directors can simultaneously hear each other during the meeting [RMBCA 8.20].

**Quorum of Directors** Unless the articles of incorporation or bylaws specify a greater number, a majority of the board of directors normally constitutes a *quorum* [RMBCA 8.24]. (A **quorum** is the minimum number of members of a body of officials or other group that must be present for business to be validly transacted.) Some state statutes specifically allow corporations to set a quorum at less than a majority but not less than one-third of the directors.[1]

**Voting** Once a quorum is present, the directors transact business and vote on issues affecting the corporation.

---

1. See, for example, Delaware Code Annotated Title 8, Section 141(b); and New York Business Corporation Law Section 707.

Each director present at the meeting has one vote.[2] Ordinary matters generally require a simple majority vote, but certain extraordinary issues may require a greater-than-majority vote.

### 6–1d Committees of the Board of Directors

When a board of directors has a large number of members and must deal with myriad complex business issues, meetings can become unwieldy. Therefore, the boards of large, publicly held corporations typically create committees of directors and delegate certain tasks to these committees. By focusing on specific subjects, committees can increase the efficiency of the board.

Two common types of committees are the *executive committee* and the *audit committee*. An executive committee handles interim management decisions between board meetings. It is limited to dealing with ordinary business matters and does not have the power to declare dividends, amend the bylaws, or authorize the issuance of stock. The audit committee is responsible for the selection, compensation, and oversight of the independent public accountants that audit the firm's financial records. *The Sarbanes-Oxley Act requires all publicly held corporations to have an audit committee.*

### 6–1e Rights of Directors

A corporate director must have certain rights to function properly in that position, including the rights of participation, inspection, and indemnification.

**Right to Participation** The *right to participation* means that directors are entitled to participate in all board of directors' meetings and have a right to be notified of these meetings. Because the dates of regular board meetings are usually specified in the bylaws, no notice of these meetings is required. If special meetings are called, however, notice is required unless waived by the director [RMBCA 8.23].

**Right of Inspection** A director also has a *right of inspection,* which means that each director can access the corporation's books and records, facilities, and premises. Inspection rights are essential for directors to make informed decisions and to exercise the necessary supervision over corporate officers and employees. This right of inspection is almost absolute and cannot be restricted (by the articles, bylaws, or any act of the board of directors).

■ **CASE IN POINT 6.1** NavLink, Inc., a Delaware corporation, provides high-end data management for customers and governments in Saudi Arabia, Qatar, Lebanon, and the United Arab Emirates. NavLink's co-founders, George Chammas and Laurent Delifer, served on its board of directors.

Chammas and Delifer were concerned about the company's 2015 annual budget and three-year operating plan. Despite repeated requests, Chammas was never given the meeting minutes from several board meetings in 2015. Chammas and Delifer believed that the other directors were withholding information and holding secret "pre-board meetings" at which plans and decisions were being made without them. They filed suit in a Delaware state court seeking inspection rights.

The court ordered NavLink to provide the plaintiffs with board meeting minutes and with communications from NavLink's secretary regarding the minutes. The plaintiffs were also entitled to inspect corporate documents and communications concerning NavLink's 2015 budget and three-year plan.[3] ■

**Right to Indemnification** When a director becomes involved in litigation by virtue of her or his position, the director may have a *right to indemnification* (reimbursement) for the legal costs, fees, and damages incurred. Most states allow corporations to indemnify and purchase liability insurance for corporate directors [RMBCA 8.51].

### 6–1f Corporate Officers and Executives

Corporate officers and other executive employees are hired by the board of directors. At a minimum, most corporations have a president, one or more vice presidents, a secretary, and a treasurer. In most states, an individual can hold more than one office, such as president and secretary, and can be both an officer and a director of the corporation.

In addition to carrying out the duties articulated in the bylaws, corporate and managerial officers act as agents of the corporation. Therefore, the ordinary rules of agency normally apply to their employment.

Corporate officers and other high-level managers are employees of the company, so their rights are defined by employment contracts. Nevertheless, the board of directors normally can remove a corporate officer at any

---

2. Except in Louisiana, which allows a director to vote by proxy under certain circumstances.

3. *Chammas v. NavLink, Inc.,* 2016 WL 767714 (Del.Ch.Ct. 2016).

time with or without cause. If the directors remove an officer in violation of the terms of an employment contract, however, the corporation may be liable for breach of contract.

For a synopsis of the roles of directors and officers, see Concept Summary 6.1.

## 6–2 Duties and Liabilities of Directors and Officers

The duties of corporate directors and officers are similar because both groups are involved in decision making and

## Concept Summary 6.1

### Roles of Directors and Officers

**Election of Directors**
- The incorporators usually appoint the first board of directors. Thereafter, shareholders elect the directors.
- Directors usually serve a one-year term, although the term can be longer. Few qualifications are required.
- A director can be a shareholder but is not required to be.
- Compensation usually is specified in the corporate articles or bylaws.

**Board of Directors' Meetings**
- The board of directors conducts business by holding formal meetings with recorded minutes.
- The dates of regular meetings are usually established in the corporate articles or bylaws.
- Special meetings can be called, with notice sent to all directors.
- Usually, a quorum is a majority of the corporate directors. Once a quorum is present, each director has one vote, and the majority normally rules in ordinary matters.

**Rights of Directors**
- Directors' rights include the rights of participation, inspection, compensation, and indemnification.

**Board of Directors' Committees**
- Directors may appoint committees and delegate some of their responsibilities to the committees and to corporate officers and executives. For instance, directors commonly appoint an *executive committee*, which handles ordinary, interim management decisions between board of directors' meetings.
- Directors may also appoint an *audit committee* to hire and supervise the independent public accountants who audit the corporation's financial records.

**Role of Corporate Officers and Executives**
- The board of directors normally hires the corporate officers and other executive employees.
- In most states, a person can hold more than one office and can be both an officer and a director of a corporation.
- The rights of corporate officers and executives are defined by employment contracts.

are in positions of control. Directors and officers are considered to be fiduciaries of the corporation because their relationship with the corporation and its shareholders is one of trust and confidence. As fiduciaries, directors and officers owe ethical—and legal—duties to the corporation and to the shareholders as a group. These fiduciary duties include the duty of care and the duty of loyalty.

## 6–2a Duty of Care

Directors and officers must exercise due care in performing their duties. The standard of *due care* has been variously described in judicial decisions and codified in many state corporation codes. Generally, it requires a director or officer to:

1. Act in good faith (honestly).
2. Exercise the care that an ordinarily prudent (careful) person would exercise in similar circumstances.
3. Do what she or he believes is in the best interests of the corporation [RMBCA 8.30(a), 8.42(a)].

If directors or officers fail to exercise due care and the corporation or its shareholders suffer harm as a result, the directors or officers can be held liable for negligence. (An exception is made if the *business judgment rule* applies, as will be discussed shortly.)

**Duty to Make Informed Decisions** Directors and officers are expected to be informed on corporate matters and to conduct a reasonable investigation of the situation before making a decision. They must, for instance, attend meetings and presentations, ask for information from those who have it, read reports, and review other written materials. In other words, directors and officers must investigate, study, and discuss matters and evaluate alternatives before making a decision. They cannot decide on the spur of the moment without adequate research.

Although directors and officers are expected to act in accordance with their own knowledge and training, they are also normally entitled to rely on information given to them by certain other persons. Under the laws of most states and Section 8.30(b) of the RMBCA, such persons include competent officers or employees, professionals such as attorneys and accountants, and committees of the board of directors. (The committee must be one on which the director does not serve, however.) The reliance must be in good faith to insulate a director from liability if the information later proves to be inaccurate or unreliable.

**Duty to Exercise Reasonable Supervision** Directors are also expected to exercise a reasonable amount of supervision when they delegate work to corporate officers and employees. ■ **EXAMPLE 6.2** Dana, a corporate bank director, fails to attend any board of directors' meetings for five years. In addition, Dana never inspects any of the corporate books or records and generally fails to supervise the activities of the bank president and the loan committee. Meanwhile, Brennan, the bank president, who is a corporate officer, makes various improper loans and permits large overdrafts. In this situation, Dana (the corporate director) can be held liable to the corporation for losses resulting from the unsupervised actions of the bank president and the loan committee. ■

**Dissenting Directors** Directors' votes at board of directors' meetings should be entered into the minutes. Sometimes, an individual director disagrees with the majority's vote (which becomes an act of the board of directors). Unless a dissent is entered in the minutes, the director is presumed to have assented. If the directors are later held liable for mismanagement as a result of a decision, dissenting directors are rarely held individually liable to the corporation. For this reason, a director who is absent from a given meeting sometimes registers a dissent with the secretary of the board regarding actions taken at the meeting.

## 6–2b The Business Judgment Rule

Directors and officers are expected to exercise due care and to use their best judgment in guiding corporate management, but they are not insurers of business success. Under the **business judgment rule,** a corporate director or officer will not be liable to the corporation or to its shareholders for honest mistakes of judgment and bad business decisions.

Courts give significant deference to the decisions of corporate directors and officers, and consider the reasonableness of a decision at the time it was made, without the benefit of hindsight. Thus, corporate decision makers are not subjected to second-guessing by shareholders or others in the corporation.

**When the Rule Applies** The business judgment rule will apply as long as the director or officer:

1. Took reasonable steps to become informed about the matter.
2. Had a rational basis for her or his decision.
3. Did not have a conflict between her or his personal interest and the interest of the corporation.

Whether these conditions were met formed the basis for the court's decision in the following case.

# Oliveira v. Sugarman

Court of Special Appeals of Maryland, 226 Md.App. 524, 130 A.3d 1085 (2016).

**Background and Facts**  iStar, Inc., a Maryland corporation, promised to award shares of company stock to employees for their performance if the stock averaged a certain target price per share over a specific period. The stock price rose 300 percent, but the target was missed. The board changed the basis for an award from performance to service—an employee who had been with iStar for a certain period was entitled to an award. It then issued additional shares to pay the awards.

Albert and Lena Oliveira, iStar shareholders, demanded that the board rescind the awards. The Oliveiras alleged misconduct and demanded that the board file a suit on the company's behalf to seek damages or other relief. The board appointed Barry Ridings, an outside director, to investigate the allegation. Ridings recommended that the board refuse the demand. The board acted on his recommendation.

The Oliveiras filed a suit in a Maryland state court against Jay Sugarman, the board chairman, and the other directors, including Ridings, alleging a breach of fiduciary duty. The court dismissed the claim. The Oliveiras appealed.

## In the Language of the Court

BURGER, J. [Judge]

\* \* \* \*

*Judicial review of a demand refusal is subject to the business judgment rule, and the court \* \* \* limits its review to whether the board acted independently, in good faith, and within the realm of sound business judgment.* [Emphasis added.]

\* \* \* \*

\* \* \* The Shareholders [the Oliveiras] assert that [Ridings's] investigation of the Shareholders' demand was rife with improper procedure. The Shareholders argue that \* \* \* Ridings lacked sufficient corporate experience to make a proper recommendation to the Board and that Ridings was not sufficiently disinterested. Both contentions are baseless. Ridings has forty years of business experience, including service on the boards of several public companies, including the American Stock Exchange. Furthermore, Ridings hired highly respected and experienced legal counsel to assist him and conducted multiple interviews.

We further reject the Shareholders' contention that Ridings was interested or lacked independence. Ridings joined the Board after the challenged conduct and had no business, personal, social, or other relationships with any other member of the Board. Although Ridings's employer [Lazard Freres & Company, where Ridings was vice chairman of investment banking] performed banking services for iStar [for two years], Lazard has no ongoing business relationship with iStar. *Furthermore, allegations of mere personal friendship or a mere outside business relationship, standing alone, are insufficient to raise a reasonable doubt about a director's independence.* [Emphasis added.]

The Shareholders' contention that Ridings lacks independence because he is compensated for his service as a Director is similarly unfounded. The Shareholders further contend that Ridings lacks independence because he is a named defendant in this lawsuit. This assertion is contrary to established law. Accordingly, we reject the Shareholders' contentions that Ridings was interested or lacked independence.

\* \* \* \*

In conclusion, the Shareholders have failed to surmount the presumption of the business judgment rule. In failing to do so, they have failed to state a claim upon which relief may be granted.

**Decision and Remedy**  *A state intermediate appellate court affirmed the lower court's dismissal of the Oliveiras' claim. "The Shareholders' bald allegations of impropriety are plainly insufficient to overcome the presumption of the business judgment rule."*

## Critical Thinking

- **Legal Environment**  *In a letter to the Oliveiras, the board explained that it saw "no upside—and much downside—to the action and lawsuit proposed in the Demand." What would the "downside" consist of?*
- **What If the Facts Were Different?**  *Only one member of the iStar board—Sugarman—received an award as an employee. The others who made the decision to change the award were, like Ridings, outside directors. Suppose that the opposite had been true. Would the result have been the same?*

**Provides Broad Protections** The business judgment rule provides broad protections to corporate decision makers. In fact, most courts will apply the rule unless there is evidence of bad faith, fraud, or a clear breach of fiduciary duties.

■ **CASE IN POINT 6.3** The board of directors of the Chugach Alaska Corporation (CAC) voted to remove Sheri Buretta as the chair and install Robert Henrichs. During his term, Henrichs acted without board approval, made decisions with only his supporters present, retaliated against directors who challenged his decisions, and ignored board rules for conducting meetings. He refused to comply with bylaws that required a special shareholders' meeting in response to a shareholder petition and personally mistreated directors, shareholders, and employees. After six months, the board voted to reinstall Buretta.

CAC filed a suit in an Alaska state court against Henrichs, alleging a breach of fiduciary duty. A jury found Henrichs liable, and the court barred him from serving on CAC's board for five years. The appellate court affirmed. Given the nature and seriousness of Henrichs's misconduct, the business judgment rule did not protect him.[4] ■

---

4. *Henrichs v. Chugach Alaska Corp.*, 250 P.3d 531 (Alaska Sup.Ct. 2011).

## 6–2c Duty of Loyalty

*Loyalty* can be defined as faithfulness to one's obligations and duties. In the corporate context, the duty of loyalty requires directors and officers to subordinate their personal interests to the welfare of the corporation. For instance, a director should not oppose a transaction that is in the corporation's best interest simply because pursuing it may cost the director his or her position. Directors cannot use corporate funds or confidential corporate information for personal advantage and must refrain from self-dealing.

Cases dealing with the duty of loyalty typically involve one or more of the following:

1. Competing with the corporation.
2. Usurping (taking personal advantage of) a corporate opportunity.
3. Pursuing an interest that conflicts with that of the corporation.
4. Using information that is not available to the public to make a profit trading securities (insider trading).
5. Authorizing a corporate transaction that is detrimental to minority shareholders.
6. Selling control over the corporation.

The following *Classic Case* illustrates the conflict that can arise between a corporate officer's personal interest and his or her duty of loyalty.

---

**Classic Case 6.2**

# Guth v. Loft, Inc.
Supreme Court of Delaware, 23 Del.Ch. 255, 5 A.2d 503 (1939).

**Background and Facts** In 1930, Charles Guth became the president of Loft, Inc., a candy-and-restaurant chain. Guth and his family also owned Grace Company, which made syrups for soft drinks. Coca-Cola Company supplied Loft with cola syrup. Unhappy with what he felt was Coca-Cola's high price, Guth entered into an agreement with Roy Megargel to acquire the trademark and formula for Pepsi-Cola and form Pepsi-Cola Corporation. Neither Guth nor Megargel could finance the new venture, however, and Grace Company was insolvent.

Without the knowledge of Loft's board, Guth used Loft's capital, credit, facilities, and employees to further the Pepsi enterprise. At Guth's direction, a Loft employee made the concentrate for the syrup, which was sent to Grace to add sugar and water. Loft charged Grace for the concentrate but allowed forty months' credit. Grace charged Pepsi for the syrup but also granted substantial credit. Grace sold the syrup to Pepsi's customers, including Loft, which paid on delivery or within thirty days. Loft also paid for Pepsi's advertising. Finally, with profits declining as a result of switching from Coca-Cola, Loft filed a suit in a Delaware state court against Guth, Grace, and Pepsi, seeking their Pepsi stock and an accounting. The court entered a judgment in the plaintiff's favor. The defendants appealed to the Delaware Supreme Court.

## In the Language of the Court
*LAYTON*, Chief Justice, delivering the opinion of the court:
* * * *

Corporate officers and directors are not permitted to use their position of trust and confidence to further their private interests. * * * They stand in a fiduciary relation to the corporation and its

**Case 6.2 Continued**

stockholders. A public policy, existing through the years, and derived from a profound knowledge of human characteristics and motives, has established *a rule that demands of a corporate officer or director, peremptorily [not open for debate] and inexorably [unavoidably], the most scrupulous observance of his duty, not only affirmatively to protect the interests of the corporation committed to his charge, but also to refrain from doing anything that would work injury to the corporation * * *.* The rule that requires an undivided and unselfish loyalty to the corporation demands that there shall be no conflict between duty and self-interest. [Emphasis added.]

* * * *

* * * *If there is presented to a corporate officer or director a business opportunity which the corporation is financially able to undertake [that] is * * * in the line of the corporation's business and is of practical advantage to it * * * and, by embracing the opportunity, the self-interest of the officer or director will be brought into conflict with that of his corporation, the law will not permit him to seize the opportunity for himself. * * * In such circumstances, * * * the corporation may elect to claim all of the benefits of the transaction for itself, and the law will impress a trust in favor of the corporation upon the property, interests and profits so acquired. [Emphasis added.]

* * * *

* * * The appellants contend that no conflict of interest between Guth and Loft resulted from his acquirement and exploitation of the Pepsi-Cola opportunity [and] that the acquisition did not place Guth in competition with Loft * * *. [In this case, however,] Guth was Loft, and Guth was Pepsi. He absolutely controlled Loft. His authority over Pepsi was supreme. As Pepsi, he created and controlled the supply of Pepsi-Cola syrup, and he determined the price and the terms. What he offered, as Pepsi, he had the power, as Loft, to accept. Upon any consideration of human characteristics and motives, he created a conflict between self-interest and duty. He made himself the judge in his own cause. * * * Moreover, a reasonable probability of injury to Loft resulted from the situation forced upon it. Guth was in the same position to impose his terms upon Loft as had been the Coca-Cola Company.

* * * The facts and circumstances demonstrate that Guth's appropriation of the Pepsi-Cola opportunity to himself placed him in a competitive position with Loft with respect to a commodity essential to it, thereby rendering his personal interests incompatible with the superior interests of his corporation; and this situation was accomplished, not openly and with his own resources, but secretly and with the money and facilities of the corporation which was committed to his protection.

**Decision and Remedy** *The Delaware Supreme Court upheld the judgment of the lower court. The state supreme court was "convinced that the opportunity to acquire the Pepsi-Cola trademark and formula, goodwill and business belonged to [Loft], and that Guth, as its President, had no right to appropriate the opportunity to himself."*

**Impact of This Case on Today's Law** *This early Delaware decision was one of the first to set forth a test for determining when a corporate officer or director has breached the duty of loyalty. The test has two basic parts: Was the opportunity reasonably related to the corporation's line of business, and was the corporation financially able to undertake the opportunity? The court also considered whether the corporation had an interest or expectancy in the opportunity. It recognized that when the corporation had "no interest or expectancy, the officer or director is entitled to treat the opportunity as his own."*

**Critical Thinking**
- **What If the Facts Were Different?** *Suppose that Loft's board of directors had approved Pepsi-Cola's use of its personnel and equipment. Would the court's decision have been different? Discuss.*

## 6–2d Conflicts of Interest

Corporate directors often have many business affiliations, and a director may sit on the board of more than one corporation. Of course, directors are precluded from entering into or supporting businesses that operate in direct competition with corporations on whose boards they serve. Their fiduciary duty requires them to make a full disclosure of any potential conflicts of interest that might arise in any corporate transaction [RMBCA 8.60].

Sometimes, a corporation enters into a contract or engages in a transaction in which an officer or director has a personal interest. The director or officer must make a *full disclosure* of the nature of the conflicting interest and all facts pertinent to the transaction. He or she must also abstain from voting on the proposed transaction. When these rules are followed, the transaction can proceed. Otherwise, directors would be prevented from ever having financial dealings with the corporations they serve.

■ **EXAMPLE 6.4** Ballo Corporation needs office space. Stephanie Colson, one of its five directors, owns the building adjoining the corporation's headquarters. Colson can negotiate a lease for the space to Ballo if she fully discloses her conflicting interest and any facts known to her about the proposed transaction to Ballo and the other four directors. If the lease arrangement is fair and reasonable, Colson abstains from voting on

it, and the other members of the corporation's board of directors unanimously approve it, the contract is valid. ■

## 6–2e Liability of Directors and Officers

Directors and officers are exposed to liability on many fronts. They can be held liable for negligence in certain circumstances, as previously discussed. They may also be held liable for the crimes and torts committed by themselves or by corporate employees under their supervision. (See this chapter's *Global Insight* feature for a discussion of how the United States criminally prosecutes corporations and their managers for bribery.)

---

## GLOBAL INSIGHT Anti-Bribery Charges Take Their Toll on U.S. and Foreign Corporations

Hitachi, Ltd., was established in 1920 in Tokyo, Japan. Among other activities, it builds and operates electrical power systems throughout the world. Almost a hundred years after its founding, Hitachi agreed to a consent decree offered by the U.S. Securities and Exchange Commission (SEC).[a] (A consent decree is a means of resolving a dispute without going to trial or admitting guilt.) Part of that decree required Hitachi to pay a fine of $19 million for violating the Foreign Corrupt Practices Act (FCPA).[b]

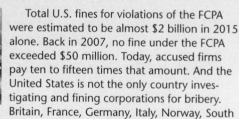

Hitachi had admitted to creating a system to bribe South Africa's ruling political party to give Hitachi preference in awarding electrical power station contracts. The SEC claimed jurisdiction over Hitachi even though the company was no longer listed on the New York Stock Exchange (NYSE). While the bribery scheme was taking place, Hitachi was a company whose shares could be traded in the United States. The long arm of U.S. anti-bribery laws had struck again.

### Anti-Bribery Lawsuits and Investigations Take Years

U.S.-owned and -based retailing giant Walmart was accused by the U.S. Department of Justice (DOJ) of bribing Mexican officials. By the time Walmart settles with the DOJ, it will have paid between $1 billion and $2 billion to forensic accountants and attorneys. Further, it will have to pay a fine. Finally, the company's managers will have spent thousands of hours conducting internal investigations.

Total U.S. fines for violations of the FCPA were estimated to be almost $2 billion in 2015 alone. Back in 2007, no fine under the FCPA exceeded $50 million. Today, accused firms pay ten to fifteen times that amount. And the United States is not the only country investigating and fining corporations for bribery. Britain, France, Germany, Italy, Norway, South Korea, and Switzerland assess bribery fines, as well.

The biggest bribery case during the decade 2000–2010 involved Siemens. That case took three years to resolve. Current cases, such as the one involving Walmart, could take up to ten years to resolve.

### Costs Continue Even after a Settlement

In most anti-bribery settlements, the accused firms must also bear the cost of being overseen for a number of years by independent compliance monitors. In addition, firms that have been involved in bribery investigations often are excluded from bidding for new business in the countries in which they allegedly offered bribes. Some accused companies have also had to defend against shareholder lawsuits.

Not surprisingly, anti-bribery compliance departments within corporations have grown in size and therefore in cost. In Germany, Siemens has spent more than $3 billion on fines and costs since it was first accused of bribery in 2008. It now has a compliance department with about four hundred employees.

**Critical Thinking** *Why do you think officers and directors of accused companies accept consent decrees rather than contest accusations at trial?*

a. *Securities and Exchange Commission v. Hitachi, Ltd.*, 2015 WL 7566666 (D.D.C. 2015).
b. 15 U.S.C. Sections 78m(b)(2)(A) and (B).

Additionally, if shareholders perceive that the corporate directors are not acting in the best interests of the corporation, they may sue the directors on behalf of the corporation. (This is known as a *shareholder's derivative suit,* which will be discussed later in this chapter.) Directors and officers can also be held personally liable under a number of statutes, such as statutes enacted to protect consumers or the environment.

See Concept Summary 6.2 for a review of the duties and liabilities of directors and officers.

## 6-3 The Role of Shareholders

The acquisition of a share of stock makes a person an owner and a shareholder in a corporation. Shareholders thus own the corporation. Although they have no legal title to corporate property, such as buildings and equipment, they do have an equitable (ownership) interest in the firm.

As a general rule, shareholders have no responsibility for the daily management of the corporation, although they are ultimately responsible for choosing the board of directors, which does have such control. Ordinarily, corporate officers and other employees owe no direct duty to individual shareholders (unless some contract or special relationship exists between them in addition to the corporate relationship).

The duty of officers and directors is to act in the best interests of the corporation and its shareholder-owners *as a whole.* In turn, as you will read later in this chapter, controlling shareholders owe a fiduciary duty to minority shareholders.

### 6-3a Shareholders' Powers

Shareholders must approve fundamental changes affecting the corporation before the changes can be implemented. Hence, shareholder approval normally is required to amend the articles of incorporation or bylaws, to conduct a merger or dissolve the corporation, and

## Concept Summary 6.2
### Duties and Liabilities of Directors and Officers

| Duties of Directors and Officers | 1. *Duty of care*—Directors and officers are obligated to act in good faith, to use prudent business judgment in the conduct of corporate affairs, and to act in the corporation's best interests. If a director or officer fails to exercise this duty of care, he or she may be answerable to the corporation and to the shareholders for breaching the duty. The *business judgment rule* immunizes a director from liability for a corporate decision as long as it was within the power of the corporation and the authority of the director to make and was an informed, reasonable, and loyal decision.<br>2. *Duty of loyalty*—Directors and officers have a fiduciary duty to subordinate their own interests to those of the corporation in matters relating to the corporation.<br>3. *Conflicts of interest*—To fulfill their duty of loyalty, directors and officers must make a full disclosure of any potential conflicts between their personal interests and those of the corporation. |
|---|---|
| Liability of Directors and Officers | 1. Corporate directors and officers are personally liable for their own torts and crimes (when not protected under the business judgment rule). Additionally, they may be held personally liable for the torts and crimes committed by corporate personnel under their direct supervision.<br>2. They may also be held personally liable for violating certain statutes, such as environmental and consumer protection laws, and can sometimes be sued by shareholders for mismanaging the corporation. |

to sell all or substantially all of the corporation's assets. Some of these powers are subject to prior board approval. Shareholder approval may also be requested (though it is not required) for certain other actions, such as to approve an independent auditor.

Shareholders also have the power to vote to elect or remove members of the board of directors. As described earlier, the first board of directors is either named in the articles of incorporation or chosen by the incorporators to serve until the first shareholders' meeting. From that time on, selection and retention of directors are exclusively shareholder functions.

Directors usually serve their full terms. If the shareholders judge them unsatisfactory, they are simply not reelected. Shareholders have the inherent power, however, to remove a director from office *for cause* (breach of duty or misconduct) by a majority vote.[5] Some state statutes (and some articles of incorporation) permit removal of directors without cause by the vote of a majority of the shareholders entitled to vote.[6]

## 6–3b Shareholders' Meetings

Shareholders' meetings must occur at least annually. In addition, special meetings can be called to deal with urgent matters.

**Notice of Meetings** A corporation must notify its shareholders of the date, time, and place of an annual or special shareholders' meeting at least ten days, but not more than sixty days, before the meeting date [RMBCA 7.05].[7] (The date and time of the annual meeting can be specified in the bylaws.) Notice of a special meeting must include a statement of the purpose of the meeting, and business transacted at the meeting is limited to that purpose.

The RMBCA does not specify how the notice must be given. Most corporations do specify in their bylaws the acceptable methods of notifying shareholders about meetings. Also, some states' incorporation statutes outline the means of notice that a corporation can use in that jurisdiction. For instance, in Alaska, notice may be

given in person, by mail, or by fax, e-mail, blog, or Web post—as long as the shareholder has agreed to that electronic method.[8]

**Proxies** It usually is not practical for owners of only a few shares of stock of publicly traded corporations to attend a shareholders' meeting. Therefore, the law allows stockholders to appoint another person as their agent to vote their shares at the meeting. The agent's formal authorization to vote the shares is called a **proxy** (from the Latin *procurare,* meaning "to manage or take care of"). Proxy materials are sent to all shareholders before shareholders' meetings.

Management often solicits proxies, but any person can solicit proxies to concentrate voting power. Proxies have been used by groups of shareholders as a device for taking over a corporation. Proxies normally are revocable (can be withdrawn), unless they are specifically designated as irrevocable and coupled with an interest. A proxy is coupled with an interest when, for instance, the person receiving the proxies from shareholders has agreed to buy their shares. Under RMBCA 7.22(c), proxies are valid for eleven months, unless the proxy agreement mandates a longer period.

**Shareholder Proposals** When shareholders want to change a company policy, they can put their ideas up for a shareholder vote. They do this by submitting a shareholder proposal to the board of directors and asking the board to include the proposal in the proxy materials that are sent to all shareholders before meetings.

**Rules for Proxies and Shareholder Proposals** The Securities and Exchange Commission (SEC) regulates the purchase and sale of securities. The SEC has special provisions relating to proxies and shareholder proposals. SEC Rule 14a-8 provides that all shareholders who own stock worth at least $1,000 are eligible to submit proposals for inclusion in corporate proxy materials. The corporation is required to include information on whatever proposals will be considered at the shareholders' meeting along with proxy materials. Only those proposals that relate to significant policy considerations, not ordinary business operations, must be included.

Under the SEC's e-proxy rules,[9] all public companies must post their proxy materials on the Internet and notify shareholders how to find that information. Although the law requires proxy materials to be posted online, public companies may also send the materials to shareholders

---

**5.** A director can often demand court review of removal for cause, however.
**6.** Most states allow *cumulative voting* for directors (described later in the chapter). If cumulative voting is authorized, a director may not be removed if the number of votes against removal would be sufficient to elect a director under cumulative voting. See, for instance, California Corporations Code Section 303A. See also Section 8.08(c) of the RMBCA.
**7.** The shareholder can waive the requirement of notice by signing a waiver form [RMBCA 7.06]. A shareholder who does not receive notice but who learns of the meeting and attends without protesting the lack of notice is said to have waived notice by such conduct.

**8.** Alaska Statutes Section 10.06.410 Notice of Shareholders' Meetings.
**9.** 17 C.F.R. Parts 240, 249, and 274.

by other means, including paper documents and DVDs sent by mail.

## 6–3c Shareholder Voting

Shareholders exercise ownership control through the power of their votes. Corporate business matters are presented in the form of *resolutions,* which shareholders vote to approve or disapprove. Each common shareholder normally is entitled to one vote per share.

The articles of incorporation can exclude or limit voting rights, particularly for certain classes of shares. For instance, owners of preferred shares are usually denied the right to vote [RMBCA 7.21]. If a state statute requires specific voting procedures, the corporation's articles or bylaws must be consistent with the statute.

**Quorum Requirements**  For shareholders to act during a meeting, a quorum must be present. Generally, a quorum exists when shareholders holding more than 50 percent of the outstanding shares are present. State laws often permit the articles of incorporation to set higher or lower quorum requirements, however. In some states,

obtaining the unanimous written consent of shareholders is a permissible alternative to holding a shareholders' meeting [RMBCA 7.25].

Once a quorum is present, voting can proceed. If a state statute requires specific voting procedures, the corporation's articles or bylaws must be consistent with the statute. A majority vote of the shares represented at the meeting usually is required to pass resolutions. At times, more than a simple majority vote is required, either by a state statute or by the corporate articles. Extraordinary corporate matters, such as a merger, consolidation, or dissolution of the corporation, require approval by a higher percentage of all corporate shares entitled to vote [RMBCA 7.27].

The corporation in the following case had eighty-four shares of voting common stock outstanding. The shareholder-appellee owned twenty shares, he and his estranged wife jointly held another sixteen shares, and three different individuals owned sixteen shares each. At a shareholders' meeting, the appellee was the only shareholder present in person. Another shareholder (not the appellee's wife) was present by proxy. Could the shares held jointly by the appellee and his wife be counted for purposes of a quorum?

---

**Case Analysis 6.3**

## Case v. Sink & Rise, Inc.

Supreme Court of Wyoming, 2013 WY 19, 297 P.3d 762 (2013).

### In the Language of the Court
*HILL,* Justice.

This case involves a dispute over corporate action during a shareholder meeting of Appellee Sink & Rise, Inc., (Sink & Rise) a Wyoming corporation. Appellee James Caleb Case (Cale Case) was the only shareholder present at the meeting. He concluded that a quorum existed and thus voted on and passed several resolutions. Cale Case also elected himself and another shareholder as the directors of the corporation, and replaced his estranged wife, Appellant Shirley Case, as the corporation's secretary.

Shirley Case took issue with her estranged husband's actions during the shareholder meeting and filed a complaint in [a Wyoming state] district court to set aside the corporate action that occurred at the shareholder meeting. * * * The district court concluded that the resolutions were passed with requisite

authority and thus they were not set aside after trial. This appeal followed.
* * * *

* * * Shirley Case argues that because her estranged husband was not entitled to vote the jointly held shares, those same shares could not be counted for quorum purposes. She reasons that because she was absent from the meeting and because only shares "entitled to vote" are to be counted in establishing a quorum, the shares in question were essentially useless at the meeting.

* * * We find the answer in the Sink & Rise corporate documents, and within Wyoming law. First, we reiterate the [district court's] characterization of the stock as being owned by husband and wife with rights of survivorship. We agree with the district court's further classification of the stock as creating a presumption of tenancy by the entirety under Wyoming law. As tenants by the

entirety, each owns an undivided 100% interest in the 16 shares.

*In an estate of the entirety, the husband and the wife during their joint lives each owns, not a part, or a separate or a separable interest, but the whole.* [Emphasis added.]

To further help us in our consideration, we turn to the corporate documents.

* * * Sink & Rise's bylaws * * * define what constitutes a "quorum," and relate the corporation's rule on voting shares:

> 6. *Quorum.* A majority of the outstanding shares entitled to vote, represented in person or by proxy, shall constitute a quorum at a meeting of Shareholders. If a quorum is present, the affirmative vote of the majority of shares entitled to vote at the meeting shall be the act of the Shareholders. * * *

**Case 6.3 Continues**

Case 6.3 Continued

7. *Voting of Shares.* * * * Each outstanding share is entitled to vote the number of shares owned by him/her on each matter submitted to a vote at a meeting of Shareholders. * * *

*According to the bylaws, for the corporation to count shares in determining a quorum, the shares must be (1) entitled to vote, and (2) represented in person or by proxy.* From our reading of the corporate documents, and because the joint stock was held by husband and wife as tenants by the entirety, we conclude that the shares held jointly by Cale Case

and Shirley Case were "entitled to vote" at the meeting. Cale Case represented the stock in person, as required by the bylaws. [Emphasis added.]

As the district court noted, and the parties agree here, the joint stock in question cannot be, and was not, voted without agreement between Cale Case and Shirley Case. * * * [But] the fact that Cale Case and Shirley Case must agree on how to vote the stock before it can actually be voted does not strip it of its voting privileges. Cale Case did not attempt to vote the stock at the meeting,

but instead considered it only for quorum purposes.

Sink & Rise's bylaws do not prevent stock owned by a husband and wife as tenants by the entirety * * * from being counted for purposes of a quorum if represented in person. The stock in question was represented in person by Cale Case at the * * * shareholder meeting, and it was properly counted to establish a quorum.

* * * *

We affirm the district court's decision.

## Legal Reasoning Questions

**1.** How many shareholders were present at the shareholders' meeting that gave rise to the dispute in this case?

**2.** How did the court "characterize" and "classify" the shares of stock that Cale and Shirley Case held jointly?

**3.** According to the court, how many shares were represented at the shareholders' meeting? Was a quorum present? Explain.

---

**Voting Lists** The corporation prepares a voting list before each shareholders' meeting. Ordinarily, only persons whose names appear on the corporation's stockholder records as owners are entitled to vote.[10]

The voting list contains the name and address of each shareholder as shown on the corporate records on a given cutoff date, or *record date.* (Under RMBCA 7.07, the bylaws or board of directors may fix a record date that is as much as seventy days before the meeting.) The voting list also includes the number of voting shares held by each owner. The list is usually kept at the corporate headquarters and must be made available for shareholder inspection [RMBCA 7.20].

**Cumulative Voting** Most states permit, and many require, shareholders to elect directors by *cumulative voting,* a voting method designed to allow minority shareholders to be represented on the board of directors.[11]

**Formula.** With cumulative voting, each shareholder is entitled to a total number of votes equal to the number of board members to be elected multiplied by the number of voting shares that the shareholder owns. The shareholder can cast all of these votes for one candidate or split them among several nominees for director. All candidates stand for election at the same time.

**How Cumulative Voting Works.** Cumulative voting can best be understood by example. ■ **EXAMPLE 6.5** A corporation has 10,000 shares issued and outstanding. The minority shareholders hold 3,000 shares, and the majority shareholders hold the other 7,000 shares. Three members of the board are to be elected. The majority shareholders' nominees are Alvarez, Beasley, and Caravel. The minority shareholders' nominee is Dovrik. Can Dovrik be elected to the board by the minority shareholders?

If cumulative voting is allowed, the answer is yes. The minority shareholders have 9,000 votes among them (the number of directors to be elected times the number of shares, or 3 × 3,000 = 9,000 votes). All of these votes can be cast to elect Dovrik. The majority shareholders have 21,000 votes (3 × 7,000 = 21,000 votes), but these votes must be distributed among their three nominees.

The principle of cumulative voting is that no matter how the majority shareholders cast their 21,000 votes, they will not be able to elect all three directors if the minority shareholders cast all of their 9,000 votes for Dovrik, as illustrated in Exhibit 6–2. ■ In contrast, when cumulative voting is not required, the entire board can be elected by a majority of shares.

---

**10.** When the legal owner of shares is deceased, bankrupt, mentally incompetent, or in some other way under a legal disability, his or her vote can be cast by a person designated by law to control and manage that owner's property.

**11.** See, for instance, California Corporations Code Section 708. Some states, such as Nebraska, require cumulative voting in their state constitutions. Under RMBCA 7.28, no cumulative voting rights exist unless the articles of incorporation so provide.

**EXHIBIT 6–2**  Results of Cumulative Voting

| Ballot | Majority Shareholder Votes | | | Minority Shareholder Votes | Directors Elected |
|---|---|---|---|---|---|
| | Alvarez | Beasley | Caravel | Dovrik | |
| 1 | 10,000 | 10,000 | 1,000 | 9,000 | Alvarez, Beasley, Dovrik |
| 2 | 9,001 | 9,000 | 2,999 | 9,000 | Alvarez, Beasley, Dovrik |
| 3 | 6,000 | 7,000 | 8,000 | 9,000 | Beasley, Caravel, Dovrik |

**Other Voting Techniques**  Before a shareholders' meeting, a group of shareholders can agree in writing to vote their shares together in a specified manner. Such agreements, called *shareholder voting agreements,* usually are held to be valid and enforceable. A shareholder can also vote by proxy, as noted earlier.

Another technique is for shareholders to enter into a *voting trust.* A **voting trust** is an agreement (a trust contract) under which a shareholder assigns the right to vote his or her shares to a trustee, usually for a specified period of time. The trustee is then responsible for voting the shares on behalf of all the shareholders in the trust. The shareholder retains all rights of ownership (for instance, the right to receive dividend payments) except the power to vote the shares [RMBCA 7.30].

# 6–4 Rights of Shareholders

Shareholders possess numerous rights in addition to the right to vote their shares, and we examine several here.

## 6–4a Stock Certificates

In the past, corporations commonly issued **stock certificates** that evidenced ownership of a specified number of shares in the corporation. Only a few jurisdictions still require physical stock certificates, and shareholders there have the right to demand that the corporation issue certificates (or replace those that were lost or destroyed). Stock is intangible personal property, however, and the ownership right exists independently of the certificate itself.

In most states and under RMBCA 6.26, a board of directors may provide that shares of stock will be uncertificated, or "paperless"—that is, no actual, physical stock certificates will be issued. Notice of shareholders' meetings, dividends, and operational and financial reports are distributed according to the ownership lists recorded in the corporation's books.

## 6–4b Preemptive Rights

Sometimes, the articles of incorporation grant preemptive rights to shareholders [RMBCA 6.30]. With **preemptive rights,** a shareholder receives a preference over all other purchasers to subscribe to or purchase a pro-rated share of a new issue of stock. Generally, preemptive rights must be exercised within a specific time period (usually thirty days).

A shareholder who is given preemptive rights can purchase a percentage of the new shares being issued that is equal to the percentage of shares she or he already holds in the company. This allows each shareholder to maintain her or his proportionate control, voting power, and financial interest in the corporation. ■ **EXAMPLE 6.6** Katlin is a shareholder who owns 10 percent of a company. Because she also has preemptive rights, she can buy 10 percent of any new issue (to maintain her 10 percent position). Thus, if the corporation issues 1,000 more shares, Katlin can buy 100 of the new shares. ■

Preemptive rights are most important in close corporations because each shareholder owns a relatively small number of shares but controls a substantial interest in the corporation. Without preemptive rights, it would be possible for a shareholder to lose his or her proportionate control over the firm. Nevertheless, preemptive rights do not exist unless provided for in the articles of incorporation.

## 6-4c Stock Warrants

**Stock warrants** are rights given by a company to buy stock at a stated price by a specified date. Usually, when preemptive rights exist and a corporation is issuing additional shares, it gives its shareholders stock warrants. Warrants are often publicly traded on securities exchanges.

## 6-4d Dividends

As mentioned, a **dividend** is a distribution of corporate profits or income *ordered by the directors* and paid to the shareholders in proportion to their shares in the corporation. Dividends can be paid in cash, property, stock of the corporation that is paying the dividends, or stock of other corporations.[12]

State laws vary, but each state determines the general circumstances and legal requirements under which dividends are paid. State laws also control the sources of revenue to be used. All states allow dividends to be paid from the undistributed net profits earned by the corporation, for instance. A number of states allow dividends to be paid out of any surplus.

**Illegal Dividends** Dividends are illegal if they are improperly paid from an unauthorized account or if their payment causes the corporation to become insolvent. Generally, shareholders must return illegal dividends only if they knew that the dividends were illegal when the payment was received (or if the dividends were paid when the corporation was insolvent). Whenever dividends are illegal or improper, the board of directors can be held personally liable for the amount of the payment.

**The Directors' Failure to Declare a Dividend** When directors fail to declare a dividend, shareholders can ask a court to compel the directors to do so. To succeed, the shareholders must show that the directors have acted so unreasonably in withholding the dividend that their conduct is an abuse of their discretion.

Often, a corporation accumulates large cash reserves for a legitimate corporate purpose, such as expansion or research. The mere fact that the firm has sufficient earnings or surplus available to pay a dividend normally is not enough to compel the directors to declare a dividend. The courts are reluctant to interfere with corporate operations and will not compel directors to declare dividends unless abuse of discretion is clearly shown.

## 6-4e Inspection Rights

Shareholders in a corporation enjoy both common law and statutory inspection rights. The RMBCA provides that every shareholder is entitled to examine specified corporate records, including voting lists [RMBCA 7.20, 16.02]. The shareholder may inspect in person, or an attorney, accountant, or other authorized assistant can do so as the shareholder's agent. In some states, a shareholder must have held her or his shares for a minimum period of time immediately preceding the demand to inspect or must hold a certain percentage of outstanding shares.

**Proper Purpose** A shareholder has a right to inspect and copy corporate books and records only for a *proper purpose,* and the request to inspect must be made in advance. A shareholder who is denied the right of inspection can seek a court order to compel the inspection.

■ **CASE IN POINT 6.7** Trading Block Holdings, Inc., offers online brokerage services. On April 1, 2013, some shareholders of Trading Block, through an attorney, sent a letter asking to inspect specific items in the corporation's books and records. The letter indicated that the purpose was to determine the financial condition of the company, how it was being managed, and whether the company's financial practices were appropriate. It also stated that the shareholders wanted to know whether Trading Block's management had engaged in any self-dealing that had negatively impacted the company as a whole.

On April 30, Trading Block responded with a letter stating that the plaintiffs were on a "fishing expedition" and did not have a proper purpose for inspecting the corporate records. Eventually, the shareholders filed a motion to compel inspection in an Illinois state court. The trial court denied the plaintiffs' motion. On appeal, the reviewing court held that the plaintiffs' allegations of self-dealing by directors and officers constituted a proper purpose for their inspection request. The trial court's decision was reversed.[13] ■

**Potential for Abuse** The power of inspection is fraught with potential abuses, and the corporation is allowed to protect itself from them. For instance, a share-

---

12. On one occasion, a distillery declared and paid a dividend in bonded whiskey.

13. *Sunlitz Holding Co., W.L.L. v. Trading Block Holdings, Inc.,* 2014 IL App (1st) 133938, 17 N.E.3d 715, 384 Ill.Dec. 733 (4 Dist. 2014).

holder can properly be denied access to corporate records to prevent harassment or to protect trade secrets or other confidential corporate information.[14]

### 6–4f Transfer of Shares

Corporate stock represents an ownership right in intangible personal property. The law generally recognizes the owner's right to transfer stock to another person unless there are valid restrictions on its transferability, such as frequently occur with close corporation stock.

When shares are transferred, a new entry is made in the corporate stock book to indicate the new owner. Until the corporation is notified and the entry is complete, all rights—including voting rights, notice of shareholders' meetings, and the right to dividend distributions—remain with the current record owner.

### 6–4g The Shareholder's Derivative Suit

When the corporation is harmed by the actions of a third party, the directors can bring a lawsuit in the name of the corporation against that party. If the corporate directors fail to bring a lawsuit, shareholders can do so "derivatively" in what is known as a **shareholder's derivative suit.**

The right of shareholders to bring a derivative action is especially important when the wrong suffered by the corporation results from the actions of the corporate directors and officers. For obvious reasons, the directors and officers would probably be unwilling to take any action against themselves.

**Written Demand Required** Before shareholders can bring a derivative suit, they must submit a written demand to the corporation, asking the board of directors to take appropriate action [RMBCA 7.40]. The directors then have ninety days in which to act. Only if they refuse to do so can the derivative suit go forward. In addition, a court will dismiss a derivative suit if a majority of the directors or an independent panel determines in good faith that the lawsuit is not in the best interests of the corporation [RMBCA 7.44].

**Any Damages Awarded Go to the Corporation** When shareholders bring a derivative suit, they are not pursuing rights or benefits for themselves personally but are acting as guardians of the corporate entity. Therefore, if the suit is successful, any damages recovered normally go into the corporation's treasury, not to the shareholders personally.[15]

## 6–5 Duties and Liabilities of Shareholders

One of the hallmarks of the corporate form of organization is that shareholders are not personally liable for the debts of the corporation. If the corporation fails, the shareholders can lose their investments, but that generally is the limit of their liability. As discussed previously, in certain instances, a court will pierce the corporate veil (disregard the corporate entity) and hold the shareholders individually liable. But these situations are the exception, not the rule.

A shareholder can also be personally liable in certain other rare instances. One relates to illegal dividends, which were mentioned previously. Another relates to *watered stock.* Finally, in certain instances, a majority shareholder who engages in oppressive conduct or attempts to exclude minority shareholders from receiving certain benefits can be held personally liable.

Concept Summary 6.3 reviews the role, rights, and liability of shareholders in a corporation.

### 6–5a Watered Stock

When a corporation issues shares for less than their fair market value, the shares are referred to as **watered stock.**[16] Usually, the shareholder who receives watered stock must pay the difference to the corporation (the shareholder is personally liable). In some states, the shareholder who receives watered stock may be liable to creditors of the corporation for unpaid corporate debts.

■ **EXAMPLE 6.8** During the formation of a corporation, Gomez, one of the incorporators, transfers his property, Sunset Beach, to the corporation for 10,000 shares of stock at a par value of $100 per share for a total price of $1 million. After the property is transferred and the shares are issued, Sunset Beach is carried on the corporate books at a value of $1 million.

On appraisal, it is discovered that the market value of the property at the time of transfer was only $500,000. The

---

14. See, for example, *United Technologies Corp. v. Treppel*, 109 A.3d 553 (Del.Ch. 2014).

15. The shareholders may be entitled to reimbursement for reasonable expenses of the derivative lawsuit, including attorneys' fees.
16. The phrase *watered stock* was originally used to describe cattle that were kept thirsty during a long drive and then were allowed to drink large quantities of water just before their sale. The increased weight of the watered stock allowed the seller to reap a higher profit.

---

## Concept Summary 6.3

### Role, Rights, and Liability of Shareholders

| | |
|---|---|
| **Shareholders' Powers** | Shareholders' powers include approval of all fundamental changes affecting the corporation and election of the board of directors. |
| **Shareholders' Meetings** | Shareholders' meetings must occur at least annually, and special meetings can be called when necessary. Notice of the time and place of a meeting (and its purpose, if the meeting is specially called) must be sent to shareholders. A minimum number of shareholders (quorum) must be present to vote. |
| **Shareholders' Rights** | Shareholders have numerous rights, which may include the following:<br>• Voting rights.<br>• Preemptive rights (depending on the corporate articles).<br>• The right to receive dividends (at the discretion of the directors).<br>• The right to inspect the corporate records.<br>• The right to transfer shares (this right may be restricted in close corporations).<br>• The right to receive a share of corporate assets when the corporation is dissolved.<br>• The right to sue on behalf of the corporation (bring a shareholder's derivative suit) when the directors fail to do so. |
| **Shareholders' Liability** | Shareholders may be liable for watered stock. In certain situations, majority shareholders may be regarded as having a fiduciary duty to minority shareholders and will be liable if that duty is breached. |

---

shares issued to Gomez are therefore watered stock, and he is liable to the corporation for the difference between the value of the shares and the value of the property. ■

### 6–5b Duties of Majority Shareholders

In some instances, a majority shareholder is regarded as having a fiduciary duty to the corporation and to the minority shareholders. This duty arises when a single shareholder (or a few shareholders acting in concert) owns a sufficient number of shares to exercise *de facto* control over the corporation. In these situations, the majority shareholder owes a fiduciary duty to the minority shareholders.

When a majority shareholder breaches her or his fiduciary duty to a minority shareholder, the minority shareholder can sue for damages. A breach of fiduciary duties by those who control a close corporation normally constitutes what is known as *oppressive conduct*. A common example of a breach of fiduciary duty occurs when the majority shareholders "freeze out" the minority shareholders and exclude them from certain benefits of participating in the firm.

■ **EXAMPLE 6.9** Brodie, Jordan, and Barbara form a close corporation to operate a machine shop. Brodie and Jordan own 75 percent of the shares in the company, but all three are directors. After disagreements arise, Brodie asks the company to purchase his shares, but his requests are refused. A few years later, Brodie dies, and his wife, Ella, inherits his shares. Jordan and Barbara refuse to perform a valuation of the company, deny Ella access to corporate information, do not declare any dividends, and refuse to elect Ella as a director. In this situation, the majority shareholders have violated their fiduciary duty to Ella. ■

# Reviewing: Corporate Directors, Officers, and Shareholders

David Brock was on the board of directors of Firm Body Fitness, Inc., which owned a string of fitness clubs in New Mexico. Brock owned 15 percent of the Firm Body stock and was also employed as a tanning technician at one of the fitness clubs. After the January financial report showed that Firm Body's tanning division was operating at a substantial net loss, the board of directors, led by Marty Levinson, discussed terminating the tanning operations. Brock successfully convinced a majority of the board that the tanning division was necessary to market the clubs' overall fitness package. By April, the tanning division's financial losses had risen. The board hired a business analyst, who conducted surveys and determined that the tanning operations did not significantly increase membership.

A shareholder, Diego Peñada, discovered that Brock owned stock in Sunglow, Inc., the company from which Firm Body purchased its tanning equipment. Peñada notified Levinson, who privately reprimanded Brock. Shortly thereafter, Brock and Mandy Vail, who owned 37 percent of the Firm Body stock and also held shares of Sunglow, voted to replace Levinson on the board of directors. Using the information presented in the chapter, answer the following questions.

1. What duties did Brock, as a director, owe to Firm Body?
2. Does the fact that Brock owned shares in Sunglow establish a conflict of interest? Why or why not?
3. Suppose that Firm Body brought an action against Brock claiming that he had breached the duty of loyalty by not disclosing his interest in Sunglow to the other directors. What theory might Brock use in his defense?
4. Now suppose that Firm Body did not bring an action against Brock. What type of lawsuit might Peñada be able to bring based on these facts?

**Debate This** . . . *Because most shareholders never bother to vote for directors, shareholders have no real control over corporations.*

## Terms and Concepts

| | | |
|---|---|---|
| business judgment rule 96 | preemptive rights 105 | stock certificate 105 |
| dividend 106 | proxy 102 | stock warrant 106 |
| inside director 93 | quorum 93 | voting trust 105 |
| outside director 93 | shareholder's derivative suit 107 | watered stock 107 |

## Issue Spotters

1. Wonder Corporation has an opportunity to buy stock in XL, Inc. The directors decide that instead of Wonder buying the stock, the directors will buy it. Yvon, a Wonder shareholder, learns of the purchase and wants to sue the directors on Wonder's behalf. Can she do it? Explain. (See *Rights of Shareholders*.)

2. Nico is Omega Corporation's majority shareholder. He owns enough stock in Omega that if he were to sell it, the sale would be a transfer of control of the firm. Discuss whether Nico owes a duty to Omega or the minority shareholders in selling his shares. (See *Duties and Liabilities of Shareholders*.)

- **Check your answers to the Issue Spotters against the answers provided in Appendix B at the end of this text.**

## Business Scenarios

**6–1. Conflicts of Interest.** Oxy Corp. is negotiating with Wick Construction Co. for the renovation of Oxy's corporate headquarters. Wick, the owner of Wick Construction Co., is also one of the five members of Oxy's board of directors. The contract terms are standard for this type of contract. Wick has previously informed two of the other directors of his interest in the construction company. Oxy's board approves the contract by a three-to-two vote, with Wick voting with the majority. Discuss whether this contract is binding on the corporation. (See *Duties and Liabilities of Directors and Officers.*)

**6–2. Liability of Directors.** AstroStar, Inc., has approximately five hundred shareholders. Its board of directors consists of three members—Eckhart, Dolan, and Macero. At a regular board meeting, the board selects Galiard as president of the corporation by a two-to-one vote, with Eckhart dissenting. The minutes of the meeting do not register Eckhart's dissenting vote. Later, an audit reveals that Galiard is a former convict and has embezzled $500,000 from the corporation that is not covered by insurance. Can the corporation hold directors Eckhart, Dolan, and Macero personally liable? Discuss. (See *Duties and Liabilities of Directors and Officers.*)

# Business Case Problems

**6–3. Fiduciary Duty of Officers.** Designer Surfaces, Inc., supplied countertops to homeowners who shopped at stores such as Lowe's and Costco. The homeowners paid the store, which then contracted with Designer to fabricate and install the countertops. Designer bought materials from Arizona Tile, LLC, on an open account. Designer's only known corporate officers were Howard Berger and John McCarthy. Designer became insolvent and could not pay Arizona Tile for all the materials it had purchased, including materials for which Designer had already received payment from the retail stores. Arizona Tile sued Designer and won a default judgment, but the company had no funds. Arizona Tile then sued Berger and McCarthy personally for diverting company funds that Designer had received in trust for payment to Arizona Tile. Arizona Tile argued that the use of the funds for other purposes was a breach of fiduciary duty. Berger and McCarthy argued that corporate law imposed neither a fiduciary duty on corporate officers nor personal liability for breach of a duty to suppliers of materials. Which argument is more credible, and why? [*Arizona Tile, LLC v. Berger*, 223 Ariz. 491, 224 P.3d 988 (Ariz.App. 2010)] (See *Role of Directors and Officers.*)

**6–4. Business Case Problem with Sample Answer— Rights of Shareholders.** Stanka Woods was the sole member of Hair Ventures, LLC. Hair Ventures owned 3 million shares of stock in Biolustré, Inc. For several years, Woods and other Biolustré shareholders did not receive notice of shareholders' meetings or financial reports. On learning that Biolustré planned to issue more stock, Woods, through Hair Ventures, demanded to see Biolustré's books and records. Biolustré asserted that the request was not for a proper purpose. Does Woods have a right to inspect Biolustré's books and records? If so, what are the limits? Do any of those limits apply in this case? Explain. [*Biolustré Inc. v. Hair Ventures, LLC*, 2011 WL 540574 (Tex.App.—San Antonio 2011)] (See *Rights of Shareholders.*)

- For a sample answer to Problem 6–4, go to Appendix C at the end of this text.

**6–5. Duty of Loyalty.** Kids International Corp. produced children's wear for Walmart and other retailers. Gila Dweck was a Kids director and its chief executive officer. Because she felt that she was not paid enough, she started Success Apparel to compete with Kids. Success operated out of Kids' premises, used its employees, borrowed on its credit, took advantage of its business opportunities, and capitalized on its customer relationships. As an "administrative fee," Dweck paid Kids 1 percent of Success's total sales. Did Dweck breach any fiduciary duties? Explain. [*Dweck v. Nasser*, 2012 WL 3194069 (Del.Ch. 2012)] (See *Duties and Liabilities of Directors and Officers.*)

**6–6. Duties of Majority Shareholders.** Bill McCann was the president and chief executive officer of McCann Ranch & Livestock Co. He and his brother Ron each owned 36.7 percent of the stock. Ron had been removed from the board of directors on their father's death, however, and was not authorized to work for the firm. Their mother, Gertrude, owned the rest of the stock, which was to pass to Bill on her death. The corporation paid Gertrude's personal expenses in an amount that represented about 75 percent of the net corporate income. Bill received regular salary increases. The corporation did not issue a dividend. Was Ron the victim of a freeze-out? Discuss. [*McCann v. McCann*, 152 Idaho 809, 275 P.3d 824 (2012)] (See *Duties and Liabilities of Shareholders.*)

**6–7. Business Judgment Rule.** Country Contractors, Inc., contracted to provide excavation services for A Westside Storage of Indianapolis, Inc., but did not complete the job and later filed for bankruptcy. Stephen Songer and Jahn Songer were Country's sole shareholders. The Songers had not misused the corporate form to engage in fraud. The firm had not been undercapitalized, personal and corporate funds had not been commingled, and Country had kept accounting records and minutes of its annual board meetings. Are the Songers personally liable for Country's failure to complete its contract? Explain. [*Country Contractors, Inc. v. A Westside Storage of Indianapolis, Inc.*, 4 N.E.3d 677 (Ind.App. 2014)] (See *Duties and Liabilities of Directors and Officers.*)

**6–8. Rights of Shareholders.** FCR Realty, LLC, and Clifford B. Green & Sons, Inc., were co-owned by three brothers—Frederick, Clifford Jr., and Richard Green. Each brother was a shareholder of the corporation. Frederick was a controlling shareholder, as well as president. Each brother owned a one-third interest in the LLC. Clifford believed that Frederick had misused LLC and corporate funds to pay nonexistent debts and liabilities and had diverted LLC assets to the corporation. He also contended that Frederick had disbursed about $1.8 million in corporate funds to Frederick's own separate business. Clifford hired an attorney and filed an action on behalf of the two companies against Frederick for breach of fiduciary duty. Frederick argued that Clifford lacked the knowledge necessary to adequately represent the companies' interest because he did not understand financial statements. Can Clifford maintain the action against Frederick? If so, and if the suit is successful, who recovers the damages? Explain. [*FCR Realty, LLC v. Green*, __ Conn.Supp. __, __ Conn.L.Rptr. __, 2016 WL 571449 (Super. 2016)] (See *Rights of Shareholders*.)

### 6–9. A Question of Ethics—Duties of Directors and Officers.

 *New Orleans Paddlewheels, Inc. (NOP), was a Louisiana corporation formed in 1982. James Smith, Sr., and Warren Reuther were its only shareholders, with each holding 50 percent of the stock. NOP was part of a sprawling enterprise of tourism and hospitality companies in New Orleans controlled by Smith and Reuther. The positions on the board of each company were split equally between the Smith and Reuther families.*

*At Smith's request, his son James Smith, Jr. (JES), became involved in the businesses. In 1999, NOP's board elected JES as president, to be in charge of day-to-day operations, and Reuther as chief executive officer (CEO), to be in charge of marketing and development. Over the next few years, animosity developed between Reuther and JES. In October 2001, JES terminated Reuther as CEO and denied him access to the offices and books of* NOP *and the other companies, literally changing the locks on the doors. At the next meetings of the boards of NOP and the overall enterprise, deadlock ensued, with the directors voting along family lines on every issue.*

*Complaining that the meetings were a "waste of time," JES began to run the entire enterprise by taking advantage of an unequal balance of power on the companies' executive committees. In NOP's subsequent bankruptcy proceeding, Reuther filed a motion for the appointment of a trustee to formulate a plan for the firm's reorganization, alleging, among other things, misconduct by NOP's management. [In re New Orleans Paddlewheels, Inc., 350 Bankr. 667 (E.D.La. 2006)] (See *Duties and Liabilities of Directors and Officers*.)*

**(a)** Was Reuther legally entitled to have access to the books and records of NOP and the other companies? JES maintained, among other things, that NOP's books were "a mess." Was JES's denial of that access unethical? Why or why not?

**(b)** How would you describe JES's attempt to gain control of NOP and the other companies? Were his actions devious and self-serving in the pursuit of personal gain or legitimate and reasonable in the pursuit of a business goal? Discuss.

## Legal Reasoning Group Activity

### 6–10. Shareholders' Duties.

Milena Weintraub and Larry Griffith were shareholders in Grand Casino, Inc., which operated a casino in South Dakota. Griffith owned 51 percent of the stock and Weintraub 49 percent. Weintraub managed the casino, which Griffith typically visited once a week. At the end of 2012, an accounting audit showed that the cash on hand was less than the amount posted in the casino's books. Later, more shortfalls were discovered. In October 2014, Griffith did a complete audit. Weintraub was unable to account for $200,500 in missing cash. Griffith then took all of the casino's most recent profits, including Weintraub's $90,447.20 share, and, without telling Weintraub, sold the casino for $400,000 and kept all of the proceeds. Weintraub filed a suit against Griffith, asserting a breach of fiduciary duty. Griffith countered with evidence of Weintraub's misappropriation of corporate cash. (See *Duties and Liabilities of Shareholders*.)

**(a)** The first group will discuss the duties that these parties owed to each other and determine whether Weintraub or Griffith, or both, breached those duties.

**(b)** The second group will decide how this dispute should be resolved and who should pay what to whom to reconcile the finances.

**(c)** A third group will discuss whether Weintraub or Griffith violated any ethical duties to each other or to the corporation.

## CHAPTER 7

# Securities Law and Corporate Governance

After the stock market crash of October 29, 1929, and the ensuing economic depression, Congress enacted legislation to regulate securities markets. The result was the Securities Act of 1933[1] and the Securities Exchange Act of 1934.[2] Both acts were designed to provide investors with more information to help them make buying and selling decisions about securities and to prohibit

deceptive, unfair, and manipulative practices. **Securities** generally include any instruments evidencing corporate ownership (stock) or debt (bonds).

Today, the sale and transfer of securities are heavily regulated by federal and state statutes and by government agencies. The Securities and Exchange Commission (SEC) is the main independent regulatory agency that administers the 1933 and 1934 securities acts. The SEC also plays a key role in interpreting the provisions of these acts (and their amendments)

and in creating regulations governing the purchase and sale of securities. The agency continually updates regulations in response to legislation, such as the Dodd-Frank Wall Street Reform and Consumer Protection Act,[3] and particular challenges, such as climate change.[4]

---

1. 15 U.S.C. Sections 77a-77aa.
2. 15 U.S.C. Sections 778a-78mm.

---

3. Pub. L. No. 111-203, July 21, 2010, 124 Stat. 1376; codified at 12 U.S.C. Sections 5301 *et seq.*
4. The SEC now requires companies to make disclosures about the potential impacts of climate change on their future profitability. See 17 C.F.R. Parts 211, 231, and 241.

---

## 7-1 The Securities Act of 1933

The Securities Act of 1933 governs initial sales of stock by businesses. The act was designed to prohibit various forms of fraud and to stabilize the securities industry by requiring that investors receive financial and other significant information concerning the securities being offered for public sale. Basically, the purpose of this act is to require disclosure. The 1933 act provides that all securities transactions must be registered with the SEC unless they are specifically exempt from the registration requirements.

### 7-1a What Is a Security?

Section 2(1) of the Securities Act contains a broad definition of securities, which generally include the following:[5]

1. Instruments and interests commonly known as securities, such as preferred and common stocks, bonds, debentures, and stock warrants.
2. Interests commonly known as securities, such as stock options, puts, and calls, that involve the right

to purchase a security or a group of securities on a national security exchange.

3. Notes, instruments, or other evidence of indebtedness, including certificates of interest in a profit-sharing agreement and certificates of deposit.
4. Any fractional undivided interest in oil, gas, or other mineral rights.
5. Investment contracts, which include interests in limited partnerships and other investment schemes.

**The *Howey* Test** In interpreting the act, the United States Supreme Court has held that an **investment contract** is any transaction in which a person (1) invests (2) in a common enterprise (3) reasonably expecting profits (4) derived *primarily* or *substantially* from others' managerial or entrepreneurial efforts. Known as the *Howey* test, this definition continues to guide the determination of what types of contracts can be considered securities.[6]

■ **CASE IN POINT 7.1** James Nistler and his wife bought undeveloped land in Jackson County, Oregon, and created an LLC to develop it. The property, called Tennessee Acres, was divided into six lots. Nistler obtained investors for the development by telling them that they would

---

5. 15 U.S.C. Section 77b(1). Amendments in 1982 added stock options.

6. *SEC v. W. J. Howey Co.*, 328 U.S. 293, 66 S.Ct. 1100, 90 L.Ed. 1244 (1946).

earn 12 to 15 percent interest on their investment and be repaid in full within a specified time. The property was never developed, the investors were never paid, and a substantial part of the funds provided by investors were used to pay Nistler and his wife.

Nistler was convicted of securities fraud. He appealed, claiming that the investments at issue did not involve "securities," but a state appellate court affirmed his conviction. The court found that there had been a pooling of funds from a group of investors whose interests had been secured by the same land. The value of that land had been highly dependent on Nistler's use of the investors' funds to develop the land. In other words, the investors had engaged in a common enterprise from which they reasonably expected to profit, and that profit would be derived from the development efforts of Nistler.[7] ■

**Many Types of Securities** For our purposes, it is convenient to think of securities in their most common form—stocks and bonds issued by corporations. Bear in mind, though, that securities can take many forms, including interests in whiskey, cosmetics, worms, beavers, boats, vacuum cleaners, muskrats, and cemetery lots. Almost any stake in the ownership or debt of a company can be considered a security. Investment contracts in condominiums, franchises, limited partnerships in real estate, and oil or gas or other mineral rights have qualified as securities.

## 7–1b Registration Statement

Section 5 of the Securities Act of 1933 broadly provides that if a security does not qualify for an exemption, that security must be *registered* before it is offered to the public. Issuing corporations must file a *registration statement* with the SEC and must provide all investors with a *prospectus.*

A **prospectus** is a disclosure document that describes the security being sold, the financial operations of the issuing corporation, and the investment or risk attaching to the security. The prospectus also serves as a selling tool for the issuing corporation. The SEC now allows an issuer to deliver its prospectus to investors electronically via the Internet.[8]

In principle, the registration statement and the prospectus supply sufficient information to enable unsophisticated investors to evaluate the financial risk involved.

**Contents of the Registration Statement** The registration statement must be written in plain English and fully describe the following:

1. The securities being offered for sale, including their relationship to the registrant's other securities.
2. The corporation's properties and business (including a financial statement certified by an independent public accounting firm).
3. The management of the corporation, including managerial compensation, stock options, pensions, and other benefits. (See this chapter's *Managerial Strategy* feature for a discussion of a new SEC rule that imposes additional requirements on the disclosure of management compensation.) Any interests of directors or officers in any material transactions with the corporation must also be disclosed.
4. How the corporation intends to use the proceeds of the sale.
5. Any pending lawsuits or special risk factors.

All companies, both domestic and foreign, must file their registration statements electronically so that they can be posted on the SEC's online EDGAR (Electronic Data Gathering, Analysis, and Retrieval) database. Investors can then access the statements via the Internet. The EDGAR database includes material on initial public offerings (IPOs), proxy statements (concerning voting authority), annual reports, registration statements, and other documents that have been filed with the SEC.

**Registration Process** The registration statement does not become effective until it has been reviewed and approved by the SEC (unless it is filed by a *well-known seasoned issuer,* as discussed shortly). The 1933 act restricts the types of activities that an issuer can engage in at each stage of the registration process. If an issuer violates these restrictions, investors can rescind their contracts to purchase the securities.

**Prefiling Period.** During the *prefiling period* (before the registration statement is filed), the issuer normally cannot sell or offer to sell the securities. Once the registration statement has been filed, a waiting period begins while the SEC reviews the registration statement for completeness.[9]

**Waiting Period.** During the waiting period, the securities can be offered for sale but cannot be sold by the issuing corporation. Only certain types of offers are allowed at this time. All issuers can distribute a *preliminary*

---

7. *State of Oregon v. Nistler,* 286 Or.App. 470, 342 P.3d 1035 (2015).
8. Basically, an electronic prospectus must meet the same requirements as a printed prospectus. The SEC rules address situations in which the graphics, images, or audio files in or accompanying a printed prospectus cannot be reproduced in an electronic form. 17 C.F.R. Section 232.304.

9. The waiting period must last at least twenty days but always extends much longer because the SEC inevitably requires numerous changes and additions to the registration statement.

## MANAGERIAL STRATEGY — The SEC's New Pay-Ratio Disclosure Rule

After the financial meltdown of recent years, Congress passed the Dodd-Frank Wall Street Reform and Consumer Protection Act.[a] One of the goals of the act was to improve accountability and transparency in the financial system. A brief section[b] in the lengthy bill requires a publicly held company to disclose the ratio of the total compensation of its chief executive officer (CEO) to the median compensation of its workers. For instance, if the annual pay of the median employee is $45,790 and the total compensation of the CEO is $12,260,000, then the pay ratio is 1 to 268. Otherwise stated, the CEO makes 268 times more than the median income for employees.

### Five Years in the Making

For five years, the Securities and Exchange Commission (SEC) hesitated to adopt a disclosure rule as mandated by the Dodd-Frank act. The SEC received almost 300,000 comments and issued its own comments on the proposed rule.[c] The commissioners indicated that they were unsure what potential economic benefits, "if any," would be realized from making this information public. The SEC has estimated that the regulation will cause companies almost 550,000 annual paperwork hours, plus about $75 million per year to hire outside professionals.

a. Pub. L. No. 111-203, July 21, 2010, 124 Stat. 1376 (2010); codified at 12 U.S.C. Sections 5301 *et seq.*
b. *Ibid.*, Section 953(b).
c. 2013 WL 6503197 (2013, S.E.C. Release Nos. 33-9452 and 34-70443).

### Dealing with the New Rule

The new rule is 1,800 words long, and managers initially may find it difficult to implement. Fortunately for them, the SEC realizes that it can only ask for "reasonable estimates" of the CEO-worker pay ratio.

The CEO's measured compensation includes salary, bonuses, stocks and options, incentive plans, and other compensation. In theory, calculating this amount is fairly straightforward.

Calculating the median income of the company's labor force is more difficult. Note that the median income is not the average income of employees. Rather, the rule requires the company to identify a "median" employee as the basis for comparison.

The rule does give companies flexibility in determining how to identify this median employee. Statistical sampling can be used, for instance. And the rule states, "Since identifying the median involves finding the employee in the middle, it may not be necessary to determine the exact compensation amounts for every employee paid more or less than that employee in the middle." The rule also permits companies to make the median employee determination only once every three years.

### Business Questions

1. *Why might the new SEC pay-ratio disclosure rule cause certain businesses to eliminate low-wage workers?*
2. *How might the new SEC pay-ratio disclosure rule help shareholders?*

---

*prospectus,*[10] which contains most of the information that will be included in the final prospectus but often does not include a price.

Most issuers can use a *free-writing prospectus* during this period (although some inexperienced issuers will need to file a preliminary prospectus first).[11] A **free-writing prospectus** is any type of written, electronic, or graphic offer that describes the issuer or its securities and includes a legend indicating that the investor may obtain the prospectus at the SEC's Web site.

**Posteffective Period.** Once the SEC has reviewed and approved the registration statement and the waiting

period is over, the registration is effective, and the *posteffective period* begins. The issuer can now offer and sell the securities without restrictions.

If the company issued a preliminary or free-writing prospectus to investors, it must provide those investors with a final prospectus either before or at the time they purchase the securities. The issuer can make the final prospectus available to investors to download from a Web site if it notifies them of the appropriate Internet address.

### 7–1c Well-Known Seasoned Issuers

A *well-known seasoned issuer* (WKSI) is a firm that has issued at least $1 billion in securities in the last three years or has outstanding stock valued at $700 million or more in the hands of the public. WKSIs have greater flexibility than other issuers. They can file registration

---

10. A preliminary prospectus may also be called a *red herring prospectus.* The name comes from the legend printed in red across the prospectus stating that the registration has been filed but has not become effective.
11. See SEC Rules 164 and 433.

statements the day they announce a new offering and are not required to wait for SEC review and approval. They can also use a free-writing prospectus at any time, even during the prefiling period.

### 7-1d Exempt Securities and Transactions

Certain types of securities are exempt from the registration requirements of the Securities Act. These securities—which generally can also be resold without being registered—are summarized under the heading "Exempt Securities" in Exhibit 7–1.[12] The exhibit also lists and describes certain transactions that are exempt from registration requirements under various SEC regulations.

The transaction exemptions are important because they are very broad and can enable an issuer to avoid the high cost and complicated procedures associated with registration. Indeed, many sales occur without registration. Even when a transaction is exempt from the registration requirements, however, the offering is still subject to the antifraud provisions of the 1933 act (as well as those of the 1934 act, to be discussed later in this chapter).

**Regulation A Offerings** An exemption from registration is available for an issuer's security offerings that do not exceed $50 million during any twelve-month period.[13] Under Regulation A,[14] the issuer must file with the SEC a notice of the issue and an offering circular, which must also be provided to investors before the sale. Additional review requirements apply to issuers raising between $20 and $50 million. Overall, Regulation A provides a much less expensive process than the procedures associated with full registration.

Note that the cap for Regulation A was $5 million until 2015, when the SEC approved rule changes to make it easier for small and mid-sized businesses to raise capital. These changes were made in connection with the Jumpstart Our Business Startups, or JOBS, Act.[15] Expanding the issuers that qualify for exemption under Regulation A will likely decrease the significance of the other exemptions listed in Exhibit 7–1. In addition, the amended Regulation A–popularly known as Reg A+— has allowed for an increase in online crowdfunding.

**Testing the Waters.** Before preparing a Regulation A offering circular, companies are allowed to "test the waters" for potential interest. To *test the waters* means to determine potential interest without actually selling any securities or requiring any commitment from those who express interest. Small-business issuers can also use an integrated registration and reporting system that requires simpler forms than the full registration system.

**Using the Internet.** Some companies have sold their securities on the Internet using Regulation A. ■ **EXAMPLE 7.2** The Spring Street Brewing Company was the first company to sell securities via an online initial public offering (IPO). Spring Street raised about $1.6 million without incurring high expenses. ■ Online IPOs are particularly attractive to small companies and start-up ventures that may find it difficult to raise capital from institutional investors or through underwriters.

**Small Offerings—Regulation D** The SEC's Regulation D contains several exemptions from registration requirements (Rules 504, 505, and 506) for offers that either involve a small dollar amount or are made in a limited manner.

**Rule 504.** Rule 504 is the exemption used by most small businesses. It provides that noninvestment company offerings up to $1 million in any twelve-month period are exempt.[16] Noninvestment companies are firms that are not engaged primarily in the business of investing or trading in securities. (In contrast, an **investment company** is a firm that buys a large portfolio of securities and professionally manages it on behalf of many smaller shareholders/owners. A **mutual fund** is a well-known type of investment company.)

■ **EXAMPLE 7.3** Zeta Enterprises is a limited partnership that develops commercial property. Zeta intends to offer $600,000 of its limited partnership interests for sale between June 1 and next May 31. The buyers will become limited partners in Zeta. Because an interest in a limited partnership meets the definition of a security (discussed earlier), this offering would be subject to the registration and prospectus requirements of the Securities Act of 1933.

Under Rule 504, however, the sales of Zeta's interests are exempt from these requirements because Zeta is a noninvestment company making an offering of less than $1 million in a given twelve-month period. Therefore, Zeta can sell its interests without filing a registration statement with the SEC or issuing a prospectus to any investor. ■

---

12. 15 U.S.C. Section 77c.
13. 15 U.S.C. Section 77c(b).
14. 17 C.F.R. Sections 230.251–230.263.
15. Pub.L.No. 112-106 (June 19, 2012).

---

16. 17 C.F.R. Section 230.504. Small businesses in California may also be exempt under SEC Rule 1001. California's rule permits limited offerings of up to $5 million *per transaction*, if they satisfy certain conditions.

**EXHIBIT 7–1** Exemptions for Securities Offerings under the 1933 Securities Act

**Rule 505.** Another exemption is available under Rule 505 for private, noninvestment company offerings up to $5 million in any twelve-month period. The offer may be made to an unlimited number of *accredited investors* and up to thirty-five unaccredited investors.

**Accredited investors** include banks, insurance companies, investment companies, employee benefit plans, the issuer's executive officers and directors, and persons whose income or net worth exceeds a certain threshold.

The SEC must be notified of the sales, and precautions must be taken, because these *restricted securities* may be resold only by registration or in an exempt transaction. No general solicitation or advertising is allowed. The issuer must provide any unaccredited investors with disclosure documents, which generally are the same as those used in registered offerings.

### Rule 506—Private Placement Exemption.

Rule 506 exempts private, noninvestment company offerings in unlimited amounts that are not generally solicited or advertised. This exemption is often referred to as the *private placement exemption* because it exempts "transactions not involving any public offering."[17] There can be an unlimited number of accredited investors and up to thirty-five unaccredited investors. To qualify for the exemption, the issuer must believe that each unaccredited investor has sufficient knowledge or experience in financial matters to be capable of evaluating the investment's merits and risks.[18]

The private placement exemption is perhaps the most important exemption for firms that want to raise funds through the sale of securities without registering them. ■ **EXAMPLE 7.4** Citco Corporation needs to raise capital to expand its operations. Citco decides to make a private $10 million offering of its common stock directly to two hundred accredited investors and a group of thirty highly sophisticated, but unaccredited, investors. Citco provides all of these investors with a prospectus and material information about the firm, including its most recent financial statements.

As long as Citco notifies the SEC of the sale, this offering will likely qualify as an exempt transaction under Rule 506. The offering is nonpublic and not generally advertised. There are fewer than thirty-five unaccredited investors, and each of them possesses sufficient knowledge and experience to evaluate the risks involved. The issuer has provided all purchasers with the material information. Thus, Citco will likely *not* be required to comply with the registration requirements of the Securities Act of 1933. ■

### Resales and Safe Harbor Rules

Most securities can be resold without registration. The Securities Act provides exemptions for resales by most persons other than issuers or underwriters. The average investor who sells shares of stock need not file a registration statement with the SEC.

Resales of restricted securities acquired under Rule 505 or Rule 506, however, trigger the registration requirements *unless the party selling them complies with Rule 144 or Rule 144A*. These rules are sometimes referred to as safe harbors.

**Rule 144.** Rule 144 exempts restricted securities from registration on resale if all of the following conditions are met:

1. There is adequate current public information about the issuer. ("Adequate current public information" refers to the reports that certain companies are required to file under the 1934 Securities Exchange Act.)
2. The person selling the securities has owned them for at least six months if the issuer is subject to the reporting requirements of the 1934 act. If the issuer is not subject to the 1934 act's reporting requirements, the seller must have owned the securities for at least one year.
3. The securities are sold in certain limited amounts in unsolicited brokers' transactions.
4. The SEC is notified of the resale.[19]

**Rule 144A.** Securities that at the time of issue were not of the same class as securities listed on a national securities exchange or quoted in a U.S. automated interdealer quotation system may be resold under Rule 144A.[20] They may be sold only to a qualified institutional buyer (an institution, such as an insurance company or a bank, that owns and invests at least $100 million in securities). The seller must take reasonable steps to ensure that the buyer knows that the seller is relying on the exemption under Rule 144A.

## 7–1e Violations of the 1933 Act

It is a violation of the Securities Act to intentionally defraud investors by misrepresenting or omitting facts in a registration statement or prospectus. Liability may also be imposed on those who are negligent with respect to the preparation of these publications. Selling securities before the effective date of the registration statement or under an exemption for which the securities do not qualify also results in liability.

Can the omission of a material fact make a statement of opinion misleading to an ordinary investor? That was the question before the United States Supreme Court in the following case.

---

**17.** 15 U.S.C. Section 77d(2).
**18.** 17 C.F.R. Section 230.506.
**19.** 17 C.F.R. Section 230.144.
**20.** 17 C.F.R. Section 230.144A.

**Case 7.1**

# Omnicare, Inc. v. Laborers District Council Construction Industry Pension Fund

Supreme Court of the United States, __ U.S. __, 135 S.Ct. 1318, 191 L.Ed.2d 253 (2015).

**Background and Facts**   Omnicare, Inc., a pharmacy services company, filed a registration statement in connection with a public offering. The statement expressed the company's opinion that it was in compliance with federal and state laws. Later, the federal government accused Omnicare of receiving kickbacks from pharmaceutical manufacturers. The Laborers District Council Construction Industry Pension Fund and others, which had bought the stock, filed a suit in a federal district court against Omnicare.

The plaintiffs alleged that Omnicare's legal-compliance opinion was "untrue" and that Omnicare had, in violation of the Securities Act, "omitted to state [material] facts necessary" to make that opinion not misleading. Omnicare argued that "no reasonable person, in any context, can understand a pure statement of opinion to convey anything more than the speaker's own mindset." The district court dismissed the pension funds' suit, but the U.S. Court of Appeals for the Sixth Circuit reversed the dismissal. Omnicare appealed to the United States Supreme Court.

## In the Language of the Court

Justice *KAGAN* delivered the opinion of the Court.

\* \* \* \*

\* \* \* Whether a statement is "misleading" depends on the perspective of a reasonable investor: The inquiry \* \* \* is objective.

\* \* \* \*

\* \* \* A reasonable person understands, and takes into account, the difference \* \* \* between a statement of fact and one of opinion. She recognizes the import of words like "I think" or "I believe," and grasps that they convey some lack of certainty as to the statement's content.

But Omnicare takes its point too far, because a reasonable investor may, depending on the circumstances, understand an opinion statement to convey facts about how the speaker has formed the opinion—or, otherwise put, about the speaker's basis for holding that view. And if the real facts are otherwise, but not provided, the opinion statement will mislead its audience. Consider an unadorned statement of opinion about legal compliance: "We believe our conduct is lawful." \* \* \* If the issuer made the statement in the face of its lawyers' contrary advice, or with knowledge that the Federal Government was taking the opposite view, the investor \* \* \* has cause to complain: He expects not just that the issuer believes the opinion (however irrationally), but that it fairly aligns with the information in the issuer's possession at the time. Thus, *if a registration statement omits material facts about the issuer's inquiry into or knowledge concerning a statement of opinion, and if those facts conflict with what a reasonable investor would take from the statement itself, then [the Securities Act] creates liability.* [Emphasis added.]

An opinion statement, however, is not necessarily misleading when an issuer knows, but fails to disclose, some fact cutting the other way. \* \* \* A reasonable investor does not expect that *every* fact known to an issuer supports its opinion statement. [Emphasis in the original.]

Moreover, *whether an omission makes an expression of opinion misleading always depends on context.* Registration statements as a class are formal documents, filed with the SEC as a legal prerequisite for selling securities to the public. Investors do not, and are right not to, expect opinions contained in those statements to reflect baseless, off-the-cuff judgments, of the kind that an individual might communicate in daily life. At the same time, an investor reads each statement within such a document, whether of fact or opinion, in light of all its surrounding text, including hedges, disclaimers, and apparently conflicting information. And the investor takes into account the customs and practices of the relevant industry. \* \* \* The reasonable investor understands a statement of opinion in its full context, and [the Securities Act] creates liability only for the omission of material facts that cannot be squared with such a fair reading. [Emphasis added.]

**Decision and Remedy**   *The United States Supreme Court concluded that "neither [lower court] considered the Funds' omissions theory with the right standard in mind." The Court therefore vacated the decision*

**Case 7.1 Continued**

*of the lower court and remanded the case "for a determination of whether the Funds have stated a viable omissions claim (or, if not, whether they should have a chance to replead)."*

**Critical Thinking**

- **Legal Environment** *Would a reasonable investor have cause to complain if an issuer, without having consulted a lawyer, states, "We believe our conduct is lawful"? Explain.*

**Remedies** Criminal violations are prosecuted by the U.S. Department of Justice. Violators may be fined up to $10,000, imprisoned for up to five years, or both.

The SEC is authorized to impose civil sanctions against those who willfully violate the 1933 act. It can request an injunction to prevent further sales of the securities involved or ask a court to grant other relief, such as ordering a violator to refund profits. Private parties who purchase securities and suffer harm as a result of false or omitted statements or other violations may bring a suit in a federal court to recover their losses and additional damages.

**Defenses** There are three basic defenses to charges of violations under the 1933 act. A defendant can avoid liability by proving any of the following:

1. The statement or omission was not material.
2. The plaintiff knew about the misrepresentation at the time the stock was purchased.
3. The defendant exercised *due diligence* in preparing or reviewing the registration and reasonably believed at the time that the statements were true. This important defense is available to an underwriter or subsequent seller but not to the issuer.

■ **CASE IN POINT 7.5** In preparation for an initial public offering (IPO), Blackstone Group, LP, filed a registration statement with the SEC. At the time, Blackstone's corporate private equity investments included FGIC Corporation (which insured investments in subprime mortgages) and Freescale Semiconductor, Inc. Before the IPO, FGIC's customers began to suffer large losses, and Freescale lost an exclusive contract to make wireless 3G chipsets for Motorola, Inc. (its largest customer). The losses suffered by these two companies would affect Blackstone. Nevertheless, Blackstone's registration statement did not mention the impact on its revenues of the investments in FGIC and Freescale.

Martin Litwin and others who had invested in Blackstone's IPO filed a suit in a federal district court against Blackstone and its officers, alleging material omissions from the statement. Blackstone argued as a defense that the omissions were not material, and the lower court

dismissed the case. The plaintiffs appealed. A federal appellate court ruled that the alleged omissions were reasonably likely to be material, and remanded the case. The plaintiffs were entitled to the opportunity to prove at a trial that Blackstone had omitted material information that it was required to disclose.[21] ■

## 7-2 The Securities Exchange Act of 1934

The 1934 Securities Exchange Act provides for the regulation and registration of securities exchanges, brokers, dealers, and national securities associations, such as the National Association of Securities Dealers (NASD). Unlike the 1933 act, which is a one-time disclosure law, the 1934 act provides for continuous periodic disclosures by publicly held corporations to enable the SEC to regulate subsequent trading.

The Securities Exchange Act applies to companies that have assets in excess of $10 million and five hundred or more shareholders. These corporations are referred to as *Section 12 companies* because they are required to register their securities under Section 12 of the 1934 act. Section 12 companies are required to file reports with the SEC annually and quarterly, and sometimes even monthly if specified events occur (such as a merger).

The act also authorizes the SEC to engage in market surveillance to deter undesirable market practices such as fraud, market manipulation, and misrepresentation. In addition, the act provides for the SEC's regulation of proxy solicitations for voting.

### 7-2a Section 10(b), SEC Rule 10b-5, and Insider Trading

Section 10(b) is one of the more important sections of the Securities Exchange Act. This section prohibits the use of any manipulative or deceptive mechanism in violation of

---

21. *Litwin v. Blackstone Group, LP,* 634 F.3d 706 (2d Cir. 2011).

SEC rules and regulations. Among the rules that the SEC has promulgated pursuant to the 1934 act is **SEC Rule 10b-5,** which prohibits the commission of fraud in connection with the purchase or sale of any security.

SEC Rule 10b-5 applies to almost all cases concerning the trading of securities, whether on organized exchanges, in over-the-counter markets, or in private transactions. Generally, the rule covers just about any form of security. The securities need not be registered under the 1933 act for the 1934 act to apply.

Private parties can sue for securities fraud under Rule 10b-5. The basic elements of a securities fraud action are as follows:

1. A *material misrepresentation* (or omission) in connection with the purchase and sale of securities.
2. *Scienter* (a wrongful state of mind).
3. *Reliance* by the plaintiff on the material misrepresentation.
4. An *economic loss.*
5. *Causation,* meaning that there is a causal connection between the misrepresentation and the loss.

**Insider Trading**  One of the major goals of Section 10(b) and SEC Rule 10b-5 is to prevent **insider trading,** which occurs when persons buy or sell securities on the basis of information that is not available to the public. Corporate directors, officers, and majority shareholders, among others, often have advance inside information that can affect the future market value of the corporate stock. Obviously, if they act on this information, their positions give them a trading advantage over the general public and other shareholders.

The 1934 act defines inside information. It also extends liability to those who take advantage of such information in their personal transactions when they know that the information is unavailable to those with whom they are dealing. Section 10(b) of the 1934 act and SEC Rule 10b-5 apply to anyone who has access to or receives information of a nonpublic nature on which trading is based—not just to corporate "insiders."

**Disclosure under SEC Rule 10b-5**  Any material omission or misrepresentation of material facts in connection with the purchase or sale of a security may violate Section 10(b) of the 1934 act and SEC Rule 10b-5. The key to liability (which can be civil or criminal) is whether the information omitted or misrepresented is *material.*

The following are some examples of material facts calling for disclosure under SEC Rule 10b-5:

1. Fraudulent trading in the company stock by a broker-dealer.
2. A dividend change (whether up or down).
3. A contract for the sale of corporate assets.
4. A new discovery, a new process, or a new product.
5. A significant change in the firm's financial condition.
6. Potential litigation against the company.

Note that any one of these facts, by itself, is not automatically considered material. It will be regarded as a material fact only if it is significant enough that it would likely affect an investor's decision as to whether to purchase or sell the company's securities.

■ **EXAMPLE 7.6**  Zilotek, Inc., is the defendant in a class-action product liability suit that its attorney, Paula Frasier, believes the company will lose. Frasier has advised Zilotek's directors, officers, and accountants that the company will likely have to pay a substantial damages award. Zilotek plans to make a $5 million offering of newly issued stock before the date when the trial is expected to end. Zilotek's potential liability and the financial consequences to the firm are material facts that must be disclosed, because they are significant enough to affect an investor's decision to purchase the stock. ■

The case that follows is a *Classic Case* interpreting materiality under SEC Rule 10b-5.

**Classic Case 7.2**

## SEC v. Texas Gulf Sulphur Co.
United States Court of Appeals, Second Circuit, 401 F.2d 833 (1968).

**Background and Facts**  Texas Gulf Sulphur Company (TGS) conducted aerial geophysical surveys over more than 15,000 square miles of eastern Canada. The operations indicated concentrations of commercially exploitable minerals. At one site near Timmins, Ontario, TGS drilled a hole that appeared to yield a core with an exceedingly high mineral content. The company did not disclose the results of the core sample to the public.

After learning of the sample, TGS officers and employees made substantial purchases of TGS's stock or accepted stock options (rights to purchase stock). On April 11, 1964, an unauthorized report

Case 7.2 Continued

of the mineral find appeared in the newspapers. On the following day, TGS issued a press release that played down the discovery and stated that it was too early to tell whether the ore find would be significant.

Several months later, TGS announced that the strike was expected to yield at least 25 million tons of ore. Subsequently, the price of TGS stock rose substantially. The Securities and Exchange Commission (SEC) brought a suit against the officers and employees of TGS for violating SEC Rule 10b-5. The officers and employees argued that the information on which they had traded had not been material at the time of their trades because the mine had not then been commercially proved. The trial court held that most of the defendants had not violated SEC Rule 10b-5, and the SEC appealed.

### In the Language of the Court

*WATERMAN*, Circuit Judge.

\* \* \* \*

\* \* \* Whether facts are material within Rule 10b-5 when the facts relate to a particular event and are undisclosed by those persons who are knowledgeable thereof *will depend at any given time upon a balancing of both the indicated probability that the event will occur and the anticipated magnitude of the event in light of the totality of the company activity.* Here, \* \* \* knowledge of the possibility, which surely was more than marginal, of the existence of a mine of the vast magnitude indicated by the remarkably rich drill core located rather close to the surface (suggesting mineability by the less expensive openpit method) within the confines of a large anomaly (suggesting an extensive region of mineralization) might well have affected the price of TGS stock and would certainly have been an important fact to a reasonable, if speculative, investor in deciding whether he should buy, sell, or hold. [Emphasis added.]

\* \* \* \*

\* \* \* A major factor in determining whether the \* \* \* discovery was a material fact is the importance attached to the drilling results by those who knew about it. \* \* \* The timing by those who knew of it of their stock purchases \* \* \*—purchases in some cases by individuals who had never before purchased \* \* \* TGS stock—virtually compels the inference that the insiders were influenced by the drilling results.

**Decision and Remedy** *The appellate court ruled in favor of the SEC. All of the trading by insiders who knew of the mineral find before its true extent had been publicly announced had violated SEC Rule 10b-5.*

**Impact of This Case on Today's Law** *This landmark case affirmed the principle that the test of whether information is "material," for SEC Rule 10b-5 purposes, is whether it would affect the judgment of reasonable investors. The corporate insiders' purchases of stock and stock options indicated that they were influenced by the drilling results and that the information about the drilling results was material. The courts continue to cite this case when applying SEC Rule 10b-5 to cases of alleged insider trading.*

**Critical Thinking**

- **What If the Facts Were Different?** *Suppose that further drilling had revealed that there was not enough ore at this site for it to be mined commercially. Would the defendants still have been liable for violating SEC Rule 10b-5? Why or why not?*

---

**Outsiders and SEC Rule 10b-5** The traditional insider-trading case involves true insiders—corporate officers, directors, and majority shareholders who have access to (and trade on) inside information. Increasingly, however, liability under Section 10(b) of the 1934 act and SEC Rule 10b-5 has been extended to include certain "outsiders"—those who trade on inside information acquired indirectly. Two theories have been developed under which outsiders may be held liable for insider trading: the *tipper/tippee theory* and the *misappropriation theory*.

**Tipper/Tippee Theory.** Anyone who acquires inside information as a result of a corporate insider's breach of his or her fiduciary duty can be liable under SEC Rule 10b-5. This liability extends to **tippees** (those who receive "tips" from insiders) and even *remote tippees* (tippees of tippees).

The key to liability under this theory is that the inside information must be obtained as a result of someone's breach of a fiduciary duty to the corporation whose shares are traded. The tippee is liable only if the following requirements are met:

1. There is a breach of a duty not to disclose inside information.
2. The disclosure is made in exchange for personal benefit.
3. The tippee knows (or should know) of this breach and benefits from it.

■ **EXAMPLE 7.7** Eric McPhail was a member of the same country club as an executive at American Superconductor. While they were golfing, the executive shared information with McPhail about the company's expected earnings, contracts, and other major developments, trusting that McPhail would keep the information confidential. Instead, McPhail tipped six of his other golfing buddies at the country club, and they all used the nonpublic information to their advantage in trading. In this situation, the executive breached his duty not to disclose the information, which McPhail knew. McPhail (the tippee) is liable under SEC Rule 10b-5, and so are his other golfing buddies (remote tippees). All traded on inside information to their benefit.[22] ■

**Misappropriation Theory.** Liability for insider trading may also be established under the misappropriation theory. This theory holds liable an individual who wrongfully obtains (misappropriates) inside information and trades on it for her or his personal gain. Basically, this individual has stolen information rightfully belonging to another.

The misappropriation theory has been controversial because it significantly extends the reach of SEC Rule 10b-5 to outsiders who ordinarily would *not* be deemed fiduciaries of the corporations in whose stock they trade. It is not always wrong to disclose material, nonpublic information about a company to a person who would not otherwise be privy to it. Nevertheless, a person who obtains the information and trades securities on it can be held liable.[23]

### Insider Reporting and Trading—Section 16(b)

Section 16(b) of the 1934 act provides for the recapture by the corporation of all profits realized by an insider on a purchase and sale, or sale and purchase, of the corporation's stock within any six-month period.[24] It is irrelevant whether the insider actually uses inside information—all such **short-swing profits** must be returned to the corporation.

In the context of Section 16(b), insiders means officers, directors, and large stockholders of Section 12 corporations. (Large stockholders are those owning 10 percent of the class of equity securities registered under Section 12 of the 1934 act.) To discourage such insiders from using nonpublic information about their companies to their personal benefit in the stock market, the SEC requires them to file reports concerning their ownership and trading of the corporation's securities.

Section 16(b) applies not only to stock but also to warrants, options, and securities convertible into stock. In addition, the courts have fashioned complex rules for determining profits. Note, though, that the SEC exempts a number of transactions under Rule 16b-3.[25]

Exhibit 7–2 compares the effects of SEC Rule 10b-5 and Section 16(b). Because of the various ways in which insiders can incur liability under these provisions, corporate insiders should seek the advice of competent counsel before trading in the corporation's stock.

### The Private Securities Litigation Reform Act

The disclosure requirements of SEC Rule 10b-5 had the unintended effect of deterring the disclosure of forward-looking information. To understand why, consider the following situation. ■ **EXAMPLE 7.8** XT Company announces that its projected earnings for a future time period will be a certain amount, but its forecast turns out to be wrong. The earnings are in fact much lower, and the price of XT's stock is affected negatively. The shareholders bring a class-action suit against XT, alleging that its directors violated SEC Rule 10b-5 by disclosing misleading financial information. ■

In an attempt to solve the problem and promote full disclosure, Congress passed the Private Securities Litigation Reform Act (PSLRA).[26] Among other things, the PSLRA provides a "safe harbor" for publicly held companies that make forward-looking statements, such as financial forecasts. Those who make such statements are protected against liability for securities fraud if they include "meaningful cautionary statements identifying important factors that could cause actual results to differ materially from those in the forward-looking statement."[27]

---

22. Three of the defendants in this case agreed to settle with the SEC and return the trading profits. See SEC press release 2014-134 "SEC Charges Group of Amateur Golfers in Insider Trading Ring."
23. See, for instance, *United States v. Gansman,* 657 F.3d 85 (2d Cir. 2011).
24. A person who expects the price of a particular stock to decline can realize profits by "selling short"—selling at a high price and repurchasing later at a lower price to cover the "short sale."
25. 17 C.F.R. Section 240.16b-3.
26. Pub.L.No. 104-67, 109 Stat. 737, codified in various sections of Title 15 of the *United States Code.*
27. 15 U.S.C. Sections 77z-2, 78u-5.

**EXHIBIT 7–2** Comparison of Coverage, Application, and Liability under SEC Rule 10b-5 and Section 16(b)

| AREA OF COMPARISON | SEC RULE 10b-5 | SECTION 16(b) |
| --- | --- | --- |
| What is the subject matter of the transaction? | Any security (does not have to be registered). | Any security (does not have to be registered). |
| What transactions are covered? | Purchase or sale. | Short-swing purchase and sale or short-swing sale and purchase. |
| Who is subject to liability? | Almost anyone with inside information under a duty to disclose—including officers, directors, controlling shareholders, and tippees. | Officers, directors, and certain shareholders who own 10 percent or more. |
| Is omission or misrepresentation necessary for liability? | Yes. | No. |
| Are there any exempt transactions? | No. | Yes, there are a number of exemptions. |
| Who may bring an action? | A person transacting with an insider, the SEC, or a purchaser or seller damaged by a wrongful act. | A corporation or a shareholder by derivative action. |

The PSLRA also affected the level of detail required in securities fraud complaints. Plaintiffs must specify each misleading statement and say how it led them to a mistaken belief.

## 7–2b Regulation of Proxy Statements

Section 14(a) of the Securities Exchange Act regulates the solicitation of proxies from shareholders of Section 12 companies. The SEC regulates the content of proxy statements. Whoever solicits a proxy must fully and accurately disclose in the proxy statement all of the facts that are pertinent to the matter on which the shareholders are to vote. SEC Rule 14a-9 is similar to the antifraud provisions of SEC Rule 10b-5. Remedies for violations range from injunctions to prevent a vote from being taken to monetary damages.

## 7–2c Violations of the 1934 Act

As mentioned earlier, violations of Section 10(b) of the Securities Exchange Act and SEC Rule 10b-5, including insider trading, may lead to both criminal and civil liability.

***Scienter* Requirement** For either criminal or civil sanctions to be imposed, *scienter* must exist—that is, the violator must have had an intent to defraud or knowledge of his or her misconduct. *Scienter* can be proved by showing that the defendant made false statements or wrongfully failed to disclose material facts. In some situations, it can even be proved by showing that the defendant was consciously reckless as to the truth or falsity of his or her statements.

■ **CASE IN POINT 7.9** Alvin Gebhart and Jack Archer started a business venture purchasing mobile home parks (MHPs) from owners and converting them to resident ownership. They formed MHP Conversions, LP, to facilitate the conversion process and issue promissory notes that were sold to investors to raise funds for the purchases. Archer ran the MHP program, and Gebhart sold the promissory notes. Gebhart sold nearly $2.4 million in MHP promissory notes to clients, who bought the notes based on Gebhart's positive statements about the investment.

During the time Gebhart was selling the notes, however, he never actually looked into the finances of the MHP program. He relied entirely on information that Archer gave him, some of which was not true. When

Gebhart was later sued for securities fraud, a federal appellate court concluded that there was sufficient evidence of *scienter*. Gebhart knew that he had no knowledge of the financial affairs of MHP, and he had been consciously reckless as to the truth or falsity of his statements about investing in MHP.[28] ■

**Complaint Must Raise an Inference of *Scienter*.** In a complaint alleging a violation, the plaintiff must state facts giving rise to an inference of *scienter*. ■ **CASE IN POINT 7.10**   Between May 4 and June 22, Boeing Company made announcements that its new plane called the Dreamliner, which had not yet flown, was on track for its first flight on June 30. Meanwhile, however, the plane failed important stress tests before and after redesign. On June 23, Boeing canceled the scheduled debut flight and warned of a delay in the delivery of the Dreamliner to the commercial airlines. Boeing's stock price dropped more than 10 percent.

A group of investors filed a suit against Boeing for securities fraud. They claimed that Boeing and its officers had known about the likely postponement of the first flight when they made public statements to the contrary. The plaintiffs argued that Boeing's "internal e-mails" would confirm this theory but did not identify the source of these messages. A federal court dismissed the suit, and that dismissal was affirmed on appeal. Allegations "merely implying unnamed confidential sources" was not sufficient to give rise to an inference of *scienter*. *Scienter* can also be established by showing a defendant's motive to commit fraud, but Boeing had nothing to gain by delaying the postponement of the first flight.[29] ■

Whether the plaintiff alleged sufficient facts to give rise to an inference of *scienter* was the question in the following case.

---

28. *Gebhart v. SEC*, 595 F.3d 1034 (9th Cir. 2010).

29. *City of Livonia Employees' Retirement System and Local 295/Local 851 v. Boeing Co.*, 711 F.3d 754 (7th Cir. 2013).

---

**Case Analysis 7.3**

# Rand-Heart of New York, Inc. v. Dolan

United States Court of Appeals, Eighth Circuit, 812 F.3d 1172 (2016).

### In the Language of the Court

*BENTON*, Circuit Judge.

\* \* \* \*

I.

[Dolan Company specializes in professional services and business information from its base in Minneapolis, Minnesota.] DiscoverReady—a subsidiary of Dolan Company—performed litigation support [discovery management and document review services, including technology services related to processing and hosting discovery data], working mostly for Bank of America. In May or June 2013, Bank of America met with James Dolan (Chief Executive Officer of Dolan Company) and other DiscoverReady representatives. Bank of America noted concerns about Dolan Company's finances \* \* \* and indicated it would send no new work to DiscoverReady until the financial concerns were resolved. \* \* \* Dolan reported what transpired at the meeting to Dolan Company's Board of Directors, which

proceeded to authorize DiscoverReady for sale. Bank of America stopped sending new work to DiscoverReady in June.

On August 1, Dolan Company released a Form 10-Q [for the second quarter], which stated:

> \* \* \* To operate profitably on a continuous basis in the future, the Company must increase revenue and eliminate costs \* \* \* . These challenges make it probable that the Company will be unable to comply with certain of its financial covenants.

Also on August 1, Dolan spoke with stock analysts. [Dolan made] the [following] statements during the conference:

> For 2013, we expect \* \* \* DiscoverReady \* \* \* to grow at double-digit rates over the prior year \* \* \*. However, we must point out that we expect DiscoverReady's third quarter revenues to be below last year's all time record revenue quarter. We make this comment not to dampen enthusiasm

about our growth prospects for DiscoverReady, but to set proper expectations for a business that may experience lumpiness on a quarter-to-quarter basis.

Asked to elaborate about "lumpiness," Dolan stated:

> Well, it's hard to be very specific about the lumpiness now without getting into details we normally do not disclose. \* \* \* These things do come and they come sometimes unexpectedly, sometimes quickly. So \* \* \* we have to be cautious in how we describe things.

On November 12, 2013, Dolan \* \* \* filed its Form 10-Q ending September 30. [Form 10-Q is a quarterly report required by the Securities and Exchange Commission.] The 10-Q reported that the decline in revenue "exceeded our expectations," largely due to "a reduction in new work from DiscoverReady's largest customer, a reduction that we identified towards the end of the quarter. We believe this reduction resulted from the customer's evaluation of the Company's overall financial condition." The closing price for Dolan Company stock fell to $2.08 on November 11, to $1.05 on November 12, to $0.90 on November 13.

On January 2, 2014, Dolan Company issued a final press release announcing the appointment of a Chief Restructuring Officer * * * . Share prices then fell by $0.14. In March, Dolan Company filed a Chapter 11 bankruptcy.

II.
* * * *

Rand-Heart [of New York, Inc.] brought a class action suit [in a federal district court on behalf of purchasers of Dolan Company's securities between August 1, 2013, and January 2, 2014,] alleging Dolan made material misrepresentations and omissions about DiscoverReady's financial stability [in violation of Section 10(b) and Rule 10b–5]. The district court granted Dolan's motion to dismiss * * * . It found that Rand-Heart failed to allege *scienter*.

[Rand-Heart appealed the dismissal to the U.S. Court of Appeals for the Eighth Circuit.]

* * * *

A.
Rand-Heart argues the district court erred in finding inadequate allegations of *scienter*.
* * * *

Rand-Heart maintains it adequately pled *scienter* by alleging that Dolan had been severely reckless. *Severe recklessness is defined as highly unreasonable omissions or misrepresentations involving an extreme departure from the standards of ordinary care, and presenting the danger of misleading buyers or sellers which is either known to the defendant or is so obvious that the defendant must have been aware of it.* [Emphasis added.]
* * * *

Rand-Heart * * * argues that Dolan was reckless in failing to disclose that Bank of America had stopped sending new work to DiscoverReady in May or June 2013. Bank of America was DiscoverReady's biggest client, providing over 50% of DiscoverReady's work. In the second half of 2013, however, Bank of America work sharply declined. The complaint quoted DiscoverReady's Chief Operating Officer's acknowledgment: "We were, our work, our revenues

were dropping and our case origination had dropped, as I said earlier, to almost nothing from Bank of America." By May or June 2013, DiscoverReady had "completed a large document review project for Bank of America" immediately causing "great concerns." This decline prompted the Company's Board in June 2013 to "authorize the marketing of DiscoverReady for sale." Taking these allegations as true, DiscoverReady's financial instability caused by the decline in Bank of America work was, at the least, so obvious that Dolan must have been aware of it. The facts pled are sufficient to survive a motion to dismiss.

B.
* * * *

The district court erred in dismissing the Section 10(b) and Rule 10b–5 claims for failure to state a claim.

III.
* * * *

The district court's decision is * * * reversed * * * and remanded for proceedings consistent with this opinion.

## Legal Reasoning Questions

1. *Scienter* can be established by showing a defendant's motive to commit fraud. In the context of the *Rand-Heart* case, what act might have established motive on Dolan's part?

2. When Bank of America met with Dolan to discuss his company's financial situation, it demanded that the company be restructured. Dolan did not disclose this fact in the Form 10-Q or in his conference with stock analysts. Was this omission misleading?

3. Suppose that Dolan had disclosed Bank of America's action with respect to DiscoverReady in the Form 10-Q and the conference. Would the result in this case have been different? Explain.

---

**Scienter Not Required for Section 16(b) Violations** Violations of Section 16(b) include the sale by insiders of stock acquired less than six months before the sale (or, for a short sale, less than six months after the sale). (Recall that a short sale involves selling securities that one does not yet own.) These violations are subject to civil sanctions. Liability under Section 16(b) is strict liability. Neither *scienter* nor negligence is required.

**Criminal Penalties** For violations of Section 10(b) and Rule 10b-5, an individual may be fined up to $5 million, imprisoned for up to twenty years, or both. A partnership or a corporation may be fined up to $25 million. Under Section 807 of the Sarbanes-Oxley Act, for a *willful* violation of the 1934 act the violator can be imprisoned for up to twenty-five years (in addition to being subject to a fine).

For a defendant to be convicted in a criminal prosecution under the securities laws, there can be no reasonable doubt that the defendant knew he or she was acting wrongfully. In other words, a jury is not allowed merely to speculate that the defendant may have acted willfully.

■ **CASE IN POINT 7.11** Douglas Newton was the president and sole director of Real American Brands, Inc. (RLAB). RLAB owned the Billy Martin's USA brand and operated a Billy Martin's retail boutique at the Trump Plaza in New York City. (Billy Martin's, a Western wear store, was co-founded by Billy Martin, the one-time manager of the New York Yankees.)

Newton agreed to pay kickbacks to Chris Russo, whom he believed to be the manager of a pension fund, to induce the fund to buy shares of RLAB stock. Newton later arranged for his friend Yan Skwara to pay similar kickbacks for the fund's purchase of stock in U.S. Farms, Inc. In reality, the pension fund was fictitious, and Newton and Skwara had been dealing with agents of the Federal Bureau of Investigation (FBI). Newton was charged with securities fraud and convicted by a jury (Skwara pled guilty). Newton appealed, but a federal appellate court upheld his conviction.

According to the court, the evidence established that in each transaction, the amount of the kickback was added to the price of the stock, which artificially increased the stock price. The evidence sufficiently proved that Newton had engaged in a scheme to defraud the supposed pension fund. His words and conduct, which were revealed on video at the trial, showed his intent to defraud the pension fund investors.[30] ■

**Civil Sanctions** The SEC can also bring a civil action against anyone who purchases or sells a security while in possession of material nonpublic information in violation of the 1934 act or SEC rules.[31] The violation must occur through the use of a national securities exchange or a broker or dealer.[32] A court can assess a penalty amounting to as much as triple the profits gained or the loss avoided by the guilty party.[33]

The Insider Trading and Securities Fraud Enforcement Act enlarged the class of persons who may be subject to civil liability for insider trading. In addition, this act gave the SEC authority to offer monetary rewards to informants.[34]

Private parties may also sue violators of Section 10(b) and Rule 10b-5. A private party can obtain rescission (cancellation) of a contract to buy securities or damages to the extent of the violator's illegal profits. Those found liable have a right to seek contribution from those who share responsibility for the violations, including accountants, attorneys, and corporations. For violations of Section 16(b), a corporation can bring an action to recover the short-swing profits.

## 7–2d Securities Fraud Online and Ponzi Schemes

A problem facing the SEC today is how to enforce the antifraud provisions of the securities laws in the online environment. Internet-related forms of securities fraud include many types of investment scams. Spam, online newsletters and bulletin boards, chat rooms, blogs, social media, and tweets can all be used to spread false information and perpetrate fraud. For a relatively small cost, fraudsters can even build sophisticated Web pages to facilitate their investment scams.

**Investment Newsletters** Hundreds of online investment newsletters provide information on stocks. Legitimate online newsletters can help investors gather valuable information, but some e-newsletters are used for fraud. The law allows companies to pay these newsletters to tout their securities. The newsletters are required to disclose who paid for the advertising, but many newsletters do not follow that law. Thus, an investor reading an online newsletter may believe that the information is unbiased, when in fact the fraudsters will directly profit by convincing investors to buy or sell particular stocks.

**Ponzi Schemes** Although much securities fraud occurs online, schemes conducted primarily offline have not disappeared. In recent years, the SEC has filed an increasing number of enforcement actions against perpetrators of *Ponzi schemes*. (Ponzi schemes are fraudulent investment operations that pay returns to investors from new capital paid to the fraudsters rather than from a legitimate investment.) Such schemes sometimes target U.S. residents and convince them to invest in offshore companies or banks.

---

30. *United States v. Newton,* 559 Fed.Appx. 902 (11th Cir. 2014).
31. 15 U.S.C. Section 78u(d)(2)(A).
32. Transactions pursuant to a public offering by an issuer of securities are exempted.
33. 15 U.S.C. Section 78u(d)(2)(C).
34. 15 U.S.C. Section 78u-1.

# 7-3 State Securities Laws

Today, every state has its own corporate securities laws, or **blue sky laws,** that regulate the offer and sale of securities within its borders. (The phrase *blue sky laws* comes from a 1917 United States Supreme Court decision. The Court stated that the purpose of such laws was to prevent "speculative schemes which have no more basis than so many feet of 'blue sky.' ")[35] Article 8 of the Uniform Commercial Code, which has been adopted by all of the states, also imposes various requirements relating to the purchase and sale of securities.

## 7-3a Requirements under State Securities Laws

State securities laws apply mainly to intrastate transactions (transactions within one state). Typically, state laws have disclosure requirements and antifraud provisions, many of which are patterned after Section 10(b) of the Securities Exchange Act of 1934 and SEC Rule 10b-5. State laws also provide for the registration of securities offered or issued for sale within the state and impose disclosure requirements.

■ **CASE IN POINT 7.12** Randall Fincke was the founder, director, and officer of Access Cardiosystems, Inc., a small start-up company that sold portable automated external heart defibrillators. Fincke prepared a business plan stating that Access's "patent counsel" had advised the firm that "its product does not infringe any patents." This statement was false—patent counsel never offered Access any opinion on the question of infringement.

Fincke gave this plan to potential investors, including Joseph Zimmel, who bought $1.5 million in Access shares. When the company later filed for Chapter 11 bankruptcy protection, Zimmel filed a complaint with the federal bankruptcy court, alleging that Fincke had violated the Massachusetts blue sky law. The court awarded Zimmel $1.5 million in damages, and the award was affirmed on appeal. Fincke had solicited investors "by means of" a false statement of material fact, in violation of the fraud provisions in the state's securities laws.[36] ■

Methods of registration, required disclosures, and exemptions from registration vary among states. Unless an exemption from registration is applicable, issuers must register or qualify their stock with the appropriate state official, often called a *corporations commissioner.* Additionally, most state securities laws regulate securities brokers and dealers.

## 7-3b Concurrent Regulation

Since the adoption of the 1933 and 1934 federal securities acts, the state and federal governments have regulated securities concurrently. Issuers must comply with both federal and state securities laws, and exemptions from federal law are not exemptions from state laws.

The dual federal and state system has not always worked well, particularly during the early 1990s, when the securities markets underwent considerable expansion. Today, many of the duplicate regulations have been eliminated, and the SEC has exclusive power to regulate most national securities activities.

The National Conference of Commissioners on Uniform State Laws has substantially revised the Uniform Securities Act to coordinate state and federal securities regulation and enforcement efforts. Nineteen states have adopted the most recent version of the Uniform Securities Act.[37]

# 7-4 Corporate Governance

**Corporate governance** can be narrowly defined as the relationship between a corporation and its shareholders. Some argue for a broader definition—that corporate governance specifies the rights and responsibilities among different participants in the corporation, such as the board of directors, managers, shareholders, and other stakeholders, and spells out the rules and procedures for making decisions on corporate affairs. Regardless of the way it is defined, effective corporate governance requires more than just compliance with laws and regulations.

Effective corporate governance is essential in large corporations because corporate ownership (by shareholders)

---

**35.** *Hall v. Geiger-Jones Co.*, 242 U.S. 539, 37 S.Ct. 217, 61 L.Ed. 480 (1917).

**36.** *In re Access Cardiosystems, Inc.*, 776 F.3d 60 (1st Cir. 2015).

**37.** At the time this book went to press, the Uniform Securities Act had been adopted in Georgia, Hawaii, Idaho, Indiana, Iowa, Kansas, Maine, Michigan, Minnesota, Mississippi, Missouri, New Hampshire, New Mexico, Oklahoma, South Carolina, South Dakota, Vermont, Wisconsin, and Wyoming, as well as in the U.S. Virgin Islands.

is separated from corporate control (by officers and managers). Under these circumstances, officers and managers may attempt to advance their own interests at the expense of the shareholders. The well-publicized corporate scandals in the early 2000s clearly illustrated how the misconduct of corporate managers can cause harm to companies and to society. Indeed, with the globalization of business, corporate governance has become even more important because a corporation's bad acts (or lack of control systems) can have far-reaching consequences.

## 7-4a Aligning the Interests of Officers and Shareholders

Some corporations have sought to align the financial interests of their officers with those of the company's shareholders by providing the officers with **stock options.** These options enable holders to purchase shares of the corporation's stock at a set price. When the market price rises above that level, the officers can sell their shares for a profit. Because a stock's market price generally increases as the corporation prospers, the options give the officers a financial stake in the corporation's well-being and supposedly encourage them to work hard for the benefit of the shareholders.

**Problems with Stock Options** Options have turned out to be an imperfect device for encouraging effective governance. Executives in some companies have been tempted to "cook" the company's books in order to keep share prices higher so that they can sell their stock for a profit. Executives in other corporations have experienced no losses when share prices dropped because their options were "repriced" so that they did not suffer from the price decline. Thus, although stock options theoretically can motivate officers to protect shareholder interests, stock option plans have sometimes become a way for officers to take advantage of shareholders.

**Outside Directors** With stock options generally failing to work as planned, there has been an outcry for more outside directors (those with no formal employment affiliation with the company). The theory is that independent directors will more closely monitor the actions of corporate officers. Hence, today we see more boards with outside directors. Note, though, that outside directors may not be truly independent of corporate officers. They may be friends or business associates of the leading officers.

## 7-4b Promoting Accountability

Effective corporate governance standards are designed to address problems such as those briefly discussed earlier and to motivate officers to make decisions that promote the financial interests of the company's shareholders. Generally, corporate governance entails corporate decision-making structures that monitor employees (particularly officers) to ensure that they are acting for the benefit of the shareholders. Thus, corporate governance involves, at a minimum:

1. The audited reporting of financial conditions at the corporation so that managers can be evaluated.
2. Legal protections for shareholders so that violators of the law who attempt to take advantage of shareholders can be punished for misbehavior and victims can recover damages for any associated losses.

**Governance and Corporate Law** State corporation statutes set up the legal framework for corporate governance. Under the corporate law of Delaware, where most major companies incorporate, all corporations must have certain structures of corporate governance in place. The most important structure, of course, is the board of directors, because the board makes the major decisions about the future of the corporation.

**The Board of Directors** Under corporate law, a corporation must have a board of directors elected by the shareholders. Directors are responsible for ensuring that the corporation's officers are operating wisely and in the exclusive interest of shareholders. Directors receive reports from the officers and give them managerial direction. In reality, though, corporate directors devote a relatively small amount of time to monitoring officers.

Ideally, shareholders would monitor the directors' supervision of the officers. In practice, however, it can be difficult for shareholders to monitor directors and hold them responsible for corporate failings. Although the directors can be sued if they fail to do their jobs effectively, directors are rarely held personally liable.

**The Audit Committee.** A crucial committee of the board of directors is the *audit committee,* which oversees the corporation's accounting and financial reporting processes, including both internal and outside auditors. Unless the committee members have sufficient expertise and are willing to spend the time to carefully examine the corporation's bookkeeping methods, however, the audit committee may be ineffective.

The audit committee also oversees the corporation's "internal controls." These controls, carried out largely by the company's internal auditing staff, are measures taken to ensure that reported results are accurate. For instance, internal controls help to determine whether a corporation's debts are collectible. If the debts are not collectible, it is up to the audit committee to make sure that the corporation's financial officers do not simply pretend that payment will eventually be made.

**The Compensation Committee.** Another important committee of the board of directors is the *compensation committee,* which determines the compensation of the company's officers. As part of this process, the committee must assess the officers' performance and attempt to design a compensation system that will align the officers' interests with those of the shareholders.

## 7-4c The Sarbanes-Oxley Act

In 2002, following a series of corporate scandals, Congress passed the Sarbanes-Oxley Act,[38] which addresses certain issues relating to corporate governance. Generally, the act attempts to increase corporate accountability by imposing strict disclosure requirements and harsh penalties for violations of securities laws. Among other things, the act requires chief corporate executives to take personal responsibility for the accuracy of financial statements and reports that are filed with the SEC.

Additionally, the act requires that certain financial and stock-transaction reports be filed with the SEC earlier than was required under the previous rules. The act also created a new entity, called the Public Company Accounting Oversight Board, to regulate and oversee public accounting firms. Other provisions of the act established private civil actions and expanded the SEC's remedies in administrative and civil actions.

Because of the importance of this act for corporate leaders and for those dealing with securities transactions, we highlight some of its key provisions relating to corporate accountability in Exhibit 7–3.

### More Internal Controls and Accountability
The Sarbanes-Oxley Act introduced direct *federal* corporate governance requirements for publicly traded companies. The law addressed many of the corporate governance procedures just discussed and created new requirements

---
**38**. 15 U.S.C. Sections 7201 *et seq.*

in an attempt to make the system work more effectively. The requirements deal with independent monitoring of company officers by both the board of directors and auditors.

Sections 302 and 404 of the Sarbanes-Oxley Act require high-level managers (the most senior officers) to establish and maintain an effective system of internal controls. The system must include "disclosure controls and procedures" to ensure that company financial reports are accurate and timely and to document financial results prior to reporting.

Senior management must reassess the system's effectiveness annually. Some companies have had to take expensive steps to bring their internal controls up to the new federal standards. Hundreds of companies have reported that they identified and corrected shortcomings in their internal control systems as a result.

### Exemptions for Smaller Companies
The act initially required all public companies to have an independent auditor file a report with the SEC on management's assessment of internal controls. Congress, however, enacted an exemption for smaller companies in 2010 in an effort to reduce compliance costs. Public companies with a market capitalization, or public float, of less than $75 million no longer need to have an auditor report on management's assessment of internal controls.

### Certification and Monitoring Requirements
Section 906 of the Sarbanes-Oxley Act requires that chief executive officers and chief financial officers certify the accuracy of the information in the corporate financial statements. The statements must "fairly represents in all material respects, the financial conditions and results of operations of the issuer." This requirement makes the officers directly accountable for the accuracy of their financial reporting and precludes any "ignorance defense" if shortcomings are later discovered.

The act also includes requirements to improve directors' monitoring of officers' activities. All members of a publicly traded corporation's audit committee, which oversees the corporation's accounting and financial reporting processes, must be outside directors. The audit committee must have a written charter that sets out its duties and provides for performance appraisal. At least one "financial expert" must serve on the audit committee, which must hold executive meetings without company officers being present. In addition to reviewing the internal controls, the committee also monitors the actions of the outside auditor.

**EXHIBIT 7–3**  Some Key Provisions of the Sarbanes-Oxley Act Relating to Corporate Accountability

## CERTIFICATION REQUIREMENTS

Under *Section 906* of the Sarbanes-Oxley Act, the chief executive officers (CEOs) and chief financial officers (CFOs) of most major companies listed on public stock exchanges must certify financial statements that are filed with the SEC. CEOs and CFOs have to certify that filed financial reports "fully comply" with SEC requirements and that all of the information reported "fairly represents in all material respects, the financial conditions and results of operations of the issuer."

Under *Section 302* of the act, CEOs and CFOs of reporting companies are required to certify that a signing officer reviewed each quarterly and annual filing with the SEC and that none contained untrue statements of material fact. Also, the signing officer or officers must certify that they have established an internal control system to identify all material information and that any deficiencies in the system were disclosed to the auditors.

## INTERNAL CONTROLS

**Financial Controls**—*Section 404(a)* requires all public companies to assess the effectiveness of their internal control over financial reporting. *Section 404(b)* requires independent auditors to report on management's assessment of internal controls, but certain companies are exempted.

**Loans to Directors and Officers**—*Section 402* prohibits any reporting company—as well as any private company that is filing an initial public offering—from making personal loans to directors and executive officers are exempted.

**Protection for Whistleblowers**—*Section 806* protects "whistleblowers"—employees who "blow the whistle" on securities violations by their employers—from being fired or in any way discriminated against by their employers.

**Blackout Periods**—*Section 306* prohibits certain types of securities transactions during "blackout periods"—periods during which the issuer's ability to purchase, sell, or otherwise transfer funds in individual account plans (such as pension funds) is suspended.

## ENHANCED PENALTIES

- *Violations of Section 906 Certification Requirements*—A CEO or CFO who certifies a financial report or statement filed with the SEC knowing that the report or statement does not fulfill all of the requirements of *Section 906* will be subject to criminal penalties of up to $1 million in fines, ten years in prison, or both. *Willful* violators of the certification requirements may be subject to $5 million in fines, twenty years in prison, or both.

- *Violations of the Securities Exchange Act of 1934*—Penalties for securities fraud under the 1934 act were also increased. Individual violators may be fined up to $5 million, imprisoned for up to twenty years, or both. *Willful* violators may be imprisoned for up to twenty-five years in addition to being fined.

- *Destruction or Alteration of Documents*—Anyone who alters, destroys, or conceals documents or otherwise obstructs any official proceeding will be subject to fines, imprisonment for up to twenty years, or both.

- *Other Forms of White-Collar Crime*—The act stiffened the penalties for certain criminal violations, such as federal mail and wire fraud, and ordered the U.S. Sentencing Commission to revise the sentencing guidelines for white-collar crimes.

## STATUTE OF LIMITATIONS FOR SECURITIES FRAUD

*Section 804* provides that a private right of action for securities fraud may be brought no later than two years after the discovery of the violation or five years after the violation, whichever is earlier.

## Reviewing: Securities Law and Corporate Governance

Dale Emerson served as the chief financial officer for Reliant Electric Company, a distributor of electricity serving portions of Montana and North Dakota. Reliant was in the final stages of planning a takeover of Dakota Gasworks, Inc., a natural gas distributor that operated solely within North Dakota. Emerson went on a weekend fishing trip with his uncle, Ernest Wallace. Emerson mentioned to Wallace that he had been putting in a lot of extra hours at the office planning a takeover of Dakota Gasworks. When he returned from the fishing trip, Wallace purchased $20,000 worth of Reliant stock. Three weeks later, Reliant made a tender offer to Dakota Gasworks stockholders and purchased 57 percent of Dakota Gasworks stock. Over the next two weeks, the price of Reliant stock rose 72 percent before leveling out. Wallace then sold his Reliant stock for a gross profit of $14,400. Using the information presented in the chapter, answer the following questions.

1. Would registration with the SEC be required for Dakota Gasworks securities? Why or why not?
2. Did Emerson violate Section 10(b) of the Securities Exchange Act of 1934 and SEC Rule 10b-5? Why or why not?
3. What theory or theories might a court use to hold Wallace liable for insider trading?
4. Under the Sarbanes-Oxley Act, who would be required to certify the accuracy of the financial statements Reliant filed with the SEC?

**Debate This** . . . *Insider trading should be legalized.*

## Terms and Concepts

accredited investor 116
blue sky laws 127
corporate governance 127
free-writing prospectus 114
insider trading 120

investment company 115
investment contract 112
mutual fund 115
prospectus 113
SEC Rule 10b-5 120

securities 112
short-swing profits 122
stock option 128
tippee 121

## Issue Spotters

1. When a corporation wishes to issue certain securities, it must provide sufficient information for an unsophisticated investor to evaluate the financial risk involved. Specifically, the law imposes liability for making a false statement or omission that is "material." What sort of information would an investor consider material? (See *The Securities Exchange Act of 1934.*)

2. Lee is an officer of Magma Oil, Inc. Lee knows that a Magma geologist has just discovered a new deposit of oil. Can Lee take advantage of this information to buy and sell Magma stock? Why or why not? (See *The Securities Exchange Act of 1934.*)

• **Check your answers to the Issue Spotters against the answers provided in Appendix B at the end of this text.**

## Business Scenarios

**7–1. Registration Requirements.** Estrada Hermanos, Inc., a corporation incorporated and doing business in Florida, decides to sell $1 million worth of its common stock to the public. The stock will be sold only within the state of Florida. José Estrada, the chair of the board, says the offering need not be registered with the Securities and Exchange Commission. His brother, Gustavo, disagrees. Who is right? Explain. (See *The Securities Act of 1933.*)

**7–2. Registration Requirements.** Huron Corp. has 300,000 common shares outstanding. The owners of these outstanding shares live in several different states. Huron has decided to split the 300,000 shares two for one. Will Huron Corp. have to file a registration statement and prospectus on the 300,000 new shares to be issued as a result of the split? Explain. (See *The Securities Act of 1933.*)

**7–3. Insider Trading.** David Gain was the chief executive officer (CEO) of Forest Media Corp., which became interested in acquiring RS Communications, Inc. To initiate negotiations, Gain met with RS's CEO, Gill Raz, on Friday, July 12. Two days later, Gain phoned his brother Mark, who bought 3,800 shares of RS stock on the following Monday. Mark discussed the deal with their father, Jordan, who bought 20,000 RS shares on Thursday. On July 25, the day before the RS bid was due, Gain phoned his parents' home, and Mark bought another 3,200 RS shares. The same routine was followed over the next few days, with Gain periodically phoning Mark or Jordan, both of whom continued to buy RS shares.

Forest's bid was refused, but on August 5, RS announced its merger with another company. The price of RS stock rose 30 percent, increasing the value of Mark's and Jordan's shares by $664,024 and $412,875, respectively. Did Gain engage in insider trading? What is required to impose sanctions for this offense? Could a court hold Gain liable? Why or why not? (See *The Securities Exchange Act of 1934*.)

# Business Case Problems

### 7–4. Business Case Problem with Sample Answer— Violations of the 1934 Act.  Matrixx Initiatives, Inc., makes and sells over-the-counter pharmaceutical products. Its core brand is Zicam, which accounts for 70 percent of its sales. Matrixx received reports that some consumers had lost their sense of smell (a condition called anosmia) after using Zicam Cold Remedy. Four product liability suits were filed against Matrixx, seeking damages for anosmia. In public statements relating to revenues and product safety, however, Matrixx did not reveal this information.

James Siracusano and other Matrixx investors filed a suit in a federal district court against the company and its executives under Section 10(b) of the Securities Exchange Act of 1934 and SEC Rule 10b-5, claiming that the statements were misleading because they did not disclose information regarding the product liability suits. Matrixx argued that to be material, information must consist of a statistically significant number of adverse events that require disclosure. Because Siracusano's claim did not allege that Matrixx knew of a statistically significant number of adverse events, the company contended that the claim should be dismissed. What is the standard for materiality in this context? Should Siracusano's claim be dismissed? Explain. [*Matrixx Initiatives, Inc. v. Siracusano*, 563 U.S. 27, 131 S.Ct. 1309, 179 L.Ed.2d 398 (2011)] (See *The Securities Exchange Act of 1934*.)

- For a sample answer to Problem 7–4, go to Appendix C at the end of this text.

### 7–5. Disclosure under SEC Rule 10b-5. Dodona I, LLC, invested $4 million in two securities offerings from Goldman, Sachs & Co. The investments were in collateralized debt obligations (CDOs). Their value depended on residential mortgage-backed securities (RMBS), whose value in turn depended on the performance of subprime residential mortgages.

Before marketing the CDOs, Goldman had noticed several "red flags" relating to investments in the subprime market, in which it had invested heavily. To limit its risk, Goldman began betting against subprime mortgages, RMBS, and CDOs, including the CDOs it had sold to Dodona. In other words, Goldman made investments based on the assumption that subprime mortgages and the securities instruments built upon them would decrease in value. In an internal e-mail, one Goldman official commented that the company had managed to "make some lemonade from some big old lemons."

Nevertheless, Goldman's marketing materials provided only boilerplate statements about the risks of investing in the securities.

The CDOs were later downgraded to junk status, and Dodona suffered a major loss while Goldman profited. Assuming that Goldman did not affirmatively misrepresent any facts about the CDOs, can Dodona still recover under SEC Rule 10b-5? If so, how? [*Dodona I, LLC v. Goldman, Sachs & Co.*, 847 F.Supp.2d 624 (S.D.N.Y. 2012)] (See *The Securities Exchange Act of 1934*.)

### 7–6. Violations of the 1933 Act. Three shareholders of iStorage sought to sell their stock through World Trade Financial Corp. The shares were *restricted securities*—that is, securities acquired in an unregistered, private sale. Restricted securities typically bear a "restrictive" legend clearly stating that they cannot be resold in the public marketplace. This legend had been wrongly removed from the iStorage shares, however. Information about the company that was publicly available included the fact that, despite a ten-year life, it had no operating history or earnings. In addition, it had net losses of about $200,000, and its stock was thinly traded. Without investigating the company or the status of its stock, World Trade sold more than 2.3 million shares to the public on behalf of the three customers. Did World Trade violate the Securities Act of 1933? Discuss. [*World Trade Financial Corp. v. Securities and Exchange Commission*, 739 F.3d 1243 (9th Cir. 2014)] (See *The Securities Act of 1933*.)

### 7–7. Securities Act of 1933. Big Apple Consulting USA, Inc., provided small publicly traded companies with a variety of services, including marketing, business planning, and Web site development and maintenance. CyberKey Corp. sold customizable USB drives. CyberKey falsely informed Big Apple that CyberKey had been awarded a $25 million contract with the Department of Homeland Security. Big Apple used this information in aggressively promoting CyberKey's stock and was compensated for the effort in the form of CyberKey shares. When the Securities and Exchange Commission (SEC) began to investigate, Big Apple sold its shares for $7.8 million. The SEC filed an action in a federal district court against Big Apple, alleging a violation of the Securities Act of 1933. Can liability be imposed on a seller for a false statement that was made by someone else? Explain. [*U.S. Securities and Exchange Commission v. Big Apple Consulting USA, Inc.*, 783 F.3d 786 (11th Cir. 2015)] (See *The Securities Act of 1933*.)

**7–8. The Securities Exchange Act of 1934.** Dilean Reyes-Rivera was the president of Global Reach Trading (GRT), a corporation registered in Puerto Rico. His brother Jeffrey was the firm's accountant. Along with GRT sales agents and other promoters, the brothers solicited funds from individuals by promising to invest the funds in low-risk, short-term, high-yield securities. The investors were guaranteed a rate of return of up to 20 percent. Through this arrangement, more than 230 persons provided the brothers with about $22 million. This money was not actually invested. Instead, the funds received from later investors were used to pay "returns" to earlier investors. The Reyes-Riveras spent $4.6 million of the proceeds to buy luxury vehicles, houses, furniture, jewelry, and trips for themselves. What is this type of scheme called? What are the potential consequences? Discuss. [*United States v. Reyes-Rivera*, 812 F.3d 79 (1st Cir. 2016)] (See *The Securities Exchange Act of 1934*.)

**7–9. A Question of Ethics—Violations of the 1934 Act.** *Melvin Lyttle told John Montana and Paul Knight about a "Trading Program" that purportedly would buy and sell securities. Lyttle said the securities deals were fully insured, as well as monitored and controlled by the Federal Reserve. Without checking the details or even verifying whether the Program existed, Montana and Knight, with Lyttle's help, began to sell interests in the Program to investors. For a minimum investment of $1 million, the investors were promised extraordinary rates of return—from 10 percent to as much as 100 percent per week—without risk. They were told, among other things, that the Program would "utilize banks that can ensure full bank integrity of The Transaction whose undertaking[s] are in complete harmony with international banking rules and protocol and who guarantee maximum security of a Funder's Capital Placement Amount." Nothing was required but the investors' funds and their silence—the Program was to be kept secret. Over a four-month period in 1999, Montana raised approximately $23 million from twenty-two investors. The promised gains did not accrue, however. Instead, Montana, Lyttle, and Knight depleted investors' funds in high-risk trades or spent the funds on themselves. [SEC v. Montana, 464 F.Supp.2d 772 (S.D.Ind. 2006)] (See The Securities Exchange Act of 1934.)*

**(a)** The Securities and Exchange Commission (SEC) filed a suit in a federal district court against Montana and the others, seeking an injunction, civil penalties, and refund of profits with interest. The SEC alleged, among other things, violations of Section 10(b) of the Securities Exchange Act of 1934 and SEC Rule 10b-5. What is required to establish such violations? Describe how and why the facts in this case meet, or fail to meet, these requirements.

**(b)** It is often remarked, "There's a sucker born every minute!" Does that phrase describe the Program's investors? Ultimately, about half of the investors recouped the amount they invested. Should the others be considered at least partly responsible for their own losses? Why or why not?

## Legal Reasoning Group Activity

**7–10. Violations of Securities Laws.** Karel Svoboda, a credit officer for Rogue Bank, evaluated and approved his employer's extensions of credit to clients. These responsibilities gave Svoboda access to nonpublic information about the clients' earnings, performance, acquisitions, and business plans from confidential memos, e-mail, and other sources. Svoboda devised a scheme with Alena Robles, an independent accountant, to use this information to trade securities. Pursuant to their scheme, Robles traded in the securities of more than twenty different companies and profited by more than $2 million. Svoboda also executed trades for his own profit of more than $800,000, despite their agreement that Robles would do all of the trading. Aware that their scheme violated Rogue Bank's policy, they attempted to conduct their trades in such a way as to avoid suspicion. When the bank questioned Svoboda about his actions, he lied, refused to cooperate, and was fired. (See *The Securities Exchange Act of 1934*.)

**(a)** The first group will determine whether Svoboda or Robles committed any crimes.

**(b)** The second group will decide whether Svoboda or Robles is subject to civil liability. If so, who could file a suit, and on what ground? What are the possible sanctions?

**(c)** A third group will identify any defenses that Svoboda or Robles could raise and determine their likelihood of success.

# Business Start-Ups Online

Hundreds of thousands of new businesses open each year in the United States. A large percentage of them fail within the first five years. But those that succeed more than offset the losses—the survivors are responsible for the creation of most new jobs.

Today, many new businesses—following in the footsteps of Facebook, Inc., Google, Inc., Twitter, Inc., and others—start online. Going into business online can be a good way to reach a wider market and experience higher sales. Generally, the steps for setting up an online business are the same as those for starting a brick-and-mortar operation. But there are added legal considerations.

## Starting an Online Business

Starting a business requires taking certain preliminary steps—for example, finding a product niche, researching potential markets, and formulating a business plan. Actually setting up the business involves additional steps. As noted, these steps are similar for all new businesses, but here we focus on online startups.

**Create a Legal Entity and Obtain a License** Creating a legal entity, such as a corporation or a limited liability company, under which to do business online can insulate the owners from personal liability. It may also give the business a greater appearance of solidity. Considerations for starting a business as a corporation, a limited liability company, or another form of organization were discussed earlier in this unit.

In any business situation, federal and state licenses and permits must be obtained if required. A license or permit is often needed to engage in an activity supervised and regulated by a federal or state administrative agency. For instance, sales of alcoholic beverages require a permit from the U.S. Treasury Department's Alcohol and Tobacco Tax and Trade Bureau.

**Select and Register a Domain Name** A domain name is the address of an online business. Once a name is selected, the registration process is simple. The Internet Corporation for Assigned Names and Numbers (ICANN), a nonprofit corporation, is responsible for coordinating the maintenance and procedures of several databases related to the namespaces of the Internet. Among other things, ICANN oversees the distribution of domain names.[1]

**Choose a Web Host and Design a Site** The Web host of an online business stores all the pages of the business's Web site and makes them available on the Internet. The Web host should be reliable, secure, and suitable for the business. Some Web hosts will perform site development and maintenance, as well as search engine registration.

The design of a site should comply with intellectual property laws. For instance, any trademark used on a site should not infringe on another's mark. Images used as part of the design should not infringe on others' copyrights.

---

1. A directory of registrars is available at https://www.internic.net.

**Application and Ethics**

## Managing an Online Business

Managing any business requires complying with federal, state, and local laws. When transacting business online in global markets, there are also international regulations to follow.

**Comply with Advertising Rules** Advertising online is subject to many of the same laws as advertising offline. Goods and services must be described truthfully, disclosures must be clear and conspicuous, and customers must understand what they are paying for. If customers must click on a link to get the information, the link must be obvious. The purpose is to provide a marketplace in which businesses can compete free of deceptive and unfair practices.

Among the regulations that apply to advertising is the Federal Trade Commission's Mail, Internet, or Telephone Order Merchandise rule, which governs representations with respect to shipping.[2] Generally, a business must ship ordered merchandise within thirty days, unless a customer agrees otherwise, or promptly refund the price of the unshipped goods.

**Protect Users' Privacy** Businesses typically collect and retain their customers' account numbers and other personal information. Keeping this data private can protect against liability for wrongful disclosure or misuse. An online business is subject to federal and state privacy laws that cover offline businesses. And wherever a firm does business, it must comply with the location's data protection laws—many foreign countries have privacy laws that apply to online businesses.

**Offer Payment Options** Online businesses generally accept credit or debit cards for payment. International sales can be increased by offering a variety of payment options, especially options that match customers' local business practices. In many European countries, for example, consumers often pay online merchants by wire transfer.

Another option is a service such as PayPal that processes payments between businesses and their customers and forwards the funds to the appropriate party. Some services specialize in processing payments from international customers. Of course, there is always some risk, but in general these services guarantee the payments.

**Collect State and Local Taxes** Federal, state, and local tax laws apply to online businesses. A tax permit must be obtained from the appropriate government agency when this is required. State and local sales taxes must be collected from customers in a state in which an online business has a *nexus*, or physical presence—a store, an office, or a warehouse, for instance.[3]

**Follow International Guidelines** An online business can make sales to, and engage in other transactions with, businesses and individuals in every continent on the globe. Even the smallest firm has the potential to reach more than a billion customers online.

The Organization for Economic Cooperation and Development, of which the United States is a member, issued a set of guidelines for doing business in international markets online. The principles expressed in the guidelines make up a voluntary code of conduct that encourages an online business to do the following:

- Use fair marketing practices.
- Offer accurate, clear information about the business's goods and services.

---

2. 16 C.F.R. Chapter I, Subchapter D, Part 435.
3. *Quill v. North Dakota*, 504 U.S. 298, 112 S.Ct. 1904, 119 L.Ed.2d 91 (1992).

- Disclose full information about the terms and costs of a transaction.
- Provide a secure method for online payment.
- Protect consumer privacy.[4]

**Comply with International Trade Laws** Doing business online in global markets requires compliance with international trade laws, including shipping and tariff and tax regulations. Customers should be informed that tariffs and taxes can significantly increase the final prices of goods and services.[5]

The United States imposes additional requirements on businesses that export products. All goods are subject to the regulations that cover economic and trade sanctions against foreign countries, companies, and individuals. Nearly every commercial transaction with any sanctioned party is prohibited.

Goods with both commercial and military applications are known as *dual-use products*. These items must be licensed by the U.S. Department of Commerce under its Export Administrative Regulations.[6] The International Traffic in Arms Regulations control sales of defense-related goods. Under these regulations, items on the U.S. Munitions List must be licensed for export.[7]

## Ethical Connection

Dealing in good faith can be more important in doing business online than in a brick-and-mortar location because Internet customers are more reliant on a business's reputation. For an online business, this involves more than minimal compliance with the relevant laws of the targeted market.

In some industries, the law imposes a repair, replace, or refund policy on merchants for some types of defects in delivered goods. In any industry, to build and maintain a customer base requires an effective customer service program. This program should go beyond what is legally required. How customer complaints are resolved is important to building trust and confidence.

**Ethics Question** *To attain success in global commerce, an online business should design its Web site with what in mind?*

**Critical Thinking** *Between 2 and 4 percent of online orders involve fraud. What can an online business do to avoid being the victim?*

---

4. A checklist of practices that follow these guidelines is in Federal Trade Commission, *Electronic Commerce: Selling Internationally A Guide for Businesses* available at https://www.ftc.gov/tips-advice/business-center/guidance/electronic-commerce-selling-internationally-guide-businesses.
5. Information on conducting business online, particularly in international markets, is provided by a number of federal agencies through BusinessUSA.gov, *Conducting Business Online*, available at business.usa.gov/export/a-guide-to-exporting-basics/conducting-business-online.
6. 15 C.F.R. Subtitle B, Chapter VII, Subchapter C.
7. 22 C.F.R. Chapter I, Subchapter M.

# Unit Two

# Human Resources

# CHAPTER 8

# Tort Law

Part of doing business today—and, indeed, part of everyday life—is the risk of being involved in a lawsuit. The list of circumstances in which businesspersons can be sued is long and varied. A customer who is injured by a security guard at a business establishment, for instance, may sue the business owner, claiming that the security guard's conduct was intentionally wrongful. A person who slips and falls at a retail store may sue the company for negligence.

Any time that one party's allegedly wrongful conduct causes injury to another, an action may arise under the law of *torts* (the word *tort* is French for "wrong"). Through tort law, society compensates those who have suffered injuries as a result of the wrongful conduct of others. Many of the lawsuits brought by or against business firms are based on various tort theories.

## 8–1 The Basis of Tort Law

Two notions serve as the basis of all **torts:** wrongs and compensation. Tort law is designed to compensate those who have suffered a loss or injury due to another person's wrongful act. In a tort action, one person or group brings a lawsuit against another person or group to obtain compensation (monetary damages) or other relief for the harm suffered.

### 8–1a The Purpose of Tort Law

Generally, the purpose of tort law is to provide remedies for the violation of various *protected interests.* Society recognizes an interest in personal physical safety. Thus, tort law provides remedies for acts that cause physical injury or that interfere with physical security and freedom of movement. Society also recognizes an interest in protecting property, and tort law provides remedies for acts that cause destruction of or damage to property.

### 8–1b Damages Available in Tort Actions

Because the purpose of tort law is to compensate the injured party for the damage suffered, you need to have an understanding of the types of damages that plaintiffs seek in tort actions. Note that legal usage distinguishes between the terms *damage* and *damages. Damage* refers to harm or injury to persons or property, while **damages** refers to monetary compensation for such harm or injury.

**Compensatory Damages** A plaintiff is awarded **compensatory damages** to compensate or reimburse the plaintiff for actual losses. Thus, the goal is to make the plaintiff whole and put her or him in the same position that she or he would have been in had the tort not occurred. Compensatory damages awards are often broken down into *special damages* and *general damages.*

**Special damages** compensate the plaintiff for quantifiable monetary losses, such as medical expenses and lost wages and benefits (now and in the future). Special damages might also be awarded to compensate for extra costs, the loss of irreplaceable items, and the costs of repairing or replacing damaged property.

■ **CASE IN POINT 8.1** Seaway Marine Transport operates the *Enterprise,* a large cargo ship, which has twenty-two hatches for storing coal. When the *Enterprise* positioned itself to receive a load of coal on the shores of Lake Erie, in Ohio, it struck a land-based coal-loading machine operated by Bessemer & Lake Erie Railroad Company. A federal court found Seaway liable and awarded $522,000 in special damages to compensate Bessemer for the cost of repairing the damage to the loading boom.[1] ■

**General damages** compensate individuals (not companies) for the nonmonetary aspects of the harm suffered, such as pain and suffering. A court might award general damages for physical or emotional pain and suffering, loss of companionship, loss of consortium (losing

---

1. *Bessemer & Lake Erie Railroad Co. v. Seaway Marine Transport,* 357 F.3d 596 (6th Cir. 2010).

the emotional and physical benefits of a spousal relationship), disfigurement, loss of reputation, or loss or impairment of mental or physical capacity.

**Punitive Damages** Occasionally, the courts also award **punitive damages** in tort cases to punish the wrongdoer and deter others from similar wrongdoing. Punitive damages are appropriate only when the defendant's conduct was particularly egregious (flagrant) or reprehensible (blameworthy).

Usually, this means that punitive damages are available in *intentional* tort actions and only rarely in negligence lawsuits (negligence actions will be discussed later in this chapter). They may be awarded, however, in suits involving *gross negligence*. Gross negligence can be defined as an intentional failure to perform a manifest duty in reckless disregard of the consequences of such a failure for the life or property of another.

Courts exercise great restraint in granting punitive damages to plaintiffs in tort actions because punitive damages are subject to limitations under the due process clause of the U.S. Constitution. The United States Supreme Court has held that to the extent that an award of punitive damages is grossly excessive, it furthers no legitimate purpose and violates due process requirements.[2] Consequently, an appellate court will sometimes reduce the amount of punitive damages awarded to a plaintiff on the ground that it is excessive and thereby violates the due process clause.

**Legislative Caps on Damages** State laws may limit the amount of damages—both punitive and general—that can be awarded to the plaintiff. More than half of the states have placed caps ranging from $250,000 to $750,000 on noneconomic general damages (such as for pain and suffering), especially in medical malpractice suits. More than thirty states have limited punitive damages, with some imposing outright bans.

### 8–1c Classification of Torts

There are two broad classifications of torts: *intentional torts* and *unintentional torts* (torts involving negligence). The classification of a particular tort depends largely on how the tort occurs (intentionally or negligently) and the surrounding circumstances. Intentional torts result from the intentional violation of person or property (fault plus intent). Negligence results from the breach of a duty to act reasonably (fault without intent).

---

**2.** *State Farm Mutual Automobile Insurance Co. v. Campbell*, 538 U.S. 408, 123 S.Ct. 1513, 155 L.Ed.2d 585 (2003).

### 8–1d Defenses

Even if a plaintiff proves all the elements of a tort, the defendant can raise a number of legally recognized *defenses* (reasons why the plaintiff should not obtain damages). A successful defense releases the defendant from partial or full liability for the tortious act.

The defenses available may vary depending on the specific tort involved. A common defense to intentional torts against persons, for instance, is *consent*. When a person consents to the act that damages her or him, there is generally no liability. The most widely used defense in negligence actions is *comparative negligence*.

In addition, most states have a *statute of limitations* that establishes the time limit (often two years from the date of discovering the harm) within which a particular type of lawsuit can be filed. After that time period has run, the plaintiff can no longer file a claim.

## 8–2 Intentional Torts against Persons

An **intentional tort,** as the term implies, requires intent. The **tortfeasor** (the one committing the tort) must intend to commit an act, the consequences of which interfere with another's personal or business interests in a way not permitted by law. An evil or harmful motive is not required—in fact, the person committing the action may even have a beneficial motive for doing what turns out to be a tortious act.

In tort law, *intent* means only that the person intended the consequences of his or her act or knew with substantial certainty that specific consequences would result from the act. The law generally assumes that individuals intend the *normal* consequences of their actions. Thus, forcefully pushing another—even if done in jest—is an intentional tort (if injury results), because the object of a strong push can ordinarily be expected to fall down.

In addition, intent can be transferred when a defendant intends to harm one individual, but unintentionally harms a second person. This is called **transferred intent.** ■ **EXAMPLE 8.2** Alex swings a bat intending to hit Blake but misses and hits Carson instead. Carson can sue Alex for the tort of battery (discussed shortly) because Alex's intent to harm Blake can be transferred to Carson. ■

### 8–2a Assault

An **assault** is any intentional and unexcused threat of immediate harmful or offensive contact—words or acts that create a reasonably believable threat. An assault can occur even if there is no actual contact with the plaintiff, provided that the defendant's conduct creates a reasonable apprehension of imminent harm in the plaintiff. Tort law aims to protect individuals from having to expect harmful or offensive contact.

## 8–2b Battery

If the act that created the apprehension is *completed* and results in harm to the plaintiff, it is a **battery**—an unexcused and harmful or offensive physical contact *intentionally* performed. ■ **EXAMPLE 8.3** Ivan threatens Jean with a gun and then shoots her. The pointing of the gun at Jean is an assault. The firing of the gun (if the bullet hits Jean) is a battery. ■

The contact can be harmful, or it can be merely offensive (such as an unwelcome kiss). Physical injury need not occur. The contact can involve any part of the body or anything attached to it—for instance, a hat, a purse, or a jacket. The contact can be made by the defendant or by some force set in motion by the defendant, such as a rock thrown by the defendant. Whether the contact is offensive is determined by the *reasonable person standard*.[3]

If the plaintiff shows that there was contact, and the jury (or judge, if there is no jury) agrees that the contact was offensive, then the plaintiff has a right to compensation. A plaintiff may be compensated for the emotional harm or loss of reputation resulting from a battery, as well as for physical harm. A defendant may assert self-defense or defense of others in an attempt to justify his or her conduct.

## 8–2c False Imprisonment

*False imprisonment* is the intentional confinement or restraint of another person's activities without justification. False imprisonment interferes with the freedom to move without restraint. The confinement can be accomplished through the use of physical barriers, physical restraint, or threats of physical force. Moral pressure does not constitute false imprisonment. It is essential that the person being restrained does not wish to be restrained. (The plaintiff's consent to the restraint bars any liability.)

Businesspersons often face suits for false imprisonment after they have attempted to confine a suspected shoplifter for questioning. Under the "privilege to detain" granted to merchants in most states, a merchant can use reasonable force to detain or delay persons suspected of shoplifting and hold them for the police. Although laws pertaining to this privilege vary from state to state, generally any detention must be conducted in a *reasonable* manner and for only a *reasonable* length of time. Undue force or unreasonable detention can lead to liability for the business.

Cities and counties may also face lawsuits for false imprisonment if they detain individuals without reason. ■ **CASE IN POINT 8.4** Police arrested Adetokunbo Shoyoye for riding the subway without a ticket and for a theft that had been committed by someone who had stolen his identity. A court ordered him to be released, but a county employee mistakenly confused Shoyoye's paperwork with that of another person who was scheduled to be sent to state prison. As a result, instead of being released, Shoyoye was held in county jail for more than two weeks. Shoyoye later sued the county for false imprisonment and won.[4] ■

## 8–2d Intentional Infliction of Emotional Distress

The tort of *intentional infliction of emotional distress* involves an intentional act that amounts to extreme and outrageous conduct resulting in severe emotional distress to another. To be **actionable** (capable of serving as the ground for a lawsuit), the act must be extreme and outrageous to the point that it exceeds the bounds of decency accepted by society.

**Outrageous Conduct** Courts in most jurisdictions are wary of emotional distress claims and confine them to situations involving truly outrageous behavior. Generally, repeated annoyances (such as those experienced by a person who is being stalked), coupled with threats, are enough. Acts that cause indignity or annoyance alone usually are not sufficient.

■ **EXAMPLE 8.5** A father attacks a man who has had consensual sexual relations with the father's nineteen-year-old daughter. The father handcuffs the man to a steel pole and threatens to kill him unless he leaves town immediately. The father's conduct may be sufficiently extreme and outrageous to be actionable as an intentional infliction of emotional distress. ■

**Limited by the First Amendment** When the outrageous conduct consists of speech about a public figure,

---

3. The *reasonable person standard* is an "objective" test of how a reasonable person would have acted under the same circumstances. See "The Duty of Care and Its Breach" later in this chapter.

4. *Shoyoye v. County of Los Angeles*, 203 Cal.App.4th 947, 137 Cal.Rptr.3d 839 (2012).

the First Amendment's guarantee of freedom of speech also limits emotional distress claims.

■ **CASE IN POINT 8.6**  *Hustler* magazine once printed a false advertisement that showed a picture of the late Reverend Jerry Falwell and described him as having lost his virginity to his mother in an outhouse while he was drunk. Falwell sued the magazine for intentional infliction of emotional distress and won, but the United States Supreme Court overturned the decision. The Court held that parodies of public figures are protected under the First Amendment from intentional infliction of emotional distress claims. (The Court uses the same standards that apply to public figures in defamation lawsuits, discussed next.)[5] ■

## 8–2e Defamation

The freedom of speech guaranteed by the First Amendment is not absolute. The courts are required to balance the vital guarantee of free speech against other pervasive

and strong social interests, including society's interest in preventing and redressing attacks on reputation.

**Defamation** of character involves wrongfully hurting a person's good reputation. The law imposes a general duty on all persons to refrain from making false, defamatory *statements of fact* about others. Breaching this duty in writing or other permanent form (such as a digital recording) involves the tort of **libel.** Breaching this duty orally involves the tort of **slander.** The tort of defamation also arises when a false statement of fact is made about a person's product, business, or legal ownership rights to property.

Establishing defamation involves proving the following elements:

1. The defendant made a false statement of fact.
2. The statement was understood as being about the plaintiff and tended to harm the plaintiff's reputation.
3. The statement was published to at least one person other than the plaintiff.
4. If the plaintiff is a public figure, she or he must also prove *actual malice,* discussed later in the chapter.

The following case involved the application of free speech guarantees to online reviews of professional services.

---

5. *Hustler Magazine, Inc. v. Falwell*, 485 U.S. 46, 108 S.Ct. 876, 99 L.Ed.2d 41 (1988). For another example of how the courts protect parody, see *Busch v. Viacom International, Inc.*, 477 F.Supp.2d 764 (N.D.Tex. 2007), involving a false endorsement of televangelist Pat Robertson's diet shake.

---

**Case Analysis 8.1**

# Blake v. Giustibelli

District Court of Appeal of Florida, Fourth District, 41 Fla. L. Weekly D122, 182 So.3d 881 (2016).

### In the Language of the Court
*CIKLIN*, C.J. [Chief Judge]

\* \* \* \*

[Ann-Marie] Giustibelli represented Copia Blake in a dissolution of marriage proceeding brought against Peter Birzon. After a breakdown in the attorney-client relationship between Giustibelli and her client[,] Blake, and oddly, Birzon as well, took to the Internet to post defamatory reviews of Giustibelli. In response, Giustibelli brought suit [in a Florida state court against Blake and Birzon], pleading a count for libel.

Blake's and Birzon's posted Internet reviews contained the following statements:

> This lawyer represented me in my divorce. She was combative and

explosive and took my divorce to a level of anger which caused major suffering of my minor children. She insisted I was an emotionally abused wife who couldn't make rational decisions which caused my case to drag on in the system for a year and a half so her FEES would continue to multiply!! She misrepresented her fees with regards to the contract I initially signed. The contract she submitted to the courts for her fees were 4 times her original quote and pages of the original had been exchanged to support her claims, only the signature page was the same. Shame on me that I did not have an original copy, but like an idiot \* \* \* I trusted my lawyer. Don't mistake sincerity for honesty because I assure you, that in this attorney's case, they are NOT the same thing. She absolutely perpetuates

the horrible image of attorneys who are only out for the money and themselves. Although I know this isn't the case and there are some very good honest lawyers out there, Mrs. Giustibelli is simply not one of the "good ones." Horrible horrible experience. Use anyone else, it would have to be a better result.

\* \* \* \*

No integrity. Will say one thing and do another. Her fees outweigh the truth. Altered her charges to 4 times the original quote with no explanation. Do not use her. Don't mistake sincerity for honesty. In her case, they're not at all the same. Will literally lie to your face if it means more money for her. Get someone else.

**Case 8.1 Continues**

**Case 8.1 Continued**

* * * Anyone else would do a superior effort for you.

* * * *

I accepted an initial VERY fair offer from my ex. Mrs. Giustibelli convinced me to "crush" him and that I could have permanent etc. Spent over a year (and 4 times her original estimate) to arrive at the same place we started at. Caused unnecessary chaos and fear with my kids, convinced me that my ex cheated (which he didn't), that he was hiding money (which he wasn't), and was mad at ME when I realized her fee circus had gone on long enough and finally said "stop." Altered her fee structures, actually replaced original documents with others to support her charges and generally gave the kind of poor service you only hear about. I'm not a disgruntled ex-wife. I'm just the foolish person who believes that a person's word should be backed by integrity. Not even remotely true in this case. I've had 2 prior attorneys and never ever have I seen ego and monies be so blatantly out of control.

Both Blake and Birzon admitted to posting the reviews on various Internet sites. The evidence showed that Blake had agreed to pay her attorney the amount reflected on the written retainer agreement—$300 an hour. Blake and Birzon both admitted at trial that Giustibelli had not charged Blake four times more than what was quoted in the agreement. The court entered judgment in favor of Giustibelli and awarded punitive damages of $350,000.

On appeal, Blake and Birzon argue that their Internet reviews constituted statements of opinion and thus were protected by the First Amendment and not actionable as defamation. We disagree. *An action for libel will lie for a false and unprivileged publication by letter, or otherwise, which exposes a person to distrust, hatred, contempt, ridicule or obloquy [censure or disgrace] or which causes such person to be avoided, or which has a tendency to injure such person in their office, occupation, business or employment.* [Emphasis added.]

Here, all the reviews contained allegations that Giustibelli lied to Blake regarding the attorney's fee. Two of the reviews contained the allegation that Giustibelli falsified a contract. These are factual allegations, and the evidence showed they were false.

* * * *

*Affirmed.*

## Legal Reasoning Questions

**1.** What is the standard for the protection of free speech guaranteed by the First Amendment?

**2.** How did this standard apply to the statements posted online by Blake and Birzon?

**3.** The First Amendment normally protects statements of opinion, and this can be an effective defense against a charge of defamation. Does it seem reasonable to disregard this defense, however, if *any* assertion of fact within a statement of opinion is false? Explain.

---

**Statement-of-Fact Requirement** Often at issue in defamation lawsuits (including online defamation) is whether the defendant made a statement of fact or a *statement of opinion.* Statements of opinion normally are not actionable, because they are protected under the First Amendment.

In other words, making a negative statement about another person is not defamation unless the statement is false and represents something as a fact rather than a personal opinion. ■ **EXAMPLE 8.7** The statement "Lane cheats on his taxes," if false, can lead to liability for defamation. The statement "Lane is a jerk" cannot constitute defamation because it is clearly an opinion. ■

**The Publication Requirement** The basis of the tort of defamation is the publication of a statement or statements that hold an individual up to contempt, ridicule, or hatred. *Publication* here means that the defamatory statements are communicated (either intentionally or accidentally) to persons other than the defamed party.

The courts have generally held that even dictating a letter to a secretary constitutes publication, although the publication may be privileged (a concept that will be explained shortly). Moreover, if a third party merely overhears defamatory statements by chance, the courts usually hold that this also constitutes publication. Defamatory statements made via the Internet are actionable as well. Note also that any individual who repeats or republishes defamatory statements normally is liable even if that person reveals the source of the statements.

■ **CASE IN POINT 8.8** Eddy Ramirez, a meat cutter at Costco Wholesale Corporation, was involved in a workplace incident with a coworker, and Costco gave him a notice of suspension. After an investigation in which coworkers were interviewed, Costco fired Ramirez. Ramirez sued, claiming that the suspension notice was defamatory. The court ruled in Costco's favor. Ramirez could not establish defamation, because he had not shown that the suspension notice was published to any third parties. Costco did nothing beyond what was necessary to investigate the events that led to Ramirez's termination.[6] ■

**Damages for Libel** Once a defendant's liability for libel is established, general damages are presumed as a matter of law. General damages are designed to compensate the plaintiff for nonspecific harms such as disgrace or dishonor in the eyes of the community, humiliation, injured reputation, and emotional distress—harms that are difficult to measure. In other words, to recover damages, the plaintiff need not prove that he or she was actually harmed in any specific way as a result of the libelous statement.

**Damages for Slander** In contrast to cases alleging libel, in a case alleging slander, the plaintiff must prove *special damages* to establish the defendant's liability. The plaintiff must show that the slanderous statement caused her or him to suffer actual economic or monetary losses.

Unless this initial hurdle of proving special damages is overcome, a plaintiff alleging slander normally cannot go forward with the suit and recover any damages. This requirement is imposed in slander cases because oral statements have a temporary quality. In contrast, a libelous (written) statement has the quality of permanence and can be circulated widely, especially through tweets and blogs. Also, libel usually results from some degree of deliberation by the author.

**Slander *Per Se*** Exceptions to the burden of proving special damages in cases alleging slander are made for certain types of slanderous statements. If a false statement constitutes "slander *per se*," it is actionable with no proof of special damages required. In most states, the following four types of declarations are considered to be slander *per se:*

1. A statement that another has a "loathsome" disease (such as a sexually transmitted disease).
2. A statement that another has committed improprieties while engaging in a profession or trade.
3. A statement that another has committed or has been imprisoned for a serious crime.

4. A statement that a person is unchaste or has engaged in serious sexual misconduct. (This usually applies only to unmarried persons and sometimes only to women.)

**Defenses to Defamation** Truth is normally an absolute defense against a defamation charge. In other words, if a defendant in a defamation case can prove that the allegedly defamatory statements of fact were true, normally no tort has been committed.

■ **CASE IN POINT 8.9** David McKee, a neurologist, went to examine a patient who had been transferred from the intensive care unit (ICU) to a private room. In the room were family members of the patient, including his son. The patient's son later made the following post on a "rate your doctor" Web site: "[Dr. McKee] seemed upset that my father had been moved [into a private room]. Never having met my father or his family, Dr. McKee said 'When you weren't in ICU, I had to spend time finding out if you transferred or died.' When we gaped at him, he said 'Well, 44 percent of hemorrhagic strokes die within 30 days. I guess this is the better option.'"

McKee filed suit for defamation but lost. The court found that all the statements made by the son were essentially true, and truth is a complete defense to a defamation action.[7] ■ In other words, true statements are not actionable no matter how disparaging. Even the presence of minor inaccuracies of expression or detail does not render basically true statements false.

Other defenses to defamation may exist if the speech is privileged or if it concerns a public figure. We discuss these defenses next. Note that the majority of defamation actions are filed in state courts, and state laws differ somewhat in the defenses they allow.

**Privileged Communications.** In some circumstances, a person will not be liable for defamatory statements because she or he enjoys a **privilege,** or immunity. Privileged communications are of two types: absolute and qualified.[8] Only in judicial proceedings and certain government proceedings is an *absolute privilege* granted. Thus, statements made by attorneys and judges in the courtroom during a trial are absolutely privileged, as are statements made by government officials during legislative debate.

6. *Ramirez v. Costco Wholesale Corp.*, 2014 WL 2696737 (Ct.Sup.Ct. 2014).

7. *McKee v. Laurion,* 825 N.W.2d 725 (Minn.Sup. 2013).
8. Note that the term *privileged communication* in this context is not the same as privileged communication between a professional, such as an attorney, and his or her client.

In other situations, a person will not be liable for defamatory statements because he or she has a *qualified, or conditional, privilege.* An employer's statements in written evaluations of employees, for instance, are protected by a qualified privilege. Generally, if the statements are made in good faith and the publication is limited to those who have a legitimate interest in the communication, the statements fall within the area of qualified privilege.

■ **EXAMPLE 8.10** Jorge has worked at Google for five years and is being considered for a management position. His supervisor, Lydia, writes a memo about Jorge's performance to those evaluating him for the position. The memo contains certain negative statements, which Lydia honestly believes are true. If Lydia limits the disclosure of the memo to company representatives, her statements will likely be protected by a qualified privilege. ■

**Public Figures.** Politicians, entertainers, professional athletes, and others in the public eye are considered **public figures.** Public figures are regarded as "fair game." False and defamatory statements about public figures that are published in the media will not constitute defamation unless the statements are made with **actual malice.**[9] To be made with actual malice, a statement must be made *with either knowledge of its falsity or a reckless disregard of the truth.*

Statements made about public figures, especially when they are communicated via a public medium, usually relate to matters of general interest. They are made about people who substantially affect all of us. Furthermore, public figures generally have some access to a public medium for answering belittling falsehoods about themselves. For these reasons, public figures have a greater burden of proof in defamation cases—to show actual malice—than do private individuals.

■ **CASE IN POINT 8.11** *In Touch* magazine published a story about a former call girl who claimed to have slept with legendary soccer player David Beckham more than once. Beckham sued *In Touch* magazine for libel, seeking $25 million in damages. He said that he had never met the woman, had not cheated on his wife with her, and had not paid her for sex. After months of litigation, a federal district court dismissed the case because Beckham could not show that the magazine had acted with actual malice. Whether or not the statements in the article were accurate, there was no evidence that the defendants had made the statements with knowledge of their falsity or reckless disregard for the truth.[10] ■

---

9. *New York Times Co. v. Sullivan,* 376 U.S. 254, 84 S.Ct. 710, 11 L.Ed.2d 686 (1964).
10. *Beckham v. Bauer Pub. Co., L.P.,* 2011 WL 977570 (2011).

## 8–2f Invasion of Privacy

A person has a right to solitude and freedom from prying public eyes—in other words, to privacy. The courts have held that certain amendments to the U.S. Constitution imply a right to privacy. Some state constitutions explicitly provide for privacy rights, as do a number of federal and state statutes.

Tort law also safeguards these rights through the tort of *invasion of privacy.* Generally, to sue successfully for an invasion of privacy, a person must have a reasonable expectation of privacy, and the invasion must be highly offensive. (See this chapter's *Digital Update* feature for a discussion of how invasion of privacy claims can arise when someone posts pictures or videos taken with digital devices.)

**Invasion of Privacy under the Common Law**
The following four acts qualify as an invasion of privacy under the common law:

1. *Intrusion into an individual's affairs or seclusion.* Invading someone's home or searching someone's briefcase or laptop without authorization is an invasion of privacy. This tort has been held to extend to eavesdropping by wiretap, unauthorized scanning of a bank account, compulsory blood testing, and window peeping. ■ **EXAMPLE 8.12** A female sports reporter for ESPN is digitally videoed while naked through the peephole in the door of her hotel room. She will probably win a lawsuit against the man who took the video and posted it on the Internet. ■

2. *False light.* Publication of information that places a person in a false light is also an invasion of privacy. For instance, writing a story that attributes to a person ideas and opinions not held by that person is an invasion of privacy. (Publishing such a story could involve the tort of defamation as well.) ■ **EXAMPLE 8.13** An Iowa newspaper prints an article saying that nineteen-year-old Yassine Alam is part of the terrorist organization Islamic State of Iraq (ISIL). Next to the article is a photo of Yassine's brother, Salaheddin. Salaheddin can sue the paper for putting him in a false light by using his photo. If the report is not true, and Yassine is not involved with ISIL, Yassine can sue the paper for defamation. ■

3. *Public disclosure of private facts.* This type of invasion of privacy occurs when a person publicly discloses private facts about an individual that an ordinary person would find objectionable or embarrassing. A newspaper account of a private citizen's sex life or financial affairs could be an actionable invasion of

## DIGITAL UPDATE — Revenge Porn and Invasion of Privacy

Nearly every digital device today takes photos and videos at virtually no cost. Software allows the recording of conversations via Skype. Many couples immortalize their "private moments" using such digital devices. One partner may take a racy selfie and send it as an attachment to a text message to the other partner, for example.

Occasionally, after a couple breaks off their relationship, one of them seeks a type of digital revenge. The result, called revenge porn, has been defined in the Cyber Civil Rights Initiative as "the online distribution of sexually explicit images of a non-consenting individual with the intent to humiliate that person."

Until relatively recently, few states had criminal statutes that covered revenge porn. Therefore, victims have sued on the basis of (1) invasion of privacy, (2) public disclosure of private facts, and (3) intentional infliction of emotional distress.

### It Is More Than Just Pictures and Videos

Perhaps the worst form of revenge porn occurs when the perpetrator provides detailed information about the victim. Such information may include the victim's name, Facebook page, address, and phone number, as well as the victim's workplace and children's names. This information, along with the sexually explicit photos and videos, are posted on hosting Web sites. Many such Web sites have been shut down, as was the case with IsAnybodyDown? and Texxxan.com. But others are still active, usually with offshore servers and foreign domain name owners.

### The Injurious Results of Revenge Porn

Of course, victims of revenge porn suffer extreme embarrassment. They may also have their reputations ruined. Some have lost their jobs. Others have been unable to obtain jobs because employers have seen their pictures online. A number of victims have been stalked in the physical world and harassed online and offline. When attempts to have offending photos removed from Web sites have failed, victims have changed their phone numbers and sometimes their names.

### A Class-Action Lawsuit

Hollie Toups, along with twenty-two other female plaintiffs, sued the domain name registrar and Web hosting company GoDaddy in a Texas court. Although GoDaddy did not create the defamatory and offensive material at issue, GoDaddy knew of the content and did not remove it. The plaintiffs asserted causes of action "for intentional infliction of emotional distress," among other claims.

Additionally, the plaintiffs argued that "by its knowing participation in these unlawful activities, GoDaddy has also committed the intentional Texas tort of invasion of privacy . . . as well as intrusion on Plaintiffs' right to seclusion, the public disclosure of their private facts, [and] the wrongful appropriation of their names and likenesses. . . ." GoDaddy sought to dismiss the case, and an appeals court eventually granted the motion to dismiss.[a]

Another Texas woman had better luck. The woman's ex-boyfriend had uploaded videos of her to YouTube and other sites. At the time she made the complaint, revenge porn was not a crime in Texas. Nevertheless, in a jury trial in 2014, she won a $500,000 award. Since then, a handful of states have made revenge porn a crime. In 2015, a California man, Kevin Bollaert, was convicted for creating a revenge porn Web site and sentenced to serve eighteen years in prison.

**Critical Thinking** *Should domain name hosting companies be liable for revenge porn?*

a. *GoDaddy.com, LLC. v. Toups*, 429 S.W.3d 752 (Tex.App.—Beaumont 2014).

---

privacy. This is so even if the information revealed is true, because it should not be a matter of public concern.

4. *Appropriation of identity.* Using a person's name, picture, likeness, or other identifiable characteristic for commercial purposes without permission is also an invasion of privacy. An individual's right to privacy normally includes the right to the exclusive use of her or his identity. ■ **EXAMPLE 8.14** An advertising agency asks a singer with a distinctive voice and stage presence to take part in a marketing campaign for a new automobile. The singer rejects the offer. If the

agency then uses someone who imitates the singer's voice and dance moves in the ad, it will be actionable as an appropriation of identity. ■

**Appropriation Statutes** Most states today have codified the common law tort of appropriation of identity in statutes that establish the distinct tort of appropriation, or right of publicity. States differ as to the degree of likeness that is required to impose liability for appropriation, however.

Some courts have held that even when an animated character in a video or a video game is made to look like an actual person, there are not enough similarities to constitute appropriation. ■ **CASE IN POINT 8.15** Robert Burck is a street entertainer in New York City who has become famous as "The Naked Cowboy." Burck performs wearing only a white cowboy hat, white cowboy boots, and white underwear. He carries a guitar strategically placed to give the illusion of nudity. Burck sued Mars, Inc., the maker of M&Ms candy, over a video it showed on billboards in Times Square that depicted a blue M&M dressed exactly like The Naked Cowboy. The court, however, held that the use of Burck's signature costume did not amount to appropriation.[11] ■

---

11. *Burck v. Mars, Inc.*, 571 F.Supp.2d 446 (S.D.N.Y. 2008).

## 8–2g Fraudulent Misrepresentation

A misrepresentation leads another to believe in a condition that is different from the condition that actually exists. Although persons sometimes make misrepresentations accidentally because they are unaware of the existing facts, the tort of **fraudulent misrepresentation (fraud),** involves *intentional* deceit for personal gain. The tort includes several elements:

1. A misrepresentation of material facts or conditions with knowledge that they are false or with reckless disregard for the truth.
2. An intent to induce another party to rely on the misrepresentation.
3. A justifiable reliance on the misrepresentation by the deceived party.
4. Damages suffered as a result of that reliance.
5. A causal connection between the misrepresentation and the injury suffered.

For fraud to occur, more than mere **puffery,** or *seller's talk,* must be involved. Fraud exists only when a person represents as a fact something he or she knows is untrue. For instance, it is fraud to claim that the roof of a building does not leak when one knows that it does. Facts are objectively ascertainable, whereas seller's talk (such as "I am the best accountant in town") is not, because the use of the word *best* is subjective.

In the following case, the court considered each of the elements of fraud.

**Case 8.2**

# Revell v. Guido

New York Supreme Court, Appellate Division, Third Department, 124 A.D.3d 1006, 2 N.Y.S.3d 252 (2015).

**Background and Facts** Joseph Guido bought a parcel of land in Stillwater, New York, that contained nine rental houses. The houses shared a waste disposal system that was defective. Guido had a new septic system installed. When town officials discovered sewage on the property, Guido had the system partially replaced. Prospective buyers, including Danny Revell, were given a property information sheet that stated, "Septic system totally new—each field totally replaced." In response to a questionnaire from the buyers' bank, Guido denied any knowledge of environmental problems.

A month after the buyers bought the houses, the septic system failed and required substantial repairs. The lender foreclosed on the property. The buyers filed a suit in a New York state court against Guido and his firm, Real Property Solutions, LLC, alleging fraud. A jury found fraud and awarded damages. The court issued a judgment in the plaintiffs' favor. The defendants appealed.

### In the Language of the Court

*EGAN,* Jr., J.: [Judge:]
  \* \* \* \*

To prevail upon their cause of action for fraud, plaintiffs were required to establish that defendants, with the intent to deceive, misrepresented or omitted a material fact that they knew to be false and that plaintiffs,

Case 8.2 Continued

*in turn, justifiably relied upon such misrepresentation or omission, thereby incurring damages.* As to the misrepresentation element, plaintiffs point to the statement made on the property information sheet * * * , as well as Guido's responses to certain of the inquiries contained on the environmental questionnaire. In this regard, the record reflects that the [replacement] septic system * * * was not "totally new," as it retained the original pump house structure and, more to the point, utilized the holding tanks that originally were part of the system * * * . There also is no question that Guido provided false answers to various inquiries posed on the environmental questionnaire. For example, Guido disavowed any knowledge of "governmental notification relating to past or recurrent violations of environmental laws with respect to the property * * * "—despite having been advised by the Town of Stillwater * * * that partially treated sewage was discovered on the property. [Emphasis added.]

As to the intent element, * * * given the arguably cavalier [offhand] manner in which Guido completed the environmental questionnaire, as well as his extensive knowledge regarding the * * * problems with the original septic system * * * , the jury could properly find that Guido made the cited misrepresentations with the intent to deceive plaintiffs.

With respect to the issue of justifiable reliance, Revell * * * conducted a visual inspection of the property prior to making an offer and did not observe any conditions indicative of a problem with the septic system. * * * If a septic system was represented to be "totally new" and a visual inspection of the property did not reveal any red flags, [that is,] boggy areas, odors or liquids bubbling up to the surface, one would assume that the system was working properly. * * * The jury [could] find that plaintiffs' reliance upon the representation contained in the property information sheet was reasonable.

* * * *

Nor are we persuaded that plaintiffs failed to tender sufficient admissible proof to substantiate the damages awarded by the jury. During the trial, the parties stipulated to the admission into evidence of a binder containing, among other things, an abundance of receipts, invoices, billing statements and canceled checks detailing plaintiffs' expenditures related to the subject property—and plaintiffs' forensic accountant, in turn, utilized such documents to arrive at a damages figure. * * * We are satisfied that plaintiffs tendered sufficient admissible proof to sustain the damages awarded by the jury.

**Decision and Remedy**  *The state intermediate appellate court affirmed the lower court's judgment in the plaintiffs' favor. The facts of the case and the plaintiffs' proof met all of the requirements for establishing fraud.*

### Critical Thinking

- **Legal Environment**  *Financing for the purchase of the property was conditioned on the bank's review of Guido's answers to the environmental questionnaire. How could the court conclude that the plaintiffs justifiably relied on misrepresentations made to the bank? Explain.*
- **What If the Facts Were Different?**  *If a visual inspection of the property had revealed "boggy areas, odors or liquids bubbling up to the surface" indicating that the septic system was not working properly, would the outcome of this case have been different?*

---

**Statement of Fact versus Opinion**  Normally, the tort of fraudulent misrepresentation occurs only when there is reliance on a *statement of fact*. Sometimes, however, reliance on a *statement of opinion* may involve the tort of fraudulent misrepresentation if the individual making the statement of opinion has superior knowledge of the subject matter. For instance, when a lawyer makes a statement of opinion about the law in a state in which the lawyer is licensed to practice, a court might treat it as a statement of fact.

**Negligent Misrepresentation**  Sometimes, a tort action can arise from misrepresentations that are made negligently rather than intentionally. The key difference between intentional and negligent misrepresentation is whether the person making the misrepresentation had actual knowledge of its falsity. Negligent misrepresentation requires only that the person making the statement or omission did not have a reasonable basis for believing its truthfulness.

Liability for negligent misrepresentation usually arises when the defendant who made the misrepresentation owed a duty of care to the plaintiff to supply correct information. (We discuss the duty of care in more detail later in the chapter.) Statements or omissions made by attorneys and accountants to their clients, for instance, can lead to liability for negligent misrepresentation.

## 8–2h Abusive or Frivolous Litigation

Tort law recognizes that people have a right not to be sued without a legally just and proper reason, and therefore it protects individuals from the misuse of litigation. Torts related to abusive litigation include malicious prosecution and abuse of process. If a party initiates a lawsuit out of malice and without a legitimate legal reason, and ends up losing the suit, that party can be sued for *malicious prosecution*. *Abuse of process* can apply to any person using a legal process against another in an improper manner or to accomplish a purpose for which the process was not designed.

The key difference between the torts of abuse of process and malicious prosecution is the level of proof. Unlike malicious prosecution, abuse of process is not limited to prior litigation and does not require the plaintiff to prove malice. It can be based on the wrongful use of subpoenas, court orders to attach or seize real property, or other types of formal legal process.

Concept Summary 8.1 reviews intentional torts against persons.

---

## Concept Summary 8.1

### Intentional Torts against Persons

| | |
|---|---|
| **Assault and Battery** | Any unexcused and intentional act that causes another person to be apprehensive of immediate harm is an assault. An assault resulting in physical contact is a battery. |
| **False Imprisonment** | An intentional confinement or restraint of another person's movement without justification. |
| **Intentional Infliction of Emotional Distress** | An intentional act that amounts to extreme and outrageous conduct resulting in severe emotional distress to another. |
| **Defamation (Libel or Slander)** | A false statement of fact, not made under privilege, that is communicated to a third person and that causes damage to a person's reputation. For public figures, the plaintiff must also prove that the statement was made with actual malice. |
| **Invasion of Privacy** | Publishing or otherwise making known or using information relating to a person's private life and affairs, with which the public has no legitimate concern, without that person's permission or approval. |
| **Fraudulent Misrepresentation (Fraud)** | A false representation made by one party, through misstatement of facts or through conduct, with the intention of deceiving another and on which the other reasonably relies to his or her detriment. |
| **Abusive or Frivolous Litigation** | The filing of a lawsuit without legitimate grounds and with malice. Alternatively, the use of a legal process in an improper manner. |

## 8–2i Wrongful Interference

The torts known as *business torts* generally involve wrongful interference with another's business rights. Public policy favors free competition, and these torts protect against tortious interference with legitimate business. Business torts involving wrongful interference generally fall into two categories: interference with a contractual relationship and interference with a business relationship.

**Wrongful Interference with a Contractual Relationship** Three elements are necessary for wrongful interference with a contractual relationship to occur:

1. A valid, enforceable contract must exist between two parties.
2. A third party must know that this contract exists.
3. This third party must *intentionally induce* a party to the contract to breach the contract.

■ **CASE IN POINT 8.16** A landmark case in this area involved an opera singer, Joanna Wagner, who was under contract to sing for a man named Lumley for a specified period of years. A man named Gye, who knew of this contract, nonetheless "enticed" Wagner to refuse to carry out the agreement, and Wagner began to sing for Gye. Gye's action constituted a tort because it interfered with the contractual relationship between Wagner and Lumley. (Wagner's refusal to carry out the agreement also entitled Lumley to sue Wagner for breach of contract.)[12] ■

The body of tort law relating to wrongful interference with a contractual relationship has increased greatly in recent years. In principle, any lawful contract can be the basis for an action of this type. The contract could be between a firm and its employees or a firm and its customers. Sometimes, a competitor of a firm lures away one of the firm's key employees. In this situation, the original employer can recover damages from the competitor only if it can be shown that the competitor knew of the contract's existence and intentionally induced the breach.

**Wrongful Interference with a Business Relationship** Businesspersons devise countless schemes to attract customers. They are prohibited, however, from unreasonably interfering with another's business in their attempts to gain a greater share of the market.

There is a difference between *competitive practices* and *predatory behavior*—actions undertaken with the intention of unlawfully driving competitors completely out of the market. Attempting to attract customers in general is a legitimate business practice, whereas specifically

targeting the customers of a competitor is more likely to be predatory. A plaintiff claiming predatory behavior must show that the defendant used predatory methods to intentionally harm an established business relationship or gain a prospective economic advantage.

■ **EXAMPLE 8.17** A shopping mall contains two athletic shoe stores: Joe's and Ultimate Sport. Joe's cannot station an employee at the entrance of Ultimate Sport's to divert customers to Joe's by telling them that Joe's will beat Ultimate Sport's prices. This type of activity constitutes the tort of wrongful interference with a business relationship, which is commonly considered to be an unfair trade practice. If this activity were permitted, Joe's would reap the benefits of Ultimate Sport's advertising. ■

**Defenses to Wrongful Interference** A person will not be liable for the tort of wrongful interference with a contractual or business relationship if it can be shown that the interference was justified or permissible. Bona fide competitive behavior—such as marketing and advertising strategies—is a permissible interference even if it results in the breaking of a contract.

■ **EXAMPLE 8.18** Taylor Meats advertises so effectively that it induces Sam's Restaurant to break its contract with Burke's Meat Company. In that situation, Burke's Meat Company will be unable to recover against Taylor Meats on a wrongful interference theory. The public policy that favors free competition through advertising outweighs any possible instability that such competitive activity might cause in contractual relations. ■

# 8–3 Intentional Torts against Property

Intentional torts against property include trespass to land, trespass to personal property, conversion, and disparagement of property. These torts are wrongful actions that interfere with individuals' legally recognized rights with regard to their land or personal property.

The law distinguishes real property from personal property. *Real property* is land and things permanently attached to the land, such as a house. *Personal property* consists of all other items, including cash and securities (such as stocks and bonds).

## 8–3a Trespass to Land

A **trespass to land** occurs when a person, without permission, does any of the following:

---

12. *Lumley v. Gye*, 118 Eng.Rep. 749 (1853).

1. Enters onto, above, or below the surface of land that is owned by another.
2. Causes anything to enter onto land owned by another.
3. Remains on land owned by another or permits anything to remain on it.

Actual harm to the land is not an essential element of this tort, because the tort is designed to protect the right of an owner to exclusive possession.

Common types of trespass to land include walking or driving on another's land, shooting a gun over another's land, and throwing rocks at a building that belongs to someone else. Another common form of trespass involves constructing a building so that part of it extends onto an adjoining landowner's property.

**Establishing Trespass** Before a person can be a trespasser, the real property owner (or another person in actual and exclusive possession of the property, such as a renter) must establish that person as a trespasser. For instance, "posted" trespass signs expressly establish as a trespasser a person who ignores these signs and enters onto the property. A guest in your home is not a trespasser, unless he or she has been asked to leave and refuses. Any person who enters onto another's property to commit an illegal act (such as a thief entering a lumberyard at night to steal lumber) is impliedly a trespasser, with or without posted signs.

**Liability for Harm** At common law, a trespasser is liable for any damage caused to the property and generally cannot hold the owner liable for injuries that the trespasser sustains on the premises. This common law rule is being modified in many jurisdictions, however, in favor of a *reasonable duty of care* rule that varies depending on the status of the parties.

For instance, a landowner may have a duty to post a notice that guard dogs patrol the property. Also, if young children are attracted to the property by some object, such a swimming pool or a sand pile, and are injured, the landowner may be held liable (under the *attractive nuisance doctrine*). Still, an owner can normally use reasonable force to remove a trespasser from the premises or detain the trespasser for a reasonable time without liability for damages.

**Defenses against Trespass to Land** One defense to a claim of trespass is to show that the trespass was warranted, such as when a trespasser enters a building to assist someone in danger. Another defense exists when the trespasser can show that she or he had a *license* to come onto the land.

A **licensee** is one who is invited (or allowed to enter) onto the property of another for the licensee's benefit. A person who enters another's property to read an electric meter, for example, is a licensee. When you purchase a ticket to attend a movie or sporting event, you are licensed to go onto the property of another to view that movie or event.

Note that licenses to enter onto another's property are *revocable* by the property owner. If a property owner asks an electric meter reader to leave and she or he refuses to do so, the meter reader at that point becomes a trespasser.

### 8–3b Trespass to Personal Property

Whenever any individual wrongfully takes or harms the personal property of another or otherwise interferes with the lawful owner's possession and enjoyment of personal property, **trespass to personal property** occurs. This tort may also be called *trespass to chattels* or *trespass to personalty*.[13] In this context, harm means not only destruction of the property, but also anything that diminishes its value, condition, or quality.

Trespass to personal property involves intentional meddling with a possessory interest (one arising from possession), including barring an owner's access to personal property. ■ **EXAMPLE 8.19** Kelly takes Ryan's business law book as a practical joke and hides it so that Ryan is unable to find it for several days before the final examination. Here, Kelly has engaged in a trespass to personal property (and also *conversion,* the tort discussed next). ■

If it can be shown that trespass to personal property was warranted, then a complete defense exists. Most states, for instance, allow automobile repair shops to hold a customer's car (under what is called an *artisan's lien*) when the customer refuses to pay for repairs already completed.

### 8–3c Conversion

Any act that deprives an owner of personal property or of the use of that property without the owner's permission and without just cause can constitute **conversion.** Even the taking of electronic records and data may form the basis of a conversion claim. Often, when conversion occurs, a trespass to personal property also occurs. The original taking of the personal property from the owner was a trespass. Wrongfully retaining the property is conversion.

---

13. Pronounced *per*-sun-ul-tee.

**Failure to Return Goods** Conversion is the civil side of crimes related to theft, but it is not limited to theft. Even when the rightful owner consented to the initial taking of the property, so no theft or trespass occurred, a failure to return the property may still be conversion. ■ **EXAMPLE 8.20** Chen borrows Mark's iPad mini to use while traveling home from school for the holidays. When Chen returns to school, Mark asks for his iPad back, but Chen says that he gave it to his little brother for Christmas. In this situation, Mark can sue Chen for conversion, and Chen will have to either return the iPad or pay damages equal to its replacement value. ■

**Intention** Conversion can occur even when a person mistakenly believed that she or he was entitled to the goods. In other words, good intentions are not a defense against conversion. Someone who buys stolen goods, for instance, may be sued for conversion even if he or she did not know the goods were stolen. If the true owner of the goods sues the buyer, the buyer must either return the property to the owner or pay the owner the full value of the property.

Conversion can also occur from an employee's unauthorized use of a credit card. ■ **CASE IN POINT 8.21** Nicholas Mora worked for Welco Electronics, Inc., but had also established his own company, AQM Supplies. Mora used Welco's credit card without permission and deposited more than $375,000 into AQM's account, which he then transferred to his personal account. Welco sued. A California court held that Mora was liable for conversion. The court reasoned that when Mora misappropriated Welco's credit card and used it, he took part of Welco's credit balance with the credit-card company.[14] ■

### 8-3d Disparagement of Property

**Disparagement of property** occurs when economically injurious falsehoods are made about another's product or property rather than about another's reputation (as in the tort of defamation). *Disparagement of property* is a general term for torts that can be more specifically referred to as *slander of quality* or *slander of title*.

**Slander of Quality** The publication of false information about another's product, alleging that it is not what its seller claims, constitutes the tort of **slander of quality,** or **trade libel.** To establish trade libel, the plaintiff must prove that the improper publication caused a third

person to refrain from dealing with the plaintiff and that the plaintiff sustained economic damages (such as lost profits) as a result.

An improper publication may be both a slander of quality and a defamation of character. For instance, a statement that disparages the quality of a product may also, by implication, disparage the character of a person who would sell such a product.

**Slander of Title** When a publication falsely denies or casts doubt on another's legal ownership of property, resulting in financial loss to the property's owner, the tort of **slander of title** occurs. Usually, this is an intentional tort in which someone knowingly publishes an untrue statement about another's ownership of certain property with the intent of discouraging a third person from dealing with the person slandered. For instance, it would be difficult for a car dealer to attract customers after competitors published a notice that the dealer's stock consisted of stolen automobiles.

See Concept Summary 8.2 for a review of intentional torts against property.

## 8-4 Unintentional Torts—Negligence

The tort of **negligence** occurs when someone suffers injury because of another's failure to live up to a required *duty of care*. In contrast to intentional torts, in torts involving negligence, the tortfeasor neither wishes to bring about the consequences of the act nor believes that they will occur. The person's conduct merely creates a risk of such consequences. If no risk is created, there is no negligence.

Moreover, the risk must be foreseeable. In other words, it must be such that a reasonable person engaging in the same activity would anticipate the risk and guard against it. In determining what is reasonable conduct, courts consider the nature of the possible harm.

Many of the actions giving rise to the intentional torts discussed earlier in the chapter constitute negligence if the element of intent is missing (or cannot be proved). ■ **EXAMPLE 8.22** Juan walks up to Maya and intentionally shoves her. Maya falls and breaks her arm as a result. In this situation, Juan is liable for the intentional tort of battery. If Juan carelessly bumps into Maya, however, and she falls and breaks her arm as a result, Juan's action constitutes negligence. In either situation, Juan has committed a tort. ■

---

**14.** *Welco Electronics, Inc. v. Mora,* 223 Cal.App.4th 202, 166 Cal.Rptr.3d 877 (2014).

## Concept Summary 8.2

### Intentional Torts against Property

| | |
|---|---|
| **Trespass to Land** | The invasion of another's real property without consent or privilege. Once a person is expressly or impliedly established as a trespasser, the property owner has specific rights, which may include the right to detain or remove the trespasser. |
| **Trespass to Personal Property** | The intentional interference with an owner's right to use, possess, or enjoy his or her personal property without the owner's consent. |
| **Conversion** | The wrongful possession or use of another person's personal property without just cause. |
| **Disparagement of Property** | Any economically injurious falsehood that is made about another's product or property; an inclusive term for the torts of *slander of quality* and *slander of title*. |

To succeed in a negligence action, the plaintiff must prove each of the following:

1. *Duty.* The defendant owed a duty of care to the plaintiff.
2. *Breach.* The defendant breached that duty.
3. *Causation.* The defendant's breach caused the plaintiff's injury.
4. *Damages.* The plaintiff suffered a legally recognizable injury.

### 8–4a The Duty of Care and Its Breach

Central to the tort of negligence is the concept of a **duty of care.** The basic principle underlying the duty of care is that people are free to act as they please so long as their actions do not infringe on the interests of others. When someone fails to comply with the duty to exercise reasonable care, a potentially tortious act may have been committed.

Failure to live up to a standard of care may be an act (accidentally setting fire to a building) or an omission (neglecting to put out a campfire). It may be a careless act or a carefully performed but nevertheless dangerous act that results in injury. In determining whether the duty of care has been breached, courts consider several factors:

1. The nature of the act (whether it is outrageous or commonplace).
2. The manner in which the act was performed (cautiously versus heedlessly).
3. The nature of the injury (whether it is serious or slight).

Creating even a very slight risk of a dangerous explosion might be unreasonable, whereas creating a distinct possibility of someone's burning his or her fingers on a stove might be reasonable.

**The Reasonable Person Standard** Tort law measures duty by the **reasonable person standard.** In determining whether a duty of care has been breached, the courts ask how a reasonable person would have acted in the same circumstances. The reasonable person standard is said to be objective. It is not necessarily how a particular person *would* act. It is society's judgment of how an ordinarily prudent person *should* act. If the so-called reasonable person existed, he or she would be careful, conscientious, even tempered, and honest.

The degree of care to be exercised varies, depending on the defendant's occupation or profession, her or his relationship with the plaintiff, and other factors. Generally, whether an action constitutes a breach of the duty of care is determined on a case-by-case basis. The outcome depends on how the judge (or jury) decides that a reasonable person in the position of the defendant would have acted in the particular circumstances of the case.

Note that the courts frequently use the reasonable person standard in other areas of law as well as in negligence cases. Indeed, the principle that individuals are required to exercise a reasonable standard of care in their activities is a pervasive concept in business law.

**The Duty of Landowners** Landowners are expected to exercise reasonable care to protect individuals coming onto their property from harm. In some jurisdictions, landowners may even have a duty to protect trespassers against certain risks. Landowners who rent or lease premises to tenants are expected to exercise reasonable care to ensure that the tenants and their guests are not harmed in common areas, such as stairways, entryways, and laundry rooms.

**The Duty to Warn Business Invitees of Risks.** Retailers and other business operators who explicitly or implicitly invite persons to come onto their premises have a duty to exercise reasonable care to protect these **business invitees.** The duty normally requires storeowners to warn business invitees of foreseeable risks, such as construction zones or wet floors, about which the owners knew or *should have known.*

■ **EXAMPLE 8.23** Liz enters Kwan's neighborhood market, slips on a wet floor, and sustains injuries as a result. If there was no sign or other warning that the floor was wet at the time Liz slipped, the owner, Kwan, would be liable for damages. A court would hold that Kwan was negligent because he failed to exercise a reasonable degree of care to protect customers against foreseeable risks about which he knew or should have known. That a patron might slip on the wet floor and be injured was a foreseeable risk, and Kwan should have taken care to avoid this risk or warn the customer of it. ■

A business owner also has a duty to discover and remove any hidden dangers that might injure a customer or other invitee. Hidden dangers might include uneven surfaces or defects in the pavement of a parking lot or a walkway, or merchandise that has fallen off shelves in a store.

**Obvious Risks Provide an Exception.** Some risks are so obvious that an owner need not warn of them. For instance, a business owner does not need to warn customers to open a door before attempting to walk through it. Other risks, however, even though they may seem obvious

to a business owner, may not be so in the eyes of another, such as a child. In addition, even if a risk is obvious, a business owner is not necessarily excused from the duty to protect customers from foreseeable harm from that risk.

■ **CASE IN POINT 8.24** Giorgio's Grill is a restaurant in Florida that becomes a nightclub after hours. At those times, traditionally, as the manager of Giorgio's knew, the staff and customers throw paper napkins into the air as the music plays. The napkins land on the floor, but no one picks them up. One night, Jane Izquierdo went to Giorgio's. Although she had been to the club on prior occasions and knew about the napkin-throwing tradition, she slipped and fell, breaking her leg. She sued Giorgio's for negligence, but lost at trial because a jury found that the risk of slipping on the napkins was obvious. A state appellate court reversed, however, holding that the obviousness of a risk does not discharge a business owner's duty to its invitees to maintain the premises in a safe condition.[15] ■

**The Duty of Professionals** Persons who possess superior knowledge, skill, or training are held to a higher standard of care than others. Professionals—including physicians, dentists, architects, engineers, accountants, and lawyers, among others—are required to have a standard minimum level of special knowledge and ability. In determining what constitutes reasonable care in the case of professionals, the law takes their training and expertise into account. Thus, an accountant's conduct is judged not by the reasonable person standard, but by the reasonable accountant standard.

If a professional violates his or her duty of care toward a client, the client may bring a suit against the professional, alleging **malpractice,** which is essentially professional negligence. For instance, a patient might sue a physician for *medical malpractice.* A client might sue an attorney for *legal malpractice.*

## 8–4b Causation

Another element necessary to a negligence action is *causation.* If a person breaches a duty of care and someone suffers injury, the person's act must have caused the harm for it to constitute the tort of negligence.

**Courts Ask Two Questions** In deciding whether the requirement of causation is met, the court must address two questions:

---

15. *Izquierdo v. Gyroscope, Inc.*, 946 So.2d 115 (Fla.App. 2007).

1. *Is there causation in fact?* Did the injury occur because of the defendant's act, or would it have occurred anyway? If the injury would not have occurred without the defendant's act, then there is causation in fact.

   **Causation in fact** usually can be determined by use of the *but for* test: "but for" the wrongful act, the injury would not have occurred. This test seeks to determine whether there was a cause-and-effect relationship between the act and the injury suffered. In theory, causation in fact is limitless. One could claim, for example, that "but for" the creation of the world, a particular injury would not have occurred. Thus, as a practical matter, the law has to establish limits, and it does so through the concept of proximate cause.

2. *Was the act the proximate, or legal, cause of the injury?* **Proximate cause,** or *legal cause,* exists when the connection between an act and an injury is strong enough to justify imposing liability. Proximate cause asks whether the injuries sustained were foreseeable or were too remotely connected to the incident to trigger liability. Judges use proximate cause to limit the scope of the defendant's liability to a subset of the total number of potential plaintiffs that might have been harmed by the defendant's actions.

   ■ **EXAMPLE 8.25** Ackerman carelessly leaves a campfire burning. The fire not only burns down the forest but also sets off an explosion in a nearby chemical plant that spills chemicals into a river, killing all the fish for twenty miles downstream and ruining the economy of a tourist resort. Should Ackerman be liable to the resort owners? To the tourists whose vacations were ruined? These are questions of proximate cause that a court must decide. ■

Both of these causation questions must be answered in the affirmative for liability in tort to arise. If there is causation in fact but a court decides that the defendant's action is not the proximate cause of the plaintiff's injury, the causation requirement has not been met. Therefore, the defendant normally will not be liable to the plaintiff.

**Foreseeability** Questions of proximate cause are linked to the concept of foreseeability because it would be unfair to impose liability on a defendant unless the defendant's actions created a foreseeable risk of injury. Generally, if the victim or the consequences of a harm done were unforeseeable, there is no proximate cause.

Probably the most cited case on the concept of foreseeability and proximate cause is the *Palsgraf* case, which established foreseeability as the test for proximate cause. ■ **CASE IN POINT 8.26** Helen Palsgraf was waiting for a train on a station platform. A man carrying a package was rushing to catch a train that was moving away from a platform across

the tracks from Palsgraf. As the man attempted to jump aboard the moving train, he seemed unsteady and about to fall. A railroad guard on the car reached forward to grab him, and another guard on the platform pushed him from behind to help him board the train.

In the process, the man's package, which (unknown to the railroad guards) contained fireworks, fell on the railroad tracks and exploded. There was nothing about the package to indicate its contents. The repercussions of the explosion caused weighing scales at the other end of the train platform to fall on Palsgraf, causing injuries for which she sued the railroad company. At the trial, the jury found that the railroad guards had been negligent in their conduct. The railroad company appealed. New York's highest state court held that the railroad company was not liable to Palsgraf. The railroad had not been negligent toward her, because injury to her was not foreseeable.[16] ■

## 8–4c The Injury Requirement and Damages

For tort liability to arise, the plaintiff must have suffered a *legally recognizable* injury. To recover damages, the plaintiff must have suffered some loss, harm, wrong, or invasion of a protected interest. Essentially, the purpose of tort law is to compensate for legally recognized harms and injuries resulting from wrongful acts. If no harm or injury results from a given negligent action, there is nothing to compensate, and no tort exists.

For instance, if you carelessly bump into a passerby, who stumbles and falls as a result, you may be liable in tort if the passerby is injured in the fall. If the person is unharmed, however, there normally can be no lawsuit for damages, because no injury was suffered.

Compensatory damages are the norm in negligence cases. A court will award punitive damages only if the defendant's conduct was grossly negligent, reflecting an intentional failure to perform a duty with reckless disregard of the consequences to others.

## 8–4d Good Samaritan Statutes

Most states now have what are called **Good Samaritan statutes.**[17] Under these statutes, someone who is aided voluntarily by another cannot turn around and sue the "Good Samaritan" for negligence. These laws were passed largely to protect physicians and medical personnel who

---

16. *Palsgraf v. Long Island Railroad Co.,* 248 N.Y. 339, 162 N.E. 99 (1928).
17. These laws derive their name from the Good Samaritan story in the Bible. In the story, a traveler who had been robbed and beaten lay along the roadside, ignored by those passing by. Eventually, a man from the region of Samaria (the "Good Samaritan") stopped to render assistance to the injured person.

volunteer their services in emergency situations to those in need, such as individuals hurt in car accidents.

### 8–4e Dram Shop Acts

Many states have also passed **dram shop acts,**[18] under which a bar's owner or bartender may be held liable for injuries caused by a person who became intoxicated while drinking at the bar. The owner or bartender may also be held responsible for continuing to serve a person who was already intoxicated.

Some states' statutes also impose liability on *social hosts* (persons hosting parties) for injuries caused by guests who became intoxicated at the hosts' homes. Under these statutes, it is unnecessary to prove that the bar owner, bartender, or social host was negligent. ■ **EXAMPLE 8.27** Jane hosts a Super Bowl party at which Brett, a minor, sneaks alcoholic drinks. Jane is potentially liable for damages resulting from Brett's drunk driving after the party. ■

## 8–5 Defenses to Negligence

Defendants often defend against negligence claims by asserting that the plaintiffs have failed to prove

---

18. Historically, a dram was a small unit of liquid, and distilled spirits (strong alcoholic liquor) were sold in drams. Thus, a dram shop was a place where liquor was sold in drams.

the existence of one or more of the required elements for negligence. Additionally, there are three basic *affirmative* defenses in negligence cases (defenses that a defendant can use to avoid liability even if the facts are as the plaintiff states): *assumption of risk, superseding cause,* and *contributory and comparative negligence.*

### 8–5a Assumption of Risk

A plaintiff who voluntarily enters into a risky situation, knowing the risk involved, will not be allowed to recover. This is the defense of **assumption of risk,** which requires two elements:

1. Knowledge of the risk.
2. Voluntary assumption of the risk.

The defense of assumption of risk is frequently asserted when the plaintiff was injured during a recreational activity that involves known risk, such as skiing or skydiving. (Courts do not apply the assumption of risk doctrine in emergency situations.)

Assumption of risk can apply not only to participants in sporting events, but also to spectators and bystanders who are injured while attending those events. In the following *Spotlight Case,* the issue was whether a spectator at a baseball game voluntarily assumed the risk of being hit by an errant ball thrown while the players were warming up before the game.

## Spotlight on the Seattle Mariners

### Case 8.3 Taylor v. Baseball Club of Seattle, LP
Court of Appeals of Washington, 132 Wash.App. 32, 130 P.3d 835 (2006).

**Background and Facts** Delinda Taylor went to a Seattle Mariners baseball game at Safeco Field with her boyfriend and her two minor sons. Their seats were four rows up from the field along the right field foul line. They arrived more than an hour before the game so that they could see the players warm up and get their autographs. When she walked in, Taylor saw that a Mariners pitcher, Freddy Garcia, was throwing a ball back and forth with José Mesa right in front of their seats.

As Taylor stood in front of her seat, she looked away from the field, and a ball thrown by Mesa got past Garcia and struck her in the face, causing serious injuries. Taylor sued the Mariners for the allegedly negligent warm-up throw. The Mariners filed a motion for summary judgment in which they argued that Taylor, a longtime Mariners fan, was familiar with baseball and the inherent risk of balls entering the stands. Thus, the motion asserted, Taylor had assumed the risk of her injury. The trial court granted the motion and dismissed Taylor's case. Taylor appealed.

### In the Language of the Court
DWYER, J. [Judge]
* * * *

* * * For many decades, courts have required baseball stadiums to screen some seats—generally those behind home plate—to provide protection to spectators who choose it.

Case 8.3 Continues

Case 8.3 Continued

A sport spectator's assumption of risk and a defendant sports team's duty of care are accordingly discerned under the doctrine of primary assumption of risk. * * * "Implied *primary* assumption of risk arises where a plaintiff has impliedly consented (often in advance of any negligence by defendant) to relieve defendant of a duty to plaintiff regarding specific *known* and appreciated risks."

* * * *

Under this implied primary assumption of risk, defendant must show that plaintiff had full subjective understanding of the specific risk, both its nature and presence, and that he or she voluntarily chose to encounter the risk.

* * * It is undisputed that the warm-up is part of the sport, that spectators such as Taylor purposely attend that portion of the event, and that the Mariners permit ticket-holders to view the warm-up.

* * * We find the fact that Taylor was injured during warm-up is not legally significant because that portion of the event is necessarily incident to the game.

* * * *

Here, there is no evidence that the circumstances leading to Taylor's injury constituted an unusual danger. It is undisputed that it is the normal, every-day practice at all levels of baseball for pitchers to warm up in the manner that led to this incident. *The risk of injuries such as Taylor's are within the normal comprehension of a spectator who is familiar with the game.* Indeed, the possibility of an errant ball entering the stands is part of the game's attraction for many spectators. [Emphasis added.]

* * * The record contains substantial evidence regarding Taylor's familiarity with the game. She attended many of her sons' baseball games, she witnessed balls entering the stands, she had watched Mariners' games both at the Kingdome and on television, and she knew that there was no screen protecting her seats, which were close to the field. In fact, as she walked to her seat she saw the players warming up and was excited about being in an unscreened area where her party might get autographs from the players and catch balls.

**Decision and Remedy**   *The state intermediate appellate court affirmed the lower court's judgment. As a spectator who chose to sit in an unprotected area of seats, Taylor voluntarily undertook the risk associated with being hit by an errant baseball thrown during the warm-up before the game.*

**Critical Thinking**

- **What If the Facts Were Different?**  *Would the result in this case have been different if it had been Taylor's minor son, rather than Taylor herself, who had been struck by the ball? Should courts apply the doctrine of assumption of risk to children? Discuss.*
- **Legal Environment**  *What is the basis underlying the defense of assumption of risk? How does that basis support the court's decision in this case?*

---

## 8–5b Superseding Cause

An unforeseeable intervening event may break the causal connection between a wrongful act and an injury to another. If so, the intervening event acts as a **superseding cause**—that is, it relieves the defendant of liability for injuries caused by the intervening event.

■ **EXAMPLE 8.28** While riding his bicycle, Derrick negligently runs into Julie, who is walking on the sidewalk. As a result of the impact, Julie falls and fractures her hip. While she is waiting for help to arrive, a small aircraft crashes nearby and explodes, and some of the fiery debris hits her, causing her to sustain severe burns. Derrick will be liable for the damages related to Julie's fractured hip, because the risk of injuring her with his bicycle was foreseeable. Normally, though, Derrick will not be liable for the burns caused by the plane crash, because he could not have foreseen the risk that a plane would crash nearby and injure Julie. ■

## 8–5c Contributory Negligence

All individuals are expected to exercise a reasonable degree of care in looking out for themselves. In the past, under the common law doctrine of **contributory negligence,** a plaintiff who was also negligent (who failed to exercise a reasonable degree of care) could not recover anything from the defendant. Under this rule, no matter how insignificant the plaintiff's negligence was relative to the defendant's negligence, the plaintiff would be precluded from recovering any damages. Today, only a few jurisdictions still follow this doctrine.

## 8–5d Comparative Negligence

In most states, the doctrine of contributory negligence has been replaced by a **comparative negligence** standard. Under this standard, both the plaintiff's and the defendant's negligence are computed, and the liability for damages is distributed accordingly.

Some jurisdictions have adopted a "pure" form of comparative negligence that allows the plaintiff to recover, even if the extent of his or her fault is greater than that of the defendant. Under pure comparative negligence, if the plaintiff was 80 percent at fault and the defendant 20 percent at fault, the plaintiff can recover 20 percent of his or her damages.

Many states' comparative negligence statutes, however, contain a "50 percent" rule that prevents the plaintiff from recovering any damages if she or he was more than 50 percent at fault. Under this rule, a plaintiff who was 35 percent at fault can recover 65 percent of his or her damages, but a plaintiff who was 65 percent (more than 50 percent) at fault can recover nothing.

## Reviewing: Tort Law

Elaine Sweeney went to Ragged Mountain Ski Resort in New Hampshire with a friend. Elaine went snow tubing down a run designed exclusively for snow tubers. There were no Ragged Mountain employees present in the snow-tube area to instruct Elaine on the proper use of a snow tube. On her fourth run down the trail, Elaine crossed over the center line between snow-tube lanes, collided with another snow tuber, and was injured. Elaine filed a negligence action against Ragged Mountain seeking compensation for the injuries that she sustained. Two years earlier, the New Hampshire state legislature had enacted a statute that prohibited a person who participates in the sport of skiing from suing a ski-area operator for injuries caused by the risks inherent in skiing. Using the information presented in the chapter, answer the following questions.

1. What defense will Ragged Mountain probably assert?
2. The central question in this case is whether the state statute establishing that skiers assume the risks inherent in the sport bars Elaine's suit. What would your decision be on this issue? Why?
3. Suppose that the court concludes that the statute applies only to skiing and not to snow tubing. Will Elaine's lawsuit be successful? Explain.
4. Now suppose that the jury concludes that Elaine was partly at fault for the accident. Under what theory might her damages be reduced in proportion to the degree to which her actions contributed to the accident and her resulting injuries?

**Debate This . . .** *Each time a state legislature enacts a law that applies the assumption of risk doctrine to a particular sport, participants in that sport suffer.*

## Terms and Concepts

actionable 140
actual malice 144
assault 139
assumption of risk 155
battery 140
business invitee 153
causation in fact 154
comparative negligence 157
compensatory damages 138

contributory negligence 156
conversion 150
damages 138
defamation 141
disparagement of property 151
dram shop act 155
duty of care 152
fraudulent misrepresentation
  (fraud) 146

general damages 138
Good Samaritan statute 154
intentional tort 139
libel 141
licensee 150
malpractice 153
negligence 151
privilege 143
proximate cause 154

## Issue Spotters

**1.** Jana leaves her truck's motor running while she enters a Kwik-Pik Store. The truck's transmission engages, and the vehicle crashes into a gas pump, starting a fire that spreads to a warehouse on the next block. The warehouse collapses, causing its billboard to fall and injure Lou, a bystander. Can Lou recover from Jana? Why or why not? (See *Unintentional Torts—Negligence*.)

**2.** A water pipe bursts, flooding a Metal Fabrication Company utility room and tripping the circuit breakers on a panel in the room. Metal Fabrication contacts Nouri, a licensed electrician with five years' experience, to check the damage and turn the breakers back on. Without testing for short circuits, which Nouri knows that he should do, he tries to switch on a breaker. He is electrocuted, and his wife sues Metal Fabrication for damages, alleging negligence. What might the firm successfully claim in defense? (See *Defenses to Negligence*.)

• **Check your answers to the Issue Spotters against the answers provided in Appendix B at the end of this text.**

## Business Scenarios

**8–1. Defamation.** Richard is an employee of the Dun Construction Corp. While delivering materials to a construction site, he carelessly backs Dun's truck into a passenger vehicle driven by Green. This is Richard's second accident in six months. When the company owner, Dun, learns of this latest accident, a heated discussion ensues, and Dun fires Richard. Dun is so angry that he immediately writes a letter to the union of which Richard is a member and to all other construction companies in the community, stating that Richard is the "worst driver in the city" and that "anyone who hires him is asking for legal liability." Richard files a suit against Dun, alleging libel on the basis of the statements made in the letters. Discuss the results. (See *Intentional Torts against Persons*.)

**8–2. Liability to Business Invitees.** Kim went to Ling's Market to pick up a few items for dinner. It was a stormy day, and the wind had blown water through the market's door each time it opened. As Kim entered through the door, she slipped and fell in the rainwater that had accumulated on the floor. The manager knew of the weather conditions but had not posted any sign to warn customers of the water hazard. Kim injured her back as a result of the fall and sued Ling's for damages. Can Ling's be held liable for negligence? Discuss. (See *Unintentional Torts—Negligence*.)

## Business Case Problems

**8–3. Spotlight on Intentional Torts—Defamation.**

 Sharon Yeagle was an assistant to the vice president of student affairs at Virginia Polytechnic Institute and State University (Virginia Tech). As part of her duties, Yeagle helped students participate in the Governor's Fellows Program. The *Collegiate Times*, Virginia Tech's student newspaper, published an article about the university's success in placing students in the program. The article's text surrounded a block quotation attributed to Yeagle with the phrase "Director of Butt Licking" under her name. Yeagle sued the *Collegiate Times* for defamation. She argued that the phrase implied the commission of sodomy and was therefore actionable. What is *Collegiate Times* defense to this claim? [*Yeagle v. Collegiate Times*, 497 S.E.2d 136 (Va. 1998)] (See *Intentional Torts against Persons*.)

**8–4. Intentional Infliction of Emotional Distress.** While living in her home country of Tanzania, Sophia Kiwanuka signed an employment contract with Anne Margareth Bakilana, a Tanzanian living in Washington, D.C. Kiwanuka traveled to the United States to work as a babysitter and maid in Bakilana's house. When Kiwanuka arrived, Bakilana confiscated her passport, held her in isolation, and forced her to work long hours under threat of having her deported. Kiwanuka worked seven days a week without breaks and was subjected to regular verbal and psychological abuse by Bakilana. Kiwanuka filed a complaint against Bakilana for intentional infliction of emotional distress, among other claims. Bakilana argued that Kiwanuka's complaint should be dismissed because the allegations were insufficient to show outrageous intentional conduct that resulted in severe emotional distress.

If you were the judge, in whose favor would you rule? Why? [*Kiwanuka v. Bakilana,* 844 F.Supp.2d 107 (D.D.C. 2012)] (See *Intentional Torts against Persons.*)

**8–5. Business Case Problem with Sample Answer—Negligence.** At the Weatherford Hotel in Flagstaff, Arizona,  in Room 59, a balcony extends across thirty inches of the room's only window, leaving a twelve-inch gap with a three-story drop to the concrete below. A sign prohibits smoking in the room but invites guests to "step out onto the balcony" to smoke. Toni Lucario was a guest in Room 59 when she climbed out of the window and fell to her death. Patrick McMurtry, her estate's personal representative, filed a suit against the Weatherford. Did the hotel breach a duty of care to Locario? What might the Weatherford assert in its defense? Explain. [*McMurtry v. Weatherford Hotel, Inc.,* 231 Ariz. 244, 293 P.3d 520 (2013)] (See *Unintentional Torts—Negligence.*)

- **For a sample answer to Problem 8–5, go to Appendix C at the end of this text.**

**8–6. Negligence.** Ronald Rawls and Zabian Bailey were in an auto accident in Bridgeport, Connecticut. Bailey rear-ended Rawls at a stoplight. Evidence showed it was more likely than not that Bailey failed to apply his brakes in time to avoid the collision, failed to turn his vehicle to avoid the collision, failed to keep his vehicle under control, and was inattentive to his surroundings. Rawls filed a suit in a Connecticut state court against his insurance company, Progressive Northern Insurance Co., to obtain benefits under an underinsured motorist clause, alleging that Bailey had been negligent. Could Rawls collect? Discuss. [*Rawls v. Progressive Northern Insurance Co.,* 310 Conn. 768, 83 A.3d 576 (2014)] (See *Unintentional Torts—Negligence.*)

**8–7. Negligence.** Charles Robison, an employee of West Star Transportation, Inc., was ordered to cover an unevenly loaded flatbed trailer with a 150-pound tarpaulin (a waterproof cloth). The load included uncrated equipment and pallet crates of different heights, about thirteen feet off the ground at its highest point. While standing on the load, manipulating the tarpaulin without safety equipment or assistance, Robison fell and sustained a traumatic head injury. He filed a suit against West Star to recover for his injury. Was West Star "negligent in failing to provide a reasonably safe place to work," as Robison claimed? Explain. [*West Star Transportation, Inc. v. Robison,* 457 S.W.3d 178 (Tex.App.—Amarillo 2015)] (See *Unintentional Torts—Negligence.*)

**8–8. Negligence.** DSC Industrial Supply and Road Rider Supply are located in North Kitsap Business Park in Seattle, Washington. Both firms are owned by Paul and Suzanne Marshall. The Marshalls had outstanding commercial loans from Frontier Bank. The bank dispatched one of its employees, Suzette Gould, to North Kitsap to "spread Christmas cheer" to the Marshalls as an expression of appreciation for their business. Approaching the entry to Road Rider, Gould tripped over a concrete "wheel stop" and fell, suffering a broken arm and a dislocated elbow. The stop was not clearly visible, it had not been painted a contrasting color, and it was not marked with a sign. Gould had not been aware of the stop before she tripped over it. Is North Kitsap liable to Gould for negligence? Explain. [*Gould v. North Kitsap Business Park Management, LLC,* 2016 WL 236455 (2016)] (See *Unintentional Torts—Negligence.*)

**8–9. A Question of Ethics—Wrongful Interference.**  White Plains Coat & Apron Co. is a New York–based linen rental business. Cintas Corp. is a competitor. White Plains had five-year exclusive contracts with some of its customers. As a result of Cintas's soliciting of business, dozens of White Plains' customers breached their contracts and entered into rental agreements with Cintas. White Plains filed a suit against Cintas, alleging wrongful interference. [ White Plains Coat & Apron Co. v. Cintas Corp., 8 N.Y.3d 422, 867 N.E.2d 381 (2007)] (See *Intentional Torts against Persons.*)

**(a)** What are the two important policy interests at odds in wrongful interference cases? Which of these interests should be accorded priority?

**(b)** The U.S. Court of Appeals for the Second Circuit asked the New York Court of Appeals to answer a question: Is a general interest in soliciting business for profit a sufficient defense to a claim of wrongful interference with a contractual relationship? What do you think? Why?

# Legal Reasoning Group Activity

**8–10. Negligence.** Donald and Gloria Bowden hosted a cookout at their home in South Carolina, inviting mostly business acquaintances. Justin Parks, who was nineteen years old, attended the party. Alcoholic beverages were available to all of the guests, even those who, like Parks, were between the ages of eighteen and twenty-one. Parks consumed alcohol at the party and left with other guests. One of these guests detained Parks at the guest's home to give Parks time to "sober up." Parks then drove himself from this guest's home and was killed in a one-car accident. At the time of death, he had a blood alcohol content of 0.291 percent, which exceeded the state's limit for driving a motor vehicle. Linda Marcum, Parks's mother, filed a suit in a South Carolina state court against the Bowdens and others, alleging that they were negligent. (See *Unintentional Torts—Negligence.*)

**(a)** The first group will present arguments in favor of holding the social hosts liable in this situation.

**(b)** The second group will formulate arguments against holding the social hosts liable based on principles in this chapter.

**(c)** The third group will determine the reasons why some courts do not treat social hosts the same as parents who serve alcoholic beverages to their underage children.

# CHAPTER 9

# Agency Formation and Duties

One of the most common, important, and pervasive legal relationships is that of **agency.** In an agency relationship involving two parties, one of the parties, called the *agent,* agrees to represent or act for the other, called the *principal.* The principal has the right to control the agent's conduct in matters entrusted to the agent.

Agency relationships are crucial in the business world. By using agents, a principal can conduct multiple business operations at the same time in different locations. Indeed, the only way that certain business entities can function is through their agents. For instance, a corporate officer is an agent who serves in a representative capacity for the corporation. The officer has the authority to bind the corporation to a contract. Only through its officers can corporations enter into contracts.

Most employees are also considered to be agents of their employers.

Today, however, the United States is experiencing a trend toward a so-called *gig economy,* which centers on short-term, independent workers who are not employees. Companies like Uber and Lyft (discussed in this chapter's feature) provide evidence of this trend. This type of on-demand employment raises questions related to agency, making agency an increasingly important topic for students of business law and the legal environment to understand.

## 9–1 Agency Relationships

Section 1(1) of the *Restatement (Third) of Agency*[1] defines *agency* as "the fiduciary relation [that] results from the manifestation of consent by one person to another that the other shall act in his [or her] behalf and subject to his [or her] control, and consent by the other so to act." In other words, in a principal-agent relationship, the parties have agreed that the agent will act *on behalf and instead of* the principal in negotiating and transacting business with third parties.

The term **fiduciary** is at the heart of agency law. This term can be used both as a noun and as an adjective. When used as a noun, it refers to a person having a duty created by his or her undertaking to act primarily for another's benefit in matters connected with the undertaking. When used as an adjective, as in the phrase *fiduciary relationship,* it means that the relationship involves trust and confidence.

Agency relationships commonly exist between employers and employees. Agency relationships may sometimes also exist between employers and independent contractors who are hired to perform special tasks or services.

### 9–1a Employer-Employee Relationships

Normally, all employees who deal with third parties are deemed to be agents. A salesperson in a department store, for instance, is an agent of the store's owner (the principal) and acts on the owner's behalf. Any sale of goods made by the salesperson to a customer is binding on the principal. Similarly, most representations of fact made by the salesperson with respect to the goods sold are binding on the principal.

Because employees who deal with third parties generally are deemed to be agents of their employers, agency law and employment law overlap considerably. Agency relationships, however, can exist outside

---

**1.** The *Restatement (Third) of Agency* is an authoritative summary of the law of agency and is often referred to by judges in their decisions and opinions.

an employer-employee relationship, so agency law has a broader reach than employment law. Additionally, agency law is based on the common law, whereas much employment law is statutory law.

Employment laws (state and federal) apply only to the employer-employee relationship. Statutes governing Social Security, withholding taxes, workers' compensation, unemployment compensation, workplace safety, and employment discrimination apply only if an employer-employee relationship exists. *These laws do not apply to independent contractors.*

## 9–1b Employer–Independent Contractor Relationships

Independent contractors are not employees because, by definition, those who hire them have no control over the details of their work performance. Section 2 of the *Restatement (Third) of Agency* defines an **independent contractor** as follows:

> [An independent contractor is] a person who contracts with another to do something for him [or her] but who is not controlled by the other nor subject to the other's right to control with respect to his [or her] physical conduct in the performance of the undertaking. He [or she] may or may not be an agent.

Building contractors and subcontractors are independent contractors. A property owner who hires a contractor and subcontractors to complete a project does not control the details of the way they perform their work. Truck drivers who own their vehicles and hire out on a per-job basis are independent contractors, but truck drivers who drive company trucks on a regular basis usually are employees. See this chapter's *Ethics Today* feature for a discussion of disputes involving the classification of drivers working for Uber and Lyft.

The relationship between a principal and an independent contractor may or may not involve an agency relationship. To illustrate: A homeowner who hires a real estate broker to sell her house has contracted with an independent contractor (the broker). The homeowner has also established an agency relationship with the broker for the specific purpose of selling the property. Another example is an insurance agent, who is both an independent contractor and an agent of the insurance company for which he sells policies. (Note that an insurance *broker,* in contrast, normally is an agent of the person obtaining insurance and not of the insurance company.)

## 9–1c Determination of Employee Status

The courts are frequently asked to determine whether a particular worker is an employee or an independent contractor. How a court decides this issue can have a significant effect on the rights and liabilities of the parties. Employers are required to pay certain taxes, such as Social Security and unemployment taxes, for employees but not for independent contractors. Therefore, workers may benefit from obtaining employee status in some situations.

**Criteria Used by the Courts** In deciding whether a worker is categorized as an employee or an independent contractor, courts often consider the following questions:

1. *How much control does the employer exercise over the details of the work?* If the employer exercises considerable control over the details of the work and the day-to-day activities of the worker, this indicates employee status. This is perhaps the most important factor weighed by the courts in determining employee status.
2. *Is the worker engaged in an occupation or business distinct from that of the employer?* If so, this points to independent-contractor, not employee, status.
3. *Is the work usually done under the employer's direction or by a specialist without supervision?* If the work is usually done under the employer's direction, this indicates employee status.
4. *Does the employer supply the tools at the place of work?* If so, this indicates employee status.
5. *For how long is the person employed?* If the person is employed for a long period of time, this indicates employee status.
6. *What is the method of payment—by time period or at the completion of the job?* Payment by time period, such as once every two weeks or once a month, indicates employee status.
7. *What degree of skill is required of the worker?* If a great degree of skill is required, this may indicate that the person is an independent contractor hired for a specialized job and not an employee.

Whether a worker is an employee or an independent contractor can affect the employer's liability for the worker's actions. An employer normally is not responsible for the actions of an independent contractor. In the following case, the court had to determine the status of an auto service company and its tow truck driver who assaulted the passenger of a vehicle the company had been hired to tow.

## Case 9.1

# Coker v. Pershad

Superior Court of New Jersey, Appellate Division, 2013 WL 1296271 (2013).

**Background and Facts** AAA North Jersey, Inc., contracted with Five Star Auto Service to perform towing and auto repair services for AAA. Terence Pershad, the driver of a tow truck for Five Star, responded to a call to AAA for assistance by the driver of a car involved in an accident in Hoboken, New Jersey. Pershad got into a fight with Nicholas Coker, a passenger in the car, and assaulted Coker with a knife.

Coker filed a suit in a New Jersey state court against Pershad, Five Star, and AAA. The court determined that Pershad was Five Star's employee and that Five Star was an independent contractor, not AAA's employee. Thus, AAA was "not responsible for the alleged negligence of its independent contractor, defendant Five Star, in hiring Mr. Pershad." Five Star entered into a settlement with Coker. Coker appealed the ruling in AAA's favor.

## In the Language of the Court

PER CURIAM [By the Whole Court].

* * * *

*The important difference between an employee and an independent contractor is that one who hires an independent contractor has no right of control over the manner in which the work is to be done.* [Emphasis added.]

* * * *

* * * Plaintiff [Coker] argues AAA controlled the means and method of the work performed by Five Star. * * * Factors * * * [that] determine whether a principal maintains the right of control over an individual or a corporation claimed to be an independent contractor [include]:

(a) the extent of control which, by the agreement, the master may exercise over the details of the work;
(b) whether or not the one employed is engaged in a distinct occupation or business;
(c) the kind of occupation, with reference to whether, in the locality, the work is usually done under the direction of the employer or by a specialist without supervision;
(d) the skill required in the particular occupation;
(e) whether the employer or the workman supplies the * * * tools * * *;
(f) the length of time for which the person is employed * * *.

Applying these factors to the facts of this case, it is clear AAA did not control the manner and means of Five Star's work. The Agreement specifically stated Five Star was an independent contractor. Five Star purchased its own trucks and any other necessary equipment. AAA assigned jobs to Five Star and Five Star completed the work without any further supervision by AAA. Five Star chose the employees to send on towing calls and the trucks and equipment the employees would use.

Five Star was also in business for itself and performed auto repair services for principals and customers other than AAA. Five Star hired and fired its own employees * * *.

* * * *

Plaintiff also argues Five Star should be considered to be controlled by AAA because "providing towing and other roadside assistance is arguably the focus of the regular business of AAA." * * * [But] AAA is an automobile club that provides a wide variety of services to its members. It contracts with numerous service providers, such as gas stations, motels and other businesses, to provide these services. Thus, AAA is not solely in the towing business.

* * * AAA had used Five Star to provide towing services for approximately eight years and there is nothing in the record to demonstrate it lacked the skill needed to provide these services.

**Decision and Remedy** *A state intermediate appellate court affirmed the lower court's ruling. AAA could not be held liable for the actions of Five Star, its independent contractor, because "AAA did not control the manner and means of Five Star's work."*

## Critical Thinking

- **Legal** *Five Star's contract with AAA required Five Star to be available to provide service for AAA members. Does this support Coker's argument that Five Star was AAA's employee? Why or why not?*

## ETHICS TODAY   Is It Fair to Classify Uber and Lyft Drivers as Independent Contractors?

The transportation-for-hire world has changed dramatically since Uber, Lyft, and other transportation-sharing companies came onto the scene. Uber started in San Francisco in 2009. Today, its services are available in one form or another in about 60 countries and more than 300 cities worldwide. Its main competitor, Lyft, was launched in 2012 and operates in more than 200 U.S. cities. The growth in transportation sharing has not been without its set-backs, though. Most of them involve laws that have prohibited Uber and Lyft from operating in certain cities, as well as lawsuits by drivers claiming that they were misclassified.

### Classification of Workers

Workers in the United States generally fall into two categories: employees and independent contractors. Employment laws, including minimum wage and anti-discrimination statutes, cover employees. Such laws do not cover most independent contractors. Enter the digital age of on-demand workers who obtain job assignments via apps.

Workers for Lyft, Uber, and similar companies choose when and where they will perform their duties. They do not choose how much they will be paid, however. For them, employment is a take-it-or-leave-it proposition. They electronically accept the platform terms of the apps, or they obtain no work assignments.

Some critics of this contractual system argue that there should be a new category of workers with "dependent-contractor" status who receive some of the protections traditionally given only to employees. Certain aspects of current labor law would be attached to the relationships between dependent contractors and their employers.

### Worker Misclassification Lawsuits

A number of former or current Uber and Lyft drivers have pursued legal remedies to change their job classification and to obtain better benefits. In California, for instance, two federal court judges allowed separate lawsuits to go before juries on the question of whether on-demand drivers should be considered employees rather than independent contractors.[a]

In a similar case, rather than go to court, Lyft settled a worker misclassification lawsuit for $12.25 million. The suit, which was settled in 2016, had been brought in 2013. The settlement did not achieve a reclassification of Lyft drivers as employees. Basically, Lyft agreed to change its terms of service to conform to California's independent contractor status regulations. For instance, the company can no longer deactivate drivers' accounts without reason and without warning the drivers. Drivers have to be given a fair hearing first. Even though the lawsuit and the agreement were California based, the new terms of service will apply to all Lyft's drivers nationwide.

### Competitors Sue Uber

In many cities, competitors, especially taxi drivers, have sued Uber. These lawsuits have involved claims of unfair competition, lack of minimum wages, and unsafe vehicles. A taxi driver sued Uber in northern California, for instance, but a federal district court ruled in favor of Uber's request for summary judgment.[b]

Another suit was brought in Pennsylvania. In this one, Checker Cab of Philadelphia claimed that Uber was violating Pennsylvania's unfair competition law. Checker Cab sought a preliminary injunction to prevent Uber from taking away its customers. The federal district court refused to grant an injunction, however, because Checker Cab failed to show irreparable harm. That decision was upheld on appeal.[c]

**Critical Thinking**  *What choices do disgruntled Uber and Lyft drivers have?*

a. *Cotter v. Lyft, Inc.,* 60 F.Supp.3d 1067 (N.D.Cal. 2015); *O'Connor v. Uber Technologies, Inc., et al.,* Case No. C-13-3826 EMC (N.D.Cal. 2015).
b. *Rosen v. Uber Technologies, Inc.,* __ F.Supp.3d __, 2016 WL 704078 (N.D.Cal. 2016).
c. *Checker Cab of Philadelphia v. Uber Technologies, Inc.,* __ Fed.Appx. __, 2016 WL 929310 (3d Cir. 2016).

**Criteria Used by the IRS**   The Internal Revenue Service (IRS) has established its own criteria for determining whether a worker is an independent contractor or an employee. The most important factor is the degree of control the business exercises over the worker.

The IRS tends to closely scrutinize a firm's classification of its workers because, as mentioned, employers can avoid certain tax liabilities by hiring independent contractors instead of employees. Even when a firm has classified a worker as an independent contractor, the IRS may decide that the worker is actually an employee. If the IRS decides that an employee is misclassified, the employer will be responsible for paying any applicable Social Security, withholding, and unemployment taxes due for that employee.

**Employee Status and "Works for Hire"**  Ordinarily, a person who creates a copyrighted work is the owner of it—unless it is a "work for hire." Under the Copyright Act, any copyrighted work created by an employee within the scope of her or his employment at the request of the employer is a "work for hire." The employer owns the copyright to the work.

In contrast, when an employer hires an independent contractor—such as a freelance artist, writer, or computer programmer—the independent contractor normally owns the copyright. An exception is made if the parties agree in writing that the work is a "work for hire" and the work falls into one of nine specific categories. The nine categories include audiovisual works, collective works (such as magazines), motion pictures, textbooks, tests, and translations.

■ **CASE IN POINT 9.1**  As a freelance contractor, Brian Cooley created two sculptures of dinosaur eggs for the National Geographic Society for use in connection with an article in its magazine, *National Geographic.* Cooley spent hundreds of hours researching, designing, and constructing the sculptures. National Geographic hired Louis Psihoyos to photograph Cooley's sculptures for the article. Cooley and Psihoyos had separate contracts with National Geographic in which each transferred the copyrights in their works to National Geographic for a limited time.

The rights to the works were returned to the artists at different times after publication. Psihoyos then began licensing his photographs of Cooley's sculptures to third parties in return for royalties. He digitized the photographs and licensed them to various online stock photography companies, and they appeared in several books published by Penguin Group. Cooley sued Psihoyos for copyright infringement.

Psihoyos argued that he owned the photos and could license them however he saw fit, but a federal district court disagreed. The court found that Psihoyos did not have an unrestricted right to use and license the photos. When Psihoyos reproduced an image of a Cooley sculpture, he reproduced the sculpture, which infringed on Cooley's copyright. Therefore, the court granted a summary judgment to Cooley.[2] ■

---

2. *Cooley v. Penguin Group (USA), Inc.,* 31 F.Supp.3d 599 (S.D.N.Y. 2014).

# 9–2 Formation of the Agency Relationship

Agency relationships normally are consensual. They come about by voluntary consent and agreement between the parties. Normally, the agreement need not be in writing, and consideration is not required.

A person must have contractual capacity to be a principal.[3] The idea is that those who cannot legally enter into contracts directly should not be allowed to do so indirectly through an agent. Any person can be an agent, however, regardless of whether he or she has the capacity to contract (including minors).

An agency relationship can be created for any legal purpose. An agency relationship created for a purpose that is illegal or contrary to public policy is unenforceable. ■ **EXAMPLE 9.2**  Archer (as principal) contracts with Burke (as agent) to sell illegal narcotics. The agency relationship is unenforceable because selling illegal narcotics is a felony and is contrary to public policy. If Burke sells the narcotics and keeps the profits, Archer cannot sue to enforce the agency agreement. ■

An agency relationship can arise in four ways: by agreement of the parties, by ratification, by estoppel, and by operation of law.

## 9–2a Agency by Agreement

Most agency relationships are based on an express or implied agreement that the agent will act for the principal and that the principal agrees to have the agent so act. An agency agreement can take the form of an express written contract or be created by an oral agreement. ■ **EXAMPLE 9.3**  Reese asks Grace, a gardener, to contract with others for the care of his lawn on a regular basis. If Grace agrees, an agency relationship exists between Reese and Grace for the lawn care. ■

An agency agreement can also be implied by conduct. ■ **CASE IN POINT 9.4**  Gilbert Bishop was admitted to a nursing home, Laurel Creek Health Care Center, suffering from various physical ailments. He was not able to use his hands well enough to write but was otherwise mentally competent. Bishop's sister offered to sign the admission papers for him, but it was Laurel Creek's

---

3. Note that some states allow a minor to be a principal. When a minor is permitted to be a principal, any resulting contracts will be voidable by the minor principal but *not* by the adult third party.

policy to have the patient's spouse sign the forms if the patient could not.

Bishop's sister then brought his wife, Anna, to the hospital to sign the paperwork, which included a mandatory arbitration clause. Later, when the family filed a lawsuit against Laurel Creek, the nursing home sought to enforce the arbitration clause. Ultimately, a Kentucky appellate court held that Bishop was bound by the contract and the arbitration clause his wife had signed. Bishop's conduct had indicated that he was giving his wife authority to act as his agent in signing the admission papers.[4] ■

## 9–2b Agency by Ratification

On occasion, a person who is in fact not an agent (or who is an agent acting outside the scope of her or his authority) makes a contract on behalf of another (a principal). If the principal approves or affirms that contract by word or by action, an agency relationship is created by *ratification.* Ratification involves a question of intent, and intent can be expressed by either words or conduct.

## 9–2c Agency by Estoppel

Sometimes, a principal causes a third person to believe that another person is the principal's agent, and the third person acts to his or her detriment in reasonable reliance on that belief. When this occurs, the principal is "estopped to deny" (prevented from denying) the agency relationship. The principal's actions have created the *appearance* of an agency that does not in fact exist, creating an agency by estoppel.

### The Third Party's Reliance Must Be Reasonable

The third person must prove that he or she *reasonably* believed that an agency relationship existed.[5] Facts and circumstances must show that an ordinary, prudent person familiar with business practice and custom would have been justified in concluding that the agent had authority.

### Created by the Principal's Conduct

Note that the acts or declarations of a purported *agent* in and of themselves do not create an agency by estoppel. Rather, it is the deeds or statements of the *principal* that create an agency by estoppel. ■ **CASE IN POINT 9.5** Francis Azur

was president and chief executive officer of ATM Corporation of America. Michelle Vanek was Azur's personal assistant. Among other duties, she reviewed his credit-card statements. For seven years, Vanek took unauthorized cash advances from Azur's credit-card account with Chase Bank. The charges appeared on at least sixty-five monthly statements.

When Azur discovered Vanek's fraud, he fired her and closed the account. He filed a suit against Chase, arguing that the bank should not have allowed Vanek to take cash advances. The court concluded that Azur (the principal) had given the bank reason to believe that Vanek (the agent) had authority. Therefore, Azur was estopped (prevented) from denying Vanek's authority.[6] ■

## 9–2d Agency by Operation of Law

The courts may find an agency relationship in the absence of a formal agreement in other situations as well. This may occur in family relationships, such as when one spouse purchases certain basic necessaries and charges them to the other spouse's account. The courts often rule that a spouse is liable for payment for the necessaries because of either a social policy or a legal duty to supply necessaries to family members.

Agency by operation of law may also occur in emergency situations. If an agent cannot contact the principal and failure to act would cause the principal substantial loss, the agent may take steps beyond the scope of her or his authority. For instance, a railroad engineer may contract on behalf of his or her employer for medical care for an injured motorist hit by the train.

Concept Summary 9.1 reviews the various ways in which agency relationships are formed.

---

## 9–3 Duties of Agents and Principals

Once the principal-agent relationship has been created, both parties have duties that govern their conduct. As discussed previously, the principal-agent relationship is *fiduciary*—based on trust. In a fiduciary relationship, each party owes the other the duty to act with the utmost good faith. In this section, we examine the various duties of agents and principals.

---

4. *Laurel Creek Health Care Center v. Bishop,* 2010 WL 985299 (Ky.App. 2010).
5. These concepts also apply when a person who is, in fact, an agent undertakes an action that is beyond the scope of her or his authority.

6. *Azur v. Chase Bank, USA, N.A.,* 601 F.3d 212 (3d Cir. 2010).

## Concept Summary 9.1

### Formation of the Agency Relationship

**By Agreement**
- The agency relationship is formed through express consent (oral or written) or implied by conduct.

**By Ratification**
- The principal either by act or by agreement ratifies the conduct of a person who is not, in fact, an agent.

**By Estoppel**
- The principal causes a third person to believe that another person is the principal's agent, and the third person acts to his or her detriment in reasonable reliance on that belief.

**By Operation of Law**
- The agency relationship is based on a social or legal duty—such as the need to support family members. Or, it is formed in emergency situations when the agent is unable to contact the principal and failure to act outside the scope of the agent's authority would cause the principal substantial loss.

## 9–3a Agent's Duties to the Principal

Generally, the agent owes the principal five duties—performance, notification, loyalty, obedience, and accounting (see Exhibit 9–1).

**Performance** An implied condition in every agency contract is the agent's agreement to use reasonable diligence and skill in performing the work. When an agent fails to perform his or her duties, liability for breach of contract may result.

**Standard of Care.** The degree of skill or care required of an agent is usually that expected of a reasonable person under similar circumstances. Generally, this is interpreted to mean ordinary care. If an agent has represented herself or himself as possessing special skills, however, the agent is expected to exercise the degree of skill claimed. Failure to do so constitutes a breach of the agent's duty.

**Gratuitous Agents.** Not all agency relationships are based on contract. In some situations, an agent acts gratuitously—that is, without payment. A gratuitous agent cannot be liable for breach of contract because there is no contract. He or she is subject only to tort liability. Once a gratuitous agent has begun to act in an agency capacity, he or she has the duty to continue to perform in that

capacity. A gratuitous agent must perform in an acceptable manner and is subject to the same standards of care and duty to perform as other agents.

■ **EXAMPLE 9.6** Bower's friend Alcott is a real estate broker. Alcott offers to sell Bower's vacation home at no charge. If Alcott never attempts to sell the home, Bower has no legal cause of action to force her to do so. If Alcott does attempt to sell the home to Friedman, but then performs so negligently that the sale falls through, Bower can sue Alcott for negligence. ■

**Notification** An agent is required to notify the principal of all matters that come to her or his attention concerning the subject matter of the agency. This is the *duty of notification,* or the duty to inform.

■ **EXAMPLE 9.7** Perez, an artist, is about to negotiate a contract to sell a series of paintings to Barber's Art Gallery for $25,000. Perez's agent learns that Barber is insolvent and will be unable to pay for the paintings. The agent has a duty to inform Perez of Barber's insolvency because it is relevant to the subject matter of the agency, which is the sale of Perez's paintings. ■

Generally, the law assumes that the principal is aware of any information acquired by the agent that is relevant to the agency—regardless of whether the agent actually passes on this information to the principal. It is a basic tenet of agency law that notice to the agent is notice to the principal.

**EXHIBIT 9-1**  Duties of the Agent

**Loyalty**  Loyalty is one of the most fundamental duties in a fiduciary relationship. Basically, the agent has the duty to act *solely for the benefit of his or her principal* and not in the interest of the agent or a third party. For instance, an agent cannot represent two principals in the same transaction unless both know of the dual capacity and consent to it.

**Maintain Confidentiality.**  The duty of loyalty also means that any information or knowledge acquired through the agency relationship is confidential. It is a breach of loyalty to disclose such information either during the agency relationship or after its termination. Typical examples of confidential information are trade secrets and customer lists compiled by the principal.

**Actions Must Benefit the Principal.**  The agent's loyalty must be undivided. The agent's actions must be strictly for the benefit of the principal and must not result in any secret profit for the agent.

■ **EXAMPLE 9.8**  Don contracts with Leo, a real estate agent, to negotiate the purchase of an office building. Leo discovers that the property owner will sell the building only as a package deal with another parcel. So Leo buys the two properties, intending to resell the building to Don. Leo has breached his fiduciary duty. As a real estate agent, Leo has a duty to communicate all offers to Don, his principal, and not to purchase the property secretly and then resell it to Don. Leo is required to act in Don's best interests and can become the purchaser in this situation only with Don's knowledge and approval. ■

In the following case, an employer alleged that a former employee had breached his duty of loyalty by planning a competing business while still working for the employer.

## Spotlight on Taser International

## Case 9.2 Taser International, Inc. v. Ward

Court of Appeals of Arizona, Division 1, 224 Ariz. 389, 231 P.3d 921 (2010).

**Background and Facts**  Taser International, Inc., develops and makes electronic control devices, commonly called stun guns, as well as accessories for electronic control devices, including a personal video and audio recording device called the TASER CAM.

Steve Ward was Taser's vice president of marketing when he began to explore the possibility of developing and marketing devices of his own design, including a clip-on camera. Ward talked to

Case 9.2 Continues

**Case 9.2 Continued**

patent attorneys and a product development company and completed most of a business plan. After he resigned from Taser, he formed Vievu, LLC, to market his clip-on camera.

Ten months after Ward resigned, Taser announced the AXON, a product that provides an audio-video record of an incident from the visual perspective of the person involved. Taser then filed a suit in an Arizona state court against Ward, alleging that he had breached his duty of loyalty to Taser. The court granted Taser's motion for a summary judgment in the employer's favor. Ward appealed.

## In the Language of the Court

*PORTLEY,* Judge.

\* \* \* \*

\* \* \* An agent is under the duty to act with entire good faith and loyalty for the furtherance of the interests of his principal in all matters concerning or affecting the subject of his agency.

One aspect of this broad principle is that an employee is precluded from actively competing with his or her employer during the period of employment.

*Although an employee may not compete prior to termination, the employee may take action during employment, not otherwise wrongful, to prepare for competition following termination of the agency relationship. Preparation cannot take the form of acts in direct competition with the employer's business.* [Emphasis added.]

\* \* \* \*

It is undisputed that, prior to his resignation, Ward did not solicit or recruit any Taser employees, distributors, customers, or vendors; he did not buy, sell, or incorporate any business; he did not acquire office space or other general business services; he did not contact or enter into any agreements with suppliers or manufacturers for his proposed clip-on camera; and he did not sell any products. However, Ward did begin developing a business plan, counseled with several attorneys, explored and abandoned the concept of an eyeglass-mounted camera device, and engaged, to some extent, in the exploration and development of a clip-on camera device.

Ward argues that his pre-termination activities did not constitute active competition but were merely lawful preparation for a future business venture. Taser contends, however, that "this case is \* \* \* about developing a rival design during employment, knowing full well TASER has sold such a device and continues to develop a second-generation product."

\* \* \* \*

\* \* \* Assuming Taser was engaged in the research and development of a recording device during Ward's employment, assuming Ward knew or should have known of those efforts, and assuming Taser's device would compete with Ward's concept, substantial design and development efforts by Ward during his employment would constitute direct competition with the business activities of Taser and would violate his duty of loyalty. In the context of a business which engages in research, design, development, manufacture, and marketing of products, we cannot limit "competition" to just actual sales of competing products.

**Decision and Remedy** *A state intermediate appellate court agreed with Taser that an employee may not actively compete with his employer before his employment is terminated. But the parties disputed the extent of Ward's pre-termination efforts, creating a genuine issue of material fact that could not be resolved on a motion for summary judgment. The appellate court thus reversed the lower court's decision in Taser's favor and remanded the case for further proceedings.*

**Critical Thinking**

- **Legal Environment** *Did Ward breach any duties owed to his employer in addition to his alleged breach of the duty of loyalty? Discuss.*
- **What If the Facts Were Different?** *Suppose that Ward's pre-termination activities focused on a product that was not designed to compete with Taser's products. Would these efforts have breached the duty of loyalty? Why or why not?*

---

**Obedience** When acting on behalf of the principal, an agent has a duty to follow all lawful and clearly stated instructions of the principal. Any deviation from such instructions is a violation of this duty.

During emergency situations, however, when the principal cannot be consulted, the agent may deviate from the instructions without violating this duty. Whenever instructions are not clearly stated, the agent can fulfill the duty of obedience by acting in good faith and in a manner reasonable under the circumstances.

**Accounting** Unless the agent and principal agree otherwise, the agent must keep and make available to the principal an account of all property and funds received and paid out on the principal's behalf. This includes gifts from third parties in connection with the agency. ■ **EXAMPLE 9.9** Marla is a salesperson for Roadway Supplies. Knife River Construction gives Marla a new tablet as a gift for prompt deliveries of Roadway's paving materials. The tablet belongs to Roadway. ■

The agent has a duty to maintain a separate account for the principal's funds and must not intermingle these funds with the agent's personal funds. If a licensed professional (such as an attorney) violates this duty, he or she may be subject to disciplinary action by the licensing authority (such as the state bar association). Of course, the professional will also be liable to his or her client (the principal) for failure to account.

### 9–3b Principal's Duties to the Agent

The principal also has certain duties to the agent (as shown in Exhibit 9–2). These duties relate to compensation, reimbursement and indemnification, cooperation, and safe working conditions.

**Compensation** In general, when a principal requests certain services from an agent, the agent reasonably expects payment. For instance, when an accountant or an attorney is asked to act as an agent, an agreement to compensate the agent for this service is implied. The principal therefore has a duty to pay the agent for services rendered.

Unless the agency relationship is gratuitous and the agent does not act in exchange for payment, the principal must pay the agreed-on value for the agent's services. If no amount has been expressly agreed on, then the principal owes the agent the customary compensation for such services. The principal also has a duty to pay that compensation in a timely manner.

■ **CASE IN POINT 9.10** Keith Miller worked as a sales representative for Paul M. Wolff Company, a subcontractor specializing in concrete-finishing services. Sales representatives at Wolff are paid a 15 percent commission on projects that meet a 35 percent gross profit threshold. The commission is paid after the projects are completed. When Miller resigned, he asked for commissions on fourteen projects for which he had secured contracts but which had not yet been completed. Wolff refused, so Miller sued.

The court found that "an agent is entitled to receive commissions on sales that result from the agent's efforts," even after the employment or agency relationship ends. Miller had met the gross profit threshold on ten of the unfinished projects, and therefore, he was entitled to more than $21,000 in commissions.[7] ■

**Reimbursement and Indemnification** Whenever an agent disburses funds at the request of the principal, the principal has a duty to reimburse the agent. The principal must also reimburse the agent (even a gratuitous

---

7. *Miller v. Paul M. Wolff Co.*, 178 Wash.App. 957, 316 P.3d 1113 (2014).

**EXHIBIT 9–2** Duties of the Principal

| DUTIES OF THE PRINCIPAL | | | |
|---|---|---|---|
| **Compensation** | **Reimbursement and Indemnification** | **Cooperation** | **Safe Working Conditions** |
| Principal must pay the agreed-on (or reasonable) value for the agent's services. | Principal must reimburse the agent for any funds paid out at the principal's request, as well as for necessary expenses. | Principal must cooperate with and assist an agent in performing his or her duties. | Principal must provide a safe working environment for agents and employees. |

agent) for any necessary expenses incurred in the course of the reasonable performance of her or his agency duties. Agents cannot recover for expenses incurred as a result of their own misconduct or negligence, though.

Subject to the terms of the agency agreement, the principal has the duty to *indemnify* (compensate) an agent for liabilities incurred because of authorized and lawful acts and transactions. For instance, if the agent, on the principal's behalf, forms a contract with a third party, and the principal fails to perform the contract, the third party may sue the agent for damages. In this situation, the principal is obligated to compensate the agent for any costs incurred by the agent as a result of the principal's failure to perform the contract.

Additionally, the principal must indemnify the agent for the value of benefits that the agent confers on the principal. The amount of indemnification usually is specified in the agency contract. If it is not, the courts will look to the nature of the business and the type of loss to determine the amount. Note that this rule applies to acts by gratuitous agents as well.

**Cooperation**   A principal has a duty to cooperate with the agent and to assist the agent in performing his or her duties. The principal must do nothing to prevent that performance.

For instance, when a principal grants an agent an exclusive territory, the principal creates an **exclusive agency,** in which the principal cannot compete with the agent or appoint or allow another agent to compete. If the principal does so, he or she violates the exclusive agency and is exposed to liability for the agent's lost profits.

■ **EXAMPLE 9.11**  Penny (the principal) creates an exclusive agency by granting Andrew (the agent) a territory within which only Andrew may sell Penny's organic skin care products. If Penny starts to sell the products herself within Andrew's territory—or permits another agent to do so—Penny has failed to cooperate with the agent. Because she has violated the exclusive agency, Penny can be held liable for Andrew's lost sales or profits. ■

In the following case, a pair of potential homebuyers entered into an agreement with a realtor to act as the buyers' exclusive agent in locating and purchasing property. Later, the buyers executed an exclusive agency agreement with a different realtor. Neither agent knew about the other until the buyers found a home that they liked and bought it.

**Case Analysis 9.3**

# NRT New England, LLC v. Jones

Appellate Court of Connecticut, 162 Conn.App. 840, 134 A.3d 632 (2016).

### In the Language of the Court

*HARPER,* J. [Judge]
    * * * *

The defendant [Christopher Jones] met Andrea Woolston, a licensed realtor working as an independent contractor [for NRT New England, LLC, doing business as Coldwell Banker Residential Brokerage], in October 2010. The defendant expressed to Woolston a desire to purchase a home for himself and his then fiancée, Katherine Wiltshire. One of the first things Woolston asked the defendant was whether he was represented by another agent. The defendant responded that he was not. After a number of conversations about the defendant's needs and wishes, the parties executed an exclusive right to represent buyer agreement (agreement), which established, among other things, that Woolston was the defendant's

exclusive agent for finding, negotiating, and purchasing property. Over the next several months, Woolston devoted a substantial amount of time searching for properties for the defendant to purchase. Specifically, Woolston researched available properties at six town halls in the communities in which the defendant was interested. She showcased a number of properties personally to the defendant and Wiltshire and introduced many more to them through e-mail. Woolston and the defendant had at least twenty appointments where they viewed multiple properties. Additionally, Woolston visited many properties alone to determine if they were suitable for the defendant. Altogether, Woolston spent hundreds of hours seeking a suitable home for the defendant.

The agreement was in effect from January 11, 2011 until July 11, 2011,

and set forth the geographical area that the defendant was interested in and the rate of compensation for the plaintiff's services. With respect to geographical area, the parties agreed that Woolston would seek properties in Killingworth, Guilford, Essex, Old Saybrook, Deep River, Lyme, and Old Lyme [Connecticut]. With respect to compensation, the defendant agreed to pay the plaintiff a commission equal to 2.5 percent of the purchase price of the property "if the [buyer] or any person or entity acting on the [buyer's] behalf purchases, options, exchanges, leases or trades any property, through the efforts of anyone, including the [buyer]." The agreement imposed the following duties on the defendant: "The [buyer] will not deal directly with any other broker, agent or licensee during the term of this agreement. The [buyer] will

**Case 9.3 Continued**

notify other brokers, agents or licensees at first contact that the [buyer] is being exclusively represented by [NRT]. The [buyer] will disclose to [NRT] any past and/or current contacts for any real property or with any other real estate broker or agent."

On May 10, 2011, the defendant informed Woolston via e-mail that he and Wiltshire purchased property at 300 Vineyard Point Road in Guilford for $1,375,000. The defendant learned of this property on May 4, 2011, from Mary Jane Burt, a realtor with H. Pearce Real Estate (H. Pearce), who previously had represented Wiltshire with the sale of her house in Hamden [Connecticut]. Woolston subsequently confronted the defendant and eventually learned that he and Wiltshire previously had executed an exclusive right to represent buyer agreement with Burt and H. Pearce. This agreement was in effect from August 1, 2010, until August 1, 2011, and contained a provision designating Burt as the exclusive agent for the defendant and Wiltshire. Thus, at the time the defendant purchased the property in Guilford, he was under contract for exclusive agency with both Woolston and Burt. The defendant never told Woolston or Burt that he had two agreements in effect at the same time. Woolston notified her superiors of what had transpired.

* * * [NRT] filed a * * * complaint [in a Connecticut state court] against the defendant [for] breach of contract * * *. After a trial * * *, the court * * * found that the plaintiff had proven * * * breach of contract * * * and damages. * * * The court awarded the plaintiff $34,375 in damages [which represented 2.5 percent of the purchase price for the Vineyard Point property] plus attorney's fees and costs. This appeal followed.

* * * *

The defendant * * * claims that the agreement was unenforceable. Specifically, he argues that the court improperly * * * found that it was inequitable to deny the plaintiff recovery.

* * * *

There is ample evidence in the record to support the court's conclusion that denying the plaintiff relief would be inequitable. Woolston testified, and the defendant himself conceded, that she rendered a significant amount of services to the defendant over several months. Specifically, Woolston researched properties at town halls for availability and encumbrances, contacted property owners, arranged personal visits, prepared and presented literature to the defendant on available properties, and attended appointments with the defendant and Wiltshire. Woolston spent hundreds of hours working for the defendant in total.

The defendant, on the other hand, accepted Woolston's services while under contract with another agent in violation of the agreement. Indeed, the defendant acknowledged that he was untruthful with Woolston at the beginning of their relationship when he told her that he was not represented by another agent. In fact, he was scheduling appointments and viewing properties with both Woolston and Burt at approximately the same time in May 2011. For example, the defendant e-mailed Woolston on May 2, 2011, thanking her for showing him a property. Approximately one week later, the defendant e-mailed Woolston to inform her that he viewed 300 Vineyard Point Road with Burt and had "put in an all cash bid that has been accepted."

The defendant nevertheless argues that it would not be inequitable to deny recovery to the plaintiff because Woolston performed no services in connection with his purchase of 300 Vineyard Point Road. We are not persuaded. *The defendant agreed to pay a commission "equal to 2.5% of the purchase price if the [buyer] or any person or entity acting on the [buyer's] behalf purchases * * * any property, through the efforts of anyone, including the [buyer], where an agreement to purchase the property was entered into during the term of this agreement."* However unjust this result may seem to the defendant in hindsight, we cannot say it is inequitable because it is precisely what he agreed to. [Emphasis added.]

* * * *

The judgment is affirmed.

**Legal Reasoning Questions**

1. What is the advantage to a principal of an exclusive agency agreement? What was the advantage to Jones of his agreement with Woolston? Discuss.

2. Why, in addition to damages, was the plaintiff awarded attorneys' fees and costs?

3. Jones's agreement with Woolston provided that on the purchase of the property, NRT "will, whenever feasible, seek compensation from the seller or the seller's agent." The court determined that it was not feasible. Why would it not be reasonable in this situation to ask the seller of the property to pay part of Woolston's commission?

---

**Safe Working Conditions** The common law requires the principal to provide safe working premises, equipment, and conditions for all agents and employees. The principal has a duty to inspect working areas and to warn agents and employees about any unsafe situations. When the agent is an employee, the employer's liability is frequently covered by state workers' compensation insurance. In addition, federal and state statutes often require the employer to meet certain safety standards.

# 9-4 Rights and Remedies of Agents and Principals

In general, for every duty of the principal, the agent has a corresponding right, and vice versa. When one party to the agency relationship violates his or her duty to the other party, the nonbreaching party is entitled to a remedy. The remedies available arise out of contract and tort law. These remedies include monetary damages, termination of the agency relationship, an injunction, and required accountings.

## 9-4a Agent's Rights and Remedies against the Principal

The agent has the right to be compensated, to be reimbursed and indemnified, and to have a safe working environment. An agent also has the right to perform agency duties without interference by the principal.

**Tort and Contract Remedies** Remedies of the agent for breach of duty by the principal follow normal contract and tort remedies. ■ **EXAMPLE 9.12** Aaron Hart, a builder who has just constructed a new house, contracts with a real estate agent, Fran Boller, to sell the house. The contract calls for the agent to have an exclusive ninety-day listing and to receive 6 percent of the selling price when the home is sold. Boller holds several open houses and shows the home to a number of potential buyers.

One month before the ninety-day listing terminates, Hart agrees to sell the house to another buyer—not one to whom Boller has shown the house—after the ninety-day listing expires. Hart and the buyer agree that Hart will reduce the price of the house by 3 percent because he will sell it directly and thus will not have to pay Boller's commission. If Boller learns of Hart's actions, she can terminate the agency relationship and sue Hart for the 6 percent commission she should have earned on the sale of the house. ■

**Demand for an Accounting** An agent can also withhold further performance and demand that the principal give an accounting. For instance, a sales agent may demand an accounting if the agent and principal disagree on the amount of commissions the agent should have received for sales made during a specific period.

**No Right to Specific Performance** When the principal-agent relationship is not contractual, the agent has no right to specific performance. An agent can recover for past services and future damages but cannot force the principal to allow him or her to continue acting as an agent.

## 9-4b Principal's Rights and Remedies against the Agent

In general, a principal has contract remedies for an agent's breach of fiduciary duties. The principal also has tort remedies if the agent engages in misrepresentation, negligence, deceit, libel, slander, or trespass. In addition, any breach of a fiduciary duty by an agent may justify the principal's termination of the agency. The main actions available to the principal are constructive trust, avoidance, and indemnification.

**Constructive Trust** Anything that an agent obtains by virtue of the employment or agency relationship belongs to the principal. An agent commits a breach of fiduciary duty if he or she secretly retains benefits or profits that, by right, belong to the principal. Therefore, the agent holds such property in a *constructive trust* (an equitable trust imposed for reasons of fairness) for the principal. ■ **EXAMPLE 9.13** Lee, a purchasing agent for Metcalf, receives cash rebates from a customer. If Lee keeps the rebates for himself, he violates his fiduciary duty to his principal, Metcalf. On finding out about the cash rebates, Metcalf can sue Lee and recover them. ■

**Avoidance** When an agent breaches the agency agreement or agency duties under a contract, the principal has a right to avoid any contract entered into with the agent. This right of avoidance is at the election of the principal.

**Indemnification** In certain situations, when a principal is sued by a third party for an agent's negligent conduct, the principal can sue the agent for indemnification—that is, for an equal amount of damages. The same holds true if the agent violates the principal's instructions.

■ **EXAMPLE 9.14** Parker (the principal) owns a used-car lot where Moore (the agent) works as a salesperson. Parker tells Moore to make no warranties for the used cars. Moore is eager to make a sale to Walters, a customer, and adds a 50,000-mile warranty for the car's engine. Parker may be liable to Walters for engine failure, but if Walters sues Parker, Parker normally can then sue Moore for indemnification for violating his instructions. ■

Sometimes, though, it is difficult to distinguish between instructions of the principal that limit an agent's authority and those that are merely advice. ■ **EXAMPLE 9.15** Gutierrez (the principal) owns an office supply company, and Logan (the agent) is the manager. Gutierrez tells Logan, "Don't purchase any more inventory this month." Gutierrez goes on vacation. A large order comes in from a local business, and the inventory on hand is insufficient to meet it. What is Logan to do? In this situation, Logan probably has the inherent authority to purchase more inventory despite Gutierrez's command. It is unlikely that Logan would be required to indemnify Gutierrez in the event that the local business subsequently canceled the order. ■

## Reviewing: Agency Formation and Duties

James Blatt hired Marilyn Scott to sell insurance for the Massachusetts Mutual Life Insurance Company. Their contract stated, "Nothing in this contract shall be construed as creating the relationship of employer and employee." The contract was terminable at will by either party. Scott financed her own office and staff, was paid according to performance, had no taxes withheld from her checks, and could legally sell products of Massachusetts Mutual's competitors. Blatt learned that Scott was simultaneously selling insurance for Perpetual Life Insurance Corporation, one of Massachusetts Mutual's fiercest competitors. Blatt therefore withheld client contact information from Scott. Scott complained to Blatt that he was inhibiting her ability to sell insurance for Massachusetts Mutual. Blatt subsequently terminated their contract. Scott filed a suit in a New York state court against Blatt and Massachusetts Mutual. Scott claimed that she had lost sales for Massachusetts Mutual—and commissions—as a result of Blatt's withholding contact information from her. Using the information presented in the chapter, answer the following questions.

1. Who is the principal and who is the agent in this scenario? By which method was an agency relationship formed between Scott and Blatt?
2. What facts would the court consider most important in determining whether Scott was an employee or an independent contractor?
3. How would the court most likely rule on Scott's employee status? Why?
4. Which of the four duties that Blatt owed Scott in their agency relationship has probably been breached?

**Debate This** . . .    *All works created by independent contractors should be considered works for hire under copyright law.*

## Terms and Concepts

agency 160
exclusive agency 170

fiduciary 160

independent contractor 161

## Issue Spotters

1. Winona contracted with XtremeCast, a broadcast media firm, to cohost an Internet-streaming sports program. Winona and XtremeCast signed a new contract for each episode. In each contract, Winona agreed to work a certain number of days for a certain salary. During each broadcast, Winona was free to improvise her performance. She had no other obligation to work for XtremeCast. Was Winona an independent contractor? (See *Agency Relationships*.)

2. Dimka Corporation wants to build a new mall on a specific tract of land. Dimka contracts with Nadine to buy the property. There is a substantial difference between the price that Dimka is willing to pay and the price at which the owner is willing to sell. When Nadine learns of this, she wants to buy the land and sell it to Dimka herself. Can she do this? Discuss. (See *Duties of Agents and Principals*.)

• **Check your answers to the Issue Spotters against the answers provided in Appendix B at the end of this text.**

# Business Scenarios

**9–1. Agency Formation.** Paul Gett is a well-known, wealthy financial expert living in the city of Torris. Adam Wade, Gett's friend, tells Timothy Brown that he is Gett's agent for the purchase of rare coins. Wade even shows Brown a local newspaper clipping mentioning Gett's interest in coin collecting. Brown, knowing of Wade's friendship with Gett, contracts with Wade to sell a rare coin valued at $25,000 to Gett. Wade takes the coin and disappears with it. On the payment due date, Brown seeks to collect from Gett, claiming that Wade's agency made Gett liable. Gett does not deny that Wade was a friend, but he claims that Wade was never his agent. Discuss fully whether an agency was in existence at the time the contract for the rare coin was made. (See *Formation of the Agency Relationship*.)

**9–2. Duty of Loyalty.** Peter hires Alice as an agent to sell a piece of property he owns. The price is to be at least $30,000. Alice discovers that the fair market value of Peter's property is actually at least $45,000 and could be higher because a shopping mall is going to be built nearby. Alice forms a real estate partnership with her cousin Carl. Then she prepares for Peter's signature a contract for the sale of the property to Carl for $32,000. Peter signs the contract. Just before closing and passage of title, Peter learns about the shopping mall and the increased fair market value of his property. Peter refuses to deed the property to Carl. Carl claims that Alice, as Peter's agent, solicited a price above that agreed on when the agency was created and that the contract is therefore binding and enforceable. Discuss fully whether Peter is bound to this contract. (See *Duties of Agents and Principals*.)

**9–3. Employee versus Independent Contractor.** Stephen Hemmerling was a driver for the Happy Cab Co. Hemmerling paid certain fixed expenses and followed various rules relating to the use of the cab, the hours that could be worked, and the solicitation of fares, among other things. Rates were set by the state. Happy Cab did not withhold taxes from Hemmerling's pay. While driving the cab, Hemmerling was injured in an accident and filed a claim for workers' compensation benefits in a state court. Such benefits are not available to independent contractors. On what basis might the court hold that Hemmerling was an employee? Explain. (See *Agency Relationships*.)

# Business Case Problems

**9–4. Agency by Ratification.** Wesley Hall, an independent contractor managing property for Acree Investments, Ltd., lost control of a fire he had set to clear ten acres of Acree land. The runaway fire burned seventy-eight acres of Earl Barrs's property. Russell Acree, one of the owners of Acree Investments, had previously owned the ten acres, but he had put it into the company and was no longer the principal owner. Hall had worked for Russell Acree in the past and had told the state forestry department that he was burning the land for Acree. Barrs sued Russell Acree for the acts of his agent, Hall. In his suit, Barrs noted that Hall had been an employee of Russell Acree, Hall had talked about burning the land "for Acree," and Russell Acree had apologized to Barrs for the fire. Barrs also pointed out that Acree Investments had not been identified as the principal property owner until Barrs filed his lawsuit. Barrs argued that those facts were sufficient to create an agency by ratification to impose liability on Russell Acree. Was Barrs's agency by ratification claim valid? Why or why not? [*Barrs v. Acree*, 691 S.E.2d 575 (Ga. App. 2010)] (See *Formation of the Agency Relationship*.)

**9–5. Employment Relationships.** William Moore owned Moore Enterprises, a wholesale tire business. William's son, Jonathan, worked as a Moore Enterprises employee while he was in high school. Later, Jonathan started his own business, called Morecedes Tire. Morecedes regrooved tires and sold them to businesses, including Moore Enterprises. A decade after Jonathan started Morecedes, William offered him work with Moore Enterprises. On the first day, William told Jonathan to load certain tires on a trailer but did not tell him how to do it. Was Jonathan an independent contractor? Discuss. [*Moore v. Moore*, 152 Idaho 245, 269 P.3d 802 (2011)] (See *Agency Relationships*.)

**9–6. Agent's Duties to Principal.** William and Maxine Miller were shareholders of Claimsco International, Inc. They filed a suit against the other shareholders, Michael Harris and Kenneth Hoxie, and the accountant who worked for all of them—John Verchota. Among other things, the Millers alleged that Verchota had breached a duty that he owed them. They claimed that at Harris's instruction, Verchota had taken various actions that placed them at a disadvantage to the other shareholders. Verchota had allegedly adjusted Claimsco's books to maximize the Millers' financial liabilities, for instance, and had falsely reported distributions of income to them without actually transferring that income. Which duty are the Millers referring to? If the allegations can be proved, did Verchota breach this duty? Explain. [*Miller v. Harris*, 2013 IL App (2d) 120512, 985 N.E.2d 671 (2 Dist. 2013)] (See *Duties of Agents and Principals*.)

**9–7. Business Case Problem with Sample Answer— Determining Employee Status.** Nelson Ovalles worked  as a cable installer for Cox Rhode Island Telecom, LLC, under an agreement with a third party, M&M Communications, Inc. The agreement stated that no employer-employee relationship existed between Cox and M&M's technicians, including Ovalles. Ovalles was required to designate his affiliation with Cox on his work van, clothing, and identification badge. Cox had minimal contact with him, however, and had limited power to control how he performed his duties. Cox supplied cable wire and similar items, but the equipment was delivered to M&M, not to Ovalles. On a workday, while Ovalles was fulfilling a work order, his van rear-ended a car driven by Barbara Cayer. Is Cox liable to Cayer? Explain. [*Cayer v. Cox*

*Rhode Island Telecom, LLC,* 85 A.3d 1140 (R.I. 2014)] (See *Agency Relationships*.)

- For a sample answer to Problem 9–7, go to Appendix C at the end of this text.

**9–8. Agency Relationships.** Standard Oil of Connecticut, Inc., sells home heating, cooling, and security systems. Standard schedules installation and service appointments with its customers and then contracts with installers and technicians to do the work. The company requires an installer or technician to complete a project by a certain time but to otherwise "exercise independent judgment and control in the execution of any work." The installers and technicians are licensed and certified by the state. Standard does not train them, provide instruction manuals, supervise them at customers' homes, or inspect their work. The installers and technicians use their own equipment and tools, and they can choose which days they work. Standard pays a set rate per project. According to criteria used by the courts, are these installers and technicians independent contractors or employees? Why? [*Standard Oil of Connecticut, Inc. v. Administrator, Unemployment Compensation Act,* 320 Conn. 611, __ A.3d __ (2016)] (See *Agency Relationships*.)

**9–9. A Question of Ethics—Agency Formation and Duties.** *Western Fire Truck, Inc., contracted with Emergency One, Inc. (EO), to be its exclusive dealer in Colorado and Wyoming through December 2003. James Costello, a Western salesperson, was authorized to order EO vehicles for his customers. Without informing Western, Costello e-mailed EO about Western's difficulties in obtaining cash to fund its operations. He asked about the viability of Western's contract and his possible employment with EO. On EO's request, and in disregard of Western's instructions, Costello sent some payments for EO vehicles directly to EO. In addition, Costello, with EO's help, sent a competing bid to a potential Western customer. EO's representative e-mailed Costello, "You have my permission to kick [Western's] ass." In April 2002, EO terminated its contract with Western. At about the same time, a Western manager discovered Costello's e-mails saying that he was dissatisfied with the company and fired Costello. Western filed a suit in a Colorado state court, alleging that Costello had breached his duty as an agent and that EO had aided and abetted the breach. [Western Fire Truck, Inc. v. Emergency One, Inc., 134 P.3d 570 (Colo.App. 2006)] (See Formation of the Agency Relationship.)*

**(a)** Was there an agency relationship between Western and Costello? Western required monthly reports from its sales staff, but Costello did not report regularly. Does this indicate that Costello was not Western's agent? In determining whether an agency relationship exists, is the right to control or the fact of control more important? Explain.

**(b)** Did Costello owe Western a duty? If so, what was the duty? Did Costello breach it? If so, how?

**(c)** A Colorado state statute allows a court to award punitive damages in "circumstances of fraud, malice, or willful and wanton conduct." Did any of these circumstances exist in this case? Should punitive damages be assessed against either defendant? Why or why not?

# Legal Reasoning Group Activity

**9–10. Agent's Duties to Principal.** John Warren wanted to buy a condominium in California. Hildegard Merrill was the agent for the seller. Because Warren's credit rating was poor, Merrill told him he needed a co-borrower to obtain a mortgage at a reasonable rate. Merrill said that her daughter Charmaine would "go on title" until the loan and sale were complete if Warren would pay her $10,000. Merrill also offered to defer her commission on the sale as a loan to Warren so that he could make a 20 percent down payment on the property. He agreed to both plans.

Merrill secured the mortgage in Charmaine's name alone by misrepresenting her daughter's address, business, and income. To close the sale, Merrill had Warren remove his name from the title to the property. In October, Warren moved into the condominium, repaid Merrill the amount of her deferred commission, and began paying the mortgage. Within a few months, Merrill had Warren evicted. Warren subsequently filed a suit against Merrill and Charmaine. (See *Duties of Agents and Principals*.)

**(a)** The first group will determine who among these parties was in an agency relationship.

**(b)** The second group will discuss the basic duty that an agent owes a principal and decide whether that duty was breached here.

## CHAPTER 10

# Agency Liability and Termination

We have already discussed how agency relationships are formed and the duties of the principal and agent in that relationship. This chapter deals with another important aspect of agency law—the liability of principals and agents to third parties.

We look first at the liability of principals for contracts formed by agents with third parties. Generally, the liability of the principal will depend on whether the agent was authorized to form the contract. The second part of the chapter deals with an agent's liability to third parties in contract and tort. It also discusses the principal's liability to third parties because of an agent's torts. The chapter concludes with a discussion of how agency relationships are terminated.

## 10–1 Scope of Agent's Authority

The liability of a principal to third parties with whom an agent contracts depends on whether the agent had the authority to enter into legally binding contracts on the principal's behalf. An agent's authority can be either *actual* (express or implied) or *apparent*. If an agent contracts outside the scope of his or her authority, the principal may still become liable by ratifying the contract.

### 10–1a Express Authority

**Express authority** is authority declared in clear, direct, and definite terms. Express authority can be given orally or in writing.

**The Equal Dignity Rule** In most states, the **equal dignity rule** requires that if the contract being executed is or must be in writing, then the agent's authority must also be in writing. (Recall that a writing includes an electronic record.) Failure to comply with the equal dignity rule can make a contract voidable *at the option of the principal*. The law regards the contract at that point as a mere offer. If the principal decides to accept the offer, the acceptance must be ratified, or affirmed, in writing.

■ **EXAMPLE 10.1** Paloma (the principal) orally asks Austin (the agent) to sell a ranch that Paloma owns. Austin finds a buyer and signs a sales contract on behalf of Paloma to sell the ranch. Because a contract for an interest in realty must be in writing, the equal dignity rule applies. The buyer cannot enforce the contract unless Paloma subsequently ratifies Austin's agency status *in a writing*. Once the sales contract is ratified, either party can enforce rights under the contract. ■

Modern business practice allows several exceptions to the equal dignity rule:

1. An executive officer of a corporation normally can conduct *ordinary* business transactions without obtaining written authority from the corporation.
2. When the agent acts in the presence of the principal, the rule does not apply.
3. When the agent's act of signing is merely a formality, then the agent does not need written authority to sign. ■ **EXAMPLE 10.2** Sandra Healy (the principal) negotiates a contract but is called out of town the day it is to be signed. If Healy orally authorizes Derek Santini to sign, the oral authorization is sufficient. ■

**Power of Attorney** Giving an agent a **power of attorney** confers express authority.[1] The power of attorney is a written document and is usually notarized. (A document is notarized when a **notary public**—a person authorized to attest to the authenticity of signatures—signs, dates, and imprints the document with her or his seal of authority.) Most states have statutory provisions for creating a power of attorney.

---

1. An agent who holds a power of attorney is called an *attorney-in-fact* for the principal. The holder does not have to be an attorney-at-law (and often is not).

A power of attorney can be *special* (permitting the agent to perform specified acts only), or it can be *general* (permitting the agent to transact all business for the principal). Because a general power of attorney (see Exhibit 10–1) grants extensive authority to the agent, it should be used with great caution and usually only in exceptional circumstances. Ordinarily, a power of attorney terminates on the incapacity or death of the person giving the power.[2]

_____

2. A *durable* power of attorney, however, continues to be effective despite the principal's incapacity or death. An elderly person, for instance, might grant a durable power of attorney to provide for the handling of property and investments or specific health-care needs should he or she become incompetent.

**EXHIBIT 10–1  A Sample General Power of Attorney**

---

## GENERAL POWER OF ATTORNEY

### Know All Men by These Presents:

That I, _____ , hereinafter referred to as PRINCIPAL, in the County of _____ State of _____ , do(es) appoint _____ as my true and lawful attorney.

In principal's name, and for principal's use and benefit, said attorney is authorized hereby;

(1) To demand, sue for, collect, and receive all money, debts, accounts, legacies, bequests, interest, dividends, annuities, and demands as are now or shall hereafter become due, payable, or belonging to principal, and take all lawful means, for the recovery thereof and to compromise the same and give discharges for the same;

(2) To buy and sell land, make contracts of every kind relative to land, any interest therein or the possession thereof, and to take possession and exercise control over the use thereof;

(3) To buy, sell, mortgage, hypothecate, assign, transfer, and in any manner deal with goods, wares and merchandise, choses in action, certificates or shares of capital stock, and other property in possession or in action, and to make, do, and transact all and every kind of business of whatever nature;

(4) To execute, acknowledge, and deliver contracts of sale, escrow instructions, deeds, leases including leases for minerals and hydrocarbon substances and assignments of leases, covenants, agreements and assignments of agreements, mortgages and assignments of mortgages, conveyances in trust, to secure indebtedness or other obligations, and assign the beneficial interest thereunder, subordinations of liens or encumbrances, bills of lading, receipts, evidences of debt, releases, bonds, notes, bills, requests to reconvey deeds of trust, partial or full judgments, satisfactions of mortgages, and other debts, and other written instruments of whatever kind and nature, all upon such terms and conditions as said attorney shall approve.

GIVING AND GRANTING to said attorney full power and authority to do all and every act and thing whatsoever requisite and necessary to be done relative to any of the foregoing as fully to all intents and purposes as principal might or could do if personally present.

All that said attorney shall lawfully do or cause to be done under the authority of this power of attorney is expressly approved.

Dated: _____        /s/ _____

State of_____  ⎫  SS.
        County of_____  ⎬
On _____ , before me, the undersigned, a Notary Public in and for said State, personally appeared _____

_____
known to me to be the person _____ whose name _____ subscribed to the within instrument and acknowledged that _____ executed the same.

Witness my hand and official seal.        (Seal) _____
                                                     Notary Public in and for said State.

---

## 10–1b  Implied Authority

An agent has the **implied authority** to do what is reasonably necessary to carry out express authority and accomplish the objectives of the agency. Authority can also be implied by custom or inferred from the position the agent occupies.

■ **EXAMPLE 10.3**  Archer is employed by Packard Grocery to manage one of its stores. Packard has not expressly stated that Archer has authority to contract with third persons. Nevertheless, authority to manage a business implies authority to do what is reasonably required (as is customary or can be inferred from a manager's position) to operate the business. This includes forming contracts to hire employees, buying merchandise and equipment, and advertising the products sold in the store. ■

Note, however, that an agent's implied authority cannot contradict his or her express authority. Thus, if a principal has limited an agent's express authority, then the fact that the agent customarily would have such authority is irrelevant. ■ **EXAMPLE 10.4**  Juanita Alvarez is the owner of six Baja Tacos restaurants. Alvarez (the principal) strictly forbids the managers (agents) of her taco shops from entering into contracts to hire additional workers. Therefore, the fact that managers customarily would have authority to hire employees is immaterial. ■

## 10–1c  Apparent Authority

Actual authority (express or implied) arises from what the principal makes clear *to the agent.* Apparent authority, in contrast, arises from what the principal causes a third party to believe. An agent has **apparent authority** when the principal, by either word or action, causes a *third party* reasonably to believe that the agent has authority to act, even though the agent has no express or implied authority.

**A Pattern of Conduct**  Apparent authority usually comes into existence through a principal's pattern of conduct over time. ■ **EXAMPLE 10.5**  Bailey is a traveling salesperson. She solicits orders for goods but does not carry them with her. She normally would not have the implied authority to collect payments from customers on behalf of the principal. Suppose that she does accept payments from Corgley Enterprises, however, and submits them to the principal's accounting department for processing. If the principal does nothing to stop Bailey from continuing this practice, a pattern develops over time, and the principal confers apparent authority on Bailey to accept payments from Corgley. ■

At issue in the following *Spotlight Case* was whether the manager of a horse breeding operation had the authority to bind the farm's owner in a contract guaranteeing breeding rights.

## Spotlight on Apparent Authority of Managers

### Case 10.1  Lundberg v. Church Farm, Inc.
Court of Appeals of Illinois, 502 N.E.2d 806, 151 Ill.App.3d (1986).

**Background and Facts**  Gilbert Church owned a horse breeding farm managed by Herb Bagley. Advertisements for the breeding rights to one of Church Farm's stallions, Imperial Guard, directed all inquiries to "Herb Bagley, Manager." Vern and Gail Lundberg bred Thoroughbred horses. The Lundbergs contacted Bagley and executed a preprinted contract giving them breeding rights to Imperial Guard "at Imperial Guard's location," subject to approval of the mares by Church. Bagley handwrote a statement on the contract that guaranteed the Lundbergs "six live foals in the first two years." He then signed it "Gilbert G. Church by H. Bagley."

The Lundbergs bred four mares, which resulted in one live foal. Church then moved Imperial Guard from Illinois to Oklahoma. The Lundbergs sued Church for breaching the contract by moving the horse. Church claimed that Bagley was not authorized to sign contracts for Church or to change or add terms, but only to present preprinted contracts to potential buyers. Church testified that although Bagley was his farm manager and the contact person for breeding rights, Bagley had never before modified the preprinted forms or signed Church's name on them. The jury found in favor of the Lundbergs and awarded $147,000 in damages. Church appealed.

#### In the Language of the Court
Justice *UNVERZAGT* delivered the opinion of the court.
     * * * *

     * * * *Defendant contends that plaintiffs have failed to establish that Bagley had apparent authority to negotiate and sign the Lundberg contract for Church Farm* * * *.

**Case 10.1 Continued**

*The party asserting an agency has the burden of proving its existence * * * but may do so by inference and circumstantial evidence. * * * Additionally, an agent may bind his principal by acts which the principal has not given him actual authority to perform, but which he appears authorized to perform. * * * An agent's apparent authority is that authority which "the principal knowingly permits the agent to assume or which he holds his agent out as possessing. It is the authority that a reasonably prudent man, exercising diligence and discretion, in view of the principal's conduct, would naturally suppose the agent to possess."* [Emphasis added.]*

Plaintiffs produced evidence at trial that Gil Church approved the Imperial Guard advertisement listing Herb Bagley as Church Farm's manager, and directing all inquiries to him. Church also permitted Bagley to live on the farm and to handle its daily operations. Bagley was the only person available to visitors to the farm. Bagley answered Church Farm's phone calls, and there was a preprinted signature line for him on the breeding rights package.

The conclusion is inescapable that Gil Church affirmatively placed Bagley in a managerial position giving him complete control of Church Farm and its dealings with the public. We believe that this is just the sort of "holding out" of an agent by a principal that justifies a third person's reliance on the agent's authority.

We cannot accept defendant's contention that the Lundbergs were affirmatively obligated to seek out Church to ascertain the actual extent of Bagley's authority. Where an agent has apparent authority to act, the principal will be liable in spite of any undisclosed limitations the principal has placed on that authority.

**Decision and Remedy**  *The state appellate court affirmed the lower court's judgment in favor of the Lundbergs for $147,000. Because Church allowed circumstances to lead the Lundbergs to believe Bagley had the authority to negotiate and sign the contract, Church was bound by Bagley's actions.*

**Critical Thinking**
- **Legal Environment**  *The court held that Church had allowed the Lundbergs to believe that Bagley was his agent. What steps could Church have taken to protect himself against a finding of apparent authority?*
- **Ethical**  *Does a principal have an ethical responsibility to inform an unaware third party that an apparent agent does not in fact have the authority to act on the principal's behalf? Explain.*

---

**Apparent Authority and Estoppel**  A court can apply the doctrine of agency by estoppel when a principal has given a third party reason to believe that an agent has authority to act. If the third party honestly relies on the principal's representations to his or her detriment, the principal may be *estopped* (prevented) from denying that the agent had authority.

### 10–1d Emergency Powers

When an unforeseen emergency demands action by the agent to protect or preserve the property and rights of the principal, but the agent is unable to communicate with the principal, the agent has emergency power. ■ **EXAMPLE 10.6**  Rob Fulsom is an engineer for Pacific Drilling Company. While Fulsom is acting within the scope of his employment, he is severely injured in an accident on an oil rig many miles from home. Acosta, the rig supervisor, directs Thompson, a physician, to give medical aid to Fulsom and to charge Pacific for the medical services.

Acosta, an agent, has no express or implied authority to bind the principal, Pacific Drilling, for Thompson's medical services. Because of the emergency situation, however, the law recognizes Acosta as having authority to act appropriately under the circumstances. ■

### 10–1e Ratification

**Ratification** occurs when the principal affirms, or accepts responsibility for, an agent's *unauthorized* act. When ratification occurs, the principal is bound to the agent's act, and the act is treated as if it had been authorized by the principal *from the outset.* Ratification can be either express or implied.

If the principal does not ratify the contract, the principal is not bound, and the third party's agreement with the agent is viewed as merely an unaccepted offer. Because the third party's agreement is an unaccepted offer, the third party can revoke it at any time, without liability, before the principal ratifies the contract. The agent, however, may be liable to the third party for misrepresenting her or his authority.

The requirements for ratification can be summarized as follows:

1. The agent must have acted on behalf of an identified principal who subsequently ratifies the action.
2. The principal must know all of the material facts involved in the transaction. If a principal ratifies a contract without knowing all of the facts, the principal can rescind (cancel) the contract.[3]
3. The principal must affirm the agent's act in its entirety.
4. The principal must have the legal capacity to authorize the transaction at the time the agent engages in the act and at the time the principal ratifies. The third party must also have the legal capacity to engage in the transaction.
5. The principal's affirmation (ratification) must occur before the third party withdraws from the transaction.

---

3. Note that if the third party has changed position in reliance on the apparent contract, the principal can still rescind the contract but must reimburse the third party for any costs.

6. The principal must observe the same formalities when ratifying the act as would have been required to authorize it initially.

Concept Summary 10.1 summarizes the rules concerning an agent's authority to bind the principal and a third party.

---

## 10–2 Liability for Contracts

Liability for contracts formed by an agent depends on how the principal is classified and on whether the actions of the agent were authorized or unauthorized. Principals are classified as disclosed, partially disclosed, or undisclosed.[4]

1. A **disclosed principal** is a principal whose identity is known by the third party at the time the contract is made by the agent.

---

4. *Restatement (Third) of Agency*, Section 1.04(2).

---

### Concept Summary 10.1

#### Authority of an Agent to Bind the Principal and a Third Party

| | | |
|---|---|---|
| **Express Authority** | **Definition:** Authority expressly given by the principal to the agent. | **Effect:** Principal and third party are bound in contract. |
| **Implied Authority** | **Definition:** Authority implied (1) by custom, (2) from the position in which the principal has placed the agent, or (3) because such authority is necessary if the agent is to carry out expressly authorized duties and responsibilities. | **Effect:** Principal and third party are bound in contract. |
| **Apparent Authority** | **Definition:** Authority created when the conduct of the principal leads a third party to believe that the principal's agent has authority. | **Effect:** Principal and third party are bound in contract. |
| **Unauthorized Acts** | **Definition:** Acts committed by an agent that are outside the scope of his or her express, implied, or apparent authority. | **Effect:** Principal and third party are not bound in contract—*unless* the principal ratifies prior to the third party's withdrawal. |

**2.** A **partially disclosed principal** is a principal whose identity is not known by the third party. Nevertheless, the third party knows that the agent is or *may* be acting for a principal at the time the contract is made. ■ **EXAMPLE 10.7** Eileen has contracted with a real estate agent to sell certain property. She wishes to keep her identity a secret, but the agent makes it clear to potential buyers of the property that he is acting in an agency capacity. In this situation, Eileen is a partially disclosed principal. ■

**3.** An **undisclosed principal** is a principal whose identity is totally unknown by the third party. In addition, the third party has no knowledge that the agent is acting in an agency capacity at the time the contract is made.

## 10–2a Authorized Acts

If an agent acts within the scope of her or his authority, normally the principal is obligated to perform the contract regardless of whether the principal was disclosed, partially disclosed, or undisclosed. Whether the *agent may also be held liable* under the contract, however, depends on the disclosed, partially disclosed, or undisclosed status of the principal.

**Disclosed or Partially Disclosed Principal** A disclosed or partially disclosed principal is liable to a third party for a contract made by the agent. If the principal is disclosed, the agent has no contractual liability for the nonperformance of the principal or the third party. If the principal is partially disclosed, in most states the agent is also treated as a party to the contract. Thus, the third party can hold the agent liable for contractual nonperformance.[5]

■ **CASE IN POINT 10.8** Stonhard, Inc., makes epoxy and urethane flooring and installs it in industrial and commercial buildings. Marvin Sussman contracted with Stonhard to install flooring at a Blue Ridge Farms food-manufacturing facility in Brooklyn, New York. Sussman did not disclose that he was acting as an agent for the facility's owner, Blue Ridge Foods, LLC, at the time of the contract.

When Stonhard was not paid for the flooring it installed, it filed a suit against the facility, its owner, and Sussman to recover damages for breach of contract. The lower court dismissed the complaint against Sussman personally, but on appeal a reviewing court reversed that decision. The contract had been signed by Sussman "of Blue Ridge Farms." That evidence indicated that

Sussman was acting as an agent for a partially disclosed principal, in that the agency relationship was known, but not the principal's identity. "As an agent for an undisclosed [or partially disclosed] principal, Sussman became personally liable under the contract."[6] ■

**Undisclosed Principal** When neither the fact of an agency relationship nor the identity of the principal is disclosed, the undisclosed principal is bound to perform just as if the principal had been fully disclosed at the time the contract was made.

■ **CASE IN POINT 10.9** Bobby Williams bought a car at Sherman Henderson's auto repair business in Louisiana for $3,000. Henderson (the agent) negotiated and made the sale for the car's owner, Joe Pike (the principal), whose name was not disclosed. Williams drove the car to Memphis, Tennessee, where his daughter was a student. Three days after the sale, the car's engine caught fire. Williams extinguished the blaze and contacted Henderson. The next day, the vehicle was stolen from a parking lot outside Williams's daughter's apartment.

Williams filed a suit in a Louisiana state court against Pike (the principal) and Henderson (the agent). The court awarded Williams $2,000, plus the costs of the suit, adding that if Williams had returned the car, it would have awarded him the entire price. A state appellate court affirmed. Both Pike and Henderson—the undisclosed principal and his agent—were liable to Williams.[7] ■

**Indemnification.** When a principal's identity is undisclosed and the agent is forced to pay the third party, the agent is entitled to be *indemnified* (compensated) by the principal. The principal had a duty to perform, even though his or her identity was undisclosed,[8] and failure to do so will make the principal ultimately liable.

**Performance.** Once the undisclosed principal's identity is revealed, the third party generally can elect to hold either the principal or the agent liable on the contract. Conversely, the undisclosed principal can require the third party to fulfill the contract, *unless* one of the following is true:

**1.** The undisclosed principal was expressly excluded as a party in the written contract.

**5.** *Restatement (Third) of Agency,* Section 6.02.

**6.** *Stonhard, Inc. v. Blue Ridge Farms, LLC,* 114 A.D.3d 757, 980 N.Y.S.2d 507 (2 Dept. 2014).
**7.** *Williams v. Pike,* 58 So.3d 525 (La.App. 2 Cir. 2011).
**8.** If the agent is a gratuitous agent, and the principal accepts the benefits of the agent's contract with a third party, then the principal will be liable to the agent on the theory of quasi contract.

**2.** The contract is a negotiable instrument signed by the agent with no indication of signing in a representative capacity.[9]

**3.** The performance of the agent is personal to the contract, thus allowing the third party to refuse the principal's performance.

## 10–2b Unauthorized Acts

If an agent has no authority but nevertheless contracts with a third party, the *principal* cannot be held liable on the contract. It does not matter whether the principal was disclosed, partially disclosed, or undisclosed. The *agent* is liable.

■ **EXAMPLE 10.10** Chu signs a contract for the purchase of a truck, purportedly acting as an agent under authority granted by Navarro. In fact, Navarro has not given Chu any such authority. Navarro refuses to pay for the truck, claiming that Chu had no authority to purchase it. The seller of the truck is entitled to hold Chu liable for payment. ■

**Implied Warranty** If the principal is disclosed or partially disclosed, and the agent contracts with a third party without authorization, the agent is liable to the third party. The agent's liability here is based on his or her breach of the *implied warranty of authority,* not on the breach of the contract itself.[10] An agent impliedly warrants that he or she has the authority to enter a contract on behalf of the principal.

■ **EXAMPLE 10.11** Pinnell, a reclusive artist, hires Auber to solicit offers for particular paintings from various galleries, but does not authorize her to enter into sales agreements. Olaf, a gallery owner, offers to buy two of Pinnell's paintings for an upcoming show. If Auber draws up a sales contract with Olaf, she impliedly warrants that she has the authority to enter into sales contracts on behalf of Pinnell. If Pinnell does not agree to ratify Auber's sales contract, Olaf cannot hold Pinnell liable, but he can hold Auber liable for breaching the implied warranty of authority. ■

**Third Party's Knowledge** Note that if the third party knows at the time the contract is made that the agent does not have authority, then the agent is not liable. Similarly, if the agent expresses to the third party *uncertainty* as to

---

**9.** Under the Uniform Commercial Code (UCC), only the agent is liable if the instrument neither names the principal nor shows that the agent signed in a representative capacity [UCC 3–402(b)(2)].

**10.** The agent is not liable on the contract because the agent was never intended personally to be a party to the contract.

the extent of her or his authority, the agent is not personally liable.

## 10–2c Actions by E-Agents

Although in the past standard agency principles applied only to *human* agents, today these same agency principles also apply to e-agents. An electronic agent, or **e-agent,** is a semiautonomous software program that is capable of executing specific tasks, such as searching through many databases and retrieving relevant information for the user.

The Uniform Electronic Transactions Act (UETA), which was discussed previously, sets forth provisions relating to the principal's liability for the actions of e-agents. According to Section 15 of the UETA, e-agents can enter into binding agreements on behalf of their principals—at least, in those states that have adopted the act. Thus, if consumers place an order over the Internet, and the company (principal) takes the order via an e-agent, the company cannot later claim that it did not receive the order.

The UETA also stipulates that if an e-agent does not provide an opportunity to prevent errors at the time of the transaction, the other party to the transaction can avoid the transaction. Therefore, if an e-agent fails to provide an on-screen confirmation of a purchase or sale, the other party can avoid the effect of any errors. ■ **EXAMPLE 10.12** Bigelow wants to purchase three copies of three different books (a total of nine items). The e-agent mistakenly records an order for thirty-three of a single book and does not provide an on-screen verification of the order. If thirty-three books are then sent to Bigelow, he can avoid the contract to purchase them. ■

---

# 10–3 Liability for Torts and Crimes

Obviously, any person, including an agent, is liable for his or her own torts and crimes. Whether a principal can also be held liable for an agent's torts and crimes depends on several factors, which we examine here. In some situations, a principal may be held liable not only for the torts of an agent but also for torts committed by an independent contractor.

## 10–3a Principal's Tortious Conduct

A principal who acts through an agent may be liable for harm resulting from the principal's own negligence or recklessness. Thus, a principal may be liable if he or she gives improper instructions, authorizes the use of improper materials or tools, or establishes improper rules that result in the agent's committing a tort.

■ **EXAMPLE 10.13**  Parker knows that Audrey's driver's license has been suspended but nevertheless tells her to use the company truck to deliver some equipment to a customer. If someone is injured as a result, Parker will be liable for his own negligence in instructing Audrey to drive without a valid license. ■

## 10–3b Principal's Authorization of Agent's Tortious Conduct

Similarly, a principal who authorizes an agent to commit a tort may be liable to persons or property injured thereby, because the act is considered to be the principal's. ■ **EXAMPLE 10.14**  Pedro directs his agent, Andy, to cut the corn on specific acreage, which neither of them has the right to do. The harvest is therefore a trespass (a tort), and Pedro is liable to the owner of the corn. ■

Note that an agent acting at the principal's direction can be liable, along with the principal, for committing the tortious act even if the agent was unaware that the act was wrong. Assume in *Example 10.14* that Andy, the agent, did not know that Pedro lacked the right to harvest the corn. Andy can nonetheless be held liable to the owner of the field for damages, along with Pedro, the principal.

## 10–3c Liability for Agent's Misrepresentation

A principal is exposed to tort liability whenever a third person sustains a loss due to the agent's misrepresentation. The principal's liability depends on whether the agent was actually or apparently authorized to make representations and whether the representations were made within the scope of the agency. The principal is always directly responsible for an agent's misrepresentation made within the scope of the agent's authority.

■ **EXAMPLE 10.15**  Ainsley is a demonstrator for Pavlovich's products. Pavlovich sends Ainsley to a home show to demonstrate the products and to answer questions from consumers. Pavlovich has given Ainsley authority to make statements about the products. If Ainsley makes only true representations, all is fine. But if he makes false claims, Pavlovich will be liable for any injuries or damages sustained by third parties in reliance on Ainsley's false representations. ■

**Apparent Implied Authority**  When a principal has placed an agent in a position of apparent authority—making it possible for the agent to defraud a third party—the principal may also be liable for the agent's fraudulent acts. For instance, partners in a partnership generally have the apparent implied authority to act as agents of the firm. Thus, if one of the partners commits a tort or a crime, the partnership itself—and often the other partners personally—can be held liable for the loss.

■ **EXAMPLE 10.16**  Saulheim & Company is a securities brokerage firm that operates as a partnership and provides various financial services. The firm's managing partner, Dan Saulheim, is caught embezzling funds that clients have turned over to the firm for investment. After he is convicted, other partners in the firm claim that they are not liable for losses resulting from his illegal activities. In this situation, other partners may be liable if a court finds that Saulheim had apparent implied authority to act in the ordinary course of the partnership's business. Thus, the firm, as principal, is liable, and the personal assets of the individual partners, as agents, can be used to pay the firm's liability. ■

**Innocent Misrepresentation**  Tort liability based on fraud requires proof that a material misstatement was made knowingly and with the intent to deceive. An agent's *innocent* misstatements in a contract or warranty transaction can also provide grounds for the third party's rescission of the contract and the award of damages. Justice dictates that when a principal knows that an agent is not accurately advised of facts but does not correct either the agent's or the third party's impressions, the principal is responsible. The point is that the principal is always directly responsible for an agent's misrepresentation made within the scope of authority.

## 10–3d Liability for Agent's Negligence

An agent is liable for his or her own torts. A principal may also be liable for harm an agent causes to a third party under the doctrine of ***respondeat superior***,[11] a Latin term meaning "let the master respond." Under the doctrine of *respondeat superior*, the principal-employer is liable for any harm caused to a third party by an agent-employee in the course or scope of employment. The doctrine imposes **vicarious liability,** or indirect liability, because the principal-employer is being held liable for torts committed by an agent-employee.

When an agent commits a negligent act in such a situation, *both* the agent and the principal are liable. ■ **EXAMPLE 10.17**  Aegis hires SDI to provide landscaping services for its property. An herbicide sprayed by

---

11. Pronounced ree-*spahn*-dee-uht soo-*peer*-ee-your. The doctrine of *respondeat superior* applies not only to employer-employee relationships but also to other principal-agent relationships in which the principal has the right of control over the agent.

SDI employee David Hoggatt enters the Aegis building through the air-conditioning system and caused Catherine Warner, an Aegis employee, to suffer a heart attack. If Warner sues, both SDI (principal) and Hoggatt (agent) can be held liable for negligence. ■

**The Doctrine of *Respondeat Superior*** The doctrine of *respondeat superior* is similar to the theory of strict liability in that liability is imposed regardless of fault. At early common law, a servant (employee) was viewed as the master's (employer's) property. The master was deemed to have absolute control over the servant's acts and was held strictly liable for them, no matter how carefully the master supervised the servant. Although employers today are not masters of their employees, control is still a central concept to liability. This chapter's *Global Insight* feature discusses whether nations that follow Islamic law recognize the doctrine of *respondeat superior.*

**Underlying Rationale.** The rationale for the doctrine of *respondeat superior* is based on the social duty that requires every person to manage his or her affairs so as not to injure another. This duty applies even when a person acts through an agent (controls the conduct of another).

**Public Policy.** Generally, public policy requires that an injured person be afforded effective relief, and a business enterprise is usually better able to provide that relief than is an individual employee. Employers normally carry liability insurance to cover any damages awarded as a result of such lawsuits. They are also able to spread the cost of risk over the entire business enterprise.

**Application Today.** The courts have applied the doctrine of *respondeat superior* for nearly two centuries. It continues to have practical implications in all situations involving principal-agent (employer-employee) relationships. Today, the small-town store with one clerk and the multinational corporation with thousands of employees are equally subject to the doctrine.

**Determining the Scope of Employment** The key to determining whether a principal may be liable for the torts of an agent under the doctrine of *respondeat superior* is whether the torts are committed within the scope of the agency. Courts may consider the following factors in determining whether a particular act occurred within the course and scope of employment:

1. Whether the employee's act was authorized by the employer.
2. The time, place, and purpose of the act.
3. Whether the act was one commonly performed by employees on behalf of their employers.
4. The extent to which the employer's interest was advanced by the act.
5. The extent to which the private interests of the employee were involved.

## GLOBAL INSIGHT   Islamic Law and *Respondeat Superior*

The doctrine of *respondeat superior* is well established in the legal systems of the United States and most Western countries. As you have already read, under this doctrine, employers can be held liable for the acts of their employees. The doctrine of *respondeat superior* is not universal, however. Most Middle Eastern countries, for example, do not follow this doctrine.

### Codification of Islamic Law

Islamic law, as codified in the *sharia*, holds to a strict belief that responsibility for human actions lies with the individual and cannot be vicariously (indirectly) extended to others. This belief and other concepts of Islamic law are based on the writings of Muhammad, the seventh-century prophet whose revelations form the basis of the Islamic religion and, by extension, the

*sharia.* Muhammad's prophecies are documented in the Koran (Qur'an), which is the principal source of the *sharia.*

### An Exception

Islamic law does allow for an employer to be responsible for an employee's actions when the actions result from a direct order given by the employer to the employee. This principle also applies to contractual obligations. Note that the master is responsible *only* if direct orders were given. Otherwise stated, unless an employee is obeying a direct order of the employer, liability for the employee's actions does not extend to the employer.

**Critical Thinking** *How would U.S. society be affected if employers could not be held vicariously liable for their employees' torts?*

**6.** Whether the employer furnished the means or instrumentality (such as a truck or a machine) by which an injury was inflicted.

**7.** Whether the employer had reason to know that the employee would perform the act in question and whether the employee had done it before.

**8.** Whether the act involved the commission of a serious crime.

In the following case, the court had to determine whether or not a dump truck operator was the employee of a concrete services contractor.

**Case 10.2**

# Asphalt & Concrete Services, Inc. v. Perry

Court of Special Appeals of Maryland, 221 Md.App. 235, 108 A.3d 558 (2015).

**Background and Facts** Asphalt & Concrete Services, Inc. (ACS), was working on a play pad at St. John Regional Catholic School in Frederick, Maryland. ACS project manager Blake Wood contacted William Johnson at Higher Power Trucking, LLC, to arrange for a dump truck to haul material from a quarry to the job site. One day, while Johnson was driving the dump truck between the job site and the quarry, the truck struck and injured Moran Perry, who was crossing an intersection.

To recover for his injuries, Perry filed a lawsuit in a Maryland state court against ACS. Perry alleged that Johnson's negligence in operating the dump truck was the proximate cause of his injuries and that Johnson was ACS's employee. ACS, however, claimed that Johnson was an independent contractor. A jury agreed with Perry and awarded him $529,500 in damages. The court issued a judgment in Perry's favor, and ACS appealed.

## In the Language of the Court

*GRAEFF,* J. [Judge]

* * * *

* * * Pursuant to the doctrine of *respondeat superior,* an employer may be found liable for torts committed by its employee while acting in the scope of employment. ACS does not dispute this well-established rule, but it argues that the evidence showed that Mr. Johnson was not its employee.

* * * Maryland courts have traditionally considered five criteria in determining whether or not an employer/employee relationship exists between two parties. *These criteria, developed from the common law standard for determining the master/servant relationship, include (1) the power to select and hire the employee, (2) the payment of wages, (3) the power to discharge, (4) the power to control the employee's conduct, and (5) whether the work is part of the regular business of the employer.* [Emphasis added.]

Of the five factors, the factor of control stands out as the most important. * * * Whether the employer has the right to control and direct the employee in the performance of the work and in the manner in which the work is to be done is the decisive, or controlling, test.

* * * *

Here, * * * the evidence indicated as follows: (1) ACS called Mr. Johnson directly to reserve his trucking services; (2) Mr. Wood spoke only to Mr. Johnson when calling Higher Power; (3) ACS directed Mr. Johnson to go to the * * * quarry to pick up materials for the play pad project and gave him the time to be there for the pick-up; (4) Mr. Johnson was required to bring the materials directly to the job site after his truck was loaded, and if Mr. Johnson did not deliver the materials promptly, ACS had the right to dock his pay or to no longer employ him; (5) ACS paid Mr. Johnson on an hourly basis from the time he picked up his first load until ACS dismissed him from the job site; (6) after Mr. Johnson delivered his first load of materials, ACS directed him to return to the quarry to pick up and bring back additional materials; and (7) at the job site, Mr. Johnson was obligated to follow ACS's directions in terms of where to drop the materials, how much material to drop, and how many times he would need to return to the quarry. Based on that evidence, a jury could find that Mr. Johnson was subject to ACS's control, and ACS was liable for Mr. Johnson's negligence pursuant to the doctrine of *respondeat superior.*

**Case 10.2 Continues**

Case 10.2 Continued

**Decision and Remedy** *The state intermediate appellate court affirmed the jury's finding with respect to Johnson's status as ACS's employee. The court disagreed, however, with the lower court's admission of certain evidence that may have influenced the jury's finding of proximate cause for Perry's injuries. As a result, the court reversed the judgment on this ground and remanded the case for a new trial.*

**Critical Thinking**
- **Economic** *Why did ACS contend that Johnson was not its employee? Discuss.*

---

### The Distinction between a "Detour" and a "Frolic"
A useful insight into the concept of "scope of employment" can be gained from Judge Baron Parke's classic distinction between a "detour" and a "frolic" in the case of *Joel v. Morison* (1834).[12] In this case, the English court held that if a servant merely took a detour from his master's business, the master will be responsible. If, however, the servant was on a "frolic of his own" and not in any way "on his master's business," the master will not be liable.

■ **EXAMPLE 10.18** While driving his employer's vehicle to call on a customer, Mandel decides to stop at a store—which is three blocks off his route—to take care of a personal matter. As Mandel approaches the store, he negligently runs into a parked vehicle owned by Chan. In this situation, because Mandel's detour from the employer's business is not substantial, he is still acting within the scope of employment, and the employer is liable.

But suppose instead that Mandel decides to pick up a few friends in another city for cocktails and in the process negligently runs his vehicle into Chan's. In this situation, the departure from the employer's business is substantial—Mandel is on a "frolic" of his own. Thus, the employer normally will not be liable to Chan for damages. ■

### Employee Travel Time
An employee going to and from work or to and from meals usually is considered to be outside the scope of employment. If travel is part of a person's position, however, as it is for a traveling salesperson, then travel time is normally considered within the scope of employment. For such an employee, the entire business trip, including the return trip home, is within the scope of employment unless there is a significant departure from the employer's business.

### Notice of Dangerous Conditions
The employer is charged with knowledge of any dangerous conditions discovered by an employee and pertinent to the employment situation.

■ **EXAMPLE 10.19** Brad, a maintenance employee in Martin's apartment building, notices a lead pipe protruding from the ground in the building's courtyard. Brad neglects either to fix the pipe or to inform Martin of the danger. John trips on the pipe and is injured. Martin is charged with knowledge of the dangerous condition regardless of whether Brad actually informed him. That knowledge is imputed to the employer by virtue of the employment relationship. ■

### 10–3e Liability for Agent's Intentional Torts
Most intentional torts that individuals commit have no relation to their employment, and their employers will not be held liable. Nevertheless, under the doctrine of *respondeat superior,* the employer can be liable for intentional torts that an employee commits within the course and scope of employment. For instance, a department store owner is liable when a security guard who is a store employee commits the tort of false imprisonment while acting within the scope of employment. Similarly, a nightclub owner is liable when a "bouncer" commits the tort of assault and battery while on the job.

In addition, an employer who knows or should know that an employee has a propensity for committing tortious acts is liable for the employee's acts even if they would not ordinarily be considered within the scope of employment. ■ **EXAMPLE 10.20** Chaz, the owner of the Comedy Club, hires Alec as a bouncer for the club even though he knows that Alec has a history of arrests for criminal assault and battery. In this situation, Chaz may be liable if Alec viciously attacks a customer in the parking lot after hours. ■

An employer is also liable for permitting an employee to engage in reckless actions that can injure others. ■ **EXAMPLE 10.21** The owner of Bates Trucking observes an employee smoking while filling containerized trucks with highly flammable liquids. Failure to stop the employee will cause the employer to be liable for

---

12. 6 Car. & P. 501, 172 Eng.Rep. 1338 (1834).

any injuries that result if a truck explodes. ■ Needless to say, most employers purchase liability insurance to cover their potential liability for employee conduct in many situations.

Whether an agent's allegedly tortious conduct fell within the scope of the agent's employment, making the principal vicariously liable, was at the heart of the dispute in the following case.

**Case Analysis 10.3**

# M.J. v. Wisan

Utah Supreme Court, 2016 UT 13, __ P.3d __ (2016).

## In the Language of the Court

Associate Chief Justice *LEE* * * * :

* * * *

[The United Effort Plan Trust ("UEP Trust" or the "Trust") was formed in Utah by members of the Fundamentalist Church of Jesus Christ of Latter-Day Saints ("FLDS Church"). The Trust] members deeded their property to the UEP Trust to be managed by Church leaders. Church leaders, who were also trustees, then used this property to minister to the needs of the members.

* * * *

[At the time of the events leading up to this case,] the Trust was operated for the express purpose of furthering the doctrines of the FLDS Church, including the practice of * * * marriage involving underage girls.

* * * *

[Later, as a result of unrelated litigation, a state court reformed the Trust] by excising the purpose of advancing the religious doctrines and goals of the FLDS Church to the degree that any of these were illegal, including * * * sexual activity between adults and minors. [The court appointed Bruce Wisan to head the Trust.]

* * * *

[Later] M.J., a former member of the FLDS Church and beneficiary of the UEP Trust, [filed this suit in a Utah state court against Wisan, as head of the Trust, alleging that] when she was fourteen years old, she was forced to marry Allen Steed, her first cousin. The wedding was performed by Warren Jeffs, who at the time was acting president of both the FLDS Church and * * * the Trust. * * * M.J. claims that Steed repeatedly sexually assaulted and raped her

* * * . She requested a divorce from Steed on multiple occasions, but Jeffs refused to allow it. He also refused to let M.J. live * * * separately from her husband.

* * * She seeks to hold * * * the Trust vicariously liable for intentional infliction of emotional distress.

* * * M.J. * * * claims that Jeffs and other trustees were acting "in furtherance of the trust administration and within the scope of their authority," and thus contends that the Trust should be liable under the doctrine of *respondeat superior.*

* * * *

The Trust filed a series of motions for summary judgment. All of those motions were denied. The Trust then filed [this] petition for review.

* * * *

* * * Under [Utah Code Section 75–7–1010, Utah's version of Section 1010 of the Uniform Trust Code,] a trust is liable for the trustee's acts performed "in the course of administering the trust."

* * * The terms of the statute, in context, are quite clear. "In the course of" *is the traditional formulation of the standard for vicarious liability under the doctrine of* respondeat superior. *We accordingly interpret the Uniform Trust Act as incorporating the established standard of* respondeat superior *liability.* Thus, under [Section 75–7–1010] a trust is liable for the acts of a trustee when the trustee was acting within the scope of his responsibility as a trustee. [Emphasis added.]

* * * *

The difficult question for the law in this field has been to define the line between a course of conduct subject to the employer's control and an

independent course of conduct not connected to the principal. *An independent course of conduct is a matter so removed from the agent's duties that the law, in fairness, eliminates the principal's vicarious liability.* Such a course of conduct is one that represents a departure from, not an escalation of, conduct involved in performing assigned work or other conduct that an employer permits or controls. [Emphasis added.]

Our cases have identified three factors of relevance to this inquiry: (1) whether the agent's conduct is of the general kind the agent is employed to perform; (2) whether the agent is acting within the hours of the agent's work and the ordinary spatial boundaries of the employment; and (3) whether the agent's acts were motivated, at least in part, by the purpose of serving the principal's interest.

* * * In the case law of a number of states, spatial and time boundaries are no longer essential hallmarks of an agency relationship. Instead, the law now recognizes that agents may interact on an employer's behalf with third parties although the employee is neither situated on the employer's premises nor continuously or exclusively engaged in performing assigned work.

A number of courts have also questioned the viability of the requirement that an agent's acts be motivated in some part by an intention to serve the principal's purposes.

* * * In [some] jurisdictions, * * * courts avoid the use of motive or intention to determine whether an employee's tortious conduct falls within the scope of employment and adopt a different

*Case 10.3 Continues*

**Case 10.3 Continued**

standard for identifying the tie between the tortfeasor's employment and the tort. One such standard is whether the tort is a generally foreseeable consequence of the enterprise undertaken by the employer or is incident to it—in other words, whether the agent's conduct is not so unusual or startling that it seems unfair to include the loss resulting from it in the employer's business costs, or whether the tort was engendered by the employment or an outgrowth of it. Another considers whether the employment furnished the specific impetus for a tort or increased the general risk that the tort would occur. These tests leave to the finder of fact the challenge of determining whether a tortfeasor's employment did more than create a happenstance opportunity to commit the tort.

* * * To resolve this case we need not choose * * * between the purpose or motive test * * * and the alternative formulations * * * because we find that the Trust's attempts to defeat its liability on summary judgment fail under any of the * * * formulations.

We do openly endorse one particular aspect of * * * the doctrine of *respondeat superior,* however. Specifically * * * we hold that an agent need not be acting within the hours of the employee's work and the ordinary spatial boundaries of the employment in order to be acting within the course of his employment. * * * We acknowledge that in today's business world much work is performed for an employer away from a defined work space and outside of a limited work shift. And we accordingly reject the Trust's attempt to escape liability on the ground that Jeffs's acts as a trustee were not performed while he was on the Trust's clock or at a work space designated for his work for the Trust. Instead we hold that the key question is whether Jeffs was acting within the scope of employment when performing work assigned by the employer or engaging in a course of conduct subject to the employer's control.

[The Trust argues] that settled case-law establishes "as a matter of law that the sexual misconduct of an employee is outside the scope of employment." Granted, there are many cases that so conclude * * * and some of those cases * * * turn principally on the ground that * * * an agent who commits a sexual assault * * * cannot be viewed as advancing, even in part, the purposes of his principal. Yet some of the cases in this field (particularly more recent ones) * * * adopt * * * a standard that turns not on motive or purpose but on foreseeability, or on whether the employee's acts were engendered by or an outgrowth of the employment, or the employment furnished the impetus for the tort.

* * * *

And we conclude that this is one of those cases. Given Jeffs's unique role as leader of the FLDS Church, and in light of the unusual, troubling function of * * * marriage involving young brides in the FLDS culture, we hold that a reasonable factfinder could conclude that Jeffs was acting within the scope of his role as a trustee in directing Steed to engage in sexual activity with M.J.

* * * *

* * * We affirm the denial of the Trust's motions for summary judgment on that basis.

**Legal Reasoning Questions**

1. Why do some courts apply a standard for imposing vicarious liability that does not rely on motive or purpose to determine whether an agent's tortious conduct falls within the scope of employment?

2. Why, in some states, are the boundaries of work time and space no longer essential factors in determining the scope of employment in an agency relationship?

3. Who does the result in this case benefit? Why?

## 10–3f Liability for Independent Contractor's Torts

Generally, an employer is not liable for physical harm caused to a third person by the negligent act of an independent contractor in the performance of the contract. This is because the employer does not have *the right to control* the details of an independent contractor's performance.

Courts make an exception to this rule when the contract involves unusually hazardous activities, such as blasting operations, the transportation of highly volatile chemicals, or the use of poisonous gases. In these situations, strict liability is imposed, and an employer cannot be shielded from liability merely by using an independent contractor.

## 10–3g Liability for Agent's Crimes

An agent is liable for his or her own crimes. A principal or employer normally is *not* liable for an agent's crime even if the crime was committed within the scope of authority or employment. An exception to this rule is made when the principal or employer participated in the crime by conspiracy or other action.

In addition, in some jurisdictions, a principal may be liable under specific statutes if an agent, in the course and scope of employment, violates certain regulations. For instance, a principal might be liable for an agent's violation of sanitation rules or regulations governing prices, weights, or the sale of liquor.

# 10–4 Termination of an Agency

Agency law is similar to contract law in that both an agency and a contract may be terminated by an act of the parties or by operation of law. Once the relationship between the principal and the agent has ended, the agent no longer has the right (*actual* authority) to bind the principal. For an agent's *apparent* authority to be terminated, though, third persons may also need to be notified that the agency has been terminated.

## 10–4a Termination by Act of the Parties

An agency may be terminated by certain acts of the parties, which are listed and described in Exhibit 10–2. Bases for termination by act of the parties include lapse of time, achievement of purpose, occurrence of a specific event, mutual agreement, and at the option of one party.

When an agency agreement specifies the time period during which the agency relationship will exist, the agency ends when that time period expires. If no definite time is stated, then the agency continues for a reasonable time and can be terminated at will by either party. What constitutes a reasonable time depends on the circumstances and the nature of the agency relationship.

The parties can, of course, mutually agree to end their agency relationship. In addition, as a general rule, either party can terminate the agency relationship without the agreement of the other. The act of termination is called *revocation* if done by the principal and *renunciation* if done by the agent. Note, however, that the terminating party may face liability if the termination is wrongful.

**EXHIBIT 10–2** Termination by Act of the Parties

| METHOD | RULES | ILLUSTRATION |
|---|---|---|
| 1. Lapse of Time. | Agency terminates automatically at the end of the stated time. | Page lists her property for sale with Alex, a real estate agent, for six months. The agency ends in six months. |
| 2. Purpose Achieved. | Agency terminates automatically on the completion of the purpose for which it was formed. | Calvin, a cattle rancher, hires Abe as his agent in the purchase of fifty breeding stock. The agency ends when the cattle have been purchased. |
| 3. Occurrence of a Specific Event. | Agency normally terminates automatically on the event's occurrence. | Meredith appoints Allen to handle her business affairs while she is away. The agency terminates when Meredith returns. |
| 4. Mutual Agreement. | Agency terminates when both parties consent to end the agency relationship. | Linda and Greg agree that Greg will no longer be her agent in procuring business equipment. |
| 5. At the Option of One Party (*revocation*, if by principal; *renunciation*, if by agent). | Either party normally has a right to terminate the agency relationship. Wrongful termination can lead to liability for breach of contract. | When Patrick becomes ill, he informs Alice that he is revoking her authority to be his agent. |

**Wrongful Termination** Although both parties have the *power* to terminate the agency, they may not always possess the *right* to do so. Wrongful termination can subject the canceling party to a lawsuit for breach of contract. ■ **EXAMPLE 10.22** Rawlins has a one-year employment contract with Munro to act as agent in return for $65,000. Munro has the *power* to discharge Rawlins before the contract period expires. But if he does so, he can be sued for breaching the contract, because he had no *right* to terminate the agency. ■

Even in an agency at will—in which either party may terminate at any time—the principal who wishes to terminate must give the agent *reasonable* notice. The notice must be at least sufficient to allow the agent to recoup his or her expenses and, in some situations, to make a normal profit.

**Agency Coupled with an Interest** A special rule applies to an *agency coupled with an interest.* In an **agency coupled with an interest,** the agent has some legal right to (an interest in) the property that is the subject of the agency. This type of agency is not an agency in the usual sense because it is created for the agent's benefit instead of for the principal's benefit.

■ **EXAMPLE 10.23** Sylvia owns Harper Hills, a vacation home. She needs some cash right away, so she enters into an agreement with Rob under which Rob will lend her $10,000. In return, she will grant Rob a one-half interest in Harper Hills and "the exclusive right to sell" it. The loan is to be repaid out of the sale's proceeds. Rob is Sylvia's agent, and their relationship is an agency coupled with an interest. The agency was created when the loan agreement was made for the purpose of securing the loan. Therefore, Rob's agency power is irrevocable. ■

An agency coupled with an interest should not be confused with a situation in which the agent merely derives proceeds or profits from the sale of the subject matter. Many agents are paid a commission for their services, but the agency relationship involved does not constitute an agency coupled with an interest. For instance, a real estate agent who merely receives a commission from the sale of real property does not have a beneficial interest in the property itself.

**Notice of Termination** When the parties terminate an agency, it is the principal's duty to inform any third parties who know of the existence of the agency that it has been terminated. No particular form is required for notice of termination to be effective. The principal can personally notify the agent, or the agent can learn of the termination through some other means.

Although an agent's actual authority ends when the agency is terminated, an agent's *apparent authority* continues until the third party receives notice (from any source) that such authority has been terminated. ■ **EXAMPLE 10.24** Manning bids on a shipment of steel, and Stone is hired as an agent to arrange transportation for the shipment. When Stone learns that Manning has lost the bid, Stone's authority to make the transportation arrangement terminates. ■

If the principal knows that a third party has dealt with the agent, the principal is expected to notify that person *directly.* For third parties who have heard about the agency but have not yet dealt with the agent, *constructive notice* is sufficient.[13] If the agent's authority is written, however, normally it must be revoked in writing (unless the written document contains an expiration date).

## 10–4b Termination by Operation of Law

Certain events terminate agency authority automatically because their occurrence makes it impossible for the agent to perform or improbable that the principal would continue to want performance. We look at these events here. Note that when an agency terminates by operation of law, there is no duty to notify third persons—unless the agent's authority is coupled with an interest.

1. *Death or insanity.* The general rule is that the death or insanity of either the principal or the agent automatically and immediately terminates an ordinary agency relationship.[14] Knowledge of the death or insanity is not required. ■ **EXAMPLE 10.25** Grey sends Bosley to Japan to purchase a rare book. Before Bosley makes the purchase, Grey dies. Bosley's agent status is terminated at the moment of Grey's death, even though Bosley does not know that Grey has died. ■ (Some states, however, have enacted statutes that change the common law rule to require an agent's knowledge of the principal's death before termination.)

---

13. With *constructive notice* of a fact, knowledge of the fact is imputed by law to a person if he or she could have discovered the fact through proper diligence. Constructive notice is often accomplished by publication in a newspaper.

14. An exception to this rule exists in the bank-customer relationship. A bank, as agent, can continue to exercise specific types of authority after the customer's death or insanity and can continue to pay checks drawn by the customer for ten days after death.

2. *Impossibility.* When the specific subject matter of an agency is destroyed or lost, the agency terminates. ■ **EXAMPLE 10.26** Pedro employs Vasquez to sell Pedro's house. Prior to any sale, the house is destroyed by fire. Vasquez's agency and authority to sell the house terminate. ■ Similarly, when it is impossible for the agent to perform the agency lawfully because of a change in the law, the agency terminates.

3. *Changed circumstances.* Sometimes, an event occurs that has such an unusual effect on the subject matter of the agency that the agent can reasonably infer that the principal will not want the agency to continue. In such situations, the agency terminates. ■ **EXAMPLE 10.27** Baird hires Joslen to sell a tract of land for $40,000. Subsequently, Joslen learns that there is oil under the land and that the land is therefore worth $1 million. The agency and Joslen's authority to sell the land for $40,000 are terminated. ■

4. *Bankruptcy.* If either the principal or the agent petitions for bankruptcy, the agency is *usually* terminated. In certain circumstances, such as when the agent's financial status is irrelevant to the purpose of the agency, the agency relationship may continue. Insolvency, as distinct from bankruptcy, does not necessarily terminate the relationship. (An *insolvent* person is one who cannot pay debts as they come due or whose liabilities exceed his or her assets.)

5. *War.* When the principal's country and the agent's country are at war with each other, the agency is terminated. In this situation, the agency is automatically suspended or terminated because there is no way to enforce the legal rights and obligations of the parties.

See Concept Summary 10.2 for a synopsis of the rules governing the termination of an agency by operation of law.

## Concept Summary 10.2

### Agency Termination by Operation of Law

| | |
|---|---|
| **Death or Insanity** | Termination of the agency is automatic on the death or insanity of either the principal or the agent—except when the agency is coupled with an interest. |
| **Impossibility** | Agency termination occurs any time the agency cannot be performed because of an event beyond the parties' control, such as the destruction of the specific subject matter. |
| **Changed Circumstances** | When events are so unusual that it would be inequitable to allow the agency to exist, the agency will terminate. |
| **Bankruptcy** | Bankruptcy petition—but not mere insolvency—usually terminates the agency. |
| **War between Countries** | War between the principal's country and the agent's country automatically suspends or terminates agency because there is no way to enforce legal rights. |

# Reviewing: Agency Liability and Termination

Lynne Meyer, on her way to a business meeting and in a hurry, stopped at a Buy-Mart store for a new car charger for her smartphone. There was a long line at one of the checkout counters, but a cashier, Valerie Watts, opened another counter and began loading the cash drawer. Meyer told Watts that she was in a hurry and asked Watts to work faster. Instead, Watts slowed her pace. At this point, Meyer hit Watts. It is not clear whether Meyer hit Watts intentionally or, in an attempt to retrieve the car charger, hit her inadvertently.

In response, Watts grabbed Meyer by the hair and hit her repeatedly in the back of the head, while Meyer screamed for help. Management personnel separated the two women and questioned them about the incident. Watts was immediately fired for violating the store's no-fighting policy. Meyer subsequently sued Buy-Mart, alleging that the store was liable for the tort (assault and battery) committed by its employee. Using the information presented in the chapter, answer the following questions.

1. Under what doctrine discussed in this chapter might Buy-Mart be held liable for the tort committed by Watts?
2. What is the key factor in determining whether Buy-Mart is liable under this doctrine?
3. How is Buy-Mart's potential liability affected by whether Watts's behavior constituted an intentional tort or a tort of negligence?
4. Suppose that when Watts applied for the job at Buy-Mart, she disclosed in her application that she had previously been convicted of felony assault and battery. Nevertheless, Buy-Mart hired Watts as a cashier. How might this fact affect Buy-Mart's liability for Watts's actions?

**Debate This** . . .  *The doctrine of* respondeat superior *should be modified to make agents solely liable for their tortious (wrongful) acts committed within the scope of employment.*

## Terms and Concepts

| | | |
|---|---|---|
| agency coupled with an interest 190 | express authority 176 | ratification 179 |
| apparent authority 178 | implied authority 178 | *respondeat superior* 183 |
| disclosed principal 180 | notary public 176 | undisclosed principal 181 |
| e-agent 182 | partially disclosed principal 181 | vicarious liability 183 |
| equal dignity rule 176 | power of attorney 176 | |

## Issue Spotters

1. Davis contracts with Estee to buy a certain horse on her behalf. Estee asks Davis not to reveal her identity. Davis makes a deal with Farmland Stables, the owner of the horse, and makes a down payment. Estee does not pay the rest of the price. Farmland Stables sues Davis for breach of contract. Can Davis hold Estee liable for whatever damages he has to pay? Why or why not? (See *Liability for Contracts*.)

2. Vivian, owner of Wonder Goods Company, employs Xena as an administrative assistant. In Vivian's absence, and without authority, Xena represents herself as Vivian and signs a promissory note in Vivian's name. In what circumstance is Vivian liable on the note? (See *Liability for Contracts*.)

• **Check your answers to the Issue Spotters against the answers provided in Appendix B at the end of this text.**

## Business Scenarios

**10–1. Unauthorized Acts.** Janell Arden is a purchasing agent–employee for the A&B Coal Supply partnership. Arden has authority to purchase the coal needed by A&B to satisfy the needs of its customers. While Arden is leaving a coal mine from which she has just purchased a large quantity of coal, her car breaks down. She walks into a small roadside grocery store for help. While there, she encounters Will Wilson, who owns 360 acres back in the mountains with all mineral rights. Wilson, in need of cash, offers to sell Arden the property for $1,500 per acre.

On inspection of the property, Arden forms the opinion that the subsurface contains valuable coal deposits. Arden contracts to purchase the property for A&B Coal Supply, signing the contract "A&B Coal Supply, Janell Arden, agent." The closing date is August 1. Arden takes the contract to the partnership. The managing partner is furious, as A&B is not in the property business. Later, just before closing, both Wilson and the partnership learn that the value of the land is at least $15,000 per acre. Discuss the rights of A&B and Wilson concerning the land contract. (See *Liability for Contracts.*)

**10–2. Respondeat Superior.** ABC Tire Corp. hires Arnez as a traveling salesperson and assigns him a geographic area and

time schedule in which to solicit orders and service customers. Arnez is given a company car to use in covering the territory. One day, Arnez decides to take his personal car to cover part of his territory. It is 11:00 A.M., and Arnez has just finished calling on all customers in the city of Tarrytown. His next appointment is at 2:00 P.M. in the city of Austex, twenty miles down the road. Arnez starts out for Austex, but halfway there he decides to visit a former college roommate who runs a farm ten miles off the main highway. Arnez is enjoying his visit with his former roommate when he realizes that it is 1:45 P.M. and that he will be late for the appointment in Austex. Driving at a high speed down the country road to reach the main highway, Arnez crashes his car into a tractor, severely injuring Thomas, the driver of the tractor. Thomas claims that he can hold ABC Tire Corp. liable for his injuries. Discuss fully ABC's liability in this situation. (See *Liability for Torts and Crimes.*)

## Business Case Problems

**10–3. Liability Based on Apparent Authority.** Summerall Electric Co. and other subcontractors were hired by National Church Services, Inc. (NCS), which was the general contractor on a construction project for the Church of God at Southaven. As work progressed, payments from NCS to the subcontractors were late and eventually stopped altogether. The church had paid NCS in full for the entire project beforehand, but apparently NCS had mismanaged the project. When payments from NCS stopped, the subcontractors filed mechanic's liens for the value of the work they had performed but for which they had not been paid. The subcontractors sued the church, contending that it was liable for the payments because NCS was its agent on the basis of either actual or apparent authority. Was NCS an agent for the church, thereby making the church liable to the subcontractors? Explain your reasoning. [*Summerall Electric Co. v. Church of God at Southaven,* 25 So.3d 1090 (Miss.App. 2010)] (See *Scope of Agent's Authority.*)

**10–4. Disclosed Principal.** To display desserts in restaurants, Mario Sclafani ordered refrigeration units from Felix Storch, Inc. Felix faxed a credit application to Sclafani. The application was faxed back with a signature that appeared to be Sclafani's. Felix delivered the units. When they were not paid for, Felix filed a suit against Sclafani to collect. Sclafani denied that he had seen the application or signed it. He testified that he referred all credit questions to "the girl in the office." Who was the principal? Who was the agent? Who is liable on the contract? Explain. [*Felix Storch, Inc. v. Martinucci Desserts USA, Inc.,* 30 Misc.3d 1217, 924 N.Y.S.2d 308 (Suffolk Co. 2011)] (See *Liability for Contracts.*)

**10–5. Liability for Contracts.** Thomas Huskin and his wife entered into a contract to have their home remodeled by House Medic Handyman Service. Todd Hall signed the contract as an authorized representative of House Medic. It turned out that House Medic was a fictitious name for Hall

Hauling, Ltd. The contract did not indicate this, however, and Hall did not inform the Huskins about Hall Hauling. When a contract dispute later arose, the Huskins sued Todd Hall personally for breach of contract. Can Hall be held personally liable? Why or why not? [*Huskin v. Hall,* 2012 WL 553136 (Ohio Ct.App. 2012)] (See *Liability for Contracts.*)

**10–6. Business Case Problem with Sample Answer— Agent's Authority.** Basic Research, L.L.C., advertised its  products on television networks owned by Rainbow Media Holdings, Inc., through an ad agency, Icebox Advertising, Inc. As Basic's agent, Icebox had the express authority to buy ads from Rainbow on Basic's behalf, but the authority was limited to buying ads with cash in advance. Despite this limit, Rainbow sold ads to Basic through Icebox on credit. Basic paid Icebox for the ads, but Icebox did not pass all of the payments on to Rainbow. Icebox filed for bankruptcy. Can Rainbow recoup the unpaid amounts from Basic? Explain. [*American Movie Classics v. Rainbow Media Holdings,* 508 Fed.Appx. 826 (10th Cir. 2013)] (See *Scope of Agent's Authority.*)

• For a sample answer to Problem 10–6, go to Appendix C at the end of this text.

**10–7. Agent's Authority.** Terry Holden's stepmother, Rosie, was diagnosed with amyotrophic lateral sclerosis (ALS), and Terry's wife, Susan, became Rosie's primary caregiver. Rosie executed a durable power of attorney appointing Susan as her agent. Susan opened a joint bank account with Rosie at Bank of America, depositing $9,643.62 of Rosie's funds. Susan used some of the money to pay for "household expenses to keep us going while we were taking care of her." Rosie died three months later. Terry's father, Charles, as executor of Rosie's estate, filed a petition in a Texas state court against Susan for an accounting. What general duty did Susan owe Rosie as her agent? What does an agent's duty of accounting require? Did Susan breach either of these duties? Explain.

[*Holden v. Holden*, 456 S.W.3d 642 (Tex.App.—Tyler 2015)] (See *Scope of Agent's Authority*.)

**10–8. Scope of Agent's Authority.** Kindred Nursing Centers East, LLC, owns and operates Whitesburg Gardens, a long-term care and rehabilitation facility, in Huntsville, Alabama. Lorene Jones was admitted to the facility following knee-replacement surgery. Jones's daughter, Yvonne Barbour, signed the admission forms required by Whitesburg Gardens as her mother's representative in her presence. Jones did not object. The forms included an "Alternative Dispute Resolution Agreement," which provided for binding arbitration in the event of a dispute between "the Resident" (Jones) and "the Facility" (Whitesburg Gardens). Six days later, Jones was transferred to a different facility. After recovering from the surgery, she filed a suit in an Alabama state court against Kindred, alleging substandard care on a claim of negligence. Can Jones be compelled to submit her claim to arbitration? Explain. [*Kindred Nursing Centers East, LLC v. Jones*, __ So.3d __, 2016 WL 762450 (Ala. 2016)] (See *Scope of Agent's Authority*.)

**10–9. A Question of Ethics—Vicarious Liability.**  *Jamie Paliath worked as a real estate agent for Home Town Realty of Vandalia, LLC (the principal, a real estate broker). Torri Auer, a California resident, relied on Paliath's advice and assistance to buy three rental properties in Ohio. Before the sales, Paliath had represented that each property was worth approximately twice as much as what Auer would pay and that there was a waiting list of prospective tenants. Paliath also stated that all of the property needed work*

*and agreed to do the work for a specified price. Nearly a year later, substantial work was still needed, and only a few of the units had been rented. Auer sued Paliath and Home Town Realty for fraudulent misrepresentation. [Auer v. Paliath, 140 Ohio St.3d 276, 17 N.E.3d 561, 2014-Ohio-3632 (2014)]* (See *Liability for Torts and Crimes*.)

**(a)** Were Paliath's representations to Auer within the scope of her employment? Explain. Will the court hold the principal (Home Town Realty) liable for the misrepresentations of the agent (Paliath)?

**(b)** What is the ethical basis for imposing vicarious liability on a principal for an agent's tort?

**10–10. Special Case Analysis—Liability for Torts and Crimes.** Go to Case Analysis 10.3, *M.J. v. Wisan*. Read the excerpt and answer the following questions.

**(a) Issue:** What conduct was at the center of the dispute in this case? Who did the plaintiff allege was liable for this conduct? Which of these parties was the principal, and which was the agent?

**(b) Rule of Law:** What rule applied to determine the liability of the parties for the conduct in dispute?

**(c) Applying the Rule of Law:** What factors did the court indicate could be considered in deciding whether to impose liability in this case?

**(d) Conclusion:** How did the court rule on the question of vicarious liability?

# Legal Reasoning Group Activity

**10–11. Liability for Independent Contractor's Torts.** Dean Brothers Corp. owns and operates a steel drum manufacturing plant. Lowell Wyden, the plant superintendent, hired Best Security Patrol, Inc. (BSP), a security company, to guard Dean property and "deter thieves and vandals." Some BSP security guards, as Wyden knew, carried firearms. Pete Sidell, a BSP security guard, was not certified as an armed guard but nevertheless came to work with his gun (in a briefcase).

While working at the Dean plant on October 31, Sidell fired his gun at Tyrone Gaines, in the belief that Gaines was an

intruder. The bullet struck and killed Gaines. Gaines's mother filed a lawsuit claiming that her son's death was the result of BSP's negligence, for which Dean was responsible. (See *Liability for Torts and Crimes*.)

**(a)** The first group will determine what the plaintiff's best argument is to establish that Dean is responsible for BSP's actions.

**(b)** The second group will discuss Dean's best defense and formulate arguments to support it.

## CHAPTER 11

# Employment, Immigration, and Labor Law

Until the early 1900s, most employer-employee relationships were governed by the common law. Even today, under the common law *employment-at-will doctrine*, private employers have considerable freedom to hire and fire workers at will, regardless of the employees' performance.

Numerous statutes and administrative agency regulations now also govern the workplace. Thus, to a large extent, statutory law has displaced common law doctrines. In this chapter and the next, we look at the most significant laws regulating employment relationships.

This chapter discusses federal statutes that regulate various aspects of the workplace, including employee wages, hours, medical leave, safety, and pension and health plans. It also examines immigration law, a topic of special importance to employers in our diverse society. The chapter concludes with coverage of labor laws, which continue to have an impact on the employment environment.

## 11–1 Employment at Will

Employment relationships have traditionally been governed by the common law doctrine of **employment at will.** Under this doctrine, either party may terminate the employment relationship at any time and for any reason, unless doing so violates an employee's statutory or contractual rights.

Today, the majority of U.S. workers continue to have the legal status of "employees at will." In other words, this common law doctrine is still in widespread use, and only one state (Montana) does not apply it.

Nonetheless, federal and state statutes governing employment relationships prevent the doctrine from being applied in a number of circumstances. An employer may not fire an employee if doing so would violate a federal or state statute, such as a law prohibiting employment discrimination.

Note that the distinction made under agency law between employee status and independent-contractor status is important here. The employment laws that will be discussed apply only to the employer-employee relationship. They do not apply to independent contractors.

### 11–1a Common Law Exceptions to the Employment-at-Will Doctrine

As noted, statutory law has affected the application of the employment-at-will doctrine. In addition, the courts have carved out various exceptions to the doctrine based on contract theory, tort theory, and public policy.

**Exceptions Based on Contract Theory** Some courts have held that an *implied* employment contract exists between the employer and the employee. If the employee is fired outside the terms of the implied contract, he or she may succeed in an action for breach of contract even though no written employment contract exists.

■ **EXAMPLE 11.1** BDI Enterprises' employment manual and personnel bulletin both state that, as a matter of policy, workers will be dismissed only for good cause. Jing Chin is an employee at BDI. If Chin reasonably expects BDI to follow this policy, a court may find that there is an implied contract based on the terms stated in the manual and bulletin. ■ Generally, the key consideration in determining whether an employment manual creates an implied contractual obligation is the employee's reasonable expectations.

An employer's oral promises to employees regarding discharge policy may also be considered part of an implied contract. If the employer fires a worker in a manner contrary to what was promised, a court may hold that the employer has violated the implied contract and is liable for damages.

**Exceptions Based on Tort Theory** In some situations, the discharge of an employee may give rise to an action for wrongful discharge (discussed shortly) under tort theories. Abusive discharge procedures may result in a lawsuit for intentional infliction of emotional distress or defamation. In addition, some courts have permitted workers to sue their employers under the tort theory of fraud. Fraud might be alleged when an employer made false promises to a prospective employee.

■ **EXAMPLE 11.2** Goldfinch Consulting, Inc., induces Brianna to leave a lucrative job and move to another state by offering her "a long-term job with a thriving business." In fact, Goldfinch is not only having significant financial problems but is also planning a merger that will result in the elimination of the position offered to Brianna. If she takes the job in reliance on Goldfinch's representations and is fired shortly thereafter, Brianna may be able to bring an action against the employer for fraud. ■

**Exceptions Based on Public Policy** The most common exception to the employment-at-will doctrine is made on the basis that the employer's reason for firing the employee violates a fundamental public policy of the jurisdiction. Generally, the courts require that the public policy involved be expressed clearly in the statutory law governing the jurisdiction.

The public-policy exception may apply to an employee discharged for **whistleblowing**—that is, telling government authorities, upper-level managers, or the media that the employer is engaged in some unsafe or illegal activity. Normally, however, whistleblowers seek protection from retaliatory discharge under federal and state statutes, such as the Whistleblower Protection Act.[1]

■ **CASE IN POINT 11.3** Donald Waddell worked for the Boyce Thompson Institute for Plant Research. Waddell did not have an employment contract for a fixed term, and the institute's employee manual said that his job was "terminable at will." Soon after he was hired, the institute implemented a whistleblower policy designed to encourage "the highest standards of financial reporting and lawful and ethical behavior."

Waddell repeatedly told his supervisor, Sophia Darling, that she needed to file certain financial documents more promptly. Darling fired Waddell, telling him that he was disrespectful and insubordinate. Waddell then sued the institute, contending that he should not have been fired because he was acting under the company's whistleblowing policy.

A New York appellate court, however, found that Waddell could be fired. Waddell was employed at will. In addition, he was not protected under the whistle-

blower policy, which had been implemented after his employment. Thus, he could not have detrimentally relied on the policy in accepting the job.[2] ■

## 11–1b Wrongful Discharge

Whenever an employer discharges an employee in violation of an employment contract or a statutory law protecting employees, the employee may bring an action for **wrongful discharge.** For instance, an employee who is terminated in retaliation for some protected activity, such as whistleblowing or participating in an employment-discrimination investigation, can sue for wrongful discharge.

Even if an employer's actions do not violate any provisions in an employment contract or statute, the employer may still be subject to liability. An employee can sue for wrongful discharge under a common law doctrine, such as a tort theory or agency. For instance, if while firing a female employee, an employer publicly discloses private facts about her sex life, that employee could sue for wrongful discharge based on an invasion of privacy.

## 11–2 Wages, Hours, and Layoffs

In the 1930s, Congress enacted several laws to regulate the wages and working hours of employees, including the following:

1. The Davis-Bacon Act[3] requires contractors and subcontractors working on federal government construction projects to pay "prevailing wages" to their employees.
2. The Walsh-Healey Act[4] applies to U.S. government contracts. It requires that a minimum wage, as well as overtime pay at 1.5 times regular pay rates, be paid to employees of manufacturers or suppliers entering into contracts with agencies of the federal government.
3. The Fair Labor Standards Act (FLSA)[5] extended wage-hour requirements to cover all employers engaged in interstate commerce or in producing goods for interstate commerce. Certain other types of businesses were included as well. The FLSA, as amended, provides the most comprehensive federal regulation of wages and hours today.

**2.** *Waddell v. Boyce Thompson Institute for Plant Research, Inc.*, 92 A.D.3d 1172, 940 N.Y.S.2d 331 (2012).
**3.** 40 U.S.C. Sections 276a–276a-5.
**4.** 41 U.S.C. Sections 35–45.
**5.** 29 U.S.C. Sections 201–260.

**1.** 5 U.S.C. Section 1201.

## 11–2a Child Labor

The FLSA prohibits oppressive child labor. Restrictions on child labor differ by age group.

Children under fourteen years of age are allowed to do only certain types of work. They can deliver newspapers, work for their parents, and be employed in entertainment and (with some exceptions) agriculture. Children aged fourteen and fifteen are allowed to work, but not in hazardous occupations. There are also restrictions on how many hours per day and per week children in these age groups can work.

Working times and hours are not restricted for persons between the ages of sixteen and eighteen, but they cannot be employed in hazardous jobs. None of these restrictions apply to those over the age of eighteen.

## 11–2b Minimum Wages

The FLSA provides that a **minimum wage** of $7.25 per hour must be paid to covered nonexempt employees. Most states also have minimum wages. More than half of the states have set their minimum wages above the federal minimum wage. When the state minimum wage is greater than the federal minimum wage, the employee is entitled to the higher wage.

■ **EXAMPLE 11.4** The Oakland Raiders paid $1.25 million in 2014 to settle wage claims made by the team's cheerleading squad (the Raiderettes) as a class action. The cheerleaders had complained that they were not being paid for hours that they spent attending other events and performing other tasks required of them by contract. After the time spent performing these other tasks was factored in, the cheerleaders were receiving wages that were well below California's minimum wage, persuading the Raiders to settle the dispute. ■

Are employees entitled to receive wages for all the time they spend at work, including times when they are taking a personal break? See this chapter's *Ethics Today* feature for a discussion of this issue.

## 11–2c Tipped Workers

When an employee receives tips while on the job, the FLSA gives employers a tip credit toward the minimum wage amount. The employer is required to pay only $2.13 an hour in direct wages—if that amount, plus the tips received, equals at least the federal minimum wage. If an employee's tips and direct wages do not equal the federal minimum wage, the employer must make up the difference. Note that some states have enacted laws to prevent employers from including tips in the minimum

wage. In these states, tipped workers receive the regular minimum wage.

If employers pay at least the federal minimum wage, the FLSA allows them to take employee tips and make other arrangements for their distribution. ■ **CASE IN POINT 11.5** Misty Cumbie worked as a waitress at a café in Portland, Oregon, that was owned and operated by Woody Woo, Inc. Woody Woo paid its servers an hourly wage that was higher than the state's minimum wage, but the servers were required to contribute their tips to a "tip pool." Approximately one-third of the tip-pool funds went to the servers, and the rest was distributed to kitchen staff members, who otherwise rarely received tips for their services. When Cumbie filed a lawsuit against Woody Woo over her tips, the court held that the tip pool did not violate the FLSA.[6] ■

## 11–2d Overtime Provisions and Exemptions

Under the FLSA, any employee who works more than forty hours per week must be paid no less than 1.5 times her or his regular pay for all hours worked over forty. The FLSA overtime provisions apply only after an employee has worked more than forty hours per *week*. Therefore, employees who work ten hours a day, four days per week, are not entitled to overtime pay.

Certain employees are exempt from the FLSA's overtime provisions. These employees generally include executive, administrative, and professional employees, as well as outside salespersons and those who create computer code. Executive and administrative employees are those whose primary duty is management and who exercise discretion and independent judgment.

■ **CASE IN POINT 11.6** Patty Lee Smith was a pharmaceutical sales representative for Johnson and Johnson (J&J). She traveled to ten physicians' offices a day to promote the benefits of J&J's drug Concerta. Smith's work was unsupervised, she controlled her own schedule, and she received an annual salary of $66,000. When she filed a claim for overtime pay, the court held that she was an administrative employee and therefore exempt from the FLSA's overtime provisions.[7] ■

An employer can voluntarily pay overtime to ineligible employees but cannot waive or reduce the overtime requirements of the FLSA. In 2016, the Department of Labor updated its overtime regulations to allow millions more employees to receive overtime pay.[8]

---

6. *Cumbie v. Woody Woo, Inc.*, 596 F.3d 577 (9th Cir. 2010).
7. *Smith v. Johnson and Johnson*, 593 F.3d 280 (3d Cir. 2010).
8. 29 C.F.R. Part 541.

## ETHICS TODAY

### Is It Fair to Dock Employees' Pay for Bathroom Breaks?

For some employees, "punching a time clock" means accounting for *all* of the time that they are not working. These employees must "punch in" when they arrive and "punch out" when they leave for the day, of course, but they also must clock out when they take breaks. That includes bathroom breaks, coffee breaks, and smoking breaks.

**What the Law Says**

The Fair Labor Standards Act[a] does not require that an employer offer its employees personal breaks. If an employer does offer them, though, employees must be compensated during those breaks. Otherwise, the employer may effectively be in violation of federal minimum wage laws.

**A Pennsylvania Publisher Faces Fines for Unpaid Bathroom Breaks**

The issue of unpaid bathroom breaks came to the fore when the U.S. Department of Labor (DOL) filed a lawsuit against American Future Systems, Inc. (doing business as Progressive Business Publications). The DOL alleged that American Future Systems had created a compensation system in which none of its six thousand employees were compensated for bathroom breaks.[b]

The DOL argued that all workday breaks of twenty minutes or less are compensable time.[c] Because American Future Systems did not compensate its employees for such breaks, those employees were not properly credited for all compensable time. The result was that they had "been paid below the minimum wage established by the Fair Labor Standards Act (FLSA)."[d] U.S. district court judge L. Felipe Restrepo agreed, finding American Future Systems liable for unpaid wages under the FLSA, plus damages. The company will have to pay past and current employees almost $2 million, according to DOL estimates.

**The Ethical Issue**

Irrespective of the illegality of not paying for personal breaks, there is an ethical issue. Should workers have to face the choice of taking a bathroom break or getting paid? Adam Welsh, a senior trial attorney for the Department of Labor, argued that the answer was no. "I think it's the rare employer who doesn't allow its employees to go to the bathroom," Welsh said.

**Critical Thinking** *Consider a company whose employees include both smokers and nonsmokers. The smokers take numerous paid smoking breaks, while the nonsmokers do not. Is there an ethical issue here? Discuss.*

a. 29 U.S.C. Sections 201 *et seq.*
b. *U.S. Department of Labor v. American Future Systems, Inc.,* Memorandum, Case No. 12-6171 (E.D.Pa. 2015).

c. 29 C.F.R. Section 785.18.
d. 29 U.S.C. Section 206(a)(1)(c).

Whereas in the past, workers making more than $23,660 a year did not qualify for overtime pay, today, that threshold has been increased to $50,440 a year.

An employee's underreporting of hours worked can undercut his or her claim for overtime. But can an employee's underreporting *support* such a claim? That question was at the center of the following case.

---

**Case 11.1**

## Bailey v. TitleMax of Georgia, Inc.

United States Court of Appeals, Eleventh Circuit, 776 F.3d 797 (2015).

**Background and Facts**   Santonias Bailey was an employee of TitleMax of Georgia, Inc., in Jonesboro, Georgia. Bailey's supervisor told him that TitleMax did not pay overtime, so he regularly worked off the clock. For example, on some Saturdays, he would work from 8:30 A.M. to 5:30 P.M., but—as ordered by his supervisor—would log only seven hours despite having worked nine. His supervisor also

**Case 11.1 Continued**

edited Bailey's time records to report fewer hours than he actually worked by, for instance, subtracting a one-hour lunch break when there had been none.

Bailey resigned from TitleMax and filed a suit in a federal district court against the employer to recover for the unpaid overtime under the Fair Labor Standards Act (FLSA). TitleMax argued that Bailey was responsible for the unpaid time. According to TitleMax, he had never complained about his supervisor, and he had violated company policy with respect to keeping accurate time records. The court issued a judgment in the defendant's favor. Bailey appealed.

## In the Language of the Court

MARTIN, Circuit Judge:

* * * *

* * * The goal of the FLSA is to counteract the inequality of bargaining power between employees and employers.

In the broadest sense, this principle * * * compels our holding here. If an employer knew or had reason to know that its employee underreported his hours, it cannot escape FLSA liability by asserting [a] defense based on that underreporting. To hold otherwise would allow an employer to wield its superior bargaining power to pressure or even compel its employees to underreport their work hours.

* * * *

If an employee has worked overtime without pay, he may bring a private FLSA action for damages. An unpaid-overtime claim has two elements: (1) an employee worked unpaid overtime, and (2) the employer knew or should have known of the overtime work. *Knowledge may be imputed [attributed] to the employer when its supervisors or management encourage artificially low reporting.* [Emphasis added.]

Mr. Bailey has shown both required elements. He worked overtime without pay. TitleMax knew or should have known he worked overtime, because Mr. Bailey's supervisor both encouraged artificially low reporting and squelched truthful timekeeping.

* * * *

* * * No one disputes that his supervisor knew he was working off the clock. *The supervisor's knowledge may be imputed to TitleMax, making it liable for the FLSA violation.* * * * TitleMax argues that * * * an employee [is] deprived of his FLSA claim because he underreported his time, even if knowledge of the underreporting is imputed to the employer. [Emphasis added.]

TitleMax has identified no case in which [any federal appellate court] approved the use of [this] defense as a total bar to an employee's FLSA claim when the employer knew the employee underreported his hours.

* * * The dearth [scarcity] of precedent supporting TitleMax's * * * argument is persuasive, if not conclusive, evidence that its argument is misguided.

**Decision and Remedy**   *The U.S. Court of Appeals for the Eleventh Circuit reversed the judgment of the lower court and remanded the case for further proceedings. "Where, as here, an employer knew or had reason to know that its employee underreported his hours, it cannot invoke [a] defense based on that underreporting to bar the employee's FLSA claim."*

**Critical Thinking**

- **Legal Environment**   *Congress enacted the FLSA in 1938. More than eight thousand FLSA suits are filed in federal district courts each year. How do these facts support the court's reasoning in this case?*

---

## 11–2e Layoffs

The Worker Adjustment and Retraining Notification (WARN) Act[9] applies to employers with at least one hundred full-time employees. The act requires these employ-

ers to provide sixty days' notice before implementing a mass layoff or closing a plant that employs more than fifty full-time workers. A mass layoff is a layoff of at least one-third of the full-time employees at a particular job site.

The WARN Act is intended to give workers advance notice so that they can start looking for new jobs while they are still employed. It is also intended to alert state

---

**9**. 29 U.S.C. Sections 2101 *et seq.*

agencies so that they can provide training and other resources for displaced workers. Employers thus must provide advance notice of the layoff both to the affected workers and to state and local government authorities. (An employer may notify the workers' union representative, if the workers are members of a labor union.) Even companies that anticipate filing for bankruptcy normally must provide notice under the WARN Act.

An employer that violates the WARN Act can be fined up to $500 for each day of the violation. Employees can recover back pay for each day of the violation (up to sixty days), plus reasonable attorneys' fees.

## 11–3 Family and Medical Leave

The Family and Medical Leave Act (FMLA)[10] allows employees to take time off work for family or medical reasons or in certain situations that arise from military service. A majority of the states have similar legislation. The FMLA does not supersede any state or local law that provides more generous protection.

### 11–3a Coverage and Application

The FMLA requires employers that have fifty or more employees to provide *unpaid* leave for specified reasons. (Some employers voluntarily offer paid family leave, but this is not a requirement of the FMLA.) The

---

10. 29 U.S.C. Sections 2601, 2611–2619, 2651–2654.

FMLA expressly covers private and public (government) employees who have worked for their employers for at least a year.

An eligible employee may take up to *twelve weeks of leave* within a twelve-month period for any of the following reasons:

1. To care for a newborn baby within one year of birth.
2. To care for an adopted or foster child within one year of the time the child is placed with the employee.
3. To care for the employee's spouse, child, or parent who has a serious health condition.
4. If the employee suffers from a serious health condition and is unable to perform the essential functions of her or his job.
5. For any qualifying exigency (nonmedical emergency) arising out of the fact that the employee's spouse, son, daughter, or parent is a covered military member on active duty.[11] For instance, an employee can take leave to arrange for child care or to deal with financial or legal matters when a spouse is being deployed overseas.

In addition, an employee may take military caregiver leave to care for a family member with a serious injury or illness incurred as a result of military duty.[12] For military caregiver leave, the employee may take up to *twenty-six weeks* of leave within a twelve-month period.

In the following case, an employee asked for medical leave to care for her mother on a trip to Las Vegas, Nevada.

---

11. 29 C.F.R. Section 825.126.
12. 29 C.F.R. Section 825.200.

**Case 11.2**

## Ballard v. Chicago Park District
United States Court of Appeals, Seventh Circuit, 741 F.3d 838 (2014).

**Background and Facts** Beverly Ballard worked for the Chicago Park District. She lived with her mother, Sarah, who suffered from end-stage congestive heart failure. Beverly served as Sarah's primary caregiver with support from Horizon Hospice & Palliative Care. The hospice helped Sarah plan and secure funds for an end-of-life goal, a "family trip" to Las Vegas. To accompany Sarah as her caretaker, Beverly asked the Park District for unpaid time off under the Family and Medical Leave Act (FMLA). The employer refused, but Beverly and Sarah took the trip as planned.

Later, the Park District terminated Beverly for "unauthorized absences." She filed a suit in a federal district court against the employer. The court issued a decision in Beverly's favor. The Park District appealed, arguing that Beverly had been absent from work on a "recreational trip."

### In the Language of the Court
*FLAUM,* Circuit Judge.
 * * * *

We begin with the text of the [FMLA]: an eligible employee is entitled to leave "in order to care for" a family member with a "serious health condition."

**Case 11.2 Continued**

\* \* \* \*

\* \* \* *The FMLA's text does not restrict care to a particular place or geographic location.* For instance, it does not say that an employee is entitled to time off "to care *at home* for" a family member. *The only limitation it places on care is that the family member must have a serious health condition.* We are reluctant, without good reason, to read in another limitation that Congress has not provided. [Emphasis added.]

\* \* \* \*

Sarah's basic medical, hygienic, and nutritional needs did not change while she was in Las Vegas, and Beverly continued to assist her with those needs during the trip. In fact, \* \* \* Beverly's presence proved quite important indeed when a fire at the hotel made it impossible to reach their room, requiring Beverly to find another source of insulin and pain medicine. Thus, at the very least, [Beverly] requested leave in order to provide physical care.

\* \* \* \*

\* \* \* The Park District describes [Beverly's] travel as a "recreational trip" or a "non-medically related pleasure trip." It also raises the specter that employees will help themselves to unpaid FMLA leave in order to take personal vacations, simply by bringing seriously ill family members along. So perhaps what the Park District means to argue is that the real reason Beverly requested leave was in order to take a free pleasure trip, and not in order to care for her mother. \* \* \* However, \* \* \* an employer concerned about the risk that employees will abuse the FMLA's leave provisions may of course require that requests be certified by the family member's health care provider. And any worries about opportunistic leave-taking in this case should be tempered by the fact that this dispute arises out of the hospice and palliative care context.

If Beverly had sought leave to care for her mother in Chicago, her request would have fallen within the scope of the FMLA. So too if Sarah had lived in Las Vegas instead of with her daughter, and Beverly had requested leave to care for her mother there. Ultimately, other than a concern that our straightforward reading will "open the door to increased FMLA requests," the Park District gives us no reason to treat the current scenario any differently.

**Decision and Remedy**  *The U.S. Court of Appeals for the Seventh Circuit affirmed the lower court's judgment. Under the FMLA, an eligible employee is entitled to take leave from work to care for a family member with a serious health condition. The care is not restricted to a particular place (such as "at home").*

**Critical Thinking**
- **What If the Facts Were Different?**  *Suppose that Beverly had requested leave to make arrangements for a change in Sarah's care, such as a transfer to a nursing home. Is it likely that the result would have been different? Explain.*
- **Legal Environment**  *Under the FMLA, an employee is eligible for leave when he or she is needed to care for a family member. Should "needed to care for" be interpreted to cover only ongoing physical care? Discuss.*

## 11–3b Benefits and Protections

When an employee takes FMLA leave, the employer must continue the worker's health-care coverage on the same terms as if the employee had continued to work. On returning from FMLA leave, most employees must be restored to their original position or to a comparable position (with nearly equivalent pay and benefits, for instance). An important exception allows the employer to avoid reinstating a *key employee*—defined as an employee whose pay falls within the top 10 percent of the firm's workforce.

## 11–3c Violations

An employer that violates the FMLA can be required to provide various remedies, including the following:

1. Damages to compensate the employee for lost wages and benefits, denied compensation, and actual monetary losses (such as the cost of providing care for a family member). Compensatory damages are available up to an amount equivalent to the employee's wages for twelve weeks.
2. Job reinstatement.
3. Promotion, if a promotion has been denied.

A successful plaintiff is also entitled to court costs and attorneys' fees. In addition, if the plaintiff shows that the employer acted in bad faith, the plaintiff can receive two times the amount of damages awarded by a judge or jury. Supervisors can also be held personally liable, as employers, for violations of the act.

Employers generally are required to notify employees when an absence will be counted against FMLA leave. If an employer fails to provide such notice, and that failure to notify causes harm to the employee, the employer can be sanctioned.[13]

# 11-4 Health, Safety, and Income Security

Under the common law, employees who were injured on the job had to file lawsuits against their employers to obtain recovery. Today, numerous state and federal statutes protect employees from the risk of accidental injury, death, or disease resulting from their employment. In addition, the government protects employees' income through Social Security, Medicare, unemployment insurance, and the regulation of pensions and health insurance plans.

## 11-4a The Occupational Safety and Health Act

At the federal level, the primary legislation protecting employees' health and safety is the Occupational Safety and Health Act,[14] which is administered by the Occupational Safety and Health Administration (OSHA). The act imposes on employers a general duty to keep the workplace safe.

To this end, OSHA has established specific safety standards that employers must follow, depending on the industry. For instance, OSHA regulations require the use of safety guards on certain mechanical equipment. It also sets maximum levels of exposure to substances in the workplace that may be harmful to workers' health.

**Notices, Records, and Reports** The act requires that employers post certain notices in the workplace, maintain specific records, and submit reports. Employers with eleven or more employees are required to keep occupational injury and illness records for each employee. Each record must be made available for inspection when requested by an OSHA compliance officer.

Whenever a work-related injury or disease occurs, employers must make reports directly to OSHA. If an employee dies or three or more employees are hospitalized because of a work-related incident, the employer must notify OSHA within eight hours. A company that fails to do so will be fined. Following the incident, a complete inspection of the premises is mandatory.

**Inspections** OSHA compliance officers may enter and inspect the facilities of any establishment covered by the Occupational Safety and Health Act. Employees may also file complaints of violations. Under the act, an employer cannot discharge an employee who files a complaint or who, in good faith, refuses to work in a high-risk area if bodily harm or death might result.

## 11-4b State Workers' Compensation Laws

State **workers' compensation laws** establish an administrative procedure for compensating workers injured on the job. Instead of suing, an injured worker files a claim with the state agency or board that administers local workers' compensation claims.

All states require employers to provide workers' compensation insurance, but the specific rules vary by state. Most states have a state fund that employers pay into for workers' compensation coverage. Usually, employers can purchase insurance from a private insurer as an alternative to paying into the state fund. Most states also allow certain employers to be *self-insured*—that is, employers that show an ability to pay claims do not need to buy insurance.

No state covers all employees under its workers' compensation statute. Typically, domestic workers, agricultural workers, temporary employees, and employees of common carriers (companies that provide transportation services to the public) are excluded. Minors are covered.

**Requirements for Receiving Workers' Compensation** In general, the only requirements to recover benefits under state workers' compensation laws are:

1. The existence of an employment relationship.
2. An *accidental* injury that *occurred on the job or in the course of employment,* regardless of fault. (An injury that occurs while an employee is commuting to or from work usually is not covered because it did not occur on the job or in the course of employment.)

**13.** This was the United States Supreme Court's holding in *Ragsdale v. Wolverine World Wide, Inc.*, 535 U.S. 81, 122 S.Ct. 1155, 152 L.Ed.2d 167 (2002).
**14.** 29 U.S.C. Sections 553, 651–678.

An injured employee must notify her or his employer promptly (usually within thirty days of the accident). Generally, an employee must also file a workers' compensation claim within a certain period (sixty days to two years) from the time the injury is first noticed, rather than from the time of the accident.

**Workers' Compensation versus Litigation** If an employee accepts workers' compensation benefits, he or she may not sue for injuries caused by the employer's negligence. By barring lawsuits for negligence, workers' compensation laws also prevent employers from avoiding liability by using defenses, such as contributory negligence or assumption of risk. A worker may sue an employer who *intentionally* injures the worker, however.

## 11–4c Income Security

Federal and state governments participate in insurance programs designed to protect employees and their families from the financial impact of retirement, disability, death, hospitalization, and unemployment. The key federal law on this subject is the Social Security Act.[15]

**Social Security** The Social Security Act provides for old-age (retirement), survivors', and disability insurance. The act is therefore often referred to as OASDI. Retired workers who are covered by Social Security receive monthly payments from the Social Security Administration, which administers the Social Security Act. Social Security benefits are fixed by statute but increase automatically with increases in the cost of living.

**Medicare** Medicare is a federal government health-insurance program administered by the Social Security Administration for people sixty-five years of age and older and for some under age sixty-five who are disabled. It originally had two parts, one pertaining to hospital costs and the other to nonhospital medical costs, such as visits to physicians' offices. It now offers additional coverage options and a prescription-drug plan. People who have Medicare hospital insurance can obtain additional federal medical insurance if they pay monthly premiums.

**Tax Contributions** Under the Federal Insurance Contributions Act (FICA),[16] both employers and employees contribute to Social Security and Medicare, although the contributions are determined differently. The employer withholds the employee's FICA contributions from the employee's wages and ordinarily matches the contributions.

For Social Security, the basis for the contributions is the employee's annual wage base—the maximum amount of the employee's wages that is subject to the tax. As of 2016, the maximum amount subject to the tax was $118,500, and the tax rate was 12.4 percent.

The Medicare tax rate is 2.9 percent. Unlike Social Security, Medicare has no cap on the amount of wages subject to the tax. So even if an employee's salary is well above the cap for Social Security, he or she will still owe Medicare tax on the total earned income.

For Social Security and Medicare together, typically the employer and the employee each pay 7.65 percent. This is equivalent to 6.2 percent (half of 12.4 percent) for Social Security plus 1.45 percent (half of 2.9 percent) for Medicare up to the maximum wage base. Any earned income above that threshold is taxed only for Medicare. Self-employed persons pay both the employer's and the employee's portions of the Social Security and Medicare taxes.

Under the Affordable Care Act, high-income earners are subject to an additional Medicare tax of 3.8 percent on most investment income. This additional tax applies to single wage earners making more than $200,000 and married couples making more than $250,000.

**Private Retirement Plans** The major federal statute that regulates employee retirement plans is the Employee Retirement Income Security Act (ERISA).[17] This act empowers a branch of the U.S. Department of Labor to enforce its provisions governing employers that have private pension funds for their employees. ERISA does *not* require an employer to establish a pension plan. When a plan exists, however, ERISA provides standards for its management.

ERISA created the Pension Benefit Guaranty Corporation (PBGC), an independent federal agency, to provide timely and uninterrupted payment of voluntary private pension benefits. The pension plans pay annual insurance premiums (at set rates adjusted for inflation) to the PBGC, which then pays benefits to participants in the event that a plan is unable to do so.

A key provision of ERISA concerns vesting. **Vesting** gives an employee a legal right to receive pension benefits when she or he stops working. Before ERISA was enacted, some employees who had worked for companies for many years received no pension benefits when their employment terminated because those benefits had not vested. Under ERISA, generally all employee contributions to pension plans vest immediately. Employee

---

**15.** 42 U.S.C. Sections 301–1397e.
**16.** 26 U.S.C. Sections 3101–3125.

**17.** 29 U.S.C. Sections 1001 *et seq.*

rights to employer contributions vest after five years of employment.

**Unemployment Insurance** The Federal Unemployment Tax Act (FUTA)[18] created a state-administered system that provides unemployment compensation to eligible individuals who have lost their jobs. The FUTA and state laws require employers that fall under the provisions of the act to pay unemployment taxes at regular intervals. The proceeds from these taxes are then paid out to qualified unemployed workers.

To be eligible for unemployment compensation, a worker must be willing and able to work. Workers who have been fired for misconduct or who have voluntarily left their jobs are not eligible for benefits. Normally, workers must be actively seeking employment to continue receiving benefits.

■ **EXAMPLE 11.7** Martha works for Baily Snowboards in Vermont. One day at work, Martha receives a text from her son saying that he has been taken to the hospital. Martha rushes to the hospital and does not return to work for several days. Bailey hires someone else for Martha's position, and Martha files for unemployment benefits. Martha's claim will be denied because she left her job voluntarily and made no effort to maintain contact with her employer. ■

**COBRA** The Consolidated Omnibus Budget Reconciliation Act (COBRA)[19] enables employees to continue, for a limited time, their health-care coverage after they are no longer eligible for group health-insurance plans. The workers—not the employers—pay the premiums for the continued coverage.

COBRA prohibits an employer from eliminating a worker's medical, vision, or dental insurance when the worker's employment is terminated or when a reduction in the worker's hours would affect coverage. Termination of employment may be voluntary or involuntary. Only workers fired for gross misconduct are excluded from protection. Employers, with some exceptions, must inform employees of COBRA's provisions before the termination or reduction of work hours.

A worker has sixty days (from the date that the group coverage would stop) to decide whether to continue with the employer's group insurance plan. If the worker chooses to continue coverage, the employer is obligated to keep the policy active for up to eighteen months (twenty-nine months if the worker is disabled). The coverage must be the same as that provided to the worker

(and his or her family members) prior to the termination or reduction of work. An employer that does not comply with COBRA risks substantial penalties, including a tax of up to 10 percent of the annual cost of the group plan or $500,000, whichever is less.

**Employer-Sponsored Group Health Plans** The Health Insurance Portability and Accountability Act (HIPAA)[20] contains provisions that affect employer-sponsored group health plans. For instance, HIPAA restricts the manner in which employers collect, use, and disclose the health information of employees and their families. Employers must designate privacy officials, distribute privacy notices, and train employees to ensure that employees' health information is not disclosed to unauthorized parties.

Failure to comply with HIPAA regulations can result in civil penalties of up to $100 per person per violation (with a cap of $25,000 per year). Employers are also subject to criminal prosecution for certain types of HIPAA violations. An employer can face up to $250,000 in criminal fines and imprisonment for up to ten years if convicted.

**Affordable Care Act** The Affordable Care Act[21] (commonly referred to as Obamacare) requires most employers with fifty or more full-time employees to offer health-insurance benefits. Under the act, any business offering health benefits to its employees (even if not legally required to do so) may be eligible for tax credits of up to 35 percent to offset the costs.

An employer who fails to provide health benefits as required under the statute can be fined up to $2,000 for each employee after the first thirty people. (This is known as the 50/30 rule: employers with fifty employees must provide insurance, and those failing to do so will be fined for each employee after the first thirty.) An employer who offers a plan that costs an employee more than 9.5 percent of the employee's income may be assessed a penalty.

## 11–5 Employee Privacy Rights

Concerns about the privacy rights of employees have arisen as employers have purportedly used invasive tactics to monitor and screen workers. Perhaps the greatest privacy concern in employment today involves electronic monitoring of employees' activities.

**18.** 26 U.S.C. Sections 3301–3310.
**19.** 29 U.S.C. Sections 1161–1169.
**20.** 29 U.S.C. Sections 1181 *et seq.*
**21.** Pub. L. No. 111-148, 124 Stat. 119, March 23, 2010, codified in various sections of 42 U.S.C.

## 11–5a Electronic Monitoring

More than half of employers engage in some form of electronic monitoring of their employees. Many employers review employees' e-mail, as well as their social media posts and other Internet messages. Employers may also make video recordings of their employees at work, record their telephone conversations, and listen to their voice mail.

**Employee Privacy Protection** Employees of private (nongovernment) employers have some privacy protection under tort law and state constitutions. In addition, state and federal statutes may limit an employer's conduct in certain respects. For instance, the Electronic Communications Privacy Act prohibits employers from intercepting an employee's personal electronic communications unless they are made on devices and systems furnished by the employer.

Nonetheless, employers do have considerable leeway to monitor employees in the workplace. In addition, private employers generally are free to use filtering software to block access to certain Web sites, such as sites containing sexually explicit images. The First Amendment's protection of free speech prevents only *government employers* from restraining speech by blocking Web sites.

**Reasonable Expectation of Privacy** When determining whether an employer should be held liable for violating an employee's privacy rights, the courts generally weigh the employer's interests against the employee's reasonable expectation of privacy. Normally, if employees have been informed that their communications are being monitored, they cannot reasonably expect those interactions to be private. In addition, a court will typically hold that employees do not have a reasonable expectation of privacy when using a system (such as an e-mail system) provided by the employer.

If employees are *not* informed that certain communications are being monitored, the employer may be held liable for invading their privacy. Most employers that engage in electronic monitoring notify their employees about the monitoring. Nevertheless, a general policy may not sufficiently protect an employer monitoring forms of communications that the policy fails to mention. For instance, notifying employees that their e-mails and phone calls may be monitored does not necessarily protect an employer who monitors social media posts or text messages.

## 11–5b Other Types of Monitoring

In addition to monitoring their employees' online activities, employers also engage in other types of employee screening and monitoring. The practices discussed next have often been challenged as violations of employee privacy rights.

**Lie-Detector Tests** At one time, many employers required employees or job applicants to take polygraph examinations (lie-detector tests). Today, the Employee Polygraph Protection Act[22] generally prohibits employers from requiring employees or job applicants to take lie-detector tests or suggesting or requesting that they do so. The act also restricts employers' ability to use or ask about the results of any lie-detector test or to take any negative employment action based on the results.

Certain employers are exempt from these prohibitions. Federal, state, and local government employers, and certain security service firms, may conduct polygraph tests. In addition, companies that manufacture and distribute controlled substances may perform lie-detector tests. Other employers may use polygraph tests when investigating losses attributable to theft, including embezzlement and the theft of trade secrets.

**Drug Testing** In the interests of public safety and to reduce unnecessary costs, many employers, including the government, require their employees to submit to drug testing.

**Public Employers.** Government (public) employers are constrained in drug testing by the Fourth Amendment to the U.S. Constitution, which prohibits unreasonable searches and seizures. Drug testing of public employees is allowed by statute for transportation workers, however. Courts normally uphold drug testing of certain employees when drug use in a particular job may threaten public safety. Also, when there is a reasonable basis for suspecting public employees of drug use, courts often find that drug testing does not violate the Fourth Amendment.

**Private Employers.** The Fourth Amendment does not apply to drug testing conducted by private employers. Hence, the privacy rights and drug testing of private-sector employees are governed by state law. Many states have statutes that allow drug testing by private employers but restrict when and how the testing may be performed. A collective bargaining agreement (discussed later in this chapter) may also provide protection against drug testing (or may authorize drug testing in certain conditions).

The permissibility of testing a private employee for drugs often hinges on whether the employer's testing was reasonable. Random drug tests and even "zero-tolerance"

---

22. 29 U.S.C. Sections 2001 *et seq.*

policies (which deny a "second chance" to employees who test positive for drugs) have been held to be reasonable. It is also reasonable to require employees of private employers who are under contract with the federal government to undergo standard background investigations to disclose potential drug use.[23]

# 11–6 Immigration Law

The United States did not have any laws restricting immigration until the late nineteenth century. Immigration law has become increasingly important in recent years, however. An estimated 12 million undocumented immigrants now live in the United States, and many of them came to find jobs. Because U.S. employers face serious penalties if they hire undocumented workers, it is necessary for businesspersons to understand immigration laws. The most important laws affecting immigration in the context of employment are the Immigration Reform and Control Act (IRCA)[24] and the Immigration Act.[25]

## 11–6a The Immigration Reform and Control Act (IRCA)

When the IRCA was enacted in 1986, it provided amnesty to certain groups of aliens living illegally in the United States at the time. It also established a system that sanctions employers that hire immigrants who lack work authorization.

The IRCA makes it illegal to hire, recruit, or refer for a fee someone not authorized to work in this country. Through Immigration and Customs Enforcement officers, the federal government conducts random compliance audits and engages in enforcement actions against employers who hire undocumented workers.

**I-9 Employment Verification** To comply with IRCA requirements, an employer must perform **I-9 verifications** for new hires, including those hired as "contractors" or "day workers" if they work under the employer's direct supervision. Form I-9, Employment Eligibility Verification, which is available from U.S. Citizenship and Immigration Services,[26] must be completed *within three*

*days* of a worker's commencement of employment. The three-day period allows the employer to check the form's accuracy and to review and verify documents establishing the prospective worker's identity and eligibility for employment in the United States.

**Documentation Requirements** The employer must declare, under penalty of perjury, that an employee produced documents establishing his or her identity and legal employability. A U.S. passport establishing the person's citizenship is acceptable documentation. So is a document authorizing a foreign citizen to work in the United States, such as a permanent resident card or an *Alien Registration Receipt*.

Most legal actions alleging violations of I-9 rules are brought against employees who provide false information or documentation. If the employee enters false information on the I-9 form or presents false documentation, the employer can fire the worker, who then may be subject to deportation. Nevertheless, employers must be honest when verifying an employee's documentation. If an employer "should have known" that the worker was unauthorized, the employer has violated the rules.

**Enforcement** U.S. Immigration and Customs Enforcement (ICE) is the largest investigative arm of the U.S. Department of Homeland Security. ICE has a general inspection program that conducts random compliance audits. Other audits may occur if the agency receives a written complaint alleging that an employer has committed violations. Government inspections include a review of an employer's file of I-9 forms. The government does not need a subpoena or a warrant to conduct such an inspection.

If an investigation reveals a possible violation, ICE will bring an administrative action and issue a Notice of Intent to Fine, which sets out the charges against the employer. The employer has a right to a hearing on the enforcement action if it files a request within thirty days. This hearing is conducted before an administrative law judge, and the employer has a right to counsel and to discovery. The typical defense in such actions is good faith or substantial compliance with the documentation provisions.

**Penalties** An employer who violates the law by hiring an unauthorized worker is subject to substantial penalties. The employer can be fined up to $2,200 for each unauthorized employee for a first offense, $5,000 per employee for a second offense, and up to $11,000 for subsequent offenses. Employers who have engaged in a "pattern or

---

**23.** *See National Aeronautics and Space Administration v. Nelson,* 562 U.S. 134, 131 S.Ct. 746, 178 L.Ed.2d 667 (2011).

**24.** 29 U.S.C. Section 1802.

**25.** This act amended various provisions of the Immigration and Nationality Act of 1952, 8 U.S.C. Sections 1101 *et seq.*

**26.** U.S. Citizenship and Immigration Services is a federal agency that is part of the U.S. Department of Homeland Security.

practice of violations" are subject to criminal penalties, which include additional fines and imprisonment for up to ten years. A company can also be barred from future government contracts.

In determining the penalty, ICE considers the seriousness of the violation (such as intentional falsification of documents) and the employer's past compliance. ICE regulations also identify factors that will mitigate (lessen) or aggravate (increase) the penalty under certain circumstances. An employer that cooperates in the investigation, for instance, may receive a lesser penalty than an uncooperative employer.

## 11–6b The Immigration Act

Often, U.S. businesses find that they cannot hire enough domestic workers with specialized skills. For this reason, U.S. immigration laws have long made provisions for businesses to hire specially qualified foreign workers.

The Immigration Act of 1990 placed caps on the number of visas (entry permits) that can be issued to immigrants each year, including employment-based visas. Employment-based visas may be classified as permanent (immigrant) or temporary (nonimmigrant). Employers who wish to hire workers with either type of visa must comply with detailed government regulations.[27]

**I-551 Alien Registration Receipts** A company seeking to hire a noncitizen worker may do so if the worker is self-authorized. To be self-authorized, a worker must either be a lawful permanent resident or have a valid temporary Employment Authorization Document. A lawful permanent resident can prove his or her status to an employer by presenting an **I-551 Alien Registration Receipt,** known as a green card, or a properly stamped foreign passport.

Many immigrant workers are not already self-authorized, and an employer that wishes to hire them can attempt to obtain labor certification, or green cards, for them. A limited number of new green cards are issued each year. A green card can be obtained only for a person who is being hired for a permanent, full-time position. (A separate authorization system provides for the temporary entry and hiring of nonimmigrant visa workers.)

To gain authorization for hiring a foreign worker, an employer must show that no U.S. worker is qualified, willing, and able to take the job. The government has detailed regulations governing the advertising of positions as well as the certification process. Any U.S. applicants who meet the stated job qualifications must be interviewed for the position. The employer must also be able to show that the qualifications required for the job are a business necessity.

**The H-1B Visa Program** The most common and controversial visa program today is the H-1B visa system. To obtain an H1-B visa, the potential employee must be qualified in a "specialty occupation," meaning that the individual has highly specialized knowledge and has attained a bachelor's or higher degree or its equivalent. Individuals with H-1B visas can stay in the United States for three to six years and can work only for the sponsoring employer.

The recipients of these visas include numerous high-tech workers. A maximum of sixty-five thousand H-1B visas are set aside each year for new immigrants.[28] That limit is typically reached within the first few weeks of the year. Consequently, tech companies often complain that Congress needs to expand the number of H-1B visas available, to encourage the best and the brightest minds to work in the United States.

Critics of the H-1B visa program, however, believe that employers are sometimes using it to replace American workers with lower-paid foreign labor. For instance, Southern California Edison let go nearly five hundred workers from its information technology (IT) department in 2015. Shortly after that, allegations surfaced that the company had illegally replaced these employees with workers with H-1B visas, leading to a government investigation.

**Labor Certification** An employer who wishes to submit an H-1B application must first file a Labor Certification application on a form known as ETA 9035. The employer must agree to provide a wage level at least equal to the wages offered to other individuals with similar experience and qualifications. The employer must also show that the hiring will not adversely affect other workers similarly employed. The employer is required to inform U.S. workers of the intent to hire a foreign worker by posting the form. The U.S. Department of Labor reviews the applications and may reject them for omissions or inaccuracies.

**H-2, O, L, and E Visas** Other specialty temporary visas are available for other categories of employees. H-2 visas provide for workers performing agricultural labor of a seasonal nature. O visas provide entry for persons who

---

27. The most relevant regulations can be found at 20 C.F.R. Section 655 (for temporary employment) and 20 C.F.R. Section 656 (for permanent employment).

28. Immigration reform proposals generally raise this annual limit on H-1B visas to more than one hundred thousand.

have "extraordinary ability in the sciences, arts, education, business or athletics which has been demonstrated by sustained national or international acclaim." L visas allow a company's foreign managers or executives to work inside the United States. E visas permit the entry of certain foreign investors or entrepreneurs.

## 11–6c State Immigration Legislation

Until 2010, federal law exclusively governed immigration and the treatment of illegal immigrants. Then Arizona enacted a law that required Arizona law enforcement officials to identify and charge immigrants in Arizona who were there illegally, potentially leading to the immigrants' deportation. Among other things, that law required immigrants to carry their papers at all times and allowed police to check a person's immigration status during any law enforcement action.

Arizona's law was challenged in *Arizona v. United States*,[29] which reached the United States Supreme Court. The Court upheld the controversial "show-me-your-papers" provision, which requires police to check the immigration status of persons stopped for other violations. All other provisions of Arizona's law were struck down as unconstitutional violations of the supremacy clause.

The fact that the Supreme Court did not strike down all parts of Arizona's immigration law opened the door for other states to enact immigration legislation, and many states have done so. The Court's decision does set limits, however. Although states may require immigrants to show their papers if stopped by law enforcement for another reason, they may not make it a crime to fail to carry documentation. States also cannot authorize law enforcement to arrest anyone based solely on a reasonable suspicion that the person is in the country illegally.

## 11–7 Labor Unions

In the 1930s, in addition to wage and hour laws, Congress also enacted the first of several labor laws. These laws protect employees' rights to join labor unions, to bargain with management over the terms and conditions of employment, and to conduct strikes.

## 11–7a Federal Labor Laws

Federal labor laws governing union-employer relations have developed considerably since the first law was enacted in 1932. Initially, the laws were concerned with protecting the rights and interests of workers. Subsequent legislation placed some restraints on unions and granted rights to employers. We look here at four major federal statutes regulating union-employer relations.

**Norris-LaGuardia Act** Congress protected peaceful strikes, picketing, and boycotts in 1932 in the Norris-LaGuardia Act.[30] The statute restricted the power of federal courts to issue injunctions against unions engaged in peaceful strikes. In effect, this act declared a national policy permitting employees to organize.

**National Labor Relations Act** One of the foremost statutes regulating labor is the 1935 National Labor Relations Act (NLRA).[31] This act established the rights of employees to engage in collective bargaining and to strike.

**Unfair Labor Practices.** The NLRA specifically defined a number of employer practices as unfair to labor:

1. Interference with the efforts of employees to form, join, or assist labor organizations or to engage in concerted activities for their mutual aid or protection.
2. An employer's domination of a labor organization or contribution of financial or other support to it.
3. Discrimination in the hiring of or the awarding of tenure to employees for reason of union affiliation.
4. Discrimination against employees for filing charges under the act or giving testimony under the act.
5. Refusal to bargain collectively with the duly designated representative of the employees.

**The National Labor Relations Board.** The NLRA created the National Labor Relations Board (NLRB) to oversee union elections and to prevent employers from engaging in unfair and illegal union activities and unfair labor practices.

The NLRB has the authority to investigate employees' charges of unfair labor practices and to file complaints against employers in response to these charges. When violations are found, the NLRB may issue a **cease-and-desist order** compelling the employer to stop engaging in the unfair practices. Cease-and-desist orders can be enforced by a federal appellate court if necessary. After the NLRB rules on claims of unfair labor practices, its decision may be appealed to a federal court.

■ **CASE IN POINT 11.8**  Roundy's, Inc., which operates a chain of stores in Wisconsin, became involved in a dispute with a local construction union. When union

---

**29.** ___ U.S. ___, 132 S.Ct. 2492, 183 L.Ed.2d 351 (2012).

**30.** 29 U.S.C. Sections 101–110, 113–115.
**31.** 20 U.S.C. Sections 151–169.

members started distributing "extremely unflattering" flyers outside the stores, Roundy's ejected them from the property. The NLRB filed a complaint against Roundy's for unfair labor practices. An administrative law judge ruled that Roundy's had violated the law by discriminating against the union, and a federal appellate court affirmed. It is an unfair labor practice for an employer to prohibit union members from distributing flyers outside a store when it allows nonunion members to do so.[32] ■

**Good Faith Bargaining.** Under the NLRA, employers and unions have a duty to bargain in good faith. Bargaining over certain subjects is mandatory, and a party's refusal to bargain over these subjects is an unfair labor practice that can be reported to the NLRB. For instance, bargaining is mandatory for subjects relating to wages or working hours.

**Workers Protected by the NLRA.** To be protected under the NLRA, an individual must be an employee or a job applicant. (If job applicants were not covered, the NLRA's ban on discrimination in regard to hiring would mean little.) Additionally, individuals who are hired by a union to organize a company (union organizers) are to be considered employees of the company for NLRA purposes.[33]

Even a temporary worker hired through an employment agency might qualify for protection under the NLRA. ■ **CASE IN POINT 11.9**  Matthew Faush was an African American employee of Labor Ready, which provides temporary employees to businesses. Faush was assigned to a job stocking shelves at a Tuesday Morning store in Pennsylvania. After he was fired by Tuesday Morning, Faush filed a suit alleging discrimination. Tuesday Morning argued that Faush was not its employee. A federal court, however, found that the NLRA's protections may extend to temporary workers and that Faush was entitled to a trial.[34] ■

**Labor-Management Relations Act**  The Labor-Management Relations Act (LMRA or Taft-Hartley Act) of 1947[35] was passed to prohibit certain unfair union practices. For instance, the act outlawed the **closed shop**—a firm that requires union membership as a condition of employment. The act preserved the legality of the union shop, however. A **union shop** does not require union membership as a prerequisite for employment but

can, and usually does, require that workers join the union after a specified time on the job.

The LMRA also prohibited unions from refusing to bargain with employers, engaging in certain types of picketing, and *featherbedding* (causing employers to hire more employees than necessary). In addition, the act allowed individual states to pass **right-to-work laws**—laws making it illegal for union membership to be required for *continued* employment in any establishment. Thus, union shops are technically illegal in the twenty-seven states that have right-to-work laws.

**Labor-Management Reporting and Disclosure Act**  The Labor-Management Reporting and Disclosure Act (LMRDA)[36] established an employee bill of rights and reporting requirements for union activities. The act also outlawed **hot-cargo agreements,** in which employers voluntarily agree with unions not to handle, use, or deal in goods of other employers produced by nonunion employees.

The LMRDA strictly regulates unions' internal business procedures, including elections. For instance, it requires unions to hold regularly scheduled elections of officers using secret ballots. Former convicts are prohibited from holding union office. Moreover, union officials are accountable for union property and funds. Members have the right to attend and to participate in union meetings, to nominate officers, and to vote in most union proceedings.

## 11–7b  Union Organization

Typically, the first step in organizing a union at a particular firm is to have the workers sign authorization cards. An **authorization card** usually states that the worker desires to have a certain union, such as the United Auto Workers, represent the workforce. If a majority of the workers sign authorization cards, the union organizers (unionizers) present the cards to the employer and ask for formal recognition of the union.

The employer is not required to recognize the union at this point in the process, but it may do so voluntarily on a showing of majority support. (Under pro-labor legislation proposed repeatedly, the employer would have to recognize the union as soon as a majority of the workers had signed authorization cards—without holding an election.)[37]

**Union Elections**  If the employer refuses to voluntarily recognize the union—or if less than a majority of the workers sign authorization cards—the union organizers

---

**32.** *Roundy's, Inc. v. NLRB*, 647 F.3d 638 (7th Cir. 2012).
**33.** See the United States Supreme Court's landmark decision in *NLRB v. Town & Country Electric, Inc.*, 516 U.S. 85, 116 S.Ct. 450, 133 L.Ed.2d 371 (1995).
**34.** *Faush v. Tuesday Morning, Inc.,* 88 F.3d 208 (3d Cir. 2015).
**35.** 29 U.S.C. Sections 141 *et seq.*

**36.** 29 U.S.C. Sections 401 *et seq.*
**37.** The proposed legislation is the Employee Free Choice Act (or Card Check Bill).

can petition for an election. The organizers present the authorization cards to the NLRB with a petition to hold an election on unionization. For an election to be held, they must demonstrate that at least 30 percent of the workers to be represented support a union or an election.

### Appropriate Bargaining Unit.

Not every group of workers can form a single union. The proposed union must represent an *appropriate bargaining unit.* One key requirement is a *mutuality of interest* among all the workers to be represented by the union. Factors considered in determining whether there is a mutuality of interest include the similarity of the jobs of the workers to be unionized and their physical location.

### New NLRB Rules Expedite Elections.

New NLRB rules that took effect in 2015 significantly reduce the time between the filing of a petition and the ensuing election. As a result, the time before an election is held has changed from an average of thirty-eight days to as little as ten days after the filing. This change favors unions because it gives employers less time to respond to organizing campaigns, which unions often spend months preparing.

The NLRB now requires that a company hold a pre-election hearing within eight days after it receives a petition for an organizing election. On the day before the hearing, the company must also submit a "statement of position" laying out every argument it intends to make against the union. Any argument that the company does not include in its position paper can be excluded from evidence at the hearing. Once the hearing is held, an election can be scheduled right away.

### Voting.

If an election is held, the NLRB supervises the election and ensures secret voting and voter eligibility. If the proposed union receives majority support in a fair election, the NLRB certifies the union as the bargaining representative for the employees.

### Union Election Campaigns

Many disputes between labor and management arise during union election campaigns. Generally, the employer has control over unionizing activities that take place on company property and during working hours. Thus, the employer may limit the campaign activities of union supporters as long as it has a legitimate business reason for doing so. The employer may also reasonably limit when and where union solicitation may occur in the workplace, provided that the employer is not discriminating against the union. (Can union organizers use company e-mail during campaigns? See this chapter's *Managerial Strategy* feature for a discussion of this topic.)

■ **EXAMPLE 11.10**  A union is seeking to organize clerks at a department store owned by Amanti Enterprises. Amanti can prohibit all union solicitation in areas of the store open to the public because the unionizing activities could interfere with the store's business. It can also restrict union-related activities to coffee breaks and lunch hours. If Amanti allows solicitation for charitable causes in the workplace, however, it may not prohibit union solicitation. ■

An employer may campaign among its workers against the union, but the NLRB carefully monitors and regulates the tactics used by management. If the employer issues threats ("If the union wins, you'll all be fired") or engages in other unfair labor practices, the NLRB may certify the union even though the union lost the election. Alternatively, the NLRB may ask a court to order a new election.

Whether an employer violated its employees' rights under the National Labor Relations Act during a union election campaign was at issue in the following case.

**Case Analysis 11.3**

# Contemporary Cars, Inc. v. National Labor Relations Board

United States Court of Appeals, Seventh Circuit, 814 F.3d 859 (2016).

### In the Language of the Court

*HAMILTON,* Circuit Judge.

\* \* \* \*

\* \* \* Contemporary Cars, Inc., \* \* \* sells and services cars in Maitland, Florida. Bob Berryhill, the dealership's general manager, is responsible for the dealership's overall operations. \* \* \* AutoNation owns the dealership, as well as over 200 other dealerships throughout the United States.

This case focuses on the dealership's service department [which the dealership had previously split into three teams].

\* \* \* The International Association of Machinists began a campaign \* \* \* to organize the service technicians.

\* \* \* The technicians talked among themselves and held off-site meetings.

\* \* \* \*

\* \* \* The union filed its representation petition. The [National Labor Relations Board] approved the proposed bargaining unit, and an election was scheduled.

In the weeks before the election, Berryhill and AutoNation vice president

**Case 11.3 Continued**

* * * Brian Davis held group [and individual] meetings [with the technicians]. * * * One week before the election, * * * Berryhill * * * announced that the dealership was working on fixing problems the technicians had and that he was replacing two team leaders, [Andre] Grobler and Oudit Manbahal, with new team leaders.

* * * Technician Anthony Roberts * * * was then playing a leading role in the union organizing. * * * About a week before the union election, the dealership laid off Roberts, though Roberts had a higher skill rating, more hours, and more seniority than many other technicians.

* * * *

* * * The technicians voted in favor of unionizing.

* * * After the election, the dealership challenged the certification of the union as the exclusive representative of a bargaining unit consisting of service technicians. * * * The [National Labor Relations] Board affirmed the certification.

* * * The Board * * * filed a complaint alleging that the dealership and AutoNation had violated * * * the National Labor Relations Act. * * * An administrative law judge found * * * that the dealership and AutoNation had indeed violated the Act by interfering with their employees' protected rights to engage in concerted activity and to organize a union [and] by firing Anthony Roberts due to anti-union animus [hostility]. [The judge ordered the dealership to cease its interference with its employees' rights and to reinstate Roberts. The judge also ordered AutoNation to post a notice at all of its dealerships that it was rescinding the no-solicitation rule.] The Board affirmed the * * * order.

The dealership and AutoNation petitioned [the U.S. Court of Appeals for Seventh Circuit] for judicial review. [The NLRB cross-petitioned for enforcement of the order.]

* * * *

The administrative law judge found, and the Board affirmed, that the dealership and AutoNation in a number of

instances acted unlawfully to frustrate their employees' protected rights to engage in concerted activity and to organize a union.

* * * *

* * * The dealership violated [the Act] in the run-up to the election by coercively creating an impression of surveillance of union activity, interrogating employees about union activity, and soliciting and promising to remedy employee grievances.

* * * *

[Team Leader] Grobler created a coercive impression of surveillance when he commented on technician Juan Cazorla's attendance of union meetings. * * * Grobler asked [Cazorla] why he was in such a rush to leave work * * *, suggesting that Cazorla had "that meeting" to go to. Cazorla pretended not to know what Grobler was talking about, although he was in fact rushing to get to a union meeting. Again [on a different occasion] Grobler commented to Cazorla that he had "better rush" since he had a meeting * * *. It would have been reasonable for Cazorla to infer from Grobler's comments that his union activities were under management surveillance.

* * * *

* * * Berryhill coercively interrogated employees [when he] called them individually into his office and asked them about union activity. The dealership's service director was also present. * * * The setting of the meetings in Berryhill's office, Berryhill's and the director's positions of authority, and the fact that each technician was alone and outnumbered by managers all support the finding of coercion.

* * * *

* * * At the * * * meetings, Berryhill asked the technicians how the dealership could improve. * * * Berryhill [stated] that he was "working on" the problems and "in progress" on the solutions. * * * The * * * meetings also included inquiries about the union effort. * * * This was an effort to frustrate the union organizing drive by soliciting and at least implicitly promising to adjust grievances.

* * * *

* * * AutoNation vice president * * * Davis coercively interrogated a * * * technician, Tumeshwar Persaud * * *. Davis * * * asked him how he felt about the union election. * * * The question forced Persaud, who had not previously disclosed his union support, either to disclose his own union sympathies or to report on his perception of his fellow employees' union support.

* * * Davis held a meeting with employees at which he solicited employee complaints and, upon hearing that management had been unresponsive to employee complaints in the past, said that employees could call him or talk to him at any time. This meeting was part of a series of * * * meetings that management held in the run-up to the union election. * * * Davis was implicitly promising to remedy grievances with the goal of frustrating the union effort.

* * * *

* * * AutoNation * * * promulgated [publicized] an overly broad no-solicitation policy in the employee handbook used at all of its facilities. * * * AutoNation's policy prohibited any solicitation on AutoNation property at any time. * * * *The policy* * * * *amounted to an unfair labor practice because of the likelihood it would chill protected concerted activity.* [Emphasis added.]

* * * *

* * * The dealership's discharge of Anthony Roberts * * * a week before the election was motivated by anti-union animus.

* * * *

* * * Berryhill's identification of Roberts as a troublemaker and instigator of the organizational campaign established that anti-union animus was a substantial factor motivating Roberts's layoff. * * * The dealership's stated reason for firing Roberts—that he lacked sufficient electronic diagnostic skills—failed to establish that Roberts would have been laid off in the absence of anti-union animus. * * * Roberts was more productive and had a higher skill rating than many technicians who were retained.

**Case 11.3 Continues**

* * * *

Substantial evidence and a reasonable basis in law support the Board's order and the administrative law judge's order to the extent affirmed by the Board. We DENY the dealership and AutoNation's petition for review and ENFORCE the Board's order in its entirety.

### Legal Reasoning Questions

**1.** What might the dealership have asserted in defense to the charge that its actions violated its employees' rights?

**2.** After the election but before the union was certified, the dealership laid off four technicians and cut others' pay without bargaining with the union, claiming economic hard times. Did these steps constitute an unfair labor practice? Discuss.

**3.** What could the employer have done to avoid the charge in this case?

---

## MANAGERIAL STRATEGY    Union Organizing Using a Company's E-Mail System

When union organizers start an organizing drive, there are certain restrictions on what they can do, particularly within the workplace. Both employers and employees must comply with Section 7 of the National Labor Relations Act (NLRA).

### Protected Concerted Activities

Under Section 7, employees have certain rights to communicate among themselves. Section 7 states, "Employees shall have the right to self-organization, . . . and to engage in other concerted activities for the purpose of collective bargaining or other mutual aid or protection. . . ."

What about communication via e-mail? Can union organizers use a company-operated e-mail system for organizing purposes? Companies typically provide e-mail systems so that employees can communicate with outsiders and among themselves as part of their jobs. Generally, company policies have prohibited the use of company-owned and -operated e-mail systems for other than job-related communications. Starting in the early 2000s, some union organizers challenged this prohibition.

### The NLRB's Perspective Evolves

The first major case concerning this issue was decided by the National Labor Relations Board (NLRB) in 2007.[a] The NLRB allowed an employer's written policy that prohibited the use of a company-provided e-mail system for non-job-related solicitations. This decision was affirmed in relevant part by a federal court two years later.[b]

In late 2014, the NLRB reversed its 2007 position. "We decide today that employee use of e-mail for statutorily protected communications on non-working time must presumptively be permitted by employers who have chosen to give employees access to their e-mail systems."[c] The NLRB argued that its 2007 decision had failed to adequately protect "employees' rights under the NLRA." The board also stated that it had a responsibility "to adapt the Act to the changing patterns of industrial life."

The new rules are clear. Once an organizing election is scheduled, a company must turn over all telephone numbers and home and e-mail addresses of the company's employees to union organizers within two days. The organizers can then communicate with employees via the company's e-mail system.

### Business Questions

**1.** *Employees meeting around the water cooler or coffee machine have always had the right to discuss work-related matters. Is an employer-provided e-mail system or social media outlet simply a digital water cooler? Why or why not?*

**2.** *If your company instituted a policy stating that employees should "think carefully about 'friending' co-workers," would that policy be lawful? Why or why not?*

---

**a.** *Register Guard,* 351 NLRB 1110 (2007).
**b.** *Guard Publishing v. NLRB,* 571 F.3d 53 (D.C. Cir. 2009).

**c.** *Purple Communications, Inc. and Communication Workers of America, AFL-CIO,* Cases 21-CA-095151, 21-RC-091531, and 21-RC-091584, March 16, 2015.

## 11–7c Collective Bargaining

If the NLRB certifies the union, the union becomes the *exclusive bargaining representative* of the workers. The central legal right of a union is to engage in collective bargaining on the members' behalf. **Collective bargaining** is the process by which labor and management negotiate the terms and conditions of employment. Collective bargaining allows the representatives elected by union members to speak on behalf of the members at the bargaining table.

**Terms and Conditions of Employment** Wages, hours of work, and certain other conditions of employment may be discussed during collective bargaining sessions. For instance, subjects for negotiation may include workplace safety, employee discounts, health-care plans, pension funds, and apprentice and scholarship programs.

**Good Faith Bargaining** Once an employer and a union sit down at the conference table, they must negotiate in good faith and make a reasonable effort to come to an agreement. They are not obligated to reach an agreement. They must, however, approach the negotiations with the idea that an agreement is possible. Both parties may engage in hard bargaining, but the bargaining process itself must be geared to reaching a compromise—not avoiding a compromise.

Although good faith is a matter of subjective intent, a party's actions can be used to evaluate the party's good or bad faith. Excessive use of delaying tactics may be proof of bad faith, for instance, as is insistence on obviously unreasonable contract terms.

If an employer (or a union) refuses to bargain in good faith without justification, it has committed an unfair labor practice. Exhibit 11–1 illustrates some differences between good faith and bad faith bargaining.

## 11–7d Strikes

Even when labor and management have bargained in good faith, they may be unable to reach a final agreement. When extensive collective bargaining has been conducted and an impasse results, the union may call a strike against the employer to pressure it into making concessions.

In a **strike,** the unionized employees leave their jobs and refuse to work. The workers also typically picket the workplace, standing outside the facility with signs stating their complaints.

A strike is an extreme action. Striking workers lose their rights to be paid, and management loses production and may lose customers when orders cannot be filled. Labor law regulates the circumstances and conduct of strikes.

Most strikes take the form of "economic strikes," which are initiated because the union wants a better contract. ■ **EXAMPLE 11.11** Teachers in Eagle Point, Oregon, engage in an economic strike after contract

**EXHIBIT 11–1** Good Faith versus Bad Faith in Collective Bargaining

| GOOD FAITH BARGAINING | BAD FAITH BARGAINING |
|---|---|
| 1. Negotiating with the belief that an agreement is possible | 1. Excessive delaying tactics |
| 2. Seriously considering the other side's positions | 2. Insistence on unreasonable contract terms |
| 3. Making reasonable proposals | 3. Rejecting a proposal without offering a counterproposal |
| 4. Being willing to compromise | 4. Engaging in a campaign among workers to undermine the union |
| 5. Sending bargainers who have the authority to enter into agreements for the company | 5. Constantly shifting positions on disputed contract terms |
| | 6. Sending bargainers who lack authority to commit the company to a contract |

negotiations with the school district fail to bring an agreement on pay, working hours, and subcontracting jobs. The unionized teachers picket outside the school building. Classes are canceled for a few weeks until the district can find substitute teachers who will fill in during the strike. ∎

**The Right to Strike**  The right to strike is guaranteed by the NLRA, within limits. Strike activities, such as picketing, are protected by the free speech guarantee of the First Amendment to the U.S. Constitution. Persons who are not employees have a right to participate in picketing an employer. The NLRA also gives workers the right to refuse to cross a picket line of fellow workers engaged in a lawful strike. Employers are permitted to hire replacement workers to substitute for the striking workers.

**Illegal Strikes**  In the following situations, the conduct of the strikers may cause the strikes to be illegal:

1.  *Violent strikes.* The use of violence (including the threat of violence) against management employees or substitute workers is illegal.
2.  *Massed picketing.* If the strikers form a barrier and deny management or other nonunion workers access to the plant, the strike is illegal.
3.  *Sit-down strikes.* Strikes in which employees simply stay in the plant without working are illegal.
4.  *No-strike clause.* A strike may be illegal if it contravenes a no-strike clause that was in the previous collective bargaining agreement between the employer and the union.
5.  *Secondary boycotts.* A **secondary boycott** is an illegal strike that is directed against someone other than the strikers' employer, such as companies that sell materials to the employer. ∎ **EXAMPLE 11.12**  The unionized workers of SemiCo go out on strike. To increase their economic leverage, the workers picket the leading suppliers and customers of SemiCo in an attempt to hurt the company's business. SemiCo is considered the primary employer, and its suppliers and customers are considered secondary employers. Picketing of the suppliers or customers is a secondary boycott. ∎
6.  *Wildcat strikes.* A wildcat strike occurs when a small number of workers, perhaps dissatisfied with a union's representation, call their own strike. The union is the exclusive bargaining representative of a group of workers, and only the union can call a strike. Therefore, a wildcat strike, unauthorized by the certified union, is illegal.

**After a Strike Ends**  In a typical strike, the employer has a right to hire permanent replacements during the strike. The employer need not terminate the replacement workers when the economic strikers seek to return to work. In other words, striking workers are not guaranteed the right to return to their jobs after the strike if satisfactory replacement workers have been found.

If the employer has not hired replacement workers to fill the strikers' positions, however, then the employer must rehire the economic strikers to fill any vacancies. Employers may not discriminate against former economic strikers, and those who are rehired retain their seniority rights.

## 11–7e  Lockouts

Lockouts are the employer's counterpart to the workers' right to strike. A **lockout** occurs when the employer shuts down to prevent employees from working. Lockouts usually are used when the employer believes that a strike is imminent or the parties have reached a stalemate in collective bargaining.

∎ **EXAMPLE 11.13**  Owners of the teams in the National Football League (NFL) imposed a lockout on the NFL players' union in 2011 after negotiations on a new collective bargaining agreement broke down. The NFL owners had proposed to reduce players' salaries and extend the season by two games because of decreased profits due to the struggling economy. A settlement was reached before the start of the 2011 football season. The players accepted a somewhat smaller proportion of the revenue generated in exchange for better working conditions and more retirement benefits. The owners agreed to keep the same number of games per season.

The owners of the teams in the National Basketball Association (NBA) also locked out their players in 2011 after the two sides failed to reach a collective bargaining agreement. The dispute involved the division of revenue and a salary cap. During the lockout, the players could not access NBA facilities, trainers, or staff, and the owners could not trade, sign, or contract with players. The lockout lasted 161 days and resulted in the cancellation of all preseason games and several weeks of regular season games. ∎

Some lockouts are illegal. An employer may not use a lockout as a tool to break the union and pressure employees into decertification, which occurs when union members vote to dissociate from the union. An employer must be able to show some economic justification for the lockout.

## Reviewing: Employment, Immigration, and Labor Law

Rick Saldona began working as a traveling salesperson for Aimer Winery in 2008. Sales constituted 90 percent of Saldona's work time. Saldona worked an average of fifty hours per week but received no overtime pay. In June 2018, Saldona's new supervisor, Caesar Braxton, claimed that Saldona had been inflating his reported sales calls and required Saldona to submit to a polygraph test. Saldona reported Braxton to the U.S. Department of Labor, which prohibited Aimer from requiring Saldona to take a polygraph test for this purpose.

In August 2018, Saldona's wife, Venita, fell from a ladder and sustained a head injury while employed as a full-time agricultural harvester. Saldona presented Aimer's Human Resources Department with a letter from his wife's physician indicating that she would need daily care for several months, and Saldona took leave until December 2018. Aimer had sixty-three employees at that time. When Saldona returned to Aimer, he was informed that his position had been eliminated because his sales territory had been combined with an adjacent territory. Using the information presented in the chapter, answer the following questions.

1. Would Saldona have been legally entitled to receive overtime pay at a higher rate? Why or why not?
2. What is the maximum length of time Saldona would have been allowed to take leave to care for his injured spouse?
3. Under what circumstances would Aimer have been allowed to require an employee to take a polygraph test?
4. Would Aimer likely be able to avoid reinstating Saldona under the *key employee* exception? Why or why not?

**Debate This** . . .   *The U.S. labor market is highly competitive, so state and federal laws that require overtime pay are unnecessary and should be abolished.*

## Terms and Concepts

authorization card 209
cease-and-desist order 208
closed shop 209
collective bargaining 213
employment at will 195
hot-cargo agreement 209
I-9 verification 206

I-551 Alien Registration
    Receipt 207
lockout 214
minimum wage 197
right-to-work law 209
secondary boycott 214

strike 213
union shop 209
vesting 203
whistleblowing 196
workers' compensation law 202
wrongful discharge 196

## Issue Spotters

1. Erin, an employee of Fine Print Shop, is injured on the job. For Erin to obtain workers' compensation, must her injury have been caused by Fine Print's negligence? Does it matter whether the action causing the injury was intentional? Explain. (See *Health, Safety, and Income Security.*)

2. Onyx applies for work with Precision Design Company, which requires union membership as a condition of employment. She also applies for work with Quality Engineering, Inc. That company does not require union membership as a condition of employment but requires employees to join a union after six months on the job. Are these conditions legal? Why or why not? (See *Labor Unions.*)

• **Check your answers to the Issue Spotters against the answers provided in Appendix B at the end of this text.**

## Business Scenarios

**11–1. Unfair Labor Practices.** Consolidated Stores is undergoing a unionization campaign. Prior to the union election, management states that the union is unnecessary to protect workers. Management also provides bonuses and wage increases to the workers during this period. The employees reject the union. Union organizers protest that the wage increases during the election campaign unfairly prejudiced the vote. Should these wage increases be regarded as an unfair labor practice? Discuss. (See *Labor Unions.*)

**11–2. Wrongful Discharge.** Denton and Carlo were employed at an appliance plant. Their job required them to perform occasional maintenance work while standing on a wire mesh twenty feet above the plant floor. Other employees had fallen through the mesh, and one of them had been killed by the fall. When their supervisor told them to perform tasks that would likely involve walking on the mesh, Denton and Carlo refused because they feared they might suffer bodily injury or death. Because they refused to do the requested work, the two employees were fired from their jobs. Was their discharge wrongful? If so, under what federal employment law? To what federal agency or department should they turn for assistance? (See *Employment at Will.*)

## Business Case Problems

**11–3. Workers' Compensation.** As a safety measure, Dynea USA, Inc., required an employee, Tony Fairbanks, to wear steel-toed boots. One of the boots caused a sore on Fairbanks's leg. The skin over the sore broke, and within a week, Fairbanks was hospitalized with a methicillin-resistant staphylococcus aureus (MRSA) infection. He filed a workers' compensation claim. Dynea argued that the MRSA bacteria that caused the infection had been on Fairbanks's skin before he came to work. What are the requirements to recover workers' compensation benefits? Does this claim qualify? Explain. [*Dynea USA, Inc. v. Fairbanks,* 241 Or.App. 311, 250 P.3d 389 (2011)] (See *Health, Safety, and Income Security.*)

**11–4. Exceptions to the Employment-at-Will Doctrine.** Li Li worked for Packard Bioscience, and Mark Schmeizl was her supervisor. In March 2000, Schmeizl told Li to call Packard's competitors, pretend to be a potential customer, and request "pricing information and literature." Li refused to perform the assignment. She told Schmeizl that she thought the work was illegal and recommended that he contact Packard's legal department. Although a lawyer recommended against the practice, Schmeizl insisted that Li perform the calls. Moreover, he later wrote negative performance reviews because she was unable to get the requested information when she called competitors and identified herself as a Packard employee. On June 1, 2000, Li was terminated on Schmeizl's recommendation. Can Li bring a claim for wrongful discharge? Why or why not? [*Li Li v. Canberra Industries,* 134 Conn.App. 448, 39 A.3d 789 (2012)] (See *Employment at Will.*)

**11–5. Collective Bargaining.** SDBC Holdings, Inc., acquired Stella D'oro Biscuit Co., a bakery in New York City. At the time, a collective bargaining agreement existed between Stella D'oro and Local 50, Bakery, Confectionary, Tobacco Workers and Grain Millers International Union. During negotiations to renew the agreement, Stella D'oro refused to give the union a copy of the company's financial statement. Stella D'oro did allow Local 50 to examine and take notes on the financial statement and offered the union an opportunity to make its own copy. Did Stella D'oro engage in an unfair labor practice? Discuss. [*SDBC Holdings, Inc. v. National Labor Relations Board,* 711 F.3d 281 (2d Cir. 2013)] (See *Labor Unions.*)

**11–6. Business Case Problem with Sample Answer— Unemployment Compensation.** Fior Ramirez worked as  a housekeeper for Remington Lodging & Hospitality, a hotel in Atlantic Beach, Florida. After her father in the Dominican Republic suffered a stroke, she asked her employer for time off to be with him. Ramirez's manager, Katie Berkowski, refused the request. Two days later, Berkowski received a call from Ramirez to say that she was with her father. He died about a week later, and Ramirez returned to work, but Berkowski told her that she had abandoned her position. Ramirez applied for unemployment compensation. Under the applicable state statute, "an employee is disqualified from receiving benefits if he or she voluntarily left work without good cause." Does Ramirez qualify for benefits? Explain. [*Ramirez v. Reemployment Assistance Appeals Commission,* 39 Fla.L.Weekly D317, 135 So.3d 408 (1 Dist. 2014)] (See *Health, Safety, and Income Security.*)

- **For a sample answer to Problem 11–6, go to Appendix C at the end of this text.**

**11–7. Labor Unions.** Carol Garcia and Pedro Salgado were bus drivers for Latino Express, Inc., a transportation company. Garcia and Salgado began soliciting signatures from other drivers to certify the Teamsters Local Union No. 777 as the official representative of the employees. Latino Express fired Garcia and Salgado. The two drivers filed a claim with the National Labor Relations Board (NLRB), alleging that the employer had committed an unfair labor practice. Which employer practice defined by the National Labor Relations Act did the plaintiffs most likely charge Latino Express with committing? Is the employer's discharge of Garcia and Salgado likely to be construed as a legitimate act in opposition to union solicitation? If a violation is found, what can the NLRB do? Discuss. [*Ohr v. Latino Express, Inc.,* 776 F.3d 469 (7th Cir. 2015)] (See *Labor Unions.*)

**11–8. Health, Safety, and Income Security.** Jefferson Partners LP entered into a collective bargaining agreement (CBA) with the Amalgamated Transit Union. Under the CBA, drivers had to either join the union or pay a fair share—85 percent—of union dues, which were used to pay for administrative costs incurred by the union. An employee who refused to pay was subject to discharge. Jefferson hired Tiffany Thompson to work as a bus driver. When told of the CBA requirement, she said that she thought it was unfair. She asserted that it was illegal to compel her to join the union and that it would be illegal to discharge her for not complying. She refused either to join the union or to pay the dues. More than two years later, she was fired on the ground that her continued refusal constituted misconduct. Is Thompson eligible for unemployment compensation? Explain. [*Thompson v. Jefferson Partners LP*, 2016 WL 953038 (Minn.App. 2016)] (See *Health, Safety, and Income Security.*)

### 11–9. A Question of Ethics—Workers' Compensation Law.

*In 1999, after working for Atchison Leather Products, Inc., for ten years, Beverly Tull began to complain of hand, wrist, and shoulder pain. Atchison recommended that she contact a certain physician, who in April 2000 diagnosed the condition as carpal tunnel syndrome "severe enough" for surgery. In August, Tull filed a claim with the state workers' compensation board. Because Atchison changed workers' compensation insurance companies every year, a dispute arose as to which company should pay Tull's claim. Fearing liability, no insurer would authorize treatment, and Tull was forced to delay surgery until December. The board granted her temporary total disability benefits for the subsequent six weeks that she missed work. On April 23, 2002, Berger Co. bought Atchison. The new employer adjusted Tull's work so that it was less demanding and stressful, but she continued to suffer pain. In July, a physician diagnosed her condition as permanent. The board granted her permanent partial disability benefits. By May 2005, bickering over the financial responsibility for Tull's claim involved five insurers—four of which had each covered Atchison for a single year and one of which covered Berger. [*Tull v. Atchison Leather Products, Inc., 37 Kan.App.2d 87, 150 P.3d 316 (2007)*] (See* Health, Safety, and Income Security.)*

(a) When an injured employee files a claim for workers' compensation, a proceeding is held to assess the injury and determine the amount of compensation. Should a dispute between insurers over the payment of the claim be resolved in the same proceeding? Why or why not?

(b) The board designated April 23, 2002, as the date of Tull's injury. What is the reason for determining the date of a worker's injury? Should the board in this case have selected this date or a different date? Why?

(c) How should the board assess liability for the payment of Tull's medical expenses and disability benefits? Would it be appropriate to impose joint and several liability on the insurers (holding each of them responsible for the full amount of damages)? Or should the individual liability of each of the insurers be determined? Explain.

# Legal Reasoning Group Activity

### 11–10. Immigration.

Nicole Tipton and Sadik Seferi owned and operated a restaurant in Iowa. Acting on a tip from the local police, agents of Immigration and Customs Enforcement executed search warrants at the restaurant and at an apartment where some restaurant workers lived. The agents discovered six undocumented aliens who worked at the restaurant and lived together. When the I-9 forms for the restaurant's employees were reviewed, none were found for the six aliens. They were paid in cash while other employees were paid by check. Tipton and Seferi were charged with hiring and harboring undocumented aliens. (See *Immigration Law.*)

(a) The first group will develop an argument that Tipton and Seferi were guilty of hiring and harboring illegal aliens.

(b) The second group will assess whether Tipton and Seferi can assert a defense by claiming that they did not know that the workers were unauthorized aliens.

# CHAPTER 12

# Employment Discrimination

Out of the 1960s civil rights movement to end racial and other forms of discrimination grew a body of law protecting employees against discrimination in the workplace. Legislation, judicial decisions, and administrative agency actions restrict employers from discriminating against workers on the basis of race, color, religion, national origin, gender, age, or disability. A class of persons defined by one or more of these criteria is known as a **protected class.**

Several federal statutes prohibit **employment discrimination** against members of protected classes. The most important is Title VII of the Civil Rights Act.[1] Title VII prohibits employment discrimination on the basis of race, color, religion, national origin, and gender. The Age Discrimination in Employment Act[2] and the Americans with Disabilities Act[3]

---
1. 42 U.S.C. Sections 2000e–2000e-17.
2. 29 U.S.C. Sections 621–634.
3. 42 U.S.C. Sections 12102–12118.

prohibit discrimination on the basis of age and disability, respectively. The protections afforded under these laws also extend to U.S. citizens who are working abroad for U.S. firms or for companies that are controlled by U.S. firms.

This chapter focuses on federal statutes, including the ones just mentioned. Many states have their own laws that protect employees against discrimination, however, and some provide more protection than federal laws do.

## 12–1 Title VII of the Civil Rights Act

Title VII of the Civil Rights Act prohibits job discrimination against employees, applicants, and union members on the basis of race, color, national origin, religion, and gender at any stage of employment. Title VII bans discrimination in the hiring process, discipline procedures, discharge, promotion, and benefits.

Title VII applies to employers with fifteen or more employees and labor unions with fifteen or more members. It also applies to labor unions that operate hiring halls (where members go regularly to be assigned jobs), employment agencies, and state and local governing units or agencies. The United States Supreme Court has ruled that an employer with fewer than fifteen employees is not automatically shielded from a lawsuit filed under Title VII.[4] In addition, the act prohibits discrimination in most federal government employment. When Title

---
4. *Arbaugh v. Y&H Corp.*, 546 U.S. 500, 126 S.Ct. 1235, 163 L.Ed.2d 1097 (2006).

VII applies to the employer, any employee—including an undocumented (alien) worker—can bring an action for employment discrimination.

### 12–1a The Equal Employment Opportunity Commission

The Equal Employment Opportunity Commission (EEOC) monitors compliance with Title VII. An employee alleging discrimination must file a claim with the EEOC before a lawsuit can be brought against the employer. The EEOC may investigate the dispute and attempt to obtain the parties' voluntary consent to an out-of-court settlement. If a voluntary agreement cannot be reached, the EEOC may file a suit against the employer on the employee's behalf.

■ **EXAMPLE 12.1** Jacqueline Cote met her wife, Diana Smithson, in Maine while they were both employees at Wal-Mart. They moved to Massachusetts and were married a few days after the state legalized same-sex marriage, and they continued working at a Wal-Mart there. Smithson eventually quit work to take care of Cote's elderly mother. Cote tried to enroll her partner in Wal-Mart's health plan, but coverage was denied. Five years later, Smithson was diagnosed with cancer.

Cote filed a claim with the EEOC arguing that Wal-Mart had intentionally discriminated against her on the basis of sex. In 2014, the commission agreed that Cote "was treated differently and denied benefits because of her sex." The EEOC ordered Wal-Mart to work with Cote to help pay Smithson's medical bills. ■

The EEOC does not investigate every claim of employment discrimination. Generally, it takes only "priority cases," such as claims that affect many workers and those involving retaliatory discharge (firing an employee in retaliation for submitting a claim to the EEOC). If the EEOC decides not to investigate a claim, the EEOC issues a "right to sue" that allows the employee to bring his or her own lawsuit against the employer.

## 12–1b Limitations on Class Actions

In an important decision, the United States Supreme Court limited the rights of employees to bring discrimination claims against their employer as a group, or class. The decision did not affect the rights of individual employees to sue under Title VII, however.

■ **CASE IN POINT 12.2** A group of female employees sued Wal-Mart, the nation's largest private employer. The employees alleged that store managers who had discretion over pay and promotions were biased against women and disproportionately favored men. The employees wished to bring a class action—a lawsuit in which a small number of plaintiffs sue on behalf of a larger group. Lower courts ruled that the employees' class-action suit could proceed, and Wal-Mart appealed. The Supreme Court ruled in favor of Wal-Mart, effectively blocking the class action. The Court held that the women had failed to prove a company-wide policy of discrimination that had a common effect on all women included in the class. Therefore, they could not maintain a class action.[5] ■

## 12–1c Intentional and Unintentional Discrimination

Title VII of the Civil Rights Act prohibits both intentional and unintentional discrimination.

---

5. *Wal-Mart Stores, Inc. v. Dukes*, 564 U.S. 338, 131 S.Ct. 2541, 180 L.Ed.2d 374 (2011).

**Intentional Discrimination** Intentional discrimination by an employer against an employee is known as **disparate-treatment discrimination.** Because intent may sometimes be difficult to prove, courts have established certain procedures for resolving disparate-treatment cases.

*Prima Facie* **Case.** A plaintiff who sues on the basis of disparate-treatment discrimination must first make out a *prima facie* **case.** *Prima facie* is Latin for "at first sight" or "on its face." Legally, it refers to a fact that is presumed to be true unless contradicted by evidence.

To establish a *prima facie* case of disparate-treatment discrimination in hiring, a plaintiff must show all of the following:

1. The plaintiff is a member of a protected class.
2. The plaintiff applied and was qualified for the job in question.
3. The plaintiff was rejected by the employer.
4. The employer continued to seek applicants for the position or filled the position with a person not in a protected class.

A plaintiff who can meet these relatively easy requirements has made out a *prima facie* case of illegal discrimination in hiring and will win in the absence of a legally acceptable employer defense.

Sometimes, current and former employees make a claim of discrimination. When the plaintiff alleges that the employer fired or took some other adverse employment action against him or her, the same basic requirements apply. To establish a *prima facie* case, the plaintiff must show that he or she was fired or treated adversely for discriminatory reasons.

**Burden-Shifting Procedure.** Once the *prima facie* case is established, the burden then shifts to the employer-defendant, who must articulate a legal reason for not hiring the plaintiff. (Again, this also applies to firing and other adverse employment actions.) If the employer did not have a legal reason for taking the adverse employment action, the plaintiff wins.

If the employer can articulate a legitimate reason for the action, the burden shifts back to the plaintiff. To prevail, the plaintiff must then show that the employer's reason is a *pretext* (not the true reason) and that the employer's decision was actually motivated by discriminatory intent.

**Unintentional Discrimination** Employers often use interviews and tests to choose from among a large number of applicants for job openings. Minimum educational requirements are also common. Some employer practices, such as those involving educational requirements, may have an unintended discriminatory impact on a protected class.

**Disparate-impact discrimination** occurs when a protected group of people is adversely affected by an employer's practices, procedures, or tests, even though they do not appear to be discriminatory. In a disparate-impact discrimination case, the complaining party must first show that the employer's practices, procedures, or tests are effectively discriminatory. Once the plaintiff has made out a *prima facie* case, the burden of proof shifts to the employer to show that the practices or procedures in question were justified.

There are two ways of showing that an employer's practices, procedures, or tests are effectively discriminatory—that is, that disparate-impact discrimination exists.

**Pool of Applicants.** A plaintiff can prove a disparate impact by comparing the employer's workforce to the pool of qualified individuals available in the local labor market. The plaintiff must show that (1) as a result of educational or other job requirements or hiring procedures, (2) the percentage of nonwhites, women, or members of other protected classes in the employer's workforce (3) does not reflect the percentage of that group in the pool of qualified applicants. If the plaintiff can show a connection between the practice and the disparity, he or she has made out a *prima facie* case and need not provide evidence of discriminatory intent.

**Rate of Hiring.** A plaintiff can also prove disparate-impact discrimination by comparing the employer's *selection rates* of members and nonmembers of a protected class (nonwhites and whites, for instance, or women and men). When an educational or other job requirement or hiring procedure excludes members of a protected class from an employer's workforce at a substantially higher rate than nonmembers, discrimination occurs.

Under EEOC guidelines, a selection rate for a protected class that is less than four-fifths, or 80 percent, of the rate for the group with the highest rate of hiring generally is regarded as evidence of disparate impact. ■ **EXAMPLE 12.3** Shady Cove District Fire Department administers an exam to applicants for the position of firefighter. At the exam session, one hundred white applicants take the test, and fifty pass and are hired. At the same exam session, sixty minority applicants take the test, but only twelve pass and are hired. Because twelve is only 20 percent of sixty, the test will be considered discriminatory under the EEOC guidelines. ■

## 12–1d Discrimination Based on Race, Color, and National Origin

Title VII prohibits employers from discriminating against employees or job applicants on the basis of race, color, or national origin. Race is interpreted broadly to apply to the ancestry or ethnic characteristics of a group of persons, such as Native Americans. National origin refers to discrimination based on a person's birth in another country or his or her ancestry or culture, such as Hispanic.

If an employer's standards or policies for selecting or promoting employees have a discriminatory effect on employees or job applicants in these protected classes, then a presumption of illegal discrimination arises. To avoid liability, the employer must show that its standards or policies have a substantial, demonstrable relationship to realistic qualifications for the job in question.

■ **CASE IN POINT 12.4** Jiann Min Chang was an instructor at Alabama Agricultural and Mechanical University (AAMU). When AAMU terminated his employment, Chang filed a lawsuit claiming discrimination based on national origin. Chang established a *prima facie* case because he (1) was a member of a protected class, (2) was qualified for the job, (3) suffered an adverse employment action, and (4) was replaced by someone outside his protected class (a non-Asian instructor).

When the burden of proof shifted to the employer, however, AAMU showed that Chang had argued with a vice president and refused to comply with her instructions. The court ruled that the university had not renewed Chang's contract for a legitimate reason—insubordination—and therefore was not liable for unlawful discrimination.[6] ■

**Reverse Discrimination** Title VII also protects against *reverse discrimination*—that is, discrimination against members of a majority group, such as white males. ■ **EXAMPLE 12.5** An African American woman fires four white men from their management positions at a school district. The men file a lawsuit for reverse discrimination. They argue that the woman was trying to eliminate white males from the district administration in violation of Title VII. The woman claims that the terminations were part of a reorganization plan to cut costs.

If the judge (or jury, in a jury trial) agrees with the men that they were fired for racially discriminatory reasons, then they will be entitled to damages. If, however, the school district can show that the real reason for the terminations was a legitimate attempt to cut costs, then normally their case will be dismissed. ■

6. *Jiann Min Chang v. Alabama Agricultural and Mechanical University,* 355 Fed.Appx. 250 (11th Cir. 2009).

**Potential Section 1981 Claims** Victims of racial or ethnic discrimination may also have a cause of action under 42 U.S.C. Section 1981. This section, which was enacted in 1866 to protect the rights of freed slaves, prohibits discrimination on the basis of race or ethnicity in the formation or enforcement of contracts. Because employment is often a contractual relationship, Section 1981 can provide an alternative basis for a plaintiff's action and is potentially advantageous because there is no limit on the damages that can be awarded.

## 12–1e Discrimination Based on Religion

Title VII of the Civil Rights Act also prohibits government employers, private employers, and unions from discriminating against persons because of their religion. (This chapter's *Digital Update* feature discusses how employers who examine prospective employees' social media posts, including posts concerning religion, might engage in unlawful discrimination.)

Employers cannot treat their employees more or less favorably based on their religious beliefs or practices. They also cannot require employees to participate in any religious activity or forbid them from participating in one. ■ **EXAMPLE 12.6** Jason Sewell claims that his employer, a car dealership, fired him for not attending the weekly prayer meetings of dealership employees. If the dealership does require its employees to attend prayer gatherings and fired Sewell for not attending, he has a valid claim of religious discrimination. ■

**Reasonable Accommodation** An employer must "reasonably accommodate" the religious practices and sincerely held religious beliefs of its employees, unless to do so would cause undue hardship to the employer's business. An employee's religion might prohibit her or him from working on a certain day of the week, for instance, or at a certain type of job. Reasonable accommodation is required even if the belief is not based on the doctrines of a traditionally recognized religion, such as Christianity or Judaism, or of a denomination, such as Baptist.

**Undue Hardship** A reasonable attempt to accommodate does not necessarily require the employer to make every change an employee requests or to make a permanent change for an employee's benefit. An employer is not required to make an accommodation that would cause the employer undue hardship. ■ **CASE IN POINT 12.7** Miguel Sánchez-Rodríguez sold cell phones at kiosks in shopping malls for AT&T in Puerto Rico. After six years, Sánchez informed his supervisors that he had become a Seventh Day Adventist and could no longer work on Saturdays for religious reasons. AT&T responded that his position required rotating Saturday shifts and that his inability to work on Saturdays would cause the company hardship.

As a reasonable accommodation, the company suggested that Sánchez swap schedules with others and offered him two alternative positions that would not require work on Saturdays. Sánchez was unable to find workers to swap shifts with him, however, and declined the other jobs because they would result in less income. He began missing work on Saturdays. After a time, AT&T indicated that it would discipline him for any additional Saturdays that he missed. Eventually, he was placed on active disciplinary status. Sánchez resigned and filed a religious discrimination lawsuit. The court found in favor of AT&T, and a federal appellate court affirmed. The company had made adequate efforts at accommodation by allowing Sánchez to swap shifts and offering him other positions that did not require work on Saturdays.[7] ■

## 12–1f Discrimination Based on Gender

Under Title VII and other federal acts, employers are forbidden from discriminating against employees on the basis of gender. Employers are prohibited from classifying or advertising jobs as male or female unless they can prove that the gender of the applicant is essential to the job. In addition, employers cannot have separate male and female seniority lists and cannot refuse to promote employees based on their gender.

**Gender Must Be a Determining Factor** Generally, to succeed in a suit for gender discrimination, a plaintiff must demonstrate that gender was a determining factor in the employer's decision to hire, fire, or promote him or her. Typically, this involves looking at all of the surrounding circumstances. ■ **CASE IN POINT 12.8** Wanda Collier worked for Turner Industries Group, LLC, in the maintenance department. She complained to her supervisor that Jack Daniell, the head of the department, treated her unfairly. Her supervisor told her that Daniell had a problem with her gender and was harder on women. The supervisor talked to Daniell about Collier's complaint but did not take any disciplinary action.

A month later, Daniell confronted Collier, pushing her up against a wall and berating her. After this incident, Collier filed a formal complaint and kept a male

---

7. *Sánchez-Rodríguez v. AT&T Mobility Puerto Rico, Inc.*, 673 F.3d 1 (1st Cir. 2012).

## DIGITAL UPDATE — Hiring Discrimination Based on Social Media Posts

Human resource officers in most companies routinely check job candidates' social media posts when deciding whom to hire. Certainly, every young person is warned not to post photos that she or he might later regret having made available to potential employers. But a more serious issue involves standard reviewing of job candidates' social media information. Specifically, do employers discriminate based on such information?

### An Experiment in Hiring Discrimination via Online Social Networks

Two researchers at Carnegie-Mellon University conducted an experiment to determine whether social media information posted by prospective employees influences employers' hiring decisions.[a] The researchers created false résumés and social media profiles. They submitted job applications on behalf of the fictional "candidates" to about four thousand U.S. employers. They then compared employers' responses to different groups—for example, to Muslim candidates versus Christian candidates.

The researchers found that candidates whose public profiles indicated that they were Muslim were less likely to be called for interviews than Christian applicants. The difference was particularly pronounced in parts of the country with more conservative residents. In those locations, Muslims received callbacks only 2 percent of the time, compared with 17 percent for Christian applicants. According to the authors of the study, "Hiring discrimination via online searches of candidates may not be widespread, but online disclosures of personal traits can significantly influence the hiring decisions of a self-selected set of employers."

a. A. Acquisti and C. N. Fong, "An Experiment in Hiring Discrimination via Online Social Networks," *Social Service Research Network*, October 26, 2014.

### Job Candidates' Perception of the Hiring Process

In another study, researchers at North Carolina State University looked at how job applicants view prospective employers' use of their social media profiles during the hiring process.[b] Job candidates appear to view the hiring process as unfair when they know that their social media profiles have been used in the selection process. This perception, according to the researchers, makes litigation more likely.

### The EEOC Speaks Up

Since 2014, the Equal Employment Opportunity Commission (EEOC) has investigated how prospective employers can use social media to engage in discrimination in the hiring process. Given that the Society for Human Resource Management estimates that more than three-fourths of its members use social media in employment screening, the EEOC is interested in regulating this procedure.

Social media sites, examined closely, can provide information to a prospective employer on the applicant's race, color, national origin, disability, religion, and other protected characteristics. The EEOC has reminded employers that such information—whether it comes from social media postings or other sources—may not legally be used to make employment decisions on prohibited bases, such as race, gender, and religion.

**Critical Thinking** *Can you think of a way a company could use information from an applicant's social media posts without running the risk of being accused of hiring discrimination?*

b. J. W. Stoughton, L. F. Thompson, and A. W. Meade, "Examining Applicant Reactions to the Use of Social Networking Websites in Pre-Employment Screening," *Journal of Business and Psychology*, November 2013, DOI: 10.1007/s10869-013-9333-6.

---

co-worker with her at all times. A month later, she was fired. She subsequently filed a lawsuit alleging gender discrimination. The court allowed Collier's claim to go to a jury because there was sufficient evidence that gender was a determining factor in Daniell's conduct.[8] ∎

8. *Collier v. Turner Industries Group, LLC*, 797 F.Supp.2d 1029 (D. Idaho 2011).

The Federal Bureau of Investigation (FBI) requires that its applicants meet certain physical fitness standards. For women, the standards include the ability to complete a minimum of fourteen push-ups. Men must be able to complete at least thirty. Whether this difference constitutes discrimination on the basis of gender was at issue in the following case.

# Bauer v. Lynch

United States Court of Appeals, Fourth Circuit, 812 F.3d 340 (2016).

## In the Language of the Court

*KING*, Circuit Judge.

* * * *

The FBI trains its Special Agent recruits at the FBI Academy in Quantico, Virginia. * * * All Trainees must pass a physical fitness test (the "PFT").

* * * The FBI requires every Special Agent recruit to pass the PFT twice: once to gain admission to the Academy, and a second time to graduate.

* * * *

* * * Trainees * * * need to satisfy the following standards * * * :

| Event | Men | Women |
|---|---|---|
| Sit-ups | 38 | 35 |
| 300-meter sprint | 52.4s | 64.9s |
| Push-ups | 30 | 14 |
| 1.5-mile run | 12m, 42s | 13m, 5s |

* * * *

After the attacks of September 11, 2001, * * * Jay Bauer resolved to contribute to the defense of our country by becoming a Special Agent in the FBI. [At the time,] he * * * served as an assistant professor at the University of Wisconsin–Milwaukee.

* * * Bauer took the PFT for the first time and failed. Although he achieved sixteen points on the test, Bauer completed only twenty-five push-ups * * * . The FBI allowed Bauer to retest [three months later] and he passed, that time completing thirty-two push-ups. With his fitness screening complete, the FBI invited Bauer to report to the Academy.

Bauer's time at the Academy largely showed great potential for a career as a Special Agent. He passed all academic tests, demonstrated proficiency in his firearms and defensive tactics training, and met all expectations for the practical applications and skills components of the Academy. Bauer's classmates also selected him as the class leader and spokesperson for the Academy

graduation. Unfortunately, Bauer faced a dilemma: he was unable to pass the PFT at Quantico.

During his twenty-two weeks at the Academy, Bauer took the PFT five times. On each occasion, he would have passed but for his failure to achieve the minimum standard for push-ups. Bauer's results, and his corresponding point scores for each event, were as follows:

| Week | Sit-ups | 300-meter sprint | Push-ups | 1.5-mile run | Total Points |
|---|---|---|---|---|---|
| Week 1 | 40 (2) | 42.6 sec. (8) | 26 (0) | 10:49 (4) | 14 |
| Week 7 | 47 (4) | 43.4 sec. (7) | 25 (0) | 10:24 (5) | 16 |
| Week 14 | 50 (6) | 43.7 sec. (7) | 28 (0) | 10:45 (4) | 17 |
| Week 18 | 51 (6) | 43.8 sec. (7) | 27 (0) | 11:09 (4) | 17 |
| Week 22 | 49 (5) | 44.1 sec. (6) | 29 (0) | 10:57 (4) | 15 |

Following his final failure of the PFT, Bauer * * * was [allowed to] resign with the possibility of future employment with the FBI * * * . Bauer * * * immediately signed a resignation letter. Two weeks later, the FBI offered Bauer a position as an Intelligence Analyst in its Chicago Field Office. He accepted and has been employed in that position since.

* * * *

* * * Bauer filed this Title VII action in [a federal district court] against [Loretta Lynch,] the Attorney General. According to the claims in Bauer's complaint, the FBI's use of the gender-normed PFT standards contravened * * * Title VII * * * which prohibits sex discrimination by federal employers.

* * * *

In his summary judgment motion, Bauer maintained that the FBI's use of the gender-normed PFT standards was facially discriminatory [involving explicit categorization, such as by sex or race].

* * * *

* * * The district court agreed with Bauer, granting his motion for summary judgment.

* * * *

The Attorney General * * * filed a timely * * * appeal.

* * * *

Title VII requires that any "personnel actions affecting employees or applicants for employment" taken by federal employers "shall be made free from any discrimination based on * * * sex." * * * *A plaintiff is entitled to demonstrate discrimination by showing that the employer uses a facially discriminatory employment practice. [The Supreme Court has outlined]* a "simple test" for identifying facial sex discrimination: such discrimination appears "where the evidence shows treatment of a person in a manner which but for that person's sex would be different."* [Emphasis added.]

* * * The district court applied [this] test and concluded that, because Bauer would have been held to a lower minimum number of push-ups had he been a woman, the gender-normed PFT standards constitute facial sex discrimination. The Attorney General maintains on appeal, however, that because the PFT assesses an overall level of physical fitness, and equally fit men and women possess innate physiological differences that lead to different performance outcomes, the PFT's gender-normed standards actually require the same level of fitness for all Trainees. In that way, the Attorney General contends, the PFT standards do not treat the sexes differently and therefore do not contravene Title VII.

* * * *

* * * The Attorney General * * * maintains that * * * some differential treatment of men and women based upon inherent physiological differences is not only lawful but also potentially required.

* * * *

Men and women simply are not physiologically the same for the purposes

Case 12.1 Continues

**Case 12.1 Continued**

of physical fitness programs. * * * Physical fitness standards suitable for men may not always be suitable for women, and accommodations addressing physiological differences between the sexes are not necessarily unlawful.

* * * The physiological differences between men and women impact their relative abilities to demonstrate the same levels of physical fitness. In other words, equally fit men and women demonstrate their fitness differently. Whether physical fitness standards discriminate based on sex, therefore, depends on whether they require men and women to demonstrate different levels of fitness.

Put succinctly, *an employer does not contravene Title VII when it utilizes physical fitness standards that distinguish between the sexes on the basis of their physiological differences but impose an equal burden of compliance on both men and women, requiring the same level of physical fitness of each.* Because the FBI purports to assess physical fitness by imposing the same burden on both men and women, this rule applies to Bauer's Title VII claims. Accordingly, the district court erred in failing to apply the rule in its disposition of Bauer's motion for summary judgment. [Emphasis added.]
* * * *

Pursuant to the foregoing, we vacate the judgment of the district court and remand for * * * further proceedings.

**Legal Reasoning Questions**

**1.** According to the reasoning of the court in the *Bauer* case, when do different employment standards for men and women satisfy Title VII's requirement of equality?

**2.** In what other circumstances might the rule in this case apply?

**3.** If Bauer had ultimately succeeded in his claim, what might the remedy have been? What else might have resulted?

---

**Pregnancy Discrimination** The Pregnancy Discrimination Act[9] expanded Title VII's definition of gender discrimination to include discrimination based on pregnancy. Women affected by pregnancy, childbirth, or related medical conditions must be treated the same as other persons not so affected but similar in ability to work. For instance, an employer cannot discriminate against a pregnant woman by withholding benefits available to others under employee benefit programs.

In the following case, an employer accommodated many of its employees who had lifting restrictions due to disabilities. The employer refused to accommodate a pregnant employee with a similar restriction. Did this refusal constitute a violation of the Pregnancy Discrimination Act?

---

9. 42 U.S.C. Section 2000e(k).

**Case 12.2**

# Young v. United Parcel Service, Inc.

Supreme Court of the United States, __ U.S. __, 135 S.Ct. 1338, 191 L.Ed.2d 279 (2015).

**Background and Facts** Peggy Young was a driver for United Parcel Service, Inc. (UPS). When she became pregnant, her doctor advised her not to lift more than twenty pounds. UPS required drivers to lift up to seventy pounds and told Young that she could not work under a lifting restriction. She filed a suit in a federal district court against UPS, claiming an unlawful refusal to accommodate her pregnancy-related lifting restriction. She alleged that UPS had multiple light-duty-for-injury categories to accommodate individuals whose non-pregnancy-related disabilities created work restrictions similar to hers.

UPS responded that, because Young did not fall into any of those categories, it had not discriminated against her. The court issued a summary judgment in UPS's favor. The U.S. Court of Appeals of the Fourth Circuit affirmed the judgment. Young appealed to the United States Supreme Court.

## In the Language of the Court

Justice *BREYER* delivered the opinion of the Court.
* * * *

* * * A plaintiff alleging that the denial of an accommodation constituted disparate treatment under the Pregnancy Discrimination Act * * * may make out a *prima facie* case by showing that she belongs to

Case 12.2 Continued

the protected class, that she sought accommodation, that the employer did not accommodate her, and that the employer did accommodate others similar in their ability or inability to work.

*The employer may then seek to justify its refusal to accommodate the plaintiff by relying on legitimate, nondiscriminatory reasons for denying her accommodation.* [Emphasis added.]

If the employer offers an apparently legitimate, nondiscriminatory reason for its actions, the plaintiff may in turn show that the employer's proffered reasons are in fact pretextual [contrived]. We believe that the plaintiff may reach a jury on this issue by providing sufficient evidence that the employer's policies impose a significant burden on pregnant workers, and that the employer's legitimate, nondiscriminatory reasons are not sufficiently strong to justify the burden, but rather—when considered along with the burden imposed—give rise to an inference of intentional discrimination.

The plaintiff can create a genuine issue of material fact as to whether a significant burden exists by providing evidence that the employer accommodates a large percentage of nonpregnant workers while failing to accommodate a large percentage of pregnant workers. Here, for example, if the facts are as Young says they are, she can show that UPS accommodates most nonpregnant employees with lifting limitations while categorically failing to accommodate pregnant employees with lifting limitations. Young might also add that the fact that UPS has multiple policies that accommodate nonpregnant employees with lifting restrictions suggests that its reasons for failing to accommodate pregnant employees with lifting restrictions are not sufficiently strong—to the point that a jury could find that its reasons for failing to accommodate pregnant employees give rise to an inference of intentional discrimination.

* * * *

* * * A party is entitled to summary judgment if there is no genuine dispute as to any material fact and the movant [that is, a person who applies to a court for a ruling in his or her favor] is entitled to judgment as a matter of law. * * * *Viewing the record in the light most favorable to Young, there is a genuine dispute as to whether UPS provided more favorable treatment to at least some employees whose situation cannot reasonably be distinguished from Young's.* [Emphasis added.]

**Decision and Remedy** *The United States Supreme Court vacated the judgment of the U.S. Court of Appeals for the Fourth Circuit and remanded the case for further proceedings. Young created a genuine dispute as to whether UPS had provided more favorable treatment to employees whose situation could not reasonably be distinguished from hers. On remand, the court must determine whether Young also created a genuine issue of material fact as to whether UPS's reasons for treating Young less favorably were a pretext.*

**Critical Thinking**
- **Legal Environment** *Could UPS have succeeded in this case if it had claimed simply that it would be more expensive or less convenient to include pregnant women among those whom it accommodates? Explain.*

**Wage Discrimination** The Equal Pay Act[10] requires equal pay for male and female employees working at the same establishment doing similar work. To determine whether the Equal Pay Act has been violated, a court looks to the primary duties of the two jobs—the job content rather than the job description controls. If a court finds that the wage differential is due to "any factor other than gender," such as a seniority or merit system, then it does not violate the Equal Pay Act.

The 2009 Lilly Ledbetter Fair Pay Act made discriminatory wages actionable under federal law regardless of when the discrimination began.[11] Previously, plaintiffs had to file a complaint within a limited time period. Today, if a plaintiff continues to work for the employer while receiving discriminatory wages, the time period for filing a complaint is practically unlimited.

**Discrimination against Transgender Persons**
In the past, most courts held that federal law (Title VII)

10. 29 U.S.C. Section 206(d).

11. Pub. L. No. 111-2, 123 Stat. 5 (January 5, 2009), amending 42 U.S.C. Section 2000e-5[e].

does not protect transgender persons from discrimination. The situation may be changing, however. A growing number of federal courts are interpreting Title VII's protections against gender discrimination to apply to transsexuals.

■ **CASE IN POINT 12.9** Dr. Deborah Fabian applied for a position as an on-call orthopedic surgeon at the Hospital of Central Connecticut. The hospital apparently declined to hire Fabian because she disclosed her identity as a transgender woman. Fabian sued the hospital alleging violations of Title VII of the Civil Rights Act and the Connecticut Fair Employment Practices Act (CFEPA).

The hospital filed a summary judgment motion, arguing that neither Title VII nor the Connecticut statute prohibits discrimination on the basis of transgender identity. The federal district court rejected this argument, however, finding that discrimination on the basis of transgender identity is discrimination on the basis of sex for Title VII purposes. Fabian was entitled to take her case to a jury and argue violations of Title VII and the CFEPA.[12] ■

## 12–1g Constructive Discharge

The majority of Title VII complaints involve unlawful discrimination in decisions to hire or fire employees. In some situations, however, employees who leave their jobs voluntarily can claim that they were "constructively discharged" by the employer. **Constructive discharge** occurs when the employer causes the employee's working conditions to be so intolerable that a reasonable person in the employee's position would feel compelled to quit.

When constructive discharge is claimed, the employee can pursue damages for loss of income, including back pay. These damages ordinarily are not available to an employee who left a job voluntarily.

**Proving Constructive Discharge** To prove constructive discharge, an employee must present objective proof of intolerable working conditions. The employee must also show that the employer knew or had reason to know about these conditions yet failed to correct them within a reasonable time period. In addition, courts generally require the employee to show causation—that the employer's unlawful discrimination caused the working conditions to be intolerable. Put in a different way, the employee's resignation must be a foreseeable result of the

employer's discriminatory action. Courts weigh the facts on a case-by-case basis.

Employee demotion is one of the most frequently cited reasons for a finding of constructive discharge, particularly when the employee was subjected to humiliation. ■ **EXAMPLE 12.10** Khalil's employer humiliates him by informing him in front of his co-workers that he is being demoted to an inferior position. Khalil's co-workers then continually insult him, harass him, and make derogatory remarks to him about his national origin (he is from Iran). The employer is aware of this discriminatory treatment but does nothing to remedy the situation, despite Khalil's repeated complaints. After several months, Khalil quits his job and files a Title VII claim. In this situation, Khalil will likely have sufficient evidence to maintain an action for constructive discharge in violation of Title VII. ■

**Applies to All Title VII Discrimination** Plaintiffs can use constructive discharge to establish any type of discrimination claim under Title VII, including race, color, national origin, religion, gender, and pregnancy. It is most commonly asserted in cases involving sexual harassment. Constructive discharge may also be used in cases involving discrimination based on age or disability (discussed later in this chapter).

## 12–1h Sexual Harassment

Title VII also protects employees against **sexual harassment** in the workplace. Sexual harassment can take two forms:

1. *Quid pro quo* harassment occurs when sexual favors are demanded in return for job opportunities, promotions, salary increases, or other benefits. *Quid pro quo* is a Latin phrase that is often translated as "something in exchange for something else."

2. *Hostile-environment* harassment occurs when a pattern of sexually offensive conduct runs throughout the workplace and the employer has not taken steps to prevent or discourage it. Such harassment exists when the workplace is permeated with discriminatory intimidation, ridicule, and insult, and this harassment is so severe or pervasive that it alters the conditions of employment.

A court considers a number of factors when determining whether the sexually offensive conduct was sufficiently severe or pervasive to create a hostile environment. As the following case shows, these factors include the nature and frequency of the conduct and whether it unreasonably interfered with the victim's work performance.

---

12. *Fabian v. Hospital of Central Connecticut,* ___ F.Supp.3d ___, 2016 WL 1089178 (D.Conn. 2016).

# Roberts v. Mike's Trucking, Ltd.

Court of Appeals of Ohio, Twelfth District, 2014 -Ohio- 766, 9 N.E.3d 483 (2014).

**Background and Facts**  Teresa Roberts worked for Mike's Trucking, Ltd., in Columbus, Ohio. Her supervisor was the company's owner, Mike Culbertson. According to Roberts, Culbertson called her his "sexretary" and constantly talked about his sex life. He often invited her to sit on "Big Daddy's" lap, rubbed against her, trapped her at the door and asked her for hugs or kisses, and inquired if she needed help in the restroom. Roberts asked him to stop this conduct, but he did not. She became less productive and began to suffer anxiety attacks and high blood pressure. Roberts filed a suit in an Ohio state court against Mike's, alleging a hostile work environment through sexual harassment in violation of Title VII. A jury decided in Roberts's favor, and Mike's appealed.

## In the Language of the Court

*HENDRICKSON*, P.J. [Presiding Judge]

\* \* \* \*

\* \* \* Conduct that is not severe or pervasive enough to create an objectively hostile or abusive work environment—an environment that a reasonable person would find hostile or abusive—is beyond Title VII's purview. Likewise, if the victim does not subjectively perceive the environment to be abusive, the conduct has not actually altered the conditions of the victim's employment, and there is no Title VII violation. Therefore, *the focus of this inquiry is: 1.) whether a reasonable person would find the environment objectively hostile; and 2.) whether the plaintiff subjectively found the conduct severe or pervasive.* [Emphasis added.]

\* \* \* \*

\* \* \* Roberts' testimony was consistent with several witnesses affirming that Culbertson frequently engaged in a variety of conduct ranging from inappropriate discussions to groping women. The witnesses stated that Culbertson often discussed his sex life, asked Roberts and the women employees if they needed help in the bathroom \* \* \*, referred to himself as "Big Daddy," asked Roberts and the women employees to sit in "Big Daddy's" lap, and asked them if they would give "Big Daddy" a hug.

The evidence established that the conduct occurred frequently. Roberts testified that throughout her employment, Culbertson's behavior became increasingly worse and that \* \* \* he talked about sex hundreds of times, and attempted to corner her and hug and kiss her at least twice a week. [Former Mike's employees] testified that Culbertson talked about sex and asked the women if they needed help with the bathroom multiple times a week. The evidence also showed that the conduct became increasingly severe as Culbertson massaged Roberts [and] rubbed up against her \* \* \*. Roberts testified that Culbertson's conduct was humiliating towards her as his remarks were in front of others and she often became "furious" with him. Other employees reported Roberts becoming angry towards Culbertson. Roberts also established that Culbertson's conduct unreasonably interfered with her work performance as she stated she did not want to go to work anymore, she became less productive, and she suffered anxiety attacks. Her fiancé testified that Roberts has lost confidence and that she is now prescribed anti-anxiety medication.

Consequently, there was sufficient and substantial evidence to support the jury's finding that a reasonable person would find Culbertson's conduct created a hostile environment and Roberts found the conduct to be sufficiently severe or pervasive to affect her employment.

**Decision and Remedy**  *A state intermediate appellate court affirmed the lower court's judgment in Roberts's favor. During the trial, other Mike's employees and Roberts's fiancé testified to corroborate Roberts's account. The evidence sufficiently established that Culbertson's conduct was severe or pervasive enough to create a hostile work environment for Roberts.*

## Critical Thinking

- **Ethical**  *Was Culbertson's conduct at any point unethical? Discuss.*
- **Legal Environment**  *Culbertson and some other witnesses testified that he did not engage in any sexually inappropriate behavior. Should an appellate court reverse a jury's decision simply due to contrary evidence? Why or why not?*

**Harassment by Supervisors** For an employer to be held liable for a supervisor's sexual harassment, the supervisor normally must have taken a *tangible employment action* against the employee. A **tangible employment action** is a significant change in employment status or benefits. Such an action occurs when an employee is fired, refused a promotion, demoted, or reassigned to a position with significantly different responsibilities, for instance. Only a supervisor, or another person acting with the authority of the employer, can cause this sort of harm. A constructive discharge also qualifies as a tangible employment action.

The United States Supreme Court issued several important rulings in cases alleging sexual harassment by supervisors that established what is known as the "*Ellerth/Faragher* affirmative defense."[13] The defense has two elements:

1. The employer must have taken reasonable care to prevent and promptly correct any sexually harassing behavior (by establishing effective harassment policies and complaint procedures, for instance).
2. The plaintiff-employee must have unreasonably failed to take advantage of preventive or corrective opportunities provided by the employer to avoid harm.

An employer that can prove both elements normally will not be liable for a supervisor's harassment.

**Retaliation by Employers** Employers sometimes retaliate against employees who complain about sexual harassment or other Title VII violations. Retaliation can take many forms. An employer might demote or fire the person, or otherwise change the terms, conditions, and benefits of employment.

Title VII prohibits retaliation, and employees can sue their employers when it occurs. In a *retaliation claim,* an individual asserts that she or he has suffered harm as a result of making a charge, testifying, or participating in a Title VII investigation or proceeding.

**Requirements for Protection.** To be protected under Title VII's retaliation provisions, the plaintiff must have opposed a practice prohibited by Title VII and suffered an adverse employment action as a result of that opposition. ■ **CASE IN POINT 12.11** Myrta Morales-Cruz had a tenure-track teaching position at the University of Puerto Rico School of Law. When her probationary period was almost over, Morales-Cruz asked the university's administrative committee to grant a one-year extension for her tenure review. The dean recommended that the extension be granted but also called her "insecure," "immature," and "fragile." Another professor commented that had she shown "poor judgment" and exhibited "personality flaws."

After Morales-Cruz complained about these comments in writing to the chancellor, the dean recommended denying the one-year extension, and the administrative committee did just that. Morales-Cruz later filed a retaliation lawsuit. She claimed that the dean had retaliated against her for complaining to the chancellor about the "discriminatory" comments made in the course of her request for an extension.

The court held that Morales-Cruz had not provided a reasonable foundation for a retaliation action. Under Title VII, an employer may not retaliate against an employee because he or she has opposed a practice prohibited by Title VII. But the court found that Morales-Cruz did not allege any facts that could be construed as gender-based discrimination. Although the comments she complained about were hardly flattering, they were entirely gender-neutral. Thus, she was not engaging in protected conduct when she opposed the remarks.[14] ■

**Protection May Extend to Others.** The Supreme Court has ruled that Title VII's retaliation protection extended to an employee who spoke out about discrimination against another employee during an employer's internal investigation.[15] The Court has also held that Title VII protected an employee who was fired after his fiancée filed a gender discrimination claim against their employer.[16]

**Harassment by Co-Workers and Others** When the harassment of co-workers, rather than supervisors, creates a hostile working environment, an employee may still have a cause of action against the employer. Normally, though, the employer will be held liable only if it knew or should have known about the harassment and failed to take immediate remedial action.

Occasionally, a court may also hold an employer liable for harassment by *nonemployees* if the employer knew about the harassment and failed to take corrective action. ■ **EXAMPLE 12.12** Jordan, who owns and manages a Great Bites restaurant, knows that one of his regular customers, Dean, repeatedly harasses Kaylia, a waitress. If Jordan does nothing and permits the harassment to continue, he may be liable under Title VII even though Dean is not an employee of the restaurant. ■

13. *Burlington Industries, Inc. v. Ellerth*, 524 U.S. 742, 118 S.Ct. 2257, 141 L.Ed.2d 633 (1998); and *Faragher v. City of Boca Raton*, 524 U.S. 775, 118 S.Ct. 2275, 141 L.Ed.2d 662 (1998).

14. *Morales-Cruz v. University of Puerto Rico*, 676 F.3d 220 (1st Cir. 2012).
15. *Crawford v. Metropolitan Government of Nashville and Davidson County, Tennessee*, 555 U.S. 271, 129 S.Ct. 846, 172 L.Ed.2d 650 (2009).
16. See *Thompson v. North American Stainless, LP*, 562 U.S. 170, 131 S.Ct. 863, 178 L.Ed.2d 694 (2011).

**Same-Gender Harassment**  In *Oncale v. Sundowner Offshore Services, Inc.,*[17] the United States Supreme Court held that Title VII protection extends to individuals who are sexually harassed by members of the same gender. Proving that the harassment in same-gender cases is "based on sex" can be difficult, though. It is easier to establish a case of same-gender harassment when the harasser is homosexual.

**Sexual-Orientation Harassment**  Federal law (Title VII) does not prohibit discrimination or harassment based on a person's sexual orientation. Nonetheless, a growing number of states have enacted laws that prohibit sexual-orientation discrimination in private employment.[18] Some states, such as Oregon, explicitly prohibit discrimination based on a person's gender identity or expression. Many companies have also voluntarily established nondiscrimination policies that include sexual orientation.

## 12–1i  Online Harassment

Employees' online activities can create a hostile working environment in many ways. Racial jokes, ethnic slurs, or other comments contained in e-mail, texts, blogs, or social media can lead to claims of hostile-environment harassment or other forms of discrimination. A worker who regularly sees sexually explicit images on a co-worker's computer screen may find the images offensive and claim that they create a hostile working environment. Nevertheless, employers may be able to avoid liability for online harassment by taking prompt remedial action.

## 12–1j  Remedies under Title VII

Employer liability under Title VII can be extensive. If the plaintiff successfully proves that unlawful discrimination occurred, he or she may be awarded reinstatement, back pay, retroactive promotions, and damages.

Several limits apply to damages. Compensatory damages are available only in cases of intentional discrimination. Punitive damages may be recovered against a private employer only if the employer acted with malice or reckless indifference to an individual's rights. The total amount of compensatory and punitive damages that plaintiffs can recover from specific employers depends on the size of the employer. For instance, there is a $50,000 cap on damages from employers with one hundred or fewer employees.

# 12–2  Discrimination Based on Age

Age discrimination is potentially the most widespread form of discrimination because anyone—regardless of race, color, national origin, or gender—could be a victim at some point in life. The Age Discrimination in Employment Act[19] (ADEA), as amended, prohibits employment discrimination on the basis of age against individuals forty years of age or older. The act also prohibits mandatory retirement for nonmanagerial workers. In addition, the ADEA protects federal and private-sector employees from retaliation based on age-related complaints.[20]

For the act to apply, an employer must have twenty or more employees, and the employer's business activities must affect interstate commerce. The EEOC administers the ADEA, but the act also permits private causes of action against employers for age discrimination.

## 12–2a  Procedures under the ADEA

The burden-shifting procedure under the ADEA differs from the procedure under Title VII. This difference resulted from a United States Supreme Court decision that dramatically changed the burden of proof in age discrimination cases.[21]

As explained earlier, if the plaintiff in a Title VII case can show that the employer was motivated, at least in part, by unlawful discrimination, the burden of proof shifts to the employer. Thus, in cases in which the employer has a "mixed motive" for discharging an employee, the employer has the burden of proving that its reason was legitimate.

Under the ADEA, in contrast, a plaintiff must show that the unlawful discrimination was not just *a* reason but *the* reason for the adverse employment action. In other words, the employee has the burden of establishing *but for* causation—that is, "but for" the employee's age, the action would not have been taken.

**Prima Facie Age Discrimination**  To establish a *prima facie* case of age discrimination, the plaintiff must show that she or he was the following:

1. A member of the protected age group.
2. Qualified for the position from which she or he was discharged.
3. Discharged because of age discrimination.

---

17. 523 U.S. 75, 118 S.Ct. 998, 140 L.Ed.2d 207 (1998).
18. See, for instance, 775 Illinois Compiled Statutes 5/1–103.

19. 29 U.S.C. Sections 621–634.
20. *Gomez-Perez v. Potter,* 553 U.S. 474, 128 S.Ct. 1931, 170 L.Ed.2d 887 (2008).
21. *Gross v. FBL Financial Services, Inc.,* 557 U.S. 167, 129 S.Ct. 2343, 174 L.Ed.2d 119 (2009).

Then the burden shifts to the employer to give a legiti-mate nondiscriminatory reason for the adverse action.

**Pretext** If the employer offers a legitimate reason for its action, then the plaintiff must show that the stated reason is only a pretext. The plaintiff is required to prove that the plaintiff's age was the real reason for the employer's decision.

■ **CASE IN POINT 12.13** Josephine Mora, a fund-raiser for Jackson Memorial Foundation, Inc., was sixty-two years old when the foundation's chief executive officer (CEO) fired her. Mora filed an age discrimination suit against the foundation. She asserted that when she was fired, the CEO told her, "I need someone younger I can pay less." A witness heard that statement and also heard the CEO say that Mora was "too old to be working here anyway." The CEO denied making these statements, and the foundation claimed that Mora had been terminated for poor job performance.

A district court granted a summary judgment in the foundation's favor, and Mora appealed. A federal appel-late court reversed, concluding that the lower court's analysis of causation was incorrect. The court held that a reasonable juror could have accepted that the CEO had made discriminatory remarks and could have found that these remarks were sufficient evidence of a discrimina-tory motive. If so, that could show that Mora was fired because of her age. The court therefore remanded the case to the lower court for a trial.[22] ■

## 12–2b Replacing Older Workers with Younger Workers

Numerous age discrimination cases have been brought against employers who, to cut costs, replaced older, higher-salaried employees with younger, lower-salaried workers. In such situations, whether a firing is discrimi-natory or simply part of a rational business decision to prune the company's ranks is not always clear.

The plaintiff must prove that the discharge was moti-vated by age bias. The plaintiff need not prove that she or he was replaced by a person "outside the protected class" (under the age of forty). The replacement worker need only be younger than the plaintiff. Nevertheless, the greater the age gap, the more likely the plaintiff will suc-ceed in showing age discrimination.

## 12–2c State Employees Not Covered by the ADEA

Generally, the states are immune from lawsuits brought by private individuals in federal court (unless a state consents to such a suit). This immunity stems from the United States Supreme Court's interpretation of the Eleventh Amendment.

State immunity under the Eleventh Amendment is not absolute. In some situations, such as when fundamental rights are at stake, Congress has the power to abrogate (abolish) state immunity to private suits through legis-lation. Such legislation must unequivocally show Con-gress's intent to subject states to private suits.[23]

Generally, though, the Court has found that state employers are immune from private suits brought by employees under the ADEA. State employers are also immune from suits brought under the Americans with Disabilities Act[24] and the Fair Labor Standards Act.[25] They are *not* immune from the requirements of the Fam-ily and Medical Leave Act.[26]

## 12–3 Discrimination Based on Disability

The Americans with Disabilities Act (ADA)[27] prohibits disability-based discrimination in all workplaces with fif-teen or more workers. An exception is state government employers, who are generally immune under the Elev-enth Amendment, as just mentioned. Basically, the ADA requires that employers "reasonably accommodate" the needs of persons with disabilities unless to do so would cause the employer to suffer an "undue hardship." The ADA Amendments Act[28] broadened the coverage of the ADA's protections, as discussed shortly.

### 12–3a Procedures under the ADA

To prevail on a claim under the ADA, a plaintiff must show that he or she (1) has a disability, (2) is otherwise qualified for the employment in question, and (3) was

---

22. *Mora v. Jackson Memorial Foundation, Inc.*, 597 F.3d 1201 (11th Cir. 2010).
23. *Tennessee v. Lane*, 541 U.S. 509, 124 S.Ct. 1978, 158 L.Ed.2d 820 (2004).
24. *Board of Trustees of the University of Alabama v. Garrett*, 531 U.S. 356, 121 S.Ct. 955, 148 L.Ed.2d 866 (2001).
25. *Alden v. Maine*, 527 U.S. 706, 119 S.Ct. 2240, 144 L.Ed.2d 636 (1999).
26. *Nevada Department of Human Resources v. Hibbs*, 538 U.S. 721, 123 S.Ct. 1972, 155 L.Ed.2d 953 (2003).
27. 42 U.S.C. Sections 12103–12118.
28. 42 U.S.C. Sections 12103 and 12205a.

excluded from the employment solely because of the disability. As in Title VII cases, the plaintiff must pursue the claim through the EEOC before filing an action in court for a violation of the ADA.

The EEOC may decide to investigate and perhaps sue the employer on behalf of the employee. The EEOC can bring a suit even if the employee previously signed an agreement with the employer to submit job-related disputes to arbitration.[29] If the EEOC decides not to sue, then the employee may do so.

Plaintiffs in lawsuits brought under the ADA may seek many of the same remedies that are available under Title VII. These include reinstatement, back pay, a limited amount of compensatory and punitive damages (for intentional discrimination), and certain other forms of relief. Repeat violators may be ordered to pay fines of up to $100,000.

## 12–3b  What Is a Disability?

The ADA is broadly drafted to cover persons with physical or mental impairments that "substantially limit" their everyday activities. Specifically, the ADA defines a *disability* as including any of the following:

1. A physical or mental impairment that substantially limits one or more of the major life activities of the affected individual.
2. A record of having such an impairment.
3. Being regarded as having such an impairment.

Health conditions that have been considered disabilities under federal law include alcoholism, acquired immune deficiency syndrome (AIDS), blindness, cancer, cerebral palsy, diabetes, heart disease, muscular dystrophy, and paraplegia. Testing positive for the human immunodeficiency virus (HIV) has qualified as a disability, as has morbid obesity. (A morbidly obese person weighs twice the normal weight for his or her height.)

**Association with Disabled Persons** A separate provision in the ADA prevents employers from taking adverse employment actions based on stereotypes or assumptions about individuals who associate with people who have disabilities.[30] An employer cannot, for instance, refuse to hire the parent of a child with a disability based on the assumption that the person will miss work too often or be unreliable.

■ **EXAMPLE 12.14** Joan, an employer, refuses to hire Edward, who has a daughter with a physical disability. She consciously bases her decision on the assumption that Edward will have to miss work frequently to care for his daughter. Edward can sue Joan for violating the ADA's provisions. ■

**Mitigating Measures** At one time, the courts focused on whether a person had a disability *after* the use of corrective devices or medication. Thus, a person with severe myopia (nearsightedness) whose eyesight could be corrected by wearing glasses did not qualify as having a disability. With the corrective lenses, the person's major life activities were not substantially impaired. Then Congress amended the ADA to strengthen its protections and prohibit employers from considering mitigating measures when determining if an individual has a disability.

Disability is now determined on a case-by-case basis. A condition may fit the definition of disability in one set of circumstances, but not in another. ■ **CASE IN POINT 12.15** Larry Rohr, a welding specialist for a power district in Arizona, was diagnosed with type 2 diabetes. To keep his condition under control, Rohr was required to follow a complex regimen of daily insulin injections and blood tests, as well as a strict diet. Therefore, his physician forbade him from taking work assignments that involved overnight, out-of-town travel, which were common in his job.

Because of these limitations, the power district asked him to transfer, apply for federal disability benefits, or take early retirement. Rohr sued for disability discrimination. The lower court granted summary judgment for the employer. Rohr appealed. A federal appellate court reversed. The court held that under the amended ADA, diabetes is a disability if it significantly restricts an individual's eating (a major life activity), as it did for Rohr. Therefore, Rohr was entitled to a trial on his discrimination claim.[31] ■

**Disclosure of Confidential Medical Information** ADA provisions also require employers to keep their employees' medical information confidential.[32] An employee who discovers that an employer has disclosed his or her confidential medical information has a right to sue the employer—even if the employee was not technically disabled. The prohibition against disclosure also applies to other employees acting on behalf of the employer.

---

**29.** This was the Supreme Court's ruling in *EEOC v. Waffle House, Inc.,* 534 U.S. 279, 122 S.Ct. 754, 151 L.Ed.2d 755 (2002).
**30.** 42 U.S.C. Section 12112(b)(4).

**31.** *Rohr v. Salt River Project Agricultural Improvement and Power District,* 555 F.3d 850 (9th Cir. 2009).
**32.** 42 U.S.C. Sections 12112(d)(3)(B), (C), and 12112(d)(4)(C).

■ **CASE IN POINT 12.16** George Shoun was working at his job at Best Formed Plastics, Inc., when he fell and injured his shoulder. Another Best Formed employee, Jane Stewart, prepared an accident report for the incident and processed Shoun's workers' compensation claim. As a result of the injury, Shoun had to take several months off work and received workers' compensation.

Stewart posted on her Facebook page a statement about how Shoun's shoulder injury "kept him away from work for 11 months and now he is trying to sue us." Shoun sued Best Formed under the ADA for wrongfully disclosing confidential information about his medical condition to other people via Facebook. He claimed that the action resulted in loss of employment and impairment of his earning capacity. The court allowed Shoun's claim to go forward to trial.[33] ■

## 12–3c Reasonable Accommodation

The ADA does not require that employers accommodate the needs of job applicants or employees with disabilities who are not otherwise qualified for the work. If a job applicant or an employee with a disability, with reasonable accommodation, can perform essential job functions, however, the employer must make the accommodation.

Required modifications may include installing ramps for a wheelchair, establishing flexible working hours, creating or modifying job assignments, and designing or improving training materials and procedures. Generally, employers should give primary consideration to employees' preferences in deciding what accommodations should be made.

**Undue Hardship** Employers who do not accommodate the needs of persons with disabilities must demonstrate that the accommodations would cause *undue hardship* in terms of being significantly difficult or expensive for the employer. Usually, the courts decide whether an accommodation constitutes an undue hardship on a case-by-case basis.

■ **EXAMPLE 12.17** Bryan Lockhart, who uses a wheelchair, works for a cell phone company that provides parking for its employees. Lockhart informs his supervisor that the parking spaces are so narrow that he is unable to extend the ramp on his van that allows him to get in and out of the vehicle. Lockhart therefore requests that the company reasonably accommodate his needs by paying a monthly fee for him to use a larger parking space in an adjacent lot. In this situation, a court will likely find that it is *not* an undue hardship for the employer to pay for additional parking for Lockhart. ■

**Job Applications and Physical Exams** Employers must modify their job-application and selection process so that those with disabilities can compete for jobs with those who do not have disabilities. For instance, a job announcement might be modified to allow applicants to respond by e-mail as well as by telephone, so that it does not discriminate against potential applicants with hearing impairments.

Employers are restricted in the kinds of questions they may ask on job-application forms and during pre-employment interviews. In addition, employers cannot require persons with disabilities to submit to preemployment physicals unless such exams are required of all other applicants. An employer can disqualify the applicant only if the medical problems discovered during a preemployment physical would make it impossible for the applicant to perform the job.

**Health-Insurance Plans** Workers with disabilities must be given equal access to any health insurance provided to other employees and cannot be excluded from coverage. An employer can put a limit, or cap, on health-care payments under its group health policy, but the cap must apply equally to all insured employees. Any group health-care plan that makes a disability-based distinction in its benefits violates the ADA (unless the employer can justify its actions under the business necessity defense, discussed shortly).

**Substance Abusers** Drug addiction is considered a disability under the ADA because it is a substantially limiting impairment. The act does not protect individuals who are actually using illegal drugs, however. Instead, the ADA protects only persons with *former* drug addictions—those who have completed or are now participating in a supervised drug-rehabilitation program. Individuals who have used drugs casually in the past also are not protected under the act. They are not considered addicts and therefore do not have a disability (addiction).

People suffering from alcoholism are also protected by the ADA. Employers cannot legally discriminate against employees simply because they suffer from alcoholism. Of course, employers can prohibit the use of alcohol in the workplace and require that employees not be under the influence of alcohol while working. Employers can also fire or refuse to hire a person who is an alcoholic if (1) the person poses a *substantial risk of harm* to himself or herself or to others, and (2) the risk cannot be reduced by reasonable accommodation.

---

33. *Shoun v. Best Formed Plastics, Inc.*, 28 F.Supp.3d 786 (N.D.Ind. 2014).

Exhibit 12–1 outlines the coverage of the employment discrimination laws discussed in this chapter.

## 12–4 Discrimination Based on Military Status

In 1994, Congress enacted the Uniformed Services Employment and Reemployment Rights Act (USERRA).[34] The USERRA protects civilian job rights and benefits for members of the military, former military personnel, and reservists. It also provides additional protections for veterans who are disabled. Most importantly, the USERRA prohibits discrimination against persons who have served in the military. In effect, it makes military service and status a protected class and gives members of this class a right to sue an employer for violations.

### 12–4a Broad Application and Provisions

The USERRA covers *all* employers, public and private, large and small. Even an employer with only one employee is subject to its provisions.[35] The act also applies to United States employers operating in foreign countries.

Under the USERRA, military plaintiffs can sue not only the employer but also individual employees who were acting in an official capacity for the employer. In other words, these employees—supervisors, for instance—can be held personally liable for violations. Additionally, there is no statute of limitations for bringing a lawsuit. The cause of action could have arisen ten weeks or ten years before the suit was filed.

The USERRA specifies that veterans can be terminated from their employment only "for cause." The employer is obligated to give employees a list of all the behaviors that would trigger a for-cause termination.

### 12–4b *Prima Facie* Case of Discrimination under the USERRA

To establish a *prima facie* case of discrimination (and retaliation) under the USERRA, the plaintiff must establish that the employer took an adverse employment action based in part on the employee's connection with the military. The connection to the military may be through the plaintiff's membership, service, or application for service, or it may be through providing testimony or statements concerning the military service of another.[36] If another similarly situated person who did not serve in the military or engage in a protected activity was treated more favorably than the plaintiff, the employer has violated the USERRA.

■ **CASE IN POINT 12.18** Baldo Bello, a staff sergeant with the United States Marine Corps Reserve, was employed by the Village of Skokie as a police officer. Police officers

---

**34.** Pub. L. No. 103-353, codified at 38 U.S.C. Sections 4301-4335.
**35.** 20 C.F.R. Section 1002.34(a).

**36.** 38 U.S.C. Section 4311(c).

**EXHIBIT 12–1**  Coverage of Employment Discrimination Laws

| Title VII of the Civil Rights Act | Age Discrimination in Employment Act | Americans with Disabilities Act (as Amended) |
|---|---|---|
| Prohibits discrimination based on race, color, national origin, religion, gender (including wage discrimination), and pregnancy; prohibits sexual harassment. | Prohibits discrimination against persons over forty years of age. | Prohibits discrimination against persons with a mental or physical impairment that substantially limits a major life activity now or in the past, or who are regarded as having such an impairment, or who are associated with a disabled person. |
| Applies to employers with fifteen or more employees. | Applies to employers with twenty or more employees. | Applies to employers with fifteen or more employees. |

in Skokie normally have nine regular days off (RDO) per month and eight sick days per year. Skokie officers who are in the reserve receive two weeks of paid leave for annual training each summer, but they do not receive pay for the required weekend military training. During his first four years as an officer at Skokie, Bello always requested RDOs to cover his weekend training drills.

After that, Bello started requesting military leave for the two to four days of drills per month, in addition to his nine RDO days. Skokie at first granted Bello military leave for monthly drills but later began to deny the requests. When Skokie officials told Bello that he needed to schedule his RDOs to cover his weekend military training, Bello filed suit in a federal district court alleging violations of the USERRA. Skokie filed a motion for summary judgment, which the court denied. The court found that Bello was meeting his employer's legitimate expectations. Bello was therefore entitled to a trial on the issue of whether Skokie had treated his leave requests less favorably than requests from other employees.[37] ■

## 12–4c Plaintiffs May Be Entitled to Promotions

Under the USERRA, returning service members are to be reemployed in the jobs that they would have attained had they not been absent for military service. Reinstatement could affect their seniority, status, pay, and other rights and benefits (such as health and pension plans). In essence, this means that if a returning service member sues an employer for violations of the USERRA and is successful, she or he could receive not only damages and reinstatement but also a promotion.

# 12–5 Defenses to Employment Discrimination

The first line of defense for an employer charged with employment discrimination is to assert that the plaintiff has failed to meet his or her initial burden of proving that discrimination occurred. As noted, plaintiffs bringing age discrimination claims may find it difficult to meet this initial burden because they must prove that age discrimination was the reason for their employer's decision.

Once a plaintiff succeeds in proving that discrimination occurred, the burden shifts to the employer to justify the discriminatory practice. Possible justifications

include that the discrimination was the result of a business necessity, a bona fide occupational qualification, or a seniority system. In some situations, as noted earlier, an effective antiharassment policy and prompt remedial action when harassment occurs may shield employers from liability for sexual harassment under Title VII.

## 12–5a Business Necessity

An employer may defend against a claim of disparate-impact (unintentional) discrimination by asserting that a practice that has a discriminatory effect is a **business necessity.** ■ **EXAMPLE 12.19** EarthFix, Inc., an international consulting agency, requires its applicants to be fluent in at least one foreign language. If this requirement is shown to have a discriminatory effect, EarthFix can defend it based on business necessity. That is, the company can argue that its workers must speak more than one language to perform their jobs at the required level of competence. If EarthFix can demonstrate a definite connection between foreign language fluency and job performance, it normally will succeed in this business necessity defense. ■

## 12–5b Bona Fide Occupational Qualification

Another defense applies when discrimination against a protected class is essential to a job—that is, when a particular trait is a **bona fide occupational qualification (BFOQ).** Note that race, color, and national origin can never be BFOQs.

Generally, courts have restricted the BFOQ defense to situations in which the employee's gender or religion is essential to the job. For instance, a women's clothing store might legitimately hire only female sales attendants if part of an attendant's job involves assisting clients in the store's dressing rooms.

## 12–5c Seniority Systems

An employer with a history of discrimination may have no members of protected classes in upper-level positions. Nevertheless, the employer may have a defense against a discrimination suit if promotions or other job benefits have been distributed according to a fair *seniority system.* In a **seniority system,** workers with more years of service are promoted first or laid off last.

■ **CASE IN POINT 12.20** Cathalene Johnson, an African American woman, was a senior service agent for Federal Express Corporation (FedEx) for more than seventeen

---

37. *Bello v. Village of Skokie,* ___ F.Supp.3d ___, 2015 WL 9582986 (N.D. Ill. 2015).

years. She resigned in 2014 and filed suit against FedEx for discrimination based on race and gender, as well as for violation of the Equal Pay Act. Johnson claimed that FedEx had paid a white male co-worker about two dollars more per hour than she had received for basically the same position. FedEx argued that the man had seniority. He had worked for FedEx for seven years longer, was the most senior employee at the station where Johnson worked, and had been a courier in addition to being a service agent. The court ruled that FedEx's seniority system was fair and provided a defense to Johnson's claims.[38] ∎

### 12-5d After-Acquired Evidence of Employee Misconduct

In some situations, employers have attempted to avoid liability for employment discrimination on the basis of "after-acquired evidence" of an employee's misconduct. After-acquired evidence refers to evidence that the employer discovers after a lawsuit has been filed.

∎ **EXAMPLE 12.21** Pratt Legal Services fires Lucy, who then sues Pratt for employment discrimination. During pretrial investigation, Pratt discovers that Lucy made material misrepresentations on her job application. Had Pratt known of these misrepresentations, it would have had grounds to fire Lucy. ∎

After-acquired evidence of wrongdoing cannot shield an employer entirely from liability for employment discrimination. It may, however, be used to limit the amount of damages for which the employer is liable.

# 12-6 Affirmative Action

Federal statutes and regulations providing for equal opportunity in the workplace were designed to reduce or eliminate discriminatory practices with respect to hiring, retaining, and promoting employees. **Affirmative action** programs go a step further and attempt to "make up" for past patterns of discrimination by giving members of protected classes preferential treatment in hiring or promotion. During the 1960s, all federal and state government agencies, private companies that contracted to do business with the federal government, and institutions that received federal funding were required to implement affirmative action policies.

Title VII of the Civil Rights Act neither requires nor prohibits affirmative action. Thus, most private companies and organizations have not been required to implement affirmative action policies, though many have done so voluntarily. Affirmative action programs have been controversial, however, particularly when they have resulted in reverse discrimination against members of a majority group, such as white males.

### 12-6a Equal Protection Issues

Because of their inherently discriminatory nature, affirmative action programs may violate the equal protection clause of the Fourteenth Amendment to the U.S. Constitution. Any federal, state, or local government affirmative action program that uses racial or ethnic classifications as the basis for making decisions is subject to strict scrutiny (the highest standard to meet) by the courts.

Today, an affirmative action program normally is constitutional only if it attempts to remedy past discrimination and does not make use of quotas or preferences. Furthermore, once such a program has succeeded in the goal of remedying past discrimination, it must be changed or eliminated.

### 12-6b State Laws Prohibiting Affirmative Action Programs

Some states have enacted laws that prohibit affirmative action programs at public institutions (colleges, universities, and state agencies) within their borders. These states include California, Maryland, Michigan, New Hampshire, Oklahoma, Virginia, and Washington. The United States Supreme Court recognized that states have the power to enact such bans in 2014.

∎ **CASE IN POINT 12.22** Michigan voters passed an initiative to amend the state's constitution to prohibit publicly funded colleges from granting preferential treatment to any group on the basis of race, sex, color, ethnicity, or national origin. The law also prohibited Michigan from considering race and gender in public hiring and contracting decisions.

A lawsuit was filed challenging the initiative as a violation of the equal protection clause in the U.S. Constitution. Although a federal appellate court held that the law violated the equal protection clause, the United States Supreme Court reversed. The Court ruled that a state has the inherent power to ban affirmative action within that state, but it did not rule on the constitutionality of any specific affirmative action program.[39] ∎

---

38. *Johnson v. Federal Express Corp.,* 996 F.Supp.2d 302 (M.D.Pa. 2014).

39. *Schuette v. Coalition to Defend Affirmative Action, Integration and Immigrant Rights,* ___ U.S. ___, 134 S.Ct. 1623, 188 L.Ed.2d 613 (2014).

# Reviewing: Employment Discrimination

Amaani Lyle, an African American woman, was hired by Warner Brothers Television Productions to be a scriptwriters' assistant for the writers of *Friends,* a popular adult-oriented television series. One of her essential job duties was to type detailed notes for the scriptwriters during brainstorming sessions in which they discussed jokes, dialogue, and story lines. The writers then combed through Lyle's notes after the meetings for script material. During these meetings, the three male scriptwriters told lewd and vulgar jokes and made sexually explicit comments and gestures. They often talked about their personal sexual experiences and fantasies, and some of these conversations were then used in episodes of *Friends.*

During the meetings, Lyle never complained that she found the writers' conduct offensive. After four months, Lyle was fired because she could not type fast enough to keep up with the writers' conversations during the meetings. She filed a suit against Warner Brothers, alleging sexual harassment and claiming that her termination was based on racial discrimination. Using the information presented in the chapter, answer the following questions.

1. Would Lyle's claim of racial discrimination be for intentional (disparate-treatment) or unintentional (disparate-impact) discrimination? Explain.
2. Can Lyle establish a *prima facie* case of racial discrimination? Why or why not?
3. When Lyle was hired, she was told that typing speed was extremely important to the position. At the time, she maintained that she could type eighty words per minute, so she was not given a typing test. It later turned out that Lyle could type only fifty words per minute. What impact might typing speed have on Lyle's lawsuit?
4. Lyle's sexual-harassment claim is based on the hostile working environment created by the writers' sexually offensive conduct at meetings that she was required to attend. The writers, however, argue that their behavior was essential to the "creative process" of writing for *Friends,* a show that routinely contained sexual innuendos and adult humor. Which defense discussed in the chapter might Warner Brothers assert using this argument?

**Debate This** . . .   *Members of minority groups and women have made enough economic progress in the last several decades that they no longer need special legislation to protect them.*

## Terms and Concepts

| | | |
|---|---|---|
| affirmative action 235 | disparate-impact | *prima facie* case 219 |
| bona fide occupational | discrimination 220 | protected class 218 |
| qualification (BFOQ) 234 | disparate-treatment | seniority system 234 |
| business necessity 234 | discrimination 219 | sexual harassment 226 |
| constructive discharge 226 | employment discrimination 218 | tangible employment action 228 |

## Issue Spotters

1. Ruth is a supervisor for a Subs & Suds restaurant. Tim is a Subs & Suds employee. The owner announces that some employees will be discharged. Ruth tells Tim that if he has sex with her, he can keep his job. Is this sexual harassment? Why or why not? (See *Title VII of the Civil Rights Act.*)

2. Koko, a person with a disability, applies for a job at Lively Sales Corporation for which she is well qualified, but she is rejected. Lively continues to seek applicants and eventually fills the position with a person who does not have a disability. Could Koko succeed in a suit against Lively for discrimination? Explain. (See *Discrimination Based on Disability.*)

- **Check your answers to the Issue Spotters against the answers provided in Appendix B at the end of this text.**

# Business Scenarios

**12–1. Title VII Violations.** Discuss fully whether either of the following actions would constitute a violation of Title VII of the 1964 Civil Rights Act, as amended: (See *Title VII of the Civil Rights Act.*)

**(a)** Tennington, Inc., is a consulting firm with ten employees. These employees travel on consulting jobs in seven states. Tennington has an employment record of hiring only white males.

**(b)** Novo Films is making a movie about Africa and needs to employ approximately one hundred extras for this picture. To hire these extras, Novo advertises in all major newspapers in Southern California. The ad states that only African Americans need apply.

**12–2. Religious Discrimination.** Gina Gomez, a devout Roman Catholic, worked for Sam's Department Stores, Inc., in Phoenix, Arizona. Sam's considered Gomez a productive employee because her sales exceeded $200,000 per year. At the time, the store gave its managers the discretion to grant unpaid leave to employees but prohibited vacations or leave during the holiday season—October through December. Gomez felt that she had a "calling" to go on a "pilgrimage" in October to a location in Bosnia where some persons claimed to have had visions of the Virgin Mary. The Catholic Church had not designated the site an official pilgrimage site, the visions were not expected to be stronger in October, and tours were available at other times. The store managers denied Gomez's request for leave, but she had a nonrefundable ticket and left anyway. Sam's terminated her employment, and she could not find another job. Can Gomez establish a *prima facie* case of religious discrimination? Explain. (See *Title VII of the Civil Rights Act.*)

# Business Case Problems

**12–3. Spotlight on Dress Code Policies—Discrimination Based on Gender.**  Burlington Coat Factory Warehouse, Inc., had a dress code that required male salesclerks to wear business attire consisting of slacks, shirt, and a necktie. Female salesclerks, by contrast, were required to wear a smock so that customers could readily identify them. Karen O'Donnell and other female employees refused to wear smocks. Instead they reported to work in business attire and were suspended. After numerous suspensions, the female employees were fired for violating Burlington's dress code policy. All other conditions of employment, including salary, hours, and benefits, were the same for female and male employees. Was the dress code policy discriminatory? Why or why not? [*O'Donnell v. Burlington Coat Factory Warehouse, Inc.,* 656 F.Supp. 263 (S.D. Ohio 1987)] (See *Title VII of the Civil Rights Act.*)

**12–4. Sexual Harassment by Co-Worker.** Billie Bradford worked for the Kentucky Department of Community Based Services (DCBS). One of Bradford's co-workers, Lisa Stander, routinely engaged in extreme sexual behavior (such as touching herself and making crude comments) in Bradford's presence. Bradford and others regularly complained about Stander's conduct to their supervisor, Angie Taylor. Rather than resolve the problem, Taylor nonchalantly told Stander to stop, encouraged Bradford to talk to Stander, and suggested that Stander was just having fun. Assuming that Bradford was subjected to a hostile work environment, could DCBS be liable? Why or why not? [*Bradford v. Department of Community Based Services,* 2012 WL 360032 (E.D.Ky. 2012)] (See *Title VII of the Civil Rights Act.*)

**12–5. Business Case Problem with Sample Answer— Age Discrimination.**  Beginning in 1986, Paul Rangel was a sales professional for the pharmaceutical company sanofi-aventis U.S. LLC (S-A). Rangel had satisfactory performance reviews until 2006, when S-A issued new "Expectations" guidelines that included sales call quotas and other standards that he failed to meet. After two years of negative performance reviews, Rangel—who was then more than forty years old—was terminated. The termination was part of a nationwide reduction in force of all sales professionals who had not met the "Expectations" guidelines, including younger workers. Did S-A engage in age discrimination? Discuss. [*Rangel v. sanofi aventis U.S. LLC,* 2013 WL 142040 (10th Cir. 2013)] (See *Discrimination Based on Age.*)

• **For a sample answer to Problem 12–5, go to Appendix C at the end of this text.**

**12–6. Discrimination Based on Disability.** Cynthia Horn worked for Knight Facilities Management–GM, Inc., in Detroit, Michigan, as a janitor. When Horn developed a sensitivity to cleaning products, her physician gave her a "no exposure to cleaning solutions" restriction. Knight discussed possible accommodations with Horn. She suggested that restrooms be eliminated from her cleaning route or that she be provided with a respirator. Knight explained that she would be exposed to cleaning solutions in any situation and concluded that there was no work available within her physician's restriction. Has Knight violated the Americans with Disabilities Act by failing to provide Horn with the requested accommodations? Explain. [*Horn v. Knight Facilities Management–GM, Inc.,* 556 Fed.Appx. 452 (6th Cir. 2014)] (See *Discrimination Based on Disability.*)

**12–7. Sexual Harassment.** Jamel Blanton was a male employee at a Pizza Hut restaurant operated by Newton Associates, Inc., in San Antonio, Texas. Blanton was subjected to sexual and racial harassment by the general manager, who was female. Newton had a clear, straightforward antidiscrimination policy and complaint procedure. The policy provided that in such a situation, an employee should complain to the harasser's supervisor. Blanton alerted a shift leader and an assistant manager about the harassment, but they were subordinate to the general manager and did not report the harassment to higher-level management. When Blanton finally complained to a manager with authority over the general manager, the employer investigated and fired the general manager within four days. Blanton filed a suit in a federal district court against Newton, seeking to impose liability on the employer for the general manager's actions. What is Newton's best defense? Discuss. [*Blanton v. Newton Associates, Inc.,* 593 Fed.Appx. 389 (5th Cir. 2015)] (See *Title VII of the Civil Rights Act.*)

**12–8. Discrimination Based on Disability.** Dennis Wallace was a deputy sheriff for Stanislaus County, California, when he injured his left knee. After surgery, he was subject to limits on prolonged standing, walking, and running. The county assigned him to work as a bailiff. The sergeants who supervised him rated his performance above average. Less than a year later, without consulting those supervisors, the county placed him on an unpaid leave of absence, under the mistaken belief that he could not safely perform the essential functions of the job. Wallace filed an action in a California state court against the county, alleging discrimination based on disability. Under state law, discriminatory intent is shown by evidence that an actual or perceived disability was a "substantial motivating factor or reason" for an employer's adverse employment action. An employee is not required to show that the action was motivated by animosity or ill will. Could Wallace likely prove the "substantial motivating factor or reason" element? Explain. [*Wallace v. County of Stanislaus,* 245 Cal.App.4th 109, 199 Cal.Rptr.3d 462 (5 Dist. 2016)] (See *Discrimination Based on Disability.*)

**12–9. A Question of Ethics—Retaliation by Employers.**
 *Shane Dawson, a male homosexual, worked for Entek International. Some of Dawson's co-workers, including his supervisor, made derogatory comments about his sexual orientation. Dawson's work deteriorated. He filed a complaint with Entek's human resources department. Two days later, he was fired. State law made it unlawful for an employer to discriminate against an individual based on sexual orientation.* [Dawson v. Entek International, *630 F.3d 928 (9th Cir. 2011)]* (See *Title VII of the Civil Rights Act.*)

**(a)** Could Dawson establish a claim for retaliation? Explain.

**(b)** Should homosexuals be a protected class under Title VII of the Civil Rights Act? Discuss the arguments for and against amending federal law to prohibit employment discrimination based on sexual orientation.

## Legal Reasoning Group Activity

**12–10. Racial Discrimination.** Two African American plaintiffs sued the producers of the reality television series *The Bachelor* and *The Bachelorette* for racial discrimination. The plaintiffs claimed that the shows had never featured persons of color in the lead roles. The plaintiffs also alleged that the producers did not provide people of color who auditioned for the lead roles with the same opportunities to compete as white people who auditioned. (See *Title VII of the Civil Rights Act.*)

**(a)** The first group will assess whether the plaintiffs can establish a *prima facie* case of disparate-treatment discrimination.

**(b)** The second group will consider whether the plaintiffs can establish disparate-impact discrimination.

**(c)** The third group will assume that the plaintiffs established a *prima facie* case and that the burden has shifted to the employer to articulate a legal reason for not hiring the plaintiffs. What legitimate reasons might the employer assert for not hiring the plaintiffs in this situation? Should the law require television producers to hire persons of color for lead roles in reality television shows? Discuss.

# Health Insurance and Small Business

Small businesses are the foundation of the U.S. economy. Increasing health-care costs and decreasing insurance coverage between 2000 and 2010 forced many small firms to stop offering health-care coverage to their employees.

Recent legislation put in place comprehensive health-insurance reforms intended to improve access, affordability, and quality in health care. An especially important law is the Patient Protection and Affordable Care Act (ACA) of 2010 (often referred to as Obamacare). The ACA sets forth responsibilities and benefits for businesses determined in part by the size of an employer's workforce.[1]

## What Is a Small Business?

The ACA defines a *small business* as a firm with fewer than fifty full-time equivalent (FTE) employees. An FTE is an employee who works thirty or more hours per week. Two half-time employees count as one FTE.

This definition fits about 96 percent of all businesses (5.8 million out of 6 million firms). In fact, 90 percent of all U.S. firms have fewer than twenty FTEs.

## What Responsibilities Does the ACA Impose on Small Businesses?

Large businesses—those with fifty or more FTEs—are required to offer health insurance to their employees or pay a penalty.[2] For a small business, there is no requirement to offer health insurance. For a small firm that chooses to do so, the ACA imposes minimum standards on health plans.

**Summary of Benefits and Coverage** All employers, including small businesses, are required to provide their employees with a "Summary of Benefits and Coverage" that includes an explanation of the costs. The summary should be in plain language. Employees can use this information to compare their employer's plan with private plans, which the employees may opt to buy instead. An employer is not required to contribute to the premium for an employee's private plan.

**Waiting Period** Employees who are eligible for employer-sponsored health insurance must not be made to wait more than ninety days for coverage.

**Notice of Marketplace Coverage Options** Small businesses that do not offer health insurance can provide their employees with a "Notice of Marketplace Coverage Options." The notice can inform employees about their options with respect to the health-insurance marketplace.

---

1. For the complete text of the ACA, see Pub. L. No. 111-148. Also significant are the health-care amendments of the Health Care and Education Reconciliation Act of 2010; see Pub. L. No. 111-152.
2. Before the ACA, more than 95 percent of these employers already offered health insurance to their employees.

**Annual Returns** All employers that provide self-insured health coverage are required to file annual information returns with the Internal Revenue Service for the individuals that are covered.[3]

## What Benefits Does the ACA Offer Small Businesses?

The ACA provides benefits to small business by expanding insurance coverage options, reducing related costs, and giving employers and employees more control over their own health care.

**Health-Insurance Marketplace** A small business can buy health-insurance coverage for its employees through the ACA's Small Business Health Options Program (SHOP). Coverage can be offered to employees any time during the year.

The SHOP marketplace offers multiple plans from private insurance companies. An employer can choose which plans to make available to its employees, whether to cover the employees' dependents, how much of the premiums the employer will pay, and other options.[4]

**Small Business Health-Care Tax Credit** Employers with fewer than twenty-five FTEs, each of whom are paid an average annual wage of less than $50,000, may be eligible for a health-care tax credit. To be eligible, an employer must cover at least 50 percent of the cost of the premiums for its employees' health insurance and buy the coverage through SHOP. Dental and vision care coverage also qualifies. An employer does not need to offer coverage to part-time employees (those working fewer than thirty hours per week) or to employees' dependents to qualify for the credit.

The amount of the credit may be as much as 50 percent of an employer's contribution toward its employees' premium costs. The smaller the business, the higher the credit—the credit is highest for firms with fewer than ten employees paid an average of $25,000 or less. And eligible small businesses can claim a business expense deduction for the premiums in excess of the credit.[5]

**Wellness Programs** A wellness program requires individuals to meet a specific standard related to health, such as a lower blood cholesterol level, to obtain a reward. Employers that promote employee health through workplace wellness programs are eligible for a reward of up to 30 percent of the cost of health coverage. The reward for a program designed to prevent or reduce the use of tobacco can be as much as 50 percent. The cost of health coverage includes employer-paid premiums and benefits.

**Rebates** The ACA requires insurance companies to spend at least 80 percent of premiums on medical care, not administrative costs. Insurers who do not meet this goal must provide rebates to policyholders.[6] This includes employers that provide group health insurance for their employees.

---

3. 26 U.S.C. Section 6055.
4. See U.S. Department of Health and Human Services, *SHOP Marketplace How-To Guides, Fact Sheets, Tools, and Other Resources for Employers* (December 11, 2015), *available at* www.healthcare.gov/small-businesses/provide-shop-coverage/resources/.
5. See Internal Revenue Service, *Small Business Health Care Tax Credit and the SHOP Marketplace* (December 11, 2015), *available at* www.irs.gov/Affordable-Care-Act/Employers/Small-Business-Health-Care-Tax-Credit-and-the-SHOP-Marketplace.
6. See Internal Revenue Service, *Medical Loss Ration (MLR) FAQs* (December 11, 2015) at www.irs.gov/uac/Medical-Loss-Ratio-(MLR)-FAQs.

**Standard Operating Rules**  The ACA accelerated the adoption of standard operating rules for health-insurance plan administration. Operating rules are the business rules and guidelines for health-insurance plans. The ACA requires one format and one set of codes for claims, remittance advice, service authorization, eligibility verification, and claims status inquiry.

**Nondiscriminatory Pricing**  The ACA ended the discriminatory insurance industry practice of increasing premiums because an employee filed a claim or got older or because a business hired a woman. At one time, premiums could increase by up to 200 percent in these circumstances.

## Ethical Connection

There has been considerable opposition to the ACA. For example, the mandate that large businesses offer health insurance to their employees or pay a penalty—called "the Obamacare effect"—has been much criticized. Detractors express concern that the mandate creates an incentive for large businesses to employ part-time workers instead of full-time employees. During the period preceding the start date of the ACA and the end of 2014, however, in the private sector the number of part-time jobs *decreased* and the number of full-time positions *increased*.

To date, there is controversial evidence that employers are reducing the hours of their employees to avoid the requirements of the ACA.[7] Many argue that the reduction in the percentage of Americans who could work but are choosing to remain out of the labor force is due to Obamacare. Why? Because good-paying full-time job opportunities have shrunk due to the higher employer cost of hiring.

**Ethics Question**  *Are small businesses ethically obligated to offer their employees health insurance? Discuss.*

**Critical Thinking**  *Should the mandate to offer employees health insurance be extended to include small businesses? Or should it be repealed altogether? Explain.*

---

7. Also, in separate legal challenges to the ACA, the United States Supreme Court has upheld key parts of the act. See *National Federation of Business v. Sebelius*, __ U.S. __, 132 S.Ct. 2566, 183 L.Ed.2d 450 (2012); and *King v. Burwell*, __ U.S. __, 135 S.Ct. 2480, 192 L.Ed.2d 483 (2015). The Court has held certain U.S. Department of Health and Human Services regulations issued under the act to be invalid, however. See *Burwell v. Hobby Lobby Stores, Inc.*, __ U.S. __, 134 S.Ct. 2751, 189 L.Ed.2d 675 (2014).

# Commercial Transactions and Credit

# CHAPTER 13

# The Formation of Sales and Lease Contracts

When we turn to contracts for the sale and lease of goods, we move away from common law principles and into the area of statutory law. State statutory law governing sales and lease transactions is based on the Uniform Commercial Code (UCC), which has been adopted as law by all of the states.[1] Of all the attempts to produce a uniform body of laws relating to commercial transactions in the United States, none has been as successful as the UCC.

The goal of the UCC is to simplify and to streamline commercial transactions. The UCC allows parties to form sales and lease contracts, including those entered into online, without observing the same degree of formality used in forming other types of contracts.

Today, businesses often engage in sales and lease transactions on a global scale. The United Nations Convention on Contracts for the International Sale of Goods (CISG) governs international sales contracts. The CISG is a model uniform law that applies only when a nation has adopted it, just as the UCC applies only to the extent that it has been adopted by a state.

---

1. Louisiana has not adopted Articles 2 and 2A, however.

## 13-1 The Uniform Commercial Code

In the early years of this nation, sales law varied from state to state, and this lack of uniformity complicated the formation of multistate sales contracts. The problems became especially troublesome in the late nineteenth century as multistate contracts became the norm. At that time, the National Conference of Commissioners on Uniform State Laws (NCCUSL) began drafting uniform laws relating to commercial transactions to address these problems.

In 1945, the NCCUSL began to work on the Uniform Commercial Code (UCC) to integrate various uniform acts into a single uniform law. The UCC was completed in 1949. Over the next several years, it was substantially accepted by almost every state in the nation.

### 13-1a Comprehensive Coverage of the UCC

The UCC is the single most comprehensive codification of the broad spectrum of laws involved in a total commercial transaction. The UCC views the entire "commercial transaction for the sale of and payment for goods" as a single legal occurrence having numerous facets. The articles and sections of the UCC are periodically revised or supplemented to clarify certain aspects or to establish new rules as needed when the business environment changes.

Article 1, titled General Provisions, sets forth definitions and general principles applicable to commercial transactions. Article 1 thus provides the basic groundwork for the remaining articles, each of which focuses on a particular aspect of commercial transactions. For instance, Article 1 sets forth an obligation to perform in "good faith" all contracts falling under the UCC [UCC 1–304]. Note, though, that many contracts do not fall under the UCC, because they do not involve commercial transactions.

■ **CASE IN POINT 13.1** Peter Amaya was a third-year medical student at Indiana University School of Medicine (IUSM) when three professors saw him cheating on an exam. He denied cheating and maintained that he was merely looking over at the clock on the wall. When he was dismissed from the school, Amaya filed suit in state court against the dean and IUSM, alleging breach of contract and breach of the duty of good faith.

The court granted IUSM's motion for summary judgment. Amaya appealed, but the reviewing court affirmed. Because a contract between a university and its students is not a sale of goods, the UCC's duty of good faith does not apply. The university's conclusion that Amaya failed to maintain acceptable professional standards was a "rational determination" arrived at after deliberation and after Amaya had numerous opportunities to be heard.[2] ■

## 13–1b A Single, Integrated Framework for Commercial Transactions

The UCC attempts to provide a consistent and integrated framework of rules to deal with all the phases *ordinarily arising* in a commercial sales transaction from start to finish. Consider the following events, all of which may occur during a single transaction:

1. *A contract for the sale or lease of goods is formed and executed.* Article 2 and Article 2A of the UCC provide rules governing all aspects of this transaction.
2. *The transaction may involve a payment—by check, electronic fund transfer, or other means.* Article 3 (on negotiable instruments), Article 4 (on bank deposits and collections), Article 4A (on fund transfers), and Article 5 (on letters of credit) cover this part of the transaction.
3. *The transaction may involve a bill of lading or a warehouse receipt that covers goods when they are shipped or stored.* Article 7 (on documents of title) deals with this subject.
4. *The transaction may involve a demand by the seller or lender for some form of security for the remaining balance owed.* Article 9 (on secured transactions) covers this part of the transaction.

# 13–2 The Scope of Articles 2 (Sales) and 2A (Leases)

Article 2 of the UCC sets forth the requirements for *sales contracts,* as well as the duties and obligations of the parties involved in the sales contract. Article 2A covers similar issues for *lease contracts.* Bear in mind, however, that the parties to sales or lease contracts are free to agree to terms different from those stated in the UCC.

## 13–2a Article 2—The Sale of Goods

Article 2 of the UCC (as adopted by state statutes) governs **sales contracts,** or contracts for the sale of goods.

To facilitate commercial transactions, Article 2 modifies some common law contract requirements. To the extent that it has not been modified by the UCC, however, the common law of contracts also applies to sales contracts. In other words, the common law requirements for a valid contract—agreement consideration, capacity, and legality—are also applicable to sales contracts.

In general, the rule is that whenever a conflict arises between a common law contract rule and the state statutory law based on the UCC, the UCC controls. Thus, when a UCC provision addresses a certain issue, the UCC rule governs. When the UCC is silent, the common law governs. The relationship between general contract law and the law governing sales of goods is illustrated in Exhibit 13–1.

In regard to Article 2, keep two points in mind.

1. Article 2 deals with the sale of *goods.* It does not deal with real property (real estate), services, or intangible property such as stocks and bonds. Thus, if the subject matter of a dispute is goods, the UCC governs. If it is real estate or services, the common law applies.
2. In some situations, the rules can vary depending on whether the buyer or the seller is a *merchant.*

We look now at how the UCC defines a *sale, goods,* and *merchant status.*

**What Is a Sale?** The UCC defines a **sale** as "the passing of title [evidence of ownership rights] from the seller to the buyer for a price" [UCC 2–106(1)]. The price may be payable in cash or in other goods or services. (For a discussion of whether states can impose taxes on online sales, see this chapter's *Digital Update* feature.)

**What Are Goods?** To be characterized as a *good,* an item of property must be *tangible,* and it must be *movable.* **Tangible property** has physical existence—it can be touched or seen. **Intangible property**—such as corporate stocks and bonds, patents and copyrights, and ordinary contract rights—has only conceptual existence and thus does not come under Article 2. A *movable* item can be carried from place to place. Hence, real estate is excluded from Article 2.

**Goods Associated with Real Estate.** Goods *associated* with real estate often do fall within the scope of Article 2, however [UCC 2–107]. For instance, a contract for the sale of minerals, oil, or gas is a contract for the sale of goods if *severance, or separation, is to be made by the seller.* Similarly, a contract for the sale of growing crops or

---

2. *Amaya v. Brater,* 981 N.E.2d 1235 (Ind.App. 2013).

### EXHIBIT 13–1 The Law Governing Contracts

This exhibit graphically illustrates the relationship between general contract law and statutory law (UCC Articles 2 and 2A) governing contracts for the sale and lease of goods. Sales contracts are not governed exclusively by Article 2 of the UCC but are also governed by general contract law whenever it is relevant and has not been modified by the UCC.

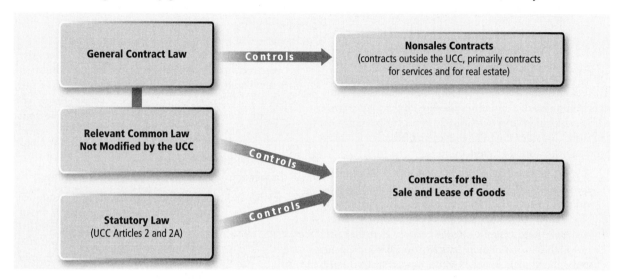

timber to be cut is a contract for the sale of goods *regardless of who severs them from the land.*

■ **CASE IN POINT 13.2** Perry Dan Cruse owned a business in Indiana that bought standing timber, cut it, and then resold it. Donald Freyberger had a contract with Cruse under which Cruse was to harvest 120 choice trees from Freyberger's land within six months. As payment, Freyberger would receive a percentage of the net proceeds from the sale of the cut timber. Cruse harvested and cut the trees but then filed for bankruptcy before the timber was sold. Freyberger filed a claim with the bankruptcy court, asserting that he had a "vendor's lien" on the timber because Cruse owed him $15,150 on the contract. (A lien would give Freyberger's claim priority over Cruse's other creditors.)

The bankruptcy court held that the timber was personal property (goods) under the UCC regardless of who cut it. Because no vendor's lien can arise on personal property under Indiana law, Freyberger's claim did not receive any special priority under bankruptcy law, and the debt could be discharged.[3] ■

**Goods and Services Combined.** When contracts involve a combination of goods and services, courts generally use the **predominant-factor test** to determine whether a contract is primarily for the sale of goods or the sale of

services.[4] If a court decides that a mixed contract is primarily a goods contract, *any* dispute, even a dispute over the services portion, will be decided under the UCC.

■ **CASE IN POINT 13.3** H & C Ag Services, LLC, entered into a contract with Ohio Fresh Eggs, LLC, that referred to "manure brokering services." H & C agreed to pay Ohio Fresh "service fees" for "all available tonnage per year of manure," which would then be resold to other parties. But the parties' contract did not specify the amount of manure. When Ohio Fresh did not carry out the contract, H & C sued for breach. A jury ruled that the primary purpose of the contract was for "manure brokering" (a service) rather than the "purchase of manure" (goods) and thus the UCC did not apply. The state trial court awarded H & C more than $2.5 million in damages. Ohio Fresh appealed.

The reviewing court held that the UCC governed the parties' contract under the predominant-factor test. The purpose of the contract was for the sale of goods—the manure—not the removal or resale of it. Despite the contract's use of the words *brokering* and *service fees,* H & C was clearly the buyer of manure from Ohio Fresh, who was the seller. Therefore, the UCC applied. Because the quantity term was left open, the parties had *not* agreed on

---

3. *In re Cruse*, 2013 WL 323275 (S.D. Indiana 2013).

4. UCC 2–314(1) does stipulate that serving food or drinks is a "sale of goods" for purposes of the implied warranty of merchantability, which will be discussed in the context of warranties. The UCC also specifies that selling unborn animals or rare coins qualifies as a "sale of goods."

## DIGITAL UPDATE    Taxing Web Purchases

In 1992, the United States Supreme Court ruled that an individual state cannot compel an out-of-state business that lacks a substantial physical presence within that state to collect and remit state taxes.[a] Congress has the power to pass legislation requiring out-of-state corporations to collect and remit state sales taxes, but it has not yet done so. Thus, only online retailers that also have a physical presence within a state must collect state taxes on Web sales made to residents of that state. (State residents are supposed to self-report their purchases and pay use taxes to the state, which they rarely do.)

### Redefining Physical Presence

A number of states have found a way to collect taxes on Internet sales made to state residents by out-of-state corporations—by redefining *physical presence*. New York started the trend in 2008 when it changed its tax laws in this manner. Now, an online retailer that pays any party within New York to solicit business for its products is considered to have a physical presence in the state and must collect state taxes. Since New York changed its law, around half of the states have made similar changes in an effort to increase their revenues by collecting sales tax from online retailers.

These new laws, often called the "Amazon tax" laws because they are largely aimed at Amazon.com, affect all online sellers, including Overstock.com and Drugstore.com. These laws especially affect retailers that pay affiliates to direct traffic to their Web sites. A federal appellate court in 2016 upheld the constitutionality of Colorado's so-called Amazon tax law, reasoning that the statute was necessary to avoid creating a tax shelter for online retailers.[b]

### Local Governments Sue Online Travel Companies

Travelocity, Priceline.com, Hotels.com, and Orbitz.com are online travel companies (OTCs) that offer, among other things, hotel booking services. By 2018, more than twenty-five cities, including Atlanta, Charleston, Philadelphia, and San Antonio, had filed suits claiming that the OTCs owed taxes on hotel reservations that they had booked. All of the cities involved in the suits impose a hotel occupancy tax, which is essentially a sales tax.

Initially, some cities won their cases, but more recently, they have been losing in court.[c] As of 2018, courts in twenty-three states have concluded that the OTCs are not subject to hotel occupancy tax, and courts in six states have found the OTCs were liable for taxes. In Wyoming, for example, the state's highest court ruled that Travelocity, Priceline, Hotwire, Expedia, and Trip Network had to collect and remit sales tax.[d]

### The Market Place Fairness Act

By the time you read this, online sales taxes may have become a reality for every online business that has annual revenues in excess of $1 million. For several years now, legislation called the Market Place Fairness Act has been introduced in the U.S. Senate. The act, if passed, would allow states to collect sales taxes from online retailers for in-state transactions.

A significant problem with such legislation is the complexity of collecting taxes for multiple jurisdictions. The current tax system involves 9,600 taxing jurisdictions. Even one zip code may cover multiple taxing entities, such as different cities and counties. Just consider that the Dallas–Fort Worth airport includes six separate taxing jurisdictions. Current software solutions for retailers that allow them to collect and remit sales taxes for different jurisdictions are extremely costly to install and operate. Overstock.com, for example, spent $1.3 million to add just one state to its sales tax collection system.

**Critical Thinking**  *Some argue that if online retailers must pay sales taxes in jurisdictions in which they have no physical presence, they have no democratic way to fight high taxes in those places. Is this an instance of taxation without representation? Discuss.*

a. *Quill Corp. v. North Dakota*, 504 U.S. 298, 112 S.Ct. 1904, 119 L.Ed.2d 91 (1992).
b. *Direct Marketing Association v. Brohl*, 814 F.3d 1129 (10th Cir. 2016).
c. *Montana Dept. of Revenue v. Priceline.com, Inc.*, 380 Mont. 352, 354 P.3d 631 (2015); and *Travelscape, LLC v. South Carolina Dept. of Revenue*, 391 S.C. 89, 705 S.E.2d 28 (2011).
d. *Travelocity.com, LP v. Wyoming Dept. of Revenue*, 329 P.3d 131 (2014). Also see *Expedia, Inc. v. District of Columbia*, 120 A.3d 623 (D.C.App. 2015).

an essential term. This meant that the contract was not enforceable under the UCC (open terms are discussed later in this chapter). Therefore, the appellate court reversed the lower court's decision and held in favor of Ohio Fresh.[5] ■

**Who Is a Merchant?** Article 2 governs the sale of goods in general. It applies to sales transactions between all buyers and sellers. In a limited number of instances, though, the UCC presumes that special business standards ought to be imposed because of merchants' relatively high degree of commercial expertise.[6] Such standards do not apply to the casual or inexperienced seller or buyer (consumer).

Section 2–104 sets forth three ways in which merchant status can arise:

1. A merchant is a person who *deals in goods of the kind* involved in the sales contract. Thus, a retailer, a wholesaler, or a manufacturer is a merchant of the goods sold in his or her business. A merchant for one type of goods is not necessarily a merchant for another type. For instance, a sporting goods retailer is a merchant when selling tennis rackets but not when selling a used computer.
2. A merchant is a person who, by occupation, *holds himself or herself out as having knowledge and skill* unique to the practices or goods involved in the transaction. This broad definition may include banks or universities as merchants.
3. A person who *employs a merchant as a broker, agent, or other intermediary* has the status of merchant in that transaction. Hence, if an art collector hires a broker to purchase or sell art for her, the collector is considered a merchant in the transaction.

In summary, a person is a **merchant** when she or he, acting in a mercantile capacity, possesses or uses an expertise specifically related to the goods being sold. This basic distinction is not always clear-cut. For instance, state courts appear to be split on whether farmers should be considered merchants.

## 13–2b Article 2A—Leases

Leases of personal property (goods such as automobiles and industrial equipment) have become increasingly common. In this context, a lease is a transfer of the right to possess and use goods for a period of time in exchange for payment. Article 2A of the UCC was created to fill the need for uniform guidelines in this area.

Article 2A covers any transaction that creates a lease of goods or a sublease of goods [UCC 2A–102, 2A–103(1)(k)]. Article 2A is essentially a repetition of Article 2, except that it applies to leases of goods rather than sales of goods and thus varies to reflect differences between sales and lease transactions. (Note that Article 2A is not concerned with leases of real property, such as land or buildings.)

**Definition of a Lease Agreement** Article 2A defines a **lease agreement** as a lessor's and lessee's bargain with respect to the lease of goods, as found in their language and as implied by other circumstances [UCC 2A–103(1)(k)]. A **lessor** is one who transfers the right to the possession and use of goods under a lease [UCC 2A–103(1)(p)]. A **lessee** is one who acquires the right to the possession and use of goods under a lease [UCC 2A–103(1)(o)]. In other words, the lessee is the party who is leasing the goods from the lessor.

Article 2A applies to all types of leases of goods. Special rules apply to certain types of leases, however, including consumer leases and finance leases.

**Consumer Leases** A *consumer lease* involves three elements:

1. A lessor who regularly engages in the business of leasing or selling.
2. A lessee (except an organization) who leases the goods "primarily for a personal, family, or household purpose."
3. Total lease payments that are less than $25,000 [UCC 2A–103(1)(e)].

To ensure special protection for consumers, certain provisions of Article 2A apply only to consumer leases. For instance, one provision states that a consumer may recover attorneys' fees if a court determines that a term in a consumer lease contract is unconscionable [UCC 2A–108(4)(a)].

**Finance Leases** A *finance lease* involves a lessor, a lessee, and a supplier. The lessor buys or leases goods from the supplier and leases or subleases them to the lessee [UCC 2A–103(1)(g)]. Typically, in a finance lease, the lessor is simply financing the transaction. ■ **EXAMPLE 13.4** Marlin Corporation wants to lease a crane for use in its construction business. Marlin's bank agrees to purchase the equipment from Jenco, Inc., and lease the equipment to Marlin. In this situation, the bank is the lessor-financer, Marlin is the lessee, and Jenco is the supplier. ■

---

5. *H & C Ag Services, LLC v. Ohio Fresh Eggs, LLC,* 41 N.E.3d 915 (Ohio App. 2015).
6. The provisions that apply only to merchants deal principally with the Statute of Frauds, firm offers, confirmatory memoranda, warranties, and contract modification. These special rules reflect expedient business practices commonly known to merchants in the commercial setting. They will be discussed later in this chapter.

Article 2A, unlike ordinary contract law, makes the lessee's obligations under a finance lease irrevocable and independent from the financer's obligations [UCC 2A–407]. In other words, the lessee must perform and continue to make lease payments even if the leased equipment turns out to be defective. The lessee must look almost entirely to the supplier for any recovery.

■ **EXAMPLE 13.5** McKessen Company obtains surgical ophthalmic equipment from a manufacturer and leases it to Vasquez for use at his medical eye center. When the equipment turns out to be defective, Vasquez stops making the lease payments. McKessen sues. Because the lease clearly qualifies as a finance lease under Article 2A, a court will hold in favor of McKessen. Vasquez is obligated to make all payments due under the lease regardless of the condition or performance of the leased equipment. Vasquez can sue the manufacturer of the defective equipment, however. ■

## 13-3 The Formation of Sales and Lease Contracts

In regard to the formation of sales and lease contracts, the UCC modifies the common law in several ways. We look here at how Articles 2 and 2A of the UCC modify common law contract rules. Remember, though, that parties to sales and lease contracts are basically free to establish whatever terms they wish.

The UCC comes into play when the parties either fail to provide certain terms in their contract or wish to change the effect of the UCC's terms in the contract's application. The UCC makes this very clear by its repeated use of such phrases as "unless the parties otherwise agree" and "absent a contrary agreement by the parties."

### 13-3a Offer

In general contract law, the moment a definite offer is met by an unqualified acceptance, a binding contract is formed. In commercial sales transactions, the verbal exchanges, correspondence, and actions of the parties may not reveal exactly when a binding contractual obligation arises. The UCC states that an agreement sufficient to constitute a contract can exist even if the moment of its making is undetermined [UCC 2–204(2), 2A–204(2)].

**Open Terms** According to general contract law, an offer must be definite enough for the parties (and the courts) to ascertain its essential terms when it is accepted. In contrast, the UCC states that a sales or lease contract will not fail for indefiniteness even if one or more terms are left open as long as *both* of the following are true:

1. The parties intended to make a contract.
2. There is a reasonably certain basis for the court to grant an appropriate remedy [UCC 2–204(3), 2A–204(3)].

The UCC provides numerous *open-term* provisions (discussed next) that can be used to fill the gaps in a contract. Thus, if a dispute occurs, all that is necessary to prove the existence of a contract is an indication (such as a purchase order) that there is a contract. Missing terms can be proved by evidence, or a court can presume that the parties intended whatever is reasonable under the circumstances.

Keep in mind, though, that if too many terms are left open, a court may find that the parties did not intend to form a contract. Also, the *quantity* of goods involved usually must be expressly stated in the contract. If the quantity term is left open, the courts will have no basis for determining a remedy.

**Open Price Term.** If the parties have not agreed on a price, the court will determine a "reasonable price at the time for delivery" [UCC 2–305(1)]. If either the buyer or the seller is to determine the price, the price is to be decided in good faith [UCC 2–305(2)]. Under the UCC, *good faith* means honesty in fact and the observance of reasonable commercial standards of fair dealing in the trade [UCC 2–103(1)(b)]. The concepts of *good faith* and *commercial reasonableness* permeate the UCC.

Sometimes, the price fails to be set through the fault of one of the parties. In that situation, the other party can treat the contract as canceled or determine a reasonable price. ■ **EXAMPLE 13.6** Perez and Merrick enter into a contract for the sale of goods and agree that Perez will determine the price. Perez refuses to specify the price. Merrick can either treat the contract as canceled or set a reasonable price [UCC 2–305(3)]. ■

**Open Payment Term.** When the parties do not specify payment terms, payment is due at the time and place at which the buyer is to receive the goods [UCC 2–310(a)]. The buyer can tender payment using any commercially normal or acceptable means, such as a check or credit card. If the seller demands payment in cash, however, the buyer must be given a reasonable time to obtain it [UCC 2–511(2)].

■ **CASE IN POINT 13.7** H. Daya International Co. is a clothing manufacturer and wholesaler based in Hong

Kong. H. Daya sold and delivered nearly $2 million worth of goods to two companies owned by Salomon Murciano. The businesses' principal place of business was in New York City. The companies, Do Denim, LLC, and Reward Jean, made only partial payments on the amounts due. After receiving discount credits, Do Denim still owed $282,029, and Reward Jean owed $721,155. H. Daya filed suit in a federal district court in New York against both companies for breach of contract. The court found in favor of H. Daya and awarded damages for the amounts due under the contract, plus prejudgment interest.

Under a New York statute, prejudgment interest of 9 percent begins accruing from "the earliest ascertainable date the cause of action existed." Because the UCC specifies that payment is due at the time the buyer receives the goods, the court held that interest started accruing from the receipt of the final shipment. Therefore, Do Denim owed an additional $44,645 in interest, and Reward Jean owed $109,181 in interest to H. Daya.[7] ■

**Open Delivery Term.** When no delivery terms are specified, the buyer normally takes delivery at the seller's place of business [UCC 2–308(a)]. If the seller has no place of business, the seller's residence is used. When goods are located in some other place and both parties know it, delivery is made there. If the time for shipment or delivery is not clearly specified in the sales contract, then the court will infer a "reasonable" time for performance [UCC 2–309(1)].

**Duration of an Ongoing Contract.** A single contract might specify successive performances but not indicate how long the parties are required to deal with each other. In this situation, either party may terminate the ongoing contractual relationship. Nevertheless, principles of good faith and sound commercial practice call for reasonable notification before termination so as to give the other party sufficient time to seek a substitute arrangement [UCC 2–309(2), (3)].

**Options and Cooperation with Regard to Performance.** When the contract contemplates shipment of the goods but does not specify the shipping arrangements, the *seller* has the right to make these arrangements. The seller must make the arrangements in good faith, using commercial reasonableness in the situation [UCC 2–311].

When a sales contract omits terms relating to the assortment of goods, the *buyer* can specify the assortment. ■ **EXAMPLE 13.8** Petry Drugs agrees to purchase one thousand toothbrushes from Marconi's Dental Supply. The toothbrushes come in a variety of colors, but the contract does not specify color. Petry, the buyer, has the right to take six hundred blue toothbrushes and four hundred green ones if it wishes. Petry, however, must exercise good faith and commercial reasonableness in making the selection [UCC 2–311]. ■

**Open Quantity Terms** Normally, as mentioned earlier, if the parties do not specify a quantity, no contract is formed. A court will have no basis for determining a remedy, because there is almost no way to determine objectively what is a reasonable quantity of goods for someone to buy. (In contrast, a court can objectively determine a reasonable price for particular goods by looking at the market for like goods.) The UCC recognizes two exceptions to this rule in requirements and output contracts [UCC 2–306(1)].

**Requirements Contracts.** Requirements contracts are common in the business world and normally are enforceable. In a **requirements contract,** the buyer agrees to purchase and the seller agrees to sell all or up to a stated amount of what the buyer requires.

■ **EXAMPLE 13.9** Newport Cannery forms a contract with Victor Tu. The cannery agrees to purchase from Tu, and Tu agrees to sell to the cannery, all of the green beans that the cannery requires during the following summer. There is implicit consideration in this contract because the buyer (the cannery) gives up the right to buy goods (green beans) from any other seller. This forfeited right creates a legal *detriment*—that is, consideration. ■

If, however, the buyer promises to purchase only if he or she *wishes* to do so, the promise is illusory (without consideration) and unenforceable by either party. Similarly, if the buyer reserves the right to buy the goods from someone other than the seller, the promise is unenforceable (illusory) as a requirements contract.

**Output Contracts.** In an **output contract,** the seller agrees to sell and the buyer agrees to buy all or up to a stated amount of what the seller produces. ■ **EXAMPLE 13.10** Ruth Sewell has planted two acres of organic tomatoes. Bella Union, a local restaurant, agrees to buy all of the tomatoes that Sewell produces that year to use at the restaurant. Again, because the seller essentially forfeits the right to sell goods to another buyer, there is implicit consideration in an output contract. ■

The UCC imposes a *good faith limitation* on requirements and output contracts. The quantity under such contracts is the amount of requirements or the amount of output that occurs during a *normal* production period.

---

7. *H. Daya Inter. Co. v. Do Denim,* 2012 WL 2524729 (S.D.N.Y. 2012).

The actual quantity purchased or sold cannot be unreasonably disproportionate to normal or comparable prior requirements or output [UCC 2–306(1)].

**Merchant's Firm Offer**   Under regular contract principles, an offer can be revoked at any time before acceptance. The major common law exception is an *option contract*, in which the offeree pays consideration for the offeror's irrevocable promise to keep the offer open for a stated period. The UCC creates a second exception for *firm offers* made by a merchant concerning the sale or lease of goods (regardless of whether or not the offeree is a merchant).

**When a Merchant's Firm Offer Arises.**   A **firm offer** arises when a merchant-offeror gives *assurances in a signed writing* that the offer will remain open. The merchant's firm offer is irrevocable without the necessity of consideration[8] for the stated period or, if no definite period is stated, a reasonable period (neither to exceed three months) [UCC 2–205, 2A–205].

■ **EXAMPLE 13.11**   Osaka, a used-car dealer, e-mails a letter to Gomez on January 1, stating, "I have a used 2016 Toyota RAV4 on the lot that I'll sell you for $22,000 any time between now and January 31." This e-mail creates a firm offer, and Osaka will be liable for breach of contract if he sells the RAV4 to another person before January 31. ■

**Requirements for a Firm Offer.**   To qualify as a firm offer, the offer must be:

1. *Written* (or electronically recorded, such as in an e-mail).
2. *Signed* by the offeror.[9]

When a firm offer is contained in a form contract prepared by the offeree, the offeror must also sign a separate assurance of the firm offer. The requirement of a separate signature ensures that the offeror will be made aware of the firm offer.

For instance, an offeree might respond to an initial offer by sending its own form contract containing a clause stating that the offer will remain open for three months. If the firm offer is buried amid copious language on the last page of the offeree's form contract, the offeror may inadvertently sign the contract without realizing that it contains a firm offer. This would defeat the purpose of

the rule—which is to give effect to a merchant's *deliberate* intent to be bound to a firm offer.

## 13–3b Acceptance

Acceptance of an offer to buy, sell, or lease goods generally may be made in any reasonable manner and by any reasonable means. The UCC permits acceptance of an offer to buy goods "either by a prompt *promise* to ship or by the prompt or current shipment of conforming or nonconforming goods" [UCC 2–206(1)(b)]. *Conforming goods* accord with the contract's terms, whereas *nonconforming goods* do not.

The prompt shipment of nonconforming goods constitutes both an acceptance, which creates a contract, and a breach of that contract. This rule does not apply if the seller **seasonably** (within a reasonable amount of time) notifies the buyer that the nonconforming shipment is offered only as an *accommodation,* or as a favor. The notice of accommodation must clearly indicate to the buyer that the shipment does not constitute an acceptance and that, therefore, no contract has been formed.

■ **EXAMPLE 13.12**   McFarren Pharmacy orders five cases of Johnson & Johnson 3-by-5-inch gauze pads from H.T. Medical Supply, Inc. If H.T. ships five cases of Xeroform 3-by-5-inch gauze pads instead, the shipment acts as both an acceptance of McFarren's offer and a breach of the resulting contract. McFarren may sue H.T. for any appropriate damages. If, however, H.T. notifies McFarren that the Xeroform pads are being shipped *as an accommodation*—because H.T. has only Xeroform pads in stock—the shipment does not act as an acceptance. Instead, it constitutes a counteroffer, and a contract will be formed only if McFarren accepts the Xeroform gauze pads. ■

**Communication of Acceptance**   Under the common law, because a unilateral offer invites acceptance by performance, the offeree need not notify the offeror of performance unless the offeror would not otherwise know about it. In other words, a unilateral offer can be accepted by beginning performance.

The UCC is more stringent than the common law in this regard because it requires notification. Under the UCC, if the offeror is not notified within a reasonable time that the offeree has accepted the contract by beginning performance, then the offeror can treat the offer as having lapsed before acceptance [UCC 2–206(2), 2A–206(2)].

**Additional Terms**   Recall that under the common law, the mirror image rule requires that the terms of the

---

8. If the offeree pays consideration, then an option contract (not a merchant's firm offer) is formed.
9. *Signed* includes any symbol executed or adopted by a party with a present intention to authenticate a writing [UCC 1–201(37)]. A complete signature is not required.

acceptance exactly match those of the offer. ■ **EXAMPLE 13.13** Adderson e-mails an offer to sell twenty Samsung Galaxy tablet model S2 to Beale. If Beale accepts the offer but changes it to require model S4 tablets, then there is no contract if the mirror image rule applies. ■

To avoid such problems, the UCC dispenses with the mirror image rule. Under the UCC, a contract is formed if the offeree's response indicates a *definite* acceptance of the offer, *even if the acceptance includes terms additional to or different from those contained in the offer* [UCC 2–207(1)]. Whether the additional terms become part of the contract depends, in part, on whether the parties are nonmerchants or merchants.

### Rules When One Party or Both Parties Are Nonmerchants.

If one (or both) of the parties is a *nonmerchant,* the contract is formed according to the terms of the original offer. The contract does not include any of the additional terms in the acceptance [UCC 2–207(2)].

■ **CASE IN POINT 13.14** OfficeSupplyStore.com sells office supplies on the Web. Employees of the Kansas City School District in Missouri ordered $17,642.54 worth of office supplies—without the authority or approval of their employer—from the Web site. The invoices accompanying the goods contained a *forum-selection clause* that required all disputes to be resolved in California.

When the goods were not paid for, Office Supply filed suit in California. The Kansas City School District objected, arguing that the forum-selection clause was not binding. The court held that the forum-selection clause was not part of the parties' contract. The clause was an additional term included in the invoices delivered to a nonmerchant buyer (the school district) with the purchased goods. Therefore, the clause did not become part of the contract unless the buyer expressly agreed, which did not happen in this case.[10] ■

### Rules When Both Parties Are Merchants.

The UCC includes a special rule for merchants to avoid the "battle of the forms," which occurs when two merchants exchange separate standard forms containing different contract terms.

Under UCC 2–207(2), in contracts *between merchants,* the additional terms *automatically* become part of the contract *unless* one of the following conditions arises:

1. The original offer expressly limited acceptance to its terms.
2. The new or changed terms materially alter the contract.
3. The offeror objects to the new or changed terms within a reasonable period of time.

When determining whether an alteration is material, courts consider several factors. Generally, if the modification does not involve any unreasonable element of surprise or hardship for the offeror, a court will hold that the modification did not materially alter the contract. Courts also consider the parties' prior dealings. As shown in the following case, however, what constitutes a material alteration is frequently a question of fact that only a court can decide.

---

10. *OfficeSupplyStore.com v. Kansas City School Board*, 334 S.W.3d 574 (Kan. 2011).

## Case 13.1

## C. Mahendra (N.Y.), LLC v. National Gold & Diamond Center, Inc.

New York Supreme Court, Appellate Division, First Department, 125 A.D.3d 454, 3 N.Y.S.3d 27 (2015).

**Background and Facts** C. Mahendra (N.Y.), LLC, is a New York wholesaler of loose diamonds. National Gold & Diamond Center, Inc., is a California seller of jewelry. Over a ten-year period, National placed orders, totaling millions of dollars, with Mahendra by phoning and negotiating the terms. Mahendra shipped diamonds "on memorandum" for National to examine. Mahendra then sent invoices for the diamonds that National chose to keep. Both the memoranda and the invoices stated, "You consent to the exclusive jurisdiction of the . . . courts situated in New York County."

When two orders totaling $64,000 went unpaid, Mahendra filed a suit in a New York state court against National, alleging breach of contract. National filed a motion to dismiss the complaint for lack of personal jurisdiction, contending that the forum-selection clause was not binding. The court granted the motion. Mahendra appealed.

**Case 13.1 Continued**

## In the Language of the Court

*SWEENY*, P.J. [Presiding Judge], *MOSKOWITZ, DEGRASSE, MANZANET-DANIELS, CLARK*, JJ. [Judges]
\* \* \* \*

\* \* \* Defendant argued the forum-selection clause in the \* \* \* memorandums was not binding because its president never signed the memorandums' terms and conditions. Defendant thus maintained that it had not signed or agreed to the forum-selection clause, nor had it otherwise consented to being sued in New York. Likewise, defendant asserted that because it had negotiated for and ordered the diamonds from California and did not sign or agree to the forum-selection clause, the consent to jurisdiction contained in the memorandums would materially alter the parties' agreements in contravention of UCC 2–207(2)(b). Thus, defendant concluded, it was not bound by the unsigned provision on the back of the \* \* \* memorandums.
\* \* \* \*

\* \* \* The [lower] court found the forum-selection clause invalid, noting that defendant did not sign the invoices. The court further found that under UCC 2–207(2), forum-selection clauses are additional terms that materially alter a contract, and must be construed as mere proposals for additions to the contract. Thus, the court concluded, the forum-selection clause was non-binding absent an express agreement. Indeed, the court noted, the complaint did not allege that defendant affirmatively expressed consent, either orally or in writing, to the forum-selection clause when it retained the invoices.
\* \* \* \*

The [lower] court correctly found that defendant is not bound by the forum-selection clause on plaintiff's invoices. UCC 2–207 contemplates situations like the one here, where parties do business through an exchange of forms such as purchase orders and invoices. As the parties did here, *merchants frequently include terms in their forms that were not discussed with the other side. UCC 2–207(2) addresses that scenario, providing, "the additional terms are to be construed as proposals for addition to the contract. Between merchants such terms become part of the contract unless: \* \* \* (b) they materially alter it."* [Emphasis added.]

Here, during telephone discussions, the parties negotiated the essential terms required for contract formation, and the invoices were merely confirmatory. Thus, the forum-selection clause is an additional term that materially altered the parties' oral contracts, and defendant did not give its consent to that additional term.

**Decision and Remedy**  *A state intermediate appellate court agreed that "the forum-selection clause is an additional term that materially altered the parties' . . . contracts, and defendant did not give its consent to that additional term." But the court reversed the dismissal of Mahendra's complaint on the ground that National's phone calls with Mahendra were sufficient contacts to subject the defendant to personal jurisdiction in New York under the state's long-arm statute.*

**Critical Thinking**

- **Legal**  *What is Mahendra's best argument that the forum-selection clause was, in fact, binding on National? Discuss.*

---

**Prior Dealings between Merchants.**  In contracts between merchants, courts also consider the parties' prior dealings.  ■ **CASE IN POINT 13.15**  WPS, Inc., submitted a proposal to manufacture equipment for Expro Americas, LLC, and Surface Production Systems, Inc. (SPS). Expro and SPS then submitted two purchase orders. WPS accepted the first purchase order in part and the second order conditionally. Among other things, WPS's acceptance required that Expro and SPS give their "full release to proceed" and agree to "pay all valid costs associated with any order cancellation." The parties' negotiations continued, and Expro and SPS eventually submitted a third purchase order.

Although the third purchase order did not comply with all of WPS's requirements, it did give WPS permission to proceed. It also specified that Expro and SPS would pay all cancellation costs. With Expro and SPS's knowledge, WPS began working on that order. Expro and SPS later canceled the order and refused to pay the cancellation costs. When the dispute ended in court,

Expro and SPS claimed that the additional terms in WPS's acceptance had materially altered the contract and rendered it unenforceable. The court found in favor of WPS. Expro and SPS had given a release to proceed that authorized WPS to go forward with manufacturing the equipment. Because "the parties operated as if they had additional time to resolve the outstanding differences," the court reasoned that Expro and SPS were contractually obligated to pay the cancellation costs.[11] ∎

**Conditioned on Offeror's Assent.** The offeree's response is not an acceptance if it contains additional or different terms and is expressly *conditioned* on the offeror's assent to those terms [UCC 2–207(1)]. This is true whether or not the parties are merchants.

∎ **EXAMPLE 13.16** Philips offers to sell Hundert 650 pounds of turkey thighs at a specified price and with specified delivery terms. Hundert responds, "I accept your offer for 650 pounds of turkey thighs *on the condition that you agree to give me ninety days to pay for them.*" Hundert's response will be construed not as an acceptance but as a counteroffer, which Philips may or may not accept. ∎

**Additional Terms May Be Stricken.** The UCC provides yet another option for dealing with conflicting terms in the parties' writings. Section 2–207(3) states that conduct by both parties that recognizes the existence of a contract is sufficient to establish a contract for sale. This is so even if the writings of the parties do not otherwise establish a contract. In this situation, "the terms of the particular contract will consist of those terms on which the writings of the parties agree, together with any supplementary terms incorporated under any other provisions of this Act." In a dispute over contract terms, this provision allows a court simply to strike from the contract those terms on which the parties do not agree.

∎ **EXAMPLE 13.17** SMT Marketing orders goods over the phone from Brigg Sales, Inc., which ships the goods to SMT with an acknowledgment form confirming the order. SMT accepts and pays for the goods. The parties' writings do not establish a contract, but there is no question that a contract exists. If a dispute arises over the terms, such as the extent of any warranties, UCC 2–207(3) provides the governing rule. ∎

As noted previously, the fact that a merchant's acceptance frequently contains terms that add to or even conflict with those of the offer is often referred to as the "battle of the forms." Although the UCC tries to eliminate this battle, the problem of differing contract terms

still arises in commercial settings, particularly when standard forms (for placing and confirming orders) are used.

## 13–3c Consideration

The common law rule that a contract requires consideration also applies to sales and lease contracts. Unlike the common law, however, the UCC does not require a contract modification to be supported by new consideration. The UCC states that an agreement modifying a contract for the sale or lease of goods "needs no consideration to be binding" [UCC 2–209(1), 2A–208(1)]. Of course, any contract modification must be made in good faith [UCC 1–304].

In some situations, an agreement to modify a sales or lease contract without consideration must be in writing to be enforceable. For instance, if the contract itself specifies that any changes to the contract must be in a signed writing, only those changes agreed to in a signed writing are enforceable.

Sometimes, when a consumer (nonmerchant) is buying goods from a merchant-seller, the merchant supplies a form that contains a prohibition against oral modification. In those situations, the consumer must sign a separate acknowledgment of the clause for it to be enforceable [UCC 2–209(2), 2A–208(2)]. Also, any modification that makes a sales contract come under Article 2's writing requirement (its Statute of Frauds, discussed next) usually requires a writing (or electronic record) to be enforceable.

See Concept Summary 13.1 for a review of the UCC's rules on offer, acceptance, and consideration.

## 13–3d The Statute of Frauds

The UCC contains Statute of Frauds provisions covering sales and lease contracts. Under these provisions, sales contracts for goods priced at $500 or more and lease contracts requiring total payments of $1,000 or more must be in writing to be enforceable [UCC 2–201(1), 2A–201(1)]. (These low threshold amounts may eventually be raised.)

**Sufficiency of the Writing** A writing, including an e-mail or other electronic record, will be sufficient to satisfy the UCC's Statute of Frauds as long as it:

1. Indicates that the parties intended to form a contract.
2. Is signed by the party (or agent of the party) against whom enforcement is sought. (Remember that a typed name can qualify as a signature on an electronic record.)

---

11. *WPS, Inc. v. Expro Americas, LLC,* 369 S.W.3d 384 (Tex.App. 2012).

---

## Concept Summary 13.1

### Offer, Acceptance, and Consideration under the UCC

**Offer**
- Not all terms have to be included for a contract to be formed.
- The price does not have to be included for a contract to be formed.
- Particulars of performance can be left open.
- An offer by a merchant in a signed writing with assurances that the offer will not be withdrawn is irrevocable without consideration (for up to three months).

**Acceptance**
- Acceptance may be made by any reasonable means of communication. It is effective when dispatched.
- An offer can be made by a promise to ship or by the shipment of conforming goods, or by prompt shipment of nonconforming goods unless accompanied by a notice of accommodation.
- Acceptance by performance requires notice within a reasonable time. Otherwise, the offer can be treated as lapsed.
- A definite expression of acceptance creates a contract even if the terms of the acceptance differ from those of the offer (unless acceptance is expressly conditioned on consent to the additional or different terms).

**Consideration**
- A *modification* of a contract for the sale or lease of goods does not require consideration as long as it is made in good faith.

---

The contract normally will not be enforceable beyond the quantity of goods shown in the writing, however. All other terms can be proved in court by oral testimony. For leases, the writing must reasonably identify and describe the goods leased and the lease term.

### Special Rules for Contracts between Merchants

The UCC provides a special rule for merchants in sales transactions (there is no corresponding rule that applies to leases under Article 2A). Merchants can satisfy the Statute of Frauds if, after the parties have agreed orally, one of the merchants sends a signed written confirmation to the other merchant within a reasonable time.

The communication must indicate the terms of the agreement, and the merchant receiving the confirmation must have reason to know of its contents. Unless the merchant who receives the confirmation gives written notice of objection to its contents within ten days after receipt, the writing is sufficient against the receiving merchant, even though she or he has not signed it [UCC 2–201(2)].

■ **EXAMPLE 13.18** Alfonso is a merchant-buyer in Cleveland. He contracts over the telephone to purchase $6,000 worth of spare aircraft parts from Goldstein, a merchant-seller in New York City. Two days later, Goldstein e-mails a signed confirmation detailing the terms of the oral contract, and Alfonso subsequently receives it. Alfonso does not notify Goldstein in writing that he objects to the contents of the confirmation within ten days of receipt. Therefore, Alfonso cannot raise the Statute of Frauds as a defense against the enforcement of the oral contract. ■

**Exceptions** The UCC defines three exceptions to the writing requirements of the Statute of Frauds. An oral contract for the sale of goods priced at $500 or more or the lease of goods involving total payments of $1,000 or more will be enforceable despite the absence of a writing in the circumstances described next [UCC 2–201(3), 2A–201(4)].

**Specially Manufactured Goods.** An oral contract for the sale or lease of custom-made goods will be enforceable if:

1. The goods are *specially manufactured* for a particular buyer or specially manufactured or obtained for a particular lessee.

**2.** The goods are *not suitable for resale or lease* to others in the ordinary course of the seller's or lessor's business.

**3.** The seller or lessor *has substantially started to manufacture* the goods or has made commitments for the manufacture or procurement of the goods.

In these situations, once the seller or lessor has taken action, the buyer or lessee cannot repudiate the agreement claiming the Statute of Frauds as a defense.

■ **EXAMPLE 13.19** Womach orders custom window treatments to use at a day spa business from Hunter Douglas for $6,000. The contract is oral. When Hunter Douglas manufactures the window coverings and tenders delivery to Womach, she refuses to pay for them, even though the job has been completed on time. Womach claims that she is not liable because the contract was oral. If the unique style, size, and color of the window treatments make it improbable that Hunter Douglas can find another buyer, Womach is liable to Hunter Douglas. ■

**Admissions.** An oral contract for the sale or lease of goods is enforceable if the party against whom enforcement is sought admits in pleadings, testimony, or other court proceedings that a sales or lease contract was made. In this situation, the contract will be enforceable even though it was oral, but enforceability will be limited to the quantity of goods admitted.

■ **CASE IN POINT 13.20** Gerald Lindgren, a farmer, agreed by phone to sell his crops to Glacial Plains Cooperative. The parties reached four oral agreements: two for the delivery of soybeans and two for the delivery of corn. Lindgren made the soybean deliveries and part of the first corn delivery, but he sold the rest of his corn to another dealer. Glacial Plains bought corn elsewhere, paying a higher price, and then sued Lindgren for breach of contract. In papers filed with the court, Lindgren acknowledged his oral agreements with Glacial Plains and admitted that he did not fully perform. The court applied the admissions exception and held that the four agreements were enforceable.[12] ■

**Partial Performance.** An oral contract for the sale or lease of goods is enforceable if payment has been made and accepted or goods have been received and accepted. This is the "partial performance" exception. The oral contract will be enforced at least to the extent that performance actually took place.

■ **EXAMPLE 13.21** Quality Meats buys food products and sells them to retail operations. Quality orally contracts with A1 Food Services, Inc., to ship three orders

of beef to Choice Processing, for which A1 agrees to pay. Quality ships the goods to Choice and sends invoices to A1. A1 bills Choice for all three orders, but pays Quality only for the first two. Quality then files a suit against A1 to recover the cost of the third order.

A1 argues that because the parties did not have a written agreement, there was no enforceable contract. But a court could find that even though A1 had not signed a written contract or purchase order, it had partially performed the contract by paying for the first two shipments. A1's conduct is likely sufficient to prove the existence of a contract, and the court could require A1 to pay for the last shipment. ■

The exceptions just discussed and other ways in which sales law differs from general contract law are summarized in Exhibit 13–2.

### 13–3e Parol Evidence

Recall that parol evidence consists of evidence outside the contract, such as evidence of the parties' prior negotiations, prior agreements, or contemporaneous oral agreements. When a contract completely sets forth all the terms and conditions agreed to by the parties and is intended as a final statement of their agreement, it is considered fully *integrated*. The terms of a **fully integrated contract** cannot be contradicted by evidence of any prior agreements or contemporaneous oral agreements.

If, however, the writing contains some of the terms the parties agreed on but not others, then the contract is not fully integrated. When a court finds that a contract is *not fully integrated,* then the court may allow evidence of *consistent additional terms* to explain or supplement the terms in the contract. The court may also allow the parties to submit evidence of *course of dealing, usage of trade,* or *course of performance* [UCC 2–202, 2A–202].

**Course of Dealing and Usage of Trade** Under the UCC, the meaning of any agreement, evidenced by the language of the parties and their actions, must be interpreted in light of commercial practices and other surrounding circumstances. In interpreting a commercial agreement, a court will assume that the course of dealing between the parties and the general usage of trade were taken into account when the agreement was phrased.

**Course of Dealing.** A **course of dealing** is a sequence of actions and communications between the parties to a particular transaction that establishes a common basis for their understanding [UCC 1–303(b)]. A course of dealing is restricted to the sequence of conduct between the parties in their transactions prior to the agreement.

---

12. *Glacial Plains Cooperative v. Lindgren*, 759 N.W.2d 661 (Min.App. 2009).

**EXHIBIT 13–2  Major Differences between Contract Law and Sales Law**

| | CONTRACT LAW | SALES LAW |
|---|---|---|
| **Contract Terms** | Contract must contain all material terms. | Open terms are acceptable if parties intended to form a contract, but the contract is not enforceable beyond quantity term. |
| **Acceptance** | Mirror image rule applies. If additional terms are added in acceptance, a counteroffer is created. | Additional terms will not negate acceptance unless acceptance is expressly conditioned on assent to the additional terms. |
| **Contract Modification** | Modification requires consideration. | Modification does not require consideration. |
| **Irrevocable Offers** | Option contracts (with consideration). | Merchants' firm offers (without consideration). |
| **Statute of Frauds Requirements** | All material terms must be included in the writing. | Writing is required only for sale of goods priced at $500 or more, but the contract is not enforceable beyond the quantity specified. Merchants can satisfy the writing by a confirmation evidencing their agreement.<br>*Exceptions:*<br>1. Specially manufactured goods.<br>2. Admissions by party against whom enforcement is sought.<br>3. Partial performance. |

Under the UCC, a course of dealing between the parties is relevant in ascertaining the meaning of the parties' agreement. It "may give particular meaning to specific terms of the agreement, and may supplement or qualify the terms of the agreement" [UCC 1–303(d)].

**Usage of Trade.** Some practices and methods of dealing are so regularly observed in a place, vocation, or trade that parties to contracts expect them to be observed in their transactions. Such a practice or method of dealing is known as a **usage of trade** [UCC 1–303(c)].

■ **EXAMPLE 13.22** Phat Khat Loans, Inc., hires Fleet Title Review Company to search the public records for prior claims on potential borrowers' assets. Fleet's invoice states, "Liability limited to amount of fee." In the title search industry, liability limits are common. After conducting many searches for Phat Khat, Fleet reports that there are no claims with respect to Main

Street Autos. Phat Khat lends $100,000 to Main, with payment guaranteed by Main's assets. When Main defaults on the loan, Phat Khat learns that another lender has priority to Main's assets under a previous claim. If Phat Khat sues Fleet for breach of contract, Fleet's liability will normally be limited to the amount of its fee. The statement in the invoice was part of the contract between Phat Khat and Fleet, according to the usage of trade in the industry and the parties' course of dealing. ■

**Course of Performance** The conduct that occurs under the terms of a particular agreement is called a **course of performance** [UCC 1–303(a)]. Presumably, the parties themselves know best what they meant by their words. Thus, the course of performance actually carried out under the parties' agreement is the best indication of what they meant [UCC 2–208(1), 2A–207(1)].

■ **EXAMPLE 13.23** Janson's Lumber Company contracts with Lopez to sell Lopez a specified number of two-by-fours. The lumber in fact does not measure exactly 2 inches by 4 inches but rather 1⅞ inches by 3¾ inches. Janson's agrees to deliver the lumber in five deliveries, and Lopez, without objection, accepts the lumber in the first three deliveries. On the fourth delivery, however, Lopez objects that the two-by-fours do not measure precisely 2 inches by 4 inches.

The course of performance in this transaction—that is, Lopez's acceptance of three deliveries without objection—is relevant in determining that here a "two-by-four" actually means a "1⅞-by-3¾." Janson's can also prove that two-by-fours need not be exactly 2 inches by 4 inches by applying usage of trade, course of dealing, or both. Janson's can, for example, show that in previous transactions, Lopez took 1⅞-inch-by-3¾-inch lumber without objection. In addition, Janson's can show that in the trade, two-by-fours are commonly 1⅞ inches by 3¾ inches. ■

Concept Summary 13.2 reviews the parol evidence rule.

**Rules of Construction** The UCC provides *rules of construction* for interpreting contracts. Express terms, course of performance, course of dealing, and usage of trade are to be construed to be consistent with each other whenever reasonable. When such a construction is unreasonable, however, the UCC establishes the following order of priority [UCC 1–303(e), 2–208(2), 2A–207(2)]:

1. Express terms.
2. Course of performance.
3. Course of dealing.
4. Usage of trade.

## 13–3f Unconscionability

An unconscionable contract is one that is so unfair and one sided that it would be unreasonable to enforce it. The UCC allows a court to evaluate a contract or any clause in a contract, and if the court deems it to have been unconscionable *at the time it was made,* the court can do any of the following [UCC 2–302, 2A–108]:

1. Refuse to enforce the contract.
2. Enforce the remainder of the contract without the unconscionable part.
3. Limit the application of the unconscionable term to avoid an unconscionable result.

The following classic case illustrates an early application of the UCC's unconscionability provisions.

---

## Concept Summary 13.2

### The Parol Evidence Rule

| Definition | • Parol evidence is evidence outside the contract, such as the parties' prior negotiations, prior agreements, or oral agreements made at the time of the contract formation. |
| --- | --- |
| | • When the contract completely sets forth all the terms and conditions agreed to by the parties and is intended as the final statement of their agreement, it is considered fully integrated. |
| | • Under the parol evidence rule, the terms of a fully integrated contract cannot be contradicted by parol evidence. |
| **When Parol Evidence Is Admissible** | • If the writing (or record) contains some of the terms that the parties agreed to but not others, the contract is not fully integrated. A court may allow consistent additional terms to explain or supplement the terms stated in the contract. |
| | • If the contract terms are ambiguous, a court might allow the parties to submit parol evidence to explain their intentions. |
| | • If evidence of course of dealing, usage of trade, or course of performance is necessary to clarify the intentions of the parties to the contract. |

# Jones v. Star Credit Corp.

Supreme Court of New York, Nassau County, 59 Misc.2d 189, 298 N.Y.S.2d 264 (1969).

**Background and Facts**  The Joneses agreed to purchase a freezer for $900 as the result of a sales-person's visit to their home. Tax and financing charges raised the total price to $1,234.80. Later, the Joneses, who had made payments totaling $619.88, brought a suit in a New York state court to have the purchase contract declared unconscionable under the UCC. At trial, the freezer was found to have a maximum retail value of approximately $300.

## In the Language of the Court

Sol M. *WACHTLER*, Justice.

    * * * *

    * * * [Section 2–302 of the UCC] authorizes the court to find, as a matter of law, that a contract or a clause of a contract was "unconscionable at the time it was made," and upon so finding the court may refuse to enforce the contract, excise the objectionable clause or limit the application of the clause to avoid an unconscionable result.

    * * * *

    * * * The question which presents itself is whether or not, under the circumstances of this case, the sale of a freezer unit having a retail value of $300 for $900 ($1,439.69 including credit charges and $18 sales tax) is unconscionable as a matter of law.

    Concededly, deciding [this case] is substantially easier than explaining it. No doubt, the mathematical disparity between $300, which presumably includes a reasonable profit margin, and $900, which is exorbitant on its face, carries the greatest weight. Credit charges alone exceed by more than $100 the retail value of the freezer. These alone may be sufficient to sustain the decision. Yet, a caveat [warning] is warranted lest we reduce the import of Section 2–302 solely to a mathematical ratio formula. It may, at times, be that; yet it may also be much more. The very limited financial resources of the purchaser, known to the sellers at the time of the sale, is entitled to weight in the balance. Indeed, the value disparity itself leads inevitably to the felt conclusion that knowing advantage was taken of the plaintiffs. In addition, *the meaningfulness of choice essential to the making of a contract can be negated by a gross inequality of bargaining power.* [Emphasis added.]

    * * * *

    * * * The defendant has already been amply compensated. In accordance with the statute, the application of the payment provision should be limited to amounts already paid by the plaintiffs and the contract be reformed and amended by changing the payments called for therein to equal the amount of payment actually so paid by the plaintiffs.

**Decision and Remedy**  *The court held that the contract was not enforceable and reformed the contract so that no further payments were required.*

**Impact of This Case on Today's Law**  *This early classic case illustrates the approach that many courts take today when deciding whether a sales contract is unconscionable—an approach that focuses on "excessive" price and unequal bargaining power. Most of the litigants who have used UCC 2–302 successfully could demonstrate both an absence of meaningful choice and contract terms that were unreasonably favorable to the other party.*

**Critical Thinking**
- **Social**  *Why would the seller's knowledge of the buyers' limited resources support a finding of unconscionability?*

## 13–4 Contracts for the International Sale of Goods

International sales contracts between firms or individuals located in different countries may be governed by the 1980 United Nations Convention on Contracts for the International Sale of Goods (CISG). The CISG governs international contracts only if the countries of the parties to the contract have ratified the CISG and if the parties have not agreed that some other law will govern their contract.

As of 2018, the CISG had been adopted by eighty-four countries, including the United States, Canada, some Central and South American countries, China, most European nations, Japan, and Mexico. That means that the CISG is the uniform international sales law of countries that account for more than two-thirds of all global trade.

Essentially, the CISG is to international sales contracts what Article 2 of the UCC is to domestic sales contracts. In domestic transactions, the UCC applies when the parties to a contract for a sale of goods have failed to specify in writing some important term, such as price or delivery. Similarly, whenever the parties to international transactions have failed to specify in writing the precise terms of a contract, the CISG will be applied.

Unlike the UCC, *the CISG does not apply to consumer sales.* Neither the UCC nor the CISG applies to contracts for services.

### 13–4a A Comparison of CISG and UCC Provisions

The provisions of the CISG, although similar for the most part to those of the UCC, differ from them in some respects. If the CISG and the UCC conflict, the CISG applies (because it is a treaty of the U.S. national government and therefore is supreme). We look here at some differences with respect to contract formation.

**The Mirror Image Rule**   Under the UCC, a definite expression of acceptance that contains additional terms can still result in the formation of a contract, unless the additional terms are conditioned on the assent of the offeror. In other words, as we have seen, the UCC does away with the mirror image rule in domestic sales contracts.

Article 19 of the CISG provides that a contract can be formed even though the acceptance contains additional terms, unless the additional terms materially alter the contract. Under the CISG, however, the definition of a "material alteration" includes almost any change in the terms. If an additional term relates to payment, quality, quantity, price, time and place of delivery, extent of one party's liability to the other, or the settlement of disputes, the CISG considers the added term a material alteration. In effect, then, the CISG requires that the terms of the acceptance mirror those of the offer.

Therefore, as a practical matter, businesspersons undertaking international sales transactions should not use the sale or purchase forms that they customarily use for transactions within the United States. Instead, they should draft specific forms to suit the needs of the particular transaction.

The court in the following case applied the CISG's mirror image rule to eighteen contracts for sales of frozen potatoes from a supplier in Canada to a company in Illinois.

---

**Case Analysis 13.3**

# VLM Food Trading International, Inc. v. Illinois Trading Co.

United States Court of Appeals, Seventh Circuit, 811 F.3d 247 (2016).

**In the Language of the Court**
SYKES, Circuit Judge.

* * * *

This [is a] contract dispute between plaintiff VLM Food Trading International, Inc., a Canadian agricultural

supplier, and Illinois Trading Company, an Illinois produce reseller.

* * * *

* * * VLM sold frozen potatoes to Illinois Trading through nine separate transactions without incident. Illinois

Trading then encountered financial difficulty and failed to pay for the next nine shipments from VLM. The parties agree that each transaction occurred the same way. First, Illinois Trading sent

Case 13.3 Continued

a purchase order specifying the item, quantity, price, and place of delivery for the potatoes. Second, VLM responded with an e-mail confirming the terms of the sale. Third, VLM shipped the order and Illinois Trading accepted it. Finally, VLM followed up by mail with an invoice. Importantly for us, the trailing invoices included a provision purporting to make Illinois Trading liable for * * * attorney's fees if it breached the contracts.

When Illinois Trading stopped paying its invoices, VLM sued Illinois Trading [in a federal district court].

* * * The answer admitted that the defendant owed VLM the purchase price for the produce * * * but contested liability for attorney's fees.

* * * The judge applied the [United Nations Convention on Contracts for the International Sale of Goods] and held that the attorney's fees provision was *not* part of the contracts. [VLM appealed, challenging the court's analysis and application of the law to reach this conclusion.]

* * * *

*The Convention's definition of the "loss" resulting from a breach of contract does not itself include attorney's fees. To succeed, VLM must show that its contracts with Illinois Trading expressly made Illinois Trading liable for VLM's attorney's fees in the event of a breach.* To determine whether the fees provision was expressly accepted by Illinois Trading, we need to know when the terms of their agreement became binding. [Emphasis added.]

A contract is formed under the Convention when there is a valid offer and acceptance. An offer is valid if it is sufficiently definite and indicates the intention of the offeror to be bound in case of acceptance. An offer is sufficiently definite if it indicates the goods and expressly or implicitly fixes or makes provision for determining the quantity and price. Once a valid offer has been extended, the offeree can accept by words or conduct, but not by silence or inactivity. An acceptance becomes effective at the moment the indication of assent reaches the offeror. Acceptance

can also be demonstrated through the offeree's conduct, if allowed as a result of practices which the parties have established between themselves or of usage.

So far so good—these contract principles are familiar and very similar to those expressed in the UCC. But * * * the Convention departs dramatically from the UCC by using the common-law "mirror image" rule * * * to resolve "battles of the forms." Under the mirror-image rule, as expressed in Article 19(1) of the Convention, "a reply to an offer which purports to be an acceptance but contains additions, limitations or other modifications is a rejection of the offer and constitutes a counter-offer."

Each Illinois Trading purchase order met all the Convention's criteria for an offer; they included sufficiently definite terms, were directed to VLM specifically, and indicated that Illinois Trading intended to be bound by VLM's acceptance. Each of VLM's confirmation e-mails was, in turn, an effective acceptance of Illinois Trading's offer because each one confirmed and accepted the terms of the purchase order. As such, the contracts were formed when Illinois Trading received VLM's confirmation e-mails. The attorney's fees provision was *not* part of the agreement described in the purchase orders and the e-mail confirmations; that term first appeared in the trailing invoices that were mailed to Illinois Trading *after* VLM delivered the produce.

Under the Convention VLM had already bound itself to the contracts proposed by Illinois Trading when it confirmed Illinois Trading's purchase offer by e-mail. The attorney's fees provision therefore could not have been a counteroffer. Rather, * * * the attorney's fees * * * provision would be a proposed modification to the contracts. Under the mirror-image rule, a party does not have to object to a proposed modification in order to keep it from being incorporated; any term that is not "mirrored" in the offer and acceptance is excluded. Contracts can only be modified by agreement of the parties.

Illinois Trading never made any statements indicating its acceptance of the proposed attorney's fees modification. Indeed, the only possible activity that could have indicated Illinois Trading's acceptance of the proposed modification was its payment of the invoices. But that conduct is just as consistent with Illinois Trading's obligations under the original agreement as it is with any new acceptance. Furthermore, since VLM had already completely performed its duties under the original proposed agreement, it had no performance left to offer in consideration for any (gratuitous) agreement by Illinois Trading to assume liability for VLM's attorney's fees in the event of breach.

* * * *

VLM contends that despite the contract-formation analysis prescribed by the Convention, the parties subjectively intended the attorney's fees provision to apply. In VLM's view the Convention "commands" judges to consider extrinsic evidence to illuminate the parties' intent. This argument relies largely on Article 8(3), which reads: "In determining the intent of a party * * * due consideration is to be given to all relevant circumstances of the case including the negotiations, any practices which the parties have established between themselves, usages and any subsequent conduct of the parties." But the purpose of this intent test is to help courts interpret the statements and conduct of parties according to their intent where the other party knew * * * what that intent was. Although VLM's conduct, sending trailing invoices containing an attorney's fees provision, clearly indicates that *VLM* intended Illinois Trading to be liable for collection fees, there was never any indication of *mutual* intent at the time of contracting. Fee-shifting was never mentioned during any negotiations, and none of Illinois Trading's subsequent conduct indicates that it agreed to pay VLM's attorney's fees.

* * * *

VLM also points to Article 9(1), which says that "parties are bound to any

Case 13.3 Continues

usage to which they have agreed and by any practices which they have established between themselves." This clause doesn't help for two reasons. First, there simply isn't any established "practice" between Illinois Trading and VLM regarding liability for attorney's fees. * * * Second, evidence of "usage" comes into play to clarify the meaning assigned to a contract term * * * . Here, no contract term is ambiguous and thus in need of clarification by evidence of usage. In other words, there's no disagreement about what the attorney's fees provision *means;* the only issue is whether it was part of the parties' agreement.

* * * *

Finally, the fact that some of Illinois Trading's contracts with other vendors included fee-shifting provisions is not relevant under the mirror-image rule, nor is the fact that Illinois Trading paid attorney's fees as part of its settlements with certain vendors. Nothing in the Convention indicates that common industry practices are automatically grafted onto contracts; rather, the content of each contract must be analyzed independently.

For all these reasons, the [district court] judge properly applied the Convention and held that the parties' contracts did not include the attorney's fees provision.

### Legal Reasoning Questions

1. How did the CISG's rules regarding the formation of contracts affect the lower court's holding in this case?

2. Did the appellate court agree with the lower court's analysis and application of the CISG's rules? Why or why not?

3. What would have been the result if the court had applied the UCC instead of the CISG?

---

**Irrevocable Offers** UCC 2–205 provides that a merchant's firm offer is irrevocable, even without consideration, if the merchant gives assurances in a signed writing. In contrast, under the CISG, an offer can become irrevocable without a signed writing. Article 16(2) of the CISG provides that an offer will be irrevocable if:

1. The offeror states orally that the offer is irrevocable.
2. The offeree reasonably relies on the offer as being irrevocable.

In both of these situations, the offer will be irrevocable even without a writing and without consideration.

**The Writing Requirement** As discussed previously, the UCC has a Statute of Frauds provision. UCC 2–201 requires contracts for the sale of goods priced at $500 or more to be evidenced by a written or electronic record signed by the party against whom enforcement is sought.

Article 11 of the CISG, however, states that a contract of sale "need not be concluded in or evidenced by writing and is not subject to any other requirements as to form. It may be proved by any means, including witnesses." Article 11 of the CISG accords with the legal customs of most nations, which no longer require contracts to meet certain formal or writing requirements to be enforceable.

**Time of Contract Formation** Under the common law of contracts and the UCC, an acceptance is effective on dispatch, so a contract is created when the acceptance is transmitted. Under the CISG, in contrast, a contract is created not at the time the acceptance is transmitted but only on its *receipt* by the offeror. (The offer becomes *irrevocable,* however, when the acceptance is sent.)

Article 18(2) states that an acceptance by return promise (a unilateral contract) "becomes effective at the moment the indication of assent reaches the offeror." Under Article 18(3), the offeree may also bind the offeror by performance even without giving any notice to the offeror. The acceptance becomes effective "at the moment the act is performed." Thus, it is the offeree's reliance, rather than the communication of acceptance to the offeror, that creates the contract.

## 13–4b Special Provisions in International Contracts

Language and legal differences among nations can create various problems for parties to international contracts when disputes arise. It is possible to avoid these problems by including in a contract special provisions relating to choice of language, choice of forum, choice of law, and the types of events that may excuse the parties from performance.

**Choice-of-Language Clause** A deal struck between a U.S. company and a company in another country frequently involves two languages. One party may not understand complex contractual terms that are written in the other party's language. Translating the terms poses its own problems, as typically many phrases are not readily translatable into another language.

To make sure that no disputes arise out of this language problem, an international sales contract should include a **choice-of-language clause.** This clause will designate the official language by which the contract will be interpreted in the event of disagreement. The clause might also specify that the agreement is to be translated into, say, Spanish, and that the translation is to be approved by both parties. If arbitration is anticipated, an additional clause must be added to indicate the official language that will be used at the arbitration proceeding.

**Forum-Selection Clause**   A **forum-selection clause** designates the forum (place, or court) in which any disputes that arise under the contract will be litigated. This clause should indicate the specific court that will have jurisdiction. The forum does not necessarily have to be within the geographic boundaries of either party's nation.

Including a forum-selection clause in an international contract is especially important because when several countries are involved, litigation may be sought in courts in different nations. There are no universally accepted rules regarding the jurisdiction of a particular court over subject matter or parties to a dispute, although the adoption of the 2005 Choice of Court Convention helped to resolve certain issues.

Under certain circumstances, a forum-selection clause will not be valid. Specifically, if the clause denies one party an effective remedy, or is the product of fraud or unconscionable conduct, the clause will not be enforced. Similarly, if the designated forum causes substantial inconvenience to one of the parties, or violates public policy, the clause may not be enforced.

**Choice-of-Law Clause**   A contractual provision designating the applicable law, called a **choice-of-law clause,** is typically included in every international contract. At common law (and in European civil law systems), parties are allowed to choose the law that will govern their contractual relationship.

There must normally be some connection between the chosen law and the contracting parties to show that the parties are not merely trying to avoid the laws of their own jurisdictions. ■ **EXAMPLE 13.24** A U.S. automaker contracts with a German company. The parties cannot choose the law of China to govern their agreement if neither the contract nor the parties have anything to do with China. The choice of Chinese law in that situation might reflect an attempt to avoid consumer, environmental, or employment laws that would otherwise apply to the transaction. ■

Under the UCC, parties may choose the law that will govern the contract as long as the choice is "reasonable." Article 6 of the CISG, however, imposes no limitation on the parties in their choice of what law will govern the contract. The 1986 Hague Convention on the Law Applicable to Contracts for the International Sale of Goods—often referred to as the Choice-of-Law Convention—allows unlimited autonomy in the choice of law. Whenever a choice of law is not specified in a contract, the Hague Convention indicates that the law of the country where the seller's place of business is located will govern.

**Force Majeure Clause**   Every contract, and particularly those involving international transactions, should have a *force majeure* **clause.** The French term *force majeure* means "impossible or irresistible force"—sometimes loosely defined as "an act of God." *Force majeure* clauses often stipulate that other events (in addition to acts of God) will excuse liability for nonperformance. Occurrences such as adverse governmental orders or regulations, embargoes, and extreme shortages of materials commonly excuse a party's nonperformance.

Note that some *force majeure* clauses require notice before a party's liability for nonperformance (or delay in performance) will be excused. ■ **CASE IN POINT 13.25** Bigge Power Constructors manufactures cranes and other heavy equipment. Bigge contracted to purchase castings from a supplier, Rexnord Industries, LLC, for $4.5 million. Bigge needed the castings for the manufacture of two large derricks that were to be used in building nuclear power plants. The parties' contract set forth a delivery schedule for the castings, which Rexnord failed to meet. Although Bigge accepted and used all of the castings Rexnord supplied, it withheld $1 million from the purchase price for costs it had incurred as a result of the supplier's delay.

Rexnord sued for breach, claiming that the delay was a *force majeure* event, which the contract defined as any event "beyond a party's reasonable control." The court held that Rexnord's delay was not excused because Rexnord had never given Bigge the required notice that events constituting a *force majeure* had occurred. Thus, Bigge was entitled to damages for Rexnord's untimely delivery of goods. (If the supplier had given the required notice, its delay normally would have been excused.)[13] ■

---

13. *Rexnord Industries, LLC v. Bigge Power Constructors,* 947 F.Supp.2d 951 (E.D.Wisconsin 2013).

# Reviewing: The Formation of Sales and Lease Contracts

Guy Holcomb owns and operates Oasis Goodtime Emporium, an adult entertainment establishment. Holcomb wanted to create an adult Internet system for Oasis that would offer customers adult-theme videos and "live" chat room programs using performers at the club. On May 10, Holcomb signed a work order authorizing Thomas Consulting Group (TCG) "to deliver a working prototype of a customer chat system, demonstrating the integration of live video and chatting in a Web browser." In exchange for creating the prototype, Holcomb agreed to pay TCG $64,697. On May 20, Holcomb signed an additional work order in the amount of $12,943 for TCG to install a customized firewall system. The work orders stated that Holcomb would make monthly installment payments to TCG, and both parties expected the work would be finished by September.

Due to unforeseen problems largely attributable to system configuration and software incompatibility, the project required more time than anticipated. By the end of the summer, the Web site was still not ready, and Holcomb had fallen behind in his payments to TCG. TCG threatened to cease work and file a suit for breach of contract unless the bill was paid. Rather than make further payments, Holcomb wanted to abandon the Web site project. Using the information presented in the chapter, answer the following questions.

1. Would a court be likely to decide that the transaction between Holcomb and TCG was covered by the Uniform Commercial Code (UCC)? Why or why not?
2. Would a court be likely to consider Holcomb a merchant under the UCC? Why or why not?
3. Did the parties have a valid contract under the UCC? Were any terms left open in the contract? If so, which terms? How would a court deal with open terms?
4. Suppose that Holcomb and TCG meet in October in an attempt to resolve their problems. At that time, the parties reach an oral agreement that TCG will continue to work without demanding full payment of the past due amounts and Holcomb will pay TCG $5,000 per week. Assuming the contract falls under the UCC, is the oral agreement enforceable? Why or why not?

**Debate This** . . . *The UCC should require the same degree of definiteness of terms, especially with respect to price and quantity, as contract law does.*

## Terms and Concepts

| | | |
|---|---|---|
| choice-of-language clause 263 | fully integrated contract 256 | predominant-factor test 246 |
| choice-of-law clause 263 | intangible property 245 | requirements contract 250 |
| course of dealing 256 | lease agreement 248 | sale 245 |
| course of performance 257 | lessee 248 | sales contract 245 |
| firm offer 251 | lessor 248 | seasonably 251 |
| *force majeure* clause 263 | merchant 248 | tangible property 245 |
| forum-selection clause 263 | output contract 250 | usage of trade 257 |

## Issue Spotters

1. E-Design, Inc., orders 150 computer desks. Fav-O-Rite Supplies, Inc., ships 150 printer stands. Is this an acceptance of the offer or a counteroffer? If it is an acceptance, is it a breach of the contract? Why or why not? What if Fav-O-Rite told E-Design it was sending the printer stands as "an accommodation"? (See *The Formation of Sales and Lease Contracts*.)
2. Truck Parts, Inc. (TPI), often sells supplies to United Fix-It Company (UFC), which services trucks. Over the

phone, they negotiate for the sale of eighty-four sets of tires. TPI sends a letter to UFC detailing the terms and two weeks later ships the tires. Is there an enforceable contract between them? Why or why not? (See *The Formation of Sales and Lease Contracts*.)

• Check your answers to the Issue Spotters against the answers provided in Appendix B at the end of this text.

# Business Scenarios

**13–1. Merchant's Firm Offer.** On May 1, Jennings, a car dealer, e-mails Wheeler and says, "I have a 1955 Thunderbird convertible in mint condition that I will sell you for $13,500 at any time before June 9. [Signed] Peter Jennings." By May 15, having heard nothing from Wheeler, Jennings sells the car to another. On May 29, Wheeler accepts Jennings's offer and tenders $13,500. When told Jennings has sold the car to another, Wheeler claims Jennings has breached their contract. Is Jennings in breach? Explain. (See *The Formation of Sales and Lease Contracts.*)

**13–2. Additional Terms.** Strike offers to sell Bailey one thousand shirts for a stated price. The offer declares that shipment will be made by Dependable truck line. Bailey replies, "I accept your offer for one thousand shirts at the price quoted. Delivery to be by Yellow Express truck line." Both Strike and Bailey are merchants. Three weeks later, Strike ships the shirts by Dependable truck line, and Bailey refuses to accept delivery. Strike sues for breach of contract. Bailey claims that there never was a contract because his reply, which included a modification of carriers, did not constitute an acceptance. Bailey further claims that even if there had been a contract, Strike would have been in breach because Strike shipped the shirts by Dependable, contrary to the contract terms. Discuss fully Bailey's claims. (See *The Formation of Sales and Lease Contracts.*)

# Business Case Problems

**13–3. Spotlight on Goods and Services—The Statute of Frauds.** Fallsview Glatt Kosher Caterers ran a business

that provided travel packages, including food, entertainment, and lectures on religious subjects, to customers during the Passover holiday at a New York resort. Willie Rosenfeld verbally agreed to pay Fallsview $24,050 for the Passover package for himself and his family. Rosenfeld did not appear at the resort and never paid the amount owed. Fallsview sued Rosenfeld for breach of contract. Rosenfeld claimed that the contract was unenforceable because it was not in writing and violated the UCC's Statute of Frauds. Is the contract valid? Explain. [*Fallsview Glatt Kosher Caterers, Inc. v. Rosenfeld,* 794 N.Y.S.2d 790 (N.Y.Super. 2005)] (See *The Formation of Sales and Lease Contracts.*)

**13–4. Business Case Problem with Sample Answer—Additional Terms.** B.S. International, Ltd. (BSI), makes

costume jewelry. JMAM, LLC, is a wholesaler of costume jewelry. JMAM sent BSI a letter with the terms for orders, including the necessary procedure for obtaining credit for items that customers rejected. The letter stated, "By signing below, you agree to the terms." Steven Baracsi, BSI's owner, signed the letter and returned it. For six years, BSI made jewelry for JMAM, which resold it. Items rejected by customers were sent back to JMAM, but were never returned to BSI. BSI filed a suit against JMAM, claiming $41,294.21 for the unreturned items. BSI showed the court a copy of JMAM's terms. Across the bottom had been typed a "PS" requiring the return of rejected merchandise. Was this "PS" part of the contract? Discuss. [*B.S. International, Ltd. v. JMAM, LLC,* 13 A.3d 1057 (R.I. 2011)] (See *The Formation of Sales and Lease Contracts.*)

- For a sample answer to Problem 13–4, go to Appendix C at the end of this text.

**13–5. Partial Performance and the Statute of Frauds.** After a series of e-mails, Jorge Bonilla, the sole proprietor of a printing company in Uruguay, agreed to buy a used printer from Crystal Graphics Equipment, Inc., in New York. Crystal Graphics, through its agent, told Bonilla that the printing press was fully operational, contained all of its parts, and was in excellent condition except for some damage to one of the printing towers. Bonilla paid $95,000. Crystal Graphics sent him a signed, stamped invoice reflecting this payment. The invoice was dated six days after Bonilla's conversation with the agent.

When the printing press arrived, Bonilla discovered that it was missing parts and was damaged. Crystal Graphics sent replacement parts, but they did not work. Crystal Graphics was never able to make the printer operational. Bonilla sued, alleging breach of contract, breach of the implied covenant of good faith and fair dealing, breach of express warranty, and breach of implied warranty. Crystal Graphics claimed that the contract was not enforceable because it did not satisfy the Statute of Frauds. Can Crystal Graphics prevail on this basis? Why or why not? [*Bonilla v. Crystal Graphics Equipment, Inc.,* 2012 WL 360145 (S.D.Fla. 2012)] (See *The Formation of Sales and Lease Contracts.*)

**13–6. The Statute of Frauds.** Kendall Gardner agreed to buy from B&C Shavings a specially built shaving mill to produce wood shavings for poultry processors. B&C faxed an invoice to Gardner reflecting a purchase price of $86,200, with a 30 percent down payment and the "balance due before shipment." Gardner paid the down payment. B&C finished the mill and wrote Gardner a letter telling him to "pay the balance due or you will lose the down payment." By then, Gardner had lost his customers for the wood shavings, could not pay the balance due, and asked for the return of his down payment. Did these parties have an enforceable contract under the Statute of Frauds? Explain. [*Bowen v. Gardner,* 2013 Ark. App. 52, 425 S.W.3d 875 (2013)] (See *The Formation of Sales and Lease Contracts.*)

**13–7. Goods and Services Combined.** Allied Shelving and Equipment, Inc., sells and installs shelving systems. National Deli, LLC, contracted with Allied to provide and install a parallel rack system (a series of large shelves) in National's warehouse. Both parties were dissatisfied with the result. National filed a suit in a Florida state court against Allied, which filed a counterclaim. Each contended that the other had materially breached the contract. The court applied common law contract principles to rule in National's favor on both claims. Allied appealed, arguing that the court should have applied the UCC. When does a court apply common law principles to a contract that involves both goods and services? In this case, why might an appellate court rule that the UCC should be applied instead? Explain. [*Allied Shelving and Equipment, Inc. v. National Deli, LLC,* 40 Fla. L. Weekly D145, 154 So.3d 482 (Dist.App. 2015)] (See *The Scope of Articles 2 and 2A.*)

**13–8. Acceptance.** New England Precision Grinding, Inc. (NEPG), sells precision medical parts in Massachusetts. NEPG agreed to supply Kyphon, Inc., with stylets and nozzles. NEPG contracted with Simply Surgical, LLC, to obtain the parts from Iscon Surgicals, Ltd. The contract did not mention Kyphon or require Kyphon's acceptance of the parts. Before shipping, Iscon would certify that the parts conformed to NEPG's specifications. On receiving the parts, NEPG would certify that they conformed to Kyphon's specifications. On delivery, Kyphon would also inspect the parts. After about half a dozen transactions, NEPG's payments to Simply Surgical lagged, and the seller refused to make further deliveries. NEPG filed a suit in a Massachusetts state court against Simply Surgical, alleging breach of contract. NEPG claimed that Kyphon had rejected some of the parts, which gave NEPG the right not to pay for them. Do the UCC's rules with respect to acceptance support or undercut the parties' actions? Discuss. [*New England Precision Grinding, Inc. v. Simply Surgical, LLC,* 89 Mass.App.Ct.176, 46 N.E.3d 590 (2016)] (See *The Formation of Sales and Lease Contracts.*)

**13–9. A Question of Ethics—Contract Terms.** *Daniel*  *Fox owned Fox & Lamberth Enterprises, Inc., a kitchen and bath remodeling business, in Dayton, Ohio. Fox leased a building from Carl and Bellulah Hussong. Craftsmen Home Improvement, Inc., also remodeled baths and kitchens. When Fox planned to close his business, Craftsmen expressed an interest in buying his showroom assets. Fox set a price of $50,000. Craftsmen's owners agreed and gave Fox a list of the desired items and "A Bill of Sale" that set the terms for payment. The parties did not discuss Fox's arrangement with the Hussongs, but Craftsmen expected to negotiate a new lease and extensively modified the premises, including removing some of the displays to its own showroom. When the Hussongs and Craftsmen could not agree on new terms, Craftsmen told Fox that the deal was off. [Fox & Lamberth Enterprises, Inc. v. Craftsmen Home Improvement, Inc., 2006-Ohio-1427 (2 Dist. 2006)] (See The Formation of Sales and Lease Contracts.)*

**(a)** In Fox's suit in an Ohio state court for breach of contract, Craftsmen raised the Statute of Frauds as a defense. What are the requirements of the Statute of Frauds? Did the deal between Fox and Craftsmen meet these requirements? Did it fall under one of the exceptions? Explain.

**(b)** Craftsmen also claimed that the predominant factor of its agreement with Fox was a lease for the Hussongs' building. What is the predominant-factor test? Does it apply here? In any event, is it fair to hold a party to a contract to buy a business's assets when the buyer cannot negotiate a favorable lease of the premises on which the assets are located? Discuss.

## Legal Reasoning Group Activity

**13–10. Parol Evidence.** Mountain Stream Trout Co. agreed to buy "market size" trout from trout grower Lake Farms, LLC. Their five-year contract did not define *market size.* At the time, in the trade, *market size* referred to fish of one-pound live weight. After three years, Mountain Stream began taking fewer, smaller deliveries of larger fish, claiming that *market size* varied according to whatever its customers demanded and that its customers now demanded larger fish. Lake Farms filed a suit for breach of contract. (See *The Formation of Sales and Lease Contracts.*)

**(a)** The first group will decide whether parol evidence is admissible to explain the terms of this contract. Are there any exceptions that could apply?

**(b)** A second group will determine the impact of course of dealing and usage of trade on the interpretation of contract terms.

**(c)** A third group will discuss how parties to a commercial contract can avoid the possibility that a court will interpret the contract terms in accordance with trade usage.

# CHAPTER 14

# Performance and Breach of Sales and Lease Contracts

The performance that is required of the parties under a sales or lease contract consists of the duties and obligations each party has under the terms of the contract. The basic obligation of the seller or lessor is to *transfer and deliver conforming goods*. The basic obligation of the buyer or lessee is to *accept and pay for conforming goods* in accordance with the contract [UCC 2–301, 2A–516(1)]. Overall performance of a sales or lease contract is controlled by the agreement between the parties. When the contract is unclear and disputes arise, the courts look to the UCC and impose standards of good faith and commercial reasonableness.

The obligations of good faith and commercial reasonableness underlie every sales and lease contract. The UCC's good faith provision, which can never be disclaimed, reads as follows: "Every contract or duty within this Act imposes an obligation of good faith in its performance or enforcement" [UCC 1–304]. *Good faith* means honesty in fact. For a merchant, it means honesty in fact and the observance of reasonable commercial standards of fair dealing in the trade [UCC 2–103(1)(b)]. In other words, merchants are held to a higher standard of performance or duty than are nonmerchants.

Sometimes, circumstances make it difficult for a party to carry out the promised performance, leading to a breach of the contract. When a breach occurs, the aggrieved (wronged) party looks for remedies. Note that in contrast to the common law of contracts, remedies under the UCC are cumulative in nature—meaning that the aggrieved party is not limited to one exclusive remedy.

## 14–1 Obligations of the Seller or Lessor

The basic duty of the seller or lessor is to deliver the goods called for under the contract to the buyer or lessee. Goods that conform to the contract description in every way are called **conforming goods.** To fulfill the contract, the seller or lessor must either deliver or tender delivery of conforming goods to the buyer or lessee.

### 14–1a Tender of Delivery

**Tender of delivery** occurs when the seller or lessor makes conforming goods available and gives the buyer or lessee whatever notification is reasonably necessary to enable the buyer or lessee to take delivery [UCC 2–503(1), 2A–508(1)].

Tender must occur at a *reasonable hour* and in a *reasonable manner*. For example, a seller cannot call the buyer at 2:00 A.M. and say, "The goods are ready. I'll give you twenty minutes to get them." Unless the parties have agreed otherwise, the goods must be tendered for delivery at a reasonable hour and kept available for a reasonable time to enable the buyer to take possession [UCC 2–503(1)(a)].

Normally, all goods called for by a contract must be tendered in a single delivery unless the parties have agreed on delivery in several lots or *installments* (discussed shortly) [UCC 2–307, 2–612, 2A–510]. ■ **EXAMPLE 14.1** An order for 1,000 Under Armour men's shirts cannot be delivered two shirts at a time. The parties may agree, however, that the shirts will be delivered in four orders of 250 each as they are produced (for summer, fall, winter, and spring inventory). Tender of delivery may then occur in this manner. ■

In the following case, the seller of a log-cabin kit gave the buyers two days' notice to arrange for their final payment on the contract and take delivery. Did this notice comply with UCC 2–503?

267

# Garziano v. Louisiana Log Home Co.

United States Court of Appeals, Fifth Circuit, 569 Fed.Appx. 292 (2014).

**Background and Facts**   Richard and Nancy Garziano contracted with Louisiana Log Home (LLH) Company for a log-cabin kit to be delivered to them in Pass Christian, Mississippi. The contract required three installment payments. The final payment, due at delivery, was to include the cost of transportation. Two days before delivery, LLH told the buyers that the final payment would be $7,686.43, plus the transportation cost of $2,625.60. The Garzianos replied that they thought they had paid off the balance for the cabin and that they expected the shipping costs to be lower. They refused to pay more, and LLH did not deliver the kit.

The Garzianos filed a claim in a federal district court against LLH, alleging that LLH had breached the contract by failing to inform them of the price of delivery in a timely manner. The court issued a judgment in LLH's favor and allowed the seller to keep the Garzianos' first two installment payments and the log-cabin kit without determining the actual amount of damages suffered. The Garzianos appealed.

## In the Language of the Court

*PER CURIAM* [By the Whole Court]:
    * * * *

The Garzianos * * * allege that LLH violated Section 75–2–503(1) of the Mississippi Code [Mississippi's version of UCC 2–503(1),] which imposes a duty to *"hold conforming goods at the buyer's disposition and give the buyer any notification reasonably necessary"* to enable the buyer to take delivery. * * * The Garzianos contend that LLH violated this statute and thereby breached the contract by failing to notify them of the amount of shipping charges until only two days before delivery, which constructively prohibited them from accepting delivery. * * * The argument seems to be that LLH's failure to inform the Garzianos of the price of delivery in a timely manner excused the Garzianos' later breach of the contract by refusing delivery. [Emphasis added.]

This argument fails.

The contracts in this case were simple and easily understood. They provided that "all costs of transportation shall be borne by the purchaser," that "shipping charges are paid directly to the trucking company at the time of delivery by cash or personal check," and specified an "F.O.B. [Free on Board] Factory Price." These contracts also made clear that the final price that would be paid, absent shipping costs, was $43,656.43. *Thus the explicit terms of the contract put the Garzianos on notice that they had both not paid off the balance on the log-home kit and that they were responsible for any shipping costs.* [Emphasis added.]
    * * * *

* * * LLH was attempting to deliver the goods when the Garzianos breached by refusing to pay either the balance on the contract or the shipping charges—both of which they were obligated to pay under the contract. * * * There was no undisclosed, expiring window of time during which the Garzianos were required to claim the log cabin. * * * They were given reasonable notice of the date of delivery. * * * [On] July 17, * * * LLH advised the Garzianos that the package would be delivered on July 19 * * *. It was at this point that LLH informed the Garzianos that they still needed to make the third installment payment and pay $2,625 for the delivery fee. While the Garzianos may have been surprised at the size of the delivery fee, the notice provided to the Garzianos was not so deficient as to prevent them from effectively taking delivery so that their refusal to pay would be excused. The only obstacle to taking delivery was the Garzianos' refusal to pay for the goods and the shipping costs. As the [lower] court correctly held, LLH's "method of tender was in compliance with the terms of the contracts."

**Decision and Remedy**   *The U.S. Court of Appeals for the Fifth Circuit affirmed the lower court's judgment. The Garzianos may have been surprised by the amount of the delivery fee, but the notice that LLH gave them was in compliance with the contract. The lower court had not determined the actual amount of LLH's damages, however. The court remanded the case to the lower court to make that finding and to remit to the Garzianos any funds paid that were in excess of LLH's actual damages.*

**Critical Thinking**

• **Legal Environment**   *How might the parties have avoided the dispute in this case?*

## 14-1b Place of Delivery

The buyer and seller (or lessor and lessee) may agree that the goods will be delivered to a particular destination where the buyer or lessee will take possession. If the contract does not indicate where the goods will be delivered, then the place for delivery will be one of the following:

1. The *seller's place of business.*
2. The *seller's residence,* if the seller has no business location [UCC 2–308(a)].
3. The *location of the goods,* if both parties know at the time of contracting that the goods are located somewhere other than the seller's business [UCC 2–308(b)].

■ **EXAMPLE 14.2** Li Wan and Boyd both live in San Francisco. In San Francisco, Li Wan contracts to sell Boyd five used trucks, which both parties know are located in a Chicago warehouse. If nothing more is specified in the contract, the place of delivery for the trucks is Chicago. Li Wan may tender delivery by giving Boyd either a negotiable or a nonnegotiable document of title. Alternatively, Li Wan may obtain the bailee's (warehouser's) acknowledgment that Boyd is entitled to possession.[1] ■

## 14-1c Delivery via Carrier

In many instances, it is clear from the surrounding circumstances or delivery terms in the contract that the parties intended the goods to be moved by a carrier. In carrier contracts, the seller fulfills the obligation to deliver the goods through either a shipment contract or a destination contract.

**Shipment Contracts** Recall that a *shipment contract* requires or authorizes the seller to ship goods by a carrier, rather than to deliver them at a particular destination [UCC 2–319, 2–509(1)(a)]. Under a shipment contract, unless otherwise agreed, the seller must do the following:

1. Place the goods into the hands of the carrier.
2. Make a contract for their transportation that is reasonable according to the nature of the goods and their value. (For instance, certain types of goods need refrigeration in transit.)
3. Obtain and promptly deliver or tender to the buyer any documents necessary to enable the buyer to obtain possession of the goods from the carrier.

4. Promptly notify the buyer that shipment has been made [UCC 2–504].

If the seller does not make a reasonable contract for transportation or notify the buyer of the shipment, the buyer can reject the goods, but only if a *material loss* or a *significant delay* results. ■ **EXAMPLE 14.3** Zigi's Organic Fruits sells strawberries to Lozier under a shipment contract. If Zigi's does not arrange for refrigerated transportation and the berries spoil during transport, a material loss to Lozier will likely result. ■ Of course, the parties are free to make agreements that alter the UCC's rules and allow the buyer to reject goods for other reasons.

**Destination Contracts** In a *destination contract,* the seller agrees to deliver conforming goods to the buyer at a particular destination. The goods must be tendered at a reasonable hour and held at the buyer's disposal for a reasonable length of time. The seller must also give the buyer appropriate notice and any necessary documents to enable the buyer to obtain delivery from the carrier [UCC 2–503].

## 14-1d The Perfect Tender Rule

The seller or lessor has an obligation to ship or tender *conforming goods.* The buyer or lessee is then obligated to accept and pay for the goods according to the contract terms [UCC 2–507].

Under the common law, the seller was obligated to deliver goods that conformed with the terms of the contract in every detail. This is called the **perfect tender rule.** The UCC preserves the perfect tender doctrine. It states that if goods or tender of delivery fails *in any respect* to conform to the contract, the buyer or lessee may accept the goods, reject the entire shipment, or accept part and reject part [UCC 2–601, 2A–509].

The corollary to this rule is that if the goods conform in every respect, the buyer or lessee does not have a right to reject the goods. ■ **CASE IN POINT 14.4** U.S. Golf & Tennis Centers, Inc., agreed to buy 96,000 golf balls from Wilson Sporting Goods Company for a total price of $20,000. Wilson represented that U.S. Golf was receiving its lowest price ($5 per two-dozen unit).

Wilson shipped golf balls to U.S. Golf that conformed to the contract in quantity and quality, but it did not receive payment. U.S. Golf claimed that it had learned that Wilson had sold the product for $2 per unit to another buyer. U.S. Golf asked Wilson to reduce the contract price of the balls to $4 per unit. Wilson refused and filed a suit. The court ruled in favor of Wilson. Because it was undisputed that the shipment of golf balls conformed to the contract specifications, U.S. Golf

---

1. Unless the buyer objects, the seller may also tender delivery by instructing the bailee in a writing to release the goods to the buyer without the bailee's acknowledgment of the buyer's rights [UCC 2–503(4)].

was obligated to accept the goods and pay the agreed-on price.[2] ∎

## 14–1e Exceptions to the Perfect Tender Rule

Because of the rigidity of the perfect tender rule, several exceptions to the rule have been created, some of which we discuss here and outline in Exhibit 14–1.

**Agreement of the Parties** Exceptions to the perfect tender rule may be established by agreement. The parties may agree, for instance, that defective goods or parts will not be rejected if the seller or lessor is able to repair or replace them within a reasonable period of time. In this situation, the perfect tender rule does not apply.

---

2. *Wilson Sporting Goods Co. v. U.S. Golf and Tennis Centers, Inc.,* 2012 WL 601804 (Tenn.App. 2012).

**Cure** The UCC does not specifically define the term **cure,** but it refers to the right of the seller or lessor to repair, adjust, or replace defective or nonconforming goods [UCC 2–508, 2A–513].

The seller or lessor has a right to attempt to "cure" a defect when the following are true:

1. A delivery is rejected because the goods were nonconforming.
2. The time for performance has not yet expired.
3. The seller or lessor provides timely notice to the buyer or lessee of the intention to cure.
4. The cure can be made within the contract time for performance.

**Reasonable Grounds.** Even if the contract time for performance has expired, the seller or lessor can still cure if he or she had *reasonable grounds to believe that the nonconforming tender would be acceptable to the buyer or lessee* [UCC 2–508(2), 2A–513(2)].

## EXHIBIT 14–1    The Perfect Tender Rule and Its Exceptions

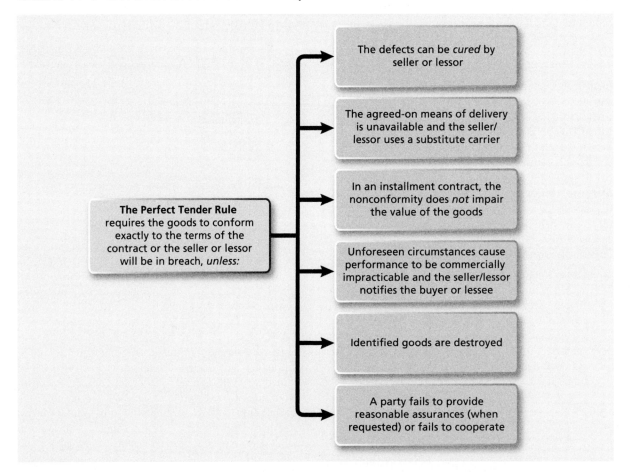

■ **EXAMPLE 14.5** In the past, Rio Electronics has frequently allowed Topps Company to substitute grey keyboards when the silver keyboards that Rio ordered were not in stock. Under a new contract for keyboards, Rio rejects a shipment of grey keyboards. In this situation, Topps had reasonable grounds to believe that Rio would accept the grey keyboards as a substitute. Therefore, normally Topps can cure within a reasonable time even if the conforming delivery will occur after the contract time for performance. ■

A seller or lessor will sometimes tender nonconforming goods with some type of price allowance (discount). A discounted price can serve as the "reasonable grounds" to believe that the buyer or lessee will accept the nonconforming tender.

**Limits the Right to Reject Goods.** The right to cure substantially restricts the right of the buyer or lessee to reject goods. To reject, the buyer or lessee must inform the seller or lessor of the particular defect. If the defect is not disclosed, the buyer or lessee cannot later assert the defect as a defense if the defect is one that the seller or lessor could have cured. Generally, buyers and lessees must act in good faith and state specific reasons for refusing to accept goods [UCC 2–605, 2A–514].

**Substitution of Carriers** Sometimes, an agreed-on manner of delivery (such as the use of a particular carrier) becomes impracticable or unavailable through no fault of either party. In that situation, if a commercially reasonable substitute is available, this substitute performance is sufficient tender to the buyer and must be used [UCC 2–614(1)]. The seller or lessor is required to arrange for a substitute carrier and normally is responsible for any additional shipping costs (unless the contract states otherwise).

■ **EXAMPLE 14.6** A sales contract calls for a large generator to be shipped by United Trucking on or before June 1. The contract terms clearly state the importance of the delivery date. The employees of United go on strike. The seller must make a reasonable substitute tender, by another trucking company or perhaps by rail, if such a substitute is available. ■

**Installment Contracts** An **installment contract** is a single contract that requires or authorizes delivery in two or more separate lots to be accepted and paid for separately. With an installment contract, a buyer or lessee can reject an installment *only if the nonconformity substantially impairs the value* of the installment and cannot be cured [UCC 2–307, 2–612(2), 2A–510(1)]. ■ **EXAMPLE 14.7**

A seller is to deliver fifteen freezers in lots of five each. In the first lot, four of the freezers have defective cooling units that cannot be repaired. The buyer in these circumstances can reject the entire lot. ■ If the buyer or lessee fails to notify the seller or lessor of the rejection, however, and subsequently accepts a nonconforming installment, the contract is reinstated [UCC 2–612(3), 2A–510(2)].

Unless the contract provides otherwise, the entire installment contract is breached only when one or more nonconforming installments *substantially* impair the value of the *whole contract*. The point to remember is that the UCC significantly alters the right of the buyer or lessee to reject the entire contract if the contract requires delivery to be made in several installments. The UCC strictly limits rejection to instances of *substantial* nonconformity.

**Commercial Impracticability** Occurrences unforeseen by either party when a contract was made may make performance commercially impracticable. When this occurs, the perfect tender rule no longer applies. The seller or lessor must, however, notify the buyer or lessee as soon as practicable that there will be a delay or nondelivery [UCC 2–615, 2A–405].

■ **EXAMPLE 14.8** Houston Oil Company obtains its oil from the Middle East. Houston enters a contract to supply Northwest Fuels with one hundred thousand barrels of oil. An oil embargo by the Organization of Petroleum Exporting Countries prevents Houston from securing oil from the Middle East or any other source to meet the terms of the contract. Assuming that the embargo was unforeseen, if Houston notifies Northwest about the problem, the nondelivery comes under the commercial impracticability exception to the perfect tender doctrine. ■

Commercial impracticability arises only when the parties, at the time the contract was made, had no reason to anticipate that the event would occur. It does not extend to problems that could have been foreseen, such as an increase in cost resulting from inflation.

■ **CASE IN POINT 14.9** In a classic 1970s case, Maple Farms, Inc., entered a contract to supply a school district in New York with milk for one school year. The contract price was the market price of milk in June, but by December, the price of raw milk had increased by 23 percent. Maple Farms stood to lose $7,350 on this contract (and more on similar contracts with other school districts). To avoid performing the contract, Maple Farms filed a suit and claimed that the unanticipated increases in a seller's costs made performance "impracticable." A

New York trial court disagreed. Because inflation and fluctuating prices could have been foreseen, they did not render performance of this contract impracticable. The court granted summary judgment in favor of the school district.[3] ■

**Commercial Impracticability and Partial Performance** Sometimes, the unforeseen event only *partially* affects the capacity of the seller or lessor to perform. Therefore, the seller or lessor can *partially* fulfill the contract but cannot tender total performance. In this event, the seller or lessor is required to distribute any remaining goods or deliveries fairly and reasonably among the parties to whom it is contractually obligated [UCC 2–615(b), 2A–405(b)]. The buyer or lessee must receive notice of the allocation and has the right to accept or reject it [UCC 2–615(c), 2A–405(c)].

■ **EXAMPLE 14.10** A Florida orange grower, Best Citrus, Inc., contracts to sell this season's crop to a number of customers, including Martin's grocery chain. Martin's contracts to purchase two thousand crates of oranges. Best Citrus has sprayed some of its orange groves with a chemical called Karmoxin. The U.S. Department of Agriculture discovers that Karmoxin poses a cancer risk and issues an order prohibiting the sale of products sprayed with the substance. Best Citrus picks all the oranges not sprayed with Karmoxin, but the quantity is insufficient to meet all the contracted-for deliveries.

In this situation, Best Citrus is required to allocate its production. It notifies Martin's that it cannot deliver the full quantity specified in the contract and indicates the amount it will be able to deliver. Martin's can either accept or reject the allocation, but Best Citrus has no further contractual liability. ■

**Destruction of Identified Goods** Sometimes, an unexpected event, such as a fire, totally destroys goods through no fault of either party before risk passes to the buyer or lessee. In such a situation, *if the goods were identified at the time the contract was formed,* the parties are excused from performance [UCC 2–613, 2A–221]. If the goods are only partially destroyed, however, the buyer or lessee can inspect them and either treat the contract as void or accept the damaged goods with a reduction in the contract price.

■ **EXAMPLE 14.11** Atlas Sporting Equipment agrees to lease to River Bicycles sixty bicycles of a particular model that has been discontinued. No other bicycles of

that model are available. River specifies that it needs the bicycles to rent to tourists. Before Atlas can deliver the bicycles, they are destroyed by a fire. In this situation, Atlas is not liable to River for failing to deliver the bicycles. Through no fault of either party, the goods were destroyed before the risk of loss passed to the lessee. The loss was total, so the contract is avoided. Clearly, Atlas has no obligation to tender the bicycles, and River has no obligation to make the lease payments for them. ■

**Assurance and Cooperation** If one party has "reasonable grounds" to believe that the other party will not perform, the first party may *in writing* "demand adequate assurance of due performance" from the other party. Until such assurance is received, the first party may "suspend" further performance without liability. What constitutes "reasonable grounds" is determined by commercial standards. If the requested assurances are not forthcoming within a reasonable time (not to exceed thirty days), the failure to respond may be treated as a repudiation of the contract [UCC 2–609, 2A–401].

Sometimes, the performance of one party depends on the cooperation of the other. When cooperation is not forthcoming, the first party can either proceed to perform the contract in any reasonable manner or suspend performance without liability and hold the uncooperative party in breach [UCC 2–311(3)].

■ **EXAMPLE 14.12** Aman is required by contract to deliver 1,200 LG washing machines to various locations in California on or before October 1. Friedman, the buyer, is to specify the locations for delivery. Aman repeatedly requests the delivery locations, but Friedman does not respond. The washing machines are ready for shipment on October 1, but Friedman still refuses to give Aman the delivery locations. If Aman does not ship on October 1, he cannot be held liable. Aman is excused for any resulting delay of performance because of Friedman's failure to cooperate. ■

Concept Summary 14.1 reviews the obligations of the seller.

---

# 14–2 Obligations of the Buyer or Lessee

The main obligation of the buyer or lessee under a sales or lease contract is to pay for the goods tendered. Once the seller or lessor has adequately tendered delivery, the

---

3. *Maple Farms, Inc. v. City School District of Elmira,* 76 Misc.2d 1080, 352 N.Y.S.2d 784 (1974).

## Concept Summary 14.1

### Obligations of the Seller or Lessor

| Tender of Delivery | • Tender of delivery occurs when the seller or lessor makes *conforming goods* available and gives the buyer or lessee whatever notification is reasonably necessary to enable the buyer or lessee to take delivery [UCC 2–503(1), 2A–508(1)].<br>• Unless the parties have agreed otherwise, the conforming goods must be tendered for delivery at a *reasonable hour* and in a *reasonable manner* [UCC 2–503(1)(a)]. |
|---|---|
| **The Perfect Tender Rule** | Under the perfect tender doctrine, the seller or lessor must tender goods that conform exactly to the terms of the contract. Exceptions to this rule are as follows:<br>• *Cure*—The right of the seller or lessor to *cure*—that is, repair, adjust, or replace—nonconforming goods within the contract time for performance [UCC 2–508, 2A–513].<br>• *Substitution of carriers*—If the agreed-on means of delivery becomes impracticable or unavailable, the seller must substitute an alternative carrier, if a reasonable one is available [UCC 2–614(1)].<br>• *Installment contracts*—Unless the contract provides otherwise, the entire installment contract is breached only when one or more nonconforming installments *substantially* impair the value of the *whole* contract [UCC 2–612(2), 2A–510(1)].<br>• *Commercial impracticability*—When performance becomes commercially impracticable owing to circumstances unforeseen when the contract was formed, the perfect tender rule no longer applies [UCC 2–615, 2A–405].<br>• *Destruction of identified goods*—When an unexpected event, such as a fire, totally destroys goods that were identified to the contract when it was formed, through no fault of either party, performance is excused [UCC 2–613, 2A–221].<br>• *Assurance and cooperation*—If a party has reasonable grounds to believe that the other party is not going to perform and demands assurances, the other party's failure to respond in a reasonable time may be treated as a repudiation (breach) and excuse further performance [UCC 2–609, 2A–401]. A party's failure to cooperate with the other party may also excuse the party from further performing [UCC 2–311(3)]. |

buyer or lessee is obligated to accept the goods and pay for them according to the terms of the contract. We discuss the obligations of the buyer or lessee under the UCC next, and they are outlined in Exhibit 14–2.

### 14–2a Payment

In the absence of any specific agreements, the buyer or lessee must make payment at the time and place the goods are *received* [UCC 2–310(a), 2A–516(1)]. When a sale is made on credit, the buyer is obligated to pay according to the specified credit terms (for example, 60, 90, or 120 days), not when the goods are received. The credit period usually begins on the *date of shipment* [UCC 2–310(d)]. Under a lease contract, a lessee must make the lease payment that was specified in the contract [UCC 2A–516(1)].

Payment can be made by any means agreed on between the parties—cash or any other method generally acceptable in the commercial world. If the seller demands

**EXHIBIT 14–2** Obligations of the Buyer or Lessee

| THE PAYMENT OF THE GOODS | THE RIGHT OF INSPECTION | THE ACCEPTANCE OF THE GOODS |
|---|---|---|
| • On tender of delivery by the seller or lessor, the buyer or lessee must pay for the goods at the time and place the goods are *received*, unless the sale is made on credit [UCC 2–310(a)].<br><br>• Payment can be made by any method generally acceptable in the commercial world, but the seller can demand cash [UCC 2–511]. | • Unless otherwise agreed or in C.O.D. (collect on delivery) shipments, the buyer or lessee has an absolute right to inspect the goods before acceptance [UCC 2–513(1), 2A–515(1)]. | • The buyer or lessee can manifest acceptance of delivered goods in words or by conduct, such as by failing to reject the goods after having had a reasonable opportunity to inspect them [UCC 2–606(1), 2A–515(1)].<br><br>• A buyer will be deemed to have accepted goods if he or she performs any act inconsistent with the seller's ownership [UCC 2–606(1)(c)]. |

cash, the seller must permit the buyer reasonable time to obtain it [UCC 2–511].

## 14–2b Right of Inspection

Unless the parties otherwise agree, or for C.O.D. (collect on delivery) transactions, the buyer or lessee has an absolute right to inspect the goods before making payment. This right allows the buyer or lessee to verify that the goods tendered or delivered conform to the contract. If the goods are not as ordered, the buyer or lessee has no duty to pay. *An opportunity for inspection is therefore a condition precedent to the right of the seller or lessor to enforce payment* [UCC 2–513(1), 2A–515(1)].

Inspection can take place at any reasonable place and time and in any reasonable manner. Generally, what is reasonable is determined by custom of the trade, past practices of the parties, and the like. The buyer bears the costs of inspecting the goods but can recover the costs from the seller if the goods do not conform and are rejected [UCC 2–513(2)].

■ **CASE IN POINT 14.13** Jessie Romero offered to deliver two trade-in vehicles to Scoggin-Dickey Chevrolet Buick, Inc., in exchange for a 2006 Silverado pickup. Scoggin-Dickey agreed. The parties negotiated a price, including a value for the trade-in vehicles, plus cash. Romero paid the cash and took the 2006 Silverado (but the dealer kept the title to it). Several weeks later, Romero delivered the two trade-in vehicles.

On inspecting the trade-in vehicles, Scoggin-Dickey found that they had little value. One of them did not even run. The dealer repossessed the Silverado. Romero sued for breach of contract, claiming that the dealer had no right to reject the trade-in vehicles after the contract was signed. The court held that the contract for the sale was not completed until Romero traded in the two vehicles. Scoggin-Dickey had a right to inspect them and did so within a reasonable time after they were delivered. The dealership was entitled to reject the trade-in vehicles and keep the 2006 Silverado, but it had to refund Romero's cash and return the trade-in vehicles.[4] ■

## 14–2c Acceptance

After having had a reasonable opportunity to inspect the goods, the buyer or lessee can demonstrate acceptance in any of the following ways:

1. The buyer or lessee indicates (by words or conduct) to the seller or lessor that the goods are conforming or that he or she will retain them in spite of their nonconformity [UCC 2–606(1)(a), 2A–515(1)(a)].
2. The buyer or lessee fails to reject the goods within a reasonable period of time [UCC 2–602(1), 2–606(1)(b), 2A–515(1)(b)].

---

4. *Romero v. Scoggin-Dickey Chevrolet Buick, Inc.,* 2010 WL 456910 (Tex. Civ.App.—Amarillo 2010).

3. In sales contracts, the buyer will be deemed to have accepted the goods if he or she performs any act inconsistent with the seller's ownership. For instance, any use or resale of the goods—except for the limited purpose of testing or inspecting the goods—generally constitutes an acceptance [UCC 2–606(1)(c)].

## 14–2d Partial Acceptance

If some of the goods delivered do not conform to the contract and the seller or lessor has failed to cure, the buyer or lessee can make a *partial* acceptance [UCC 2–601(c), 2A–509(1)]. The same is true if the nonconformity was not reasonably discoverable before acceptance. (In the latter situation, the buyer or lessee may be able to revoke the acceptance, as will be discussed later in this chapter.)

A buyer or lessee cannot accept less than a single commercial unit, however. The UCC defines a *commercial unit* as a unit of goods that, by commercial usage, is viewed as a "single whole" for purposes of sale. A commercial unit cannot be divided without materially impairing the character of the unit, its market value, or its use [UCC 2–105(6), 2A–103(1)(c)]. A commercial unit can be a single article (such as a machine), a set of articles (such as a suite of furniture), a quantity (such as a bale, a gross, or a carload), or any other unit treated in the trade as a single whole.

## 14–2e Anticipatory Repudiation

What if, before the time for contract performance, one party clearly communicates to the other the intention *not* to perform? Such an action is a breach of the contract by *anticipatory repudiation.*

**Suspension of Performance Obligations** When anticipatory repudiation occurs, the nonbreaching party has a choice of two responses:

1. Treat the repudiation as a final breach by pursuing a remedy.
2. Wait to see if the repudiating party will decide to honor the contract despite the avowed intention to renege [UCC 2–610, 2A–402].

In either situation, the nonbreaching party may suspend performance.

**A Repudiation May Be Retracted** The UCC permits the breaching party to "retract" his or her repudiation (subject to some limitations). This can be done by any method that clearly indicates the party's intent to perform. Once retraction is made, the rights of the repudiating party under the contract are reinstated. There can be no retraction, however, if since the time of the repudiation the other party has canceled or materially changed position or otherwise indicated that the repudiation is final [UCC 2–611, 2A–403].

■ **EXAMPLE 14.14** On April 1, Cora Lyn, who owns a small inn, purchases a suite of furniture from Tom Horton, proprietor of Horton's Furniture Warehouse. The contract states that "delivery must be made on or before May 1." On April 10, Horton informs Lyn that he cannot make delivery until May 10 and asks her to consent to the modified delivery date.

In this situation, Lyn has two options. She can either treat Horton's notice of late delivery as a final breach of contract and pursue a remedy or agree to the later delivery date. Suppose that Lyn does neither for two weeks. On April 24, Horton informs Lyn that he will be able to deliver the furniture by May 1 after all. In effect, Horton has retracted his repudiation, reinstating the rights and obligations of the parties under the original contract. Note that if Lyn had told Horton that she was canceling the contract after he repudiated, he would not have been able to retract his repudiation. ■

# 14–3 Remedies of the Seller or Lessor

Note that remedies for breach under the UCC are *cumulative* in nature—meaning that the aggrieved (wronged) party is not limited to one exclusive remedy. When the buyer or lessee is in breach, the remedies available to the seller or lessor depend on the circumstances existing at the time of the breach. The most pertinent considerations are which party has possession of the goods, whether the goods are in transit, and whether the buyer or lessee has rejected or accepted the goods.

## 14–3a When the Goods Are in the Possession of the Seller or Lessor

If the buyer or lessee breaches the contract *before the goods have been delivered*, the seller or lessor has the right to pursue the following remedies:

1. Cancel (rescind) the contract.
2. Withhold delivery of the goods.
3. Resell the goods and sue to recover damages.

4. Sue to recover the purchase price or lease payments due.
5. Sue to recover damages for the buyer's nonacceptance of goods.

**The Right to Cancel the Contract** If the buyer or lessee breaches the contract, the seller or lessor can choose to simply cancel the contract [UCC 2–703(f), 2A–523(1)(a)]. The seller or lessor must notify the buyer or lessee of the cancellation, and at that point all remaining obligations of the seller or lessor are discharged. The buyer or lessee is not discharged from all remaining obligations, however. She or he is in breach, and the seller or lessor can pursue remedies available under the UCC for breach.

**The Right to Withhold Delivery** In general, sellers and lessors can withhold delivery or discontinue performance of their obligations under sales or lease contracts when the buyers or lessees are in breach [UCC 2–703(a), 2A–523(1)(c)]. This is true whether a buyer or lessee has wrongfully rejected or revoked acceptance of contract goods (discussed later), failed to make a payment, or repudiated the contract. The seller or lessor can also refuse to deliver the goods to a buyer or lessee who is insolvent (unable to pay debts as they become due) unless the buyer or lessee pays in cash [UCC 2–702(1), 2A–525(1)].

**The Right to Resell or Dispose of the Goods** When a buyer or lessee breaches or repudiates the contract while the seller or lessor is in possession of the goods, the seller or lessor can resell or dispose of the goods. Any resale of the goods must be made in good faith and in a commercially reasonable manner. The seller must give the original buyer reasonable notice of the resale, unless the goods are perishable or will rapidly decline in value [UCC 2–706(2), (3)].

The seller can retain any profits made as a result of the sale and can hold the buyer or lessee liable for any loss [UCC 2–703(d), 2–706(1), 2A–523(1)(e), 2A–527(1)]. (Here, a loss is any deficiency between the resale price and the contract price.) In lease transactions, the lessor can lease the goods to another party and recover damages from the original lessee. Damages include any unpaid lease payments up to the time the new lease begins. The lessor can also recover any deficiency between the lease payments due under the original lease and those due under the new lease, along with incidental damages [UCC 2A–527(2)].

When the goods contracted for are *unfinished at the time of the breach*, the seller or lessor can do either of the following:

1. Cease manufacturing the goods and resell them for scrap or salvage value.
2. Complete the manufacture and resell or dispose of the goods, and hold the buyer or lessee liable for any deficiency.

In choosing between these two alternatives, the seller or lessor must exercise reasonable commercial judgment in order to mitigate the loss and obtain maximum value from the unfinished goods [UCC 2–704(2), 2A–524(2)].

**The Right to Recover the Purchase Price or Lease Payments Due** Under the UCC, an unpaid seller or lessor can bring an action to recover the purchase price or the payments due under the lease contract, plus incidental damages [UCC 2–709(1), 2A–529(1)]. If a seller or lessor is unable to resell or dispose of the goods and sues for the contract price or lease payments due, the goods must be held for the buyer or lessee. The seller or lessor can resell the goods at any time before collecting the judgment from the buyer or lessee. If the goods are resold, the net proceeds from the sale must be credited to the buyer or lessee because of the duty to mitigate damages.

■ **EXAMPLE 14.15** Cascade School contracts with Stickme.com to purchase ten thousand bumper stickers with the school's name and logo on them. Stickme tenders delivery of the stickers, but Cascade wrongfully refuses to accept them. In this situation, Stickme can bring an action for the purchase price. Stickme has delivered conforming goods, and Cascade has refused to accept or pay for the goods. Obviously, Stickme will not likely be able to resell the stickers, so this situation falls under UCC 2–709. Stickme is required to make the bumper stickers available for Cascade. In the unlikely event that it can find another buyer, it can sell the stickers at any time prior to collecting the judgment from Cascade. ■

**The Right to Recover Damages for the Buyer's Nonacceptance** If a buyer or lessee repudiates a contract or wrongfully refuses to accept the goods, a seller or lessor can bring an action to recover the damages sustained. Ordinarily, the amount of damages equals the difference between the contract price or lease payments and the market price or lease payments at the time and place of tender of the goods, plus incidental damages [UCC 2–708(1), 2A–528(1)].

When the ordinary measure of damages is inadequate to put the seller or lessor in as good a position as the buyer's or lessee's performance would have, the UCC provides an alternative. In that situation, the proper measure of damages is the lost profits of the seller or lessor, including a reasonable allowance for overhead and other expenses [UCC 2–708(2), 2A–528(2)].

### 14–3b When the Goods Are in Transit

When the seller or lessor has delivered the goods to a carrier or a bailee but the buyer or lessee has not yet received them, the goods are said to be *in transit.*

**Effect of Insolvency and Breach** If the seller or lessor learns that the buyer or lessee is insolvent, the seller or lessor can stop the delivery of the goods still in transit, regardless of the quantity of goods shipped. A different rule applies if the buyer or lessee is in breach but is not insolvent. In this situation, the seller or lessor can stop the goods in transit only if the quantity shipped is at least a carload, a truckload, a planeload, or a larger shipment [UCC 2–705(1), 2A–526(1)].

■ **EXAMPLE 14.16** Arturo Ortega orders a truckload of lumber from Timber Products, Inc., to be shipped to Ortega six weeks later. Ortega, who has not paid Timber Products for a past shipment, promises to pay the debt immediately and to pay for the current shipment as soon as it is received. After the lumber has been shipped, a bankruptcy court judge notifies Timber Products that Ortega has filed a petition in bankruptcy and listed Timber Products as one of his creditors. If the goods are still in transit, Timber Products can stop the carrier from delivering the lumber to Ortega. ■

**Requirements for Stopping Delivery** To stop delivery, the seller or lessor must *timely notify* the carrier or other bailee that the goods are to be returned or held for the seller or lessor. If the carrier has sufficient time to stop delivery, the goods must be held and delivered according to the instructions of the seller or lessor. The seller or lessor is liable to the carrier for any additional costs incurred [UCC 2–705(3), 2A–526(3)].

The seller or lessor has the right to stop delivery of the goods under UCC 2–705(2) and 2A–526(2) until the time when:

1. The buyer or lessee receives the goods.
2. The carrier or the bailee acknowledges the rights of the buyer or lessee in the goods (by reshipping or holding the goods for the buyer or lessee, for example).
3. A negotiable document of title covering the goods has been properly transferred to the buyer in a sales transaction, giving the buyer ownership rights in the goods [UCC 2–705(2)].

Once the seller or lessor reclaims the goods in transit, she or he can pursue the remedies allowed to sellers and lessors when the goods are in their possession.

### 14–3c When the Goods Are in the Possession of the Buyer or Lessee

When the buyer or lessee breaches the contract while the goods are in his or her possession, the seller or lessor can sue. The seller or lessor can recover the purchase price of the goods or the lease payments due, plus incidental damages [UCC 2–709(1), 2A–529(1)].

In some situations, a seller may also have a right to reclaim the goods from the buyer. For instance, in a sales contract, if the buyer has received the goods on credit and the seller discovers that the buyer is insolvent, the seller can demand the return of the goods [UCC 2–702(2)]. Ordinarily, the demand must be made within ten days of the buyer's receipt of the goods.[5] The seller's right to reclaim the goods is subject to the rights of a good faith purchaser or other subsequent buyer in the ordinary course of business who purchases the goods from the buyer before the seller reclaims them.

In regard to lease contracts, if the lessee is in default (fails to make payments that are due, for instance), the lessor may reclaim leased goods that are in the lessee's possession [UCC 2A–525(2)].

# 14–4 Remedies of the Buyer or Lessee

When the seller or lessor breaches the contract, the buyer or lessee has numerous remedies available under the UCC. Like the remedies available to sellers and lessors, the remedies available to buyers and lessees depend on the circumstances at the time of the breach. Relevant factors include whether the seller has refused to deliver conforming goods or has delivered nonconforming goods.

### 14–4a When the Seller or Lessor Refuses to Deliver the Goods

If the seller or lessor refuses to deliver the goods to the buyer or lessee, the basic remedies available to the buyer or lessee include the right to:

---

5. The seller can demand and reclaim the goods at any time if the buyer misrepresented his or her solvency in writing within three months prior to the delivery of the goods.

1. Cancel (rescind) the contract.
2. Obtain goods that have been paid for if the seller or lessor is insolvent.
3. Sue to obtain specific performance if the goods are unique or if damages are an inadequate remedy.
4. Buy other goods (obtain *cover*) and recover damages from the seller.
5. Sue to obtain identified goods held by a third party (*replevy* goods).
6. Sue to obtain damages.

**The Right to Cancel the Contract** When a seller or lessor fails to make proper delivery or repudiates the contract, the buyer or lessee can cancel, or rescind, the contract. The buyer or lessee is relieved of any further obligations under the contract but retains all rights to other remedies against the seller or lessor [UCC 2–711(1), 2A–508(1)(a)]. (The right to cancel the contract is also available to a buyer or lessee who has rightfully rejected goods or revoked acceptance, as will be discussed shortly.)

**The Right to Obtain the Goods upon Insolvency** If a buyer or lessee has partially or fully paid for goods that are in the possession of a seller or lessor who becomes insolvent, the buyer or lessee can obtain the goods. The seller or lessor must have become insolvent within ten days after receiving the first payment, and the goods must be identified to the contract. To exercise this right, the buyer or lessee must pay the seller or lessor any unpaid balance of the purchase price or lease payments [UCC 2–502, 2A–522].

**The Right to Obtain Specific Performance** A buyer or lessee can obtain specific performance if the goods are unique or the remedy at law (monetary damages) is inadequate [UCC 2–716(1), 2A–521(1)]. Ordinarily, an award of damages is sufficient to place a buyer or lessee in the position she or he would have occupied if the seller or lessor had fully performed.

When the contract is for the purchase of a particular work of art or a similarly unique item, however, damages may not be sufficient. Under these circumstances, equity requires that the seller or lessor perform exactly by delivering the particular goods identified to the contract (the remedy of specific performance).

■ **CASE IN POINT 14.17** Together, Doreen Houseman and Eric Dare bought a house and a pedigreed dog. When the couple separated, they agreed that Dare would keep the house (and pay Houseman for her interest in it) and that Houseman would keep the dog. Houseman

allowed Dare to take the dog for visits, but after one visit, Dare kept the dog. Houseman filed a lawsuit seeking specific performance of their agreement. The court found that because pets have special subjective value to their owners, a dog can be considered a unique good. Thus, an award of specific performance was appropriate.[6] ■

**The Right of Cover** In certain situations, buyers and lessees can protect themselves by obtaining **cover**—that is, by buying or leasing substitute goods for those that were due under the contract. This option is available when the seller or lessor repudiates the contract or fails to deliver the goods, or when a buyer or lessee has rightfully rejected goods or revoked acceptance. In purchasing or leasing substitute goods, the buyer or lessee must act in good faith and without unreasonable delay [UCC 2–712, 2A–518].

After obtaining substitute goods, the buyer or lessee can recover from the seller or lessor:

1. The difference between the cost of cover and the contract price (or lease payments).
2. Incidental damages that resulted from the breach.
3. *Consequential damages* to compensate for indirect losses (such as lost profits) resulting from the breach that were reasonably foreseeable at the time of contract formation. The amount of consequential damages is reduced by any amount the buyer or lessee saved as a result of the breach. (For instance, the buyer might obtain cover without having to pay delivery charges that were part of the original sales contract.)

Buyers and lessees are not required to cover, and failure to do so will not bar them from using any other remedies available under the UCC. A buyer or lessee who fails to cover, however, risks collecting a lower amount of consequential damages. A court may reduce the consequential damages by the amount of the loss that could have been avoided had the buyer or lessee purchased or leased substitute goods.

**The Right to Replevy Goods** Buyers and lessees also have the right to replevy goods. **Replevin**[7] is an action to recover identified goods in the hands of a party who is unlawfully withholding them. Under the UCC, a buyer or lessee can replevy goods identified to the contract if the seller or lessor has repudiated or breached the contract. To maintain an action to replevy goods, buyers and lessees must usually show that they were unable to cover for the

---

6. *Houseman v. Dare*, 405 N.J.Super. 538, 966 A.2d 24 (2009).
7. Pronounced ruh-*pleh*-vun, derived from the Old French word *plevir*, meaning "to pledge."

goods after making a reasonable effort [UCC 2–716(3), 2A–521(3)].

**The Right to Recover Damages** If a seller or lessor repudiates the contract or fails to deliver the goods, the buyer or lessee can sue for damages. For the buyer, the measure of recovery is the difference between the contract price and the market price of the goods at the time the buyer *learned* of the breach. For the lessee, the measure is the difference between the lease payments and the lease payments that could be obtained for the goods at the time the lessee learned of the breach. The market price or market lease payments are determined at the place where the seller or lessor was supposed to deliver the goods. The buyer or lessee can also recover incidental and consequential damages less the expenses that were saved as a result of the breach [UCC 2–713, 2A–519].

■ **CASE IN POINT 14.18** Les Entreprises Jacques Defour & Fils, Inc., contracted to buy a thirty-thousand-gallon industrial tank from Dinsick Equipment Corporation for $70,000. Les Entreprises hired Xaak Transport, Inc., to pick up the tank, but when Xaak arrived at the pickup location, there was no tank. Les Entreprises paid Xaak $7,459 for its services and filed a suit against Dinsick.

The court awarded compensatory damages of $70,000 for the tank and incidental damages of $7,459 for the transport. To establish a breach of contract requires an enforceable contract, substantial performance by the nonbreaching party, a breach by the other party, and damages. In this case, Les Entreprises agreed to buy a tank and paid the price. Dinsick failed to tender or deliver the tank, or to refund the price. The shipping costs were a necessary part of performance, so this was a reasonable expense.[8] ■

## 14–4b When the Seller or Lessor Delivers Nonconforming Goods

When the seller or lessor delivers nonconforming goods, the buyer or lessee has several remedies available under the UCC.

**The Right to Reject the Goods** If either the goods or their tender fails to conform to the contract in any respect, the buyer or lessee can reject all of the goods or any commercial unit of the goods [UCC 2–601, 2A–509]. On rejecting the goods, the buyer or lessee may obtain cover or cancel the contract, and may seek damages just as if the seller or lessor had refused to deliver the goods.

**Timeliness and Reason for Rejection Are Required.** The buyer or lessee must reject the goods within a reasonable amount of time after delivery or tender of delivery and must seasonably notify the seller or lessor [UCC 2–602(1), 2A–509(2)]. If the buyer or lessee fails to reject the goods within a reasonable amount of time, acceptance will be presumed.

When rejecting goods, the buyer or lessee must also designate defects that are ascertainable by reasonable inspection. Failure to do so precludes the buyer or lessee from using such defects to justify rejection or to establish breach if the seller or lessor could have cured the defects [UCC 2–605, 2A–514].

**Duties of Merchant-Buyers and Lessees When Goods Are Rejected.** Sometimes, a *merchant-buyer or lessee* rightfully rejects goods, and the seller or lessor has no agent or business at the place of rejection. In that situation, the merchant-buyer or lessee has a good faith obligation to follow any reasonable instructions received from the seller or lessor with respect to the goods [UCC 2–603, 2A–511]. The buyer or lessee is entitled to be reimbursed for the care and cost entailed in following the instructions. The same requirements apply if the buyer or lessee rightfully revokes her or his acceptance of the goods at some later time [UCC 2–608(3), 2A–517(5)]. (Revocation of acceptance will be discussed shortly.)

If no instructions are forthcoming and the goods are perishable or threaten to decline in value quickly, the buyer or lessee can resell the goods. The buyer or lessee must exercise good faith and can take appropriate reimbursement and a selling commission (not to exceed 10 percent of the gross proceeds) from the proceeds [UCC 2–603(1), (2); 2A–511(1)]. If the goods are not perishable, the buyer or lessee may store them for the seller or lessor or reship them to the seller or lessor [UCC 2–604, 2A–512].

**Revocation of Acceptance** Acceptance of the goods precludes the buyer or lessee from exercising the right of rejection. It does not necessarily prevent the buyer or lessee from pursuing other remedies, however. In certain circumstances, a buyer or lessee is permitted to *revoke* his or her acceptance of the goods.

**Revoking Acceptance of a Commercial Unit.** Acceptance of a lot or a commercial unit can be revoked if the nonconformity *substantially* impairs the value of the lot or unit *and* if one of the following factors is present:

1.  Acceptance was based on the reasonable assumption that the nonconformity would be cured, and it has not been cured within a reasonable period of time [UCC 2–608(1)(a), 2A–517(1)(a)].

---

8. *Les Entreprises Jacques Defour & Fils, Inc. v. Dinsick Equipment Corp.*, 2011 WL 307501 (N.D.Ill. 2011).

**2.** The failure of the buyer or lessee to discover the nonconformity was reasonably induced either by the difficulty of discovery before acceptance or by assurances made by the seller or lessor [UCC 2–608(1)(b), 2A–517(1)(b)].

■ **CASE IN POINT 14.19** Armadillo Distribution Enterprises, Inc., is a major distributor of musical instruments. Armadillo contracted with a Chinese corporation, Hai Yun Musical Instruments Manufacture Co., Ltd., to manufacture one thousand drum kits. Hai Yun had made drums for Armadillo in the past. Hai Yun furnished samples for Armadillo's approval prior to manufacturing the kits. After Armadillo inspected and approved the samples, Hai Yun delivered five shipping containers of drum kits, and Armadillo began distribution.

Armadillo soon started receiving numerous complaints from its retail outlet customers concerning product returns due to cosmetic and structural defects in the drum kits. Armadillo immediately inspected the remaining four shipment containers and discovered that a high percentage of the drum kits were defective and unfit for commercial distribution. Armadillo revoked its acceptance of the kits and filed a suit in federal court for breach of contract. The district court ruled that Hai Yun

had breached the contract by delivering nonconforming goods. The court awarded Armadillo nearly $90,000 in direct and incidental damages.[9] ■

**Notice of Revocation.** Revocation of acceptance is not effective until notice is given to the seller or lessor. Notice must occur within a reasonable time after the buyer or lessee either discovers or *should have discovered* the grounds for revocation. Additionally, revocation must occur before the goods have undergone any substantial change (such as spoilage) not caused by their own defects [UCC 2–608(2), 2A–517(4)]. Once acceptance is revoked, the buyer or lessee can pursue remedies, just as if the goods had been rejected.

To effectively revoke acceptance, a buyer must "relinquish dominion over the goods." This requires a buyer to return the goods or at least to stop using them, unless the use is necessary to avoid substantial hardship. At issue in the following case was whether the purchaser of lights for a commercial building sufficiently relinquished dominion over the goods to revoke acceptance.

---

9. *Armadillo Distribution Enterprises, Inc. v. Hai Yun Musical Instruments Manufacture Co. Ltd.*, 142 F.Supp.3d 1245 (M.D.Fla. 2015).

---

**Case Analysis 14.2**

# Genesis Health Clubs, Inc. v. LED Solar & Light Co.

United States Court of Appeals, Tenth Circuit, __ F.3d __, 2016 WL 373699 (2016).

### In the Language of the Court
*HARRIS L. HARTZ*, Circuit Judge.

* * * *

Genesis [Health Clubs, Inc.], based in Kansas, operates health clubs. LED Solar & Light Company], based in Virginia, manufactures and sells LED lighting.

* * * LED Solar submitted a proposed contract "to furnish the replacement lamps for Genesis's building" for $82,271.50. LED Solar "warranted watt for watt exchange a minimum of 35% deduction in wattage consumption." * * * Genesis executed the contract later that month.

Soon after installation began, Genesis encountered problems with the lights. [Genesis] complained that "the defect rate on these lamps is * * * 73% * * *," "the LED tubes * * * are not consistent in color," [and there are] multiple light failures throughout Genesis's facility.

* * * [LED Solar] found "no fault with [the] lamps" and instructed [Genesis] to return problem lights for a refund.

* * * Genesis returned a shipment of lights, seeking a $3,777 refund.

* * * [A later e-mail to LED Solar explained] that Genesis would be "returning all of the lights" one shipment at a time in exchange for a refund, "allowing Genesis to phase out the faulty lamps."

But the return/refund process never got off the ground because of a dispute regarding whether Genesis had been properly credited for its [previous] shipment of lights * * * . On the same day as [the] email saying that Genesis would return the lights one shipment at a time, [LED Solar] responded by email, telling [Genesis]:

* * * Everything you have shipped back that was not damaged in handling works fine. If you ship those

items back not damaged we will credit the account without any problem. * * * Right now [Genesis] * * * owes more [on the contract] than the credit on the returned items * * * . [We] have been waiting for several months for the returns that you have been saying you are returning. Yet nothing has shown up.

[Genesis] replied * * * :

* * * You have not been prompt in your commitment to refund for returned items. * * * You have your money for the entire order that was pre-paid. * * * We are trying to replace the defective lights with the refund dollars for the product returned.

* * * [LED Solar] never paid Genesis the $3,777 and Genesis never returned any more lights.

**Case 14.2 Continued**

* * * Genesis filed a * * * petition [in a Kansas state court] asserting claims of breach of * * * warranty. LED Solar removed the case to federal court based on diversity jurisdiction.

* * * *

* * * The court concluded that Genesis could not recover the purchase price because it failed to reject or revoke acceptance of the lights. [Genesis appealed.]

* * * *

Under the * * * Uniform Commercial Code, a buyer may cancel the contract and recover the purchase price by rightfully rejecting or justifiably revoking acceptance. *Rejection is available for goods that fail in any respect to conform to the contract, and it must be communicated to the seller within a reasonable time after the goods' delivery or tender. What constitutes a reasonable time depends on the nature, purpose, and circumstances of the action.* [Emphasis added.]

Even after the goods have been accepted, the buyer may revoke his acceptance of a lot or commercial unit whose nonconformity substantially impairs its value to him if he has accepted it * * * on the reasonable assumption that its nonconformity would be cured and it has not been seasonably cured. A buyer who revokes has the same rights and duties with regard to the goods involved as if he had rejected them. Thus, revocation requires notification to the seller within a reasonable time after the buyer discovers or should have discovered the ground for it and before any substantial change in condition of the goods which is not caused by their own defects.

In the case of both remedies, the buyer's exercise of ownership or dominion over the goods may negate an attempt to cancel the contract and recover the purchase price. * * * *A buyer's act of dominion over the goods * * * is inconsistent with a claim by the buyer that acceptance has been revoked.* [Emphasis added.]

In the case before us, Genesis did not effectively reject or revoke acceptance of the lights because it never relinquished dominion over them. Despite allegedly agreeing with LED Solar to return all the lights in stages, it never returned any after reaching the agreement and continued to use them.

Genesis argues that without the $3,777 refund for an earlier (preagreement) shipment of lights to LED Solar, it was unable "to continue the return and replacement process. * * * [LED Solar] was aware that Genesis * * * would have to find and purchase new lights to replace LED Solar's * * * bulbs prior to removing them all from the facility."

True, a buyer's continued use of the goods after the supposed revocation is not inconsistent with revocation if such use was necessary to avoid substantial hardship. But Genesis made no showing of substantial hardship. It offered no financial evidence that it could not afford to return any more lights without the $3,777 refund * * *. It cites no evidence that it attempted to resolve the impasse and reach some accommodation with LED Solar for future returns. It did not even produce evidence that LED Solar was incorrect in saying that the $3,777 had been credited toward what Genesis still owed. Nor does it explain why it could not afford to return lights that were not functioning. In short, no reasonable jury could find that Genesis reasonably continued using the lights after it informed LED Solar that it wanted to return them. Genesis had no excuse for using the bulbs until LED Solar accepted the * * * financial terms demanded by Genesis to govern the returns. There was no proper rejection or revocation of acceptance of the bulbs.

We conclude that summary judgment was properly entered on Genesis's claim for a refund of the purchase price.

**Legal Reasoning Questions**

1. According to the UCC, if delivered goods do not conform to a sales contract, how can the buyer revoke acceptance?

2. In this case, what was the dispute between the buyer and the seller? How did this dispute end in litigation?

3. On what key point did the lower and appellate courts agree? Why?

**The Right to Recover Damages for Accepted Goods** A buyer or lessee who has accepted nonconforming goods may also keep the goods and recover damages [UCC 2–714(1), 2A–519(3)]. To do so, the buyer or lessee must notify the seller or lessor of the breach within a reasonable time after the defect was or should have been discovered. Failure to give notice of the defects (breach) to the seller or lessor normally bars the buyer or lessee from pursuing any remedy [UCC 2–607(3), 2A–516(3)]. In addition, the parties to a sales or lease contract can insert into the contract a provision requiring the buyer or lessee to give notice of any defects in the goods within a prescribed period.

When the goods delivered are not as promised, the measure of damages generally equals the difference between the value of the goods as accepted and their value if they had been delivered as warranted. An exception occurs if special circumstances show proximately caused damages of a different amount [UCC 2–714(2), 2A–519(4)]. The buyer or lessee is also entitled to incidental and consequential damages when appropriate

[UCC 2–714(3), 2A–519]. With proper notice to the seller or lessor, the buyer or lessee can also deduct all or any part of the damages from the price or lease payments still due under the contract [UCC 2–717, 2A–516(1)].

Is two years after a sale of goods a reasonable time period in which to discover a defect in those goods and notify the seller of a breach? That was the question in the following case.

## Spotlight on Baseball Cards

## Case 14.3 Fitl v. Strek

Supreme Court of Nebraska, 269 Neb. 51, 690 N.W.2d 605 (2005).

**Background and Facts** In 1995, James Fitl attended a sports-card show in San Francisco, California, where he met Mark Strek, doing business as Star Cards of San Francisco, an exhibitor at the show. Later, on Strek's representation that a certain 1952 Mickey Mantle Topps baseball card was in near-mint condition, Fitl bought the card from Strek for $17,750. Strek delivered it to Fitl in Omaha, Nebraska, and Fitl placed it in a safe-deposit box.

In May 1997, Fitl sent the card to Professional Sports Authenticators (PSA), a sports-card grading service. PSA told Fitl that the card was ungradable because it had been discolored and doctored. Fitl complained to Strek, who replied that Fitl should have initiated a return of the card sooner. According to Strek, "a typical grace period for the unconditional return of a card [was within] 7 days to 1 month" of its receipt. In August, Fitl sent the card to ASA Accugrade, Inc. (ASA), another grading service, for a second opinion of the value. ASA also concluded that the card had been refinished and trimmed. Fitl filed a suit in a Nebraska state court against Strek, seeking damages. The court awarded Fitl $17,750, plus his court costs. Strek appealed to the Nebraska Supreme Court.

### In the Language of the Court
*WRIGHT*, J. [Judge]
* * * *

Strek claims that the [trial] court erred in determining that notification of the defective condition of the baseball card 2 years after the date of purchase was timely pursuant to [UCC] 2–607(3)(a).

* * * The [trial] court found that Fitl had notified Strek within a reasonable time after discovery of the breach. Therefore, our review is whether the [trial] court's finding as to the reasonableness of the notice was clearly erroneous.

Section 2–607(3)(a) states: "Where a tender has been accepted * * * the buyer must within a reasonable time after he discovers or should have discovered any breach notify the seller of breach or be barred from any remedy." [Under UCC 1–204(2),] *"what is a reasonable time for taking any action depends on the nature, purpose and circumstances of such action."* [Emphasis added.]

The notice requirement set forth in Section 2–607(3)(a) serves three purposes.

* * * The most important one is to enable the seller to make efforts to cure the breach by making adjustments or replacements in order to minimize the buyer's damages and the seller's liability. A second policy is to provide the seller a reasonable opportunity to learn the facts so that he may adequately prepare for negotiation and defend himself in a suit. A third policy * * * is the same as the policy behind statutes of limitation: to provide a seller with a terminal point in time for liability.

* * * *A party is justified in relying upon a representation made to the party as a positive statement of fact when an investigation would be required to ascertain its falsity.* In order for Fitl to have determined that the baseball card had been altered, he would have been required to conduct an investigation. We find that he was not required to do so. Once Fitl learned that the baseball card had been altered, he gave notice to Strek. [Emphasis added.]

* * * One of the most important policies behind the notice requirement * * * is to allow the seller to cure the breach by making adjustments or replacements to minimize the buyer's damages and the seller's liability. However, even if Fitl had learned immediately upon taking possession of the baseball card that it was not authentic and had notified Strek at that time, there is no evidence that Strek could have made any adjustment or taken any action that would have minimized his liability. In its altered condition, the baseball card was worthless.

**Case 14.3 Continued**

\* \* \* Earlier notification would not have helped Strek prepare for negotiation or defend himself in a suit because the damage to Fitl could not be repaired. Thus, the policies behind the notice requirement, to allow the seller to correct a defect, to prepare for negotiation and litigation, and to protect against stale claims at a time beyond which an investigation can be completed, were not unfairly prejudiced by the lack of an earlier notice to Strek. Any problem Strek may have had with the party from whom he obtained the baseball card was a separate matter from his transaction with Fitl, and an investigation into the source of the altered card would not have minimized Fitl's damages.

**Decision and Remedy** *The state supreme court affirmed the decision of the lower court. Under the circumstances, notice of a defect in the card two years after its purchase was reasonable. The buyer had reasonably relied on the seller's representation that the card was "authentic" (which it was not), and when the defects were discovered, the buyer had given timely notice.*

**Critical Thinking**
- **What If the Facts Were Different?** *Suppose that Fitl and Strek had included in their deal a written clause requiring Fitl to give notice of any defect in the card within "7 days to 1 month" of its receipt. Would the result have been different? Why or why not?*
- **Legal Environment** *What might a court award to a buyer who prevails in a dispute such as the one in this case?*

# 14–5 Additional Provisions Affecting Remedies

The parties to a sales or lease contract can vary their respective rights and obligations by contractual agreement. For instance, a seller and buyer can expressly provide for remedies in addition to those provided in the UCC. They can also specify remedies in lieu of those provided in the UCC (including liquidated damages clauses), or they can change the measure of damages. A seller can provide that the buyer's only remedy on the seller's breach will be repair or replacement of the item. Alternatively, the seller can limit the buyer's remedy to return of the goods and refund of the purchase price.

In sales and lease contracts, an agreed-on remedy is in addition to those provided in the UCC unless the parties expressly agree that the remedy is exclusive of all others [UCC 2–719(1), 2A–503(1),(2)].

## 14–5a Exclusive Remedies

If the parties state that a remedy is *exclusive,* then it is the sole remedy. ■ **EXAMPLE 14.20** Standard Tool Company agrees to sell a pipe-cutting machine to United Pipe & Tubing Corporation. The contract limits United's remedy exclusively to repair or replacement of any defective parts. Thus, repair or replacement of defective parts is the buyer's only remedy under this contract. ■

When circumstances cause an exclusive remedy to fail in its essential purpose, it is no longer exclusive, and the buyer or lessee may pursue other remedies available under

the UCC [UCC 2–719(2), 2A–503(2)]. In *Example 14.20,* suppose that Standard Tool Company was unable to repair a defective part, and no replacement parts were available. In this situation, because the exclusive remedy failed in its essential purpose (to provide recovery), the buyer could pursue other remedies available under the UCC.

## 14–5b Consequential Damages

As discussed earlier, consequential damages are special damages that compensate for indirect losses (such as lost profits) resulting from a breach of contract that were reasonably foreseeable. Under the UCC, parties to a contract can limit or exclude consequential damages, provided the limitation is not unconscionable. When the buyer or lessee is a consumer, any limitation of consequential damages for personal injuries resulting from consumer goods is presumed to be unconscionable. The limitation of consequential damages is not necessarily unconscionable when the loss is commercial in nature—for instance, lost profits and property damage [UCC 2–719(3), 2A–503(3)].

## 14–5c Statute of Limitations

An action for breach of contract under the UCC must be commenced *within four years after the cause of action accrues* [UCC 2–725(1)]. This means that a buyer or lessee must file the lawsuit within four years after the breach occurs.[10] Thus, the buyer or lessee has four years from

---

10. For breach of warranty, the cause of action arises when the seller or lessor delivers the contracted goods [UCC 2–725(2), 2A–506(2)].

the delivery date to file a suit for breach of warranty. The parties can agree in their contract to reduce this period to not less than one year, but cannot extend it beyond four years [UCC 2–725(1), 2A–506(1)].

If a buyer or lessee has accepted nonconforming goods, that party has a reasonable time to notify the seller or lessor of the breach. Failure to provide notice will bar the buyer or lessee from pursuing any remedy [UCC 2–607(3)(a), 2A–516(3)].

# 14–6 Dealing with International Contracts

Buyers and sellers (or lessees and lessors) engaged in international business transactions may be separated by thousands of miles. Therefore, special precautions are often taken to ensure performance under international contracts. Sellers and lessors want to avoid delivering goods for which they might not be paid. Buyers and lessees desire the assurance that sellers and lessors will not be paid until there is evidence that the goods have been shipped. Thus, **letters of credit** frequently are used to facilitate international business transactions.

## 14–6a Letter-of-Credit Transactions

In a simple letter-of-credit transaction, the *issuer* (a bank or other financial institution) agrees to issue a letter of credit and to ascertain whether the *beneficiary* (seller or lessor) performs certain acts. In return, the *account party* (buyer or lessee) promises to reimburse the issuer for the amount paid to the beneficiary. The transaction may also involve an *advising bank* that transmits information and a *paying bank* that expedites payment under the letter of credit. See Exhibit 14–3 for an illustration of a letter-of-credit transaction.

**EXHIBIT 14–3  A Letter-of-Credit Transaction**

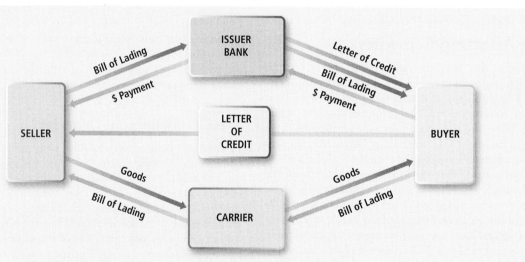

**CHRONOLOGY OF EVENTS**

1. Buyer contracts with issuer bank to issue a letter of credit. This sets forth the bank's obligation to pay on the letter of credit and buyer's obligation to pay the bank.

2. Letter of credit is sent to seller informing seller that on compliance with the terms of the letter of credit (such as presentment of necessary documents—in this example, a bill of lading), the bank will issue payment for the goods.

3. Seller delivers goods to carrier and receives a bill of lading.

4. Seller delivers the bill of lading to issuer bank and, if the document is proper, receives payment.

5. Issuer bank delivers the bill of lading to buyer.

6. Buyer delivers the bill of lading to carrier.

7. Carrier delivers the goods to buyer.

8. Buyer settles with issuer bank.

**Payment under a Letter of Credit** Under a letter of credit, the issuer is bound to pay the beneficiary (seller or lessor) when the beneficiary has complied with the terms and conditions of the letter of credit. The letter of credit assures the beneficiary of payment at the same time as it assures the account party (buyer or lessee) of performance. Typically, a letter of credit will require that the beneficiary deliver a *bill of lading* (the carrier's contract) to prove that shipment has been made.

**The Value of a Letter of Credit** The basic principle behind letters of credit is that payment is made against the documents presented by the beneficiary and not against the facts that the documents purport to reflect. Thus, in a letter-of-credit transaction, the issuer (bank) does not police the underlying contract. The letter of credit is independent of the underlying contract between the buyer and the seller. Eliminating the need for the bank (issuer) to inquire into whether actual contractual conditions have been satisfied greatly reduces the costs of letters of credit. Moreover, the use of a letter of credit protects both buyers and sellers.

## 14–6b  Remedies for Breach of International Sales Contracts

The United Nations Convention on Contracts for the International Sale of Goods (CISG) provides international sellers and buyers with remedies very similar to those available under the UCC. Article 74 of the CISG provides for money damages, including foreseeable consequential damages, on a contract's breach. As under the UCC, the measure of damages normally is the difference between the contract price and the market price of the goods.

Under Article 49, the buyer is permitted to avoid obligations under the contract if the seller breaches the contract or fails to deliver the goods during the time specified in the contract or later agreed on by the parties. Similarly, under Article 64, the seller can avoid obligations under the contract if the buyer breaches the contract, fails to accept delivery of the goods, or fails to pay for the goods.

The CISG also allows for specific performance as a remedy under Article 28, which provides that "one party is entitled to require performance of any obligation by the other party." Nevertheless, a court may grant specific performance under Article 28 only if it would do so "under its own [national] law." As already discussed, U.S. courts normally grant specific performance only if no adequate remedy at law (monetary damages) is available and the goods are unique in nature. In other countries, such as Germany, however, specific performance is a commonly granted remedy for breach of contract.

## Reviewing: Performance and Breach of Sales and Lease Contracts

GFI, Inc., a Hong Kong company, makes audio decoder chips, an essential component in the manufacture of smartphones. Egan Electronics contracts with GFI to buy 10,000 chips on an installment contract, with 2,500 chips to be shipped every three months, F.O.B. Hong Kong, via Air Express. At the time for the first delivery, GFI delivers only 2,400 chips. GFI explains, however, that although the shipment is 4 percent short, the chips are of a higher quality than those specified in the contract and are worth 5 percent more. Egan accepts the shipment and pays GFI the contract price.

At the time for the second shipment, GFI makes a shipment identical to the first. Egan again accepts and pays for the chips. At the time for the third shipment, GFI ships 2,400 of the same chips, but this time GFI sends them via Hong Kong Air instead of Air Express. While in transit, the chips are destroyed. When it is time for the fourth shipment, GFI again sends 2,400 chips, but this time Egan rejects the chips without explanation. Using the information presented in the chapter, answer the following questions.

1. Did GFI have a legitimate reason to expect that Egan would accept the fourth shipment? Why or why not?
2. Did the substitution of carriers in the third shipment constitute a breach of the contract by GFI? Explain.
3. Suppose that the silicon used for the chips becomes unavailable for a period of time. Consequently, GFI cannot manufacture enough chips to fulfill the contract but does ship as many as it can to Egan. Under what doctrine might a court release GFI from further performance of the contract?
4. Under the UCC, does Egan have a right to reject the fourth shipment? Why or why not?

**Debate This** . . .  *If a contract specifies a particular carrier, then the shipper must use that carrier or be in breach of the contract—no exceptions should ever be allowed.*

## Terms and Concepts

| | | |
|---|---|---|
| conforming goods 267 | installment contract 271 | replevin 278 |
| cover 278 | letter of credit 284 | tender of delivery 267 |
| cure 270 | perfect tender rule 269 | |

## Issue Spotters

1. Country Fruit Stand orders eighty cases of peaches from Downey Farms. Without stating a reason, Downey delivers thirty cases instead of eighty and delivers at the wrong time. Does Country have the right to reject the shipment? Explain. (See *Obligations of the Seller or Lessor*.)

2. Brite Images agrees to sell Poster Planet five thousand posters of celebrities, to be delivered on May 1. On April 1, Brite repudiates the contract. Poster Planet informs Brite that it expects delivery. Can Poster Planet sue Brite without waiting until May 1? Why or why not? (See *Obligations of the Buyer or Lessee*.)

• Check your answers to the Issue Spotters against the answers provided in Appendix B at the end of this text.

## Business Scenarios

**14–1. Anticipatory Repudiation.** Moore contracted in writing to sell her 2017 Hyundai Santa Fe to Hammer for $18,500. Moore agreed to deliver the car on Wednesday, and Hammer promised to pay the $18,500 on the following Friday. On Tuesday, Hammer informed Moore that he would not be buying the car after all. By Friday, Hammer had changed his mind again and tendered $18,500 to Moore. Moore, although she had not sold the car to another party, refused the tender and refused to deliver. Hammer claimed that Moore had breached their contract. Moore contended that Hammer's repudiation released her from her duty to perform under the contract. Who is correct, and why? (See *Obligations of the Buyer or Lessee*.)

**14–2. Remedies of the Buyer or Lessee.** Lehor collects antique cars. He contracts to purchase spare parts for a 1938 engine from Beem. These parts are not made anymore and are scarce. To obtain the contract with Beem, Lehor agrees to pay 50 percent of the purchase price in advance. Lehor sends the payment on May 1, and Beem receives it on May 2. On May 3, Beem, having found another buyer willing to pay substantially more for the parts, informs Lehor that he will not deliver as contracted. That same day, Lehor learns that Beem is insolvent. Discuss fully any possible remedies available to Lehor to enable him to take possession of these parts. (See *Remedies of the Buyer or Lessee*.)

## Business Case Problems

**14–3. Spotlight on Revocation of Acceptance—Remedies of the Buyer.** L.V.R.V., Inc., sells recreational vehicles (RVs) in Las Vegas, Nevada, as Wheeler's Las Vegas RV. In September 1997, Wheeler's sold a Santara RV made by Coachmen Recreational Vehicle Co. to Arthur and Roswitha Waddell. The Waddells hoped to spend two or three years driving around the country, but almost immediately—and repeatedly—they experienced problems with the RV. Its entry door popped open. Its cooling and heating systems did not work properly. Its batteries did not maintain a charge. Most significantly, its engine overheated when ascending a moderate grade. The Waddells brought it to Wheeler's service department for repairs. Over the next year and a half, the RV spent more than seven months at Wheeler's. In March 1999, the Waddells filed a complaint in a Nevada state court against the dealer to revoke their acceptance of the RV. What are the requirements for a buyer's revocation of acceptance? Were the requirements

met in this case? In whose favor should the court rule? Why? [*Waddell v. L.V.R.V., Inc.*, 122 Nev. 15, 125 P.3d 1160 (2006)] (See *Remedies of the Buyer or Lessee*.)

**14–4. The Right to Recover Damages.** Woodridge USA Properties, L.P., bought eighty-seven commercial truck trailers from Southeast Trailer Mart, Inc. (STM). Gerald McCarty, an independent sales agent who arranged the deal, showed Woodridge the documents of title. They did not indicate that Woodridge was the buyer. Woodridge asked McCarty to sell the trailers, and within three months they were sold, but McCarty did not give the proceeds to Woodridge. Woodridge—without mentioning the title documents—asked STM to refund the contract price. STM refused. Does Woodridge have a right to recover damages from STM? Explain. [*Woodridge USA Properties, L.P. v. Southeast Trailer Mart, Inc.*, 412 Fed.Appx. 218 (11th Cir. 2011)] (See *Remedies of the Buyer or Lessee*.)

**14–5. Business Case Problem with Sample Answer—Nonconforming Goods.**  Padma Paper Mills, Ltd., converts waste paper into usable paper. In 2007, Padma entered into a contract with Universal Exports, Inc., under which Universal Exports certified that it would ship white envelope cuttings. Padma paid $131,000 for the paper. When the shipment arrived, however, Padma discovered that Universal Exports had sent multicolored paper plates and other brightly colored paper products. Padma accepted the goods but notified Universal Exports that they did not conform to the contract. Can Padma recover even though it accepted the goods knowing that they were nonconforming? If so, how? [*Padma Paper Mills, Ltd. v. Universal Exports, Inc.,* 34 Misc.3d 1236(A) (N.Y.Sup. 2012)] (See *Remedies of the Buyer or Lessee.*)

• **For a sample answer for Problem 14–5, go to Appendix C at the end of this text.**

**14–6. The Right of Rejection.** Erb Poultry, Inc., is a distributor of fresh poultry products in Lima, Ohio. CEME, LLC, does business as Bank Shots, a restaurant in Trotwood, Ohio. CEME ordered chicken wings and "dippers" from Erb, which were delivered and for which CEME issued a check in payment. A few days later, CEME stopped payment on the check. When contacted by Erb, CEME alleged that the products were beyond their freshness date, mangled, spoiled, and the wrong sizes. CEME did not provide any evidence to support the claims or arrange to return the products. Is CEME entitled to a full refund of the amount paid for the chicken? Explain. [*Erb Poultry, Inc. v. CEME, LLC,* 20 N.E.3d 1228 (Ohio App. 2 Dist. 2014)] (See *Remedies of the Buyer or Lessee.*)

**14–7. Remedies for Breach.** LO Ventures, LLC, doing business as Reefpoint Brewhouse in Racine, Wisconsin, contracted with Forman Awnings and Construction, LLC, for the fabrication and installation of an awning system over an outdoor seating area. After the system was complete, Reefpoint expressed concerns about the workmanship but did not give Forman a chance to make repairs. The brewhouse used the awning for two months and then had it removed so that siding on the building could be replaced. The parties disagreed about whether cracked and broken welds observed after the removal of the system were due to shoddy workmanship. Reefpoint paid only $400 on the contract price of $8,161. Can Reefpoint rescind the contract and obtain a return of its $400? Is Forman entitled to recover the difference between Reefpoint's payment and the contract price? Discuss. [*Forman Awnings*

*and Construction, LLC v. LO Ventures, LLC,* 360 Wis.2d 492, 864 N.W.2d 121 (2015)] (See *Remedies of the Buyer or Lessee.*)

**14–8. Remedies of the Buyer or Lessee.** M. C. and Linda Morris own a home in Gulfport, Mississippi, that was extensively damaged in Hurricane Katrina. The Morrises contracted with Inside Outside, Inc. (IO), to rebuild their kitchen. When the new kitchen cabinets were delivered, some defects were apparent, and as installation progressed, others were revealed. IO ordered replacement parts to cure the defects. Before the parts arrived, however, the parties' relationship deteriorated, and IO offered to remove the cabinets and refund the price. The Morrises also asked to be repaid for the installation fee. IO refused but emphasized that it was willing to fulfill its contractual obligations. At this point, are the Morrises entitled to revoke their acceptance of the cabinets? Why or why not? [*Morris v. Inside Outside, Inc.,* 185 So.3d 413 (Miss.App. 2016)] (See *Remedies of the Buyer or Lessee.*)

**14–9. A Question of Ethics—Revocation of Acceptance.**  Scotwood Industries, Inc., sells calcium chloride flake for use in ice melt products. Between July and September 2004, Scotwood delivered thirty-seven shipments of flake to Frank Miller & Sons, Inc. After each delivery, Scotwood billed Miller, which paid thirty-five of the invoices and processed 30 to 50 percent of the flake. In August, Miller began complaining about the product's quality. Scotwood assured Miller that it would remedy the situation. Finally, in October, Miller told Scotwood, "This is totally unacceptable. We are willing to discuss Scotwood picking up the material." Miller claimed that the flake was substantially defective because it was chunked. Calcium chloride maintains its purity for up to five years, but if it is exposed to and absorbs moisture, it chunks and becomes unusable. Scotwood sued to collect payment on the unpaid invoices. In response, Miller filed a counterclaim in a federal district court for breach of contract, seeking to recover based on revocation of acceptance, among other things. [Scotwood Industries, Inc. v. Frank Miller & Sons, Inc., 435 F.Supp.2d 1160 (D.Kan. 2006)] (See *Remedies of the Buyer or Lessee.*)

**(a)** What is revocation of acceptance? How does a buyer effectively exercise this option? Do the facts in this case support this theory as a ground for Miller to recover damages? Why or why not?

**(b)** Is there an ethical basis for allowing a buyer to revoke acceptance of goods and recover damages? If so, is there an ethical limit to this right? Discuss.

# Legal Reasoning Group Activity

**14–10. Performance Obligations.** Kodiak agrees to sell one thousand espresso machines to Lin to be delivered on May 1. Due to a strike during the last week of April, there is a temporary shortage of delivery vehicles. Kodiak can deliver the espresso makers two hundred at a time over a period of ten days, with the first delivery on May 1. (See *Obligations of the Buyer or Lessee.*)

**(a)** The first group will determine if Kodiak has the right to deliver the goods in five lots. What happens if Lin objects to delivery in lots?

**(b)** A second group will analyze whether the doctrine of commercial impracticability applies to this scenario and, if it does, what the result will be.

## CHAPTER 15

# Negotiable Instruments

Most commercial transactions would be inconceivable without negotiable instruments. A **negotiable instrument** is a signed writing that contains an unconditional promise or order to pay an exact amount, either on demand or at a specific future time. Recall that writings include electronic records.

A negotiable instrument can function as a substitute for cash or as an extension of credit. The checks that you receive are negotiable instruments that act as substitutes for cash. The promissory note that you probably signed to obtain an educational loan is a negotiable instrument that functions as an extension of credit. Because negotiable instruments originally were paper documents, they are sometimes referred to as *commercial paper*.

For a negotiable instrument to operate *practically* as either a cash substitute or a credit device, it is essential that the instrument be *easily transferable without danger of being uncollectible*. This is a fundamental function of negotiable instruments.

The law governing negotiable instruments grew out of commercial necessity. In the medieval world, merchants developed their own set of rules, which eventually became known as the *Lex Mercatoria* (Law Merchant). The Law Merchant was later codified in England and is the forerunner of Article 3 of the Uniform Commercial Code (UCC). Article 3 imposes special requirements for the form and content of negotiable instruments. It also governs their negotiation, or transfer.

## 15–1 Types of Negotiable Instruments

UCC 3–104(b) defines an *instrument* as a "negotiable instrument."[1] For that reason, whenever the term *instrument* is used in this book, it refers to a negotiable instrument. As mentioned, negotiable instruments are also sometimes referred to as *commercial paper*.

The UCC specifies four types of negotiable instruments: *drafts, checks, notes,* and *certificates of deposit* (CDs). These instruments, which are summarized briefly in Exhibit 15–1, frequently are divided into two classifications: *orders to pay* (drafts and checks) and *promises to pay* (promissory notes and CDs). We will discuss both classifications in the following subsections.

Negotiable instruments may also be classified as either demand instruments or time instruments. A *demand instrument* is payable on demand—that is, it is payable immediately after it is issued and thereafter for a reasonable period of time.[2] **Issue** is "the first delivery of an instrument by the maker or drawer . . . for the purpose of giving rights on the instrument to any person" [UCC 3–105]. All checks are demand instruments because, by definition, they must be payable on demand. A *time instrument* is payable at a future date.

### 15–1a Drafts and Checks (Orders to Pay)

A **draft** is an unconditional written order that involves *three parties*. The party creating the draft (the **drawer**) orders another party (the **drawee**) to pay money, usually to a third party (the **payee**). The most common type of draft is a check, but drafts other than checks may be used in commercial transactions.

---

1. Note that all of the references to Article 3 of the UCC in this chapter are to the 1990 version of Article 3, which has been adopted by almost all of the states.

2. "A promise or order is 'payable on demand' if it (i) states that it is payable on demand or at sight, or otherwise indicates that it is payable at the will of the holder, or (ii) does not state any time of payment" [UCC 3–108(a)]. The UCC defines a *holder* as "the person in possession of a negotiable instrument that is payable either to bearer or to an identified person [who] is the person in possession" [UCC 1–201(21)(A)]. The term *bearer* will be defined later in this chapter.

**EXHIBIT 15–1**  Basic Types of Negotiable Instruments

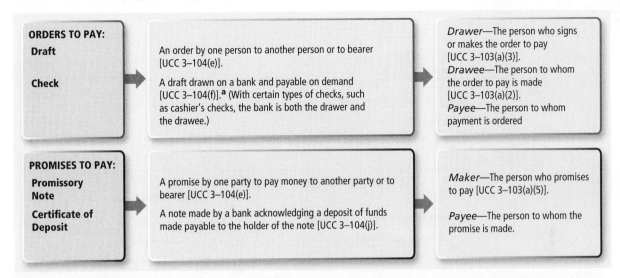

| ORDERS TO PAY: Draft | An order by one person to another person or to bearer [UCC 3–104(e)]. | *Drawer*—The person who signs or makes the order to pay [UCC 3–103(a)(3)]. |
| Check | A draft drawn on a bank and payable on demand [UCC 3–104(f)].ᵃ (With certain types of checks, such as cashier's checks, the bank is both the drawer and the drawee.) | *Drawee*—The person to whom the order to pay is made [UCC 3–103(a)(2)]. *Payee*—The person to whom payment is ordered |
| PROMISES TO PAY: Promissory Note | A promise by one party to pay money to another party or to bearer [UCC 3–104(e)]. | *Maker*—The person who promises to pay [UCC 3–103(a)(5)]. |
| Certificate of Deposit | A note made by a bank acknowledging a deposit of funds made payable to the holder of the note [UCC 3–104(j)]. | *Payee*—The person to whom the promise is made. |

a. Under UCC 4–105(1), banks include savings banks, savings and loan associations, credit unions, and trust companies (organizations that perform the fiduciary functions of trusts and agencies).

**Time Drafts and Sight Drafts**  A *time draft* is payable at a definite future time. A *sight draft* (or demand draft) is payable on sight—that is, when it is presented to the drawee (usually a bank or financial institution) for payment. A sight draft may be payable on acceptance.

**Acceptance** is the drawee's written promise to pay the draft when it comes due. Usually, an instrument is accepted by writing the word *accepted* across its face, followed by the date of acceptance and the signature of the drawee. A draft can be both a time and a sight draft. Such a draft is payable at a stated time after sight. An example would be a draft that states that it is payable ninety days after sight.

Exhibit 15–2 shows a typical time draft. For the drawee to be obligated to honor the order, the drawee must be obligated to the drawer either by agreement or through a debtor-creditor relationship. ■ **EXAMPLE 15.1** On January 16, OurTown Real Estate orders $1,000 worth of office supplies from Eastman Supply Company, with payment due April 16. Also on January 16, OurTown sends Eastman a draft drawn on its account with the First National Bank of Whiteacre as payment. In this scenario, the drawer is OurTown, the drawee is OurTown's bank (First National Bank of Whiteacre), and the payee is Eastman Supply Company. First National Bank is obligated to honor the draft because of its account agreement with OurTown Real Estate. ■

**Trade Acceptances**  A trade acceptance is a type of draft that is frequently used in the sale of goods. In a **trade acceptance,** the seller of the goods is both the drawer and the payee. The buyer to whom credit is extended is the drawee. Essentially, the draft orders the buyer to pay a specified amount to the seller, usually at a stated time in the future.

■ **EXAMPLE 15.2** Jackson Street Bistro buys its restaurant supplies from Osaka Industries. When Jackson requests supplies, Osaka creates a draft ordering Jackson to pay Osaka for the supplies within ninety days and sends it along with the supplies. When the supplies arrive, Jackson accepts the draft by signing its face and is then obligated to make the payment. This signed draft is a trade acceptance and can be sold to a third party if Osaka needs cash before the payment is due. (Osaka would sell the draft through the *commercial money market*—the market that businesses use for short-term borrowing.) ■

When a draft orders the buyer's bank to pay, it is called a **banker's acceptance.** Banker's acceptances are commonly used in international trade.

**Checks**  As mentioned, the most commonly used type of draft is a **check.** Although fewer checks are written today and most transactions are electronic, checks are still more common than promissory notes or other types of negotiable instruments. (For a discussion of mobile payment

**EXHIBIT 15–2  A Typical Time Draft**

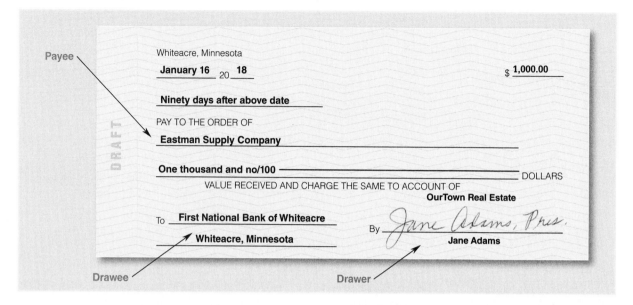

apps, which are increasingly popular as alternatives to checks, see this chapter's *Digital Update* feature.)

Checks are demand instruments because they are payable on demand. Most commonly, the writer of the check is the drawer, the bank on which the check is drawn is the drawee, and the person to whom the check is made payable is the payee. On certain types of checks, such as *cashier's checks,* the bank is both the drawer and the drawee. A cashier's check functions the same as cash because the bank has committed itself to paying the stated amount on demand.

### 15–1b  Promissory Notes (Promises to Pay)

A **promissory note** is a written promise made by one person (the **maker** of the promise) to pay another (usually a payee) a specified sum. A promissory note, which is often referred to simply as a *note,* can be made payable at a definite time or on demand. It can name a specific payee or merely be payable to bearer (bearer instruments will be discussed later in this chapter).

■ **EXAMPLE 15.3**  On April 30, Laurence and Margaret Roberts sign a writing unconditionally promising to pay "to the order of" the First National Bank of Whiteacre $3,000 (with 8 percent interest) on or before June 29. This writing is a promissory note. Laurence and Margaret Roberts are the note's co-makers, and the First National Bank of Whiteacre is the payee. ■ A typical promissory note is shown in Exhibit 15–3.

Promissory notes are commonly assigned (negotiated, or transferred) from one lender, or payee, to another. Assignment does not affect the maker's obligation to pay the note as promised. Promissory notes are also used in a variety of credit transactions. ■ **EXAMPLE 15.4**  Nadine Fuller signs a promissory note to purchase an Ultra HD television. The note, which is payable in installments over a twelve-month period, is called an *installment note.* ■

A promissory note is not a debt—it is only the evidence of a debt. But does the loss of a note affect the rights of the owner? That was the question in the following case.

**Case 15.1**

# Silicon Valley Bank v. Miracle Faith World Outreach, Inc.

Appellate Court of Connecticut, 140 Conn.App. 827, 60 A.3d 343 (2013).

**Company Profile**  *Miracle Faith World Outreach, Inc., a religious corporation, was founded by Bobby and Christine Davis in 1964. The Miracle Faith World Outreach Church started with prayer meetings in Christine's mother's home in Stamford, Connecticut. As its numbers grew, the church expanded first into*

**Case 15.1 Continued**

*the basement of a three-family house and later into churches in Springdale and Stamford before buying a new facility in Monroe. The twenty-acre property included a two-story church building and a fellowship hall totaling more than twenty thousand square feet.*

**Background and Facts**  Miracle Faith World Outreach borrowed $1,962,000 to buy the buildings and land in Monroe, signing a note payable to Silicon Valley Bank in Santa Clara, California. In the seventh year of the note's ten-year term, with more than $1,600,000 owing on the principal and almost $60,000 owing on unpaid interest, Miracle Faith defaulted. Silicon Valley filed an action in a Connecticut state court to foreclose. Eugene Wong, an associate at the bank, provided the court with only a copy of the note. Wong said that he had looked for the original at several of the bank's offices and at a third-party storage facility, but had been unable to find it. The court decided in the bank's favor, and Miracle Faith appealed. The church argued that "the court abused its discretion by determining that the plaintiff was the owner and holder of the note" even though the bank could produce only a copy.

## In the Language of the Court
*BEACH,* J. [Judge]
\* \* \* \*

A bill or note is not a debt; it is only primary evidence of a debt; and where this is lost, impaired or destroyed bona fide, it may be supplied by secondary evidence \* \* \*. The loss of a bill or note alters not the rights of the owner, but merely renders secondary evidence necessary and proper. [Emphasis added.]

The Uniform Commercial Code \* \* \* addresses situations \* \* \* where the instrument sought to be enforced is unavailable, by creating an exception to the general rule that one must hold an instrument in order to enforce its payment. General Statutes Section 42a–3–309(a) [Connecticut's version of UCC 3–309(a)] provides:

> "A person not in possession of an instrument is entitled to enforce the instrument if (i) the person was in possession of the instrument and entitled to enforce it when loss of possession occurred, (ii) the loss of possession was not the result of a transfer by the person or a lawful seizure, and (iii) the person cannot reasonably obtain possession of the instrument because the instrument was destroyed, its whereabouts cannot be determined, or it is in the wrongful possession of an unknown person or a person that cannot be found or is not amenable to service of process."

Here, the court found that the plaintiff had sustained its burden of showing that the note was lost and that the copy it produced was authentic.

The plaintiff established that it had entered into a transaction including a promissory note secured by a mortgage, a term loan agreement, and a mortgage with the defendant. Wong testified that ordinarily the original note would have been kept in the plaintiff's California headquarters. After a period of time, it would have been sent to a third-party storage facility. Wong testified that he checked "all the places where the note could possibly be," but he was unable to locate it. Although the original was lost, a copy of the note had been kept in the plaintiff's credit file for the subject loan. Although the defendant takes issue with the admission of the copy of the note, it does not claim that the copy was in any way inaccurate. The court, therefore, did not abuse its discretion in admitting a copy of the note.

**Decision and Remedy**  *A state intermediate appellate court concluded that the lower court did not abuse its discretion in admitting a copy of the note and affirmed the judgment. A note is not a debt—it is only evidence of a debt—and its loss does not alter the rights of the owner. The bank showed that the note was lost and that the copy it produced was authentic.*

### Critical Thinking
- **Legal Environment**  *Wong testified that he had looked for the note at a third-party storage facility. If the note had been found there, would that mean that the note had been "transferred" to the facility, making the storage company the holder of the instrument? Explain.*
- **Technological**  *If a note is the best primary evidence of the existence of a debt, what might be the best evidence of the amount of the debt and the interest calculation?*

**EXHIBIT 15–3** A Typical Promissory Note

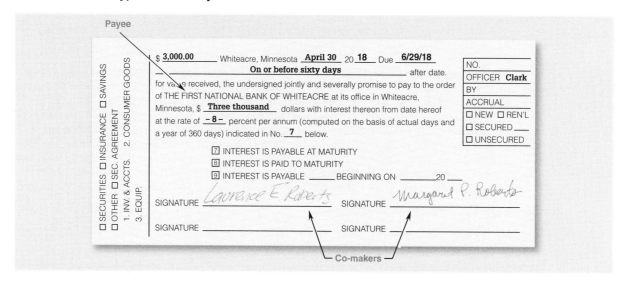

## 15–1c Certificates of Deposit (Promises to Pay)

A **certificate of deposit (CD)** is another type of note. A CD is issued when a party deposits funds with a bank and the bank promises to repay the funds, with interest, on a certain date [UCC 3–104(j)]. The bank is the maker of the note, and the depositor is the payee. ■ **EXAMPLE 15.5** On February 15, Sara Levin deposits $5,000 with the First National Bank of Whiteacre. The bank promises to repay the $5,000, plus 3.25 percent annual interest, on August 15. ■ Exhibit 15–4 shows an example of a small CD.

Because CDs are time deposits, the purchaser-payee typically is not allowed to withdraw the funds before the date of maturity (except in limited circumstances, such as disability or death). If a payee wants to access the funds before the maturity date, he or she can sell (negotiate) the CD to a third party. CDs in small denominations (for amounts up to $100,000) are often sold by savings and loan associations, savings banks, commercial banks, and credit unions.

## 15–2 Requirements for Negotiability

For an instrument to be negotiable, it must meet the following requirements:

1. Be in writing.
2. Be signed by the maker or the drawer.

3. Be an unconditional promise or order to pay.
4. State a fixed amount of money.
5. Be payable on demand or at a definite time.
6. Be payable to order or to bearer.

## 15–2a Written Form

Negotiable instruments must be in written form (but may be evidenced by electronic record) [UCC 3–103(a) (6), (9)].[3] Clearly, an oral promise can create the danger of fraud or make it difficult to determine liability.

1. The writing must be on material that lends itself to *permanence.* Promises carved in blocks of ice or inscribed in the sand or on other impermanent surfaces would not qualify as negotiable instruments. The UCC nevertheless gives considerable leeway as to what can be a negotiable instrument. ■ **EXAMPLE 15.6** Checks and notes have been written on napkins, menus, tablecloths, shirts, and a variety of other materials. Courts will enforce negotiable instruments written on these odd types of materials. ■

2. The writing must also have *portability.* Although the UCC does not explicitly state this requirement, if an instrument is not movable, it obviously cannot meet the requirement that it be freely transferable. ■ **EXAMPLE 15.7** Cullen writes on the side of

---

3. Under the Uniform Electronic Transactions Act (UETA), an electronic record may be sufficient to constitute a negotiable instrument (see UETA Section 16). A small number of states have also adopted amendments to Article 3 that explicitly authorize electronic negotiable instruments.

**EXHIBIT 15–4** A Sample Certificate of Deposit

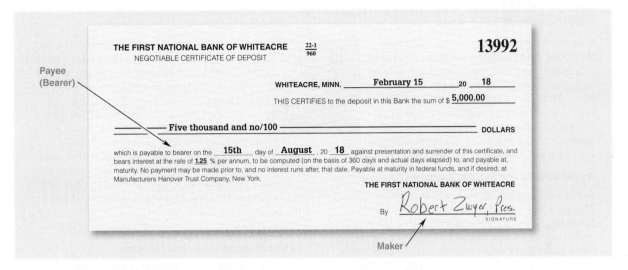

a cow, "I, Cullen, promise to pay $500 to the order of Merrill." Technically, this would meet the requirements of a negotiable instrument—except for portability. Because a cow cannot easily be transferred in the ordinary course of business, the "instrument" is nonnegotiable. ■

### 15–2b Signatures

For an instrument to be negotiable, it must be signed by (1) the maker if it is a note or a certificate of deposit or (2) the drawer if it is a draft or a check [UCC 3–103(a)(3), (5)]. If a person signs an instrument as an authorized *agent* for the maker or drawer, the maker or drawer has effectively signed the instrument [UCC 3–402].

**Signature Requirements** The UCC is quite lenient with regard to what constitutes a signature. Nearly any symbol executed or adopted by a person with the intent to authenticate a written or electronic document can be a **signature** [UCC 1–201(37)]. A signature can be made by a device, such as a rubber stamp, or a thumbprint, and can consist of any name, including a trade or assumed name, or a word, mark, or symbol [UCC 3–401(b)]. If necessary, parol evidence (such as oral testimony) is admissible to identify the signer. When the signer is identified, the signature becomes effective.

Although there are almost no limitations on the manner in which a signature can be made, one should be careful about receiving an instrument that has been signed in an unusual way. Oddities on a negotiable instrument can open the door to disputes and lead to litigation. Furthermore, an unusual signature clearly will decrease the *marketability* of an instrument because it creates uncertainty.

**Placement of the Signature** The location of the signature on the document is unimportant, although the usual place is the lower right-hand corner. ■ **EXAMPLE 15.8** A *handwritten* statement on the body of the instrument, such as "I, Kammie Orlik, promise to pay Janis Tan," is sufficient to act as a signature. ■

### 15–2c Unconditional Promise or Order to Pay

The terms of the promise or order must be included in the writing on the face of a negotiable instrument. The terms must also be *unconditional*—that is, they cannot be conditioned on the occurrence or nonoccurrence of some other event or agreement [UCC 3–104(a)].

**Promises** For an instrument to be negotiable, it must contain an express promise or order to pay. ■ **EXAMPLE 15.9** Kyra executes a promissory note that says "I promise to pay Alvarez $1,000 on demand for the purchase of these goods." These words satisfy the promise-to-pay requirement. ■

A mere acknowledgment of the debt, such as an I.O.U. ("I owe you"), might logically *imply* a promise, but it is *not* sufficient under the UCC. This is because the UCC requires that a promise be an *affirmative* (express) undertaking [UCC 3–103(a)(9)]. In contrast, if such words as

## DIGITAL UPDATE — Pay with Your Smartphone

A payment revolution is going on right now. Starting in 2009, customers at certain Starbucks locations in New York, San Francisco, and Seattle could use an iPhone app to pay for their lattes. By 2016, thousands of Starbucks locations were accepting payments from all types of smartphone-based operating systems. Some experts estimate that smartphone point-of-sale payments will total more than $61 billion in 2017.

### Apple Enters the Mobile Payments Arena

Apple, Inc., provides its own mobile payment and "digital wallet" service, called Apple Pay. Owners of Apple iPhones and iPads sold after 2014, along with its Apple Watch, have access to the service. Apple Pay enables these devices to communicate wirelessly with special point-of-sale systems using near field communication (NFC) technology. A person using an iPhone holds it close to the point-of-sale terminal and authenticates the transaction by holding a fingerprint to the phone's Touch ID sensor. Customers' payment information is kept private from the retailer. The system generates a "dynamic security code" for each transaction.

### Google and Samsung Provide Competition

Google created the Google Wallet wireless payment system even before Apple Pay was launched. Then, in 2015, Google and the mobile payments company Softcard contracted with AT&T, T-Mobile USA, and Verizon Wireless to preinstall Google Wallet in smartphones sold by those three companies.

Google's Android system is used on most Samsung smartphones. Samsung, a fierce competitor of Apple, announced in 2015 its purchase of LoopPay, a mobile payments startup. Also in 2015, Samsung created a direct competitor to Apple Pay called Samsung Pay. It was designed to work with existing magnetic-strip credit-card machines as well as the newer NFC technology.

### Linking Digital Wallets to Other Apps on a Smartphone

The ultimate goal in this modern payment system world is a link from a digital wallet to another app within a single smartphone. For instance, Google allows its Google Wallet to link to its Google Offers, which is a discount-deal app. Mobile payment systems will eventually be tied to rewards programs and special offers at individual stores.

**Critical Thinking** *Does having a digital wallet in a smartphone entail more security risks than carrying a physical wallet? Explain.*

---

"to be paid on demand" or "due on demand" are added to an I.O.U., the need for an express promise is satisfied.

A certificate of deposit is exceptional in this respect because no express promise is required. The bank's acknowledgment of the deposit and the other terms of the instrument clearly indicate a promise by the bank to repay the sum of money [UCC 3–104(j)].

**Orders** An *order* is associated with three-party instruments, such as checks, drafts, and trade acceptances. An order directs a third party to pay the instrument as drawn. In the typical check, for instance, the word *pay* (to the order of a payee) is a command to the drawee bank to pay the check when presented, and thus it is an order.

A command, such as "pay," is mandatory in an order even if it is accompanied by courteous words, as in "Please pay" or "Kindly pay." Generally, the language used must indicate that a command, or order, is being given. Stating "I wish you would pay" does not fulfill this requirement.

An order may be addressed to one person or to more than one person, either jointly ("to A *and* B") or alternatively ("to A *or* B") [UCC 3–103(a)(6)].

**Unconditionality of the Promise or Order** Only *unconditional* promises or orders can be negotiable [UCC 3–104(a)]. A promise or order is conditional (and *not* negotiable) if it states *any* of the following:

1. An express condition to payment.
2. That the promise or order is subject to or governed by another writing.
3. That the rights or obligations with respect to the promise or order are stated in another writing.

A mere *reference* to another writing or record does not of itself make the promise or order conditional [UCC 3–106(a)]. For instance, including the phrase "as per contract" or "This debt arises from the sale of goods X and Y" does not render an instrument nonnegotiable. Similarly, a statement in the instrument that payment can be made only out of a particular fund or source (such as the proceeds of a particular crop) will not render the instrument nonnegotiable [UCC 3–106(b)(ii)].

■ **CASE IN POINT 15.10**   Sam and Odalis Groome entered into two contracts to buy a pair of alpacas from Alpacas of America, LLC (AOA). To finance the purchases, the buyers signed two notes, one for $18,750 and one for $20,250. Each note included a reference to a contract, a payment schedule, and a security agreement, which provided an interest in the alpacas to secure payment. Within a few months, the Groomes stopped making payments. When AOA sued to collect the unpaid amounts, the Groomes argued that the notes were nonnegotiable because they referred to and were governed by other writings (the contracts). Ultimately, a state appellate court ruled that the Groomes' notes did contain unconditional promises to pay and thus were negotiable.[4] ■

In contrast, if the payment is to be made from a fund that does not yet exist, or is conditioned on the occurrence of some future event, the instrument will be non-negotiable.   ■ **EXAMPLE 15.11**   Duffy's note promises to pay Sherman from the trust account that Duffy will establish when he receives the proceeds from his father's estate. This promise is conditional, and the note is non-negotiable. ■

In the following case, the court considered the negotiability of a note that included a reference to a mortgage. The makers of the note argued that this reference rendered the note nonnegotiable.

4. *Alpacas of America, LLC v. Groome,* 179 Wash.App. 391, 317 P.3d 1103 (2014).

**Case Analysis 15.2**

## OneWest Bank, FSB v. Nunez

District Court of Appeal of Florida, Fourth District, 41 Fla.L.Weekly D540, __ So.3d __ (2016).

### In the Language of the Court
WARRER, J. [Judge]
* * * *

* * * Jose and Jessica Nunez, and Felipa Delrio, executed [a] note to America's Wholesale Lender [Countrywide Home Loans, Inc.] together with a mortgage [to buy property in Hallandale, Florida]. The note and mortgage were assigned * * * to OneWest [Bank]. The [Nunezes and Delrio] defaulted, and OneWest filed a complaint [in a Florida state court] to foreclose on the mortgage [and collect on the note]. The [defendants] filed an answer * * *, including a claim that OneWest was not entitled to enforce the promissory note because it was not a negotiable instrument. They claimed that the note referred to and incorporated provisions of the mortgage, thus destroying its negotiability.

The promissory note in this case contains language that is standard in mortgage notes across the country. Specifically, Section 11 of the promissory note contains the following provision:

In addition to the protections given to the Note Holder under this Note, a Mortgage * * * dated the same date as this Note, protects the Note Holder from possible losses that might result

if I do not keep the promises that I make in this Note. That * * * Instrument describes how and under what conditions I may be required to make immediate payment in full of all amounts I owe under this Note.

The promissory note then includes a provision from the mortgage relating to transfer of the property, including that the lender may require immediate payment of all sums secured by the mortgage if the borrower transfers the property without the lender's consent.

At the foreclosure trial, the court held that the note was not negotiable, and thus, OneWest * * * could not maintain the action on the note or the foreclosure action. The court entered an order * * * dismissing the complaint. [OneWest appealed.]
* * * *

* * * The trial court erred in concluding that the note in question was non-negotiable. Florida has adopted the Uniform Commercial Code, including its provision on negotiability and enforcement of negotiable instruments. Under Florida Statutes Section 673.1041(1) [Florida's version of UCC 3–104(a)] the term "negotiable instrument" means:

An unconditional promise or order to pay a fixed amount of money, with or without interest or other charges described in the promise or order, if it:
* * * *

(c) Does not state any other undertaking or instruction by the person promising or ordering payment to do any act in addition to the payment of money.

Florida Statutes Section 673.1061 [UCC 3–106(a)] defines "unconditional" by stating those conditions that prevent it from being unconditional:

(1) Except as provided in this section, for the purposes of [Florida Statutes] Section 673.1041(1), a promise or order is unconditional unless it states:
(a) An express condition to payment;
(b) That the promise or order is subject to or governed by another writing; or
(c) That rights or obligations with respect to the promise or order are stated in another writing. A reference to another writing does not of itself make the promise or order conditional.
(2) A promise or order is not made conditional:

Case 15.2 Continues

(a) By a reference to another writing for a statement of rights with respect to collateral, prepayment, or acceleration.

The UCC comments to this section address the inclusion of language regarding collateral and acceleration, and confirm that the inclusion of such language does not make the note conditional:

Many notes issued in commercial transactions are secured by collateral, are subject to acceleration in the event of default, or are subject to prepayment, or acceleration does not prevent the note from being an instrument if the statement is in the note itself. * * * In some cases it may be convenient not to include a statement concerning collateral, prepayment, or acceleration in the note, but rather to refer to an accompanying loan agreement,

security agreement or mortgage for that statement. [Florida Statutes Section 673.1061(2)(a)] allows a reference to the appropriate writing for a statement of these rights. * * *

*Thus, the mention of the mortgage instrument as to the * * * rights of acceleration in the promissory note does not destroy the unconditional nature of the note.* [Emphasis added.]

Two cases from other jurisdictions have considered the exact language contained in the promissory note in this case and concluded that it did not render the note non-negotiable. In [the first case], the court relied on the UCC comment to the statutory provision to conclude that "the reference to the mortgage, in Section 11 of the note, with respect to rights of acceleration does not render the note nonnegotiable." * * * [The

second case] * * * dealt with nearly identical language, including the incorporation of the acceleration on transfer provisions of the mortgage in the note. The bankruptcy judge found that the provisions were conditions regarding acceleration, permissible under Section 3-106(b) of the UCC and not destroying negotiability. *We agree with the foregoing authority that Section 11 of the note refers to the mortgage for a statement of rights with respect to * * * acceleration and thus does not render the note nonnegotiable.* [Emphasis added.]
* * * *

Because the court erred in dismissing the foreclosure proceeding based upon the non-negotiability of the promissory note, we reverse and remand for further proceedings.

**Legal Reasoning Questions**

1. The lower court concluded that the note was nonnegotiable and dismissed the bank's attempt to enforce it. Was this an error?

2. Suppose that the note in this case had stated, "The terms of the mortgage are by this reference made a part hereof." Would the result have been different?

3. How did the fact that "the promissory note in this case contains language that is standard in mortgage notes across the country" affect the court's reasoning?

## 15–2d A Fixed Amount of Money

Negotiable instruments must state with certainty a fixed amount of money to be paid at the time the instrument is payable [UCC 3–104(a)]. This requirement ensures that the value of the instrument can be determined with clarity and certainty.

**Fixed Amount** The term *fixed amount* (sometimes called *sum certain*) means that the amount must be ascertainable from the face of the instrument. Interest may be stated as a fixed or variable rate. A demand note payable with 10 percent interest meets the requirement of a fixed amount because its amount can be determined at the time it is payable [UCC 3–104(a)].

The rate of interest may also be determined with reference to information that is not contained in the instrument itself but is described by it, such as a formula or a source [UCC 3–112(b)]. For instance, an instrument that is payable at the *legal rate of interest* (a rate of interest

fixed by statute) is negotiable. Mortgage notes tied to a variable rate of interest (a rate that fluctuates as a result of market conditions) are also negotiable.

■ **CASE IN POINT 15.12** Alta Logistics, Inc., executed a promissory note to Bank of America (BOA) for the purpose of obtaining a revolving line of credit. The note stated the amount due as "the principal amount of One Hundred Twenty-Five Thousand 00/100 Dollars ($125,000.00) or so much as may be outstanding, together with interest on the unpaid outstanding principal balance of each advance." The note also indicated that the unpaid balance could be determined by indorsements on the note and BOA's internal records (including daily printouts).

Five years after the note came due, BOA filed an action against Alta to enforce the note. The court held that the note was not negotiable because it did not state a fixed amount on its face. This finding affected the statute of limitations for filing an action on the note. Since the note was not negotiable, UCC Article 3's six-year statute of limitations did not apply. The claim instead had to be treated as a breach of contract claim, which must be filed within four years. The court dismissed BOA's case because BOA did not file within this four-year statute of limitations period.[5] ■

**Payable in Money** UCC 3–104(a) provides that a fixed amount is to be *payable in money*. The UCC defines money as "a medium of exchange authorized or adopted by a domestic or foreign government as a part of its currency" [UCC 1–201(24)]. Gold is not a medium of exchange adopted by the U.S. government, so a note made payable in gold is nonnegotiable. An instrument payable in the United States with a face amount stated in a foreign currency can be paid in the foreign money or in the equivalent in U.S. dollars [UCC 3–107].

## 15–2e Payable on Demand or at a Definite Time

A negotiable instrument must "be payable on demand or at a definite time" [UCC 3–104(a)(2)]. To determine the value of a negotiable instrument, it is necessary to know when the maker, drawee, or *acceptor* is required to pay. (An **acceptor** is a drawee who has accepted, or agreed to pay, an instrument when it is presented later for payment.) It is also necessary to know when the obligations of secondary parties, such as *indorsers*,[6] will arise.

Furthermore, it is necessary to know when an instrument is due in order to calculate when the statute of limitations may apply [UCC 3–118(a)]. Finally, with an interest-bearing instrument, it is necessary to know the exact interval during which the interest will accrue to determine the instrument's value at the present time.

**Payable on Demand** Instruments that are payable on demand include those that contain the words "Payable at sight" or "Payable upon presentment." **Presentment** occurs when a demand to either pay or accept an instrument is made by or on behalf of a person entitled to enforce the instrument [UCC 3–501]. In other words, presentment occurs when a person brings the instrument to the appropriate party for payment or acceptance.

The very nature of the instrument may indicate that it is payable on demand. For instance, a check, by definition, is payable on demand [UCC 3–104(f)]. If no time

5. *Bank of America, N.A. v. Alta Logistics, Inc.*, 2015 WL 505373 (Tex. App.—Dallas 2015).
6. We should note that because the UCC uses the spelling *indorse* (*indorsement*, and the like), rather than the more common spelling *endorse* (*endorsement*, and the like), we adopt the UCC's spelling here and in other chapters in this text.

for payment is specified and the person responsible for payment must pay on the instrument's presentment, the instrument is payable on demand [UCC 3–108(a)].

■ **CASE IN POINT 15.13** National City Bank gave Reger Development, LLC, a line of credit to finance potential development opportunities. Reger signed a promissory note requiring it to "pay this loan in full immediately upon Lender's demand." About a year later, the bank asked Reger to pay down the loan and stated that it would be reducing the amount of cash available through the line of credit. Reger sued, alleging that the bank had breached the terms of the note. The court ruled in the bank's favor. The promissory note was a demand instrument because it explicitly set forth the lender's right to demand payment at any time. Thus, National City had the right to collect payment from Reger at any time on demand.[7] ■

**Payable at a Definite Time** If an instrument is not payable on demand, to be negotiable it must be payable at a definite time. An instrument is payable at a definite time if it states *any* of the following:

1. That it is payable on a specified date.
2. That it is payable within a definite period of time (such as thirty days) after being presented for payment.
3. That it is payable on a date or time readily ascertainable at the time the promise or order is issued [UCC 3–108(b)].

The maker or drawee is under no obligation to pay until the specified date.

When an instrument is payable by the maker or drawer *on or before* a stated date, it is clearly payable at a definite time. The maker or drawer has the *option* of paying before the stated maturity date, but the payee can still rely on payment being made by the maturity date. The option to pay early does not violate the definite-time requirement. ■ **EXAMPLE 15.14** Ari gives Ernesto an instrument dated May 1, 2017, that indicates on its face that it is payable *on or before* May 1, 2018. This instrument satisfies the definite-time requirement. ■

In contrast, an instrument that is undated and made payable "one month after date" is clearly nonnegotiable. There is no way to determine the maturity date from the face of the instrument. Whether the time period is a month or a year, if the date is uncertain, the instrument is not payable at a definite time. ■ **EXAMPLE 15.15** An instrument states, "One year after the death of my grandfather, Jerome Adams, I promise to pay $5,000 to

7. *Reger Development, LLC v. National City Bank*, 592 F.3d 759 (7th Cir. 2010).

the order of Lucy Harmon. [Signed] Jacqueline Wells." It is nonnegotiable. The date that the instrument becomes payable is uncertain. ■

**Acceleration Clause** An **acceleration clause** allows a payee or other holder of a time instrument to demand payment of the entire amount due, with interest, if a specified event occurs. (A **holder** is any person in possession of a negotiable instrument that is payable either to the bearer or to an identified person that is the person in possession [UCC 1–201(20)].)

■ **EXAMPLE 15.16** Marta lends $1,000 to Ruth, who makes a negotiable note promising to pay $100 per month for eleven months. The note contains an acceleration provision. This provision permits Marta or any holder to immediately demand all the payments plus the interest owed to date if Ruth fails to pay an installment in any given month. Ruth fails to make the third payment. Marta accelerates the unpaid balance, and the note becomes due and payable in full. Ruth owes Marta the remaining principal plus any unpaid interest to that date. ■

Instruments that include acceleration clauses are negotiable because the exact value of the instrument can be ascertained. In addition, the instrument will be payable on a specified date if the event allowing acceleration does not occur [UCC 3–108(b)(ii)]. Thus, the specified date is the outside limit used to determine the value of the instrument.

**Extension Clause** The reverse of an acceleration clause is an **extension clause,** which allows the date of maturity to be extended into the future [UCC 3–108(b) (iii), (iv)]. To keep the instrument negotiable, the interval of the extension must be specified if the right to extend the time of payment is given to the maker or the drawer of the instrument. If, however, the holder of the instrument can extend the time of payment, the extended maturity date need not be specified.

■ **EXAMPLE 15.17** Alek executes a note that reads, "The maker has the right to postpone the time of payment of this note beyond its definite maturity date of January 1, 2018. This extension, however, shall be for no more than a reasonable time." A note with this language is not negotiable, because it does not satisfy the definite-time requirement. The right to extend is the maker's, and the maker has not indicated when the note will become due after the extension.

In contrast, suppose that Alek's note reads, "The holder of this note at the date of maturity, January 1, 2018, can extend the time of payment until the following June 1 or later, if the holder so wishes." This note is negotiable. The length of the extension does not have to

be specified, because the option to extend is solely that of the holder. After January 1, 2018, the note is, in effect, a demand instrument. ■

## 15–2f Payable to Order or to Bearer

Because one of the functions of a negotiable instrument is to serve as a substitute for cash, freedom to transfer is essential. To ensure a proper transfer, the instrument must be "payable to order or to bearer" at the time it is issued or first comes into the possession of the holder [UCC 3–104(a)(1)]. An instrument is not negotiable unless it meets this requirement.

**Order Instruments** An **order instrument** is an instrument that is payable (1) "to the order of an identified person" or (2) "to an identified person or order" [UCC 3–109(b)]. An identified person is the person "to whom the instrument is initially payable" as determined by the intent of the maker or drawer [UCC 3–110(a)]. The identified person, in turn, may transfer the instrument to whomever he or she wishes.

Thus, the maker or drawer is agreeing to pay either the person specified on the instrument or whomever that person might designate. In this way, the instrument retains its transferability. ■ **EXAMPLE 15.18** An instrument states, "Payable to the order of James Yung" or "Pay to James Yung or order." Clearly, the maker or drawer has indicated that payment will be made to Yung or to whomever Yung designates. The instrument is negotiable. ■

Note that with order instruments, the person specified must be identified with *certainty,* because the transfer of an order instrument requires the indorsement, or signature, of the payee. An *indorsement* is a signature placed on an instrument, such as on the back of a check, generally for the purpose of transferring one's ownership rights in the instrument. An order instrument made "Payable to the order of my nicest cousin," for instance, is not negotiable, because it does not clearly specify the payee.

**Bearer Instruments** A **bearer instrument** is an instrument that does not designate a specific payee [UCC 3–109(a)]. The term **bearer** refers to a person in possession of an instrument that is payable to bearer or indorsed in blank (with a signature only) [UCC 1–201(5), 3–109(a), 3–109(c)]. This means that the maker or drawer agrees to pay anyone who presents the instrument for payment.

Any instrument containing terms such as the following is a bearer instrument:

1. "Payable to the order of bearer."
2. "Payable to Simon Reed or bearer."
3. "Payable to bearer."

**4.** "Pay cash."

**5.** "Pay to the order of cash."

■ **CASE IN POINT 15.19** Amine Nehme applied for credit at the Venetian Resort Hotel Casino in Las Vegas, Nevada, and was granted $500,000 in credit. He signed a gambling marker—that is, a promise to pay a gambling debt—for $500,000. Nehme quickly lost that amount gambling. The Venetian presented the marker for payment to Nehme's bank, Bank of America, which returned it for insufficient funds. The casino's owner, Las Vegas Sands, LLC, filed a suit against Nehme for failure to pay a negotiable instrument.

The court held that the marker fit the UCC's definitions of negotiable instrument and check. It was a means for payment of $500,000 from Bank of America to the order of the Venetian. It did not state a time for payment and thus was payable on demand. It was also unconditional—that is, it stated no promise by Nehme other than the promise to pay a fixed amount of money. Therefore, the marker was a negotiable instrument, and the Venetian was entitled to enforce it.[8] ■

**Can Be Payable to Nonexistent Person.** In addition, an instrument that "indicates that it is not payable to an identified person" is a bearer instrument [UCC 3–109(a)(3)]. Thus, an instrument that is "payable to X" can be negotiated as a bearer instrument, as though it were payable to cash. Similarly, an instrument that is "payable to Captain America" is negotiable as a bearer instrument because it is obvious that it is payable to a *nonexistent person.*

**Cannot Be Payable to Nonexistent Organization.** The UCC does not accept an instrument issued to a *nonexistent organization* as payable to bearer, however [UCC 3–109, Comment 2]. Therefore, an instrument "payable to the order of the Camrod Company," if no such company exists, would not be a bearer instrument or an order instrument. In fact, the instrument would not qualify as a negotiable instrument at all.

See Concept Summary 15.1 for a convenient review of the basic rules governing negotiability.

## 15–3 Factors That Do Not Affect Negotiability

Certain ambiguities or omissions will not affect the negotiability of an instrument. Article 3's rules for interpreting ambiguous terms include the following:

8. *Las Vegas Sands, LLC v. Nehme*, 632 F.3d 526 (9th Cir. 2011).

**1.** Unless the date of an instrument is necessary to determine a definite time for payment, the fact that an instrument is undated does not affect its negotiability. A typical example is an undated check, which is still negotiable. If a check is not dated, under the UCC its date is the date of its issue [UCC 3–113(b)]. The issue date is the date on which the drawer first delivers the check to another person to give that person rights in the check.

**2.** Antedating or postdating an instrument does not affect its negotiability [UCC 3–113(a)]. *Antedating* occurs when a party puts a date on an instrument that precedes the actual calendar date. *Postdating* occurs when a party puts a date on an instrument that is after the actual date. ■ **EXAMPLE 15.20** Crenshaw draws a check on his account at First Bank, payable to Sirah Imports. He postdates the check by fifteen days. Sirah Imports can immediately negotiate the check, and, unless Crenshaw tells First Bank otherwise, the bank can charge the amount of the check to Crenshaw's account [UCC 4–401(c)]. ■

**3.** Handwritten terms outweigh typewritten and printed terms (preprinted terms on forms, for example), and typewritten terms outweigh printed terms [UCC 3–114]. ■ **EXAMPLE 15.21** Most checks are preprinted "Pay to the order of" followed by a blank line, making them order instruments. In handwriting, Travis inserts in the blank "Anita Delgado or bearer." The handwritten terms will outweigh the printed form, and the check will be a bearer instrument. ■

**4.** Words outweigh figures unless the words are ambiguous [UCC 3–114]. This rule becomes important when the numerical amount and the written amount on a check differ. ■ **EXAMPLE 15.22** Reirson issues a check payable to Reliable Appliance Company. For the amount, she fills in the number "$100" but writes out the words "One thousand and 00/100" dollars. The check is payable in the amount of $1,000. ■

**5.** When an instrument simply states "with interest" and does not specify a particular interest rate, the interest rate is the *judgment rate of interest* [UCC 3–112(b)]. The judgment rate of interest refers to a rate of interest fixed by statute that applies to court judgments.

**6.** A check is negotiable even if there is a notation on it stating that it is "nonnegotiable" or "not governed by Article 3." Any other instrument, however, can be made nonnegotiable by the maker's or drawer's conspicuously noting on it that it is "nonnegotiable" or "not governed by Article 3" [UCC 3–104(d)].

In the following case, the court was asked to compare the words and figures in a promissory note to determine its amount.

## Case 15.3

# Charles R. Tips Family Trust v. PB Commercial, LLC

Court of Appeals of Texas, Houston, First District, 459 S.W.3d 147 (2015).

**Background and Facts**   The Charles R. Tips Family Trust signed a promissory note in favor of Patriot Bank to obtain a loan to buy a house in Harris County, Texas. The note identified the principal amount of the loan as "ONE MILLION SEVEN THOUSAND AND NO/100 ($1,700,000.00) DOLLARS." (Note the inconsistency between the spelled-out amount, $1,007,000, and the numerals, $1,700,000.). The family trust then made payments totaling only $595,586. PB Commercial, LLC (PBC), acquired the note, sold the residence for $874,125, and pursued litigation in a Texas state court against the borrower, alleging default.

The defendant, Charles R. Tips Family Trust, argued that the written words in an instrument control. Thus, the note had been satisfied in full by the amount of the payments plus the sale price of the house. In fact, the trust pointed out that PBC had collected a surplus of $189,111. The court entered a judgment in PBC's favor. The trust appealed, arguing one issue—that the amount of the loan must be determined from the printed words in the note and not the numerals.

## In the Language of the Court

Michael *MASSENGALE*, Justice.

* * * *

* * * To recover on a promissory note on which the borrower has defaulted, PBC was required to prove that * * * a certain balance was due and owing on the note.

* * * *

* * * Under the Uniform Commercial Code, which governs negotiable instruments such as the Note, "if an instrument contains contradictory terms, * * * words prevail over numbers." * * * *This rule derives from the principle that writing words more likely represents the parties' true intentions than writing numbers.* [Emphasis added.]

* * * *

The Note * * * describes the original amount of the loan obligation as "ONE MILLION SEVEN THOUSAND AND NO/100 ($1,700,000.00) DOLLARS." The phrase "one million seven thousand and no/100 dollars" has a plain, unambiguous meaning, namely the sum of $1,007,000.00. Thus, the words and the numerals in the [Note] are in conflict, differing by $693,000.

* * * *

* * * It does not matter that the discrepancy between the words and numbers here is a large one. Neither [Texas Business & Commercial Code] Section 3.114 [Texas's version of UCC 3–114] nor Texas case law makes a distinction on the basis of the size of the obligation or the significance of the conflict in terms.

PBC argues that this case presents a unique circumstance in that the omission of a single word transforms "one million seven hundred thousand" into "one million seven thousand." If the former phrase were modified in any other way, according to PBC, we would be faced with either an ambiguous term or an unambiguous but absurd one. For example, PBC [proposes] a scenario in which a [clerk's] error rendered the phrase as "one seven hundred thousand," omitting the word "million." According to PBC, such an amount would be ambiguous, and the court would have to refer to the numerals and extrinsic [outside] evidence to resolve the ambiguity. But this hypothetical scenario has no bearing on this case because there is no ambiguity in the text here.

* * * *

*Here, the words "one million seven thousand" control over the numerals "$1,700,000" to set the amount of the promissory note.* [Emphasis added.]

**Decision and Remedy**   *A state intermediate appellate court reversed the judgment of the lower court. Under the UCC, "if an instrument contains contradictory terms, . . . words prevail over numbers." In this case, the note's words and numerals were in conflict. Thus, the words "one million seven thousand" controlled over the numerals "$1,700,000" as the amount of the promissory note.*

Case 15.3 Continued **Critical Thinking**

• **What If the Facts Were Different?** *Suppose that the note had described the amount of the loan as "ONE MILLION SEVEN HUNDRED THOUSAND AND NO/100 ($1,007,000.00) DOLLARS." What would have been the result?*

---

## Concept Summary 15.1

### Requirements for Negotiability

| | |
|---|---|
| **Must Be in Writing** | • A writing can be on anything that is readily transferable and that has a degree of permanence. |
| **Must Be Signed by the Maker or Drawer** | • The signature can be anywhere on the face of the instrument.<br>• It can be in any form (such as a word, mark, or rubber stamp) that purports to be a signature and authenticates the writing.<br>• A signature may be made in a representative capacity. |
| **Must Be a Definite Promise or Order** | • A promise must be more than a mere acknowledgment of a debt.<br>• The words "I/We promise" or "Pay" meet this criterion. |
| **Must Be Unconditional** | • Payment cannot be expressly conditional on the occurrence of an event.<br>• Payment cannot be made subject to or governed by another agreement. |
| **Must Be an Order or Promise to Pay a Fixed Amount** | • An amount may be considered a fixed sum even if payable in installments, with a fixed or variable rate of interest, or at a foreign exchange rate. |
| **Must Be Payable in Money** | • Any medium of exchange recognized as the currency of a government is money. |
| **Must Be Payable on Demand or at a Definite Time** | • Any instrument that is payable on sight, presentment, or issue or that does not state any time for payment is a demand instrument.<br>• An instrument is still payable at a definite time, even if it is payable on or before a stated date or within a fixed period after sight or if the drawer or maker has the option to extend the time for a definite period.<br>• Acceleration clauses do not affect the negotiability of the instrument. |
| **Must Be Payable to Order or to Bearer** | • An order instrument must identify the payee with reasonable certainty.<br>• An instrument whose terms indicate payment to no particular person is payable to bearer. |

## Reviewing: Negotiable Instruments

Robert Durbin, a student, borrowed funds from a bank for his education and signed a promissory note for their repayment. The bank lent the funds under a federal program designed to assist students at postsecondary institutions. Under this program, repayment ordinarily begins nine to twelve months after the student borrower fails to carry at least one-half of the normal full-time course load at his or her school. The federal government guarantees that the note will be fully repaid. If the student defaults on the repayment, the lender presents the current balance—principal, interest, and costs—to the government. When the government pays the balance, it becomes the lender, and the borrower owes the government directly.

Durbin defaulted on his note, and the government paid the lender the balance due and took possession of the note. Durbin then refused to pay the government, claiming that the government was not the holder of the note. The government filed a suit in a federal district court against Durbin to collect the amount due. Using the information presented in the chapter, answer the following questions.

1. Using the categories discussed in the chapter, what type of negotiable instrument was the note that Durbin signed (an order to pay or a promise to pay)? Explain.
2. Suppose that the note did not state a specific interest rate but instead referred to a statute that established the maximum interest rate for government-guaranteed school loans. Would the note fail to meet the requirements for negotiability in that situation? Why or why not?
3. For the government to be a holder, which method must have been used to transfer the instrument from the bank to the government?
4. Suppose that, in court, Durbin argues that because the school closed down before he could finish his education, there was a failure of consideration. That is, he did not get something of value in exchange for his promise to pay. Assuming that the government is a holder of the promissory note, would this argument likely be successful against it? Why or why not?

**Debate This** . . .   *Congress should pass a law disallowing all negotiable instruments that are not written on paper.*

## Terms and Concepts

| | | |
|---|---|---|
| acceleration clause 298 | draft 288 | negotiable instrument 288 |
| acceptance 289 | drawee 288 | order instrument 298 |
| acceptor 297 | drawer 288 | payee 288 |
| banker's acceptance 289 | extension clause 298 | presentment 297 |
| bearer 298 | holder 298 | promissory note 290 |
| bearer instrument 298 | issue 288 | signature 293 |
| certificate of deposit (CD) 292 | maker 290 | trade acceptance 289 |
| check 289 | | |

## Issue Spotters

1. Sasha owes $600 to Dale, who asks her to sign an instrument for the debt. Consider each of the following alternatives for the wording on that instrument:
   (a) "I.O.U. $600,"
   (b) "I promise to pay $600."
   (c) An instruction to Sasha's bank stating, "I wish you would pay $600 to Dale."
   Which of these phrases would prevent the instrument's negotiability? Why? (See *Requirements for Negotiability*.)

2. Marit worked for Town & Garden, a landscape design service owned by Donald. Marit signed a note payable to Donald to become a co-owner of Town & Garden. The note, which was undated, required installment payments, but Donald never asked for them. Is Marit's note a demand note? Explain. (See *Requirements for Negotiability*.)

• **Check your answers to the Issue Spotters against the answers provided in Appendix B at the end of this text.**

# Business Scenarios

**15–1. Negotiable Instruments.** Sabrina Runyan writes the following note on a sheet of paper: "I, the undersigned, do hereby acknowledge that I owe Leo Woo one thousand dollars, with interest, payable out of the proceeds of the sale of my horse, Lightning, next month. Payment is to be made on or before six months from date." Discuss specifically why this is not a negotiable instrument. (See *Types of Negotiable Instruments*.)

**15–2. Negotiability.** Juan Sanchez writes the following note on the back of an envelope: "I, Juan Sanchez, promise to pay Kathy Martin or bearer $500 on demand." Is this a negotiable instrument? Discuss fully. (See *Requirements for Negotiability*.)

**15–3. Promissory Notes.** A college student, Austin Keynes, wished to purchase a new entertainment system from Friedman Electronics, Inc. Because Keynes did not have the cash to pay for the entertainment system, he offered to sign a note promising to pay $150 per month for the next six months. Friedman Electronics, eager to sell the system to Keynes, agreed to accept the promissory note, which read, "I, Austin Keynes, promise to pay to Friedman Electronics or its order the sum of $150 per month for the next six months." The note was signed by Austin Keynes. A week later, Friedman Electronics, which was badly in need of cash, signed the back of the note and sold it to the First National Bank of Halston. Give the specific designation of each of the three parties on this note. (See *Types of Negotiable Instruments*.)

**15–4. Bearer Instruments.** Adam's checks are imprinted with the words "Pay to the order of" followed by a blank. Adam fills in an amount on one of the checks and signs it, but he does not write anything in the blank following the phrase "Pay to the order of." Adam gives this check to Beth. On another check, Adam writes in the blank "Carl or bearer." Which, if either, of these checks is a bearer instrument, and why? (See *Requirements for Negotiability*.)

# Business Case Problems

**15–5. Negotiability.** Michael Scotto borrowed $2,970 from Cindy Vinueza. Both of their signatures appeared at the bottom of a note. The note stated, "I Michael Scotto owe Cindy Vinueza $2,970 (two thousand and nine-hundred & seventy dollars) & agree to pay her back in full. Signed on this 26th day of September 2009." More than a year later, Vinueza filed a suit against Scotto to recover on the note. Scotto admitted that he had borrowed the funds, but he contended—without proof—that he had paid Vinueza in full. Is this note negotiable? Which party is likely to prevail? Why? [*Vinueza v. Scotto*, 30 Misc.3d 1229, 924 N.Y.S.2d 312 (1 Dist. 2011)] (See *Requirements for Negotiability*.)

**15–6. Business Case Problem with Sample Answer—Payable on Demand or at a Definite Time.** Abby Novel

signed a handwritten note that read, "Glen Gallwitz 1-8-2002 loaned me $5,000 at 6 percent interest a total of $10,000.00." The note did not state a time for repayment. Novel used the funds to manufacture and market a patented jewelry display design. More than seven years after Novel signed the note, Gallwitz filed a suit to recover the stated amount. Novel claimed that she did not have to pay because the note was not negotiable—it was incomplete. Is she correct? Explain. [*Gallwitz v. Novel*, 2011-Ohio-297 (5 Dist. 2011)] (See *Requirements for Negotiability*.)

- **For a sample answer to Problem 15–6, go to Appendix C at the end of this text.**

**15–7. Bearer Instruments.** Eligio Gaitan borrowed the funds to buy real property in Downers Grove, Illinois, and signed a note payable to Encore Credit Corp. Encore indorsed the note in blank. Later, when Gaitan defaulted on the payments, an action to foreclose on the property was filed in an Illinois state court by U.S. Bank, N.A. The note was in the bank's possession, but there was no evidence that the note had been transferred or negotiated to the bank. Can U.S. Bank enforce payment of the note? Why or why not? [*U.S. Bank National Association v. Gaitan*, 2013 IL App (2d) 120105-U, 2013 WL 160378 (2013)] (See *Requirements for Negotiability*.)

**15–8. Payable to Order or to Bearer.** Thomas Caraccia signed a note and mortgage in favor of VirtualBank to obtain funds to buy property in Palm Beach Gardens, Florida. VirtualBank indorsed the note in blank, making it bearer paper, and transferred possession of the note to Bank of America. Bank of America transferred the note to U.S. Bank, which later gave the note back to Bank of America to collect Caraccia's payments on behalf of U.S. Bank. When Caraccia defaulted on the payments, U.S. Bank filed a suit in a Florida state court against him, seeking to enforce the note and foreclose on the property. Caraccia contended that because the note was indorsed in blank and was not in the physical possession of U.S. Bank, the bank could not enforce it. Could the bank successfully argue that although it did not *physically* possess the note, it *constructively* possessed (exercised legal control over) it? Explain. [*Caraccia v. U.S. Bank, National Association*, 41 Fla.L.Weekly. D476, 185 So.3d 1277 (Dist.Ct.App. 2016)] (See *Requirements for Negotiability*.)

**15–9. A Question of Ethics—Promissory Notes.** In

*November 2000, Monay Jones signed a promissory note in favor of a mortgage company in the amount of $261,250. Jones used the deed to her home in Denver, Colorado, as collateral. Fifth Third Bank soon became the holder of the note. After Jones defaulted on a payment, in September 2001 she and the bank agreed to raise the note's balance to $280,231.23. She again defaulted. In November, the bank received a check from a third party as payment on Jones's note. It was the bank's policy to refuse personal checks in payoffs of large debts. The bank representative who worked on Jones's account noted receipt of the check in the bank's records and*

*forwarded it to the "payoff department." A week later, the bank discovered that the check had been lost without having been posted to Jones's account or submitted for payment. The bank notified Jones, and both parties searched, without success, for a copy of the check or evidence of the identity of its maker, the drawee bank, or the amount. In late 2002, the bank filed a suit in a Colorado state court to foreclose on Jones's home. She insisted that the note had been paid in full by a cashier's check issued by an Arkansas bank at the request of her deceased aunt. [Fifth Third Bank v. Jones, 168 P.3d 1 (Colo.App. 2007)] (See Types of Negotiable Instruments.)*

**(a)** What evidence supports a finding that Jones gave the bank a check? Does it seem more likely that the check was a cashier's check or a personal check? Would it be fair for a court to find that the check had paid the note in full?

**(b)** Under UCC 3–310, if a cashier's check or other certified check "is taken for an obligation, the obligation is discharged." The bank argued that it had not "taken [Jones's check] for an obligation" because the bank's internal administrative actions were still pending when the check was lost. Would it be fair for the court to rule in the bank's favor based on this argument? Why or why not?

## Legal Reasoning Group Activity

**15–10. Requirements for Negotiability.** Peter Gowin was an employee of a granite countertop business owned by Joann Stathis. In November 2015, Gowin signed a promissory note agreeing to pay $12,500 to become a co-owner of the business. The note was dated January 15, 2015—ten months before it was signed—and required Gowin to make installment payments starting in February 2015. Stathis told Gowin not to worry about the note and never requested any payments. Gowin continued to work at the business until 2017, when he quit, claiming that he owned half of the business. Stathis argued that Gowin was not a co-owner because he had never paid the $12,500 into the business. (See *Requirements for Negotiability.*)

**(a)** The first group will formulate an argument in favor of Stathis that Gowin did not own any interest in the business because he had not paid the $12,500.

**(b)** The second group will evaluate the strength of Gowin's argument. Gowin claimed that, because compliance with the stated dates was impossible, the note effectively did not state a date for its payment. It was thus a demand note under UCC 3–108(a). Gowin further argued that no demand for payment had been made. Therefore, his obligation to pay had not arisen, and the termination of his ownership interest in the granite business was improper.

## CHAPTER 16

# Transferability and Holder in Due Course

Once issued, a negotiable instrument can be transferred to others by *assignment* or by *negotiation*. Recall that an assignment is a transfer of rights under a contract. Under contract law principles, a transfer by assignment to an assignee gives the assignee only those rights that the assignor possessed. Any defenses that can be raised against an assignor can normally be raised against the assignee. This same rule applies when a negotiable instrument, such as a promissory note, is transferred by assignment to an assignee. The assignee receives only those rights in the instrument that the assignor had prior to the assignment.

In contrast, when an instrument is transferred by **negotiation,** the Uniform Commercial Code (UCC) provides that the transferee (the person to whom the instrument is transferred) becomes a *holder* [UCC 3–201(a)]. A holder receives, at the very least, the rights of the previous possessor [UCC 3–203(b), 3–305]. But unlike an assignment, a transfer by negotiation can make it possible for a holder to receive *more* rights in the instrument than the prior possessor had [UCC 3–305]. A holder who receives greater rights is known as a *holder in due course.*

## 16–1 Negotiation

As just described, negotiation is the transfer of an instrument in such form that the transferee becomes a holder. There are two methods of negotiating an instrument so that the receiver becomes a holder. The method used depends on whether the instrument is an *order instrument* or a *bearer instrument.*

### 16–1a Negotiating Order Instruments

An order instrument contains the name of a payee capable of indorsing, as in "Pay to the order of Jamie Fowler." If an instrument is an order instrument, it is negotiated by delivery with any necessary indorsements (discussed shortly). ■ **EXAMPLE 16.1** Welpac Corporation issues a payroll check "to the order of Elliot Goodseal." Goodseal takes the check to the bank, signs his name on the back (an indorsement), gives it to the teller (a delivery), and receives cash. Goodseal has negotiated the check to the bank [UCC 3–201(b)]. ■

Negotiating order instruments requires both delivery and indorsement. If Goodseal had taken the check to the bank and delivered it to the teller without signing it, the transfer would not qualify as a negotiation. In that situation, the transfer would be treated as an assignment, and the bank would become an assignee rather than a holder. In fact, whenever a transfer fails to qualify as a negotiation because it fails to meet one or more of the requirements of a negotiable instrument, it is treated as an assignment.

### 16–1b Negotiating Bearer Instruments

If an instrument is payable to bearer, it is negotiated by delivery—that is, by transfer into another person's possession. Indorsement is not necessary [UCC 3–201(b)]. The use of bearer instruments thus involves a greater risk of loss or theft than the use of order instruments.

■ **EXAMPLE 16.2** Alonzo Cruz writes a check payable to "cash," thus creating a bearer instrument. Cruz then hands the check to Blaine Parrington (a delivery). Parrington puts the check in his wallet, which is subsequently stolen. The thief now has possession of the check. At this point, the thief has no rights in the check. If the thief "delivers" the check to an innocent third person, however, negotiation will be complete. All rights to the check will pass *absolutely* to that third person, and Parrington will lose all right to recover the proceeds of the check from that person [UCC 3–306]. Of course, Parrington can recover his funds from the thief—if the thief can be found. ■

## 16–2 Indorsements

An indorsement is required whenever an order instrument is negotiated. An **indorsement** is a signature with or without additional words or statements. It is most often written on the back of the instrument itself. If there is no room on the instrument, the indorsement can be written on a separate piece of paper (called an *allonge*). That paper must be firmly affixed to the instrument, such as with staples. A paper firmly attached to a negotiable instrument is part of the instrument [UCC 3–204(a)].

A person who transfers a note or a draft by signing (indorsing) it and delivering it to another person is an **indorser.** The person to whom the check is indorsed and delivered is the **indorsee.** ■ **EXAMPLE 16.3** Luisa Perez receives a graduation check for $100. She can transfer the check to her mother (or to anyone) by signing it on the back. Luisa is an indorser. If Luisa indorses the check by writing "Pay to Avery Perez," Avery Perez is the indorsee. ■

There are four main categories of indorsements: blank, special, qualified, and restrictive. Note that a single indorsement may have characteristics of more than one category. In other words, these categories are not mutually exclusive.

### 16–2a Blank Indorsements

A **blank indorsement** does not specify a particular indorsee and can consist of a mere signature [UCC

**EXHIBIT 16–1** A Blank Indorsement

*Mark Deitsch*

3–205(b)]. ■ **EXAMPLE 16.4** A check payable "to the order of Mark Deitsch" can be indorsed in blank simply by writing Deitsch's signature on the back of the check. ■ Exhibit 16–1 shows a blank indorsement.

An order instrument indorsed in blank becomes a bearer instrument and can be negotiated by delivery alone [UCC 3–205(b)]. In other words, as will be discussed later, a blank indorsement converts an order instrument to a bearer instrument, which anybody can cash. ■ **EXAMPLE 16.5** Rita Chou indorses in blank a check payable to her order and then loses it on the street. If Schaefer finds the check, he can sell it to Duncan for value without indorsing it. This constitutes a negotiation because Schaefer has made delivery of a bearer instrument (which was an order instrument until it was indorsed in blank). ■

Does an instrument that requires an indorsement for negotiation need to contain the written signature of an individual's name? That was the question in the following case.

Case 16.1

## *In re* Bass
Supreme Court of North Carolina, 738 S.E.2d 173 (2013).

**Background and Facts** Tonya Bass signed a note with Mortgage Lenders Network USA, Inc., to borrow $139,988, repayable with interest in monthly installments of $810.75, to buy a house in Durham County, North Carolina. The note was transferred by stamped imprints to Emax Financial Group LLC, then to Residential Funding Corporation, and finally to U.S. Bank N.A. When Bass stopping paying on the note, U.S. Bank filed an action in a North Carolina state court to foreclose. The court issued an order permitting the foreclosure to proceed, and Bass appealed. She argued that the stamp transferring the note from Mortgage Lenders to Emax was invalid because it was not accompanied by a signature. A state intermediate appellate court issued a decision in Bass's favor based on the lack of a "proper indorsement." U.S. Bank appealed.

### In the Language of the Court
*MARTIN,* Justice.
　　* * * *

　　The UCC defines "signature" broadly, as "any symbol executed or adopted with present intention to adopt or accept a writing." The official comment explains that

**Case 16.1 Continued**

as the term "signed" is used in the Uniform Commercial Code, a complete signature is not necessary. The symbol may be printed, stamped or written; it may be by initials or by thumbprint. It may be on any part of the document and in appropriate cases may be found in a billhead or letterhead. No catalog of possible situations can be complete and the court must use common sense and commercial experience in passing upon these matters. The question always is whether the symbol was executed or adopted by the party with present intention to adopt or accept the writing.

Thus, the UCC does not limit a signature to a long-form writing of an individual person's name. Under this broad definition, the authenticating intent is sufficiently shown by the fact that the name of a party is written on the line which calls for the name of that party. Even if there might be some irregularities in the signature, the necessary intent can still be found based on the signature itself and other attendant circumstances. [Emphasis added.]

* * * [Bass] asserts the stamp by Mortgage Lenders does not qualify as an indorsement under [North Carolina General Statutes (N.C.G.S.)] Section 25–3–204(a) [North Carolina's version of UCC 3–204(a)]. She [contends] that an indorsement must include some representation of an individual signature to be valid.

The contested stamp indicates on its face an intent to transfer the debt from Mortgage Lenders to Emax:

Pay to the order of:
Emax Financial Group, LLC
without recourse
By: Mortgage Lenders Network USA, Inc.

In addition, the stamp appears on the page of the Note where other, uncontested indorsements were placed. We also observe that the original Note was indeed transferred in accordance with the stamp's clear intent. The stamp evidences that it was executed or adopted by the party with present intention to adopt or accept the writing. Under the broad definition of "signature" and the accompanying official comment, the stamp by Mortgage Lenders constitutes a signature.

* * * With no unambiguous evidence indicating the signature was made for any other purpose, the stamp was an indorsement that transferred the Note from Mortgage Lenders to Emax.

**Decision and Remedy** *The North Carolina Supreme Court reversed the decision of the lower court and held that U.S. Bank was the holder of the note. The indorsements on the note unambiguously indicated the intent of each creditor to transfer the note to a succeeding lender and finally to U.S. Bank.*

**Critical Thinking**

- **Legal Environment** *Even though forged or unauthorized signatures on negotiable instruments are uncommon, should U.S. Bank have had to prove that the indorsements on this note were valid and authorized? Why or why not?*
- **Economic** *How does the presumption that an indorsement is legitimate "without unambiguous evidence to the contrary" protect the transferability of a negotiable instrument?*

---

## 16–2b Special Indorsements

A **special indorsement** contains the signature of the indorser and identifies the person to whom the indorser intends to make the instrument payable—that is, it names the indorsee [UCC 3–205(a)]. ■ **EXAMPLE 16.6** Words such as "Pay to the order of Russell Clay" or "Pay to Russell Clay," followed by the signature of the indorser, are sufficient to identify the indorsee. ■ When an instrument is indorsed in this way, it is an order instrument.

To avoid the risk of loss from theft, a holder may convert a blank indorsement to a special indorsement by writing, above the signature of the indorser, words identifying the indorsee [UCC 3–205(c)]. This changes the bearer instrument back to an order instrument.

■ **EXAMPLE 16.7** A check is made payable to Hal Cohen. He signs his name on the back of the check—a blank indorsement—and negotiates the check by delivering it to William Hunter. Hunter is not able to cash the check immediately but wants to avoid any risk should he lose the check. He therefore writes "Pay to William Hunter" above Cohen's blank indorsement. In this manner, Hunter has converted Cohen's blank indorsement into a special indorsement. Further negotiation now requires William Hunter's indorsement, plus delivery. ■ Exhibit 16–2 shows a special indorsement.

In the following case, a note bore a series of special indorsements, ending in an assignment of the note to

**EXHIBIT 16–2 A Special Indorsement**

Pay to William Hunter

Hal Cohen

its holder at the time of the maker's default. The question was whether this indorsement and supporting evidence were sufficient to establish the holder's standing to enforce the note.

**Case Analysis 16.2**

# AS Peleus, LLC v. Success, Inc.
Appellate Court of Connecticut, 162 Conn.App. 750, 133 A.3d 503 (2016).

### In the Language of the Court
*GRUENDEL*, J. [Judge]
* * * *

This appeal concerns real property owned by the defendant [Success, Inc.] and known as 520 Success Avenue (property). That property is partially situated in Stratford and partially situated in Bridgeport [Connecticut]. * * * The defendant executed a promissory note (note) in favor of Greenpoint Mortgage Funding, Inc. (Greenpoint), in the principal amount of $525,000. The note was secured by two identical mortgage deeds on the property.

* * * When the defendant failed to make its * * * payments, the plaintiff [AS Peleus, LLC,] provided the defendant with written notice that it was in default of those obligations. The notice further stated that the plaintiff was "exercising its right under the loan documents to accelerate payment of the note" and therefore demanded "immediate payment and performance of all obligations under those documents * * * ." The defendant failed to comply with that demand, and the plaintiff commenced the present foreclosure action in [a Connecticut state court against the defendant].

* * * The court * * * found that the plaintiff "has proven through documents and testimony that it is the owner and

holder of the note * * * ." Accordingly, the court rendered a judgment of * * * foreclosure, and this appeal followed.
* * * *

The defendant claims that the court erroneously found that the plaintiff was the owner and holder of the note * * * in question.
* * * *

* * * *The holder of a note seeking to enforce the note through foreclosure must produce the note. The note must be endorsed so as to demonstrate that the foreclosing party is a holder, either by a specific endorsement to that party or by means of a blank endorsement to bearer* * * * . If the foreclosing party produces a note demonstrating that it is a valid holder of the note, the court is to presume that the foreclosing party is the rightful owner of the debt * * * . The defending party may rebut the presumption that the holder is the rightful owner of the debt, but bears the burden to prove that the holder of the note is not the owner of the debt * * * . The defending party does not carry its burden by merely identifying some documentary lacuna [gap] in the chain of title that might give rise to the possibility that a party other than the foreclosing party owns the debt * * * . *To rebut the presumption that the holder of a note endorsed specifically or to bearer is the rightful owner of the debt, the defending*

*party must prove that another party is the owner of the note and debt* * * * . Without such proof, the foreclosing party may rest its standing to foreclose * * * on its status as the holder of the note. [Emphasis added.]

In the present case, the plaintiff introduced the original note into evidence at trial * * * . The note contains a series of allonges, under which ownership of the note was transferred by special endorsement to various entities. In the first allonge appended thereto, Greenpoint assigned the note to "Citigroup Global Markets Realty Corp." In the second such allonge, the note was assigned to "Waterfall Victoria Master Fund, Ltd." In the third allonge, the note was assigned to "Waterfall Victoria Depositor, LLC." In the fourth allonge, the note was assigned to "Waterfall Victoria Mortgage Trust 2011–SBC1." In the fifth allonge, the note was assigned to "Citibank, N.A., as Trustee for CMLTI Asset Trust." In the sixth and final allonge, the note was assigned to the plaintiff.

The record thus demonstrates that the plaintiff produced the original note, which bore a special endorsement to the plaintiff. In so doing, the plaintiff established its *prima facie* case against the defendant. The plaintiff also submitted

Case 16.2 Continued

into evidence the * * * default notice that it provided to the defendant. * * * The defendant introduced no evidence in response.

Furthermore, the plaintiff offered the testimony of Russell Schaub at trial. Schaub was the chief operating officer of Gregory Funding, LLC, the plaintiff's mortgage servicing company. * * * Schaub indicated that he was personally familiar with the books and records of the plaintiff, which were maintained in the ordinary course of business by Gregory Funding, LLC. Schaub also testified that the plaintiff purchased the note from "an affiliate of Citigroup" * * * approximately six months prior to the commencement of this action. On that basis, Schaub testified that the plaintiff was the owner and holder of the note * * * at issue in this case.

* * * *

The record before us contains documentary and testimonial evidence that substantiates the court's finding that the plaintiff was the owner and holder of the note * * * in question. That finding, therefore, is not clearly erroneous.

* * * *

The judgment is affirmed.

### Legal Reasoning Questions

**1.** What evidence did the plaintiff offer to establish standing to enforce the note? Was this sufficient proof? Explain.

**2.** What might have been the result if the assignments of the note had ended with the indorsement on the fifth allonge?

**3.** If the series of indorsements on the note had ended with a blank indorsement, would the lower court's holding have been in error?

---

## 16–2c Qualified Indorsements

Generally, an indorser, *merely by indorsing,* impliedly promises to pay the holder, or any subsequent indorser, the amount of the instrument in the event that the drawer or maker defaults on the payment [UCC 3–415(a)]. Usually, then, indorsements are *unqualified indorsements.* In other words, the indorser is guaranteeing payment of the instrument in addition to transferring title to it.

An indorser who does not wish to be liable on an instrument can use a **qualified indorsement** to disclaim this liability [UCC 3–415(b)]. The notation "without recourse" is commonly used to create a qualified indorsement.

■ **EXAMPLE 16.8**  A check is made payable to the order of Sarah Jacobs. Sarah wants to negotiate the check to Allison Jong but does not want to assume liability for the check's payment. Sarah could create a qualified indorsement by indorsing the check as follows: "Pay to Allison Jong, without recourse, [signed] Sarah Jacobs" (see Exhibit 16–3). ■

**The Effect of Qualified Indorsements**  Qualified indorsements are often used by persons acting in a representative capacity (agents). For instance, insurance agents sometimes receive checks payable to them that are really intended as payment to the insurance company. The agent is merely indorsing the payment through to the insurance company and should not be required to make good on a check if it is later dishonored.

**EXHIBIT 16–3**  A Qualified Indorsement

> Pay to Allison Jong,
> without recourse
> Sarah Jacobs

The "without recourse" indorsement relieves the agent from any liability on the check. If the instrument is dishonored, the holder cannot recover from the agent who indorsed "without recourse" unless the indorser breached one of the transfer warranties. (Transfer warranties, which relate to such matters as good title and authorized signature, will be discussed in a later chapter.)

### Special versus Blank Qualified Indorsements

A qualified indorsement ("without recourse") can be accompanied by either a special indorsement or a blank indorsement. In either situation, the instrument still transfers title and can be further negotiated.

A special qualified indorsement includes the name of the indorsee as well as the words "without recourse," as shown in Exhibit 16–3. The special indorsement makes the instrument an order instrument, and it requires an indorsement, plus delivery, for negotiation.

A blank qualified indorsement ("without recourse, [signed] Jennie Cole") makes the instrument a bearer instrument, and only delivery is required for negotiation. ■ **CASE IN POINT 16.9** Thomas Brandt executed a promissory note with MortgageIT, Inc., to finance a home. Seven years later, Brandt still owed $132,000 on the note, and Green Tree Servicing, LLC, filed a suit to foreclose on the property. Brandt argued that MortgageIT had canceled the note because the note included an undated indorsement—"without recourse" to Wells Fargo Bank, NA—that had been crossed out and marked VOID. Another paper was attached to the note, however. It contained indorsements without recourse from MortgageIT to Countrywide Bank FSB, from Countrywide Bank FSB to Countrywide Home Loans, and from Countrywide Home Loans to blank. A state appellate court held that the note was payable to bearer. Because Green Tree Servicing was in possession of the note, it had title to, and was a holder of, the note. Therefore, the court ordered foreclosure on the property to pay Brandt's debt on the note to Green Tree.[1] ■

### 16–2d Restrictive Indorsements

A **restrictive indorsement** requires the indorsee to comply with certain instructions regarding the funds involved but does not prohibit further negotiation of the instrument [UCC 3–206(a)]. Although most indorsements are nonrestrictive, many forms of restrictive indorsements exist, including those discussed here.

**Indorsements to Pay Only a Named Payee** An indorsement such as "Pay to Julie Diaz only, [signed] Thomas Fasulo" does not destroy negotiability. Diaz can negotiate the paper to a holder just as if it had read "Pay to Julie Diaz, [signed] Thomas Fasulo" [UCC 3–206(a)]. If the holder gives value, this type of restrictive indorsement has the same legal effect as a special indorsement.

**Conditional Indorsements** When payment depends on the occurrence of some event specified in the indorsement, the instrument has a conditional indorsement [UCC 3–204(a)]. ■ **EXAMPLE 16.10** Keenan Barton indorses a check as follows: "Pay to Lars Johansen if he completes the renovation of my kitchen by June 1, 2019, [signed] Keenan Barton." Barton has created a conditional indorsement. ■

Article 3 states that an indorsement conditioning the right to receive payment "does not affect the right of the

indorsee to enforce the instrument" [UCC 3–206(b)]. A person paying or taking an instrument for value (*taking for value* will be discussed later in the chapter) can disregard the condition without liability.

The effect of a conditional indorsement, which appears on the back of an instrument, differs from the effect of conditional language that appears on the *face* (front) of an instrument. As noted, conditional indorsements need not prevent further negotiation. In contrast, an instrument with conditional language on its face is not negotiable, because it does not meet the requirement that a negotiable instrument must contain an unconditional promise to pay.

**Indorsements for Deposit or Collection** A common type of restrictive indorsement makes the indorsee (almost always a bank) a collecting agent of the indorser [UCC 3–206(c)]. In particular, the indorsements "For deposit only" and "For collection only" have the effect of locking the instrument into the bank collection process. Only a bank can acquire the rights of a holder following one of these indorsements until the item has been specially indorsed by a bank to a person who is not a bank [UCC 3–206(c), 4–201(b)]. Exhibit 16–4 illustrates this type of indorsement on a check payable and issued to Marcel Dumont.

**Trust (Agency) Indorsements** Indorsements to persons who are to hold or use the funds for the benefit of the indorser or a third party are called **trust indorsements** (also known as *agency indorsements*) [UCC 3–206(d), (e)]. ■ **EXAMPLE 16.11** Raj Gupta asks his accountant, Stephanie Malik, to pay some bills for him while he is out of the country. Gupta indorses his payroll check to Stephanie Malik "as agent for Raj Gupta." This trust (agency) indorsement obligates Malik to use the funds only for the benefit of Gupta. ■

**EXHIBIT 16–4** "For Deposit Only" and "For Collection Only" Indorsements

---

1. *Green Tree Servicing, LLC v. Brandt,* 2015 -Ohio- 4636, 2015 WL 6951589 (Ohio App. 2015).

The result of a trust indorsement is that legal rights in the instrument are transferred to the original indorsee. If the original indorsee pays or applies the proceeds consistently with the indorsement, the indorsee is a holder and can become a holder in due course (as described shortly). Sample trust (agency) indorsements are shown in Exhibit 16–5.

As noted, the original indorsee has a duty to use the funds only for the benefit of the indorser. This is a *fiduciary* duty—a duty mandated by a relationship involving trust and loyalty. The fiduciary restrictions on the instrument do not reach beyond the original indorsee, however [UCC 3–206(d), (e)]. Any subsequent purchaser can qualify as a holder in due course unless he or she has actual notice that the instrument was negotiated in breach of a fiduciary duty.

For a synopsis of the various indorsements and the consequences of using each type, see Concept Summary 16.1.

**EXHIBIT 16–5**  Trust (Agency) Indorsements

> Pay to Stephanie Malik as Agent for Raj Gupta
>
> Raj Gupta

or

> Pay to Ellen Cook in trust for Roger Callahan
>
> Roger Callahan

---

## Concept Summary 16.1

### Types of Indorsements and Their Effect

**Blank Indorsements**
- **Definition:** Indorser does not identify the person to whom the instrument is payable. This can merely consist of a signature, such as "Mary Bennett."
- **Effect:** Creates a bearer instrument, which can be negotiated by delivery alone.

**Special Indorsements**
- **Definition:** Indorser identifies the person to whom the instrument is payable, such as "Pay to the order of Roy Clark."
- **Effect:** Creates an order instrument. Negotiation requires indorsement and delivery.

**Qualified Indorsements**
- **Definition:** Indorser includes words indicating that he or she is not guaranteeing or assuming liability for payment, such as "Pay to Jack Leist without Recourse, Sarah Wu."
- **Effect:** Relieves indorser of any liability for payment of the instrument; frequently used by agents or others acting on behalf of another.

**Restrictive Indorsements**
- **Definition:** Indorser includes specific instructions regarding the funds involved or states a condition to the right of the indorsee to receive payment, such as "For Deposit (or Collection) Only."
- **Effect:** Only a bank can become a holder of instruments indorsed for deposit or collection. (In a trust indorsement, the agent has the rights of a holder but has a duty to use the funds consistent with the indorsement.)

## How Indorsements Can Convert Order Instruments to Bearer Instruments and Vice Versa

Earlier, we saw that order instruments and bearer instruments are negotiated differently. The method used for negotiation depends on the character of the instrument *at the time the negotiation takes place.* Indorsement can convert an order instrument into a bearer instrument and vice versa.

As mentioned earlier, an instrument payable to the order of a named payee and indorsed in blank becomes a bearer instrument [UCC 3–205(b)]. ■ **EXAMPLE 16.12** A check is made payable to the order of Jessie Arnold. Arnold indorses it by signing her name on the back. The instrument, which is now a bearer instrument, can be negotiated by delivery without indorsement. Arnold can negotiate the check to whomever she wishes merely by delivery, and that person can negotiate by delivery without indorsement. If Arnold loses the check after she indorses it, anyone who finds the check can negotiate it further. ■

Similarly, a bearer instrument can be converted into an order instrument through indorsement. ■ **EXAMPLE 16.13** Jessie Arnold takes the check that she indorsed in blank (now a bearer instrument) and negotiates it, by delivery, to Jonas Tolling. Tolling indorses the check "Pay to Mark Hyatt, [signed] Jonas Tolling." By adding this special indorsement, Tolling has converted the check into an order instrument. The check can be further negotiated only by indorsement (by Mark Hyatt) and delivery [UCC 3–205(b)]. ■ Exhibit 16–6 illustrates how an indorsement can convert an order instrument into a bearer instrument and vice versa.

## 16–2e Miscellaneous Indorsement Problems

Of course, difficulties can arise with indorsements, such as when a party's name is misspelled or ambiguous. The UCC provides rules that attempt to resolve these issues.

**Misspelled Names**  An indorsement should be identical to the name that appears on the instrument. A payee or indorsee whose name is misspelled can indorse with the misspelled name, the correct name, or both [UCC 3–204(d)]. ■ **EXAMPLE 16.14** Marley Ellison receives a check payable to the order of Mary Ellison. She can indorse the check either "Marley Ellison" or "Mary Ellison." ■ The usual practice is to indorse with the name as it appears on the instrument followed by the correct name.

**Instruments Payable to Entities**  A negotiable instrument can be drawn payable to an entity such as an estate, a partnership, or an organization. In this situation, an authorized representative of the entity can negotiate the instrument. ■ **EXAMPLE 16.15** A check states "Pay to the order of the Red Cross." An authorized representative of the Red Cross can negotiate this check. ■

Similarly, negotiable paper can be payable to a public officer. For instance, checks reading "Pay to the order of the County Tax Collector" or "Pay to the order of Larry White, Receiver of Taxes" can be negotiated by whoever holds the office [UCC 3–110(c)].

**EXHIBIT 16–6  Converting an Order Instrument to a Bearer Instrument and Vice Versa**

### Indorsement Converting an Order Instrument to a Bearer Instrument

A check payable to the order of Jessie Arnold is an order instrument. Arnold indorses the check in blank (by simply signing her name), thus converting the instrument to a bearer instrument, and delivers the check to Jonas Tolling.

### Indorsement Converting a Bearer Instrument to an Order Instrument

Jonas Tolling adds a special indorsement and negotiates the check to Mark Hyatt. The special indorsement, because it makes the instrument payable to a specific indorsee (Mark Hyatt), converts the bearer instrument back into an order instrument. To negotiate the instrument further, Mark Hyatt must indorse and deliver the instrument.

**Alternative or Joint Payees** An instrument payable to two or more persons *in the alternative* (for instance, "Pay to the order of Ying or Tuan") requires the indorsement of only one of the payees [UCC 3–110(d)]. If, however, an instrument is made payable to two or more persons *jointly* (for instance, "Pay to the order of Bridgette and Tony Van Horn"), all of the payees' indorsements are necessary for negotiation.

**If the Instrument Is Ambiguous.** What if an instrument payable to two or more persons does not clearly indicate whether it is payable in the alternative or payable jointly? In this situation, "the instrument is payable to the persons alternatively" [UCC 3–110(d)]. The same principles apply to special indorsements that identify more than one person to whom the indorser intends to make the instrument payable [UCC 3–205(a)].

■ **CASE IN POINT 16.16** Hyatt Corporation hired Skyscraper Building Maintenance, LLC, to perform maintenance. Skyscraper asked Hyatt to make checks for the services payable to Skyscraper and J&D Financial Corporation. Two of the checks issued by Hyatt were made payable to "J&D Financial Corp. Skyscraper Building Maint." Parties listed in this manner—without an "and" or "or" between them—are referred to as *stacked payees.* The checks were indorsed only by Skyscraper and negotiated by a bank.

J&D and Hyatt filed a lawsuit against the bank claiming that the checks were payable *jointly* and thus required indorsement by both payees. The bank argued that the checks were payable to J&D and Skyscraper *alternatively.* The court found that the bank was not liable. A check payable to stacked payees is ambiguous and thus payable *alternatively,* with indorsement by only one of the payees, under UCC 3–110(d).[2] ■

**Suspension of the Drawer's Obligation.** When a drawer gives one alternative or joint payee a check, the drawer's obligation on the check to other payees is suspended [UCC 3–310(b)(1)]. The payee who has possession of the check holds it for the benefit of all of the payees. In other words, the drawer has no obligation to make sure that the funds are allocated or distributed among the joint payees.

■ **CASE IN POINT 16.17** Vernon and Shirley Graves owned a building that they leased to John and Tamara Johnson to use for their towing business. The Johnsons insured the property and business through Westport Insurance Company. When a fire destroyed the building, Westport Insurance agreed to pay $98,000 in three payments, with the checks co-payable to Johnson's Towing

and Vernon Graves. Westport issued two checks, for $30,000 and $29,000, and delivered them to Graves. A third check was given to the Johnsons.

The Johnsons did not remit the funds from this third check to the Graveses, who subsequently filed a lawsuit against the Johnsons and Westport. The court dismissed the lawsuit, holding that the parties had agreed that the insurance company would issue the checks to joint payees and that Westport had complied with this agreement. Once Westport sent the checks to one of the joint payees, its obligation to the other joint payees was suspended until the check was either paid or dishonored.[3] ■

# 16–3 Holder in Due Course (HDC)

One of the most important distinctions in the law governing negotiable instruments is that between a holder and a *holder in due course* (HDC). Often, whether a holder is entitled to obtain payment will depend on whether she or he is an HDC.

## 16–3a Holder versus Holder in Due Course

When an instrument is transferred, an ordinary holder obtains only those rights that the transferor had in the instrument, as mentioned previously. In this respect, a holder has the same status as an assignee. Like an assignee, a holder normally is subject to the same defenses that could be asserted against the transferor.

In contrast, a **holder in due course (HDC)** takes an instrument *free* of most of the defenses and claims that could be asserted against the transferor. An HDC is a holder who meets certain acquisition requirements and therefore receives a higher level of protection from defenses and claims asserted by other parties.

■ **EXAMPLE 16.18** Shanna Morrison buys a BMW X3 SUV for her business from Heritage Motors in Irvine, California, signing a promissory note for $50,000 as part of the deal. Heritage negotiates the note to Apollo Financial Services, which promises to pay Heritage for it in six months. During the next two months, Morrison has significant problems with the SUV and sues Heritage for breach of contract. She also refuses to make further payments on the note.

Whether Apollo can hold Morrison liable on the note depends on whether it has met the requirements for HDC status. If Apollo has met these requirements and thus has HDC status, it is entitled to payment on the note. If

---

2. *Hyatt Corp. v. Palm Beach National Bank*, 840 So.2d 300 (Fla.App. 2003).

3. *Graves v. Johnson*, 862 N.E.2d 716 (Ind.App. 2007); see also *First Bank and Trust v. Scottsdale Insurance Company*, 2015 WL 7015419 (E.D.La. 2015).

Apollo has not met these requirements, it has the status of an ordinary holder, and Morrison's defense against payment to Heritage will also be effective against Apollo. ■

## 16–3b Requirements for HDC Status

The basic requirements for attaining HDC status are set forth in UCC 3–302. An HDC must be a holder of a negotiable instrument and must have taken the instrument (1) for value, (2) in good faith, and (3) without notice that it is defective. (An instrument is defective when, for instance, it is overdue, dishonored, irregular, or incomplete.) We now examine each of these requirements.

**Taking for Value**   An HDC must have given value for the instrument [UCC 3–302(a)(2)(i), 3–303]. A person who receives an instrument as a gift or inherits it has *not* met the requirement of value. In these situations, the person normally becomes an ordinary holder and does not possess the rights of an HDC.

Under UCC 3–303(a), a holder takes an instrument for value if the holder has done any of the following:

1. Performed the promise for which the instrument was issued or transferred.
2. Acquired a security interest or other lien in the instrument, excluding a lien obtained by a judicial proceeding.
3. Taken the instrument in payment of, or as security for, a preexisting obligation (sometimes called an **antecedent claim**).   ■ **EXAMPLE 16.19**  Zon owes Dwyer $2,000 on a past-due account. Zon negotiates a $2,000 note signed by Gordon to Dwyer. If Dwyer accepts it to discharge the overdue account balance, Dwyer has given value for the instrument. ■

4. Given a negotiable instrument as payment.   ■ **EXAMPLE 16.20**  Justin issued a $5,000 negotiable promissory note to Paige. The note is due six months from the date issued. Paige needs cash and does not want to wait until the maturity date to collect. She negotiates the note to her friend Lexi, who pays $2,000 in cash and writes Paige a check—a negotiable instrument—for the balance of $3,000. Lexi has given full value for the note by paying $2,000 in cash and issuing Paige the check for $3,000. ■
5. Given an irrevocable commitment (such as a letter of credit) as payment.

**Value Is Distinguishable from Consideration.**   The concept of *value* in the law of negotiable instruments is not the same as the concept of *consideration* in the law of contracts. Although a promise to give value in the future is valid consideration to support a contract, it does not constitute sufficient value to make the promisor an HDC. If a person promises to perform or give value in the future, that person is not an HDC.

A holder takes an instrument for value *only to the extent that the promise has been performed* [UCC 3–303(a)(1)]. Let's return to *Example 16.18*, in which Heritage Motors negotiates Shanna Morrison's promissory note to Apollo Financial Services in return for Apollo's promise to pay in six months. In this example, Apollo is not an HDC. At the time of Morrison's breach of contract lawsuit against Heritage, Apollo has not yet paid Heritage for the note. Thus, it did not take the note for value. If Apollo had paid Heritage for the note at the time of transfer (given value), it would be an HDC and could have held Morrison liable on the note. Exhibit 16–7 illustrates these concepts further.

## EXHIBIT 16–7   Taking for Value

By exchanging defective goods (a defective BMW X3 SUV) for a promissory note, Heritage Motors breached its contract with Morrison. Morrison could assert this breach as a defense if Heritage presented the note to her for payment. Heritage exchanged the note for Apollo Financial Services' promise to pay in six months, however. Because Apollo did not take the note for value, it is not a holder in due course. Thus, Morrison can assert against Apollo the defense of Heritage's breach when Apollo submits the note to Morrison for payment. In contrast, if Apollo had taken the note for value, Morrison could not assert that defense and would be liable to pay the note.

Shanna Morrison — $50,000 Note → Heritage Motors — Morrison's $50,000 Note → Apollo Financial Services
← Defective Goods — ← Promise to Pay in Six Months

(Photos from Shutterstock.com: Left, Yuri Areurs; center, Tupungato; right, wavebreakmedia)

**Exceptions.** In a few situations, the holder may pay for the instrument but not acquire HDC status. For instance, when the instrument is purchased at a judicial sale, such as a bankruptcy or creditor's sale, the holder will not be an HDC. Similarly, if the instrument is acquired as a result of taking over a trust or estate (as administrator), or as part of a corporate purchase of assets, the holder will have only the rights of an ordinary holder [UCC 3–302(c)].

**Taking in Good Faith** The second requirement for HDC status is that the holder must take the instrument in *good faith* [UCC 3–302(a)(2)(ii)]. This means that the holder must have acted honestly in the process of acquiring the instrument. UCC 3–103(a)(4) defines *good faith* as "honesty in fact and the observance of reasonable commercial standards of fair dealing" [UCC 3–103(a)(4)].

The good faith requirement applies only to the *holder*. It is immaterial whether the transferor acted in good faith. Thus, even a person who takes a negotiable instrument from a thief may become an HDC if the person acquired the instrument in good faith and had no reason to be suspicious of the transaction. The purchaser must honestly believe that the instrument was not defective, however. If a person purchases a $10,000 note for $300 from a stranger on a street corner, the issue of good faith can be raised. Both the suspicious circumstances and the grossly inadequate consideration (value) should make the purchaser suspicious.

In the following case, the court had to determine whether a check had been accepted in good faith.

## Spotlight on Holder in Due Course

### Case 16.3 Georg v. Metro Fixtures Contractors, Inc.
Supreme Court of Colorado, 178 P.3d 1209 (2008).

**Background and Facts** Cassandra Demery worked as a bookkeeper at Clinton Georg's business, Freestyle, until Georg discovered that she had embezzled more than $200,000 and had failed to pay $240,000 in state and federal taxes owed by Freestyle. Georg fired Demery and said that if she did not repay the embezzled funds, he would notify the authorities.

Demery went to work as a bookkeeper for Metro Fixtures, a company owned by her parents. Without authorization, she wrote a check to Freestyle for $189,000 out of Metro's account and deposited it to Freestyle's checking account. She told Georg that the check was a loan to her from her family to enable her to repay him. Georg used the funds to pay his back taxes.

Two years later, Metro discovered Demery's theft and sued Georg and Freestyle for conversion because Demery had no authority to take the funds. The trial court held that Freestyle was a holder in due course (HDC) and granted summary judgment. Metro appealed. The appeals court reversed, holding that because Demery had deposited the check directly into Freestyle's account, Freestyle could not have been an HDC, as it never had actual possession of the check. Georg and Freestyle appealed.

### In the Language of the Court
*HOBBS,* Justice.
    * * * *

A check is a negotiable instrument. The holder in due course doctrine is designed to encourage the transfer and usage of checks and facilitate the flow of capital. *An entity may qualify as a holder in due course even if the instrument at issue may have passed through the hands of a thief.* A holder in due course must meet five conditions: (1) be a holder; (2) of a negotiable instrument who took it; (3) for value; (4) in good faith; (5) without notice of certain problems with the instrument. [Emphasis added.]

To be a holder one must meet two conditions * * * : (1) he or she must have possession (2) of an instrument drawn, issued, or indorsed to him or her. Possession is an element designed to prevent two or more claimants from qualifying as holders who could take free of the other party's claim of ownership. With rare exceptions, those claiming to be holders have physical ownership of the instrument in question.

An otherwise authorized signature on a negotiable instrument is not converted into an unauthorized forgery when an agent, authorized to sign negotiable instruments in his principal's name, abuses that authority by negotiating the instrument to a holder in due course for the agent's own personal benefit.

Case 16.3 Continues

**Case 16.3 Continued**

Section 4–201(a) [of Colorado's UCC statute] states that a collecting bank "is an agent or sub-agent of the owner of the item." Further, the statute states, "This provision applies regardless of the form of indorsement or lack of indorsement * * *." A check payable to a party and deposited in that party's account makes the party the "owner" of the check under the UCC. Further, the [well-known] treatise on the UCC speaks to a collecting bank as an agent for the owner's possession:

> Sometimes the one claiming to be a holder in due course will not have possession of the instrument at the time of the suit. When a collecting bank holds the check, the solution is simple for section 4-201 makes that bank the agent of the owner of the check. *Under traditional analysis, the agent's possession would be the owner's possession and thus the owner would have "possession."*

Thus, there are circumstances wherein requiring actual physical possession of the instrument would be problematic and constructive possession applies. *Nevertheless, a determination of constructive possession should occur only when delivery is clearly for an identifiable person under circumstances excluding any other party as a holder in due course.* [Emphasis added.]

* * * *

Colorado's UCC intends to promote reliability on issued instruments, not to undermine their efficacy by placing the burden on the person to whom it is issued to determine a check's validity. Metro's recourse is not against Freestyle, but rather against its agent employee for breaching her fiduciary duty to the company.

Having reviewed the holder in due course elements in light of the undisputed facts of the case, we determine that Freestyle was a holder with constructive possession of a negotiable instrument, which was given for value and taken in good faith without notice of a forgery or an unauthorized signature. Accordingly, we reverse the judgment of the court of appeals and remand with directions that the court of appeals return this case to the district court for entry of judgment in favor of Freestyle.

**Decision and Remedy** *The Colorado Supreme Court reinstated the verdict of the trial court and held that Freestyle had received the check in good faith, not knowing it involved theft. Demery was the wrongdoer in this case, and either Metro or Freestyle would have to absorb the loss. Because Freestyle had no reason to know of the theft and Metro did not take steps to prevent it, the loss should fall on Metro.*

**Critical Thinking**

- **What If the Facts Were Different?** *Suppose that Demery had gone to work for a company with which she had no relationship and had stolen funds from it to pay Georg. Would Georg then be the more innocent party? Why or why not?*
- **Ethical** *Georg knew that Demery had embezzled funds from Freestyle when she was an employee. Shouldn't he have been suspicious about the source of the funds that Demery was using to repay Freestyle? Why did the court conclude that Freestyle acted in good faith in accepting the check?*

---

**Taking without Notice** The final requirement for HDC status concerns notice of defects. A person cannot be an HDC if she or he knows or has reason to know that the instrument is defective in any one of the following ways [UCC 3–302(a)]:

1. It is overdue.
2. It has been dishonored.
3. It is part of a series in which at least one instrument has an uncured (uncorrected) default.
4. The instrument contains an unauthorized signature or has been altered.
5. There is a defense against the instrument or a claim to the instrument.

6. The instrument is so incomplete or irregular as to call into question its authenticity.

**What Constitutes Notice?** Under UCC 1–201(25), a person is considered to have notice in any of the following circumstances:

1. The person has actual knowledge of the defect.
2. The person has received a notice or notification about the defect (such as a letter from a bank identifying the serial numbers of stolen bearer instruments).
3. The person has reason to know that a defect exists, given all the facts and circumstances known at the time in question.

The holder must also have received the notice "at a time and in a manner that gives a reasonable opportunity to act on it" [UCC 3–302(f)]. A purchaser's knowledge of certain facts, such as insolvency proceedings against the maker or drawer of the instrument, does *not* constitute notice that the instrument is defective [UCC 3–302(b)].

**Overdue Demand Instruments.** What constitutes notice that an instrument is overdue depends on whether it is a demand instrument (payable on demand) or a time instrument (payable at a definite time).

A purchaser has notice that a *demand instrument* is overdue in two situations. One situation occurs when a person takes a demand instrument knowing that demand already has been made.

The other situation occurs when a person takes a demand instrument an unreasonable length of time after its date. For a check, a "reasonable time" is ninety days after the date of the check. For all other demand instruments, what will be considered a reasonable time depends on the circumstances [UCC 3–304(a)].

**Overdue Time Instruments.** Normally, a *time instrument* is overdue on the day after its due date. Anyone who takes a time instrument after the due date is on notice that it is overdue [UCC 3–304(b)].[4] Therefore, if a promissory note due on May 15 is purchased on May 16, the purchaser will be an ordinary holder, not an HDC.

If an instrument states that it is "Payable in thirty days," counting begins the day *after* the instrument is dated. For instance, a note dated December 1 that is payable in thirty days is due by midnight on December 31. If the payment date falls on a Sunday or holiday, the instrument is payable on the next business day.

A series of notes issued at the same time with successive maturity dates is overdue when any note in the series is overdue. This serves to notify prospective purchasers that they cannot qualify as HDCs [UCC 3–302(a)(2)(iii)].

If the principal is to be paid in installments, the default or nonpayment of any one installment will make the instrument overdue and provide notice to prospective purchasers of the default. The instrument will remain overdue until the default is cured [UCC 3–304(b)(1)].

An instrument does not become overdue if there is a default on a payment of interest only, however [UCC 3–304(c)]. For this reason, most installment notes provide that any payment will be applied first to interest, and the remainder will then be applied to the principal. This serves as notice that any installment payment for less than the full amount results in a default on an installment payment toward the principal.

**Dishonored Instruments.** An instrument is *dishonored* when the party to whom the instrument is presented refuses to pay it. If a holder knows or has reason to know that an instrument has been dishonored, the holder is on notice and cannot claim HDC status [UCC 3–302(a)(2)]. Thus, a person who takes a check clearly stamped "insufficient funds" is put on notice. Conversely, if a person purchasing an instrument does not know and has no reason to know that it has been dishonored, the person is *not* put on notice. Therefore, that person can become an HDC.

■ **EXAMPLE 16.21** Lucinda Gonzalez holds a demand note dated September 1 on Apex, Inc., a local business firm. On September 17, she demands payment, and Apex refuses (that is, dishonors the instrument). On September 22, Gonzalez negotiates the note to Brenner, a purchaser who lives in another state. Brenner does not know, and has no reason to know, that the note has been dishonored. Because Brenner is *not* put on notice, Brenner can become an HDC. ■

**Notice of Claims or Defenses.** A holder cannot become an HDC if he or she has notice of any claim to the instrument or defense against it [UCC 3–302(a)(2)(v), (vi)]. A purchaser has notice if the claims or defenses are apparent on the instrument's face or if the purchaser had reason to know of them from facts surrounding the transaction.[5] For instance, a potential purchaser who knows that the maker of a note has breached the underlying contract with the payee cannot thereafter purchase the note as an HDC.

Knowledge of one defense precludes a holder from asserting HDC status in regard to all other defenses. ■ **EXAMPLE 16.22** James Wu, knowing that the note he has taken has a forged indorsement, presents it to the maker for payment. The maker refuses to pay on the ground of breach of the underlying contract. The maker can assert this defense against Wu even though Wu had no knowledge of the breach. Wu's knowledge

---

4. A time instrument also becomes overdue the day after an accelerated due date, unless the purchaser has no reason to know that the due date has been accelerated [UCC 3–302(a)(2)(iii), 3–304(b)(3)].

5. If an instrument contains a statement required by a statute or an administrative rule to the effect that the rights of a holder or transferee are subject to the claims or defenses that the issuer could assert against the original payee, the instrument is negotiable. There cannot be an HDC of the instrument, however. See UCC 3–106(d).

of the forgery prevents him from being an HDC in any circumstances. ∎

**Incomplete Instruments.** A purchaser cannot become an HDC of an instrument so incomplete on its face that an element of negotiability is lacking (for example, the amount is not filled in) [UCC 3–302(a)(1)]. Minor omissions (such as the omission of the date) are permissible because these do not call into question the validity of the instrument [UCC 3–113(b)].

Similarly, when a person accepts an instrument that has been completed without knowing that it was incomplete when issued, that person can take it as an HDC [UCC 3–115(b), 3–302(a)(1)]. Even if an instrument that is originally incomplete is later completed in an unauthorized manner, an HDC can still enforce the instrument as completed [UCC 3–407(c)].

∎ **EXAMPLE 16.23** Peyton asks Brittany to buy a textbook for him when she goes to the campus bookstore. Peyton writes a check payable to the campus store, leaves the amount blank, and tells Brittany to fill in the price of the textbook. The cost of the textbook is $85. If Brittany fills in the check for $150 before she gets to the bookstore, the bookstore cashier sees only a properly completed instrument. Therefore, because the bookstore had no notice that the check was incomplete when it was issued, the bookstore can take the check for $150 and become an HDC. ∎

**Irregular Instruments.** Any irregularity on the face of an instrument (such as an obvious forgery or alteration) that calls into question its validity or ownership will bar HDC status. In addition, any irregularity that creates an ambiguity as to the party to pay prevents a holder from becoming an HDC.

A difference between the handwriting used in the body of a check and that used in the signature will not by itself make an instrument irregular. Nor will antedating or postdating a check or stating the amount in digits but failing to write out the numbers. Visible evidence that a maker's or drawer's signature is forged, however, will disqualify a purchaser from HDC status.

Nevertheless, a good forgery of a signature or a careful alteration can go undetected by reasonable examination. In that situation, the purchaser can qualify as an HDC [UCC 3–302(a)(1)]. Losses that result from well-crafted forgeries usually fall on the party to whom the forger transferred the instrument (assuming, of course, that the forger cannot be found). Typically, this means the bank that accepts a check despite evidence on the check's face that it is irregular will bear the loss if the check later turns out to be forged.

# 16–4 Holder through an HDC

A person who does not qualify as an HDC but who derives his or her title through an HDC can acquire the rights and privileges of an HDC. This rule, which is sometimes called the **shelter principle,** is set out in UCC 3–203(b):

> Transfer of an instrument, whether or not the transfer is a negotiation, vests in the transferee any right of the transferor to enforce the instrument, including any right as a holder in due course, but the transferee cannot acquire rights of a holder in due course by a transfer, directly or indirectly, from a holder in due course if the transferee engaged in fraud or illegality affecting the instrument.

## 16–4a The Purpose of the Shelter Principle

The shelter principle extends the benefits of HDC status and is designed to aid the HDC in readily disposing of the instrument. Anyone, no matter how far removed from an HDC, who can ultimately trace her or his title back to an HDC comes within the shelter principle. The idea is based on the legal theory that the transferee of an instrument receives at least the rights that the transferor had. By extending the benefits of HDC status, the shelter principle promotes the marketability and free transferability of negotiable instruments.

## 16–4b Limitations on the Shelter Principle

There are some limitations on the shelter principle. If a holder participated in fraud or illegality affecting the instrument, that holder is not allowed to improve her or his status by repurchasing the instrument from a later HDC. Similarly, a holder who had notice of a claim or defense against an instrument cannot gain HDC status by later reacquiring the instrument from an HDC [UCC 3–203(b)].

∎ **EXAMPLE 16.24** Matthew and Carla collaborate to defraud Dina. Dina is induced to give Carla a negotiable note payable to Carla's order. Carla then specially indorses the note for value to Ling, an HDC. Matthew and Carla split the proceeds. Ling negotiates the note to Stuart, another HDC. Stuart then negotiates the note for value to Matthew. Matthew, even though he obtained the note through an HDC, is not a holder through an HDC because he participated in the original fraud and can never acquire HDC rights in this note. ∎

See Concept Summary 16.2 for a review of the requirements for HDC status.

## Concept Summary 16.2

### Requirements for HDC Status

| | |
|---|---|
| **Must Be a *Holder*** | A *holder* is defined as a person in possession of an instrument "if the instrument is payable to bearer or, in the cases of an instrument payable to an identified person, if the identified person is in possession"[UCC 1–201(20)]. |
| **Must Take for Value** | A holder gives *value* by performing the promise for which the instrument was issued or transferred; acquiring a security interest or other lien in the instrument; taking the instrument in payment of, or as security for, an antecedent debt; giving a negotiable instrument as payment; or giving an irrevocable commitment as payment [UCC 3–303]. |
| **Must Take in Good Faith** | *Good faith* is defined for purposes of revised Article 3 as "honesty in fact and the observance of reasonable commercial standards of fair dealing" [UCC 3–103(a)(4)]. |
| **Must Take without Notice** | A holder must not be *on notice* that the instrument is defective in any of the following ways: (1) The instrument is overdue, (2) the instrument has been dishonored, (3) there is an uncured default with respect to another instrument issued as part of the same series, (4) the instrument contains an unauthorized signature or has been altered, (5) there is a defense against the instrument or a claim to the instrument, and (6) the instrument is so irregular or incomplete as to call into question its authenticity [UCC 3–302, 3–304]. |
| **The Shelter Principle** | A holder who cannot qualify as an HDC has the rights of an HDC if he or she derives title through an HDC [UCC 3–203(b)]. |

## Reviewing: Transferability and Holder in Due Course

The Brown family owns several companies, including the J. H. Stevedoring Company and Penn Warehousing and Distribution, Inc. Many aspects of the companies' operations and management are intertwined. Dennis Bishop worked for J. H. and Penn for more than ten years until, by 2017, he had become the financial controller at J. H. His responsibilities included approving invoices for payment and reconciling the corporate checkbook. In December 2018, Bishop began stealing from Penn and J. H. by writing checks on the corporate accounts and using the funds for his own benefit (committing the crime of embezzlement). Several members of the Brown family signed the checks for Bishop without hesitation because he was a longtime, trusted employee. Over the next two years, Bishop embezzled $1,209,436. He used $670,632 to buy horses from the Fasig-Tipton Company and Fasig-Tipton Midlantic, Inc., with Penn and J. H. checks made payable to those firms. When Bishop's fraud was revealed, J. H. and Penn filed a suit in a federal district court against the Fasig-Tipton firms (the defendants) to recover the amounts of the checks made payable to them. Using the information presented in the chapter, answer the following questions.

Continues

1. What method was most likely used to negotiate the instruments described here?
2. Suppose that all of the checks issued to the defendants were made payable to "Fasig-Tipton Co., Fasig-Tipton Midlantic, Inc." Under the Uniform Commercial Code, were the instruments payable jointly or in the alternative? Why is this significant?
3. Do the defendants in this situation (the two Fasig-Tipton firms) meet the requirements of an HDC? Why or why not?
4. In whose favor should the court rule, and why?

**Debate This** . . . *We should eliminate the status of holder in due course for those who possess negotiable instruments.*

## Terms and Concepts

| | | |
|---|---|---|
| antecedent claim 314 | indorsement 306 | restrictive indorsement 310 |
| blank indorsement 306 | indorser 306 | shelter principle 318 |
| holder in due course (HDC) 313 | negotiation 305 | special indorsement 307 |
| indorsee 306 | qualified indorsement 309 | trust indorsement 310 |

## Issue Spotters

1. Kurt receives from Nabil a check that is made out "Pay to the order of Kurt." Kurt turns it over and writes on the back, "Pay to Adam. [Signed] Kurt." What type of indorsement is this? What effect does this indorsement have on whether the check is considered an order instrument or a bearer instrument? Explain. (See *Negotiation.*)

2. Ben contracts with Amy to fix her roof. Amy writes Ben a check, but Ben never makes the repairs. Carl knows Ben breached the contract but cashes the check anyway. Can Carl become an HDC? Why or why not? (See *Holder in Due Course.*)

• **Check your answers to the Issue Spotters against the answers provided in Appendix B at the end of this text.**

## Business Scenarios

**16–1. Indorsements.** A check drawn by Cullen for $500 is made payable to the order of Jordan and issued to Jordan. Jordan owes his landlord $500 in rent and transfers the check to his landlord with the following indorsement: "For rent paid, [signed] Jordan." Jordan's landlord has contracted to have Deborah do some landscaping on the property. When Deborah insists on immediate payment, the landlord transfers the check to Deborah without indorsement. Later, to pay for some palm trees purchased from Better-Garden Nursery, Deborah transfers the check with the following indorsement: "Pay to Better-Garden Nursery, without recourse, [signed] Deborah." Better-Garden Nursery sends the check to its bank indorsed "For deposit only, [signed] Better-Garden Nursery." (See *Indorsements.*)

(a) Classify each of these indorsements.

(b) Was the transfer from Jordan's landlord to Deborah, without indorsement, an assignment or a negotiation? Explain.

**16–2. Holder in Due Course.** Through negotiation, Emilio has received from dishonest payees two checks with the following histories:

(a) The drawer issued a check to the payee for $9. The payee cleverly altered the numeral amount on the check from $9 to $90 and the written word from "nine" to "ninety."

(b) The drawer issued a check to the payee without filling in the amount. The drawer authorized the payee to fill in the amount for no more than $90. The payee filled in the amount of $900.

Discuss whether Emilio, by giving value to the payees, can qualify as a holder in due course of these checks. (See *Holder in Due Course.*)

**16–3. Negotiation.** Bertram writes a check for $200 payable to "cash." He puts the check in his pocket and drives to the bank to cash the check. As he gets out of his car in the bank's parking lot, the check slips out of his pocket and falls to the pavement. Jerrod walks by moments later, picks up the check, and later that day delivers it to Amber, to whom he owes $200. Amber indorses the check "For deposit only, [signed] Amber Dowel" and deposits it into her checking account. In light of these circumstances, answer the following questions:

**(a)** Is the check a bearer instrument or an order instrument?

**(b)** Did Jerrod's delivery of the check to Amber constitute a valid negotiation? Why or why not?

**(c)** What type of indorsement did Amber make?

**(d)** Does Bertram have a right to recover the $200 from Amber? Explain. (See *Negotiation*.)

# Business Case Problems

**16–4. Transfer and Holder in Due Course.** Germanie Fequiere executed and delivered a promissory note in the principal amount of $240,000 to BNC Mortgage. As security for the note, Fequiere executed and delivered a mortgage on real property. BNC indorsed the promissory note in blank. Later, Chase Home Finance, LLC, became the holder in due course of the note and holder of the mortgage. When Fequiere failed to make payments on the note, Chase sought to foreclose on the property. Fequiere asserted that Chase could not foreclose on the property because the mortgage on the property had not been properly transferred from BNC to Chase. Assuming that is true, does it mean that Chase, as holder of the negotiable note, cannot foreclose on the collateral (the property secured by the mortgage)? Explain your answer. [*Chase Home Finance, LLC v. Fequiere*, 119 Conn.App. 570, 989 A.2d 606 (2010)] (See *Holder in Due Course*.)

**16–5. Business Case Problem with Sample Answer—Negotiation.**

Sandra Ford signed a note and a mortgage on her home in Westwood, New Jersey, to borrow $403,750 from Argent Mortgage Co. Argent transferred the note and mortgage to Wells Fargo Bank, N.A., without indorsement. The following spring, Ford stopped making payments on the note. Wells Fargo filed a suit in a New Jersey state court against Ford to foreclose on the mortgage. Ford asserted that Argent had committed fraud in connection with the note by providing misleading information and charging excessive fees. Ford contended that Wells Fargo was subject to these defenses because the bank was not a holder in due course of the note. Was the transfer of the note from Argent to Wells Fargo a negotiation or an assignment? What difference does that make? If Argent indorsed the note to Wells Fargo now, would the bank's status change? Discuss. [*Wells Fargo Bank, N.A. v. Ford*, 418 N.J.Super. 592, 15 A.3d 327 (App.Div. 2011)] (See *Negotiation*.)

- For a sample answer to Problem 16–5, go to Appendix C at the end of this text.

**16–6. Indorsements.** Angela Brock borrowed $544,000 and signed a note payable to Amerifund Mortgage Services, LLC, to buy a house in Silver Spring, Maryland. The note was indorsed in blank and transferred several times "without recourse" before Brock fell behind on the payments. On behalf of Deutsche Bank National Trust Co., BAC Home Loans Servicing LP initiated foreclosure. Brock filed an action in a Maryland state court to block it, arguing that BAC could not foreclose because Deutsche Bank, not BAC, owned the note. Can BAC enforce the note? Explain. [*Deutsche Bank National Trust Co. v. Brock*, 430 Md. 714, 63 A.3d 40 (2013)] (See *Indorsements*.)

**16–7. Transfer by Negotiation.** Thao Thi Duong signed a note in the amount of $200,000 in favor of Country Home Loans, Inc., to obtain a loan to buy a house in Marrero, Louisiana. The note was indorsed "PAY TO THE ORDER OF [blank space] WITHOUT RECOURSE COUNTRY HOME LOANS, INC." Almost five years later, Duong defaulted on the payments. The Federal National Mortgage Association (Fannie Mae) had come into possession of the note. Fannie Mae wanted to foreclose on the house and sell it to recover the balance due. Duong argued that the words "to the order of [blank space]" in the indorsement made the note an incomplete order instrument and that Fannie Mae thus could not enforce it. What is Fannie Mae's best response to this argument? [*Federal National Mortgage Association v. Thao Thi Duong*, 167 So.3d 920 (La.App. 5 Cir. 2015)] (See *Negotiation*.)

**16–8. Indorsements.** Denise and Nick Purificato signed a note secured by real property in Florida. The note was transferred through several parties to Aurora Loan Services, LLC. The Purificatos defaulted on the payments. Aurora filed a suit in a Florida state court against them, seeking a judgment of foreclosure to recover the unpaid debt. While proceedings were pending, Nationstar Mortgage, LLC, succeeded Aurora and became the plaintiff in the suit. At trial, Nationstar provided a screen shot of the note and an allonge, which had been imaged as a single document before Aurora filed the complaint against the Purificatos. Nationstar also provided the original note and allonge, which ended in a blank indorsement. The allonge stated that it was "affixed and a permanent part of said note." Did this evidence establish that the allonge was sufficiently affixed to the note to prove Nationstar's status as the holder with the right to enforce it? Discuss. [*Purificato v. Nationstar Mortgage, LLC*, 41 Fla.L.Weekly. D104, 182 So.3d 821 (Dist.Ct.App. 4 Dist. 2016)] (See *Indorsements*.)

**16–9. A Question of Ethics—Indorsements.**

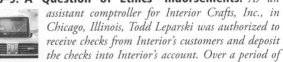

*As an assistant comptroller for Interior Crafts, Inc., in Chicago, Illinois, Todd Leparski was authorized to receive checks from Interior's customers and deposit the checks into Interior's account. Over a period of five months, Leparski stole more than $500,000 from Interior by indorsing the checks "Interior Crafts—For Deposit Only" but then depositing some of them into his own account at Marquette Bank. Leparski used an automated teller machine owned by Pan American Bank to make the deposits into Marquette. Marquette alerted Interior, which was able to recover about $250,000 from Leparski. Interior also recovered $250,000 under its policy with American Insurance Co. To collect the rest of the missing funds, Interior filed a suit in an Illinois state court against Leparski*

*and the banks. The court ruled in favor of Interior, and Pan American appealed to a state intermediate appellate court. [Interior Crafts, Inc. v. Leparski, 366 Ill.App.3d 1148, 853 N.E.2d 1244, 304 Ill.Dec. 878 (3 Dist. 2006)]* (See *Indorsements.*)

**(a)** What type of indorsement is "Interior Crafts—For Deposit Only"? What is the obligation of a party that receives a check with this indorsement? Does the fact that Interior authorized Leparski to indorse its checks but not to deposit those checks into his own account absolve Pan American of liability? Explain.

**(b)** From an ethical perspective, how might a business firm such as Interior discourage an employee's thievery such as Leparski's acts in this case? Discuss.

## Legal Reasoning Group Activity

**16–10. Holder in Due Course.** Celine issues a ninety-day negotiable promissory note payable to the order of Hayden. The amount of the note is left blank, pending a determination of the amount that Hayden will need to purchase a used car for Celine. Celine authorizes any amount not to exceed $2,000. Hayden, without authority, fills in the note in the amount of $5,000 and thirty days later sells the note to First National Bank of Oklahoma for $4,850. Hayden does not buy the car and leaves the state. First National Bank has no knowledge that the instrument was incomplete when issued or that Hayden had no authority to complete the instrument in the amount of $5,000. (See *Holder in Due Course.*)

**(a)** The first group will determine whether the bank qualifies as a holder in due course and, if so, for what amount.

**(b)** The second group will decide what would have happened if Hayden had sold the note to a stranger in a bar for $500. Would the stranger qualify as a holder in due course? Explain.

## CHAPTER 17

# Liability, Defenses, and Discharge

iability on a negotiable instrument can arise either from a person's signature on the instrument (*signature liability*) or from the warranties that are implied when the person presents the instrument for negotiation (*warranty liability*). A person who signs a negotiable instrument is potentially liable for payment of the amount stated on the instrument. Unlike signature liability, warranty liability does not require a signature and

extends to both signers and nonsigners. A breach of warranty can occur when the instrument is transferred or presented for payment.

This chapter focuses on the liability *of the instrument itself or the warranties connected with the transfer or presentment of the instrument.* Suppose that Donna agrees to buy one thousand wearable fitness activity trackers from Luis and issues a check to Luis in payment. The liability

discussed in this chapter does not relate directly to the contract (for instance, whether the fitness monitors are of proper quality or fit for their intended purpose). Instead, the chapter discusses the liability connected with the *check* (such as what recourse Luis will have if Donna's bank refuses to pay the check due to insufficient funds in her account).

## 17-1 Signature Liability

The key to liability on a negotiable instrument is a signature. The Uniform Commercial Code (UCC) broadly defines a signature to include any name, word, mark, or symbol that is executed or adopted by a person [UCC 1–201(37), 3–401(b)].

The general rule is that every party, except a qualified indorser,[1] who signs a negotiable instrument is either primarily or secondarily liable for payment of that instrument when it comes due. A person is *not* liable on an instrument unless he or she has signed it personally or through an authorized representative (agent) [UCC 3–401(a)].

### 17-1a Primary Liability

Primary liability is unconditional. A person who is primarily liable on a negotiable instrument is absolutely required to pay the instrument—unless, of course, he or she has a valid defense to payment. Liability is immediate when the instrument is signed or issued. No action by the holder of the instrument is required. Only *makers*

(who promise to pay) and *acceptors* (such as a bank that has agreed to pay an instrument when presented later) are primarily liable [UCC 3–412, 3–413].

**Makers** The maker of a promissory note unconditionally promises to pay the note according to its terms. It is the maker's promise to pay that renders the instrument negotiable. Even if the promissory note was incomplete at the time the maker signed it, the maker is still obligated to pay. The maker must pay it according to either its stated terms or terms that were agreed on and later filled in to complete the instrument [UCC 3–115, 3–407, 3–412].

■ **EXAMPLE 17.1** Tristan executes a preprinted promissory note to Sharon without filling in the due-date blank. If Sharon does not complete the form by adding the date, the note will be payable on demand. If Sharon subsequently writes in a due date that Tristan authorized, the note is payable on the stated due date. In either situation, Tristan (the maker) is obligated to pay the note. (Note that if Sharon fills in a date that Tristan did not authorize, Tristan can claim material alteration as a defense to payment.) ■

**Acceptors** An *acceptor* is a drawee that promises to pay an instrument when it is presented later for payment [UCC 3–409(a)]. ■ **EXAMPLE 17.2** Premier Electric,

---

1. A qualified indorser—one who indorses "without recourse"—undertakes no obligation to pay [UCC 3–415(b)]. A qualified indorser merely assumes warranty liability, which will be discussed later in this chapter.

LLC, brings a draft made payable to R&C Services to Banner Bank for acceptance. Banner Bank accepts the draft by stamping "accepted" on its face, signing it, and dating it. Banner Bank is now obligated to pay the draft when it is presented for payment. ■ The drawee's acceptance is a promise to pay that places the drawee in almost the same position as the maker of a promissory note [UCC 3–413]. Failure to pay an accepted draft when presented leads to primary signature liability for the drawee-acceptor.

## 17–1b Secondary Liability

*Drawers* and *indorsers* are secondarily liable. On a negotiable instrument, secondary liability is *contingent liability*. In other words, a drawer or an indorser will be liable *only if* the party that is primarily responsible for paying the instrument refuses to do so—that is, **dishonors** the instrument.

On drafts and checks, a drawer's secondary liability does not arise until the drawee fails to pay or to accept the instrument, whichever is required. With regard to promissory notes, an indorser's secondary liability does not arise until the maker, who is primarily liable, has defaulted on the instrument [UCC 3–412, 3–415].

Thus, dishonor of an instrument triggers the liability of parties who are secondarily liable on the instrument—that is, the drawer and *unqualified* indorsers. ■ **EXAMPLE 17.3** Nina Lee writes a check for $1,000 on her account at Western Bank payable to the order of Rick Carerra. Carerra indorses and delivers the check, for value, to Eric Deere. Deere deposits the check into his account at Universal Bank, but the bank returns the check to Deere marked "insufficient funds," thus dishonoring the check. The question for Deere is whether the drawer (Lee) or the drawee-indorser (Carerra) can be held liable on the check after the bank has dishonored it. The answer to the question depends on whether certain conditions for secondary liability (outlined next) have been satisfied. ■

Parties are secondarily liable on a negotiable instrument *only if* the following events occur:[2]

1. The instrument is properly and timely presented.
2. The instrument is dishonored.
3. Timely notice of dishonor is given to the secondarily liable party.[3]

---

2. An instrument can be drafted to include a waiver of the presentment and notice of dishonor requirements [UCC 3–504]. Presume, for simplicity's sake, that such waivers have *not* been incorporated into the instruments described in this chapter.
3. These requirements are necessary for a secondarily liable party to have *signature* liability on a negotiable instrument, but they are not necessary for a secondarily liable party to have *warranty* liability.

**Presentment** Recall that *presentment* occurs when a person presents an instrument either to the party liable on the instrument for payment or to a drawee for acceptance. The holder must present the instrument to the appropriate party, in a timely fashion, and give reasonable identification if requested [UCC 3–414(f), 3–415(e), 3–501].

**Proper Presentment.** Presentment can be made by any commercially reasonable means, including oral, written, or electronic communication [UCC 3–501(b)].

The party to whom the instrument must be presented depends on the type of instrument involved. A note or certificate of deposit (CD) must be presented to the maker for payment. A check is presented to the drawee (bank) for payment [UCC 3–501(a), 3–502(b)]. A draft is presented to the drawee for payment or acceptance.

■ **EXAMPLE 17.4** Urban Furnishings receives a draft that is payable thirty days from the date of issue. Urban can present the draft to the drawee, Elmore Credit Union, the next day for acceptance. Alternatively, Urban can wait thirty days and present the draft to Elmore for payment. ■

**Timely Presentment.** Timeliness is important for proper presentment [UCC 3–414(f), 3–415(e), 3–501(b)(4)]. Failure to present an instrument on time is a common reason for improper presentment and can discharge unqualified indorsers from secondary liability. The appropriate time for presentment is determined by the nature of the instrument, any usage of banking or trade, and the facts of the particular case.

If the instrument is payable on demand, the holder must present it for payment or acceptance within a reasonable time. If it is a promissory note, the holder must present it to the maker on the note's due date. The holder of a domestic check must present it for payment or collection within thirty days of its *date* to make the drawer secondarily liable. With respect to indorsers, the holder must present a check within thirty days after its indorsement to make the indorser secondarily liable [UCC 3–414(f), 3–415(e)].

The time for proper presentment for different types of instruments is shown in Exhibit 17–1.

**Dishonor** As mentioned, an instrument is dishonored when the required payment or acceptance is refused or cannot be obtained within the prescribed time. An instrument is also dishonored when the required presentment is excused (as it is, for instance, if the maker has died) and the instrument is not properly accepted or paid [UCC 3–502(e), 3–504].

**EXHIBIT 17–1** Time for Proper Presentment

|  | **TIME INSTRUMENT** | **DEMAND INSTRUMENT** | **CHECK** |
|---|---|---|---|
| **For Acceptance** | On or before due date. | Within a reasonable time (after date of issue or after secondary party becomes liable on the instrument). | Not applicable. |
| **For Payment** | On due date. | Within a reasonable time. | Within thirty days of its date to hold drawer secondarily liable. Within thirty days of indorsement to hold indorser secondarily liable. |

In the following situations, a delay in payment or a refusal to pay an instrument will *not dishonor* the instrument:

1. When presentment is made after an established cutoff hour (not earlier than 2:00 P.M.), a bank can postpone payment until the following business day without dishonoring the instrument [UCC 3–501(b)(4)].
2. When the holder refuses to exhibit the instrument, to give reasonable identification, or to sign a receipt for the payment on the instrument, a bank's refusal to pay does not dishonor the instrument [UCC 3–501(b)(2)].
3. When an instrument is returned because it lacks a proper indorsement, the instrument is not dishonored [UCC 3–501(b)(3)(i)].

**Proper Notice** Once an instrument has been dishonored, proper notice must be given to secondary parties (drawers and indorsers) for them to be held liable. ■ **EXAMPLE 17.5** Oman writes a check on his account at People's Bank payable to Leah. Leah indorses the check in blank and cashes it at Midwest Grocery, which transfers it to People's Bank for payment. If People's Bank refuses to pay it, Midwest must timely notify Leah to hold her liable. ■

Notice can be given in any reasonable manner, including an oral, written, or electronic communication, as well as a notice written or stamped on the instrument itself

[UCC 3–503(b)].[4] Any necessary notice must be given by a bank before its midnight deadline (midnight of the next banking day after receipt) [UCC 3–503(c)]. Any party other than a bank must give notice within thirty days following the day of dishonor (or the day on which the person learned of the dishonor) [UCC 3–503(c)].

## 17–1c Accommodation Parties

An **accommodation party** is one who signs an instrument for the purpose of lending his or her name as credit to another party on the instrument [UCC 3–419(a)]. Banks may require an accommodation party—a cosigner—to secure against nonpayment of a negotiable instrument. A parent who cosigns a promissory note with her or his son or daughter, for instance, is an accommodation party, and the child (the maker) is the accommodated party.

**Accommodation Makers** If the accommodation party signs on behalf of the *maker*, he or she is an *accommodation maker* and is primarily liable on the instrument. ■ **CASE IN POINT 17.6** Anis Algahmee co-signed a $10,000 promissory note enabling Louis Irizarry to obtain

---

4. Written notice is preferable because a secondary party may claim that an oral notice was never received. Also, to give proper notice of the dishonor of a foreign draft (a draft drawn in one country and payable in another), a formal notice called a *protest* is required [UCC 3–505(b)].

a student loan to attend Ohio State University. The terms of the note stated that both the borrower and the cosigner "individually and collectively" promised to pay the debt with 6.36 percent interest and a finance charge.

When Irizarry stopped making payments on the note, the National Collegiate Student Loan Trust filed a lawsuit against both Irizarry and Algahmee. The court held that under the terms of the note, Algahmee was primarily liable as an accommodation maker. Therefore, the court granted a summary judgment against Algahmee for balance due on the student loan (more than $17,000).[5] ■

**Accommodation Indorsers** If the accommodation party signs on behalf of a *payee or other holder* (usually to make the instrument more marketable), she or he is an *accommodation indorser.* As an indorser, she or he is secondarily liable. ■ **EXAMPLE 17.7** Frank Huston applies to Northeast Bank for a $20,000 loan to start a small business. Huston's lender (which has possession of the note) asks Susan Smith, who has invested in Huston's business, to sign the note. In this situation, Smith is an indorser and thus has secondary liability—that is, the lender must pursue Huston first before seeking payment from Smith. If Smith ends up paying the amount due on the note, she has a right to reimbursement from Huston (the accommodated party) [UCC 3–419(e)]. ■

## 17–1d Authorized Agents' Signatures

Agency law applies to negotiable instruments. Questions often arise as to the liability on an instrument signed by an agent. An **agent** is a person who agrees to represent or act for another, called the **principal.**

Agents can sign negotiable instruments, just as they can sign contracts, and thereby bind their principals [UCC 3–401(a)(ii), 3–402(a)]. Without such a rule, all corporate commercial business would stop, as every corporation can and must act through its agents. Certain requirements must be met, however, before the principal becomes liable on the instrument. A basic requirement to hold the principal liable on the instrument is that the agent must be *authorized* to sign the instrument on the principal's behalf.

**Liability of the Principal** Generally, an authorized agent binds a principal on an instrument if the agent *clearly names* the principal in the signature (in handwriting or by some mark or symbol). In this situation, the UCC presumes that the signature is authorized and

genuine [UCC 3–308(a)]. The agent can add his or her own name, but if the signature shows clearly that it is made on behalf of a specific principal, the agent is not liable on the instrument [UCC 3–402(b)(1)]. ■ **EXAMPLE 17.8** Either of the following signatures by Sandra Binney as agent for Bob Aronson will bind Aronson on the instrument: "Aronson, by Binney, agent" or "Aronson." ■

An agent who signs only his or her own name, however, will be personally liable to a holder in due course (HDC) who has no notice of his or her agency status. For ordinary holders, an agent can escape liability by proving that the original parties did not intend the agent to be liable on the instrument [UCC 3–402(a), (b)(2)].[6] In either situation, the principal is bound if the party entitled to enforce the instrument can prove the agency relationship.

**Liability of the Agent** An authorized agent may be held personally liable on a negotiable instrument in the following three situations.

1. When the agent signs his or her own name on the instrument with no indication of agency status, an HDC can hold the agent personally liable, as noted above.

2. When the agent signs in both the agent's name and the principal's name, but nothing on the instrument indicates the agency relationship, the agent may be liable.

3. When the agent indicates his or her agency status in signing a negotiable instrument but fails to name the principal (such as, "Sandra Binney, agent"), the agent may be liable [UCC 3–402(b)(2)].

Obviously, to protect against potential liability, an authorized agent should disclose on the instrument the identity of the principal and also indicate that the agent is signing in a representative capacity. Failure to do so can lead to personal liability.

■ **EXAMPLE 17.9** Hugh Carter, the president of International Supply, Inc., hires Greenscape Design to landscape International's office complex. Carter signs a promissory note as "Hugh Carter, International Supply, Inc." International does not make any payments on the note, so Greenscape files a suit against both Carter and International. Carter argues that he signed the note as an agent and therefore should not be personally liable for the debt. But a court in this situation will likely decide that Carter is personally liable because nothing on the note indicates that Carter was signing it as an agent for International. ■

Corporate officers often act as agents on behalf of their employers. Like a corporation, a limited liability

---

5. *National College Student Loan Trust 2004-1 v. Irizarry,* 2015 -Ohio- 1798 (Ohio App. 2015).

6. See UCC 3–402, Comment 1.

company (LLC) is a business entity that can protect its officers from personal liability for obligations entered into on the company's behalf. But an officer may be personally liable for an LLC's business debts if the officer personally guaranties payment. Whether that occurred in the following case was the question before the court.

## Case Analysis 17.1

# Envision Printing, LLC v. Evans

Court of Appeals of Georgia, 336 Ga.App. 635, 786 S.E.2d 250 (2016).

### In the Language of the Court

*MERCIER, Judge.*

Envision Printing, LLC sued Bernie Evans [in a Georgia state court], alleging that he defaulted on a promissory note. Evans moved for summary judgment, asserting that he was not personally responsible for the debt because he had signed the promissory note solely in his capacity as an officer of a limited liability company. * * *

* * * The record shows that Evans was the CEO [chief executive officer] of Red Rhino Market Group, LLC ("Red Rhino"), that Red Rhino was a customer of Envision Printing, and that Red Rhino was in arrears on its account with Envision Printing. * * * Evans executed a promissory note (hereafter, the "note") in favor of Envision Printing. In pertinent part, the note states:

> FOR VALUE RECEIVED, the undersigned (hereinafter referred to as "Maker") promises to pay to the order of Envision Printing, LLC * * * .

The terms of the note are set out thereafter, and [a signature block follows. Beneath the words "Red Rhino Market Group, LLC" are] the signatures of Evans and one witness * * * . There are no other signatures on the note.

In moving for summary judgment, Evans pointed to the following evidence: the note contained no language indicating that Evans would be personally responsible for the debt; the note used the singular term "Maker" throughout, and the signature box was titled "Red Rhino Market Group, LLC," under which were spaces for several signatures; the only address listed in the note as the Maker's address was Red Rhino's

corporate address; Evans averred in an affidavit that he had signed the note solely in his capacity as CEO of Red Rhino; prior to signing the note, a Red Rhino employee sent an e-mail to Envision Printing stating that "Bernie [has] full authorization under the LLC documents to sign for Red Rhino Market Group;" an Envision Printing employee replied to that e-mail, also by e-mail, instructing the Red Rhino employee to "have Bernie sign it," and did not object to the "to sign for Red Rhino" statement; Envision Printing sent the note to Red Rhino's e-mail address for signatures; and a Red Rhino employee witnessed Evans's signing of the note.

In its response, Envision Printing argued that Evans was personally responsible for the debt. Envision Printing pointed to, among other things, the affidavit of * * * Envision Printing's president wherein the latter averred that Evans had "signed the Note personally, and Envision accepted the Note as a personal obligation of Bernie Evans and continued to do business with Red Rhino after receiving the Note." Envision Printing also asserted that Evans had signed the note without indicating thereon that he was doing so in a representative capacity.

In its order granting summary judgment to Evans, the trial court found that Evans had signed the promissory note solely in his representative capacity and was not personally liable. The court further found that Envision Printing knew that Evans had not signed in his personal capacity.

[Envision Printing appealed.] Envision Printing contends that the trial court erred by granting summary

judgment to Evans when he was personally liable under the note. We disagree.

*Generally, a corporation's officers and the corporation are entirely separate and distinct entities. Contracts may be signed by one acting in a representative capacity, or a representative may make himself liable for the debt of the corporation;* this Court examines the language of the contract to determine in what capacity the representative is bound. [Emphasis added.]

The construction of contracts involves three steps. At least initially, construction is a matter of law for the court. First, the trial court must decide whether the language is clear and unambiguous. If it is, no construction is required, and the court simply enforces the contract according to its clear terms. Next, if the contract is ambiguous in some respect, the court must apply the rules of contract construction to resolve the ambiguity. Finally, if the ambiguity remains after applying the rules of construction, the issue of what the ambiguous language means and what the parties intended must be resolved by a jury.

The cardinal rule of contract construction is to ascertain the intention of the parties. * * * In this case, looking at the whole contract, we conclude that there is ambiguity as to the capacity in which Evans signed, but, as discussed below, that ambiguity can be resolved by applying the rules of contract construction.

[Official Code of Georgia Annotated (OCGA)] Section 11–3–402(b)(2) [Georgia's version of UCC 3–402(b)(2)] prescribes the conditions under which an authorized representative's signature

*Case 17.1 Continues*

Case 17.1 Continued

on a note may make the representative personally liable for the obligation. That statute provides, in pertinent part:

> * * * if the form of the signature does not show unambiguously that the signature is made in a representative capacity or the represented person is not identified in the instrument, the representative is liable on the instrument to a holder in due course

that took the instrument without notice that the representative was not intended to be liable on the instrument.

In this case, the form of Evans's signature does not show unambiguously that he signed the instrument in a representative capacity. At the same time, the represented person (Red Rhino Market Group, LLC) is clearly identified in the

instrument. Thus, under OCGA Section 11–3–402(b)(2), Evans is liable if Envision Printing took the note "without notice that [he] was not intended to be liable on the instrument." We conclude that Envision Printing had notice that Evans was not intended to be personally liable on the note.

* * * *

*Judgment affirmed.*

**Legal Reasoning Questions**

1. On Evans's motion for summary judgment, what evidence did the opposing parties emphasize? Based on this evidence, what did the court conclude?

2. How did the rules of contract construction apply in this case?

3. Suppose that the name Red Rhino Market Group, LLC, had not been included on the note. Would Evans have been personally liable for its payment? Discuss.

---

**Checks Signed by Agents** An important exception to the rules on agent liability is made for checks that are signed by agents. If an agent signs his or her own name on a *check that is payable from the account of the principal,* and the principal is identified on the check, the agent will not be personally liable on the check [UCC 3–402(c)]. ■ **EXAMPLE 17.10** Sandra Binney, who is *authorized* to draw checks on Aronson Company's account, signs a check that is preprinted with Aronson Company's name. The signature reads simply "Sandra Binney." In this situation, Binney will not be personally liable on the check. ■

## 17–1e Unauthorized Signatures

Unauthorized signatures arise in two situations:

1. When a person forges another person's name on a negotiable instrument.

2. When an agent who lacks the authority signs an instrument on behalf of a principal.

**The General Rule** The general rule is that an unauthorized signature is wholly inoperative and will not bind the person whose name is signed or forged. ■ **EXAMPLE 17.11** Parker finds Dolby's checkbook lying in the street, writes out a check to himself, and forges Dolby's signature. Banks normally have a duty to determine whether a person's signature on a check is forged. If a bank fails to determine that Dolby's signature is not genuine and

cashes the check for Parker, the bank will generally be liable to Dolby for the amount. ■

The general rule also applies to agents' signatures. If an agent lacks the authority to sign the principal's name or has exceeded the authority given by the principal, the signature does not bind the principal but will bind the "unauthorized signer" [UCC 3–403(a)]. ■ **EXAMPLE 17.12** Maya Campbell is the principal, and Lena Shem is her agent. Shem, without authority, signs a promissory note as follows: "Maya Campbell, by Lena Shem, agent." Because Maya Campbell's "signature" is unauthorized, Campbell cannot be held liable, but Shem is liable to a holder of the note. This would be true even if Shem had signed the note "Maya Campbell," without indicating any agency relationship. In either situation, the unauthorized signer, Shem, is liable on the instrument. ■

**Exceptions to the General Rule** There are two exceptions to the general rule that an unauthorized signature will not bind the person whose name is signed:

1. *Ratification.* When the person whose name is signed *ratifies* (affirms) the signature, he or she will be bound [UCC 3–403(a)]. The parties involved need not be principal and agent for this section of the UCC to apply. For instance, a mother may ratify her daughter's forgery of the mother's signature so that the daughter will not be prosecuted for forgery.

A person can ratify an unauthorized signature either expressly (by affirming the signature) or impliedly (by other conduct, such as keeping any benefits received in the transaction or failing to repudiate the signature).

2. *Negligence.* When the negligence of the person whose name was forged substantially contributed to the forgery, a court may not allow the person to deny the effectiveness of an unauthorized signature [UCC 3–115, 3–406, 4–401(d)(2)].

■ **EXAMPLE 17.13** Roger writes and signs a check, leaves blank the amount and the name of the payee, and then sets the check in a place available to the public. Joan finds the check, fills it in, and cashes it. Roger, on the basis of his negligence, can be estopped (prevented) from denying liability for payment of the check. Whatever loss occurs may be allocated between the parties on the basis of *comparative negligence,* however [UCC 3–406(b)]. If Roger can demonstrate that the bank was negligent in paying the check, a court may require the bank to bear a portion of the loss. ■

### When the Holder Is a Holder in Due Course

A person who forges a check or signs an instrument without authorization can be held personally liable for payment by a holder in due course, or HDC [UCC 3–403(a)]. This is true even if the name of the person signing the instrument without authorization does not appear on the instrument.

■ **EXAMPLE 17.14** If Michel Vuillard signs "Paul Richman" without Richman's authorization, Vuillard is personally liable just as if he had signed his own name. Vuillard's liability is limited, however, to persons who in good faith pay the instrument or take it for value. A holder who knew the signature was unauthorized would not qualify as an HDC (because of the good faith requirement) and thus could not recover from Vuillard on the instrument. (The defenses that are effective against ordinary holders versus HDCs will be discussed later in this chapter.) ■

## 17–1f Special Rules for Unauthorized Indorsements

Generally, when an indorsement is forged or unauthorized, the burden of loss falls on the first party to take the instrument with the forged or unauthorized indorsement. The reason for this general rule is that the first party to take an instrument is in the best position to prevent the loss.

■ **EXAMPLE 17.15** Jen Nilson steals a check drawn on Universal Bank and payable to the order of Inga Leed. Nilson indorses the check "Inga Leed" and presents the check to Universal Bank for payment. The bank, without

asking Nilson for identification, pays the check, and Nilson disappears. In this situation, Leed will not be liable on the check. because her indorsement was forged. The bank will bear the loss, which it might have avoided if it had asked Nilson for identification. ■

This general rule has two important exceptions that cause the loss to fall on the maker or drawer. These exceptions arise when an indorsement is made by an *imposter* or by a *fictitious payee.*

**Imposter Rule** An **imposter** is one who, through deception, induces a maker or drawer to issue an instrument in the name of an impersonated payee. The imposter may carry out the deception by her or his personal appearance or by use of mail, Internet, telephone, or other communication.

**Focus Is on the Maker's or Drawer's Intent.** If the maker or drawer believes the imposter to be the named payee at the time of issue, the imposter's indorsement is not treated as unauthorized when the instrument is transferred to an innocent party. This is because the maker or drawer *intended* the imposter to receive the instrument.

In these situations, the unauthorized indorsement of a payee's name can be as effective as if the real payee had signed. The UCC's *imposter rule* provides that an imposter's indorsement will be effective—that is, not a forgery—insofar as the drawer or maker is concerned [UCC 3–404(a)].

**Comparative Negligence Applies.** The comparative negligence standard mentioned previously also applies to situations involving imposters [UCC 3–404(d)]. Thus, if a bank fails to exercise ordinary care in cashing a check made out to an imposter, the drawer may be able to recover a portion of the loss from the bank.

■ **EXAMPLE 17.16** Carol impersonates Donna and induces Edward to write a check payable to the order of Donna. Carol, continuing to impersonate Donna, negotiates the check to First National Bank as payment on her loan there. As the drawer of the check, Edward is liable for its amount to First National. If the bank failed to use due care when taking the check from Carol, however, Edward may be able to recover a portion of his loss from First National. ■

**Fictitious Payees** When a person causes an instrument to be issued to a payee who will have *no interest* in the instrument, the payee is referred to as a **fictitious payee.** A fictitious payee can be a person or firm that does not truly exist, or it may be an identifiable party that will not acquire any interest in the instrument.

Under the UCC's *fictitious payee rule,* the payee's indorsement is not treated as a forgery, and an innocent holder can hold the maker or drawer liable on the instrument [UCC 3–404(b), 3–405]. Basically, the loss falls on the maker or drawer of the instrument rather than on the third party that accepts it or on the bank that cashes it.

Fictitious payees most often arise in two situations:

1. When a dishonest employee deceives the employer into signing an instrument payable to a party with no right to receive payment on the instrument.
2. When a dishonest employee or agent has the authority to issue an instrument on behalf of the employer and issues a check to a party who has no interest in the instrument.

**■ CASE IN POINT 17.17** Braden Furniture Company gave its bookkeeper, Bonnie Manning, general authority to access the company's accounting program and create checks. Over the course of seven years, Manning created more than two hundred unauthorized checks, totaling $470,000, which she deposited in her own account at Union State Bank. Braden Furniture was not a customer of Union State Bank.

The majority of the checks did not identify a payee (the payee line on the check was left blank). Braden Furniture (the drawer) sued Union State Bank for the loss, claiming that the bank was negligent in accepting and paying the blank checks. The court, however, held that the fictitious payee rule applied. Therefore, under the UCC, the loss fell on Braden Furniture, not on Union State Bank.[7] ■

For a synopsis of the rules relating to signature liability, see Concept Summary 17.1.

# 17–2 Warranty Liability

In addition to signature liability, transferors make certain implied warranties regarding the instruments that they are negotiating. Warranty liability arises even when a transferor does not indorse (sign) the instrument [UCC 3–416, 3–417].

Warranty liability is particularly important when a holder cannot hold a party liable on her or his signature, such as when a person delivers a bearer instrument. *Unlike secondary signature liability, warranty liability is not*

subject to the conditions of proper presentment, dishonor, or notice of dishonor.

Warranties fall into two categories: those that arise from the *transfer* of a negotiable instrument and those that arise on *presentment.* Both transfer and presentment warranties attempt to shift liability back to the wrongdoer or to the person who dealt face to face with the wrongdoer and thus was in the best position to prevent the wrongdoing.

## 17–2a Transfer Warranties

A person who transfers an instrument *for consideration* makes the following five **transfer warranties** to all subsequent transferees and holders who take the instrument in good faith [UCC 3–416]:

1. The transferor is entitled to enforce the instrument.
2. All signatures are authentic and authorized.
3. The instrument has not been altered.
4. The instrument is not subject to a defense or claim of any party that can be asserted against the transferor.
5. The transferor has no knowledge of any bankruptcy proceedings against the maker, the acceptor, or the drawer of the instrument.[8]

Note that for transfer warranties to arise, an instrument *must be transferred for consideration.* **■ EXAMPLE 17.18** Quality Products Corporation sells goods to Royal Retail Stores and receives in payment Royal Retail's promissory note. Quality then sells the note, for value, to Superior Finance Company. In this situation, the instrument has been transferred for consideration. ■

### Parties to Whom Warranty Liability Extends
The manner of transfer and the type of negotiation that are used determine how far a transfer warranty will run and whom it will cover. Transfer of an order instrument by indorsement and delivery extends warranty liability to any subsequent holder who takes the instrument in good faith. The warranties of a person who, for consideration, transfers *without indorsement* (by delivery of a bearer instrument), however, will extend only to the immediate transferee [UCC 3–416(a)].

---

7. *Braden Furniture Co. v. Union State Bank,* 109 So.3d 625 (Ala. 2012).

8. A 2002 amendment to UCC 3–416(a) adds a sixth warranty. It involves "a remotely created consumer item," such as an electronic check, drawn on a customer's account, which is not created by the payor bank and does not contain the drawer's handwritten signature. This amendment has been adopted in only a few states. Under this amendment, a bank that accepts and pays the instrument warrants to the next bank in the collection chain that the consumer authorized the item in that amount.

# Concept Summary 17.1

## Signature Liability

| | |
|---|---|
| **Primary and Secondary Liability** | • *Primary Liability*—Makers and acceptors are primarily liable [UCC 3–409, 3–412, 3–413].<br>• *Secondary Liability*—Drawers and indorsers are secondarily liable. Parties who are secondarily liable on an instrument promise to pay on that instrument only if the instrument is properly and timely presented, the instrument is dishonored, or timely notice of dishonor is given [UCC 3–414, 3–415, 3–501, 3–502, 3–503]. |
| **Accommodation Parties** | • An *accommodation party* is one who signs an instrument for the purpose of lending his or her name as credit to another party on the instrument [UCC 3–419].<br>• Accommodation *makers* are primarily liable; accommodation *indorsers* are secondarily liable. |
| **Agents' Signatures** | • An *agent* is a person who agrees to represent or act for another, called the *principal*. Agents can sign negotiable instruments and thereby bind their principals.<br>• Liability on the instrument depends on whether the agent is authorized and on whether the agent's representative capacity and the principal's identity are both indicated on the instrument [UCC 3–401, 3–402, 3–403].<br>• Agents need not indicate their representative capacity on *checks*—provided the checks clearly identify the principal and are drawn on the principal's account. |
| **Unauthorized Signatures** | • An unauthorized signature is wholly inoperative as the signature of the person whose name is signed *unless:*<br>  1. The person whose name is signed ratifies (affirms) it or is precluded from denying it [UCC 3–115, 3–403, 3–406, 4–401].<br>  2. The instrument has been negotiated to a holder in due course [UCC 3–403]. |
| **Special Rules for Unauthorized Indorsements** | • An unauthorized indorsement will not bind the maker or drawer of the instrument except in the following circumstances:<br>  1. When an imposter induces the maker or drawer of an instrument to issue it to the imposter *(imposter rule)* [UCC 3–404(a)].<br>  2. When a person causes an instrument to be issued to a payee who will have *no interest* in the instrument *(fictitious payee rule)* [UCC 3–404(b), 3–405]. |

■ **EXAMPLE 17.19** Lyle forges Kim's name as a maker of a promissory note. The note is made payable to Lyle. Lyle indorses the note in blank, negotiates it for consideration to Bret, and then leaves the country. Bret, without indorsement, delivers the note for consideration to Fern. Fern, also without indorsement, delivers the note for consideration to Rick. On Rick's presentment of the note to Kim, the forgery is discovered. Rick can hold Fern (the immediate transferor) liable for breach of the warranty that all signatures are genuine. Rick cannot hold Bret liable, because Bret is not Rick's immediate transferor. Rather, Bret is a prior nonindorsing transferor.

Note that if Lyle had added a special indorsement ("Payable to Bret") instead of a blank indorsement, the instrument would have remained an order instrument. In that situation, Bret would have had to indorse the instrument to negotiate it to Fern, and his transfer warranties would extend to all subsequent holders, including Rick. This example shows the importance of the distinction between transfer by indorsement and delivery (of an order instrument) and transfer by delivery only, without indorsement (of a bearer instrument). ■

Concept Summary 17.2 illustrates the rules on transfer warranty liability.

**Recovery for Breach of Warranty** A holder who takes an instrument in good faith can sue for breach of a warranty as soon as he or she has reason to know of the breach [UCC 3–416(d)]. The transferee or holder must notify the warrantor of the breach of warranty claim within thirty days of discovering the breach [UCC 3–416(c)]. Failure to give notice relieves the warrantor from liability for any loss caused by a delay.

The transferee or holder can recover damages for the breach in an amount equal to the loss suffered (but not more than the amount of the instrument). Damages can also include expenses and any loss of interest caused by the breach [UCC 3–416(b)].

These warranties cannot be disclaimed with regard to checks [UCC 3–416(c)]. In the check-collection process, banks rely on these warranties. For all other instruments, the immediate parties can agree to a disclaimer, and an indorser can disclaim by including in the indorsement such words as "without warranties."

### 17–2b Presentment Warranties

Any person who presents an instrument for payment or acceptance makes the following **presentment warranties** to any other person who in good faith pays or accepts the instrument [UCC 3–417(a), (d)]:

1. The person obtaining payment or acceptance is entitled to enforce the instrument or is authorized to

---

## Concept Summary 17.2

### Transfer Warranty Liability for Transferors Who Receive Consideration

**TRANSFER WARRANTIES**
1. The transferor is entitled to enforce the instrument.
2. All signatures are authentic and authorized.
3. The instrument has not been altered.
4. The instrument is not subject to a defense or claim of any party that can be asserted against the transferor.
5. The transferor has no knowledge of insolvency proceedings against the maker, acceptor, or drawer of the instrument.

**Indorser who receives consideration** obtains transfer warranties that extend *to any subsequent holder* who takes the instrument in good faith.

**Nonindorser who receives consideration** obtains the same transfer warranties, but they extend *only to the immediate transferee*.

obtain payment or acceptance on behalf of a person who is entitled to enforce the instrument. (This is, in effect, a warranty that there are no missing or unauthorized indorsements.)

2. The instrument has not been altered.
3. The person obtaining payment or acceptance has no knowledge that the signature of the drawer of the instrument is unauthorized.[9]

**Protect the Transferee**  These warranties are referred to as *presentment warranties* because they protect the person to whom the instrument is presented. They often have the effect of shifting liability back to the party that was in the best position to prevent the wrongdoing.

**Limitations**  The second and third warranties do not apply to makers, acceptors, and drawers. It is assumed that a drawer or a maker will recognize his or her own signature and that a maker or an acceptor will recognize whether an instrument has been materially altered.

Presentment warranties cannot be disclaimed with respect to checks. Also, a party claiming breach of warranty must notify the warrantor within thirty days after the claimant knows or has reason to know of the breach. If the claim is made after thirty days, the warrantor is not liable for any loss caused by the delay [UCC 3–417(e)].

---

9. As mentioned, 2002 amendments to Article 3 of the UCC provide additional protection for "a remotely created consumer item."

# 17–3 Defenses and Limitations

Certain defenses can bar collection from persons who would otherwise be liable on an instrument. There are two general categories of defenses—*universal defenses* and *personal defenses*—as shown in Exhibit 17–2.

## 17–3a Universal Defenses

**Universal defenses** (also called *real defenses*) are valid against *all* holders, including HDCs and holders through HDCs. Universal defenses include those listed next and described in the following subsections.

1. Forgery of a signature on the instrument.
2. Fraud in the execution.
3. Material alteration.
4. Discharge in bankruptcy.
5. Minority.
6. Illegality, mental incapacity, or extreme duress.

**Forgery**  A forged signature will not bind the person whose name is used. Thus, when a person forges an instrument, the person whose name is forged has no liability to pay any holder or any HDC the value of the forged instrument. If the person whose name is forged ratifies (approves or validates) the signature, however, he or she may be liable. Similarly, a maker or drawer who is barred from denying a forgery (because it was made possible by

**EXHIBIT 17–2**  Defenses against Liability on Negotiable Instruments

| UNIVERSAL (REAL) DEFENSES | PERSONAL (LIMITED) DEFENSES |
|---|---|
| Valid against all holders, including holders in due course | Valid against ordinary holders but not against holders in due course |
| 1. Forgery.<br>2. Fraud in the execution.<br>3. Material alteration.<br>4. Discharge in bankruptcy.<br>5. Minority, if the contract is voidable.<br>6. Illegality, mental incapacity, or duress, if the contract is void under state law. | 1. Breach of contract (including breach of contract warranties).<br>2. Lack or failure of consideration.<br>3. Fraud in the inducement (ordinary fraud).<br>4. Illegality, mental incapacity, or duress, if the contract is voidable.<br>5. Previous payment or cancellation of the instrument.<br>6. Unauthorized completion of an incomplete instrument and nondelivery of the instrument. |

his or her negligence, for instance) may also be held liable [UCC 3–401(a), 3–403(a)].

**Fraud in the Execution** If a person is deceived into signing a negotiable instrument by being told that it is something else, *fraud in the execution* (or inception) is committed against the signer [UCC 3–305(a)(1)(iii)]. ■ **EXAMPLE 17.20** Connor, a salesperson, asks Javier, a customer, to sign a paper. Connor says that it is a receipt for the delivery of goods that Javier is picking up from the store. In fact, it is a promissory note, but Javier is unfamiliar with the English language and does not realize this. In this situation, even if the note is negotiated to an HDC, Javier has a valid defense against payment. ■

This defense cannot be raised if a reasonable inquiry would have revealed the nature and terms of the instrument. Thus, the signer's age, experience, and intelligence are relevant because they frequently determine whether the signer should have understood the nature of the transaction before signing.

**Material Alteration** An alteration is *material* if it changes the contract terms between two parties *in any way*. Examples include any unauthorized addition of words or numbers or other changes to complete an incomplete instrument that affect the obligation of a party to the instrument [UCC 3–407(a)]. Making any change in the amount, the date, or the rate of interest—even if the change is only one penny, one day, or 1 percent—is material.

It is not a material alteration, however, to correct the maker's address or to draw a red line across the instrument to indicate that an auditor has checked it. It is also not a material alteration to change the figures on a check so that they agree with the written amount. If the alteration is not material, any holder is entitled to enforce the instrument according to its original terms.

**A Complete or Partial Defense.** Material alteration is a *complete defense* against an ordinary holder but only a *partial defense* against an HDC. An ordinary holder can recover nothing on an instrument that has been materially altered [UCC 3–407(b)]. In contrast, when an original term has been altered, an HDC can enforce the instrument against the maker or drawer—but only according to the original terms [UCC 3–407(c)(i)]. For instance, if the amount payable has been altered, the HDC can enforce the instrument for the original amount but not the altered amount.

Note that if an alteration is readily apparent (such as a number changed on the face of a check), then obviously the holder has notice of some defect or defense. Thus, the

holder cannot be an HDC (and therefore cannot enforce the instrument) [UCC 3–302(a)(1), (2)(iv)].

**An HDC Can Enforce an Incomplete Instrument That Was Subsequently Altered.** If an instrument was originally incomplete and was later completed in an unauthorized manner, alteration can no longer be claimed as a defense against an HDC [UCC 3–407(b), (c)]. The HDC can enforce the instrument as completed because a drawer or maker who issued an incomplete instrument normally will be held responsible for such an alteration. A drawer or maker could have avoided the alteration by the exercise of greater care in completing the instrument.

**Discharge in Bankruptcy** Discharge in bankruptcy is an absolute defense on any instrument regardless of the status of the holder [UCC 3–305(a)(1)(iv)]. This defense exists because the purpose of bankruptcy is to settle finally all of the insolvent party's debts.

**Minority** Minority, or infancy, is a universal defense only to the extent that state law recognizes it as a defense to a simple contract. Because state laws on minority vary, so do determinations of whether minority is a universal defense against an HDC [UCC 3–305(a)(1)(i)].

**Illegality** Certain types of illegality constitute universal defenses, whereas others are personal defenses. If a statute provides that an illegal transaction is void, then the defense is universal—that is, absolute against both an ordinary holder and an HDC. If the law merely makes the instrument voidable, then the illegality is a personal defense against an ordinary holder, but not against an HDC [UCC 3–305(a)(1)(ii)].

**Mental Incapacity** If a court has declared a person to be mentally incompetent, then any instrument issued by that person is void. The instrument is void *ab initio* (from the beginning) and unenforceable by any holder or HDC [UCC 3–305(a)(1)(ii)]. Mental incapacity in these circumstances is a universal defense. If a court has not declared a person to be mentally incompetent, then mental incapacity operates as a personal defense against ordinary holders but not against HDCs.

**Extreme Duress** When a person signs and issues a negotiable instrument under extreme duress, the instrument is void and unenforceable by any holder or HDC [UCC 3–305(a)(1)(ii)]. An immediate threat of force or violence (for instance, at gunpoint) would qualify as extreme duress. (Ordinary duress is a defense against ordinary holders but not against HDCs.)

## 17–3b Personal Defenses

**Personal defenses** (sometimes called *limited defenses*) are used to avoid payment to an ordinary holder of a negotiable instrument. They are not a defense against an HDC or a holder through an HDC. Personal defenses include the following:

1. Breach of contract or breach of warranty.
2. Lack or failure of consideration.
3. Fraud in the inducement (ordinary fraud).
4. Illegality.
5. Mental incapacity.
6. Ordinary duress or undue influence rendering the contract voidable [UCC 3–305(a)(1)(ii)].
7. Previous payment or cancellation [UCC 3–601(b), 3–602(a), 3–603, 3–604].
8. Unauthorized completion of an incomplete instrument [UCC 3–115, 3–302, 3–407, 4–401(d)(2)].
9. Nondelivery of the instrument [UCC 1–201(14), 3–105(b), 3–305(a)(2)].

**Breach of Contract or Breach of Warranty** A breach of the underlying contract for which the negotiable instrument was issued is a personal defense. If a breach occurs, the maker of a note can refuse to pay it, or the drawer of a check can order his or her bank to stop payment on the check. Breach of warranty can also be claimed as a defense to liability on the instrument.

■ **EXAMPLE 17.21** Elias purchases two dozen pairs of athletic shoes from De Soto. The shoes are to be delivered in six weeks. Elias gives De Soto a promissory note for $1,000, which is the price of the shoes. The shoes arrive, but many of them are discolored, and the soles of several pairs are coming apart. Elias has a defense to liability on the note on the basis of breach of contract and breach of warranty. (A seller impliedly promises that the goods being sold are at least merchantable.)

If, however, the note is no longer in the hands of the payee-seller (De Soto) but is presented for payment by an HDC, the result is different. The maker-buyer (Elias) in that situation will not be able to plead breach of contract or warranty as a defense against liability on the note. ■

**Lack or Failure of Consideration** The absence of consideration (value) may be a successful defense in some instances [UCC 3–303(b), 3–305(a)(2)]. ■ **EXAMPLE 17.22** Tony gives Cleo, as a gift, a note that states, "I promise to pay you $100,000," and Cleo accepts the note. No consideration is given in return for Tony's promise, and a court will not enforce the promise. ■

Similarly, if delivery of goods becomes impossible, a party who has issued a draft or note under the contract has a defense for not paying it. Thus, in *Example 17.21*, if the shoes were lost in an accident and delivery became impossible, De Soto could not subsequently enforce Elias's promise to pay the $1,000 promissory note. (If the note was in the hands of an HDC, however, Elias's defense would not be available against the HDC.)

In the following case, a party asserted lack of consideration as a defense for not paying a promissory note.

---

**Case Analysis 17.2**

## Mills v. Chauvin

Supreme Court of New York, Appellate Division, Third Department, 103 A.D.3d 1041, 962 N.Y.S.2d 412 (2013).

### In the Language of the Court
*PER CURIAM.*
* * * *

Plaintiff, Gregory Mills, and defendant, Robert Chauvin, are two experienced attorneys who shared both a friendship and a professional/business relationship. Those longstanding relationships deteriorated and gave rise to this action.
* * * *

* * * The parties formed a partnership and took ownership of a commercial office building located on Crescent Road in the Town of Clifton Park, Saratoga County. * * * After Chauvin

decided, for a variety of reasons, that he no longer wished to maintain his ownership of the Crescent Road property, the parties agreed that Mills would purchase Chauvin's one-half interest in such property and they executed a purchase and sale agreement establishing a purchase price of $261,176.67 and a closing date.
* * * *

Chauvin was an investor in the Amelia Village [real estate development] project [in Virginia]. Over a course of time, Mills made multiple monetary payments to Chauvin—totaling $395,750—which Chauvin claims were investments in the project and Mills claims were loans.

Ultimately, Mills requested that Chauvin return the payments he had advanced. In connection therewith, Chauvin executed a promissory note * * * that obligated him to pay Mills $395,750. However, Chauvin later challenged the validity of the promissory note and claimed that Mills was not entitled to a return of his investments.
* * * *

Mills subsequently filed [a] complaint [in a New York state court against Chauvin] to recover the payments Mills had made with respect to the Amelia Village project, based upon claims of breach

**Case 17.2 Continues**

of contract and unjust enrichment, respectively.

* * * *

The action proceeded to a nonjury trial * * * . At the conclusion thereof, Supreme Court [the trial court] found * * * that the promissory note was valid and enforceable and that Mills was entitled to recover pursuant to its terms. Chauvin now appeals from the judgment entered upon that decision.

* * * *

* * * Initially, we reject Chauvin's claim that Supreme Court erred in concluding that the * * * promissory note was enforceable. Chauvin does not dispute that Mills had previously paid him $395,750 in connection with the Amelia Village project, that he signed the promissory note promising to repay that amount to Mills, or that he tendered the note to Mills for the purpose of providing documentation to Mills' lending institution in support of Mills'

application for financing of the purchase of the Crescent Road property. Instead, Chauvin claims that the promissory note was not enforceable because it was not given to secure a debt and, therefore, lacked consideration.

In this regard, Mills testified that * * * the parties * * * agreed that Chauvin would repay Mills all of the money that Mills had contributed to the Amelia Village project and that the promissory note confirmed their agreement. On the other hand, Chauvin claims that the payments that Mills made to the Amelia Village project were investments that could not be returned when Mills withdrew from that project, and that the promissory note was not intended to be a promise of repayment.

* * * *

The record amply supports Supreme Court's finding that the consideration for the promissory note was the $395,750 that Mills had provided to

Chauvin in connection with the Amelia Village project and that the promissory note represented security for Chauvin's antecedent obligation to repay such funds. *The note itself—which was drafted by Chauvin, signed by him, notarized and transmitted to Mills clearly states that it was executed in return for a loan received by Chauvin and contained an unconditional promise or order to pay a sum certain in money. In addition, Mills took the note as a holder in due course.* Based upon our independent evaluation of the evidence and, giving due deference to the trial court's credibility determinations concerning witnesses, we conclude that Supreme Court's determination that Chauvin failed to establish a bona fide defense of lack of consideration is supported by the record. [Emphasis added.]

* * * *

ORDERED that the order and judgments are affirmed, with costs to plaintiff.

**Legal Reasoning Questions**

1. If the court had accepted Chauvin's claim that Mills's funds represented an investment, would the result in this case have been different? Explain.

2. Do the facts in this case support the court's conclusion that Mills took Chauvin's note as an HDC? Why or why not?

3. How did Mills's status as an HDC affect Chauvin's asserted defense?

**Fraud in the Inducement (Ordinary Fraud)** A person who issues a negotiable instrument based on false statements by the other party will be able to avoid payment on that instrument, unless the holder is an HDC. ■ **CASE IN POINT 17.23** New Houston Gold Exchange, Inc. (HGE), issued a $3,500 postdated check to Shelly McKee to buy a purportedly genuine Rolex watch. McKee indorsed the check and presented it to RR Maloan Investments, Inc., a check-cashing service. RR Maloan cashed the check. Meanwhile, HGE issued a stop-payment order on the check based on information that the watch was counterfeit. When RR Maloan presented the check to HGE's bank for payment, the bank refused to honor it. HGE claimed that RR Maloan was not a holder in due course because of McKee's fraud in selling an allegedly fake Rolex. RR Maloan filed a suit in a Texas state

court against HGE to recover the funds, asserting that it was an HDC entitled to collect on the check.

Ultimately, a state appellate court found that McKee's ostensible fraud toward HGE did not prevent RR Maloan from obtaining the status of an HDC. The check-cashing service took the check in good faith and for fair value, unaware of McKee's alleged fraud in inducing HGE to issue the check. Therefore, RR Maloan was entitled to payment on the check.[10] ■

**Illegality** As mentioned, if a statute provides that an illegal transaction is voidable, the defense is personal. For instance, some states make contracts in restraint of trade

---

10. *RR Maloan Investments, Inc. v. New HGE, Inc.,* 428 S.W.3d 355 (Tex. App.—Houston 2014).

voidable. Thus, an instrument given in payment of a contract to restrain trade in those states is voidable and operates as a personal defense.

**Mental Incapacity**  If a maker or drawer issues a negotiable instrument while mentally incompetent but before a court has declared him or her to be so, the instrument is voidable. In this situation, mental incapacity serves as a personal defense.

### 17–3c Federal Limitations on the Rights of HDCs

The federal government limits the rights of HDCs in certain circumstances because of the harsh effects that the HDC rules can sometimes have on consumers. Under the HDC doctrine, a consumer who purchased a defective product (such as a defective automobile) would continue to be liable to HDCs even if the consumer returned the defective product to the retailer.

■ **EXAMPLE 17.24**  To buy a used truck with a one-year warranty, Brian pays $5,000 down and signs a promissory note to the dealer for the remaining $15,000. The truck turns out to be defective, and Brian returns it to the dealer, but the dealer has already sold the note to an HDC. Under the HDC doctrine, Brian would remain liable to the HDC for $15,000 in this situation because his claim of breach of warranty is a personal defense, not a universal defense. ■

To protect consumers who purchase defective products, the Federal Trade Commission (FTC) adopted Rule 433, which effectively abolished the HDC doctrine in consumer transactions.[11]

**FTC Rule 433**  FTC Rule 433 severely limits the rights of HDCs that purchase instruments arising out of *consumer credit* transactions. The rule applies to consumers who purchase goods or services for personal, family, or household use using a consumer credit contract. The regulation prevents a consumer from being required to make payment for a defective product to a third party HDC who has acquired a promissory note that formed part of the consumer's contract with the dealer who sold the defective good.

Rule 433 requires the following provision to be included in boldface type in consumer credit contracts:

---

### NOTICE

ANY HOLDER OF THIS CONSUMER CREDIT CONTRACT IS SUBJECT TO ALL CLAIMS AND DEFENSES WHICH THE DEBTOR COULD ASSERT AGAINST THE SELLER OF GOODS OR SERVICES OBTAINED PURSUANT HERETO OR WITH THE PROCEEDS HEREOF. RECOVERY HEREUNDER BY THE DEBTOR SHALL NOT EXCEED AMOUNTS PAID BY THE DEBTOR HEREUNDER.

**Effect of the Rule**  When a negotiable instrument contains the required notice, a consumer can bring any defense that she or he has against the seller of a product against a subsequent holder as well. In essence, FTC Rule 433 places an HDC of the instrument in the position of a contract assignee.

The rule makes the buyer's duty to pay conditional on the seller's full performance of the contract. It also clearly reduces the degree of transferability of negotiable instruments resulting from consumer credit contracts. An instrument that contains this notice or a similar statement required by law remains negotiable, but there cannot be an HDC of such an instrument [UCC 3–106(d)].

There is a loophole, however. FTC Rule 433 does not prohibit third parties from purchasing notes or credit contracts that do *not* contain the required notice. If a third party purchases an instrument arising from a consumer credit transaction that lacks the notice, that third party normally is not subject to the buyer's defenses against the seller. Thus, some consumers remain unprotected by the FTC rule.[12]

---

## 17–4 Discharge

Discharge from liability on an instrument can come from payment, cancellation, or material alteration. Discharge can also occur if a party reacquires an instrument, if a holder impairs another party's right of recourse, or if a holder surrenders collateral without consent.

---

11. 16 C.F.R. Section 433.2. The rule was enacted in 1976 pursuant to the FTC's authority under the Federal Trade Commission Act, 15 U.S.C. Sections 41–58.

12. A 2002 amendment to UCC 3–305(e) closes this loophole, but only a minority of the states have adopted the amendment. The amendment makes a third party holder in possession of a note or other instrument that was supposed to include this notice subject to a buyer's defenses against a seller even if the instrument did not include the notice.

## 17-4a Discharge by Payment or Tender of Payment

All parties to a negotiable instrument will be discharged when the party primarily liable on it pays to a holder the full amount due [UCC 3–602, 3–603]. The liability of all parties is also discharged when the drawee of an unaccepted draft or check makes payment in good faith to the holder.

Payment by any other party (for instance, an indorser) discharges only the liability of that party and subsequent parties. The party making such a payment still has the right to recover on the instrument from any prior parties.[13]

**Good Faith Required**   A party will not be discharged if that party knowingly (in bad faith) pays a holder who acquired the instrument by theft or who obtained the instrument from someone else who acquired it by theft [UCC 3–602(b)(2)]. An exception to this rule is made if the person has the rights of an HDC.

**Tender of Payment**   Sometimes, a tender (offer) of payment is made to a person entitled to enforce the instrument, and the tender is refused. In that situation, the rights of indorsers and accommodation parties to seek reimbursement are impaired (impairment of the right of recourse is discussed shortly). Therefore, the indorsers and accommodation parties are discharged to the extent of the amount of the tender [UCC 3–603(b)].

■ **EXAMPLE 17.25**   Megan Caldwell is entitled to enforce a $15,000 promissory note, which was indorsed by Bret Reznor and Jill Sanchez. Omni Ventures, LLC, tenders a $10,000 payment on the note, but Caldwell refuses. In this situation, Reznor's and Sanchez's liability on the note is discharged to the extent of the tender ($10,000). ■

When a tender of payment of the amount due on an instrument is made to a person entitled to enforce the instrument, the obligation to pay interest after the date of tender is discharged [UCC 3–603(c)].

## 17-4b Discharge by Cancellation or Surrender

Intentional cancellation of an instrument discharges the liability of all parties [UCC 3–604]. Destruction or mutilation of a negotiable instrument is considered cancellation only if it is done with the intention of eliminating obligation on the instrument [UCC 3–604(a)(i)]. Thus, if an instrument is destroyed or mutilated by accident, the instrument is not discharged, and the original terms can be established by parol evidence [UCC 3–309].

Any of the following acts—if done by the holder *with the intent to cancel* the obligation—will discharge liability:

1. Writing "Paid" across the face of an instrument.
2. Intentionally tearing up an instrument.
3. Crossing out a party's signature. Doing this will discharge that party's liability and the liability of subsequent indorsers who have already signed the instrument.
4. Surrendering the instrument (such as a promissory note) to the party to be discharged.

■ **CASE IN POINT 17.26**   Edith Mark bought a Ford pickup and signed a loan contract and promissory note with Huntington National Bank to finance the purchase. She had made twenty of the sixty-six payments required on the loan when she received the original agreement, stamped "PAID," in the mail, along with the title certificate. Mark stopped making payments on the loan, and the bank filed a lawsuit. Mark argued that the note had been discharged by surrender, but the bank claimed that the documents had been returned to her due to an inadvertent clerical error. The court held that because the bank did not intend to discharge the note when it returned the documents to Mark, the surrender did not constitute a valid cancellation of the note.[14] ■

## 17-4c Discharge by Material Alteration

Materially altering an instrument may discharge the liability of all parties, as previously discussed [UCC 3–407(b)]. (An HDC may be able to enforce a materially altered instrument against its maker or drawer according to the instrument's *original* terms, however.)

## 17-4d Discharge by Reacquisition

The reacquisition of an instrument by a person who held it previously discharges all intervening indorsers against subsequent holders who do not qualify as HDCs [UCC 3–207]. Of course, the person reacquiring the instrument may be liable to subsequent holders if the instrument is dishonored.

---

13. Under a 2002 amendment to UCC 3–602(b), when a party entitled to enforce an instrument transfers it without giving notice to the parties obligated to pay it, and one of those parties pays the transferor, that payment is effective. For instance, Roberto borrows $5,000 from Consumer Finance Company on a note payable to the lender. Consumer Finance transfers the note to Delta Investment Corporation but continues to collect payments from Roberto. Under this amendment, those payments effectively discharge Roberto to the extent of their amount.

14. *Huntington National Bank v. Mark*, 2004 -Ohio- 3856 (Ohio App. 2004).

## 17–4e Discharge by Impairment of Recourse

Discharge can also occur when a party's right of recourse is impaired [UCC 3–605]. A *right of recourse* is a right to seek reimbursement. Ordinarily, when a holder collects the amount of an instrument from an indorser, the indorser has a right of recourse against prior indorsers, the maker or drawer, and accommodation parties.

If the holder has adversely affected the indorser's right to seek reimbursement from these other parties, however, the indorser is not liable on the instrument (to the extent that the indorser's right of recourse is impaired). This occurs when, for instance, the holder releases or agrees not to sue a party against whom the indorser has a right of recourse. It also occurs when a holder agrees to an extension of the instrument's due date or to some other material modification that results in an impairment of the indorser's right of recourse [UCC 3–605(c), (d)].[15]

---

15. The 2002 amendments to UCC 3–605 essentially apply the principles of suretyship and guaranty to circumstances involving the impairment of the right of recourse of "secondary obligors." These obligors include indorsers and accommodation parties. Amended UCC 3–605(a) differs from these principles, however, in that the release of a principal obligor by a person entitled to enforce a check grants a complete discharge to an indorser of the check without requiring proof of harm.

## 17–4f Discharge by Impairment of Collateral

Sometimes, a party to an instrument gives collateral as security that her or his performance will occur. When a holder "impairs the value" of that collateral without the consent of the parties who would benefit from it in the event of nonpayment, those parties are discharged to the extent of the impairment [UCC 3–605(e), (f)].

■ **EXAMPLE 17.27**   Jerome and Myra sign a note as co-makers, putting up Jerome's property as collateral. The note is payable to Montessa. Montessa is required by law to file a *financing statement* with the state to put others on notice of her interest in Jerome's property. If Montessa fails to file the financing statement and Jerome goes through bankruptcy, the property may be sold to pay other debts. Jerome will be unable to pay anything on the note.

In other words, Montessa's failure to file the statement prevents her from taking possession of the collateral, selling it, and crediting the amount owed on the note. This impairs the value of the collateral to Myra, because the proceeds from the sale would have discharged her liability on the note. Myra, as co-maker, is discharged to the extent of this impairment. She is responsible only for any remaining indebtedness, not for the entire unpaid balance. ■

---

# Reviewing: Liability, Defenses, and Discharge

Nancy Mahar was the office manager at Golden Years Nursing Home, Inc. She was given a signature stamp to issue checks to the nursing home's employees for up to $100 as advances on their pay. The checks were drawn on Golden Years' account at First National Bank. Over a seven-year period, Mahar wrote a number of checks to employees exclusively for the purpose of embezzling funds for herself. She forged the employees' indorsements on the checks, signed her name as a second indorser, and deposited the checks in her personal account at Star Bank. The employees whose names were on the checks never actually requested them. When the scheme was uncovered, Golden Years filed a suit against Mahar, Star Bank, and others to recover the funds. Using the information presented in the chapter, answer the following questions.

1. With regard to signature liability, which provision of the Uniform Commercial Code (UCC) discussed in this chapter applies to this scenario?
2. What is the rule set forth by that provision?
3. Under the UCC, which party, Golden Years or Star Bank, must bear the loss in this situation? Why?
4. Based on these facts, describe any transfer or presentment warranties that Mahar may have violated.

---

**Debate This** . . .   *Because signature stamps create so many opportunities for embezzlement, they should be banned.*

## Terms and Concepts

accommodation party 325
agent 326
dishonor 324
fictitious payee 329

imposter 329
personal defense 335
presentment warranty 332
principal 326

transfer warranty 330
universal defense 333

## Issue Spotters

**1.** Rye signs corporate checks for Suchin Corporation. Rye writes a check payable to U-All Company, even though Suchin does not owe U-All anything. Rye signs the check, forges U-All's indorsement, and cashes the check at Viceroy Bank, the drawee. Does Suchin have any recourse against the bank for the payment? Why or why not? (See *Signature Liability.*)

**2.** Skye asked Jim to buy a textbook for her at the campus bookstore. Skye wrote a check payable to the bookstore and left the amount blank for Jim to fill in the price of the book. The cost of the book was $100. Jim filled in the check for $200 before he got to the bookstore. The clerk at the bookstore took the check for $200 and gave Jim the book, plus $100 in cash. Was the bookstore a holder in due course on Skye's check? (See *Discharge.*)

• Check your answers to the Issue Spotters against the answers provided in Appendix B at the end of this text.

## Business Scenarios

**17–1. Material Alteration.** Williams purchased a used car from Stein for $1,000. Williams paid for the car with a check (written in pencil) payable to Stein for $1,000. Stein, through careful erasures and alterations, changed the amount on the check to read $10,000 and negotiated the check to Boz. Boz took the check for value, in good faith, and without notice of the alteration. He thus met the Uniform Commercial Code's requirements for the status of a holder in due course. Can Williams successfully raise the universal (real) defense of material alteration to avoid payment on the check? Explain. (See *Defenses and Limitations.*)

**17–2. Signature Liability.** Waldo makes out a negotiable promissory note payable to the order of Grace. Grace indorses the note by writing on it "Without recourse, Grace" and transfers the note for value to Adam. Adam, in need of cash, negotiates the note to Keith by indorsing it with the words "Pay to Keith, Adam." On the due date, Keith presents the note to Waldo for payment, only to learn that Waldo has filed for bankruptcy and will have all debts (including the note) discharged. Discuss fully whether Keith can hold Waldo, Grace, or Adam liable on the note. (See *Signature Liability.*)

**17–3. Defenses.** Niles sold Kennedy a small motorboat for $1,500, telling Kennedy that the boat was in excellent condition. Kennedy gave Niles a check for $1,500, which Niles indorsed and gave to Frazier for value. When Kennedy took the boat for a trial run, she discovered that the boat leaked, needed to be painted, and required a new motor. Kennedy stopped payment on her check, which had not yet been cashed. Niles had disappeared. Can Frazier recover from Kennedy as a holder in due course? Discuss. (See *Defenses and Limitations.*)

## Business Case Problems

**17–4. Business Case Problem with Sample Answer— Defenses.** Thomas Klutz obtained a franchise from Kahala Franchise Corp. to operate a Samurai Sam's restaurant. Under their agreement, Klutz could transfer the franchise only if he obtained Kahala's approval and paid a transfer fee. Without telling Kahala, Klutz sold the restaurant to William Thorbecke. Thorbecke signed a note for the price. When Kahala learned of the deal, the franchisor told Thorbecke to stop using the Samurai Sam's name. Thorbecke stopped paying on the note, and Klutz filed a claim for the unpaid amount. In defense, Thorbecke asserted breach of contract and fraud. Are these defenses effective against Klutz? Explain. [*Kahala Franchise Corp. v. Hit*

*Enterprises, LLC,* 159 Wash.App. 1013 (Div. 2 2011)] (See *Defenses and Limitations.*)

• For a sample answer to Problem 17–4, go to Appendix C at the end of this text.

**17–5. Defenses.** Damion and Kiya Carmichael took out a loan from Ameriquest Mortgage Co. to refinance their mortgage. They signed a note to make monthly payments on the loan. Later, Deutsche Bank National Trust Co. acquired the note. The Carmichaels stopped making payments and filed for bankruptcy. Deutsche asked the court to foreclose on the mortgage. The Carmichaels asserted that they had been fraudulently induced to make the loan and sign the note. Was the bank free of this defense? Explain. *[In re Carmichael,* 443 Bankr. 698 (E.D.Pa. 2011)] (See *Defenses and Limitations.*)

**17–6. Unauthorized Indorsements.** Angela Brock borrowed $544,000 and signed a note payable to Amerifund Mortgage Services, LLC, to buy a house in Silver Spring, Maryland. The note was indorsed in blank and transferred several times "without recourse" before Brock fell behind on the payments. On behalf of Deutsche Bank National Trust Co., BAC Home Loans Servicing LP initiated foreclosure. Brock filed an action in a Maryland state court to block it, arguing that BAC could not foreclose because Deutsche Bank, not BAC, owned the note. Can BAC enforce the note? Explain. [*Deutsche Bank National Trust Co. v. Brock,* 63 A.3d 40 (Md. 2013)] (See *Signature Liability.*)

**17–7. Signature Liability.** Guillermo and Guadalupe Albarran and their sons, Ruben and Rolando, owned R. Cleaning Impact, Inc. (RCI). Neresh Kumar owned Amba II, Inc., a check-cashing business. The Albarrans cashed checks through Amba on a regular basis, often delivering a stack of employee paychecks to Amba for cashing. Later, the Albarrans' bank refused payment on some of the checks. Kumar learned that some of these items were payable to fictitious payees with fictitious addresses. Others had been filled out for amounts greater than real employees' pay. Meanwhile, RCI became insolvent and closed its account, and Guillermo and Guadalupe filed for bankruptcy. Amba was left with many unpaid checks. Among these parties, who can be held liable for the loss on the unpaid checks? Explain. [*Albarran v. Amba II, Inc.,* 2016 WL 688924 (2016)] (See *Signature Liability.*)

**17–8. Special Case Analysis—Defenses.** Go to Case Analysis 17.2, *Mills v. Chauvin.* Read the excerpt and answer the following questions.

**(a) Issue:** What document was at the center of the dispute in this case?

**(b) Rule of Law:** What are the elements of consideration? What are the requirements for attaining the status of a holder in due course (HDC)?

**(c) Applying the Rule of Law:** Did the document at the center of the dispute in this case satisfy the elements of consideration? Did the party in possession of the document take it as an HDC? Explain.

**(d) Conclusion:** Who did the court determine was liable? Why?

**17–9. A Question of Ethics—Primary and Secondary Liability.** *Clarence Morgan, Jr., owned Easy Way Automotive, a*  *car dealership in D'Lo, Mississippi. Easy Way sold a truck to Loyd Barnard, who signed a note for the amount of the price payable to Trustmark National Bank in six months. Before the note came due, Barnard returned the truck to Easy Way, which sold it to another buyer. Using some of the proceeds from the second sale, Easy Way sent a check to Trustmark to pay Barnard's note. Meanwhile, Barnard obtained another truck from Easy Way, financed through another six-month note payable to Trustmark. After eight of these deals, some of which involved more than one truck, an Easy Way check to Trustmark was dishonored. In a suit in a Mississippi state court, Trustmark sought to recover the amounts of two of the notes from Barnard. Trustmark had not secured titles to two of the trucks covered by the notes, however, and this complicated Barnard's efforts to reclaim the vehicles from the later buyers. [Trustmark National Bank v. Barnard, 930 So.2d 1281 (Miss.App. 2006)]* (See *Signature Liability.*)

**(a)** On what basis might Barnard be liable on the Trustmark notes? Would he be primarily or secondarily liable? Could this liability be discharged on the theory that Barnard's right of recourse had been impaired when Trustmark did not secure titles to the trucks covered by the notes? Explain.

**(b)** Easy Way's account had been subject to other recent overdrafts, and a week after the check to Trustmark was returned for insufficient funds, Morgan committed suicide. At the same time, Barnard was unable to obtain a mortgage because the unpaid notes affected his credit rating. How do the circumstances of this case underscore the importance of practicing business ethics?

# Legal Reasoning Group Activity

**17–10. Agents' Signatures.** Robert Helmer and Percy Helmer, Jr., were authorized signatories on the corporate checking account of Event Marketing, Inc. The Helmers signed a check drawn on Event Marketing's account and issued to Rummel Technologies, Inc. (RTI), in the amount of $84,965. The check was signed on July 13, 2015, but dated August 14. When RTI presented the check for payment, it was dishonored due to insufficient funds. RTI filed a suit in a

Georgia state court against the Helmers to collect the amount of the check. (See *Signature Liability.*)

**(a)** The first group will determine whether an authorized signatory on a corporate account can be held personally liable for corporate checks returned for insufficient funds.

**(b)** The second group will decide if the Helmers were personally liable on Event Marketing's check in this situation.

# CHAPTER 18

# Banking in the Digital Age

Many people today use debit cards rather than checks for their retail transactions, and payments are increasingly being made via smartphones, tablets, and other mobile devices. Nonetheless, commercial checks remain an integral part of the U.S. economic system. In fact, checks are the most common type of negotiable instruments regulated by the Uniform Commercial Code (UCC).

Articles 3 and 4 of the UCC govern issues relating to checks. Article 3 sets forth the requirements for all negotiable instruments, including checks. Article 4 establishes a framework for deposit and checking agreements between a bank and its customers.

Article 4 also governs the relationships of banks with one another as they process checks for payment. A check therefore may fall within the scope of Article 3 and yet be subject to the provisions of Article 4 while in the course of collection. If a conflict arises between Articles 3 and 4, Article 4 controls [UCC 4–102(a)].

## 18–1 Checks

A **check** is a special type of draft that is drawn on a bank, ordering the bank to pay a fixed amount of money on demand [UCC 3–104(f)]. Article 4 defines a *bank* as "a person engaged in the business of banking, including a savings bank, savings and loan association, credit union or trust company" [UCC 4–105(1)]. If any other institution (such as a brokerage firm) handles a check for payment or for collection, then the check is not covered by Article 4.

A person who writes a check is called the *drawer.* The drawer is usually a depositor in the bank on which the check is drawn. The person to whom the check is payable is the *payee.* The bank or financial institution on which the check is drawn is the *drawee.* Thus, if Anne Tomas writes a check on her checking account to pay her college tuition, she is the drawer, her bank is the drawee, and her college is the payee.

Between the time a check is drawn and the time it reaches the drawee, the effectiveness of the check may be altered in some way. For instance, the account on which the check is drawn may no longer have sufficient funds to pay the check. To avoid such problems, a payee may insist on payment by an instrument that has already been accepted by the drawee, such as a cashier's check, a traveler's check, or a certified check.

### 18–1a Cashier's Checks

Checks are usually three-party instruments, but on some checks, the bank serves as both the drawer *and* the drawee. For instance, when a bank draws a check on itself, the check is called a **cashier's check** and is a negotiable instrument on issue (see Exhibit 18–1) [UCC 3–104(g)]. Normally, a cashier's check identifies a specific payee. In effect, with a cashier's check, the bank assumes responsibility for paying the check, thus making the check more readily acceptable as a substitute for cash.

■ **EXAMPLE 18.1** Blake needs to pay a moving company $8,000 for moving his household goods to his new home in another state. The moving company requests payment in the form of a cashier's check. Blake goes to a bank (he need not have an account at the bank) and purchases a cashier's check, payable to the moving company, in the amount of $8,000. Blake has to pay the bank the $8,000 for the check, plus a small service fee. He then gives the check to the moving company. ■

Cashier's checks are sometimes used in the business community as nearly the equivalent of cash. Except in very limited circumstances, the issuing bank *must* honor its cashier's checks when they are presented for payment. If a bank wrongfully dishonors a cashier's check, a holder can recover from the bank all expenses incurred, interest, and consequential damages [UCC 3–411].

■ **CASE IN POINT 18.2** James Berwick purchased a $250,000 cashier's check from Bank of Colorado that

**EXHIBIT 18–1**  A Cashier's Check

*The abbreviation *NT&SA* stands for National Trust and Savings Association. The Bank of America NT&SA is a subsidiary of Bank of America Corporation.

was made payable to Ron Bryant. Berwick instructed the bank to give the check to James Kalhorn, who was to deliver the check to Bryant. The next day, Bryant presented the cashier's check to a Las Vegas Sands casino, which called Bank of Colorado to verify that it had issued the cashier's check. Las Vegas Sands then deposited the check into its bank account. Before the cashier's check was returned to Bank of Colorado for payment, however, Berwick claimed that it was lost and requested the bank to stop payment on it. The bank refused to pay the cashier's check, and litigation followed. A court found that Bank of Colorado had improperly honored Berwick's stop-payment order and was liable for wrongfully refusing to pay the cashier's check.[1] ■

## 18–1b Traveler's Checks

A **traveler's check** is an instrument that is payable on demand, drawn on or payable at a financial institution (such as a bank), and designated as a traveler's check. The issuing institution is directly obligated to accept and pay its traveler's check according to the check's terms.

Traveler's checks are designed to be a safe substitute for cash when a person is on vacation or traveling. Each check is issued for a fixed amount, such as $20, $50, or $100. The purchaser is required to sign the check at the time it is purchased and again at the time it is used

[UCC 3–104(i)]. Instead of issuing traveler's checks, most major banks purchase and issue American Express traveler's checks for their customers (see Exhibit 18–2).

## 18–1c Certified Checks

A **certified check** is a check that has been *accepted* by the bank on which it is drawn [UCC 3–409(d)]. When a drawee bank *certifies* (accepts) a check, it immediately charges the drawer's account with the amount of the check and transfers those funds to its own certified-check account. In effect, the bank is agreeing in advance to accept that check when it is presented for payment and to make payment from those funds reserved in the certified-check account. Certification, then, is a promise that sufficient funds are on deposit and *have been set aside* to cover the check.

To certify a check, the bank writes or stamps the word *certified* on the face of the check and typically indicates the amount that it will pay.[2] Once a check is certified, the drawer and any prior indorsers are completely discharged from liability on the check [UCC 3–414(c), 3–415(d)]. Only the certifying bank is required to pay the instrument.

Either the drawer or the holder (payee) of a check can request certification. The drawee bank is not required

---

1. *Bank of Colorado v. Berwick,* 2011 WL 1135349 (D.Colo. 2011).

2. If the certification does not state an amount, and the amount is later increased and the instrument negotiated to a holder in due course (HDC), the certifying bank must pay the amount of the instrument when it was taken by the HDC [UCC 3–413(b)].

**EXHIBIT 18–2  An American Express Traveler's Check**

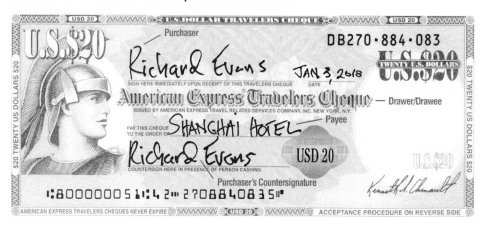

to certify a check, however. A bank's refusal to certify a check is not a dishonor of the check [UCC 3–409(d)].

# 18–2 The Bank-Customer Relationship

The bank-customer relationship begins when the customer opens a checking account and deposits funds. Essentially, three types of relationships arise at this time—creditor-debtor, agency, and contractual.

## 18–2a Creditor-Debtor Relationship

A creditor-debtor relationship is created between a customer and a bank when, for instance, the customer makes cash deposits into a checking account. When a customer makes a deposit, the customer becomes a creditor, and the bank a debtor, for the amount deposited.

## 18–2b Agency Relationship

An agency relationship also arises between the customer and the bank when the customer writes a check on his or her account. In effect, the customer is ordering the

bank to pay the amount specified on the check to the holder when the holder presents the check to the bank for payment. In this situation, the bank becomes the customer's agent and is obligated to honor the customer's request.

Similarly, when the customer deposits a check into his or her account, the bank, as the customer's agent, is obligated to collect payment on the check from the bank on which the check was drawn. Thus, when checking account funds are transferred among different banks, each bank acts as the collection agent for its customers [UCC 4–201(a)].

## 18–2c Contractual Relationship

Whenever a bank-customer relationship is established, certain contractual rights and duties arise. The contractual rights and duties of the bank and the customer depend on the nature of the transaction. These rights and duties are discussed in detail in the sections that follow.

The following case arose when a company realized that the balance in its corporate bank account was depleted. In fact, service charges had resulted in a negative balance. Under the parties' account agreement, was the bank liable for the loss of the funds?

**Case 18.1**

# Royal Arcanum Hospital Association of Kings County, Inc. v. Herrnkind

New York Supreme Court, Appellate Division, Second Department, 113 A.D.3d 672, 978 N.Y.S.2d 355 (2014).

**Background and Facts**  The board of the Royal Arcanum Hospital Association of Kings County, Inc., passed a resolution to require that all corporate checks be signed by two of three officers. These officers were Frank Vassallo, Joseph Rugilio, and William Herrnkind. The three were also named as

**Case 18.1 Continued**

signatories on the firm's account with Capital One Bank, but the terms of the account did not include the two-signature requirement. After Vassallo and Rugilio died, Herrnkind opened a new account in the corporate name that expressly permitted checks to be drawn on it with only one signature. Only Herrnkind's name appeared on the signature card. The account statements were sent to Royal Arcanum "care of William Herrnkind."

Over the next four years, a series of transactions reduced the balance of the account from nearly $200,000 to zero. Royal Arcanum filed a suit in a New York state court against Herrnkind and Capital One to recover the funds. The court dismissed the complaint against the bank. Royal Arcanum appealed.

### In the Language of the Court

Thomas A. *DICKERSON*, J.P. [Judge Presiding], Cheryl E. *CHAMBERS*, Sheri S. *ROMAN*, and Robert J. *MILLER*, JJ. [Judges]

* * * *

A bank and its depositor have the contractual relationship of debtor and creditor, with an implicit understanding that the bank will pay out a customer's funds only in accordance with its instructions. Contrary to the plaintiff's contention, in support of its motion, *the Bank established*, prima facie, *that [it] * * * did not agree to a two-signature requirement when the plaintiff opened the initial account * * *, or when it opened the subsequent account, and therefore that the [Bank] * * * did not breach any such requirement in allowing the withdrawals to be made in the absence of the approval of two officers.* Moreover, as the [lower] Court correctly concluded, insofar as the Bank's transactions with the plaintiff were concerned, the plaintiff conferred, at the least, apparent authority on Herrnkind to act on its behalf. The Bank established, *prima facie,* that it exercised due care and diligence under the circumstances, and that the circumstances surrounding the subject transactions were not such as would arouse the suspicion of its employees. In opposition to the Bank's *prima facie* showing of its entitlement to judgment as a matter of law, the plaintiff failed to raise a triable issue of fact. [Emphasis added.]

* * * *

Accordingly, the [lower] Court properly granted the Bank's motion for summary judgment dismissing the complaint insofar as asserted against it.

**Decision and Remedy**  *The state intermediate appellate court affirmed the decision of the lower court to dismiss Royal Arcanum's complaint against Capital One. The bank was not liable for the payment of unauthorized withdrawals on the firm's corporate accounts because the terms never included a two-signature requirement for the transactions.*

### Critical Thinking

- **Legal Environment**  *What circumstances indicated that Herrnkind had Royal Arcanum's authority to act on its behalf?*

# 18–3 The Bank's Duty to Honor Checks

When a banking institution provides checking services, it agrees to honor the checks written by its customers, with the usual stipulation that sufficient funds must be available in the account. When a drawee bank *wrongfully* fails to honor a check, it is liable to its customer for damages resulting from its refusal to pay [UCC 4–402(b)]. The customer does not have to prove that the bank breached its contractual commitment or was negligent.

The customer's agreement with the bank includes a general obligation to keep sufficient funds on deposit to cover all checks written. The customer is liable to the payee or to the holder of a check in a civil suit if a check is dishonored for insufficient funds. If intent to defraud can be proved, the customer can also be subject to criminal prosecution for writing a bad check.

When the bank properly dishonors a check for insufficient funds, it has no liability to the customer. The bank may rightfully refuse payment on a customer's check in other circumstances as well. Next, we examine the rights and duties of both the bank and its customers in specific situations.

## 18–3a Overdrafts

When the bank receives an item properly payable from its customer's checking account but the account contains insufficient funds to cover the check, the bank has two options. It can either dishonor the item, or it can pay the item and charge the customer's account, thus creating an **overdraft** [UCC 4–401(a)]. The bank can subtract the difference (plus a service charge) from the customer's next deposit because the check carries with it an enforceable implied promise to reimburse the bank.

With a joint account, however, the bank cannot hold any joint-account owner liable for payment of the overdraft unless that customer signed the check or benefited from its proceeds [UCC 4–401(b)]. ■ **EXAMPLE 18.3** Aaron and Sarah are married and have a joint bank account. Aaron writes a check to pay the electric bill for their apartment. If the check results in an overdraft, both Aaron and Sarah will be liable, because both obviously benefited from having electricity in their apartment. ■

A bank can expressly agree with a customer to accept overdrafts through an "overdraft protection agreement." If such an agreement is formed, any failure of the bank to honor a check because it would create an overdraft breaches this agreement and is considered a wrongful dishonor [UCC 4–402(a), (b)].

If a bank posts items to a customer's account only once a day, several items of different amounts may accumulate before the posting. Depending on the order in which the items are posted, an overdraft may occur earlier or later in the sequence. If the bank charges its customer a separate fee for honoring each item after an overdraft occurs, the sequencing of items can significantly impact the amount of fees that the customer is charged. At the center of the following case was one bank's decision to switch its sequencing to post items of the highest amount first.

## Case Analysis 18.2

# Legg v. West Bank
Supreme Court of Iowa, 873 N.W.2d 763 (2016).

### In the Language of the Court
ZAGER, Justice.
* * * *

West Bank is a state-chartered Iowa bank.

West Bank issues bank cards to its customers. Customers use their bank cards in one of two ways: automatic teller machine withdrawals (ATM withdrawals) or point of sale purchases (POS purchases). Customers may also make electronic payments using their West Bank accounts that are processed in the same way as ATM withdrawals and POS purchases. All three of these transactions are classified as "bank card transactions."
* * * *

If West Bank is called upon to pay a Bank Card transaction when there are insufficient funds in the account, the bank advances sufficient money to cover the amount by which the account is short, and assesses a non-sufficient funds (NSF) fee. Those advances are automatically deducted from the customer account and repaid to the bank the next time a deposit sufficient to cover the advances is made to the account.

* * * The NSF fee West Bank charged customers was originally $27.00. It was later raised to $30.00.

West Bank does not post customer account balances in real time. Rather, transactions are posted in a batch at the end of the day. Prior to July 1, 2006, West Bank posted bank card transactions with the lowest amount for each day's debits posted first and the highest amount posted last (low-to-high sequencing). After July 1, 2006, West Bank reversed its posting sequencing and posted bank card transactions with the highest amount posted first and the lowest amount posted last (high-to-low sequencing). Beginning October 1, 2010, West Bank changed its posting order back to low-to-high sequencing.
* * * *

[Darla and Jason Legg had a joint checking account with West Bank. Over a three-week period] the Leggs were charged [separate] NSF fees [for each of five transactions that resulted in overdrafts under West Bank's] new high-to-low sequencing.

* * * If the bank card transactions had been posted in the low-to-high sequence, the Leggs would have only been charged one NSF fee. [A few months later] the Leggs were charged four NSF fees for bank card transactions. The Leggs would have only been charged two NSF fees if

the transactions were posted low-to-high.
* * * *

The Leggs filed this action [in an Iowa state court against West Bank, claiming that West Bank breached its duty to act in good faith when it changed the sequencing order of bank card transactions to high-to-low. West Bank filed a motion for summary judgment.]
* * * *

* * * The * * * court denied West Bank's motion for summary judgment * * * . West Bank [appealed to this court.]
* * * *

*When the Leggs opened their account with West Bank, they were provided with a [Deposit Account] Agreement that included the statement that West Bank "shall have an obligation to Depositor to exercise good faith and ordinary care in connection with each account." Before West Bank initiated the sequencing change, it consulted with an Iowa Bankers Association Compliance Officer. After this consultation, West Bank concluded in an internal memo that the previous practice of posting low-to-high created a business expectation with customers and it would be necessary to notify them of the change.*

**Case 18.2 Continued**

Although West Bank's memo specifically discussed notifying its customers of the sequencing change with regard to bank card transactions, West Bank nonetheless made the change without notifying customers. [Emphasis added.]

The [lower] court, relying on the opinions of other courts that have heard similar issues, concluded that the plaintiffs could pursue their good-faith claim. One case the * * * court discussed addressed whether express contract terms were being carried out in good faith. In [another case,] the plaintiffs argued that the banks violated express contractual provisions to act in good faith by reordering postings to high-to-low sequencing. The court found that the plaintiffs

were not asking to vary the terms of the express contract. Rather, they were asking that the bank carry out its express agreement to exercise its discretion regarding the posting sequencing in good faith. The court cited to a number of cases where other courts held that when one party is given discretion to act under a contract, said discretion must be exercised in good faith.

Similarly, West Bank has discretion with regard to the sequencing order of bank card transactions in its agreements with the Leggs and its other customers. *The bank wrote the duty of good faith into its contract with customers.* The Leggs could reasonably argue that the change in sequencing of bank card transactions,

coupled with the lack of notification, violated the reasonable expectations of customers that the bank act in good faith when exercising its discretion to sequence transactions. [Emphasis added.]

* * * *

We conclude that the [lower] court [did not err] when it denied summary judgment to West Bank on * * * the [Leggs'] claim based on a potential breach of the express duty of good faith in the sequencing of postings of bank card transactions. The case is remanded for further proceedings consistent with this opinion.

**Legal Reasoning Questions**

1. After the initial sequencing change, West Bank provided its customers with a document titled "Miscellaneous Fees." A footnote in that document stated, "Checks written on your account will be paid in order daily with the largest check paid first and the smallest check paid last." Was this adequate notice to the customers of the change? Explain.

2. How did the decisions of other courts in similar cases affect the rulings of the courts in this case?

3. Suppose that West Bank's "Deposit Account Agreement" had not included "an obligation to Depositor to exercise good faith and ordinary care in connection with each account." Would the result have been different? Discuss.

## 18–3b Postdated Checks

A bank may charge a postdated check against a customer's account unless the customer notifies the bank, in a timely manner, not to pay the check until the stated date. (Indeed, banks typically ignore the dates on checks and treat them as demand instruments unless a customer has notified the bank that a check was postdated.) The notice of postdating must be given in time to allow the bank to act on the notice before committing itself to pay on the check. A bank that fails to act on the customer's notice and charges the account before the date on the postdated check may be liable for any damages the customer incurred [UCC 4–401(c)].

## 18–3c Stale Checks

Commercial banking practice regards a check that is presented for payment more than six months from its date as a **stale check.** A bank is not obligated to pay an uncertified check presented more than six months from its date [UCC 4–404]. When it receives a stale check for payment,

the bank has the option of paying or not paying the check. If a bank pays a stale check in good faith without consulting the customer, the bank has the right to charge the customer's account for the amount of the check.

## 18–3d Stop-Payment Orders

A **stop-payment order** is an order by a customer to her or his bank not to pay a certain check.[3] Only a customer (or a person authorized to draw on the account) can order the bank not to pay the check when it is presented for payment [UCC 4–403(a)].

A customer has no right to stop payment on a check that has already been certified (or accepted) by a bank, however. A person who wrongfully stops payment on a check will be liable to the payee for the amount of the check. In addition, the customer-drawer must have a *valid legal ground* for issuing a stop-payment order, or the holder can sue the customer-drawer for payment.

---

3. Note that the right to stop payment is not limited to checks. It extends to any item payable by any bank. See Official Comment 3 to UCC 4–403.

**Reasonable Time and Manner** The customer-drawer must issue the stop-payment order within a reasonable time and in a reasonable manner to permit the bank to act on it [UCC 4–403(a)].

Although a stop-payment order can be given orally over the phone, it is generally binding on the bank for only fourteen calendar days unless confirmed in writing.[4] (Recall that an electronic record, such as a stop-payment order submitted via the bank's Web site, is a writing.) A written stop-payment order is effective for six months, at which time it must be renewed in writing [UCC 4–403(b)].

**Bank's Liability for Wrongful Payment** If the bank pays the check in spite of a stop-payment order, the bank will be obligated to recredit the customer's account. In addition, if the bank's payment over a stop-payment order causes subsequent checks written on the drawer's account to "bounce," the bank will be liable for the resultant costs the drawer incurs. The bank is liable only for the amount of the actual loss suffered by the drawer because of the wrongful payment, however [UCC 4–403(c)].

■ **EXAMPLE 18.4** Mike Murano orders one hundred smartphones from Advanced Communications, Inc., at $100 each. Murano pays in advance with a check for $10,000. Later that day, Advanced Communications tells Murano that it will not deliver the smartphones as arranged. Murano immediately calls the bank and stops payment on the check. Two days later, in spite of this stop-payment order, the bank inadvertently honors Murano's check to Advanced Communications for the undelivered phones. The bank will be liable to Murano for the full $10,000.

The result would be different, however, if Advanced Communications had delivered and Murano had accepted ninety phones. Because Murano would have owed Advanced Communications $9,000 for the goods delivered, Murano's actual loss would be only $1,000. Consequently, the bank would be liable to Murano for only $1,000. ■

## 18–3e Incompetence or Death of a Customer

A customer's mental incompetence or death does not automatically revoke a bank's authority to accept, pay, or collect an item. Only after the bank is notified of the

customer's incompetence or death and has reasonable time to act on the notice will the bank's authority be ineffective [UCC 4–405]. Without this provision, banks would constantly be required to verify the continued competence and life of their drawers.

Thus, if a bank is unaware that the customer who wrote a check has been declared incompetent or has died, the bank can pay without incurring liability. Even when a bank knows of the death of its customer, for ten days after the *date of death* it can pay or certify checks drawn on or before the date of death. An exception is made if a person claiming an interest in the account of the deceased customer, such as an heir, orders the bank to stop payment.

## 18–3f Forged Drawers' Signatures

When a bank pays a check on which the drawer's signature is forged, generally the bank suffers the loss. A bank may be able to recover at least some of the loss from the customer, however, if the customer's negligence substantially contributed to the forgery. A bank may also obtain partial recovery from the forger of the check (if the forger can be found) or from the holder who presented the check for payment (if the holder knew that the signature was forged).

**The General Rule** A forged signature on a check has no legal effect as the signature of a customer-drawer [UCC 3–403(a)]. The general rule is that the bank must recredit the customer's account when it pays on a forged signature.

For this reason, banks require a signature card from each customer who opens a checking account. Signature cards allow a bank to verify whether the signatures on its customers' checks are genuine. Banks today normally verify signatures only on checks that exceed a certain threshold, such as $2,500 or some higher amount, because it would be too costly to verify every signature.

Note that a bank may contractually shift to the customer the risk of forged checks created electronically or by the use of nonmanual signatures. For instance, the contract might stipulate that the customer is solely responsible for maintaining security over any signature stamp.

**Customer Negligence** When a customer's negligence substantially contributes to a forgery, the bank normally will *not* be obligated to recredit the customer's

---

4. Some states do not recognize oral stop-payment orders. The orders must be in writing.

account for the amount of the check [UCC 3–406(a)]. The customer's liability may be reduced, however, by the amount of the loss caused by negligence on the part of the bank [UCC 3–406(b)].

■ **CASE IN POINT 18.5**   Kenneth Wulf worked for Auto-Owners Insurance Company for ten years. During that time, Wulf opened a checking account at Bank One in the name of "Auto-Owners, Kenneth B. Wulf." Over a period of eight years, he deposited $546,000 worth of checks that he had stolen from Auto-Owners and indorsed with a stamp that read "Auto-Owners Insurance Deposit Only." When the thefts were finally discovered, Auto-Owners sued Bank One for negligence.

The insurance company claimed that the bank should not have allowed Wulf to open an account in Auto-Owners' name without proof that he was authorized to do so. The court ruled in favor of the bank, though, finding that Bank One's conduct was not a significant factor in bringing about the loss. Instead, the negligence of Auto-Owners contributed substantially to its own losses. Therefore, the bank did not have to recredit the customer's account.[5] ■

**Timely Examination of Bank Statements Required.** Banks typically send or provide online monthly statements that detail the activity in their customers' checking accounts. The statements provide the customer with information (check number, amount, and date of payment) that allows them to reasonably identify each check that the bank has paid [UCC 4–406(a), (b)].

In the past, banks routinely included the canceled checks themselves (or copies of them) with the statement, but that practice is unusual today. If the bank does retain the canceled checks, it must keep the checks—or legible images of them—for seven years [UCC 4–406(b)].

The customer has a duty to promptly examine bank statements (and canceled checks or copies, if they are included) with reasonable care and to report any alterations or forged signatures [UCC 4–406(c)]. The customer is also obligated to report any alteration or apparent forgery in the signatures of indorsers. If the customer fails to fulfill her or his duty and the bank suffers a loss as a result, the customer will be liable for the loss [UCC 4–406(d)].

**Consequences of Failure to Detect Forgeries.** Sometimes, the same wrongdoer forges the customer's signature on a series of checks. To recover for all of the forged items, the customer must discover and report the first forged check to the bank within thirty calendar days of the receipt or availability of the bank statement [UCC 4–406(d)(2)]. Failure to notify the bank within this time period discharges the bank's liability for all forged checks that it pays prior to notification.

■ **CASE IN POINT 18.6**   Denise Kaplan opened two bank accounts with JPMorgan Chase Bank (JPMC) in 2009. Her agreement with JPMC stated that she would review her monthly statements for accuracy and report any unauthorized transactions or discrepancies within thirty days. Later that same year, her husband, Joel Kaplan, submitted new signature cards that added his name to the accounts.

In 2012, Denise notified JPMC that she was not able to access her monthly bank statements, which were being sent to her husband's e-mail address. When JPMC provided the statements to her, she discovered that her husband had been making withdrawals from her accounts. Denise obtained a court order preventing Joel from further accessing the accounts. She claimed that the signature cards that gave him this access had been forged and that she had not consented to the addition of his name to the accounts.

Denise sued JPMC for accepting the allegedly forged signature cards from Joel, but the court ruled in favor of JPMC. Because Denise did not notify the bank until 2012 that she had not been receiving her monthly statements, she was well beyond the thirty-day time period for detecting and reporting forgeries. Therefore, the bank was not liable for any unauthorized transactions.[6] ■

**Negligence and the Bank's Duty of Care.** In one situation, a bank customer can escape liability, at least in part, for failing to notify the bank of forged or altered checks within the required thirty-day period. When the customer can prove that the bank was also negligent—that is, that the bank failed to exercise ordinary care—then the bank, too, will be liable. The loss will be allocated between the bank and the customer on the basis of comparative negligence [UCC 4–406(e)].

The UCC defines *ordinary care* as the "observance of reasonable commercial standards, prevailing in the area in which [a] person is located, with respect to the business

---

**5.** *Auto-Owners Insurance Co. v. Bank One*, 879 N.E.2d 1086 (Ind.Sup.Ct. 2008).

**6.** *Kaplan v. JPMorgan Chase Bank, N.A.*, 2015 WL 2358240 (N.D.Ill. 2015).

in which that person is engaged" [UCC 3–103(a)(7)]. As mentioned earlier, it is customary in the banking industry to examine signatures only on checks that exceed a certain amount. Thus, if a bank fails to examine a signature on a particular check, the bank has not necessarily breached its duty to exercise ordinary care.

**One-Year Time Limit.** Regardless of the degree of care exercised by the customer or the bank, the UCC places an absolute time limit on the liability of a bank for paying a check with a customer's forged signature. A customer who fails to report a forged signature within one year loses the legal right to have the bank recredit her or his account [UCC 4–406(f)]. The year runs from the date on which the statement was made available for inspection. The parties can agree in their contract to a lower time limit, but the UCC stipulates that the bank has no liability on forged instruments after one year.

**Other Parties from Whom the Bank May Recover** As noted, a forged signature on a check has no legal effect as the signature of a drawer. Instead, the person who forged the signature is liable [UCC 3–403(a)]. Therefore, when a bank pays a check on which the drawer's signature is forged, the bank has a right to recover from the party who forged the signature (if he or she can be found).

The bank may also have a right to recover from a party who transferred a check bearing a forged drawer's signature and received payment. This right is limited, however, in that the bank cannot recover from a person who took the check in good faith and for value. A bank also cannot recover from a person who in good faith changed position in reliance on the payment or acceptance [UCC 3–418(c)].

## 18–3g Checks Bearing Forged Indorsements

A bank that pays a customer's check bearing a forged indorsement must recredit the customer's account or be liable to the customer (drawer) for breach of contract. ■ **EXAMPLE 18.7** Cameron issues a $500 check "to the order of Sophia Alonzo." Margo steals the check, forges Alonzo's indorsement, and cashes the check. When the check reaches Cameron's bank, the bank pays it and debits Cameron's account.

In this situation, the bank must recredit Cameron's account for the $500 because it failed to carry out

Cameron's order to pay "to the order of Sophia Alonzo" [UCC 4–401(a)]. Cameron's bank can in turn recover—for breach of warranty—from the bank that cashed the check when Margo presented it [UCC 4–207(a)(2)]. ■

Eventually, *the loss usually falls on the first party to take the instrument bearing the forged indorsement* because a forged indorsement does not transfer title. Thus, whoever takes an instrument with a forged indorsement cannot become a holder.

The customer, in any event, has a duty to report forged indorsements promptly. The bank is relieved of liability if the customer fails to report the forged indorsements within three years of receiving the bank statement that contained the forged items [UCC 4–111].[7]

■ **CASE IN POINT 18.8** The Michigan Basic Property Insurance Association (MBP) banked with Fifth Third Bank. MBP issued a check from its account to Joyce Washington, Countrywide Home Loans, and T & C Federal Credit Union as co-payees. Washington indorsed the check by signing all three payees' names and deposited it into her own account. When the check reached Fifth Third Bank, it notified MBP of the payment through a daily account statement. MBP did not object, so Fifth Third debited the funds from MBP's account. After MBP received its monthly account statement showing the payment, it again did not object.

When MBP was forced to issue a second check to Countrywide, it sued Fifth Third Bank seeking to have its account recredited. Ultimately, a state appellate court found that Fifth Third Bank was not liable to MBP. Under the UCC, the check was not properly payable because it had two forged indorsements. Thus, the bank would normally be required to recredit the amount of the check. But in this case, the parties had agreed by contract that if the bank was not promptly notified of forgery, the loss would fall on the customer. Because MBP did not promptly notify the bank of the forgeries as required under its account agreement, MBP was liable for any forged indorsements.[8] ■

## 18–3h Altered Checks

The customer's instruction to the bank is to pay the exact amount on the face of the check to the holder. The bank has an implicit duty to examine checks before making final payments. If it fails to detect an alteration, it is liable

---

7. This is a general statute of limitations for all actions under Article 4. It provides that any lawsuit must be brought within three years of the time that the cause of action arises.
8. *Michigan Basic Property Insurance Association v. Washington,* 2012 WL 20573 (Mich.App. 2012).

to its customer for the loss because it did not pay as the customer ordered.

The bank's loss is the difference between the original amount of the check and the amount actually paid. ■ **EXAMPLE 18.9** Hailey Lyonne writes a check for $11 that is increased to $111. Lyonne's account will be charged $11 (the amount the customer ordered the bank to pay). The bank will normally be responsible for the remaining $100 [UCC 4–401(d)(1)]. ■

**Customer Negligence** As in a situation involving a forged drawer's signature, a customer's negligence can shift the loss when payment is made on an altered check (unless the bank was also negligent). For instance, a person may carelessly write a check and leave large gaps around the numbers and words where additional numbers and words can be inserted.

Similarly, a person who signs a check and leaves the dollar amount for someone else to fill in is barred from protesting when the bank unknowingly and in good faith pays whatever amount is shown [UCC 4–401(d)(2)]. Finally, if the bank can trace its loss on successive altered checks to the customer's failure to discover the initial alteration, then the bank can reduce its liability for reimbursing the customer's account [UCC 4–406].

In every situation involving a forged drawer's signature or an alteration, a bank must observe reasonable commercial standards of care in paying on a customer's checks [UCC 4–406(e)]. The customer's contributory negligence can be asserted only if the bank has exercised ordinary care.

**Other Parties from Whom the Bank May Recover** The bank is entitled to recover the amount of loss (including expenses) from the transferor who presented the check for payment. A transferor, by presenting a check for payment, warrants that the check has not been altered.

There are two exceptions to this rule. First, if the bank is also the drawer (as it is on a cashier's check), it cannot recover from the presenting party if the party is a holder in due course (HDC) acting in good faith [UCC 3–417(a)(2), 4–208(a)(2)]. The reason is that an instrument's drawer is in a better position than an HDC to know whether the instrument has been altered.

Second, an HDC who presents a certified check for payment in good faith does not warrant to the check's certifier that the check was unaltered before the HDC acquired it [UCC 3–417(a)(2), 4–208(a)(2)]. ■ **EXAMPLE 18.10** Alan, the drawer, draws a check for

$500 payable to Rachel, the payee. Rachel alters the amount to $5,000. National City Bank, the drawee, certifies the check for $5,000. Rachel negotiates the check to Jordan, an HDC. The drawee bank pays Jordan $5,000. On discovering the mistake, the bank cannot recover from Jordan the $4,500 paid by mistake, even though the bank was not in a superior position to detect the alteration. This result is in accord with the purpose of certification, which is to obtain the definite obligation of a bank to honor a definite instrument. ■

For a synopsis of the rules governing the honoring of checks, see Concept Summary 18.1.

## 18–4 The Bank's Duty to Accept Deposits

A bank has a duty to its customer to accept the customer's deposits of cash and checks. When checks are deposited, the bank must make the funds represented by those checks available within certain time frames. A bank also has a duty to collect payment on any checks payable or indorsed to its customer and deposited by the customer into his or her account. Cash deposits made in U.S. currency are received into the customer's account without being subject to further collection procedures.

### 18–4a Availability Schedule for Deposited Checks

The Expedited Funds Availability Act (EFAA)[9] and Regulation CC[10] (the regulation implementing the act) establish when funds from deposited checks must be made available to the customer. The rules are as follows:

1. Any local check (drawn on a bank in the same area) deposited must be available for withdrawal by check or as cash within one business day from the date of deposit.
2. For nonlocal checks, the funds must be available for withdrawal within not more than five business days.
3. Under the Check Clearing in the 21st Century Act[11] (Check 21), a bank must credit a customer's account as soon as the bank receives the funds.
4. For cash deposits, wire transfers, and government checks, funds must be available on the next business day.

---

9. 12 U.S.C. Sections 4001–4010.
10. 12 C.F.R. Sections 229.1–229.42.
11. 12 U.S.C. Sections 5001–5018.

## Concept Summary 18.1

### Basic Rules for Honoring Checks

**Wrongful Dishonor**
- The bank is liable to its customer for actual damages proved if it wrongfully dishonors a check due to its own mistake [UCC 4–402].

**Overdraft**
- The bank has a right to charge a customer's account for any item properly payable, even if the charge results in an overdraft [UCC 4–401].

**Postdated Check**
- The bank may charge a postdated check against a customer's account, unless the customer notifies the bank of the postdating in time to allow the bank to act on the notice before the bank commits itself to pay on the check [UCC 4–401].

**Stale Check**
- The bank is not obligated to pay an uncertified check presented more than six months after its date, but the bank may do so in good faith without liability [UCC 4–404].

**Stop-Payment Order**
- The customer (or a person authorized to draw on the account) must institute a stop-payment order in time for the bank to have a reasonable opportunity to act.
- A customer has no right to stop payment on a check that has been certified or accepted by the bank, however, and can be held liable for stopping payment on any check without a valid legal ground [UCC 4–403].

**Death or Incompetence of a Customer**
- So long as the bank does not know of the death or incompetence of a customer, the bank can pay an item without liability. Even with knowledge of a customer's death, a bank can honor or certify checks (in the absence of a stop-payment order) for ten days after the date of the customer's death [UCC 4–405].

**Forged Signature or Alteration**
- The customer has a duty to examine account statements with reasonable care on receipt and to notify the bank promptly of any unauthorized signatures or alterations.
- The customer's failure to report promptly an unauthorized signature or alteration will discharge the bank's liability—unless the bank failed to exercise reasonable care (and then the bank may be responsible for some portion of the loss).
- The customer is prevented from holding the bank liable after one year for unauthorized customer signatures or alterations and after three years for unauthorized indorsements [UCC 4–406].

---

**5.** The first $100 of any deposit must be available for cash withdrawal on the opening of the *next business day* after deposit.

A different availability schedule applies to deposits made at *nonproprietary* automated teller machines (ATMs). These are ATMs that are not owned or operated by the bank receiving the deposits. Basically, a five-day hold is permitted on all deposits, including cash deposits, made at nonproprietary ATMs. Other exceptions also exist. For instance, a banking institution has eight days to make funds available in new accounts (those open less than thirty days).

A bank that places a longer hold on a deposited check than that specified by the rules must notify the customer. A credit union's failure to provide this notice to its customer was at the center of the following case.

# Shahin v. Delaware Federal Credit Union

United States Court of Appeals, Third Circuit, 602 Fed.Appx. 50 (2015).

**Background and Facts**  Nina Shahin deposited a check in the amount of $2,500 into her checking account at the Delaware Federal Credit Union (DelOne). DelOne placed a two-business-day "local hold" on the check, pending verification. Concerned that the drawer's signature did not match the handwriting on the rest of the check, the bank placed it on a fifteen-day "nonverified" hold. Meanwhile, a payment from Shahin's checking account to Bank of America was denied for insufficient funds (NSF), and DelOne transferred funds from her savings account to cover other payments. DelOne then imposed two $30 penalties for NSF, as well as transfer fees totaling $6.

Shahin filed a suit in a federal district court against DelOne, alleging that the credit union had failed to give her proper notice of the extended hold. The court issued a summary judgment in Shahin's favor. She was awarded the amount of the NSF and transfer fees, plus $1,000, the maximum amount of liability for a notice violation under Regulation CC. Shahin appealed, claiming that the amount of damages was insufficient.

## In the Language of the Court

*PER CURIAM* [By the Whole Court].

* * * *

* * * *Proper notice of the extended hold [is] required under 12 C.F.R. Section 229.13 [of Regulation CC].* [Emphasis added.]

* * * *

Shahin claims on appeal that the District Court failed to award sufficient * * * damages. * * * Pursuant to 12 C.F.R. Section 229.21, a depository institution that fails to comply with the notice provision of Section 229.13 with respect to any person:

(a) * * * is liable to that person in an amount equal to the sum of—

(1) Any actual damage sustained by that person as a result of the failure;

(2) Such additional amount as the court may allow, except that—

(i) In the case of an individual action, liability under this paragraph shall not be less than $100 nor greater than $1,000 * * * .

* * * In her motion for summary judgment, Shahin asserted * * * that DelOne imposed $60 in NSF charges and $6.00 in transfer fees. The summary judgment record supported the District Court's finding that DelOne was liable to Shahin for the NSF and "overdraft" fees it imposed; those actual damages totaled $66.00. * * * Shahin failed to argue or provide evidence to support any other claim for actual damages.

DelOne was subject to liability to Shahin for penalties under Section 229.21(a)(2). * * * The amount of $1,000 was the maximum amount allowable under that provision.

**Decision and Remedy**  *The U.S. Court of Appeals for the Third Circuit affirmed the lower court's judgment and its award to Shahin of the amount of DelOne's NSF and transfer fees, plus $1,000. The court denied Shahin's claim for further damages.*

## Critical Thinking

- **Economic**  *Is $1,000 an appropriate penalty for the failure of a depository institution to comply with Regulation CC's notice provision? Why or why not?*

---

## 18–4b  Interest-Bearing Accounts

Under the Truth-in-Savings Act (TISA)[12] and Regulation DD,[13] the act's implementing regulation, banks must pay interest based on the full balance of a customer's interest-bearing account over the relevant period.

12. 12 U.S.C. Sections 4301–4313.
13. 12 C.F.R. Sections 230.1–230.9.

■ **EXAMPLE 18.11**  Nigel has an interest-bearing checking account with First National Bank. Nigel keeps a $500 balance in the account for most of the month but withdraws all but $50 the day before the bank posts the interest. The bank cannot pay interest on only the $50. The interest must be adjusted to account for the entire month, including those days when Nigel's balance was higher. ■

Before opening a deposit account, new customers must be provided certain information, including the following:

1. The minimum balance required to open an account and to be paid interest.
2. The interest, stated in terms of the annual percentage yield on the account.
3. How interest is calculated.
4. Any fees, charges, and penalties and how they are calculated.

Also, a customer's monthly statement must disclose the interest earned on the account, any fees that were charged, how the fees were calculated, and the number of days that the statement covers.

## 18–4c The Traditional Collection Process

Usually, deposited checks involve parties who do business at different banks, but sometimes checks are written between customers of the same bank. Either situation brings into play the bank collection process as it operates under Article 4 of the UCC. The check-collection process described in the following subsections has been modified as the banking industry continues to implement Check 21, which will be discussed shortly.

**Designations of Banks** The first bank to receive a check for payment is the **depositary bank.**[14] For instance, when a person deposits a tax-refund check from the Internal Revenue Service into a personal checking account at the local bank, that bank is the depositary bank.

The bank on which a check is drawn (the drawee bank) is called the **payor bank.** Any bank except the payor bank that handles a check during some phase of the collection process is a **collecting bank.** Any bank except the payor bank or the depositary bank to which an item is transferred in the course of this collection process is called an **intermediary bank.**

During the collection process, any bank can take on one or more of the various roles of depositary, payor, collecting, or intermediary bank. ■ **EXAMPLE 18.12** Brooke, a buyer in New York, writes a check on her New York bank and sends it to David, a seller in San Francisco. David deposits the check in his San Francisco bank account. David's bank is both a *depositary bank* and a *collecting bank.* Brooke's bank in New York is the *payor bank.* As the check travels from San Francisco to New York, any

*collecting bank* handling the item in the collection process (other than the ones acting as depositary bank and payor bank) is also called an *intermediary bank.* ■

Exhibit 18–3 illustrates how various banks function in the check-collection process.

### Check Collection between Customers of the Same Bank

An item that is payable by the depositary bank that receives it (which in this situation is also the payor bank) is called an "on-us item." Usually, a bank issues a "provisional credit" for on-us items within the same day. If the bank does not dishonor the check by the opening of the second banking day following its receipt, the check is considered paid [UCC 4–215(e)(2)].

### Check Collection between Customers of Different Banks

Once a depositary bank receives a check, it must arrange to present the check, either directly or through intermediary banks, to the appropriate payor bank. When the check reaches the payor bank, that bank is liable for the face amount of the check, unless the payor bank dishonors it [UCC 4–302].[15]

Each bank in the collection chain must pass the check on before midnight of the next banking day following its receipt [UCC 4–202(b)].[16] A "banking day" is any part of a day on which the bank is open to carry on substantially all of its banking functions. Thus, if only a bank's drive-through facilities are open, a check deposited on Saturday will not trigger a bank's midnight deadline until the following Monday.

The UCC permits what is called *deferred posting.* According to UCC 4–108, "a bank may fix an afternoon hour of 2:00 P.M. or later as a cutoff hour for the handling of money and items and the making of entries on its books." Any checks received after that hour "may be treated as being received at the opening of the next banking day." Thus, if a bank's "cutoff hour" is 3:00 P.M., a check received by a payor bank at 4:00 P.M. on Monday will be deferred for posting until Tuesday. In this situation, the payor bank's deadline will be midnight Wednesday.

### How the Federal Reserve System Clears Checks

The **Federal Reserve System** is a network of twelve district banks located around the country and headed by the Federal Reserve Board of Governors. Most

---

14. All definitions in this section are found in UCC 4–105. The terms *depositary* and *depository* have different meanings in the banking context. A depository bank is a *physical place* (a bank or other institution) in which deposits or funds are held or stored.

15. Most checks are cleared by a computerized process. If a bank fails to meet its midnight deadline because of an electrical outage or equipment malfunction, the bank is "excused" from liability if the bank has exercised "such diligence as the circumstances require" [UCC 4–109(d)].

16. A bank may take a "reasonably longer time" in certain circumstances, such as a power failure that disrupts the bank's computer system [UCC 4–202(b)].

**EXHIBIT 18–3  The Check-Collection Process**

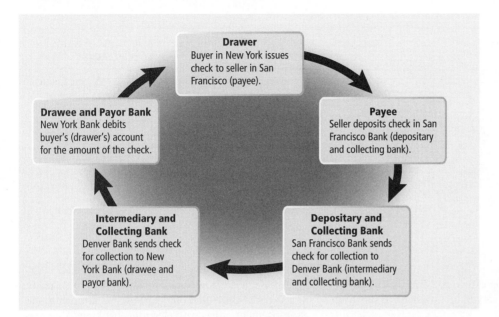

banks in the United States have Federal Reserve accounts. The Federal Reserve System acts as a **clearinghouse**—a place where banks exchange checks drawn on each other and settle daily balances.

■ **EXAMPLE 18.13** Tami Moy, who lives in Cleveland, Ohio, writes a check to Jeanne Sutton of Boston, Massachusetts. When Jeanne receives the check in the mail, she deposits it in her bank. Her bank then deposits the check in the Federal Reserve Bank of Boston, which transfers it to the Federal Reserve Bank of Cleveland. That Federal Reserve bank then sends the check to Moy's bank, which deducts the amount of the check from Moy's account. ■

**Electronic Check Presentment** In the past, most checks were processed manually. Today, most checks are processed electronically—a practice that has been facilitated by Check 21. Whereas manual check processing can take days, *electronic check presentment* can be done on the day of the deposit. Check information is encoded, transmitted electronically, and processed by other banks' computers. After encoding a check, a bank may retain it and present only its image or description for payment under an electronic presentment agreement [UCC 4–110].

A bank that encodes information for electronic presentment warrants to any subsequent bank or payor that the encoded information is correct [UCC 4–209]. Similarly, a bank that retains a check and presents its image or description for payment warrants that the image or description is accurate.

Regulation CC provides that a returned check must be encoded with the routing number of the depositary bank, the amount of the check, and other information. The regulation further states that a check must still be returned within the deadlines required by the UCC.

## 18–4d Check Clearing and the Check 21 Act

To streamline the costly and time-consuming traditional method of check collection, Congress enacted the Check Clearing in the 21st Century Act (Check 21). Check 21 changed the collection process by creating a new negotiable instrument called a **substitute check.** Although the act does not require banks to change their current check-collection practices, its creation of substitute checks facilitates the use of electronic check processing.

**Substitute Checks** A substitute check is a reproduction of the front and back of an original check that contains all of the same information required on checks for automated processing. A bank creates substitute checks from digital images of original checks (see Exhibit 18–4). It can then process the check information electronically or deliver substitute checks to banks that wish to continue receiving paper checks.

The original check can be destroyed after a substitute check is created, helping to prevent the check from being

**EXHIBIT 18–4 A Sample Substitute Check**

paid twice and reducing expenses. Nevertheless, at least for a while, not all checks will be converted to substitute checks.

**Faster Access to Funds** The Expedited Funds Availability Act requires the Federal Reserve Board to revise the availability schedule for funds from deposited checks to correspond to reductions in check-processing time. Therefore, as the speed of check processing increases under Check 21, the Federal Reserve Board will reduce the maximum time that a bank can hold funds from deposited checks before making them available to the depositor.

That means, of course, that account holders will have faster access to their deposited funds. It also means they will also have less *float time*—the time between when a check is written and when the amount is actually deducted from the account. Consequently, to avoid overdrafts, account holders need to make sure that funds are available to cover checks when they are written.

# 18–5 Electronic Fund Transfers

An **electronic fund transfer (EFT)** is a transfer of funds made through the use of an electronic terminal, smartphone, tablet, computer, or telephone. The law governing EFTs depends on the type of transfer involved. Consumer fund transfers are governed by the Electronic Fund Transfer Act (EFTA).[17] Commercial fund transfers are governed by Article 4A of the UCC.

Although electronic banking offers numerous benefits, it also poses difficulties on occasion. It is difficult to issue stop-payment orders with electronic banking. Also, fewer records are available to prove or disprove that a transaction took place, and the possibilities for tampering with a person's private banking information have increased.

## 18–5a Types of EFT Systems

Most banks offer EFT services to their customers. The following are the most common types of EFT systems used by bank customers:

1. *Automated teller machines* (ATMs)—The machines are connected online to the bank's computers. A customer inserts a plastic card (called an ATM or debit card) issued by the bank and keys in a *personal identification number* (PIN) to access her or his accounts and conduct banking transactions.

2. *Point-of-sale systems*—Online terminals allow consumers to transfer funds to merchants to pay for purchases using a debit card.

3. *Direct deposits and withdrawals*—Customers can authorize the bank to allow another party, such as the government or an employer, to make direct deposits into their accounts. Similarly, a customer can ask the bank to make automatic payments to a third party at regular, recurrent intervals from the customer's funds (insurance premiums or loan payments, for instance).

4. *Online payment systems*—Most financial institutions permit their customers to access the institution's computer system via the Internet and direct a transfer of funds between accounts or pay a particular bill. Payments can be made on a one-time or a recurring basis.

---

17. 15 U.S.C. Sections 1693–1693r. The EFTA amended Title IX of the Consumer Credit Protection Act.

## 18–5b Consumer Fund Transfers

The Electronic Fund Transfer Act (EFTA) provides a basic framework for the rights, liabilities, and responsibilities of users of EFT systems. The act gave the Federal Reserve Board authority to issue rules and regulations to help implement the act's provisions. The Federal Reserve Board's implemental regulation is called **Regulation E.**

The EFTA governs financial institutions that offer electronic transfers of funds involving customer accounts. The types of accounts covered include checking accounts, savings accounts, and any other asset accounts established for personal, family, or household purposes.

**Disclosure Requirements** The EFTA is essentially a disclosure law benefiting consumers. The act requires financial institutions to inform consumers of their rights and responsibilities, including those listed here, with respect to EFT systems.

1. The bank must provide a monthly statement for every month in which there is an electronic transfer of funds. The statement must show the amount and date of the transfer, the names of the retailers or other third parties involved, the location or identification of the terminal, and the fees.
2. If a customer's debit card is lost or stolen and used without her or his permission, the customer shall be required to pay no more than $50. The customer, however, must notify the bank of the loss or theft within two days of learning about it. Otherwise, the customer's liability increases to $500. The customer may be liable for more than $500 if she or he does not report the unauthorized use within sixty days after it appears on the customer's statement. (If a customer voluntarily gives her or his debit card to another, who then uses it improperly, the protections just mentioned do not apply.)
3. The customer must discover any error on the monthly statement within sixty days and notify the bank. The bank then has ten days to investigate and must report its conclusions to the customer in writing. If the bank takes longer than ten days, it must return the disputed amount to the customer's account until it finds the error. If there is no error, the customer is required to return the funds to the bank.
4. The bank must make receipts available for transactions made through computer terminals, but it is not obligated to do so for telephone transfers.

**Violations and Damages** EFT systems are vulnerable to fraud when someone uses another's card, code, or other means to make unauthorized transfers. Unauthorized access to an EFT system constitutes a federal felony,

and those convicted may be fined up to $10,000 and sentenced to as long as ten years in prison. Banks must strictly comply with the terms of the EFTA and are liable for any failure to adhere to its provisions.

For a bank's violation of the EFTA, a consumer may recover both actual damages (including attorneys' fees and costs) and punitive damages of not less than $100 and not more than $1,000.[18] Failure to investigate an error in good faith makes the bank liable for treble damages (three times the amount of damages). Even when a customer has sustained no actual damage, the bank may be liable for legal costs and punitive damages if it fails to follow the proper procedures outlined by the EFTA for error resolution.

## 18–5c Commercial Fund Transfers

Funds are also transferred electronically "by wire" between commercial parties. In fact, the dollar volume of payments made by wire transfer is more than $1 trillion a day—an amount that far exceeds the dollar volume of payments made by other means. The two major wire payment systems are the Federal Reserve wire transfer network (Fedwire) and the New York Clearing House Interbank Payments Systems (CHIPS).

Commercial wire transfers are governed by Article 4A of the UCC, which has been adopted by most of the states. Article 4A uses the term *funds transfer* rather than *wire transfer* to describe the overall payment transaction.

■ **EXAMPLE 18.14** Jellux, Inc., owes $5 million to Perot Corporation. Instead of sending Perot a check or some other instrument that would enable Perot to obtain payment, Jellux instructs its bank, North Bank, to credit $5 million to Perot's account in South Bank. North Bank debits Jellux's North Bank account and wires $5 million to South Bank with instructions to credit $5 million to Perot's South Bank account. In more complex transactions, additional banks would be involved. ■

# 18–6 Online Banking and E-Money

Online banking is common in today's world. Within a few minutes, anybody with the proper software can access his or her account, transfer funds, write "checks," pay bills, monitor investments, and even buy and sell stocks.

Also commonplace is the use of **digital cash,** or **e-money,** which consists of funds stored on microchips in

---

18. In a class-action suit, a court can award up to $500,000 or 1 percent of the institution's net worth as punitive damages. 15 U.S.C. Section 1693m.

laptops, smartphones, tablets, and other devices. E-money replaces *physical* cash—coins and paper currency—with *virtual* cash in the form of electronic impulses.

All these developments are part of a general trend toward making payments electronically. Electronic payment systems are often replacing checks, as discussed in this chapter's *Digital Update* feature.

## 18–6a Online Banking

Most customers use three kinds of online banking services:

1. Consolidating bills and making payments.
2. Transferring funds among accounts.
3. Applying for loans and credit cards.

Withdrawing and depositing funds are two banking functions not yet widely available online. Nevertheless, there are software applications (apps) that enable customers to make deposits into their accounts using electronic devices. For instance, JPMorgan Chase has an app that allows customers to deposit checks via their smartphones or tablets. The customer simply takes a photo of the check's front and back (showing proper indorsement) with a smartphone or tablet and then sends that image to the bank.

Mobile payment apps, such as Apple Pay, Android Pay, and Samsung Pay, are also popular. These apps allow people to use a smartphone, smart watch, or tablet to make purchases at a growing number of establishments. The person simply holds an iPhone or other device close to the point-of-sale terminal to authenticate the transaction. Customers' payment information is kept private while the system generates a "dynamic security code" for each transaction. Some experts estimate that smartphone point-of-sale payments will total more than $70 billion in 2018.

---

## DIGITAL UPDATE    Electronic Payment Systems Are Reducing the Use of Checks

Most young people no longer use checks. Businesses, in contrast, use checks regularly. Indeed, businesses are still using checks for more than half of their transactions. Issuing checks is costly, though. A typical business spends $5 to $25 to issue a paper check. That same transaction, if done electronically, costs between $1 and $2. Nevertheless, U.S. businesses account for over two-thirds of the 22 billion checks written each year worldwide.

### eBills on the Rise

In some areas of the world, such as within the European Union and parts of Latin America, businesses have been required to switch to digital invoices. That has not been the case in the United States.

Still, the use of electronic billing is on the rise in the United States. An electronic bill, or eBill, is simply an electronic version of a paper bill. eBills contain the same information as paper bills. The difference is that you can view and pay them online.

An increasing number of banks offer online banking services that enable customers to pay bills online. Such services include electronic bill payment and presentment (EBPP). One type of EBPP is offered directly by the company that provides goods or services to consumers. Another type allows consumers to pay multiple bills electronically through their bank's online banking system.

### Business-to-Business (B2B) Bill Paying and the Cloud

As U.S. businesses have grown more comfortable with cloud computing, they have also grown more comfortable with digital payments. The Association of Financial Professionals estimates that approximately 60 percent of today's businesses are very likely or somewhat likely to convert to electronic payments for their suppliers within the next few years. Whereas the use of checks for business-to-business payments was 80 percent of all transactions in 2004, it is estimated that by 2020, that figure will drop to 20 percent.

Several companies offer Internet-based payment systems for B2B bill paying. Typical companies of this kind charge a monthly subscription cost plus a small per-unit transaction fee. These companies carry out the payment process without any additional input from the companies requesting the transaction payments. A growing number of cloud-based companies, such as eBill.com and inHance Cloud, offer these services.

**Critical Thinking** *Are there additional risks in using electronic payment systems instead of checks?*

## 18–6b Stored-Value and Smart Cards

The simplest kind of e-money system uses *stored-value cards*. These are plastic cards embossed with magnetic strips containing magnetically encoded data. Frequently, a stored-value card can be used only to purchase specific goods and services offered by the card issuer. An example is a gift card that is redeemable only at a particular retail store or restaurant.

**Smart cards** are plastic cards containing microchips that can hold much more information than magnetic strips can. A smart card carries and processes security programming. This capability gives smart cards a technical advantage over stored-value cards. The microprocessors on smart cards can also authenticate the validity of transactions. Retailers can program electronic cash registers to confirm the authenticity of a smart card by examining a unique digital signature stored on its microchip. Common uses for smart cards are as credit cards and ATM cards.

## Reviewing: Banking in the Digital Age

RPM Pizza, Inc., issued a check for $96,000 to Systems Marketing for an advertising campaign. A few days later, RPM decided not to go through with the deal and placed a written stop-payment order on the check. RPM and Systems had no further contact for many months. Three weeks after the stop-payment order expired, however, Toby Rierson, an employee at Systems, cashed the check. Bank One Cambridge, RPM's bank, paid the check with funds from RPM's account. The amount of the check was large, and the check was more than six months old (stale). The bank should therefore have verified the signature on the check according to standard banking procedures and the bank's own policies. Bank One did not do so, however. RPM filed a suit in a federal district court against Bank One to recover the amount of the check. Using the information presented in the chapter, answer the following questions.

1.  How long is a written stop-payment order effective? What else could RPM have done to prevent this check from being cashed?
2.  What would happen if it turned out that RPM did not have a legitimate reason for stopping payment on the check?
3.  What are a bank's obligations with respect to stale checks? Should Bank One have contacted RPM before paying the check? Why or why not?
4.  Assume that Rierson's indorsement on the check was a forgery. Would a court be likely to hold the bank liable for the amount of the check because it failed to verify the signature on the check? Why or why not?

**Debate This . . .** *To reduce fraud, checks that utilize mechanical or electronic signature systems should not be honored.*

## Terms and Concepts

| | | |
|---|---|---|
| cashier's check 342 | electronic fund transfer (EFT) 356 | Regulation E 357 |
| certified check 343 | e-money 357 | smart card 359 |
| check 342 | Federal Reserve System 354 | stale check 347 |
| clearinghouse 355 | intermediary bank 354 | stop-payment order 347 |
| collecting bank 354 | overdraft 346 | substitute check 355 |
| depositary bank 354 | payor bank 354 | traveler's check 343 |
| digital cash 357 | | |

## Issue Spotters

1.  Lyn writes a check for $900 to Mac, who indorses the check in blank and transfers it to Nan. She presents the check to Omega Bank, the drawee bank, for payment. Omega does not honor the check. Is Lyn liable to Nan? Could Lyn be subject to criminal prosecution? Why or why not? (See *The Bank's Duty to Honor Checks*.)

**2.** Herb steals a check from Kay's checkbook, forges Kay's signature, and transfers the check to Will for value. Unaware that the signature is not Kay's, Will presents the check to First State Bank, the drawee. The bank cashes the check. Kay discovers the forgery and insists that the bank recredit her account. Can the bank refuse to recredit Kay's account? If not, can the bank recover the amount paid to Will? Why or why not? (See *The Bank's Duty to Honor Checks.*)

• **Check your answers to the Issue Spotters against the answers provided in Appendix B at the end of this text.**

## Business Scenarios

**18–1. Forged Signatures.** Roy Supply, Inc., and R. M. R. Drywall, Inc., had checking accounts at Wells Fargo Bank. Both accounts required all checks to carry two signatures—that of Edward Roy and that of Twila June Moore, both of whom were executive officers of both companies. Between January 2015 and March 2016, the bank honored hundreds of checks on which Roy's signature was forged by Moore. On January 31, 2017, Roy and the two corporations notified the bank of the forgeries and then filed a suit in a California state court against the bank, alleging negligence. Who is liable for the amounts of the forged checks? Why? (See *The Bank's Duty to Honor Checks.*)

**18–2. Customer Negligence.** Gary goes grocery shopping and carelessly leaves his checkbook in his shopping cart. His checkbook, with two blank checks remaining, is stolen by Dolores. On May 5, Dolores forges Gary's name on a check for $100 and cashes the check at Gary's bank, Citizens Bank of Middletown. Gary has not reported the loss of his blank checks to his bank. On June 1, Gary receives his monthly bank statement from Citizens Bank. The statement shows the forged check, but Gary does not examine it. On June 20, Dolores forges Gary's last check for $1,000 and cashes it at Eastern City Bank, a bank with which she has previously done business. Citizens Bank honors the check. On July 1, Gary receives another bank statement, discovers both forgeries, and immediately notifies Citizens Bank. Dolores cannot be found. Gary claims that Citizens Bank must recredit his account for both checks, as his signature was forged. Discuss fully Gary's claim. (See *The Bank's Duty to Honor Checks.*)

## Business Case Problems

**18–3. Spotlight on Embezzlement—Forged Drawers' Signatures.** In December 1999, Spacemakers of America,  Inc., hired Jenny Triplett as a bookkeeper. Triplett was responsible for maintaining the company checkbook and reconciling it with the monthly statements from SunTrust Bank. She also handled invoices from vendors. Spacemakers' president, Dennis Rose, reviewed the invoices and signed the checks to pay them, but no other employee checked Triplett's work.

By the end of her first full month of employment, Triplett had forged six checks totaling more than $22,000, all payable to Triple M Entertainment, which was not a Spacemakers vendor. By October 2000, Triplett had forged fifty-nine more checks, totaling more than $475,000. A SunTrust employee became suspicious of an item that required sight inspection under the bank's fraud detection standards, which exceeded those of other banks in the area. Triplett was arrested. Spacemakers filed a suit in a Georgia state court against SunTrust. The bank filed a motion for summary judgment. On what basis could the bank avoid liability? In whose favor should the court rule, and why? [*Spacemakers of America, Inc. v. SunTrust Bank,* 271 Ga.App. 335, 609 S.E.2d 683 (2005)] (See *The Bank's Duty to Honor Checks.*)

**18–4. Forged Drawers' Signatures.** Debbie Brooks and Martha Tingstrom lived together. Tingstrom handled their finances. For five years, Brooks did not look at any statements concerning her accounts. When she finally reviewed the statements, she discovered that Tingstrom had taken $85,500

through Brooks's checking account with Transamerica Financial Advisors. Tingstrom had forged Brooks's name on six checks paid between one and two years earlier. Another year passed before Brooks filed a suit against Transamerica. Who is most likely to suffer the loss for the checks paid with Brooks's forged signature? Why? [*Brooks v. Transamerica Financial Advisors,* 57 So.3d 1153 (La.App. 2 Cir. 2011)] (See *The Bank's Duty to Honor Checks.*)

**18–5. Business Case Problem with Sample Answer— Honoring Checks.** Adley Abdulwahab (Wahab) opened an  account on behalf of W Financial Group, LLC, with Wells Fargo Bank. Wahab was one of three authorized signers on the account. Five months later, Wahab withdrew $1,701,250 from W Financial's account to buy a cashier's check payable to Lubna Lateef. Wahab visited a different Wells Fargo branch and deposited the check into the account of CA Houston Investment Center, LLC. Wahab was the only authorized signer on this account. Lateef never received or indorsed the check. W Financial filed a suit to recover the amount. Applying the rules for payment on a forged indorsement, who is liable? Explain. [*Jones v. Wells Fargo Bank,* 666 F.3d 955 (5th Cir. 2012)] (See *The Bank's Duty to Honor Checks.*)

• **For a sample answer to Problem 18–5, go to Appendix C at the end of this text.**

**18–6. Consumer Fund Transfers.** Stephen Patterson held an account with Suntrust Bank in Alcoa, Tennessee. Juanita

Wehrman—with whom Patterson was briefly involved in a romantic relationship—stole his debit card. She used it for sixteen months (well beyond the length of their relationship) to make unauthorized purchases in excess of $30,000. When Patterson learned what was happening, he closed his account. The bank would reimburse Patterson only $677.46—the amount of unauthorized transactions that occurred within sixty days of the transmittal of the bank statement that revealed the first unauthorized transaction. Is the bank's refusal justifiable? Explain. [*Patterson v. Suntrust Bank,* 2013 WL 139315 (Tenn. App. 2013)] (See *Electronic Fund Transfers.*)

**18–7. Forged Drawers' Signatures.** Victor Nacim had a checking account at Compass Bank. The "Deposit Agreement" required him to report an unauthorized transaction within thirty days of his receipt of the statement on which it appeared to obtain a recredit. When Nacim moved to a new residence, he asked the bank to update the address on his account. Compass continued to mail his statements to his previous address, however, and Nacim did not receive them. In the meantime, Compass officer David Peterson made an unauthorized withdrawal of $34,000 from Nacim's account. A month later, Peterson told Nacim what he had done. The next month, Nacim asked the bank for a recredit. Compass refused on the ground that he had reported the withdrawal more than thirty days after the bank mailed the statement on which it appeared—a statement that Nacim never received. Is Nacim entitled to a recredit? Explain. [*Compass Bank v. Nacim,* 459 S.W.3d 95 (Tex.App.—El Paso 2015)] (See *The Bank's Duty to Honor Checks.*)

**18–8. The Bank-Customer Relationship.** Euro International Mortgage, Inc. (EIM), held two accounts—Account 9378 and Account 3998—at Bank of America. Ravi Kadiyala was an authorized signatory on Account 9378 but not on Account 3998. Through EIM, Kadiyala obtained a username and password to gain access to Account 3998, from which he transferred $200,000 to Account 9378. He then instructed the bank to issue cashier's checks against the new balance in Account 9378. Meanwhile, Mark Pupke, an authorized signatory on both accounts, learned what Kadiyala had done and told the bank to cancel the checks and reverse the transfer. Does the bank have a duty to honor either party's request? If so, whose? Why? [*Kadiyala v. Bank of America,* 630 Fed.Appx. 633 (7th Cir. 2016)] (See *The Bank-Customer Relationship.*)

**18–9. A Question of Ethics—Death or Incompetence of a Customer.**  *New York resident Esther Braunstein worked as an usher at Lincoln Center, held an administrative position with Citibank, was a school crossing guard, and assisted disabled persons and others as a volunteer. Before her death, she drew a $5,000 check payable to each of two of her daughters, Sandra Braunstein and Carol Russo. The checks were drawn on a joint account held in the names of Esther and Sandra. Carol did not cash her check until five months after Esther's death. Sandra filed a suit in a New York state court against Carol to recover the funds.* [*Braunstein v. Russo,* 988 N.Y.S.2d 521 (2 Dept. 2014)] (See *The Bank's Duty to Honor Checks.*)

**(a)** Is one sister's attempt to recover funds given to another sister by their mother always unethical? Who is legally entitled to the funds? Discuss.

**(b)** If the check that Carol cashed five months after Esther's death had not been a gift from Esther, but instead had contained a forged drawer's signature, on whom could liability have been imposed? How might that circumstance have affected the ethics of the situation? Explain.

# Legal Reasoning Group Activity

**18–10. Bank's Duty to Honor Checks.** On January 5, Brian drafts a check for $3,000 drawn on Southern Marine Bank and payable to his assistant, Shanta. Brian puts last year's date on the check by mistake. On January 7, before Shanta has had a chance to go to the bank, Brian is killed in an automobile accident. Southern Marine Bank is aware of Brian's death. On January 10, Shanta presents the check to the bank, and the bank honors the check by payment to Shanta. Later, Brian's widow, Joyce, claims that the bank acted wrongfully when it paid Shanta. Joyce points out that the bank knew of Brian's death and that the check was by date over one year old. As executor of Brian's estate and sole heir by his will, Joyce demands that Southern Marine Bank recredit Brian's estate for the check paid to Shanta. (See *The Bank's Duty to Honor Checks.*)

**(a)** The first group will determine whether the bank acted wrongfully by honoring Brian's check and paying Shanta.

**(b)** The second group will assess whether Joyce has a valid claim against Southern Marine Bank for the amount of the check paid to Shanta.

**(c)** A third group will assume that the check Brian drafted was on his business account rather than his personal account and that he had two partners in the business. Would a business partner be in a better position to force Southern Marine Bank to recredit Brian's account than his widow? Why or why not?

# CHAPTER 19

# Creditors' Rights and Remedies

Normally, creditors have no problem collecting the debts owed to them. When disputes arise over the amount owed, however, or when the debtor simply cannot or will not pay, what happens? What remedies are available to creditors when a debtor **defaults** (fails to pay as promised)? In this chapter, we focus on some basic laws that assist the debtor and creditor in resolving their dispute without resorting to bankruptcy.

The remedies we discuss in this chapter are available regardless of whether a creditor is secured or unsecured. *Secured creditors* are those whose loans are backed by *collateral*, which is specific property (such as a car or a house) pledged by a borrower to ensure repayment. The loans made by *unsecured creditors,* such as companies that provide credit cards, are not backed by collateral. Under Article 9 of the Uniform Commercial Code (UCC), certain remedies are available only to secured creditors.

## 19–1 Laws Assisting Creditors

Both the common law and statutory laws other than Article 9 of the UCC create various rights and remedies for creditors. Next, we discuss some of these rights and remedies, including liens, garnishment, and creditors' composition agreements.

### 19–1a Liens

A **lien** is an encumbrance on (claim against) property to satisfy a debt or protect a claim for the payment of a debt. Liens may arise under the common law (usually by possession of the property) or under statutory law. *Mechanic's liens* are statutory liens, whereas *artisan's liens* were recognized at common law. *Judicial liens* may be used by a creditor to collect on a debt before or after a judgment is entered by a court. Liens are a very important tool for creditors because they generally take priority over other claims against the same property.

**Mechanic's Liens** Sometimes, a person who has contracted for labor, services, or materials to be furnished for making improvements on real property does not immediately pay for the improvements. When that happens, the creditor can place a **mechanic's lien** on the property.

**Real Property Secures the Debt.** A mechanic's lien creates a special type of debtor-creditor relationship in which the real estate itself becomes security for the debt. ■ **EXAMPLE 19.1** Kirk contracts to paint Tanya's house for an agreed-on price to cover labor and materials. If Tanya refuses to pay or pays only a portion of the charges after the work is completed, a mechanic's lien against the property can be created. Kirk is then a lienholder, and the real property is encumbered (burdened) with the mechanic's lien for the amount owed. ■

If the property owner fails to pay the debt, the lienholder is technically entitled to foreclose on the real estate and sell it. (*Foreclosure* is the process by which a creditor legally takes a debtor's property to satisfy a debt.) The sale proceeds are then used to pay the debt and the costs of the legal proceedings. The surplus, if any, is paid to the former owner.

In the real world, however, small-amount mechanic's liens are rarely the basis of foreclosure. Rather, these liens simply remain on the books of the state until the house is sold. At closing (when the sale is finalized), the seller agrees to pay any mechanic's liens out of the proceeds of the sale before the seller receives any of the funds.

**Governed by State Law.** State law governs the procedures that must be followed to create a mechanic's (or other statutory) lien. Generally, the lienholder must file a written notice of lien within a specific time period (usually within 60 to 120 days) from the last date that material or labor was provided.

In the following case, the state mechanic's lien statute required the lien to be filed no more than 90 days after "the completion of the work." The contractor that filed the lien and the owner of the project against which the lien was filed disputed the meaning of the term "completion."

**Case Analysis 19.1**

# Picerne Construction Corp. v. Villas

California Court of Appeal, Third District, 244 Cal.App.4th 1201, 199 Cal.Rptr.3d 257 (2016).

### In the Language of the Court

*MAURO*, J. [Judge]

* * * *

Castellino [Villas, LLC] and Picerne [Construction Corporation] entered into an agreement in which Picerne would build an apartment complex called Castellino Villas at Laguna West (project or property) in the City of Elk Grove [California] (the City). The project consisted of 11 apartment buildings, separate garages, a clubhouse, and other facilities.

* * * *

The City issued certificates of occupancy for the 11 buildings within the project * * * after a city inspector conducted a final inspection of each building. The first certificates of occupancy were issued on May 3, 2006. The final certificate of occupancy was issued on July 25, 2006.

Picerne employees and subcontractors continued to perform work at the project after July 25, 2006.

* * * *

[John] Olsen [Castellino's representative for the project] signed a document titled "Owner's Acceptance of Site" for Castellino on September 8, 2006.

* * * *

Castellino began renting apartments at the property in October 2006.

Picerne recorded a claim of mechanic's lien on November 28, 2006.

Picerne filed a complaint [in a California state court] to foreclose its mechanic's lien on December 29, 2006.

* * * *

* * * The trial court * * * determined * * * Picerne is entitled to foreclose its lien.

* * * *

[On appeal to this court] Castellino * * * contends Picerne does not have a valid mechanic's lien because Picerne did not record a claim of mechanic's lien within 90 days after substantial completion of the project.

* * * *

*In order to have a valid mechanic's lien, a claimant must record a claim of lien within a prescribed period of time after completion of the work of improvement * * *. The failure of a claimant to timely record a claim of lien precludes the enforcement of a mechanic's lien.* [Emphasis added.]

[When Picerne filed its lien, mechanic's liens were governed by California Civil Code Section 3115, which] provided, "Each original contractor [a contractor who has a direct contractual relationship with the owner for the work], in order to enforce a lien, must record his claim of lien after he completes his contract and before the expiration of 90 days after the completion of the work of improvement." [According to Section 3116, the term "work of improvement" means the entire structure or scheme of improvement as a whole.]

* * * The [California State] Legislature defined the term completion as "actual completion of the work of improvement." In addition, * * * deemed to be equivalent to a completion [was] the acceptance by the owner or his

agent of the work of improvement.

Substantial evidence supports the trial court's finding that the owner accepted the project as of September 8, 2006. * * * Picerne timely recorded its claim of mechanic's lien within 90 days after September 8, 2006.

* * * *

Castellino * * * nevertheless claims that the time for Picerne to record its claim of mechanic's lien began to run before September 8, 2006. [Castellino] asserts the phrase "completion of the work of improvement" in Section 3115 means substantial completion of the work of improvement, and the project was substantially completed by July 25, 2006, when the City issued the final certificate of occupancy.

There are cases construing the * * * mechanic's lien statute which interpreted "completion" as substantial completion.

* * * *

[But these cases were decided before the Legislature amended Section 3115 to define] completion of the work of improvement as actual completion of the work of improvement * * *. The Legislature did not define "completion of the work of improvement" as substantial completion. Courts have looked at whether the work at issue was required under the claimant's contract in determining whether a work of improvement was completed.

Castellino argues that interpreting the term "completion" * * * to mean substantial completion would be sound

**Case 19.1 Continues**

public policy because it would ensure transparency, visibility, objectivity, and certainty in the relationship between the contractor and the owner in the filing of mechanic's liens. However, following the language of the statute by construing "completion" as "actual completion" does not create uncertainty when reference can be made to the parties' agreement and the labor and materials furnished. Moreover, * * * deemed equivalent to completion [is] acceptance of the work of improvement.

In addition, contrary to Castellino's argument, public policy supports the interpretation of completion as actual completion in this specific context. *The mechanic's lien statute is intended [primarily to benefit] persons who perform labor or furnish materials for works of improvement, and it is to be liberally construed for the protection of laborers and material suppliers, with doubts concerning the meaning of the statute generally resolved in favor of the lien claimant.* Interpreting completion as actual completion gives lien claimants the maximum amount of time

to assert their rights before such rights are cut off, whereas interpreting completion as substantial completion could cut off mechanic's lien rights much earlier. The interpretation espoused by Castellino would contravene the purpose of California's mechanic's lien law to protect the right to payment of those who have furnished labor or materials to works of improvement. Our construction of the term "completion" * * * effectuates the intent of the mechanic's lien law. [Emphasis added.]

Substantial evidence supports the trial court's findings that even though the City had issued certificates of occupancy for the 11 buildings within the project, roof and stairway work required under the general contract continued between July 25, 2006 and September 19, 2006. Elizar Ortiz [an installer employed by Picerne's stairway subcontractor] testified he worked 22½ hours on September 15, 18, and 19, 2006, installing grip tape on all of the stairs at the project. The general contract called for the installation of anti-slip grip tape

on all concrete stair treads. Ortiz's testimony established the work he performed on September 15, 18, and 19, 2006 was not corrective or repair work.

The president of Picerne's roofing subcontractor testified his company performed roofing work at the project after July 25, 2006. He said such work included straightening out some of the valleys in the roofs, installing nailers and hips on the roof ridges, and nailing trim. * * * The roof and stairway work performed after July 25, 2006, is not comparable to adding a few strokes of paint or turning a screw.

Picerne recorded a claim of mechanic's lien * * * within 90 days of the date Castellino accepted the project and when the stairway and roofing subcontractors performed work required under their contracts. Accordingly, the trial court did not err in concluding Picerne timely recorded its claim of mechanic's lien.

* * * *

* * * The judgment is affirmed.

### Legal Reasoning Questions

1. How did the California legislature define the term "completion"? Was this definition clear? Discuss.
2. How did the owner of the project at the center of this case want the court to interpret "completion"? What arguments support this contention?
3. Ultimately, how did the court define "completion"? Why?

---

**Artisan's Liens** When a debtor fails to pay for labor and materials furnished for the repair or improvement of *personal* property, a creditor can recover payment through an **artisan's lien.** As mentioned, artisan's liens usually take priority over other creditors' claims to the same property.[1]

**Lienholder Must Retain Possession.** In contrast to a mechanic's lien, an artisan's lien is *possessory.* That is, the lienholder ordinarily must have retained possession of the property and have expressly or impliedly agreed to provide the services on a cash, not a credit, basis. The lien remains

in existence as long as the lienholder maintains possession, and the lien is terminated once possession is *voluntarily* surrendered, unless the surrender is only temporary.[2]

■ **CASE IN POINT 19.2** Carrollton Exempted Village School District (in Ohio) hired Clean Vehicle Solutions America, LLC (CVSA, based in New York) to convert ten school buses from diesel to compressed natural gas. The contract price was $660,000. The district paid a $400,000 deposit and agreed to pay installments of $26,000 to CVSA after the delivery of each converted bus. After the first two buses were delivered, the district

---

1. An artisan's lien has priority over a filed statutory lien (such as a title lien on an automobile or a lien filed under Article 9 of the UCC) and a bailee's lien (such as a storage lien).

2. Involuntary surrender of possession by a lienholder, such as when a police officer seizes goods from a lienholder, does not terminate the lien.

refused to continue the contract, claiming that the conversion made the two buses unsafe to drive.

Both parties filed breach of contract lawsuits. CVSA also asserted an artisan's lien over two other buses that it still had in its possession because it had started converting them to natural gas and spent $65,000 doing so. Regardless of the outcome in the parties' lawsuits, CVSA has an artisan's lien that gives it a priority claim to those two buses so long as they remain in its possession. The buses will act as security for the district's payment of at least the amount CVSA has spent converting them to natural gas.[3] ∎

**Foreclosure on Personal Property.** Modern statutes permit the holder of an artisan's lien to foreclose and sell the property subject to the lien to satisfy the debt. As with a mechanic's lien, the lienholder is required to give notice to the owner of the property before the foreclosure and sale. The sale proceeds are used to pay the debt and the costs of the legal proceedings, and the surplus, if any, is paid to the former owner.

**Judicial Liens** When a debt is past due, a creditor can bring a legal action against the debtor to collect the debt. If the action is successful, the court awards the creditor a judgment against the debtor (usually for the amount of the debt plus any interest and legal costs incurred). Frequently, however, the creditor is unable to collect the awarded amount.

To ensure that a judgment in the creditor's favor will be collectible, the creditor may request that certain property of the debtor be seized to satisfy the debt. (As will be discussed, under state or federal statutes, some kinds of property are exempt from attachment by creditors.) A court's order to seize the debtor's property is known as a *writ of attachment* if it is issued before a judgment. If the order is issued after a judgment, it is referred to as a *writ of execution.*

**Writ of Attachment.** In the context of judicial liens, **attachment** refers to a court-ordered seizure and taking into custody of property before a judgment is obtained on a past-due debt. (Attachment has a different meaning in the context of secured transactions.[4]) Because attachment is a *prejudgment* remedy, it occurs either at the time a lawsuit is filed or immediately afterward.

A creditor must comply with the specific state's statutory restrictions and requirements. The due process clause of the Fourteenth Amendment to the U.S. Constitution requires that the debtor be given notice and an opportunity to be heard. The creditor must have an enforceable right to payment of the debt under law and must follow certain procedures. Otherwise, the creditor can be liable for damages for wrongful attachment.

The typical procedure for attachment is as follows:

1. The creditor files with the court an *affidavit* (a written statement, made under oath). The affidavit states that the debtor has failed to pay and indicates the statutory grounds under which attachment is sought.
2. The creditor must post a bond to cover at least the court costs, the value of the property attached, and the value of the loss of use of that property suffered by the debtor.
3. When the court is satisfied that all the requirements have been met, it issues a **writ of attachment.** The writ directs the sheriff or other officer to seize the debtor's nonexempt property. If the creditor prevails at trial, the seized property can be sold to satisfy the judgment.

**Writ of Execution.** If a creditor wins a judgment against a debtor and the debtor will not or cannot pay the amount due, the creditor can request a **writ of execution** from the court. A writ of execution is an order that directs the sheriff to seize (levy) and sell any of the debtor's nonexempt real or personal property. The writ applies only to property that is within the court's geographic jurisdiction (usually the county in which the courthouse is located).

The proceeds of the sale are used to pay the judgment, accrued interest, and costs of the sale. Any excess is paid to the debtor. The debtor can pay the judgment and redeem the nonexempt property at any time before the sale takes place. (Because of exemption laws and bankruptcy laws, however, many judgments are practically uncollectible.)

## 19-1b Garnishment

An order for **garnishment** permits a creditor to collect a debt by seizing property of the debtor that is being held by a third party. As a result of a garnishment proceeding, for instance, the debtor's employer may be ordered by the court to turn over a portion of the debtor's wages to pay the debt. Many other types of property can be garnished as well, including funds in a bank account, tax refunds, pensions, and trust funds. It is only necessary that the property is not exempt from garnishment and is in the possession of a third party.

---

3. *Clean Vehicle Solutions America, LLC v. Carrollton Exempted Village School District Board of Education,* 2015 WL 5459852 (S.D.N.Y. 2015).
4. In secured transactions, *attachment* refers to the process through which a security interest becomes effective and enforceable against a debtor with respect to the debtor's collateral [UCC 9–203].

■ **CASE IN POINT 19.3** When Edward G. Tinsley divorced Michelle Townsend, they entered into a marital settlement contract. They agreed to sell the marital home and split the proceeds evenly. But Tinsley refused to cooperate with the sale. A court therefore appointed a trustee to sell the house for them and ordered the sheriff to evict Tinsley. Tinsley then conveyed the house to a trust established in his name. Even after the sheriff evicted Tinsley from the house and changed the locks, Tinsley managed to move back in and change the locks again.

Tinsley was arrested for trespassing and charged with contempt of court (for disobeying court orders). In the meantime, Tinsley secretly sold the home for $150,000 and deposited the proceeds into a bank account held in the name of Edward G. Tinsley Living Trust at SunTrust Bank. After learning of the sale, the court-appointed trustee obtained a writ of garnishment on all of Tinsley's and his trust's bank accounts at SunTrust Bank. Despite numerous objections from Tinsley (and a trial and appeal), SunTrust eventually complied with the garnishment order and sent all the funds to the trustee.[5] ■

**Procedures** Garnishment can be a prejudgment remedy, requiring a hearing before a court, but it is most often a postjudgment remedy. State law governs garnishment actions, so the specific procedures vary from state to state.

In some states, the judgment creditor needs to obtain only one order of garnishment, which will then apply continuously to the judgment debtor's wages until the entire debt is paid. In other states, the judgment creditor must go back to court for a separate order of garnishment for each pay period.

See this chapter's *Ethics Today* feature for a discussion of how creditors can obtain garnishment even when a debtor crosses state lines in an attempt to avoid paying the debt.

**Laws Limiting the Amount of Wages Subject to Garnishment** Both federal and state laws limit the amount that can be taken from a debtor's weekly take-home pay through garnishment proceedings.[6] Federal law provides a minimal framework to protect debtors from losing all their income to pay judgment debts.[7] State laws also provide dollar exemptions, and these amounts are often larger than those provided by federal law.

Under federal law, an employer cannot dismiss an employee because his or her wages are being garnished.

### 19–1c Creditors' Composition Agreements

Creditors may contract with the debtor for discharge of the debtor's liquidated debts (debts that are definite, or fixed, in amount) on payment of a sum less than that owed. These agreements are referred to as **creditors' composition agreements** (or *composition agreements*) and usually are held to be enforceable unless they are formed under duress.

## 19–2 Mortgages

When individuals purchase real property, they typically make a **down payment** in cash and borrow the remaining funds from a financial institution. The borrowed funds are secured by a **mortgage**—a written instrument that gives the creditor a lien on the debtor's real property as security for payment of a debt. The creditor is the *mortgagee,* and the debtor is the *mortgagor.*

### 19–2a Fixed-Rate versus Adjustable-Rate Mortgages

Lenders offer various types of mortgages to meet the needs of different borrowers, but a basic distinction is whether the interest rate is fixed or variable. A *fixed-rate mortgage* has a fixed, or unchanging, rate of interest, so the payments remain the same for the duration of the loan. Lenders determine the interest rate for a standard fixed-rate mortgage loan based on a variety of factors, including the borrower's credit history, credit score, income, and debts.

With an *adjustable-rate mortgage (ARM),* the rate of interest paid by the borrower changes periodically. Typically, the initial interest rate for an ARM is set at a relatively low fixed rate for a specified period, such as a year or three years. After that time, the interest rate adjusts annually or by some other period, such as biannually or monthly. The interest rate adjustment is calculated by adding a certain number of percentage points (called the margin) to an index rate (one of various government interest rates).

ARMs contractually shift the risk that the interest rate will change from the lender to the borrower. Borrowers will have lower initial payments if they are willing to assume the risk of interest rate increases.

---

5. *Tinsley v. SunTrust Bank,* 2016 WL 687545 (Md.App. 2016).
6. A few states (such as Texas) do not permit garnishment of wages by private parties except under a child-support order.
7. For instance, the federal Consumer Credit Protection Act, 15 U.S.C. Sections 1601–1693r, provides that a debtor can retain either 75 percent of his or her disposable earnings per week or an amount equivalent to thirty hours of work paid at federal minimum wage rates, whichever is greater.

## ETHICS TODAY — Creditors' Rights When Debtors Move to Another State

Creditors have rights when debtors default. The former often go to court and win judgments against the latter. But what can creditors do when judgment debtors simply "pack up and leave"? That is to say, when debtors engage in the ethically suspect action of crossing state lines to avoid judgments, is there recourse for creditors?

### Full Faith and Credit

The Constitution of the United States provides that full faith and credit shall be given in each state to the public acts, records, and judicial proceedings of every other state.[a] Among other things, this means that judgments made in one state will be honored in other states. Fortunately for creditors, there is a long judicial history of the application of judgments to debtors who have moved to another state.[b]

### The Uniform Enforcement of Foreign Judgments Act

Most states have adopted the Uniform Enforcement of Foreign Judgments Act.[c] The act allows judgments obtained in one jurisdiction (such as a state) to be "domesticated" (recognized and enforced) in a different jurisdiction (such as another state). One goal is to prevent judgment debtors from evading payment of their obligations by relocating to another state.

In most states, domestication of a foreign judgment can be accomplished rapidly. The judgment creditor files an authenticated copy of the judgment in the "foreign" state, along with an affidavit and a notice of foreign judgment. The notice of domestication action then is provided to the debtor. A local court enters an order affirming that the foreign judgment has been domesticated.

The equivalent at the federal level involves registering judgments between federal courts.[d] Unlike state court domestication procedures, federal court domestication procedures do not require that notice be given to the judgment debtor.

### Time Is of the Essence

Once domestication of a foreign judgment has occurred, judgment creditors must record the domestication order with the proper authorities within the jurisdiction to put others on notice. Thus, if real property is involved, a title search will show the foreign judgment against the debtor who has an ownership interest in the real property.

All states have specific lifespans (statutes of limitations) for foreign judgments. Often, a judgment debtor will attempt to counter a foreign judgment by claiming that the lifespan of the foreign judgment had lapsed.[e] Domestications of foreign judgments can be renewed, however.

### Garnishment Actions

When a judgment debtor moves to another state, one method of obtaining repayment for debts owed is through the process of garnishment. The benefit for the creditor in such cases is that judgment debtors are often surprised when their bank accounts are frozen or their regular salaries are reduced. Garnishments are typically served against a bank, which then has to freeze any accounts belonging the debtor.

**Critical Thinking** *Is it fair that property or wage garnishments may "surprise" a judgment debtor?*

a. U.S. Const., Art. IV, Section 1.
b. See, for example, *Aultman, Miller & Co. v. Mills*, 9 Wash. 68, 36 P.1046 (Wash. S. Ct. 1894).
c. Originally issued by the National Conference of Commissioners on Uniform State Laws (NCCUSL) in 1948. Revised in 1964.
d. 28 U.S.C. Section 1963.
e. See, for instance, *Independent Bank v. Pandy*, __ P.3d __, 2015 WL 188988 (Colo.App. 2015).

## 19–2b Mortgage Provisions

Because a mortgage involves a transfer of real property, it must be in writing to comply with the Statute of Frauds. Mortgages normally are lengthy and formal documents containing many provisions, including the following:

1. *The terms of the underlying loan.* These include the loan amount, the interest rate, the period of repayment, and other important financial terms, such as the margin and index rate for an ARM.

2. *A prepayment penalty clause.* A **prepayment penalty clause** requires the borrower to pay a penalty if the mortgage is repaid in full within a certain period. A prepayment penalty helps to protect the lender should the borrower refinance within a short time after obtaining a mortgage.

3. *Provisions relating to the maintenance of the property.* Because the mortgage conveys an interest in the property to the lender, the lender often requires the

borrower to maintain the property to protect the lender's investment.

4. *A statement obligating the borrower to maintain homeowner's insurance on the property.* **Homeowner's insurance** protects the lender's interest in the event of a loss due to certain hazards, such as fire or storm damage.

5. *A list of the non-loan financial obligations to be borne by the borrower.* For instance, the borrower typically is required to pay all property taxes, assessments, and other claims against the property.

6. *Creditor protections.* When creditors extend mortgages, they are advancing a significant amount of funds for a number of years. Consequently, creditors usually require debtors to obtain **mortgage insurance** if they do not make a down payment of at least 20 percent of the purchase price.

Creditors record the mortgage with the appropriate office in the county where the property is located, so that their interest in the property is officially on record.

## 19–2c Mortgage Foreclosure

If the homeowner *defaults,* or fails to make the mortgage payments, the lender has the right to foreclose on the mortgaged property. **Foreclosure** is the legal process by which the lender repossesses and auctions off the property that has secured the loan.

Foreclosure is expensive and time consuming. It generally benefits neither the borrowers, who lose their homes, nor the lenders, which face the prospect of losses on their loans. Therefore, both lenders and borrowers are motivated to avoid foreclosure proceedings if possible.

**Ways to Avoid Foreclosure** Possible methods of avoiding foreclosure include forbearance, workout agreements, and short sales (see Exhibit 19–1).

A **forbearance** is a postponement of part or all of the payments on a loan for a limited time. This option works well when the debtor can solve the problem by securing a new job, selling the property, or finding another acceptable solution.

**EXHIBIT 19–1** Methods of Avoiding Foreclosure

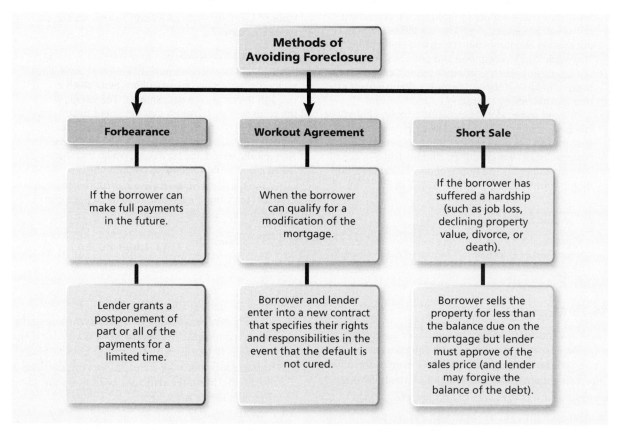

A **workout agreement** is a contract that describes the respective rights and responsibilities of the borrower and the lender as they try to resolve the default. Usually, the lender agrees to delay seeking foreclosure. In exchange, the borrower provides additional financial information that might be used to modify the mortgage.

A lender may sometimes agree to a **short sale,** which is a sale of the property for less than the balance due on the mortgage loan. Typically, the borrower has to show some hardship, such as the loss of a job, a decline in the value of the home, a divorce, or a death in the household. The lender often has approval rights in a short sale, so the sale process may take much longer than an ordinary real estate transaction.

**Foreclosure Procedure** If all efforts to find another solution fail, the lender will proceed to foreclosure. The lender must strictly comply with the state statute governing foreclosures. Many problems arose in the last ten years because lenders, facing a record number of foreclosures during the recent recession, had difficulty complying with the required statutory formalities.

To bring a foreclosure action, a bank must have standing to sue. In the following case, the court had to decide whether a bank could foreclose a mortgage even though the bank could not prove when it became the owner of the borrower's promissory note.

## Spotlight on Foreclosures

## Case 19.2 McLean v. JPMorgan Chase Bank, N.A.
District Court of Appeal of Florida, Fourth District, 79 So.3d 170 (2012).

**Background and Facts** On May 11, 2009, JPMorgan Chase Bank (Chase) filed a foreclosure action against Robert McLean. The complaint alleged that Chase was entitled to enforce the mortgage and promissory note on which McLean had defaulted. Nevertheless, the attached mortgage identified a different mortgagee and lender, and Chase claimed that the note had been "lost, stolen, or destroyed." When McLean filed a motion to dismiss, Chase produced a mortgage assignment dated May 14, 2009, which was three days after it had filed the lawsuit. Eventually, Chase also filed the original note. Although the indorsement to Chase was undated, Chase then filed a motion for summary judgment. The trial court granted Chase's motion even though the accompanying affidavit failed to show that Chase had owned the mortgage or note when it filed the complaint. McLean appealed.

### In the Language of the Court
*PER CURIAM* [By the Whole Court].
    * * * *

A crucial element in any mortgage foreclosure proceeding is that the party seeking foreclosure must demonstrate that it has standing to foreclose.
    * * * *

* * * A party's standing is determined at the time the lawsuit was filed. Stated another way, *"the plaintiff's lack of standing at the inception of the case is not a defect that may be cured by the acquisition of standing after the case is filed." Thus, a party is not permitted to establish the right to maintain an action retroactively by acquiring standing to file a lawsuit after the fact.* [Emphasis added.]
    * * * *

In the present case, as is common in recent foreclosure cases, Chase did not attach a copy of the original note to its complaint, but instead [filed a claim] to re-establish a lost note. Later, however, Chase filed * * * the original promissory note, which bore a special endorsement in favor of Chase. [Thus,] * * * it obtained standing to foreclose, at least at some point.

Nonetheless, the record evidence is insufficient to demonstrate that Chase had standing to foreclose *at the time the lawsuit was filed.* [Emphasis in original.] The mortgage was assigned to Chase three days after Chase filed the instant foreclosure complaint. While the original note contained an undated special endorsement in Chase's favor, the affidavit filed in support of summary judgment did not state when the endorsement was made to Chase. Furthermore, the affidavit, which was dated after the

*Case 19.2 Continues*

**Case 19.2 Continued**

lawsuit was filed, did not specifically state when Chase became the owner of the note, nor did the affidavit indicate that Chase was the owner of the note before suit was filed.

We therefore reverse the summary judgment and corresponding final judgment of foreclosure. On remand, in order for Chase to be entitled to summary judgment, it must show * * * that it was the holder of the note on the date the complaint was filed (that the note was endorsed to Chase on or before the date the lawsuit was filed). By contrast, if the evidence shows that the note was endorsed to Chase after the lawsuit was filed, then Chase had no standing at the time the complaint was filed, in which case the trial court should dismiss the instant lawsuit and Chase must file a new complaint.

**Decision and Remedy** *The Florida appellate court held that Chase had not proved that it had standing to foreclose against McLean. The court therefore reversed the trial court's grant of summary judgment.*

**Critical Thinking**

- **Legal Environment** *If Chase cannot prove that it owned the note at the time of its complaint, what will happen next? Will Chase prevail? Why or why not?*

---

**Redemption Rights** Every state allows a defaulting borrower to redeem the property before the foreclosure sale by paying the full amount of the debt, plus any interest and costs that have accrued. This **equitable right of redemption** gives the defaulting buyer a chance to regain title and possession after default.

The *statutory right of redemption,* in contrast, entitles the borrower to repurchase property *after* a judicial foreclosure. In other words, in states that provide for statutory redemption, the homeowner has a right to buy the property back from a third party who bought it at a foreclosure sale. Generally, the borrower may exercise this right for up to one year from the time the house is sold at a foreclosure sale.[8] The borrower may retain possession of the property after the foreclosure sale until the statutory redemption period ends. If the borrower does not exercise the right of redemption, the new buyer receives title to and possession of the property.

Concept Summary 19.1 provides a synopsis of the remedies available to creditors.

---

# 19-3 Suretyship and Guaranty

When a third person promises to pay a debt owed by another in the event that the debtor does not pay, either a *suretyship* or a *guaranty* relationship is created. Exhibit 19–2 illustrates these relationships. The third person's creditworthiness becomes the security for the debt owed.

Suretyship and guaranty provide creditors with the right to seek payment from the third party if the primary debtor, or *principal,* defaults on her or his obligations. Normally a guaranty must be in writing to be enforceable under the Statute of Frauds, unless its main purpose is to benefit the guarantor. Traditionally, a suretyship agreement did not require a writing to be enforceable, and oral surety agreements were sufficient. Today, however, some states require a writing to enforce a suretyship.

At common law, there were significant differences in the liability of a surety and a guarantor. Today, however, the distinctions outlined here have been abolished in some states.

## 19-3a Suretyship

A contract of strict **suretyship** is a promise made by a third person to be responsible for the debtor's obligation. It is an express contract between the **surety** (the third party) and the creditor.

In the strictest sense, the surety is primarily liable for the debt of the principal. The creditor can demand payment from the surety from the moment the debt is due. The creditor need not exhaust all legal remedies against the principal debtor before holding the surety responsible for payment.

■ **EXAMPLE 19.4** Roberto Delmar wants to borrow from the bank to buy a used car. Because Roberto is still in college, the bank will not lend him the funds without a cosigner. Roberto's father, José Delmar, who has dealt with the bank before, agrees to cosign the note, thereby becoming a surety who is jointly liable for payment of the debt. When José Delmar cosigns the note, he becomes primarily liable to the bank. On the note's due

---

8. Some states do not allow a borrower to waive the statutory right of redemption. This means that a buyer at auction must wait one year to obtain title to, and possession of, a foreclosed property.

## Concept Summary 19.1

### Remedies Available to Creditors

| | |
|---|---|
| **Liens** | • *Mechanic's lien*—A lien placed on an owner's real estate for labor, services, or materials furnished for improvements made to the realty (real property).<br>• *Artisan's lien*—A lien placed on an owner's personal property for labor performed or value added to that property.<br>• *Judicial liens*—Including the following:<br>**a.** Writ of attachment: A court-ordered seizure of property prior to a court's final determination of the creditor's rights to the property. Creditors must strictly comply with applicable state statutes to obtain a writ of attachment.<br>**b.** Writ of execution: A court order directing the sheriff to seize (levy) and sell a debtor's nonexempt real or personal property to satisfy a court's judgment in the creditor's favor. |
| **Garnishment** | • A collection remedy that allows the creditor to attach a debtor's funds—such as wages owed or bank accounts—and property that are held by a third person. |
| **Creditors' Composition Agreement** | • A contract between a debtor and her or his creditors by which the debtor's debts are discharged by payment of a sum less than the amount that is actually owed. |
| **Mortgage Foreclosure** | • On the debtor's default, the entire mortgage debt is due and payable, allowing the creditor to foreclose on the realty by selling it to satisfy the debt. |

**EXHIBIT 19–2  Suretyship and Guaranty Parties**

In a suretyship or guaranty arrangement, a third party promises to be responsible for a debtor's obligations. A third party who agrees to be responsible for the debt even if the primary debtor does not default is known as a *surety*. A third party who agrees to be *secondarily* responsible for the debt—that is, responsible only if the primary debtor defaults—is known as a *guarantor*. Normally, a promise of guaranty (a collateral, or secondary, promise) must be in writing to be enforceable.

**Principal Debtor**

**Creditor**

**Surety** (Primary Liability to Creditor) or **Guarantor** (Secondary Liability to Creditor) date, the bank can seek payment from either Roberto or José Delmar, or both jointly. ∎

## 19-3b Guaranty

With a suretyship arrangement, the surety is *primarily* liable for the debtor's obligation. With a guaranty arrangement, the **guarantor**—the third person making the guaranty—is *secondarily* liable.

The guarantor can be required to pay the obligation *only after the principal debtor defaults,* and usually only after the creditor has made an attempt to collect from the debtor. The guaranty contract terms determine the extent and time of the guarantor's liability.

∎ **EXAMPLE 19.5** BX Enterprises, a small corporation, needs to borrow funds to meet its payroll. BX's president is Dawson, a wealthy businessperson who owns 70 percent of the company. The bank is skeptical about the creditworthiness of BX and requires Dawson to sign an agreement making herself personally liable for payment if BX does not pay off the loan. As a guarantor of the loan, Dawson cannot be held liable until BX is in default. ∎

The following case concerned a lender's attempt to recover on a loan guaranty.

### Case 19.3

# HSBC Realty Credit Corp. (USA) v. O'Neill

United States Court of Appeals, First Circuit, 745 F.3d 564 (2014).

**Background and Facts** To finance a development project in Delaware, Brandywine Partners, LLC, borrowed $15.9 million from HSBC Realty Credit Corp. (USA). As part of the deal, Brian O'Neill, principal for Brandywine, signed a guaranty that designated him the "primary obligor" for $8.1 million of the loan. Brandywine defaulted, and HSBC filed a suit in a federal district court against O'Neill to recover on the guaranty. O'Neill filed a counterclaim, alleging fraud.

O'Neill based his fraud claim on two provisions in the loan agreement. The first provision expressed the loan-to-value ratio. O'Neill alleged that this clause valued the property at $26.5 million and that HSBC knew this was not the property's real value. The second provision stated that if Brandywine defaulted, HSBC could recover its loan by selling the property. According to O'Neill, this clause represented that HSBC would try to recover by selling the property before trying to collect from the guaranty.

The court granted HSBC's motion to dismiss O'Neill's counterclaim and issued a judgment in HSBC's favor. O'Neill appealed, still arguing that HSBC had fraudulently induced him to sign the guaranty.

### In the Language of the Court

*THOMPSON,* Circuit Judge.

\* \* \* \*

O'Neill loudly protests that his fraudulent-inducement claim should have been enough to defeat HSBC's dismissal efforts. His theory rises or falls on his belief that two provisions in the project-loan agreement constitute false statements of material fact made to induce him to sign the guaranty and that he reasonably relied on those false statements to his detriment.

The first provision he points to involves the \* \* \* loan-to-value ratio, which he alleges put the collateral property's value at $26.5 million and is an HSBC representation that the chance of its having to call the $8.1 million guaranty was basically zero. HSBC made that representation, he adds, even though HSBC—and not he—knew that this was not the property's real value.

The second project-loan-agreement provision he harps on provides that if Brandywine defaults, HSBC "can recover the obligations" by selling the property. He reads this contract language as an HSBC representation that it would move against the property before turning to his guaranty \* \* \* . [But] we are unmoved. Merely to state the obvious, that proviso says that HSBC "can" proceed first against the property, not that it must do so.

Ultimately—and unhappily for O'Neill—we must enforce the guaranty according to its terms, with the parties' rights ascertained [determined] from the written text. \* \* \* *Reliance on supposed misrepresentations that contradict the terms of the parties' agreement is unreasonable as a matter of law and so cannot support a fraudulent-inducement claim.* \* \* \* The contract-inducing misrepresentations that O'Neill trumpets

**Case 19.3 Continued**

are irreconcilably at odds with the guaranty's express terms. * * * O'Neill specifically warranted in the guaranty that he was familiar with the collateral property's value, that the property did not operate as an inducement for him to make the guaranty, and that HSBC said nothing to induce him to execute the guaranty—all of which destroys his fraudulent-inducement thesis centered on the project-loan agreement's loan-to-value-ratio provision. He also agreed with the guaranty's tagging him as the primary obligor and with its allowing HSBC to go after him first to recoup the debt—provisions that put the kibosh on [put an end to] his other suggestion that HSBC must first seek recourse against the property. [Emphasis added.]

* * * *

The net result of all this is that O'Neill's inducement-based arguments fail.

**Decision and Remedy** *The U.S. Court of Appeals for the First Circuit affirmed the lower court's judgment in favor of HSBC. The guaranty stated that O'Neill was familiar with the value of the property, that he was not relying on it as an inducement to sign the guaranty, and that HSBC made no representations to induce him to sign. The guaranty also provided that HSBC could enforce its rights against him without trying to recover on the property first.*

**Critical Thinking**

- **E-Commerce** *Do the principles applied to a written guaranty in this case also govern electronically recorded agreements and contracts entered into online? Why or why not?*
- **What If the Facts Were Different?** *Suppose that O'Neill had alleged a history of performance with HSBC that would have made his reliance on the complained-of representations reasonable. Could this have changed the result? Explain.*

## 19–3c Actions That Release the Surety and the Guarantor

Basically, the same actions will release either a surety or a guarantor from an obligation. For simplicity, this subsection and the following subsections will refer just to sureties, but remember that the same rules generally apply to guarantors.

1. *Material modification.* Making any material modification to the terms of the original contract without the surety's consent will discharge the surety's obligation. (The extent to which the surety is discharged depends on whether he or she was compensated and the amount of loss suffered from the modification. For instance, a father who receives no consideration for acting as a surety on his daughter's loan will be completely discharged if the loan contract is modified without his consent.)

2. *Surrender of property.* If a creditor surrenders the collateral to the debtor or impairs the collateral without the surety's consent, these acts can reduce the obligation of the surety. If the creditor's actions reduce the value of the property used as collateral, the surety is released to the extent of any loss suffered.

3. *Payment or tender of payment.* Naturally, any payment of the principal obligation by the debtor or by another person on the debtor's behalf will discharge the surety from the obligation. Even if the creditor refused to accept the payment when it was tendered, if the creditor knew about the suretyship, the obligation of the surety can be discharged.

## 19–3d Defenses of the Surety and the Guarantor

Generally, the surety or guarantor can also assert any of the defenses available to the principal debtor to avoid liability on the obligation to the creditor. A few exceptions do exist, however. They apply to both sureties and guarantors, but again, for simplicity, we refer just to sureties.

1. *Incapacity and bankruptcy.* Incapacity and bankruptcy are personal defenses, which can be asserted only by the person who is affected. Therefore, the surety cannot assert the principal debtor's incapacity or bankruptcy as a defense. (A surety may assert his or her own incapacity or bankruptcy as a defense, of course.)

2. *Statute of limitations.* The surety cannot assert the statute of limitations as a defense. (In contrast, the principal debtor can claim the statute of limitations as a defense to payment.)

3. *Fraud.* If the creditor fraudulently induced the person to act as a surety on the debt, the surety or guarantor can assert fraud as a defense. In most states, the creditor must inform the surety, before the formation of the suretyship contract, of material facts known by the creditor that would substantially increase the surety's risk. Failure to so inform may constitute fraud and render the suretyship obligation voidable.

## 19–3e Rights of the Surety and the Guarantor

When the surety or guarantor pays the debt owed to the creditor, he or she acquires certain rights, as discussed next. Again, for simplicity, the discussion refers just to sureties.

**The Right of Subrogation** The surety has the legal **right of subrogation.** Simply stated, this means that any right that the creditor had against the debtor now becomes the right of the surety. Included are creditor rights in bankruptcy, rights to collateral possessed by the creditor, and rights to judgments obtained by the creditor. In short, the surety now stands in the shoes of the creditor and may pursue any remedies that were available to the creditor against the debtor.

■ **CASE IN POINT 19.6** Guerrero Brothers, Inc. (GBI), contracted with the Public School System (PSS) to build a high school. Century Insurance Company (CIC) agreed to provide GBI with the required payment and performance bonds on the project. Thus, CIC acted as a surety of GBI's performance and promised to finish the project if GBI defaulted.

Four years after construction began, PSS canceled GBI's contract, and CIC fulfilled GBI's obligations by finishing construction of the school. Numerous disputes arose, and litigation ensued. Ultimately, PSS agreed to pay GBI $500,000 in contract funds. CIC then filed an action against GBI and PSS to recover the $867,000 it claimed PSS owed it for finishing the school. The court found that CIC, as a performing surety, was entitled to the remaining contract funds through the right of subrogation. It had performed GBI's obligations and therefore stepped into GBI's shoes and had the right to obtain payment from PSS.[9] ■

---

9. *Century Insurance Co. v. Guerrero Brothers, Inc.,* 2010 WL 997112 (N.Mariana Islands 2010).

**The Right of Reimbursement** The surety has a **right of reimbursement** from the debtor. Basically, the surety is entitled to receive from the debtor all outlays made on behalf of the suretyship arrangement. Such outlays can include expenses incurred as well as the actual amount of the debt paid to the creditor.

**The Right of Contribution** Two or more sureties are called **co-sureties.** When a co-surety pays more than her or his proportionate share on a debtor's default, she or he has a **right of contribution.** That means the co-surety is entitled to recover from the other co-sureties the amount paid above the surety's obligation. Generally, a co-surety's liability either is determined by agreement or, in the absence of agreement, is set at the maximum liability under the suretyship contract.

■ **EXAMPLE 19.7** Yasser and Itzhak, two co-sureties, are obligated under a suretyship contract to guarantee Jules's debt. Itzhak's maximum liability is $15,000, and Yasser's is $10,000. Jules owes $10,000 and is in default. Itzhak pays the creditor the entire $10,000.

In the absence of an agreement to the contrary, Itzhak can recover $4,000 from Yasser. The amount of the debt that Yasser agreed to cover ($10,000) is divided by the total amount that he and Itzhak together agreed to cover ($25,000). The result is multiplied by the amount of the default, yielding the amount that Yasser owes—($10,000 ÷ $25,000) × $10,000 = $4,000. ■

---

# 19–4 Protection for Debtors

The law protects debtors as well as creditors. Consumer protection statutes protect debtors' rights, for instance, and bankruptcy laws are designed specifically to assist debtors in need of help. In addition, in most states, certain types of real and personal property are exempt from execution or attachment. State exemption statutes usually include both real and personal property.

## 19–4a Exempted Real Property

Probably the most familiar exemption is the **homestead exemption.** The purpose of the homestead exemption is to ensure that the debtor will retain some form of shelter.

**The General Rule** Each state permits the debtor to retain the family home, either in its entirety or up to a specified dollar amount, free from the claims of unsecured creditors or trustees in bankruptcy. (Note that federal bankruptcy law places a cap on the amount that debtors filing bankruptcy can claim is exempt under their states' homestead exemption.)

■ **EXAMPLE 19.8** Vince Beere owes Chris Veltman $40,000. The debt is the subject of a lawsuit, and the court awards Veltman a judgment of $40,000 against Beere. Beere's homestead is valued at $50,000, and the homestead exemption is $25,000. There are no outstanding mortgages or other liens on his homestead. To satisfy the judgment debt, Beere's family home is sold at public auction for $45,000. The proceeds of the sale are distributed as follows:

1. Beere is given $25,000 as his homestead exemption.
2. Veltman is paid $20,000 toward the judgment debt, leaving a $20,000 deficiency judgment (that is, "leftover debt"). The deficiency judgment can be satisfied from any other nonexempt property (personal or real) that Beere may own, if permitted by state law. ■

**Limitations** In a few states, statutes allow the homestead exemption only if the judgment debtor has a family.

If a judgment debtor does not have a family, a creditor may be entitled to collect the full amount realized from the sale of the debtor's home. In addition, the homestead exemption interacts with other areas of law and can sometimes operate to cancel out a portion of a lien on a debtor's real property.

## 19–4b Exempted Personal Property

Personal property that is most often exempt from satisfaction of judgment debts includes the following:

1. Household furniture up to a specified dollar amount.
2. Clothing and certain personal possessions, such as family pictures or a Bible.
3. A vehicle (or vehicles) for transportation (at least up to a specified dollar amount).
4. Certain classified animals, usually livestock but including pets.
5. Equipment that the debtor uses in a business or trade, such as tools or professional instruments, up to a specified dollar amount.

## Reviewing: Creditors' Rights and Remedies

Air Ruidoso, Ltd., operated a commuter airline and air charter service between Ruidoso, New Mexico, and airports in Albuquerque and El Paso. Executive Aviation Center, Inc., provided services for airlines at the Albuquerque International Airport. Air Ruidoso failed to pay more than $10,000 that it owed Executive Aviation on its account for fuel, oil, and oxygen. Executive Aviation then took possession of Air Ruidoso's plane, claiming that it had a lien on the plane. Using the information presented in the chapter, answer the following questions.

1. Can Executive Aviation establish an artisan's lien on the plane? Why or why not?
2. Suppose that Executive Aviation files a lawsuit in court against Air Ruidoso for the $10,000 past-due debt. What two methods discussed in this chapter would allow the court to order the seizure of Air Ruidoso's plane to satisfy the debt?
3. Suppose that Executive Aviation discovers that Air Ruidoso has sufficient assets in one of its bank accounts to pay the past-due amount. How might Executive Aviation attempt to obtain access to these funds?
4. Suppose that the contract between the companies provides that "if the airline becomes insolvent, Braden Fasco, the chief executive officer of Air Ruidoso, agrees to cover its outstanding debts." Is this a suretyship or a guaranty agreement?

**Debate This . . .**   *Because writs of attachment are a prejudgment remedy for nonpayment of a debt, they are unfair and should be abolished.*

## Terms and Concepts

Continues

## Issue Spotters

**1.** Jorge contracts with Larry of Midwest Roofing to fix Jorge's roof. Jorge pays half of the contract price in advance. Larry and Midwest complete the job, but Jorge refuses to pay the rest of the price. What can Larry and Midwest do? (See *Laws Assisting Creditors*.)

**2.** Alyssa owes Don $5,000 and refuses to pay. Don obtains a garnishment order and serves it on Alyssa's employer. If the employer complies with the order and Alyssa stays on the job, is one order enough to garnish Alyssa's wages for each pay period until the debt is paid? Explain. (See *Laws Assisting Creditors*.)

• **Check your answers to the Issue Spotters against the answers provided in Appendix B at the end of this text.**

## Business Scenarios

**19–1. Liens.** Kanahara is employed part-time by the Cross-Bar Packing Corp. and earns take-home pay of $400 per week. He is $2,000 in debt to the Holiday Department Store for goods purchased on credit over the past eight months. Most of this property is nonexempt and is now in Kanahara's apartment. Kanahara is in default on his payments to Holiday. Holiday learns that Kanahara has a girlfriend in another state and that he plans to give her most of this property for Christmas. Discuss what actions can be taken by Holiday to collect the debt owed by Kanahara. (See *Laws Assisting Creditors*.)

**19–2. Liens.** Nabil is the owner of a relatively old home valued at $105,000. The home's electrical system is failing, and the wiring needs to be replaced. Nabil contracts with Kandhari Electrical to replace the electrical system. Kandhari performs the repairs, and on June 1 submits a bill of $10,000 to Nabil. Because of financial difficulties, Nabil does not pay the bill. Nabil's only asset is his home, but his state's homestead exemption is $60,000. Discuss fully Kandhari's remedies in this situation. (See *Laws Assisting Creditors*.)

## Business Case Problems

**19–3. Foreclosure on Mortgages and Liens.** LaSalle Bank loaned $8 million to Cypress Creek 1, LP, to build an apartment complex. The loan was secured by a mortgage. Cypress Creek hired contractors to provide concrete work, plumbing, carpentry, and other construction services. Cypress Creek later went bankrupt owing LaSalle $3 million. The contractors recorded mechanic's liens when they were not paid for their work. The property was sold to LaSalle at a sheriff's sale for $1.3 million. The contractors claimed that their mechanic's liens should be satisfied out of the $1.3 million before any funds were distributed to LaSalle for its mortgage. The trial court distributed the $1.3 million primarily to LaSalle, with only a small fraction going to the contractors. Do the liens come before the mortgage in priority of payment? Discuss. [*LaSalle Bank National Association v. Cypress Creek 1, LP*, 242 Ill.2d 231, 950 N.E.2d 1109 (2011)] (See *Mortgages*.)

**19–4. Guaranty.** Timothy Martinez, owner of Koenig & Vits, Inc. (K&V), guaranteed K&V's debt to Community Bank & Trust. The guaranty stated that the bank was not required to seek payment of the debt from any other source before enforcing the guaranty. K&V defaulted. Through a Wisconsin state court, the bank sought payment of $536,739.40, plus interest at the contract rate of 7.5 percent, from Martinez. Martinez argued that the bank could not enforce his guaranty while other funds were available to satisfy K&V's debt. For example, the debt might be paid out of the proceeds of a sale of corporate assets. Is this an effective defense to a guaranty? Why or why not? [*Community Bank & Trust v. Koenig & Vits, Inc.*, 346 Wis.2d 279 (Wis.App. 2013)] (See *Suretyship and Guaranty*.)

**19–5. Business Case Problem with Sample Answer— Liens.**  Daniel and Katherine Balk asked Jirak Construction, LLC, to remodel their farmhouse in Lawler, Iowa. Jirak provided the Balks with an initial estimate of $45,975 for the cost. Over the course of the work, the Balks made significant changes to the plan. Jirak agreed to the changes and regularly advised the Balks about the increasing costs. In mid-project, Jirak provided an itemized breakdown at their request. The Balks paid Jirak $67,000, but refused to pay more. Jirak claimed that they still owed $55,000 in labor and materials. Jirak filed a suit in an Iowa state court against the Balks to collect. Which of the liens discussed in this chapter would be most effective to Jirak in its attempt to collect? How does that type of lien work? Is the court likely to enforce it in this case? Explain. [*Jirak Construction, LLC v. Balk*, 863 N.W.2d 35 (Iowa App. 2015)] (See *Laws Assisting Creditors*.)

- For a sample answer to Problem 19–5, go to Appendix C at the end of this text.

**19–6. Laws Assisting Creditors.** Grand Harbour Condominium Owners Association, Inc., obtained a judgment in an Ohio state court against Gene and Nancy Grogg for $45,458.86. To satisfy the judgment, Grand Harbour filed a notice of garnishment with the court, seeking funds held by the Groggs in various banks. The Groggs disputed Grand Harbour's right to garnish the funds. They claimed that the funds were exempt Social Security and pension proceeds, but they offered no proof of this claim. The banks responded by depositing $23,911.97 with the court. These funds were delivered to Grand Harbour. Later, the Groggs filed a petition for bankruptcy in a federal bankruptcy court. After they were granted a discharge, they filed a "motion to return funds to debtors" but provided no evidence that their debt to Grand Harbour had been included in the discharge. What is Grand Harbour's best argument in response to the Groggs' motion? [*Grand Harbour Condominium Owners Association, Inc. v. Grogg*, 2016-Ohio-1386, __ Ohio App.3d __, __ N.E.2d __ (2016)] (See *Laws Assisting Creditors*.)

**19–7. A Question of Ethics: Guaranty.** *73-75 Main Avenue, LLC, agreed to lease a portion of the commercial property at 73 Main Avenue, Norwalk, Connecticut, to PP Door Enterprise, Inc. Nan Zhang, as manager of PP Door, signed the lease agreement. The lessor required the principal officers of PP Door to execute personal guaranties. In addition, the principal officers agreed to provide the lessor with credit information. Apparently, both the lessor and the principals of PP Door signed the lease and guaranty agreements that were sent to PP Door's office. When PP Door failed to make monthly payments, 73-75 Main Avenue filed a suit against PP Door and its owner, Ping Ying Li. At trial, Li testified that she was the sole owner of PP Door but denied that Zhang was its manager. She also denied signing the guaranty agreement. She claimed that she had signed the credit authorization form because Zhang had told her he was too young to have good credit. Li claimed to have no knowledge of the lease agreement. She did admit, however, that she had paid the rent. She claimed that Zhang had been in a car accident and had asked her to help pay his bills, including the rent at 73 Main Avenue. Li further testified that she did not see the name PP Door on the storefront of the leased location. [73-75 Main Avenue, LLC v. PP Door Enterprise Inc., 120 Conn.App. 150, 991 A.2d 650 (2010)] (See Suretyship and Guaranty.)*

**(a)** Li argued that she was not liable on the lease agreement because Zhang was not authorized to bind her to the lease. Do the facts support Li? Why or why not?

**(b)** Li claimed that the guaranty for rent was not enforceable against her. Why might the court agree?

**19–8. Special Case Analysis—Liens.** Go to Case Analysis 19.1, *Picerne Construction Corp. v. Villas*. Read the excerpt, and answer the following questions.

**(a) Issue:** What statutory term was the focus of the dispute in this case? Why?

**(b) Rule of Law:** Under the state statute that applied in this case, what must a party show to enforce a lien?

**(c) Applying the Rule of Law:** What proof supported the plaintiff's attempt to enforce its lien? What did the defendant argue in opposition?

**(d) Conclusion:** How did the court resolve the dispute between the creditor and debtor here? Who benefited from this decision?

# Legal Reasoning Group Activity

**19–9. Attachment.** Brent Avery, on behalf of his law firm—The Law Office of Brent Avery—contracted with Marlin Broadcasting to air commercials on KRTV, a local radio station. Avery, who was the sole member of his firm, helped to create the commercials. The ads featured his voice, focused on his name and experience, and solicited direct contact with "defense attorney Brent Avery." When KRTV was not paid for the broadcasts, Marlin filed a lawsuit against Avery and his firm, alleging an outstanding balance of $35,250.

Pending the court's hearing of the suit, Marlin filed a request for a writ of attachment. Marlin offered in evidence the parties' contracts, the ads' transcripts, and KRTV's invoices. Avery contended that he could not be held personally liable for the cost of the ads. Marlin countered that the ads unjustly enriched Avery by conferring a personal benefit on him to Marlin's detriment. (See *Laws Assisting Creditors*.)

**(a)** The first group will explain the purpose of attachment.

**(b)** The second group will outline what a creditor must prove to obtain a writ of attachment.

**(c)** The third group will determine whether Marlin Broadcasting is entitled to attachment in this scenario.

# CHAPTER 20

# Secured Transactions

Whenever the payment of a debt is guaranteed, or *secured,* by personal property owned or held by the debtor, the transaction becomes known as a **secured transaction.** The concept of the secured transaction is as basic to modern business practice as the concept of credit. Logically, sellers and lenders do not want to risk nonpayment, so they usually will not sell goods or lend funds unless the promise of payment is somehow guaranteed. Indeed, business as we know it could not exist without laws permitting and governing secured transactions.

Article 9 of the Uniform Commercial Code (UCC) governs secured transactions in personal property. Personal property includes accounts, agricultural liens, and *chattel paper* (any documents or records evidencing a debt secured by personal property). It also includes commercial assignments of $1,000 or more, *fixtures* (certain property that is attached to land), instruments, and other types of intangible property, such as patents. Article 9 does not cover creditor-collection devices such as liens and mortgages on real property.

## 20–1 The Terminology of Secured Transactions

In every state, the UCC's terminology is now uniformly used in all documents that involve secured transactions. The following is a brief summary of the UCC's definitions of terms relating to secured transactions:

1. A **secured party** is any creditor who has a *security interest* in the debtor's *collateral.* This creditor can be a seller, a lender, a cosigner, or even a buyer of accounts or chattel paper [UCC 9–102(a)(72)].
2. A **debtor** is the party who *owes payment* or other performance of a secured obligation [UCC 9–102(a)(28)].
3. A **security interest** is the interest in the collateral (such as personal property, fixtures, or accounts) that *secures payment or performance* of an obligation [UCC 1–201(37)].
4. A **security agreement** is an *agreement* that creates or provides for a security interest [UCC 9–102(a)(73)].
5. **Collateral** is the *subject* of the *security interest* [UCC 9–102(a)(12)].
6. A **financing statement**—referred to as the UCC-1 form—is the *instrument normally filed to give public notice to third parties* of the secured party's security interest [UCC 9–102(a)(39)].

Together, these basic definitions form the concept under which a debtor-creditor relationship becomes a secured transaction relationship (see Exhibit 20–1).

## 20–2 Creation of a Security Interest

A creditor has two main concerns if the debtor defaults: (1) Can the debt be satisfied through the possession and (usually) sale of the collateral? (2) Will the creditor have priority over any other creditors or buyers who may have rights in the same collateral? These two concerns are met through the creation and perfection of a security interest. We begin by examining how a security interest is created.

### 20–2a Basic Requirements

To become a secured party, the creditor must obtain a security interest in the collateral of the debtor. Three requirements must be met for a creditor to have an enforceable security interest:

1. Unless the creditor has possession of the collateral, there must be a written or authenticated security agreement that clearly describes the collateral subject

**EXHIBIT 20–1  Secured Transactions—Concept and Terminology**

In a security agreement, a debtor and a creditor agree that the creditor will have a security interest in collateral in which the debtor has rights. In essence, the collateral secures the loan and ensures the creditor of payment should the debtor default.

to the security interest. This agreement must be signed or authenticated by the debtor.

2. The secured party must give the debtor something of value.

3. The debtor must have rights in the collateral.

Once these requirements have been met, the creditor's rights are said to *attach* to the collateral. **Attachment** gives the creditor an enforceable security interest in the collateral [UCC 9–203].[1]

■ **EXAMPLE 20.1**  To furnish his new office suite, Abdul applies for a credit card at an office supply store. The application contains a clause stating that the store will retain a security interest in the goods purchased with the card until the goods have been paid for in full. This application is considered a *written security agreement*, which is the first requirement for an enforceable security interest. The goods that Abdul buys with the card are the *something of value* from the secured party (the second requirement). Abdul's ownership interest in those goods is the *right* that he has in them (the third requirement). Thus, the requirements for an enforceable security

interest are met. When Abdul buys something with the card, the store's rights attach to the purchased goods. ■

## 20–2b Written or Authenticated Security Agreement

When the collateral is not in the possession of the secured party, the security agreement must be either written or authenticated. Here, **authenticate** means to sign or, on an electronic record, to adopt any symbol that verifies the intent to adopt or accept the record [UCC 9–102(a)(7)]. Authentication thus provides for electronic filing (the filing process will be discussed later). See this chapter's *Digital Update* feature for a discussion of a type of secured transaction that is performed online.

A security agreement must also contain a description of the collateral that reasonably identifies it. Generally, such phrases as "all the debtor's personal property" or "all the debtor's assets" would *not* constitute a sufficient description [UCC 9–108(c)].

If the debtor signs, or otherwise authenticates, a security agreement, does he or she also have to sign an attached list of the collateral to create a valid security interest? That was the question before the court in the following case.

---

1. The term *attachment* has a different meaning in secured transactions than in the context of judicial liens, where it refers to a court-ordered seizure of property.

**Case 20.1**

# Royal Jewelers, Inc. v. Light

Supreme Court of North Dakota, 2015 ND 44, 859 N.W.2d 921 (2015).

**Background and Facts**  Steven Light bought a $55,050 wedding ring for his wife, Sherri Light, on credit from Royal Jewelers, Inc., a store in Fargo, North Dakota. The receipt granted Royal a security interest in the ring. Later, Royal assigned its interest to GRB Financial Corp. Steven and GRB signed a

Case 20.1 Continues

**Case 20.1 Continued**

modification agreement changing the repayment terms. An attached exhibit listed the items pledged as security for the modification, including the ring. Steven did not separately sign the exhibit.

A year later, Steven died. Royal and GRB filed a suit in a North Dakota state court against Sherri, alleging that GRB had a valid security interest in the ring. Sherri cited UCC 9–203, under which there is an enforceable interest only if "the debtor has authenticated a security agreement that provides a description of the collateral." Sherri argued that the modification agreement did not "properly authenticate" the description of the collateral, including the ring, because Steven had not signed the attached exhibit. The court issued a judgment in GRB's favor. Sherri appealed.

### In the Language of the Court

*CROTHERS*, Justice.

* * * *

Sherri Light * * * claims the * * * modification agreement signed by Steven Light * * * did not properly authenticate the agreement describing the collateral under [North Dakota Commercial Code (NDCC)] Section 41–09–13(2)(c)(1) [North Dakota's version of UCC 9–203] because he did not separately sign the exhibit identifying secured collateral, including the ring.

Section 41–09–13(2)(c)(1) provides:

2. * * * A security interest is enforceable against the debtor and third parties with respect to the collateral only if:

* * * *

c. One of the following conditions is met:

(1) The debtor has authenticated a security agreement that provides a description of the collateral * * *.

The plain language of that statute requires a debtor to authenticate a security agreement providing a description of the collateral. [Under NDCC Section 41–09–02(1)(g) [North Dakota's version of UCC 9–102(1)(g),] "authenticate" means "to sign" or "to execute or otherwise adopt a symbol, or encrypt or similarly process a record in whole or in part, with the present intent of the authenticating person to identify the person and adopt or accept a record." NDCC Section 41–09–08(2) [North Dakota's version of UCC 9–108(2)] says a description of collateral is sufficient if it reasonably identifies the collateral and may include a specific listing or any other method by which the collateral is objectively determinable.

* * * No authority [requires] a debtor to separately sign an exhibit attached to and referenced in a signed security agreement * * *. *A security agreement is not unenforceable merely because a description of collateral in an exhibit was attached to the security agreement * * *. Several documents may be considered together as a security agreement * * *.* [Emphasis added.]

Steven Light signed the * * * modification agreement which referenced an attached exhibit listing assets pledged as security for the note. * * * The attached exhibit listing the ring was part of the * * * agreement signed by Steven Light, and the [lower] court determined the modification agreement was properly executed by Steven Light. Evidence establishes Steven Light initially granted a valid security interest in the ring and the ring had not been fully paid for * * *. GRB Financial received an assignment of the security interest from Royal Jewelers * * *, and the court did not err in finding GRB Financial had a valid and enforceable security interest in the ring.

**Decision and Remedy** *The North Dakota Supreme Court affirmed the lower court's judgment. The court stated, "No authority [requires] a debtor to separately sign an exhibit attached to and referenced in a signed security agreement."*

### Critical Thinking

- **Ethical** *Under the circumstances, is it ethical for GRB to enforce its security interest in the ring to recover the unpaid amount of the price? Discuss.*

## 20–2c Secured Party Must Give Value

The secured party must give something of value to the debtor. Under the UCC, value can include a binding commitment to extend credit and, in general, any consideration sufficient to support a simple contract [UCC 1–204]. Normally, the value given by a secured party involves a direct loan or a commitment to sell goods on credit.

## DIGITAL UPDATE    Secured Transactions—Escrow Services Online

When you buy something online, you typically must use your credit card, make an electronic fund transfer, or send a check before the goods you bought are sent to you. If you are buying an expensive item, such as a car, you are not likely to send funds without being assured that you will receive the item in the condition promised. Enter the concept of escrow.

### Escrow Accounts

Escrow accounts are commonly used in real estate transactions, but they are also useful for smaller transactions, particularly those done on the Internet. An escrow account involves three parties—the buyer, the seller, and a trusted third party that collects, holds, and disperses funds according to instructions from the buyer and seller.

Escrow services are provided by licensed and regulated escrow companies. For example, if you buy a car on the Internet, you and the seller will agree on an escrow company to which you send the funds. When you receive the car and are satisfied with it, the escrow company will release the funds to the seller. This is a type of secured transaction.

### Escrow.com

One of the best-known online escrow firms is Escrow.com, which had processed more than $2.7 billion in secured transactions by 2017. All of its escrow services are offered via its Web site and provided independently by Internet Escrow Services, one of its operating subsidiaries. Escrow.com is particularly useful for transactions that involve an international buyer or seller. It has become the recommended transaction settlement service for AutoTrader, Resale Weekly, Cars.com, eBay Motors, and Flippa.com.

**Critical Thinking** *How could online escrow services reduce Internet fraud?*

## 20–2d Debtor Must Have Rights in the Collateral

The debtor must have rights in the collateral. That is, the debtor must have some ownership interest or right to obtain possession of that collateral. The debtor's rights can represent either a current or a future legal interest in the collateral. For instance, a retailer-debtor can give a secured party a security interest not only in existing inventory owned by the retailer but also in *future* inventory that the retailer will acquire. (A common misconception is that the debtor must have title to the collateral to have rights in it, but this is not a requirement.)

For a synopsis of the rules for creating a security interest, see Concept Summary 20.1.

## 20–3 Perfection of a Security Interest

**Perfection** is the legal process by which secured parties protect themselves against the claims of third parties who may wish to have their debts satisfied out of the same collateral. Whether a secured party's security interest is

---

### Concept Summary 20.1

#### Creating a Security Interest

| Requirements for Creating a Security Interest | 1. Unless the creditor has possession of the collateral, there must be a written or authenticated security agreement signed or authenticated by the debtor that describes the collateral subject to the security interest. <br> 2. The secured party must give value to the debtor. <br> 3. The debtor must have rights in the collateral—that is, some ownership interest or right to obtain possession of the specified collateral. |
| --- | --- |

perfected or unperfected can have serious consequences for the secured party.

What if a debtor has borrowed from two different creditors and used the same property as collateral for both loans? If the debtor defaults on both loans, which of the two creditors has first rights to the collateral? In this situation, the creditor with a perfected security interest will prevail.

Perfection usually is accomplished by filing a financing statement. In some circumstances, however, a security interest becomes perfected even though no financing statement is filed.

## 20–3a Perfection by Filing

The most common means of perfection is by filing a *financing statement* with the office of the appropriate government official. A financing statement gives public notice to third parties of the secured party's security interest. The security agreement itself can also be filed to perfect the security interest. The financing statement must provide the names of the debtor and the secured party, and it must indicate the collateral covered by the financing statement.

A uniform financing statement form (see Exhibit 20–2) is used in all states [UCC 9–521]. It must be filed in the appropriate office, together with payment of the correct

**EXHIBIT 20–2** A Uniform Financing Statement Sample

UCC FINANCING STATEMENT
FOLLOW INSTRUCTIONS

A. NAME & PHONE OF CONTACT AT FILER (optional)

B. E-MAIL CONTACT AT FILER (optional)

C. SEND ACKNOWLEDGMENT TO: (Name and Address)

THE ABOVE SPACE IS FOR FILING OFFICE USE ONLY

1. DEBTOR'S NAME: Provide only one Debtor name (1a or 1b) (use exact, full name; do not omit, modify, or abbreviate any part of the Debtor's name); if any part of the Individual Debtor's name will not fit in line 1b, leave all of item 1 blank, check here ☐ and provide the Individual Debtor information in item 10 of the Financing Statement Addendum (Form UCC1Ad)

1a. ORGANIZATION'S NAME

OR

| 1b. INDIVIDUAL'S SURNAME | FIRST PERSONAL NAME | ADDITIONAL NAME(S)/INITIAL(S) | SUFFIX |
|---|---|---|---|
| 1c. MAILING ADDRESS | CITY | STATE | POSTAL CODE | COUNTRY |

2. DEBTOR'S NAME: Provide only one Debtor name (2a or 2b) (use exact, full name; do not omit, modify, or abbreviate any part of the Debtor's name); if any part of the Individual Debtor's name will not fit in line 2b, leave all of item 2 blank, check her ☐ and provide the Individual Debtor information in item 10 of the Financing Statement Addendum (Form UCC1Ad)

2a. ORGANIZATION'S NAME

OR

| 2b. INDIVIDUAL'S SURNAME | FIRST PERSONAL NAME | ADDITIONAL NAME(S)/INITIAL(S) | SUFFIX |
|---|---|---|---|
| 2c. MAILING ADDRESS | CITY | STATE | POSTAL CODE | COUNTRY |

3. SECURED PARTY'S NAME (or NAME of ASSIGNEE of ASSIGNOR SECURED PARTY): Provide only one Secured Party name (3a or 3b)

3a. ORGANIZATION'S NAME

OR

| 3b. INDIVIDUAL'S SURNAME | FIRST PERSONAL NAME | ADDITIONAL NAME(S)/INITIAL(S) | SUFFIX |
|---|---|---|---|
| 3c. MAILING ADDRESS | CITY | STATE | POSTAL CODE | COUNTRY |

4. COLLATERAL: This financing statement covers the following collateral:

filing fee [UCC 9–516(a)]. The filing can be accomplished electronically [UCC 9–102(a)(18)]. Once completed, filings are indexed by the name of the debtor so that they can be located by subsequent searches. A financing statement may be filed even before a security agreement is made or a security interest attaches [UCC 9–502(d)].

**The Debtor's Name**  The UCC requires that a financing statement be filed under the name of the debtor [UCC 9–502(a)(1)]. Slight variations in names normally will not be considered misleading if a search of the filing office's records, using a standard search engine routinely used by that office, would find the filings [UCC 9–506(c)].[2] If the debtor is identified by the correct name at the time the financing statement is filed, the secured party's interest retains its priority even if the debtor's name later changes.

Because most states use electronic filing systems, UCC 9–503 sets out detailed rules for determining when the debtor's name as it appears on a financing statement is sufficient.

1. *Corporations.* For corporations, which are organizations that have registered with the state, the debtor's name on the financing statement must be "the name of the debtor indicated on the public record of the debtor's jurisdiction of organization" [UCC 9–503(a)(1)].

2. *Trusts.* If the debtor is a trust or a trustee for property held in trust, the financing statement must disclose this information and provide the trust's name as specified in its official documents [UCC 9–503(a)(3)].

3. *Individuals and organizations.* For all others, the financing statement must disclose "the individual or organizational name of the debtor" [UCC 9–503(a) (4)(A)]. The word *organization* includes unincorporated associations, such as clubs and some churches, as well as joint ventures and general partnerships. If an organizational debtor does not have a group name, the names of the individuals in the group must be listed.

4. *Trade names.* Providing only the debtor's trade name (or a fictitious name) in a financing statement is *not* sufficient for perfection [UCC 9–503(c)]. Thus, the name Pete's Plumbing (if Pete's Plumbing is not a distinct legal entity) is not sufficient. The financing statement must also include the owner-debtor's actual name—Pete Hanson.

**Changes in the Debtor's Name**  What if the debtor's name changes, and the financing statement becomes seriously misleading because of the name change? In this situation, the financing statement remains effective only for collateral the debtor acquired before or within four months after the name change. Unless an amendment to the financing statement is filed, the secured party's interest in goods that the debtor acquired after the four-month period is unperfected [UCC 9–507(b) and (c)].

A one-page uniform financing statement amendment form is available for filing name changes and for other purposes [UCC 9–521]. (See the discussion of amendments later in this chapter.)

**Description of the Collateral**  Both the security agreement and the financing statement must describe the collateral in which the secured party has a security interest. (For land-related security interests, a legal description of the realty is also required [UCC 9–502(b)].)

The security agreement must describe the collateral because no security interest in goods can exist unless the parties agree on which goods are subject to the security interest. The financing statement must describe the collateral to provide public notice of the fact that certain goods of the debtor are subject to a security interest.

Sometimes, the descriptions in the two documents vary. The description in the security agreement must be more precise than the description in the financing statement. The UCC permits broad, general descriptions in the financing statement, such as "all assets" or "all personal property." Usually, if a financing statement accurately describes the agreement between the secured party and the debtor, the description is sufficient [UCC 9–504].

■ **EXAMPLE 20.2**  A security agreement for a commercial loan to a manufacturer of automotive parts may list all of the manufacturer's equipment subject to the loan by serial number. The financing statement, in contrast, may simply state "all equipment owned or hereafter acquired." ■

**Where to File**  In most states, a financing statement must be filed centrally in the appropriate state office in the state where the debtor is located. An exception occurs when the collateral consists of timber to be cut, fixtures, or items to be extracted—such as oil, coal, gas, and minerals [UCC 9–301(3) and (4), 9–502(b)]. In those

---

2. If the name listed in the financing statement is so inaccurate that a search using the standard search engine will not find the debtor's name, the financing statement is deemed seriously misleading under UCC 9–506. See also UCC 9–507, which governs the effectiveness of financing statements found to be seriously misleading.

circumstances, the financing statement is filed in the county where the collateral is located.

Note that the state in which a financing statement should be filed depends on the debtor's location, not the location of the collateral (with the exception of the collateral just mentioned) [UCC 9–301]. The debtor's location is determined as follows [UCC 9–307]:

1. For an *individual debtor,* it is the state of the debtor's principal residence.
2. For an organization registered with the state, such as a corporation, it is the state in which the organization is registered. Thus, if a debtor is incorporated in Delaware and has its chief executive office in New York, a secured party would file the financing statement in Delaware.
3. For *all other entities,* it is the state in which the business is located or, if the debtor has more than one office, the place from which the debtor manages its business operations and affairs.

**Consequences of an Improper Filing** Any improper filing renders the secured party's interest unperfected and reduces the secured party's claim to that of an unsecured creditor. For instance, if the debtor's name is incorrect or if the collateral is not sufficiently described on the financing statement, the filing may not be effective.

■ **EXAMPLE 20.3** Arthur Mendez Juarez, a strawberry farmer, leased farmland from Glendale Fruits, Inc., and borrowed funds from Glendale for payroll and production expenses. The sublease and other documents set out Juarez's full name, but Juarez generally went by the name "Mendez," and he signed the sublease "Arthur Mendez." To perfect its interests, Glendale filed financing statements that identified the debtor as "Arthur Mendez."

Some time later, Juarez contracted to sell strawberries to Frozun Fruits, LLC, which also advanced him funds secured by a financing statement. This statement identified the debtor as "Arthur Juarez." By the following year, Juarez was unable to pay his debts. He owed Glendale more than $200,000 and Frozun nearly $50,000. Both Glendale and Frozun filed suits against Juarez claiming to have priority under a perfected security interest.

In this situation, a properly filed financing statement would identify the debtor's true name (Arthur Juarez). Because a debtor name search for "Arthur Juarez" would not disclose a financing statement in the name of "Arthur Mendez," Glendale's financing statement was seriously misleading. Therefore, Frozun's security interest

would have priority because its financing statement was recorded properly. ■

## 20–3b Perfection without Filing

In two types of situations, security interests can be perfected without filing a financing statement. The first occurs when the collateral is transferred into the possession of the secured party. The second occurs when the security interest is one of a limited number under the UCC that can be perfected on attachment [UCC 9–309].

The phrase *perfected on attachment* means that these security interests are automatically perfected at the time of their creation, without a filing and without possession of the goods. Two of the most common security interests that are perfected on attachment are a *purchase-money security interest* in consumer goods (explained shortly) and an assignment of a beneficial interest in an estate of a deceased person [UCC 9–309(1), (13)].

**Perfection by Possession** In the past, one of the most frequently used means of obtaining financing under the common law was to pledge certain collateral as security for the debt. The collateral was then transferred into the creditor's possession. When the debt was paid, the collateral was returned to the debtor. Although the debtor usually entered into a written security agreement, oral security agreements were also enforceable as long as the secured party possessed the collateral.

The UCC retained the common law pledge and the principle that the security agreement need not be in writing if the collateral is transferred to the secured party [UCC 9–310, 9–312(b), 9–313]. ■ **EXAMPLE 20.4** Sheila needs cash to pay for a medical procedure. She obtains a loan for $4,000 from Trent. As security on the loan, she gives him a promissory note on which she is the payee. Even though the agreement to hold the note as collateral was oral, Trent has a perfected security interest. He does not need to file a financing statement, because he has possession of the note. No other creditor of Sheila's can attempt to recover the note from Trent in payment for other debts. ■

Certain items—such as stocks, bonds, negotiable instruments, and jewelry—are commonly transferred into the creditor's possession when they are used as collateral for loans. For most collateral, however, possession by the secured party is impractical because it would prevent the debtor from using or deriving income from the property to pay off the debt. ■ **EXAMPLE 20.5** Jeb, a farmer, takes out a loan to finance the purchase of a corn harvester and uses the equipment as collateral. Clearly, the purpose of the purchase would be defeated if Jeb transferred the collateral into the creditor's possession. ■

### Perfection by Attachment—The Purchase-Money Security Interest in Consumer Goods

Under the UCC, fourteen types of security interests are perfected automatically at the time they are created [UCC 9–309]. The most common is the **purchase-money security interest (PMSI)** in *consumer goods* (items bought primarily for personal, family, or household purposes).

A PMSI in consumer goods is created when a seller or lender agrees to extend credit to a buyer for part or all of the purchase price of the goods in a sales transaction. The entity that extends the credit can be either the seller (a store, for instance) or a financial institution that lends the buyer the funds with which to purchase the goods [UCC 9–102(a)(2)].

**Automatic Perfection.** A PMSI in consumer goods is perfected automatically at the time of a credit sale—that is, at the time the PMSI is created. The seller in this situation does not need to do anything more to perfect her or his interest.

■ **EXAMPLE 20.6** Jami purchases a Whirlpool washer and dryer from West Coast Appliance for $2,500. Unable to pay the entire amount in cash, Jami signs a purchase agreement to pay $1,000 down and $100 per month until the balance, plus interest, is fully paid. West Coast Appliance is to retain a security interest in the appliances until full payment has been made. Because the security interest was created as part of the purchase agreement with a consumer, it is a PMSI, and West Coast Appliance's security interest is automatically perfected. ■

**Exceptions to Automatic Perfection.** There are two exceptions to the rule of automatic perfection for PMSIs:

1. Certain types of security interests that are subject to other federal or state laws may require additional steps to be perfected [UCC 9–311]. Many jurisdictions, for instance, have certificate-of-title statutes that establish perfection requirements for security interests in certain goods, including automobiles, trailers, boats, mobile homes, and farm tractors.

   ■ **EXAMPLE 20.7** Martin Sedek purchases a boat at a Florida dealership. Florida has a certificate-of-title statute. Sedek obtains financing for his purchase through General Credit Corporation. General Credit Corporation will need to file a certificate of title with the appropriate state official to perfect the PMSI. ■

2. PMSIs in nonconsumer goods, such as a business's inventory or livestock, are not automatically perfected [UCC 9–324]. These types of PMSIs will be discussed later in this chapter in the context of priorities.

## 20–3c Perfection and the Classification of Collateral

Where or how to perfect a security interest sometimes depends on the classification or definition of the collateral. Collateral is generally divided into two classifications: *tangible collateral* (collateral that can be seen, felt, and touched) and *intangible collateral* (collateral that consists of or generates rights). Exhibit 20–3 summarizes various classifications of collateral and the methods of perfecting a security interest in collateral falling within each of those classifications.[3]

## 20–3d Effective Time Duration of Perfection

A financing statement is effective for five years from the date of filing [UCC 9–515]. If a **continuation statement** is filed *within six months prior to the expiration date,* the effectiveness of the original statement is continued for another five years. The continuation period starts with the expiration date of the first five-year period [UCC 9–515(d), (e)]. The effectiveness of the statement can be continued in the same manner indefinitely. Any attempt to file a continuation statement outside the six-month window will render the continuation ineffective, and the perfection will lapse at the end of the five-year period.

If a financing statement lapses, the security interest that had been perfected by the filing now becomes unperfected. A purchaser for value can take the property that was used as collateral as if the security interest had never been perfected [UCC 9–515(c)].

To review the ways of perfecting a security interest, see Concept Summary 20.2.

---

3. There are additional classifications, such as agricultural liens, commercial tort claims, and investment property. For definitions of these types of collateral, see UCC 9–102(a)(5), (a)(13), and (a)(49).

**EXHIBIT 20–3** Selected Types of Collateral and Methods of Perfection

| TANGIBLE COLLATERAL | | METHOD OF PERFECTION |
|---|---|---|
| All things that are movable at the time the security interest attaches or that are attached to land, including timber and crops. | | |
| **Consumer Goods** | Items bought primarily for personal, family, or household purposes, such as a home theatre system. | A purchase-money security interest (PMSI) in consumer goods is automatically perfected at the time it is created (except for certain vehicles that also must comply with certificate-of-title statutes). For other consumer goods, general rules of filing or possession apply. |
| **Equipment** | Goods bought for or used primarily in business (and not part of inventory or farm products)—for example, a delivery truck. | Filing or (rarely) possession by secured party. |
| **Farm Products** | Crops (including aquatic goods), livestock, or supplies produced in a farming operation —for example, ginned cotton, milk, eggs, and maple syrup. | Filing or (rarely) possession by secured party. |
| **Inventory** | Goods held by a person for sale or under a contract of service or lease; raw materials held for production and work in progress. | Filing or (rarely) possession by secured party. |
| INTANGIBLE COLLATERAL | | METHOD OF PERFECTION |
| Nonphysical property that exists only in connection with something else. | | |
| **Chattel Paper** | A writing or electronic record that evidences both a monetary obligation and a security interest in goods and software used in goods—for example, a security agreement. | Filing or possession or control by secured party. |
| **Instruments** | A negotiable instrument—such as a check, note, certificate of deposit, draft, or other writing—that evidences a right to the payment of money and is not a security agreement or lease, but rather a type that can ordinarily be transferred (after indorsement, if necessary) by delivery. | Normally, filing or possession. For the sale of promissory notes, perfection can be by attachment (automatically on the creation of the security interest). |
| **Accounts** | Any right to receive payment for property (real or personal), including intellectual licensed property, services, insurance policies, and certain other receivables. | Filing required except for certain assignments that can be perfected by attachment (automatically on the creation of the security interest). |
| **Deposit Accounts** | Any demand, time, savings, passbook, or similar account maintained with a bank. | Perfection by control, such as when the secured party is the bank in which the account is maintained or when the parties have agreed that the secured party can direct the disposition of funds in a particular account. |

## Concept Summary 20.2

### Perfecting a Security Interest

| | |
|---|---|
| **Perfecting a Security Interest by Filing** | The most common method of perfection is *by filing* a financing statement containing the names of the secured party and the debtor and indicating the collateral covered by the financing statement. <br>• Communication of the financing statement to the appropriate filing office, together with the correct filing fee, constitutes a filing. <br>• The financing statement must be filed under the name of the debtor. Fictitious (trade) names normally are not sufficient. |
| **Perfecting a Security Interest without Filing** | Two common methods to perfect a security interest *without filing* include the following: <br>1. *By transfer of collateral*—The debtor can transfer possession of the collateral to the secured party. For example, a *pledge* is this type of transfer. <br>2. *By attachment*—A limited number of security interests are perfected by attachment, such as a purchase-money security interest (PMSI) in consumer goods. If the secured party has a PMSI in consumer goods (for personal or household purposes, for example), the secured party's security interest is perfected automatically. |

# 20–4 The Scope of a Security Interest

A security interest can cover property in which the debtor has either present or future ownership or possessory rights. Therefore, security agreements can cover the proceeds of the sale of collateral, after-acquired property, and future advances, as discussed next.

## 20–4a Proceeds

**Proceeds** are the cash or property received when collateral is sold or disposed of in some other way [UCC 9–102(a)(64)]. A security interest in the collateral gives the secured party a security interest in the proceeds acquired from the sale of that collateral.

■ **EXAMPLE 20.8** People's Bank has a perfected security interest in the inventory of a retail seller of heavy farm machinery. The retailer sells a tractor out of this inventory to Jacob Lamensdorf. Lamensdorf agrees, in a security agreement, to make monthly payments to the retailer for a period of twenty-four months. If the retailer goes into default on the loan from the bank, the bank is entitled to the remaining payments Lamensdorf owes to the retailer as proceeds. ■

A security interest in proceeds is automatically perfected at the same time as the secured party perfected its security interest in the original collateral. It remains perfected for twenty days after the debtor receives the proceeds from the sale of the collateral.

The parties can agree to extend the twenty-day automatic perfection period in the original security agreement [UCC 9–315(c), (d)]. Extensions are typically done when the collateral is the type that is likely to be sold, such as a retailer's inventory of tablets or smartphones. The UCC also permits a security interest in identifiable cash proceeds to remain perfected after twenty days [UCC 9–315(d)(2)].

The dispute in the following case focused on proceeds. The court was asked to decide whether the actions taken by the debtor and another creditor had stripped a secured creditor of its interest in certain proceeds.

# *In re* Tusa–Expo Holdings, Inc.

United States Court of Appeals, Fifth Circuit, 811 F.3d 786 (2016).

**Background and Facts** Tusa Office Solutions, Inc., a subsidiary of Tusa–Expo Holdings, Inc., was the largest retail dealer in new furniture made by Knoll, Inc. A customer ordered Knoll furniture from Tusa Office, which ordered it from Knoll and delivered it to the customer. The customer paid Tusa Office, which then paid Knoll. Knoll set a limit on the amount of the payments that could be outstanding before it would stop filling new orders. As part of the deal, Tusa Office granted Knoll a first-priority security interest in specified accounts receivable.

Meanwhile, Tusa Office obtained a loan from Textron Financial, Inc. Knoll and Textron agreed separately that Textron would have a first-priority security interest in all of Tusa Office's assets except Knoll's collateral.

The terms of the loan required Tusa Office to establish a bank account—called the lockbox—into which its customers made payments directly. Textron could withdraw funds from the lockbox and use them to increase the credit available to Tusa Office on its loan. Tusa Office used the increased credit to pay Knoll. By paying Knoll, Tusa Office kept its debt to Knoll below the furniture maker's limit, which enabled Tusa Office to fill new orders for its customers.

Ultimately, Tusa Office filed a bankruptcy petition in a federal bankruptcy court. Marilyn Garner, the bankruptcy trustee, sought to recapture some of the funds that Knoll had received through the lockbox.[a] To do this, Garner had to establish that Knoll had received more by these transfers than it would receive on Tusa Office's bankruptcy. The court issued a ruling against the trustee, who appealed.

## In the Language of the Court

*WIENER,* Circuit Judge:

* * * *

* * * *A creditor who merely recovers its own collateral receives no more * * * than it would have received anyway.* [Emphasis added.]

The Trustee asserts that the transfers from Tusa Office to Knoll were not made from the proceeds of Knoll's collateral.

* * * *

The Trustee does not dispute that the payments Tusa Office's customers deposited into the lockbox were proceeds of Tusa Office's accounts receivable. She argues * * * that * * * Knoll's first-priority security interest in the payments was stripped by operation of [Texas Business and Commerce Code] Section 9.332(a) [Texas's version of UCC 9–332(a)]: "A transferee of money takes the money free of a security interest * * * ." Section 9.332(a) does not apply if such a transfer of money was made to the debtor. The Trustee therefore insists that Textron, not Tusa Office, was the transferee. In so doing, the Trustee contends that the lockbox was "owned * * * by Textron."

* * * *

* * * The Loan Agreement is clear. It specifies that * * * "Tusa Office shall have established a * * * lockbox * * * for its collections and the transfer thereof to Textron * * * ." The Loan Agreement also states that "Tusa Office shall have possession of Textron's Collateral."

Because Tusa Office, not Textron, owned the lockbox, Section 9.332(a) does not apply. Therefore, Knoll's first-priority security interest in the proceeds of Tusa Office's accounts receivable survived the deposit into the lockbox.

* * * *

The Trustee next contends that Section 9.332(b) [Texas's version of UCC 9–332(b)] stripped Knoll's first-priority security interest when they were transferred from the lockbox to Textron.

* * * *

---

**a.** A debtor files a petition in a federal bankruptcy court to liquidate its assets, pay its creditors with the proceeds, and obtain a discharge of any remaining debt. It is the job of the bankruptcy trustee to collect those assets and distribute them fairly among the debtor's creditors.

Case 20.2 Continued

The plain language of Section 9.332(b) states that a "transferee of funds from a deposit account takes the funds free of a security interest in the deposit account."

\* \* \* \*

The plain language of Section 9.332(b) is unambiguous. Knoll's first-priority security interest in the proceeds of Tusa Office's accounts receivable survived the transfer from the lockbox to Textron. Not only is this consistent with Section 9.332(b), but it is also consistent with the \* \* \* Agreement between Knoll and Textron.

**Decision and Remedy** *The U.S. Court of Appeals for the Fifth Circuit affirmed the ruling of the lower court. The trustee could not recover the funds that were transferred to Knoll from Tusa Office through the lockbox because those funds were the proceeds of Knoll's own collateral.*

**Critical Thinking**
- **Legal Environment** *Why does UCC 9–332 permit transferees to take funds "free of a security interest"? How did this provision work to protect the parties in this case?*
- **Ethical** *Office Expo, Inc., a dealer in used furniture, was, like Tusa Office, a subsidiary of Tusa–Expo Holdings. Tusa Office operated profitably, but Office Expo did not. To bolster Office Expo, funds were transferred from Tusa Office to Office Expo on a regular basis, which caused problems for Tusa Office. Were these transfers unethical? Discuss.*

## 20–4b After-Acquired Property

**After-acquired property** is property that the debtor acquired after the execution of the security agreement. The security agreement may provide for a security interest in after-acquired property, such as a debtor's inventory [UCC 9–204(1)].

Generally, the debtor will purchase new inventory to replace the inventory sold. The secured party wants this newly acquired inventory to be subject to the original security interest. Thus, the after-acquired property clause continues the secured party's claim to any inventory acquired thereafter. (This is not to say that the original security interest will take priority over the rights of all other creditors with regard to this after-acquired inventory, as will be discussed later.)

■ **EXAMPLE 20.9** Amato buys factory equipment from Bronson on credit, giving as security an interest in all of her equipment—both what she is buying and what she already owns. The security agreement with Bronson contains an after-acquired property clause. Six months later, Amato pays cash to another seller of factory equipment for additional equipment. Six months after that, Amato goes out of business before she has paid off her debt to Bronson. Bronson has a security interest in all of Amato's equipment, even the equipment bought from the other seller. ■

## 20–4c Future Advances

Often, a debtor will arrange with a bank to have a *continuing line of credit* under which the debtor can borrow funds intermittently. Advances against lines of credit can be subject to a properly perfected security interest in certain collateral.

The security agreement may provide that any future advances made against that line of credit are also subject to the security interest in the same collateral [UCC 9–204(c)]. Future advances need not be of the same type or otherwise related to the original advance to benefit from this type of **cross-collateralization.**[4] Cross-collateralization occurs when an asset that is not the subject of a loan is used to collateralize that loan.

■ **EXAMPLE 20.10** Stroh is the owner of a small manufacturing plant with equipment valued at $1 million. He has an immediate need for $40,000 of working capital. He obtains a loan from Midwestern Bank and signs a security agreement, putting up all of his equipment as security. The bank properly perfects its security interest. The security agreement provides that Stroh can borrow up to $500,000 in the future, using the same equipment as collateral for any future advances. Midwestern Bank does not have to execute a new security agreement and perfect a security interest each time an advance is made, up to a cumulative total of $500,000. For priority purposes, each advance is perfected as of the date of the *original* perfection. ■

## 20–4d The Floating-Lien Concept

A security agreement that provides for a security interest in proceeds, in after-acquired property, or in collateral subject

---

4. See Official Comment 5 to UCC 9–204.

to future advances by the secured party is often characterized as a **floating lien.** This type of security interest continues in the collateral or proceeds even if the collateral is sold, exchanged, or disposed of in some other way.

**A Floating Lien in Inventory** Floating liens commonly arise in the financing of inventories. A creditor is not interested in specific pieces of inventory, which are constantly changing, so the lien "floats" from one item to another as the inventory changes.

■ **EXAMPLE 20.11** Cascade Sports, Inc., an Oregon corporation, operates as a cross-country ski dealer. The company has a line of credit with Portland First Bank to finance its inventory of cross-country skis. Cascade and Portland First enter into a security agreement that provides for coverage of proceeds, after-acquired inventory, present inventory, and future advances. Portland First perfects its security interest in the inventory by filing centrally with the office of the secretary of state in Oregon. One day, Cascade sells a new pair of the latest cross-country skis and receives a used pair in trade. That same day, Cascade purchases two new pairs of cross-country skis from a local manufacturer for cash. Later that day, to meet its payroll, Cascade borrows $8,000 from Portland First Bank under the security agreement.

Portland First has a perfected security interest in the used pair of skis under the proceeds clause. It also has a perfected security interest in the two new pairs of skis purchased from the local manufacturer under the after-acquired property clause. The new amount of funds advanced to Cascade is secured on all of the above-mentioned collateral by the future-advances clause. All of this is accomplished under the original perfected security interest. The various items in the inventory have changed, but Portland First still has a perfected security interest in Cascade's inventory. Hence, it has a floating lien in the inventory. ■

**A Floating Lien in a Shifting Stock of Goods** The concept of the floating lien can also apply to a shifting stock of goods. The lien can start with raw materials, follow them as they become finished goods and inventories, and continue as the goods are sold and are turned into accounts receivable, chattel paper, or cash.

# 20–5 Priorities

When more than one party claims an interest in the same collateral, which has priority? The UCC sets out detailed rules to answer this question. In many situations the party who has a perfected security interest will have priority. There are, however, exceptions that give priority rights to another party, such as a buyer in the ordinary course of business.

## 20–5a General Rules of Priority

The basic rule is that when more than one security interest has been perfected in the same collateral, the first to be perfected (or filed) has priority over any perfected later. If only one of the conflicting security interests has been perfected, then that security interest has priority. If none of the security interests have been perfected, then the first security interest that attaches has priority.

The UCC's rules of priority can be summarized as follows:

1. *Perfected security interest versus unsecured creditors and unperfected security interests.* When two or more parties have claims to the same collateral, a perfected secured party's interest has priority over the interests of most other parties [UCC 9–322(a)(2)]. This includes priority to the proceeds from a sale of collateral resulting from a bankruptcy (giving the perfected secured party rights superior to those of the bankruptcy trustee).

2. *Conflicting perfected security interests.* When two or more secured parties have perfected security interests in the same collateral, generally the first to perfect (by filing or taking possession of the collateral) has priority [UCC 9–322(a)(1)].

3. *Conflicting unperfected security interests.* When two conflicting security interests are unperfected, the first to attach (be created) has priority [UCC 9–322(a)(3)]. This is sometimes called the "first-in-time" rule.

■ **EXAMPLE 20.12** Rick Morales and his wife and son own a dairy farm called Lost Creek Heifers (LCH) that has received multiple loans through Ag Services, Inc. Morales executes a promissory note and security agreement in favor of Ag Services. The note lists all of LCH's accounts, equipment, farm products, inventory, livestock, and proceeds as collateral. A year later, Morales and his wife separate, and he signs a separation agreement giving her some cash and land.

The following year, Morales buys out his son's interest in LCH by giving him a promissory note for $100,000. The note lists all of LCH's equipment, inventory, livestock, and proceeds as collateral. Morales also sells a herd of dairy cows for $500,000 and gives his former wife a check for $240,000. LCH files for bankruptcy shortly thereafter. A dispute arises over which party (Ag Services, Morales's son, or Morales's former wife) is entitled to the proceeds from the sale of the cows. In this situation, a court will likely find that because Ag Services' security interest in the proceeds was the first in time to *attach*, Ag Services has first priority to the proceeds. ■

## 20–5b Exceptions to the General Priority Rules

In some situations, on the debtor's default, the perfection of a security interest will not protect a secured party against certain other third parties having claims to the collateral. For instance, the UCC provides that in certain circumstances a PMSI, properly perfected,[5] will prevail over another security interest in after-acquired collateral, even though the other was perfected first.

**Buyers in the Ordinary Course of Business** A major exception to the priority rules exists for a buyer in the ordinary course of business. A *buyer in the ordinary course of business* is a person who, in good faith, buys goods from a party in the business of selling such goods [UCC 1–201(9)].

A buyer in the ordinary course takes the goods free from any security interest created by the seller *even if the security interest is perfected and the buyer knows of its existence* [UCC 9–320(a)]. In other words, a buyer in the ordinary course will have priority even if a previously perfected security interest exists as to the goods. The rationale for this rule is obvious. If buyers could not obtain the goods free and clear of any security interest the merchant had created, the free flow of goods in the marketplace would be hindered.

■ **EXAMPLE 20.13** Dubbs Auto grants a security interest in its inventory to Heartland Bank for a $300,000 line of credit. Heartland perfects its security interest by filing financing statements with the appropriate state offices. Dubbs uses $9,000 of its credit to buy two used trucks and delivers the certificates of title, which designate Dubbs as the owner, to Heartland.

Later, Dubbs sells one of the trucks to Samuel Murdoch and another to Michael Laxton. National City Bank finances both purchases. New certificates of title designate the buyers as the owners and Heartland as the "first lienholder," but Heartland receives none of the funds from the sales. If Heartland sues National City, claiming that its security interest in the vehicles takes priority, it

will lose. Because Murdoch and Laxton are buyers in the ordinary course of business, Heartland's security interest in the motor vehicles was extinguished when the vehicles were sold to them. ■

**PMSI in Goods Other than Inventory and Livestock** An important exception to the first-in-time rule involves a perfected PMSI in certain types of collateral, such as equipment, that is not inventory or livestock [UCC 9–324(a)]. (Remember that a PMSI that is *not* in consumer goods must still be perfected.) ■ **EXAMPLE 20.14** Piper Sandoval borrows funds from West Bank, signing a security agreement in which she puts up all of her present and after-acquired equipment as security. On May 1, West Bank perfects this security interest (which is not a PMSI). On July 1, Sandoval purchases a new piece of equipment from Zylex Company on credit, signing a security agreement. The delivery date for the new equipment is August 1.

Zylex thus has a PMSI in the new equipment (which is not part of its inventory), but the PMSI is not in consumer goods and thus is not automatically perfected. If Sandoval defaults on her payments to both West Bank and Zylex, which of them has priority with regard to the new piece of equipment? Generally, West Bank would have priority because its interest perfected first in time. In this situation, however, as long as Zylex perfected its PMSI in the new equipment within twenty days after Sandoval took possession on August 1, Zylex has priority. ■

**PMSI in Inventory** Another important exception to the first-in-time rule has to do with security interests in inventory. A perfected PMSI in inventory has priority over a conflicting security interest in the same inventory. To maintain this priority, the holder of the PMSI must notify the holder of the conflicting security interest on or before the time the debtor takes possession of the inventory [UCC 9–324(b)].

■ **EXAMPLE 20.15** On May 1, SNS Electronics borrows funds from Key Bank. SNS signs a security agreement that puts up all of its present inventory and any after-acquired inventory as collateral. Key Bank perfects its interest (not a PMSI) on that date. On June 10, SNS buys new inventory from Martin, Inc., a manufacturer, to use for its Fourth of July sale. SNS makes a down payment for the new inventory and signs a security agreement giving Martin a PMSI in the new inventory as collateral for the remaining debt. Martin delivers the inventory to SNS on June 28, but SNS's Fourth of July sale is a disaster, and most of its inventory remains unsold. In August, SNS defaults on its payments to both Key Bank and Martin.

---

5. Recall that, with some exceptions (such as motor vehicles), a PMSI in *consumer goods* is automatically perfected—no filing is necessary. A PMSI that is *not* in consumer goods must still be perfected, however.

Does Key Bank or Martin have priority with respect to the new inventory delivered to SNS on June 28? If Martin has not perfected its security interest by June 28, Key Bank's after-acquired collateral clause has priority because it was the first to be perfected (on May 1). If, however, Martin has perfected *and* gives proper notice of its security interest to Key Bank before SNS takes possession of the goods on June 28, Martin has priority. ■

**Buyers of the Collateral** The UCC recognizes that there are certain types of buyers whose interest in purchased goods could conflict with those of a perfected secured party on the debtor's default. These include buyers in the ordinary course of business (as discussed), as well as buyers of farm products, instruments, documents, or securities. The UCC sets down special rules of priority for these types of buyers.

Exhibit 20–4 describes the various rules regarding the priority of claims to a debtor's collateral.

# 20–6 Rights and Duties of Debtors and Creditors

The security agreement itself determines most of the rights and duties of the debtor and the secured party. The UCC, however, imposes some rights and duties that apply unless the security agreement states otherwise.

## 20–6a Information Requests

At the time of filing a financing statement, a secured party can also furnish a *copy* of the financing statement to the filing officer. The secured party can request that the officer note the file number, date, and hour of the original filing on the copy [UCC 9–523(a)]. The filing officer must send this copy to the person designated by the secured party or to the debtor, if the debtor makes the request.

The filing officer must also give information to a person who is contemplating obtaining a security interest from a prospective debtor [UCC 9–523(c), (d)]. If requested, the filing officer must issue a certificate (for a fee) that provides information on possible perfected financing statements with respect to the named debtor.

## 20–6b Release, Assignment, and Amendment

A secured party can release all or part of any collateral described in the financing statement, thereby terminating its security interest in that collateral. The release is recorded by filing a uniform amendment form [UCC 9–512, 9–521(b)].

A secured party can also assign all or part of the security interest to a third party (the assignee). The assignee becomes the secured party of record if the assignment is filed by use of a uniform amendment form [UCC 9–514, 9–521(a)].

If the debtor and the secured party agree, they can amend the information in the filed financing statement and can add or substitute new collateral. They do so by filing a uniform amendment form that indicates the file number of the initial financing statement [UCC 9–512(a)]. An amendment does not extend the time period of perfection. If new collateral is added, however, the perfection date (for priority purposes) for the new collateral begins on the date the amendment is filed [UCC 9–512(b), (c)].

## 20–6c Confirmation or Accounting Request by Debtor

The debtor may believe that the amount of the unpaid debt or the list of the collateral subject to the security interest is inaccurate. The debtor has the right to request a confirmation of the unpaid debt or list of collateral [UCC 9–210]. The debtor is entitled to one request without charge every six months.

The secured party must comply with the debtor's confirmation request by authenticating and sending to the debtor an accounting within fourteen days after the request is received. Otherwise, the secured party can be held liable for any loss suffered by the debtor, plus $500 [UCC 9–210, 9–625(f)].

## 20–6d Termination Statement

When the debtor has fully paid the debt, if the secured party perfected the security interest by filing, the debtor is entitled to have a termination statement filed. Such a statement demonstrates to the public that the filed perfected security interest has been terminated [UCC 9–513].

Whenever consumer goods are involved, the secured party *must* file a termination statement (or, alternatively,

**EXHIBIT 20-4  Priority of Claims to a Debtor's Collateral**

| PARTIES | PRIORITY |
|---|---|
| **Perfected Secured Party** versus **Unsecured Parties and Creditors** | A perfected secured party's interest has priority over the interests of most other parties, including unsecured creditors, unperfected secured parties, subsequent lien creditors, trustees in bankruptcy, and buyers who do not purchase the collateral in the ordinary course of business. |
| **Perfected Secured Party** versus **Perfected Secured Party** | Between two perfected secured parties in the same collateral, the general rule is that the first in time of perfection is the first in right to the collateral [UCC 9–322(a)(1)]. |
| **Perfected Secured Party** versus **Perfected PMSI** | A PMSI, even if second in time of perfection, has priority providing that the following conditions are met: <br> 1. *Other collateral*—A PMSI has priority, providing it is perfected within twenty days after the debtor takes possession [UCC 9–324(a)]. <br> 2. *Inventory*—A PMSI has priority if it is perfected and proper written or authenticated notice is given to the other security-interest holder on or before the time the debtor takes possession [UCC 9–324(b)]. <br> 3. *Software*—Applies to a PMSI in software only if used in goods subject to a PMSI. If the goods are inventory, priority is determined the same as for inventory. If they are not, priority is determined as for goods other than inventory [UCC 9–103(c), 9–324(f)]. |
| **Perfected Secured Party** versus **Purchaser of Debtor's Collateral** | 1. *Buyer of goods in the ordinary course of the seller's business*—Buyer prevails over a secured party's security interest, even if perfected and even if the buyer knows of the security interest [UCC 9–320(a)]. <br> 2. *Buyer of consumer goods purchased outside the ordinary course of business*—Buyer prevails over a secured party's interest, even if perfected by attachment, providing the buyer purchased as follows: <br>    a. For value. <br>    b. Without actual knowledge of the security interest. <br>    c. For use as a consumer good. <br>    d. Prior to the secured party's perfection by filing [UCC 9–320(b)]. <br> 3. *Buyer of chattel paper*—Buyer prevails if the buyer: <br>    a. Gave new value in making the purchase. <br>    b. Took possession in the ordinary course of the buyer's business. <br>    c. Took without knowledge of the security interest [UCC 9–330]. <br> 4. *Buyer of instruments, documents, or securities*—Buyer who is a holder in due course, a holder to whom negotiable documents have been duly negotiated, or a bona fide purchaser of securities has priority over a previously perfected security interest [UCC 9–330(d), 9–331(a)]. <br> 5. *Buyer of farm products*—Buyer from a farmer takes free and clear of perfected security interests unless, where permitted, a secured party files centrally an effective financing statement (EFS) or the buyer receives proper notice of the security interest before the sale. |
| **Unperfected Secured Party** versus **Unsecured Creditor** | An unperfected secured party prevails over unsecured creditors and creditors who have obtained judgments against the debtor but who have not begun the legal process to collect on those judgments [UCC 9–201(a)]. |

a release). The statement must be filed within one month of the final payment or within twenty days of receiving the debtor's authenticated demand, whichever is earlier [UCC 9–513(b)].

When the collateral is not consumer goods, the secured party is not required to file or to send a termination statement unless the debtor demands one [UCC 9–513(c)]. Whenever a secured party fails to file or send the termination statement as requested, the debtor can recover $500 plus any additional loss suffered [UCC 9–625(e)(4), (f)].

# 20–7 Default

Article 9 defines the rights, duties, and remedies of the secured party and of the debtor on the debtor's default. If the secured party fails to comply with his or her duties, the debtor is afforded particular rights and remedies under the UCC.

## 20–7a What Constitutes Default

What constitutes *default* is not always clear. In fact, Article 9 does not define the term. Instead, the UCC encourages the parties to include in their security agreements the standards under which their rights and duties will be measured [UCC 9–601, 9–603]. In so doing, parties can stipulate the conditions that will constitute a default. Often, these critical terms are shaped by creditors themselves in an attempt to provide the maximum protection possible.

The UCC does impose some requirements, however. The parties cannot agree to waive or alter certain UCC provisions, such as those involving the debtor's right to an accounting or disposition of collateral [UCC 9–602]. In addition, the terms may not run counter to the UCC's provisions regarding good faith and unconscionability.

Any breach of the terms of the security agreement can constitute default. Nevertheless, default occurs most commonly when the debtor fails to meet the scheduled payments that the parties have agreed on or when the debtor becomes bankrupt.

## 20–7b Basic Remedies

The rights and remedies of secured parties under Article 9 are *cumulative* [UCC 9–601(c)]. Therefore, if a creditor is unsuccessful in enforcing rights by one method, she

or he can pursue another method. Generally, a secured party's remedies can be divided into two basic categories: repossession and litigation.

**Repossession of the Collateral—The Self-Help Remedy** On the debtor's default, a secured party can take peaceful possession of the collateral covered by the security agreement without the use of the judicial process [UCC 9–609(b)]. This provision is referred to as the "self-help" provision of Article 9.

The UCC does not define what constitutes *peaceful possession*. The general rule is that the secured party must repossess the collateral without any breach of the peace (without trespassing or breaking and entering, for instance).

**Judicial Remedies** Alternatively, a secured party can relinquish the security interest and use any judicial remedy available, such as obtaining a judgment on the underlying debt, followed by execution and levy [UCC 9–601(a)]. **Execution** is the implementation of a court's decree or judgment. **Levy** is the legal process of obtaining of funds through the seizure and sale of nonexempt property, usually done after a writ of execution has been issued.

## 20–7c Disposition of Collateral

Once default has occurred and the secured party has obtained possession of the collateral, the secured party can:

1. Retain the collateral in full or partial satisfaction of the debt (subject to limitations, discussed next).
2. Sell, lease, license, or otherwise dispose of the collateral in any commercially reasonable manner and apply the proceeds toward satisfaction of the debt [UCC 9–602(7), 9–603, 9–610(a), 9–613, 9–620]. Any sale is always subject to procedures established by state law.

**Retention of Collateral by the Secured Party** Parties are sometimes better off if they do not sell the collateral. Therefore, the UCC generally allows secured parties to choose not to sell. A secured party may retain the collateral unless it consists of consumer goods and the debtor has paid 60 percent or more of the purchase price in a PMSI or debt in a non-PMSI [UCC 9–620(e)]. This general right to retain the collateral is subject to several limitations.

**Notice Requirements.** The secured party must notify the debtor of its proposal to retain the collateral. Notice is required unless the debtor has signed a statement renouncing or modifying her or his rights *after default* [UCC 9–620(a), 9–621].

If the collateral is consumer goods, the secured party does not need to give any other notice. In all other situations, the secured party must also send notice to any other secured party from whom the secured party has received notice of a claim of interest in the collateral. The secured party must also send notice to any *junior lienholder* who held a security interest (or statutory lien) in the collateral ten days before the debtor consented to the retention [UCC 9–621]. (A **junior lienholder** is a party holding a lien that is subordinate to one or more other liens on the same property.)

**Objections.** The debtor or other party notified of the retention has the right to object. If, within twenty days after the notice is sent, the secured party receives a written objection, the secured party must sell or otherwise dispose of the collateral. If no written objection is received, the secured party may retain the collateral in full or partial satisfaction of the debtor's obligation [UCC 9–620(a), 9–621].

**Consumer Goods** When the collateral is consumer goods and the debtor has paid 60 percent of the purchase price on a PMSI or loan amount, the secured party must sell or otherwise dispose of the repossessed collateral within ninety days [UCC 9–620(e), (f)]. Failure to comply opens the secured party to an action for conversion or other liability under UCC 9–625(b) and (c). A secured party will not be liable, however, if the consumer-debtor signed a written statement *after default* renouncing or modifying the right to demand the sale of the goods [UCC 9–624].

**Disposition of Collateral by the Secured Party**
A secured party who does not choose to retain the collateral or who is required to sell it must dispose of it in a *commercially reasonable* manner. The secured party must notify the debtor and other specified parties in writing ahead of time about the sale or disposition of the collateral. Notification is not required if the collateral is perishable, will decline rapidly in value, or is of a type customarily sold on a recognized market [UCC 9–611(b), (c)].[6]

**Sale Can Be Public or Private.** The UCC allows substantial flexibility with regard to disposition. The sale can be public or private. The collateral can be disposed of in its present condition or following any commercially reasonable preparation or processing [UCC 9–610(a)]. The secured party may purchase the collateral at a public sale, but normally not at a private sale [UCC 9–610(c)].

**Must Be Commercially Reasonable.** Every aspect of the disposition's method, manner, time, and place must be commercially reasonable [UCC 9–610(b)]. If the secured party does not dispose of the collateral in a commercially reasonable manner, the price paid for the collateral at the sale may be negatively affected. In that situation, a court can reduce the amount of any deficiency that the debtor owes to the secured party [UCC 9–626(a)(3)].

Although the purpose of requiring a commercially reasonable disposition is to obtain a satisfactory price, the courts look at many factors to determine reasonableness. ■ **CASE IN POINT 20.16** Shannon Hicklin bought a used Ford Explorer under an installment sales contract. When she fell three payments behind—still owing $5,741.65—Onyx Acceptance Corporation repossessed the car and sold it for $1,500 at a private auction. After deducting the costs of repossession and sale, there was a deficiency under the contract of $5,018.88. Onyx filed a suit to collect this amount from Hicklin.

Onyx claimed that the sale was commercially reasonable because the auction price ($1,500) was more than 50 percent of the estimated market value ($2,335). The court, however, found that the price alone was not enough to prove reasonableness. Onyx needed to show that every aspect of the sale was conducted in a commercially reasonable manner. Alternatively, under UCC 9–627(b)(3), Onyx could show that the sale conformed with the reasonable commercial practices among dealers in that type of property. Because Onyx did not do either, it could not collect any deficiency from Hicklin.[7] ■

In the following case, two defaulting debtors alleged that their creditor's sale of the debtors' shares of stock was commercially unreasonable. The debtors contended that a different type of sale or a different "inducement" might have attracted a higher price.

---

**6.** The debtor may waive the right to receive a notice of disposition, but only after default [UCC 9–624(a)].

**7.** *Hicklin v. Onyx Corp.*, 970 A.2d 244 (Del.Sup.Ct. 2009).

# Smith v. Firstbank Corp.

Court of Appeals of Michigan, 2013 WL 951377 (2013).

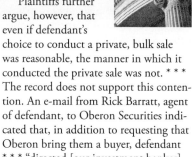

## In the Language of the Court

*PER CURIAM.*

* * * *

The facts in this secured transactions case are not in dispute. Plaintiffs [Bradley Smith, on his own behalf and on behalf of the John J. Smith Revocable Living Trust] borrowed funds from [defendant Firstbank Corporation] in 2002; the notes to defendant were secured with pledges of Sparton Corporation stock as well as other collateral. Plaintiffs defaulted on these loans. Eventually, after many modifications and extensions, defendant took possession of the pledged shares of Sparton stock. Shortly thereafter, defendant sold the stock in two private transactions: on January 12, 2010, it sold 602,170 shares to a brokerage firm at $4.84 per share, and on February 19, 2010, it sold 450,000 shares to a brokerage firm at $5.05 per share. The parties agree that the closing price for Sparton stock on the New York Stock Exchange on both sale dates was $6.05 per share. Defendant then released the remaining collateral to plaintiffs and remitted to plaintiffs by cashier's check the excess funds collected in the private sales. The value of the collateral retained by plaintiffs was over five million dollars.

Plaintiffs filed suit [in a Michigan state court] against defendant, alleging that the sales violated defendant's contractual duties to plaintiffs because they were "commercially unreasonable" * * *. Defendant moved the trial court for summary disposition [judgment]. * * * The trial court issued an Opinion and Order granting defendant's motion * * *. This appeal followed.

* * * *

At issue in the instant case is the secured party's disposition of collateral after the debtors' default. Defendant, the secured party, was authorized by MCL [Michigan Compiled Laws] 440.9609 [Michigan's version of UCC 9–609] to take possession of the collateral following plaintiffs' default. The parties agree that plaintiffs defaulted in the instant case, and that defendant was within its rights to take possession of the pledged shares.

MCL 440.9610 [Michigan's version of UCC 9–610] governs the disposition of collateral after default, and provides in relevant part: * * *

> Every aspect of a disposition of collateral, including the method, manner, time, place, and other terms, must be commercially reasonable.

Further, MCL 440.9627 [Michigan's version of UCC 9–627] provides guidance for determination of whether the disposition of collateral was commercially reasonable, and provides in relevant part: * * *

> The fact that a greater amount could have been obtained by a collection, enforcement, disposition, or acceptance at a different time or in a different method from that selected by the secured party is not of itself sufficient to preclude the secured party from establishing that the collection, enforcement, disposition, or acceptance was made in a commercially reasonable manner.

* * * *

* * * *The circumstances surrounding previous sales of Sparton stock on the public market, and concerns about what public sales would do to the share price, rendered defendant's choice to sell in private transactions reasonable.* * * * In 2008, Wachovia [Bank] sold approximately 400,000 shares of Sparton to satisfy plaintiff Smith's debts. The sale required 18 separate transactions over a two-month period; during that period the share price declined by almost 50 percent. * * * *It was not commercially unreasonable for defendant to seek a private sale to avoid this risk.* [Emphasis added.]

Plaintiffs further argue, however, that even if defendant's choice to conduct a private, bulk sale was reasonable, the manner in which it conducted the private sale was not. * * * The record does not support this contention. An e-mail from Rick Barratt, agent of defendant, to Oberon Securities indicated that, in addition to requesting that Oberon bring them a buyer, defendant * * * "directed [our investment banker] to bring similar type offers to us as well." In addition, defendant's Chief Executive Officer testified * * * that "discounts in large transactions, in thinly traded stocks, were common" and that he was advised by employees of Oberon Securities that selling a "block this large would require a discount of 15 to 20 percent."

The evidence thus does not support the contention that defendant did not seek multiple offers or seek to get the best price for the stock. Rather, the evidence shows that defendant * * * received one offer for Smith's stock, at a discount. Rather than risk public sales and a repeat of what happened in 2008, defendant made the sale. In fact, plaintiffs' contention that defendant did not attempt to garner the best sale price it could is contradicted by the fact that defendant was able to sell the second block of shares (the shares pledged by the trust) for 21 cents more per share, notwithstanding that the closing price for Sparton was exactly the same on the day of both the first and second sales.

* * * *

* * * Although plaintiffs speculate that public sales would have resulted in a higher price, or that the private buyer could have been induced to pay a higher price, speculation and conjecture are insufficient to allow an opposing party to survive a motion for summary disposition.

Affirmed.

## Legal Reasoning Questions

1. What type of property was at the center of the dispute in this case? How did that property become involved in the dispute?

2. On what ground did the plaintiffs argue that the bank should not have been granted a summary judgment?

3. Why does collateral have to be disposed of in a commercially reasonable manner? Is price alone enough to prove reasonableness? Why or why not?

---

**Proceeds from Disposition** Proceeds from the disposition of collateral after default on the underlying debt are distributed in the following order:

1. Reasonable expenses incurred by the secured party in repossessing, storing, and reselling the collateral.
2. Balance of the debt owed to the secured party.
3. Junior lienholders who have made written or authenticated demands.
4. Any surplus to the debtor, unless the collateral consists of accounts, payment intangibles, promissory notes, or chattel paper [UCC 9–608(a); 9–615(a), (e)].

**Noncash Proceeds** Sometimes, the secured party receives noncash proceeds from the disposition of collateral after default. Whenever that occurs, the secured party must make a value determination and apply this value in a commercially reasonable manner [UCC 9–608(a)(3), 9–615(c)].

**Deficiency Judgment** Often, after proper disposition of the collateral, the secured party still has not collected all that the debtor owes. Unless otherwise agreed, the debtor normally is liable for any deficiency, and the creditor can obtain a **deficiency judgment** from a court to collect the deficiency. Practically speaking, though, debtors who have defaulted on a loan rarely have the cash to pay any deficiency.

Note that if the underlying transaction is a sale of accounts, chattel paper, or promissory notes, the debtor is *not* liable for any deficiency. The debtor is also not entitled to any surplus from the disposition of these types of collateral, unless that right is granted by the security agreement [UCC 9–615(e)].

**Redemption Rights** The debtor or any other secured party can exercise the right of *redemption* of the collateral. Redemption may occur at any time before the secured party disposes of the collateral, enters into a contract for its disposition, or discharges the debtor's obligation by retaining the collateral. To redeem the collateral, the debtor or other secured party must tender the entire obligation that is owed, plus any reasonable expenses and attorneys' fees incurred by the secured party in retaking and maintaining the collateral [UCC 9–623].

Concept Summary 20.3 provides a review of the secured party's remedies on the debtor's default.

## Concept Summary 20.3

### Remedies of the Secured Party on the Debtor's Default

| **Repossession of the Collateral** | The secured party may take possession (peacefully or by court order) of the collateral covered by the security agreement and then pursue one of two alternatives: |
|---|---|

1.  *Retain the collateral*—unless the collateral is consumer goods and the debtor has paid 60 percent of the selling price on a PMSI or 60 percent of the debt on a non-PMSI. To retain the collateral, the secured party must—
    a.  Give notice to the debtor if the debtor has not signed a statement renouncing or modifying his or her rights after default. With consumer goods, no other notice is necessary.
    b.  Send notice to any other secured party who has given written or authenticated notice of a claim to the same collateral or who has filed a security interest or a statutory lien ten days before the debtor consented to the retention. If an objection is received within twenty days from the debtor or any other secured party given notice, the creditor must dispose of the collateral according to the requirements of UCC 9–602, 9–603, 9–610, and 9–613. Otherwise, the creditor may retain the collateral in full or partial satisfaction of the debt.
2.  *Dispose of the collateral*—in accordance with the requirements of UCC 9–602(7), 9–603, 9–610(a), and 9–613. To do so, the secured party must—
    a.  Dispose of (sell, lease, or license) the goods in a commercially reasonable manner.
    b.  Notify the debtor and (except in sales of consumer goods) other identified persons, including those who have given notice of claims to the collateral to be sold (unless the collateral is perishable or will decline rapidly in value).
    c.  Apply the proceeds in the following order:
        i.  Expenses incurred by the secured party in repossessing, storing, and reselling the collateral.
        ii.  The balance of the debt owed to the secured party.
        iii.  Junior lienholders who have made written or authenticated demands.
        iv.  Surplus to the debtor (unless the collateral consists of accounts, payment intangibles, promissory notes, or chattel paper).

| **Judicial Remedies** | The secured party may relinquish the security interest and proceed with any judicial remedy available, such as obtaining a judgment on the underlying debt, followed by execution and levy on the nonexempt assets of the debtor. |
|---|---|

## Reviewing: Secured Transactions

Paul Barton owned a small property-management company, doing business as Brighton Homes. In October, Barton went on a spending spree. First, he bought a Bose surround-sound system for his home from KDM Electronics. The next day, he purchased a Wilderness Systems kayak and roof rack from Outdoor Outfitters, and the day after that he bought a new Toyota 4-Runner financed through Bridgeport Auto. Two weeks later, Barton purchased six new iMac computers for his office, also from KDM Electronics. Barton bought each of these items under an installment sales contract. Six months later, Barton's property-management business was failing. He could not make the payments due on any of these purchases and thus defaulted on the loans. Using the information presented in the chapter, answer the following questions.

1. For which of Barton's purchases (the surround-sound system, the kayak, the 4-Runner, and the iMacs) would the creditor need to file a financing statement to perfect its security interest?
2. Suppose that Barton's contract for the office computers mentioned only the name *Brighton Homes.* What would be the consequences if KDM Electronics filed a financing statement that listed only Brighton Homes as the debtor's name?
3. Which of these purchases would qualify as a PMSI in consumer goods?
4. Suppose that after KDM Electronics repossesses the surround-sound system, it decides to keep the system rather than sell it. Can KDM do this under Article 9? Why or why not?

**Debate This** . . .   *A financing statement that does not have the debtor's exact name should still be effective because creditors should always be protected when debtors default.*

## Terms and Concepts

| | | |
|---|---|---|
| after-acquired property 389 | deficiency judgment 397 | proceeds 387 |
| attachment 379 | execution 394 | purchase-money security |
| authenticate 379 | financing statement 378 | interest (PMSI) 385 |
| collateral 378 | floating lien 390 | secured party 378 |
| continuation statement 385 | junior lienholder 395 | secured transaction 378 |
| cross-collateralization 389 | levy 394 | security agreement 378 |
| debtor 378 | perfection 381 | security interest 378 |

## Issue Spotters

1. Nero needs $500 to buy textbooks and other supplies. Olivia agrees to loan Nero $500, accepting Nero's computer as collateral. They put their agreement in writing. How can Olivia let other creditors know of her interest in the computer? (See *Creation of a Security Interest.*)
2. Liberty Bank loans Michelle $5,000 to buy a car, which is used as collateral to secure the loan. After repaying less than 50 percent of the loan, Michelle defaults. Liberty could repossess and keep the car, but the bank does not want it. What are the alternatives? (See *Default.*)

• **Check your answers to the Issue Spotters against the answers provided in Appendix B at the end of this text.**

# Business Scenarios

**20–1. Priorities.** Redford is a seller of electric generators. He purchases a large quantity of generators from a manufacturer, Mallon Corp., by making a down payment and signing an agreement to make the balance of payments over a period of time. The agreement gives Mallon Corp. a security interest in the generators and the proceeds. Mallon Corp. properly files a financing statement on its security interest. Redford receives the generators and immediately sells one of them to Garfield on an installment contract, with payment to be made in twelve equal installments. At the time of the sale, Garfield knows of Mallon's security interest. Two months later, Redford goes into default on his payments to Mallon. Discuss Mallon's rights against Garfield in this situation. (See *Priorities.*)

**20–2. Perfection of a Security Interest.** Marsh has a prize horse named Arabian Knight. Marsh is in need of working capital. She borrows $50,000 from Mendez, who takes possession of Arabian Knight as security for the loan. No written agreement is signed. Discuss whether, in the absence of a written agreement, Mendez has a security interest in Arabian Knight. If Mendez does have a security interest, is it a

perfected security interest? Explain. (See *Perfection of a Security Interest.*)

**20–3. The Scope of a Security Interest.** Edward owned a retail sporting goods shop. A new ski resort was being constructed in his area, and to take advantage of the potential business, Edward decided to expand his operations. He borrowed a large sum from his bank, which took a security interest in his present inventory and any after-acquired inventory as collateral for the loan. The bank properly perfected the security interest by filing a financing statement. Edward's business was profitable, so he doubled his inventory. A year later, just a few months after the ski resort had opened, an avalanche destroyed the ski slope and lodge. Edward's business consequently took a turn for the worse, and he defaulted on his debt to the bank. The bank then sought possession of his entire inventory, even though the inventory was now twice as large as it had been when the loan was made. Edward claimed that the bank had rights to only half of his inventory. Was Edward correct? Explain. (See *The Scope of a Security Interest.*)

# Business Case Problems

**20–4. Spotlight on Radio Shack—Priorities.** In June  1995, Michael and Debra Boudreaux, doing business as D&J Enterprises, Inc., bought a retail electronics store operated under a franchise from Radio Shack. They borrowed from Cabool State Bank to pay for the business and signed loan documents and a financing statement, which identified them as "Debtors." Elsewhere on the financing statement, the bank identified "D&J Enterprises, Inc., Radio Shack, Dealer, Debra K. Boudreaux, Michael C. Boudreaux" as "Debtors." The statement covered, in part, the store inventory.

Before the end of the year, Michael and Debra changed the name of their business to Tri-B Enterprises, Inc. In January 1998, the store closed. The next month, Radio Shack terminated the franchise. Despite the lack of a security interest, Radio Shack took possession of the inventory, claiming that the couple and Tri-B owed the company $6,394.73. The bank filed a suit in a Missouri state court against Radio Shack, claiming a perfected security interest in the inventory with priority over Radio Shack's claim. Did the bank's security interest take priority over Radio Shack's claim? Why or why not? [*Cabool State Bank v. Radio Shack,* 65 S.W.3d 613 (Mo. App. 2002)] (See *Priorities.*)

**20–5. Default.** Primesouth Bank issued a loan to Okefenokee Aircraft, Inc. (OAI), to buy a plane. OAI executed a note in favor of Primesouth in the amount of $161,306.25 plus interest. The plane secured the note. When OAI defaulted, Primesouth repossessed the plane. Instead of disposing of the collateral and seeking a deficiency judgment, however, the bank retained possession of the plane and filed a suit in

a Georgia state court against OAI to enforce the note. OAI did not deny that it had defaulted on the note or dispute the amount due. Instead, OAI argued that Primesouth Bank was not acting in a commercially reasonable manner. According to OAI, the creditor must sell the collateral and apply the proceeds against the debt. What is a secured creditor's obligation in these circumstances? Can the creditor retain the collateral and seek a judgment for the amount of the underlying debt, or is a sale required? Discuss. [*Okefenokee Aircraft, Inc. v. Primesouth Bank,* 296 Ga.App. 782, 676 S.E.2d 394 (2009)] (See *Default.*)

**20–6. Disposition of Collateral.** PRA Aviation, LLC, borrowed $3 million from Center Capital Corp. to buy a Gates Learjet 55B. Center perfected a security interest in the plane. Later, PRA defaulted on the loan, and Center obtained possession of the jet. The market, design, and mechanical condition of similar aircraft were reviewed to estimate the jet's value at $1.45 million. The jet was marketed in trade publications, on the Internet, and by direct advertising to select customers for $1.595 million. There were three offers. Center sold the jet to the high bidder for $1.3 million. Was the sale commercially reasonable? Explain. [*Center Capital Corp. v. PRA Aviation, LLC,* 2011 WL 867516 (E.D.Pa. 2011)] (See *Default.*)

**20–7. Business Case Problem with Sample Answer— Perfecting a Security Interest.** Thomas Tille owned  M.A.T.T. Equipment Co. To operate the business, Tille borrowed funds from Union Bank. For each loan, Union filed a financing statement that included Tille's signature and address, the bank's address, and a description of the collateral. The first loan covered all of Tille's equipment, including "any after-acquired property." The second loan covered a truck crane "whether owned now or acquired later." The third loan covered a "Bobcat mini-excavator." Did these financing statements perfect Union's security interests? Explain. [*Union Bank Co. v. Heban*, 2012-Ohio-30 (Ohio App. 2012)] (See *Perfection of a Security Interest.*)

- **For a sample answer for Problem 20–7, go to Appendix C at the end of this text.**

**20–8. Disposition of Collateral.** With a loan of 1.4 million euros from Barclays Bank, PLC, Thomas Poynter bought a yacht. The loan agreement gave Barclays multiple stand-alone options on default. One option required the lender to give ten days' advance notice of a sale. A different option permitted the lender to avoid this requirement. When Poynter did not repay the loan, Barclays repossessed the yacht and notified Poynter that it would be sold—but did not specify a date, time, or place. Two months later, the yacht was sold. The sale price was less than Poynter owed, and Barclays filed a suit in a federal district court for the deficiency. Is Barclays entitled to collect even though it did not give Poynter ten days' advance notice of the sale? Explain. [*Barclays Bank PLC v. Poynter*, 710 F.3d 16 (1st Cir. 2013)] (See *Default.*)

**20–9. Perfection of a Security Interest.** G&K Farms, a North Dakota partnership, operated a farm in Texas. G&K was insured under the Supplemental Revenue Assistance Payments Program (SURE), through which the federal government provides financial assistance for crop losses caused by natural disasters. PHI Financial Services, Inc., loaned G&K $6.6 million. PHI filed a financing statement that described the collateral as the debtor's interest in "Government Payments." The document did not refer to the farm's crops. G&K defaulted on the loan. Later, G&K received a SURE payment for crop losses and transferred some of the funds to its law firm, Johnston Law Office, P.C., in payment for services. PHI brought an action against Johnston to recover those funds as partial payment on its loan to G&K. Johnston argued that PHI did not have a perfected security interest in the SURE payment because the financing statement did not identify the crops. Was the description of the collateral in the financing statement sufficient? Why or why not? [*PHI Financial Services, Inc. v. Johnston Law Office, P.C.*, 2016 ND 20, 874 N.W.2d 910 (2016)] (See *Perfection of a Security Interest.*)

**20–10. A Question of Ethics—Priorities.** *Mark Denton cosigned a $101,250 loan issued by the First Interstate Bank (FIB) in Missoula, Montana, to Denton's friend Eric Anderson. Denton's business assets—a mini-warehouse operation—secured the loan. On his own, Anderson obtained a $260,000 U.S. Small Business Administration (SBA) loan from FIB at the same time. The purpose of both loans was to buy logging equipment so that Anderson could start a business. Two years after the loan was made, the business failed. As a consequence, FIB repossessed and sold the equipment and applied the proceeds to the SBA loan. FIB then asked Denton to pay the other loan's outstanding balance ($98,460), plus interest. When Denton refused, FIB initiated proceedings to obtain his business assets. Denton filed a suit in a Montana state court against FIB. He claimed, in part, that Anderson's equipment was the collateral for the loan that FIB was attempting to collect from Denton. [Denton v. First Interstate Bank of Commerce, 2006 MT 193, 333 Mont. 169, 142 P.3d 797 (2006)] (See Priorities.)*

**(a)** Denton's assets served as the security for Anderson's loan because Anderson had nothing to offer. When the loan was obtained, Dean Gillmore, FIB's loan officer, explained to them that if Anderson defaulted, the proceeds from the sale of the logging equipment would be applied to the SBA loan first. Under these circumstances, is it fair to hold Denton liable for the unpaid balance of Anderson's loan? Why or why not?

**(b)** Denton argued that the loan contract was unconscionable and constituted a "contract of adhesion." What makes a contract unconscionable? Did the transaction between the parties in this case qualify? What is a "contract of adhesion"? Was this deal unenforceable on that basis? Explain.

# Legal Reasoning Group Activity

**20–11. Security Interests.** Nick Sabol, doing business in the recording industry as Sound Farm Productions, applied to Morton Community Bank for a $58,000 loan to expand his business. Besides the loan application, Sabol signed a promissory note that referred to the bank's rights in "any collateral." Sabol also signed a letter authorizing Morton Community Bank to execute, file, and record all financing statements, amendments, and other documents required by Article 9 to establish a security interest. Sabol did not sign any other documents, including the financing statement, which contained a description of the collateral. Two years later, without having repaid the loan, Sabol filed for bankruptcy. The bank claimed a security interest in Sabol's sound equipment. (See *Creation of a Security Interest.*)

**(a)** The first group will list all the requirements of an enforceable security interest and explain why each of these elements is necessary.

**(b)** The second group will determine if Morton Community Bank had a valid security interest.

**(c)** The third group will discuss whether a bank should be able to execute financing statements on a debtor's behalf without the debtor being present or signing them. Are there are any drawbacks to this practice? Explain.

# CHAPTER 21

# Bankruptcy Law

**M**any people in today's economy are struggling to pay their debts. Although in the old days, debtors were punished and sometimes even sent to prison for failing to pay what they owed, debtors today rarely go to jail. They have many other options, including *bankruptcy*—the last resort in resolving debtor-creditor problems.

The right to petition for bankruptcy relief under federal law is an essential aspect of our capitalistic society, in which we have great opportunities for financial success but may also encounter financial difficulties. Therefore, every businessperson should have some understanding of this topic.

## 21-1 The Bankruptcy Code

Bankruptcy relief is provided under federal law. Although state laws may play a role in bankruptcy proceedings, particularly state laws governing property, the governing law is based on federal legislation.

Article I, Section 8, of the U.S. Constitution gave Congress the power to establish "uniform laws on the subject of bankruptcies throughout the United States." Federal bankruptcy legislation was first enacted in 1898 and since then has undergone several modifications, most recently in the 2005 Bankruptcy Reform Act.[1] Federal bankruptcy laws (as amended) are called the Bankruptcy Code or, more simply, the Code.

### 21-1a Goals of Bankruptcy Law

Bankruptcy law in the United States has two main goals:

1. To protect a debtor by giving him or her a fresh start without creditors' claims.
2. To ensure equitable treatment of creditors who are competing for a debtor's assets.

Thus, the law attempts to balance the rights of the debtor and of the creditors.

Although the twin goals of bankruptcy remain the same, the balance between them shifted somewhat after the 2005 reform legislation. That law was enacted, in part, because of the growing concern that the law allowed too many debtors to avoid paying their debts. Thus, a major goal of the reforms was to require more consumers to pay as many of their debts as possible instead of having those debts fully extinguished in bankruptcy.

### 21-1b Bankruptcy Courts

Bankruptcy proceedings are held in federal bankruptcy courts, which are under the authority of U.S. district courts. Rulings from bankruptcy courts can be appealed to the district courts.

A bankruptcy court can conduct a jury trial if the appropriate district court has authorized it and the parties to the bankruptcy consent. Bankruptcy courts follow the Federal Rules of Bankruptcy Procedure rather than the Federal Rules of Civil Procedure. Bankruptcy court judges are appointed for terms of fourteen years.

### 21-1c Types of Bankruptcy Relief

The Bankruptcy Code is contained in Title 11 of the *United States Code* and has eight chapters. Chapters 1, 3, and 5 of the Code contain general definitional provisions, as well as provisions governing case administration, creditors, the debtor, and the estate. These three chapters normally apply to all kinds of bankruptcies.

Four chapters of the Code set forth the most important types of relief that debtors can seek:

1. Chapter 7 provides for **liquidation** proceedings (the selling of all nonexempt assets and the distribution of the proceeds to the debtor's creditors).

---

1. The full title of the act was the Bankruptcy Abuse Prevention and Consumer Protection Act, Pub. L. No. 109-8, 119 Stat. 23 (April 20, 2005).

**2.** Chapter 11 governs reorganizations.

**3.** Chapter 12 (for family farmers and family fishermen) and 13 (for individuals) provide for the adjustment of debts by persons with regular incomes.[2]

Note that a debtor (except for a municipality) need not be insolvent[3] to file for bankruptcy relief under the Bankruptcy Code. Anyone obligated to a creditor can declare bankruptcy.

## 21–1d Special Requirements for Consumer-Debtors

A **consumer-debtor** is a debtor whose debts result primarily from the purchase of goods for personal, family, or household use. The Bankruptcy Code requires that the clerk of the court give all consumer-debtors written notice of the general purpose, benefits, and costs of each chapter under which they might proceed. In addition, the clerk must provide consumer-debtors with information on the types of services available from credit counseling agencies.

# 21–2 Liquidation Proceedings

Liquidation under Chapter 7 of the Bankruptcy Code is probably the most familiar type of bankruptcy proceeding and is often referred to as an *ordinary,* or *straight, bankruptcy.* Put simply, a debtor in a liquidation bankruptcy turns all assets over to a **bankruptcy trustee,** a person appointed by the court to manage the debtor's funds. The trustee sells the nonexempt assets and distributes the proceeds to creditors. With certain exceptions, the remaining debts are then **discharged** (extinguished), and the debtor is relieved of the obligation to pay the debts.

Any "person"—defined as including individuals, partnerships, and corporations[4]—may be a debtor in a liquidation proceeding. A husband and wife may file jointly

for bankruptcy under a single petition. Railroads, insurance companies, banks, savings and loan associations, investment companies licensed by the Small Business Administration, and credit unions *cannot* be debtors in a liquidation bankruptcy, however. Other chapters of the Bankruptcy Code or other federal or state statutes apply to them.

A straight bankruptcy can be commenced by the filing of either a voluntary or an involuntary **petition in bankruptcy**—the document that is filed with a bankruptcy court to initiate bankruptcy proceedings. If a debtor files the petition, the bankruptcy is voluntary. If one or more creditors file a petition to force the debtor into bankruptcy, the bankruptcy is involuntary. We discuss both voluntary and involuntary bankruptcy proceedings under Chapter 7 in the following subsections.

## 21–2a Voluntary Bankruptcy

To bring a voluntary petition in bankruptcy, the debtor files official forms designated for that purpose in the bankruptcy court. The law now requires that *before* debtors can file a petition, they must receive credit counseling from an approved nonprofit agency within the 180-day period preceding the date of filing. Debtors filing a Chapter 7 petition must include a certificate proving that they have received individual or group counseling from an approved agency within the last 180 days.

A consumer-debtor who is filing for liquidation bankruptcy must confirm the accuracy of the petition's contents. The debtor must also state in the petition, at the time of filing, that he or she understands the relief available under other chapters of the Code and has chosen to proceed under Chapter 7.

Attorneys representing the consumer-debtors must file an affidavit stating that they have informed the debtors of the relief available under each chapter of the Bankruptcy Code. In addition, the attorneys must reasonably attempt to verify the accuracy of the consumer-debtors' petitions and schedules (described next). Failure to do so is considered perjury.

**Chapter 7 Schedules** The voluntary petition must contain the following schedules:

**1.** A list of both secured and unsecured creditors, their addresses, and the amount of debt owed to each.

**2.** A statement of the financial affairs of the debtor.

**3.** A list of all property owned by the debtor, including property that the debtor claims is exempt.

**4.** A list of current income and expenses.

---

**2.** There are no Chapters 2, 4, 6, 8, or 10 in Title 11. Such "gaps" are not uncommon in the *United States Code.* They occur because chapter numbers (or other subdivisional unit numbers) are sometimes reserved for future use when a statute is enacted. (A gap may also appear if a law has been repealed.)

**3.** The inability to pay debts as they become due is known as *equitable* insolvency. *Balance sheet* insolvency, which exists when a debtor's liabilities exceed assets, is not the test. Thus, debtors whose cash-flow problems become severe may petition for bankruptcy voluntarily or be forced into involuntary bankruptcy even though their assets far exceed their liabilities.

**4.** The definition of *corporation* includes unincorporated companies and associations. It also covers labor unions.

**5.** A certificate of credit counseling (as mentioned previously).

**6.** Proof of payments received from employers within sixty days prior to the filing of the petition.

**7.** A statement of the amount of monthly income, itemized to show how the amount is calculated.

**8.** A copy of the debtor's federal income tax return for the most recent year ending immediately before the filing of the petition.

The official forms must be completed accurately, sworn to under oath, and signed by the debtor. To conceal assets or knowingly supply false information on these schedules is a crime under the bankruptcy laws.

With the exception of tax returns, failure to file the required schedules within forty-five days after the filing of the petition will result in an automatic dismissal of the petition. (An extension may be granted, however.) The debtor has up to seven days before the date of the first creditors' meeting to provide a copy of the most recent tax returns to the trustee.

**Tax Returns during Bankruptcy** In addition, a debtor may be required to file a tax return at the end of each tax year while the case is pending and to provide a copy to the court. This may be done at the request of the court or the **U.S. trustee**—a government official who performs administrative tasks that a bankruptcy judge would otherwise have to perform. Any *party in interest* (a party, such as a creditor, who has a valid interest in the outcome of the proceedings) may make this request as well. Debtors may also be required to file tax returns during Chapter 11 and 13 bankruptcies.

**Substantial Abuse—Means Test** In the past, a bankruptcy court could dismiss a Chapter 7 petition if the use of Chapter 7 would constitute a "substantial abuse" of bankruptcy law. Today, the law provides a *means test* to determine a debtor's eligibility for Chapter 7.

The purpose of the test is to keep upper-income people from abusing the bankruptcy process by filing for Chapter 7, as was thought to have happened in the past. The test forces more people to file for Chapter 13 bankruptcy rather than have their debts discharged under Chapter 7.

**The Basic Formula.** A debtor wishing to file for bankruptcy must complete the means test to determine whether she or he qualifies for Chapter 7. The debtor's average monthly income in recent months is compared with the median income in the geographic area in which the person lives. (The U.S. Trustee Program provides these data at its Web site.) If the debtor's income is below

the median income, the debtor usually is allowed to file for Chapter 7 bankruptcy, as there is no presumption of bankruptcy abuse.

**Applying the Means Test to Future Disposable Income.** If the debtor's income is above the median income, then further calculations must be made. The calculations are meant to determine whether the person will have sufficient disposable income in the future to repay at least some of his or her unsecured debts.

As a basis for the calculations, it is presumed that the debtor's recent monthly income will continue for the next sixty months. *Disposable income* is then calculated by subtracting living expenses and secured debt payments, such as mortgage payments, from monthly income.

Living expenses are amounts allowed under formulas used by the Internal Revenue Service (IRS). The IRS allowances include modest allocations for food, clothing, housing, utilities, transportation (including a car payment), health care, and other necessities. (The U.S. Trustee Program's Web site also provides these amounts.) The allowances do not include expenditures for items such as cell phones and cable television service.

**Can the Debtor Afford to Pay Unsecured Debts?** Once future disposable income has been estimated, that amount is used to determine whether the debtor will have income that could be applied to unsecured debts. The courts may also consider the debtor's bad faith or other circumstances indicating abuse.

■ **CASE IN POINT 21.1** Christopher Dean Ng and his wife filed for Chapter 7 bankruptcy, hoping primarily to discharge their mortgage debt of $464,830. At the time the petition was filed, Ng was forty-three years old and worked as an electronic technician. He earned a monthly salary of $7,439.47, as well as a military pension of $1,439.88 a month. His wife was not employed. From Ng's monthly salary, he made a voluntary contribution of $520 to an employer 401(k) plan and a $343 payment on a pension loan. In calculating his disposable income, Ng excluded these amounts.

The U.S. trustee filed a motion to dismiss Ng's petition due to substantial abuse, claiming that the retirement contributions should be disallowed. The court agreed and dismissed the Chapter 7 petition. The Ngs appealed, and the appellate court affirmed. Ng's retirement contributions were not reasonably necessary based on his age, his financial circumstances, and his testimony that he was not planning to retire for at least twenty years. The Ngs could afford to repay some of their debts before they made monthly contributions toward retirement.[5] ■

5. *In re Ng*, 422 Bankr. 118 (9th Cir. 2012).

**Additional Grounds for Dismissal** As already noted, a court can dismiss a debtor's voluntary petition for Chapter 7 relief for substantial abuse or for failure to provide the necessary documents within the specified time.

In addition, a court might dismiss a Chapter 7 in two other situations. First, if the debtor has been convicted of a violent crime or a drug-trafficking offense, the victim can file a motion to dismiss the voluntary petition.[6] Second, if the debtor fails to pay postpetition domestic-support obligations (which include child and spousal support), the court may dismiss the debtor's petition.

**Order for Relief** If the voluntary petition for bankruptcy is found to be proper, the filing of the petition will itself constitute an **order for relief.** (An order for relief is a court's grant of assistance to a petitioner.) Once a consumer-debtor's voluntary petition has been filed, the trustee and creditors must be given notice of the order for relief by mail not more than twenty days after entry of the order.

## 21–2b Involuntary Bankruptcy

An involuntary bankruptcy occurs when the debtor's creditors force the debtor into bankruptcy proceedings. An involuntary case cannot be filed against a charitable institution or a farmer (an individual or business that receives more than 50 percent of gross income from farming operations).

An involuntary petition should not be used as an everyday debt-collection device, and the Code provides penalties for the filing of frivolous petitions against debtors. If the court dismisses an involuntary petition, the petitioning creditors may be required to pay the costs and attorneys' fees incurred by the debtor in defending against the petition. If the petition was filed in bad faith, damages can be awarded for injury to the debtor's reputation. Punitive damages may also be awarded.

**Requirements** For an involuntary action to be filed, the following requirements must be met:

1. If the debtor has twelve or more creditors, three or more of these creditors having unsecured claims totaling at least $15,325 must join in the petition.
2. If a debtor has fewer than twelve creditors, one or more creditors having a claim totaling $15,325 or more may file.[7]

---

6. Note that the court may not dismiss a case on this ground if the debtor's bankruptcy is necessary to satisfy a claim for a domestic-support obligation.
7. 11 U.S.C. Section 303. The amounts stated in this chapter are in accordance with those computed on April 1, 2016.

**Order for Relief** If the debtor challenges the involuntary petition, a hearing will be held, and the bankruptcy court will enter an order for relief if it finds either of the following:

1. The debtor is not paying debts as they come due.
2. A general receiver, assignee, or custodian took possession of, or was appointed to take charge of, substantially all of the debtor's property within 120 days before the filing of the petition.

If the court grants an order for relief, the debtor will be required to supply the same information in the bankruptcy schedules as in a voluntary bankruptcy.

## 21–2c Automatic Stay

The moment a petition, either voluntary or involuntary, is filed, an **automatic stay,** or suspension, of all actions by creditors against the debtor or the debtor's property normally goes into effect. The automatic stay prohibits creditors from taking any act to collect, assess, or recover a claim against the debtor that arose before the filing of the petition. The stay normally continues until the bankruptcy proceeding is closed or dismissed. (In some circumstances, it is possible to petition the bankruptcy court for relief from the automatic stay, as will be discussed shortly.)

If a creditor *knowingly* violates the automatic stay (a willful violation), any injured party, including the debtor, is entitled to recover actual damages, costs, and attorneys' fees. Punitive damages may be awarded as well.

■ **CASE IN POINT 21.2** Stefanie Kuehn filed for bankruptcy. When she requested a transcript from the university at which she had obtained her master's degree, the university refused because she owed more than $6,000 in tuition. Kuehn complained to the court. The court ruled that the university had violated the automatic stay by refusing to provide a transcript because it was attempting to collect an unpaid tuition debt.[8] ■

**The Adequate Protection Doctrine** Underlying the Code's automatic-stay provision for a secured creditor is a concept known as *adequate protection*. The **adequate protection doctrine,** among other things, protects secured creditors from losing their security as a result of the automatic stay.

The bankruptcy court can provide adequate protection by requiring the debtor or trustee to make periodic cash payments or a one-time cash payment. The court can also require the debtor or trustee to provide additional collateral or replacement liens to the extent that

---

8. *In re Kuehn*, 563 F.3d 289 (7th Cir. 2009).

the stay may actually cause the value of the property to decrease.

**Exceptions to the Automatic Stay** The Code provides the following exceptions to the automatic stay:

1. Collection efforts can continue for domestic-support obligations. These obligations include any debt owed to or recoverable by a spouse, a former spouse, a child of the debtor, that child's parent or guardian, or a governmental unit.
2. Proceedings against the debtor related to divorce, child custody or visitation, domestic violence, and support enforcement are not stayed.
3. Investigations by a securities regulatory agency (such as an investigation into insider trading) can continue.
4. Certain statutory liens for property taxes are not stayed.

**Requests for Relief from the Automatic Stay** A secured creditor or other party in interest can petition the bankruptcy court for relief from the automatic stay. If a creditor or other party requests relief from the stay, the stay will automatically terminate sixty days after the request, unless the court grants an extension[9] or the parties agree otherwise.

**Secured Property** The automatic stay on secured property terminates forty-five days after the creditors' meeting unless the debtor redeems or reaffirms certain debts. (Creditors' meetings and reaffirmation will be discussed later in this chapter.) In other words, the debtor cannot keep the secured property (such as a financed automobile), even if she or he continues to make payments on it, without reinstating the rights of the secured party to collect on the debt.

**Bad Faith** If the debtor had two or more bankruptcy petitions dismissed during the prior year, the Code presumes bad faith. In such a situation, the automatic stay does *not* go into effect until the court determines that the petition was filed in good faith.

In addition, the automatic stay on secured debts will terminate thirty days after the petition is filed if the debtor filed a bankruptcy petition that was dismissed within the prior year. Any party in interest can request that the court extend the stay by showing that the filing is in good faith.

## 21–2d Estate in Bankruptcy

On the commencement of a liquidation proceeding under Chapter 7, an *estate in bankruptcy* (sometimes called an *estate in property*) is created. The estate consists of all the debtor's interests in property currently held, wherever located. The estate in bankruptcy includes all of the following:

1. *Community property* (property jointly owned by married persons in certain states).
2. Property transferred in a transaction voidable by the trustee.
3. Proceeds and profits from the property of the estate.

Certain after-acquired property to which the debtor becomes entitled *within 180 days after filing* may also become part of the estate. Such after-acquired property includes gifts, inheritances, property settlements (from divorce), and life insurance death proceeds.

Generally, though, the filing of a bankruptcy petition fixes a dividing line. Property acquired prior to the filing of the petition becomes property of the estate, and property acquired after the filing of the petition, except as just noted, remains the debtor's.

## 21–2e The Bankruptcy Trustee

Promptly after the order for relief in the liquidation proceeding has been entered, a trustee is appointed. The basic duty of the trustee is to collect the debtor's available estate and reduce it to cash for distribution, preserving the interests of both the debtor and the unsecured creditors. The trustee is held accountable for administering the debtor's estate.

To enable the trustee to accomplish this duty, the Code gives the trustee certain powers, stated in both general and specific terms. These powers must be exercised within two years of the order for relief.

**Duties for Means Testing** The trustee is required to promptly review all materials filed by the debtor to determine if there is substantial abuse. Within ten days after the first meeting of the creditors (discussed shortly), the trustee must file a statement indicating whether the case is presumed to be an abuse under the means test. The trustee must provide a copy of this statement to all creditors within five days.

When there is a presumption of abuse, the trustee must either file a motion to dismiss the petition (or convert it to a Chapter 13 petition) or file a statement explaining why a motion would not be appropriate. If the debtor owes a domestic-support obligation (such as

---

9. The court might grant an extension, for example, on a motion by the trustee that the property is of value to the estate.

child support), the trustee must provide written notice of the bankruptcy to the claim holder (a former spouse, for instance).

**The Trustee's Powers** The trustee has the power to require persons holding the debtor's property at the time the petition is filed to deliver the property to the trustee.[10] To enable the trustee to implement this power, the Code provides that the trustee has rights *equivalent* to those of certain other parties, such as a creditor who has a judicial lien. This power of a trustee, which is equivalent to that of a lien creditor, is known as *strong-arm power*.

In addition, the trustee has specific *powers of avoidance*. They enable the trustee to set aside (avoid) a sale or other transfer of the debtor's property and take the property back for the debtor's estate. These powers apply to voidable rights available to the debtor, preferences, and fraudulent transfers by the debtor. Each power is discussed in more detail next. In addition, a trustee can avoid certain statutory liens (creditors' claims against the debtor's property).

The debtor shares most of the trustee's avoidance powers. Thus, if the trustee does not take action to enforce one of the rights just mentioned, the debtor in a liquidation bankruptcy can enforce that right.[11]

**Voidable Rights** A trustee steps into the shoes of the debtor. Thus, any reason that a debtor can use to obtain the return of her or his property can be used by the trustee as well. These grounds include fraud, duress, incapacity, and mutual mistake.

■ **EXAMPLE 21.3** Ben sells his boat to Tara. Tara gives Ben a check, knowing that she has insufficient funds in her bank account to cover the check. Tara has committed fraud. Ben has the right to avoid that transfer and recover the boat from Tara. If Ben files for bankruptcy relief under Chapter 7, the trustee can exercise the same right to recover the boat from Tara, and the boat becomes a part of the debtor's estate. ■

**Preferences** A debtor is not permitted to transfer property or to make a payment that favors—or gives a **preference** to—one creditor over others. The trustee is allowed to recover payments made both voluntarily and involuntarily to one creditor in preference over another.

To have made a recoverable preferential payment, an *insolvent* debtor must have transferred property, for a *preexisting* debt, within *ninety days* before the filing of the bankruptcy petition. The transfer must have given the creditor more than the creditor would have received as a result of the bankruptcy proceedings. The Code presumes that a debtor is insolvent during the ninety-day period before filing a petition.

If a **preferred creditor** (one who has received a preferential transfer) has sold the property to an innocent third party, the trustee cannot recover the property from the innocent party. The preferred creditor, however, generally can be held liable for the value of the property.

**Preferences to Insiders.** Sometimes, the creditor receiving the preference is an insider. An **insider** is an individual, partner, partnership, corporation, or officer or director of a corporation (or a relative of one of these) who has a close relationship with the debtor. In this situation, the avoidance power of the trustee extends to transfers made within *one year* before filing. (If the transfer was fraudulent, as will be discussed shortly, the trustee can avoid transfers made within *two years* before filing.) The trustee must, however, prove that the debtor was insolvent when the transfer occurred and that it was made to or for the benefit of an insider.

**Transfers That Do Not Constitute Preferences.** Not all transfers are preferences. Most courts generally assume that payment for services rendered *within fifteen days* before the payment is not a preference. If a creditor receives payment in the ordinary course of business from a debtor, such as payment of last month's cell phone bill, the bankruptcy trustee cannot recover the payment.

To be recoverable, a preference must be a transfer for an antecedent (preexisting) debt, such as a year-old landscaping bill. In addition, the Code permits a consumer-debtor to transfer any property to a creditor up to a total value of $6,225 without the transfer's constituting a preference. Payment of domestic-support debts does not constitute a preference.

**Fraudulent Transfers** The trustee may avoid fraudulent transfers or obligations if they (1) were made within two years prior to the filing of the petition or (2) were made with actual intent to hinder, delay, or defraud a creditor. ■ **EXAMPLE 21.4** Amy is planning to petition for bankruptcy, so she sells her gold jewelry, worth $10,000, to a friend for $500. The friend agrees that in

---

10. Usually, though, the trustee takes constructive, rather than actual, possession of the debtor's property. For instance, to obtain control of a debtor's business inventory, a trustee might change the locks on the doors to the business and hire a security guard.

11. Under a Chapter 11 bankruptcy, for which no trustee other than the debtor generally exists, the debtor has the same avoidance powers as a trustee under Chapter 7. Under Chapters 12 and 13, a trustee must be appointed.

the future he will "sell" the jewelry back to Amy for the same amount. This is a fraudulent transfer that the trustee can undo. ∎

Transfers made for less than reasonably equivalent consideration are also vulnerable if the debtor thereby became insolvent or was left engaged in business with an unreasonably small amount of capital. When a fraudulent transfer is made outside the Code's two-year limit, creditors may seek alternative relief under state laws. Some state laws may allow creditors to recover transfers made up to three years before the filing of a petition.

## 21–2f Exemptions

As just described, the trustee takes control of the debtor's property in a Chapter 7 bankruptcy, but an individual debtor is entitled to exempt (exclude) certain property from the bankruptcy.

**Federal Exemptions** The Bankruptcy Code exempts the following property, up to a specified dollar amount that changes every three years:[12]

1. A portion of equity in the debtor's home (the homestead exemption).
2. Motor vehicles, up to a certain value (usually just one vehicle).
3. Reasonably necessary clothing, household goods and furnishings, and household appliances (the aggregate value not to exceed a certain amount).
4. Jewelry, up to a certain value.
5. Tools of the debtor's trade or profession, up to a certain value.
6. A portion of unpaid but earned wages.
7. Pensions.
8. Public benefits, including public assistance (welfare), Social Security, and unemployment compensation, accumulated in a bank account.
9. Damages awarded for personal injury up to a certain amount.

Property that is *not* exempt under federal law includes bank accounts, cash, family heirlooms, collections of stamps and coins, second cars, and vacation homes.

**State Exemptions** Individual states have the power to pass legislation precluding debtors from using the federal exemptions within the state. A majority of the states have done this. In those states, debtors may use only state,

not federal, exemptions. In the rest of the states, debtors may choose either the exemptions provided under state law or the federal exemptions.

**Limitations on the Homestead Exemption** The Bankruptcy Code limits the amount of equity that can be claimed under the homestead exemption. In general, if the debtor acquired the homestead within three and a half years preceding the date of filing, the maximum equity exempted is $155,675, even if state law would permit a higher amount.

In addition, the state homestead exemption is available only if the debtor has lived in a state for two years before filing the bankruptcy petition. Furthermore, a debtor who has violated securities laws, been convicted of a felony, or engaged in certain other intentional misconduct may not be permitted to claim the homestead exemption.

## 21–2g Creditors' Meeting

Within a reasonable time after the order for relief has been granted (not more than forty days), the trustee must call a meeting of the creditors listed in the schedules filed by the debtor. The bankruptcy judge does not attend this meeting. The debtor is required to attend (unless excused by the court) and to submit to examination under oath by the creditors and the trustee. At the meeting, the trustee ensures that the debtor is aware of the potential consequences of bankruptcy and of the possibility of filing under a different chapter of the Code.

## 21–2h Creditors' Claims

To be entitled to receive a portion of the debtor's estate, each creditor normally files a *proof of claim* with the bankruptcy court within ninety days of the creditors' meeting. A proof of claim is necessary if there is any dispute concerning the claim. The proof of claim lists the creditor's name and address, as well as the amount that the creditor asserts is owed to the creditor by the debtor.

When the debtor has no assets—called a "no-asset case"—creditors are notified of the debtor's petition for bankruptcy but are instructed not to file a claim. In no-asset cases, the unsecured creditors will receive no payment, and most, if not all, of these debts will be discharged.

## 21–2i Distribution of Property

The Code provides specific rules for the distribution of the debtor's property to secured and unsecured creditors.

---

12. The dollar amounts stated in the Bankruptcy Code are adjusted automatically every three years on April 1 based on changes in the Consumer Price Index. The adjusted amounts are rounded to the nearest $25.

If any amount remains after the priority classes of creditors have been satisfied, it is turned over to the debtor.

### Distribution to Secured Creditors

The Code requires that consumer-debtors file a statement of intention with respect to secured collateral. They can choose to pay off the debt and redeem the collateral, claim it is exempt, reaffirm the debt and continue making payments, or surrender the property to the secured party.

If the collateral is surrendered to the secured party, the secured creditor can enforce the security interest. The secured party can either (1) accept the property in full satisfaction of the debt or (2) sell the collateral and use the proceeds to pay off the debt. Thus, the secured party has priority over unsecured parties as to the proceeds from the disposition of the collateral. Should the collateral be insufficient to cover the secured debt owed, the secured creditor becomes an unsecured creditor for the difference (deficiency).

There are limited exceptions to these rules. For instance, certain unsecured creditors can sometimes step into the shoes of secured tax creditors in Chapter 7 liquidation proceedings. In such situations, when the collateral securing the tax claims is sold, the unsecured creditors are paid first. This exception does not include holders of unsecured claims for administrative expenses incurred in Chapter 11 cases that are converted to Chapter 7 liquidations. In the following case, the plaintiff argued that it should.

## Case 21.1

# *In re* Anderson

United States Court of Appeals, Fourth Circuit, 811 F.3d 166 (2016).

**Background and Facts**   Henry Anderson filed a voluntary petition in a federal bankruptcy court for relief under Chapter 11 of the Bankruptcy Code. The U.S. Department of the Treasury, through the Internal Revenue Service (IRS), filed a proof of claim against the bankruptcy estate for $997,551.80, of which $987,082.88 was secured by the debtor's property. Stubbs & Perdue, P.A., served as Anderson's counsel. During the proceedings, the court approved compensation of $200,000 to Stubbs for its services. These fees constituted an unsecured claim against the estate for administrative expenses. Later, Anderson's case was converted to a Chapter 7 liquidation. The trustee accumulated $702,630.25 for distribution to the estate's creditors—not enough to pay the claims of both the IRS and Stubbs. The trustee excluded Stubbs's claim. Stubbs objected. The court dismissed Stubbs's objection. A federal district court upheld the dismissal. Stubbs appealed, arguing that the IRS's claim should be subordinated to Stubbs's claim for fees.

### In the Language of the Court

Pamela *HARRIS,* Circuit Judge:

\* \* \* \*

\* \* \* Before any of the events at issue here, Section 724(b)(2) \* \* \* provided all holders of administrative expense claims, like Stubbs, with the right to subordinate secured tax creditors in Chapter 7 liquidations. But that statutory scheme was criticized on the ground that it created perverse incentives, encouraging Chapter 11 debtors and their representatives to incur administrative expenses even where there was no real hope for a successful reorganization, to the detriment of secured tax creditors when Chapter 7 liquidation ultimately proved necessary.

\* \* \* Congress responded with a fix \* \* \* to limit the class of administrative expenses covered by Section 724(b)(2) \* \* \*. *In order to provide greater protection for holders of tax liens* \* \* \*, *unsecured Chapter 11 administrative expense claims would no longer take priority over secured tax claims in Chapter 7 liquidations.* [Emphasis added.]

\* \* \* \*

\* \* \* The Bankruptcy Technical Corrections Act [BTCA] \* \* \* clarified that Chapter 11 administrative expense claimants do not hold subordination rights under Section 724(b)(2).

\* \* \* Eleven months later, the Debtor's bankruptcy case converted from Chapter 11 to Chapter 7, implicating Section 724(b)(2) for the first time.

\* \* \* \*

\* \* \* *As a general rule, a court is to apply the law in effect at the time it renders its decision.* [Emphasis added.]

Case 21.1 Continues

* * * *

Stubbs argues, however, that it would be unjust to apply the BTCA version of Section 724(b)(2) * * * to disallow payment on its unsecured claim for Chapter 11 fees. Prior to the BTCA, Stubbs contends, it was entitled to subordinate the IRS's secured claim.

The problem with Stubbs's argument is its premise: that Stubbs held subordination rights under Section 724(b)(2) before the BTCA was enacted * * * . Before the BTCA was enacted, Section 724(b)(2) had no application to the Debtor's case at all. It afforded Stubbs no entitlement to subordinate the IRS's secured tax claim for the threshold reason that it simply did not apply in the Chapter 11 proceedings that began in this case * * * and did not end until * * * eleven months *after* the BTCA's passage. The pre-BTCA version of Section 724(b)(2) that Stubbs invokes, in other words, never controlled this case.

**Decision and Remedy** *The U.S. Court of Appeals for the Fourth Circuit affirmed the dismissal of Stubbs's claim. Under Section 724(b)(2), "it is clear that Stubbs is not entitled to subordinate the IRS's secured tax claim in favor of its unsecured claim to Chapter 11 administrative expenses."*

**Critical Thinking**
- **Legal Environment** *Why, as a general rule, should a court apply the law that is in effect at the time the court renders its decision?*
- **What If the Facts Were Different?** *Suppose that Anderson had filed his initial bankruptcy petition under Chapter 7, not under Chapter 11. Would the result have been different? Discuss.*

---

**Distribution to Unsecured Creditors** Bankruptcy law establishes an order of priority for debts owed to *unsecured* creditors, and they are paid in the order of their priority. Claims for domestic-support obligations, such as child support and alimony, have the highest priority among unsecured creditors, so these claims must be paid first. Each class, or group, must be fully paid before the next class is entitled to any of the remaining proceeds.

If there are insufficient proceeds to fully pay all the creditors in a class, the proceeds are distributed *proportionately* to the creditors in that class. Classes lower in priority receive nothing. In almost all Chapter 7 bankruptcies, the funds will be insufficient to pay all creditors.

Exhibit 21–1 illustrates the collection and distribution of property in most voluntary bankruptcies. The exhibit includes a listing of the classes of unsecured creditors.

## 21–2j Discharge

From the debtor's point of view, the primary purpose of liquidation is to obtain a fresh start through a discharge of debts. A discharge voids, or sets aside, any judgment on a discharged debt and prevents any action to collect it. Certain debts, however, are not dischargeable in bankruptcy. Also, certain debtors may not qualify to have all debts discharged in bankruptcy. These situations are discussed next.

**Exceptions to Discharge** Claims that are not dischargeable in bankruptcy include the following:

1. Claims for back taxes accruing within two years prior to bankruptcy.
2. Claims for amounts borrowed by the debtor to pay federal taxes or any nondischargeable taxes.[13]
3. Claims against property or funds obtained by the debtor under false pretenses or by false representations.
4. Claims by creditors who were not notified of the bankruptcy. These claims did not appear on the schedules the debtor was required to file.
5. Claims based on fraud[14] or misuse of funds by the debtor while acting in a fiduciary capacity or claims involving the debtor's embezzlement or larceny.
6. Domestic-support obligations and property settlements as provided for in a separation agreement or divorce decree.
7. Claims for amounts due on a retirement account loan.
8. Claims based on willful or malicious conduct by the debtor toward another or the property of another. ■ **CASE IN POINT 21.5** Anthony Mickletz owned a pizza restaurant that employed John Carmello.

---

13. Taxes accruing within three years prior to bankruptcy are nondischargeable, including federal and state income taxes, employment taxes, taxes on gross receipts, property taxes, excise taxes, customs duties, and any other taxes for which the government claims the debtor is liable in some capacity. See 11 U.S.C. Sections 507(a)(8) and 523(a)(1).

14. Even if a debtor who is sued for fraud settles the lawsuit, the settlement agreement may not be discharged in bankruptcy because of the underlying fraud. See *Archer v. Warner*, 538 U.S. 314, 123 S.Ct. 1462, 155 L.Ed.2d 454 (2003); and *In re Sager*, ___ Bankr. ___, 2015 WL 1650654 (E.D. Pa. 2015).

**EXHIBIT 21–1** Collection and Distribution of Property in Most Voluntary Bankruptcies

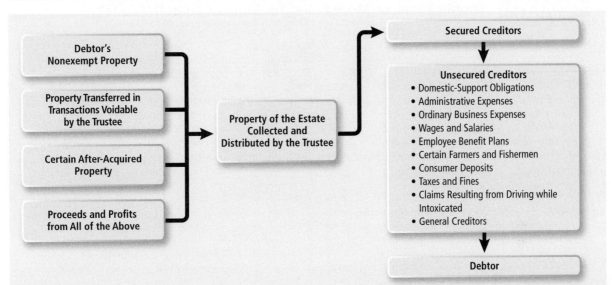

One night after Carmello had finished his shift, Mickletz called him back into the restaurant and accused him of stealing. An argument ensued, and Mickletz shoved Carmello, causing him to fall and injure his back. Because Mickletz did not provide workers' compensation coverage as required by law, the state prosecuted him criminally. He was ordered to pay more than $45,000 in restitution to Carmello for his injuries. Carmello also filed a civil suit against Mickletz, which the parties agreed to settle for $175,000. Later, Mickletz filed a petition for bankruptcy. Carmello argued that these debts were nondischargeable, and the court agreed. The exception from discharge includes any debts for willful (deliberate or intentional) injury, and Mickletz's actions were deliberate.[15] ■

9. Certain government fines and penalties.
10. Student loans, unless payment of the loans imposes an undue hardship on the debtor and the debtor's dependents. (For an example of what constitutes undue hardship, see *Case in Point 21.6*, which follows this list.)
11. Consumer debts of more than $650 for luxury goods or services owed to a single creditor incurred within ninety days of the order for relief.
12. Cash advances totaling more than $925 that are extensions of open-end consumer credit obtained by the debtor within seventy days of the order for relief.
13. Judgments against a debtor as a result of the debtor's operation of a motor vehicle while intoxicated.

14. Fees or assessments arising from property in a homeowners' association, as long as the debtor retained an interest in the property.
15. Taxes with respect to which the debtor failed to provide required or requested tax documents.

■ **CASE IN POINT 21.6** At the time he filed for Chapter 7 bankruptcy, Terence Wolfe had not been consistently employed for twenty years. He had been fired from numerous positions for behavioral issues and had difficulty finding and holding a job. Wolfe had been diagnosed with personality disorders and ultimately was granted disability status by the U.S. government. He was living on disability payments of $1,126 per month at the time he filed for Chapter 7 bankruptcy.

Among Wolfe's debts were more than $131,000 in student loan debts. Wolfe sought to have these debts discharged because repaying them would constitute undue hardship. The court agreed and granted a discharge. According to the court, although Wolfe is intelligent, "he has been unable, for more than two decades, to maintain full-time employment for any meaningful length of time. He is living at a minimal standard of living and it is unlikely that he will ever be able to repay these loans."[16] ■

See this chapter's *Ethics Today* feature for a discussion of whether the law should make it easier to obtain a discharge of student loan debts.

15. *In re Mickletz*, 544 Bankr. 804 (E.D.Pa. 2016).

16. *In re Wolfe*, 501 Bankr. 426, 24 Fla.L.WeeklyFed. B235 (M.D.Fla. 2011).

## ETHICS TODAY    Should There Be More Relief for Student Loan Defaults?

According to many observers, student loan debt has reached crisis levels in the United States. Outstanding student loan balances total $1.2 *trillion* nationally and are growing by around $3,000 *per second*. About 20 percent are ninety or more days' delinquent or are in default. That is the highest delinquency rate among all forms of debt, including credit cards, automobile loans, and mortgages. The average student loan debt is more than $30,000.

### Consequences of Default

Any student borrower who has not made regular payments for nine months is in default. If you are in default on a student loan, the U.S. Department of Education can do any of the following to collect:

1. Keep your tax refund if you were supposed to receive one.
2. Garnish your paycheck without obtaining a court judgment.
3. Take your federal benefits, such as Social Security retirement payments or disability payments.

In addition, in some states any professional license that you have can be revoked. The Department of Education can also bring a lawsuit against you. If it wins, it can collect the judgment from your bank accounts or place a lien on any real property that you own.

### Caps on Interest Rates, Forgiveness, and Income-Based Plans

Recently, Congress attempted to ease the burden on student loan debtors by reducing the interest rates they can be charged. In addition, President Barack Obama signed an executive order putting into place an income-based repayment plan. This plan caps

payments at no more than 10 percent of disposable income. Any balance not paid off after twenty years will be forgiven.

Should the federal government go further? Yes, at least according to President Obama. In 2015, Obama signed a presidential memorandum titled "Student Aid Bill of Rights."

The memorandum directs the Department of Education to implement actions to ensure that the debt collection process for defaulted student loans "is fair, transparent, [and] charges reasonable fees to defaulted borrowers."

Critics point out that such student loan debt forgiveness could have a cost. They claim that colleges and universities might "hint" to potential students that they need not worry about taking on higher student loans because some portion will be forgiven by the federal government.

### Political Impetus

Politicians are increasingly discussing student loan debt and the costs of higher education. Some are asking Congress to allow federal student loans to be discharged in most bankruptcy proceedings. Others advocate making college education free or at least reducing the costs charged to certain students. One plan calls for allowing students to refinance their loans at very low interest rates. Another proposal is to prohibit the federal government from profiting from student loan debt (the government brings in more than $41 billion a year from student loans).

**Critical Thinking** *Why does the Bankruptcy Code provide that student loans should not be dischargeable unless there is undue hardship? What argument can be made in favor of allowing student loans to be dischargeable?*

---

Today, however, the federal government guarantees many student loans (similar to the way the government backs certain mortgages). When student loans are guaranteed, the lenders are not affected by default in the same way and have no reason to refuse to finance education. This bolsters the argument that student loan debts should be dischargeable in the same way as other types of debts.

**Objections to Discharge** In addition to the exceptions to discharge previously discussed, a bankruptcy court may also deny discharge based on the debtor's *conduct.* Grounds for denial of discharge of the debtor include the following:

1. The debtor's concealment or destruction of property with the intent to hinder, delay, or defraud a creditor.
2. The debtor's fraudulent concealment or destruction of financial records.
3. The grant of a discharge to the debtor within eight years before the petition was filed.
4. The debtor's failure to complete the required consumer education course.
5. The debtor's involvement in proceedings in which the debtor could be found guilty of a felony. (Basically, a court may not discharge any debt until the completion of felony proceedings against the debtor.)

When a discharge is denied under any of these circumstances, the debtor's assets are still distributed to the creditors. After the bankruptcy proceeding, however, the debtor remains liable for the unpaid portion of all claims.

In addition, a discharge may be revoked (taken back) within one year if it is discovered that the debtor acted fraudulently or dishonestly during the bankruptcy proceeding. If that occurs, a creditor whose claim was not satisfied in the distribution of the debtor's property can proceed with his or her claim against the debtor.

Whether a bankruptcy court properly denied a discharge based on the debtors' conduct was the issue in the following case.

## Case 21.2

## *In re* Cummings
United States Court of Appeals, Ninth Circuit, 595 Fed.Appx. 707 (2015).

**Background and Facts**  Clarence and Pamela Cummings filed a petition for a Chapter 7 bankruptcy in a federal bankruptcy court. After the debtors filed two amended versions of the required schedules, the trustee asked for additional time to investigate. The court granted the request. The debtors then filed a third amended schedule. In it, they disclosed for the first time the existence of First Beacon Management Company, a corporation that they planned to use as part of their postbankruptcy "fresh start."

The trustee claimed that the Cummingses' failure to disclose their interest in First Beacon was a "false oath relating to a material fact made knowingly and fraudulently" in violation of the Bankruptcy Code. The court agreed and denied the debtors a discharge. The Bankruptcy Appellate Panel (BAP) affirmed the court's decision. The Cummingses appealed.

### In the Language of the Court
*MEMORANDUM.*
\* \* \* \*

Chapter 7 debtors Clarence Thomas Cummings and Pamela K. Cummings appeal the judgment of the Bankruptcy Appellate Panel ("BAP") affirming \* \* \* the bankruptcy court's order denying discharge on the ground that the debtors made false oaths \* \* \* . The bankruptcy court rejected the explanatory testimony of Mr. Cummings as "not credible" and "beyond not credible" and the BAP found that "there is ample evidence to support the bankruptcy court's findings.
\* \* \* \*

\* \* \* Debtors claim that the bankruptcy court failed to consider other "voluminous independent and undisputed documentary evidence" introduced at trial that, they assert, "completely obliterated any suggestion of fraudulent intent."

\* \* \* These materials do not advance debtors' claim of inadvertence [lack of intent] or otherwise suggest bankruptcy court error. To the contrary, *the documents corroborate the obviousness of debtors' fraud and the objective it advanced, [namely], to insulate First Beacon Management Co.,* \* \* \* *the new corporate anchor of their post-petition fresh start, from the stigma of bankruptcy.* [Emphasis added.]

Debtors' eventual disclosure of their interest in First Beacon on their third amended Schedule \* \* \* does not negate their initial fraud. To the contrary, the sequence of debtors' filings substantiates the presence of fraud: they elected, twice, to amend their Schedule \* \* \* without adding First Beacon, and disclosed First Beacon only after the issuance of an order granting the Trustee additional time to investigate.
\* \* \* \*

The Trustee fully carried its burden of proving by a preponderance of the evidence \* \* \* that under the circumstances, debtors' failure to disclose their interest in First Beacon as debtor property was a "false oath" relating to a material fact made knowingly and fraudulently.

**Decision and Remedy**  The U.S. Court of Appeals for the Ninth Circuit affirmed the ruling of the Bankruptcy Appellate Panel. The Cummingses' bankruptcy filings revealed the presence of fraud. Thus, their Chapter 7 petition for discharge of their debts was denied.

### Critical Thinking
• **Economic**  *Why would a debtor risk the denial of a discharge to conceal assets? Discuss.*

## 21–2k Reaffirmation of Debt

An agreement to pay a debt dischargeable in bankruptcy is called a **reaffirmation agreement.** A debtor may wish to pay a debt—such as a debt owed to a family member, physician, bank, or some other creditor—even though the debt could be discharged in bankruptcy. Also, as noted previously, a debtor cannot retain secured property while continuing to pay without entering into a reaffirmation agreement.

**Procedures** To be enforceable, reaffirmation agreements must be made before the debtor is granted a discharge. The agreement must be signed and filed with the court. Court approval is required unless the debtor is represented by an attorney during the negotiation of the reaffirmation and submits the proper documents and certifications. Even when the debtor is represented by an attorney, court approval may be required if it appears that the reaffirmation will result in undue hardship to the debtor.

When court approval is required, a separate hearing will take place. The court will approve the reaffirmation only if it finds that the agreement will not result in undue hardship to the debtor and that the reaffirmation is consistent with the debtor's best interests.

**Required Disclosures** To discourage creditors from engaging in abusive reaffirmation practices, the law provides specific language for disclosures that must be given to debtors entering into reaffirmation agreements. Among other things, these disclosures explain that the debtor is not required to reaffirm any debt. They also inform the debtor that liens on secured property, such as mortgages and cars, will remain in effect even if the debt is not reaffirmed.

The reaffirmation agreement must disclose the amount of the debt reaffirmed, the rate of interest, the date payments begin, and the right to rescind. The disclosures also caution the debtor: "Only agree to reaffirm a debt if it is in your best interest. Be sure you can afford the payments you agree to make."

The original disclosure documents must be signed by the debtor, certified by the debtor's attorney, and filed with the court at the same time as the reaffirmation agreement. A reaffirmation agreement that is not accompanied by the original signed disclosures will not be effective.

■ **CASE IN POINT 21.7** Howard Lapides, who owned a seafood import business, signed a secured promissory note for $400,000 with Venture Bank for a revolving line-of-credit loan. Part of the collateral for that loan was a third mortgage on the Lapideses' home (two other

banks held prior mortgages). Eventually, Howard and his wife filed for Chapter 7 bankruptcy protection, and their personal debts were discharged. Afterward, Venture Bank convinced the Lapideses to sign a reaffirmation agreement by telling them that it would refinance all three mortgages so that they could keep their house.

The Lapideses made twelve $3,500 payments to Venture Bank, but when the bank did not refinance the other mortgages, they stopped making payments. Venture Bank filed suit, but a court refused to enforce the reaffirmation agreement because it violated the Bankruptcy Code. The agreement had never been signed by Lapideses' attorney or filed with the bankruptcy court.[17] ■

# 21–3 Reorganizations

The type of bankruptcy proceeding most commonly used by corporate debtors is the Chapter 11 *reorganization*. In a reorganization, the creditors and the debtor formulate a plan under which the debtor pays a portion of the debts and is discharged of the remainder. The debtor is allowed to continue in business.

As noted, this type of bankruptcy generally involves a corporate reorganization. Nevertheless, any debtor (except a stockbroker or a commodities broker) who is eligible for Chapter 7 relief is eligible for relief under Chapter 11. Railroads are also eligible.

Congress has established a "fast-track" Chapter 11 procedure for small-business debtors whose liabilities do not exceed $2.49 million and who do not own or manage real estate. The fast track enables a debtor to avoid the appointment of a creditors' committee and also shortens the filing periods and relaxes certain other requirements. Because the process is shorter and simpler, it is less costly.

The same principles that govern the filing of a liquidation (Chapter 7) petition apply to reorganization (Chapter 11) proceedings. The case may be brought either voluntarily or involuntarily. The automatic-stay provision and its exceptions (such as substantial abuse), as well as the adequate protection doctrine, apply in reorganizations.

## 21–3a Workouts

In some instances, to avoid bankruptcy proceedings, creditors may prefer private, negotiated adjustments of creditor-debtor relations, also known as **workouts.** Often, these out-of-court workouts are much more

---

17. *Venture Bank v. Lapides,* 800 F.3d 442 (8th Cir. 2015).

flexible and thus more conducive to a speedy settlement. Speed is critical because delay is one of the most costly elements in any bankruptcy proceeding. Another advantage of workouts is that they avoid the various administrative costs of bankruptcy proceedings.

## 21-3b  Best Interests of the Creditors

Once a Chapter 11 petition has been filed, a bankruptcy court can dismiss or suspend proceedings at any time if dismissal or suspension would better serve the interests of the creditors. Before taking such an action, the court must give notice and conduct a hearing. The Code also allows a court, after notice and a hearing, to dismiss a case under reorganization "for cause" when there is no reasonable likelihood of rehabilitation. Similarly, a court can dismiss when there is an inability to effect a plan or an unreasonable delay by the debtor that may harm the interests of creditors. A debtor whose petition is dismissed for these reasons can file a subsequent Chapter 11 petition in the future.[18]

## 21-3c  Debtor in Possession

On entry of the order for relief, the debtor generally continues to operate the business as a **debtor in possession (DIP).** The court, however, may appoint a trustee (often referred to as a *receiver*) to operate the debtor's business. The court will choose this action if gross mismanagement of the business is shown or if appointing a trustee is in the best interests of the estate.

The DIP's role is similar to that of a trustee in a liquidation bankruptcy.[19] The DIP is entitled to avoid preferential payments made to creditors and fraudulent transfers of assets. The DIP can also exercise a trustee's strong-arm powers. The DIP has the power to decide whether to cancel or assume prepetition executory contracts (contracts that are not yet performed) or unexpired leases.

Cancellation of executory contracts or unexpired leases can be of substantial benefit to a Chapter 11 debtor. ■ **EXAMPLE 21.8**  Five years ago, APT Corporation leased an office building for a twenty-year term. Now, APT can no longer pay the rent due under the lease and has filed for Chapter 11 reorganization. In this situation, the debtor in possession can cancel the lease, and APT will not be required to continue paying the substantial rent due for fifteen more years. ■

## 21-3d  Creditors' Committees

As soon as practicable after the entry of the order for relief, a creditors' committee of unsecured creditors is appointed.[20] The business's suppliers may serve on the committee. The committee can consult with the trustee or the DIP concerning the administration of the case or the formulation of the plan. Additional creditors' committees may be appointed to represent special interest creditors.

Generally, no orders affecting the estate will be entered without the consent of the committee or after a hearing in which the judge is informed of the committee's position. As mentioned earlier, businesses with debts of less than $2.49 million that do not own or manage real estate can avoid creditors' committees. In these fast-track proceedings, orders can be entered without a committee's consent.

## 21-3e  The Reorganization Plan

A reorganization plan to rehabilitate the debtor is a plan to conserve and administer the debtor's assets in the hope of an eventual return to successful operation and solvency. The plan must be fair and equitable and must do the following:

1.  Designate classes of claims and interests.
2.  Specify the treatment to be afforded to the classes of creditors. (The plan must provide the same treatment for all claims in a particular class.)
3.  Provide an adequate means for the plan's execution. (Individual debtors are required to utilize postpetition assets as necessary to execute the plan.)
4.  Provide for payment of tax claims over a five-year period.

The plan need not provide for full repayment to unsecured creditors. Instead, creditors receive a percentage of each dollar owed to them by the debtor.

**Filing the Plan**  Only the debtor may file a plan within the first 120 days after the date of the order for relief. This period may be extended, but not beyond eighteen months from the date of the order for relief. If the debtor does not meet the 120-day deadline or obtain an extension, any party may propose a plan. If a small-business debtor chooses to avoid a creditors' committee, the time for the debtor's filing is 180 days.

**Acceptance of the Plan**  Once the plan has been developed, it is submitted to each class of creditors for

---

**18.** See 11 U.S.C. Section 1112(b).
**19.** 11 U.S.C. Section 544(a).

**20.** If the debtor has filed a reorganization plan accepted by the creditors, the trustee may decide not to call a meeting of the creditors.

acceptance. For the plan to be adopted, each class must accept it. A class has accepted the plan when a majority of the creditors in the class, representing two-thirds of the amount of the total claim, vote to approve it. If the debtor fails to procure creditor consent of the plan within 180 days, any party may propose a plan.

**Confirmation of the Plan** Confirmation is conditioned on the debtor's certifying that all postpetition domestic-support obligations have been paid in full. In addition, even when all classes of creditors accept the plan, the court may refuse to confirm it if it is not "in the best interests of the creditors." For small-business debtors, if the plan meets the listed requirements, the court must confirm the plan within forty-five days (unless this period is extended).

The plan can be modified on the request of the debtor, the DIP, the trustee, the U.S. trustee, or a holder of an unsecured claim. If an unsecured creditor objects to the plan, specific rules apply to the value of property to be distributed under the plan. Tax claims must be paid over a five-year period.

Even if only one class of creditors has accepted the plan, the court may still confirm the plan under the Code's so-called **cram-down provision.** In other words, the court may confirm the plan over the objections of a class of creditors. Before the court can exercise the right of cram-down confirmation, it must be demonstrated that the plan does not discriminate unfairly against any creditors and is fair and equitable.

**Discharge** The plan is binding on confirmation. Nevertheless, the law provides that confirmation of a plan does not discharge an individual debtor. *For individual debtors, the plan must be completed before discharge will be granted,* unless the court orders otherwise. For all other debtors, the court may order discharge at any time after the plan is confirmed.

On discharge, the debtor is given a reorganization discharge from all claims not protected under the plan. This discharge does not apply to any claims that would be denied discharge under liquidation.

# 21–4 Bankruptcy Relief under Chapter 12 and Chapter 13

In addition to bankruptcy relief through liquidation and reorganization, the Code also provides for family-farmer and family-fisherman debt adjustments (Chapter 12) and

individuals' repayment plans (Chapter 13). The procedures for filing Chapter 12 and Chapter 13 plans are very similar. Because Chapter 13 plans are the more commonly used of the two types, we discuss Chapter 13 first.

## 21–4a Individuals' Repayment Plans—Chapter 13

Chapter 13 of the Bankruptcy Code provides for "Adjustment of Debts of an Individual with Regular Income." Individuals with regular income who owe fixed (liquidated) unsecured debts of less than $383,175 or fixed secured debts of less than $1,149,525 may take advantage of bankruptcy repayment plans. Partnerships and corporations are excluded.

Among those eligible are salaried employees and sole proprietors, as well as individuals who live on welfare, Social Security, fixed pensions, or investment income. Many small-business debtors have a choice of filing under either Chapter 11 or Chapter 13. Repayment plans offer some advantages because they are less expensive and less complicated than reorganization or liquidation proceedings.

**Filing the Petition** A Chapter 13 repayment plan case can be initiated only by the debtor's filing of a voluntary petition or by court conversion of a Chapter 7 petition. Recall that a court may convert a Chapter 7 petition because of a finding of substantial abuse under the means test. In addition, certain liquidation and reorganization cases may be converted to repayment plan cases with the consent of the debtor.[21]

A trustee, who will make payments under the plan, must be appointed. On the filing of a repayment plan petition, the automatic stay previously discussed takes effect. Although the stay applies to all or part of the debtor's consumer debt, it does not apply to any business debt incurred by the debtor or to any domestic-support obligations.

**Good Faith Requirement** The Bankruptcy Code imposes the requirement of good faith on a debtor at both the time of the filing of the petition and the time of the filing of the plan. The Code does not define good faith, but if the circumstances on the whole indicate bad faith, a court can dismiss a debtor's Chapter 13 petition.

---

21. A Chapter 13 repayment plan may be converted to a Chapter 7 liquidation at the request of the debtor or, under certain circumstances, by a creditor "for cause." A Chapter 13 case may be converted to a Chapter 11 case after a hearing.

In determining whether a Chapter 13 plan was proposed in good faith, should the bankruptcy court consider whether the debtor included his Social Security income in the amount of disposable income available for payment of unsecured creditors? That was the issue in the following case.

**Case Analysis 21.3**

# *In re* Welsh

United States Court of Appeals, Ninth Circuit, 711 F.3d 1120 (2013).

## In the Language of the Court

*RIPPLE,* Senior Circuit Judge:

\* \* \* \*

[David and Sharon Welsh] filed a voluntary Chapter 13 petition [in a federal bankruptcy court]. Their required schedules revealed the following assets: a home in Missoula, Montana, valued at $400,000, encumbered by a secured claim of $330,593.66; a Ford F-250 valued at $10,000, encumbered by a secured claim of $18,959; a 2006 Subaru Outback valued at of $9,500, encumbered by a secured claim of $12,211; a 2005 Toyota Matrix valued at $2,200, encumbered by a secured claim of $1,996; a 2005 Airstream trailer valued at $23,000, encumbered by a secured claim of $39,000; and two 2007 Honda ATVs each valued at $2,700, encumbered by secured claims of $3,065 and $4,500. In addition to their secured debts, the schedules revealed unsecured claims totaling approximately $180,500, the largest of which were their daughter's student loan debt in the amount of $60,000 and a joint debt owed to Bank of America on a line of credit in the amount of $50,000.

Mrs. Welsh is employed as a nurse and reported on Schedule I a monthly income of $6,975.40. She also draws a pension of $1,100 per month. Mr. Welsh is retired, but listed a monthly income of $358.03 from wages, salary and commissions, as well as Social Security income in the amount of $1,165.

Because their income exceeds the median for the state of Montana, the debtors calculated their disposable income according to the means test. \* \* \* They listed their current monthly income as $8,116.31; their current monthly income did not include Mr.

Welsh's Social Security income of $1,165 because Social Security income is excluded from the current monthly income calculation. After deducting future payments on secured claims, the debtors were left with a disposable income of $218.12 per month.

The Welshes proposed a plan that provided for payments of $125 per month to unsecured creditors for the first thirty months of the plan. After their vehicle loans were paid, the payments would increase to $500 per month for the last thirty months of the plan. The proposed plan would pay off approximately $14,700 of the debtors' $180,500 unsecured debt.

The [Bankruptcy] Trustee objected on the ground that the debtors had not proposed their plan in good faith \* \* \* because [they failed] to commit one hundred percent of their disposable income to the plan.

\* \* \* \*

The bankruptcy court \* \* \* rejected the Trustee's argument.

[On the Trustee's appeal] the [Bankruptcy Appellate Panel (BAP) for the Ninth Circuit] affirmed the bankruptcy court's judgment.

\* \* \* \*

In this appeal, the Trustee \* \* \* maintains that, in determining whether the Welshes proposed their Chapter 13 plan in good faith, the bankruptcy court \* \* \* should have considered Mr. Welsh's Social Security income.

\* \* \* \*

In 2005, Congress \* \* \* enacted the Bankruptcy Abuse Prevention and Consumer Protection Act ("BAPCPA"). The good faith requirement \* \* \* remained the same, but there were significant changes with respect to the calculation

of disposable income. Before the BAP-CPA, bankruptcy judges had authority to determine a debtor's ability to pay based on the individual circumstances of each case and each debtor. Congress replaced this discretion with a detailed, mechanical means test, which requires debtors with above-median income to calculate their "disposable income" by subtracting specific expenses from "current monthly income," as defined by the Bankruptcy Code. For our purposes, several elements of this calculation are important. *The debtor begins with his "current monthly income," which, by definition, explicitly "excludes benefits received under the Social Security Act."* The debtor then subtracts living expenses based on the Internal Revenue Service's "Collection Financial Standards," a detailed series of averages for living expenses that the Service uses to calculate necessary expenditures for delinquent taxpayers. The debtor also subtracts his averaged payments to secured creditors due during the following sixty months. [Emphasis added.]

As is the case here, the manner in which the means test calculates "disposable income" may underestimate the amount of actual funds that a taxpayer has available to pay unsecured creditors. A debtor who receives Social Security income \* \* \* does not have to account for that income when calculating "disposable income" according to the means test. \* \* \* The result may be that \* \* \* little "disposable income," as that figure is calculated, remains to pay unsecured creditors.

\* \* \* \*

Here, the Trustee does not contend, of course, that the calculation of

Case 21.3 Continues

disposable income should have incorporated Social Security income; the statutory language is clearly to the contrary. Instead, he concedes that disposable income was calculated correctly under the BAPCPA, but nevertheless maintains that the Welshes' failure to dedicate Mr. Welsh's Social Security income to the payment of unsecured creditors requires a conclusion that the plan was not proposed in good faith * * * . We cannot conclude, however, that a plan prepared completely in accordance with the very detailed calculations that Congress set forth is not proposed in good faith. To hold otherwise would be to allow the bankruptcy court to substitute its judgment of how much and what kind of income should be dedicated to the payment of unsecured creditors for the judgment of Congress. Such an approach would not only flout the express language of Congress, but also one of Congress's purposes in enacting the BAPCPA, namely to reduce the amount of discretion that bankruptcy courts previously had over the calculation of an above-median debtor's income and expenses.

* * * *

We conclude that Congress's adoption of the BAPCPA forecloses a court's consideration of a debtor's Social Security income * * * as part of the inquiry into good faith * * * . We therefore affirm the judgment of the BAP.

**Legal Reasoning Questions**

1. On what ground did the trustee contend that the debtors had not proposed their Chapter 13 plan in good faith?
2. How did the court rule with respect to the trustee's argument? Why?
3. In evaluating a debtor's petition, what factors should be part of a good faith analysis? Should consideration of the calculation of disposable income play a role? Why or why not?

**The Repayment Plan** A plan of rehabilitation by repayment must provide for the following:

1. The turning over to the trustee of such future earnings or income of the debtor as is necessary for execution of the plan.
2. Full payment through deferred cash payments of all claims entitled to priority, such as taxes.[22]
3. Identical treatment of all claims within a particular class. (The Code permits the debtor to list co-debtors, such as guarantors or sureties, as a separate class.)

The repayment plan may provide either for payment of all obligations in full or for payment of a lesser amount. The debtor must begin making payments under the proposed plan within thirty days after the plan has been filed and must continue to make "timely" payments.[23] If the debtor fails to make timely payments or to commence payments within the thirty-day period, the court can convert the case to a Chapter 7 bankruptcy or dismiss the petition.

**Allowable Expenses.** In putting together a repayment plan, a debtor must apply the means test to identify the amount of disposable income that will be available to repay creditors. The debtor is allowed to deduct certain expenses from monthly income to arrive at this amount, but only if they are appropriate.

■ **CASE IN POINT 21.9** Jason Ransom filed a Chapter 13 bankruptcy petition. Among his assets, he listed a Toyota Camry that he owned free of any debt. In his monthly expenses, he claimed a car-ownership deduction of $471 and a separate $388 deduction for costs to operate the car. He proposed a five-year plan that would repay about 25 percent of his unsecured debt.

FIA Card Services, N.A., an unsecured creditor, objected to the plan. FIA argued that Ransom was not entitled to the car-ownership allowance because he did not owe money on the car. Ultimately, the United States Supreme Court ruled in FIA's favor. A deduction is appropriate only if the debtor will incur that expense during the life of the Chapter 13 plan. A debtor who does not make loan or lease payments may not take a car-ownership deduction.[24] ■

**Length of the Plan.** The length of the payment plan can be three or five years, depending on the debtor's family income. If the family income is greater than the median family income in the relevant geographic area under the

---

22. As with a Chapter 11 reorganization plan, full repayment of all claims is not always required.
23. The bankruptcy trustee holds on to these payments until the court either confirms or denies the debtor's plan. If the court confirms the plan, the trustee distributes the funds to creditors as stated in the plan. If the court denies the debtor's plan, the trustee returns the funds, minus administrative expenses, to the debtor.
24. *Ransom v. FIA Card Services, N.A.,* 562 U.S. 61, 131 S.Ct. 716, 178 L.Ed.2d 603 (2011).

means test, the term of the proposed plan must be three years.[25] The term may not exceed five years.

**Confirmation of the Plan.** After the plan is filed, the court holds a confirmation hearing, at which interested parties (such as creditors) may object to the plan. The hearing must be held at least twenty days, but no more than forty-five days, after the meeting of the creditors. The debtor must have filed all prepetition tax returns and paid all postpetition domestic-support obligations before a court will confirm any plan.

The court will confirm a plan with respect to each claim of a secured creditor under any of the following circumstances:

1. If the secured creditors have accepted the plan.
2. If the plan provides that secured creditors retain their liens until there is payment in full or until the debtor receives a discharge.
3. If the debtor surrenders the property securing the claims to the creditors.

In addition, for a motor vehicle purchased within 910 days before the petition is filed, the plan must provide that a creditor with a purchase-money security interest (PMSI) retains its lien until the entire debt is paid. For PMSIs on other personal property, the payment plan must cover debts incurred within a one-year period preceding the filing.

**Discharge** After the debtor has completed all payments, the court grants a discharge of all debts provided for by the repayment plan. Generally, all debts are dischargeable except the following:

1. Allowed claims not provided for by the plan.
2. Certain long-term debts provided for by the plan.
3. Certain tax claims and payments on retirement accounts.
4. Claims for domestic-support obligations.
5. Debts related to injury or property damage caused while driving under the influence of alcohol or drugs.

An order granting discharge is final as to the debts listed in the repayment plan. ■ **CASE IN POINT 21.10** Francisco Espinosa filed a petition for an individual repayment plan under Chapter 13 of the Bankruptcy Code. His plan proposed to pay only the principal on his student loan and to discharge the interest. United Student Aid Funds, Inc. (the creditor), had notice of the plan and did not object. The court confirmed the plan without finding that payment of the student loan

interest would cause undue hardship (as required under the Code).

Years later, United filed a motion asking the bankruptcy court to rule that its order confirming the plan was void because it was in violation of the rules governing bankruptcy. The court denied United's petition and ordered the creditor to cease its collection efforts. The case ultimately reached the United States Supreme Court, which affirmed the lower court's holding that the student loan debt was discharged.[26] ■

## 21-4b Family Farmers and Fishermen—Chapter 12

Congress created Chapter 12 of the Bankruptcy Code to help relieve economic pressure on small farmers. In 2005, Congress extended this protection to family fishermen, modified its provisions somewhat, and made it a permanent chapter in the Bankruptcy Code. (Previously, the statutes authorizing Chapter 12 had to be periodically renewed by Congress.)

Concept Summary 21.1 compares bankruptcy procedures under Chapters 7, 11, 12, and 13.

**Definitions** For purposes of Chapter 12, a *family farmer* is one whose gross income is at least 50 percent farm dependent and whose debts are at least 50 percent farm related. The total debt for a family farmer must not exceed $4,031,575. A partnership or close corporation that is at least 50 percent owned by the farm family can also qualify as a family farmer.[27]

A *family fisherman* is one whose gross income is at least 50 percent dependent on commercial fishing operations[28] and whose debts are at least 80 percent related to commercial fishing. The total debt for a family fisherman must not exceed $1,868,200. As with family farmers, a partnership or close corporation can also qualify.

**Filing the Petition** The procedure for filing a family-farmer or family-fisherman bankruptcy plan is similar to the procedure for filing a repayment plan under Chapter 13. The debtor must file a plan not later than ninety days after the order for relief has been entered. The filing of the

---

25. See 11 U.S.C. Section 1322(d) for details on when the court will find that the Chapter 13 plan should extend to a five-year period.

26. *United Student Aid Funds, Inc. v. Espinosa*, 559 U.S. 260, 130 S.Ct. 1367, 176 L.Ed.2d 158 (2010).
27. Note that for a corporation or partnership to qualify under Chapter 12, at least 80 percent of the value of the firm's assets must consist of assets related to the farming operation.
28. Commercial fishing operations include catching, harvesting, or raising fish, shrimp, lobsters, urchins, seaweed, shellfish, or other aquatic species or products.

# Concept Summary 21.1

## Forms of Bankruptcy Relief Compared

| FORM | CHAPTER 7 | CHAPTER 11 | CHAPTERS 12 AND 13 |
|---|---|---|---|
| Purpose | Liquidation. | Reorganization. | Adjustment. |
| Who Can Petition | Debtor (voluntary) or creditors (involuntary). | Debtor (voluntary) or creditors (involuntary). | Debtor (voluntary) only. |
| Who Can Be a Debtor | Any "person" (including partnerships, corporations, and municipalities) except railroads, insurance companies, banks, savings and loan institutions, investment companies licensed by the Small Business Administration, and credit unions. Farmers and charitable institutions cannot be involuntarily petitioned. If the court finds the petition to be a substantial abuse of the use of Chapter 7, the debtor may be required to convert to a Chapter 13 repayment plan. | Any debtor eligible for Chapter 7 relief. Railroads are also eligible. Individuals have specific rules and limitations. | **Chapter 12**—Any family farmer (one whose gross income is at least 50 percent farm dependent and whose debts are at least 50 percent farm related) or family fisherman (one whose gross income is at least 50 percent dependent on commercial fishing operations and whose debts are at least 80 percent related to commercial fishing) or any partnership or close corporation at least 50 percent owned by a family farmer or fisherman, when total debt does not exceed a specified amount ($4,031,575 for farmers and $1,868,200 for fishermen).<br><br>**Chapter 13**—Any individual (not partnerships or corporations) with regular income who owes fixed (liquidated) unsecured debts of less than $383,175 or fixed secured debts of less than $1,149,525. |
| Procedure Leading to Discharge | Nonexempt property is sold, and the proceeds are distributed (in order) to priority groups. Dischargeable debts are terminated. | Plan is submitted. If the plan is approved and followed, debts are discharged. | Plan is submitted and must be approved if the value of the property to be distributed equals the amount of the claims or if the debtor turns over disposable income for a three-year or five-year period. If the plan is followed, debts are discharged. |
| Advantages | On liquidation and distribution, most or all debts are discharged, and the debtor has an opportunity for a fresh start. | Debtor continues in business. Creditors can either accept the plan, or it can be "crammed down" on them. The plan allows for the reorganization and liquidation of debts over the plan period. | Debtor continues in business or possession of assets. If the plan is approved, most debts are discharged after the plan period. |

petition acts as an automatic stay against creditors' and co-obligors' actions against the estate.

A farmer or fisherman who has already filed a reorganization or repayment plan may convert it to a Chapter 12 plan. The debtor may also convert a Chapter 12 plan to a liquidation plan.

**Content and Confirmation of the Plan** The content of a plan under Chapter 12 is basically the same as that of a Chapter 13 repayment plan. Generally, the plan must be confirmed or denied within forty-five days of filing.

The plan must provide for payment of secured debts at the value of the collateral. If the secured debt exceeds the value of the collateral, the remaining debt is unsecured.

For unsecured debtors, the plan must be confirmed in either of the following circumstances: (1) the value of the property to be distributed under the plan equals the amount of the claim, or (2) the plan provides that all of the debtor's disposable income to be received in a three-year period (or longer, by court approval) will be applied to making payments. Disposable income is all income received less amounts needed to support the farmer or fisherman and his or her family and to continue the farming or commercial fishing operation. Completion of payments under the plan discharges all debts provided for by the plan.

## Reviewing: Bankruptcy Law

Three months ago, Janet Hart's husband of twenty years died of cancer. Although he had medical insurance, he left Janet with outstanding medical bills of more than $50,000. Janet has two teenage daughters to support. She has worked at the local library for the past ten years, earning $1,500 per month. Since her husband's death, she has also received $1,500 in Social Security benefits and $1,100 in life insurance proceeds every month, for a total monthly income of $4,100. After making the mortgage payment of $1,500 and paying the amounts due on other debts, Janet has barely enough left to buy groceries for her family. She decides to file for Chapter 7 bankruptcy, hoping for a fresh start. Using the information presented in the chapter, answer the following questions.

1. What must Janet do *before* filing a petition for relief under Chapter 7?
2. How much time does Janet have after filing the bankruptcy petition to submit the required schedules? What happens if Janet does not meet the deadline?
3. Assume that Janet files a petition under Chapter 7. Further assume that the median family income in the geographic area in which Janet lives is $49,300. What steps would a court take to determine whether Janet's petition is presumed to be "substantial abuse" using the means test?
4. Suppose that the court determines that no *presumption* of substantial abuse applies in Janet's case. Nevertheless, the court finds that Janet does have the ability to pay at least a portion of the medical bills out of her disposable income. What would the court likely order in that situation?

**Debate This** . . . *Rather than being allowed to file Chapter 7 bankruptcy petitions, individuals and couples should always be forced to make an effort to pay off their debts through Chapter 13.*

## Terms and Concepts

adequate protection doctrine 405
automatic stay 405
bankruptcy trustee 403
consumer-debtor 403
cram-down provision 416
debtor in possession (DIP) 415

discharge 403
insider 407
liquidation 402
order for relief 405
petition in bankruptcy 403

preference 407
preferred creditor 407
reaffirmation agreement 414
U.S. trustee 404
workout 414

# Issue Spotters

1. After graduating from college, Tina works briefly as a salesperson before filing for bankruptcy. Tina's petition states that her only debts are student loans, taxes accruing within the last year, and a claim against her based on her misuse of customers' funds during her employment. Are these debts dischargeable in bankruptcy? Explain. (See *Liquidation Proceedings*.)

2. Ogden is a vice president of Plumbing Service, Inc. (PSI). On May 1, Ogden loans PSI $10,000. On June 1, the firm repays the loan. On July 1, PSI files for bankruptcy. Quentin is appointed trustee. Can Quentin recover the $10,000 paid to Ogden on June 1? Why or why not? (See *Liquidation Proceedings*.)

- **Check your answers to the Issue Spotters against the answers provided in Appendix B at the end of this text.**

# Business Scenarios

### 21–1. Voluntary versus Involuntary Bankruptcy. Burke
has been a rancher all her life, raising cattle and crops. Her ranch is valued at $500,000, almost all of which is exempt under state law. Burke has eight creditors and a total indebtedness of $70,000. Two of her largest creditors are Oman ($30,000 owed) and Sneed ($25,000 owed). The other six creditors have claims of less than $5,000 each. A drought has ruined all of Burke's crops and forced her to sell many of her cattle at a loss. She cannot pay off her creditors. (See *Liquidation Proceedings*.)

**(a)** Under the Bankruptcy Code, can Burke, with a $500,000 ranch, voluntarily petition herself into bankruptcy? Explain.

**(b)** Could either Oman or Sneed force Burke into involuntary bankruptcy? Explain.

### 21–2. Distribution of Property. Montoro petitioned
himself into voluntary bankruptcy. There were three major claims against his estate. One was made by Carlton, a friend who held Montoro's negotiable promissory note for $2,500. Another was made by Elmer, Montoro's employee, who claimed that Montoro owed him three months' back wages of $4,500. The last major claim was made by the United Bank of the Rockies on an unsecured loan of $5,000. In addition, Dietrich, an accountant retained by the trustee, was owed $500, and property taxes of $1,000 were owed to Rock County. Montoro's nonexempt property was liquidated, with proceeds of $5,000. Discuss fully what amount each party will receive, and why. (See *Liquidation Proceedings*.)

# Business Case Problems

### 21–3. Discharge in Bankruptcy. Caroline McAfee loaned
$400,000 to Carter Oaks Crossing. Joseph Harman, president of Carter Oaks Crossing, signed a promissory note providing that the company would repay the amount with interest in installments beginning in 1999 and ending by 2006. Harman signed a personal guaranty for the note. Carter Oaks Crossing defaulted on the note, so McAfee sued Harman for payment under the guaranty. Harman moved for summary judgment on the ground that McAfee's claim against him had been discharged in his Chapter 7 bankruptcy case. The case had been filed after 1999 but before the default on the note. The guaranty was not listed among Harman's debts in the bankruptcy filing. Would the obligation under the guaranty have been discharged in bankruptcy, as Harman claimed? Why or why not? [*Harman v. McAfee*, 302 Ga.App. 698, 691 S.E.2d 586 (2010)] (See *Liquidation Proceedings*.)

### 21–4. Automatic Stay. Michelle Gholston leased a Chevy
Impala from EZ Auto Van Rentals. In November 2011, Gholston filed for bankruptcy. Around November 21, the bankruptcy court notified EZ Auto of Gholston's bankruptcy and the imposition of an automatic stay. Nevertheless, because Gholston had fallen behind on her payments, EZ Auto repossessed the vehicle on November 28. Gholston's attorney then

reminded EZ Auto about the automatic stay, but the company failed to return the car. As a result of the car's repossession, Gholston suffered damages that included emotional distress, lost wages, attorneys' fees, and car rental expenses. Can Gholston recover from EZ Auto? Why or why not? [*In re Gholston*, 2012 WL 639288 (M.D.Fla. 2012)] (See *Liquidation Proceedings*.)

### 21–5. Business Case Problem with Sample Answer— Discharge in Bankruptcy. Like many students, Barbara
 Hann financed her education partially through loans. These loans included three federally insured Stafford Loans of $7,500 each ($22,500 in total). Hann believed that she had repaid the loans, but when she filed a Chapter 13 petition, Educational Credit Management Corp. (ECMC) filed an unsecured proof of claim based on the loans. Hann objected. At a hearing at which ECMC failed to appear, Hann submitted correspondence from the lender that indicated the loans had been paid. The court entered an order sustaining Hann's objection. Despite the order, can ECMC resume its effort to collect on Hann's loans? Explain. [*In re Hann*, 711 F.3d 235 (1st Cir. 2013)] (See *Liquidation Proceedings*.)

- **For a sample answer to Problem 21–5, go to Appendix C at the end of this text.**

**21–6. Discharge.** Michael and Dianne Shankle divorced. An Arkansas state court ordered Michael to pay Dianne alimony and child support, as well as half of the $184,000 in their investment accounts. Instead, Michael withdrew more than half of the investment funds and spent them. Over the next several years, the court repeatedly held Michael in contempt for failing to pay Dianne. Six years later, Michael filed for Chapter 7 bankruptcy, including in the petition's schedule the debt to Dianne of unpaid alimony, child support, and investment funds. Is Michael entitled to a discharge of this debt, or does it qualify as an exception? Explain. [*In re Shankle,* 554 Fed.Appx. 264 (5th Cir. 2014)] (See *Liquidation Proceedings.*)

**21–7. Discharge under Chapter 13.** James Thomas and Jennifer Clark married and had two children. They bought a home in Ironton, Ohio, with a loan secured by a mortgage. Later, they took out a second mortgage. On their divorce, the court gave Clark custody of the children and required Clark to pay the first mortgage. The divorce decree also required Thomas and Clark to make equal payments on the second mortgage and provided that Clark would receive all proceeds on the sale of the home. Thomas failed to make any payments, and Clark sold the home. At that point, she learned that Auto Now had a lien on the home because Thomas had not made payments on his car. Clark used all the sale proceeds to pay off the lien and the mortgages. When Thomas filed a petition for a Chapter 13 bankruptcy in a federal bankruptcy court, Clark filed a proof of claim for the mortgage and lien debts. Clark claimed that Thomas should not be able to discharge these debts because they were part of his domestic-support obligations. Are these debts dischargeable? Explain. [*In re Thomas,* 591 Fed.Appx. 443 (6th Cir. 2015)] (See *Bankruptcy Relief under Chapter 12 and Chapter 13.*)

**21–8. Liquidation Proceedings.** Jeffrey Krueger and Michael Torres, shareholders of Cru Energy, Inc., were embroiled in litigation in a Texas state court. Both claimed to act on Cru's behalf, and each charged the other with attempting to obtain control of Cru through fraud and other misconduct. Temporarily prohibited from participating in Cru's business, Krueger formed Kru, a company with the same business plan and many of the same shareholders as Cru. Meanwhile, to delay the state court proceedings, Krueger filed a petition for a Chapter 7 liquidation in a federal bankruptcy court. He did not reveal his interest in Kru to the bankruptcy court. Ownership of Krueger's Cru shares passed to the bankruptcy trustee, but Krueger ignored this. He called a meeting of Cru's shareholders—except Torres—and voted those shares to remove Torres from the board and elect himself chairman, president, chief executive officer, and treasurer. The Cru board then dismissed all of Cru's claims against Krueger in his suit with Torres. Are there sufficient grounds for the bankruptcy court to dismiss Krueger's bankruptcy petition? Discuss. [*In re Krueger,* 812 F.3d 365 (5th Cir. 2016)] (See *Liquidation Proceedings.*)

**21–9. A Question of Ethics—Discharge in Bankruptcy.**  *Monica Sexton filed a petition for Chapter 13 reorganization. One of her creditors was Friedman's Jewelers. Her petition misclassified Friedman's claim as $800 of unsecured debt. Within days, Friedman's filed proof of a secured claim for $300 and an unsecured claim for $462. Eventually, Friedman's was sent payments of about $300 by check. None of the checks were cashed. By then, Friedman's had filed its own petition under Chapter 11, Bankruptcy Receivables Management (BRM) had bought Friedman's unpaid accounts, and the checks had not been forwarded. Sexton received a discharge on the completion of her plan. BRM was not notified. BRM wrote to Sexton's attorney to ask about the status of her case, but received no response. BRM demanded that Sexton surrender the collateral on its claim. Sexton asked the court to impose sanctions on BRM for violating the discharge order. [*In re Sexton, 2011 WL 284180 (E.D.N.C. 2011)] (See Liquidation Proceedings.)*

**(a)** Was Sexton's debt to Friedman's dischargeable? Discuss.

**(b)** Should BRM be sanctioned for willfully violating the discharge order? Why or why not?

# Legal Reasoning Group Activity

**21–10. Discharge in Bankruptcy.** Cathy Coleman took out loans to complete her college education. After graduation, Coleman was irregularly employed as a teacher before filing a petition in a federal bankruptcy court under Chapter 13. The court confirmed a five-year plan under which Coleman was required to commit all of her disposable income to paying the student loans. Less than a year later, when Coleman was laid off, she still owed more than $100,000 to Educational Credit Management Corp. Coleman asked the court to discharge the debt on the ground that it would be an undue hardship for her to pay it. (See *Liquidation Proceedings.*)

**(a)** The first group will determine when a debtor normally is entitled to a discharge under Chapter 13.

**(b)** The second group will discuss whether student loans are dischargeable and when "undue hardship" is a legitimate ground for an exception to the general rule.

**(c)** The third group will outline the goals of bankruptcy law and make an argument, based on these facts and principles, in support of Coleman's request.

Application and Ethics

# Federal Student Loans—Default and Discharge

Ruby borrows $16,000 from the U.S. Department of Education (DOE) to help pay for her education at State University. To obtain the funds, she signs a note for the borrowed amount plus interest payable to DOE. She does not make payments on the loan when they come due.

Has Ruby defaulted on the loan? What will happen?

## Federal Student Loan Programs

Federal government loans make up about 93 percent of the $1.2 trillion student loan market. Loans from private lenders make up the rest. It is important for borrowers to know which type of loan they owe. The collection methods available to private lenders are different from the methods available to federal lenders.

Federal student loan programs include the following.[1]

- *William D. Ford Federal Direct Loans*, which are made by the DOE.[2]
- *Federal Perkins Loans*, which are made by schools to students who demonstrate financial need.[3]
- *Federal Family Education Loans (FFEL)*, which were made by banks or other private lenders before July 1, 2010. The federal government guaranteed these loans. This program has been discontinued, but the outstanding amounts of any of the loans must still be paid.[4]

## Default

A borrower is in default on a federal student loan if he or she fails to repay it according to the terms in the note. For most federal student loans, this occurs if a payment has not been made for more than 270 days (330 days for FFELs).[5]

## Consequences of Default on a Federal Student Loan

If a borrower defaults on a federal student loan, the entire balance of the loan, including both principal and interest, can become due in a single payment.

**Transfer of the Note to a Collection Agency** Once default occurs, the holder of the note—which may be the DOE, the school that made the loan, a state agency, or a private nonprofit organization—can transfer the note to a collection agency to recover the unpaid debt.

Any additional costs to collect payment can then be added to the outstanding principal.[6] These expenses can be up to 18.5 percent of the defaulted amount of the principal and interest for Federal Direct Loans and FFELs, and more for Federal Perkins Loans.

---

1. Each program has eligibility requirements, interest rates, loan limits, and other stipulations that are subject to change. See U.S. Department of Education, *Loans* (Dec. 7, 2015) available at https://studentaid.ed.gov/sa/types/loans.
2. 20 U.S.C. Sections 1087a–1087j.
3. 20 U.S.C. Sections 1087aa–1087ii.
4. 20 U.S.C. Sections 1071–1087-4.
5. U.S. Department of Education, *Understanding Default* (Dec. 7, 2015) available at https://studentaid.ed.gov/sa/repay-loans/default.
6. *Marx v. General Revenue Corp.*, __ U.S. __, 133 S.Ct. 1166, 185 L.Ed.2d 242 (2013).

**Treasury Offset**  There are other actions that the holder of the note might take. The DOE has the authority to collect the amount of the loan. This can be done by withholding funds from the defaulted borrower's sources of income. For instance, the DOE can ask the Department of the Treasury to withhold a defaulted debtor's federal income tax refund and other payments of federal funds, including Social Security payments.[7] This is known as a *Treasury offset.*

**Garnishment**  The DOE or any other holder of the note can order the debtor's employer to withhold up to 15 percent of the debtor's disposable pay. No court order is necessary (unlike with a garnishment to recover the unpaid amount of a *private* student loan, which requires a court order). The withholding can continue until the debt is paid or otherwise taken out of default.[8] The DOE can arrange for a similar amount to be withheld from a federal employee's wages through the *federal salary offset program.*

Whether a debtor's employer is a private business or the federal government, the debtor has rights with regard to garnishment or offset. The debtor has a right to be notified of a proposed garnishment or offset, a right to object to it, and a right to a hearing on the objection.

## Forgiveness, Cancellation, and Discharge

A federal student loan must be repaid. This is true even for borrowers who do not finish school, do not find a job related to their program of study, or are not satisfied with the education they received.

In certain circumstances, however, some or all of a loan may be forgiven, canceled, or discharged. For all federal student loans, these circumstances include the following.

- *Closed school*—A debtor may be entitled to a discharge if the school closes while the student is enrolled or within 120 days after he or she withdraws.
- *Total and permanent disability*—To prove total and permanent disability, the debtor must show that he or she is unable to engage in any substantial gainful activity due to a physical or mental impairment.
- *Death*—If a borrower dies, his or her federal student loan will be discharged.
- *Bankruptcy*—A loan may be discharged in bankruptcy if its repayment would cause undue hardship. Undue hardship requires that repaying the loan would prevent the debtor from maintaining a minimal standard of living, the situation would continue for a significant portion of the repayment period, and good faith efforts to repay the loan were made before the bankruptcy filing.

Federal Direct Loans and FFELs may be discharged or forgiven in the following additional circumstances.

- *False certification of student eligibility*—This can happen when a school falsely certifies a student's eligibility to benefit from its program. It can also happen when the student does not qualify for the occupation in which he or she paid to be educated (because of a health condition, for instance). Finally, it can result from forgery or identity theft.
- *Unauthorized payment*—A loan may be discharged if a school signed a student's name on the loan application or endorsed the loan check without the student's knowledge. An exception exists when the proceeds were paid to the student or applied against charges owed by the student to the school.

Continues

---

7. *Lockhart v. United States*, 548 U.S. 142, 126 S.Ct. 699, 163 L.Ed.2d 557 (2005).
8. *Sanon v. Department of Higher Education*, 453 Fed.Appx. 28 (2d Cir. 2011).

- *Unpaid refund*—An unpaid refund occurs when a student takes out a loan to attend a school and withdraws, but the school does not refund the appropriate amount to the DOE.
- *Full-time teacher*—A teacher who has been teaching full-time in a low-income school or educational service agency for five consecutive years may have some or all of a loan forgiven.

Some or all of a Federal Perkins Loan may be canceled for those who are employed in certain occupations. These include the following.

- Volunteers in the Peace Corps or VISTA.
- Military personnel (serving in areas of hostilities).
- Nurses and other medical technicians.
- Law enforcement and corrections officers.
- Workers for Head Start, and other child and family services.
- Professional providers of early intervention services for disabled persons.
- Teachers who have been teaching full-time in low-income schools or in certain subject areas.[9]

Finally, a Federal Direct Loan may be forgiven if the borrower is employed in a particular public service job and has made 120 payments on the loan.

## Ethical Connection

Many of the ways to avoid paying a federal student loan without defaulting are ethical, and even laudable. For example, a loan may be forgiven for a debtor who is a teacher, a military serviceperson, a law enforcement officer, a nurse, or a child-care provider. Individuals who pursue these occupations are likely to have high ethical standards. Their contribution to the public good may exceed any amount that they borrowed to go to school. Ultimately, the public may accrue the greatest benefit from their service. Thus, it will be *us* who owe *them*—a debt of gratitude.

**Ethics Question** *In addition to the borrowers listed in this feature, who deserves to have their federal student loans forgiven? Why?*

**Critical Thinking** *What are the consequences in addition to those stated in this feature of failing to make timely payments on federal student loans? Discuss.*

---

9. For more information on these options, see U.S. Department of Education, *Forgiveness, Cancellation, and Discharge* (Dec. 7, 2015) available at https://studentaid.ed.gov/sa/repay-loans/forgiveness-cancellation.

# Government Regulation

## CHAPTER 22

# Professional Liability and Accountability

Professionals, such as accountants, attorneys, physicians, and architects, are increasingly faced with the threat of liability. In part, this is because the public has become more aware that professionals are required to deliver competent services and adhere to certain standards of performance within their professions.

The failure of several major companies and leading public accounting firms in the past twenty years has focused attention on the importance of abiding by professional accounting standards. Numerous corporations and former corporations have been accused of engaging in accounting fraud. These include American International Group (AIG, the world's largest insurance company), HealthSouth, Goldman Sachs, Lehman Brothers, Tyco International, and India-based Satyam Computer Services, to name a few. These companies may have reported fictitious revenues, concealed liabilities or debts, or artificially inflated their assets.

Considering the many potential sources of legal liability that they face, accountants, attorneys, and other professionals should be very aware of their legal obligations. In this chapter, we look at the potential liability of professionals under both the common law and statutory law. We conclude the chapter with a brief examination of the relationships of professionals, particularly accountants and attorneys, with their clients.

## 22–1 Potential Liability to Clients

Under the common law, professionals may be liable to clients for breach of contract, negligence, or fraud.

### 22–1a Liability for Breach of Contract

Accountants and other professionals face liability under the common law for any breach of contract. A professional owes a duty to her or his client to honor the terms of their contract and to perform the contract within the stated time period. If the professional fails to perform as agreed in the contract, then she or he has breached the contract, and the client has the right to seek to recover damages from the professional.

Damages can include expenses incurred by the client to hire another professional to provide the contracted-for services and any other reasonable and foreseeable losses that arise from the professional's breach. For instance, if the client had to pay liquidated damages or penalties for failing to meet deadlines, the court may order the professional to pay an equivalent amount in damages to the client.

### 22–1b Liability for Negligence

Accountants and other professionals may also be held liable under the common law for negligence in the performance of their services. Recall that to establish negligence, the plaintiff must prove four elements: duty, breach, causation, and damages.

Negligence cases against professionals often focus on the standard of care exercised by the professionals. All professionals are subject to the standards of conduct and the ethical codes established by their profession, by state statutes, and by judicial decisions. They are also governed by the contracts they enter into with their clients.

In performing their contracts, professionals must exercise the established standards of care, knowledge, and judgment generally accepted by members of their professional group. How do those standards apply when an attorney stores confidential client information and other data on the cloud? See this chapter's *Ethics Today* feature for a discussion of this issue.

**Accountant's Duty of Care** Accountants play a major role in a business's financial system. Accountants

## What Are an Attorney's Responsibilities for Protecting Data Stored in the Cloud?

To achieve both cost savings and better security, more and more attorneys are storing their data, including confidential client information, on the cloud. Sometimes, professionals assume that once their data have migrated to the cloud, they no longer have to be concerned with keeping the information secure. But cloud computing is simply the virtualization of the computing process. In other words, the professional is still ultimately responsible for the information.

### Rules of Professional Conduct and Stored Information

Attorneys' obligations for their clients' information are spelled out in the American Bar Association's Model Rules of Professional Conduct, which serve as the basis for the ethics rules for attorneys adopted by most states. Comment 17 to Model Rule 1.6 states, "The lawyer must take reasonable precautions to prevent the [client's] information from coming into the hands of unintended recipients." Thus, lawyers have an ethical duty to safeguard confidential client information. It makes no difference whether the information is stored as documents in a filing cabinet or as electromagnetic impulses on a server that might be located anywhere. (Note that Rule 1.6 does not require an attorney to guarantee that a breach of confidentiality will never occur.)

Certainly, it is harder to maintain control over information stored on the cloud. Although the attorney "owns" the data, he or she probably does not even know the location of the computer where the information is stored. Furthermore, a provider of cloud computing services may move data from one server to another. Attorneys should be aware of jurisdictional issues and make sure that their cloud computing provider is complying with data protection regulations and privacy notification requirements wherever the provider's servers are located.

### Litigation Issues

The problems presented by e-discovery become even more complex when information is stored in the cloud. Not only will adequate data maps have to be readily available during discovery and subsequent litigation, but the attorney will have to ascertain who will have access to sensitive information.

Attorneys must be particularly careful to avoid spoliation, or the negligent altering or destruction of evidence relevant to the litigation. Preserving information in the cloud can be more difficult if the data are spread across multiple physical storage sites. Sometimes, attorneys can be required to isolate the relevant data within their cloud computing provider's cloud resources.

**Critical Thinking** *To what extent must attorneys reveal to their clients where confidential data are stored?*

have the expertise and experience necessary to establish and maintain accurate financial records, and to design, control, and audit record-keeping systems. They also prepare reliable statements reflecting an individual's or a business's financial status, give tax advice, and prepare tax returns.

Generally, an accountant is expected to possess the skills that an ordinarily prudent accountant would have and to exercise the degree of care that an ordinarily prudent accountant would exercise. The level of skill expected of accountants and the degree of care that they should exercise in performing their services are reflected in the standards discussed next.

**GAAP and GAAS.** When performing their services, accountants must comply with **generally accepted accounting principles (GAAP)** and **generally accepted auditing standards (GAAS).** The Financial Accounting Standards Board (FASB, usually pronounced "faz-bee") determines what accounting conventions, rules, and procedures constitute GAAP at a given point in time. Similarly, the American Institute of Certified Public Accountants established GAAS to identify the professional qualities and the judgment that an auditor should exercise in auditing financial records.

A violation of GAAP and GAAS is considered *prima facie* evidence of negligence on the part of the accountant. Compliance with GAAP and GAAS, however, does not *necessarily* relieve an accountant from potential legal liability. An accountant may be held to a higher standard of conduct established by state statutes or by judicial decisions.

**Global Accounting Rules.** Although the United States has used the GAAP standards for many years, they are being replaced by global accounting rules. The Securities and Exchange Commission (SEC) now requires U.S. companies to use global accounting rules for all financial reports filed with the SEC. These rules, known as **International Financial Reporting Standards (IFRS),** are established by the London-based International Accounting Standards Board.

The SEC decided to replace GAAP with IFRS for several reasons. GAAP are rule based, whereas IFRS focus more on general principles. As a result, GAAP are very detailed and fill nearly 25,000 pages. IFRS are simpler, more straightforward, and shorter, filling only 2,500 pages. Consequently, companies should find it less difficult to comply with IFRS.

Another benefit is that investors will find it easier to make cross-country comparisons between the financial statements of, say, a technology company in Silicon Valley and one in Japan. Furthermore, having uniform accounting rules that apply to all nations makes sense in a global economy. The members of the European Union and more than one hundred other nations—including nearly all of the trading partners of the United States—use IFRS.

**Discovering Improprieties.** An accountant is not required to discover every impropriety, **defalcation**[1] (embezzlement), or fraud in a client's books. If, however, an impropriety goes undiscovered because of the accountant's negligence or failure to perform a duty, the accountant will be liable for any resulting losses suffered by the client. Therefore, an accountant who uncovers suspicious financial transactions and fails to investigate the matter fully or to inform the client of the discovery can be held liable to the client for the resulting loss.

**Audits.** One of the more important tasks that an accountant may perform for a business is an audit. An *audit* is a systematic inspection, by analyses and tests, of a business's financial records. An accountant qualified to perform audits is often called an **auditor.** After performing an audit, the auditor issues an opinion letter stating whether, in his or her opinion, the financial statements fairly present the business's financial position.

The purpose of an audit is to provide the auditor with evidence to support an opinion on the reliability of the business's financial statements. A normal audit is not intended to uncover fraud or other misconduct.

Nevertheless, an accountant may be liable for failing to detect misconduct if a normal audit would have revealed it. Also, if the auditor agreed to examine the records for evidence of fraud or other obvious misconduct and then failed to detect it, he or she may be liable.

**Qualified Opinions and Disclaimers.** In issuing an opinion letter, an auditor may *qualify* the opinion or include a *disclaimer.* In a qualified opinion, the auditor approves the financial statements overall but identifies one or two issues that are still in question. In a disclaimer, the auditor basically states that she or he does not have sufficient information to issue an opinion. A qualified opinion or a disclaimer must be specific and identify the reason for the qualification or disclaimer.

■ **EXAMPLE 22.1** Richard Zehr performs an audit of Lacey Corporation's financial statements. In the opinion letter, Zehr qualifies his opinion by stating that there is uncertainty about how a lawsuit against the firm will be resolved. In this situation, Zehr will not be liable if the outcome of the suit is unfavorable for the firm. Zehr could still be liable, however, if he failed to discover other problems that an audit in compliance with GAAS and IFRS would have revealed. ■

**Unaudited Financial Statements.** Sometimes, accountants are hired to prepare unaudited financial statements. (A financial statement is considered unaudited if incomplete auditing procedures have been used in its preparation or if insufficient procedures have been used to justify an opinion.) Lesser standards of care are typically required in this situation.

Nevertheless, accountants may be liable for omissions from unaudited statements. Accountants may be subject to liability for failing, in accordance with standard accounting procedures, to designate a balance sheet as "unaudited." An accountant will also be held liable for failure to disclose to a client facts or circumstances suggesting that misstatements have been made or that fraud has been committed.

**Defenses to Negligence.** If an accountant is found guilty of negligence, the client can collect damages for losses that arose from the accountant's negligence. An accountant facing a negligence claim, however, has several possible defenses, including the following:

1. The accountant was not negligent.
2. If the accountant was negligent, this negligence was not the proximate cause of the client's losses.
3. The client was also negligent (depending on whether the state applies contributory negligence or comparative negligence).

---

1. This term, pronounced deh-ful-*kay*-shun, is derived from the Latin *de* ("off") and *falx* ("sickle"—a tool for cutting grain or tall grass). In law, the term refers to the act of a defaulter or of an embezzler. As used here, it means embezzlement.

■ **EXAMPLE 22.2** Coopers & Peterson, LLP, provide accounting services for Bandon Steel Mills, Inc. (BSM). Coopers advises BSM to report a certain transaction as a $12.3 million gain on its financial statements. Later, BSM plans to make a public offering of its stock. The SEC reviews its financial statements and determines that the accounting treatment of the transaction has to be corrected before the sale.

Because of the delay, the public offering does not occur as planned on May 2, when BSM's stock is selling for $16 per share. It takes place instead on June 13, when, due to unrelated factors, the price has fallen to $13.50. If BSM files a lawsuit against Coopers claiming that the negligent accounting resulted in the stock's being sold at a lower price, BSM is unlikely to prevail. Although the accountant's negligence may have delayed the stock offering, the negligence was not the proximate cause of the decline in the stock price. Coopers would not be liable for damages based on the price decline. ■

**Attorney's Duty of Care** The conduct of attorneys is governed by rules established by each state and by the American Bar Association's Model Rules of Professional Conduct. All attorneys owe a duty to provide competent and diligent representation. Attorneys are required to be familiar with well-settled principles of law applicable to a case and to find relevant law that can be discovered through a reasonable amount of research. They must also investigate and discover facts that could materially affect clients' legal rights.

Normally, an attorney's performance is expected to be that of a reasonably competent general practitioner of ordinary skill, experience, and capacity. Often, an attorney holds himself or herself out as having expertise in a particular area of law (such as intellectual property). In this instance, the attorney is held to a higher standard of care in that area of law than attorneys without such knowledge.

**Misconduct.** Typically, state rules of professional conduct for attorneys provide that committing a criminal act that reflects adversely on the attorney's "honesty or trustworthiness, or fitness as a lawyer" is professional misconduct. The rules often further provide that a lawyer should not engage in conduct involving "dishonesty, fraud, deceit, or misrepresentation." Under these rules, state authorities can discipline attorneys for many types of misconduct.

Note, though, that states do not frequently discipline attorneys if their misconduct does not reflect on their honesty and trustworthiness.   ■ **CASE IN POINT 22.3** Daniel Johns, a Wisconsin attorney, was the driver in a one-vehicle drunk driving accident in which his brother

was killed. He pleaded guilty to homicide by use of a vehicle while driving with a blood alcohol level over the legal limit. Johns served 120 days in jail and was released on five years' probation. The court terminated his probation early because of his good behavior, and he went back to practicing law.

The state's office of lawyer regulation (OLR) then initiated disciplinary proceedings seeking to suspend Johns's license to practice for sixty days for professional misconduct. The court, however, explained that the "commission of a criminal act by a Wisconsin licensed lawyer does not, *per se,* constitute professional misconduct." The OLR had not proved that Johns's crime reflected adversely on his honesty, trustworthiness, or fitness as a lawyer in other respects. In fact, except for this one tragic event, Johns had led an exemplary life without a hint of professional misconduct. The court therefore dismissed the disciplinary complaint.[2] ■

**Liability for Malpractice.** When an attorney fails to exercise reasonable care and professional judgment, she or he breaches the duty of care and can be held liable for *malpractice* (professional negligence). In malpractice cases—as in all cases involving allegations of negligence—the plaintiff must prove that the attorney's breach of the duty of care actually caused the plaintiff to suffer some injury.

■ **CASE IN POINT 22.4** The law firm of Husch Blackwell Sanders, LLP, represented Brian Nail in a dispute with his former employer over stock options. When Nail left the company, he acquired options to purchase his former employer's stock within eighteen months. But then the former employer merged with another company, and the stock was "locked up" for twelve months after the merger. The value of the stock declined significantly during this period. Husch Blackwell eventually negotiated a settlement that extended Nail's option period. When Nail attempted to exercise his options under the settlement agreement, however, complications arose that prevented him from immediately obtaining the stock.

Nail sued Husch Blackwell in a Missouri state court for malpractice, alleging that the firm had negligently drafted the settlement agreement and negligently delayed advising him to exercise the options. Nail sought to recover damages equal to the difference between the highest value of the stock during the lock-up period and his cost to acquire the stock. The trial court granted a summary judgment in favor of the law firm, and the Missouri Supreme Court affirmed. Nail had failed to prove that Husch Blackwell's alleged negligence was the proximate

---

2. *In re Disciplinary Proceedings against Johns,* 2014 WI 32, 353 Wis.2d 746, 847 N.W.2d 179 (2014).

cause of his damages. The decline in the stock price was unrelated to the law firm's alleged misconduct.[3] ■

## 22–1c Liability for Fraud

Fraud, or misrepresentation, involves the following elements:

1. A misrepresentation of a material fact.
2. An intent to deceive.
3. Justifiable reliance by the innocent party on the misrepresentation.

In addition, to obtain damages, the innocent party must have been injured. Both actual and constructive fraud are potential sources of legal liability for an accountant or other professional.

**Actual Fraud** A professional may be held liable for *actual* fraud when (1) he or she intentionally misstates a material fact to mislead a client and (2) the client is injured as a result of justifiably relying on the misstated fact. A material fact is one that a reasonable person would consider important in deciding whether to act.

Among other penalties, an accountant guilty of fraudulent conduct may suffer penalties imposed by a state board of accountancy. ■ **CASE IN POINT 22.5** Michael Walsh, a certified public accountant (CPA), impersonated his brother-in-law, Stephen Teiper, on the phone to obtain financial information from Teiper's insurance company. Teiper wrote a letter reporting Walsh's conduct to the Nebraska Board of Public Accountancy. After a hearing, the board reprimanded Walsh, placed him on probation for three months, and ordered him to attend four hours of ethics training. He also had to pay the costs of the hearing. The Nebraska Supreme Court affirmed the board's decision on appeal.[4] ■

**Constructive Fraud** A professional may sometimes be held liable for **constructive fraud** whether or not he or she acted with fraudulent intent. Constructive fraud may be found when a professional is grossly negligent in performing his or her duties. ■ **EXAMPLE 22.6** Paula, an accountant, is conducting an audit of ComCo, Inc. Paula accepts the explanations of Ron, a ComCo officer, regarding certain financial irregularities, despite evidence that contradicts those explanations and indicates that the irregularities may be illegal. Paula's conduct could be characterized as an intentional failure to perform a duty

in reckless disregard of the consequences of such failure. This would constitute gross negligence and could be held to be constructive fraud. ■

## 22–2 Potential Liability to Third Parties

Traditionally, a professional owed a duty only to those with whom she or he had a direct contractual relationship—that is, those with whom she or he was in *privity of contract*. A professional's duty was only to her or his client. Violations of statutes, fraud, and other intentional or reckless acts of wrongdoing were the only exceptions to this general rule.

Today, this situation has changed, perhaps most noticeably with respect to accountants who conduct audits (auditors). Numerous third parties—including investors, shareholders, creditors, corporate managers and directors, and regulatory agencies—rely on the opinions of auditors when making decisions. In view of this extensive reliance, many courts have all but abandoned the privity requirement in regard to accountants' liability to third parties.

In this discussion, we focus primarily on the potential liability of auditors to third parties. Understanding an auditor's common law liability to third parties is critical. Often, when a business fails, its independent auditor may be one of the few defendants still *solvent*—that is, able to pay expenses and debts. The majority of courts now hold that auditors can be held liable to third parties for negligence, but the standard for the imposition of this liability varies.

### 22–2a The *Ultramares* Rule

The traditional rule regarding an accountant's liability to third parties based on privity of contract was enunciated by Chief Judge Benjamin Cardozo in 1931. ■ **CASE IN POINT 22.7** Fred Stern & Company had hired the public accounting firm of Touche, Niven & Company to review Stern's financial records and prepare a balance sheet for the year ending December 31, 1923.[5] Touche prepared the balance sheet and supplied Stern with thirty-two certified copies. According to the certified balance sheet, Stern had a net worth (assets less liabilities) of $1,070,715.26.

---

3. *Nail v. Husch Blackwell Sanders, LLP*, 436 S.W.3d 556 (2014).
4. *Walsh v. State*, 276 Neb. 1034, 759 N.W.2d 100 (2009).

5. Banks, creditors, stockholders, purchasers, and sellers often rely on balance sheets when making decisions related to a company's business.

In reality, however, Stern's liabilities exceeded its assets—the company's records had been falsified by insiders at Stern to reflect a positive net worth. In reliance on the certified balance sheets, Ultramares Corporation loaned substantial amounts to Stern. After Stern was declared bankrupt, Ultramares brought an action against Touche for negligence in an attempt to recover damages.

The New York Court of Appeals (that state's highest court) refused to impose liability on Touche. The court concluded that Touche's accountants owed a duty of care only to those persons for whose "primary benefit" the statements were intended. In this case, the statements were intended only for the primary benefit of Stern. The court held that in the absence of privity or a relationship "so close as to approach that of privity," a party could not recover from an accountant.[6] ∎

**The Requirement of Privity** The requirement of privity has since been referred to as the *Ultramares* rule, or the New York rule. It continues to be used in some states. ∎ **CASE IN POINT 22.8** Toro Company supplied equipment and credit to Summit Power Equipment Distributors and required Summit to submit audited reports indicating its financial condition. Accountants at Krouse, Kern & Company prepared the reports, which allegedly contained mistakes and omissions regarding Summit's financial condition.

Toro extended large amounts of credit to Summit in reliance on the audited reports. When Summit was unable to repay these amounts, Toro brought a negligence action against Krouse and proved that the accountants knew the reports would be used by Summit to induce Toro to extend credit. Nevertheless, under the *Ultramares* rule, the court refused to hold the accounting firm liable because the firm was not in privity with Toro.[7] ∎

**Modification to Allow "Near Privity"** The *Ultramares* rule was restated and somewhat modified in a 1985 New York case, *Credit Alliance Corp. v. Arthur Andersen & Co.*[8] In that case, the court held that if a third party has a sufficiently close relationship or *nexus* (connection) with an accountant, then the *Ultramares* privity requirement may be satisfied without the establishment of an accountant-client relationship. The rule enunciated in the *Credit Alliance* case is often referred to as the "near privity"

rule. Only a minority of states have adopted this rule of accountants' liability to third parties.

## 22–2b The *Restatement* Rule

The *Ultramares* rule has been severely criticized. Much of the work performed by auditors is intended for use by persons who are not parties to the contract. Critics of the *Ultramares* rule assert that auditors should owe a duty to these third parties. As support for this position has grown, there has been an erosion of the *Ultramares* rule, and accountants may now be liable to third parties in some situations.

The majority of courts have adopted the position taken by the *Restatement (Third) of Torts*. This rule states that accountants are subject to liability for negligence not only to their clients but also to foreseen, or known, users of their reports or financial statements. Under the *Restatement (Third) of Torts,* an accountant's liability extends to:

1. Persons for whose benefit and guidance the accountant intends to supply the information or knows that the recipient intends to supply it.
2. Persons whom the accountant intends the information to influence or knows that the recipient so intends.

∎ **EXAMPLE 22.9** Steve, an accountant, prepares a financial statement for Tech Software, Inc., a client, knowing that Tech will submit that statement when it applies for a loan from First National Bank. If the statement includes negligent misstatements or omissions, the bank may hold Steve liable, because he knew that the bank would rely on his work when deciding whether to make the loan. ∎

## 22–2c The "Reasonably Foreseeable Users" Rule

A small minority of courts hold accountants liable to any users whose reliance on an accountant's statements or reports was *reasonably foreseeable*. This standard has been criticized as extending liability too far and exposing accountants to massive liability.

The majority of courts have concluded that the *Restatement's* approach is more reasonable because it allows accountants to control their exposure to liability. Liability is "fixed by the accountants' particular knowledge at the moment the audit is published," not by the foreseeability of the harm that might occur to a third party after the report is released.

Exhibit 22–1 summarizes the three different views of accountants' liability to third parties.

---

6. *Ultramares Corp. v. Touche*, 255 N.Y. 170, 174 N.E. 441 (1931).
7. *Toro Co. v. Krouse, Kern & Co.*, 827 F.2d 155 (7th Cir. 1987). See also *Citibank, F.S.B. v. McGladrey & Pullen, LLP,* 2007 WL 7134666 (Ill. 2007).
8. 65 N.Y.2d 536, 483 N.E.2d 110 (1985). A "relationship sufficiently intimate to be equated with privity" is enough for a third party to sue another's accountant for negligence.

**EXHIBIT 22–1** Three Basic Rules of an Accountant's Liability to Third Parties

| RULE | DESCRIPTION | APPLICATION |
|------|-------------|-------------|
| The *Ultramares* Rule | Liability will be imposed only if the accountant is in privity, or near privity, with the third party. | A minority of courts apply this rule. |
| The *Restatement* Rule | Liability will be imposed only if the third party's reliance is foreseen, or known, or if the third party is among a class of foreseen, or known, users. | The majority of courts have adopted this rule. |
| The "Reasonably Foreseeable Users" Rule | Liability will be imposed only if the third party's use was reasonably foreseeable. | A small minority of courts use this rule. |

## 22–2d Liability of Attorneys to Third Parties

Like accountants, attorneys may be held liable under the common law to third parties who rely on legal opinions to their detriment. Generally, an attorney is not liable to a nonclient unless the attorney has committed fraud (or

malicious conduct). The liability principles stated in the *Restatement (Third) of Torts,* however, may apply to attorneys as well as to accountants.

Should an attorney's duty of care extend to third party beneficiaries whose rights were harmed by the attorney's malpractice? That question was at issue in the following case.

**Case Analysis 22.1**

## Perez[a] v. Stern

Nebraska Supreme Court, 279 Neb. 187, 777 N.W.2d 545 (2010).

### In the Language of the Court

GERRARD, J. [Justice]

\* \* \* \*

[Reyna] Guido is the mother of two minor children. [Domingo] Martinez, the children's father, died after he was run over by a car on July 8, 2001. Martinez was the victim of a hit-and-run accident.

Guido, as personal representative of Martinez's estate, retained [Sandra] Stern to file a wrongful death lawsuit. On July 8, 2003, Stern filed a wrongful death complaint in the district court. But Stern admits that she never perfected service of the complaint, and because the complaint was not served within six months of filing, the case was dismissed by operation of law.

\* \* \* On February 6, 2007, Guido filed these legal malpractice claims against Stern on behalf of herself, the children, and the estate. Guido alleged that the wrongful death claim expired as a result of Stern's failure to timely perfect service of the complaint. Stern moved for summary judgment on the ground that the malpractice claims were barred by the two-year statute of limitations for professional negligence. Before the court ruled on the motion, Guido voluntarily dismissed her individual claim, but maintained claims as personal representative of the estate and next friend of the children.

The district court found that the malpractice claims accrued on May 7, 2004, when the wrongful death claim was dismissed. The court found that the estate's claim against Stern was time barred. In response to Guido's argument that the children's minority tolled

[suspended] the statute of limitations with respect to them, the court found that because the children could not have brought the underlying wrongful death claim in their own names, the statute of limitations for the legal malpractice claims was not tolled by reason of the children's minority. The court granted summary judgment in favor of Stern and dismissed the complaint.

\* \* \* \*

Guido [appealed, claiming] that the district court erred in granting Stern's motion for summary judgment on her affirmative defense of the statute of limitations and, specifically, determining that the children had no independent standing to sue Stern and that Stern owed no independent duty to the minor children to protect their rights and interests.

---

a. Estaban Perez was one of the minor children of Domingo Martinez, the man killed in the accident.

**Case 22.1 Continued**

We note that neither Guido's assignments of error nor the argument in her appellate brief challenges the district court's dismissal of Guido's claims as an individual and as personal representative of Martinez's estate. Therefore, those aspects of the court's judgment will be affirmed.

* * * *

The issue in this case is whether Stern owed an independent duty to the children, as Martinez's next of kin, to timely prosecute the underlying wrongful death claim.

* * * *

In Nebraska, *a lawyer owes a duty to his or her client to use reasonable care and skill in the discharge of his or her duties, but ordinarily this duty does not extend to third parties, absent facts establishing a duty to them.* [Emphasis added.]

But that does not end our analysis. * * * We have never said that privity [of contract] is an absolute requirement of a legal malpractice claim. Instead, we have said that a lawyer's duty to use reasonable care and skill in the discharge of his or her duties *ordinarily* does not extend to third parties, *absent facts establishing a duty to them.* On the facts of this case, we conclude, as have other courts to have addressed this issue in the context of a wrongful death action, that the facts establish an independent legal duty from Stern to Martinez's statutory beneficiaries. [Emphasis in the original]

* * * Courts have repeatedly emphasized that *the starting point for analyzing an attorney's duty to a third party is determining whether the third party was a direct and intended beneficiary of the attorney's services.* [Emphasis added.]

* * * *

In this case, we conclude that Stern owed a duty to the children, as direct and intended beneficiaries of her services, to competently represent their interests. To hold otherwise would deny legal recourse to the children for whose benefit Stern was hired in the first place.

* * * Stern owed a legal duty to Martinez's minor children to exercise reasonable care in representing their interests. Therefore, they have standing to sue Stern for neglecting that duty, and their claims against Stern were tolled by their minority. The district court erred in concluding that their claims were time barred. We affirm the court's dismissal of Guido's individual claim and its determination that the estate's claim against Stern was time barred. But with respect to the children, this cause is reversed and remanded for further proceedings to fully adjudicate Guido's claims on behalf of the children * * * .

Affirmed in part, and in part reversed and remanded for further proceedings.

**Legal Reasoning Questions**

1. If the children had suffered no harm as a result of the attorney's malpractice, would the outcome of this case have been different? Why or why not?

2. Why did the court affirm the dismissal of Guido's individual claim but not the claims that she had brought on behalf of the children?

3. If one of the children had not been a minor at the time of the father's death, the court would have dismissed that child's claims against Stern, even though the child was an intended beneficiary. Is it fair for the law to treat minors differently from other children with regard to a statute of limitations? Why or why not?

---

Concept Summary 22.1 reviews the common law rules under which accountants, attorneys, and other professionals may be held liable.

# 22-3 The Sarbanes-Oxley Act

The Sarbanes-Oxley Act imposes a number of strict requirements on both domestic and foreign public accounting firms. These requirements apply to firms that provide auditing services to companies ("issuers") whose securities are sold to public investors. The act defines the term *issuer* as a company (1) that has securities registered under Section 12 of the Securities Exchange Act of 1934, (2) that is required to file reports under Section 15(d) of the 1934 act, or (3) that has filed a registration statement that has not yet become effective under the Securities Act of 1933.

## 22-3a The Public Company Accounting Oversight Board

The Sarbanes-Oxley Act increased government oversight of public accounting practices by creating the Public Company Accounting Oversight Board, which reports to the Securities and Exchange Commission. The board oversees the audit of public companies that are subject to securities laws. The goal is to protect public investors and to ensure that public accounting firms comply with the provisions of the act. The act defines *public accounting*

## Concept Summary 22.1

### Common Law Liability of Accountants and Other Professionals

| Liability to Clients | • *Breach of contract*—A professional who fails to perform according to his or her contractual obligations can be held liable for breach of contract and resulting damages.<br>• *Negligence*—An accountant, attorney, or other professional, in performing her or his duties, must use the care, knowledge, and judgment generally used by professionals in the same or similar circumstances. Failure to do so is negligence. An accountant's violation of generally accepted accounting principles and generally accepted auditing standards is *prima facie* evidence of negligence.<br>• *Fraud*—Intentionally misrepresenting a material fact to a client, when the client relies on the misrepresentation, is actual fraud. Gross negligence in performance of duties is constructive fraud. |
|---|---|
| Liability to Third Parties | • *Liability of accountants*—An accountant may be liable for negligence to any third person the accountant knows or should have known will benefit from the accountant's work. The standard for imposing this liability varies, but generally courts follow the *Ultramares* rule, the *Restatement* rule, or the "Reasonably Foreseeable Users" rule.<br>• *Liability of attorneys*—An attorney generally is not liable to a nonclient unless the attorney committed fraud or other malicious conduct. In some situations, an attorney may be liable to persons whose reliance is foreseen or known. |

*firms* as firms "engaged in the practice of public accounting or preparing or issuing audit reports." Smaller companies—those with less than $75 million in publicly held shares—no longer need to file an auditor's report on management's assessment of internal controls under Section 404(b). The key provisions relating to the duties of the oversight board and the requirements relating to public accounting firms are summarized in Exhibit 22–2.

## 22-3b Requirements for Maintaining Working Papers

In performing an audit for a client, an accountant accumulates various **working papers**—the documents used and developed during the audit. These include notes, computations, memoranda, copies, and other papers that make up the work product of an accountant's services to a client.

Under the common law, which in this instance has been codified in a number of states, working papers remain the accountant's property. It is important for accountants to retain such records in the event that they need to defend against lawsuits for negligence or other actions in which their competence is challenged. The client also has a right to access an accountant's working papers because they reflect the client's financial situation. On a client's request, an accountant must return any of the client's records or journals to the client, and failure to do so may result in liability.

The Sarbanes-Oxley Act initially provided that accountants must maintain working papers relating to an audit or review for five years from the end of the fiscal period in which the audit or review was concluded. The period was subsequently increased to seven years. A knowing violation of this requirement will subject the accountant to a fine, imprisonment for up to ten years, or both.

**EXHIBIT 22–2**  Key Provisions of the Sarbanes-Oxley Act Relating to Public Accounting Firms

### AUDITOR INDEPENDENCE

To help ensure that auditors remain independent of the firms that they audit, Title II of the Sarbanes-Oxley Act does the following:

1. Makes it unlawful for Registered Public Accounting Firms (RPAFs) to perform both audit and nonaudit services for the same company at the same time. Nonaudit services include the following:

   - Bookkeeping or other services related to the accounting records or financial statements of the audit client.
   - Financial information systems design and implementation.
   - Appraisal or valuation services.
   - Fairness opinions.
   - Management functions.
   - Broker or dealer, investment adviser, or investment banking services.

2. Requires preapproval for most auditing services from the issuer's (the corporation's) audit committee.

3. Requires audit partner rotation by prohibiting RPAFs from providing audit services to an issuer if either the lead audit partner or the audit partner responsible for reviewing the audit has provided such services to that corporation in each of the prior five years.

4. Requires RPAFs to make timely reports to the audit committees of the corporations. The report must indicate all critical accounting policies and practices to be used; all alternative treatments of financial information within generally accepted accounting principles that have been discussed with the corporation's management officials, the ramifications of the use of such alternative treatments, and the treatment preferred by the auditor; and other material written communications between the auditor and the corporation's management.

5. Makes it unlawful for an RPAF to provide auditing services to an issuer if the corporation's chief executive officer, chief financial officer, chief accounting officer, or controller was previously employed by the auditor and participated in any capacity in the audit of the corporation during the one-year period preceding the date when the audit began.

### DOCUMENT DESTRUCTION

The Sarbanes-Oxley Act provides that anyone who destroys, alters, or falsifies records with the intent to obstruct or influence a federal investigation or in relation to bankruptcy proceedings can be criminally prosecuted and sentenced to a fine, imprisonment for up to twenty years, or both.

### DOCUMENT RETENTION

The Sarbanes-Oxley Act also requires accountants who audit or review publicly traded companies to retain all working papers related to the audit or review for a period of five years (now amended to seven years). Violators can be sentenced to a fine, imprisonment for up to ten years, or both.

# 22–4 Potential Liability of Accountants under Securities Laws

Both civil and criminal liability may be imposed on accountants under the Securities Act of 1933, the Securities Exchange Act of 1934, and the Private Securities Litigation Reform Act of 1995.[9]

## 22–4a Liability under the Securities Act of 1933

The Securities Act of 1933 requires registration statements to be filed with the Securities and Exchange Commission (SEC) prior to an offering of securities.[10] Accountants frequently prepare and certify the issuer's financial statements that are included in the registration statement.

---

9. Civil and criminal liability may also be imposed on accountants and other professionals under other statutes, including the Racketeer Influenced and Corrupt Organizations Act (RICO).

---

10. Many securities and transactions are expressly exempted from the 1933 act.

**Liability under Section 11** Section 11 of the Securities Act imposes civil liability on accountants for misstatements and omissions of material facts in registration statements. Accountants may be held liable if a financial statement they prepared for inclusion "contained an untrue statement of a material fact or omitted to state a material fact required to be stated therein or necessary to make the statements therein not misleading."[11]

An accountant may be liable to anyone who acquires a security covered by the registration statement. A purchaser of a security need only demonstrate that she or he has suffered a loss on the security. Proof of reliance on the materially false statement or misleading omission ordinarily is not required. Nor is there a requirement of privity between the accountant and the security purchaser.

**The Due Diligence Standard.** Section 11 imposes a duty on accountants to use **due diligence** in preparing financial statements included in the filed registration statements. Once a purchaser has proved a loss on a security, the accountant has the burden of showing that he or she exercised due diligence.

To prove due diligence, the accountant must demonstrate that she or he followed generally accepted standards and did not commit negligence or fraud. The accountant must show that he or she:

1. Conducted a reasonable investigation.
2. Had reasonable grounds to believe and did believe, at the time the registration statement became effective, that the statements therein were true and that there was no omission of a material fact that would be misleading.[12]

In particular, the due diligence standard places a burden on accountants to verify information furnished by a corporation's officers and directors. Merely asking questions is not always sufficient to satisfy the requirement of due diligence. Accountants may be held liable, for instance, for failing to detect danger signals in documents furnished by corporate officers that required further investigation.

**Other Defenses to Liability.** Besides proving that he or she has acted with due diligence, an accountant may raise the following defenses to Section 11 liability:

1. There were no misstatements or omissions.
2. The misstatements or omissions were not of material facts.

3. The misstatements or omissions had no causal connection to the plaintiff's loss.
4. The plaintiff-purchaser invested in the securities knowing of the misstatements or omissions.

**Liability under Section 12(2)** Section 12(2) of the 1933 Securities Act imposes civil liability for fraud in relation to offerings or sales of securities.[13] Liability arises when the offeror or seller makes an oral statement to an investor or provides a written prospectus[14] that includes an untrue statement or omits a material fact. Accountants may be liable under Section 12(2) if they participated in preparing materials in which the false misrepresentation or omission was made.

Those who purchase securities and suffer harm as a result of a false or omitted statement, or some other violation, may bring a suit in a federal court to recover their losses and other damages. The U.S. Department of Justice brings criminal actions against those who commit willful violations.

The penalties include fines up to $10,000, imprisonment up to five years, or both. The SEC is authorized to seek an injunction against a willful violator to prevent further violations. The SEC can also ask a court to grant other relief, such as an order to a violator to refund profits derived from an illegal transaction.

## 22-4b Liability under the Securities Exchange Act of 1934

Under Sections 18 and 10(b) of the 1934 Securities Exchange Act and SEC Rule 10b-5, an accountant may be found liable for fraud. A plaintiff has a substantially heavier burden of proof under the 1934 act than under the 1933 act because an accountant does not have to prove due diligence to escape liability under the 1934 act. The 1934 act relieves an accountant from liability if the accountant acted in "good faith."

**Liability under Section 18** Section 18 of the 1934 act imposes civil liability on an accountant who makes or causes to be made in any application, report, or document a statement that at the time and in light of the circumstances was false or misleading with respect to any material fact.[15]

Section 18 liability is narrow in that it applies only to applications, reports, documents, and registration

---

11. 15 U.S.C. Section 77k(a).
12. 15 U.S.C. Section 77k(b)(3).

13. 15 U.S.C. Section 77*l*.
14. A *prospectus* contains financial disclosures about the corporation for the benefit of potential investors.
15. 15 U.S.C. Section 78r(a).

statements filed with the SEC. In addition, it applies only to sellers and purchasers. Under Section 18, a seller or purchaser must prove one of the following:

1. The false or misleading statement affected the price of the security.
2. The purchaser or seller relied on the false or misleading statement in making the purchase or sale and was not aware of the inaccuracy of the statement.

Sellers and purchasers must bring a cause of action "within one year after the discovery of the facts constituting the cause of action and within three years after such cause of action accrued."[16] A court has the discretion to assess reasonable costs, including attorneys' fees, against accountants who violate Section 18.

**Good Faith Defense.** An accountant will not be liable for violating Section 18 if he or she acted in good faith in preparing the financial statement. To demonstrate good faith, an accountant must show that he or she had no knowledge that the financial statement was false or misleading. Also, the accountant must have had no intent to deceive, manipulate, defraud, or seek unfair advantage over another party.

**Other Defenses.** In addition to the good faith defense, accountants can escape liability by proving that the buyer or seller of the security in question knew that the financial statement was false and misleading. Note, too, that "mere" negligence in preparing a financial statement does not lead to liability under the 1934 act. This differs from the 1933 act, under which an accountant is liable for all negligent acts.

**Liability under Section 10(b) and SEC Rule 10b-5** Accountants additionally face potential legal liability under the antifraud provisions contained in the Securities Exchange Act and SEC Rule 10b-5. The scope of these antifraud provisions is very broad and allows private parties to bring civil actions against violators.

**Prohibited Conduct.** Section 10(b) makes it unlawful for any person, including an accountant, to use, in connection with the purchase or sale of any security, any manipulative or deceptive device or plan that is counter to SEC rules and regulations.[17] Rule 10b-5 further makes it unlawful for any person, by use of any means or instrumentality of interstate commerce, to do the following:

1. Employ any device, scheme, or strategy to defraud.
2. Make any untrue statement of a material fact or omit to state a material fact necessary to make the statements made, in light of the circumstances, not misleading.
3. Engage in any act, practice, or course of business that operates or would operate as a fraud or deceit on any person, in connection with the purchase or sale of any security.[18]

**Extent of Liability.** Accountants may be held liable only to sellers or purchasers of securities under Section 10(b) and Rule 10b-5. Privity is not necessary for a recovery. An accountant may be liable not only for fraudulent misstatements of material facts in written material filed with the SEC, but also for any fraudulent oral statements or omissions made in connection with the purchase or sale of any security.

For a plaintiff to succeed in recovering damages under these antifraud provisions, he or she must prove intent (*scienter*) to commit the fraudulent or deceptive act. Ordinary negligence is not enough.

Do accountants have a duty to correct misstatements that they discover in *previous* financial statements if they know that potential investors are relying on those statements? That was the question in the following case.

---

**16.** 15 U.S.C. Section 17r(c).

**17.** 15 U.S.C. Section 78j(b).
**18.** 17 C.F.R. Section 240.10b-5.

## Spotlight on Accountant's Duty to Correct Mistakes

### Case 22.2 Overton v. Todman & Co., CPAs

United States Court of Appeals, Second Circuit, 478 F.3d 479 (2007).

**Background and Facts** From 1999 through 2002, Todman & Company, CPAs, P.C., audited the financial statements of Direct Brokerage, Inc. (DBI), a broker-dealer in New York registered with the Securities and Exchange Commission (SEC). Each year, Todman issued an unqualified opinion that DBI's financial statements were accurate. DBI filed its statements and Todman's opinions with the SEC.

Case 22.2 Continues

Despite the certifications of accuracy, Todman made significant errors that concealed DBI's largest liability—its payroll taxes—in the 1999 and 2000 audits. The errors came to light in 2003 when the New York State Division of Taxation subpoenaed DBI's payroll records. It became clear that the company had not filed or paid its payroll taxes for 1999 and 2000. This put DBI in a precarious financial position, owing the state more than $3 million in unpaid taxes, interest, and penalties.

To meet its needs, DBI sought outside investors, including David Overton, who relied on DBI's statements and Todman's opinion for 2002 to invest in DBI. When DBI collapsed under the weight of its liabilities in 2004, Overton and others filed a suit in a federal district court against Todman. Among other things, the plaintiffs asserted fraud under Section 10(b) and Rule 10b-5. The court dismissed the complaint. The plaintiffs appealed to the U.S. Court of Appeals for the Second Circuit.

### In the Language of the Court

*STRAUB*, Circuit Judge.

* * * *

*A fundamental principle of securities law is that before an individual becomes liable for his silence, he must have an underlying duty to speak.* [Emphasis added.]

* * * *

* * * The Supreme Court [has] held that [Section] 10(b) does not authorize aiding and abetting liability. In order to be liable under [Section] 10(b), the Court held, an actor must himself "mak[e] * * * a material misstatement (or omission) or * * * commit * * * a manipulative act." The rationale underpinning this holding was that (1) by its terms, [Section] 10(b) requires the making of a statement or omission and (2) without such a statement or omission, the "critical" element of reliance would be absent.

Although the Court did not specifically discuss an auditor's duty to correct, it made clear that * * * secondary actors such as accountants may incur primary liability based on their omissions * * * .

* * * For many years we have recognized the existence of an accountant's duty to correct its certified opinions, but never squarely held that such a duty exists for the purposes of primary liability under [Section] 10(b) of the 1934 Act and Rule 10b-5. Presented with an opportunity to do so, we now so hold. *Specifically, we hold that an accountant violates the "duty to correct" and becomes primarily liable under [Section] 10(b) and Rule 10b-5 when it (1) makes a statement in its certified opinion that is false or misleading when made; (2) subsequently learns or was reckless in not learning that the earlier statement was false or misleading; (3) knows or should know that potential investors are relying on the opinion and financial statements; yet (4) fails to take reasonable steps to correct or withdraw its opinion and/or the financial statements; and (5) all the other requirements for liability are satisfied.* [Emphasis added.]

* * * *

In light of the above principles, we conclude that the District Court erred in dismissing the complaint. Plaintiffs pled that Todman's certified opinion and DBI's 2002 financial statements were misleading at the time they were issued, especially with respect to DBI's payroll tax liability; Todman * * * subsequently learned that its certified opinion was false; Todman also knew that DBI was soliciting outside investors based in part on its 2002 certified financial statements and Todman's accompanying opinion; and that despite this knowledge, Todman took no action to correct or withdraw its opinion and/or DBI's financial statements. These allegations adequately state a claim of primary accountant liability under [Section] 10(b) and Rule 10b-5.

**Decision and Remedy** *The U.S. Court of Appeals for the Second Circuit held that an accountant is liable in these circumstances under Section 10(b) and Rule 10b-5. The court vacated the lower court's dismissal and remanded the case.*

### Critical Thinking

- **What If the Facts Were Different?** *If Todman had conducted an audit for DBI but had not issued a certified opinion about DBI's financial statements, would the result in this case have been the same? Explain.*
- **Legal Environment** *Did Overton have a valid reason to sue DBI's auditors? Why or why not?*

## 22–4c The Private Securities Litigation Reform Act of 1995

The Private Securities Litigation Reform Act made some changes to the potential liability of accountants and other professionals in securities fraud cases. Among other things, the act imposed a statutory obligation on accountants. An auditor must use adequate procedures in an audit to detect any illegal acts of the company being audited. If something illegal is detected, the auditor must disclose it to the company's board of directors, the audit committee, or the SEC, depending on the circumstances.[19]

**Proportionate Liability** The act provides that, in most situations, a party is liable only for the proportion of damages for which he or she is responsible.[20] In other words, the parties are subject to proportionate liability rather than joint and several liability. An accountant who participates in, but is unaware of, illegal conduct may not be liable for the entire amount of the loss caused by the illegality.

■ **EXAMPLE 22.10** Nina Chavez, an accountant, helped the president and owner of Midstate Trucking Company draft financial statements that misrepresented Midstate's financial condition. If Nina was not actually aware of the fraud, she can still be held liable, but the amount of her liability could be less than the entire loss. ■

**Aiding and Abetting** The act also made it a crime to aid and abet a violation of the 1934 Securities Exchange Act. Aiding and abetting might include knowingly participating or assisting in some improper activity or keeping quiet about it. If an accountant knowingly aids and abets a primary violator, the SEC can seek an injunction or monetary damages.

■ **EXAMPLE 22.11** Smith & Jones, an accounting firm, performs an audit for Belco Sales Company that is so inadequate as to constitute gross negligence. Belco uses the financial statements provided by Smith & Jones as part of a scheme to defraud investors. When the scheme is uncovered, the SEC can bring an action against Smith & Jones for aiding and abetting. The firm knew or should have known that its audited statements contained material misrepresentations on which investors were likely to rely. ■

## 22–4d Potential Criminal Liability of Accountants

An accountant may be found criminally liable for violations of securities laws and tax laws. In addition, most states make it a crime to (1) knowingly certify false reports, (2) falsify, alter, or destroy books of account, and (3) obtain property or credit through the use of false financial statements.

**Criminal Violations of Securities Laws** Accountants may be subject to criminal penalties for *willful* violations of the 1933 Securities Act and the 1934 Securities Exchange Act. If convicted, they face imprisonment for up to five years and/or a fine of up to $10,000 under the 1933 act and imprisonment for up to ten years and a fine of $100,000 under the 1934 act.

Under the Sarbanes-Oxley Act, if an accountant's false or misleading certified audit statement is used in a securities filing, the accountant may be held criminally liable. The accountant may be fined up to $5 million, imprisoned for up to twenty years, or both.

**Criminal Violations of Tax Laws** The Internal Revenue Code makes it a felony to aid or assist in the preparation of a false tax return. Violations are punishable by a fine of $100,000 ($500,000 for a corporation's return) and imprisonment for up to three years.[21] This provision applies to anyone who prepares tax returns for others for compensation, not just to accountants.[22]

A penalty of $250 per tax return is levied on tax preparers for negligent understatement of the client's tax liability. For willful understatement of tax liability or reckless or intentional disregard of rules or regulations, a penalty of $1,000 is imposed.[23]

A tax preparer may also be subject to penalties for failing to furnish the taxpayer with a copy of the return, failing to sign the return, or failing to furnish the appropriate tax identification numbers.[24] In addition, those who prepare tax returns for others may be fined $1,000 per document for aiding and abetting another's understatement of tax liability (the penalty is increased to $10,000 for corporate returns).[25] The tax preparer's liability is limited to one penalty per taxpayer per tax year.

Concept Summary 22.2 outlines the potential statutory liability of accountants and other professionals.

---

19. 15 U.S.C. Section 78j-1.
20. 15 U.S.C. Section 78u-4(g).
21. 26 U.S.C. Section 7206(2).
22. 26 U.S.C. Section 7701(a)(36).
23. 26 U.S.C. Section 6694.
24. 26 U.S.C. Section 6695.
25. 26 U.S.C. Section 6701.

## Concept Summary 22.2

### Statutory Law Liability of Accountants and Other Professionals

**Sarbanes-Oxley Act**
- See Exhibit 22–2 for key the provisions of the act.

**Securities Act of 1933, Sections 11 and 12(2)**
- Under Section 11 of the 1933 Securities Act, an accountant who makes a false statement or omits a material fact in audited financial statements required for registration of securities under the law may be liable to anyone who acquires securities covered by the registration statement.
- The accountant's defense is basically the use of due diligence and the reasonable belief that the work was complete and correct. The burden of proof is on the accountant.
- Willful violations of this act may be subject to criminal penalties.
- Section 12(2) of the 1933 act imposes civil liability for fraud on anyone who makes an untrue statement or omits a material fact when offering or selling a security to any purchaser of the security.

**Securities Exchange Act of 1934, Sections 10(b) and 18**
- Under Sections 10(b) and 18 of the 1934 Securities Exchange Act, accountants are held liable for false and misleading applications, reports, and documents required under the act.
- The burden is on the plaintiff, and the accountant has numerous defenses, including good faith and lack of knowledge that what was submitted was false.
- Willful violations of this act may be subject to criminal penalties.

**Internal Revenue Code**
- Aiding or assisting in the preparation of a false tax return is a felony. Aiding and abetting an individual's understatement of tax liability is a separate crime.
- Tax preparers who negligently or willfully understate a client's tax liability or who recklessly or intentionally disregard Internal Revenue Code rules or regulations are subject to penalties.
- Tax preparers who fail to provide a taxpayer with a copy of the return, fail to sign the return, or fail to furnish the appropriate tax identification numbers may also be subject to penalties.

# 22–5 Confidentiality and Privilege

Professionals are restrained by the ethical tenets of their professions to keep all communications with their clients confidential.

## 22–5a Attorney-Client Relationships

The confidentiality of attorney-client communications is protected by law, which confers a *privilege* on such communications. This privilege exists because of the client's need to fully disclose the facts of his or her case to the attorney.

To encourage frankness, confidential attorney-client communications relating to representation are normally held in strictest confidence and protected by law. The attorney and her or his employees may not discuss the client's case with anyone—even under court order—without the client's permission. The client holds the privilege, and only the client may waive it—by disclosing privileged information to someone outside the privilege, for example.

Note, however, that the SEC has implemented rules requiring attorneys who become aware that a client has violated securities laws to report the violation to the SEC. Reporting a client's misconduct could be a breach of the attorney-client privilege, so these rules have created a potential conflict for some attorneys.

Once an attorney-client relationship arises, all communications between the parties are privileged. The question in the following case was whether communications between an attorney and an individual *before* that individual was informed that the attorney was *not* his counsel were privileged.

**Case 22.3**

# Commonwealth of Pennsylvania v. Schultz

Superior Court of Pennsylvania, 133 A.3d 294 (2016).

**Background and Facts**  An investigation into allegations of sexual misconduct involving minors and Jerry Sandusky, former defensive coordinator for the Pennsylvania State University football team, led a grand jury to subpoena Gary Schultz. Schultz, a retired vice president of the university, had overseen the campus police at the time of the alleged events.

Before testifying, Schultz met with Cynthia Baldwin, counsel for Penn State. He told her that he did not have any documents relating to the two incidents, believing this disclosure to be in the strictest confidence between attorney and client. Baldwin, however, saw her role as counsel only for Penn State, representing Schultz as an agent of the university, not personally. She did not explain this to him, and she appeared with him during his testimony.

Later, a file was found in Schultz's office containing notes pertaining to the two incidents. When Baldwin was called to testify, she revealed what he had told her at their meeting. On the basis of this testimony, the grand jury charged Schultz with the crimes of perjury, obstruction of justice, and conspiracy. Before a trial was held on these charges, Schultz filed a motion to preclude Baldwin's testimony and quash (suppress) the charges, arguing that her testimony violated the attorney-client privilege. The court denied the motion. Schulz appealed.

## In the Language of the Court

Opinion by *BOWES*, J. [Judge]

 * * * *

*Communications between a putative [assumed] client and corporate counsel are generally privileged prior to counsel informing the individual of the distinction between representing the individual as an agent of the corporation and representing the person in his or her personal capacity.* [Emphasis added.]

When corporate counsel clarifies the potential inherent conflict of interest in representing the corporation and an individual and explains that the attorney may divulge the communications between that person and the attorney because they do not represent the individual, the individual may then make a knowing, intelligent, and voluntary decision whether to continue communicating with corporate counsel.

 * * * *

 * * * Where an attorney purports to offer only limited representation before and at a grand jury proceeding, * * * a putative client must be made expressly aware of that fact.

As Schultz consulted with Ms. Baldwin for purposes of preparing for his grand jury testimony * * * , and reasonably believed she represented him, and Ms. Baldwin neglected to adequately explain the distinction between personal representation and agency representation * * * , we conclude that all the communications between Schultz and Ms. Baldwin were protected by the attorney-client privilege.

 * * * Accordingly, we preclude Ms. Baldwin from testifying in future proceedings regarding privileged communications between her and Schultz, absent a waiver by Schultz.

 * * * *

 * * * Schultz * * * was not aware that Ms. Baldwin was not appearing with him [during his grand jury testimony] in order to protect his interests and therefore unable to provide advice concerning whether he should answer potentially incriminating questions or invoke his right against self-incrimination. Since Schultz was constructively without counsel during his grand jury testimony, and he did not provide

Case 22.3 Continues

informed consent as to limited representation, * * * his right against self-incrimination was not protected by Ms. Baldwin's agency representation, and the appropriate remedy is to quash the perjury charge.
* * * *

[Finally] since the obstruction of justice and related conspiracy charges in this matter relied extensively on a presentment from an investigating grand jury privy to impermissible privileged communications, we quash the counts of obstruction of justice and the related conspiracy charge.

**Decision and Remedy** *A state intermediate appellate court reversed the order of the lower court regarding Schultz's pretrial motion. Baldwin was precluded from testifying about Schultz's privileged communications with her, and the charges of perjury, obstruction of justice, and conspiracy against Schultz were quashed.*

**Critical Thinking**
- **Legal Environment** *How does the result in this case further the purpose of the attorney-client privilege?*
- **What If the Facts Were Different?** *Suppose that a hearing had been held on the question of the attorney-client privilege before Baldwin testified. Would the result have been different?*

## 22–5b Accountant-Client Relationships

In a few states, accountant-client communications are privileged by state statute. In these states, accountant-client communications may not be revealed even in court or in court-sanctioned proceedings without the client's permission.

The majority of states, however, abide by the common law, which provides that, if a court so orders, an accountant must disclose information about his or her client to the court. Physicians and other professionals may similarly be compelled to disclose in court information given to them in confidence by patients or clients.

Communications between professionals and their clients—other than those between an attorney and her or his client—are not privileged under federal law. *In cases involving federal law, state-provided rights to confidentiality of accountant-client communications are not recognized.* Thus, in those cases, in response to a court order, an accountant must provide the information sought.

# Reviewing: Professional Liability and Accountability

Superior Wholesale Corporation planned to purchase Regal Furniture, Inc., and wished to determine Regal's net worth. Superior hired Lynette Shuebke, of the accounting firm Shuebke Delgado, to review an audit that had been prepared by Norman Chase, the accountant for Regal. Shuebke advised Superior that Chase had performed a high-quality audit and that Regal's inventory on the audit dates was stated accurately on the general ledger. As a result of these representations, Superior went forward with its purchase of Regal.

After the purchase, Superior discovered that the audit by Chase had been materially inaccurate and misleading, primarily because the inventory had been grossly overstated on the balance sheet. Later, a former Regal employee who had begun working for Superior exposed an e-mail exchange between Chase and former Regal chief executive officer Buddy Gantry. The exchange revealed that Chase had cooperated in overstating the inventory and understating Regal's tax liability. Using the information presented in the chapter, answer the following questions.

1. If Shuebke's review was conducted in good faith and conformed to generally accepted accounting principles, can Superior hold Shuebke Delgado liable for negligently failing to detect material omissions in Chase's audit? Why or why not?
2. According to the rule adopted by the majority of courts to determine accountants' liability to third parties, could Chase be liable to Superior? Explain.
3. Generally, what requirements must be met before Superior can recover damages under Section 10(b) of the 1934 Securities Exchange Act and SEC Rule 10b-5? Can Superior meet these requirements? Why or why not?

**4.** Suppose that a court determined that Chase had aided Regal in willfully understating its tax liability. What is the maximum penalty that could be imposed on Chase?

**Debate This** . . .   *Only the largest publicly held companies should be subject to the Sarbanes-Oxley Act.*

## Terms and Concepts

| | | |
|---|---|---|
| auditor 430 | generally accepted accounting | International Financial Reporting |
| constructive fraud 432 | principles (GAAP) 429 | Standards (IFRS) 430 |
| defalcation 430 | generally accepted auditing | working papers 436 |
| due diligence 438 | standards (GAAS) 429 | |

## Issue Spotters

**1.** Dave, an accountant, prepares a financial statement for Excel Company, a client, knowing that Excel will use the statement to obtain a loan from First National Bank. Dave makes negligent omissions in the statement that result in a loss to the bank. Can the bank successfully sue Dave? Why or why not? (See *Potential Liability to Third Parties.*)

**2.** Nora, an accountant, prepares a financial statement as part of a registration statement that Omega, Inc., files with the Securities and Exchange Commission before making a public offering of securities. The statement contains a misstatement of material fact that is not attributable to Nora's fraud or negligence. Pat relies on the misstatement, buys some of the securities, and suffers a loss. Can Nora be held liable to Pat? Explain. (See *Potential Liability of Accountants under Securities Laws.*)

• Check your answers to the Issue Spotters against the answers provided in Appendix B at the end of this text.

## Business Scenarios

**22–1. The *Ultramares* Rule.** Larkin, Inc., retains Howard Patterson to manage its books and prepare its financial statements. Patterson, a certified public accountant, lives in Indiana and practices there. After twenty years, Patterson has become a bit bored with generally accepted accounting principles (GAAP) and has adopted more creative accounting methods. Now, though, Patterson has a problem, as he is being sued by Molly Tucker, one of Larkin's creditors. Tucker alleges that Patterson either knew or should have known that Larkin's financial statements would be distributed to various individuals. Furthermore, she asserts that these financial statements were negligently prepared and seriously inaccurate. What are the consequences of Patterson's failure to follow GAAP? Under the traditional *Ultramares* rule, can Tucker recover damages from Patterson? Explain. (See *Potential Liability to Third Parties.*)

**22–2. The *Restatement* Rule.** The accounting firm of Goldman, Walters, Johnson & Co. prepared financial statements for Lucy's Fashions, Inc. After reviewing the various financial statements, Happydays State Bank agreed to loan Lucy's Fashions $35,000 for expansion. When Lucy's Fashions declared bankruptcy under Chapter 11 six months later, Happydays State Bank promptly filed an action against Goldman, Walters, Johnson & Co., alleging negligent preparation of financial statements. Assuming that the court has abandoned the *Ultramares* approach, what is the result? What are the policy reasons for holding accountants liable to third parties with whom they are not in privity? (See *Potential Liability to Third Parties.*)

**22–3. Accountant's Liability under Rule 10b-5.** In early 2014, Bennett, Inc., offered a substantial number of new common shares to the public. Harvey Helms had a long-standing interest in Bennett because his grandfather had once been president of the company. On receiving a prospectus prepared and distributed by Bennett, Helms was dismayed by the pessimism it embodied. Helms decided to delay purchasing stock in the company. Later, Helms asserted that the prospectus prepared by the accountants was overly pessimistic and contained materially misleading statements. Discuss fully how successful Helms would be in bringing a cause of action under Rule 10b-5 against the accountants of Bennett, Inc. (See *Potential Liability of Accountants under Securities Laws.*)

# Business Case Problems

**22–4. Accountant's Liability for Audit.** A West Virginia bank ran its asset value from $100 million to $1 billion over seven years by aggressively marketing subprime loans. The Office of the Comptroller of the Currency, a federal regulator, audited the bank and discovered that the books had been falsified for several years and that the bank was insolvent. The Comptroller closed the bank and brought criminal charges against its managers.

The Comptroller fined Grant Thornton, the bank's accounting firm, $300,000 for recklessly failing to meet generally accepted auditing standards during the years it audited the bank. The Comptroller claimed Thornton violated federal law by "participating in . . . unsafe and unsound banking practice." Thornton appealed, contending that it was not involved in bank operations to that extent based on its audit function. What would be the key to determining if the accounting firm could be held liable for that violation of federal law? [*Grant Thornton, LLP v. Office of the Comptroller of the Currency,* 514 F.3d 1328 (D.C. Cir. 2008)] (See *Potential Liability to Clients.*)

**22–5. Professional's Liability.** Soon after Teresa DeYoung's husband died, her mother-in-law also died, leaving an inheritance of more than $400,000 for DeYoung's children. DeYoung hired John Ruggerio, an attorney, to ensure that her children would receive it. Ruggerio advised her to invest the funds in his real estate business. She declined. A few months later, $300,000 of the inheritance was sent to Ruggerio. Without telling DeYoung, he deposited the $300,000 in his account and began to use the funds in his real estate business. Nine months later, $109,000 of the inheritance was sent to Ruggerio. He paid this to DeYoung. She asked about the remaining amount. Ruggerio lied to hide his theft. Unable to access these funds, DeYoung's children changed their college plans to attend less expensive institutions. Nearly three years later, DeYoung learned the truth. Can she bring a suit against Ruggerio? If so, on what ground? If not, why not? Did Ruggerio violate any standard of professional ethics? Discuss. [*DeYoung v. Ruggerio,* 185 Vt. 267, 971 A.2d 627 (2009)] (See *Potential Liability to Clients.*)

**22–6. Professional Malpractice.** Jeffery Guerrero hired James McDonald, a certified public accountant, to represent him and his business in an appeal to the Internal Revenue Service. The appeal was about audits that showed Guerrero owed more taxes. When the appeal failed, McDonald helped Guerrero prepare materials for an appeal to the Tax Court, which was also unsuccessful. Guerrero then sued McDonald for professional negligence in the preparation of his evidence for the court. Guerrero claimed that McDonald had failed to adequately prepare witnesses and to present all the arguments that could have been made on his behalf so that he could have won the case. Guerrero contended that McDonald was liable for all of the additional taxes he was required to pay. Is Guerrero's claim likely to result in liability on McDonald's part? What factors would the court consider? [*Guerrero v. McDonald,* 302 Ga.App. 164, 690 S.E.2d 486 (2010)] (See *Potential Liability to Clients.*)

**22–7. Business Case Problem with Sample Answer—Potential Liability to Third Parties.**  In 2006, twenty-seven entities became limited partners in two hedge funds that had invested with Bernard Madoff and his investment firm. The partners' investment adviser gave them various investment information, including a memorandum indicating that an independent certified public accountant, KPMG, LLP, had audited the hedge funds' annual reports. Since 2004, KPMG had also prepared annual reports addressed to the funds' "Partners." Each report stated that KPMG had investigated the funds' financial statements, had followed generally accepted auditing principles, and had concluded that the statements fairly summarized the funds' financial conditions. Moreover, KPMG used the information from its audits to prepare individual tax statements for each fund partner.

In 2008, Madoff was charged with securities fraud for running a massive Ponzi scheme. In a 2009 report, the Securities and Exchange Commission identified numerous "red flags" that should have been discovered by investment advisers and auditors. Unfortunately, the auditors did not find them, and the hedge funds' partners lost millions of dollars. Is KPMG potentially liable to the funds' partners under the *Restatement (Third) of Torts?* Why or why not? [*Askenazy v. Tremont Group Holdings, Inc.,* 2012 WL 440675 (Mass.Super. 2012)] (See *Potential Liability to Third Parties.*)

- **For a sample answer to Problem 22–7, go to Appendix C at the end of this text.**

**22–8. Attorney's Duty of Care.** Luis and Maria Rojas contracted to buy a house in Westchester County, New York, from Andrew and Karen Paine. The house was on property designated as "Lot No. 8" on a subdivision map filed in the county clerk's office. The Paines had acquired the property in two parts by the transfer of two separate deeds. At the closing, they delivered a deed stating that it covered "the same property." In fact, however, the legal description attached to the deed covered only the portion of Lot No. 8 described in one of the two previous deeds. Attorney Paul Herrick represented the Rojases in the deal with the Paines. When the Rojases sought to sell the property two years later, the title search revealed that they owned only part of Lot No. 8, and the buyer refused to go through with the sale. Is Herrick liable for malpractice? Explain. [*Rojas v. Paine,* 125 A.D.3d 745, 4 N.Y.S.3d 223 (2 Dept. 2015)] (See *Potential Liability to Clients.*)

**22–9. A Question of Ethics—Liability for Negligence.**  *Portland Shellfish Co. processes live shellfish in Maine. As one of the firm's two owners, Frank Wetmore held 300 voting and 150 nonvoting shares of the stock. Donna Holden held the other 300 voting shares. Donna's husband, Jeff, managed the company's daily operations, including production, procurement, and sales. The board of directors consisted of Frank and Jeff. In 2001, disagreements* arose over the company's management. *The Holdens invoked the "Shareholders' Agreement," which provided that "[i]n the event of a deadlock, the directors shall hire an accountant at [Macdonald, Page, Schatz, Fletcher & Co., LLC] to determine the value of the outstanding shares. . . . [E]ach shareholder shall have the right to buy out the other shareholder(s)' interest."*

*Macdonald Page estimated the stock's "fair market value" at $1.09 million. Donna offered to buy Frank's shares at a price equal to his proportionate share. Frank countered by offering $1.25 million for Donna's shares. Donna rejected Frank's offer and insisted that he sell his shares to her or she would sue. In the face of this threat, Frank sold his shares to Donna for $750,705. Believing the stock to be worth more than twice Macdonald Page's estimate, Frank filed a suit in a federal district court against the accounting firm. [Wetmore v. Macdonald, Page, Schatz, Fletcher & Co., LLC, 476 F.3d 1 (1st Cir. 2007)] (See Potential Liability to Clients.)*

**(a)** Frank claimed that in valuing the stock, the accounting firm had disregarded "commonly accepted and reliable methods of valuation in favor of less reliable methods." He alleged negligence, among other things. Macdonald Page filed a motion to dismiss the complaint. What are the elements that establish negligence? Which is the most critical element in this case?

**(b)** Macdonald Page evaluated the company's stock by identifying its "fair market value," defined as "the price at which the property would change hands between a willing buyer and a willing seller, neither being under a compulsion to buy or sell and both having reasonable knowledge of relevant facts." The firm knew that the shareholders would use its estimate to determine the price that one would pay to the other. Under these circumstances, was Frank's injury foreseeable? Discuss.

**(c)** What factor might have influenced Frank to sell his shares to Donna even though he thought that Macdonald Page's "fair market value" figure was less than half of what it should have been? Does this factor represent an unfair, or unethical, advantage? Explain.

## Legal Reasoning Group Activity

**22–10. Attorney-Client Privilege.** Napster, Inc., offered a service that allowed its users to browse digital music files on other users' computers and download selections for free. Music industry principals sued Napster for copyright infringement, and the court ordered Napster to remove from its service files that were identified as infringing. When Napster failed to comply, it was shut down.

A few months later, Bertelsmann, a German corporation, loaned Napster $85 million to fund its anticipated transition to a licensed digital music distribution system. The terms allowed Napster to spend the loan on "general, administrative and overhead expenses." In an e-mail, Napster's chief executive officer referred to a "side deal" under which Napster could use up to $10 million of the loan to pay litigation expenses. Napster failed to launch the new system before declaring bankruptcy. The plaintiffs filed a suit against Bertelsmann, alleging that its loan had prolonged Napster's infringement. The plaintiffs asked the court to order the disclosure of all attorney-client communications related to the loan. (See *Confidentiality and Privilege.*)

**(a)** The first group will identify the principle that Bertelsmann could assert to protect these communications and outline the purpose of this protection.

**(b)** The second group will decide whether this principle should protect a client who consults an attorney for advice that will help the client commit fraud.

**(c)** A third group will determine whether the court should grant the plaintiffs' request.

# CHAPTER 23

# Administrative Agencies

Government agencies established to administer the law have a great impact on the day-to-day operations of businesses. In its early years, the United States had a simple, nonindustrial economy with little regulation. As the economy has grown and become more complex, the size of government has also increased, and so has the number, size, and power of administrative agencies.

In some instances, new agencies have been created in response to a crisis. In the wake of the financial crisis that led to the latest economic recession, for instance, Congress enacted the Dodd-Frank Wall Street Reform and Consumer Protection Act. Among other things, this statute created the Financial Stability Oversight Council to identify and respond to emerging risks in the financial system. It also created the Consumer Financial Protection Bureau (CFPB) to protect consumers from alleged abusive practices by financial institutions, mortgage lenders, and credit-card companies.

As the number of agencies has multiplied, so have the rules, orders, and decisions that they issue. Today, there are rules covering almost every aspect of a business's operations. These regulations make up the body of *administrative law.*

## 23–1 The Practical Significance of Administrative Law

Whereas statutory law is created by legislatures, administrative law is created by administrative agencies. When Congress—or a state legislature—enacts legislation, it typically adopts a rather general statute and leaves its implementation to an **administrative agency.** The agency then creates the detailed rules and regulations necessary to carry out the statute. The administrative agency, with its specialized personnel, has the time, resources, and expertise to make the detailed decisions required for regulation.

### 23–1a Administrative Agencies Exist at All Levels of Government

Administrative agencies are spread throughout the government. At the federal level, the Securities and Exchange Commission regulates a firm's capital structure and financing, as well as its financial reporting. The National Labor Relations Board oversees relations between a firm and any unions with which it may deal. The Equal Employment Opportunity Commission also regulates employer-employee relationships. The Environmental Protection Agency and the Occupational Safety and Health Administration affect the way a firm manufactures its products, and the Federal Trade Commission influences the way it markets those products.

There are administrative agencies at the state and local levels as well. Commonly, a state agency (such as a state pollution-control agency) is created as a parallel to a federal agency (such as the Environmental Protection Agency). Just as federal statutes take precedence over conflicting state statutes, so do federal agency regulations take precedence over conflicting state regulations. Because the rules of state and local agencies vary widely, we focus here exclusively on federal administrative law.

### 23–1b Agencies Provide a Comprehensive Regulatory Scheme

Often, administrative agencies at various levels of government work together and share the responsibility of creating and enforcing particular regulations. ■ **EXAMPLE 23.1** When Congress enacted the Clean Air Act, it provided only general directions for the prevention of air pollution. The specific pollution-control requirements imposed on businesses are almost entirely the product of decisions made by the Environmental Protection Agency (EPA). Moreover, the EPA works with parallel environmental agencies at the state level to analyze existing data and determine the appropriate pollution-control standards. ■

Legislation and regulations have significant benefits—in the example of the Clean Air Act, a cleaner environment than existed in decades past. At the same time, these benefits entail considerable costs for business. The EPA has estimated the costs of compliance with the Clean Air Act at many tens of billions of dollars yearly. Although the agency has calculated that the overall benefits of its regulations often exceed their costs, the burden on business is substantial. Business therefore has a strong incentive to try to influence the regulatory environment through lobbying.

## 23-2 Agency Creation and Powers

Congress creates federal administrative agencies. By delegating some of its authority to make and implement laws, Congress can indirectly monitor a particular area in which it has passed legislation. Delegation enables Congress to avoid becoming bogged down in the details relating to enforcement—details that are often best left to specialists.

To create an administrative agency, Congress passes **enabling legislation,** which specifies the name, purposes, functions, and powers of the agency being created. Federal administrative agencies can exercise only those powers that Congress has delegated to them in enabling legislation. Through similar enabling acts, state legislatures create state administrative agencies.

An agency's enabling statute defines its legal authority. An agency cannot regulate beyond the powers granted by the statute, and it may be required to take some regulatory action by the terms of that statute. When regulated groups oppose a rule adopted by an agency, they often bring a lawsuit arguing that the rule was not authorized by the enabling statute and is therefore void. Conversely, a group may file a suit claiming that an agency has illegally *failed* to pursue regulation required by the enabling statute.

### 23-2a Enabling Legislation—An Example

Congress created the Federal Trade Commission (FTC) in the Federal Trade Commission Act.[1] The act prohibits unfair methods of competition and deceptive trade practices. It also describes the procedures that the FTC must follow to charge persons or organizations with violations of the act, and it provides for judicial review of agency orders. The act grants the FTC the power to do the following:

1. Create "rules and regulations for the purpose of carrying out the Act."
2. Conduct investigations of business practices.
3. Obtain reports from interstate corporations concerning their business practices.
4. Investigate possible violations of federal antitrust statutes. (The FTC shares this task with the Antitrust Division of the U.S. Department of Justice.)
5. Publish findings of its investigations.
6. Recommend new legislation.
7. Hold trial-like hearings to resolve certain trade disputes that involve FTC regulations or federal antitrust laws.

The commission that heads the FTC is composed of five members. The president, with the advice and consent of the Senate, appoints each of the FTC commissioners for a term of seven years. The president also designates one of the commissioners to be the chair.

### 23-2b Types of Agencies

There are two basic types of administrative agencies: executive agencies and independent regulatory agencies. Federal *executive agencies* include the cabinet departments of the executive branch, which assist the president in carrying out executive functions, and the subagencies within the cabinet departments. The Occupational Safety and Health Administration, for instance, is a subagency within the U.S. Department of Labor.

Executive agencies usually have a single administrator, director, or secretary who is appointed by the president to oversee the agency and can be removed by the president at any time. Exhibit 23–1 lists the cabinet departments and some of their most important subagencies.

*Independent regulatory agencies,* such as the Federal Trade Commission and the Securities and Exchange Commission (SEC), are outside the federal executive departments (those headed by a cabinet secretary). The president's power is less pronounced in regard to independent agencies, whose officers serve for fixed terms and cannot be removed without just cause. See Exhibit 23–2 for a list of selected independent regulatory agencies and their principal functions.

### 23-2c Agency Powers and the Constitution

Administrative agencies occupy an unusual niche in the U.S. governmental structure, because they exercise powers that normally are divided among the three branches of government. Agencies' powers include functions

1. 15 U.S.C. Sections 41–58.

**EXHIBIT 23–1 Executive Departments and Important Subagencies**

| DEPARTMENT | SELECTED SUBAGENCIES |
| --- | --- |
| State | Passport Office; Bureau of Diplomatic Security; Foreign Service; Bureau of Intelligence and Research |
| Treasury | Internal Revenue Service; U.S. Mint |
| Interior | U.S. Fish and Wildlife Service; National Park Service; Bureau of Indian Affairs; Bureau of Land Management |
| Justice[a] | Federal Bureau of Investigation; Drug Enforcement Administration; Bureau of Prisons; U.S. Marshals Service |
| Agriculture | Soil Conservation Service; Agricultural Research Service; Food Safety and Inspection Service |
| Commerce[b] | Bureau of the Census; Bureau of Economic Analysis; U.S. Patent and Trademark Office; National Oceanic and Atmospheric Administration |
| Labor[b] | Occupational Safety and Health Administration; Bureau of Labor Statistics; Employment Standards Administration; Office of Labor-Management Standards |
| Defense[c] | National Security Agency; Joint Chiefs of Staff; Departments of the Air Force, Navy, Army |
| Housing and Urban Development | Government National Mortgage Association; Office of Fair Housing and Equal Opportunity |
| Transportation | Federal Aviation Administration; Federal Highway Administration; National Highway Traffic Safety Administration |
| Energy | Office of Civilian Radioactive Waste Management; Office of Nuclear Energy; Energy Information Administration |
| Health and Human Services[d] | Food and Drug Administration; Centers for Medicare and Medicaid Services; Centers for Disease Control and Prevention; National Institutes of Health |
| Education[d] | Office of Elementary and Secondary Education; Office of Postsecondary Education; Office of Vocational and Adult Education |
| Veterans Affairs | Veterans Health Administration; Veterans Benefits Administration; National Cemetery Administration |
| Homeland Security | U.S. Citizenship and Immigration Services; Directorate of Border and Transportation Services; U.S. Coast Guard; Federal Emergency Management Agency |

**a.** Formed from the Office of the Attorney General.
**b.** Formed from the Department of Commerce and Labor.
**c.** Formed from the Department of War and the Department of the Navy.
**d.** Formed from the Department of Health, Education, and Welfare.

associated with the legislature *(rulemaking)*, the executive branch *(enforcement)*, and the courts *(adjudication)*.

The constitutional principle of *checks and balances* allows each branch of government to act as a check on the actions of the other two branches. Furthermore, the U.S. Constitution authorizes only the legislative branch to create laws. Yet administrative agencies, to which the Constitution does not specifically refer, can make **legislative rules,** or *substantive rules,* that are as legally binding as laws that Congress passes.

Administrative agencies also issue **interpretive rules,** which simply declare policy and do not affect legal rights or obligations. ■ **EXAMPLE 23.2** The Equal Employment Opportunity Commission periodically issues interpretive rules indicating how it plans to interpret the provisions of certain statutes, such as the Americans with

**EXHIBIT 23–2** Selected Independent Regulatory Agencies

| NAME OF AGENCY | PRINCIPAL DUTIES |
|---|---|
| Federal Reserve System (the Fed) Board of Governors | Determines policy with respect to interest rates, credit availability, and the money supply (including various "bailouts" in the financial sector). |
| Federal Trade Commission (FTC) | Prevents businesses from engaging in unfair trade practices; stops the formation of monopolies in the business sector. |
| Securities and Exchange Commission (SEC) | Regulates the nation's stock exchanges, in which shares of stock are bought and sold; enforces the securities laws. |
| Federal Communications Commission (FCC) | Regulates communications by telegraph, cable, telephone, radio, satellite, Internet, and television. |
| National Labor Relations Board (NLRB) | Protects employees' rights to join unions and bargain collectively with employers; attempts to prevent unfair labor practices by both employers and unions. |
| Equal Employment Opportunity Commission (EEOC) | Works to eliminate discrimination in employment based on religion, gender, race, color, disability, national origin, or age; investigates claims of discrimination. |
| Environmental Protection Agency (EPA) | Undertakes programs aimed at reducing air and water pollution; works with state and local agencies to help fight environmental hazards. |
| Nuclear Regulatory Commission (NRC) | Ensures that electricity-generating nuclear reactors in the United States are built and operated safely; regularly inspects operations of such reactors. |

Disabilities Act. These informal rules provide enforcement guidelines for agency officials. ■

**The Delegation Doctrine** Courts generally hold that Article I of the U.S. Constitution is the basis for all administrative law. Section 1 of that article grants all legislative powers to Congress and requires Congress to oversee the implementation of all laws. Article I, Section 8, gives Congress the power to make all laws necessary for executing its specified powers. Under what is known as the **delegation doctrine,** courts interpret these passages as granting Congress the power to establish administrative agencies and delegate to them the power to create rules for implementing those laws.

The three branches of government exercise certain controls over agency powers and functions, as discussed next, but in many ways administrative agencies function independently. For this reason, administrative agencies, which constitute the **bureaucracy,** are sometimes referred to as the fourth branch of the U.S. government.

**Executive Controls** The executive branch of government exercises control over agencies both through the president's power to appoint federal officers and through the president's veto power. The president may veto enabling legislation passed by Congress or congressional attempts to modify an existing agency's authority.

**Legislative Controls** Congress exercises authority over agency powers through legislation. Congress gives power to an agency through enabling legislation and can take power away—or even abolish an agency altogether—through subsequent legislation. Legislative authority is required to fund an agency, and enabling legislation usually sets certain time and monetary limits on the funding of particular programs. Congress can always revise these limits.

In addition to its power to create and fund agencies, Congress has the authority to investigate the implementation of its laws and the agencies that it has created. Congress also has the power to "freeze" the enforcement of most federal regulations before the regulations take effect. (Another legislative check on agency actions is the Administrative Procedure Act, discussed shortly.)

The question that a court faces when confronted with an agency's interpretation of a statute it administers is always whether the agency has acted within its statutory authority. At issue in the following case was an agency's authority under a statute enacted in the nineteenth century.

**Case 23.1**

# Loving v. Internal Revenue Service

United States Court of Appeals, District of Columbia Circuit, 742 F.3d 1013 (2014).

**Background and Facts** The Internal Revenue Service (IRS) is a subagency of the U.S. Department of the Treasury. Responding to concerns about the performance of some paid tax-return preparers, the IRS issued a new rule. The rule required paid preparers to pass an initial certification exam, pay annual fees, and complete at least fifteen hours of continuing education courses each year. As authority for the rule, the IRS relied on a statute enacted in 1884 and recodified in 1982. The statute authorizes the agency to "regulate the practice of representatives of persons before the Department of the Treasury." Three independent preparers filed a suit in a federal district court against the IRS, contending that the rule exceeded the agency's authority. The court ruled in the plaintiffs' favor. The IRS appealed.

## In the Language of the Court

*KAVANAUGH,* Circuit Judge.

\* \* \* \*

In our view, at least six considerations foreclose the IRS's interpretation of the statute.

*First* is the meaning of the key statutory term "representatives." \* \* \* \* The term "representative" is traditionally and commonly defined as an agent with authority to bind others, a description that does not fit tax-return preparers.

Put simply, *tax-return preparers are not agents. They do not possess legal authority to act on the taxpayer's behalf. They cannot legally bind the taxpayer by acting on the taxpayer's behalf.* [Emphasis added.]

\* \* \* \*

*Second* is the meaning of the phrase "practice \* \* \* before the Department of the Treasury."

\* \* \* To "practice before" a court or agency ordinarily refers to practice during an investigation, adversarial hearing, or other adjudicative proceeding.

That is quite different from the process of filing a tax return. \* \* \* *Tax-return preparers do not practice before the IRS when they simply assist in the preparation of someone else's tax return.* [Emphasis added.]

\* \* \* \*

*Third* is the history of [the statute]. The language [in the original statute included the phrase] "agents, attorneys, or other persons representing claimants."

That original language plainly would not encompass tax-return preparers. \* \* \* When Congress re-codified the statute in 1982, Congress simplified the phrase \* \* \* to the current "representatives of persons." But \* \* \* Congress made clear in the statute itself that \* \* \* the 1982 Act was designed "to revise, codify, and enact" the amended provisions "without substantive change."

\* \* \* \*

*Fourth* is the broader statutory framework.

\* \* \* \*

\* \* \* [By enacting other statutes specific to tax-return preparers,] multiple Congresses have acted as if [the statute at the center of this case] did not extend so broadly as to cover tax-return preparers. \* \* \* The meaning of one statute may be affected by other Acts, particularly where Congress has spoken \* \* \* more specifically to the topic at hand. So it is here.

*Fifth* is the nature and scope of the authority being claimed by the IRS.

If we were to accept the IRS's interpretation of [the statute,] the IRS would be empowered for the first time to regulate hundreds of thousands of individuals in the multi-billion dollar tax-preparation industry. Yet nothing in the statute's text or the legislative record contemplates that vast expansion of the IRS's authority.

*Sixth* is the IRS's past approach to this statute. Until [now] the IRS never interpreted the statute to give it authority to regulate tax-return preparers.

\* \* \* In light of the text, history, structure, and context of the statute, it becomes apparent that the IRS never before adopted its current interpretation for a reason: It is incorrect.

**Case 23.1 Continued**

**Decision and Remedy** *The U.S. Court of Appeals for the District of Columbia Circuit affirmed the lower court's ruling. Under the IRS's interpretation of the statute, the agency "would be empowered for the first time to regulate hundreds of thousands of individuals in the multi-billion dollar tax-preparation indus- try." Nothing in the statute's text, history, structure, or context "contemplates that vast expansion of the IRS's authority."*

**Critical Thinking**

- **Legal Environment** *As a policy matter, some observers might argue that the IRS should be allowed to regulate tax-return preparers more strictly. Under the reasoning of the court, who has the authority to give effect to such a policy, and how would it be accomplished?*

**Judicial Controls** The judicial branch exercises con- trol over agency powers through the courts' review of agency actions. As you will read shortly, the Administra- tive Procedure Act provides for judicial review of most agency decisions. Agency actions are not automatically subject to judicial review, however. The party seeking court review must first exhaust all administrative rem- edies under what is called the **exhaustion doctrine.** In other words, the complaining party normally must have exhausted all available administrative remedies before seeking court review.[2]

■ **EXAMPLE 23.3** The Federal Trade Commis- sion (FTC) claims that Sysco Industries used deceptive advertising and orders it to run new ads correcting the misstatements. Sysco contends that its ads were not deceptive. Under the exhaustion doctrine, Sysco must go through the entire FTC process before it can bring a suit against the FTC in court to challenge the order. ■

## 23–2d The Administrative Procedure Act

Sometimes, Congress specifies certain procedural requirements in an agency's enabling legislation. In the absence of any directives from Congress concerning a particular agency procedure, the Administrative Proce- dure Act (APA)[3] applies.

**The Arbitrary and Capricious Test** One of Con- gress's goals in enacting the APA was to provide for more judicial control over administrative agencies. To that end, the APA provides that courts should "hold unlaw- ful and set aside" agency actions found to be "arbitrary, capricious, an abuse of discretion, or otherwise not in accordance with law."[4] Under this standard, parties can

challenge regulations as contrary to law or as so irrational that they are arbitrary and capricious.

There is no precise definition of what makes a rule arbitrary and capricious, but the standard includes fac- tors such as whether the agency has done any of the following:

1. Failed to provide a rational explanation for its decision.
2. Changed its prior policy without justification.
3. Considered legally inappropriate factors.
4. Entirely failed to consider a relevant factor.
5. Rendered a decision plainly contrary to the evidence.

See this chapter's *Digital Update* feature for a discus- sion of administrative rules for broadband operators that have been challenged as arbitrary and capricious.

**Fair Notice** The APA also includes many requirements concerning the notice that regulatory agencies must give to those affected by its regulations. For instance, an agency may change the way it applies a certain regulatory prin- ciple. Before the change can be carried out, the agency must give fair notice of what conduct will be expected in the future.

■ **CASE IN POINT 23.4** The 1934 Communica- tions Act established a system of limited-term broadcast licenses subject to various conditions. One condition was the indecency ban, which prohibited the uttering of "any obscene, indecent, or profane language by means of radio communication." For nearly thirty years, the Fed- eral Communications Commission (FCC) invoked this ban only when the offensive language had been repeated, or "dwelled on," in the broadcast. It was not applied to "fleeting expletives" (offensive words used only briefly).

Then the FCC changed its policy, declaring that an offensive term, such as the F-word, was actionably indecent even if it was used only once. In 2006, the FCC applied this new rule to two Fox Television broadcasts, each of which

2. The plaintiff must also have *standing to sue* the agency.
3. 5 U.S.C. Sections 551–706.
4. 5 U.S.C. Section 706(2)(A).

## DIGITAL UPDATE — Imposing a 1930s Regulatory Law on Broadband Operators

Since the advent of the Internet, it has remained largely unregulated. President Bill Clinton (1993–2001) said clearly and often that the Internet should remain lightly regulated, at most. During the Obama administration, however, pressure from the president himself applied to the Federal Communications Commission (FCC) started to change that thinking.

### An Unsuccessful Attempt to Impose Regulation on Internet Service Providers

In 2010, under the authority of the Telecommunications Act of 1996,[a] the FCC attempted to regulate Internet service providers (ISPs) by enacting the "Open Internet Order." Under this order, the FCC would have required broadband ISPs to transfer data files equally, without consideration of the size or source of the files—so-called net neutrality. The policy prohibited providers from transmitting certain content at slower speeds or higher costs than other types of content. Challenged in court, the order was overturned.[b]

### The Advent of "Obamanet"

In early 2015, the FCC commissioners voted to regulate ISPs as "common carriers" under Title II of the Communications Act of 1934.[c] Normally, a common carrier is a business that transports items from one place to another, such as a trucking company. Under the 1934 act, this definition was widened to include telephone companies. Under the new FCC rules, the Internet would fall under the act as well. The new rules are still under discussion, and legal challenges have been filed.

### What the New FCC Rules Mean

Here is a summary of the new rules:
- No Internet service provider can prevent a user from accessing "legal content, applications, services, or non-harmful devices" on the Internet. The goal to is prevent censorship and discrimination.
- No Internet service provider can deliberately reduce the speed of data from particular sites or applications.
- No Internet service provider can charge content providers more to provide them with faster service.

**Critical Thinking** *Some observers predict that numerous lawsuits will be filed against the FCC. Why would this be likely?*

a. 47 U.S.C. Sections 1302(a), (b).
b. *Verizon v. Federal Communications Commission*, 740 F.3d 623 (D.C. Cir. 2014).
c. 47 U.S.C. Sections 201 *et seq.*

---

contained a single use of the F-word. The broadcasts had aired before the FCC's change in policy. The FCC ruled that these two broadcasts were indecent, and Fox appealed the ruling. Ultimately, the case reached the United States Supreme Court, and the Court determined that the FCC's order should be set aside. Because the FCC did not provide fair notice prior to the broadcasts in question that fleeting expletives could constitute actionable indecency, the standards were unconstitutionally vague.[5] ∎

## 23–3 The Administrative Process

All federal agencies must follow specific procedural requirements as they go about fulfilling their three basic functions: rulemaking, enforcement, and adjudication. These three functions make up what is known as the **administrative process.** As mentioned, the APA imposes requirements that all federal agencies must follow in the absence of contrary provisions in the enabling legislation. This act is an integral part of the administrative process.

### 23–3a Rulemaking

The major function of an administrative agency is **rulemaking**—the formulation of new regulations, or rules. The APA defines a *rule* as "an agency statement of general or particular applicability and future effect designed to implement, interpret, or prescribe law and policy."[6]

Regulations are sometimes said to be *legislative* because, like statutes, they have a binding effect. Thus, violators of agency rules may be punished. Because

5. *Federal Communications Commission v. Fox Television Stations, Inc.*, __ U.S. __, 132 S.Ct. 2307, 183 L.Ed.2d 234 (2012).

6. 5 U.S.C. Section 551(4).

agency rules have such significant legal force, the APA established procedures for agencies to follow in creating rules.

Many rules must be adopted using the APA's **notice-and-comment rulemaking,** which involves three basic steps:

1. Notice of the proposed rulemaking.
2. A comment period.
3. The final rule.

The APA recognizes some limited exceptions to its procedural requirements, but they are seldom invoked. ■ **EXAMPLE 23.5** The Occupational Safety and Health Act authorized the Occupational Safety and Health Administration (OSHA) to develop and issue rules governing safety in the workplace. When OSHA wants to formulate rules regarding safety in the steel industry, it has to follow the specific procedures outlined by the APA. ■

The impetus for rulemaking may come from various sources, including Congress and the agency itself. In addition, private parties may petition an agency to begin a rulemaking (or repeal a rule). For instance, environmental groups have petitioned for stricter air-pollution controls to combat emissions that may contribute to climate change.

**Notice of the Proposed Rulemaking** When a federal agency decides to create a new rule, the agency publishes a notice of the proposed rulemaking proceedings in the *Federal Register*. The *Federal Register* is a daily publication of the executive branch that prints government orders, rules, and regulations.

The agency's notice states where and when the proceedings will be held, the agency's legal authority for making the rule (usually its enabling legislation), and the terms or subject matter of the rule. The agency must also make available to the public certain other information, such as the key scientific data underlying the proposal. The proposed rule is often reported by the news media and published in the trade journals of the industries that will be affected.

**Comment Period** Following the publication of the notice of the proposed rulemaking proceedings, the agency must allow ample time for persons to comment in writing on the proposed rule. The purpose of this comment period is to give interested parties the opportunity to express their views on the proposed rule in an effort to influence agency policy. The comments can be made in writing or, if a hearing is held, orally. All comments become a public record that others can examine.

■ **EXAMPLE 23.6** Brown Trucking learns that the U.S. Department of Transportation is considering a new regulation that will have a negative impact on its ability to do business and on its profits. A notice of the rulemaking is published in the *Federal Register*. Later, a public hearing is held so that proponents and opponents can offer evidence and question witnesses. At this hearing, Brown's owner orally expresses his opinion about the pending rule. ■

The agency need not respond to all comments, but it must respond to any significant comments that bear directly on the proposed rule. The agency responds by either modifying its final rule or explaining, in a statement accompanying the final rule, why it did not make any changes. In some circumstances, particularly when less formal procedures are used, an agency may accept comments after the comment period is closed.

**The Final Rule** After the agency reviews the comments, it drafts the final rule and publishes it in the *Federal Register*. A final rule must contain a "concise general statement of . . . basis and purpose" that describes the reasoning behind the rule.[7] The final rule can include modifications based on the public comments. If substantial changes are made, however, a new proposal and a new opportunity for comment are required.

The final rule is later compiled along with the rules and regulations of other federal administrative agencies in the *Code of Federal Regulations*. Final rules have binding legal effect unless the courts later overturn them.

**Failure to Follow Rulemaking Procedures** If an agency fails to follow proper rulemaking procedures, the resulting rule may not be binding. ■ **EXAMPLE 23.7** Members of the Hemp Industries Association (HIA) manufacture and sell food products made from hemp seed and oil. These products may contain trace amounts of THC, a component of marijuana. Without following formal rulemaking procedures, the Drug Enforcement Administration (DEA) publishes rules that effectively ban the possession and sale of HIA's food products, treating them as controlled substances. A court will most likely overturn the rules because the DEA did not follow formal rulemaking procedures. ■

**Informal Agency Actions** Rather than take the time to conduct notice-and-comment rulemaking, agencies have increasingly been using more informal methods of policymaking, such as issuing interpretive rules and guidance documents. As mentioned earlier, unlike

---

7. 5 U.S.C. Section 555(c).

legislative rules, interpretive rules simply declare policy and do not affect legal rights or obligations. Guidance documents advise the public on the agencies' legal and policy positions.

Informal agency actions are exempt from the APA's requirements because they do not establish legal rights. A party cannot be directly prosecuted for violating an interpretive rule or a guidance document. Nevertheless, an informal action can be important because it warns regulated entities that the agency may engage in formal rulemaking if they ignore its informal policymaking.

## 23–3b Enforcement

Although rulemaking is the most prominent agency activity, rule enforcement is also critical. Often, an agency enforces its own rules. After a final rule is issued, agencies conduct investigations to monitor compliance with the rule or the terms of the enabling statute.

An agency investigation of this kind might begin when the agency receives a report of a possible violation. In addition, many agency rules require compliance reporting from regulated entities, and such a report may trigger an enforcement investigation.

**Inspections and Tests**   In conducting investigations, many agencies gather information through on-site inspections. Sometimes, inspecting an office, a factory, or some other business facility is the only way to obtain the evidence needed to prove a regulatory violation. At other times, an inspection or test is used in place of a formal hearing to show the need to correct or prevent an undesirable condition.

Administrative inspections and tests cover a wide range of activities, including safety inspections of underground coal mines, safety tests of commercial equipment and automobiles, and environmental monitoring of factory emissions. An agency may also ask a firm or individual to submit certain documents or records to the agency for examination.

Normally, business firms comply with agency requests to inspect facilities or business records because it is in any firm's interest to maintain a good relationship with regulatory bodies. In some instances, however, such as when a firm thinks an agency's request is unreasonable and disruptive, the firm may refuse to comply with the request. In such situations, an agency may resort to the use of a subpoena or a search warrant.

**Subpoenas**   There are two basic types of subpoenas. The subpoena *ad testificandum*[8] ("to testify") is an ordi-

nary subpoena. It is a writ, or order, compelling a witness to appear at an agency hearing. The subpoena *duces tecum*[9] ("bring it with you") compels an individual or organization to hand over books, papers, records, or documents to the agency. An administrative agency may use either type of subpoena to obtain testimony or documents.

There are limits on what an agency can demand. To determine whether an agency is abusing its discretion in pursuing information as part of an investigation, a court may consider such factors as the following:

1. *The purpose of the investigation.* An investigation must have a legitimate purpose. Harassment is an example of an improper purpose. An agency may not issue an administrative subpoena to inspect business records if the motive is to harass or pressure the business into settling an unrelated matter.
2. *The relevance of the information being sought.* Information is relevant if it reveals that the law is being violated or if it assures the agency that the law is not being violated.
3. *The specificity of the demand for testimony or documents.* A subpoena must, for instance, adequately describe the material being sought.
4. *The burden of the demand on the party from whom the information is sought.* For instance, the cost to the company of copying requested documents or providing digital information may become burdensome. (Note that a business generally is protected from revealing information such as trade secrets.)

**Search Warrants**   The Fourth Amendment protects against unreasonable searches and seizures by requiring that in most instances a physical search for evidence must be conducted under the authority of a search warrant. An agency's search warrant is an order directing law enforcement officials to search a specific place for a specific item and seize it for the agency. It was once thought that administrative inspections were exempt from the warrant requirement, but the United States Supreme Court has held that the requirement does apply to the administrative process.[10]

Nevertheless, agencies can conduct warrantless searches in several situations. Warrants are not required to conduct searches in highly regulated industries. Firms that sell firearms or liquor, for instance, are automatically subject to inspections without warrants. Sometimes, a statute permits warrantless searches of certain types of hazardous operations, such as coal mines. Also, a warrantless inspection in an emergency situation is normally considered reasonable.

---

8. Pronounced ad tes-te-fe-*kan*-dum.

9. Pronounced *doo*-suhs *tee*-kum.
10. *Marshall v. Barlow's, Inc.,* 436 U.S. 307, 98 S.Ct. 1816, 56 L.Ed.2d 305 (1978).

## 23–3c Adjudication

After conducting an investigation of a suspected rule violation, an agency may initiate an administrative action against an individual or organization. Most administrative actions are resolved through negotiated settlements at their initial stages. Sometimes, though, an action ends in formal **adjudication**—the resolution of the dispute through a hearing conducted by the agency.

**Negotiated Settlements** Depending on the agency, negotiations may involve a simple conversation or a series of informal conferences. Whatever form the negotiations take, their purpose is to rectify the problem to the agency's satisfaction and eliminate the need for additional proceedings.

Settlement is an appealing option to firms for two reasons: to avoid appearing uncooperative and to avoid the expense involved in formal adjudication proceedings and in possible later appeals. Settlement is also an attractive option for agencies. To conserve their resources and avoid formal actions, administrative agencies devote a great deal of effort to giving advice and negotiating solutions to problems.

**Formal Complaints** If a settlement cannot be reached, the agency may issue a formal complaint against the suspected violator. ■ **EXAMPLE 23.8** The Environmental Protection Agency (EPA) finds that Acme Manufacturing, Inc., is polluting groundwater in violation of federal pollution laws. The EPA issues a complaint against Acme in an effort to bring the plant into compliance with federal regulations. This complaint is a public document, and a press release may accompany it. Acme will respond by filing an answer to the EPA's allegations. If Acme and the EPA cannot agree on a settlement, the case will be adjudicated. ■

**The Hearing** Agency adjudication may involve a trial-like arbitration procedure before an **administrative law judge (ALJ).** The Administrative Procedure Act (APA) requires that before the hearing takes place, the agency must issue a notice that includes the facts and law on which the complaint is based, the legal authority for the hearing, and its time and place. The administrative agency adjudication process is described next and illustrated graphically in Exhibit 23–3.

**The Role of the Administrative Law Judge** An ALJ presides over the hearing and has the power to administer oaths, take testimony, rule on questions of evidence, and make determinations of fact. Technically, the ALJ, who works for the agency prosecuting the case, is not an

**EXHIBIT 23–3** The Formal Administrative Agency Adjudication Process

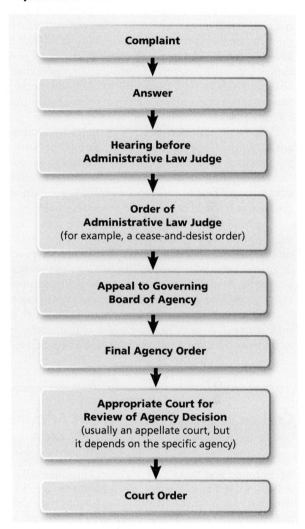

independent judge. Nevertheless, the law requires an ALJ to be unbiased.

Certain safeguards prevent bias on the part of the ALJ and promote fairness in the proceedings. For instance, the APA requires that the ALJ be separate from an agency's investigative and prosecutorial staff. The APA also prohibits *ex parte* (private) communications between the ALJ and any party to an agency proceeding, including the agency and the company involved. Finally, provisions of the APA protect the ALJ from agency disciplinary actions unless the agency can show good cause for such an action.

**Hearing Procedures** Hearing procedures vary widely from agency to agency. Administrative agencies generally exercise substantial discretion over the type of procedure that will be used. Frequently, disputes are resolved through informal adjudication proceedings. ■ **EXAMPLE 23.9** The Federal Trade Commission (FTC) charges Good Foods, Inc., with deceptive advertising. Representatives of Good Foods and the FTC, their counsel, and the ALJ meet at a table in a conference room to resolve the dispute informally. ■

A formal adjudicatory hearing, in contrast, resembles a trial in many respects. Prior to the hearing, the parties are permitted to undertake discovery—involving depositions, interrogatories, and requests for documents or other information. The discovery process usually is not quite as extensive as it would be in a court proceeding, however.

The hearing itself must comply with the procedural requirements of the APA and must also meet the constitutional standards of due process. The burden of proof in an enforcement proceeding is placed on the agency. During the hearing, the parties may give testimony, present other evidence, and cross-examine adverse witnesses.

Trials and administrative agency hearings do differ in some respects. A significant difference is that normally much more information, including hearsay (secondhand

information), can be introduced as evidence during an administrative hearing.

**Agency Orders** Following a hearing, the ALJ renders an **initial order,** or decision, on the case. Either party can appeal the ALJ's decision to the board or commission that governs the agency. If displeased with the result, the party can appeal that decision to a federal appellate court.

■ **EXAMPLE 23.10** The EPA issues a complaint against Acme Manufacturing, Inc., for polluting groundwater. The complaint results in a hearing before an ALJ, who rules in the EPA's favor. If Acme is dissatisfied with the decision, it can appeal to the EPA commission and then to a federal appellate court. ■

If no party appeals the case, the ALJ's decision becomes the **final order** of the agency. The ALJ's decision also becomes final if a party appeals and the commission and the court decline to review the case. If a party appeals and the case is reviewed, the final order comes from the commission's decision or (if that decision is appealed) the decision of the reviewing court.

In the following case, a federal appeals court reviewed the Drug Enforcement Administration's denial of a university professor's application to register to cultivate marijuana.

---

## Case 23.2

## Craker v. Drug Enforcement Administration

United States Court of Appeals, First Circuit, 714 F.3d 17 (2013).

**Background and Facts** Dr. Lyle Craker, a professor in the University of Massachusetts's Department of Plant, Soil and Insect Sciences, applied to the Drug Enforcement Administration (DEA) for permission to register to manufacture marijuana for clinical research. He stated that "a second source of plant material is needed to facilitate privately funded Food and Drug Administration (FDA)-approved research into medical uses of marijuana, ensuring a choice of sources and an adequate supply of quality, research-grade marijuana for medicinal applications."

An administrative law judge recommended that Craker's application be granted, but a DEA deputy administrator issued an order denying his application. Under the DEA's interpretation, the Controlled Substances Act (CSA) requires an applicant to prove both that effective controls against diversion of the marijuana for unapproved purposes are in place and that its supply and the competition to supply it are inadequate. The administrator determined that the professor had not proved that effective controls against the marijuana's diversion were in place or that supply and competition were inadequate. Craker petitioned the U.S. Court of Appeals for the First Circuit to review the order.

### In the Language of the Court
*HOWARD,* Circuit Judge.
    * * *

    Since 1968, the National Center for Natural Products Research ("NCNPR") at the University of Mississippi has held the necessary registration and a government contract to grow marijuana for research purposes. The contract is administered by the National Institute on Drug Abuse ("NIDA"), a component of the National Institutes of Health ("NIH"), which, in turn, is a component of the [U.S.]

Case 23.2 Continued

Department of Health and Human Services ("HHS"). The contract is opened for competitive bidding every five years. The NCNPR is the only entity registered by the DEA to manufacture marijuana.
\* \* \* \*

Dr. Craker's argument with respect to competition is essentially that there cannot be "adequately competitive conditions" when there is only one manufacturer of marijuana.

The Administrator \* \* \* observed that NIDA had provided marijuana manufactured by the University of Mississippi either at cost or free to researchers, and that Dr. Craker had made no showing of how he could provide it for less \* \* \*. Additionally, the Administrator noted that Dr. Craker is free to bid on the contract when it comes up for renewal.

*We see nothing improper in the Administrator's approach. The [CSA's] term "adequately competitive conditions" is not necessarily as narrow as the petitioner suggests. \* \* \* That the current regime may not be the most competitive situation possible does not render it "inadequate."* [Emphasis added.]
\* \* \* \*

In finding that Dr. Craker failed to demonstrate that the current supply of marijuana was not adequate and uninterrupted, the Administrator observed that there were over 1,000 kilograms of marijuana in NIDA possession, an amount which far exceeds present research demands and "any foreseeable" future demand. Dr. Craker does not dispute this finding, or that the current amount is more than ninety times the amount he proposes to supply. Instead, he argues that the adequacy of supply must not be measured against NIDA-approved research, but by whether the supply is adequate to supply projects approved by the FDA. But even if we were to accept his premise—which we don't—Dr. Craker fails to demonstrate that the supply is inadequate for those needs, either. He merely states that certain projects were rejected as "not bona-fide" by NIDA, a claim which does not address the adequacy of supply. The fact that Dr. Craker disagrees with the method by which marijuana research is approved does not undermine the substantial evidence that supports the Administrator's conclusion.

**Decision and Remedy**  *The U.S. Court of Appeals for the First Circuit denied Craker's petition to review the agency's order "because the Administrator's interpretation of the CSA is permissible and her findings are reasonable and supported by the evidence."*

**Critical Thinking**
- **Economic**  *Why should a court wait to review an agency's order until the order has gone through the entire procedural process and can be considered final?*
- **Legal Environment**  *Under what standard does a court defer to an agency's interpretation of a statute? Did the court in this case appear to have applied that standard to the DEA's interpretation of the Controlled Substances Act? Discuss.*

# 23–4 Judicial Deference to Agency Decisions

When asked to review agency decisions, courts historically granted deference to the agency's judgment. In other words, the courts tended to accept the agency's judgment, often citing the agency's great expertise in the subject area of the regulation. This deference seems especially appropriate when applied to an agency's analysis of factual questions, but should it also extend to an agency's interpretation of its own legal authority? In *Chevron U.S.A., Inc. v. Natural Resources Defense Council, Inc.,*[11] the United States Supreme Court held that it should.

11. 467 U.S. 837, 104 S.Ct. 2778, 81 L.Ed.2d 694 (1984).

By so ruling, the Court created a standard of broadened deference to agencies on questions of legal interpretation.

## 23–4a The Holding of the *Chevron* Case

At issue in the *Chevron* case was whether the courts should defer to an agency's interpretation of a statute giving it authority to act. The Environmental Protection Agency (EPA) had interpreted the phrase "stationary source" in the Clean Air Act as referring to an entire manufacturing plant, and not to each facility within a plant. The agency's interpretation enabled it to adopt the so-called bubble policy, which allowed companies to offset increases in emissions in part of a plant with decreases elsewhere in the plant. This interpretation reduced pollution-control compliance costs to manufacturers. An environmental group challenged the legality of the EPA's interpretation.

The Supreme Court held that the courts should defer to an agency's interpretation of law as well as fact. The Court found that the agency's interpretation of the statute was reasonable. The Court's decision in the *Chevron* case created a new standard for courts to use when reviewing agency interpretations of law. This standard involves the following two questions:

1. Did Congress directly address the issue in dispute in the statute? If so, the statutory language prevails.
2. If the statute is silent or ambiguous, is the agency's interpretation "reasonable"? If it is, a court should uphold the agency's interpretation even if the court would have interpreted the law differently.

### 23-4b When Courts Will Give *Chevron* Deference to Agency Interpretation

The notion that courts should defer to agencies on matters of law was controversial. Under the holding of the *Chevron* case, when the meaning of a particular statute's language is unclear and an agency interprets it, the court must follow the agency's interpretation as long as it is reasonable. This led to considerable discussion and litigation to test the boundaries of the *Chevron* holding.

For instance, are courts required to give deference to all agency interpretations or only to those that result from adjudication or formal rulemaking procedures? The United States Supreme Court has held that in order for agency interpretations to be assured *Chevron* deference, they must meet the formal legal standards for notice-and-comment

rulemaking. Nevertheless, there are still gray areas, and many agency interpretations are challenged in court.

■ **CASE IN POINT 23.11**  The Federal Insurance Contributions Act (FICA) requires employees and employers to pay Social Security taxes on all wages. The FICA excludes wages paid for any service to a school "performed by a student who is enrolled and regularly attending classes." The Mayo Foundation for Medical Education and Research offers educational residency programs to physicians who seek instruction in a chosen specialty. In addition to receiving instruction, the physicians are paid to spend fifty to eighty hours a week caring for patients. The U.S. Treasury Department issued a rule providing that anyone who works forty or more hours per week is an employee, not a student. The Mayo Foundation asserted that the rule did not apply to its residents.

The United States Supreme Court upheld the rule. Congress gave the Treasury Department the authority to make rules to enforce the Internal Revenue Code. The employee rule was issued after notice-and-comment procedures, and it was based on a reasonable determination that imposing Social Security taxes on medical residents would further the purpose of the statute. The physicians were "the kind of workers that Congress intended to both contribute to and benefit from the Social Security system."[12] ■

The following case involves a federal agency's role in determining whether alien pilots may be certified to operate large, U.S.-registered aircraft.

---

12. *Mayo Foundation for Medical Education and Research v. United States,* 562 U.S. 44, 131 S.Ct. 704, 178 L.Ed.2d 588 (2011).

---

**Case Analysis 23.3**

## Olivares v. Transportation Security Administration

United States Court of Appeals, District of Columbia Circuit, 819 F.3d 454 (2016).

### In the Language of the Court
*EDWARDS,* Senior Circuit Judge:
\* \* \* \*

I. BACKGROUND
In the aftermath of the tragic terrorist attacks on September 11, 2001, Congress created the Transportation Security Administration [TSA] to shore up our nation's civil aviation security. [TSA is part of the U.S.] Department of Homeland Security under the direction of the Secretary of Homeland Security.

\* \* \* No pilot may serve in any capacity as an airman with respect to a civil aircraft \* \* \* without an airman certificate from FAA [Federal Aviation Administration]. For large aircraft, pilots must obtain additional certification known as a Type Rating. [Under the Aviation and Transportation Security Act of 2001,] aliens who seek training and certification to operate large, U.S.-registered aircraft must first secure clearance by TSA. If TSA determines that an alien applicant presents a risk to aviation or national

security, then that applicant is ineligible to receive the training necessary to secure a large aircraft Type Rating from FAA.
\* \* \* \*

[Alberto Olivares (Petitioner), a citizen of Venezuela,] received [an] opportunity to pilot a large, U.S.-registered aircraft. \* \* \* Petitioner applied to attend an FAA-certified flight school in France, and TSA conducted a background investigation.

Case 23.3 Continued

* * * *

* * * TSA concluded that Petitioner was a "Threat to Transportation/ National Security" [and] sent an email to Petitioner denying his application.

* * * Petitioner filed his petition for review with this court. * * * Andrea Vara executed a sworn declaration explaining TSA's grounds for denying Petitioner's application for training. Ms. Vara is employed by [TSA] as the Alien Flight Student Program Manager. She has been responsible for managing TSA's Alien Flight Student Program, which conducts security threat assessments on individuals who are not U.S. citizens or nationals who seek flight instruction or recurrent training from FAA-certified flight training providers.

The Vara Declaration makes it clear that Ms. Vara was the Government official who made the determination that Petitioner's application should be denied * * * . The Vara Declaration states:

* * * Petitioner submitted Training Request # 565192, seeking to train at FlightSafety International—Paris Learning Center.

* * * Petitioner was subject to an investigation, which revealed the following. In 2007, Petitioner pled guilty to conspiracy to possess with intent to distribute controlled substances and the U.S. District Court for the Northern District of Illinois sentenced him to eighty (80) months imprisonment. Petitioner's conviction made him inadmissible to the United States and led to the revocation of his FAA Airman's Certificate. Petitioner was deported to his home country of Venezuela in March 2010.

A public news article published after Petitioner was deported provided a U.S. address for Petitioner. Further, records indicated that Petitioner was a suspected international trafficker in firearms. There was evidence that Petitioner had previously been involved in the export of weapons and U.S. currency to Venezuela by private aircraft, was the second pilot of an aircraft from which several weapons and $500,000 was seized by local

authorities in Aruba, and that one of his associates was arrested in Aruba for smuggling firearms.

This information, viewed as a whole, demonstrated Petitioner's willingness to consistently disregard the law and to use an aircraft for criminal activity, in opposition to U.S. security interests. The information also raised concerns that Petitioner may use his flight training to advance the interests of a criminal enterprise, which could include an enterprise that seeks to do harm to the United States.

Based on all the foregoing information, I concluded Petitioner posed a threat to aviation and national security and * * * denied his training request.

* * * *

## II. ANALYSIS
### A. THE COURT'S JURISDICTION

* * * An action taken by TSA on behalf of the Secretary of Homeland Security is clearly subject to review.

* * * *

### B. STANDARD OF REVIEW

Pursuant to the Administrative Procedure Act, we must uphold TSA's decisions unless they are arbitrary, capricious, an abuse of discretion, or otherwise not in accordance with law.

What is important here is that, because Congress has entrusted TSA with broad authority over civil aviation security, it is TSA's job—not * * * ours— to strike a balance between convenience and security. Therefore, *in cases of this sort, we must defer to TSA actions that reasonably interpret and enforce the safety and security obligations of the agency. * * * Courts do not second-guess expert agency judgments on potential risks to national security. Rather, we defer to the informed judgment of agency officials whose obligation it is to assess risks to national security.* [Emphasis added.]

* * * *

### D. PETITIONER'S * * * CLAIM

* * * *

* * * Petitioner argues that TSA should not have used his suspected firearms trafficking or his Massachusetts

address to support its decision. [TSA had discovered that, even though Olivares had been deported with no right to return to the United States, he maintained a local address in Massachusetts.] Petitioner claims that the Massachusetts address actually belongs to his brother, and Petitioner insists that he has never illegally entered the United States. Petitioner also points out that the firearms incident occurred nearly two decades ago and that he was merely suspected of being involved. In light of the limited standard of review that controls the disposition of this case, these arguments are not persuasive. It was rational for TSA to find it suspicious and thus consider information indicating that a deported individual appeared to maintain a current U.S. address and had been suspected of involvement in firearms trafficking. The agency's weighing of this information, along with the information regarding Petitioner's known criminal history, was not inconsistent with reasoned decision making.

Given TSA's broad authority to assess potential risks to aviation and national security, the agency's clear and reasonable explanation offered in the Vara Declaration, and the limited standard of review [under the holding in the *Chevron* case], we are in no position to second-guess TSA's judgment in denying Petitioner's application. In assessing risks to national security, conclusions must often be based on informed judgment rather than concrete evidence, and that reality affects what we may reasonably insist on from the Government. When it comes to collecting evidence and drawing factual inferences in this area, the lack of competence on the part of the courts is marked, and respect for the Government's conclusions is appropriate. Where no factual certainties exist or where facts alone do not provide the answer * * * we require only that the agency so state and go on to identify the considerations it found persuasive.

*It is self-evident that TSA's action against Petitioner was related to the agency's goals of improving the safety of air*

Case 23.3 Continues

Case 23.3 Continued

*travel.* TSA was not required to show that Petitioner would engage in activities designed to compromise aviation or national security. Rather, the agency was merely required to give a reasonable explanation as to why it believed that Petitioner presented a risk to aviation or national security. The Vara Declaration satisfies this legal obligation. [Emphasis added.]

III. CONCLUSION

For the reasons set forth above, the petition for review is denied.

**Legal Reasoning Questions**

1. What impact did the Vara Declaration have on the court's ruling in this case?

2. Is a court's evaluation of an agency's assessment of a risk to national security different from a review of other agency determinations? Explain.

3. Should the agency at the center of this case have revealed the reasons for its decision before Olivares filed a suit challenging it? Explain.

# 23–5 Public Accountability

As a result of growing public concern over the powers exercised by administrative agencies, Congress passed several laws to make agencies more accountable through public scrutiny. Here, we discuss the most significant of these laws.

## 23–5a Freedom of Information Act

The Freedom of Information Act (FOIA)[13] requires the federal government to disclose certain records to any person or entity on written request, even if no reason is given for the request. All federal government agencies must make their records available electronically on the Internet and in other electronic formats.

The FOIA exempts certain types of records, such as those pertaining to national security and those containing information that is confidential or personal. ■ **EXAMPLE 23.12** Juanita, a reporter from an online health magazine, makes an FOIA request to the Centers for Disease Control and Prevention for a list of people who have contracted a highly contagious virus. The Centers for Disease Control and Prevention will not have to comply, because the requested information is confidential and personal. ■

For other records, a request that complies with the FOIA procedures need only contain a reasonable description of the information sought. An agency's failure to comply with an FOIA request can be challenged in a federal district court. The media, industry trade associations, public-interest groups, and even companies seeking information about competitors rely on these FOIA provisions to obtain information from government agencies.

## 23–5b Government in the Sunshine Act

The Government in the Sunshine Act,[14] or open meeting law, requires that "every portion of every meeting of an agency" be open to "public observation." The act also requires that the public be provided with adequate advance notice of scheduled meetings and agendas.

Like the FOIA, the Sunshine Act contains certain exceptions. Closed meetings are permitted in the following situations:

1. The subject of the meeting concerns accusing any person of a crime.

2. Open meetings would frustrate implementation of future agency actions.

3. The subject of the meeting involves matters relating to future litigation or rulemaking.

Courts interpret these exceptions to allow open access whenever possible.

## 23–5c Regulatory Flexibility Act

Concern over the effects of regulation on the efficiency of businesses, particularly smaller ones, led Congress to pass the Regulatory Flexibility Act[15] in 1980. Under this act, whenever a new regulation will have a "significant impact upon a substantial number of small entities," the

---

13. 5 U.S.C. Section 552.

14. 5 U.S.C. Section 552b.

15. 5 U.S.C. Sections 601–612.

agency must conduct a regulatory flexibility analysis. The analysis must measure the cost that the rule would impose on small businesses and consider less burdensome alternatives. The act also contains provisions to alert small businesses about forthcoming regulations. The act relieved small businesses of some record-keeping burdens, especially with regard to hazardous waste management.

### 23–5d Small Business Regulatory Enforcement Fairness Act

The Small Business Regulatory Enforcement Fairness Act[16] includes various provisions intended to ease the regulatory burden on small businesses:

16. 5 U.S.C. Sections 801 *et seq.*

1. Federal agencies must prepare guides that explain in plain English how small businesses can comply with federal regulations.
2. Congress may review new federal regulations for at least sixty days before they take effect, giving opponents of the rules time to present their arguments.
3. The courts may enforce the Regulatory Flexibility Act. This provision helps to ensure that federal agencies will consider ways to reduce the economic impact of new regulations on small businesses.
4. The Office of the National Ombudsman at the Small Business Administration was set up to receive comments from small businesses about their dealings with federal agencies. Based on these comments, Regional Small Business Fairness Boards rate the agencies and publicize their findings.

## Reviewing: Administrative Agencies

Assume that the Securities and Exchange Commission (SEC) has a rule that it will enforce statutory provisions prohibiting insider trading only when the insiders make monetary profits for themselves. Then the SEC makes a new rule, declaring that it will now bring enforcement actions against individuals for insider trading even if the individuals did not personally profit from the transactions. In making the new rule, the SEC does not conduct a rulemaking procedure but simply announces its decision. A stockbrokerage firm objects that the new rule was unlawfully developed without opportunity for public comment. The brokerage firm challenges the rule in an action that ultimately is reviewed by a federal appellate court. Using the information presented in the chapter, answer the following questions.

1. Is the SEC an executive agency or an independent regulatory agency? Does it matter to the outcome of this dispute? Explain.
2. Suppose that the SEC asserts that it has always had the statutory authority to pursue persons for insider trading regardless of whether they personally profited from the transactions. This is the only argument the SEC makes to justify changing its enforcement rules. Would a court be likely to find that the SEC's action was arbitrary and capricious under the Administrative Procedure Act (APA)? Why or why not?
3. Would a court be likely to give *Chevron* deference to the SEC's interpretation of the law on insider trading? Why or why not?
4. Now assume that a court finds that the new rule is merely "interpretive." What effect would this determination have on whether the SEC had to follow the APA's rulemaking procedures?

**Debate This** . . .  *Because an administrative law judge (ALJ) acts as both judge and jury, there should always be at least three ALJs in each administrative hearing.*

## Terms and Concepts

adjudication 457
administrative agency 448
administrative law judge (ALJ) 457
administrative process 454
bureaucracy 451

delegation doctrine 451
enabling legislation 449
exhaustion doctrine 453
final order 458
initial order 458

interpretive rule 450
legislative rule 450
notice-and-comment
  rulemaking 454
rulemaking 454

## Issue Spotters

1. The U.S. Department of Transportation (DOT) sometimes hears an appeal from a party whose contract with the DOT has been canceled. An administrative law judge (ALJ) who works for the DOT hears this appeal. What safeguards promote the ALJ's fairness? (See *The Administrative Process*.)

2. Techplate Corporation learns that a federal administrative agency is considering a rule that will have a negative impact on the firm's ability to do business. Does the firm have any opportunity to express its opinion about the pending rule? Explain. (See *The Administrative Process*.)

• **Check your answers to the Issue Spotters against the answers provided in Appendix B at the end of this text.**

## Business Scenarios

**23–1. Rulemaking and Adjudication Powers.** For decades, the Federal Trade Commission (FTC) resolved fair trade and advertising disputes through individual adjudications. In the 1960s, the FTC began promulgating rules that defined fair and unfair trade practices. In cases involving violations of these rules, the due process rights of participants were more limited and did not include cross-examination. Although anyone charged with violating a rule would receive a full adjudication, the legitimacy of the rule itself could not be challenged in the adjudication. Furthermore, a party charged with violating a rule was almost certain to lose the adjudication. Affected parties complained to a court, arguing that their rights before the FTC were unduly limited by the new rules. What would the court examine to determine whether to uphold the new rules? (See *The Administrative Process*.)

**23–2. Informal Rulemaking.** Assume that the Food and Drug Administration (FDA), using proper procedures, adopts a rule describing its future investigations. This new rule covers all future circumstances in which the FDA wants to regulate food additives. Under the new rule, the FDA is not to regulate food additives without giving food companies an opportunity to cross-examine witnesses. Later, the FDA wants to regulate methylisocyanate, a food additive. The FDA undertakes an informal rulemaking procedure, without cross-examination, and regulates methylisocyanate. Producers protest, saying that the FDA promised them the opportunity for cross-examination. The FDA responds that the Administrative Procedure Act does not require such cross-examination and that it is free to withdraw the promise made in its new rule. If the producers challenge the FDA in court, on what basis would the court rule in their favor? Explain. (See *The Administrative Process*.)

## Business Case Problems

**23–3. Rulemaking.** The Investment Company Act prohibits a mutual fund from engaging in certain transactions when there may be a conflict of interest between the manager of the fund and its shareholders. Under rules issued by the Securities and Exchange Commission (SEC), however, a fund that meets certain conditions may engage in an otherwise prohibited transaction. In June 2004, the SEC added two new conditions. A year later, the SEC reconsidered the new conditions in terms of the costs that they would impose on the funds. Within eight days, and without asking for public input, the SEC readopted the conditions. The Chamber of Commerce of the United States asked a federal appellate court to review the new rules. The Chamber argued that in readopting the rules, the SEC relied on materials not in the "rulemaking record" without providing an opportunity for public comment. The SEC countered that the information was otherwise "publicly available." In adopting a rule, should an agency consider information that is not part of the rulemaking record? Why or why not? [*Chamber of Commerce of the United States v. Securities and Exchange Commission*, 443 F.3d 890 (D.C.Cir. 2006)] (See *The Administrative Process*.)

**23–4. Business Case Problem with Sample Answer—Agency Powers.** A well-documented rise in global temperatures has coincided with a significant increase in the concentration of carbon dioxide in the atmosphere. Many scientists believe that the two trends are related, because when carbon dioxide is released into the atmosphere, it produces a greenhouse effect, trapping solar heat. Under the Clean Air Act (CAA), the Environmental Protection Agency (EPA) is authorized to regulate "any" air pollutants "emitted into . . . the ambient air" that in its "judgment cause, or contribute to, air pollution."

A group of private organizations asked the EPA to regulate carbon dioxide and other "greenhouse gas" emissions from new motor vehicles. The EPA refused, stating, among other things, that Congress last amended the CAA in 1990 without authorizing new, binding auto emissions limits. Nineteen states, including Massachusetts, asked a district court to review the EPA's denial. Did the EPA have the authority to regulate greenhouse gas emissions from new motor vehicles? If so, was its stated reason for refusing to do so consistent with that authority? Discuss. [*Massachusetts v. Environmental*

*Protection Agency,* 549 U.S. 497, 127 S.Ct. 1438, 167 L.Ed.2d 248 (2007)] (See *Agency Creation and Powers.*)

• **For a sample answer to Problem 23–4, go to Appendix C at the end of this text.**

**23–5. Judicial Deference.** After Dave Conley died of lung cancer, his widow filed for benefits under the Black Lung Benefits Act. To qualify for benefits under the act, she had to show that exposure to coal dust was a substantial contributing factor to her husband's death. Conley had been a coal miner, but he had also been a longtime smoker. At the benefits hearing, a physician testified that coal dust was a substantial factor in Conley's death. No evidence was presented to support this conclusion, however. The administrative law judge awarded benefits. On appeal, should a court defer to this decision? Discuss. [*Conley v. National Mines Corp.,* 595 F.3d 297 (6th Cir. 2010)] (See *Judicial Deference to Agency Decisions.*)

**23–6. Arbitrary and Capricious Test.** Michael Manin, an airline pilot, was twice convicted of disorderly conduct, a minor misdemeanor. To renew his flight certification with the National Transportation Safety Board (NTSB), Manin filed an application that asked him about his criminal history. He did not disclose his two convictions. When these came to light more than ten years later, Manin argued that he had not known that he was required to report convictions for minor misdemeanors. The NTSB's policy was to consider an applicant's understanding of what information a question sought before determining whether an answer was false. But without explanation, the agency departed from this policy, refused to consider Manin's argument, and revoked his certification. Was this action arbitrary or capricious? Explain. [*Manin v. National Transportation Safety Board,* 627 F.3d 1239 (D.C.Cir. 2011)] (See *Agency Creation and Powers.*)

**23–7. Adjudication.** Mechanics replaced a brake assembly on the landing gear of a CRJ-700 plane operated by GoJet Airlines, LLC. The mechanics installed gear pins to lock the assembly in place during the repair but failed to remove one of the pins after they had finished. On the plane's next flight, a warning light alerted the pilots that the landing gear would not retract after takeoff. There was a potential for danger, but the pilots flew the CRJ-700 safely back to the departure airport. No one was injured, and no property was damaged. The Federal Aviation Administration (FAA) cited GoJet for violating FAA regulations by "carelessly or recklessly operating an unairworthy airplane." GoJet objected to the citation. To which court can GoJet appeal for review? On what ground might that court decline to review the case? [*GoJet Airlines, LLC v. F.A.A.,* 743 F.3d 1168 (8th Cir. 2014)] (See *The Administrative Process.*)

**23–8. Judicial Deference to Agency Decisions.** Knox Creek Coal Corporation operates coal mines in West Virginia. The U.S. Department of Labor charged Knox's Tiller No. 1 Mine with "significant and substantial" (S&S) violations of the Federal Mine Safety and Health Act. According to the charges, inadequately sealed enclosures of electrical equipment in the mine created the potential for an explosion. The Mine Act designates a violation as S&S when it "*could* significantly and substantially contribute to the cause and effect of a coal or other mine safety or health hazard." Challenging the S&S determination, Knox filed a suit against the secretary of labor. The secretary argued that "could" means "merely possible"—if there is a violation, the existence of a hazard is assumed. This position was consistent with agency and judicial precedent and the Mine Act's history and purpose. Knox argued that "could" requires proof of the likelihood of a hazard. When does a court defer to an agency's interpretation of law? Do those circumstances exist in this case? Discuss. [*Knox Creek Coal Corp v. Secretary of Labor,* 811 F.3d 148 (4th Cir. 2016)] (See *Judicial Deference to Agency Decisions.*)

**23–9. A Question of Ethics—Rulemaking.** *To ensure highway safety and protect driver health, Congress charged federal agencies with regulating the hours of service of commercial motor vehicle operators. Between 1940 and 2003, the regulations that applied to long-haul truck drivers were mostly unchanged. (Long-haul drivers are those who operate beyond a 150-mile radius of their base.) In 2003, the Federal Motor Carrier Safety Administration (FMCSA) revised the regulations significantly, increasing the number of daily and weekly hours that drivers could work. The agency had not considered the impact of the changes on the health of the drivers, however, and the revisions were overturned.*

*The FMCSA then issued a notice that it would reconsider the revisions and opened them up for public comment. The agency analyzed the costs to the industry and the crash risks due to driver fatigue under different options. It concluded that the safety benefits of not increasing the hours were less than the economic costs. In 2005, the agency issued a rule that was nearly identical to the 2003 version. Public Citizen, Inc., and others, including the Owner-Operator Independent Drivers Association, asked the U.S. Court of Appeals for the District of Columbia Circuit to review the 2005 rule as it applied to long-haul drivers. [Owner-Operator Independent Drivers Association, Inc. v. Federal Motor Carrier Safety Administration, 494 F.3d 188 (D.C.Cir. 2007)] (See The Administrative Process.)*

**(a)** The FMCSA's cost-benefit analysis included new methods that were not disclosed to the public in time for comments. Was this unethical? Should the agency have disclosed the new methodology sooner? Why or why not?

**(b)** The FMCSA created a graph to show the risk of a crash as a function of the time a driver spent on the job. The graph plotted the first twelve hours of a day individually, but the rest of the time was depicted with an aggregate figure at the seventeenth hour. This made the risk at those hours appear to be lower. Is it unethical for an agency to manipulate data? Explain.

# Legal Reasoning Group Activity

**23–10. Investigation.** Maureen Droge was a flight attendant for United Air Lines, Inc. (UAL). After being assigned to work in Paris, France, she became pregnant. Because UAL does not allow its flight attendants to fly during their third trimester of pregnancy, Droge was placed on involuntary leave. She applied for temporary disability benefits through the French social security system. Her request was denied because UAL does not contribute to the French system on behalf of its U.S.-based flight attendants. Droge filed a charge of discrimination with the U.S. Equal Employment Opportunity Commission (EEOC), alleging that UAL had discriminated against her and other Americans. The EEOC issued a subpoena, asking UAL to detail all benefits received by all UAL employees living outside the United States. UAL refused to provide the information on the ground that it was irrelevant and compliance would be unduly burdensome. The EEOC filed a suit in a federal district court against UAL. (See *The Administrative Process.*)

**(a)** The first group will decide whether the court should enforce the subpoena and explain why.

**(b)** The second group will discuss whether the EEOC should be able to force a U.S. company operating overseas to provide the same disability benefits to employees located there as it does to employees in the United States. Should UAL be required to contribute to the French social security system for employees who reside in France?

# CHAPTER 24

# Consumer Law

All statutes, agency rules, and common law judicial decisions that serve to protect the interests of consumers are classified as **consumer law.** Traditionally, in disputes involving consumers, it was assumed that the freedom to contract carried with it the obligation to live by the deal made. Over time, this attitude has changed considerably.

Today, countless federal and state laws attempt to protect consumers from unfair trade practices, unsafe products, discriminatory or unreasonable credit requirements, and other problems related to consumer transactions. Nearly every agency and department of the federal government has an office of consumer affairs, and most states have one or more such offices to help consumers. Also, typically the attorney general's office assists consumers at the state level.

In recent years, there has been a renewed interest in attempting to protect consumers in their dealings with credit-card companies, financial institutions, and insurance companies. Congress has enacted new credit-card regulations and financial reforms to regulate the nation's largest banks. It has also enacted health-care reforms and revised food safety laws.

## 24–1 Advertising, Marketing, and Sales

Numerous federal laws have been passed to define the duties of sellers and the rights of consumers. Exhibit 24–1 shows many of the areas of consumer law that are regulated by federal statutes. We begin our discussion of this legislation by examining some of the laws and regulations relating to advertising, marketing, and sales. Although we focus on federal law, realize that state consumer protection laws in these and other areas often provide more sweeping and significant protections than do federal laws.

### 24–1a Deceptive Advertising

One of the most important federal consumer protection laws is the Federal Trade Commission Act.[1] The act created the Federal Trade Commission (FTC) to carry out the broadly stated goal of preventing unfair and deceptive trade practices, including deceptive advertising.

Generally, **deceptive advertising** occurs if a reasonable consumer would be misled by the advertising claim. Vague generalities and obvious exaggerations are permissible. These claims are known as *puffery*. When a claim

takes on the appearance of authenticity, however, it may create problems.

**Claims That Appear to Be Based on Factual Evidence** Advertising that *appears* to be based on factual evidence but, in fact, is not reasonably supported by evidence will be deemed deceptive. ■ **CASE IN POINT 24.1** MedLab, Inc., advertised that its weight-loss supplement ("The New Skinny Pill") would cause users to lose substantial amounts of weight rapidly. The ads claimed that "clinical studies prove" that people who take the pill lose "as much as 15 to 18 pounds per week and as much as 50 percent of all excess weight in just 14 days, without dieting or exercising." The FTC sued MedLab for deceptive advertising.

An expert hired by the FTC to evaluate the claim testified that to lose this much weight, "a 200-pound individual would need to run between 57 and 68 miles every day"—the equivalent of more than two marathons per day. The court concluded that the advertisement was false and misleading, granted the FTC a summary judgment, and issued a permanent injunction to stop MedLab from running the ads.[2] ■

The following case involved an advertising claim based on limited scientific evidence.

<hr>

1. 15 U.S.C. Sections 41–58.

2. *Federal Trade Commission v. MedLab, Inc,* 615 F.Supp.2d 1068 (N.D.Cal. 2009).

**EXHIBIT 24–1  Selected Areas of Consumer Law Regulated by Statutes**

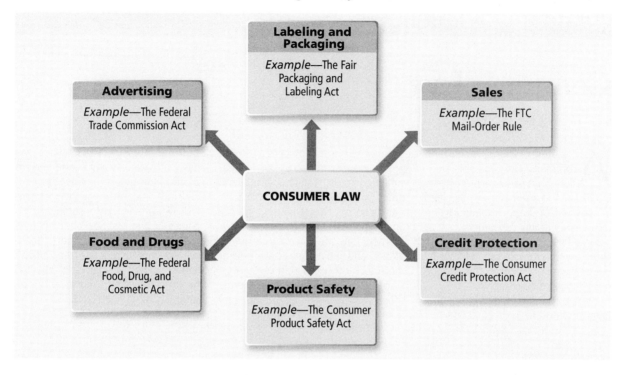

**Labeling and Packaging**
*Example*—The Fair Packaging and Labeling Act

**Advertising**
*Example*—The Federal Trade Commission Act

**Sales**
*Example*—The FTC Mail-Order Rule

**CONSUMER LAW**

**Food and Drugs**
*Example*—The Federal Food, Drug, and Cosmetic Act

**Product Safety**
*Example*—The Consumer Product Safety Act

**Credit Protection**
*Example*—The Consumer Credit Protection Act

---

Case **24.1**

# POM Wonderful, LLC v. Federal Trade Commission

United States Court of Appeals, District of Columbia Circuit, 777 F.3d 478 (2015).

**Background and Facts**  POM Wonderful, LLC, makes and sells pomegranate-based products. In ads, POM touted medical studies claiming to show that daily consumption of its products could treat, prevent, or reduce the risk of heart disease, prostate cancer, and erectile dysfunction. These ads mischaracterized the scientific evidence.

The Federal Trade Commission (FTC) charged POM with, and held POM liable for, making false, misleading, and unsubstantiated representations in violation of the FTC Act. POM was barred from running future ads asserting that its products treat or prevent any disease unless "randomized, controlled, human clinical trials" (RCTs, for "randomized controlled trials") demonstrated statistically significant results. POM petitioned the U.S. Court of Appeals for the District of Columbia Circuit to review this injunctive order.

## In the Language of the Court

*SRINIVASAN, Circuit Judge:*
    * * * *

* * * POM's ads * * * convey the net impression that clinical studies or trials show that a causal relation has been established between the consumption of the challenged POM products and its efficacy to treat, prevent or reduce the risk of the serious diseases in question. The Commission found that experts in the relevant fields would require RCTs * * * to establish such a causal relationship.

The Commission examined each of the studies invoked by petitioners in their ads, concluding that the referenced studies fail to qualify as RCTs of the kind that could afford adequate substantiation. Petitioners' claims therefore were deceptive.

Case 24.1 Continued   * * * *

* * * The Commission's finding is supported by substantial record evidence. That evidence includes written reports and testimony from medical researchers stating that experts in the fields of cardiology and urology require randomized, double-blinded, placebo-controlled clinical trials to substantiate any claim that a product treats, prevents, or reduces the risk of disease.

The Commission drew on that expert testimony to explain why the attributes of well-designed RCTs are necessary to substantiate petitioners' claims. A control group, for example, allows investigators to distinguish between real effects from the intervention, and other changes, including those due to the mere act of being treated (placebo effect) and the passage of time. Random assignment of a study's subjects to treatment and control groups increases the likelihood that the treatment and control groups are similar in relevant characteristics, so that any difference in the outcome between the two groups can be attributed to the treatment. And when a study is double-blinded ([that is,] when neither the study participants nor the investigators know which patients are in the treatment group and which patients are in the control group), it is less likely that participants or investigators will consciously or unconsciously take actions potentially biasing the results.

* * * *

* * * The need for RCTs is driven by the claims petitioners have chosen to make. * * * *An advertiser* * * *may assert a health-related claim backed by medical evidence falling short of an RCT if it includes an effective disclaimer disclosing the limitations of the supporting research.* Petitioners did not do so. [Emphasis added.]

**Decision and Remedy**  *The U.S. Court of Appeals for the District of Columbia Circuit enforced the FTC's order with respect to POM's ads. The court pointed out that "An advertiser who makes express representations about the level of support for a particular claim must possess the level of proof claimed in the ad and must convey that information to consumers in a non-misleading way."*

**Critical Thinking**

• **Ethical**  *POM claimed that it is unethical to require RCTs to substantiate disease-related claims about food products. It argued that, for instance, "doctors cannot . . . ethically deprive a control group of patients of all Vitamin C for a decade to determine whether Vitamin C helps prevent cancer." Is this a valid argument? Why or why not?*

**Claims Based on Half-Truths**  Some advertisements contain "half-truths," meaning that the presented information is true but incomplete and may therefore lead consumers to a false conclusion.  ■ **EXAMPLE 24.2**  The maker of Campbell's soups advertised that "most" Campbell's soups are low in fat and cholesterol and thus helpful in fighting heart disease. What the ad did not say was that many Campbell's soups are high in sodium and that high-sodium diets may increase the risk of heart disease. Hence, the FTC ruled that Campbell's claims were deceptive. ■ In addition, advertising that contains an endorsement by a celebrity may be deemed deceptive if the celebrity does not actually use the product.

**Bait-and-Switch Advertising**  The FTC has issued rules that govern specific advertising techniques. One of the most important rules is contained in the FTC's "Guides Against Bait Advertising."[3]

Some retailers systematically advertise merchandise at low prices to get customers into their stores. But when the customers arrive, they find that the merchandise is not in stock. Salespersons then encourage them to purchase more expensive items instead. This practice, known as **bait-and-switch advertising,** is a form of deceptive advertising. The low price is the "bait" to lure the consumer into the store. The salesperson is instructed to "switch" the consumer to a different, more expensive item.

Under the FTC guidelines, bait-and-switch advertising occurs if the seller does any of the following:

1. Refuses to show the advertised item.
2. Fails to have a reasonable quantity of the item in stock.
3. Fails to promise to deliver the advertised item within a reasonable time.
4. Discourages employees from selling the advertised item.

---

**3.** 16 C.F.R. Part 238.

**Online Deceptive Advertising** Deceptive advertising occurs in the online environment as well as offline. The FTC actively monitors online advertising. It has identified hundreds of Web sites that have made false or deceptive claims for products and services ranging from medical treatments to exercise equipment and weight-loss aids.

The FTC has issued guidelines to help online businesses comply with existing laws prohibiting deceptive advertising. These guidelines include the following requirements:

1. All ads—both online and offline—must be truthful and not misleading.
2. The claims made in an ad must be substantiated—that is, advertisers must have evidence to back up their claims.
3. Ads cannot be unfair, which the FTC defines as "likely to cause substantial consumer injury that consumers could not reasonably avoid and that is not outweighed by the benefit to consumers or competition."
4. Ads must disclose relevant limitations and qualifying information concerning the claims advertisers are making.
5. Required disclosures must be "clear and conspicuous." For instance, because consumers may not read an entire Web page, an online disclosure should be placed as close as possible to the claim being qualified. Generally, hyperlinks to a disclosure are recommended only for lengthy disclosures. If hyperlinks are used, they should be obvious and should be placed as close as possible to the relevant information it qualifies.

The FTC creates additional guidelines as needed to respond to new issues that arise with online advertising. One new issue involves so-called native ads, which are discussed in this chapter's *Digital Update* feature.

**Federal Trade Commission Actions** The FTC receives complaints from many sources, including competitors of alleged violators, consumers, trade associations, Better Business Bureaus, and government organizations and officials. When the agency receives numerous and widespread complaints about a particular problem, it will investigate.

**Formal Complaint.** If the FTC concludes that a given advertisement is unfair or deceptive, it drafts a formal complaint, which is sent to the alleged offender. The company may agree to settle the complaint without further proceedings. If not, the FTC can conduct a hearing in which the company can present its defense.

**FTC Orders and Remedies.** If the FTC succeeds in proving that an advertisement is unfair or deceptive, it usually issues a **cease-and-desist order** requiring the company to stop the challenged advertising. In some circumstances, it may also impose a sanction known as **counteradvertising.** This requires the company to advertise anew—in print, on the Internet, on radio, and on television—to inform the public about the earlier misinformation. The FTC sometimes institutes a **multiple product order,** which requires a firm to stop false advertising for all of its products, not just the product involved in the original action.

**Damages When Consumers Are Injured.** When a company's deceptive ad involves wrongful charges to consumers, the FTC may seek other remedies, including damages. ■ **CASE IN POINT 24.3** The FTC sued Bronson Partners, LLC, for deceptively advertising two products—Chinese Diet Tea and Bio-Slim Patch. Bronson's ads claimed that the diet tea "eliminates 91 percent of absorbed sugars," "prevents 83 percent of fat absorption," and "doubles your metabolic rate to burn calories fast." The Bio-Slim Patch ads promised "lasting weight loss" and claimed that "ugly fatty tissue will disappear at a spectacular rate" as product users wear the patch while carrying on their normal lifestyle.

Eventually, Bronson conceded that it had engaged in deceptive advertising, and the FTC sought damages. The court awarded the FTC $1,942,325, which was the amount of Bronson's revenues from the two products.[4] ■

**Restitution Possible.** When a company's deceptive ad leads to wrongful payments by consumers, the FTC may seek other remedies, including restitution. ■ **CASE IN POINT 24.4** Verity International, Ltd., billed phone-line subscribers who accessed certain online pornography sites at the rate for international calls to Madagascar. When consumers complained about the charges, Verity told them that the charges were valid and had to be paid, or the consumers would face further collection actions. A federal appellate court held that this representation of "uncontestability" was deceptive and a violation of the FTC act. The court ordered Verity to pay nearly $18 million in restitution to consumers.[5] ■

---

4. *Federal Trade Commission v. Bronson Partners, LLC,* 664 F.3d 359 (2d Cir. 2011).
5. *Federal Trade Commission v. Verity International, Ltd.,* 443 F.3d 48 (2d Cir. 2006).

## DIGITAL UPDATE    Regulating "Native" Ads on the Internet

Sponsored content on the Internet—content that someone pays to put there—is everywhere. One particular type of sponsored content is the "native" ad. Here, *native* describes advertisements that follow the natural form and function of the user experience into which they are placed. Thus, such an ad matches the rest of a Web page's content, including the visual design, as if it were "native" to the page.

### Native Ad Integration on Desktops and Mobile Devices

Perhaps the most obvious native ads are in search engine results. When you type "native ads" in a Google search box, you will find that the first several "hits" listed in the search results are actually sponsored ads. Yet they have the look and feel of the rest of the search results.

Additionally, native ads are often placed within stories in online publications. Suppose, for instance, that you are reading a story on new fashions on your smartphone. You will likely see a native ad that looks as if it is part of the story but that is actually sponsored and perhaps written by a clothing company.

Some native ads are delivered via "recommendation widgets." Usually, the widgets are integrated into a page but do not mimic the appearance of the page. Rather, they direct you to a different Web page—perhaps telling you that "you might like" that site. Clicking the widget takes you to the site.

Native ads have become increasingly popular because desktop, smartphone, and tablet users have figured out how to block traditional online ads. Moreover, native ads are less intrusive than traditional online

ads—important because of the increasing number of consumers who most often access small screens, such as those on smartphones.

### The Federal Trade Commission Takes Action

In response to the growth in native advertising, the Federal Trade Commission (FTC) has issued guidelines.[a] The FTC starts out with the basic question "[A]s native advertising evolves, are consumers able to differentiate advertising from other content?" In its guidance document,[b] the FTC suggests the following:

- Disclosures should be placed where consumers will notice them.
- Disclosures should be placed not after the native ad, but before or above it.
- Disclosures should remain with native ads if the ads are republished.
- Once consumers arrive on a click- or tap-into page where the complete native ad appears, disclosures should be placed as close as possible to where consumers will look first.
- Disclosures should stand out and should be understandable.

**Critical Thinking** *What is the equivalent of native advertising in commercially released movies?*

a. Federal Trade Commission, *Native Advertising: A Guide to Business,* December 2015.
b. Federal Trade Commission, *.com Disclosures: How to Make Effective Disclosures in Digital Advertising,* March 2013, available at www.ftc.gov/tips-advice/business-center/guidance/com-disclosures-how-make-effective-disclosures-digital.

**False Advertising Claims under the Lanham Act** The Lanham Act[6] protects trademarks, as discussed elsewhere. The act also covers false advertising claims. To state a successful claim for false advertising under this act, a business must establish each of the following elements:

1. An injury to a commercial interest in reputation or sales.

6. 15 U.S.C. Sections 1051–1128.

2. Direct causation of the injury by false or deceptive advertising.
3. A loss of business from buyers who were deceived by the advertising.

The dispute between the parties in the following case focused initially on a mimicked microchip. When the case reached the United States Supreme Court, the question was whether Static Control Components, Inc., could sue Lexmark International, Inc., for false advertising under the Lanham Act.

Case 24.2

# Lexmark International, Inc.
# v. Static Control Components, Inc.

Supreme Court of the United States, __ U.S. __, 134 S.Ct. 1377, 188 L.Ed.2d 392 (2014).

**Background and Facts** Lexmark International, Inc., sells the only style of toner cartridges that work with the company's laser printers. Other businesses—known as remanufacturers—acquire and refurbish used Lexmark cartridges to sell in competition with the cartridges sold by Lexmark. To deter remanufacturing, Lexmark introduced a program that gave customers a 20 percent discount on new toner cartridges if they agreed to return the empty cartridges to Lexmark. Static Control Components, Inc., makes and sells components for the remanufactured cartridges, including microchips that mimic the chips in Lexmark's cartridges.

Lexmark released ads that claimed Static Control's microchips illegally infringed Lexmark's patents. Lexmark then filed a suit in a federal district court against Static Control, alleging violations of intellectual property law. Static Control counterclaimed, alleging that Lexmark had engaged in false advertising in violation of the Lanham Act. The court dismissed the counterclaim. It held that Static Control lacked standing to bring that claim. On Static Control's appeal, the U.S. Court of Appeals for the Sixth Circuit reversed the dismissal. Lexmark appealed to the United States Supreme Court.

## In the Language of the Court

Justice *SCALIA* delivered the opinion of the Court.

\* \* \* \*

First, \* \* \* a statutory cause of action extends only to plaintiffs whose interests fall within the zone of interests protected by the law invoked.

\* \* \* \*

\* \* \* To come within the zone of interests in a suit for false advertising under [the Lanham Act,] a plaintiff must allege an injury to a commercial interest in reputation or sales.

\* \* \* \*

Second, \* \* \* a statutory cause of action is limited to plaintiffs whose injuries are proximately caused by violations of the statute.

\* \* \* \*

\* \* \* A plaintiff suing under [the Lanham Act] ordinarily must show economic or reputational injury flowing directly from the deception wrought by the defendant's advertising; and that occurs when deception of consumers causes them to withhold trade from the plaintiff.

\* \* \* \*

Applying those principles to Static Control's false-advertising claim, we conclude that Static Control comes within the class of plaintiffs whom Congress authorized to sue under [the Lanham Act].

To begin, Static Control's alleged injuries—lost sales and damage to its business reputation—are injuries to precisely the sorts of commercial interests the Act protects. *Static Control is suing not as a deceived consumer, but [in the words of the statute] as a "person engaged in \* \* \* commerce within the control of Congress" whose position in the marketplace has been damaged by Lexmark's false advertising.* There is no doubt that it is within the zone of interests protected by the statute. [Emphasis added.]

Static Control also sufficiently alleged that its injuries were proximately caused by Lexmark's misrepresentations.

First, Static Control alleged that Lexmark disparaged its business and products by asserting that Static Control's business was illegal. *When a defendant harms a plaintiff's reputation by casting aspersions [abuse] on its business, the plaintiff's injury flows directly from the audience's belief in the disparaging statements.* [Emphasis added.]

\* \* \* \*

The District Court emphasized that Lexmark and Static Control are not direct competitors [since Static Control is not itself a remanufacturer]. But when a party claims reputational injury from disparagement, competition is not required for proximate cause; and that is true even if the defendant's aim was to harm its immediate competitors, and the plaintiff merely suffered collateral damage.

**Case 24.2 Continued**

In addition, Static Control adequately alleged proximate causation by alleging that it designed, manufactured, and sold microchips that both (1) were necessary for, and (2) had no other use than, refurbishing Lexmark toner cartridges. It follows from that allegation that any false advertising that reduced the remanufacturers' business necessarily injured Static Control as well.

**Decision and Remedy** *The United States Supreme Court affirmed the lower court's ruling. Static Control had adequately pleaded the elements of a cause of action under the Lanham Act for false advertising. The Court's decision clarified that businesses do not need to be direct competitors to bring an action for false advertising under the act.*

**Critical Thinking**
- **What If the Facts Were Different?** *Suppose that Lexmark had issued a retraction of its advertising claims before this case reached the Supreme Court. Would the outcome have been different? Discuss.*
- **Legal Environment** *Under the Court's ruling in this case, is Static Control now entitled to relief? Explain your answer.*

## 24–1b Marketing

In addition to regulating advertising practices, Congress has passed several laws to protect consumers against other marketing practices.

**Telephone Solicitation** The Telephone Consumer Protection Act (TCPA)[7] prohibits telephone solicitation using an automatic telephone dialing system or a prerecorded voice. In addition, most states have statutes regulating telephone solicitation. The TCPA also makes it illegal to transmit ads via fax without first obtaining the recipient's permission. (Most states also have laws regulating telephone solicitation.)

The Federal Communications Commission (FCC) enforces the TCPA. The FCC imposes substantial fines ($11,000 each day) on companies that violate the junk fax provisions of the act.[8] The TCPA also gives consumers a right to sue for either $500 for each violation of the act or for the actual monetary losses resulting from a violation, whichever is greater. If a court finds that a defendant willfully or knowingly violated the act, the court has the discretion to treble (triple) the amount of damages awarded.

**Fraudulent Telemarketing** The Telemarketing and Consumer Fraud and Abuse Prevention Act[9] directed the FTC to establish rules governing telemarketing and to bring actions against fraudulent telemarketers.

The FTC's Telemarketing Sales Rule (TSR)[10] requires a telemarketer to identify the seller's name, describe the product being sold, and disclose all material facts related to the sale (such as the total cost). The TSR makes it illegal for telemarketers to misrepresent information or facts about their goods or services. A telemarketer must also remove a consumer's name from its list of potential contacts if the customer so requests.

An amendment to the TSR established the national Do Not Call Registry. Telemarketers must refrain from calling those consumers who have placed their names on the list. Significantly, the TSR applies to any offer made to consumers in the United States—even if the offer comes from a foreign firm. Thus, the TSR helps to protect consumers from illegal cross-border telemarketing operations.

## 24–1c Sales

A number of statutes protect consumers by requiring the disclosure of certain terms in sales transactions and providing rules governing unsolicited merchandise. The FTC has regulatory authority in this area, as do some other federal agencies.

Many states and the FTC have **"cooling-off" laws** that permit the buyers of goods sold door to door to cancel their contracts within three business days. The FTC rule also requires that consumers be notified in Spanish of this right if the oral negotiations for the sale were in that language.

The contracts that fall under these cancellation rules include trade show sales contracts, contracts for home

---

**7.** 47 U.S.C. Sections 227 *et seq.*
**8.** See, for instance, *Imhoff Investment, LLC v. Alfoccinio, Inc.*, 792 F.3d 627 (6th Cir. 2015).
**9.** 15 U.S.C. 6101–6108.

**10.** 16 C.F.R. Sections 310.1–310.8.

equity loans, Internet purchase contracts, and home (door-to-door) sales contracts. In addition, certain states have passed laws allowing consumers to cancel contracts for dating services, gym memberships, and weight loss programs.

The FTC Mail or Telephone Order Merchandise Rule[11] protects consumers who purchase goods via mail, Internet, phone, or fax. Merchants are required to ship orders within the time promised in their advertisements and to notify consumers when orders cannot be shipped on time. If the seller does not give an estimated shipping time, it must ship within thirty days. Merchants must also issue a refund within a specified period of time when a consumer cancels an order.

# 24–2 Labeling and Packaging Laws

A number of federal and state laws deal specifically with the information given on labels and packages. In general, labels must be accurate, and they must use words that are easily understood by the ordinary consumer. In some instances, labels must specify the raw materials used in the product, such as the percentage of cotton, nylon, or other fiber used in a garment. In other instances, the product must carry a warning, such as those required on cigarette packages and advertising.[12]

## 24–2a Automobile Fuel Economy Labels

The Energy Policy and Conservation Act (EPCA)[13] requires automakers to attach an information label to every new car. The label must include the Environmental Protection Agency's fuel economy estimate for the vehicle. ■ **CASE IN POINT 24.5** Gaetano Paduano bought a new Honda Civic Hybrid in California. The information label on the car included the fuel economy estimate from the Environmental Protection Agency (EPA). Honda's sales brochure added, "Just drive the Hybrid like you would a conventional car and save on fuel bills."

When Paduano discovered that the car's fuel economy was less than half of the EPA's estimate, he sued Honda for deceptive advertising under a California law. The automaker claimed that the federal law (the EPCA) preempted the state's deceptive advertising law. The court held in Paduano's favor, finding that the federal statute did not preempt a claim for deceptive advertising made under state law.[14] ■

## 24–2b Food Labeling

Because the quality and safety of food are so important to consumers, several statutes deal specifically with food labeling. The Fair Packaging and Labeling Act requires that food product labels identify (1) the product, (2) the net quantity of the contents (and, if the number of servings is stated, the size of a serving), (3) the manufacturer, and (4) the packager or distributor. The act includes additional requirements concerning descriptions on packages, savings claims, components of nonfood products, and standards for the partial filling of packages.

**Nutritional Content of Food Products** Food products must bear labels detailing the nutritional content, including the number of calories and the amounts of various nutrients that the food contains. The Nutrition Labeling and Education Act[15] requires food labels to provide standard nutrition facts and regulates the use of such terms as *fresh* and *low fat*.

The U.S. Food and Drug Administration (FDA) and the U.S. Department of Agriculture (USDA) are the primary agencies that issue regulations on food labeling. These rules are published in the *Federal Register* and updated annually.

**Caloric Content of Restaurant Foods** The health-care reforms enacted in 2010 (the Affordable Care Act, or Obamacare) included provisions aimed at combating the problem of obesity in the United States. All restaurant chains with twenty or more locations are now required to post the caloric content of the foods on their menus so that customers will know how many calories the foods contain.[16] Foods offered through vending machines must also be labeled so that their caloric content is visible to would-be purchasers.

In addition, restaurants must post guidelines on the number of calories that an average person requires daily so that customers can determine what portion of a day's calories a particular food will provide. The hope is that consumers, armed with this information, will consider the number of calories when they make their food choices. The federal law on menu labeling supersedes all previous state and local laws in this area.

11. 16 C.F.R. Sections 435.1–435.2.
12. 15 U.S.C. Sections 1331–1341.
13. 49 U.S.C. Section 32908(b)(1).
14. *Paduano v. American Honda Motor Co.*, 169 Cal.App.4th 1453, 88 Cal. Rptr.3d 90 (2009).
15. 21 U.S.C. Section 343.1.
16. See Section 4205 of the Patient Protection and Affordable Care Act, Pub. L. No. 111-148, 124 Stat. 119 (March 23, 2010).

# 24–3 Protection of Health and Safety

Although labeling and packaging laws promote consumer health and safety, there is a significant distinction between regulating the information dispensed about a product and regulating the actual content of the product. The classic example is tobacco products. Producers of tobacco products must use labels that warn consumers about the health hazards associated with their use, but the sale of tobacco products has not been subjected to significant restrictions. We now examine various laws that regulate the actual products made available to consumers.

## 24–3a The Federal Food, Drug, and Cosmetic Act

The most important federal legislation regulating food and drugs is the Federal Food, Drug, and Cosmetic Act (FDCA).[17] The act protects consumers against adulterated (contaminated) and misbranded foods and drugs. The FDCA establishes food standards, specifies safe levels of potentially hazardous food additives, and provides classifications of foods and food advertising. Most of these statutory requirements are monitored and enforced by the Food and Drug Administration (FDA).

Interestingly, the European Union and a number of other countries, such as Canada, have banned some foods that the FDA assumes to be safe. These foods include brominated vegetable oil (a common ingredient in sports drinks, such as Gatorade) and Olestra/Olean (a cholesterol-free fat substitute found in certain potato chips). Food products containing such substances may not be sold in the European Union. Similarly, certain food colorings found in processed foods in the United States (in M&Ms and Kraft macaroni and cheese, for instance) are not allowed in foods in some other countries.

**Tainted Foods** In the last twenty years or so, many people in the United States have contracted food poisoning from eating foods that were contaminated, often with salmonella or *E. coli* bacteria. ■ **EXAMPLE 24.6** During 2015 and 2016, hundreds of people across the United States were sickened by eating tainted food at the popular restaurant chain Chipotle Mexican Grill. Causes of illness in these outbreaks included *E-coli* and salmonella, as well as the highly contagious norovirus. ■

In response to the problem of food contamination, Congress enacted the Food Safety Modernization Act (FSMA)[18] to provide greater government control over the U.S. food safety system. The act gives the FDA authority to directly recall any food products that it suspects are tainted, rather than relying on the producers to recall items.

The FSMA requires anyone who manufactures, processes, packs, distributes, receives, holds, or imports food products to pay a fee and register with the U.S. Department of Health and Human Services. (There are some exceptions for small farmers.) Owners and operators of such facilities are required to analyze and identify food safety hazards, implement preventive controls, monitor effectiveness, and take corrective actions. The FSMA places additional restrictions on importers of food and requires them to verify that imported foods meet U.S. safety standards.

**Drugs and Medical Devices** The FDA is also responsible under the FDCA for ensuring that drugs are safe and effective before they are marketed to the public. Because the FDA must ensure the safety of new medications, there is always a delay before drugs are available to the public, and this sometimes leads to controversy.

■ **CASE IN POINT 24.7** A group of citizens petitioned the FDA to allow everyone access to "Plan B"—the morning-after birth control pill—without a prescription. The FDA denied the petition and continued to require women under the age of seventeen to obtain a prescription. The group appealed to a federal district court, claiming that the prescription requirement can delay access to the pill. The pill should be taken as soon as possible after sexual intercourse, preferably within twenty-four hours. The court ruled in favor of the plaintiffs and ordered the FDA to make the morning-after pill available to people of any age without a prescription.[19] ■

## 24–3b The Consumer Product Safety Act

The Consumer Product Safety Act[20] created a comprehensive regulatory scheme over consumer safety matters and established the Consumer Product Safety Commission (CPSC).

**The CPSC's Authority** The CPSC conducts research on the safety of individual consumer products and maintains a clearinghouse on the risks associated with various products. The Consumer Product Safety Act authorizes the CPSC to do the following:

---

17. 21 U.S.C. Sections 301–393.

18. Pub. L. No. 111-353, 124 Stat. 3885 (January 4, 2011). This statute affected numerous parts of Title 21 of the U.S.C.
19. *Tummino v. Hamburg,* 936 F.Supp.2d 162 (E.D.N.Y. 2013).
20. 15 U.S.C. Sections 2051–2083.

1. Set safety standards for consumer products.
2. Ban the manufacture and sale of any product that the commission believes poses an "unreasonable risk" to consumers. (Products banned by the CPSC have included various types of fireworks, cribs, and toys, as well as many products containing asbestos or vinyl chloride.)
3. Remove from the market any products it believes to be imminently hazardous. The CPSC frequently works in conjunction with manufacturers to conduct voluntary recalls of defective products from stores. ■ **EXAMPLE 24.8** In cooperation with the CPSC, the Scandinavian company IKEA recalled three million baby bed canopies and thirty million wall-mounted children's lamps because they posed a strangulation risk to children. ■
4. Require manufacturers to report on any products already sold or intended for sale if the products have proved to be hazardous.
5. Administer other product-safety legislation, including the Child Protection and Toy Safety Act[21] and the Federal Hazardous Substances Act.[22]

**Notification Requirements** The Consumer Product Safety Act requires the distributors of consumer products to notify the CPSC immediately if they receive information that a product "contains a defect which . . . creates a substantial risk to the public" or "an unreasonable risk of serious injury or death."

■ **EXAMPLE 24.9** A company that sells juicers receives twenty-three letters from customers complaining that during operation the juicer suddenly exploded, sending pieces of glass and razor-sharp metal across the room. The company must immediately notify the CPSC because the alleged defect creates a substantial risk to the public. ■

### 24–3c Health-Care Reforms

The health-care reforms enacted in 2010 gave Americans new rights and benefits with regard to health care.[23] The legislation also prohibited certain insurance company practices.

**Expanded Coverage for Children and Seniors**
The reforms enabled more children to obtain health-insurance coverage and allowed young adults (under age twenty-six) to remain on their parents' health insurance policies. The legislation also ended lifetime limits and most annual limits on care, and gave insured persons access to recommended preventive services (such as cancer screening and vaccinations) without cost. People can no longer be denied insurance because of preexisting conditions. Medicare recipients now receive a 50 percent discount on name-brand drugs, and the reforms will eliminate a gap in Medicare's prescription drug coverage by 2020.

**Controlling Costs of Health Insurance** In an attempt to control the rising costs of health insurance, certain restrictions were placed on insurance companies. Insurance companies must spend at least 85 percent of all premium dollars collected from large employers (80 percent of the premiums collected from individuals and small employers) on benefits and quality improvement. If insurance companies do not meet these goals, they must provide rebates to consumers. Additionally, states can require insurance companies to justify any premium increases to be eligible to participate in the new health-insurance exchanges. In spite of the legislation, health insurance costs have continued to increase.

## 24–4 Credit Protection

Credit protection is one of the more important aspects of consumer protection legislation. Nearly 80 percent of U.S. consumers have credit cards, and most carry a balance on these cards—a total of about $2.5 trillion of debt nationwide. The Consumer Financial Protection Bureau (CFPB) is the agency that oversees the credit practices of banks, mortgage lenders, and credit-card companies.[24]

### 24–4a The Truth-in-Lending Act

A key statute regulating the credit and credit-card industries is the Truth-in-Lending Act (TILA), the name commonly given to Title I of the Consumer Credit Protection Act, as amended.[25] The TILA is basically a *disclosure law*. It is administered by the Federal Reserve Board and requires sellers and lenders to disclose credit terms and loan terms so that individuals can shop around for the best financing arrangements.

---

**21.** 15 U.S.C. Section 1262(e).
**22.** 15 U.S.C. Sections 1261–1273.
**23.** Patient Protection and Affordable Health Care Act of 2010, Pub. L. No.111-148, 124 Stat. 119 (March 23, 2010); and the Health Care and Education Reconciliation Act of 2010, Pub. L. No. 111-152, 124 Stat. 1029 (March 30, 2010).
**24.** Title 10 of the Restoring American Financial Stability Act of 2010, S.B. 3217, April 15, 2010.
**25.** 15 U.S.C. Sections 1601–1693r.

**Application** TILA requirements apply only to those who, in the ordinary course of business, lend funds, sell on credit, or arrange for the extension of credit. Thus, sales or loans made between two consumers do not come under the protection of the act. Additionally, this law protects only debtors who are natural persons (as opposed to the artificial "person" of a corporation). It does not extend to other legal entities.

**Disclosure Requirements** The TILA's disclosure requirements are contained in **Regulation Z,** issued by the Federal Reserve Board of Governors. If the contracting parties are subject to the TILA, the requirements of Regulation Z apply to any transaction involving an installment sales contract that calls for payment to be made in more than four installments. Transactions subject to Regulation Z typically include installment loans, retail and installment sales, car loans, home-improvement loans, and certain real estate loans if the amount of financing is less than $25,000.

Under the provisions of the TILA, all of the terms of a credit instrument must be clearly and conspicuously disclosed. A lender must disclose the annual percentage rate (APR), finance charge, amount financed, and total payments (the sum of the amount loaned, plus any fees, finance charges, and interest). If a creditor fails to follow the *exact* procedures required by the TILA, the creditor risks contract rescission (cancellation) under the act.

**Equal Credit Opportunity** Congress enacted the Equal Credit Opportunity Act (ECOA)[26] as an amendment to the TILA. The ECOA prohibits the denial of credit solely on the basis of race, religion, national origin, color, gender, marital status, or age. The act also prohibits credit discrimination on the basis of whether an individual receives certain forms of income, such as public-assistance benefits.

Under the ECOA, a creditor may not require a cosigner on a credit instrument if the applicant qualifies under the creditor's standards of creditworthiness for the amount and terms of the credit request. **■ CASE IN POINT 24.10** T.R. Hughes, Inc., and Summit Pointe, LLC, obtained financing from Frontenac Bank to construct two real estate developments near St. Louis, Missouri. The bank also required the builder, Thomas R. Hughes, and his wife, Carolyn Hughes, to sign personal guaranty agreements for the loans.

When the borrowers failed to make the loan payments, the bank sued the two companies and Thomas and Carolyn Hughes personally, and foreclosed on the properties. Carolyn claimed that the personal guaranty contracts that she signed were obtained in violation of the ECOA. The court held that because the applicant, Thomas R. Hughes, was creditworthy, the personal guarantys of Carolyn Hughes were obtained in violation of the ECOA and therefore unenforceable.[27] ■

**Credit-Card Rules** The TILA also contains provisions regarding credit cards. One provision limits the liability of a cardholder to $50 per card for unauthorized charges made before the creditor is notified that the card has been lost. If a consumer receives an *unsolicited* credit card in the mail that is later stolen, the company that issued the card cannot charge the consumer for any unauthorized charges.

Another provision requires credit-card companies to disclose the balance computation method that is used to determine the outstanding balance and to state when finance charges begin to accrue. Other provisions set forth procedures for resolving billing disputes with the credit-card company. These procedures are used if, for instance, a cardholder thinks that an error has occurred in billing or wishes to withhold payment for a faulty product purchased by credit card.

**Amendments to Credit-Card Rules** Amendments to the TILA's credit-card rules added the following protections:

1. A company may not retroactively increase the interest rates on existing card balances unless the account is sixty days delinquent.
2. A company must provide forty-five days' advance notice to consumers before changing its credit-card terms.
3. Monthly bills must be sent to cardholders twenty-one days before the due date.
4. The interest rate charged on a customer's credit-card balance may not be increased except in specific situations, such as when a promotional rate ends.
5. A company may not charge over-limit fees except in specified situations.
6. When the customer has balances at different interest rates, payments in excess of the minimum amount due must be applied first to the balance with the highest rate. (For instance, a higher interest rate is commonly charged for cash advances.)
7. A company may not compute finance charges based on the previous billing cycle (a practice known as double-cycle billing). This practice hurts consumers because they are charged interest for the previous cycle even if they have paid the bill in full.

---

26. 15 U.S.C. Sections 1691–1691f.

27. *Frontenac Bank v. T.R. Hughes, Inc.,* 404 S.W.3d 272 (Mo.App. 2012).

## 24–4b The Fair Credit Reporting Act

The Fair Credit Reporting Act (FCRA)[28] protects consumers against inaccurate credit reporting and requires that lenders and other creditors report correct, relevant, and up-to-date information. The act provides that con-

28. 15 U.S.C. Sections 1681–1681t.

sumer credit reporting agencies may issue credit reports to users only for specified purposes. Legitimate purposes include the extension of credit, the issuance of insurance policies, and responding to the consumer's request.

Whether an Internet service provider had a legitimate purpose to pull a customer's credit report was at issue in the following case.

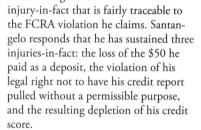

**Case Analysis 24.3**

# Santangelo v. Comcast Corporation

United States District Court, Northern District of Illinois, Eastern Division, __ F.Supp.3d __, 2016 WL 464223 (2016).

### In the Language of the Court

John Z. *LEE*, United States District Judge
* * * *

I. Factual and Procedural Background
[Keith Santangelo filed a complaint in a federal district court against Comcast Corporation, alleging a violation of the Fair Credit Reporting Act (FCRA).] Santangelo alleges * * * that he contacted Comcast through the company's online customer service "Chat" function * * * and requested Internet service for his new apartment. During the chat session, a Comcast representative asked Santangelo for permission to run a credit inquiry. Santangelo asked if any option was available to avoid the credit inquiry. The Comcast representative told him that the company would forgo the inquiry if he paid a $50 deposit.

The option to pay a $50 deposit in order to avoid a credit inquiry was an explicit part of Comcast's official Risk Management Policy * * * .The policy also required a $50 deposit from any prospective customer who agreed to a credit inquiry but whose credit score proved to be unsatisfactory. According to Santangelo, the deposit policy "reflects Comcast's calculated business decision and belief that the collection of a $50 deposit is sufficient to cover the risk presented by a person with bad credit and is sufficient to cover the risk presented by a person who refuses a credit pull."

Santangelo opted to pay the $50 deposit in lieu of a credit inquiry. * * * Nevertheless, Comcast, without Santangelo's authorization, pulled his credit

report * * * . This credit inquiry depleted [lowered] Santangelo's credit score.
* * * *

* * * Comcast now moves to dismiss the * * * complaint.
II. Analysis
* * * *

*FCRA prohibits the obtaining of a "consumer report," commonly known as a credit report, except for purposes authorized by that statute. The statute lists specific permissible purposes, such as * * * any * * * "legitimate business need * * * in connection with a business transaction that is initiated by the consumer."* These limitations are intended to produce a balance between consumer privacy and the needs of a modern, credit-driven economy. [Emphasis added.]

Santangelo contends that Comcast did not have a permissible purpose for obtaining his credit report after he paid the $50 deposit in exchange for the company's promise not to check his credit. If he is correct and the company's violation was willful, he would be entitled to recover attorney's fees and either actual damages or statutory damages between $100 and $1,000. If the company's violation was merely negligent, Santangelo would be permitted to recover only attorney's fees and actual damages.
1. Standing
Comcast first argues that Santangelo lacks standing to bring his FCRA claim. To establish standing * * * a plaintiff must show * * * the injury is fairly traceable to the challenged action of the defendant.

According to Comcast, Santangelo has not alleged an injury-in-fact that is fairly traceable to the FCRA violation he claims. Santangelo responds that he has sustained three injuries-in-fact: the loss of the $50 he paid as a deposit, the violation of his legal right not to have his credit report pulled without a permissible purpose, and the resulting depletion of his credit score.
* * * *

* * * It was the very fact that Comcast received the $50 from Santangelo before it performed the credit check that made it illegal. * * * And once Comcast checked Santangelo's credit, it should have refunded the deposit immediately, rather than keeping it. Comcast's receipt and withholding of the $50, therefore, is inextricable [inseparable] from the FCRA violation and can be said to be fairly traceable to the FCRA violation. * * * Even if the $50.00 deposit were fully refundable, Santangelo still has standing based on the lost time-value of the money.

* * * Santangelo also has sufficiently alleged an injury-in-fact by alleging that Comcast obtained his credit report without a permissible purpose in violation of the FCRA.

*Because the FCRA grants consumers a legally protected interest in limiting access to their credit reports and provides redress for violations, * * * Santangelo's allegations about Comcast's interference with that legally protected interest are sufficient*

**Case 24.3 Continued**

*to establish* * * * *standing.* [Emphasis added.]

* * * Santangelo also alleges that the FCRA violation in this case depleted his credit score. In response, Comcast contends that a reduced credit score, without resulting damages, does not constitute an injury.

* * * The Court agrees with Santangelo that a depleted credit score is sufficient to constitute an injury * * *. Credit scores are of great importance in our economy, and a depleted credit score could affect a consumer in numerous ways, inflicting harm that often may be difficult to prove or quantify. Congress has the power to discourage the needless depletion of consumers' credit scores even when the depleted score cannot be neatly tied to a financial harm.

2. Sufficiency of Santangelo's allegations

Comcast next argues that Santangelo's allegations do not state an FCRA claim.

* * * *

In his * * * complaint, Santangelo * * * alleges that Comcast's deposit policies demonstrate its lack of a legitimate need to run credit checks with respect to consumers who paid a $50 deposit. According to the * * * complaint, Comcast's established policy is to forgo a credit check in exchange for a $50 deposit. The company also has a policy of accepting a $50 deposit from consumers who opt for a credit check but prove to have poor credit. Santangelo compares this situation to that of a car dealer who accepts a cash payment for the full purchase price of a car. * * * The car dealer * * * does not have a legitimate need to obtain the purchaser's credit report. Similarly, a landlord does not have a legitimate need to obtain a tenant's credit report if the tenant is entitled to a lease renewal without regard to creditworthiness.

In response, Comcast * * * argues that it had a legitimate business need to establish Santangelo's creditworthiness despite his deposit because—unlike in the car dealer example—his $50 deposit would cover less than two months of service in a long-term contract. * * * [Santangelo] contends that, under company policy, his creditworthiness was irrelevant to Comcast's determination of his eligibility for service once the deposit was collected, much like the tenants in [the landlord example].

* * * *

* * * Comcast's mere violation of its alleged agreement not to pull Santangelo's credit report does not support an FCRA claim. But the possibility that the company itself believed that its customers' creditworthiness was irrelevant if they paid a deposit is enough.

Comcast's final argument for dismissing Santangelo's FCRA claim is that he neither explicitly alleges that the company's actions were willful, which is necessary to trigger statutory damages, nor identifies any actual damages that he could recover if Comcast acted only negligently. Although [Santangelo] does not use the word willful in his complaint, he alleges that the company obtained his credit report despite that it "knew that it did not have a legitimate business need." This allegation implies recklessness at the very least, and reckless conduct qualifies as willful conduct under the FCRA.

* * * *

III. Conclusion

* * * The Court denies Comcast's motion to dismiss.

**Legal Reasoning Questions**

1. Comcast argued that it had refunded Santangelo's $50, plus interest in the amount of $10, four months after pulling his credit report. Does this argument undercut the plaintiff's claim to have standing? Why or why not?

2. What might discovery reveal that would affect the outcome in this case? Explain.

3. What damages might Santangelo be able to prove based on the depletion of his credit score?

**Consumer Notification and Inaccurate Information** Any time a consumer is denied credit or insurance on the basis of her or his credit report, the consumer must be notified of that fact. The notice must include the name and address of the credit-reporting agency that issued the report. The same notice must be sent to consumers who are charged more than others ordinarily would be for credit or insurance because of their credit reports.

Under the FCRA, consumers may request the source of any information used by the credit agency, as well as the identity of anyone who has received an agency's report. Consumers are also permitted to access the information about them contained in a credit reporting agency's files.

If a consumer discovers that an agency's files contain inaccurate information, he or she should report the problem to the agency. On the consumer's written (or electronic) request, the agency must conduct a systematic examination of its records. Any unverifiable or erroneous information must be deleted within a reasonable period of time.

**Remedies for Violations** A credit reporting agency that fails to comply with the act is liable for actual damages, plus additional damages not to exceed $1,000 and attorneys' fees.[29] Creditors and other companies that use information from credit reporting agencies may also be liable for violations of the FCRA. The United States Supreme Court has held that an insurance company's failure to notify new customers that they were paying higher insurance rates as a result of their credit scores was a *willful* violation of the FCRA.[30]

■ **CASE IN POINT 24.11** Branch Banking & Trust Company of Virginia (BB&T) gave Rex Saunders an auto loan but failed to give him a payment coupon book and refused his attempts to make payments on the loan. In fact, BB&T told him that it had not extended a loan to him. Eventually, BB&T discovered its mistake and demanded full payment, plus interest and penalties.

When payment was not immediately forthcoming, BB&T declared that Saunders was in default. It then repossessed the car and forwarded adverse credit information about Saunders to credit reporting agencies, without noting that Saunders disputed the information. Saunders filed a lawsuit alleging violations of the FCRA and was awarded $80,000 in punitive damages. An appellate court found that the damages award was reasonable, given BB&T's willful violation.[31] ■

## 24–4c The Fair and Accurate Credit Transactions Act

Congress passed the Fair and Accurate Credit Transactions (FACT) Act in an effort to combat identity theft.[32] The act established a national fraud alert system. Consumers who suspect that they have been or may be victimized by identity theft can place an alert on their credit files. When a consumer establishes that identify theft has occurred, the credit reporting agency must stop reporting allegedly fraudulent account information.

The act also requires the major credit reporting agencies to provide consumers with free copies of their own credit reports every twelve months. Another provision requires account numbers on credit-card receipts to be truncated (shortened). Merchants, employees, or others who may have access to the receipts can no longer obtain the consumers' names and full credit-card numbers. Financial institutions must work with the FTC to identify

"red flag" indicators of identity theft and to develop rules for the disposal of sensitive credit information.

## 24–4d The Fair Debt Collection Practices Act

The Fair Debt Collection Practices Act (FDCPA)[33] attempts to curb perceived abuses by collection agencies. The act applies only to specialized debt-collection agencies and attorneys who regularly attempt to collect debts on behalf of someone else, usually for a percentage of the amount owed. Creditors attempting to collect debts are not covered by the act unless, by misrepresenting themselves, they cause debtors to believe they are collection agencies.

**Requirements of the Act**   Under the FDCPA, a collection agency may not do any of the following:

1. Contact the debtor at the debtor's place of employment if the debtor's employer objects.
2. Contact the debtor at inconvenient or unusual times (such as three o'clock in the morning), or at any time if the debtor is being represented by an attorney.
3. Contact third parties other than the debtor's parents, spouse, or financial adviser about payment of a debt unless a court authorizes such action.
4. Harass or intimidate the debtor (by using abusive language or threatening violence, for instance) or make false or misleading statements (such as posing as a police officer).
5. Communicate with the debtor at any time after receiving notice that the debtor is refusing to pay the debt, except to advise the debtor of further action to be taken by the collection agency.

The FDCPA also requires a collection agency to include a **validation notice** when it initially contacts a debtor for payment of a debt or within five days of that initial contact. The notice must state that the debtor has thirty days in which to dispute the debt and to request a written verification of the debt from the collection agency.

**Enforcement of the Act**   The Federal Trade Commission is primarily responsible for enforcing the FDCPA. A debt collector who fails to comply with the act is liable for actual damages, plus additional damages not to exceed $1,000 and attorneys' fees.

---

**29.** 15 U.S.C. Section 1681n.

**30.** *Safeco Insurance. Co. of America v. Burr,* 551 U.S. 47, 127 S.Ct. 2201, 167 L.Ed.2d 1045 (2007).

**31.** *Saunders v. Branch Banking & Trust Co. of Virginia,* 526 F.3d 142 (4th Cir. 2008).

**32.** Pub. L. No. 108-159, 117 Stat. 1952.

**33.** 15 U.S.C. Section 1692.

Debt collectors who violate the act are exempt from liability if they can show that the violation was not intentional and resulted from a bona fide error. Furthermore, the error must have occurred in spite of procedures the company had already put in place to avoid such errors. The "bona fide error" defense typically has been applied to mistakes of fact or clerical errors. A few courts have gone further and allowed the good faith error defense in other circumstances.[34]

---

34. See, for instance, *Zortman v. J.C. Christensen & Associates, Inc.*, 2012 WL 1563918 (D.Minn. 2012); see also *Mbaku v. Bank of America, N.A.*, 2013 WL 425981 (D.Colo. 2013).

## Reviewing: Consumer Law

Leota Sage saw a local motorcycle dealer's newspaper advertisement offering a MetroRider EZ electric scooter for $1,699. When she went to the dealership, however, she learned that the EZ model had been sold out. The salesperson told Sage that he still had the higher-end MetroRider FX model in stock for $2,199 and would sell her one for $1,999. Sage was disappointed but decided to purchase the FX model.

When Sage said that she wished to purchase the scooter on credit, she was directed to the dealer's credit department. As she filled out the credit forms, the clerk told Sage, who is an Asian American, that she would need a cosigner to obtain a loan. Sage could not understand why she would need a cosigner and asked to speak to the store manager. The manager apologized, told her that the clerk was mistaken, and said that he would "speak to" the clerk. The manager completed Sage's credit application, and Sage then rode the scooter home. Seven months later, Sage received a letter from the manufacturer informing her that a flaw had been discovered in the scooter's braking system and that the model had been recalled. Using the information presented in the chapter, answer the following questions.

1. Did the dealer engage in deceptive advertising? Why or why not?
2. Suppose that Sage had ordered the scooter through the dealer's Web site but the dealer was unable to deliver it by the date promised. What would the FTC have required the merchant to do in that situation?
3. Assuming that the clerk required a cosigner based on Sage's race or gender, what act prohibits such credit discrimination?
4. What organization has the authority to ban the sale of scooters based on safety concerns?

**Debate This** . . . *Laws against bait-and-switch advertising should be abolished because no consumer is ever forced to buy anything.*

## Terms and Concepts

| | | |
|---|---|---|
| bait-and-switch advertising 469 | "cooling-off" laws 473 | multiple product order 470 |
| cease-and-desist order 470 | counteradvertising 470 | Regulation Z 477 |
| consumer law 467 | deceptive advertising 467 | validation notice 480 |

## Issue Spotters

1. United Pharmaceuticals, Inc., believes that it has developed a new drug that will be effective in the treatment of patients with AIDS. The drug has had only limited testing, but United wants to make the drug widely available as soon as possible. To market the drug, what must United prove to the U.S. Food and Drug Administration? (See *Protection of Health and Safety.*)

2. Gert buys a notebook computer from EZ Electronics. She pays for it with her credit card. When the computer proves defective, she asks EZ to repair or replace it, but EZ refuses. What can Gert do? (See *Credit Protection.*)

• **Check your answers to the Issue Spotters against the answers provided in Appendix B at the end of this text.**

# Business Scenarios

**24–1. Unsolicited Merchandise.** Andrew, a resident of California, received an advertising circular in the U.S. mail announcing a new line of regional cookbooks distributed by the Every-Kind Cookbook Co. Andrew didn't want any books and threw the circular away. Two days later, Andrew received in the mail an introductory cookbook entitled *Lower Mongolian Regional Cookbook*, as announced in the circular, on a "trial basis" from Every-Kind. Andrew was not interested but did not go to the trouble to return the cookbook. Every-Kind demanded payment of $20.95 for the *Lower Mongolian Regional Cookbook*. Discuss whether Andrew can be required to pay for the book. (See *Advertising, Marketing, and Sales*.)

**24–2. Credit-Card Rules.** Maria Ochoa receives two new credit cards on May 1. She has solicited one of them from Midtown Department Store, and the other arrives unsolicited from High-Flying Airlines. During the month of May, Ochoa makes numerous credit-card purchases from Midtown Department Store, but she does not use the High-Flying Airlines card. On May 31, a burglar breaks into Ochoa's home and steals both credit cards, along with other items. Ochoa notifies the Midtown Department Store of the theft on June 2, but she fails to notify High-Flying Airlines. Using the Midtown credit card, the burglar makes a $500 purchase on June 1 and a $200 purchase on June 3. The burglar then charges a vacation flight on the High-Flying Airlines card for $1,000 on June 5. Ochoa receives the bills for these charges and refuses to pay them. Discuss Ochoa's liability for the charges. (See *Credit Protection*.)

# Business Case Problems

### 24–3. Spotlight on McDonald's—Food Labeling.

McDonald's Corp.'s Happy Meal® meal selection consists of an entrée, a small order of french fries, a small drink, and a toy. In the early 1990s, McDonald's began to aim its Happy Meal marketing at children aged one to three. In 1995, McDonald's began making nutritional information for its food products available in documents known as "McDonald's Nutrition Facts." Each document lists the food items that the restaurant serves and provides a nutritional breakdown, but the Happy Meal is not included.

Marc Cohen filed a suit against McDonald's in an Illinois state court. Among other things, Cohen alleged that McDonald's had violated a state law prohibiting consumer fraud and deceptive business practices by failing to adhere to the Nutrition Labeling and Education Act (NLEA). The NLEA sets out different requirements for products specifically intended for children under the age of four—for instance, the products' labels cannot declare the percent of daily value of nutritional components. Does it make sense to have different requirements for children of this age? Why or why not? Should a state court impose such regulations? Explain. [*Cohen v. McDonald's Corp.*, 347 Ill.App.3d 627, 808 N.E.2d 1, 283 Ill.Dec. 451 (1 Dist. 2004)] (See *Labeling and Packaging Laws*.)

**24–4. Deceptive Advertising.** Brian Cleary and Rita Burke filed a suit against cigarette maker Philip Morris USA, Inc., seeking class-action status for a claim of deceptive advertising. Cleary and Burke claimed that "light" cigarettes, such as Marlboro Lights, were advertised as safer than regular cigarettes, even though the health effects are the same. They contended that the tobacco companies concealed the true nature of light cigarettes. Philip Morris correctly claimed that it was authorized by the government to advertise cigarettes, including light cigarettes. Assuming that is true, should the plaintiffs still be able to bring a deceptive advertising claim against the

tobacco company? Why or why not? [*Cleary v. Philip Morris USA, Inc.*, 683 F.Supp.2d 730 (N.D.Ill. 2010)] (See *Advertising, Marketing, and Sales*.)

### 24–5. Business Case Problem with Sample Answer— Fair Debt-Collection Practices.

Bank of America hired Atlantic Resource Management, LLC, to collect a debt from Michael E. Engler. Atlantic called Engler's employer and asked his supervisor about the company's policy concerning the execution of warrants. The caller then told the supervisor that, to stop process of the warrant, Engler needed to call Atlantic about "Case Number 37291 NY0969" during the first three hours of his next shift. When Engler's supervisor told him about the call, Engler feared that he might be arrested, and he experienced discomfort, embarrassment, and emotional distress at work. Can Engler recover under the Fair Debt Collection Practices Act? Why or why not? [*Engler v. Atlantic Resource Management, LLC*, 2012 WL 464728 (W.D.N.Y. 2012)] (See *Credit Protection*.)

• **For a sample answer to Problem 24–5, go to Appendix C at the end of this text.**

**24–6. Deceptive Advertising.** Innovative Marketing, Inc. (IMI), sold "scareware"—computer security software. IMI's Internet ads redirected consumers to sites where they were told that a scan of their computers had detected dangerous files— viruses, spyware, and "illegal" pornography. In fact, no scans were conducted. Kristy Ross, an IMI cofounder and vice president, reviewed and edited the ads, and was aware of the many complaints that consumers had made about them. An individual can be held liable under the Federal Trade Commission Act's prohibition of deceptive practices if the person (1) participated directly in the deceptive practices or had the authority to control them and (2) had or should have had knowledge of them. Were IMI's ads deceptive? If so, can Ross be held liable?

Explain. [*Federal Trade Commission v. Ross*, 743 F.3d 886 (4th Cir. 2014)] (See *Advertising, Marketing, and Sales.*)

**24–7. A Question of Ethics—Fair Debt-Collection Practices.** *Barry Sussman graduated from law school, but also served time in prison for attempting to collect debts by posing as an FBI agent. He theorized that if a debt-collection business collected only debts that it owned as a result of buying checks written on accounts with insufficient funds (NSF checks), it would not be subject to the Fair Debt Collection Practices Act (FDCPA). Sussman formed Check Investors, Inc., to act on his theory. Check Investors bought more than 2.2 million NSF checks, with an estimated face value of about $348 million, for pennies on the dollar. Check Investors added a fee of $125 or $130 (more than the legal limit in most states) to the face amount of each check and aggressively pursued its drawer to collect. The firm's employees were told to accuse drawers of being criminals and to threaten them with arrest and prosecution. The threats were false. Check Investors never took steps to initiate a prosecution. The employees contacted the drawers' family members and used "saturation phoning"—phoning a drawer numerous times in a short period. They used abusive language, referring to drawers as "deadbeats," "retards," "thieves," and "idiots." Between January 2000 and January 2003, Check Investors netted more than $10.2 million from its efforts. [Federal Trade Commission v. Check Investors, Inc., 502 F.3d 159 (3d Cir. 2007)]* (See *Credit Protection.*)

**(a)** The Federal Trade Commission filed a suit in a federal district court against Check Investors and others, alleging, in part, violations of the FDCPA. Was Check Investors a "debt collector," collecting "debts," within the meaning of the FDCPA? If so, did its methods violate the FDCPA? Were its practices unethical? What might Check Investors argue in its defense? Discuss.

**(b)** Are "deadbeats" the primary beneficiaries of laws such as the FDCPA? If not, how would you characterize debtors who default on their obligations?

# Legal Reasoning Group Activity

**24–8. Consumer Protections.** Many states have enacted laws that go even further than federal law to protect consumers. These laws vary tremendously from state to state. (See *Advertising, Marketing, and Sales.*)

**(a)** The first group will decide whether having different laws is fair to sellers who may be prohibited from engaging in a practice in one state that is legal in another.

**(b)** The second group will consider how these different laws might affect a business.

**(c)** A third group will determine whether it is fair that residents of one state have more protection than residents of another.

## CHAPTER 25

# Environmental Protection

Concern over the degradation of the environment has increased over time in response to the environmental effects of population growth, urbanization, and industrialization. Environmental protection is not without a price, however. For many businesses, the costs of complying with environmental regulations are high, and for some they may seem too high. A constant tension exists between the desire to increase profits and productivity and the need to protect the environment.

To a great extent, environmental law consists of statutes passed by federal, state, or local governments and regulations issued by administrative agencies. Before examining statutory and regulatory environmental laws, however, we look at the remedies against environmental pollution that are available under the common law.

## 25–1 Common Law Actions

Common law remedies against environmental pollution originated centuries ago in England. Those responsible for operations that created dirt, smoke, noxious odors, noise, or toxic substances were sometimes held liable under common law theories of nuisance or negligence. Today, individuals who have suffered a harm from pollution continue to rely on the common law to obtain damages and injunctions against business polluters.

### 25–1a Nuisance

Under the common law doctrine of **nuisance,** persons may be held liable if they use their property in a manner that unreasonably interferes with others' rights to use or enjoy their own property. Courts typically balance the harm caused by the pollution against the costs of stopping it.

Courts have often denied injunctive relief on the ground that the hardships that would be imposed on the polluter and on the community are greater than the hardships suffered by the plaintiff. ■ **EXAMPLE 25.1** Hewitt's factory causes neighboring landowners to suffer from smoke, soot, and vibrations. But if the factory is the core of the local economy, a court may leave it in operation and award monetary damages to the injured parties. Damages can include compensation for any decline in the value of their property caused by Hewitt's operation. ■

To obtain relief from pollution under the nuisance doctrine, a property owner may have to identify a distinct harm separate from that affecting the general public. This harm is referred to as a "private" nuisance. Under the common law, individuals were denied standing (access to the courts) unless they suffered a harm distinct from that suffered by the public at large. Some states still require this. A public authority (such as a state's attorney general), however, can sue to stop a "public" nuisance.

### 25–1b Negligence and Strict Liability

An injured party may sue a business polluter in tort under negligence and strict liability theories. A negligence action is based on a business's alleged failure to use reasonable care toward a party whose injury was foreseeable and was caused by the lack of reasonable care. For instance, employees might sue an employer whose failure to use proper pollution controls has contaminated the air, causing the employees to suffer respiratory illnesses. Lawsuits for personal injuries caused by exposure to a toxic substance, such as asbestos, radiation, or hazardous waste, have given rise to a growing body of tort law known as **toxic torts.**

Businesses that engage in ultrahazardous activities—such as the transportation of radioactive materials—are strictly liable for any injuries the activities cause. In a strict liability action, the injured party does not have to prove that the business failed to exercise reasonable care.

# 25–2 Federal, State, and Local Regulations

All levels of government in the United States regulate some aspect of the environment. In this section, we look at some of the ways in which the federal, state, and local governments control business activities and land use in the interests of environmental preservation and protection.

## 25–2a State and Local Regulations

In addition to the federal regulations to be discussed shortly, many states have enacted laws to protect the environment. State laws may restrict a business's discharge of chemicals into the air or water or regulate its disposal of toxic wastes. States may also regulate the disposal or recycling of other wastes, including glass, metal, plastic containers, and paper. Additionally, states may restrict emissions from motor vehicles.

City, county, and other local governments also regulate some aspects of the environment. For instance, local zoning laws may be designed to inhibit or regulate the growth of cities and suburbs. In the interest of safeguarding the environment, such laws may prohibit certain land uses. Even when zoning laws permit a business's proposed development plan, the plan may have to be altered to lessen the development's environmental impact. In addition, cities and counties may impose rules regulating methods of waste removal, the appearance of buildings, the maximum noise level, and other aspects of the local environment.

State and local regulatory agencies also play a significant role in implementing federal environmental legislation. Typically, the federal government relies on state and local governments to enforce federal environmental statutes and regulations, such as those regulating air quality.

## 25–2b Federal Regulations

Congress has passed a number of statutes to control the impact of human activities on the environment. Exhibit 25–1 lists and summarizes the major federal environmental statutes discussed in this chapter. Most of these statutes are designed to address pollution in the air, water, or land. Some specifically regulate toxic chemicals, including pesticides, herbicides, and hazardous wastes.

**Environmental Regulatory Agencies** The primary federal agency regulating environmental law is the Environmental Protection Agency (EPA). Other federal agencies with authority to regulate specific environmental matters include the Department of the Interior, the Department of Defense, the Department of Labor, the Food and Drug Administration, and the Nuclear Regulatory Commission. In addition, as mentioned, state and local agencies play an important role in enforcing federal environmental legislation.

Most federal environmental laws provide that citizens can sue to enforce environmental regulations if government agencies fail to do so. Similarly, citizens can sue to limit enforcement actions if agencies go too far in their actions. Typically, a threshold hurdle in such suits is meeting the requirements for standing to sue.

In the following case, an animal advocacy organization brought a suit to stop the "taking" (killing or capture) of migratory birds at New York City's John F. Kennedy International Airport (JFK). Birds had been involved in several near-catastrophes at JFK. A collision between herring gulls and a passenger jet, for instance, had caused the jet's engine to explode and the aircraft to catch fire.

To reduce the risks, the Port Authority of New York and New Jersey—which operates JFK—obtained a permit from the U.S. Fish and Wildlife Service (FWS) to "take" certain birds that threatened to interfere with aircraft at JFK. The advocacy organization, Friends of Animals, challenged the issuance of this permit.

**Case Analysis 25.1**

## Friends of Animals v. Clay
United States Court of Appeals, Second Circuit, 811 F.3d 94 (2016).

### In the Language of the Court
José A. *CABRANES*, Circuit Judge.
    * * * *
BACKGROUND
    The taking of migratory birds is governed by the Migratory Bird Treaty Act ("MBTA"). The MBTA, which

implements a series of treaties as federal law, prohibits the taking of any bird protected by those treaties unless and except as permitted by regulations promulgated [declared] under the statute. * * * One such regulation is 50 C.F.R. [Code of Federal Regulations] Section

21.41. Under Section 21.41, FWS may issue "depredation permits" that authorize the taking (or possession or transport) of migratory birds that are causing injury to certain human interests.

Case 25.1 Continues

**Case 25.1 Continued**

* * * *

[Friends of Animals (FOA) filed a suit in a federal district court against William Clay, Deputy Administrator in the U.S. Department of Agriculture and others, including the U.S. Fish and Wildlife Service (FWS), challenging the issuance of the permit. The court issued a summary judgment in favor of the defendants. FOA appealed to the U.S. Court of Appeals for the Second Circuit.]

The permit * * * identifies eighteen species of migratory birds that have, in the past, compromised public safety at JFK, and authorizes the Port Authority to take a quota of birds of each species.

In addition to setting out these species-specific quotas, the challenged permit contains an "emergency-take" provision. This provision empowers the Port Authority, "in emergency situations only," to take any migratory bird (except bald eagles, golden eagles, or endangered or threatened species) that poses a "direct threat to human safety"—defined as a "threat of serious bodily injury or a risk to human life"—even if it is of a species not listed on the permit. FWS rarely includes an emergency take provision in its migratory bird permits, but—mindful of the grave risks that arise when birds congregate near aircraft—it makes an exception for airports.

DISCUSSION

FOA directs its challenge at the * * * permit's emergency-take provision. According to FOA, Section 21.41 does not authorize FWS to issue a permit that allows the emergency take of a migratory bird irrespective of its species. Instead, FOA argues, permit applicants like the Port Authority must provide species-specific information to FWS, and FWS may authorize the taking of only those species specifically listed on the permit.

Contending that FWS's alleged failure to abide by the requirements of Section 21.41 has resulted in the Port Authority's unlawful taking of a number of migratory birds, * * * FOA asks us to invalidate the operative permit as the product of agency action that was arbitrary, capricious, an abuse of discretion, or otherwise not in accordance with law.

* * * *

FWS's authority to issue depredation permits under Section 21.41 is limited in certain respects by subsections (c) and (d) of that provision. Subsection (d) provides, for instance, that a permit's duration is limited to one year. Subsection (c) sets forth conditions common to all permits, such as the prohibition of certain hunting practices and mandatory steps for disposing of birds that have been killed; it also states that depredation permits are subject to the general conditions set forth in 50 C.F.R. Part 13. Various provisions in Part 13, in turn, further hem in the agency's permitting authority. *But among the express limitations on FWS's discretion imposed by Section 21.41(c)–(d) and Part 13, we find nothing to indicate that FWS may not issue a permit that contains an emergency-take provision. Accordingly, unless some other feature of the regulatory regime counsels otherwise, we must conclude that FWS has authority to issue permits of the type challenged here.* [Emphasis added.]

FOA argues that this other feature is found in Section 21.41(b). This provision states that an application for a depredation permit must [identify] * * * "the particular species of migratory birds committing [an] injury." According to FOA, that regulation, when read in connection with Section 21.41(c)(1)—which provides that "permittees may not kill migratory birds unless specifically authorized on the permit"—makes

clear that a depredation permit may not authorize the taking of bird species not listed on the permit's face.

We disagree. Section 21.41(b) by its terms governs the conduct of applicants, not FWS, and specifies what information must be included in the permit application, not the permit itself. Indeed, the provision is styled as a direct address to applicants, to whom it gives point-by-point instructions for seeking a permit. FOA identifies no particular reason why we should read this subsection, contrary to its plain language, as a limit on FWS's authority to issue permits rather than as a means to ensure that applicants provide FWS with information germane to the permitting determination. Section 21.41(b) is a hopelessly slender reed on which to rest the argument that FWS is powerless to authorize the Port Authority to take migratory birds that threaten air safety.

Nor does the language of Section 21.41(c)(1) alter this conclusion. True, this subsection provides that permittees must "not kill migratory birds unless specifically authorized on the permit." But this is in no way inconsistent with the * * * permit's emergency-take provision. *The permit authorizes the Port Authority, in emergency situations, to "take * * * any migratory birds * * * when the migratory birds * * * are posing a direct threat to human safety."* The permit thus specifically authorizes the taking of migratory birds if certain conditions are met—and one method of taking a bird is killing it. [Emphasis added.]

* * * *

CONCLUSION

In sum, we hold that FWS did not run afoul of Section 21.41 in issuing to the Port Authority the * * * depredation permit. The * * * order of the District Court is accordingly AFFIRMED.

**Legal Reasoning Questions**

**1.** In what circumstance might the Port Authority—or anyone else—take a migratory bird without a permit and *not* be sanctioned?

**2.** Under the plaintiff's suggested reading of the regulation at issue in this case, what difficult choice would the Port Authority face?

**3.** Why is the taking of birds, or any wildlife, protected by treaty and federal law? What should be the limit to this protection?

**EXHIBIT 25–1** Major Federal Environmental Statutes

| POPULAR NAME | PURPOSE | STATUTE REFERENCE |
|---|---|---|
| Rivers and Harbors Appropriations Act | To prohibit ships and manufacturers from discharging and depositing refuse in navigable waterways. | 33 U.S.C. Sections 401–418. |
| Federal Insecticide, Fungicide, and Rodenticide Act | To control the use of pesticides and herbicides. | 7 U.S.C. Sections 136–136y. |
| Federal Water Pollution Control Act | To eliminate the discharge of pollutants from major sources into navigable waters. | 33 U.S.C. Sections 1251–1387. |
| Clean Air Act | To control air pollution from mobile and stationary sources. | 42 U.S.C. Sections 7401–7671q. |
| National Environmental Policy Act | To limit environmental harm from federal government activities. | 42 U.S.C. Sections 4321–4370d. |
| Ocean Dumping Act | To prohibit the dumping of radiological, chemical, and biological warfare agents and high-level radioactive waste into the ocean. | 16 U.S.C. Sections 1401–1445. |
| Endangered Species Act | To protect species that are threatened with extinction. | 16 U.S.C. Sections 1531–1544. |
| Safe Drinking Water Act | To regulate pollutants in public drinking water systems. | 42 U.S.C. Sections 300f–300j-25. |
| Toxic Substances Control Act | To regulate toxic chemicals and chemical compounds. | 15 U.S.C. Sections 2601–2692. |
| Comprehensive Environmental Response, Compensation, and Liability Act | To regulate the clean-up of hazardous waste–disposal sites. | 42 U.S.C. Sections 9601–9675. |
| Small Business Liability Relief and Brownfields Revitalization Act | To allow developers who comply with state voluntary clean-up programs to avoid federal liability for the properties that they decontaminate and develop. | 42 U.S.C. Section 9628. |

**Environmental Impact Statements** All agencies of the federal government must take environmental factors into consideration when making significant decisions. The National Environmental Policy Act[1] requires that an **environmental impact statement (EIS)** be prepared for every major federal action that significantly affects the quality of the environment. (See Exhibit 25–2.) An EIS must analyze the following:

1. The impact that the action will have on the environment.
2. Any adverse effects on the environment and alternative actions that might be taken.
3. Any irreversible effects the action might generate.

An action qualifies as "major" if it involves a substantial commitment of resources (monetary or otherwise). An action is "federal" if a federal agency has the power to control it. ■ **EXAMPLE 25.2** Development of a ski resort by a private developer on federal land may require an EIS. Construction or operation of a nuclear plant, which requires a federal permit, necessitates an EIS, as does creation of a dam as part of a federal project. ■

If an agency decides that an EIS is unnecessary, it must issue a statement supporting this conclusion. Private individuals, consumer interest groups, businesses, and others who believe that a federal agency's activities threaten the environment often use EISs as a means to challenge those activities.

1. 42 U.S.C. Sections 4321–4370d.

**EXHIBIT 25–2** Environmental Impact Statements

# 25–3 Air Pollution

Federal involvement with air pollution goes back to the 1950s and 1960s, when Congress authorized funds for air-pollution research and enacted the Clean Air Act.[2] The Clean Air Act provides the basis for issuing regulations to control multistate air pollution. It covers both mobile sources (such as automobiles and other vehicles) and stationary sources (such as electric utilities and industrial plants) of pollution.

## 25–3a Mobile Sources

Regulations governing air pollution from automobiles and other mobile sources specify pollution standards and establish time schedules for meeting the standards. The EPA periodically updates the pollution standards in light of new developments and data, usually reducing the amount of emissions allowed.

**Reducing Emissions** The Obama administration set a long-term goal of reducing emissions, including those from cars and sport utility vehicles, by 80 percent by 2050. The administration also ordered the EPA to develop national standards regulating fuel economy and

emissions for medium- and heavy-duty trucks starting with 2014 models.

**Authority to Regulate Greenhouse Gases** A growing concern among many scientists and others around the world is that greenhouse gases, such as carbon dioxide ($CO_2$), contribute to climate change. The Clean Air Act, as amended, however, does not specifically mention $CO_2$ emissions. Therefore, the EPA did not regulate $CO_2$ emissions from motor vehicles until 2009, after the Supreme Court ruled that it had the authority to do so.

■ **CASE IN POINT 25.3** Environmental groups and several states, including Massachusetts, sued the EPA in an effort to force the agency to regulate $CO_2$ emissions from motor vehicles. The case eventually reached the United States Supreme Court. The EPA argued that the plaintiffs lacked standing because global climate change has widespread effects, so the individual plaintiffs could not show particularized harm. Furthermore, the agency claimed that it did not have authority under the Clean Air Act to address global climate change and regulate $CO_2$.

The Court, however, ruled that Massachusetts had standing because its coastline, including state-owned lands, faced an imminent threat from rising sea levels purportedly caused by climate change. The Court also held that the Clean Air Act's broad definition of "air pollutant" gives the EPA authority to regulate $CO_2$. The Clean Air Act requires the EPA to regulate any air

---

2. 42 U.S.C. Sections 7401–7671q.

pollutants that might "endanger public health or welfare." Accordingly, the Court ordered the EPA to determine whether $CO_2$ was a pollutant that endangered public health.[3] ∎

The EPA later concluded that greenhouse gases, including $CO_2$ emissions, *do* constitute a public danger. In fact, in 2015, the EPA started regulating greenhouse gas emissions from airplanes.

**Controlling Climate Change** In 2016, a federal district court in Oregon allowed an unprecedented lawsuit to go forward against the U.S. government for doing too little to control climate change. ■ **CASE IN POINT 25.4** A group of young people (aged eight to nineteen) filed a suit against the federal government, as well as the fossil fuel industry. The plaintiffs argued that the government has known for years that $CO_2$ pollution causes climate change and threatens catastrophic consequences. By failing to address the causes of this pollution, they claimed, the government has violated their constitutional rights.

The court found that the plaintiffs had alleged particular, concrete harms to young people and future generations sufficient to give them standing to pursue their claims in court. Of course, this ruling means only that the plaintiffs have met their threshold burden of establishing standing. The court simply denied the government's motion to dismiss—it did not decide the merits of the case or grant relief to the plaintiffs. Those issues have yet to be resolved.[4] ∎

## 25–3b Stationary Sources

The Clean Air Act also authorizes the EPA to establish air-quality standards for stationary sources (such as manufacturing plants). But the act recognizes that the primary responsibility for implementing these standards rests with state and local governments. The standards are aimed at controlling hazardous air pollutants—those likely to cause death or a serious, irreversible, or incapacitating condition, such as cancer or neurological or reproductive damage.

The EPA sets primary and secondary levels of ambient standards—that is, maximum permissible levels of certain pollutants—and the states formulate plans to achieve

those standards. Different standards apply depending on whether the sources of pollution are located in clean areas or polluted areas and whether they are existing sources or major new sources.

**Hazardous Air Pollutants** The Clean Air Act requires the EPA to list all hazardous air pollutants (HAPs) on a prioritized schedule. In all, nearly two hundred substances—including asbestos, benzene, beryllium, cadmium, mercury, and vinyl chloride—have been classified as hazardous. They are emitted from stationary sources by a variety of business activities, including smelting (melting ore to produce metal), dry cleaning, house painting, and commercial baking.

**Maximum Achievable Control Technology** Instead of establishing specific emissions standards for each hazardous air pollutant, the Clean Air Act requires major *new* sources[5] to use pollution-control equipment that represents the *maximum achievable control technology,* or MACT, to reduce emissions. The EPA issues guidelines as to what equipment meets this standard.[6]

## 25–3c Violations of the Clean Air Act

For violations of emission limits under the Clean Air Act, the EPA can assess civil penalties of up to $25,000 per day. Additional fines of up to $5,000 per day can be assessed for other violations, such as failure to maintain the required records. To penalize those who find it more cost-effective to violate the act than to comply with it, the EPA is authorized to impose a penalty equal to the violator's economic benefits from noncompliance. Persons who provide information about violators may be paid up to $10,000. Private citizens can also sue violators.

Those who knowingly violate the act, including corporate officers, may be subject to criminal penalties. For instance, knowingly making false statements or failing to report violations may be punishable by fines of up to $1 million and imprisonment for up to two years.

In the following case, the phrase "knowingly violate" was at the center of the dispute in an individual's appeal of his conviction for Clean Air Act violations.

---

3. *Massachusetts v. Environmental Protection Agency*, 549 U.S. 497, 127 S.Ct. 1438, 167 L.Ed.2d 248 (2007).
4. *Juliana v. United States*, ___ F.Supp.3d ___, 2016 WL 1442435 (D.Or. 2016).
5. The term *major new sources* includes existing sources modified by a change in a method of operation that increases emissions.
6. The EPA has also issued rules to regulate hazardous air pollutants emitted by landfills. See 40 C.F.R. Sections 60.750–60.759.

# United States v. O'Malley

United States Court of Appeals, Seventh Circuit, 739 F.3d 1001 (2014).

**Background and Facts**  Duane O'Malley owned and operated Origin Fire Protection. Michael Pinski hired Origin to remove and dispose of 2,200 feet of insulation from a building Pinski owned in Kankakee, Illinois. The insulation contained asbestos, which Pinski, O'Malley, and O'Malley's employees recognized. O'Malley did not have a license to remove asbestos, and none of his employees were trained in complying with federal asbestos regulations. Nevertheless, Origin removed the debris and disposed of it at various sites, including a vacant lot where it spilled onto the soil, resulting in clean-up costs of nearly $50,000.

In a federal district court, a jury convicted O'Malley of removing, transporting, and dumping asbestos in violation of the Clean Air Act. The court sentenced him to 120 months of imprisonment, three years of supervised release, a fine of $15,000, and $47,085.70 in restitution to the Environmental Protection Agency (EPA). O'Malley appealed.

## In the Language of the Court

*TINDER, Circuit Judge.*

\* \* \* \*

On appeal to this court, O'Malley \* \* \* claims that because the [EPA's regulations] define "asbestos-containing material" as only six types of regulated asbestos, the government was required to prove that O'Malley knew that the asbestos in the building was one of the six forms of regulated asbestos. He asserts that the government did not present evidence to demonstrate O'Malley's knowledge of the type of asbestos in the building.

\* \* \* \*

O'Malley is correct that not all forms of asbestos are subject to regulation. The Clean Air Act [under Section 7412] authorizes the regulation of hazardous air pollutants, one of which is asbestos. "Because asbestos is not typically emitted through a conveyance designed and constructed to emit or capture it, such as a pipe or smokestack, but rather escapes from more diffuse sources such as open construction or demolition sites, EPA adopted a work-practice standard for the handling of asbestos in building demolition and renovation." \* \* \* The work practice standard promulgated for the handling of asbestos applies only to the six types of "regulated asbestos-containing material (RACM)," [which includes "friable asbestos material"]. "Friable asbestos material" is defined as "any material containing more than 1 percent asbestos \* \* \* that, when dry, can be crumbled, pulverized, or reduced to powder by hand pressure." Thus, there is no question that the material in [this case]—which was both friable and contained asbestos at concentrations ranging from four percent to forty-eight percent—was indeed "regulated asbestos-containing material."

\* \* \* \*

*The Clean Air Act makes it a crime for any person to "knowingly violate any \* \* \* requirement or prohibition of \* \* \* Section 7412, \* \* \* including a requirement of any rule" promulgated under Section 7412.* \* \* \* The district court instructed the jury on the knowledge elements as follows: "The government must prove \* \* \* the defendant knew that asbestos-containing material was in the building." [Emphasis added.]

O'Malley argues that the knowledge element instruction should have required the government to prove that the defendant knew that regulated asbestos-containing material, not simply asbestos-containing material, was in the building. But this cannot be correct. \* \* \* The phrase "knowingly violates" does not "carv[e] out an exception to the general rule that ignorance of the law is no excuse." The *mens rea* [criminal intent] required by the phrase is one that is higher than strict liability \* \* \*. But it is certainly much lower than specific intent, especially when, as here, "dangerous \* \* \* materials are involved," because "the probability of regulation is so great that anyone who is aware that he is in possession of them or dealing with them must be presumed to be aware of the regulation." The very fact that O'Malley was knowingly working with asbestos-containing material met the *mens rea* requirement.

**Case 25.2 Continued**     **Decision and Remedy** *The U.S. Court of Appeals for the Seventh Circuit affirmed the lower court's judgment. The appellate court disagreed with O'Malley's claim that the government was required to prove he knew the asbestos was one of the six types of regulated asbestos. "The very fact that O'Malley was knowingly working with asbestos-containing material met the* mens rea *requirement."*

**Critical Thinking**
- **What If the Facts Were Different?** *Suppose that O'Malley had been licensed to remove the asbestos. Would the result have been different? Why or why not?*

# 25-4 Water Pollution

Water pollution stems mostly from industrial, municipal, and agricultural sources. Pollutants entering streams, lakes, and oceans include organic wastes, heated water, sediments from soil runoff, nutrients (including fertilizers and human and animal wastes), and toxic chemicals and other hazardous substances.

Federal regulations governing water pollution can be traced back to the 1899 Rivers and Harbors Appropriations Act.[7] These regulations prohibited ships and manufacturers from discharging or depositing refuse in navigable waterways without a permit.[8] In 1948, Congress passed the Federal Water Pollution Control Act (FWPCA),[9] but its regulatory system and enforcement powers proved to be inadequate.

## 25-4a The Clean Water Act

In 1972, Congress passed amendments to the FWPCA, and the amended act became known as the Clean Water Act (CWA). The CWA established the following goals: (1) make waters safe for swimming, (2) protect fish and wildlife, and (3) eliminate the discharge of pollutants into the water. The CWA also set specific schedules, which were later extended by amendment and by the Water Quality Act.[10] Under these schedules, the EPA limits the discharge of various types of pollutants based on the technology available for controlling them.

**Permit System for Point-Source Emissions** The CWA established a permit system for regulating discharges from "point sources" of pollution, which include industrial, municipal (such as sewage pipes and treatment plants), and agricultural facilities.[11] Under this system, called the National Pollutant Discharge Elimination System (NPDES), any point source emitting pollutants into water must have a permit. Pollution not from point sources, such as runoff from small farms, is not subject to much regulation.

NPDES permits can be issued by the EPA and authorized state agencies and Indian tribes. The permits may be issued only if the discharge will not violate water-quality standards, and they must be reissued every five years. Although initially the NPDES system focused mainly on industrial wastewater, it was later expanded to cover stormwater discharges.

In practice, the NPDES system under the CWA includes the following elements:

1. National effluent (pollution) standards set by the EPA for each industry.
2. Water-quality standards set by the states under EPA supervision.
3. A discharge permit program that sets water-quality standards to limit pollution.
4. Special provisions for toxic chemicals and for oil spills.
5. Construction grants and loans from the federal government for publicly owned treatment works, primarily sewage treatment plants.

**Standards for Equipment** Regulations generally specify that the *best available control technology,* or BACT, be installed. The EPA issues guidelines as to what equipment meets this standard. Essentially, the guidelines require the most effective pollution-control equipment available.

New sources must install BACT equipment before beginning operations. Existing sources are subject to

---

7. 33 U.S.C. Sections 401–418.
8. The term *navigable waters* is interpreted today as including *intra*state lakes and streams used by interstate travelers and industries, as well as coastal and freshwater wetlands.
9. 33 U.S.C. Sections 1251–1387.
10. This act amended 33 U.S.C. Section 1251.

11. 33 U.S.C. Section 1342.

**EXHIBIT 25–3** Pollution-Control Equipment Standards under the Clean Air Act and the Clean Water Act

| THE CLEAN AIR ACT |
| --- |
| • Major sources of pollution must use pollution-control equipment that represents the *maximum achievable control technology*, or MACT, to reduce emissions. |

| THE CLEAN WATER ACT |
| --- |
| • New sources of pollution must install the *best available control technology*, or BACT, before beginning operations.<br>• Existing sources must immediately install equipment that utilizes the *best practical control technology*, or BPCT, and meet a timetable for installing BACT equipment. |

timetables for the installation of BACT equipment and must immediately install equipment that utilizes the *best practical control technology*, or BPCT. The EPA also issues guidelines as to what equipment meets this standard.

Exhibit 25–3 graphically illustrates the pollution-control equipment standards required under the Clean Air Act and the Clean Water Act.

The EPA must take into account many factors when issuing and updating its rules. Some provisions of the CWA instruct the EPA to weigh the cost of the technology required relative to the benefits achieved. The provision that covers power plants, however, neither requires nor prohibits a cost-benefit analysis. The question in the following case was whether the EPA could base its decision on such an analysis.

**Case 25.3**

# Entergy Corp. v. Riverkeeper, Inc.
Supreme Court of the United States, 556 U.S. 208, 129 S.Ct. 1498, 173 L.Ed.2d 369 (2009).

**Background and Facts** As part of its implementation of the Clean Water Act, the Environmental Protection Agency (EPA) developed two sets of rules that apply to the cooling systems of power plants. Phase I rules require new power plants to restrict their inflow of water "to a level commensurate with that which can be attained by a closed-cycle recirculating cooling water system." Phase II rules apply "national performance standards" to more than five hundred existing plants but do not require closed-cycle systems.

The EPA had found that converting these existing facilities to closed-cycle operations would cost $3.5 billion per year. The facilities would then produce less power while burning the same amount of coal. Moreover, other technologies can attain nearly the same results as closed-cycle systems. Phase II rules also allow a variance from the national performance standards if a facility's cost of compliance "would be significantly greater than the benefits."

Environmental organizations, including Riverkeeper, Inc., challenged the Phase II regulations, arguing that existing plants should be required to convert to closed-cycle systems. The U.S. Court of Appeals for the Second Circuit issued a ruling in the plaintiffs' favor. Power-generating companies, including Entergy Corporation, appealed to the United States Supreme Court.

## In the Language of the Court
Justice *SCALIA* delivered the opinion of the Court.
* * * *

In setting the Phase II national performance standards and providing for site-specific cost-benefit variances, the EPA relied on its view that [the] "best technology available" standard permits consideration of the technology's costs and of the relationship between those costs and the environmental benefits produced.

* * * The "best" technology—that which is "most advantageous"—may well be the one that produces the most of some good, here a reduction in adverse environmental impact. But "best technology" may also describe the technology that most efficiently produces some good. *In common parlance one could*

Case 25.3 Continued

*certainly use the phrase "best technology" to refer to that which produces a good at the lowest per-unit cost, even if it produces a lesser quantity of that good than other available technologies.* [Emphasis added.]

* * * This latter reading is [not] precluded by the statute's use of the phrase "for minimizing adverse environmental impact." *Minimizing* * * * *is a term that admits of degree and is not necessarily used to refer exclusively to the "greatest possible reduction."* [Emphasis added.]

Other provisions in the Clean Water Act also suggest the agency's interpretation. When Congress wished to mandate the greatest feasible reduction in water pollution, it did so in plain language: The provision governing the discharge of toxic pollutants into the Nation's waters requires the EPA to set "effluent limitations which shall require the elimination of discharges of all pollutants * * * ." The less ambitious goal of "minimizing adverse environmental impact" suggests, we think, that the agency retains some discretion to determine the extent of reduction that is warranted under the circumstances. That determination could plausibly involve a consideration of the benefits derived from reductions and the costs of achieving them.

* * * [Under other Clean Water Act provisions that impose standards on sources of pollution,] the EPA is instructed to consider, among other factors, "the total cost of application of technology in relation to the * * * benefits to be achieved."

* * * *

This * * * comparison of * * * statutory factors * * * leads us to the conclusion that it was well within the bounds of reasonable interpretation for the EPA to conclude that cost-benefit analysis is not categorically forbidden.

* * * *

While not conclusive, it surely tends to show that the EPA's current practice is a reasonable and hence legitimate exercise of its discretion to weigh benefits against costs that the agency has been proceeding in essentially this fashion for over 30 years.

**Decision and Remedy** *The United States Supreme Court concluded that the EPA had permissibly relied on a cost-benefit analysis to set national performance standards and to allow for variances from those standards. The Court reversed the lower court's judgment and remanded the case.*

**Critical Thinking**
- **Ethical** *In this case, aquatic organisms were most directly at risk. Is it acceptable to apply cost-benefit analyses to situations in which the lives of people are directly affected? Explain.*
- **Global** *In analyzing the costs and benefits of an action that affects the environment, should a line be drawn at a nation's borders? Why or why not?*

---

**Wetlands** The CWA prohibits the filling or dredging of **wetlands** unless a permit is obtained from the Army Corps of Engineers. The EPA defines *wetlands* as "those areas that are inundated or saturated by surface or ground water at a frequency and duration sufficient to support . . . vegetation typically adapted for life in saturated soil conditions." Wetlands are thought to be vital to the ecosystem because they filter streams and rivers and provide habitat for wildlife.

■ **CASE IN POINT 25.5** To build a home in Idaho, Michael and Chantell Sackett filled part of their residential lot with dirt and rock. A few months later, they received a compliance order from the EPA that required them to restore their property immediately or face fines of $75,000 a day. The EPA order claimed that, because their property was near a major lake, the Sacketts had polluted wetlands in violation of the Clean Water Act.

The Sacketts requested a hearing with the EPA, but it was denied. They then sued the EPA in federal district court, asserting, among other things, that the compliance order was "arbitrary and capricious" under the Administrative Procedure Act. The district court held that it could not review the EPA's compliance order because it was not a final agency action. An appellate court affirmed, but the United States Supreme Court reversed. The Court held that the Sacketts could challenge the EPA's compliance order in federal court. The government could not force them to comply with the EPA order without providing an opportunity for judicial review.[12] ■

---

12. *Sackett v. Environmental Protection Agency*, ___ U.S. ___, 132 S.Ct. 1367, 182 L.Ed.2d 367 (2012).

**Violations of the Clean Water Act** Because point-source water pollution control is based on a permit system, the permits are the key to enforcement. States have primary responsibility for enforcing the permit system, subject to EPA monitoring.

Discharging emissions into navigable waters without a permit, or in violation of pollution limits under a permit, violates the CWA. Violators are subject to a variety of civil and criminal penalties. Depending on the violation, civil penalties range from $10,000 to $25,000 per day, but not more than $25,000 per violation. Lying about a violation is more serious than admitting the truth about improper discharges.

Criminal penalties apply only if a violation was intentional. Criminal penalties range from a fine of $2,500 per day and imprisonment for up to one year to a fine of $1 million and fifteen years' imprisonment. Injunctive relief and damages can also be imposed. The polluting party can be required to clean up the pollution or pay for the cost of doing so.

## 25–4b Drinking Water

The Safe Drinking Water Act[13] requires the EPA to set maximum levels for pollutants in public water systems. The operators of public water systems must come as close as possible to meeting the EPA's standards by using the best available technology that is economically and technologically feasible.

Under the act, each supplier of drinking water is required to send an annual statement describing the source of its water to every household it supplies. The statement must also disclose the level of any contaminants in the water and any possible health concerns associated with the contaminants.

■ **EXAMPLE 25.6** In 2014, Flint, Michigan, changed its source of drinking water from the Detroit water system to the Flint River. Detroit's water had been treated to prevent lead from leaching from aging lead pipes into the water. Flint River water was not treated, which allowed lead to leach into the water from the pipes. Flint's drinking water became contaminated with lead—a serious public health hazard. By the time Flint sent out the required EPA notices, thousands of children had been exposed to drinking water with high lead levels. Several civil lawsuits have been filed against government officials as a result of the incident, and three individuals face criminal prosecution. The city will end up paying millions to fix the problem. ■

## 25–4c Ocean Dumping

The Marine Protection, Research, and Sanctuaries Act[14] (popularly known as the Ocean Dumping Act) regulates the transportation and dumping of pollutants into ocean waters. It prohibits the ocean dumping of any radiological, chemical, and biological warfare agents and high-level radioactive waste.

The act also established a permit program for transporting and dumping other materials, and designated certain areas as marine sanctuaries. Each violation of any provision or permit requirement in the Ocean Dumping Act may result in a civil penalty of up to $50,000. A knowing violation is a criminal offense that may result in a $50,000 fine, imprisonment for not more than a year, or both. A court may also grant an injunction to prevent an imminent or continuing violation.

## 25–4d Oil Pollution

When more than 10 million gallons of oil leaked into Alaska's Prince William Sound from the *Exxon Valdez* supertanker in 1989, Congress responded by passing the Oil Pollution Act.[15] (At that time, the *Exxon Valdez* disaster was the worst oil spill in U.S. history, but the British Petroleum oil spill in the Gulf of Mexico in 2010 surpassed it.)

Under the Oil Pollution Act, any oil facility, oil shipper, vessel owner, or vessel operator that discharges oil into navigable waters or onto an adjoining shore may be liable for clean-up costs and damages. The polluter can also be ordered to pay for damage to natural resources, private property, and the local economy, including the increased cost of providing public services.

## 25–5 Toxic Chemicals and Hazardous Waste

Originally, most environmental clean-up efforts were directed toward reducing smog and making water safe for fishing and swimming. Today, control of toxic chemicals and hazardous waste has become increasingly important. If not properly disposed of, these substances may seriously endanger human health and the environment—for instance, by contaminating public drinking water.

**13.** 42 U.S.C. Sections 300f to 300j-25.

**14.** 16 U.S.C. Sections 1401–1445.
**15.** 33 U.S.C. Sections 2701–2761.

## 25–5a Pesticides and Herbicides

The Federal Insecticide, Fungicide, and Rodenticide Act (FIFRA)[16] regulates the use of pesticides and herbicides. These substances must be (1) registered before they can be sold, (2) certified and used only for approved applications, and (3) used in limited quantities when applied to food crops.

**EPA Actions** The EPA can cancel or suspend registration of substances that it has identified as harmful and can inspect the factories where the chemicals are made. A substance is deemed harmful if human exposure to the substance, including exposure through eating food, results in a risk of one in a million (or higher) of developing cancer.[17]

**Violations and Penalties** It is a violation of FIFRA to sell a pesticide or herbicide that is either unregistered or has had its registration canceled or suspended. It is also a violation to sell a pesticide or herbicide with a false or misleading label. For instance, it is an offense to sell a substance that has a chemical strength that is different from the concentration described on the label. It is also a violation to destroy or deface any labeling required under the act.

Penalties for commercial dealers include imprisonment for up to one year and a fine of up to $25,000 (producers can be fined up to $50,000). Farmers and other private users of pesticides or herbicides who violate the act are subject to a $1,000 fine and incarceration for up to thirty days.

Note that a state can also regulate the sale and use of federally registered pesticides. ■ **CASE IN POINT 25.7** The EPA conditionally registered Strongarm, a weed-killing pesticide made by Dow Agrosciences, LLC. Dow sold Strongarm to Texas peanut farmers. When the farmers applied it, Strongarm damaged their crops and failed to control the growth of weeds. The farmers sued Dow for violations of Texas law, but the lower courts ruled that FIFRA preempted their claims. The farmers appealed to the United States Supreme Court. The Court held that under a specific provision of FIFRA, a state can regulate the sale and use of federally registered pesticides so long as the regulation does not permit anything that FIFRA prohibits.[18] ■

## 25–5b Toxic Substances

The Toxic Substances Control Act[19] regulates chemicals and chemical compounds that are known to be toxic, such as asbestos and polychlorinated biphenyls (PCBs). The act also controls the introduction of new chemical compounds by requiring investigation of any possible harmful effects from these substances.

Under the act, the EPA can require that manufacturers, processors, and other entities planning to use chemicals first determine their effects on human health and the environment. The EPA can regulate substances that could pose an imminent hazard or an unreasonable risk of injury to health or the environment. The EPA can also require special labeling, limit the use of a substance, set production quotas, or prohibit the use of a substance altogether.

## 25–5c The Resource Conservation and Recovery Act

The Resource Conservation and Recovery Act (RCRA)[20] was Congress's response to growing concerns about the effects of hazardous waste materials on the environment. The RCRA required the EPA to determine which forms of solid waste should be considered hazardous and to establish regulations to monitor and control hazardous waste disposal.

Among other things, the act requires all producers of hazardous waste materials to label and package properly any hazardous waste to be transported. Amendments to the RCRA decrease the use of land containment in the disposal of hazardous waste and require smaller generators of hazardous waste to comply with the act.

Under the RCRA, a company may be assessed a civil penalty of up to $25,000 for each violation.[21] The penalty is based on the seriousness of the violation, the probability of harm, and the extent to which the violation deviates from RCRA requirements. Criminal penalties include fines of up to $50,000 for each day of violation, imprisonment for up to two years (in most instances), or both. Criminal fines and the time of imprisonment can be doubled for certain repeat offenders.

## 25–5d Superfund

The Comprehensive Environmental Response, Compensation, and Liability Act (CERCLA),[22] commonly known

**16.** 7 U.S.C. Sections 136–136y.
**17.** 21 U.S.C. Section 346a.
**18.** *Bates v. Dow Agrosciences, LLC*, 544 U.S. 431, 125 S.Ct. 1788, 161 L.Ed.2d 687 (2005).
**19.** 15 U.S.C. Sections 2601–2692.
**20.** 42 U.S.C. Sections 6901–6986.
**21.** 42 U.S.C. Section 6928(a).
**22.** 42 U.S.C. Sections 9601–9675.

as Superfund, regulates the clean-up of disposal sites in which hazardous waste is leaking into the environment. CERCLA, as amended, has four primary elements:

1. It established an information-gathering and analysis system that enables the government to identify chemical dump sites and determine the appropriate action.
2. It authorized the EPA to respond to emergencies and to arrange for the clean-up of a leaking site directly if the persons responsible fail to clean up the site.
3. It created a Hazardous Substance Response Trust Fund (also called *Superfund*) to pay for the clean-up of hazardous sites using funds obtained through taxes on certain businesses.
4. It allowed the government to recover the cost of clean-up from persons who were (even remotely) responsible for hazardous substance releases.

**Potentially Responsible Parties**  Superfund provides that when a release or a potential release of hazardous chemicals from a site occurs, the following persons may be held responsible for cleaning up the site:

1. The person who generated the wastes disposed of at the site.
2. The person who transported the waste to the site.
3. The person who owned or operated the site at the time of the disposal.
4. The current owner or operator.

A person falling within one of these categories is referred to as a **potentially responsible party (PRP).** If the PRPs do not clean up the site, the EPA can clean up the site and recover the clean-up costs from the PRPs.

**Strict Liability of PRPs.**  Superfund imposes strict liability on PRPs, and that liability cannot be avoided through transfer of ownership. Thus, selling a site where hazardous wastes were disposed of does not relieve the seller of liability, and the buyer also becomes liable for the clean-up.

Liability also extends to businesses that merge with or buy corporations that have violated CERCLA. A parent corporation is not automatically liable for the violations of its subsidiary. It can be held liable, however, if the subsidiary was merely a shell company or if the parent corporation participated in or controlled the facility.[23]

**Joint and Several Liability of PRPs.**  Liability under Superfund is usually joint and several. In other words, a PRP who generated *only a fraction of the hazardous waste* disposed of at a site may nevertheless be liable for *all* of

the clean-up costs. CERCLA authorizes a party who has incurred clean-up costs to bring a "contribution action" against any other person who is liable or potentially liable for a percentage of the costs.

**Minimizing Liability**  One way for a business to minimize its potential liability under Superfund is to conduct environmental compliance audits of its own operations regularly. That is, the business can investigate its own operations and property to determine whether any environmental hazards exist.

The EPA encourages companies to conduct self-audits and promptly detect, disclose, and correct wrongdoing. Companies that do so are subject to lighter penalties for violations of environmental laws. (Fines may be reduced as much as 75 percent.)

In addition, under EPA guidelines, the EPA will waive all fines if a small company corrects environmental violations within 180 days after being notified of the violations (or 360 days if pollution-prevention techniques are involved). The policy does not apply to criminal violations of environmental laws, though, or to violations that pose a significant threat to public health, safety, or the environment.

**Defenses**  There are a few defenses to liability under CERCLA. The most important is the *innocent landowner defense.*[24] This defense may protect a landowner who acquired the property after it was used for hazardous waste disposal.

The landowner claiming the innocent landowner defense must not have had a contractual or employment relationship with the person (or other entity) who owned the land when the contamination occurred. Because land is often transferred by contract, it would seem that this defense would not normally be available. However, a landowner who can show that he or she had no knowledge of the hazardous waste disposal at the time of purchase can still assert the defense.

To succeed, the landowner must show that at the time the property was acquired, she or he had no reason to know that it had been used for hazardous waste disposal. The landowner must also show that at the time of the purchase, she or he undertook "all appropriate inquiries." That is, he or she investigated the previous ownership and uses of the property to determine whether there was reason for concern about hazardous substances. In effect, then, this defense protects only property owners who took precautions and investigated the possibility of environmental hazards before buying the property.

---

**23.** The landmark case establishing the liability of a parent corporation under CERCLA is *United States v. Bestfoods,* 524 U.S. 51, 118 S.Ct. 1876, 141 L.Ed.2d 43 (1998).

**24.** 42 U.S.C. Section 9601(35)(B).

## Reviewing: Environmental Protection

Residents of Lake Caliopa, Minnesota, began noticing an unusually high number of lung ailments among the local population. Several concerned citizens pooled their resources and commissioned a study to compare the frequency of these health conditions in Lake Caliopa with national averages. The study concluded that residents of Lake Caliopa experienced four to seven times the rate of frequency of asthma, bronchitis, and emphysema as the population nationwide.

During the study period, citizens began expressing concerns about the large volume of smog emitted by the Cotton Design apparel manufacturing plant on the outskirts of town. The plant had a production facility two miles east of town beside the Tawakoni River and employed seventy full-time workers. Just downstream on the Tawakoni River, the city of Lake Caliopa operated a public water works facility, which supplied all city residents with water.

The Minnesota Pollution Control Agency required Cotton Design to install new equipment to control air and water pollution. Later, citizens sued Cotton Design for various respiratory ailments allegedly caused or compounded by smog from Cotton Design's factory. Using the information presented in the chapter, answer the following questions.

1. Under the common law, what would each plaintiff be required to identify in order to be given relief by the court?

2. What standard for limiting emissions into the air does Cotton Design's pollution-control equipment have to meet?

3. If Cotton Design's emissions violated the Clean Air Act, how much can the EPA assess in fines per day?

4. What information must the city send to every household that it supplies with water?

**Debate This** . . .    *The courts should reject all cases in which the wetlands in question do not consist of actual bodies of water that exist during the entire year.*

## Terms and Concepts

environmental impact
  statement (EIS) 487
nuisance 484

potentially responsible
  party (PRP) 496
toxic tort 484

wetlands 493

## Issue Spotters

1. Resource Refining Company's plant emits smoke and fumes. Resource's operation includes a short railway system, and trucks enter and exit the grounds continuously. Constant vibrations from the trains and trucks rattle nearby residential neighborhoods. The residents sue Resource. Are there any reasons why the court might refuse to issue an injunction against Resource's operation? Explain. (See *Common Law Actions.*)

2. ChemCorp generates hazardous wastes from its operations. Disposal Trucking Company transports those wastes to Eliminators, Inc., which owns a site for hazardous waste disposal. Eliminators sells the property on which the disposal site is located to Fluid Properties, Inc. If the Environmental Protection Agency cleans up the site, from whom can it recover the cost? (See *Toxic Chemicals and Hazardous Waste.*)

• **Check your answers to the Issue Spotters against the answers provided in Appendix B at the end of this text.**

## Business Scenarios

**25–1. The Clean Water Act.** Fruitade, Inc., is a processor of a soft drink called Freshen Up. Fruitade uses returnable bottles, which it cleans with a special acid to allow for further beverage processing. The acid is diluted with water and then allowed to pass into a navigable stream. Fruitade crushes its broken bottles and throws the crushed glass into the stream. Discuss fully any environmental laws that Fruitade has violated. (See *Water Pollution.*)

**25–2. Environmental Protection.** Moonbay is a home-building corporation that primarily develops retirement communities. Farmtex owns a number of feedlots in Sunny Valley. Moonbay purchases 20,000 acres of farmland in the same area and begins building and selling homes on this acreage. In the meantime, Farmtex continues to expand its feedlot business, and eventually only 500 feet separate the two operations.

Because of the odor and flies from the feedlots, Moonbay finds it difficult to sell the homes in its development. Moonbay wants to enjoin (prevent) Farmtex from operating its feedlot in the vicinity of the retirement home development. Under what common law theory would Moonbay file this action? Has Farmtex violated any federal environmental laws? Discuss. (See *Common Law Actions*.)

# Business Case Problems

**25–3. Spotlight on the Grand Canyon—Environmental Impact Statement.** The U.S. National Park Service

(NPS) manages the Grand Canyon National Park in Arizona under a management plan that is subject to periodic review. In 2006, after nine years of background work and the completion of a comprehensive environmental impact statement, the NPS issued a new management plan for the park. The plan allowed for the continued use of rafts on the Colorado River, which runs through the Grand Canyon. The number of rafts was limited, however. Several environmental groups criticized the plan because they felt that it still allowed too many rafts on the river. The groups asked a federal appellate court to overturn the plan, claiming that it violated the wilderness status of the national park. When can a federal court overturn a determination by an agency such as the NPS? Explain. [*River Runners for Wilderness v. Martin,* 593 F.3d 1064 (9th Cir. 2010)] (See *Federal, State, and Local Regulations*.)

**25–4. Superfund.** A by-product of phosphate fertilizer production is pyrite waste, which contains arsenic and lead. From 1884 to 1906, seven phosphate fertilizer plants operated on a forty-three-acre site in Charleston, South Carolina. Planters Fertilizer & Phosphate Co. bought the site in 1906 and continued to make fertilizer. In 1966, Planters sold the site to Columbia Nitrogen Corp. (CNC), which also operated the fertilizer plants. In 1985, CNC sold the site to James Holcombe and J. Henry Fair. Holcombe and Fair subdivided and sold the site to Allwaste Tank Cleaning Inc., Robin Hood Container Express, the city of Charleston, and Ashley II of Charleston, Inc. Ashley spent almost $200,000 cleaning up the contaminated soil. Who can be held liable for the cost? Why? [*PCS Nitrogen Inc. v. Ashley II of Charleston LLC,* 714 F.3d 161 (4th Cir. 2013)] (See *Toxic Chemicals and Hazardous Waste*.)

**25–5. Business Case Problem with Sample Answer—Environmental Impact Statements.** The U.S. Forest Ser-

vice (USFS) proposed a travel management plan (TMP) for the Beartooth Ranger District in the Pryor and Absaroka Mountains in the Custer National Forest of southern Montana. The TMP would convert unauthorized user-created routes within the wilderness to routes authorized for motor vehicle use. It would also permit off-road "dispersed vehicle camping" within 300 feet of the routes, with some seasonal restrictions. The TMP would ban cross-country motorized travel outside the designated routes. Is an environmental impact statement required before

the USFS implements the TMP? If so, what aspects of the environment should the USFS consider in preparing it? Discuss. [*Pryors Coalition v. Weldon,* 551 Fed.Appx. 426 (9th Cir. 2014)] (See *Federal, State, and Local Regulations*.)

- **For a sample answer to Problem 25–5, go to Appendix C at the end of this text.**

**25–6. The Clean Water Act.** ICG Hazard, LLC, operates the Thunder Ridge surface coal mine in Leslie County, Kentucky, under a National Pollutant Discharge Elimination System permit issued by the Kentucky Division of Water (KDOW). As part of the operation, ICG discharges selenium into the surrounding water. Selenium is a naturally occurring element that endangers aquatic life once it reaches a certain concentration. KDOW knew when it issued the permit that mines in the area could produce selenium but did not specify discharge limits for the element in ICG's permit. Instead, the agency imposed a one-time monitoring requirement, which ICG met. Does ICG's discharge of selenium violate the Clean Water Act? Explain. [*Sierra Club v. ICG Hazard, LLC,* 781 F.3d 281 (6th Cir. 2015)] (See *Water Pollution*.)

**25–7. Special Case Analysis—Environmental Regulatory Agencies.** Go to Case Analysis 25.1, *Friends of Animals v. Clay.* Read the excerpt and answer the following questions.

**(a) Issue:** What regulation was at issue in this case? What activity does it regulate?

**(b) Rule of Law:** What rule of statutory interpretation did the court apply to construe this regulation?

**(c) Applying the Rule of Law:** How did the plaintiff want the regulation to be interpreted? What was the court's response?

**(d) Conclusion:** What were the results of the court's interpretation of the regulation?

**25–8. A Question of Ethics—Clean Air Act.** *In the Clean*

*Air Act, Congress allowed California, which has particular problems with clean air, to adopt its own standard for emissions from cars and trucks. California's standard is subject to the approval of the Environmental Protection Agency (EPA) based on certain criteria. Congress also allowed other states to adopt California's standard after the EPA's approval.*

*In 2004, in an effort to address climate change, the California Air Resources Board amended the state's standard to attain "the maximum feasible and cost-effective reduction of GHG [greenhouse gas] emissions from motor vehicles." The regulation, which applies to new passenger vehicles and light-duty trucks for 2009 and later, imposes decreasing limits on emissions of carbon dioxide through 2016. While EPA approval was pending, Vermont and other states adopted similar standards.*

*Green Mountain Chrysler Plymouth Dodge Jeep and other auto dealers, automakers, and associations of automakers filed a suit in a federal district court against George Crombie (then the secretary of the Vermont Agency of Natural Resources) and others, seeking relief from the state regulations. [Green Mountain Chrysler Plymouth Dodge Jeep v. Crombie, 508 F.Supp.2d 295 (D.Vt. 2007)]* (See *Air Pollution.*)

**(a)** Under the Environmental Policy and Conservation Act (EPCA) of 1975, the National Highway Traffic Safety Administration sets fuel economy standards for new cars. The plaintiffs argued, among other things, that the EPCA, which prohibits states from adopting separate fuel economy standards, preempts Vermont's GHG regulation. Do the GHG rules equate to the fuel economy standards? Discuss.

**(b)** Do Vermont's rules tread on the efforts of the federal government to address climate change internationally? Who should regulate GHG emissions? The federal government? The state governments? Both? Neither? Why?

**(c)** The plaintiffs claimed that they would go bankrupt if they were forced to adhere to the state's GHG standards. Should they be granted relief on this basis? Does history support their claim? Explain.

## Legal Reasoning Group Activity

**25–9. Clean-Up Costs.** It has been estimated that for every dollar spent cleaning up hazardous waste sites, administrative agencies spend seven dollars in overhead. (See *Toxic Chemicals and Hazardous Waste.*)

**(a)** The first group will list and explain possible ways to trim these administrative costs.

**(b)** The second group will evaluate whether the laws pertaining to hazardous waste clean-up can or should be changed to reduce the costs to government.

## CHAPTER 26

# Antitrust Law

After the Civil War (1861–1865), the American public became increasingly concerned about declining competition in the marketplace. Large corporate enterprises were attempting to reduce or eliminate competition by legally tying themselves together in *business trusts*.

The most famous trust was the Standard Oil trust of the late 1800s. Participants in the trust transferred their stock to a trustee. The trustee then fixed prices, controlled production, and established exclusive geographic markets for all of the oil companies that were members of the

---

**1.** 49 U.S.C. Sections 501–526

trust. Some observers began to argue that the trust wielded so much economic power that corporations outside the trust could not compete effectively.

Eventually, legislators at both the state and the federal level began to enact laws to rein in the trusts. Hence, the laws regulating economic competition in the United States today are referred to as **antitrust laws.** At the national level, antitrust legislation began when Congress passed the Interstate Commerce Act[1] in 1887, followed by the Sherman Antitrust

Act[2] in 1890. In 1914, Congress passed the Clayton Act[3] and the Federal Trade Commission Act.[4] We examine these major federal antitrust statutes in this chapter.

The purpose of antitrust legislation was—and still is—to foster competition. Behind these laws lies our society's belief that competition leads to lower prices, better products, a wider selection of goods, and more product information.

---

**2.** 15 U.S.C. Sections 1–7.
**3.** 15 U.S.C. Sections 12–27.
**4.** 15 U.S.C. Sections 41–58a.

## 26–1 The Sherman Antitrust Act

The author of the Sherman Antitrust Act, Senator John Sherman, was the brother of the famed Civil War general William Tecumseh Sherman. He was also a recognized financial authority. He had been concerned for years about what he saw as diminishing competition within U.S. industry and the emergence of monopolies. He told Congress that the Sherman Act "does not announce a new principle of law, but applies old and well-recognized principles of the common law."[5]

Indeed, today's antitrust laws are the direct descendants of common law actions intended to limit **restraints of trade** (agreements between or among firms that have the effect of reducing competition in the marketplace). Such actions date to the fifteenth century in England. The common law was not always consistent, however, and had not been effective in curbing the trusts. That is why Sherman proposed the Sherman Antitrust Act, often simply called the Sherman Act.

---

**5.** 21 *Congressional Record* 2456 (1890).

### 26–1a Major Provisions of the Sherman Act

Sections 1 and 2 contain the main provisions of the Sherman Act:

1. Every contract, combination in the form of trust or otherwise, or conspiracy, in restraint of trade or commerce among the several States, or with foreign nations, is hereby declared to be illegal [and is a felony punishable by fine and/or imprisonment].
2. Every person who shall monopolize, or attempt to monopolize, or combine or conspire with any other person or persons, to monopolize any part of the trade or commerce among the several States, or with foreign nations, shall be deemed guilty of a felony [and is similarly punishable].

### 26–1b Differences between Section 1 and Section 2

The two sections of the Sherman Act are quite different. Section 1 requires two or more persons, because a person cannot contract, combine, or conspire alone. Thus, the essence of the illegal activity is *the act of joining together.* Section 2, though, can apply either to one person or to two or more persons because it refers to "every person." Thus, unilateral conduct can result in a violation of Section 2.

It follows that the cases brought to the courts under Section 1 of the Sherman Act differ from those brought under Section 2. Section 1 cases are often concerned with whether an agreement (written or oral) leads to a restraint of trade. Section 2 cases deal with the structure of a monopoly that exists in the marketplace.

The term **monopoly** generally is used to describe a market in which there is a single seller or a very limited number of sellers. Whereas Section 1 focuses on agreements that are restrictive—that is, agreements that have a wrongful purpose—Section 2 looks at the so-called misuse of **monopoly power** in the marketplace. Monopoly power exists when a firm has an extreme amount of **market power**—the ability to affect the market price of its product.

Both Section 1 and Section 2 seek to curtail market practices that result in undesired monopoly pricing and output behavior. For a case to be brought under Section 2, however, the "threshold" or "necessary" amount of monopoly power must already exist. We illustrate the different requirements for violating these two sections of the Sherman Act in Exhibit 26–1.

## 26–1c Jurisdictional Requirements

The Sherman Act applies only to restraints that have a significant impact on interstate commerce. Courts have generally held that any activity that substantially affects interstate commerce falls within the scope of the Sherman Act. As will be discussed later in this chapter, the Sherman Act also extends to U.S. nationals abroad who are engaged in activities that affect U.S. foreign commerce.

Federal courts have exclusive jurisdiction over antitrust cases brought under the Sherman Act. State laws regulate local restraints on competition, and state courts decide claims brought under those laws.

# 26–2 Section 1 of the Sherman Act

The underlying assumption of Section 1 of the Sherman Act is that society's welfare is harmed if rival firms are permitted to join in an agreement that consolidates their market power or otherwise restrains competition. The types of trade restraints that Section 1 of the Sherman Act prohibits generally fall into two broad categories: *horizontal restraints* and *vertical restraints,* both of which will be discussed shortly. First, though, we look at the rules that the courts may apply when assessing the anticompetitive impact of alleged restraints of trade.

## 26–2a *Per Se* Violations versus the Rule of Reason

Some restraints are so substantially anticompetitive that they are deemed ***per se* violations**—illegal *per se* (inherently)—under Section 1. Other agreements, however, even though they result in enhanced market power, do not *unreasonably* restrain trade and are therefore lawful. Using the **rule of reason,** the courts analyze anticompetitive agreements that allegedly violate Section 1 of the Sherman Act to determine whether they actually constitute reasonable restraints of trade.

**Rationale for the Rule of Reason** The need for a rule-of-reason analysis of some agreements in restraint of trade is obvious. If the rule of reason had not been

**EXHIBIT 26–1** Required Elements of a Sherman Act Violation

| SECTION 1 VIOLATION REQUIREMENTS | SECTION 2 VIOLATION REQUIREMENTS |
|---|---|
| 1. An agreement between two or more parties that<br>2. Unreasonably restrains competition and<br>3. Affects interstate commerce. | 1. The possession of monopoly power in the relevant market, and<br>2. The willful acquisition or maintenance of that power as distinguished from its growth or development as a consequence of a superior product, business acumen, or historic accident. |

developed, almost any business agreement could conceivably be held to violate the Sherman Act. United States Supreme Court Justice Louis Brandeis effectively phrased this sentiment in *Chicago Board of Trade v. United States,* a case decided in 1918:

> Every agreement concerning trade, every regulation of trade, restrains. To bind, to restrain, is of their very essence. The true test of legality is whether the restraint imposed is such as merely regulates and perhaps thereby promotes competition or whether it is such as may suppress or even destroy competition.[6]

**Factors That Courts Consider** When analyzing an alleged Section 1 violation under the rule of reason, a court will consider the following factors:

1. The purpose of the agreement.
2. The parties' ability to implement the agreement to achieve that purpose.
3. The effect or potential effect of the agreement on competition.
4. Whether the parties could have relied on less restrictive means to achieve their purpose.

■ **CASE IN POINT 26.1** A group of consumers sued NBC Universal, the Walt Disney Company, and other broadcasters, as well as cable and satellite distributors. The consumers claimed that the bundling together of high-demand and low-demand television channels in cable and satellite programming packages violates the Sherman Act. Bundling forces consumers to pay for channels they do not watch to have access to channels they watch regularly.

The consumers argued that the defendants, through their control of high-demand programming, exercised market power that made it impossible for any distributor to offer unbundled programs. A federal appellate court ruled in favor of the defendants and dismissed the case. The court reasoned that the Sherman Act applies to actions that diminish competition and that the bundling of channels does not injure competition.[7] ■

## 26–2b Horizontal Restraints

The term **horizontal restraint** is encountered frequently in antitrust law. A horizontal restraint is any agreement that in some way restrains competition between rival firms competing in the same market. Horizontal restraints may include price-fixing, group boycotts, market divisions, and trade associations.

**Price Fixing** Any **price-fixing agreement**—an agreement among competitors to fix prices—constitutes a *per se* violation of Section 1. The agreement on price need not be explicit. As long as it restricts output or artificially fixes price, it violates the law.

**The Reason Behind the Agreement Is Not a Defense.** A price-fixing agreement is always a violation of Section 1, even if there are good reasons behind it. ■ **CASE IN POINT 26.2** In a classic price-fixing case, independent oil producers in Texas and Louisiana were caught between falling demand due to the Great Depression of the 1930s and increasing supply from newly discovered oil fields. A group of the major refining companies agreed to buy "distress" gasoline (excess supplies) from the independents so as to dispose of it in an "orderly manner." Although there was no explicit agreement as to price, it was clear that the purpose of the agreement was to limit the supply of gasoline on the market and thereby raise prices.

There may have been good reasons for the agreement. Nonetheless, the United States Supreme Court recognized the potentially adverse effects that such an agreement could have on open and free competition. The Court held that the reasonableness of a price-fixing agreement is never a defense. Any agreement that restricts output or artificially fixes price is a *per se* violation of Section 1.[8] ■

**Price-Fixing Cartels Today.** Price-fixing cartels (groups) are still commonplace in today's business world, particularly among global companies. The U.S. government actively pursues companies that it suspects of being involved in price-fixing cartels. International price-fixing cartels have been alleged in numerous industries, including air freight, auto parts, computer monitors, digital commerce, and drug manufacturers.

■ **CASE IN POINT 26.3** After Amazon.com released the Kindle e-book reader, it began selling e-book downloads at $9.99 (lower than the actual cost) and made up the difference by selling more Kindles. When the iPad entered the e-book scene, Apple and some book publishers agreed to use Apple's "agency" model, which Apple was already using for games and apps. The agency model allowed the book publishers to set their own prices while Apple kept 30 percent as a commission.

The U.S. government sued Apple and the publishers for price fixing. Because the publishers involved in the arrangement chose prices that were relatively similar, the government argued that price fixing was evident

---

6. 246 U.S. 231, 38 S.Ct. 242, 62 L.Ed. 683 (1918).
7. *Brantley v. NBC Universal, Inc.,* 675 F.3d 1192 (9th Cir. 2012).

8. *United States v. Socony-Vacuum Oil Co.,* 310 U.S. 150, 60 S.Ct. 811, 84 L.Ed. 1129 (1940).

and "would not have occurred without the conspiracy among the defendants." Ultimately, a federal appellate court held that Apple's agreement with publishers to raise e-book prices was a *per se* illegal price-fixing conspiracy. As a result, Apple was ordered to pay $400 million to consumers and $50 million in attorneys' fees.[9] ■

**Group Boycotts** A **group boycott** is an agreement by two or more sellers to refuse to deal with (that is, to boycott) a particular person or firm. Because they involve concerted action, group boycotts have been held to constitute *per se* violations of Section 1 of the Sherman Act.

To prove a violation of Section 1, the plaintiff must demonstrate that the boycott or joint refusal to deal was undertaken with the intention of eliminating competition or preventing entry into a given market. Although most boycotts are illegal, a few, such as group boycotts against a supplier for political reasons, may be protected under the First Amendment right to freedom of expression.

**Horizontal Market Division** It is a *per se* violation of Section 1 of the Sherman Act for competitors to divide up territories or customers. ■ **EXAMPLE 26.4** Axm Electronics Basics, Halprin Servo Supplies, and Aicarus Prime Electronics compete against each other in the states of Kansas, Nebraska, and Oklahoma. The three firms agree that Axm will sell products only in Kansas, Halprin will sell only in Nebraska, and Aicarus will sell only in Oklahoma.

This concerted action violates Section 1 of the Sherman Act. It reduces marketing costs and allows all three firms (assuming there is no other competition) to raise the price of the goods sold in their respective states. The same violation would take place if the three firms divided up their customers by class rather than region. They might agree that Axm would sell only to institutional purchasers (such as governments and schools) in all three states, Halprin only to wholesalers, and Aicarus only to retailers. The result would be the same. ■

**Trade Associations** Businesses in the same general industry or profession frequently organize trade associations to pursue common interests. A trade association may engage in various joint activities, such as exchanging information, representing the members' business interests before governmental bodies, and conducting advertising campaigns. Trade associations also frequently are involved in setting regulatory standards to govern the industry or profession.

Generally, the rule of reason is applied to many of these horizontal actions. If a court finds that a trade association practice or agreement that restrains trade is sufficiently beneficial both to the association and to the public, it may deem the restraint reasonable.

In *concentrated industries,* however, trade associations can be, and have been, used as a means to facilitate anticompetitive actions, such as fixing prices or allocating markets. A **concentrated industry** is one in which either a single firm or a small number of firms control a large percentage of market sales. When trade association agreements have substantially anticompetitive effects, a court will consider them to be in violation of Section 1 of the Sherman Act.

**Joint Ventures** Joint ventures undertaken by competitors are also subject to antitrust laws. If a joint venture does not involve price fixing or market divisions, the agreement will be analyzed under the rule of reason. Whether the joint undertaking violates Section 1 will then depend on the factors stated earlier in this chapter. A court will look at the venture's purpose, the potential benefits relative to the likely harms, and whether there are less restrictive alternatives for achieving the same goals.

## 26–2c Vertical Restraints

A **vertical restraint** of trade results from an agreement between firms at different levels in the manufacturing and distribution process. In contrast to horizontal relationships, which occur at the same level of operation, vertical relationships encompass the entire chain of production.

The chain of production normally includes the purchase of inventory, basic manufacturing, distribution to wholesalers, and eventual sale of a product at the retail level. For some products, these distinct phases are carried on by different firms. In other instances, a single firm carries out two or more of the separate functional phases. Such enterprises are said to be **vertically integrated firms.**

Even though firms operating at different functional levels are not in direct competition with one another, they are in competition with other firms. Thus, agreements between firms standing in a vertical relationship may affect competition. Some vertical restraints are *per se* violations of Section 1. Others are judged under the rule of reason.

**Territorial or Customer Restrictions** In arranging for the distribution of its products, a manufacturing firm often wishes to insulate dealers from direct

---

9. *United States v. Apple, Inc.,* 791 F.3d 290 (2d Cir. 2015). Apple had previously agreed to settle the case for these amounts if its appeal was unsuccessful.

competition with other dealers selling its products. To do so, the manufacturer may institute territorial restrictions or attempt to prohibit wholesalers or retailers from reselling the products to certain classes of buyers, such as competing retailers.

**May Have Legitimate Purpose.** A firm may have legitimate reasons for imposing territorial or customer restrictions. For instance, an electronics manufacturer may wish to prevent a dealer from reducing costs and undercutting rivals by offering its products without promotion or customer service. In this situation, the cost-cutting dealer reaps the benefits (sales of the product) paid for by other dealers who undertake promotion and arrange for customer service. By not providing customer service (and relying on a nearby dealer to provide these services), the cost-cutting dealer may also harm the manufacturer's reputation.

**Judged under the Rule of Reason.** Territorial and customer restrictions were once considered *per se* violations of Section 1.[10] In 1977, the United States Supreme Court held that they should be judged under the rule of reason. ■ **CASE IN POINT 26.5** The Supreme Court case involved GTE Sylvania, Inc., a manufacturer of television sets. Sylvania limited the number of retail franchises that it granted in any given geographic area. It also required each franchisee to sell only Sylvania products from the location at which it was franchised. Sylvania retained sole discretion to increase the number of retailers in an area.

When Sylvania decided to open a new franchise, it terminated the franchise of Continental T.V., Inc., an existing franchisee in that area that would have been in competition with the new franchise. Continental filed a lawsuit claiming that Sylvania's vertically restrictive franchise system violated Section 1 of the Sherman Act. The United States Supreme Court found that "vertical restrictions promote interbrand competition by allowing the manufacturer to achieve certain efficiencies in the distribution of his products." Therefore, Sylvania's vertical system, which was not price restrictive, did not constitute a *per se* violation of Section 1 of the Sherman Act.[11] ■

The decision in the *Continental* case marked a definite shift from rigid characterization of territorial and customer restrictions to a more flexible, economic analysis

of these vertical restraints under the rule of reason. This rule is still applied in most vertical restraint cases.

**Resale Price Maintenance Agreements** An agreement between a manufacturer and a distributor or retailer in which the manufacturer specifies what the retail prices of its products must be is known as a **resale price maintenance agreement.** Such agreements were once considered to be *per se* violations of Section 1 of the Sherman Act.

Today, however, both *maximum* resale price maintenance agreements and *minimum* resale price maintenance agreements are judged under the rule of reason.[12] The setting of a maximum price that retailers and distributors can charge for a manufacturer's products may sometimes increase competition and benefit consumers.

## 26–3 Section 2 of the Sherman Act

Section 1 of the Sherman Act proscribes certain concerted, or joint, activities that restrain trade. In contrast, Section 2 condemns "every person who shall monopolize, or attempt to monopolize." Thus, two distinct types of behavior are subject to sanction under Section 2: *monopolization* and *attempts to monopolize.*

One tactic that may be involved in either offense is predatory pricing. **Predatory pricing** occurs when one firm (the predator) attempts to drive its competitors from the market by selling its product at prices substantially *below* the normal costs of production. Once the competitors are eliminated, the predator presumably will raise its prices far above their competitive levels to recapture its losses and earn higher profits.

### 26–3a Monopolization

The United States Supreme Court has defined **monopolization** as involving the following two elements:

1. The possession of monopoly power in the relevant market.
2. "The willful acquisition or maintenance of the power as distinguished from growth or development as a

---

10. See *United States v. Arnold, Schwinn & Co.*, 388 U.S. 365, 87 S.Ct. 1856, 18 L.Ed.2d 1249 (1967).
11. *Continental T.V., Inc. v. GTE Sylvania, Inc.*, 433 U.S. 36, 97 S.Ct. 2549, 53 L.Ed.2d 568 (1977).

12. The United States Supreme Court ruled that maximum resale price agreements should be judged under the rule of reason in *State Oil Co. v. Khan*, 522 U.S. 3, 118 S.Ct. 275, 139 L.Ed.2d 199 (1997). In *Leegin Creative Leather Products, Inc. v. PSKS, Inc.*, 551 U.S. 877, 127 S.Ct. 2705, 168 L.Ed.2d 623 (2007), the Supreme Court found that the rule of reason also applies to minimum resale price agreements.

consequence of a superior product, business acumen, or historic accident."[13]

To establish a violation of Section 2, a plaintiff must prove both of these elements—monopoly power and an *intent* to monopolize.

**Defining Monopoly Power** The Sherman Act does not define *monopoly.* In economic theory, monopoly refers to control of a specific market by a single entity. It is well established in antitrust law, however, that a firm may be a monopolist even though it is not the sole seller in a market.

Additionally, size alone does not determine whether a firm is a monopoly. ■ **EXAMPLE 26.6** A "mom and pop" grocery located in the isolated town of Happy Camp, Idaho, is a monopolist if it is the only grocery serving that particular market. Size in relation to the market is what matters, because monopoly involves the power to affect prices. ■

**Proving Monopoly Power** Monopoly power can be proved by direct evidence that the firm used its power to control prices and restrict output.[14] Usually, though, there is not enough evidence to show that the firm intentionally controlled prices, so the plaintiff has to offer indirect, or circumstantial, evidence of monopoly power.

To prove monopoly power indirectly, the plaintiff must show that the firm has a dominant share of the relevant market and that there are significant barriers for new competitors entering that market. ■ **CASE IN POINT 26.7** DuPont manufactures and sells para-aramid fiber, a synthetic fiber used to make body armor, fiber-optic cables, and tires, among other things. Although several companies around the world manufacture this fiber, only three sell in the U.S. market—DuPont (based in the United States), Teijin (based in the Netherlands), and Kolon Industries, Inc. (based in Korea). DuPont is the industry leader, and at times has produced 60 percent of all para-aramid fibers purchased in the United States.

After DuPont brought suit against Kolon for theft and misappropriation of trade secrets, Kolon counterclaimed that DuPont had illegally monopolized and attempted to monopolize the U.S. para-aramid market in violation of Section 2. Kolon claimed that, to deter competition, DuPont had illegally used multiyear supply agreements for all of its high-volume para-aramid customers. A

federal appellate court, however, found that there was insufficient proof that DuPont had possessed monopoly power in the U.S. market during the relevant time period (between 2006 and 2009). Additionally, the court concluded that Kolon had not shown that the supply agreements foreclosed competition. Therefore, the court held in favor of DuPont on the antitrust claims.[15] ■

**Relevant Market** Before a court can determine whether a firm has a dominant market share, it must define the relevant market. The relevant market consists of two elements: (1) a relevant product market and (2) a relevant geographic market.

**Relevant Product Market.** The relevant product market includes all products that have identical attributes (all brands of tea, for instance), as well as products that are reasonably interchangeable with them. Products are considered reasonably interchangeable if consumers treat them as acceptable substitutes. For instance, tea and coffee are reasonably interchangeable, so they may be included in the same relevant product market.

Establishing the relevant product market is often the key issue in monopolization cases because the way the market is defined may determine whether a firm has monopoly power. When the product market is defined narrowly, the degree of a firm's market power appears greater.

■ **EXAMPLE 26.8** White Whale Apps acquires Springleaf Apps, its main competitor in nationwide Android-based mobile phone apps. White Whale maintains that the relevant product market consists of all online retailers of mobile phone apps. The Federal Trade Commission (FTC), however, argues that the relevant product market consists of retailers that sell only apps for Android mobile phones. Under the FTC's narrower definition, White Whale can be seen to have a dominant share of the relevant product market. Thus, the FTC can take appropriate actions against White Whale. ■

In the following case, the FTC alleged that the leading U.S. producer of domestic ductile iron pipe fittings sought to maintain monopoly power in violation of antitrust law. The FTC filed this action under Section 5 of the Federal Trade Commission Act. Section 5, like Section 2 of the Sherman Act, requires proof of both the possession of monopoly power in the relevant market and the willful acquisition or maintenance of that power.

---

13. *United States v. Grinnell Corp.*, 384 U.S. 563, 86 S.Ct. 1698, 16 L.Ed.2d 778 (1966).
14. See, for example, *Broadcom Corp. v. Qualcomm, Inc.*, 501 F.3d 297 (3d Cir. 2007).
15. *Kolon Industries, Inc. v. E.I. DuPont de Nemours & Co.*, 748 F.3d 160 (4th Cir. 2014).

# McWane, Inc. v. Federal Trade Commission

United States Court of Appeals, Eleventh Circuit, 783 F.3d 814 (2015).

### In the Language of the Court

*MARCUS,* Circuit Judge:

* * * *

* * * Pipe fittings join together pipes and help direct the flow of pressurized water in pipeline systems. They are sold primarily to municipal water authorities and their contractors. Although there are several thousand unique configurations of fittings (different shapes, sizes, coatings, etc.), approximately 80% of the demand is for about 100 commonly used fittings.

Fittings are commodity products produced to American Water Works Association ("AWWA") standards, and any fitting that meets AWWA specifications is interchangeable, regardless of the country of origin.

* * * Certain municipal, state, and federal laws require [government] waterworks projects to use domestic-only fittings. Domestic fittings sold for use in projects with domestic-only specifications command higher prices than imported fittings.

* * * *

* * * In late 2009, McWane [Inc., headquartered in Birmingham, Alabama,] was the only supplier of domestic fittings.

* * * Looking to take advantage of the increased demand for domestic fittings prompted by [the passage of the American Recovery and Reinvestment Act of 2009 (ARRA), which provided a large infusion of money for waterworks projects that required domestic pipe fittings, Star Pipe Products] decided to enter the market for domestic [fittings].

In response to Star's forthcoming entry into the * * * market, McWane implemented its "Full Support Program" in order "to protect its domestic brands and market position." * * * McWane informed customers that if they did not "fully support McWane branded

products for their domestic fitting and accessory requirements," they "may forgo participation in any unpaid rebates they had accrued for domestic fittings and accessories or shipment of their domestic fitting and accessory orders of McWane products for up to 12 weeks."

* * * *

* * * The FTC issued a * * * complaint charging * * * that McWane's * * * Full Support Program constituted unlawful maintenance of a monopoly over the domestic fittings market.

* * * *

* * * The Commission found that the relevant market was the supply of domestically manufactured fittings for use in domestic-only waterworks projects, because imported fittings are not a substitute for domestic fittings for such projects. The Commission noted that this conclusion was bolstered by the higher prices charged for domestic fittings used in domestic-only projects. The Commission also found that McWane had monopoly power in that market, with 90–95% market share * * * and [that there were] substantial barriers to entry in the form of major capital outlays required to produce domestic fittings.

The Commission [also found] that McWane's Full Support Program * * * foreclosed Star's access to distributors for domestic fittings and harmed competition, thereby contributing significantly to the maintenance of McWane's monopoly power in the market. It noted that * * * the country's two largest waterworks distributors (with a combined 60% market share), prohibited their branches from purchasing domestic fittings from Star after the Full Support Program was announced * * * . Unable to attract [customers], Star was prevented from generating the revenue needed to acquire its own foundry, a

more efficient means of producing domestic fittings; thus, its growth into a rival that could challenge McWane's monopoly power was artificially stunted.

Moreover, the Commission found that * * * McWane's * * * conduct had an impact on price: after the Full Support Program was implemented, McWane raised domestic fittings prices and increased its gross profits despite flat production costs, and it did so across states, regardless of whether Star had entered the market as a competitor.

* * * *

[The Commission issued an order directing McWane to stop requiring exclusivity from its customers.] McWane filed a timely petition in this Court seeking review of the Commissioner's order.

* * * *

* * * *Given the identification of persistent price differences between domestic fittings and imported fittings, the distinct customers, and the lack of reasonable substitutes in this case, there was sufficient evidence to support the Commission's market definition.* [Emphasis added.]

* * * *

* * * The evidence of McWane's overwhelming market share (90%), the large capital outlays required to enter the domestic fittings market, and McWane's undeniable continued power over domestic fittings prices amount to sufficient evidence that a reasonable mind might accept as adequate to support the Commission's conclusion [that McWane possessed monopoly power in the relevant market].

* * * *

* * * We agree that [McWane's] conduct amounts to a violation of Section 5 of the Federal Trade Commission Act.

Accordingly, we AFFIRM.

Case 26.1 Continued

### Legal Reasoning Questions

**1.** How did McWane's Full Support Program harm competition? Explain.

**2.** What did the Federal Trade Commission conclude? What "factual and economic" evidence supported this conclusion?

**3.** Instead of imposing an exclusivity policy, what action might McWane have taken to benefit its customers and compete with Star?

---

**Relevant Geographic Market.** The second component of the relevant market is the geographic extent of the market in which the firm and its competitors sell the product or services. For products that are sold nationwide, the geographic boundaries of the market can encompass the entire United States.

If transportation costs are significant or a producer and its competitors sell in only a limited area (one in which customers have no access to other sources of the product), then the geographic market is limited to that area. A national firm may thus compete in several distinct areas and have monopoly power in one geographic area but not in another.

Generally, the geographic market is that section of the country within which a firm can increase its price a bit without attracting new sellers or losing many customers to alternative suppliers outside that area. Of course, the Internet is changing perceptions of the size and limits of a geographic market. It may become difficult to perceive any geographic market as local, except for products that are not easily transported, such as concrete.

**The Intent Requirement** Monopoly power, in and of itself, does not constitute the offense of monopolization under Section 2 of the Sherman Act. The offense also requires an *intent* to monopolize.

A dominant market share may be the result of good business judgment or the development of a superior product. It may simply be the result of a historical accident. In these situations, the acquisition of monopoly power is not an antitrust violation. Indeed, it would be contrary to society's interest to condemn every firm that acquired a position of power because it was well managed and efficient and marketed a product desired by consumers.

If a firm possesses market power as a result of carrying out some purposeful act to acquire or maintain that power through anticompetitive means, then it is in violation of

Section 2. In most monopolization cases, intent may be inferred from evidence that the firm had monopoly power and engaged in anticompetitive behavior.

**Unilateral Refusals to Deal** As discussed previously, joint refusals to deal (group boycotts) are subject to close scrutiny under Section 1 of the Sherman Act. A single manufacturer acting unilaterally, though, normally is free to deal, or not to deal, with whomever it wishes.[16]

Nevertheless, in some instances, a unilateral refusal to deal will violate Section 2 of the Sherman Act. These instances occur only if (1) the firm refusing to deal has—or is likely to acquire—monopoly power and (2) the refusal is likely to have an anticompetitive effect on a particular market.

■ **EXAMPLE 26.9** Clark Industries owns three of the four major downhill ski areas in Blue Hills, Idaho. Clark refuses to continue participating in a jointly offered six-day "all Blue Hills" lift ticket. Clark's refusal to cooperate with its smaller competitor is a violation of Section 2 of the Sherman Act. Because Clark owns three-fourths of the local ski areas, it has monopoly power. Thus, its unilateral refusal to deal has an anticompetitive effect on the market. ■

### 26–3b Attempts to Monopolize

Section 2 also prohibits **attempted monopolization** of a market, which requires proof of the following three elements:

**1.** Anticompetitive conduct.

**2.** The specific intent to exclude competitors and garner monopoly power.

---

**16.** For a classic case in this area, see *United States v. Colgate & Co.*, 250 U.S. 300, 39 S.Ct. 465, 63 L.Ed. 992 (1919). See also *Pacific Bell Telephone Co. v. Linkline Communications, Inc.*, 555 U.S. 438, 129 S.Ct. 1109, 172 L.Ed.2d 836 (2009).

**3.** A "dangerous" probability of success in achieving monopoly power. The probability cannot be dangerous unless the alleged offender possesses some degree of market power. Only serious threats of monopolization are condemned as violations.

As mentioned earlier, predatory pricing is a form of anticompetitive conduct that, in theory, could be used by firms that are attempting to monopolize. Related to predatory pricing is *predatory bidding*. This practice involves the acquisition and use of *monopsony power,* which is market power on the *buy* side of a market. Predatory bidding occurs when a buyer bids up the price of an input too high for its competitors to pay, causing them to leave the market. The predatory bidder then attempts to drive down input prices to reap above-competitive profits and recoup any losses it suffered in bidding up the input prices.

The question in the following *Spotlight Case* was whether a claim of predatory bidding was sufficiently similar to a claim of predatory pricing that the same antitrust test should apply to both.

## Spotlight on Weyerhaeuser

### Case 26.2 Weyerhaeuser Co. v. Ross-Simmons Hardwood Lumber Co.
Supreme Court of the United States, 549 U.S. 312, 127 S.Ct. 1069, 166 L.Ed.2d 911 (2007).

**Background and Facts** Weyerhaeuser Company entered the Pacific Northwest's hardwood lumber market in 1980. By 2000, Weyerhaeuser owned six mills processing 65 percent of the red alder logs in the region. Meanwhile, Ross-Simmons Hardwood Lumber Company operated a single competing mill. When the prices of the logs rose and those for the lumber fell, Ross-Simmons suffered heavy losses. Several million dollars in debt, the mill closed in 2001.

Ross-Simmons filed a suit in a federal district court against Weyerhaeuser, alleging attempted monopolization under Section 2 of the Sherman Act. Ross-Simmons claimed that Weyerhaeuser used its dominant position in the market to bid up the prices of logs and prevent its competitors from being profitable. Weyerhaeuser argued that the antitrust test for predatory pricing applies to a claim of predatory bidding and that Ross-Simmons had not met this standard. The district court ruled in favor of the plaintiff, the U.S. Court of Appeals for the Ninth Circuit affirmed, and Weyerhaeuser appealed to the United States Supreme Court.

#### In the Language of the Court
Justice *THOMAS* delivered the opinion of the Court.
        * * * *

Predatory-pricing and predatory-bidding claims are analytically similar. This similarity results from the close theoretical connection between monopoly and monopsony. The kinship between monopoly and monopsony suggests that similar legal standards should apply to claims of monopolization and to claims of monopsonization.

* * * Both claims involve the deliberate use of unilateral pricing measures for anticompetitive purposes. And both claims logically require firms to incur short-term losses on the chance that they might reap supracompetitive [above-competitive] profits in the future.
        * * * *

* * * *"Predatory pricing schemes are rarely tried, and even more rarely successful." Predatory pricing requires a firm to suffer certain losses in the short term on the chance of reaping supracompetitive profits in the future. A rational business will rarely make this sacrifice.* The same reasoning applies to predatory bidding. [Emphasis added.]
        * * * *

* * * A failed predatory-pricing scheme may benefit consumers. * * * Failed predatory-bidding schemes can also * * * benefit consumers.

In addition, predatory bidding presents less of a direct threat of consumer harm than predatory pricing. A predatory-pricing scheme ultimately achieves success by charging higher prices to consumers. By

Case 26.2 Continued

contrast, a predatory-bidding scheme could succeed with little or no effect on consumer prices because a predatory bidder does not necessarily rely on raising prices in the output market to recoup its losses.

* * * *

* * * [Thus,] our two-pronged [predatory pricing] test should apply to predatory-bidding claims.

* * * A plaintiff must prove that the alleged predatory bidding led to below-cost pricing of the predator's outputs. That is, the predator's bidding on the buy side must have caused the cost of the relevant output to rise above the revenues generated in the sale of those outputs. * * * Given the multitude of procompetitive ends served by higher bidding for inputs, the risk of chilling procompetitive behavior with too lax a liability standard is * * * serious * * *. Consequently, only higher bidding that leads to below-cost pricing in the relevant output market will suffice as a basis for liability for predatory bidding.

A predatory-bidding plaintiff also must prove that the defendant has a dangerous probability of recouping the losses incurred in bidding up input prices through the exercise of monopsony power. Absent proof of likely recoupment, a strategy of predatory bidding makes no economic sense because it would involve short-term losses with no likelihood of offsetting long-term gains.

Ross-Simmons has conceded that it has not satisfied [this] standard. Therefore, its predatory-bidding theory of liability cannot support the jury's verdict.

**Decision and Remedy** The United States Supreme Court held that the antitrust test that applies to claims of predatory pricing also applies to claims of predatory bidding. Because Ross-Simmons conceded that it had not met this standard, the Court vacated the lower court's judgment and remanded the case.

**Critical Thinking**
- **Social** *Do predatory-bidding schemes ever benefit consumers? Explain your answer.*
- **Economic** *Why does a plaintiff alleging predatory bidding have to prove that the defendant's "bidding on the buy side caused the cost of the relevant output to rise above the revenues generated in the sale of those outputs"?*

# 26–4 The Clayton Act

Congress enacted the Clayton Act to strengthen federal antitrust laws. The act was aimed at specific anticompetitive or monopolistic practices that the Sherman Act did not cover. The substantive provisions of the act—set out in Sections 2, 3, 7, and 8—deal with four distinct forms of business behavior, which are declared illegal but not criminal. For each provision, the act states that the behavior is *illegal only if it tends to substantially lessen competition or to create monopoly power.*

## 26–4a Section 2—Price Discrimination

Section 2 of the Clayton Act prohibits **price discrimination,** which occurs when a seller charges different prices to competing buyers for identical goods or services. Congress strengthened this section by amending it with the passage of the Robinson-Patman Act in 1936. As amended, Section 2 prohibits price discrimination that cannot be justified by differences in production costs, transportation costs, or cost differences due to other reasons. In short, a seller cannot charge one buyer a lower price than it charges that buyer's competitor.

**Requirements** To violate Section 2, the seller must be engaged in interstate commerce, the goods must be of like grade and quality, and the goods must have been sold to two or more purchasers. In addition, the effect of the price discrimination must be to substantially lessen competition, tend to create a monopoly, or otherwise injure competition. Without proof of an actual injury resulting from the price discrimination, the plaintiff cannot recover damages.

Note that price discrimination claims can arise from discounts, offsets, rebates, or allowances given to one buyer over another. Moreover, giving favorable credit terms, delivery, or freight charges to some buyers, but not others, can also lead to allegations of price discrimination. For instance, when a seller offers goods to different customers at the same price but includes free delivery for certain buyers, it may violate Section 2 in some circumstances.

**Defenses** There are several statutory defenses to liability for price discrimination.

1. *Cost justification.* If the seller can justify the price reduction by demonstrating that a particular buyer's purchases saved the seller costs in producing and selling the goods, the seller will not be liable for price discrimination.

2. *Meeting a competitor's prices.* If the seller charged the lower price in a good faith attempt to meet an equally low price of a competitor, the seller will not be liable for price discrimination. ■ **EXAMPLE 26.10** Rogue, Inc., is a retail dealer of Mercury Marine outboard motors in Shady Cove, Oregon. Mercury Marine also sells its motors to other dealers in the Shady Cove area. When Rogue discovers that Mercury is selling its outboard motors at a substantial discount to Rogue's largest competitor, it files a price discrimination lawsuit. Mercury Marine can defend itself by showing that the discounts given to Rogue's competitor were made in good faith to meet the low price charged by another manufacturer of marine motors. ■

3. *Changing market conditions.* A seller may lower its price on an item in response to changing conditions affecting the market for or the marketability of the goods concerned. Sellers are allowed to readjust their prices to meet the realities of the market without liability for price discrimination. Thus, if an advance in technology makes a particular product less marketable than it was previously, a seller can lower the product's price.

## 26–4b Section 3—Exclusionary Practices

Under Section 3 of the Clayton Act, sellers or lessors cannot condition the sale or lease of goods on the buyer's or lessee's promise not to use or deal in the goods of the seller's competitor. In effect, this section prohibits two types of vertical agreements involving exclusionary practices—exclusive-dealing contracts and tying arrangements.

**Exclusive-Dealing Contracts** A contract under which a seller forbids a buyer to purchase products from the seller's competitors is called an **exclusive-dealing contract.** A seller is prohibited from making an exclusive-dealing contract under Section 3 if the effect of the contract is "to substantially lessen competition or tend to create a monopoly."

In the past, courts were more inclined to find that exclusive-dealing contracts substantially lessened competition. ■ **CASE IN POINT 26.11** In one classic case, Standard Oil Company, the largest gasoline seller in the nation in the late 1940s, made exclusive-dealing contracts with independent stations in seven western states.

The contracts involved 16 percent of all retail outlets, whose sales were approximately 7 percent of all retail sales in that market. The United States Supreme Court ruled that the market was substantially concentrated because the seven largest gasoline suppliers all used exclusive-dealing contracts with their independent retailers and together controlled 65 percent of the market.

Looking at market conditions after the arrangements were instituted, the Court found that market shares were extremely stable and that entry into the market was apparently restricted. Thus, the Court held that the Clayton Act had been violated because competition was "foreclosed in a substantial share" of the relevant market.[17] ■ Note that since the Supreme Court's 1949 decision, a number of subsequent decisions have called the holding in this case into doubt.[18]

Today, it is clear that to violate antitrust law, an exclusive-dealing agreement (or a tying arrangement, discussed next) must qualitatively and substantially harm competition. To prevail, a plaintiff must present affirmative evidence that the performance of the agreement will foreclose competition and harm consumers.

**Tying Arrangements** When a seller conditions the sale of a product (the tying product) on the buyer's agreement to purchase another product (the tied product) produced or distributed by the same seller, a **tying arrangement** results. The legality of a tying arrangement (or *tie-in sales agreement*) depends on several factors, such as the purpose of the agreement. Courts also focus on the agreement's likely effect on competition in the relevant markets (the market for the tying product and the market for the tied product).

Section 3 of the Clayton Act has been held to apply only to commodities, not to services. Tying arrangements, however, can also be considered agreements that restrain trade in violation of Section 1 of the Sherman Act. Thus, cases involving tying arrangements of services have been brought under Section 1 of the Sherman Act. Although earlier cases condemned tying arrangements as illegal *per se,* courts now evaluate tying agreements under the rule of reason.[19]

---

17. *Standard Oil Co. of California v. United States,* 337 U.S. 293, 69 S.Ct. 1051, 93 L.Ed. 1371 (1949).

18. See, for example, *Illinois Tool Works, Inc. v. Independent Ink, Inc.,* 547 U.S. 28, 126 S.Ct. 1281, 164 L.Ed.2d 26 (2006); and *Stop & Shop Supermarket Co. v. Blue Cross & Blue Shield of Rhode Island,* 373 F.3d 57 (1st Cir. 2004).

19. *Illinois Tool Works, Inc. v. Independent Ink, Inc.,* 547 U.S. 28, 126 S.Ct. 1281, 164 L.Ed.2d 26 (2006). This decision was the first time the Supreme Court recognized that tying arrangements can have legitimate business justifications.

**■ CASE IN POINT 26.12** James Batson bought a nonrefundable ticket from Live Nation Entertainment, Inc., to attend a rock concert at the Charter One Pavilion in Chicago. The front of the ticket noted that the price included a nine-dollar parking fee. Batson did not have a car to park, however. In fact, he had walked to the concert venue and had bought the ticket just before the performance.

Frustrated at being charged for parking that he did not need, Batson filed a suit in a federal district court against Live Nation. He argued that the bundled parking fee was unfair because consumers were forced to pay it or forego the concert. He asserted that this was a tying arrangement in violation of Section 1 of the Sherman Act. The court dismissed the suit, and a federal appellate court affirmed. The court was unable to identify a product market in which Live Nation had sufficient power to force consumers who wanted to attend a concert (the tying product) to buy "useless parking rights" (the tied product). While such bundles may be annoying, there was no evidence that Live Nation's parking tie-in restrained competition for parking in Chicago.[20] ■

## 26–4c Section 7—Mergers

Under Section 7 of the Clayton Act, a person or business organization cannot hold stock or assets in more than one business when "the effect . . . may be to substantially lessen competition." Section 7 is the statutory authority for preventing mergers or acquisitions that could result in monopoly power or a substantial lessening of competition in the marketplace. Section 7 applies to both horizontal and vertical mergers, as discussed in the following subsections.

A crucial consideration in most merger cases is **market concentration.** Determining market concentration involves allocating percentage market shares among the various companies in the relevant market. When a small number of companies share a large part of the market, the market is concentrated. **■ EXAMPLE 26.13** If the four largest grocery stores in Chicago account for 80 percent of all retail food sales, the market is concentrated in those four firms. If one of these stores absorbs the assets and liabilities of another, so that the other ceases to exist, the result is a merger that further concentrates the market and possibly diminishes competition. ■

Competition is not necessarily diminished solely as a result of market concentration, however. Courts will consider other factors in determining if a merger violates

Section 7. One factor of particular importance is whether the merger will make it more difficult for *potential* competitors to enter the relevant market.

**Horizontal Mergers** Mergers between firms that compete with each other in the same market are called **horizontal mergers.** If a horizontal merger creates an entity with a significant market share, the merger may be considered illegal because it increases market concentration. The Federal Trade Commission (FTC) and the U.S. Department of Justice (DOJ) have established guidelines for determining which mergers will be challenged.[21]

When analyzing the legality of a horizontal merger, the courts consider three additional factors. The first factor is the overall concentration of the relevant market. The second is the relevant market's history of tending toward concentration. The final factor is whether the merger is apparently designed to establish market power or restrict competition.

**Vertical Mergers** A **vertical merger** occurs when a company at one stage of production acquires a company at a higher or lower stage of production. An example of a vertical merger is a company merging with one of its suppliers or retailers.

Whether a vertical merger will be deemed illegal generally depends on several factors, such as whether the merger creates a single firm that controls an undue percentage share of the relevant market. The courts also analyze the concentration of firms in the market, barriers to entry into the market, and the apparent intent of the merging parties. If a merger does not prevent competitors of either of the merging firms from competing in a segment of the market, the merger will not be condemned as foreclosing competition and thus is legal.

## 26–4d Section 8— Interlocking Directorates

Section 8 of the Clayton Act deals with *interlocking directorates*—that is, the practice whereby individuals serve as directors on the boards of two or more competing companies simultaneously. Specifically, no person may be a director for two or more competing corporations at the same time if either of the corporations has capital, surplus, or undivided profits aggregating more than $31,841,000

---

20. *Batson v. Live Nation Entertainment, Inc.,* 746 F.3d 827 (7th Cir. 2014).

21. These guidelines include a formula for assessing the degree of concentration in the relevant market called the *Herfindahl-Hirschman Index* (HHI), which is available at **www.justice.gov.**

or competitive sales of $3,184,100 or more. The Federal Trade Commission adjusts these threshold amounts each year. (The amounts given here are those announced by the commission in 2016.)

## 26-5 Enforcement and Exemptions

The federal agencies that enforce the federal antitrust laws are the U.S. Department of Justice (DOJ) and the Federal Trade Commission (FTC), which was established by the Federal Trade Commission Act. Section 5 of that act condemns all forms of anticompetitive behavior that are not covered under other federal antitrust laws.

### 26-5a Agency Actions

Only the DOJ can prosecute violations of the Sherman Act, which can be either criminal or civil offenses. Violations of the Clayton Act are not crimes, but the act can be enforced by either the DOJ or the FTC through civil proceedings.

The DOJ or the FTC may ask the courts to impose various remedies, including **divestiture** (making a company give up one or more of its operations) and dissolution. A meatpacking firm, for instance, might be forced to divest itself of control or ownership of butcher shops.

The FTC has sole authority to enforce violations of Section 5 of the Federal Trade Commission Act. FTC actions are effected through administrative orders, but if a firm violates an FTC order, the FTC can seek court sanctions for the violation.

### 26-5b Private Actions

A private party who has been injured as a result of a violation of the Sherman Act or the Clayton Act can sue

for **treble damages** (three times the actual damages suffered) and attorneys' fees. In some instances, private parties may also seek injunctive relief to prevent antitrust violations. A party wishing to sue under the Sherman Act must prove that:

1. The antitrust violation either caused or was a substantial factor in causing the injury that was suffered.
2. The unlawful actions of the accused party affected business activities of the plaintiff that were protected by the antitrust laws.

Additionally, the United States Supreme Court has held that to pursue antitrust lawsuits, private parties must present some evidence suggesting that an illegal agreement was made.[22]

A private party can bring an action under Section 2 of the Sherman Act based on the attempted enforcement of a fraudulently obtained patent. This is called a *Walker Process* claim.[23] To prevail, the plaintiff must first show that the defendant obtained the patent by fraud on the U.S. Patent and Trademark Office and enforced the patent with knowledge of the fraud. The plaintiff must then establish all the other elements of a Sherman Act monopolization claim—anticompetitive conduct, an intent to monopolize, and a dangerous probability of achieving monopoly power.

In the following case, a respiratory filter maker was accused of patent infringement. The maker sought a declaratory judgment of non-infringement, asserting a *Walker Process* claim. One of the primary issues was whether attorney fees were an appropriate basis for damages.

22. *Bell Atlantic Corp. v. Twombly*, 550 U.S. 544, 127 S.Ct. 1955, 167 L.Ed.2d 929 (2007).
23. The name of the claim comes from the title of the case in which the claim originated—*Walker Process Equipment v. Food Machine and Chemical Corp.*, 382 U.S. 172, 86 S.Ct. 347, 15 L.Ed.2d 247 (1965).

**Case 26.3**

## TransWeb, LLC v. 3M Innovative Properties Co.

United States Court of Appeals, Federal Circuit, 812 F.3d 1295 (2016).

**Background and Facts** TransWeb, LLC, makes respirator filters made of nonwoven fibrous material to be worn by workers at contaminated worksites. At a filtration industry exposition, TransWeb's founder, Kumar Ogale, handed out samples of TransWeb's filter material. At the time, 3M Innovative Products Company was experimenting with filter materials. At the expo, 3M employees obtained the TransWeb samples.

More than a year later, 3M obtained patents for its filter products and filed a suit against TransWeb, claiming infringement. 3M asserted that it had not received the TransWeb samples until after its patent application had been filed. The suit was dismissed.

TransWeb then filed a suit in a federal district court, seeking a declaratory judgment of non-infringement and asserting a *Walker Process* claim. A jury found that 3M had obtained its patents through fraud, that its assertion of the patents against TransWeb violated antitrust law, and that Trans-Web was entitled to attorney fees as damages. TransWeb had incurred $7.7 million defending against 3M's infringement suit. The court trebled this to $23 million. 3M appealed.

## In the Language of the Court
*HUGHES,* Circuit Judge.
* * * *

3M argues that the district court erred in awarding the $23 million of attorney-fees damages, because TransWeb failed to show any link between those attorney fees and an impact on competition. 3M argues that those attorney fees had no effect on competition because they did not force TransWeb out of the market or otherwise affect prices in the market.
* * * *

3M's argument focuses on the fact that the harmful effect on competition proven by TransWeb at trial never actually came about. TransWeb proved at trial that increased prices for fluorinated filter * * * respirators would have resulted had 3M succeeded in its suit.
* * * *

* * * 3M's unlawful act was * * * aimed at reducing competition and would have done so had the suit been successful. 3M's unlawful act was the bringing of suit based on a patent known to be fraudulently obtained. What made this act unlawful under the antitrust laws was its attempt to gain a monopoly based on this fraudulently obtained patent. TransWeb's attorney fees flow directly from this unlawful aspect of 3M's act. * * * The attorney fees are precisely the type of loss that the claimed violations would be likely to cause.
* * * *

* * * *It is the abuse of the legal process by the antitrust-defendant that makes the attorney fees incurred by the antitrust-plaintiff during that legal process a relevant antitrust injury.* [Emphasis added.]

No assertion of a patent known to be fraudulently obtained can be a proper use of legal process. No successful outcome of that litigation, regardless of how much the patentee subjectively desires it, would save that suit from being improper due to its tainted origin.

* * * The antitrust laws exist to protect competition. If we were to hold that TransWeb can seek antitrust damages only [by] forfeiture of competition, but not [by] defending the anticompetitive suit, then we would be incentivizing the former over the latter. * * * This is not in accord with the purpose of those very same antitrust laws.

Furthermore, it furthers the purpose of the antitrust laws to encourage TransWeb to bring its antitrust suit * * * instead of waiting to be excluded from the market * * * . If TransWeb proceeds only after being excluded from the market * * * , then the [injury] will no longer be borne by TransWeb alone, but rather would be shared by all consumers in the relevant markets.

**Decision and Remedy**  *The U.S. Court of Appeals for the Federal Circuit affirmed the lower court's judgment and award of trebled attorney fees. "TransWeb's attorney fees appropriately flow from the unlawful aspect of 3M's antitrust violation and thus are an antitrust injury that can properly serve as the basis for antitrust damages."*

## Critical Thinking
- **Legal Environment**  *How would TransWeb's injury have been "shared by all consumers in the relevant markets" if TransWeb had not sued until* after *it had been driven out of those markets by 3M's actions?*
- **Ethical**  *What does 3M's conduct suggest about its corporate ethics?*

## 26-5c Exemptions from Antitrust Laws

There are many legislative and constitutional limitations on antitrust enforcement. Most of the statutory and judicially created exemptions to the antitrust laws apply only in certain areas (see Exhibit 26–2). One of the most significant exemptions covers joint efforts by businesspersons to obtain legislative, judicial, or executive action. Under this exemption, for example, DVD producers can jointly lobby Congress to change the copyright laws without being held liable for attempting to restrain trade.

**EXHIBIT 26–2** Exemptions to Antitrust Enforcement

| EXEMPTION | SOURCE AND SCOPE |
|---|---|
| Labor | The Clayton Act—Permits unions to organize and bargain without violating antitrust laws and specifies that strikes and other labor activities normally do not violate any federal law. |
| Agricultural Associations | The Clayton Act and the Capper-Volstead Act—Allow agricultural cooperatives to set prices. |
| Fisheries | The Fisheries Cooperative Marketing Act—Allows the fishing industry to set prices. |
| Insurance Companies | The McCarran-Ferguson Act—Exempts the insurance business in states in which the industry is regulated. |
| Exporters | The Webb-Pomerene Act—Allows U.S. exporters to engage in cooperative activity to compete with similar foreign associations. The Export Trading Company Act—Permits the U.S. Department of Justice to exempt certain exporters. |
| Professional Baseball | The United States Supreme Court—Has held that professional baseball is exempt because it is not "interstate commerce."[a] |
| Oil Marketing | The Interstate Oil Compact—Allows states to set quotas on oil to be marketed in interstate commerce. |
| Defense Activities | The Defense Production Act—Allows the president to approve, and thereby exempt, certain activities to further the military defense of the United States. |
| Small Businesses' Cooperative Research | The Small Business Administration Act—Allows small firms to undertake cooperative research. |
| State Actions | The United States Supreme Court—Has held that actions by a state are exempt if the state clearly articulates and actively supervises the policy behind its action.[b] |
| Regulated Industries | Federal Agencies—Industries (such as airlines) are exempt when a federal administrative agency (such as the Federal Aviation Administration) has primary regulatory authority. |
| Businesspersons' Joint Efforts to Seek Government Action | The United States Supreme Court—Cooperative efforts by businesspersons to obtain legislative, judicial, or executive action are exempt unless it is clear that an effort is "objectively baseless" and is an attempt to make anticompetitive use of government processes.[c] |

a. *Federal Baseball Club of Baltimore, Inc. v. National League of Professional Baseball Clubs,* 259 U.S. 200, 42 S.Ct. 465, 66 L.Ed. 898 (1922). See *City of San Jose v. Office of the Commissioner of Baseball,* 776 F.3d 686 (9th Cir. 2015).
b. See *Parker v. Brown,* 317 U.S. 341, 63 S.Ct. 307, 87 L.Ed. 315 (1943).
c. *Eastern Railroad Presidents Conference v. Noerr Motor Freight, Inc.,* 365 U.S. 127, 81 S.Ct. 523, 5 L.Ed.2d 464 (1961); and *United Mine Workers of America v. Pennington,* 381 U.S. 657, 89 S.Ct. 1585, 14 L.Ed.2d 626 (1965). These two cases established the exception often referred to as the *Noerr-Pennington* doctrine.

# 26–6 U.S. Antitrust Laws in the Global Context

U.S. antitrust laws have a broad application. Not only may persons in foreign nations be subject to their provisions, but the laws may also be applied to protect foreign consumers and competitors from violations committed by U.S. business firms. Consequently, *foreign persons,* a term that by definition includes foreign governments, may sue under U.S. antitrust laws in U.S. courts.

## 26–6a The Extraterritorial Application of U.S. Antitrust Laws

Section 1 of the Sherman Act provides for the extraterritorial effect of the U.S. antitrust laws. Any conspiracy that has a *substantial effect* on U.S. commerce is within the reach of the Sherman Act. The violation may even occur outside the United States, and foreign governments as well as individuals can be sued for violation of U.S. antitrust laws.

Before U.S. courts will exercise jurisdiction and apply antitrust laws, it must be shown that the alleged violation had a substantial effect on U.S. commerce. U.S. jurisdiction is automatically invoked, however, when a *per se* violation occurs.

If a domestic firm, for instance, joins a foreign cartel to control the production, price, or distribution of goods, and this cartel has a *substantial effect* on U.S. commerce, a *per se* violation may arise. Hence, both the domestic firm and the foreign cartel could be sued for violation of the U.S. antitrust laws.

Likewise, if a foreign firm doing business in the United States enters into a price-fixing or other anticompetitive agreement to control a portion of U.S. markets, a *per se* violation may exist. ■ **CASE IN POINT 26.14** Carrier Corporation is a U.S. firm that manufactures air-conditioning and refrigeration (ACR) equipment. To make these products, Carrier uses ACR copper tubing it buys from Outokumpu Oyj, a Finnish company. Carrier is one of the world's largest purchasers of ACR copper tubing.

After the Commission of the European Communities found that Outokumpu had conspired with other companies to fix ACR tubing prices in Europe, Carrier filed a suit in a U.S. court. Carrier alleged that the cartel had also conspired to fix prices in the United States by agreeing that only Outokumpu would sell ACR tubing in the U.S. market. The district court dismissed the case for lack of jurisdiction, but a federal appellate court reversed. The reviewing court found that the alleged anticompetitive conspiracy had a substantial effect on U.S. commerce. Therefore, the U.S. courts had jurisdiction over the Finnish defendant.[24] ■

## 26–6b The Application of Foreign Antitrust Laws

Large U.S. companies increasingly must be concerned about the application of foreign antitrust laws. The European Union (EU), in particular, has stepped up its enforcement actions against antitrust violators.

**European Union Enforcement** The EU's laws promoting competition are stricter in many respects than those of the United States and define more conduct as anticompetitive. The EU actively pursues antitrust violators, especially individual companies and cartels that allegedly engage in monopolistic conduct. EU investigations of possible antitrust violations often take years. See this chapter's *Digital Update* feature for a discussion of how the EU is pursuing Google, Inc., for antitrust violations.

**Increased Enforcement in Asia and Latin America** Many other nations also have laws that promote competition and prohibit trade restraints. Japanese antitrust laws forbid unfair trade practices, monopolization, and restrictions that unreasonably restrain trade. China's antitrust rules restrict monopolization and price fixing (except that the Chinese government can set prices on exported goods). Indonesia, Malaysia, South Korea, and Vietnam all have statutes protecting competition. Argentina, Brazil, Chile, Peru, and several other Latin American countries have adopted modern antitrust laws as well.

Most of the antitrust laws apply extraterritorially, as U.S. antitrust laws do. This means that a U.S. company may be subject to another nation's antitrust laws if the company's conduct has a substantial effect on that nation's commerce. For instance, in 2015, China fined the U.S. chipmaker Qualcomm, Inc., $975 million for violating antitrust laws. China has also targeted Microsoft, Inc., in its antitrust investigations and has searched Microsoft's company servers in China for evidence of violations.

---

24. *Carrier Corp. v. Outokumpu Oyj,* 673 F.3d 430 (6th Cir. 2012).

## DIGITAL UPDATE   Google Faces an Antitrust Complaint from the European Union

"Just google it." Google's search engine is so dominant that the company name has become a verb synonymous with conducting an Internet search. According to the European Commissioner for Competition, Margrethe Vestager, Google has become too dominant, at least with respect to comparison shopping and product search. For that reason, the European Union (EU) has formally charged Google with an antitrust violation. The charges relate specifically to Google operations in the EU.

### The EU's Antitrust Objections

According to the EU, Google is abusing a dominant position—a breach of EU antitrust rules. The EU has alleged that Google promotes its own comparison shopping service at the expense of competitors. It does this by "positioning and prominently displaying its comparison shopping service in its general search result pages, irrespective of its merits." As a result, "users do not necessarily see the most relevant results in response to queries—to the detriment of consumers and rival comparison shopping services." Presumably, this conduct started in 2008.

### What the EU Wants Google to Do and Google's Response

Now that the EU has established its complaint against Google, here is what it wants Google to do: change the way it displays search results in the EU. When Google shows comparison shopping services in response to a user's query, the search results should show the most relevant services first.

In response to both the complaint and the suggested remedy, Google offered a 130-page rebuttal. It contends that it cannot change its core software. It also claims that the results in its search algorithms are based on relevance. In addition, Google contends that it has actually boosted traffic to its Web competitors. Therein lies the major argument against the EU's antitrust complaint. Search engines have proliferated on the Web, suggesting that Google's success has not eliminated competition.

### The Compartmentalization of Search on the Web

More and more frequently, Internet users do not engage in general searches. Rather, they know exactly where to go to obtain product information. When they want information on movies, for instance, they go to the Internet Movie Data Base (IMDB) rather than Google. When they want information on music, they go to iTunes. When they want to search for the cheapest airfares, they go to Kayak or similar sites. When they want to find the best rates on hotels, they go to sites such as hotels.com. And when they are interested in buying a product, they frequently go to Amazon or eBay. Amazon, in particular, has fine-tuned its ability to generate advertising revenues through its Amazon-sponsored links.

And, of course, social media must be considered. More people are on social media sites than ever before, particularly on their mobile devices. Users spend four times more time on Facebook than they do on Google. These users often "crowdsource"—that is, look for answers from Facebook friends rather than search on Google. Facebook is also becoming increasingly competitive with Google in the services it offers, including mobile payments and the Facebook Messenger instant messaging service.

Whether the European Antitrust Commission accepts Google's arguments will determine Google's fate. Will it pay billions of dollars in fines and be forced to make significant changes in how it does business? That probably will not be decided any time soon. Experts estimate that the case could go on for years.

**Critical Thinking** *Which companies in Europe do you think may have pressured the European Union to lodge its antitrust complaint against Google?*

## Reviewing: Antitrust Law

The Internet Corporation for Assigned Names and Numbers (ICANN) is a nonprofit entity that organizes Internet domain names. It is governed by a board of directors elected by various groups with commercial interests in the Internet. One of ICANN's functions is to authorize an entity to serve as a registry for certain "Top Level Domains" (TLDs). ICANN and VeriSign entered into an agreement that authorized VeriSign to serve as a registry for the ".com" TLD and provide registry services in accordance with ICANN's specifications. VeriSign complained that ICANN was restricting the services that it could make available as a registrar, blocking new services, imposing unnecessary conditions on those services, and setting the prices at which the services were offered. VeriSign claimed that ICANN's control of the registry services for domain names violated Section 1 of the Sherman Act. Using the information presented in the chapter, answer the following questions.

1. Should ICANN's actions be judged under the rule of reason or be deemed *per se* violations of Section 1 of the Sherman Act? Why?
2. Should ICANN's actions be viewed as a horizontal or a vertical restraint of trade? Why?
3. Does it matter that ICANN's directors are chosen by groups with a commercial interest in the Internet? Explain.
4. If the dispute is judged under the rule of reason, what might be ICANN's defense for having a standardized set of registry services that must be used?

**Debate This** . . .   *The Internet and the rise of e-commerce have rendered our current antitrust concepts and laws obsolete.*

## Terms and Concepts

antitrust law 500
attempted monopolization 507
concentrated industry 503
divestiture 512
exclusive-dealing contract 510
group boycott 503
horizontal merger 511
horizontal restraint 502
market concentration 511
market power 501

monopolization 504
monopoly 501
monopoly power 501
*per se* violation 501
predatory pricing 504
price discrimination 509
price-fixing agreement 502
resale price maintenance
   agreement 504

restraint of trade 500
rule of reason 501
treble damages 512
tying arrangement 510
vertical merger 511
vertical restraint 503
vertically integrated firm 503

## Issue Spotters

1. Under what circumstances would Pop's Market, a small store in a small, isolated town, be considered a monopolist? If Pop's is a monopolist, is it in violation of Section 2 of the Sherman Act? Why or why not? (See *Section 2 of the Sherman Act.*)
2. Maple Corporation conditions the sale of its syrup on the buyer's agreement to buy Maple's pancake mix. What factors would a court consider to decide whether this arrangement violates the Clayton Act? (See *The Clayton Act.*)

• **Check your answers to the Issue Spotters against the answers provided in Appendix B at the end of this text.**

# Business Scenarios

**26–1. Group Boycott.** Jorge's Appliance Corp. was a new retail seller of appliances in Sunrise City. Because of its innovative sales techniques and financing, Jorge's attracted many customers. As a result, the appliance department of No-Glow Department Store, a large chain store with a great deal of buying power, lost a substantial number of sales. No-Glow told a number of appliance manufacturers from whom it made large-volume purchases that if they continued to sell to Jorge's, No-Glow would stop buying from them. The manufacturers immediately stopped selling appliances to Jorge's. Jorge's filed a suit against No-Glow and the manufacturers, claiming that their actions constituted an antitrust violation. No-Glow and the manufacturers were able to prove that Jorge's was a small retailer with a small market share. They claimed that because the relevant market was not substantially affected, they were not guilty of restraint of trade. Discuss fully whether there was an antitrust violation. (See *Section 1 of the Sherman Act.*)

**26–2. Antitrust Laws.** Allitron, Inc., and Donovan, Ltd., are interstate competitors selling similar appliances, principally in the states of Illinois, Indiana, Kentucky, and Ohio. Allitron and Donovan agree that Allitron will no longer sell in Indiana and Ohio and that Donovan will no longer sell in Illinois and Kentucky. Have Allitron and Donovan violated any antitrust laws? If so, which law? Explain. (See *Section 1 of The Sherman Act.*)

# Business Case Problems

**26–3. Section 2 of the Sherman Act.** While Deer Valley Resort Co. (DVRC) was developing its ski resort in the Wasatch Mountains near Park City, Utah, it sold parcels of land in the resort village to third parties. Each sales contract reserved the right of approval over the conduct of certain businesses on the property, including ski rentals. For fifteen years, DVRC permitted Christy Sports, LLC, to rent skis in competition with DVRC's ski rental outlet. Then DVRC opened a new midmountain ski rental outlet and revoked Christy's permission to rent skis. This meant that most skiers who flew into Salt Lake City and shuttled to Deer Valley had few choices. They could carry their ski equipment with them on their flights, take a shuttle into Park City and look for cheaper ski rentals there, or rent from DVRC. Christy filed a suit in a federal district court against DVRC. Was DVRC's action an attempt to monopolize in violation of Section 2 of the Sherman Act? Why or why not? [*Christy Sports, LLC v. Deer Valley Resort Co.,* 555 F.3d 1188 (10th Cir. 2009)] (See *Section 2 of the Sherman Act.*)

**26–4. Price Fixing.** Together, EMI, Sony BMG Music Entertainment, Universal Music Group Recordings, Inc., and Warner Music Group Corp. produced, licensed, and distributed 80 percent of the digital music sold in the United States. The companies formed MusicNet to sell music to online services that sold the songs to consumers. MusicNet required all of the services to sell the songs at the same price and subject to the same restrictions. Digitization of music became cheaper, but MusicNet did not change its prices. Did MusicNet violate the antitrust laws? Explain. [*Starr v. Sony BMG Music Entertainment,* 592 F.3d 314 (2d Cir. 2010)] (See *Section 1 of the Sherman Act.*)

**26–5. Business Case Problem with Sample Answer— Price Discrimination.** Dayton Superior Corp. sells its

products in interstate commerce to several companies, including Spa Steel Products, Inc. The purchasers often compete directly with each other for customers. From 2005 to 2007, one of Spa Steel's customers purchased Dayton Superior's products from two of Spa Steel's competitors. According to the customer, Spa Steel's prices were always 10 to 15 percent higher for the same products. As a result, Spa Steel lost sales to at least that customer and perhaps others. Spa Steel wants to sue Dayton Superior for price discrimination. Which requirements for such a claim under Section 2 of the Clayton Act does Spa Steel satisfy? What additional facts will it need to prove? [*Dayton Superior Corp. v. Spa Steel Products, Inc.,* 2012 WL 113663 (N.D.N.Y. 2012)] (See *The Clayton Act.*)

- **For a sample answer to Problem 26–5, go to Appendix C at the end of this text.**

**26–6. Section 1 of the Sherman Act.** The National Collegiate Athletic Association (NCAA) and the National Federation of State High School Associations (NFHS) set a new standard for non-wood baseball bats. Their goal was to ensure that aluminum and composite bats performed like wood bats in order to enhance player safety and reduce technology-driven home runs and other big hits. Marucci Sports, LLC, makes non-wood bats. Under the new standard, four of Marucci's eleven products were decertified for use in high school and collegiate games. Marucci filed suit against the NCAA and the NFHS under Section 1 of the Sherman Act. At trial, Marucci's evidence focused on injury to its own business. Did the NCAA and NFHS's standard restrain trade in violation of the Sherman Act? Explain. [*Marucci Sports, L.L.C. v. National Collegiate Athletic Association,* 751 F.3d 368 (5th Cir. 2014)] (See *Section 1 of the Sherman Act.*)

**26–7. Mergers.** St. Luke's Health Systems, Ltd., operated an emergency clinic in Nampa, Idaho. Saltzer Medical Group, P.A., had thirty-four physicians practicing at its offices in Nampa. Saint Alphonsus Medical Center operated the only hospital in Nampa. St. Luke's acquired Saltzer's assets and entered into a five-year professional service agreement with the Saltzer physicians. This affiliation resulted in a combined share of two-thirds of the Nampa adult primary care provider market. Together, the two entities could impose a significant increase in the prices charged to patients and insurers, and correspondence between the parties indicated that they would. Saint Alphonsus filed a suit against St. Luke's to block the merger. Did this affiliation violate antitrust law? Explain. [*Saint Alphonsus Medical Center-Nampa, Inc. v. St. Luke's Health System, Ltd.*, 778 F.3d 775 (9th Cir. 2015)] (See *The Clayton Act*.)

**26–8. Section 1 of the Sherman Act.** Manitou North America, Inc., makes and distributes telehandlers (forklifts with extendable telescopic booms) to dealers throughout the United States. Manitou agreed to make McCormick International, LLC, its exclusive dealer in the state of Michigan. Later, Manitou entered into an agreement with Gehi Company, which also makes and sells telehandlers. The companies agreed to allocate territories within Michigan among certain dealers for each manufacturer, limiting the dealers' selection of competitive products to certain models. Under this agreement, McCormick was precluded from buying or selling Gehi telehandlers. What type of trade restraint did the agreement between Manitou and Gehi represent? Is this a violation of antitrust law? If so, who was injured, and how were they injured? Explain. [*Manitou North America, Inc. v. McCormick International, LLC,* __ N.W.2d __, 2016 WL 439354 (2016)] (See *Section 1 of the Sherman Act*.)

**26–9. A Question of Ethics—Section 1 of the Sherman**
 **Act.** *In the 1990s, DuCoa, L.P., made choline chloride, a B-complex vitamin essential for the growth and development of animals. DuCoa, Bioproducts, Inc., and Chinook Group, Ltd., each had*

*one-third of the U.S. market for choline chloride. To stabilize the market and keep the price of the vitamin higher than it would otherwise have been, the companies took action. They agreed to fix the price and allocate market share by deciding which of them would offer the lowest price to each customer. At times, however, the companies disregarded the agreement.*

*During an increase in competitive activity in August 1997, Daniel Rose became president of DuCoa. The next month, a subordinate advised him of the conspiracy. By February 1998, Rose had begun to implement a strategy to persuade DuCoa's competitors to rejoin the conspiracy. By April, the three companies had reallocated their market shares and increased their prices. In June, the U.S. Department of Justice began to investigate allegations of price fixing in the vitamin market. Ultimately, a federal district court convicted Rose of conspiracy to violate Section 1 of the Sherman Act. [*United States v. Rose,* 449 F.3d 627 (5th Cir. 2006)] (See *Section 1 of the Sherman Act*.)

**(a)** The court "enhanced" Rose's sentence to thirty months' imprisonment, one year of supervised release, and a $20,000 fine. Among other things, the court based this enhancement on Rose's role as "a manager or supervisor" in the conspiracy. Rose appealed the enhancement to the U.S. Court of Appeals for the Fifth Circuit. Was it fair to increase Rose's sentence on this ground? Why or why not?

**(b)** Was Rose's participation in the conspiracy unethical? If so, how might Rose have behaved ethically instead? If not, could any of the participants' conduct be considered unethical? Explain.

## Legal Reasoning Group Activity

**26–10. Antitrust Violations.** Residents of the city of Madison, Wisconsin, became concerned about overconsumption of liquor near the campus of the University of Wisconsin (UW). The city initiated a new policy, imposing conditions on area bars to discourage reduced-price "specials" that were believed to encourage high-volume and dangerous drinking. Later, the city began to draft an ordinance to ban all drink specials. Bar owners responded by announcing that they had "voluntarily" agreed to discontinue drink specials on Friday and Saturday nights after 8:00 P.M. The city put its ordinance on hold. Several UW students filed a lawsuit against the local

bar owners' association, alleging violations of antitrust law. (See *Section 1 of the Sherman Act*.)

**(a)** The first group will identify the grounds on which the plaintiffs might base their claim for relief and formulate an argument on behalf of the plaintiffs.

**(b)** The second group will determine whether the defendants are exempt from the antitrust laws.

**(c)** The third group will decide how the court should rule in this dispute and provide reasons for the ruling.

Application and Ethics

## Climate Change

Our planet's average temperature has risen by 1.5 degrees Fahrenheit over the last hundred years. It is predicted that it will rise another 0.5 to 4.5 degrees over the next century. These seemingly small increases in the average temperature can result in significant change to our climate.

### What Are the Causes?

Over the last century, our atmosphere experienced a large increase in carbon dioxide and other *greenhouse gases (GHGs)*. GHGs act like a blanket around our planet, absorbing radiation from the surface, trapping it as heat in the atmosphere, and reflecting it back to the surface.

This process, known as the *greenhouse effect*, is necessary to support life. The recent increase in GHGs, however, may be changing our climate. Deforestation, industrial processes, and agricultural practices emit these gases, but the majority of GHGs come from burning fossil fuels to produce energy.[1]

### What Are the Effects?

The warmer it gets, the greater the risk for more change to the climate. Ultimately, the climate that we are used to may no longer be a guide for what to expect in the future.

**Changes in Weather** Rising global temperatures have sometimes coincided with changes in weather. Some locations have seen altered rainfall, resulting in heavier rains and more floods, or more frequent and intense heat waves and droughts. The rising temperatures may also be making our planet's oceans warmer and more acidic. Some glaciers and ice caps are melting, which may cause sea levels to rise.

**Impacts on Society** The warmer temperatures and changes in weather can affect society in many ways. Agricultural yields, human health, and the supply of energy are affected. More severe weather can lead to higher food and energy prices and increasing insurance costs. (Note, though, that higher average temperatures could lead to more agricultural output and hence lower food prices.) Of course, any impact in one area of human activity can have widespread and unforeseen effects throughout society.

### What Can We Do about It?

The effects of climate change may be lessened by choices that reduce GHGs. About half of the states have set statewide GHG emission goals.[2] In the areas of transportation and power generation, two of the options for reducing emissions are the use of low-emission fuels and increased energy efficiency.

**Reduce Emissions at the Pump and the Plant** Motor vehicles and transportation fuels are sources for nearly a third of U.S. GHG emissions. To reduce these emissions, the federal

---

1. Fossil fuel-burning power plants are the largest single source of U.S. GHG emissions at 33 percent.
2. California established the first statewide goals in 2006 in the Global Warming Solutions Act.

government and the states impose emission standards on cars and trucks, and encourage the use of fuel-efficient vehicles and alternative fuels.

The federal Environmental Protection Agency (EPA) and National Highway Transportation Safety Administration have established standards for GHG emissions and fuel economy for new light-duty cars and trucks through the model year 2025.[3] The standards are projected to save about 4 billion barrels of oil and avoid 2 billion metric tons of GHG emissions per year.

Some states have set low-emission fuel standards. More than a dozen states have set renewable fuel standards to encourage the use of low-emission fuels. Incentives to use alternative fuels include tax exemptions, tax credits, and grants.

To reduce GHG emissions from coal- and gas-fired power plants, the EPA issued the Clean Power Plan (CPP).[4] It is projected that, when the CPP is fully in place in 2030, carbon pollution from the power sector will be 32 percent below 2005 levels. Emissions of sulfur dioxide from power plants will be 90 percent lower than 2005 levels, and emissions of nitrogen oxides will be 72 percent lower.

About two-thirds of the states will require power companies to generate a certain percentage or amount of power from renewable energy sources by a specific date, which varies by state. These targets aim to reduce emissions and to improve air quality, diversify energy sources, and create jobs in the renewable energy industry.

**Become More Energy Efficient** More than half of the states have set standards requiring power companies to save specified amounts of energy. To attain these goals, the utilities must adopt more efficient technology in their operations and encourage their customers to become more energy efficient.

About half of the states dedicate funds to the support of renewable energy projects. More than a dozen of these states formed the Clean Energy States Alliance to coordinate their investments.

Nearly all states permit utility customers to sell electricity back to the grid. In most states, utilities offer their customers the opportunity to have a portion of their power provided from renewable sources.

Many states participate in regional climate initiatives. For example, nine states in the northeastern United States formed the Regional Greenhouse Gas Initiative to implement a market-based program to reduce GHG emissions from power plants. The initiative sets an emissions budget, or cap, for each member state. Credits that exceed the actual emissions can be sold. The proceeds are generally invested in energy-efficient renewable energy programs.

**Adapt to the Changes** The EPA's State and Local Climate and Energy Program provides technical assistance, analytical tools, and outreach support on climate change issues to state, local, and tribal governments.[5] The program directs resource managers to set priorities and to design and implement climate and energy policies tailored to the particular circumstances of their locations.

Part of the process is to assess an area's vulnerability to the effects of climate change and to consider approaches for adapting to the effects. For example, a coastal estuary that is subject to

---

3. 40 C.F.R. Parts 85, 86, and 600, and 49 C.F.R. Parts 523, 531, 533, 600 *et al.* The United States Supreme Court has made clear that the Environmental Protection Agency can regulate GHGs under the Clean Air Act. See *Massachusetts v. E.P.A.*, 549 U.S. 497, 127 S.Ct. 1438, 167 L.Ed.2d 248 (2007).

4. 40 C.F.R. Part 60. This act is being challenged in court.

5. See Environmental Protection Agency, *State and Local Climate and Energy Program* (December 28, 2015) available at http://www3.epa.gov/statelocalclimate/index.html.

Continues

salt-water inundation as a consequence of rising sea levels might benefit from a coastal restoration project.

The U.S. Interagency Climate Change Adaptation Task Force coordinates the efforts for adaptation across government agencies.[6] The task force recommends actions that the federal government can take to respond to the needs of states and local communities. The top priority is to enhance the resilience of natural resources to absorb the impacts of climate change.

**Agree to More Limits on Emissions** The European Union and 195 nations, including the United States, participated in the 2015 United Nations Climate Change Conference in Paris, France. The parties negotiated the Paris Agreement to encourage the reduction of GHG emissions.[7] The agreement sets a goal of limiting the global temperature increase to less than 2 degrees Celsius. The parties agreed to make "nationally determined contributions" (NDCs) to this goal and to pursue domestic measures designed to achieve the NDCs.[8] None of these agreements are binding, however, and therefore rely on voluntary actions by governments throughout the world.

## Ethical Connection

Have all these efforts had an effect? It seems that they have. The transition to clean energy is happening faster than anticipated, and GHG emissions and air pollution have decreased somewhat.

Furthermore, climate change could have some positive effects. For example, the goals to lessen the impact and adapt to the changes create economic opportunities. There are new markets for alternative sources of power and sales of GHG emission credits, for instance. Climate change also represents a political opportunity to improve air quality and develop domestic sources of clean energy.

A business that takes advantage of these opportunities is not acting unethically. Such a business is, in fact, acting in the best interest of all of us.

**Ethics Question** *Is it ethical to continue to use fossil fuels? Explain.*

**Critical Thinking** *What are the advantages of fossil fuels? What are the disadvantages? Discuss.*

---

6. Executive Order, *Preparing the United States for the Impacts of Climate Change* (November 11, 2013) available at https://www.whitehouse.gov/the-press-office/2013/11/01/executive-order-preparing-united-states-impacts-climate-change.

7. United Nations Framework Convention on Climate Change, Conference of the Parties, *Adoption of the Paris Agreement. Proposal by the President*, FCCC/CP/2015/L.9/Rev. 1 (December 12, 2015) available at http://unfccc.int/resource/docs/2015/cop21/eng/l09r01.pdf.

8. There are, however, no binding emission targets or financial commitments. And the agreement itself will not become binding until fifty-five of the participants who produce more than 55 percent of global GHGs have ratified it.

# Property and Its Protection

## CHAPTER 27

# Personal Property and Bailments

**P**roperty consists of the legally protected rights and interests a person has in anything with an ascertainable value that is subject to ownership. For instance, virtual property has become quite valuable in today's world, as you will read later in this chapter. Property would have little value, however, if the law did not define the rights of owners to use, sell, dispose of, and control their property and prevent others from trespassing on it.

In the United States, a substantial body of law protects the rights of property owners, but that protection is not absolute. Property owners may have to prove that their ownership rights in a particular item of property are superior to the claims of others. In addition, through its police powers, the government can impose regulations and taxes on property, and can take or seize private property under certain circumstances.

In this chapter, we examine the differences between personal and real property and look at the methods of acquiring ownership of personal property. We also consider issues relating to mislaid, lost, and abandoned personal property. In the remainder of the chapter, we discuss bailment relationships. A *bailment* is created when personal property is temporarily delivered into the care of another without a transfer of title, such as when a person takes an item of clothing to the dry cleaners. The fact that there is no passage of title and no intent to transfer title is what distinguishes a bailment from a sale or a gift.

## 27–1 Personal Property versus Real Property

Property is divided into real property and personal property. **Real property** (sometimes called *realty* or *real estate*) means the land and everything permanently attached to it, including structures and anything permanently attached to the structures. Everything else is **personal property** (sometimes referred to as *personalty* or **chattel**). In essence, real property is immovable, whereas personal property is capable of being moved.

Personal property can be tangible or intangible. *Tangible* personal property, such as a flat-screen TV, heavy construction equipment, or a car, has physical substance.

*Intangible* personal property represents some set of rights and interests, but it has no physical existence. Stocks and bonds, patents, trademarks, and copyrights—as well as digital and virtual property—are examples of intangible personal property.

Both personal property and real property can be owned by an individual person or by some other entity. When two or more persons own real or personal property together, concurrent ownership exists. (The different types of joint or concurrent ownership will be discussed in the chapter on real property.)

In the following case, a concurrent owner of a copyright to an unpublished autobiography contended that she was entitled to an accounting for the use of the work to create a successful theatrical production.

**Case 27.1**

## Corbello v. DeVito

United States Court of Appeals, Ninth Circuit, 777 F.3d 1058 (2015).

**Background and Facts** Rex Woodward contracted with Thomas DeVito, one of the original members of The Four Seasons rock band, to ghostwrite DeVito's autobiography. Before it was published, Woodward died, and his interest in the manuscript's copyright passed to his widow, Donna Corbello. Later, DeVito agreed to grant former bandmates Frankie Valli and Bob Gaudio the right to use "aspects of his life related to The Four Seasons, including . . . his creative contributions, biographies, events in

**Case 27.1 Continued**

his life, name and likeness (the Materials)" to develop a musical about The Four Seasons. The result was a Broadway hit called *Jersey Boys.*

Actors and others involved in the show attributed their inspiration, in part, to DeVito's unpublished autobiography. Corbello filed a suit in a federal district court against DeVito and his bandmates for an accounting of the profits earned from this use of the work. The court issued a judgment in the defendants' favor. Corbello appealed.

### In the Language of the Court

*O'SCANNLAIN,* Circuit Judge:

* * * *

A co-owner of a copyright must account to other co-owners for any profits he earns from * * * use of the copyright.

* * * *

Pursuant to [DeVito's agreement with former Four Seasons band members Frankie Valli and Bob Gaudio,] DeVito "granted to Valli and Gaudio the exclusive right to use and incorporate the Materials in one or more theatrical productions, and any and all ancillary and subsidiary exploitations thereof." As defined in the Agreement, "Materials" includes * * * DeVito's "biographies."

* * * *

In the context of the * * * Agreement, the term "biographies" is not ambiguous [confusing or uncertain]. [Under] standard dictionary definitions * * * a "biography" is a "history of a person's life" * * * that is "usually written" * * *. As an account of DeVito's life that has been reduced to writing, [Woodward's] Work, on its face, qualifies under these straightforward definitions as a "biography."

* * * *

* * * DeVito granted Valli and Gaudio the "exclusive right to use" his "biographies," unambiguously including [Woodward's] Work, to create a play. Such play constitutes a "derivative work," the right to create which resides in each copyright holder of the underlying work and may be transferred by that holder to a third party. Thus, in granting this exclusive right to create, * * * the * * * Agreement constitutes a transfer of ownership of DeVito's derivative-work right in the Work to Valli and Gaudio.

* * * *

* * * *A joint-owner cannot transfer more than he himself holds; thus, [a transfer] from one joint-owner to a third party cannot bind the other joint-owners or limit their rights in the copyright without their consent.* In other words, the third party's right is "exclusive" as to the [transferring] co-owner, but not as to the other co-owners. [Emphasis added.]

* * * *

* * * Because the Agreement unambiguously transfers DeVito's derivative-work right to Valli and Gaudio, and copyright co-owners must account to one another for any profits earned by exploiting that copyright, the district court erred in rejecting Corbello's claim for [an] accounting.

**Decision and Remedy**  *The U.S. Court of Appeals for the Ninth Circuit reversed the lower court's judgment. Woodward's work qualified as a biography, the use of which DeVito granted to Valli and Gaudio to develop the Broadway play* Jersey Boys. *This grant constituted a transfer of DeVito's right in the work. As Woodward's widow and thus as a concurrent owner of the work's copyright, Corbello was entitled to an accounting of the profits from the play.*

**Critical Thinking**

- **Legal Environment**  *Under what circumstances would Corbello* not *be entitled to an accounting? Why?*

---

## 27–1a Why Is the Distinction Important?

How property is taxed and what is required to transfer or acquire the property is determined by whether the property is classified as real or personal property.

**Taxation**  The two types of property are usually subject to different types of taxes. Generally, each state assesses property taxes on real property. Typically, the tax rate is based on the market value of the real property and the services provided by the city, state, and county in which the property is located. For instance, higher taxes may be imposed on real property located within the city limits to pay for schools, roads, and libraries.

Businesses also often pay taxes on the personal property they own, use, or lease, including office or farm equipment and supplies. Individuals may pay sales tax when purchasing personal property, but generally they are not required to pay annual taxes on personal property that is not used for business.

**Acquisition** Another reason for distinguishing between real and personal property has to do with the way the property is acquired or transferred. Personal property can be transferred with a minimum of formality. In contrast, real property transfers generally involve a written sales contract and a *deed* that is recorded with the state.

Similarly, establishing ownership rights is simpler for personal property than for real property. ■ **EXAMPLE 27.1** If Mia gives Shawn an iPad Air as a gift, Shawn does not need to have any paperwork evidencing title, as he would if she had given him real property. (The ways to acquire ownership of personal property will be discussed shortly.) ■

### 27–1b  Conversion of Real
###         Property to Personal Property

Sometimes, real property can be turned into personal property by detaching it from the land. For instance, the trees, bushes, and plants growing on land are considered part of the real property (with the exception of crops that must be planted every year). If the property is sold, all the vegetation growing on the land normally is transferred to the new owner of the real property.

Once the items are severed (removed) from the land, however, they become personal property. If the trees are cut from the land, the timber is personal property. If apples, grapes, or raspberries are picked from trees or vines growing on real property, they become personal property. Similarly, if land contains minerals (including oil) or other natural resources (such as marble), the resources are part of the real property. But once removed, they become personal property.

Conversely, personal property may be converted into real property by permanently attaching it to the real property. When personal property is affixed to real property in a permanent way, as when tile is installed in a house, it is known as a *fixture*. (Fixtures will be discussed in the context of real property in the next chapter.)

## 27–2  Acquiring Ownership
##         of Personal Property

The most common way of acquiring personal property is by purchasing it. (Today, even virtual property is often purchased, as discussed in this chapter's *Digital Update*

---

### DIGITAL UPDATE    The Exploding World of Digital Property

Jon Jacobs took out a real mortgage on his real house so that he could pay $100,000 in real dollars for a virtual asteroid near the virtual Planet Calypso in the virtual world Entropia Universe. A few years later, he sold Club Neverdie, the virtual space resort he had constructed on the virtual asteroid, for more than $600,000. At the time, Jacobs was making $200,000 per year from players' purchases of virtual goods at the resort.

If the prospect of paying real funds for virtual property seems disconcerting, remember that property does not have to be tangible. Property consists of a bundle of rights in anything that has an ascertainable value and is subject to ownership—a definition that encompasses virtual property, including all the intangible objects used in virtual worlds like Entropia Universe and Second Life.

**Digital Goods Have Value, Too**

Digital goods include virtual goods, but more important, they include digital books, music libraries, and movie downloads, as well as domain names and expensively created Web sites. This digital property has real value. Some digital music libraries, for example, cost thousands of dollars.

**Who Keeps the Digital Goods?**

The growing value of digital goods raises some legal questions. For instance, what are the respective rights of the creator/owner of a virtual-world Web site and the players at that site? And what happens when a husband and wife decide to divorce after they have purchased virtual real estate or digital goods with real-world dollars? The couple—or a court—will have to figure out a way to divide the goods. Property and divorce laws will have to adapt to take into account this changing world.

**Critical Thinking** *How might a couple who enjoys purchasing digital goods together avoid property division issues in the event of a divorce?*

feature.) Another way in which personal property is often acquired is by will or inheritance. Here, we look at additional ways in which ownership of personal property can be acquired, including acquisition by possession, production, gift, accession, and confusion.

## 27–2a Possession

Sometimes, a person can become the owner of personal property merely by possessing it. For instance, one way to acquire ownership through possession is the capture of wild animals. Wild animals belong to no one in their natural state, and the first person to take possession of a wild animal normally owns it. A hunter who kills a deer, for instance, has assumed ownership of it (unless he or she acted in violation of the law). Those who find lost or abandoned property can also acquire ownership rights through mere possession of the property, as will be discussed later in this chapter.

## 27–2b Production

Production—the fruits of labor—is another means of acquiring ownership of personal property. For instance, writers, inventors, manufacturers, and others who produce personal property may thereby acquire title to it. (In some situations, though, as when a researcher is hired to invent a new product or technique, the researcher may not own what is produced.)

## 27–2c Gift

A **gift** is a fairly common means of acquiring or transferring ownership of property. A gift is essentially a *voluntary* transfer of property ownership for which no consideration is given. The presence of consideration is what distinguishes a contractual obligation to transfer ownership of property from a gift.

For a gift to be effective, the following three elements are required:

1. Donative intent on the part of the *donor* (the one giving the gift).
2. Delivery.
3. Acceptance by the *donee* (the one receiving the gift).

Until these three requirements are met, no effective gift has been made. ■ **EXAMPLE 27.2** Gary's Aunt Celia tells him that she is going to give him a new Mercedes-Benz for his next birthday. Aunt Celia has simply made a promise to make a gift. There is no gift until the Mercedes-Benz is delivered and accepted. ■

**Donative Intent** When a gift is challenged in court, the court will determine whether donative intent exists by looking at the language of the donor and the surrounding circumstances. A court may look at the relationship between the parties and the size of the gift in relation to the donor's other assets. When a person has given away a large portion of her or his assets, the court will scrutinize the transaction closely. The court will analyze the donor's mental capacity and look for indications of fraud or duress.

■ **CASE IN POINT 27.3** Over a period of three months, Jean Knowles Goodman, who was eighty-five years old, gave Steven Atwood several checks that totaled $56,100. Atwood was a veterinarian who had cared for Goodman's dogs for nearly twenty years, and he and Goodman had become friends. Shortly after writing the last check, Goodman was hospitalized and diagnosed with dementia (loss of brain function) and alcohol dependency.

The guardian who was appointed to represent Goodman filed a lawsuit to invalidate the gifts, claiming that Goodman had lacked mental capacity and donative intent. At trial, a psychiatrist who had examined Goodman testified on behalf of Atwood that while Goodman lacked the capacity to care for herself, she would have understood that she was giving away her funds. Therefore, the court concluded that Goodman had donative intent to make the gifts to Atwood.[1] ■

**Delivery** The gift must be delivered to the donee. Delivery may be accomplished by means of a third person who is the agent of either the donor or the donee. Naturally, no delivery is necessary if the gift is already in the hands of the donee (provided there is donative intent and acceptance). Delivery is obvious in most cases, but some objects cannot be relinquished physically. Then the question of delivery depends on the surrounding circumstances.

**Constructive Delivery.** When the object itself cannot be physically delivered, a symbolic, or constructive, delivery will be sufficient. **Constructive delivery** confers the right to take possession (rather than actual possession) of the object in question. It is a general term for all of those acts that the law holds to be equivalent to acts of real delivery.

■ **EXAMPLE 27.4** Teresa wants to make a gift of rare coins that she has stored in a safe-deposit box at her bank. Teresa certainly cannot deliver the box itself to the donee, and she does not want to take the coins out of the bank. In this situation, she can simply deliver the key to the box to the donee and authorize the donee's access to the box and its contents. This constitutes symbolic, or constructive, delivery of the contents of the box. ■

Constructive delivery is always necessary for gifts of intangible personal property—such as stocks, bonds,

---

1. *Goodman v. Atwood,* 78 Mass.App.Ct. 655, 940 N.E.2d 514 (2011).

insurance policies, and contracts. What will be delivered are documents that represent rights and are not, in themselves, the true property.

**Relinquishing Dominion and Control.** An effective delivery also requires that the donor give up complete control and **dominion** (power, ownership rights) over the subject matter of the gift. The outcome of disputes often turns on whether control has actually been relinquished. The Internal Revenue Service carefully examines transactions between relatives, especially when one has given income-producing property to another who is in a lower marginal tax bracket. Unless complete control over the property has been relinquished, the "donor"—not the family member who received the "gift"—will have to pay taxes on the income from that property.

In the following *Classic Case*, the court focused on the requirement that a donor must relinquish complete control and dominion over property before a gift can be effectively delivered.

**Classic Case 27.2**

## *In re* Estate of Piper
Missouri Court of Appeals, 676 S.W.2d 897 (1984).

**Background and Facts** Gladys Piper died intestate (without a will). At the time of her death, she owned miscellaneous personal property worth $5,150 and had in her purse $206.75 in cash and two diamond rings. Wanda Brown, Piper's niece, took the contents of her purse, allegedly to preserve the items for the estate. Clara Kauffman, a friend of Gladys Piper, filed a claim against the estate for $4,800. For several years before Piper's death, Kauffman had taken Piper to the doctor, beauty salon, and grocery store. She had also written Piper's checks to pay her bills and helped her care for her home.

Kauffman maintained that Piper had promised to pay her for these services and that Piper had given her the diamond rings as a gift. The trial court denied Kauffman's request for payment of $4,800 on the basis that the services had been voluntary. Kauffman then filed a petition for delivery of personal property (the rings), which was granted by the trial court. The defendants—Piper's heirs and the administrator of Piper's estate—appealed.

### In the Language of the Court
*GREENE,* Judge.
\* \* \* \*

While no particular form is necessary to effect a delivery, and while the delivery may be actual, constructive, or symbolical, there must be some evidence to support a delivery theory. What we have here, at best, \* \* \* was an intention on the part of Gladys, at some future time, to make a gift of the rings to Clara. Such an intention, no matter how clearly expressed, which has not been carried into effect, confers no ownership rights in the property in the intended donee. *Language written or spoken, expressing an intention to give, does not constitute a gift, unless the intention is executed by a complete and unconditional delivery of the subject matter, or delivery of a proper written instrument evidencing the gift.* There is no evidence in this case to prove delivery, and, for such reason, the trial court's judgment is erroneous. [Emphasis added.]

**Decision and Remedy** *The judgment of the trial court was reversed. No effective gift of the rings had been made, because Piper had never delivered the rings to Kauffman.*

**Impact of This Case on Today's Law** *This classic case clearly illustrates the delivery requirement for making a gift. Assuming that Piper did, indeed, intend for Kauffman to have the rings, it was unfortunate that Kauffman had no right to receive them after Piper's death. Yet the alternative might lead to even more unfairness. The policy behind the delivery requirement is to protect alleged donors and their heirs from fraudulent claims based solely on parol evidence. If not for this policy, an alleged donee could easily claim that a gift had been made when, in fact, it had not.*

Case 27.2 Continued    **Critical Thinking**
- **What If the Facts Were Different?** *Suppose that Piper had told Kauffman that she was giving the rings to Kauffman but wished to keep them in her possession for a few more days. Would this have affected the court's decision in this case? Explain.*

---

**Acceptance** The final requirement of a valid gift is acceptance by the donee. This rarely presents any problems, because most donees readily accept their gifts. The courts generally assume acceptance unless the circumstances indicate otherwise.

**Gifts *Inter Vivos* and Gifts *Causa Mortis*** A gift made during the donor's lifetime is called a **gift *inter vivos.*** A gift made in contemplation of imminent death is a **gift *causa mortis*** (a so-called *deathbed gift*). To be effective, a gift *causa mortis* must meet the three requirements of intent, delivery, and acceptance.

In addition, a gift *causa mortis* does not become absolute until the donor dies from the contemplated illness or event, and it is automatically revoked if the donor survives.[2] ■ **EXAMPLE 27.5** Yang, who is about to undergo surgery to remove a cancerous tumor, delivers an envelope to Chao, a close business associate. The envelope contains a letter saying, "I want to give you $1 million in U.S. government bonds in the event of my death from this operation." Chao redeems (cashes in) the bonds. The surgeon performs the operation and removes the tumor. Yang recovers fully from the operation, but the day after he leaves the hospital, he is killed when his home is struck by a tornado.

If the administrator of Yang's estate tries to recover the $1 million, she will normally succeed. The gift *causa mortis* to Chao is automatically revoked if Yang survives the operation. The *specific event* that was contemplated in making the gift was death from a particular operation. Because Yang's death was not the result of this event, the gift is revoked, and the $1 million passes to Yang's estate. ■

A gift *causa mortis* may also be revoked if the prospective donee dies before the donor. Therefore, even if Yang in *Example 27.5* had died during the operation, the gift would have been revoked if Chao had died a few minutes earlier. In that event, the $1 million would have passed to Yang's estate, and not to Chao's heirs.

### 27–2d Accession

**Accession** means "something added." Accession occurs when someone adds value to an item of personal property by the use of either labor or materials.

Generally, there is no dispute about who owns the property after accession occurs, especially when the accession is accomplished with the owner's consent. ■ **EXAMPLE 27.6** Hays buys all the materials necessary to customize his Corvette. He hires Zach, a customizing specialist, to come his house to perform the work. Hays pays Zach for the value of the labor, obviously retaining title to the property. ■

If an improvement is made wrongfully—without the permission of the owner—the owner retains title to the property and normally does not have to pay for the improvement. This is true even if the accession increased the value of the property substantially. ■ **EXAMPLE 27.7** Colton steals a truck and puts expensive new tires on it. If the rightful owner later recovers the truck, the owner obviously will not be required to compensate Colton, a thief, for the value of the new tires. ■

### 27–2e Confusion

**Confusion** is the commingling (mixing together) of goods to such an extent that one person's personal property cannot be distinguished from another's. Confusion frequently occurs with *fungible goods,* such as grain or oil, which consist of identical units.[3]

If confusion occurs as a result of agreement, an honest mistake, or the act of some third party, the owners share ownership in the commingled goods in proportion to the amount each contributed. ■ **EXAMPLE 27.8** Five farmers in a small Iowa community enter into a cooperative arrangement. Each fall, the farmers harvest the same amount of number 2–grade yellow corn and store it in silos that are held by the cooperative. Each farmer thus owns one-fifth of the total corn in the silos. If a fire burns down one of the silos, each farmer will bear one-fifth of the loss. ■ If goods are confused due to an intentional

---

2. For a classic case on the requirement that the donor must die from the contemplated peril, see *Brind v. International Trust Co.*, 66 Colo. 60, 179 P. 148 (1919).

3. See Section 1–201(17) of the Uniform Commercial Code (UCC).

wrongful act, then the innocent party ordinarily acquires title to the whole.

Concept Summary 27.1 reviews various ways in which personal property can be acquired.

something and holding onto it, however, does not *necessarily* give the finder any legal rights in the property. Different rules apply, depending on whether the property was mislaid, lost, or abandoned.

# 27–3 Mislaid, Lost, and Abandoned Property

As already noted, one of the methods of acquiring ownership of property is to possess it. Simply finding

## 27–3a Mislaid Property

Property that has been voluntarily placed somewhere by the owner and then inadvertently forgotten is **mislaid property.** A person who finds mislaid property does not obtain title to the goods. Instead, the owner of the place where the property was mislaid becomes the caretaker

## Concept Summary 27.1

### Acquisition of Personal Property

| | |
|---|---|
| **By Purchase or by Will** | The most common means of acquiring ownership in personal property is by purchasing it. Another way in which personal property is often acquired is by will or inheritance. |
| **Possession** | Ownership may be acquired by possession if no other person has ownership title, such as capturing wild animals or finding abandoned property. |
| **Production** | Any product or item produced by an individual (with minor exceptions) becomes the property of that individual. |
| **Gift** | An effective gift is made when the following three requirements are met:<br>• There is evidence of *intent* to make a gift of the property in question.<br>• The gift is *delivered* (physically or constructively) to the donee or the donee's agent.<br>• The gift is *accepted* by the donee. |
| **Accession** | When value is added to personal property by use of labor or materials, the owner of the original property generally retains title to the property and benefits from the added value. |
| **Confusion** | If confusion occurs as a result of agreement, an honest mistake, or the act of some third party, the owners share ownership in the commingled goods in proportion to the amount each contributed. If goods are confused due to an intentional wrongful act, the innocent party ordinarily acquires title to the whole. |

of the property, because it is highly likely that the true owner will return.[4]

■ **EXAMPLE 27.9** Maya goes to a movie theater. While paying for popcorn at the concessions stand, she sets her smartphone on the counter and then leaves it there. The smartphone is mislaid property, and the theater owner is entrusted with the duty of reasonable care for it. ■

## 27–3b Lost Property

Property that is *involuntarily* left is **lost property.** A finder of lost property can claim title to the property against the whole world—*except the true owner.*[5] If the true owner is identified and demands that the lost property be returned, the finder must return it. In contrast, if a third party attempts to take possession of the lost property, the finder will have a better title than the third party.

■ **EXAMPLE 27.10** Kayla works in a large library at night. As she crosses the courtyard on her way home, she finds a gold bracelet set with what seem to be precious stones. She takes the bracelet to a jeweler to have it appraised. While pretending to weigh the bracelet, the jeweler's employee removes several of the stones. If Kayla brings an action to recover the stones from the jeweler, she normally will win, because she found lost property and holds title against everyone *except the true owner.* ■

**Conversion of Lost Property** When a finder of lost property knows the true owner and fails to return the property to that person, the finder is guilty of the tort of *conversion.* In *Example 27.10,* if Kayla knows that the gold bracelet she found belongs to Geneva and does not return the bracelet, Kayla is guilty of conversion. Many states require the finder to make a reasonably diligent search to locate the true owner of lost property.

**Estray Statutes** Many states have **estray statutes,** which encourage and facilitate the return of property to its true owner and reward the finder for honesty if the property remains unclaimed. These laws provide an incentive for finders to report their discoveries by enabling them, at the end of a specified time, to acquire legal title to the found property.

Generally, the item must be lost property, not merely mislaid property, for estray statutes to apply. Estray statutes usually require the finder or the county clerk to advertise the property in an attempt to help the owner recover what has been lost.

■ **CASE IN POINT 27.11** Drug smugglers often enter the United States illegally from Canada via a frozen river that flows through Van Buren, Maine. When two railroad employees in Van Buren found a duffel bag that contained $165,580 in cash, they reported their find to U.S. Customs agents, who took custody of it. A drug-sniffing dog gave a positive alert on the bag for the scent of drugs. The federal government filed a lawsuit claiming title to the property under criminal forfeiture laws (because the property was involved in illegal drug transactions).

The two employees argued that they were entitled to the $165,580 under Maine's estray statute. That statute required finders to (1) provide written notice to the town clerk within seven days after finding the property, (2) post a public notice, and (3) advertise in the town's newspaper. Because the employees had not fulfilled these requirements, the court ruled that they had not acquired title to the property. Thus, the U.S. government had a right to seize the cash.[6] ■

## 27–3c Abandoned Property

Property that has been *discarded* by the true owner, who has *no intention* of reclaiming title to it, is **abandoned property.** Someone who finds abandoned property acquires title to it, and that title is good against the whole world, *including the original owner.* If a person finds abandoned property while trespassing on another's property, however, the trespasser will not acquire title.

The owner of lost property who eventually gives up any further attempt to find it is frequently held to have abandoned the property. ■ **EXAMPLE 27.12** While Alekis is hiking in the redwoods, her expensive watch falls off. She retraces her route and searches for the watch but cannot find it. She finally gives up her search and returns home some five hundred miles away. When Frye later finds the watch, he acquires title to it that is good even against Alekis. By completely giving up her search, Alekis abandoned the watch just as effectively as if she had intentionally discarded it. ■

Exhibit 27–1 summarizes the distinctions among these types of property.

---

4. The finder of mislaid property is an *involuntary bailee* (as will be discussed later in this chapter).
5. For a landmark English case establishing finders' rights in property, see *Armory v. Delamirie,* 93 Eng.Rep. 664 (K.B. [King's Bench] 1722).

---

6. *United States v. One Hundred Sixty-Five Thousand Five Hundred Eighty Dollars ($165,580) in U.S. Currency,* 502 F.Supp.2d 114 (D.Me. 2007).

**EXHIBIT 27–1**  Mislaid, Lost, and Abandoned Property

| TYPE OF PROPERTY | DESCRIPTION |
| --- | --- |
| Mislaid Property | Property that is placed somewhere voluntarily by the owner and then inadvertently forgotten. A finder of mislaid property will not acquire title to the goods, and the owner of the place where the property was mislaid becomes a caretaker of the mislaid property. |
| Lost Property | Property that is involuntarily left by the owner. A finder of lost property can claim title to the property against the whole world except the true owner. |
| Abandoned Property | Property that has been discarded by the true owner, who has no intention of reclaiming title to the property in the future. A finder of abandoned property can claim title to it against the whole world, including the original owner. |

# 27–4 Bailments

Many routine personal and business transactions involve bailments. A **bailment** is formed by the delivery of personal property, without transfer of title, by one person (called a **bailor**) to another (called a **bailee**). What distinguishes a bailment from a sale or a gift is that possession is transferred without passage of title or intent to transfer title.

Bailment agreements usually are made for a particular purpose—for example, to loan, lease, store, repair, or transport the property. On completion of the purpose, the bailee is obligated to return the bailed property in the same or better condition to the bailor or a third person or to dispose of it as directed.

Although bailments typically arise by agreement, not all of the elements of a contract must necessarily be present for a bailment to be created. ■ **EXAMPLE 27.13** If Amy lends her bicycle to a friend, a bailment is created, but not by contract, because there is no consideration. Note, though, that many commercial bailments, such as the delivery of clothing to the cleaners for dry cleaning, are based on contract. ■

## 27–4a Elements of a Bailment

Not all transactions involving the delivery of property from one person to another create a bailment. For such a transfer to become a bailment, the following three elements must be present:

1. Personal property.
2. Delivery of possession (without title).
3. Agreement that the property will be returned to the bailor or otherwise disposed of according to its owner's directions.

**Personal Property Requirement** Only personal property, not real property or persons, can be the subject of a bailment. ■ **EXAMPLE 27.14** When you check your bags at the airport, a bailment of your luggage is created because it is personal property. When you board the plane as a passenger, no bailment is created. ■

Bailments commonly involve *tangible* items—jewelry, cattle, automobiles, and the like. Nevertheless, *intangible* personal property, such as promissory notes and shares of stock, may also be bailed.

**Delivery of Possession** *Delivery of possession* means transfer of possession of the property to the bailee. For delivery to occur, the bailee must be given *exclusive possession and control* over the property, and the bailee must *knowingly* accept the property.[7] In other words, the bailee must *intend* to exercise control over it.

If either delivery of possession or knowing acceptance is lacking, there is no bailment relationship. ■ **EXAMPLE 27.15** Delacroix goes to a five-star restaurant and checks her coat. She forgets that there is a $20,000 diamond necklace in the coat pocket. In accepting the coat, the bailee does not *knowingly* also accept the necklace. Thus, a bailment of the coat exists—because the restaurant has exclusive possession and control over the coat and knowingly accepted it—but not a bailment of the necklace. ■

**Physical versus Constructive Delivery.** Either *physical* or *constructive delivery* will result in the bailee's exclusive possession of and control over the property. As discussed earlier (in the context of gifts), constructive delivery is a substitute, or symbolic, delivery. What is delivered to the bailee is not the actual property bailed (such as a car) but something so related to the property (such as the car keys) that the requirement of delivery is satisfied.

---

7. This rule applies to *voluntary bailments*, not to *involuntary bailments*.

**Involuntary Bailments.** In certain situations, a court will find that a bailment exists despite the apparent lack of the requisite elements of control and knowledge. One situation in which this occurs is when the bailee acquires the property accidentally or by mistake—as in finding someone else's lost or mislaid property. A bailment is created even though the bailor did not voluntarily deliver the property to the bailee. Such bailments are referred to as *constructive* or *involuntary* bailments.

■ **EXAMPLE 27.16** Several corporate managers attend a meeting at the law firm of Jacobs & Matheson. One of the corporate officers, Kyle Gustafson, inadvertently leaves his briefcase behind at the conclusion of the meeting. In this situation, a court could find that an involuntary bailment was created even though Gustafson did not voluntarily deliver the briefcase and the law firm did not intentionally accept it. If an involuntary bailment exists, the firm is responsible for taking care of the briefcase and returning it to Gustafson. ■

### 27–4b The Bailment Agreement

A bailment agreement can be express or implied. Although a written contract is not required for bailments for less than one year, it is a good idea to have one, especially when valuable property is involved.

The bailment agreement expressly or impliedly provides for the return of the bailed property to the bailor or to a third person, or for disposal of the property by the bailee. It is assumed that the bailee will return the identical goods originally given by the bailor. In certain types of bailments, though, such as bailments of fungible goods,[8] the property returned need only be equivalent property.

■ **EXAMPLE 27.17** A bailment is created when Holman stores his grain (fungible goods) in Joe's Warehouse. At the end of the storage period, however, the warehouse is not obligated to return to Holman exactly the same grain that he stored. As long as the warehouse returns grain of the same *type, grade,* and *quantity,* the warehouse—the bailee—has performed its obligation. ■

# 27–5 Ordinary Bailments

Bailments are either *ordinary* or *special (extraordinary).* There are three types of ordinary bailments. They are distinguished according to *which party receives a benefit*

*from the bailment.* This factor will dictate the rights and liabilities of the parties. In addition, the courts may use it to determine the standard of care required of the bailee in possession of the personal property.

The three types of ordinary bailments are listed below and described in the following subsections:

1. Bailment for the sole benefit of the bailor.
2. Bailment for the sole benefit of the bailee.
3. Bailment for the mutual benefit of the bailee and the bailor.

### 27–5a Bailment for the Sole Benefit of the Bailor

A bailment for the sole benefit of the bailor is a type of *gratuitous bailment*—meaning that it involves no consideration. The bailment is for the convenience and benefit of the bailor. Basically, the bailee is caring for the bailor's property as a favor. Therefore, the bailee owes only a slight duty of care and will be liable only if she or he is grossly negligent in caring for the property.

■ **EXAMPLE 27.18** Allen asks Sumi to store his car in her garage while he is away. If Sumi agrees to do so, then a gratuitous bailment is created, because the bailment is for the sole benefit of the bailor (Allen). If the car is damaged while in Sumi's garage, Sumi will not be responsible for the damage unless it was caused by her gross negligence. ■

### 27–5b Bailment for the Sole Benefit of the Bailee

When one person lends an item to another person (the bailee) solely for that person's convenience and benefit, a bailment for the sole benefit of the bailee is created. Because the bailee is borrowing the item for her or his own benefit, the bailee owes a duty to exercise the utmost care and will be liable for even slight negligence.

■ **EXAMPLE 27.19** Jeremy asks to borrow Sumi's boat so that he can take his girlfriend sailing over the weekend. The bailment of the boat is for Jeremy's (the bailee's) sole benefit. If Jeremy fails to pay attention and runs the boat aground, damaging its hull, he is liable for the costs of repairing the boat. ■

### 27–5c Mutual-Benefit Bailments

The most common kind of bailment is for the mutual benefit of the bailee and the bailor, and involves some form of compensation for storing items or holding

---

8. As mentioned earlier, *fungible goods* are goods that consist of identical particles, such as wheat. Fungible goods are defined in UCC 1–201(17).

property. It is a contractual bailment and is often referred to as a *bailment for hire* or a *commercial bailment.*

In a commercial bailment, the bailee must exercise ordinary care, which is the care that a reasonably prudent person would use under the circumstances. If the bailee fails to exercise reasonable care, he or she will be liable for ordinary negligence.

■ **EXAMPLE 27.20** Allen leaves his car at Midas for an oil change. Because Midas will be paid to change Allen's oil, this is a mutual-benefit bailment. If Midas fails to put the correct amount of oil back into Allen's car and the engine is damaged as a result, Midas will be liable for failure to have exercised reasonable care. ■

### 27–5d  Rights of the Bailee

Certain rights are implicit in the bailment agreement. Generally, the bailee has the right to take possession of the property and to utilize it for accomplishing the purpose of the bailment. The bailee also has a right to receive compensation (unless the bailment is intended to be gratuitous). In addition, the bailee may have the right to limit her or his liability for the bailed goods. These rights of the bailee are present (with some limitations) in varying degrees in all bailment transactions.

**Right of Possession**  A hallmark of the bailment agreement is that the bailee acquires the *right to control and possess the property temporarily.* The duration of a bailment depends on the terms of the agreement. If the agreement specifies its duration, then the bailment continues for that time period, and an earlier termination by the bailor is a breach of contract. If no duration is stated, the bailment ends when either the bailor or the bailee requests its termination and the bailed property is returned to the bailor.

A bailee's right of possession, even though temporary, permits the bailee to recover damages from any third parties for damage or loss to the property. ■ **EXAMPLE 27.21** No-Spot Dry Cleaners sends all suede leather garments to Cleanall Company for special processing. If Cleanall loses or damages any leather goods, No-Spot has the right to recover from Cleanall. ■ If the bailed property is stolen, the bailee has a legal right to regain possession of it.

**Right to Use Bailed Property**  In some bailments, a bailee may have a right to use the bailed property. When no express provision is made, the extent of use depends on how necessary it is for the goods to be at the bailee's disposal for the ordinary purpose of the bailment to be carried out.

■ **EXAMPLE 27.22**  If Lauren borrows a car to drive a friend to the airport, she, as the bailee, will obviously be expected to use the car. In contrast, if Devin drives his own car to the airport and places it in long-term storage nearby, the storage company, as the bailee, will not be expected to use the car. The ordinary purpose of a storage bailment does not include use of the property. The bailee will, however, be expected to use or move the car if necessary in an emergency (such as a hurricane or flood) to protect it from harm. ■

**Right of Compensation**  Except in a gratuitous bailment, a bailee has a right to be compensated as provided for in the bailment agreement. The bailee also has the right to be reimbursed for costs incurred and services rendered in keeping the bailed property (even in a gratuitous bailment).

To enforce the right of compensation, the bailee has a right to place a *possessory lien* on the specific bailed property until she or he has been fully compensated. Such a lien is sometimes referred to as a **bailee's lien,** or artisan's lien. If the bailor refuses to pay or cannot pay, in most states the bailee is entitled to foreclose on the lien and sell the property to recover the amount owed.

■ **EXAMPLE 27.23**  Liam leaves his car at Dusty's Automotive for repairs. Dusty's informs Liam that the car needs a new transmission, and Liam authorizes Dusty's to perform the work. When Liam returns to pick up the car, he refuses to pay the amount due for the transmission work. Dusty's has a right to keep the car and place a lien on it until Liam pays for the repairs. If Liam continues to refuse to pay, Dusty's can follow the state's statutory process for foreclosing on the lien and selling the car to recover what is owed. ■

**Right to Limit Liability**  In ordinary bailments, bailees have the right to limit their liability provided that both of the following are true:

1. *The limitations are called to the attention of the bailor.* It is essential that the bailor be informed of the limitation in some way. ■ **EXAMPLE 27.24** A sign in Nikolai's garage states that Nikolai will not be responsible "for loss due to theft, fire, or vandalism." Whether the sign will constitute notice will depend on the size of the sign, its location, and any other circumstances affecting the likelihood that customers will see it. ■

2. *The limitations are not against public policy.* Courts consider certain types of disclaimers of liability to be against public policy and therefore illegal, whether or not the bailor is aware of them. As previously discussed, the courts carefully scrutinize *exculpatory*

*clauses,* which limit a person's liability for her or his own wrongful acts. In bailments, especially mutual-benefit bailments, exculpatory clauses are often held to be illegal. ■ **EXAMPLE 27.25** A receipt from a parking garage expressly disclaims liability for any damage to parked cars, regardless of the cause. Because the bailee (the garage) has attempted to exclude liability for the bailee's own negligence, the clause will likely be deemed unenforceable because it is against public policy. ■

## 27–5e Duties of the Bailee

The bailee's duties are based on a mixture of tort law and contract law, and include the following two basic responsibilities:

1. To take appropriate care of the property.
2. To surrender the property to the bailor or dispose of it in accordance with the bailor's instructions at the end of the bailment.

**The Duty of Care** The bailee must exercise reasonable care in preserving the bailed property. What constitutes reasonable care in a bailment situation normally depends on the nature and specific circumstances of the bailment.

As already mentioned, the courts determine the appropriate standard of care on the basis of the type of bailment involved. In a bailment for the sole benefit of the bailor, the bailee need exercise only a slight degree of care, whereas in a bailment for the sole benefit of the bailee, the bailee must exercise great care.

Exhibit 27–2 illustrates the degree of care required of bailees in bailment relationships. Determining whether a bailee exercised an appropriate degree of care is usually a question of fact for the jury or for the judge (in a non-jury trial). A bailee's failure to exercise appropriate care in handling the bailor's property results in tort liability. ■ **CASE IN POINT 27.26** Bridge Tower Dental contracted with Meridian Computer Center to develop a computer system for its dental practice. Bridge Tower paid a computer consultant, Al Colson, to install the

system and to provide maintenance and support. When Colson noticed that one of the server's two hard drives had stopped working, he informed Bridge Tower and took the server to Meridian Computer to be repaired. Meridian's owner, Jason Patten, agreed to replace the failing hard drive under the warranty. In attempting to copy data from the mirrored hard drive, however, Patten accidentally erased all the data, which he had not backed up. As a result, Bridge Tower lost all of its patients' records and contact information.

Bridge Tower sued Meridian for negligence. The Supreme Court of Idaho ruled in favor of Bridge Tower. Colson had entrusted Meridian with a server containing a failing hard drive (which was to be replaced) and a fully functional mirrored hard drive containing data. Meridian had a duty to protect and safeguard this bailed property in order to return it in the same condition it was in when delivered. Patten mistakenly erased the data on the mirrored hard drive, which constituted negligence.[9] ■

**Duty to Return Bailed Property** At the end of the bailment, the bailee normally must hand over the original property to either the bailor or someone the bailor designates, or must otherwise dispose of it as directed.[10] Failure to give up possession at the time the bailment ends is a breach of contract and could result in a tort lawsuit for conversion or negligence.

■ **CASE IN POINT 27.27** SANY America, Inc., loaned a crane to Turner Brothers, LLC, a construction contractor, for demonstration purposes. SANY wanted to sell the crane to Turner and continued to allow Turner to use it during their negotiations, but the parties never came to an agreement on a price. After the negotiations ended, SANY asked Turner for the crane's location to arrange retrieval. Before SANY retrieved the crane from Turner,

---

9. *Bridge Tower Dental, P.A. v. Meridian Computer Center, Inc.,* 272 P.3d 541 (Idaho Sup.Ct. 2012).
10. As mentioned earlier, if the bailment involves fungible goods, such as grain, then the bailee is not required to return exactly the same goods to the bailor. Instead, the bailee must return goods of the same type, grade, and quantity.

**EXHIBIT 27–2 Degree of Care Required of a Bailee**

however, it was severely damaged while being operated at Turner's construction site.

Turner removed the inoperable crane from the site at its own expense and then notified SANY that it expected compensation for the transportation expenses. In addition, Turner refused to return the crane to SANY and began billing SANY for daily storage costs. SANY sued for conversion, and Turner counterclaimed. A federal district court held that the parties' transaction was a bailment. Because Turner had wrongfully retained the crane after SANY demanded its return, SANY was entitled to summary judgment for conversion.[11] ■

A bailee may be liable for conversion or misdelivery if the goods are given to the wrong person. Hence, a bailee should verify that any person other than the bailor to whom the goods are given is authorized to take possession.

**Lost or Damaged Property** If the bailed property has been lost or is returned damaged, a court will presume that the bailee was negligent. The bailee's obligation is excused, however, if the property was destroyed, lost, or stolen through no fault of the bailee (or claimed by a third party with a superior claim). In other words, the bailee can rebut the presumption of negligence by showing that he or she exercised due care.

■ **CASE IN POINT 27.28**   Hornbeck Offshore Service engaged R&R Marine, Inc., to repair the ship *Erie*

*Service* at R&R's shipyard on Lake Sabine in Port Arthur, Texas. While repairs were being made, a tropical storm warning was issued for Port Arthur. R&R's personnel left the shipyard without securing or preparing the *Erie Service* for the storm. During the night, rain and water from Lake Sabine swamped the vessel. R&R's insurer, National Liability & Fire Insurance Company, asked a federal district court to declare that it was not required to pay the salvage cost. Hornbeck filed a counterclaim with the court alleging that R&R had been negligent. The lower court issued a decision in Hornbeck's favor, and R&R appealed.

A federal appellate court affirmed the lower court's ruling. The ship had been delivered to R&R afloat, R&R had full custody of the vessel, and it sank while in R&R's care. This gave rise to a presumption of negligence. The severity of the weather conditions in Port Arthur had been foreseeable, and R&R showed no evidence that it had exercised ordinary care. The court held that R&R—not the insurer—was liable for the salvage cost because R&R had been negligent in failing to protect the ship from damage from the storm.[12] ■

In the following case, the court had to determine whether a constructive bailment existed over the personal property of tenants who were evicted. If so, was the landlord-bailor negligent for removing the tenants' personal property and leaving it outside?

---

11. *SANY America, Inc. v. Turner Brothers, LLC,* ___ F.Supp.3d ___, 2016 WL 1452341 (D.Mass. 2016).

12. *National Liability & Fire Insurance Co. v. R&R Marine, Inc.,* 756 F.3d 825 (5th Cir. 2014).

---

**Case Analysis 27.3**

# Zissu v. IH2 Property Illinois, L.P.

United States District Court, Northern District of Illinois, Eastern Division, ___ F.Supp.3d ___, 2016 WL 212937 (2016).

## In the Language of the Court

John Z. *LEE,* United States District Judge

Plaintiffs Pavel Zissu and Aise Zissu bring suit [in this federal district court] against the owner of the property where they resided, IH2 Property Illinois, L.P. The Zissus claim that after a Cook County [Illinois] Sheriff turned over possession of the premises to IH2 pursuant to an eviction order, the company removed all of their personal property from the premises and put it outside. In their complaint, the Zissus assert [that the company's actions

constituted] negligence [and a constructive] bailment.

FACTUAL BACKGROUND
* * * The Zissus resided at a property in the City of Chicago owned by IH2. * * * [An Illinois state court judge] issued an order for possession, allowing IH2 to evict the Zissus. The order was executed by a Cook County Sheriff.

Once IH2 was given possession of the premises, its agents took all of the Zissus' personal property that was in the apartment and placed it outside on the curb. The property, which included

jewelry, furniture, and personal documents, was then either stolen or damaged.

LEGAL STANDARD
A motion [to dismiss under the Federal Rules of Procedure] challenges the sufficiency of the complaint.

*A complaint * * * must * * * allege sufficient factual matter, accepted as true, to state a claim to relief that is plausible on its face. For a claim to have facial plausibility, a plaintiff must plead factual content that allows the court to draw the reasonable*

Case 27.3 Continued

*inference that the defendant is liable for the misconduct alleged.* [Emphasis added.]

ANALYSIS

This is a diversity suit. As such, we apply state substantive law and federal procedural law. Both parties cite Illinois law in their briefing, so the Court will apply Illinois law.

I. Negligence

The Zissus allege that IH2 negligently removed their personal property from the premises following the eviction, causing much of it to be damaged or stolen. * * * In its motion to dismiss, IH2 argues that the Zissus cannot state a claim for negligence because IH2, as the landlord, did not owe a duty to protect personal property left on the premises following the eviction.

* * * *

Because [the statutes of Illinois are silent on this issue and] the Illinois Supreme Court has not addressed this issue, this Court must attempt to divine [guess] how the [Illinois] Supreme Court would rule. In fact, only two courts have addressed the question of a landlord's duty under Illinois law. [In] *Centagon, Inc. v. Board of Directors of 1212 Lake Shore Drive Condominium Association,* __ F.Supp.2d __, 2001 WL 1491523 (N.D.Ill. 2001), a condo association had obtained a judgment granting exclusive possession of a unit that had belonged to the plaintiff. The sheriff's office executed the eviction and * * * removed the personal property onto the curb and sidewalk.

* * * The court held that the facts in that case were insufficient to impose an affirmative duty upon defendants to care for any personal property left in the Unit after eviction. The mere fact that the representatives of the condo association had been present and had observed the eviction and removal of the property was not enough to establish a duty of care.

* * * An Illinois appellate court applied a similar analytical framework in *Dargis v. Paradise Park, Inc.,* 354 Ill. App.3d 171, 819 N.E.2d 1220 (2004). There, the court concluded that, while a landlord has no duty in such situations as a general matter, an exception is created when the landlord chooses to care for the property. * * * This decision is helpful because state appellate court decisions, although not binding, constitute persuasive authority.

In the end, the Court agrees with the reasoning in these cases and finds that the Illinois Supreme Court would hold that, although a landlord does not have a general duty under common law to care for the personal property of a former tenant after a proper and legal eviction, a duty of care does arise when a landlord acts as an actual or constructive bailee with respect to the tenant's property. [If] the complaint states a claim for bailment as further discussed below, the Court finds that Plaintiffs have sufficiently alleged the existence of a duty and a breach of that duty to survive a motion to dismiss as to their negligence claim.

II. Bailment

* * * The Zissus allege that a constructive (or implied) bailment was created when IH2 took control over the personal property that had been left behind. In its motion to dismiss, IH2 argues that the Zissus have failed to state a claim because IH2 never took possession of the personal property.

*A bailment occurs when goods, or other personal property, are delivered to another, who under contract either express or implied has agreed to accept delivery and deal with the property in a particular way.* To recover under a bailment theory, the plaintiff must allege: (1) an express or implied agreement to create a bailment, (2) delivery of the property, (3) the bailee's acceptance of the property, and (4) the bailee's failure to return the property or the bailee's delivery of the property in a damaged condition. [Emphasis added.]

An implied bailment—also called a constructive bailment—may be found where the property of one person is voluntarily received by another for some purpose other than that of obtaining ownership. The implied bailment may be deduced from the circumstances surrounding the transaction, including the benefits received by the parties, their intentions, the kind of property involved, and the opportunities of each to exercise control over the property.

The Zissus contend that, by actively removing the property from the premises and putting it on the street, IH2 assumed control over the property. Unlike in *Centagon*, in which the defendants had watched the sheriff take out the property, IH2 itself took possession of the property and put it outside. * * * It was IH2's alleged actions after the sheriff had turned over possession of the premises to IH2 that gave rise to the bailment relationship. * * * The allegations are sufficient [to establish this claim] at the pleading stage.

* * * *

CONCLUSION

For the reasons stated herein, the Court denies IH2's motion to dismiss.

**Legal Reasoning Questions**

1. How did related cases addressing the issue of a landlord's duty under Illinois law affect the court's reasoning in this case?

2. Besides negligence, are there other tort claims that the Zissus might have successfully alleged in their complaint? Discuss.

3. Suppose that instead of putting the Zissus' personal property outside, IH2 had taken it to a storage facility. Would the result have been different?

## 27–5f Duties of the Bailor

The duties of a bailor are essentially the same as the rights of a bailee. A bailor has a duty to compensate the bailee, as discussed earlier. A bailor also has an all-encompassing duty to provide the bailee with goods that are free from known defects that could cause injury to the bailee.

**Bailor's Duty to Reveal Defects** The bailor's duty to reveal defects to the bailee translates into two rules:

1. In a *mutual-benefit bailment,* the bailor must notify the bailee of all known defects and any hidden defects that the bailor knows of or could have discovered with reasonable diligence and proper inspection.
2. In a *bailment for the sole benefit of the bailee,* the bailor must notify the bailee of any known defects.

The bailor's duty to reveal defects is based on a negligence theory of tort law. A bailor who fails to give the appropriate notice is liable to the bailee and to any other person who might reasonably be expected to come into contact with the defective article.

■ **EXAMPLE 27.29** Rentco (the bailor) rents a tractor to Hal Iverson. Unknown to Rentco (but *discoverable* by reasonable inspection), the brake mechanism on the tractor is defective at the time the bailment is made. Iverson uses the defective tractor without knowledge of the brake problem and is injured along with two other field workers when the tractor rolls out of control. In this situation, Rentco is liable for the injuries sustained by Iverson and the other workers because it negligently failed to discover the defect and notify Iverson. ■

**Warranty Liability for Defective Goods** A bailor can also incur warranty liability under contract law for injuries resulting from the bailment of defective articles. Property that is leased from a bailor must be *fit for the intended purpose of the bailment.* The bailor's knowledge of or ability to discover any defects is immaterial.

Warranties of fitness arise by law in sales contracts, and courts have held that these warranties apply to bailments "for hire." Article 2A of the Uniform Commercial Code (UCC) extends the implied warranties of merchantability and fitness for a particular purpose to bailments that include rights to use the bailed goods.[13]

---

13. UCC 2A–212, 2A–213.

# 27–6 Special Types of Bailments

A business is likely to engage in some special types of bailment transactions. These include bailments in which the bailee's duty of care is *extraordinary* and the bailee's liability for loss or damage to the property is absolute. Such situations usually involve common carriers and hotel operators. Warehouse companies have the same duty of care as ordinary bailees, but like carriers, they are subject to extensive federal and state laws, including Article 7 of the UCC.

## 27–6a Common Carriers

*Common carriers* are publicly licensed to provide transportation services to the general public. They are legally bound to carry all passengers or freight as long as there is enough space, the fee is paid, and there are no reasonable grounds to refuse service. Common carriers differ from private carriers, which operate transportation facilities for only a select clientele. A private carrier is not required to provide service to every person or company making a request.

**Strict Liability Applies** The delivery of goods to a common carrier creates a bailment relationship between the shipper (bailor) and the common carrier (bailee). Unlike ordinary bailees, the common carrier is held to a standard of care based on *strict liability,* rather than reasonable care, in protecting the bailed personal property. This means that the common carrier is absolutely liable, regardless of care, for all loss or damage to goods except when damage was caused by a natural disaster or war.

**Limitations on Liability** Common carriers cannot contract away their liability for damaged goods. Subject to government regulations, however, they are permitted to limit their dollar liability to an amount stated on the shipment contract or rate filing. Carriers may also limit the value of property that they will transport.

■ **CASE IN POINT 27.30** Treiber & Straub, Inc., a jewelry store, used UPS to ship a diamond ring worth $105,000. The owner of the jewelry store arranged for the shipment on UPS's Web site, which required him to click on two on-screen boxes to agree to "My UPS Terms and Conditions." In these terms, UPS and its insurer limited their liability and the amount of insurance coverage on packages to $50,000, and refused to ship items worth more than $50,000. Both UPS and its insurer disclaimed liability *entirely* for such items. Nevertheless, the store owner purchased $50,000 in insurance for the package.

When the ring was lost, the jewelry store filed suit against UPS to recover $50,000 under the insurance policy. The court held that UPS's disclaimer of liability was enforceable. It also found that the jewelry store had breached the contract by indicating that the shipment was worth less than $50,000 when the ring was worth much more.[14] ■

## 27–6b Warehouse Companies

Warehousing is the business of providing storage of property for compensation. Like ordinary bailees, warehouse companies are liable for loss or damage to property resulting from *negligence*. But because a warehouse company is a professional bailee, it is expected to exercise a high degree of care to protect and preserve the goods.

**Limitations on Liability** A warehouse company can limit the dollar amount of its liability. Under the UCC, however, it must give the bailor the option of paying a higher storage rate for an increase in the liability limit.[15]

**Warehouse Receipts** Unlike ordinary bailees, a warehouse company can issue *documents of title*—in particular, *warehouse receipts*.[16] A warehouse receipt describes the bailed property and the terms of the bailment contract. It can be negotiable or nonnegotiable, depending on how it is written. It is negotiable if its terms provide that the warehouse company will deliver the goods "to the bearer" of the receipt or "to the order of" a person named on the receipt.[17]

---

**14.** *Treiber & Straub, Inc. v. United Parcel Service, Inc.*, 474 F.3d 379 (7th Cir. 2007).

**15.** UCC 7–204(1), (2).

**16.** A *document of title* is defined in UCC 1–201(15) as any "document which in the regular course of business or financing is treated as adequately evidencing that the person in possession of it is entitled to receive, hold, and dispose of the document and the goods it covers." A *warehouse receipt* is a document of title issued by a person engaged for hire in the business of storing goods.

**17.** UCC 7–104.

The warehouse receipt represents the goods (that is, it indicates title) and hence has value and utility in financing commercial transactions. ■ **EXAMPLE 27.31** Ossip delivers 6,500 cases of canned corn to Chaney, the owner of a warehouse. Chaney issues a negotiable warehouse receipt payable "to bearer" and gives it to Ossip. Ossip sells and delivers the warehouse receipt to Better Foods, Inc. Better Foods is now the owner of the corn and can obtain the cases by simply presenting the warehouse receipt to Chaney. ■

## 27–6c Hotel Operators

At common law, hotel owners were strictly liable for the loss of any cash or property that guests brought into their rooms. Today, state statutes continue to apply strict liability to hotel operators for any loss or damage to their guests' personal property. In many states, however, hotel operators can avoid strict liability for loss of guests' cash and valuables by:

**1.** Providing a safe in which to keep guests' valuables.
**2.** Notifying guests that a safe is available.

In addition, statutes often limit the liability of innkeepers with regard to articles that are not kept in the safe and may limit the availability of damages in the absence of negligence. Most statutes require that the hotel post these limitations on the doors of the rooms or otherwise notify guests.

■ **EXAMPLE 27.32** A guest at Crown Place hotel is traveling with jewelry valued at $1 million. She puts the jewelry in the safe in her room, but someone comes into the room and removes the jewelry from the safe without the use of force. The woman sues the hotel, which claims that it is not liable under the state statute. If Crown Place did not comply with statutory requirements that it post the legal limitations in the guest rooms, however, it will not be protected from liability. Crown Place will be strictly liable for the loss of the woman's jewelry. ■

Concept Summary 27.2 reviews the rights and duties of bailees and bailors.

## Concept Summary 27.2

### Rights and Duties of the Bailee and the Bailor

**Rights of a Bailee (Duties of a Bailor)**

- The right of possession allows a bailee to sue any third parties who damage, lose, or convert the bailed property.
- The right to use the property to the extent it is necessary to carry out the purpose of the bailment.
- The right to be compensated or reimbursed for keeping bailed property. In the event of nonpayment, the bailee has a right to place a possessory (bailee's) lien on the bailed property.
- The right to limit liability. An ordinary bailee can limit the types of risk, monetary amount, or both, provided proper notice is given and the limitation is not against public policy. In special bailments, limitations on liability for negligence usually are not allowed, but limitations on the monetary amount of loss are permitted.

**Duties of a Bailee (Rights of a Bailor)**

- A bailee must exercise appropriate care over property entrusted to her or him. What constitutes appropriate care normally depends on the nature and circumstances of the bailment. A common carrier (special bailee) is held to a standard of care based on strict liability except when damage was caused by a natural disaster or war.
- Bailed goods in a bailee's possession must be returned to the bailor or be disposed of according to the bailor's directions. Failure to return the property gives rise to a presumption of negligence.

## Reviewing: Personal Property and Bailments

Vanessa Denai purchased forty acres of land in rural Louisiana. On the property were a 1,600-square-foot house and a metal barn. Denai later met Lance Finney, who had been seeking a small plot of rural property to rent. After several meetings, Denai invited Finney to live on a corner of her property in exchange for Finney's assistance in cutting wood and tending the property. Denai agreed to store Finney's sailboat in her barn.

With Denai's consent, Finney constructed a concrete and oak foundation on Denai's property. Finney then purchased a 190-square-foot dome from Dome Baja for $3,395. The dome was shipped by Doty Express, a transportation company licensed to serve the public. When it arrived, Finney installed the dome frame and fabric exterior so that the dome was detachable from the foundation. A year after Finney installed the dome, Denai wrote Finney a note stating, "I've decided to give you four acres of land surrounding your dome as drawn on this map." This gift violated no local land-use restrictions. Using the information presented in the chapter, answer the following questions.

1. Is the dome real property or personal property? Explain.
2. Is Denai's gift of land to Finney a testamentary gift, a gift *causa mortis,* or a gift *inter vivos?*
3. What type of bailment relationship was created when Denai agreed to store Finney's boat? What degree of care was Denai required to exercise in storing the boat?
4. What standard of care applied to the shipment of the dome by Doty Express?

**Debate This . . .**   *Common carriers should not be able to limit their liability.*

## Terms and Concepts

## Issue Spotters

**1.** Quintana Corporation sends important documents to Regal Nursery, Inc., via Speedy Messenger Service. While the documents are in Speedy's care, a third party causes an accident to Speedy's delivery vehicle that results in the loss of the documents. Does Speedy have a right to recover from the third party for the loss of the documents? Why or why not? (See *Ordinary Bailments.*)

**2.** Rosa de la Mar Corporation ships a load of goods via Southeast Delivery Company. The load of goods is lost in a hurricane in Florida. Who suffers the loss? Explain your answer. (See *Special Types of Bailments.*)

• **Check your answers to the Issue Spotters against the answers provided in Appendix B at the end of this text.**

## Business Scenarios

**27–1. Duties of the Bailee.** Atka owns a valuable speedboat. She is going on vacation and asks her neighbor, Regina, to store the boat in one stall of Regina's double garage. Regina consents, and the boat is moved into the garage. Regina, in need of some grocery items for dinner, drives to the store. She leaves the garage door open, as is her custom. While she is at the store, the speedboat is stolen. What standard of care is required in this situation? Has Regina breached that duty? (See *Ordinary Bailments.*)

**27–2. Duties of the Bailee.** Orlando borrows a gasoline-driven lawn edger from his neighbor, Max. Max has not used the lawn edger for two years. Orlando has never owned a lawn edger and is not familiar with its use. Max previously used this edger often, and if he had made a reasonable inspection, he would have discovered that the blade was loose. Orlando is injured when the blade becomes detached while he is edging his yard. (See *Ordinary Bailments.*)

**(a)** Can Orlando hold Max liable for his injuries? Why or why not?

**(b)** Would your answer be different if Orlando had rented the edger from Max and paid a fee? Explain.

## Business Case Problems

**27–3. Gifts.** John Wasniewski opened a brokerage account with Quick and Reilly, Inc., in his son James's name. Twelve years later, when the balance was $52,085, the account was closed, and the funds were transferred to a joint account in the names of John and James's brother. James did not learn of the existence of the account in his name until the transfer, when he received a tax form for the account's final year. He filed a suit in a Connecticut state court against Quick and Reilly, alleging breach of contract and seeking to recover the account's principal and interest. What are the elements of a valid gift? Did John's opening of the account with Quick and Reilly constitute a gift to James? What is the likely result in this case, and why? [*Wasniewski v. Quick and Reilly, Inc.,* 292 Conn. 98, 971 A.2d 8 (2009)] (See *Acquiring Ownership of Personal Property.*)

**27–4. Business Case Problem with Sample Answer— Bailment Obligation.** Bob Moreland left his plane at Don  Gray's aircraft repair shop to be painted. When Moreland picked up the airplane, he was disappointed in the quality of the work and pointed out numerous defects. Moreland refused to pay Gray and flew the plane to another shop to have the work redone. Gray sued to collect, contending that Moreland had no right to take the plane to another shop without giving Gray a chance to fix any defects. Gray further argued that by taking the plane, Moreland had accepted Gray's work. Moreland counterclaimed for his expenses. Which party should be awarded damages, and why? [*Gray v. Moreland,* 2010 Ark. App. 207, 374 S.W.3d 178 (2010)] (See *Bailments.*)

• For a sample answer to Problem 27–4, go to Appendix C at the end of this text.

**27–5. Gifts.** Jennifer Koerner adopted a dog—called the Stig—from the Anti-Cruelty Society in Chicago, Illinois, for $95. Koerner wrote a poem and presented it to Kent Nielsen, her live-in boyfriend. In the poem, she expressed her intent to give the Stig to him as a gift. While Koerner and Nielsen lived together, they were both involved in the Stig's day-to-day care. They ended their relationship a year later, and Nielsen agreed to leave their shared residence. Can Nielsen take the Stig with him, or is Koerner the Stig's rightful owner? Explain. [*Koerner v. Nielsen,* 8 N.E.3d 161 (Ill.App. 1 Dist. 2014)] (See *Acquiring Ownership of Personal Property.*)

**27–6. Lost Property.** Sara Simon misplaced her Galaxy cell phone in Manhattan, Kansas. Days later, Shawn Vargo contacted her, claiming to have bought the phone from someone else. He promised to mail it to Simon if she would wire $100 to him through a third party, Mark Lawrence. When Simon spoke to Lawrence about the wire transfer, she referred to the phone as hers and asked, "Are you going to send my phone to me?" Simon paid, but she did not get the phone. Instead, Lawrence took it to a Best Buy store and traded it in for credit. Charged with the theft of lost property, Lawrence claimed that he did not know Simon was the owner of the phone. Was Simon's phone lost, mislaid, or abandoned? What is the finder's responsibility with respect to this type of property? Can Lawrence successfully argue that he did not know the phone was Simon's? Explain. [*State of Kansas v. Lawrence,* 347 P.3d 240 (Kan.App. 2015)] (See *Mislaid, Lost, and Abandoned Property.*)

**27–7. Bailments.** Christie's Fine Art Storage Services Inc. (CFASS) is in the business of storing fine works of art at its warehouse in Brooklyn, New York. The warehouse is next to the East River in a flood zone. Boyd Sullivan owns works of art by Alberto Vargas, including *Beauty and the Beast* and *Miss Universe.* Sullivan contracted to store the works at CFASS's facility under an agreement that limited the warehouser's liability for damage to the goods to $200,000. A few months later, as Hurricane Sandy approached, CFASS was warned, along with the other businesses in the flood zone, of the potential for damage from the storm. CFASS e-mailed its clients that extra precautions were being taken. Despite this assurance, Sullivan's works were left exposed on a ground floor and sustained severe damage in the storm. Who is most likely to suffer the loss? Why? [*Sullivan v. Christie's Fine Art Storage Services, Inc.,* 2016 WL 427615 (N.Y.Sup. Trial Order 2016)] (See *Bailments.*)

**27–8. A Question of Ethics—Gifts.**  *Jason Crippen and Catharyn Campbell of Knoxville, Tennessee, were involved in a romantic relationship for many months. Their relationship culminated in an engagement on December 25, 2005, when Crippen placed an engagement ring on Campbell's finger and simultaneously proposed marriage. Campbell accepted the proposal, and the parties were engaged to be married. The engagement did not last, however. The parties broke up, their romantic relationship ended, and neither had any intent to marry the other. Crippen asked Campbell to return the ring. She refused. Crippen filed a suit in a Tennessee state court against Campbell to recover the ring. Both parties filed motions for summary judgment. The court ruled in Campbell's favor. Crippen appealed to a state intermediate appellate court. [Crippen v. Campbell, 2007 WL 2768076 (Tenn. App. 2007)] (See Acquiring Ownership of Personal Property.)*

**(a)** Under what reasoning could the court affirm the award of the ring to Campbell? On what basis could the court reverse the judgment and order Campbell to return the ring? (Hint: Is an engagement ring a completed gift immediately on its delivery?) Which principle do you support, and why?

**(b)** Should the court determine who was responsible for breaking off the engagement before awarding ownership of the ring? Why or why not?

**(c)** If, instead of Crippen, one of his creditors had sought the ring in satisfaction of one of his debts, how should the court have ruled? Why?

## Legal Reasoning Group Activity

**27–9. Bailments.** On learning that Sébastien planned to travel abroad, Roslyn asked him to deliver $25,000 in cash to her family in Mexico. During a customs inspection at the border, Sébastien told the customs inspector that he carried less than $10,000. The officer discovered the actual amount of cash that Sébastien was carrying, seized it, and arrested Sébastien. Roslyn asked the government to return what she claimed were her funds, arguing that the arrangement with Sébastien was a bailment and that she still held title to the cash. (See *Bailments.*)

**(a)** The first group will argue that Roslyn is entitled to the cash.

**(b)** The second group will take the position of the government and develop an argument that Roslyn's agreement with Sébastien does not qualify as a bailment.

COMMERCIAL LAW FOR ACCOUNTANTS · MILLER

# CHAPTER 28

# Real Property and Landlord-Tenant Law

From the earliest times, property has provided a means for survival. Primitive peoples lived off the fruits of the land, eating the vegetation and wildlife. Later, as the wildlife was domesticated and the vegetation cultivated, property provided pastures and farmland. Throughout history, property has continued to be an indicator of family wealth and social position. In the Western world, the protection of an individual's right to his or her property has become one of our most important rights.

In this chapter, we look at the nature of real property and the ways in which it can be owned. We examine the legal requirements involved in the transfer of real property. We even consider, in this chapter's *Spotlight Case,* whether the buyer of a haunted house can rescind the sale.

Realize that real property rights are never absolute. There is a higher right—that of the government to take, for compensation, private land for public use. Later in the chapter, we discuss this right, as well as other restrictions on the ownership or use of property, including zoning laws. We conclude the chapter with a discussion of landlord-tenant relationships.

## 28-1 The Nature of Real Property

Real property (or realty) consists of land and everything permanently attached to it, including structures and other fixtures. Real property encompasses airspace and subsurface rights, as well as rights to plants and vegetation. In essence, real property is immovable.

### 28-1a Land and Structures

Land includes the soil on the surface of the earth and the natural products or artificial structures that are attached to it. Land further includes all the waters contained on or under its surface and much, but not necessarily all, of the airspace above it. The exterior boundaries of land extend down to the center of the earth and up to the farthest reaches of the atmosphere (subject to certain qualifications).

### 28-1b Airspace and Subsurface Rights

The owner of real property has rights to both the airspace above the land and the soil and minerals underneath it. Any limitations on either airspace rights or subsurface rights, called *encumbrances,* normally must be indicated on the document that transfers title at the time of purchase. The ways in which ownership rights in real property can be limited will be examined later in this chapter.

**Airspace Rights** Disputes concerning airspace rights may involve the right of commercial and private planes to fly over property and the right of individuals and governments to seed clouds and produce artificial rain. Flights over private land normally do not violate property rights unless the flights are so low and so frequent that they directly interfere with the owner's enjoyment and use of the land. Leaning walls or projecting eave spouts or roofs may also violate the airspace rights of an adjoining property owner.

**Subsurface Rights** In many states, ownership of land can be separated from ownership of its subsurface. In other words, the owner of the surface may sell subsurface rights to another person. When ownership is separated into surface and subsurface rights, each owner can pass title to what she or he owns without the consent of the other owner.

Subsurface rights can be extremely valuable, as these rights include the ownership of minerals, oil, or natural gas. But a subsurface owner's rights would be of little value if he or she could not use the surface to exercise those rights. Hence, a subsurface owner has a right (called a *profit,* discussed later in this chapter) to go onto

543

the surface of the land to, for instance, find and remove minerals.

Of course, conflicts can arise between the surface owner's use of the property and the subsurface owner's need to extract minerals, oil, or natural gas. In that situation, one party's interest may become subservient (secondary) to the other party's interest either by statute or by case law. If the owners of the subsurface rights excavate, they are absolutely (strictly) liable if their excavation causes the surface to collapse. Many states have statutes that also make the excavators liable for any damage to structures on the land. Typically, these statutes set out precise requirements for excavations of various depths.

## 28–1c Plant Life and Vegetation

Plant life, both natural and cultivated, is also considered to be real property. In many instances, the natural vegetation, such as trees, adds greatly to the value of realty. When a parcel of land is sold and the land has growing crops on it, the sale includes the crops, unless otherwise specified in the sales contract. When crops are sold by themselves, however, they are considered to be personal property, or goods. Consequently, the sale of crops is a sale of goods and is governed by the Uniform Commercial Code (UCC) rather than by real property law.

## 28–1d Fixtures

Certain personal property can become so closely associated with the real property to which it is attached that the law views it as real property. Such property is known as a **fixture**—an item affixed to realty, meaning that it is attached to the real property in a permanent way. The item may be embedded in the land or permanently attached to the property or to another fixture on the property by means of cement, plaster, bolts, nails, or screws. An item, such as a statue, may even sit on the land without being attached, as long as the owner *intends* it to be a fixture.

Fixtures are included in the sale of land unless the sales contract specifies otherwise. The issue of whether an item is a fixture (and thus real estate) or not a fixture (and thus personal property) often arises with respect to land sales, real property taxation, insurance coverage, and divorces. How the issue is resolved can have important consequences for the parties involved.

**Typical Fixtures** Some items can only be attached to property permanently—such as tile floors, cabinets, and carpeting. Because such items are attached permanently, it is assumed that the owner intended them to be fixtures. Also, when an item of property is custom-made for installation on real property, as storm windows are, the item usually is classified as a fixture.

In addition, an item that is firmly attached to the land and integral to its use may be deemed a fixture. For instance, a mobile home or a complex irrigation system bolted to a cement slab on a farm can be a fixture. The courts assume that owners, in making such installations, intend the objects to become part of their real property.

**The Role of Intent** Generally, when the courts need to determine whether a certain item is a fixture, they examine the intention of the party who placed the object on the real property. When the intent of that party is in dispute, the courts will usually deem that the item is a fixture if either or both of the following are true:

- The property attached cannot be removed without causing substantial damage to the remaining realty.
- The property attached is so adapted to the rest of the realty as to have become a part of it.

■ **CASE IN POINT 28.1** Terminal 5, a facility owned by the Port of Seattle (Port), was used in loading and unloading the shipping containers used to transport goods by ship. APL Limited entered into a long-term lease with the Port for use of Terminal 5 and for use of Port-owned container cranes. Terminal 5 was substantially rebuilt, and steel cranes were constructed and installed. The cranes were 100 feet apart, 198 feet tall, and 85 feet wide, and were mounted on rails embedded in concrete. They were hard-wired to a dedicated high-voltage electrical system built specifically for Terminal 5 and were attached to the power substation by cables.

APL later filed a lawsuit against the state of Washington for a refund of sales tax it had paid on the lease of the cranes. The state argued that the cranes were personal property and, as such, subject to sales tax. The trial court ruled in favor of the state, but a Washington appellate court reversed. The reviewing court found that the trial court had not sufficiently taken the Port's intent into account in determining that the cranes were personal property, not fixtures. "When the owner and the person that [attaches property to realty] are one and the same, a rebuttable presumption arises that the owner's intention was for the [property] to become part of the realty." The reviewing court remanded the case so the lower court could examine evidence of the Port's intent.[1] ■

---

1. *APL Limited v. Washington State Department of Revenue,* 154 Wash.App. 1020 (2010).

**Trade Fixtures Are Personal Property** Trade fixtures are an exception to the rule that fixtures are a part of the real property to which they are attached. A **trade fixture** is personal property that is installed for a commercial purpose *by a tenant* (one who rents real property from the owner, or landlord).

Trade fixtures remain the property of the tenant unless removal would irreparably damage the building or realty. A walk-in cooler, for instance, purchased and installed by a tenant who uses the premises for a restaurant, is a trade fixture. The tenant can remove the cooler from the premises when the lease terminates but ordinarily must repair any damage that the removal causes or compensate the landlord for the damage.

# 28–2 Ownership and Other Interests in Real Property

Ownership of property is an abstract concept that cannot exist independently of the legal system. No one can actually possess, or *hold*, a piece of land, the air above it, the earth below it, and all the water contained on it. One can only possess *rights* in real property.

Numerous rights are involved in real property ownership, which is why property ownership is often viewed as a bundle of rights. One who possesses the entire bundle of rights is said to hold the property in *fee simple*, which is the most complete form of ownership. When only some of the rights in the bundle are transferred to another person, the effect is to limit the ownership rights of both the transferor of the rights and the recipient.

Ownership interests in real property have traditionally been referred to as *estates in land*, which include fee simple estates, life estates, and leasehold estates. We examine these types of estates in this section, and we also discuss several forms of concurrent ownership of property. Finally, we describe certain interests in real property that is owned by others.

## 28–2a Ownership in Fee Simple

In a **fee simple absolute**, the owner has the greatest aggregation of rights, privileges, and power possible. The owner can give the property away or dispose of the property by *deed* or by *will*. When there is no will, the fee simple passes to the owner's legal heirs on her or his death. A fee simple absolute is potentially infinite in duration and is assigned forever to a person and

her or his heirs without limitation or condition.[2] The owner has the rights of *exclusive* possession and use of the property.

The rights that accompany a fee simple absolute include the right to use the land for whatever purpose the owner sees fit. Of course, other laws, including applicable zoning, noise, and environmental laws, may limit the owner's ability to use the property in certain ways. A person who uses his or her property in a manner that unreasonably interferes with others' right to use or enjoy their own property can be liable for the tort of *nuisance*.

■ **CASE IN POINT 28.2** Nancy and James Biglane owned and lived in a building next door to the Under the Hill Saloon, a popular bar that featured live music. During the summer, the Saloon, which had no air-conditioning, opened its windows and doors, and live music echoed up and down the street. The Biglanes installed extra insulation, thicker windows, and air-conditioning units in their building. Nevertheless, the noise from the Saloon kept the Biglanes awake at night. Eventually, they sued the owners of the Saloon for nuisance. The court held that the noise from the bar unreasonably interfered with the Biglanes' right to enjoy their property and prohibited the Saloon from opening its windows and doors while playing music.[3] ■

## 28–2b Life Estates

A **life estate** is an estate that lasts for the life of some specified individual. A **conveyance**, or transfer of real property, "to A for his life" creates a life estate.[4] The life tenant's ownership rights cease to exist on the life tenant's death.

The life tenant has the right to use the land, provided that he or she commits no **waste** (injury to the land). In other words, the life tenant cannot use the land in a manner that would adversely affect its value. The life tenant can use the land to harvest crops or, if mines and oil wells are already on the land, can extract minerals and oil from it, but the life tenant cannot establish new wells or mines. The life tenant can also create liens, *easements* (discussed shortly), and leases, but none can extend beyond the life

---

2. In another type of estate, the *fee simple defeasible*, ownership in fee simple automatically terminates if a stated event occurs. For instance, property might be conveyed (transferred) to a school only as long as it is used for school purposes. In addition, the fee simple may be subject to a *condition subsequent*. This means that if a stated event occurs, the prior owner of the property can bring an action to regain possession of the property.

3. *Biglane v. Under the Hill Corp.*, 949 So.2d 9 (Miss.Sup. 2007).

4. A less common type of life estate is created by the conveyance "to A for the life of B." This is known as an estate *pur autre vie*—that is, an estate for the duration of the life of another.

of the tenant. In addition, with few exceptions, the life tenant has an exclusive right to possession during his or her lifetime.

Along with these rights, the life tenant also has some duties—to keep the property in repair and to pay property taxes. In short, the owner of the life estate has the same rights as a fee simple owner except that she or he must maintain the value of the property during her or his tenancy.

In the following case, the life tenant refused to pay the taxes and the premiums for the insurance on the property. Was this waste?

## Case 28.1

# Main Omni Realty Corp. v. Matus

New York Supreme Court, Appellate Division, Second Department, 124 A.D.3d 604, 1 N.Y.S.3d 319 (2015).

**Background and Facts**   Craig Matus held a life estate in certain residential real property in Huntington, New York. On the termination of the life estate, title to the property was to transfer to Main Omni Realty Corporation, a wholly owned subsidiary of New York Community Bank. For a dozen years, Matus refused to pay premiums for insurance on the property. He also refused to pay the property taxes, resulting in tax liens.

To preserve its interest in the property, Main Omni paid the premiums and the liens, which avoided a foreclosure and sale of the property. Main Omni then filed a suit in a New York state court against Matus, seeking to recover the amount of the premiums and taxes on the ground of unjust enrichment. In addition, it sought to extinguish (end) the life estate on the ground of waste based on Matus's refusal to pay the taxes. The court denied Main Omni's motion for summary judgment. Main Omni appealed.

## In the Language of the Court

Ruth C. *BALKIN,* J.P. [Judge Presiding], L. Priscilla *HALL,* Leonard B. *AUSTIN,* and Betsey *BARROS,* JJ. [Judges].
      * * * *

The essential inquiry in any action for unjust enrichment or restitution is whether it is against equity and good conscience to permit the defendant to retain what is sought to be recovered. *A plaintiff must show that (1) the other party was enriched, (2) at the plaintiff's expense, and (3) that it is against equity and good conscience to permit the other party to retain what is sought to be recovered.* [Emphasis added.]

The plaintiffs established their *prima facie* entitlement to judgment as a matter of law on their first cause of action, which alleged unjust enrichment and sought restitution, and their second cause of action, which alleged waste and sought to extinguish the defendant's life estate. As life tenant, the defendant was obligated to pay the property taxes and * * * insurance on the subject property, and the intentional failure to do so constitutes waste. It is undisputed that the defendant intentionally failed to pay the property taxes and * * * insurance on the subject property, and he has clearly expressed his intention not to do so in the future. Under these circumstances, the remainder interest in the subject property is in constant danger of forfeiture in a tax lien sale, unless the plaintiffs continue paying the property taxes and * * * insurance premiums the defendant is otherwise obligated to pay. The plaintiffs therefore demonstrated, *prima facie,* that the defendant was unjustly enriched by the plaintiffs' payment of these expenses for the defendant, and that equity warrants extinguishing his life estate in the subject property.

**Decision and Remedy**   *A state intermediate appellate court reversed the lower court's denial of Main Omni's motion and ordered a summary judgment in the plaintiff's favor. Because Matus continued to refuse to pay the taxes on the property, the court ended his life estate.*

## Critical Thinking

- **Economic**   *Why would the owner of a life estate refuse to pay the taxes and insurance premiums on the property of the estate? Should any reason for this refusal have influenced the court's decision in this case?*

## 28–2c Concurrent Ownership

Persons who share ownership rights simultaneously in particular property (including real property and personal property) are said to have **concurrent ownership.** There are two principal types of concurrent ownership: *tenancy in common* and *joint tenancy.* Concurrent ownership rights can also be held in a *tenancy by the entirety* or as *community property,* but these types of concurrent ownership are less common.

**Tenancy in Common**   The term **tenancy in common** refers to a form of co-ownership in which each of two or more persons owns an undivided interest in the property. The interest is undivided because each tenant shares rights in the whole property. On the death of a tenant in common, that tenant's interest in the property passes to her or his heirs.

■ **EXAMPLE 28.3**   Four friends purchase a condominium unit in Hawaii together as tenants in common. This means that each of them has a one-fourth ownership interest in the whole. If one of the four owners dies a year after the purchase, his ownership interest passes to his heirs (his wife and children, for example) rather than to the other tenants in common. ■

Unless the co-tenants have agreed otherwise, a tenant in common can transfer her or his interest in the property to another without the consent of the remaining co-owners. In most states, it is presumed that a co-tenancy is a tenancy in common unless there is specific language indicating the intent to establish a joint tenancy.

**Joint Tenancy**   In a **joint tenancy,** each of two or more persons owns an undivided interest in the property, but a deceased joint tenant's interest passes to the surviving joint tenant or tenants.

**Right of Survivorship.**   The right of a surviving joint tenant to inherit a deceased joint tenant's ownership interest—referred to as a *right of survivorship*—distinguishes a joint tenancy from a tenancy in common. ■ **EXAMPLE 28.4** Jerrold and Eva are married and purchase a house as joint tenants. The title to the house clearly expresses the intent to create a joint tenancy because it refers to Jerrold and Eva as "joint tenants with right of survivorship." Jerrold has three children from a prior marriage. If Jerrold dies, his interest in the house automatically passes to Eva rather than to his children from the prior marriage. ■

**Termination of a Joint Tenancy.**   A joint tenant can transfer her or his rights by sale or gift to another without the consent of the other joint tenants. Doing so terminates the joint tenancy, however. The person who purchases the property or receives it as a gift becomes a tenant in common, not a joint tenant. ■ **EXAMPLE 28.5** Three brothers, Brody, Saul, and Jacob, own a parcel of land as joint tenants. Brody is experiencing financial difficulties and sells his interest in the real property to Beth. The sale terminates the joint tenancy, and now Beth, Saul, and Jacob hold the property as tenants in common. ■

A joint tenant's interest can also be levied against (seized by court order) to satisfy the tenant's judgment creditors. If this occurs, the joint tenancy terminates, and the remaining owners hold the property as tenants in common. (Judgment creditors can also seize the interests of tenants in a tenancy in common.)

**Tenancy by the Entirety**   A less common form of shared ownership of real property by married persons is a **tenancy by the entirety.** It differs from a joint tenancy in that neither spouse may separately transfer his or her interest during his or her lifetime unless the other spouse consents. In some states in which statutes give the wife the right to convey her property, this form of concurrent ownership has effectively been abolished. A divorce, either spouse's death, or mutual agreement will terminate a tenancy by the entirety.

**Community Property**   A limited number of states[5] allow married couples to own property as **community property.** If property is held as community property, each spouse technically owns an undivided one-half interest in the property. This type of ownership applies to most property acquired by the husband or the wife during the course of the marriage. It generally does *not* apply to property acquired prior to the marriage or to property acquired by gift or inheritance as separate property during the marriage. After a divorce, community property is divided equally in some states and according to the discretion of the court in other states.

## 28–2d Leasehold Estates

A **leasehold estate** is created when a real property owner or lessor (landlord) agrees to convey the right to possess and use the property to a lessee (tenant) for a certain period of time. The tenant's right to possession is

---

5. These states include Alaska, Arizona, California, Idaho, Louisiana, Nevada, New Mexico, Texas, Washington, and Wisconsin. Puerto Rico allows property to be owned as community property as well.

*temporary*, which is what distinguishes a tenant from a purchaser, who acquires title to the property.

In every leasehold estate, the tenant has a *qualified* right to exclusive possession. It is qualified because the landlord has a right to enter onto the premises to ensure that no waste is being committed. In addition, the tenant can use the land—for instance, by harvesting crops—but cannot injure it by such activities as cutting down timber to sell or extracting oil.

**Fixed-Term Tenancy** A **fixed-term tenancy,** also called a *tenancy for years,* is created by an express contract stating that the property is leased for a specified period of time, such as a month, a year, or a period of years. Signing a one-year lease to occupy an apartment, for instance, creates a fixed-term tenancy. Note that the term need not be specified by date and can be conditioned on the occurrence of an event, such as leasing a cabin for the summer or an apartment during Mardi Gras.

At the end of the period specified in the lease, the lease ends (without notice), and possession of the property returns to the lessor. If the tenant dies during the period of the lease, the lease interest passes to the tenant's heirs as personal property. Often, leases include renewal or extension provisions.

**Periodic Tenancy** A **periodic tenancy** is created by a lease that does not specify a term but does specify that rent is to be paid at certain intervals, such as weekly, monthly, or yearly. The tenancy is automatically renewed for another rental period unless properly terminated. ■ **EXAMPLE 28.6** Jewel, LLC, enters into a lease with Capital Properties. The lease states, "Rent is due on the tenth day of every month." This provision creates a periodic tenancy from month to month. ■ A periodic tenancy sometimes arises after a fixed-term tenancy ends when the landlord allows the tenant to retain possession and continue paying monthly or weekly rent.

Under the common law, to terminate a periodic tenancy, the landlord or tenant must give at least one period's notice to the other party. If the tenancy is month to month, for instance, one month's notice must be given prior to the last month's rent payment. Today, however, state statutes often require a different period of notice before the termination of a tenancy.

**Tenancy at Will** With a **tenancy at will,** either party can terminate the tenancy without notice. This type of tenancy can arise if a landlord rents property to a tenant "for as long as both agree" or allows a person to live on the premises without paying rent. Tenancy at will is rare today because most state statutes require a landlord to provide some period of notice to terminate a tenancy. States may also require a landowner to have sufficient cause (a legitimate reason) to end a residential tenancy.

**Tenancy at Sufferance** The mere possession of land without right is called a **tenancy at sufferance.** A tenancy at sufferance is not a true tenancy because it is created when a tenant *wrongfully* retains possession of property. Whenever a tenancy for years or a periodic tenancy ends and the tenant continues to retain possession of the premises without the owner's permission, a tenancy at sufferance is created.

### 28–2e Nonpossessory Interests

In contrast to the types of property interests just described, some interests in land do not include any rights to possess the property. These interests are therefore known as **nonpossessory interests.** They include *easements, profits,* and *licenses.*

An **easement** is the right of a person to make limited use of another person's real property without taking anything from the property. The right to walk across another's property, for example, is an easement. In contrast, a **profit** is the right to go onto land owned by another and take away some part of the land itself or some product of the land. ■ **EXAMPLE 28.7** Shawn owns real property known as the Dunes. Shawn gives Carmen the right to go there and remove all of the sand and gravel that she needs for her cement business. Carmen has a profit. ■

Easements and profits can be classified as either *appurtenant* or *in gross.* Because easements and profits are similar and the same rules apply to both, we discuss them together.

**Easement or Profit Appurtenant** An easement (or profit) *appurtenant* arises when the owner of one piece of land has a right to go onto (or remove something from) an adjacent piece of land owned by another. The land that is benefited by the easement is called the *dominant estate,* and the land that is burdened is called the *servient estate.*

Because easements appurtenant are intended to *benefit the land,* they run (are conveyed) with the land when it is transferred. ■ **EXAMPLE 28.8** Owen has a right to drive his car across Green's land, which is adjacent to Owen's property. This right-of-way over Green's property is an easement appurtenant to Owen's land. If Owen sells his land, the easement runs with the land to benefit the new owner. ■

**Easement or Profit in Gross** In an easement or profit *in gross,* the right to use or take things from another's land is given to one who does not own an adjacent tract of land. These easements are intended to *benefit a particular person or business,* not a particular piece of land, and cannot be transferred.

■ **EXAMPLE 28.9** Avery owns a parcel of land with a marble quarry. Avery conveys to Classic Stone Corporation the right to come onto her land and remove up to five hundred pounds of marble per day. Classic Stone owns a profit in gross and cannot transfer this right to another. ■ Similarly, when a utility company is granted an easement to run its power lines across another's property, it obtains an easement in gross.

**Creation of an Easement or Profit** Most easements and profits are created by an express grant in a contract, deed, or will. This allows the parties to include terms defining the extent and length of time of use. In some situations, however, an easement or profit can be created without an express agreement.

An easement or profit may arise by **implication** when the circumstances surrounding the division of a parcel of property imply its creation. ■ **EXAMPLE 28.10** Barrow divides a parcel of land that has only one well for drinking water. If Barrow conveys the half without a well to Dean, a profit by implication arises because Dean needs drinking water. ■

An easement may also be created by **necessity.** An easement by necessity does not require division of property for its existence. A person who rents an apartment, for instance, has an easement by necessity in the private road leading up to it.

An easement arises by **prescription** when one person exercises an easement, such as a right-of-way, on another person's land without the landowner's consent. The use must be apparent and continue for the length of time required by the applicable statute of limitations. (In much the same way, title to property may be obtained by adverse possession, as will be discussed later in this chapter.)

■ **CASE IN POINT 28.11** Junior and Wilma Thompson sold twenty-one of their fifty acres of land in Missouri to Walnut Bowls, Inc. The deed expressly reserved an easement to the Thompsons' remaining twenty-nine acres, but it did not fix a precise location for the easement. James and Linda Baker subsequently bought the remaining acreage of the Thompsons' land.

Many years later—on learning of the easement to the Bakers' property—a potential buyer of Walnut Bowls' property refused to go through with the sale. Walnut

Bowls then put steel cables across its driveway entrances, installed a lock and chain on an access gate, and bolted a "No Trespassing" sign facing the Bakers' property. The Bakers filed a suit in a Missouri state court to determine the location of the easement. Citing the lack of an express location, the court held that there was no easement.

The Bakers appealed, and a state intermediate appellate court reversed that decision. The reviewing court held that an easement existed and instructed the trial court to determine its location. An easement can be created by deed even though its specific location is not identified. The location can later be fixed by agreement between the parties or inferred from use. If the easement is not identified in either of these ways, a court must determine the location.[6] ■

**Termination of an Easement or Profit** An easement or profit can be terminated or extinguished in several ways. The simplest way is to deed it back to the owner of the land that is burdened by it. Similarly, if the owner of an easement or profit acquires the property burdened by it, then it is merged into the property.

Another way to terminate an easement or profit is to abandon it and provide evidence of the intent to relinquish the right to use it. Mere nonuse will not extinguish an easement or profit, however, *unless the nonuse is accompanied by an overt act showing the intent to abandon.* An overt act might be, for instance, installing and using a different access road to one's property and discontinuing using an easement across the neighboring property. In any case, a court must be convinced that there was an intent to abandon the easement or profit.

**License** In the context of real property, a **license** is the revocable right of a person to come onto another person's land. It is a personal privilege that arises from the consent of the owner of the land and can be revoked by the owner. A ticket to attend a movie at a theater or a concert is an example of a license.

In essence, a license grants a person the authority to enter the land of another and perform a specified act or series of acts without obtaining any permanent interest in the land. When a person with a license exceeds the authority granted and undertakes some action on the property that is not permitted, the property owner can sue that person for the tort of trespass.

■ **CASE IN POINT 28.12** A Catholic church granted Prince Realty Management, LLC, a three-month license to use a three-foot strip of its property adjacent to

6. *Baker v. Walnut Bowls, Inc.,* 423 S.W.3d 293 (Mo.App. 2014).

Prince's property. The license authorized Prince to "put up plywood panels," creating a temporary fence to protect Prince's property during the construction of a new building. During the license's term, Prince installed steel piles and beams on the licensed property. When Prince ignored the church's demands that these structures be removed, the church sued Prince for trespass. The court concluded that the license allowed only temporary structures and that Prince had exceeded its authority by installing steel piles and beams. Therefore, the church was entitled to damages.[7] ■

Exhibit 28–1 illustrates the various interests in real property discussed in this chapter.

## 28–3 Transfer of Ownership

Ownership interests in real property are frequently transferred by sale, and the terms of the transfer are specified in a real estate sales contract. When real property is sold, the type of interest being transferred and the conditions of the transfer normally are set forth in a *deed* executed by the person who is conveying the property. Real property ownership can also be transferred by gift, by will or inheritance, by adverse possession, or by eminent domain.

---

7. *Roman Catholic Church of Our Lady of Sorrows v. Prince Realty Management, LLC*, 47 A.D.3d 909, 850 N.Y.S.2d 569 (2008).

### 28–3a Real Estate Sales Contracts

In some ways, a sale of real estate is similar to a sale of goods because it involves a transfer of ownership, often with specific warranties. A sale of real estate, however, is a more complicated transaction that involves certain formalities that are not required in a sale of goods. In part because of these complications, real estate brokers or agents who are licensed by the state assist the buyers and sellers during the sales transaction.

Usually, after substantial negotiation (offers, counteroffers, and responses), the parties enter into a detailed contract setting forth their agreement. A contract for a sale of land includes such terms as the purchase price, the type of deed the buyer will receive, the condition of the premises, and any items that will be included.

Unless the buyer pays cash for the property, the buyer must obtain financing through a mortgage loan. Real estate sales contracts are often contingent on the buyer's ability to obtain financing at or below a specified rate of interest. The contract may also be contingent on certain events, such as the completion of a land survey or the property's passing one or more inspections. Normally, the buyer is responsible for having the premises inspected for physical or mechanical defects and for insect infestation.

**Closing Date and Escrow**   The contract usually fixes a date for performance, or **closing,** that frequently is four to twelve weeks after the contract is signed. On this day,

**EXHIBIT 28–1**   Interests in Real Property

| TYPE OF INTEREST | DESCRIPTION |
|---|---|
| Ownership Interests | 1. *Fee simple*—The most complete form of ownership.<br>2. *Life estate*—An estate that lasts for the life of a specified individual.<br>3. *Concurrent ownership*—When two or more persons hold title to property together, concurrent ownership exists.<br>  a. Tenancy in common<br>  b. Joint tenancy<br>  c. Tenancy by the entirety<br>  d. Community property |
| Leasehold Estates | 1. Fixed-term tenancy (tenancy for years)<br>2. Periodic tenancy<br>3. Tenancy at will<br>4. Tenancy at sufferance |
| Nonpossessory Interests | 1. Easements<br>2. Profits<br>3. Licenses |

the seller conveys the property to the buyer by delivering the deed to the buyer in exchange for payment of the purchase price.

Deposits toward the purchase price normally are held in a special account, called an **escrow account,** until all of the conditions of sale have been met. Once the closing takes place, the funds in the escrow account are transferred to the seller.

**Marketable Title** The title to a particular parcel of property is especially important to the buyer. A grantor (seller) is obligated to transfer **marketable title,** or good title, to the grantee (buyer). Marketable title means that the grantor's ownership is free from encumbrances (except those disclosed by the grantor) and free of defects.

If the buyer signs a purchase contract and then discovers that the seller does not have a marketable title, the buyer can withdraw from the contract. ■ **EXAMPLE 28.13** Chan enters into an agreement to buy Fortuna Ranch from Hal. Chan then discovers that Hal has given Pearl an option to purchase the ranch and the option has not expired. In this situation, the title is not marketable, because Pearl could exercise the option and Hal would be compelled to sell the ranch to her. Therefore, Chan can withdraw from the contract to buy the property. ■

The most common way of ensuring title is through **title insurance,** which insures the buyer against loss from defects in title to real property. When financing the purchase of real property, almost all lenders require title insurance to protect their interests in the collateral for the loan.

**Implied Warranties in the Sale of New Homes**
The common law rule of *caveat emptor* ("let the buyer beware") held that the seller of a home made no warranty as to its soundness or fitness (unless the contract or deed stated otherwise). Today, however, most states imply a warranty—the **implied warranty of habitability**—in the sale of new homes.

Under this warranty, the seller of a new house warrants that it will be fit for human habitation even if the deed or contract of sale does not include such a warranty. Essentially, the seller is warranting that the house is in reasonable working order and is of reasonably sound construction. The seller can be liable if the home is defective. In some states, the warranty protects not only the first purchaser but any subsequent purchaser as well.

**Seller's Duty to Disclose Hidden Defects** In most jurisdictions, courts impose on sellers a duty to disclose any known defect that materially affects the value of the property and that the buyer could not reasonably discover. Failure to disclose such a defect gives the buyer a right to rescind the contract and to sue for damages based on fraud or misrepresentation.

There is normally a limit to the time within which the buyer can bring a suit against the seller based on the defect. Time limits run from either the date of the sale or the day that the buyer discovered (or should have discovered) the defect. ■ **EXAMPLE 28.14** Ian Newson partially renovates a house in Louisiana and sells it to Jerry and Tabitha Moreland for $87,000. Two months after the Morelands move in, they discover rotten wood behind the tile in the bathroom and experience problems with the plumbing. The state statute specifies that the Morelands have one year from the date of the sale or the discovery of the defect to file a lawsuit. Therefore, the Morelands must file suit within twelve months of discovering the defects (which would be fourteen months from the date of the sale). ■

In the following *Spotlight Case,* the court had to decide whether the buyer of a house had the right to rescind the sales contract because he was not told that the house was allegedly haunted.

## Spotlight on Sales of Haunted Houses

### Case 28.2 Stambovsky v. Ackley
Supreme Court, Appellate Division, New York, 572 N.Y.S.2d 672, 169 A.D.2d 254 (1991).

**Background and Facts** Jeffrey Stambovsky signed a contract to buy Helen Ackley's home in Nyack, New York. After the contract was signed, Stambovsky discovered that the house was widely reputed to be haunted. The Ackley family claimed to have seen poltergeists on numerous occasions over the prior nine years. The Ackleys had been interviewed and quoted in both a national publication (*Reader's Digest*) and the local newspaper. The house was described as "a riverfront Victorian (with ghost)" when it was part of a walking tour of Nyack, New York. When Stambovsky discovered the house's reputation, he sued to rescind the contract and recover his down payment. He alleged that Ackley and

Case 28.2 Continues

**Case 28.2 Continued**

her real estate agent made material misrepresentations when they failed to disclose Ackley's belief that the home was haunted. Ackley argued that, under the doctrine of *caveat emptor,* she was under no duty to disclose to the buyer the home's haunted reputation. The trial court dismissed Stambovsky's case. Stambovsky appealed.

## In the Language of the Court
Justice *RUBIN* delivered the opinion of the court.
* * * *

While I agree with [the trial court] that the real estate broker, as agent for the seller, is under no duty to disclose to a potential buyer the phantasmal reputation of the premises and that, in his pursuit of a legal remedy for fraudulent misrepresentation against the seller, plaintiff hasn't a ghost of a chance, I am nevertheless moved by the spirit of equity to allow the buyer to seek rescission of the contract of sale and recovery of his down payment. New York law fails to recognize any remedy for damages incurred as a result of the seller's mere silence, applying instead the strict rule of *caveat emptor.* Therefore, the theoretical basis for granting relief, even under the extraordinary facts of this case, is elusive if not ephemeral [short-lived].
* * * *

*The doctrine of* caveat emptor *requires that a buyer act prudently to assess the fitness and value of his purchase and operates to bar the purchaser who fails to exercise due care from seeking the equitable remedy of rescission.* * * * Applying the strict rule of *caveat emptor* to a contract involving a house possessed by poltergeists conjures up visions of a psychic or medium routinely accompanying the structural engineer and Terminix man on an inspection of every home subject to a contract of sale. It portends [warns] that the prudent attorney will establish an escrow account lest the subject of the transaction come back to haunt him and his client—or pray that his malpractice insurance coverage extends to supernatural disasters. In the interest of avoiding such untenable consequences, the notion that a haunting is a condition which can and should be ascertained upon reasonable inspection of the premises is a hobgoblin which should be exorcised from the body of legal precedent and laid quietly to rest. [Emphasis added.]
* * * *

In the case at bar [under consideration], defendant seller deliberately fostered the public belief that her home was possessed. Having undertaken to inform the public at large, to whom she has no legal relationship, about the supernatural occurrences on her property, she may be said to owe no less a duty to her contract vendee. It has been remarked that the occasional modern cases, which permit a seller to take unfair advantage of a buyer's ignorance so long as he is not actively misled are "singularly unappetizing." Where, as here, the seller not only takes unfair advantage of the buyer's ignorance but has created and perpetuated a condition about which he is unlikely to even inquire, enforcement of the contract (in whole or in part) is offensive to the court's sense of equity. Application of the remedy of rescission, within the bounds of the narrow exception to the doctrine of *caveat emptor* set forth herein, is entirely appropriate to relieve the unwitting purchaser from the consequences of a most unnatural bargain.

**Decision and Remedy** *The New York appellate court found that the doctrine of* caveat emptor *did not apply in this case. The court allowed Stambovsky to rescind the purchase contract and recover the down payment.*

**Critical Thinking**
- **Ethical** *In not disclosing the house's reputation to Stambovsky, was Ackley's behavior unethical? If so, was it unethical because she knew something he did not, or was it unethical because of the nature of the information she omitted? What if Ackley had failed to mention that the roof leaked or that the well was dry—conditions that a buyer would normally investigate? Explain your answer.*
- **Legal Environment** *Why did the court decide that applying the strict rule of* caveat emptor *was inappropriate in this case? How would applying this doctrine increase costs for the purchaser?*

## 28–3b Deeds

Possession and title to land are passed from person to person by means of a **deed**—the instrument used to transfer real property. Deeds must meet certain requirements, but unlike a contract, a deed does not have to be supported by legally sufficient consideration. Gifts of real property are common, and they require deeds even though there is no consideration for the gift.

To be valid, a deed must include the following:

1. The names of the grantor (the giver or seller) and the grantee (the donee or buyer).
2. Words evidencing the intent to convey (for instance, "I hereby bargain, sell, grant, or give"). No specific words are necessary. If the deed does not specify the type of estate being transferred, it presumptively transfers the property in fee simple absolute.
3. A legally sufficient description of the land. The description must include enough detail to distinguish the property being conveyed from every other parcel of land. The property can be identified by reference to an official survey or recorded plat map, or each boundary can be described by metes and bounds. **Metes and bounds** is a system of measuring boundary lines by the distance between two points, often using physical features of the local geography. A property description might say, for instance, "beginning at the southwesterly intersection of Court and Main Streets, then West 40 feet to the fence, then South 100 feet, then Northeast approximately 120 feet back to the beginning."
4. The grantor's (and usually his or her spouse's) signature.
5. Delivery of the deed.

Different types of deeds provide different degrees of protection against defects of title, as discussed next.

**Warranty Deeds** A **warranty deed** contains the greatest number of warranties and thus provides the most extensive protection against defects of title. In most states, special language is required to create a general warranty deed. Warranty deeds commonly include the following covenants:

1. A covenant that the grantor has the title to, and the power to convey, the property.
2. A covenant of quiet enjoyment (a warranty that the buyer will not be disturbed in her or his possession of the land).
3. A covenant that transfer of the property is made without knowledge of adverse claims of third parties.

Generally, the warranty deed makes the grantor liable for all defects of title during the time that the property was held by the grantor and previous titleholders. ■ **EXAMPLE 28.15** Sanchez sells a two-acre lot and office building by warranty deed to Fast Tech, LLC. Subsequently, Amy shows that she has better title than Sanchez had and evicts Fast Tech. Here, Fast Tech can sue Sanchez for breaching the covenant of quiet enjoyment. Fast Tech can recover the purchase price of the land, plus any other damages incurred as a result. ■

**Special Warranty Deed** A **special warranty deed,** or *limited warranty deed,* in contrast, warrants only that the grantor or seller held good title during his or her ownership of the property. In other words, the seller does not guarantee that there are no adverse claims by third parties against any previous owners of the property.

If the special warranty deed discloses all liens or other encumbrances, the seller will not be liable to the buyer if a third person subsequently interferes with the buyer's ownership. If the third person's claim arises out of, or is related to, some act of the seller, however, the seller will be liable to the buyer for damages.

**Quitclaim Deed** A **quitclaim deed** offers the least protection against defects in the title. Basically, a quitclaim deed conveys to the grantee whatever interest the grantor had. If the grantor had no interest, then the grantee receives no interest. (Naturally, if the grantor had a defective title or no title at all, a conveyance by warranty deed or special warranty deed would not cure the defect. Such a deed, however, would give the buyer a cause of action to sue the seller.)

Quitclaim deeds are often used when the seller, or grantor, is uncertain as to the extent of his or her rights in the property. They may also be used to release a party's interest in a particular parcel of property. This may be necessary, for instance, in divorce settlements or business dissolutions when the grantors are dividing up their interests in real property.

**Grant Deed** With a **grant deed,** the grantor simply states, "I grant the property to you" or "I convey, or bargain and sell, the property to you." By state statute, grant deeds carry with them an implied warranty that the grantor owns the property and has not previously transferred it to someone else or encumbered it, except as set out in the deed.

## 28–3c Recording Statutes

Once the seller delivers the deed to the buyer (at closing), legal title to the property is conveyed. Nevertheless, the buyer should promptly record the deed with the state records office. Every state has a **recording statute,** which allows deeds to be recorded in the public record for a fee. Deeds generally are recorded in the county in which the property is located. Many state statutes require that the grantor sign the deed in the presence of two witnesses before it can be recorded.

Recording a deed gives notice to the public that a certain person is now the owner of a particular parcel of real estate. By putting everyone on notice as to the true owner, recording a deed prevents the previous owners from fraudulently conveying the land to other purchasers.

## 28–3d Adverse Possession

A person who wrongfully possesses the real property of another (by occupying or using the property) may eventually acquire title to it through adverse possession. **Adverse possession** is a means of obtaining title to land without delivery of a deed and without the consent of—or payment to—the true owner. Thus, adverse possession is a method of *involuntarily* transferring title to the property from the true owner to the adverse possessor.

Essentially, when one person possesses the real property of another for a certain statutory period of time, that person acquires title to the land. The statutory period varies from three to thirty years, depending on the state, with ten years being most common.

**Requirements for Adverse Possession**  For property to be held adversely, four elements must be satisfied:

1. *Possession must be actual and exclusive.* The possessor must physically occupy the property. This requirement is clearly met if the possessor lives on the property, but it may also be met if the possessor builds fences, erects structures, plants crops, or even grazes animals on the land.

2. *The possession must be open, visible, and notorious, not secret or clandestine.* The possessor must occupy the land for all the world to see. This requirement ensures that the true owner is on notice that someone is possessing the owner's property wrongfully.

3. *Possession must be continuous and peaceable for the required period of time.* This requirement means that the possessor must not be interrupted in the occupancy by the true owner or by the courts. Continuous does not mean constant. It simply means that the possessor has continuously occupied the property in some fashion for the statutory time. Peaceable means that no force was used to possess the land.

4. *Possession must be hostile and adverse.* In other words, the possessor cannot be living on the property with the owner's permission and must claim the property as against the whole world.

■ **CASE IN POINT 28.16**  Charles Scarborough and Mildred Rollins were adjoining landowners, sharing one common boundary. Based on Rollins's survey of the property, Rollins believed that she owned a portion of a gravel road located to the south of the apartment buildings she owned. In contrast, Scarborough believed that the gravel road was located totally on his property and that he owned some property north of the gravel road toward Rollins's apartment buildings.

Scarborough filed a complaint seeking a court order stating that he had title to the property and was its sole owner. The court, however, ruled that Rollins owned a portion of the gravel road by adverse possession. She had used it openly for more than thirty-five years, it was generally thought to be part of her apartment complex, and she had paid taxes on it.[8] ■

The following case raises the question of whether a landowner next to a rail line can acquire a portion of the right-of-way by adverse possession.

---

8. *Scarborough v. Rollins,* 44 So.3d 381 (Miss.App. 2010).

**Case Analysis 28.3**

# Montgomery County v. Bhatt

Court of Appeals of Maryland, 446 Md. 79, 130 A.3d 424 (2016).

### In the Language of the Court
Glenn T. HARRELL, Jr., J. [Judge]

Driving that train, high on cocaine,
Casey Jones you better watch your speed.
Trouble ahead, trouble behind,

And you know that notion just
crossed my mind.

—The Grateful Dead, *Casey Jones,* on
Workingman's Dead (Warner Bros.
Records 1970).

Although the
record of the present case does not
reflect a comparable level of drama as
captured by the refrain of "Casey Jones,"

it hints at plenty of potential trouble, both ahead and behind, for a pair of public works projects (one in place and the other incipient [in development]) cherished by the government and some citizens of Montgomery County.

The Capital Crescent Trail is a well-known hiker/biker route that runs between Georgetown in the District of Columbia and Silver Spring, Maryland. Its path was used formerly as the Georgetown Branch of the Baltimore & Ohio (B&O) Railroad. After the trains stopped running in 1985, the property was transferred in 1988 to the government of Montgomery County, Maryland, via a quitclaim deed for a consideration of $10 million. It is planned that the Maryland portion of the former rail line (and current interim hiker/biker trail) will become the proposed Purple Line, a commuter light rail project.

BACKGROUND
* * * Ajay Bhatt owns 3313 Coquelin Terrace (a subdivided, single-family residential lot—"Lot 8"—improved by a dwelling) in Chevy Chase, Montgomery County, Maryland. He purchased this property in 2006 from his aunt, who owned the property since at least the 1970s. The lot abuts the Georgetown Branch of the B&O Railroad/Capital Crescent Trail. In 1890, the right-of-way that was the rail line (and is today the hiker/biker trail) was conveyed in a fee-simple deed from George Dunlop, grantor, to the Metropolitan Southern Railroad Company ("the Railroad"), grantee.

The right-of-way was obtained by the County * * * from the Railroad pursuant to the federal Rails-to-Trails Act. [Federal regulations] allow the County to preserve the land as a hiker/biker trail until the County chooses whether and when to restore a form of rail service within the right-of-way.

On 18 October 2013, Montgomery County issued to Bhatt a civil citation asserting a violation of Section 49-10(b) of the Montgomery County Code, which prohibits a property owner from

erecting or placing "any structure, fence, post, rock, or other object in a public right-of-way." The * * * claimed violation was the placement and maintenance by Bhatt's predecessors-in-interest of Lot 8 of a fence and shed within the former rail line (and current hiker/biker trail) right-of-way, without a permit. * * * The District Court of Maryland, sitting in Montgomery County, * * * found Bhatt guilty * * * and ordered him to remove the fence and shed encroaching upon the County's right-of-way.

The appeal was heard *de novo* by the [Maryland] Circuit Court. [When a court hears a case *de novo*, it decides the issues without reference to the legal conclusions or assumptions made by the previous court.]
* * * *

Bhatt's defense to the charged violation of Section 28–10(b) was that he owned the encroached-upon land by adverse possession.

Bhatt argued that, because the fence had been located beyond the property line of Lot 8 since at least 1963, the Railroad was obliged to take action to remove it prior to the maturation of the twenty-year period for adverse possession.

* * * The Circuit Court vacated the District Court's judgment and dismissed the violation citation. * * * The Circuit Court concluded ultimately that Bhatt had a creditable claim for adverse possession.

The County petitioned this Court for a writ of *certiorari.* * * * We granted the Petition.
* * * *

DISCUSSION
I. Contentions
* * * The County contends * * * that, because this Court has considered previously a railroad line to be analogous to a public highway for most purposes, the land in question is not subject to an adverse possession claim.

* * * Bhatt rejects the public highway-railroad line analogy because the land was in private, not public, use during its operation as a rail line.

II. Analysis

a. Railroads as Public Highways
A railroad is in many essential respects a public highway, and the rules of law applicable to one are generally applicable to the other. Railroads are owned frequently by private corporations, but this has never been considered a matter of any importance * * * because the function performed is that of the State. Railroad companies operate as a public use and are not viewed strictly as private corporations since they are publicly regulated common carriers. *Essentially, a railroad is a highway dedicated to the public use.* [Emphasis added.]
* * * *

b. May a public highway (or any portion of its right-of-way, no matter the type of real property interest by which it is held) be possessed adversely by an abutting private citizen?
* * * *Nothing is more solidly established than the rule that title to property held by a municipal corporation in its governmental capacity, for a public use, cannot be acquired by adverse possession.* [Emphasis added.]
* * * *

* * * Because time does not run against the state, or the public, * * * public highways are not subject to a claim for adverse possession, except in the limited circumstances of a clear abandonment by the State. By parity [equivalence] of reasoning applied to the present case, railway lines [are] also not * * * subject to a claim for adverse possession, without evidence of clear abandonment or a clear shift away from public use.

c. Use of the right-of-way
* * * We do not find in this record, however, that there is any evidence of abandonment by the rail line operator (or Montgomery County) or that the right-of-way was taken out of public use such that a claim for adverse possession could ripen within this right-of-way.
* * * *

The 1890 Dunlop Deed shows that the purchase made by the Railroad was from a private landowner. There was no evidence adduced [offered] by Bhatt supporting a conclusion that the right-of-way was abandoned and was not being used by the public, even during the period from 1985 when the freight service ended and 1988 when the property was conveyed to the County and became a hiker/biker trail as an interim public use.

* * * *

Because no evidence was presented by Bhatt to show that the current use of the right-of-way by Montgomery County is unreasonable or that the Railroad or the County abandoned the right-of-way, no claim for adverse possession will lie. Accordingly, we shall reverse the judgment of the Circuit Court. Bhatt's fence and shed encroached upon the right-of-way in violation of Montgomery

County Code Section 28–10(b). The District Court got it right.

JUDGMENT OF THE CIRCUIT COURT FOR MONTGOMERY COUNTY REVERSED. CASE REMANDED TO THAT COURT WITH INSTRUCTIONS TO AFFIRM THE JUDGMENT OF THE DISTRICT COURT OF MARYLAND, SITTING IN MONTGOMERY COUNTY.

**Legal Reasoning Questions**

1. Bhatt claimed to have met all of the requirements to acquire a strip of public land through adverse possession. Which element did the court find had *not* been met? Why?

2. What is the "potential trouble, both ahead and behind, for a pair of public works projects" hinted at in this case? In whose favor is that "trouble" likely to be resolved?

3. Should a private party, by encroaching on a public right-of-way, be able to acquire title adverse to the public rights? Discuss.

---

**Purpose of the Doctrine** There are a number of public-policy reasons for the adverse possession doctrine. These include society's interest in resolving boundary disputes, in determining title when title to property is in question, and in assuring that real property remains in the stream of commerce. More fundamentally, the doctrine punishes owners who do not take action when they see adverse possession and rewards possessors for putting land to productive use.

---

# 28–4 Limitations on the Rights of Property Owners

No ownership rights in real property can ever really be absolute—that is, an owner of real property cannot always do whatever she or he wishes on or with the property. Nuisance and environmental laws, for instance, restrict certain types of activities. Property ownership is also conditional on the payment of property taxes. Zoning laws and building permits frequently restrict the use of realty. In addition, if a property owner fails to pay debts, the property may be seized to satisfy judgment creditors. In short, the rights of every property owner are subject to certain conditions and limitations.

## 28–4a Eminent Domain

Even ownership in fee simple absolute is limited by a superior ownership. Just as the king was the ultimate landowner in medieval England, today the government has an ultimate ownership right in all land in the United States. This right, known as **eminent domain,** is sometimes referred to as the *condemnation power* of government to take land for public use. It gives the government the right to acquire possession of real property in the manner directed by the U.S. Constitution and the laws of the state whenever the public interest requires it.

The power of eminent domain generally is invoked through **condemnation** proceedings. ■ **EXAMPLE 28.17** When a new public highway is to be built, the government decides where to build it and how much land to condemn. After the government determines that a particular parcel of land is necessary for the highway, it will first offer to buy the property. If the owner refuses the offer, the government brings a judicial (*condemnation*) proceeding to obtain title to the land. ■

Condemnation proceedings usually involve two distinct phases. The first seeks to establish the government's right to take the property, and the second determines the fair value of the property.

**The Taking** When the government takes land owned by a private party for public use, it is referred to as a **taking.** Under the *takings clause* of the Fifth Amendment to the U.S. Constitution, the government may take private property for public use, but it must pay "just compensation" to the owner. State constitutions contain similar provisions. In the first phase of condemnation proceedings, the government must prove that it needs to acquire privately owned property for a public use.

■ **EXAMPLE 28.18**  Franklin County, Iowa, engages Bosque Systems to build a liquefied natural gas pipeline that crosses the property of more than two hundred landowners. Some property owners consent to this use and accept the Bosque's offer of compensation. Others refuse the offer. A court will likely deem the pipeline to be a public use. Therefore, the government can exert its eminent domain power to "take" the land, provided that it pays just compensation to the property owners. ■

**The Compensation**  The U.S. Constitution and state constitutions require that the government pay just compensation to the landowner when invoking its condemnation power. Just compensation means fair value. In the second phase of the condemnation proceeding, the court determines the fair value of the land, which usually is approximately equal to its market value.

Property may be taken by the government only for public use, not for private benefit. But can eminent domain be used to promote private development when the development is deemed to be in the public interest? See this chapter's *Ethics Today* for a discussion of this issue.

## 28–4b Inverse Condemnation

Typically, a government agency exercises the power of eminent domain in the manner just discussed. **Inverse condemnation,** in contrast, occurs when a government simply takes private property from a landowner without paying any compensation, thereby forcing the landowner to sue the government for compensation.

The taking can be physical, as when a government agency uses or occupies the land, or it may be constructive, as when an agency regulation results in loss of property value. The United States Supreme Court has held that even temporary flooding of land by the government may result in liability under the takings clause.[9]

■ **CASE IN POINT 28.19**  In Walton County, Florida, water flows through a ditch from Oyster Lake to the Gulf of Mexico. When Hurricane Opal caused the water to rise in Oyster Lake, Walton County reconfigured the drainage to divert the overflow onto the nearby property of William and Patricia Hemby. The flow was eventually

---

9. *Arkansas Game and Fish Commission v. United States*, ___ U.S. ___, 133 S.Ct. 511, 184 L.Ed.2d 417 (2012).

---

## ETHICS TODAY

### Should Eminent Domain Be Used to Promote Private Development?

Issues of fairness often arise when the government takes private property for public use. One issue is whether it is fair for a government to take property by eminent domain and then convey it to private developers.

For instance, suppose a city government decides that it is in the public interest to have a larger parking lot for a local, privately owned sports stadium. Or suppose it decides that its citizens would benefit from having a manufacturing plant locate in the city to create more jobs. The government may condemn certain tracts of existing housing or business property and then convey the land to the privately owned stadium or manufacturing plant.

Such actions may bring in private developers and businesses that provide jobs and increase tax revenues, thus revitalizing communities. But is the land really being taken for "public use," as required by the Fifth Amendment to the U.S. Constitution?

**The Supreme Court's Ruling**

In 2005, the United States Supreme Court ruled that the power of eminent domain may be used to further

economic development.[a] At the same time, the Court recognized that individual states have the right to pass laws that prohibit takings for economic development.

**The States' Responses**

Since then, the vast majority of the states have passed laws to curb the government's ability to take private property and subsequently give it to private developers. Nevertheless, loopholes in some state legislation still allow takings for redevelopment of slum areas. Thus, the debate over whether (and when) it is fair for the government to take citizens' property for economic development continues.

**Critical Thinking**  *At what point might the predicted benefits of a new private commercial endeavor outweigh the constitutional requirement of a taking only for public use?*

---

a. *Kelo v. City of New London, Connecticut*, 545 U.S. 469, 125 S.Ct. 2655, 162 L.Ed.2d 439 (2005).

restored to pre-hurricane conditions, but during a later emergency, water was diverted onto the Hembys' property again. This diversion was not restored.

The Hembys filed a suit against the county. After their deaths, their daughter Cozette Drake pursued the claim. The court found that by allowing the water diversion to remain on Drake's property long after the emergency had passed, the county had engaged in a permanent or continuous physical invasion. This invasion rendered Drake's property useless and deprived her of its beneficial enjoyment. Drake was therefore entitled to receive compensation from the county.[10] ■

### 28–4c Restrictive Covenants

A private restriction on the use of land is known as a **restrictive covenant.** If the restriction is binding on the party who initially purchases the property and on subsequent purchasers as well, it is said to "run with the land." A covenant running with the land must be in writing (usually it is in the deed), and subsequent purchasers must have reason to know about it.

■ **EXAMPLE 28.20** In the course of developing a fifty-lot suburban subdivision, Levitt records a declaration of restrictions effectively limiting construction on each lot to one single-family house. Each lot's deed includes a reference to the declaration with a provision that the purchaser and her or his successors are bound to those restrictions. Thus, each purchaser assumes ownership with notice of the restrictions. If an owner attempts to build a duplex (or any noncompliant structure) on a lot, the other owners may obtain a court order to prevent the construction.

Alternatively, Levitt might simply have included the restrictions on the subdivision's map, filed the map in the appropriate public office, and included a reference to the map in each deed. Under these circumstances, each owner would still have been held to have constructive notice of the restrictions. ■

## 28–5 Zoning and Government Regulations

The rules and regulations that collectively manage the development and use of land are known as **zoning laws.** Zoning laws were first used in the United States to segregate slaughterhouses, distilleries, kilns, and other businesses that might pose a nuisance to nearby residences.

The growth of modern urban areas led to an increased need to organize uses of land. Today, zoning laws enable municipalities to control the speed and type of development within their borders by creating different zones and regulating the use of property allowed in each zone.

The United States Supreme Court has held that zoning is a constitutional exercise of a government's police powers.[11] Therefore, as long as zoning ordinances are rationally related to the health, safety, or welfare of the community, a municipal government has broad discretion to carry out zoning as it sees fit.

### 28–5a Purpose and Scope of Zoning Laws

The purpose of zoning laws is to manage the land within a community in a way that encourages sustainable and organized development while controlling growth in a manner that serves the interests of the community. One of the basic elements of zoning is the classification of land by permissible use, but zoning extends to other aspects of land use as well.

**Permissible Uses of Land** Municipalities generally divide their available land into districts according to the land's present and potential future uses. Typically, land is classified into the following types of permissible uses:

1. *Residential.* In areas dedicated for **residential use,** landowners can construct buildings for human habitation.
2. *Commercial.* Land assigned for business activities is designated as being for **commercial use,** sometimes called business use. An area with a number of retail stores, offices, supermarkets, and hotels might be designated as a commercial or business district. Land used for entertainment purposes, such as movie theaters and sports stadiums, also falls into this category, as does land used for government activities.
3. *Industrial.* Areas designated for **industrial use** typically encompass light and heavy manufacturing, shipping, and heavy transportation. For instance, undeveloped land with easy access to highways and railroads might be classified as suitable for future use by industry. Although industrial uses can be profitable for a city seeking to raise tax revenue, such uses can also result in noise, smoke, or vibrations that interfere with others' enjoyment of their property. Consequently, areas zoned for industrial use generally are kept as far as possible from residential districts and some commercial districts.

---

10. *Drake v. Walton County,* 6 So.3d 717 (Fla.App. 2009).

11. *Village of Euclid v. Ambler Realty Co.,* 272 U.S. 365, 47 S.Ct. 114, 71 L.Ed. 303 (1926).

**4.** *Conservation districts.* Some municipalities also establish certain areas that are dedicated to carrying out local soil and water conservation efforts. For instance, wetlands might be designated as a conservation district.

A city's residential, commercial, and industrial districts may be divided, in turn, into subdistricts. For instance, zoning ordinances may regulate the type, density, size, and approved uses of structures within a given district. Thus, a residential district may be divided into low-density (single-family homes with large lots), high-density (single- and multiple-family homes with small lots), and planned-unit (condominiums or apartments) subdistricts.

**Other Zoning Restrictions** Zoning rules extend to much more than the permissible use of land. In residential districts, for instance, an ordinance may require a house or garage to be set back a specific number of feet from a neighbor's property line.

In commercial districts, zoning rules may attempt to maintain a certain visual aesthetic. Therefore, businesses may be required to construct buildings of a certain height and width so that they conform to the style of other commercial buildings in the area.

Businesses may also be required to provide parking for patrons or take other measures to manage traffic. Sometimes, municipalities limit construction of new businesses to prevent traffic congestion.

Zoning laws may even attempt to regulate the public morals of the community. For instance, cities commonly impose severe restrictions on the location and operation of adult businesses and medical (or recreational) marijuana dispensaries.

## 28–5b  Exceptions to Zoning Laws

Zoning restrictions are not absolute. It is impossible for zoning laws to account for every contingency. The purpose of zoning is to control development, not to prevent it altogether or to limit the government's ability to adapt to changing circumstances or unforeseen needs. Hence, legal processes have been developed to allow for exceptions to zoning laws, such as *variances* and *special-use permits*.

**Variances** A property owner who wants to use his or her land in a manner not permitted by zoning rules can request a **variance,** which allows an exception to the rules. The property owner making the request must demonstrate that the requested variance:

**1.** Is necessary for reasonable development.
**2.** Is the least intrusive solution to the problem.
**3.** Will not alter the essential character of the neighborhood.

**Hardship Situations.** Property owners normally request variances in *hardship situations*—that is, when complying with the zoning rules would be too difficult or costly due to existing property conditions. ■ **EXAMPLE 28.21** Lin, a homeowner, wants to replace her single-car garage with a two-car garage. If she does so, however, the garage will be closer to her neighbor's property than is permitted by the zoning rules. In this situation, she may ask for a variance. She can claim that the configuration of her property would make it difficult and costly to comply with the zoning code, so compliance would create a hardship for her. ■

Similarly, a church might request a variance from height restrictions in order to erect a new steeple. Or a furniture store might ask for a variance from *footprint* limitations so that it can expand its showroom. (A building's footprint is the area of ground that it covers.)

Note that the hardship may not be self-created. In other words, a person who buys property with zoning restrictions in effect cannot usually then argue that he or she needs a variance in order to use the property as intended.

**Public Hearing.** In almost all instances, before a variance is granted, there must be a public hearing with adequate notice to neighbors who may object to the exception. After the public hearing, a hearing examiner appointed by the municipality (or the local zoning board or commission) determines whether to grant the exception. When a variance is granted, it applies only to the specific parcel of land for which it was requested and does not create a regulation-free zone.

**Special-Use Permits** Sometimes, zoning laws permit a certain use only if the property owner complies with specific requirements to ensure that the proposed use does not harm the immediate neighborhood. In such instances, the zoning board can issue **special-use permits,** also called conditional-use permits.

■ **EXAMPLE 28.22** An area is designated as a residential district, but small businesses are permitted to operate there so long as they do not affect the characteristics of the neighborhood. A bank asks the zoning board for a special-use permit to open a branch in the area. At the public hearing, the bank demonstrates that the branch will be housed in a building that conforms to the style of other structures in the area. The bank also shows that adequate parking will be available and that landscaping will shield the parking lot from public view. Unless there are strong objections from the branch's prospective neighbors, the board will likely grant the permit. ■

**Special Incentives** In addition to granting exceptions to zoning regulations, municipalities may also wish to encourage certain kinds of development. To do so, they offer incentives, often in the form of lower tax rates or tax credits. For instance, to attract new businesses that will provide jobs and increase the tax base, a city may offer lower property tax rates for a period of years. Similarly, homeowners may receive tax credits for historic preservation if they renovate and maintain older homes.

# 28–6 Landlord-Tenant Relationships

A landlord-tenant relationship is established by a lease contract. A **lease** contract arises when a property owner (landlord) agrees to give another party (the tenant) the exclusive right to possess the property for a limited time. In most states, statutes require leases for terms exceeding one year to be in writing. The lease should describe the property and indicate the length of the term, the amount of the rent, and how and when it is to be paid.

State or local law often dictates permissible lease terms. For instance, a statute or ordinance might prohibit the leasing of a structure that is in a certain physical condition or is not in compliance with local building codes. As in other areas of law, the National Conference of Commissioners on Uniform State Laws has issued a model act to create more uniformity in the law governing landlord-tenant relations. Twenty-one states have adopted variations of the Uniform Residential Landlord and Tenant Act (URLTA).

## 28–6a Rights and Duties

The rights and duties of landlords and tenants generally pertain to four broad areas of concern—the possession, use, maintenance, and, of course, rent of leased property.

**Possession** A landlord is obligated to give a tenant possession of the property that the tenant has agreed to lease. After obtaining possession, the tenant retains the property exclusively until the lease expires, unless the lease states otherwise.

**Quiet Enjoyment.** The covenant of quiet enjoyment mentioned previously also applies to leased premises. Under this covenant, the landlord promises that during the lease term, neither the landlord nor anyone having a superior title to the property will disturb the tenant's use and enjoyment of the property. This covenant forms the essence of the landlord-tenant relationship, and if it is breached, the tenant can terminate the lease and sue for damages.

**Eviction.** If the landlord deprives the tenant of possession of the leased property or interferes with the tenant's use or enjoyment of it, an **eviction** occurs. An eviction occurs, for instance, when the landlord changes the lock and refuses to give the tenant a new key.

A **constructive eviction** occurs when the landlord wrongfully performs or fails to perform any of the duties the lease requires, thereby making the tenant's further use and enjoyment of the property exceedingly difficult or impossible. Examples of constructive eviction include a landlord's failure to provide heat in the winter, light, or other essential utilities.

**Use of the Premises** The tenant normally may make any use of the leased property, provided the use is legal and does not injure the landlord's interest. The parties are free to limit by agreement the uses to which the property may be put. A tenant is not entitled to create a nuisance by substantially interfering with others' quiet enjoyment of their property rights.

**Maintenance of the Premises** The tenant is responsible for any damage to the premises that he or she causes, intentionally or negligently. The landlord can hold the tenant liable for the cost of returning the property to the physical condition it was in at the lease's inception. The tenant usually is not responsible for ordinary wear and tear, and the property's consequent depreciation in value.

In some jurisdictions, landlords of residential property are required by statute to maintain the premises in good repair. Landlords must also comply with applicable state statutes and city ordinances regarding maintenance and repair of commercial buildings.

In addition, the implied warranty of habitability discussed earlier may apply to *residential* leases. The warranty requires a landlord who leases residential property to ensure that the premises are habitable—that is, safe and suitable to live in. Also, the landlord must make repairs to maintain the premises in that condition for the lease's duration. Generally, this warranty applies to major, or *substantial,* physical defects that the landlord knows or should know about and has had a reasonable time to repair. A large hole in the roof, for instance, would be a substantial defect.

■ **EXAMPLE 28.23**   Carol and Ken Galprin own a house within the city limits of Redmond. A city regulation states that a residence must be connected to the city sewer system before anyone, including tenants, can live in the residence. The Galprins' house is not connected to the city system. Thus, it is not legally habitable, and they cannot lease it to tenants. ■

**Rent**   *Rent* is the tenant's payment to the landlord for the tenant's occupancy or use of the landlord's real property. Usually, the tenant must pay the rent even if she or he refuses to occupy the property or moves out for unjustified reasons while the lease is in force.

Under the common law, if the leased premises were destroyed by fire or flood, the tenant still had to pay rent. Today, however, if an apartment building burns down, most states' laws do not require tenants to continue to pay rent.

In some situations, such as when a landlord breaches the implied warranty of habitability, a tenant may be allowed to withhold rent as a remedy. When rent withholding is authorized under a statute, the tenant must usually put the amount withheld into an *escrow account.* The funds are held in the name of the tenant and are returned to the tenant if the landlord fails to make the premises habitable.

## 28-6b  Transferring Rights to Leased Property

Either the landlord or the tenant may wish to transfer her or his rights to the leased property during the term of the lease. If the landlord sells the leased property, the tenant becomes the tenant of the new owner. The new owner may collect subsequent rent but must abide by the terms of the existing lease.

**Assignment**   The tenant's transfer of his or her entire interest in the leased property to a third person is an *assignment of the lease.* Many leases require that an assignment have the landlord's written consent. The landlord can nullify (avoid) an assignment made without the required consent. State statutes may specify that the landlord may not unreasonably withhold consent, however. Also, a landlord who knowingly accepts rent from the assignee may be held to have waived the consent requirement.

When an assignment is valid, the assignee acquires all of the tenant's rights under the lease. An assignment, however, does not release the original tenant (assignor) from the obligation to pay rent if the assignee defaults. Also, if the assignee exercises an option under the original lease to extend the term, the original tenant remains liable for the rent during the extension, unless the landlord agrees otherwise.

**Sublease**   The tenant's transfer of all or part of the premises for a period shorter than the lease term is a **sublease.** The same restrictions that apply to an assignment of the tenant's interest in leased property apply to a sublease. If the landlord's consent is required, a sublease without such permission is ineffective. Also, like an assignment, a sublease does not release the tenant from her or his obligations under the lease.

■ **EXAMPLE 28.24**   Derek, a student, leases an apartment for a two-year period. Although Derek had planned on attending summer school, he decides to accept a job offer in Europe for the summer months instead. Derek therefore obtains his landlord's consent to sublease the apartment to Ava. Ava is bound by the same terms of the lease as Derek, and the landlord can hold Derek liable if Ava violates the lease terms. ■

## 28-6c  Termination of the Lease

Usually, a lease terminates when its term ends. The tenant surrenders the property to the landlord, who retakes possession. If the lease states the time it will end, the landlord is not required to give the tenant notice. The lease terminates automatically.

A lease can also be terminated in several other ways. If the tenant purchases the leased property from the landlord during the term of the lease, for instance, the lease will be terminated. The parties may also agree to end a tenancy before it would otherwise terminate. Finally, the tenant may *abandon* the premises—move out completely with no intention of returning before the lease term expires.

At common law, a tenant who abandoned leased property was still obligated to pay the rent for the full term of the lease. The landlord could let the property stand vacant and charge the tenant for the remainder of the term. This is still the rule in some states. In most states today, however, the landlord has a duty to *mitigate* his or her damages—that is, to make a reasonable attempt to lease the property to another party. Consequently, the tenant's liability for unpaid rent is restricted to the period of time that the landlord would reasonably need to lease the property to another tenant. Damages may also be allowed for the landlord's costs in leasing the property again.

## Reviewing: Real Property and Landlord-Tenant Law

Vern Shoepke purchased a two-story home from Walter and Eliza Bruster in the town of Roche, Maine. The warranty deed did not specify what covenants would be included in the conveyance. The property was adjacent to a public park that included a popular Frisbee golf course. (Frisbee golf is a sport similar to golf but using Frisbees.) Wayakichi Creek ran along the north end of the park and along Shoepke's property. The deed allowed Roche citizens the right to walk across a five-foot-wide section of the lot beside Wayakichi Creek as part of a two-mile public trail system. Teenagers regularly threw Frisbee golf discs from the walking path behind Shoepke's property over his yard to the adjacent park. Shoepke habitually shouted and cursed at the teenagers, demanding that they not throw objects over his yard. Two months after moving into his Roche home, Shoepke leased the second floor to Lauren Slater for nine months. After three months of tenancy, Slater sublet the second floor to a local artist, Javier Indalecio. (The lease agreement did not specify that Shoepke's consent would be required to sublease the second floor.) Over the remaining six months, Indalecio's use of oil paints damaged the carpeting in Shoepke's home. Using the information presented in the chapter, answer the following questions.

1. What is the term for the right of Roche citizens to walk across Shoepke's land on the trail?
2. What covenants would most courts infer were included in the warranty deed that was used in the property transfer from the Brusters to Shoepke?
3. Suppose that Shoepke wants to file a trespass lawsuit against some teenagers who continually throw Frisbees over his land. Shoepke discovers, however, that when the city put in the Frisbee golf course, the neighborhood homeowners signed an agreement that limited their right to complain about errant Frisbees. What is this type of promise or agreement called in real property law?
4. Can Shoepke hold Slater financially responsible for the damage to the carpeting caused by Indalecio? Why or why not?

**Debate This** . . .   *Under no circumstances should a local government be able to condemn property in order to sell it later to real estate developers for private use.*

## Terms and Concepts

| | | |
|---|---|---|
| adverse possession 554 | fixture 544 | periodic tenancy 548 |
| closing 550 | grant deed 553 | prescription 549 |
| commercial use 558 | implication 549 | profit 548 |
| community property 547 | implied warranty of habitability 551 | quitclaim deed 553 |
| concurrent ownership 547 | industrial use 558 | recording statute 554 |
| condemnation 556 | inverse condemnation 557 | residential use 558 |
| constructive eviction 560 | joint tenancy 547 | restrictive covenant 558 |
| conveyance 545 | lease 560 | special-use permit 559 |
| deed 553 | leasehold estate 547 | special warranty deed 553 |
| easement 548 | license 549 | sublease 561 |
| eminent domain 556 | life estate 545 | taking 556 |
| escrow account 551 | marketable title 551 | tenancy at sufferance 548 |
| eviction 560 | metes and bounds 553 | tenancy at will 548 |
| fee simple absolute 545 | necessity 549 | tenancy by the entirety 547 |
| fixed-term tenancy 548 | nonpossessory interest 548 | tenancy in common 547 |

## Issue Spotters

1. Bernie sells his house to Consuela under a warranty deed. Later, Delmira appears, holding a better title to the house than Consuela has. Delmira wants to have Consuela evicted from the property. What can Consuela do? (See *Transfer of Ownership.*)

2. Grey owns a commercial building in fee simple. Grey transfers temporary possession of the building to Haven Corporation. Can Haven transfer possession for even less time to Idyll Company? Explain. (See *Ownership and Other Interests in Real Property.*)

• **Check your answers to the Issue Spotters against the answers provided in Appendix B at the end of this text.**

## Business Scenarios

**28–1. Property Ownership.** Madison owned a tract of land, but he was not sure that he had full title to the property. When Rafael expressed an interest in buying the land, Madison sold it to Rafael and executed a quitclaim deed. Rafael properly recorded the deed immediately. Several months later, Madison learned that he had had full title to the tract of land. He then sold the land to Linda by warranty deed. Linda knew of the earlier purchase by Rafael but took the deed anyway and later sued to have Rafael evicted from the land. Linda claimed that because she had a warranty deed, her title to the land was better than that conferred by Rafael's quitclaim deed. Will Linda succeed in claiming title to the land? Explain. (See *Transfer of Ownership.*)

**28–2. Eviction.** James owns a three-story building. He leases the ground floor to Juan's Mexican restaurant. The lease is to run for a five-year period and contains an express covenant of quiet enjoyment. One year later, James leases the top two stories to the Upbeat Club, a dance club for teens. The club's hours run from 5:00 P.M. to 11:00 P.M. The noise from the Upbeat Club is so loud that it is driving customers away from Juan's restaurant. Juan has notified James of the interference and has called the police on a number of occasions. James refuses to talk to the owners of the Upbeat Club or to do anything to remedy the situation. Juan abandons the premises. James files a suit for breach of the lease agreement and for the rental payments still due under the lease. Juan claims that he was constructively evicted and files a countersuit for damages. Discuss who will be held liable. (See *Landlord-Tenant Relationships.*)

## Business Case Problems

**28–3. Commercial Lease Terms.** Gi Hwa Park entered into a lease with Landmark HHH, LLC, for retail space in the Plaza at Landmark, a shopping center in Virginia. The lease required the landlord to keep the roof "in good repair" and the tenant to obtain insurance on her inventory and absolve the landlord from any losses to the extent of the insurance proceeds. Park opened a store—The Four Seasons—in the space, specializing in imported men's suits and accessories. Within a month and continuing for nearly eight years, water intermittently leaked through the roof, causing damage. Landmark eventually had a new roof installed, but water continued to leak into The Four Seasons. On a night of record rainfall, the store suffered substantial water damage, and Park was forced to close. On what basis might Park seek to recover from Landmark? What might Landmark assert in response? Which party's argument is more likely to succeed, and why? [*Landmark HHH, LLC v. Gi Hwa Park,* 277 Va. 50, 671 S.E.2d 143 (2009)] (See *Landlord-Tenant Relationships.*)

**28–4. Business Case Problem with Sample Answer— Adverse Possession.**  The McKeag family operated a marina on their lakefront property in Bolton, New York. For more than forty years, the McKeags used a section of property belonging to their neighbors, the Finleys, as a beach for the marina's customers. The McKeags also stored a large float on the beach during the winter months, built their own retaining wall, and planted bushes and flowers there. The McKeags prevented others from using the property, including the Finleys. Nevertheless, the families always had a friendly relationship, and one of the Finleys gave the McKeags permission to continue using the beach in 1992. He also reminded them of his ownership several times, to which they said nothing. The McKeags also asked for permission to mow grass on the property and once apologized for leaving a jet ski there. Can the McKeags establish adverse possession over the statutory period of ten years? Why or why not? [*McKeag v. Finley,* 939 N.Y.S.2d 644 (N.Y.App.Div. 2012)] (See *Transfer of Ownership.*)

• For a sample answer to Problem 28–4, go to Appendix C at the end of this text.

**28–5. Rent.** Flawlace, LLC, leased unfinished commercial real estate in Las Vegas, Nevada, from Francis Lin to operate a beauty salon. The lease required Flawlace to obtain a "certificate of occupancy" from the city to commence business. This required the installation of a fire protection system. The lease did not allocate responsibility for the installation to either party. Lin voluntarily undertook to install the system. After a month of delays, Flawlace moved out. Three months later, the installation was complete, and Lin leased the premises to a new tenant. Did Flawlace owe rent for the three months between the time that it moved out and the time that the new tenant moved in? Explain. [*Tri-Lin Holdings, LLC v. Flawlace, LLC,* 2014 WL 1101577 (Nev.Sup.Ct. 2014)] (See *Landlord-Tenant Relationships.*)

**28–6. Landlord-Tenant Relationships.** Bhanmattie Kumar was walking on a sidewalk in Flushing, New York, when she tripped over a chipped portion of the sidewalk and fell. The defective sidewalk was in front of a Pretty Girl store—one of a chain of apparel stores headquartered in Brooklyn—on premises leased from PI Associates, LLC. Kumar filed a claim in a New York state court against PI, seeking to recover damages for her injuries. PI filed a cross-claim against Pretty Girl. On what basis would the court impose liability on PI? In what situation would Pretty Girl be the liable party? Is there any circumstance in which Kumar could be at least partially responsible for her injury? Discuss. [*Bhanmattie Rajkumar Kumar v. PI Associates, LLC,* 125 A.D.3d 609, 3 N.Y.S.3d 372 (2 Dept. 2015)] (See *Landlord-Tenant Relationships.*)

**28–7. Ownership and Other Interests in Real Property.** Arthur and Diana Ebanks owned three properties in the Cayman Islands in joint tenancy. With respect to joint tenancies, Cayman law is the same as U.S. law. When the Ebanks

divorced, the decree did not change the tenancy in which the properties were held. On the same day as the divorce filing, Arthur executed a will providing that "any property in my name and that of another as joint tenants . . . will pass to the survivor, and I instruct my Personal Representative to make no claim thereto." Four years later, Arthur died. His brother Curtis, the personal representative of his estate, asserted that Arthur's interest in the Cayman properties was part of the estate. Diana said that the sole interest in the properties was hers. Who do the Cayman properties belong to? Why? [*Ebanks v. Ebanks,* 41 Fla. L. Weekly D291, __ So.3d __ (2 Dist. 2016)] (See *Ownership and Other Interests in Real Property.*)

**28–8. Special Case Analysis—Adverse Possession.** Go to Case Analysis 28.3, *Montgomery County v. Bhatt.* Read the excerpt, and answer the following questions.

**(a) Issue:** What conflict, and between which parties, did this case highlight?

**(b) Rule of Law:** On which specific requirement of what rule of law did the outcome in this case depend?

**(c) Applying the Rule of Law:** What exception to the applied rule of law might have resulted in a decision in the plaintiff's favor? Why did that exception not apply in this case?

**(d) Conclusion:** In light of the rule of law applied in this case, what was the judgment?

**28–9. A Question of Ethics—Adverse Possession.**
 Alana Mansell built a garage on her property that encroached on the property of her neighbor, Betty Hunter, by fourteen feet. Hunter knew of the encroachment and informally agreed to it, but she did not transfer ownership of the property to Mansell. A survey twenty-eight years later confirmed the encroachment, and Hunter sought the removal of the garage. Mansell asked a court to declare that she was the owner of the property by adverse possession. [Hunter v. Mansell, *240 P.3d 469 (Colo.App. 2010)] (See Transfer of Ownership.)

**(a)** Did Mansell obtain title by adverse possession? Would the open occupation of the property for nearly thirty years be in Mansell's favor? Why or why not?

**(b)** Was Mansell's conduct in any way unethical? Discuss.

# Legal Reasoning Group Activity

**28–10. Adverse Possession.** The Wallen family owned a cabin on Lummi Island in the state of Washington. A driveway ran from the cabin across their property to South Nugent Road. Floyd Massey bought the adjacent lot and built a cabin on it in 1980. To gain access to his property, Massey used a bulldozer to extend the driveway, without

the Wallens' permission but also without their objection. In 2005, the Wallens sold their property to Wright Fish Company. Massey continued to use and maintain the driveway without permission or objection. In 2011, Massey sold his property to Robert Drake. Drake and his employees continued to use and maintain the driveway without permission or objection, although Drake knew it was located largely on Wright's property. In 2013, Wright sold its lot to Robert Smersh. The next year, Smersh told Drake to stop using the driveway. Drake filed a suit against Smersh, claiming an easement by prescription (which is created by meeting the same requirements as adverse possession). (See *Transfer of Ownership*.)

**(a)** The first group will decide whether Drake's use of the driveway meets all of the requirements for adverse possession (easement by prescription).

**(b)** The second group will determine how the court should rule in this case and why. Does it matter that Drake knew the driveway was located largely on Wright's (and then Smersh's) property? Should it matter? Why or why not?

**(c)** A third group will evaluate the underlying policy and fairness of adverse possession laws. Should the law reward persons who take possession of someone else's land for their own use? Does it make sense to punish owners who allow someone else to use their land without complaint? Explain.

# CHAPTER 29

# Intellectual Property

**I**ntellectual property is any property that results from intellectual, creative processes—the products of an individual's mind. Although it is an abstract term for an abstract concept, intellectual property is nonetheless familiar to almost everyone. The apps for your iPhone, iPad, or Samsung Galaxy, the movies you see, and the music you listen to are all forms of intellectual property.

More than two hundred years ago, the framers of the U.S. Constitution recognized the importance of protecting creative works in Article I, Section 8. Statutory protection of these rights began in the 1940s and continues to evolve to meet the needs of modern society. In today's global economy, however, protecting intellectual property in one country is no longer sufficient. The United States is participating in various international agreements to secure ownership rights in intellectual property in other countries.

Whether locally or globally, businesspersons have a vital need to protect their rights in intellectual property, which may be more valuable than their physical property, such as machines and buildings. Consider, for instance, the importance of intellectual property rights to technology companies, such as Apple, Inc., and Samsung. These two companies have been involved in patent litigation over the designs of their smartphones for several years.

## 29–1 Trademarks and Related Property

A **trademark** is a distinctive mark, motto, device, or implement that a manufacturer stamps, prints, or otherwise affixes to the goods it produces so that they can be identified on the market and their origins made known. In other words, a trademark is a source indicator. At common law, the person who used a symbol or mark to identify a business or product was protected in the use of that trademark. Clearly, by using another's trademark, a business could lead consumers to believe that its goods were made by the other business. The law seeks to avoid this kind of confusion.

In the following classic case, the defendants argued that the Coca-Cola trademark was entitled to no protection under the law because the term did not accurately represent the product.

## The Coca-Cola Co. v. The Koke Co. of America
Supreme Court of the United States, 254 U.S. 143, 41 S.Ct. 113, 65 L.Ed.189 (1920).

**Company Profile** *John Pemberton, an Atlanta pharmacist, invented a caramel-colored, carbonated soft drink in 1886. His bookkeeper, Frank Robinson, named the beverage Coca-Cola after two of the ingredients, coca leaves and kola nuts. Asa Candler bought the Coca-Cola Company in 1891, and within seven years, he had made the soft drink available throughout the United States, as well as in parts of Canada and Mexico. Candler continued to sell Coke aggressively and to open up new markets, reaching Europe before 1910. In doing so, however, he attracted numerous competitors, some of which tried to capitalize directly on the Coke name.*

**Background and Facts**   The Coca-Cola Company sought to enjoin (prevent) the Koke Company of America and other beverage companies from, among other things, using the word *Koke* for their products. The Koke Company of America and other beverage companies contended that the Coca-Cola trademark was a fraudulent representation and that Coca-Cola was therefore not entitled to any help from the courts. The Koke Company and the other defendants alleged that the Coca-Cola Company, by its use of the Coca-Cola name, represented that the beverage contained cocaine (from coca leaves), which it no longer did. The trial court granted the injunction against the Koke Company, but the appellate court reversed the lower court's ruling. Coca-Cola then appealed to the United States Supreme Court.

## In the Language of the Court

Mr. Justice *HOLMES* delivered the opinion of the Court.

* * * *

* * * Before 1900 the beginning of [Coca-Cola's] good will was more or less helped by the presence of cocaine, a drug that, like alcohol or caffeine or opium, may be described as a deadly poison or as a valuable [pharmaceutical item, depending on the speaker's purposes]. The amount seems to have been very small,[a] but it may have been enough to begin a bad habit and after the Food and Drug Act of June 30, 1906, if not earlier, long before this suit was brought, it was eliminated from the plaintiff's compound.

* * * Since 1900 the sales have increased at a very great rate corresponding to a like increase in advertising. The name now characterizes a beverage to be had at almost any soda fountain. It means a single thing coming from a single source, and well known to the community. It hardly would be too much to say that the drink characterizes the name as much as the name the drink. In other words *Coca-Cola probably means to most persons the plaintiff's familiar product to be had everywhere rather than a compound of particular substances.* * * * Before this suit was brought the plaintiff had advertised to the public that it must not expect and would not find cocaine, and had eliminated everything tending to suggest cocaine effects except the name and the picture of [coca] leaves and nuts, which probably conveyed little or nothing to most who saw it. It appears to us that it would be going too far to deny the plaintiff relief against a palpable [readily evident] fraud because possibly here and there an ignorant person might call for the drink with the hope for incipient cocaine intoxication. The plaintiff's position must be judged by the facts as they were when the suit was begun, not by the facts of a different condition and an earlier time. [Emphasis added.]

**Decision and Remedy**   *The district court's injunction was allowed to stand. The competing beverage companies were enjoined from calling their products Koke.*

**Impact of This Case on Today's Law**   *In this early case, the United States Supreme Court made it clear that trademarks and trade names (and nicknames for those marks and names, such as the nickname "Coke" for "Coca-Cola") that are in common use receive protection under the common law. This holding is significant historically because it is the predecessor to the federal statute later passed to protect trademark rights—the Lanham Act of 1946. In many ways, this act represented a codification of common law principles governing trademarks.*

**Critical Thinking**

- **What If the Facts Were Different?**  *Suppose that Coca-Cola had been trying to make the public believe that its product contained cocaine. Would the result in this case likely have been different? Why or why not?*

---

a. In reality, until 1903 the amount of active cocaine in each bottle of Coke was equivalent to one "line" of cocaine.

## 29–1a Statutory Protection of Trademarks

Statutory protection of trademarks and related property is provided at the federal level by the Lanham Act of 1946.[1] The Lanham Act was enacted, in part, to protect manufacturers from losing business to rival companies that used confusingly similar trademarks. The act incorporates the common law of trademarks and provides remedies for owners of trademarks who wish to enforce their claims in federal court. Many states also have trademark statutes.

**Trademark Dilution**  In 1995, Congress amended the Lanham Act by passing the Federal Trademark Dilution Act,[2] which allowed trademark owners to bring suits in federal court for trademark **dilution.** In 2006, Congress further amended the law on trademark dilution by passing the Trademark Dilution Revision Act (TDRA).[3]

Under the TDRA, to state a claim for trademark dilution, a plaintiff must prove the following:

1. The plaintiff owns a famous mark that is distinctive.
2. The defendant has begun using a mark in commerce that allegedly is diluting the famous mark.
3. The similarity between the defendant's mark and the famous mark gives rise to an *association* between the marks.
4. The association is likely to impair the distinctiveness of the famous mark or harm its reputation.

Trademark dilution laws protect "distinctive" or "famous" trademarks (such as Rolls Royce, McDonald's, Starbucks, and Apple) from certain unauthorized uses. Such a mark is protected even when the use is on noncompeting goods or is unlikely to cause confusion. More than half of the states have also enacted trademark dilution laws.

**Marks Need Not Be Identical**  Note that a famous mark may be diluted by the use of an *identical* mark or by the use of a *similar* mark.[4] A similar mark is more likely to lessen the value of a famous mark when the companies using the marks provide related goods or compete against each other in the same market.

■ **CASE IN POINT 29.1**  Samantha Lundberg opened a business called "Sambuck's Coffeehouse," in Astoria, Oregon, even though she knew that "Starbucks" was one of the largest coffee chains in the nation. Starbucks Corporation filed a dilution lawsuit, and a federal court ruled that use of the "Sambuck's" mark constituted trademark dilution because it created confusion for consumers. Not only was there a "high degree" of similarity between the marks, but also both companies provided coffee-related services and marketed their services through "stand-alone" retail stores. Therefore, the use of the similar mark (Sambuck's) reduced the value of the famous mark (Starbucks).[5] ■

## 29–1b Trademark Registration

Trademarks may be registered with the state or with the federal government. To register for protection under federal trademark law, a person must file an application with the U.S. Patent and Trademark Office in Washington, D.C. Under current law, a mark can be registered (1) if it is currently in commerce or (2) if the applicant intends to put it into commerce within six months.

In special circumstances, the six-month period can be extended by thirty months. Thus, the applicant would have a total of three years from the date of notice of trademark approval to make use of the mark and file the required use statement. Registration is postponed until the mark is actually used. During this waiting period, any applicant can legally protect his or her trademark against a third party who previously has neither used the mark nor filed an application for it.

Registration is renewable between the fifth and sixth years after the initial registration and every ten years thereafter (every twenty years for those trademarks registered before 1990).

## 29–1c Trademark Infringement

Registration of a trademark with the U.S. Patent and Trademark Office gives notice on a nationwide basis that the trademark belongs exclusively to the registrant. The registrant is also allowed to use the symbol ® to indicate that the mark has been registered. Whenever that trademark is copied to a substantial degree or used in its entirety by another, intentionally or unintentionally, the trademark has been *infringed* (used without authorization).

When a trademark has been infringed, the owner of the mark has a cause of action against the infringer. To succeed in a trademark infringement action, the owner must show that the defendant's use of the mark created a likelihood of confusion about the origin of the defendant's goods or services. The owner need not prove that

1. 15 U.S.C. Sections 1051–1128.
2. 15 U.S.C. Section 1125.
3. Pub. L. No. 103-312, 120 Stat. 1730 (2006).
4. See *Louis Vuitton Malletier S.A. v. Haute Diggity Dog, LLC*, 507 F.3d 252 (4th Cir. 2007); and *Moseley v. V Secret Catalogue, Inc.*, 537 U.S. 418, 123 S.Ct. 1115, 155 L.Ed.2d 1 (2003).
5. *Starbucks Corp. v. Lundberg*, 2005 WL 3183858 (D.Or. 2005).

the infringer acted intentionally or that the trademark was registered (although registration does provide proof of the date of inception of the trademark's use).

The most commonly granted remedy for trademark infringement is an *injunction* to prevent further infringement. Under the Lanham Act, a trademark owner that successfully proves infringement can recover actual damages, plus the profits that the infringer wrongfully received from the unauthorized use of the mark. A court can also order the destruction of any goods bearing the unauthorized trademark. In some situations, the trademark owner may also be able to recover attorneys' fees.

At the center of the following case was an injunction granted in an earlier dispute between two brothers prohibiting one of them from using trademarks owned by the other, including a mark featuring their shared last name.

## Case 29.2

# LFP IP, LLC v. Hustler Cincinnati, Inc.
United States Court of Appeals, Sixth Circuit, 810 F.3d 424 (2016).

**Background and Facts**  Brothers Jimmy and Larry Flynt owned "The Hustler Club," a bar and night-club in Cincinnati, Ohio. Larry opened Hustler clubs in other Ohio cities. Within a few years, he also began publishing *Hustler,* a sexually explicit magazine. Larry formed LFP IP, Inc., and other corporations to conduct his enterprises. Many of them used the trademarks "HUSTLER" and "LARRY FLYNT," which LFP owned. Jimmy opened his own store, Hustler Cincinnati, and paid LFP licensing fees to use the "HUSTLER" mark.

When the store stopped paying the fees, LFP filed a suit in a federal district court against the store's corporate owner, alleging trademark infringement. The court issued an injunction prohibiting Jimmy from using the "HUSTLER" mark. Later, he opened a store called "FLYNT Sexy Gifts." LFP claimed that this name was likely to cause confusion with the "LARRY FLYNT" mark. The court modified the injunction to limit Jimmy's use of the "Flynt" name without "Jimmy." Jimmy appealed.

## In the Language of the Court
*SUTTON,* Circuit Judge.
* * * *

Courts * * * may exercise their sound judicial discretion to modify an injunction if the circumstances, whether of law or fact, obtaining at the time of its issuance have changed, or new ones have since arisen.

* * * The [district] court * * * applied the traditional test for trademark infringement under federal law, asking whether (1) Larry and his companies owned the LARRY FLYNT trademark, (2) Jimmy used the mark in commerce, and (3) the use was likely to cause confusion. The court found all three elements satisfied * * * . Because the original injunction was tailored to prevent trademark infringement by [Jimmy] and because Jimmy had committed new violations, the district court acted appropriately when it modified its initial grant of relief to cover Jimmy's conduct at the [new] outlet.

The district court's modified injunction was also suitably tailored to the changed circumstances. Balancing the competing interests of Larry and Jimmy, the court permitted Jimmy to use his full name while protecting Larry's interest in the LARRY FLYNT trademark.
* * * *

Jimmy * * * takes issue with some of the factual findings that the district court used to justify the modified injunction.

But none of the district court's factual findings is clearly erroneous. * * * Larry * * * presented evidence that he used the mark in connection with a wide range of adult entertainment products, including the kinds of products sold at Jimmy's store. Because *product use * * * marks the salient [most noticeable] indicator of ownership in trademark-infringement actions*, the district court reasonably found that Larry * * * owned the LARRY FLYNT trademark with respect to retail goods. The court also reasonably found that Larry began using the mark on adult entertainment products before Jimmy did. * * * And * * * Larry's company * * * continued to use that mark in commerce. [Emphasis added.]

In claiming an absence of evidence of consumer confusion, Jimmy missteps. Some of the evidence comes from Jimmy himself. When asked about instances where a consumer has been confused, in terms of whether or not Jimmy was the owner of the store, Jimmy responded, "I have experienced the

Case 29.2 Continues

Case 29.2 Continued

confusion in the names, you know. Jimmy and Larry Flynt, in this market area, is somewhat synonymous with Hustler or with Flynt. You're not going to get around that."

**Decision and Remedy** *The U.S. Court of Appeals for the Sixth Circuit affirmed the lower court's modification of the injunction. The injunction was initially tailored to prevent Jimmy's infringement of his brother's marks. When Jimmy committed a new violation by opening "FLYNT Sexy Gifts," the district court acted appropriately in modifying the injunction to cover this conduct.*

**Critical Thinking**
- **E-Commerce** *Could Jimmy use his last name—the name that he shares with his brother—as a domain name? Why or why not?*
- **What If the Facts Were Different?** *Suppose that Jimmy had used the marks at the center of this case on an entirely different line of goods, not adult entertainment products. Would the result have been the same? Explain.*

## 29-1d Distinctiveness of the Mark

A trademark must be sufficiently distinctive to enable consumers to identify the manufacturer of the goods easily and to distinguish between those goods and competing products.

**Strong Marks** Fanciful, arbitrary, or suggestive trademarks are generally considered to be the most distinctive (strongest) trademarks. These marks receive automatic protection because they serve to identify a particular product's source, as opposed to describing the product itself.

**Fanciful and Arbitrary Trademarks.** Fanciful trademarks use invented words, such as "Xerox" for one manufacturer's copiers and "Google" for a search engine. Arbitrary trademarks use common words in an uncommon way that is not descriptive of the product, such as "Dutch Boy" as a name for paint.

Even a single letter used in a particular style can be an arbitrary trademark. ■ **CASE IN POINT 29.2** Sports entertainment company ESPN sued Quiksilver, Inc., a maker of youth-oriented clothing, alleging trademark infringement. ESPN claimed that Quiksilver's clothing used the stylized "X" mark that ESPN uses in connection with the "X Games" ("extreme" sports competitions).

Quiksilver filed counterclaims for trademark infringement and dilution, arguing that it had a long history of using the stylized X on its products. ESPN had created the X Games in the mid-1990s, and Quiksilver had been using the X mark since 1994. ESPN asked the court to dismiss Quiksilver's counterclaims, but the court refused, holding that the X on Quiksilver's clothing is clearly an arbitrary mark. The court found that the two Xs are

"similar enough that a consumer might well confuse them." Therefore, Quicksilver could continue its claim for trademark infringement.[6] ■

**Suggestive Trademarks.** Suggestive trademarks indicate something about a product's nature, quality, or characteristics, without describing the product directly. These marks require imagination on the part of the consumer to identify the characteristic.

"Dairy Queen," for instance, suggests an association between its products and milk, but it does not directly describe ice cream. "Blu-ray" is a suggestive mark that is associated with the high-quality, high-definition video contained on a particular type of optical data storage disc. Although blue-violet lasers are used to read blu-ray discs, the term *blu-ray* does not directly describe the disc.

**Secondary Meaning** Descriptive terms, geographic terms, and personal names are not inherently distinctive and do not receive protection under the law until they acquire a secondary meaning. A secondary meaning may arise when customers begin to associate a specific term or phrase (such as *London Fog*) with specific trademarked items (coats with "London Fog" labels) made by a particular company.

Whether a secondary meaning becomes attached to a name usually depends on how extensively the product is advertised, the market for the product, the number of sales, and other factors. ■ **CASE IN POINT 29.3** Unity Health Plans Insurance Corporation has been a health maintenance organization (HMO) insurer in Wisconsin since 1955. In 2013, another health-care provider, Iowa

6. *ESPN, Inc. v. Quiksilver, Inc.*, 586 F.Supp.2d 219 (S.D.N.Y. 2008).

Health System, began rebranding itself (changing its name and marketing) as UnityPoint Health. When the company expanded into Wisconsin, where Unity Health already had an established presence, Unity Health filed a trademark infringement suit in federal court.

The court found that Unity Health was a descriptive mark, and thus not inherently distinctive. But the court also held that the Unity Health mark had acquired a secondary meaning, largely because it had been used for so long and so exclusively by one health insurer in Wisconsin. It made no difference to the court that only one part of the mark (Unity) was common to both trademarks. To allow Iowa Health Systems to use the mark UnityPoint Health in Wisconsin would likely create confusion for consumers. Therefore, the court issued an injunction and blocked Iowa Health from using the trademark Unity-Point Health.[7] ■

Once a secondary meaning is attached to a term or name, a trademark is considered distinctive and is protected. Even a color can qualify for trademark protection, as did the color schemes used by some state university sports teams, including Ohio State University and Louisiana State University.[8]

■ **CASE IN POINT 29.4** Federal Express Corporation (FedEx) provides transportation and delivery services worldwide using the logo FedEx in a specific color combination. FedEx sued a competitor, JetEx Management Services, Inc., for using the same color combination and a similar name and logo. JetEx also mimicked FedEx's trademarked slogan ("The World on Time" for FedEx, and "Keeping the World on Time" for JetEx). FedEx alleged trademark infringement and dilution, among other claims. A federal district court in New York granted a permanent injunction to block JetEx from using the infringing mark in FedEx colors.[9] ■

**Generic Terms** Generic terms that refer to an entire class of products, such as *bicycle* and *computer,* receive no protection, even if they acquire secondary meanings. A particularly thorny problem arises when a trademark acquires generic use. For instance, *aspirin* and *thermos* were originally the names of trademarked products, but today the words are used generically. Other trademarks that have acquired generic use are *escalator, trampoline, raisin bran, dry ice, lanolin, linoleum, nylon,* and *cornflakes.*

A trademark does not become generic simply because it is commonly used, however. ■ **CASE IN POINT 29.5** In 2014, David Elliot and Chris Gillespie sought to register numerous domain names, including "googledisney.com" and "googlenewstvs.com." (A *domain name* is part of an Internet address, such as "cengage.com.") They were unable to register the names because all of them used the word *google,* a trademark of Google, Inc.

Elliot and Gillespie brought an action in federal court to have the Google trademark cancelled because it had become a generic term. They argued that because most people now use *google* as a verb ("to google") when referring to searching the Internet with any search engine (not just Google), the term should no longer be protected. The court held that even if people do use the word *google* as a verb, it is still a protected trademark if consumers associate the noun with one company. The court concluded that "the primary significance of the word *google* to a majority of the public who utilize Internet search engines is a designation of the Google search engine."[10] ■

## 29–1e Service, Certification, and Collective Marks

A **service mark** is essentially a trademark that is used to distinguish the *services* (rather than the products) of one person or company from those of another. For instance, each airline has a particular mark or symbol associated with its name. Titles and character names used in radio and television are frequently registered as service marks.

Other marks protected by law include certification marks and collective marks. A **certification mark** is used by one or more persons, other than the owner, to certify the region, materials, mode of manufacture, quality, or other characteristic of specific goods or services. Certification marks include "Good Housekeeping Seal of Approval" and "UL Tested."

When used by members of a cooperative, association, or other organization, a certification mark is referred to as a **collective mark.** ■ **EXAMPLE 29.6** Collective marks appear at the ends of motion picture credits to indicate the various associations and organizations that participated in the making of the films. The union marks found on the tags of certain products are also collective marks. ■

## 29–1f Trade Dress

The term **trade dress** refers to the image and overall appearance of a product. Trade dress is a broad concept

---

7. *Unity Health Plans Insurance Co. v. Iowa Health System,* 995 F.Supp.2d 874 (W.D.Wis. 2014).
8. *Board of Supervisors of Louisiana State University v. Smack Apparel Co.,* 438 F.Supp.2d 653 (E.D.La. 2006). See also *Abraham v. Alpha Chi Omega,* 781 F.Supp.2d 396 (N.D.Tex. 2011).
9. *Federal Express Corp. v. JetEx Management Services, Inc.,* 2014 WL 4628983 (E.D.N.Y. 2014).

10. *Elliot v. Google,* 45 F.Supp.3d 1156 (D.Ariz. 2014).

and can include either all or part of the total image or overall impression created by a product or its packaging.

■ **EXAMPLE 29.7**  The distinctive decor, menu, layout, and style of service of a particular restaurant may be regarded as trade dress. Trade dress can also include the layout and appearance of a catalogue, the use of a lighthouse as part of the design of a golf hole, the fish shape of a cracker, or the G-shaped design of a Gucci watch. ■

Basically, trade dress is subject to the same protection as trademarks. In cases involving trade dress infringement, as in trademark infringement cases, a major consideration is whether consumers are likely to be confused by the allegedly infringing use.

## 29–1g Counterfeit Goods

Counterfeit goods copy or otherwise imitate trademarked goods, but they are not the genuine trademarked goods. The importation of goods that bear counterfeit (fake) trademarks poses a growing problem for U.S. businesses, consumers, and law enforcement. In addition to the negative financial effects on legitimate businesses, certain counterfeit goods, such as pharmaceuticals and nutritional supplements, can present serious public health risks.

**The Stop Counterfeiting in Manufactured Goods Act**  The Stop Counterfeiting in Manufactured Goods Act[11] (SCMGA) was enacted to combat counterfeit goods. The act makes it a crime to traffic intentionally in or attempt to traffic in counterfeit goods or services, or to knowingly use a counterfeit mark on or in connection with goods or services.

Before this act, the law did not prohibit the creation or shipment of counterfeit labels that were not attached to any product. Therefore, counterfeiters would make labels and packaging bearing another's trademark, ship the labels to another location, and then affix them to an inferior product to deceive buyers. The SCMGA closed this loophole by making it a crime to knowingly traffic in counterfeit labels, stickers, packaging, and the like, regardless of whether the items are attached to any goods.

**Penalties for Counterfeiting**  Persons found guilty of violating the SCMGA may be fined up to $2 million or imprisoned for up to ten years (or more if they are repeat offenders). If a court finds that the statute was violated, it must order the defendant to forfeit the counterfeit products (which are then destroyed), as well as any property

used in the commission of the crime. The defendant must also pay restitution to the trademark holder or victim in an amount equal to the victim's actual loss.

■ **CASE IN POINT 29.8**  Charles Anthony Jones pleaded guilty to trafficking of counterfeit prescription erectile dysfunction drugs. The court sentenced Jones to thirty-seven months in prison and ordered him to pay $633,019 in restitution. Jones appealed, arguing that the amount awarded was more than the pharmaceutical companies' actual losses. The court agreed. The pharmaceutical companies were entitled only to their lost net profits rather than the retail price of the genuine drugs.[12] ■

**Combating Foreign Counterfeiters**  Although Congress has enacted statutes against counterfeit goods, the United States cannot prosecute foreign counterfeiters because our national laws do not apply to them. One effective tool that U.S. officials have used to combat online sales of counterfeit goods is to obtain a court order to close down the domain names of Web sites that sell such goods. For instance, U.S. agents have shut down hundreds of domain names on the Monday after Thanksgiving ("Cyber Monday"). Shutting down the Web sites, particularly on key shopping days, prevents some counterfeit goods from entering the United States. Europol, an international organization, has also used this tactic.

## 29–1h Trade Names

Trademarks apply to *products*. A **trade name** indicates part or all of a business's name, whether the business is a sole proprietorship, a partnership, or a corporation. Generally, a trade name is directly related to a business and its goodwill.

A trade name may be protected as a trademark if the trade name is also the name of the company's trademarked product—for example, Coca-Cola. Unless it is also used as a trademark or service mark, a trade name cannot be registered with the federal government. Trade names are protected under the common law, but only if they are unusual or fancifully used. The word *Safeway*, for example, was sufficiently fanciful to obtain protection as a trade name for a grocery chain.

## 29–1i Licensing

One way to avoid litigation and still make use of another's trademark or other form of intellectual property is to obtain a license to do so. A **license** in this context

11. Pub. L. No. 109-181 (2006), which amended 18 U.S.C. Sections 23129–2320.

12. *United States v. Jones*, 616 Fed.Appx. 726 (5th Cir. 2015).

is an agreement, or contract, permitting the use of a trademark, copyright, patent, or trade secret for certain purposes. The party that owns the intellectual property rights and issues the license is the *licensor,* and the party obtaining the license is the *licensee.* The licensee generally pays fees, or *royalties,* for the privilege of using the intellectual property.

A license grants only the rights expressly described in the license agreement. A licensor might, for example, allow the licensee to use the trademark as part of its company or domain name, but not otherwise use the mark on any products or services. Disputes frequently arise over licensing agreements, particularly when the license involves Internet uses.

■ **CASE IN POINT 29.9**  George V Restauration S.A. and others owned and operated the Buddha Bar Paris, a restaurant with an Asian theme in Paris, France. One of the owners allowed Little Rest Twelve, Inc., to use the Buddha Bar trademark and its associated concept in New York City under the name *Buddha Bar NYC.* Little Rest paid royalties for its use of the Buddha Bar mark and advertised Buddha Bar NYC's affiliation with Buddha Bar Paris. This connection was also noted on its Web site and in the media.

When a dispute arose, the owners of Buddha Bar Paris withdrew their permission for Buddha Bar NYC's use of their mark, but Little Rest continued to use it. The owners of the mark filed a suit in a New York state court against Little Rest. The court granted an injunction to prevent Little Rest from using the mark.[13] ■

# 29–2 Patents

A **patent** is a grant from the government that gives an inventor the exclusive right to make, use, or sell his or her invention for a period of twenty years. Patents for designs, as opposed to those for inventions, are given for a fourteen-year period. The applicant must demonstrate to the satisfaction of the U.S. Patent and Trademark Office that the invention, discovery, process, or design is novel, useful, and not obvious in light of current technology.

Until recently, U.S. patent law differed from the laws of many other countries because the first person to invent a product obtained the patent rights rather than the first person to file for a patent. It was often difficult to prove who invented an item first, however, which prompted Congress to change the system in 2011 by passing the America Invents Act.[14] Now the first person to file an application for a patent on a product or process will receive patent protection. In addition, the new law established a nine-month limit for challenging a patent on any ground.

The period of patent protection begins on the date the patent application is filed, rather than when the patent is issued, which may sometimes be years later. After the patent period ends (either fourteen or twenty years later), the product or process enters the public domain, and anyone can make, sell, or use the invention without paying the patent holder.

## 29–2a Searchable Patent Databases

A significant development relating to patents is the availability online of the world's patent databases. The Web site of the U.S. Patent and Trademark Office (www.uspto.gov) provides searchable databases covering U.S. patents granted since 1976. The Web site of the European Patent Office (www.epo.org) provides online access to 50 million patent documents in more than seventy nations through a searchable network of databases.

Businesses use these searchable databases in many ways. Companies may conduct patent searches to list or inventory their patents, which are valuable assets. Patent searches may also be conducted to study trends and patterns in a specific technology or to gather information about competitors in the industry.

## 29–2b What Is Patentable?

Under federal law, "[w]hoever invents or discovers any new and useful process, machine, manufacture, or composition of matter, or any new and useful improvement thereof, may obtain a patent therefor, subject to the conditions and requirements of this title."[15] Thus, to be patentable, the applicant must prove that the invention, discovery, process, or design is *novel, useful,* and *not obvious* in light of current technology.

In sum, almost anything is patentable, except the laws of nature, natural phenomena, and abstract ideas (including algorithms[16]). Even artistic methods and works of art, certain business processes, and the structures of storylines

13. *George V Restauration S.A. v. Little Rest Twelve, Inc.,* 58 A.D.3d 428, 871 N.Y.S.2d 65 (2009).

14. The full title of this law is the Leahy-Smith America Invents Act, Pub. L. No. 112-29 (2011), which amended 35 U.S.C. Sections 1, 41, and 321.

15. 35 U.S.C. Section 101.

16. An *algorithm* is a step-by-step procedure, formula, or set of instructions for accomplishing a specific task. An example is the set of rules used by a search engine to rank the listings contained within its index in response to a query.

are patentable, provided that they are novel and not obvious.[17]

Plants that are reproduced asexually (by means other than from seed), such as hybrid or genetically engineered plants, are patentable in the United States, as are genetically engineered (or cloned) microorganisms and animals. ■ **CASE IN POINT 29.10** Monsanto, Inc., sells its patented genetically modified (GM) seeds to farmers to help them achieve higher yields from crops using fewer pesticides. It requires farmers who buy GM seeds to sign licensing agreements promising to plant the seeds for only one crop and to pay a technology fee for each acre planted. To ensure compliance, Monsanto has many full-time employees whose job is to investigate and prosecute farmers who use the GM seeds illegally. Monsanto has filed nearly 150 lawsuits against farmers in the United States and has been awarded more than $15 million in damages (not including out-of-court settlement amounts).[18] ■

### 29–2c Patent Infringement

If a firm makes, uses, or sells another's patented design, product, or process without the patent owner's permission, that firm commits the tort of patent infringement. Patent infringement may occur even though the patent owner has not put the patented product into commerce. Patent infringement may also occur even though not all features or parts of a product are copied. (To infringe the patent on a process, however, all steps or their equivalent must be copied.) To read about an important issue in patent infringement today, see this chapter's *Digital Update* feature.

**Patent Infringement Lawsuits and High-Tech Companies** Obviously, companies that specialize in developing new technology stand to lose significant profits if someone "makes, uses, or sells" devices that incorporate their patented inventions. Because these firms are the holders of numerous patents, they are frequently involved in patent infringement lawsuits (as well as other types of intellectual property disputes).

■ **CASE IN POINT 29.11** Apple sued Samsung in federal court alleging that Samsung's Galaxy smartphones and tablets that use Google's HTC Android operating system infringe on Apple's patents. Apple has design patents that cover its devices' graphical user interface (the display of icons on the home screen), shell, and screen and button design. Apple has also patented the way information is displayed on iPhones and other devices, the way windows pop open, and the way information is scaled and rotated.

A jury found that Samsung had willfully infringed five of Apple's patents and awarded damages. The parties appealed. A judge later reduced the amount of damages awarded on the patent claims, but litigation between the two companies has continued. In 2015, a federal appellate court held that elements of the physical design of these two manufacturers' mobile devices and their on-screen icons were functional and thus not protected under the Lanham Act. A product feature is functional and not protected as trade dress if it is essential to the article's use or purpose or affects the cost or quality of the article.[19] ■

**Patent Infringement and Foreign Sales** Many companies that make and sell electronics and computer software and hardware are based in foreign nations (for instance, Samsung Electronics Company is a Korean firm). Foreign firms can apply for and obtain U.S. patent protection on items that they sell within the United States. Similarly, U.S. firms can obtain protection in foreign nations where they sell goods.

In the United States, the Supreme Court has narrowly construed patent infringement as it applies to exported software, however. As a general rule, under U.S. law, no patent infringement occurs when a patented product is made and sold in another country. ■ **CASE IN POINT 29.12** AT&T Corporation holds a patent on a device used to digitally encode, compress, and process recorded speech. AT&T brought an infringement case against Microsoft Corporation, which admitted that its Windows operating system incorporated software code that infringed on AT&T's patent.

The United States Supreme Court held that Microsoft was liable only for infringement in the United States and not for the Windows-based computers produced in foreign locations. The Court reasoned that Microsoft had not "supplied" the software for the computers but had only electronically transmitted a master copy, which the foreign manufacturers copied and loaded onto the computers.[20] ■

---

**17.** For a United States Supreme Court case discussing the obviousness requirement, see *KSR International Co. v. Teleflex, Inc.*, 550 U.S. 398, 127 S.Ct. 1727, 167 L.Ed.2d 705 (2007).

**18.** See, for example, *Monsanto Co. v. Bowman*, 657 F.3d 1341 (Fed.Cir. 2011); and *Monsanto Co. v. Scruggs*, 2009 WL 1228318 (Fed.Cir. 2009).

**19.** *Apple, Inc. v. Samsung Electronics Co.*, 926 F.Supp.2d 1110 (N.D.Cal. 2013); 786 F.3d 983 (Fed. Cir. 2015).

**20.** *Microsoft Corp. v. AT&T Corp.*, 550 U.S. 437, 127 S.Ct. 1746, 167 L.Ed.2d 737 (2007).

## DIGITAL UPDATE   The Problem of Patent Trolls

In recent years, a huge number of patent infringement lawsuits have been filed against software and technology firms. Many patent cases involve companies defending real innovations, but some lawsuits are "shakedowns" by patent trolls.

*Patent trolls*—more formally called nonpracticing entities (NPEs) or patent assertion entities (PAEs)—are firms that do not make or sell products or services but are in the business of patent litigation. These firms buy patents and then try to enforce them against companies that *do* sell products or services, demanding licensing fees and threatening infringement lawsuits. Patent trolls usually target online businesses.

### "I'm Going to Sue You Unless You Pay Me to Go Away"

Patent trolls literally bank on the fact that when threatened with infringement suits, most companies would rather pay to settle than engage in costly litigation, even if they believe they could win.

Consider an example. Soverain Software, LLC, sued dozens of online retailers, including Amazon, Avon, Home Depot, Macy's, Nordstrom, Kohl's, RadioShack, The Gap, and Victoria's Secret. Soverain claimed that it owned patents that covered nearly any use of online shopping-cart technology and that all these retailers had infringed on its patents. Amazon paid millions to settle with Soverain, as did most of the other defendants.

Interestingly, one online retailer, Newegg, Inc., refused to pay Soverain and ultimately won in court. In 2013, a federal appellate court held that the shopping-cart patent claim was invalid on the ground of obviousness because the technology for it had already existed before Soverain obtained its patent.[a]

### The Role of Software Patents

The patent troll problem is concentrated in software patents, which often include descriptions of what the software does rather than the computer code involved. Many software patents are vaguely worded and overly broad. In the United States, both the patent system and the courts have had difficulty evaluating and protecting such patents.

As a result, nearly any business that uses basic technology can be a target of patent trolls. In fact, *more than 60 percent of all new patent cases* are filed by patent trolls. The firms most commonly targeted by patent trolls are large technology companies, including AT&T, Google, Apple, Samsung, Amazon, and Verizon. In one recent year, "AT&T was sued for patent infringement by patent trolls 54 times—more than once a week."[b]

**Critical Thinking** *Some argue that the best way to stop patent trolls from taking advantage of the system would be to eliminate software patents completely and pass a law that makes software unpatentable. Would this be fair to software and technology companies? Why or why not?*

a. *Soverain Software, LLC v. Newegg, Inc.*, 728 F.3d 1332 (Fed. Cir. 2013), *cert.* denied, 134 S.Ct. 910 (2014).
b. Roger Parloff, "Taking on the Patent Trolls," *Fortune*, February 27, 2014.

## 29–2d Remedies for Patent Infringement

If a patent is infringed, the patent holder may sue for relief in federal court. The patent holder can seek an injunction against the infringer and can also request damages for royalties and lost profits. In some cases, the court may grant the winning party reimbursement for attorneys' fees and costs. If the court determines that the infringement was willful, the court can triple the amount of damages awarded (treble damages).

In the past, permanent injunctions were routinely granted to prevent future infringement. Today, however, according to the United States Supreme Court, a patent holder must prove that it has suffered irreparable injury and that the public interest would not be *disserved* by a permanent injunction.[21] Thus, courts have discretion to decide what is equitable in the circumstances and to consider what is in the public interest rather than just the interests of the parties.

■ **CASE IN POINT 29.13** Cordance Corporation developed some of the technology and software that automates Internet communications. Cordance sued Amazon.com, Inc., for patent infringement, claiming that Amazon's one-click purchasing interface infringed on one of Cordance's patents. After a jury found Amazon guilty of infringement, Cordance requested the court to issue a permanent injunction against Amazon's infringement or,

21. *eBay, Inc. v. MercExchange, LLC*, 547 U.S. 388, 126 S.Ct. 1837, 164 L.Ed.2d 641 (2006).

alternatively, to order Amazon to pay Cordance an ongoing royalty.

The court refused to issue a permanent injunction because Cordance had not proved that it would otherwise suffer irreparable harm. Cordance and Amazon were not direct competitors in the relevant market. Cordance had never sold or licensed the technology infringed by Amazon's one-click purchasing interface and had presented no market data or evidence to show how the infringement negatively affected Cordance. The court also refused to impose an ongoing royalty on Amazon.[22] ∎

# 29–3 Copyrights

A **copyright** is an intangible property right granted by federal statute to the author or originator of a literary or artistic production of a specified type. The Copyright Act of 1976,[23] as amended, governs copyrights. Works created after January 1, 1978, are automatically given statutory copyright protection for the life of the author plus 70 years. For copyrights owned by publishing houses, the copyright expires 95 years from the date of publication or 120 years from the date of creation, whichever comes first. For works by more than one author, the copyright expires 70 years after the death of the last surviving author.[24]

When copyright protection ends, works enter into the *public domain*. Intellectual property, such as songs and other published works, that have entered into the public domain belong to everyone and are not protected by copyright or patent laws.

∎ **CASE IN POINT 29.14** The popular character Sherlock Holmes originated in stories written by Arthur Conan Doyle and published from 1887 through 1927. Over the years, elements of the characters and stories created by Doyle have appeared in books, movies, and television series, including *Elementary* on CBS and *Sherlock* on BBC.

Before 2013, those who wished to use the copyrighted Sherlock material had to pay a licensing fee to Doyle's estate. Then, in 2013, the editors of a book of Holmes-related stories filed a lawsuit in federal court claiming that the basic Sherlock Holmes story elements introduced before 1923 should no longer be protected. The

court agreed and ruled that these elements have entered the public domain—that is, the copyright has expired, and they can be used without permission.[25] ∎

## 29–3a Registration

Copyrights can be registered with the U.S. Copyright Office (www.copyright.gov) in Washington, D.C. Registration is not required, however. A copyright owner no longer needs to place the symbol © or the term *Copr.* or *Copyright* on the work to have the work protected against infringement. Chances are that if somebody created it, somebody owns it.

Generally, copyright owners are protected against the following:

1. Reproduction of the work.
2. Development of derivative works.
3. Distribution of the work.
4. Public display of the work.

## 29–3b What Is Protected Expression?

Works that are copyrightable include books, records, films, artworks, architectural plans, menus, music videos, product packaging, and computer software. To be protected, a work must be "fixed in a durable medium" from which it can be perceived, reproduced, or communicated. As noted, protection is automatic, and registration is not required.

Section 102 of the Copyright Act explicitly states that it protects original works that fall into one of the following categories:

1. Literary works (including newspaper and magazine articles, computer and training manuals, catalogues, brochures, and print advertisements).
2. Musical works and accompanying words (including advertising jingles).
3. Dramatic works and accompanying music.
4. Pantomimes and choreographic works (including ballets and other forms of dance).
5. Pictorial, graphic, and sculptural works (including cartoons, maps, posters, statues, and even stuffed animals).
6. Motion pictures and other audiovisual works (including multimedia works).
7. Sound recordings.
8. Architectural works.

22. *Cordance Corp. v. Amazon.com, Inc.*, 730 F.Supp.2d 333 (D.Del. 2010).
23. 17 U.S.C. Sections 101 *et seq.*
24. These time periods reflect the extensions of the length of copyright protection enacted by Congress in the Copyright Term Extension Act of 1998, 17 U.S.C. Section 302. The United States Supreme Court upheld the constitutionality of the act in 2003. See *Eldred v. Ashcroft*, 537 U.S. 186, 123 S.Ct. 769, 154 L.Ed.2d 683 (2003).

25. *Klinger v. Conan Doyle Estate, Ltd.*, 988 F.Supp.2d 879 (N.D.Ill. 2013).

**Section 102 Exclusions** Generally, anything that is not an original expression will not qualify for copyright protection. Facts widely known to the public are not copyrightable. Page numbers are not copyrightable because they follow a sequence known to everyone. Mathematical calculations are not copyrightable.

Furthermore, it is not possible to copyright an *idea.* Section 102 of the Copyright Act specifically excludes copyright protection for any "idea, procedure, process, system, method of operation, concept, principle, or discovery, regardless of the form in which it is described, explained, illustrated, or embodied." Thus, anyone can freely use the underlying ideas or principles embodied in a work.

What is copyrightable is the particular way in which an idea is *expressed.* Whenever an idea and an expression are inseparable, the expression cannot be copyrighted. An idea and its expression, then, must be separable to be copyrightable. Thus, for the design of a useful item to be copyrightable, the way it looks must be separate from its utilitarian (functional) purpose.

■ **CASE IN POINT 29.15** Inhale, Inc., registered a copyright on a hookah—a device for smoking tobacco by filtering the smoke through water held in a container at the base. Starbuzz Tobacco, Inc., sold hookahs with water containers shaped exactly like the Inhale containers.

Inhale filed a suit in a federal district court against Starbuzz for copyright infringement. The court determined that the shape of the water container on Inhale's hookahs was not copyrightable. The U.S. Court of Appeals for the Ninth Circuit affirmed the judgment. "The shape of a container is not independent of the container's utilitarian function—to hold the contents within its shape—because the shape accomplishes the function."[26] ■

---

26. *Inhale, Inc. v. Starbuzz Tobacco, Inc.*, 755 F.3d 1038 (2014).

**Compilations of Facts** Unlike ideas, *compilations* of facts are copyrightable. Under Section 103 of the Copyright Act, a compilation is "a work formed by the collection and assembling of preexisting materials or data that are selected, coordinated, or arranged in such a way that the resulting work as a whole constitutes an original work of authorship."

The key requirement in the copyrightability of a compilation is originality. If the facts are selected, coordinated, or arranged in an original way, they can qualify for copyright protection. Therefore, the White Pages of a telephone directory do not qualify for copyright protection, because they simply list alphabetically names and telephone numbers. The Yellow Pages of a directory can be copyrightable, provided the information is selected, coordinated, or arranged in an original way. Similarly, a compilation of information about yachts listed for sale has qualified for copyright protection.[27]

### 29–3c Copyright Infringement

Whenever the form or expression of an idea is copied, an infringement of copyright has occurred. The reproduction does not have to be exactly the same as the original, nor does it have to reproduce the original in its entirety. If a substantial part of the original is reproduced, the copyright has been infringed.

In the following case, rapper Curtis Jackson—better known as "50 Cent"—was the defendant in a suit that claimed his album *Before I Self-Destruct,* and the film of the same name, infringed the copyright of Shadrach Winstead's book *The Preacher's Son—But the Streets Turned Me into a Gangster.*

---

27. *BUC International Corp. v. International Yacht Council, Ltd.*, 489 F.3d 1129 (11th Cir. 2007).

**Case Analysis 29.3**

# Winstead v. Jackson
United States Court of Appeals, Third Circuit, 509 Fed.Appx. 139 (2013).

### In the Language of the Court
*PER CURIAM.* [By the Whole Court]
* * * *

* * * Winstead filed his * * * complaint in the United States District Court for the District of New Jersey, claiming that Jackson's album/CD and film derived their contents from, and infringed the copyright of, his book.
* * * *

* * * The District Court dismissed Winstead's * * * complaint * * * , concluding that Jackson * * * did not improperly copy protected aspects of Winstead's book.
* * * *

Winstead appeals.
* * * *

Here, it is not disputed that Winstead is the owner of the copyrighted

property * * * . However, *not all copying is copyright infringement, so even if actual copying is proven, the court must decide, by comparing the allegedly infringing work with the original work, whether the copying was unlawful. Copying may be proved inferentially by showing that the allegedly infringing work is substantially similar to the copyrighted*

Case 29.3 Continues

*work.* A court compares the allegedly infringing work with the original work, and considers whether a "lay-observer" would believe that the copying was of protectable aspects of the copyrighted work. The inquiry involves distinguishing between the author's expression and the idea or theme that he or she seeks to convey or explore, because the former is protected and the latter is not. The court must determine whether the allegedly infringing work is similar because it appropriates the unique expressions of the original work, or merely because it contains elements that would be expected when two works express the same idea or explore the same theme. [Emphasis added.]

* * * A lay observer would not believe that Jackson's album/CD and film copied protectable aspects of Winstead's book. Jackson's album/CD is comprised of 16 individual songs, which explore drug-dealing, guns and money, vengeance, and other similar clichés of hip hop gangsterism. Jackson's fictional film is the story of a young man who turns to violence when his mother is killed in a drive-by shooting. The young man takes revenge by killing the man who killed his mother, and then gets rich by becoming an "enforcer" for a powerful criminal. He takes up with a woman who eventually betrays him, and is shot to death by her boyfriend, who has just been released from prison. The movie ends with his younger brother vowing to seek vengeance. Winstead's book purports to be autobiographical and tells the story of a young man whose beloved father was a Bishop in the church. The protagonist was angry as a child because his stepmother abused him, but he found acceptance and self-esteem on the streets of Newark because he was physically

powerful. He earned money robbing and beating people, went to jail, returned to crime upon his release, and then made even more money. The protagonist discusses his time at Rahway State Prison in great and compelling detail. The story ends when the protagonist learns that his father has passed away; he conveys his belief that this tragedy has led to his redemption, and he hopes that others might learn from his mistakes.

* * * Although Winstead's book and Jackson's works share similar themes and setting, the story of an angry and wronged protagonist who turns to a life of violence and crime has long been a part of the public domain [and is therefore not protected by copyright law]. Winstead argues * * * that a protagonist asking for God's help when his father dies, cutting drugs with mixing agents to maximize profits, and complaining about relatives who are addicts and steal the product, are protectable, but these things are not unique. To the extent that Jackson's works contain these elements, they are to be expected when two works express the same idea about "the streets" or explore the same theme. Winstead argues that not every protagonist whose story concerns guns, drugs, and violence in an urban setting winds up in prison or loses a parent, but this argument only serves to illustrate an important difference between his book and Jackson's film. Jackson's protagonist never spends any time in prison, whereas Winstead's protagonist devotes a considerable part of his story to his incarcerations.

In addition, Winstead's book and Jackson's works are different with respect to character, plot, mood, and sequence of events. Winstead's protagonist embarks on a life of crime at a very young age, but is redeemed by the death of his beloved

father. Jackson's protagonist turns to crime when he is much older and only after his mother is murdered. He winds up dead at a young age, unredeemed. Winstead's book is hopeful; Jackson's film is characterized * * * by moral apathy. It is true that both works involve the loss of a parent and the protagonist's recognition of the parent's importance in his life, but nowhere does Jackson appropriate anything unique about Winstead's expression of this generic topic.

Winstead contends that direct phrases from his book appear in Jackson's film. * * * He emphasizes these phrases: "Yo, where is my money at," "I would never have done no shit like that to you," "my father, my strength was gone," "he was everything to me," and "I did not know what to do," but, like the phrases "putting the work in," "get the dope, cut the dope," "let's keep it popping," and "the strong take from the weak but the smart take from everybody," they are either common in general or common with respect to hip hop culture, and do not enjoy copyright protection. The average person reading or listening to these phrases in the context of an overall story or song would not regard them as unique and protectable. Moreover, words and short phrases do not enjoy copyright protection. The similarity between Winstead's book and the lyrics to Jackson's songs on the album/CD is even more tenuous. "Stretching the dope" and "bloodshot red eyes" are common phrases that do not enjoy copyright protection. A side-by-side comparison of Winstead's book and the lyrics from Jackson's album/CD do not support a claim of copyright infringement.

For the foregoing reasons, we will affirm the order of the District Court dismissing [Winstead's] complaint.

## Legal Reasoning Questions

1. Which expressions of an original work are protected by copyright law?

2. Is all copying copyright infringement? If not, what is the test for determining whether a creative work has been unlawfully copied?

3. How did the court in this case determine whether the defendant's work infringed on the plaintiff's copyright?

**Remedies for Copyright Infringement** Those who infringe copyrights may be liable for damages or criminal penalties. These range from actual damages or statutory damages, imposed at the court's discretion, to criminal proceedings for willful violations.

Actual damages are based on the harm caused to the copyright holder by the infringement, while statutory damages, not to exceed $150,000, are provided for under the Copyright Act. Criminal proceedings may result in fines and/or imprisonment. A court can also issue a permanent injunction against a defendant when the court deems it necessary to prevent future copyright infringement.

■ **CASE IN POINT 29.16** Rusty Carroll operated an online term paper business, R2C2, Inc., that offered up to 300,000 research papers for sale at nine Web sites. Individuals whose work was posted on these Web sites without their permission filed a lawsuit against Carroll for copyright infringement. Because Carroll had repeatedly failed to comply with court orders regarding discovery, the court found that the copyright infringement was likely to continue unless an injunction was issued. The court therefore issued a permanent injunction prohibiting Carroll and R2C2 from selling any term paper without sworn documentary evidence that the paper's author had given permission.[28] ■

**The "Fair Use" Exception** An exception to liability for copyright infringement is made under the "fair use" doctrine. In certain circumstances, a person or organization can reproduce copyrighted material without paying royalties. Section 107 of the Copyright Act provides as follows:

> [T]he fair use of a copyrighted work, including such use by reproduction in copies or phonorecords or by any other means specified by [Section 106 of the Copyright Act], for purposes such as criticism, comment, news reporting, teaching (including multiple copies for classroom use), scholarship, or research, is not an infringement of copyright. In determining whether the use made of a work in any particular case is a fair use the factors to be considered shall include—
>
> (1) the purpose and character of the use, including whether such use is of a commercial nature or is for nonprofit educational purposes;
> (2) the nature of the copyrighted work;
> (3) the amount and substantiality of the portion used in relation to the copyrighted work as a whole; and
> (4) the effect of the use upon the potential market for or value of the copyrighted work.

**What Is Fair Use?** Because these guidelines are very broad, the courts determine whether a particular use is fair on a case-by-case basis. Thus, anyone who reproduces copyrighted material may be committing a violation. In determining whether a use is fair, courts have often considered the fourth factor to be the most important.

■ **CASE IN POINT 29.17** A number of research universities, in partnership with Google, Inc., agreed to digitize books from their libraries and create a repository for them. Eighty member institutions (including many colleges and universities) contributed more than ten million works into the HathiTrust Digital Library. Some authors complained that this book scanning violated their rights and sued the HathiTrust and several associated entities for copyright infringement.

The court, however, sided with the defendants and held that making digital copies for the purposes of online search was a fair use. The library's searchable database enabled researchers to find terms of interest in the digital volumes—but not to read the volumes online. Therefore, the court concluded that the digitization did not provide a substitute that damaged the market for the original works.[29] ■

**The First Sale Doctrine** Section 109(a) of the Copyright Act provides that the owner of a particular item that is copyrighted can, without the authority of the copyright owner, sell or otherwise dispose of it. This rule is known as the first sale doctrine.

Under this doctrine, once a copyright owner sells or gives away a particular copy of a work, the copyright owner no longer has the right to control the distribution of that copy. Thus, for instance, a person who buys a copyrighted book can sell it to someone else. The first sale doctrine also applies to a person who receives promotional CDs, such as a music critic or radio programmer.[30]

■ **CASE IN POINT 29.18** Supap Kirtsaeng, a citizen of Thailand, was a graduate student at the University of Southern California. He enlisted friends and family in Thailand to buy copies of textbooks there and ship them to him in the United States. Kirtsaeng resold the textbooks on eBay, where he eventually made about $100,000.

John Wiley & Sons, Inc., had printed eight of those textbooks in Asia. Wiley sued Kirtsaeng in federal district court for copyright infringement. Kirtsaeng argued that Section 109(a) of the Copyright Act allows the first purchaser-owner of a book to sell it without the copyright owner's permission. The trial court held in favor of Wiley, and that decision was affirmed on appeal. Kirtsaeng then appealed to the United States Supreme Court, which ruled

---

**28.** *Weidner v. Carroll*, 2010 WL 310310 (S.D.Ill. 2010).

**29.** *Authors Guild, Inc., v. HathiTrust*, 755 F.3d 87 (2d Cir. 2014).
**30.** See, for example, *UMG Recordings, Inc. v. Augusto*, 628 F.3d 1175 (9th Cir. 2011).

in Kirtsaeng's favor. The first sale doctrine applies even to goods purchased abroad and resold in the United States.[31] ■

## 29-3d Copyright Protection for Software

The Computer Software Copyright Act amended the Copyright Act to include computer programs in the list of creative works protected by federal copyright law.[32] Generally, copyright protection extends to those parts of a computer program that can be read by humans, such as the "high-level" language of a source code. Protection also extends to the binary-language object code, which is readable only by the computer, and to such elements as the overall structure, sequence, and organization of a program.

Not all aspects of software are protected, however. Courts typically have not extended copyright protection to the "look and feel"—the general appearance, command structure, video images, menus, windows, and other screen displays—of computer programs. (Note that copying the "look and feel" of another's product may be a violation of trade dress or trademark laws, however.) Sometimes it can be difficult for courts to decide which particular aspects of software are protected.

■ **CASE IN POINT 29.19** Oracle America, Inc., is a software company that owns numerous application programming interfaces, or API packages. Oracle grants licenses to others to use these API packages to write applications in the Java programming language. Java is open and free for anyone to use, but using it requires an interface. When Google began using some of Oracle's API packages to run Java on its Android mobile devices, Oracle sued for copyright infringement. Google argued that the software packages were command structure and, as such, not protected under copyright law. Ultimately, a federal appellate court concluded that the API packages were source code and were entitled to copyright protection.[33] ■

## 29-4 Trade Secrets

The law of trade secrets protects some business processes and information that are not, or cannot be, patented, copyrighted, or trademarked. A **trade secret** is basically information of commercial value, such as customer lists, plans, and research and development. Trade secrets may also include pricing information, marketing methods, production techniques, and generally anything that makes an individual company unique and that would have value to a competitor.

Unlike copyright and trademark protection, protection of trade secrets extends to both ideas and their expression. For this reason, and because there are no registration or filing requirements for trade secrets, trade secret protection may be well suited for software.

Of course, a company's trade secrets must be disclosed to some persons, particularly to key employees. Businesses generally attempt to protect their trade secrets by having all employees who use a protected process or information agree in their contracts, or in confidentiality agreements, never to divulge it.

## 29-4a State and Federal Law on Trade Secrets

Under Section 757 of the *Restatement of Torts,* those who disclose or use another's trade secret, without authorization, are liable to that other party if either of the following is true:

1. They discovered the secret by improper means.
2. Their disclosure or use constitutes a breach of a duty owed to the other party.

Stealing confidential business data by industrial espionage, such as by tapping into a competitor's computer, is a theft of trade secrets without any contractual violation and is actionable in itself.

Trade secrets have long been protected under the common law. Today, nearly every state has enacted trade secret laws based on the Uniform Trade Secrets Act.[34] Additionally, the Economic Espionage Act[35] makes the theft of trade secrets a federal crime.

## 29-4b Trade Secrets in Cyberspace

Computer technology is undercutting many business firms' ability to protect their confidential information, including trade secrets. For example, a dishonest employee could e-mail trade secrets in a company's computer to a competitor or a future employer. If e-mail is not an option, the employee might walk out with the information on a flash drive.

Misusing a company's social media account is yet another way in which employees may appropriate trade secrets. ■ **CASE IN POINT 29.20** Noah Kravitz worked for a company called PhoneDog for four years as a product reviewer and video blogger. PhoneDog provided him with the Twitter account "@PhoneDog_Noah." Kravitz's popularity grew, and he had approximately 17,000

---

**31.** *Kirtsaeng v. John Wiley & Sons, Inc.,* ___ U.S. ___, 133 S.Ct. 1351, 185 L.Ed.2d 392 (2013).
**32.** Pub. L. No. 96-517 (1980), amending 17 U.S.C. Sections 101, 117.
**33.** *Oracle America, Inc. v. Google Inc.,* 750 F.3d 1339 (Fed.Cir. 2014).

**34.** The Uniform Trade Secrets Act, as drafted by the National Conference of Commissioners on Uniform State Laws (NCCUSL), can be found at uniformlaws.org.
**35.** 18 U.S.C. Sections 1831–1839.

followers by the time he quit. PhoneDog requested that Kravitz stop using the Twitter account. Although Kravitz changed his handle to "@noahkravitz," he continued to use the account. PhoneDog subsequently sued Kravitz for misappropriation of trade secrets, among other things. Kravitz moved for a dismissal, but the court found that the complaint adequately stated a cause of action for

misappropriation of trade secrets and allowed the suit to continue.[36] ∎

Exhibit 29–1 outlines trade secrets and other forms of intellectual property discussed in this chapter.

36. *PhoneDog v. Kravitz*, 2011 WL 5415612 (N.D.Cal. 2011). See also *Mintel Learning Technology, Inc. v. Ambrow Education Holding Ltd.*, 2012 WL 762126 (N.D.Cal. 2012).

**EXHIBIT 29–1   Forms of Intellectual Property**

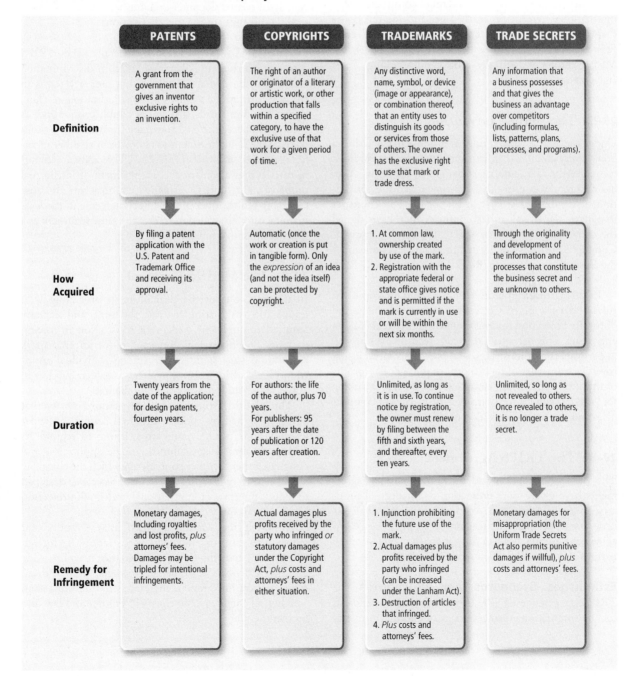

# 29–5 International Protection for Intellectual Property

For many years, the United States has been a party to various international agreements relating to intellectual property rights. For instance, the Paris Convention of 1883, to which almost 180 countries are signatory, allows parties in one country to file for patent and trademark protection in any of the other member countries. Other international agreements in this area include the Berne Convention, the Trade-Related Aspects of Intellectual Property Rights (known as the TRIPS agreement), the Madrid Protocol, and the Anti-Counterfeiting Trade Agreement.

## 29–5a The Berne Convention

Under the Berne Convention, if a U.S. citizen writes a book, every country that has signed the convention must recognize the U.S. author's copyright in the book. Also, if a citizen of a country that has not signed the convention first publishes a book in one of the 169 countries that have signed, all other countries that have signed the convention must recognize that author's copyright. Copyright notice is not needed to gain protection under the Berne Convention for works published after March 1, 1989.

In 2011, the European Union altered its copyright rules under the Berne Convention to extend the period of royalty protection for musicians from fifty years to seventy years. This decision aids major record labels as well as performers and musicians who previously faced losing royalties from sales of their older recordings. The profits of musicians and record companies have been shrinking for years because of the sharp decline in sales of compact discs and the rise in illegal downloads.

## 29–5b The TRIPS Agreement

The Berne Convention and other international agreements have given some protection to intellectual property on a worldwide level. None of them, however, has been as significant and far reaching in scope as the TRIPS agreement. Representatives from more than one hundred nations signed the TRIPS agreement in 1994.

**Establishes Standards and Procedures** The TRIPS agreement established, for the first time, standards for the international protection of intellectual property rights, including patents, trademarks, and copyrights for movies, computer programs, books, and music. Each member country of the World Trade Organization must include in its domestic laws broad intellectual property rights and effective remedies (including civil and criminal penalties) for violations of those rights.

Each member nation must also ensure that legal procedures are available for parties who wish to bring actions for infringement of intellectual property rights. Additionally, a related document established a mechanism for settling disputes among member nations.

**Prohibits Discrimination** Generally, the TRIPS agreement forbids member nations from discriminating against foreign owners of intellectual property rights in the administration, regulation, or adjudication of those rights. In other words, a member nation cannot give its own nationals (citizens) favorable treatment without offering the same treatment to nationals of all other member countries. ■ **EXAMPLE 29.21** A U.S. software manufacturer brings a suit for the infringement of intellectual property rights under Germany's national laws. Because Germany is a member of the TRIPS agreement, the U.S. manufacturer is entitled to receive the same treatment as a German manufacturer. ■

## 29–5c The Madrid Protocol

In the past, one of the difficulties in protecting U.S. trademarks internationally was the time and expense required to apply for trademark registration in foreign nations. The filing fees and procedures for trademark registration vary significantly among individual countries. The Madrid Protocol, which was signed into law in 2003, may help to resolve these problems.

The Madrid Protocol is an international treaty that has been signed by about a hundred countries. Under its provisions, a U.S. company wishing to register its trademark abroad can submit a single application and designate other member countries in which the company would like to register its mark. The treaty was designed to reduce the costs of international trademark protection by more than 60 percent.

Although the Madrid Protocol may simplify and reduce the cost of trademark registration in foreign countries, it remains to be seen whether it will provide significant benefits to trademark owners. Even with an easier registration process, there are still questions as to whether all member countries will enforce the law and protect the mark.

## 29–5d The Anti-Counterfeiting Trade Agreement

In 2011, Australia, Canada, Japan, Korea, Morocco, New Zealand, Singapore, and the United States signed the Anti-Counterfeiting Trade Agreement (ACTA), an international treaty to combat global counterfeiting and piracy. Other nations have since signed the agreement.

**Goals and Provisions** The goals of the treaty are to increase international cooperation, facilitate the best law enforcement practices, and provide a legal framework to combat counterfeiting. ACTA applies not only to counterfeit physical goods, such as medications, but also to pirated copyrighted works being distributed via the Internet. The idea is to create a new standard of enforcement for intellectual property rights that goes beyond the TRIPS agreement and encourages international cooperation and information sharing among signatory countries.

**Border Searches** Under ACTA, member nations are required to establish border measures that allow officials, on their own initiative, to search commercial shipments of imports and exports for counterfeit goods. The treaty neither requires nor prohibits random border searches of electronic devices, such as laptops, tablet devices, and smartphones, for infringing content.

If border authorities reasonably believe that any goods in transit are counterfeit, the treaty allows them to keep the suspect goods unless the owner proves that the items are authentic and noninfringing. The treaty allows member nations, in accordance with their own laws, to order online service providers to furnish information about suspected trademark and copyright infringers, including their identities.

# Reviewing: Intellectual Property

Two computer science majors, Trent and Xavier, have an idea for a new video game, which they propose to call Hallowed. They form a business and begin developing their idea. Several months later, Trent and Xavier run into a problem with their design and consult a friend, Brad, who is an expert in designing computer source codes. After the software is completed but before Hallowed is marketed, a video game called Halo 2 is released for both the Xbox and the Playstation systems. Halo 2 uses source codes similar to those of Hallowed and imitates Hallowed's overall look and feel, although not all the features are alike. Using the information presented in the chapter, answer the following questions.

1. Would the name *Hallowed* receive protection as a trademark or as trade dress? Explain.
2. If Trent and Xavier had obtained a patent on Hallowed, would the release of Halo 2 have infringed on their patent? Why or why not?
3. Based only on the facts described above, could Trent and Xavier sue the makers of Halo 2 for copyright infringement? Why or why not?
4. Suppose that Trent and Xavier discover that Brad took the idea of Hallowed and sold it to the company that produced Halo 2. Which type of intellectual property issue does this raise?

**Debate This** . . .   *Congress has amended copyright law several times so that copyright holders now have protection for many decades. Was Congress right in extending these copyright time periods?*

# Terms and Concepts

| | | |
|---|---|---|
| certification mark 571 | intellectual property 566 | trade dress 571 |
| collective mark 571 | license 572 | trade name 572 |
| copyright 576 | patent 573 | trade secret 580 |
| dilution 568 | service mark 571 | trademark 566 |

## Issue Spotters

**1.** Roslyn, a food buyer for Organic Cornucopia Food Company, decides to go into business for herself as Roslyn's Kitchen. She contacts Organic's suppliers, offering to buy their entire harvest for the next year. She also contacts Organic's customers, offering to sell her products at prices lower than Organic's prices. Has Roslyn violated any of the intellectual property rights discussed in this chapter? Explain. (See *Trade Secrets.*)

**2.** Global Products develops, patents, and markets software. World Copies, Inc., sells Global's software without the maker's permission. Is this patent infringement? If so, how might Global save the cost of suing World for infringement and at the same time profit from World's sales? (See *Patents.*)

• **Check your answers to the Issue Spotters against the answers provided in Appendix B at the end of this text.**

## Business Scenarios

**29–1. Fair Use.** Professor Wise is teaching a summer seminar in business torts at State University. Several times during the course, he makes copies of relevant sections from business law texts and distributes them to his students. Wise does not realize that the daughter of one of the textbook authors is a member of his seminar. She tells her father about Wise's copying activities, which have taken place without her father's or his publisher's permission. Her father sues Wise for copyright infringement. Wise claims protection under the fair use doctrine. Who will prevail? Explain. (See *Copyrights.*)

**29–2. Patent Infringement.** John and Andrew Doney invented a hard-bearing device for balancing rotors. Although they obtained a patent for their invention from the U.S. Patent and Trademark Office, it was never used as an automobile wheel balancer. Some time later, Exetron Corp. produced an automobile wheel balancer that used a hard-bearing device with a support plate similar to that of the Doneys' device. Given that the Doneys had not used their device for automobile wheel balancing, does Exetron's use of a similar device infringe on the Doneys' patent? Why or why not? (See *Patents.*)

## Business Case Problems

### 29–3. Spotlight on Macy's—Copyright Infringement.

 United Fabrics International, Inc., bought a fabric design from an Italian designer and registered a copyright to it with the U.S. Copyright Office. When Macy's, Inc., began selling garments with a similar design, United filed a copyright infringement suit against Macy's. Macy's argued that United did not own a valid copyright to the design and so could not claim infringement. Does United have to prove that the copyright is valid to establish infringement? Explain. [*United Fabrics International, Inc. v. C&J Wear, Inc.,* 630 F.3d 1255 (9th Cir. 2011)] (See *Copyrights.*)

**29–4. Theft of Trade Secrets.** Hanjuan Jin, a citizen of China, worked as a software engineer for Motorola for many years in a division that created proprietary standards for cellular communications. Contrary to Motorola's policies, Jin also secretly began working as a consultant for Lemko Corp., as well as with Sun Kaisens, a Chinese software company, and with the Chinese military. She started corresponding with Sun Kaisens's management about a possible full-time job in China. Jin took several medical leaves of absence from Motorola to return to Beijing and work with Sun Kaisens and the military.

After one of these medical leaves, Jin returned to Motorola. Over a period of several days, Jin accessed and downloaded thousands of documents on her personal laptop and on pen drives. When, later, she attempted to board a flight to China

from Chicago, she was randomly searched by U.S. Customs and Border Protection officials at the airport. U.S. officials discovered the downloaded Motorola documents. Are there any circumstances under which Jin could avoid being prosecuted for theft of trade secrets? If so, what are these circumstances? Discuss fully. [*United States v. Hanjuan Jin,* 833 F.Supp.2d 977 (N.D.Ill. 2012)] (See *Trade Secrets.*)

**29–5. Copyright Infringement.** SilverEdge Systems Software hired Catherine Conrad to perform a singing telegram. SilverEdge arranged for James Bendewald to record Conrad's performance of her copyrighted song to post on its Web site. Conrad agreed to wear a microphone to assist in the recording, told Bendewald what to film, and asked for an additional fee only if SilverEdge used the video for a commercial purpose. Later, the company chose to post a video of a different performer's singing telegram instead. Conrad filed a suit in a federal district court against SilverEdge and Bendewald for copyright infringement. Are the defendants liable? Explain. [*Conrad v. Bendewald,* 500 Fed.Appx. 526 (7th Cir. 2013)] (See *Copyrights.*)

### 29–6. Business Case Problem with Sample Answer—

 **Patents.** The U.S. Patent and Trademark Office (PTO) denied Raymond Gianelli's application for a patent for a "Rowing Machine"—an exercise machine on which a user *pulls* on handles to perform a rowing motion against a selected resistance. The PTO considered the device obvious in light of a previously patented "Chest Press Apparatus for Exercising

Regions of the Upper Body"—an exercise machine on which a user *pushes* on handles to overcome a selected resistance. On what ground might this result be reversed on appeal? Discuss. [*In re Gianelli*, 739 F.3d 1375 (Fed. Cir. 2014)] (See *Patents*.)

- **For a sample answer to Problem 29–6, go to Appendix C at the end of this text.**

**29–7. Patents.** Rodney Klassen was employed by the U.S. Department of Agriculture (USDA). Without the USDA's authorization, Klassen gave Jim Ludy, a grape grower, plant material for two unreleased varieties of grapes. For almost two years, most of Ludy's plantings bore no usable fruit, none of the grapes were sold, and no plant material was given to any other person. The plantings were visible from publicly accessible roads, but none of the vines were labeled, and the variety could not be identified by simply viewing the vines. Under patent law, an applicant may not obtain a patent for an invention that is in public use for more than one year before the date of the application. Could the USDA successfully apply for patents on the two varieties given to Ludy? Explain. [*Delano Farms Co. v. California Table Grape Commission*, 778 F.3d 1243 (Fed. Cir. 2015)] (See *Patents*.)

**29–8. Copyright.** Savant Homes, Inc., is a custom home designer and builder. Using what it called the "Anders Plan," Savant built a model house in Windsor, Colorado. This was a ranch house with two bedrooms on one side and a master suite on the other, separated by a combined family room, dining room, and kitchen. Ron and Tammie Wagner toured the Savant house. The same month, the Wagners hired builder Douglas Collins and his firm, Douglas Consulting, LLC, to build a house for them in Windsor. After it was built, Savant filed a suit in a federal district court against Collins for copyright infringement, alleging that the builder had copied the Anders Plan in the design and construction of the Wagner house. Collins showed that the Anders Plan consisted of standard elements and standard arrangements of elements. In these circumstances, has infringement occurred? Explain.

*[Savant Homes, Inc. v. Collins*, 809 F.3d 1133 (10th Cir. 2016)] (See *Copyrights*.)

**29–9. A Question of Ethics—Copyright Infringement.**

 *Custom Copies, Inc.*, prepares and sells coursepacks, which contain compilations of readings for college courses. A teacher selects the readings and delivers a syllabus to the copy shop, which obtains the materials from a library, copies them, and binds the copies. Blackwell Publishing, Inc., which owns the copyright to some of the materials, filed a suit, alleging copyright infringement. Custom Copies filed a motion to dismiss for failure to state a claim. [*Blackwell Publishing, Inc. v. Custom Copies, Inc.*, 2006 WL 1529503 (N.D.Fla. 2006)] (See *Copyrights*.)

**(a)** Custom Copies argued, in part, that creating and selling did not "distribute" the coursepacks. Does a copy shop violate copyright law if it only copies materials for coursepacks? Does the copying fall under the "fair use" exception? Should the court grant the defendant's motion? Why or why not?

**(b)** What is the potential impact of copying and selling a book or journal without the permission of, and the payment of royalties or a fee to, the copyright owner? Explain.

**29–10. Special Case Analysis—Copyright Infringement.** Go to Case Analysis 29.3, *Winstead v. Jackson*. Read the excerpt, and answer the following questions. (See *Copyrights*.)

**(a) Issue:** This case focused on an allegation of copyright infringement involving what parties and which creative works?

**(b) Rule of Law:** What is the test for determining whether a creative work infringes the copyright of another work?

**(c) Applying the Rule of Law:** How did the court determine whether the claim of copyright infringement was supported in this case?

**(d) Conclusion:** Was the defendant liable for copyright infringement? Why or why not?

# Legal Reasoning Group Activity

**29–11. Patents.** After years of research, your company develops a product that might revolutionize the green (environmentally conscious) building industry. The product is made from relatively inexpensive and widely available materials combined in a unique way that can substantially lower the heating and cooling costs of residential and commercial buildings. The company has registered the trademark it intends to use on the product and has filed a patent application with the U.S. Patent and Trademark Office. (See *Patents*.)

**(a)** One group should provide three reasons why this product does or does not qualify for patent protection.

**(b)** Another group should develop a four-step procedure for how your company can best protect its intellectual property rights (trademark, trade secret, and patent) and prevent domestic and foreign competitors from producing counterfeit goods or cheap knockoffs.

**(c)** Another group should list and explain three ways your company can utilize licensing.

## CHAPTER 30

# Insurance

Protecting against loss is a foremost concern of all property owners. No one can predict whether an accident or a fire will occur, so individuals and businesses typically protect their personal and financial interests by obtaining insurance.

**Insurance** is a contract in which the insurance company (the insurer) promises to pay or otherwise compensate another (either the insured or the beneficiary) for a particular loss.

Insurance may provide for compensation in the event of (1) the injury or death of the insured or another, (2) damage to the insured's property, or (3) other types of losses, such as those resulting from lawsuits. Basically, insurance is an arrangement for *transferring and allocating risk.* In general, **risk** can be described as a prediction concerning potential loss based on known and unknown factors.

**Risk management** normally involves the transfer of certain risks from the individual to the insurance company by a contractual agreement. We examine the insurance contract and its provisions in this chapter. First, however, we look at some basic insurance terminology and concepts.

## 30–1 Insurance Terminology and Concepts

Like other legal areas, insurance has its own special concepts and terminology. An insurance contract is called a **policy.** The consideration paid to the insurer is called a **premium,** and the insurance company is sometimes called an **underwriter.** The parties to an insurance policy are the *insurer* (the insurance company) and the *insured* (the person covered by its provisions).

Insurance contracts usually are obtained through an *agent,* who normally works for the insurance company, or through a *broker,* who is ordinarily an *independent contractor.* When a broker deals with an applicant for insurance, the broker is, in effect, the applicant's agent (and not an agent of the insurance company).

In contrast, an insurance agent is an agent of the insurance company, not an agent of the applicant. Thus, the agent owes fiduciary duties to the insurer (the insurance company), but not to the person who is applying for insurance. As a general rule, the insurance company is bound by the acts of its agents when they act within the scope of the agency relationship. In most situations, state law determines the status of all parties writing or obtaining insurance.

## 30–1a Classifications of Insurance

Insurance is classified according to the nature of the risk involved. Fire insurance, casualty insurance, life insurance, and title insurance apply to different types of risk and protect different persons and interests. This is reasonable because the types of losses that are expected and the types that are foreseeable or unforeseeable vary with the nature of the activity. Exhibit 30–1 provides a list of common insurance classifications.

## 30–1b Insurable Interest

A person must have an **insurable interest** in something in order to insure it. Without an insurable interest, there is no enforceable contract, and a transaction to purchase insurance coverage would have to be treated as a wager. The existence of an insurable interest is a primary concern in determining liability under an insurance policy.

**Life Insurance** In regard to life insurance, a person must have a reasonable expectation of benefit from the continued life of another to have an insurable interest in that person's life. The insurable interest must exist *at the time the policy is obtained.*

**EXHIBIT 30–1   Selected Insurance Classifications**

| TYPE OF INSURANCE | COVERAGE |
| --- | --- |
| Accident | Covers expenses, losses, and suffering incurred by the insured because of accidents causing physical injury and any consequent disability; sometimes includes a specified payment to heirs of the insured if death results from an accident. |
| All-Risk | Covers all losses that the insured may incur except those that are specifically excluded. Typical exclusions are losses due to war, pollution, earthquakes, and floods. |
| Automobile | May cover damage to automobiles resulting from specified hazards or occurrences (such as fire, vandalism, theft, or collision); normally provides protection against liability for personal injuries and property damage resulting from the operation of the vehicle. |
| Casualty | Protects against losses incurred by the insured as a result of being held liable for personal injuries or property damage sustained by others. |
| Disability | Replaces a portion of the insured's monthly income from employment in the event that illness or injury causes a short- or long-term disability. Some states require employers to provide short-term disability insurance. Benefits typically last a set period of time, such as six months for short-term coverage or five years for long-term coverage. |
| Fire | Covers losses to the insured caused by fire. |
| Floater | Covers movable property, as long as the property is within the territorial boundaries specified in the contract. |
| Homeowners' | Protects homeowners against some or all risks of loss to their residences and the residences' contents or liability arising from the use of the property. |
| Key-Person | Protects a business in the event of the death or disability of a key employee. |
| Liability | Protects against liability imposed on the insured as a result of injuries to the person or property of another. |
| Life | Covers the death of the policyholder. On the death of the insured, the insurer pays the amount specified in the policy to the insured's beneficiary. |
| Major Medical | Protects the insured against major hospital, medical, or surgical expenses. |
| Malpractice | A form of liability insurance that protects professionals (physicians, lawyers, and others) against malpractice claims brought against them by their patients or clients. |
| Term Life | Provides life insurance for a specified period of time (term) with no cash surrender value. It usually is renewable. |

**Life Insurance on Family Members.** Close family relationships give a person an insurable interest in the life of another. For instance, a husband can take out an insurance policy on his wife and vice versa, or parents can take out life insurance policies on their children. A policy that a person takes out on his or her spouse remains valid even if they divorce, unless a specific provision in the policy calls for its termination on divorce.

**Key-Person Life Insurance.** *Key-person insurance* is insurance obtained by an organization on the life of a person who is important to that organization. Because the organization expects to experience financial gain from the continuation of the key person's life or financial loss from the key person's death, the organization has an insurable interest.

Typically, a small company will insure the lives of its important employees. Similarly, a corporation has an insurable interest in the life of a key executive (such as a talented CEO) whose death would result in financial loss to the company. If a firm insures a key person's life and that person leaves the firm and subsequently dies, the firm can collect on the insurance policy, provided that it has continued to pay the premiums.

**Property Insurance** For property insurance, an insurable interest exists when the insured derives a monetary benefit from the preservation and continued existence of the property. The insurable interest must exist at the time the loss occurs but need not exist when the policy is purchased.

■ **CASE IN POINT 30.1** ABM Industries, Inc., operated the heating, ventilation, and air-conditioning systems at the World Trade Center (WTC) in New York City in 2001. ABM also maintained all of the WTC's common areas. At the time, ABM employed more than eight hundred workers at the WTC. Zurich American Insurance Company insured ABM against losses resulting from "business interruption" caused by direct physical loss or damage "to property owned, controlled, used, leased or intended for use" by ABM.

After the terrorist attacks on September 11, ABM filed a claim to recover for the loss of all income derived from its WTC operations. Zurich argued that the recovery should be limited to the income lost as a result of the destruction of ABM's office and storage space and supplies. A federal appellate court, however, ruled that ABM was entitled to compensation for the loss of all of its WTC operations. The court reasoned that the "policy's scope expressly includes real or personal property that the insured 'used,' 'controlled,' or 'intended for use.'" Because ABM's income depended on "the common areas and leased premises in the WTC complex," it had an insurable interest in that property at the time of the loss.[1] ■

In the following case, the plaintiff sought to retain his insurable interest in a home he no longer owned.

---

1. *Zurich American Insurance Co. v. ABM Industries, Inc.*, 397 F.3d 158 (2d Cir. 2005).

**Case 30.1**

# Breeden v. Buchanan

Court of Appeals of Mississippi, 164 So.3d 1057 (2015).

**Background and Facts** Donald Breeden and Willie Buchanan were married in Marion County, Mississippi. They lived in a home in Sandy Hook. Nationwide Property & Casualty Insurance Company insured the home under a policy bought by Breeden that named him as the insured. The policy provided that the spouse of the named insured was covered as an insured. After eight years of marriage, Breeden and Buchanan divorced. Breeden transferred his interest in the home to Buchanan as part of the couple's property settlement.

Less than a year later, a fire completely destroyed the home. An insurance claim was filed with Nationwide. Nationwide paid Buchanan. Breeden then filed a suit in a Mississippi state court against Buchanan and Nationwide. The plaintiff asserted claims for breach of contract and bad faith, and sought to recover the proceeds under the policy. The court dismissed the suit. Breeden appealed.

## In the Language of the Court

*GRIFFIS*, P.J. [Presiding Judge], for the Court:

* * * *

Breeden's claims for breach of contract [and] bad-faith denial of insurance benefits * * * are based on the insurance policy. The [lower] court ruled that Breeden had no "insurable interest" in the Nationwide policy and had no right to the proceeds of the policy. Specifically, the * * * court ruled:

> The court finds that the pleadings reflect no insurable interest in Breeden in and to the policy or to the proceeds, as Breeden transferred and conveyed his right, title, and interest in and to the insured property to his former spouse, Buchanan, as part and parcel of their divorce proceeding and property settlement agreement, this transfer and conveyance having transpired several months before the occurrence of the loss, which is the subject matter of Breeden's complaint.
>
> Finding that Breeden had no insurable interest in and to the property—and thus no entitlement to any of the insurance proceeds—it follows that Nationwide did not breach the insurance contract by failing to pay Breeden any insurance proceeds from the loss, nor did it act in bad faith.

**Case 30.1 Continued**   * * * *

Breeden argues that the [lower] court was in error to determine that he had no insurable interest in the home. The home, which was Breeden's and Buchanan's marital residence, was insured under a Nationwide homeowners' insurance policy. The policy was effective from May 27, 2010, to May 27, 2011. The policy insured the home and its contents. At the beginning of the policy period, May 27, 2010, both Breeden and Buchanan had an insurable interest in the home because they were married and lived together in the home. The policy provided that the spouse of the named insured who resides at the same premises is covered as an insured. Based on the allegations of the complaint, the documents attached to the complaint, and Nationwide's motion [to dismiss], the * * * judge determined that Breeden did not have an insurable interest in the home at the time of the fire loss.

The fire loss occurred in April 2011. *At that time, Breeden did not have an insurable interest in the home. * * * The factual allegations of the complaint indicated that he did not have any ownership interest in the home at the time of the loss.* [Emphasis added.]
* * * *

Based on the complaint and the accompanying documents, there was simply nothing further that Nationwide owed under the insurance policy.

**Decision and Remedy** *A state intermediate appellate court affirmed the lower court's dismissal of Breeden's suit. Buchanan, not Breeden, was entitled to the proceeds of the insurance claim filed with Nationwide. At the time of the fire, the insurable interest in the property existed solely with Buchanan.*

**Critical Thinking**
- **Economic** *Why is an insurable interest required for the enforcement of an insurance contract?*

---

# 30–2 The Insurance Contract

An insurance contract is governed by the general principles of contract law, although the insurance industry is heavily regulated by each state.[2] Thus, for the insurance contract to be binding, consideration (in the form of a premium) must be given. In addition, the parties forming the contract must have the required contractual capacity to do so.

## 30–2a Application for Insurance

Customarily, a party offers to purchase insurance by submitting an application to the insurance company. The company can either accept or reject the offer. Sometimes, the insurance company's acceptance is conditional—on the results of a life insurance applicant's medical examination, for instance.

The filled-in application form is usually attached to the policy and made a part of the insurance contract. Thus, an insurance applicant is bound by any false statements that appear in the application (subject to certain exceptions). Insurance companies evaluate their risk

based on the information included in the application. Therefore, an applicant's misstatements or misrepresentations can void a policy, especially if the insurance company can show that it would not have extended insurance if it had known the facts.

## 30–2b Effective Date

The effective date of an insurance contract—that is, the date on which the insurance coverage begins—is important. Any loss sustained before the effective date will not be covered by the policy.

In some situations, the insurance applicant is not protected until a formal written policy is issued. In other situations, the applicant is protected between the time an application is received and the time the insurance company either accepts or rejects it. In these situations, a *binder* may be written.

**Binder** Recall that a broker is an agent of the applicant, not an agent of the insurance company. Therefore, if a person hires a broker to obtain insurance, and the broker fails to procure a policy, the applicant normally is not insured.

In contrast, a person who is obtaining insurance from an insurance company's agent is usually protected from

---

2. The states were given authority to regulate the insurance industry by the McCarran-Ferguson Act of 1945, 15 U.S.C. Sections 1011–1015.

the moment the application is made, provided that some form of premium has been paid. Usually, the agent will write a memorandum, or **binder,** indicating that a policy is pending and stating its essential terms. The binder provides temporary coverage until a formal policy is accepted or denied.

**Life Insurance** Parties may agree that a life insurance policy will be binding at the time the insured pays the first premium. The policy may, however, be expressly contingent on the applicant's passing a physical examination. If the applicant pays the premium and passes the examination, then the policy coverage is continuously in effect. If the applicant pays the premium but dies before having the physical examination, the policy may still be effective. In order to collect, the applicant's estate normally must show that the applicant would have passed the examination had he or she not died.

## 30–2c Provisions and Clauses

Some of the important provisions and clauses contained in insurance contracts are discussed in the following subsections and listed in Exhibit 30–2.

**Provisions Mandated by Statute** If a statute mandates that a certain provision be included in insurance contracts, a court will interpret the insurance policy as containing that provision. If a statute requires that any limitations on coverage be stated in the contract, a court will not allow an insurer to avoid liability by relying on an unexpressed restriction.

**Incontestability Clauses** Statutes commonly require that a policy for life or health insurance include an **incontestability clause**. Such a clause provides that after the policy has been in force for a specified length of time—often two or three years—the insurer cannot contest statements made in the application.

Once a policy becomes incontestable, the insurer cannot later avoid a claim on the basis of, for instance, fraud on the part of the insured, unless the clause provides an exception for that circumstance. The clause does not prevent an insurer from asserting other defenses to a claim, such as the nonpayment of premiums, failure to file proof of death, or lack of an insurable interest.

**Coinsurance Clauses** Often, when taking out fire insurance policies, property owners insure their property

## EXHIBIT 30–2 Insurance Contract Provisions and Clauses

| TYPE OF CLAUSE | DEFINITION |
| --- | --- |
| Antilapse Clause | An antilapse clause provides that a life insurance policy will not automatically lapse if no payment is made on the date due. Ordinarily, under such a provision, the insured has a *grace period* of thirty or thirty-one days within which to pay an overdue premium before the policy is canceled. |
| Appraisal Clause | Insurance policies frequently provide that if the parties cannot agree on the amount of a loss covered under the policy or the value of the property lost, an appraisal, or estimate, by an impartial and qualified third party can be demanded. |
| Arbitration Clause | Many insurance policies include clauses that call for arbitration of any disputes that arise between the insurer and the insured concerning the settlement of claims. |
| Coinsurance Clause | Many property insurance policies include a coinsurance clause that applies in the event of a partial loss and determines what percentage of the value of the property must be insured for an owner to be fully reimbursed for a loss. If the owner insures the property up to a specified percentage (typically 80 percent) of its value, she or he will recover any loss up to the face amount of the policy. |
| Incontestability Clause | An incontestability clause provides that after a policy has been in force for a specified length of time—usually two or three years—the insurer cannot contest statements made in the application. |
| Multiple Insurance Clause | Many insurance policies include a clause providing that if the insured has multiple insurance policies that cover the same property and the amount of coverage exceeds the loss, the loss will be shared proportionately by the insurance companies. |

for less than full value because most fires do not result in a total loss. To encourage owners to insure their property for an amount as close to full value as possible, fire insurance policies generally include a coinsurance clause.

Typically, a **coinsurance clause** provides that if the owner insures the property up to a specified percentage—usually 80 percent—of its value, she or he will recover any loss up to the face amount of the policy. If the insurance is for less than the specified percentage, the owner is responsible for a proportionate share of the loss. In effect, the owner becomes a coinsurer.

Coinsurance applies only in instances of partial loss. The amount of the recovery is calculated by using the following formula:

$$\text{Loss} \times \left( \frac{\text{Amount of Insurance Coverage}}{\text{Coinsurance Percentage} \times \text{Property Value}} \right) = \text{Amount of Recovery}$$

■ **EXAMPLE 30.2** Madison, who owns property valued at $200,000, takes out a policy in the amount of $100,000. If Madison then suffers a loss of $80,000, her recovery will be $50,000. Madison will be responsible for (coinsure) the balance of the loss, or $30,000, which is the amount of loss ($80,000) minus the amount of recovery ($50,000).

$$\$80{,}000 \times \left( \frac{\$100{,}000}{0.8 \times \$200{,}000} \right) = \$50{,}000$$

Suppose that, instead, Madison had taken out a policy in the amount of 80 percent of the value of the property, or $160,000. Then, according to the same formula, she would have recovered the full amount of the loss (the face amount of the policy). ■

**Appraisal and Arbitration Clauses** Most fire insurance policies provide that if the parties cannot agree on the amount of a loss covered under the policy or on the value of the property lost, an *appraisal* can be demanded. An appraisal is an estimate of the property's value determined by a suitably qualified individual who has no interest in the property. Typically, two appraisers are used, with one appointed by each party. A third party, or umpire, may be called on to resolve differences. Other types of insurance policies also contain provisions for appraisal and arbitration when the insured and insurer disagree on the value of a loss.

**Multiple Insurance Coverage** Sometimes, an insured has *multiple insurance coverage*—that is, policies

with several companies covering the same insurable interest. If the amount of coverage exceeds the loss, the insured can collect from each insurer only the company's proportionate share of the liability relative to the total amount of insurance.

Many fire insurance policies include a pro rata clause, which requires that all carriers proportionately share in any loss. ■ **EXAMPLE 30.3** Green insured $50,000 worth of property with two companies. Each policy had a liability limit of $40,000. If the property is totally destroyed, Green can collect only $25,000 from each insurer. ■

**Antilapse Clauses** A life insurance policy may provide, or a statute may require a policy to provide, that it will not automatically lapse if no payment is made on the date due. Ordinarily, under an **antilapse provision,** the insured has a *grace period* of thirty or thirty-one days within which to pay an overdue premium.

If the insured fails to pay a premium altogether, there are alternatives to cancellation:

1. The insurer may be required to extend the insurance for a period of time.
2. The insurer may issue a policy with less coverage to reflect the amount of the payments made.
3. The insurer may pay to the insured the policy's **cash surrender value**—the amount the insurer has agreed to pay on the policy's cancellation before the insured's death. (This value depends on the type of policy. It also depends on the period that the policy has already run, the amount of the premium, the insured's age and life expectancy, and amounts to be repaid on any outstanding loans taken out against the policy.)

When the insurance contract states that the insurer cannot cancel the policy, these alternatives are important.

## 30–2d Interpreting Provisions of an Insurance Contract

The courts recognize that most people do not have the special training necessary to understand the intricate terminology used in insurance policies. Therefore, when disputes arise, the courts will interpret the words used in an insurance contract according to their ordinary meanings in light of the nature of the coverage involved.

When there is an ambiguity in the policy, the provision generally is interpreted *against the insurance company.* Also, when it is unclear whether an insurance contract actually exists because the written policy has not been delivered, the uncertainty normally is resolved against the insurance company. The court presumes that the policy is in effect unless the company can show otherwise. Similarly, an insurer must make sure that the insured is adequately notified of any change in coverage under an existing policy.

Disputes over insurance often focus on the application of exclusions in the policy. ■ **CASE IN POINT 30.4** Alberto and Karelli Mila were insured under a liability policy that contained a list of twelve exclusions. "Exclusion k" stated that coverage did not apply to "bodily injury arising out of sexual molestation, corporal punishment or physical or mental abuse." Verushka Valero, on behalf of her child, filed a suit against the Milas, charging them with negligent supervision of a perpetrator who sexually molested Valero's child.

The Milas filed a claim with their insurer to provide a defense against the charges. The insurer refused and sought a court order declaring that it had no obligation under the policy to provide such a defense. The court ruled in favor of the insurer, and the decision was affirmed on appeal. The language in the Milas' policy excluding coverage for "bodily injury arising out of sexual molestation" was clear and unambiguous. The exclusion applied to preclude coverage.[3] ■

## 30–2e Cancellation

The insured can cancel a policy at any time, and the insurer can cancel under certain circumstances. When an insurance company can cancel its insurance contract, the policy or a state statute usually requires that the insurer give advance written notice of the cancellation. The same requirement applies when only part of a policy is canceled. Any premium paid in advance and not yet earned may be refundable on the policy's cancellation. The insured may also be entitled to a life insurance policy's cash surrender value.

The insurer may cancel an insurance policy for various reasons, depending on the type of insurance. For example:

1. Automobile insurance can be canceled for nonpayment of premiums or suspension of the insured's driver's license.
2. Property insurance can be canceled for nonpayment of premiums or for other reasons, including the insured's fraud or misrepresentation, gross negligence, or conviction for a crime that increases the risk assumed by the insurer.

3. Life and health policies can be canceled because of false statements made by the insured in the application, but the cancellation must take place before the effective date of an incontestability clause.

An insurer cannot cancel—or refuse to renew—a policy for discriminatory reasons or other reasons that violate public policy. Also, an insurer cannot cancel a policy because the insured has appeared as a witness in a case brought against the company.

## 30–2f Duties and Obligations of the Parties

Both parties to an insurance contract are responsible for the obligations they assume under the contract. In addition, both the insured and the insurer have an implied duty to act in good faith.

**Duties of the Insured**   Good faith requires the party who is applying for insurance to reveal everything necessary for the insurer to evaluate the risk of issuing the policy. In other words, the applicant must disclose all facts that an insurer would consider in determining whether to charge a higher premium or to refuse to issue a policy altogether. Many insurance companies require that an applicant give the company permission to access other information, such as private medical records and credit ratings, for the purpose of evaluating risk.

Once the insurance policy is issued, the insured has three basic duties under the contract:

1. To pay the premiums as stated in the contract.
2. To notify the insurer within a reasonable time if an event occurs that gives rise to a claim.
3. To cooperate with the insurer during any investigation or litigation.

**Duties of the Insurer**   Once the insurer has accepted the risk, and some event occurs that gives rise to a claim, the insurer has a *duty to investigate* to determine the facts. When a policy provides insurance against third party claims, the insurer is obligated to make reasonable efforts to settle any such claim.

If a settlement cannot be reached, then regardless of the claim's merit, the insurer has a *duty to defend* any suit against the insured. Usually, a policy provides that in this situation the insured must *cooperate* in the defense and attend hearings and trials if necessary.

The insurer also owes a *duty to pay* any legitimate claims up to the face amount of the policy. An insurer has a duty to provide or pay an attorney to defend its insured when a complaint alleges facts that could, if

---

3. *Valero v. Florida Insurance Guaranty Association, Inc.,* 59 So.3d 1166 (Fla. App. 2011).

proved, impose liability on the insured within the policy's coverage.

■ **CASE IN POINT 30.5** Dentist Robert Woo installed implants for one of his employees, Tina Alberts, whose family raised potbellied pigs. As a joke, while Alberts was anesthetized, Woo installed a set of "flippers" (temporary partial bridges) shaped like boar tusks and took photos. A month later, Woo's staff showed the photos to Alberts at a party. Alberts refused to return to work. She filed a suit against Woo for battery.

Woo's insurance company refused to defend him in the suit, and he ended up paying Alberts $250,000 to settle her claim. Woo then sued the insurance company and won. The court held that the insurance company had a duty to defend Woo under the professional liability provision of his policy because Woo's practical joke took place during a routine dental procedure.[4] ■

**Bad Faith Actions** Although insurance law generally follows contract law, most states now recognize a "bad faith" tort action against insurers. Thus, if an insurer in bad faith denies coverage of a claim, the insured may sue. If successful, the insured can recover an amount exceeding the policy's coverage limits and may also recover punitive damages. Some courts have held insurers liable for a bad faith refusal to settle claims for reasonable amounts within the policy limits.

## 30–2g Defenses against Payment

An insurance company can raise any of the defenses that would be valid in an ordinary action on a contract, as well as the following defenses:

1. *Fraud or misrepresentation.* If the insurance company can show that the policy was procured through fraud or misrepresentation, it may have a valid defense for not paying on a claim. (The insurance company may also have the right to disaffirm or rescind the insurance contract.)
2. *Lack of insurable interest.* An absolute defense exists if the insurer can show that the insured lacked an insurable interest—thus rendering the policy void from the beginning.
3. *Illegal actions of the insured.* Improper actions, such as those that are against public policy or that are otherwise illegal, can also give the insurance company a defense against the payment of a claim or allow it to rescind the contract.

---

4. *Woo v. Fireman's Fund Insurance Co.,* 161 Wash.2d 43, 164 P.3d 454 (2007).

In some situations, the insurance company may be prevented, or estopped, from asserting defenses that normally are available. For instance, an insurance company ordinarily cannot escape payment on the death of an insured on the ground that the person's age was stated incorrectly on the application. Also, incontestability clauses prevent the insurer from asserting certain defenses.

---

# 30–3 Types of Insurance

There are four general types of insurance coverage: life insurance, fire and homeowners' insurance, automobile insurance, and business liability insurance. We now examine briefly the coverage available under each of these types of insurance.

## 30–3a Life Insurance

There are five basic types of life insurance:

1. **Whole life** provides protection with an accumulated cash surrender value that can be used as collateral for a loan. The insured pays premiums during his or her entire lifetime, and the beneficiary receives a fixed payment on the death of the insured. (It is also sometimes referred to as straight life, ordinary life, or cash-value insurance.)
2. **Limited-payment life** is a type of policy under which premiums are paid for a stated number of years. After that time, the policy is paid up and fully effective during the insured's lifetime. For instance, a policy might call for twenty payments. Naturally, premiums are higher than for whole life. Like whole life, this insurance also has a cash surrender value.
3. **Term insurance** is a type of policy for which premiums are paid for a specified term. Payment on the policy is due only if death occurs within the term period. Premiums are lower than for whole life or limited-payment life, and there usually is no cash surrender value. Frequently, this type of insurance can be converted to another type of life insurance.
4. **Endowment insurance** involves fixed premium payments that are made for a definite term. At the end of the term, a fixed amount is paid to the insured or, if the insured dies during the specified term, to a beneficiary. Endowment insurance has a rapidly increasing cash surrender value, but premiums are high because a payment must be made at the end of the term even if the insured is still living.

5. **Universal life** combines aspects of both term insurance and whole life insurance. From every payment, usually called a "contribution," the issuing life insurance company makes two deductions. The first is a charge for term insurance protection. The second is for company expenses and profit. The funds that remain after these deductions earn interest for the policyholder at a rate determined by the company. The interest-earning amount is called the policy's *cash value*, but that term does not mean the same thing as it does for a traditional whole life insurance policy. With a universal life policy, the cash value grows at a variable interest rate rather than at a predetermined rate.

The rights and liabilities of the parties to life insurance contracts are basically dependent on the specific contract. A few features deserve special attention.

**Insurer's Liability** The life insurance contract determines not only the extent of the insurer's liability but also, generally, whether the insurer is liable on the death of the insured. Many life insurance contracts exclude liability for death caused by suicide, and some contain other exclusions, such as liability for death caused by military action during war. In the absence of contractual exclusion, most courts today construe any cause of death to be one of the insurer's risks.

**Adjustment Due to Misstatement of Age** The insurance policy constitutes the agreement between the parties. As noted earlier, the application for insurance is part of the policy and is usually attached to the policy. When the insured misstates his or her age on the application, an error is introduced, particularly as to the amount of premiums paid. As mentioned, misstatement of age is not a material error sufficient to allow the insurer to void the policy. Instead, on discovery of the error, the insurer will adjust the premium payments and/or benefits accordingly.

**Assignment** Most life insurance policies allow the insured to change beneficiaries. When this is permitted, in the absence of any prohibition or notice requirement, the insured can assign the rights to the policy without the consent of the insurer or the beneficiary. The insured may, for instance, wish to assign the rights to the policy as security for a loan.

If the beneficiary's right is *vested*—that is, has become absolute, entitling the beneficiary to payment of the proceeds—the policy cannot be assigned without the beneficiary's consent. For the most part, life insurance contracts permit assignment and require notice only to the insurer to be effective.

**Creditors' Rights** Unless insurance proceeds are exempt under state law, the insured's interest in life insurance is an asset that is subject to the rights of judgment creditors. These creditors generally can reach all of the following:

1. Insurance proceeds payable to the insured's estate.
2. Insurance proceeds payable to anyone if the payment of premiums constituted a fraud on creditors.
3. Insurance proceeds payable to a named beneficiary unless the beneficiary's rights have vested.

Creditors, however, cannot compel the insured to make available the cash surrender value of the policy or to change the named beneficiary to that of the creditor. Almost all states exempt at least a part of the proceeds of life insurance from creditors' claims.

**Termination** Although the insured can cancel and terminate the policy, the insurer generally cannot do so. Therefore, termination usually takes place only if one of the following occurs:

1. Default in premium payments, which causes the policy to lapse.
2. Death and payment of benefits.
3. Expiration of the term of the policy.
4. Cancellation by the insured.

## 30–3b Fire and Homeowners' Insurance

There are basically two types of insurance policies for a home: standard fire insurance policies and homeowners' policies.

**Standard Fire Insurance Policies** The standard fire insurance policy protects the homeowner against fire and lightning, as well as damage from smoke and water caused by the fire or the fire department. Most fire insurance policies are classified according to the type of property covered and the extent of the issuer's liability. Exhibit 30–3 lists typical fire insurance policies.

**Liability.** The insurer's liability is determined from the terms of the policy. Most policies limit recovery to losses resulting from *hostile* fires—basically, those that break out or begin in places where no fire was intended to burn. A *friendly* fire—one burning in a place where it was intended to burn—is often not covered. Therefore, smoke from a fireplace is not covered, but smoke from a fire caused by a defective electrical outlet is covered. Sometimes, owners add "extended coverage" to the fire policy to cover losses from "friendly" fires.

**EXHIBIT 30–3   Typical Fire Insurance Policies**

| TYPE OF POLICY | COVERAGE |
| --- | --- |
| Blanket | Covers a class of property rather than specific property, because the property is expected to shift or vary in nature. A policy covering the inventory of a business is an example. |
| Floater | Usually supplements a specific policy. It is intended to cover property that may change in either location or quantity. For instance, if a painting is to be exhibited during the year at numerous locations throughout the state, a floater policy would be desirable. |
| Open | A policy that does not state an agreed-on value for the property. The policy usually provides for a maximum liability of the insurer, but payment for loss is restricted to the fair market value of the property at the time of loss or to the insurer's limit, whichever is less. |
| Specific | Covers a specific item of property at a specific location. An example is a particular painting located in a residence or a piece of machinery located in a factory or business. |
| Valued | A policy that, by agreement, places a specific value on the subject to be insured to cover the eventuality of its total loss. |

If the policy is a *valued* policy (see Exhibit 30–3) and the subject matter is completely destroyed, the insurer is liable for the amount specified in the policy. If it is an *open* policy, then the extent of the actual loss must be determined. The insurer is liable only for the amount of the loss or for the maximum amount specified in the policy, whichever is less. For partial losses, actual loss must always be determined, and the insurer's liability is limited to that amount. Most insurance policies permit the insurer either to restore or replace the property destroyed or to pay for the loss.

**Proof of Loss.** As a condition for recovery, fire insurance policies require the insured to file a proof of loss with the insurer within a specified period or immediately (within a reasonable time). Failure to comply

*could* allow the insurance carrier to avoid liability. Courts vary somewhat on the enforcement of such clauses.

**Occupancy Clause.** Most standard policies include clauses that require that the premises be occupied at the time of the loss. If the premises are vacant or unoccupied for a given period and the insurer has not consented to the vacancy, then coverage is suspended until the premises are reoccupied. Persons going on extended vacations should check their policies regarding this point.

In the following case, the court had to consider how long a house must be left vacant before it can be considered "unoccupied." The court also addressed the question of whether the risk of hazard is always greater when a home is unoccupied.

**Case Analysis 30.2**

# Estate of Luster v. Allstate Insurance Co.

United States Court of Appeals, Seventh Circuit, 598 F.3d 903 (2010).

### In the Language of the Court
*POSNER,* Circuit Judge.
\* \* \* \*

This diversity suit for breach of an insurance contract was dismissed on summary judgment \* \* \*, and the plaintiff's [Estate of Luster's] appeal presents issues of both contract interpretation and Indiana insurance law.

[Wavie] Luster was a widow living alone in her house in Merrillville, Indiana. She had a homeowner's insurance policy from Allstate [Insurance Company]. In October 2001, when she was eighty-three, she was injured in a fall, and after being released from the hospital moved into an extended-care facility. She executed a power of attorney to her

lawyer, Rick Gikas, who is the representative of her estate in this litigation. She never returned home and died in April 2006, some four and a half years after her fall. Gikas had notified Allstate of his power of attorney and had directed the company to bill the insurance premiums to his law

**Case 30.2 Continues**

**Case 30.2 Continued**

office. No one lived in the house after she left it.

Three months after her death—her house still unoccupied—a fire caused extensive damage. Gikas submitted a claim on behalf of the estate. An investigation indicated that the fire may well have been started by burglars, but the plaintiff denies this and the district judge made no finding.

In the course of the investigation Allstate discovered that the house had been unoccupied for four and a half years before Mrs. Luster's death and denied the claim, precipitating this suit. Allstate continued billing Gikas for premiums, however, and he continued paying them until October 2008, more than two years after the fire, when Allstate—which claims not to have known that the policy was still in force until its lawyers read the estate's summary-judgment brief that month—purported to cancel the policy retroactively to November 2001, and returned the premiums for the subsequent period to the estate.

The appeal requires us to consider [certain] provisions of the insurance policy: [The policy required the insured to notify Allstate of any change in occupancy of the premises and excluded coverage for property loss caused by "any substantial change or increase in hazard" or by "vandalism or malicious mischief" if the insured's dwelling was unoccupied for more than thirty consecutive days immediately prior to the vandalism or malicious mischief.]

* * * *

Gikas argues that * * * the house was *not* unoccupied, because right up until her death Luster expressed the intention of returning to live there when her health permitted.

*Regardless of the owner's intentions, * * * four and a half years of continuous absence of human occupation constitutes a change in occupancy.* [Emphasis added.]

The duty-to-notify provision entitled Allstate to cancel the policy in the event the house became unoccupied.

Although the policy expressly authorizes the insurer to cancel it for a violation of any of its terms, it also requires the insurer to give thirty days' notice of intention to cancel, and Allstate failed to do that after discovering in the wake of the fire that the house had been unoccupied for years. *The requirement of notice of intent to cancel is important; it gives the insured an opportunity to prevent a lapse of coverage, by taking steps to reinstate the policy or obtain a substitute policy from another insurer. Retroactive termination is inconsistent with the requirement of advance notice.* [Emphasis added.]

* * * *

The district judge ruled that leaving the house unoccupied constituted a "substantial change or increase in hazard" within the meaning [of the policy]. The judge seems to have thought that to leave a house unoccupied for however short a time causes an "increase in hazard" as a matter of law. Allstate takes the more moderate position that any gap in occupation of more than thirty days increases hazard as a matter of law.

Neither position is correct. Houses are rarely occupied continuously. A homeowner might take a thirty-one-day trip; Allstate implies that if a fire occurred during that period the insured would be uncovered. That is not the law.

Allstate's argument thus implies that if you have a second home the homeowner's policy on your primary residence is illusory; you're away a lot

and so coverage lapses. That's nonsense. And even if the house is unoccupied in the relevant sense—the sense that triggers the duty to notify the insurance company of a change in occupancy—it doesn't follow that you have created a "substantial * * * increase in hazard." Maybe you fitted the house with an array of locks and alarms and hired a security company to check on the house daily and so made the house more secure than when you were living there—an especially plausible inference if you happen to be an elderly person who might if in residence damage it inadvertently by leaving appliances on or failing to remove combustibles [flammable items] like cans containing paint or oil-soaked rags or to attend to defects in the electrical wiring of the house. *There is no rule that moving out of a house per se [in itself] increases the hazards against which the insurance company has insured you.* [Emphasis added.]

* * * *

There may well have been vandalism, by burglars, and if so it occurred more than thirty days after the house became unoccupied, whenever precisely occupancy ceased—sometime during the four and a half years between Luster's fall and her death. But we do not know whether the vandalism caused the loss—there is no judicial finding that the fire that was the immediate cause of the loss was the result of vandalism. To decide whether it was will require an evidentiary hearing, as will Allstate's alternative ground that nonoccupancy substantially increased the risk of loss.

* * * *

REVERSED AND REMANDED.

## Legal Reasoning Questions

**1.** Why did the court conclude that an unoccupied house did not necessarily create a substantial increase in hazard?

**2.** Why did the court hold that Allstate's cancellation of the policy, retroactive to November 2001 (when Luster moved to an extended-care facility), was ineffective?

**3.** Was Luster's intent to return to her home when her health permitted sufficient to constitute occupancy? Why or why not?

**Assignment.** Before a loss has occurred, a fire insurance policy is not assignable without the consent of the insurer. The theory is that the fire insurance policy is a personal contract between the insured and the insurer. The non-assignability of a policy is extremely important when a house is purchased. It means that the purchaser must procure his or her own insurance. If the purchaser wishes to assume the seller's remaining period of insurance coverage, the insurer's consent is essential.

■ **EXAMPLE 30.6** Kiana is selling her home and lot to Jayden. Kiana has a one-year fire policy with Ajax Insurance Company, with six months of coverage remaining at the date on which the sale is to close. Kiana agrees to assign the balance of her policy, but Ajax has not given its consent. One day after passage of the deed, a fire totally destroys the house. Can Jayden recover from Ajax?

The answer is no. The policy is actually voided on the closing of the transaction and the deeding of the property. The reason the policy is voided is that Kiana no longer has an insurable interest at the time of loss, and Jayden has no rights in a nonassignable policy. ■

**Homeowners' Policies** A homeowners' policy provides protection against a number of risks under a single policy, allowing the policyholder to avoid the cost of buying each protection separately. There are two basic types of homeowners' coverage: property coverage and liability coverage.

**Property Coverage.** *Property coverage* includes the house, garage, and other private buildings on the policyholder's lot. It also includes the personal possessions and property of the policyholder at home, at work, or while traveling. If the policyholder is forced to live away from home because of a fire or some other covered peril, the policy covers additional living expenses.

Perils insured under property coverage often include fire, lightning, wind, hail, vandalism, and theft (of personal property). Standard homeowners' insurance typically does not cover flood damage. In the absence of a specific provision, such items of personal property as motor vehicles, farm equipment, airplanes, and boats normally are not included under property coverage. Coverage for other property, such as jewelry and securities, usually is limited to a specified dollar amount.

**Liability Coverage.** *Liability coverage* under a homeowners' policy is for personal liability in the event that someone is injured on the insured's property because of an unsafe condition on the property. It also applies when the insured damages someone else's property or injures someone else (unless the injury involves an automobile,

as noted below). In addition, it applies when the policyholder is negligent.

Similar to liability coverage is coverage for the medical payments of others who are injured on the policyholder's property and for the property of others that is damaged by a member of the policyholder's family.

Liability coverage normally does not apply to a liability that arises from business or professional activities or from the operation of a motor vehicle, which are subjects for separate policies. Also excluded is liability arising from intentional misconduct.

**Renters' Policies.** Renters also take out insurance policies to protect against losses to personal property. Renters' insurance covers personal possessions against various perils and includes coverage for additional living expenses and liability.

### 30–3c Automobile Insurance

There are two basic kinds of automobile insurance: liability insurance and collision and comprehensive insurance.

**Liability Insurance** Automobile liability insurance covers liability for bodily injury and property damage. Liability limits are usually described by a series of three numbers, such as 100/300/50. This means that, for one accident, the policy will pay a maximum of $100,000 for bodily injury to one person, a maximum of $300,000 for bodily injury to more than one person, and a maximum of $50,000 for property damage. Many insurance companies offer liability coverage in amounts up to $500,000 and sometimes higher.

Individuals who are dissatisfied with the maximum liability limits offered by regular automobile insurance coverage can purchase separate coverage under an *umbrella policy.* Umbrella limits sometimes go as high as $10 million. Umbrella policies also cover personal liability in excess of the liability limits of a homeowners' policy.

**Collision and Comprehensive Insurance** Collision insurance covers damage to the insured's car in any type of collision. Usually, it is not advisable to purchase full collision coverage (otherwise known as *zero deductible*). The price per year is relatively high because it is likely that some small repair jobs will be required each year. Most people prefer to take out policies with a deductible of $250, $500, or $1,000, which cost substantially less than zero-deductible coverage.

Comprehensive insurance covers loss, damage, and destruction due to fire, hurricane, hail, vandalism, and theft. It can be obtained separately from collision insurance.

**Other Automobile Insurance** Other types of automobile insurance coverage include the following:

1. *Uninsured motorist coverage.* Uninsured motorist coverage insures the driver and passengers against injury caused by any driver without insurance or by a hit-and-run driver. Some states require that it be included in all auto insurance policies sold.
2. *Accidental death benefits.* Sometimes referred to as *double indemnity,* accidental death benefits provide for a payment of twice the policy's face amount if the policyholder dies in an accident. This coverage generally costs very little, but it may not be necessary if the insured has a sufficient amount of life insurance.
3. *Medical payment coverage.* Medical payment coverage provided by an auto insurance policy pays hospital and other medical bills and sometimes funeral expenses. This type of insurance protects all the passengers in the insured's car when the insured is driving.
4. *Other-driver coverage.* An **omnibus clause,** or *other-driver clause,* protects the vehicle owner who has taken out the insurance and anyone who drives the vehicle with the owner's permission. This coverage may be held to extend to a third party who drives the vehicle with the permission of the person to whom the owner gave permission.

## 30–3d Business Liability Insurance

A business may be vulnerable to all sorts of risks. A key employee may die or become disabled, a customer may be injured when using a manufacturer's product, or a professional may overlook some important detail and be liable for malpractice. If a key employee (such as the company president) dies, the firm may have some protection under a key-person insurance policy, discussed earlier. In the other circumstances, other types of insurance may apply.

**General Liability** Comprehensive general liability insurance can encompass as many risks as the insurer agrees to cover. It can protect a business from liability for injuries arising from on-premises events held after work hours, such as company social functions. It can protect bars and liquor stores, which in many jurisdictions are liable when a buyer of liquor becomes intoxicated as a result of the sale and injures a third party. General liability insurance can protect a business not only from liability for physical injuries, but also from liability for the loss of financial support suffered by a family because of the injuries.

**Product Liability** Manufacturers and retailers may be subject to liability for injuries resulting from the products they sell, and product liability insurance can be written to match specific products' risks. Coverage can be procured under a comprehensive general liability policy or under a separate policy. The coverage may include payment for expenses incurred to recall and replace a product that has proved to be defective.

**Professional Malpractice** Attorneys, physicians, architects, engineers, and other professionals often become the targets of negligence suits. Professionals purchase malpractice insurance to protect themselves against such claims. The large judgments in some malpractice suits have contributed to a significant increase in malpractice insurance premiums.

**Workers' Compensation** Workers' compensation insurance covers payments to employees who are injured in accidents arising out of and in the course of employment (that is, on the job). State statutes govern workers' compensation.

## Reviewing: Insurance

Provident Insurance, Inc., issued an insurance policy to a company providing an employee, Steve Matlin, with disability insurance. Soon thereafter, Matlin was diagnosed with "panic disorder and phobia of returning to work." He lost his job and sought disability coverage. Provident denied coverage, doubting the diagnosis of disability. Matlin and his employer sued Provident.

During pretrial discovery, the insurer learned that Matlin had stated on the policy application that he had never been treated for any "emotional, mental, nervous, urinary, or digestive disorder" or any kind of heart disease. In fact, before Matlin filled out the application, he had visited a physician for chest pains and general anxiety, and the physician had prescribed an antidepressant and recommended that Matlin stop smoking. Using the information presented in the chapter, answer the following questions.

1. Did Matlin commit a misrepresentation on his policy application? Explain.
2. If there was any ambiguity on the application, should it be resolved in favor of the insured or the insurer? Why?
3. Assuming that the policy is valid, does Matlin's situation fall within the terms of the disability policy? Why or why not?
4. If Matlin is covered by the policy but is also disqualified by his misrepresentation on the application for coverage, might the insurer still be liable for bad faith denial of coverage? Explain.

**Debate This . . .**  *Whenever an insurance company can prove that the applicant committed fraud during the application process, it should not have to pay on the policy.*

## Terms and Concepts

antilapse provision 591
binder 590
cash surrender value 591
coinsurance clause 591
endowment insurance 593
incontestability clause 590

insurable interest 586
insurance 586
limited-payment life 593
omnibus clause 598
policy 586
premium 586

risk 586
risk management 586
term insurance 593
underwriter 586
universal life 594
whole life 593

## Issue Spotters

1. Neal applies to Farm Insurance Company for a life insurance policy. On the application, Neal understates his age. Neal obtains the policy, but for a lower premium than he would have had to pay had he disclosed his actual age. The policy includes an incontestability clause. Six years later, Neal dies. Can the insurer refuse payment? Why or why not? (See *The Insurance Contract*.)

2. Al is divorced and owns a house. Al has no reasonable expectation of benefit from the life of Bea, his former spouse, but applies for insurance on her life anyway. Al obtains a fire insurance policy on the house and then sells the house. Al continues to pay the premiums on both the life insurance policy and the fire insurance policy. Ten years later, Bea dies and the house is destroyed by fire. Can Al obtain payment for these events? Explain your answers. (See *Insurance Terminology and Concepts*.)

• **Check your answers to the Issue Spotters against the answers provided in Appendix B at the end of this text.**

## Business Scenarios

**30–1. Insurable Interest.** Adia owns a house and has an elderly third cousin living with her. Adia decides she needs fire insurance on the house and a life insurance policy on her third cousin to cover funeral and other expenses that will result from her cousin's death. Adia takes out a fire insurance policy from Ajax Insurance Co. and a $10,000 life insurance policy from Beta Insurance Co. on her third cousin. Six months later, Adia sells the house to John and transfers title to him. Adia and her cousin move into an apartment. With two months remaining on the Ajax policy, a fire totally destroys the house. At the same time, Adia's third cousin dies. Both insurance companies say that they have no liability under the insurance contracts because Adia did not have an insurable interest, and they return the premiums. Discuss the companies' claims. (See *Insurance Terminology and Concepts*.)

**30–2. Insurer's Defenses.** Patrick contracts with an Ajax Insurance Co. agent for a $50,000 ordinary life insurance policy. The application form is filled in to show Patrick's age as thirty-two. In addition, the application form asks whether Patrick has ever had any heart ailments or problems. Patrick answers no, forgetting that as a young child he was diagnosed as having a slight heart murmur. A policy is issued. Three years later, Patrick becomes seriously ill and dies. A review of the policy discloses that Patrick was actually thirty-three at the time of the application and the issuance of the policy and that he erred in answering the question about a history of heart ailments. Discuss whether Ajax can void the policy and escape liability on Patrick's death. (See *The Insurance Contract*.)

**30–3. Assignment.** Sapata has an ordinary life insurance policy on her life and a fire insurance policy on her house.

Both policies have been in force for a number of years. Sapata's life insurance names her son, Rory, as beneficiary. Sapata has specifically removed her right to change beneficiaries, and the life insurance policy is silent on the right of assignment. Sapata is going on a one-year European vacation and borrows money from Leonard to finance the trip. Leonard takes an assignment of the life insurance policy as security for the loan, as the policy has accumulated a substantial cash surrender value. Sapata also rents out her house to Leonard and assigns her fire insurance policy to him. Discuss fully whether Sapata's assignment of these policies is valid. (See *Types of Insurance.*)

## Business Case Problems

**30–4. Interpreting Provisions.** Richard Vanderbrook's home in New Orleans, Louisiana, was insured through Unitrin Preferred Insurance Co. His policy excluded coverage for "flood, surface water, waves, tidal water, overflow of a body of water, or spray from any of these, whether or not driven by wind." The policy did not define the term *flood.* In 2005, Hurricane Katrina struck along the coast of the Gulf of Mexico, devastating portions of Louisiana. In New Orleans, some of the most significant damage occurred when the levees along three canals ruptured, and water submerged about 80 percent of the city, including Vanderbrook's home. He filed a claim for the loss, but Unitrin refused to pay.

Vanderbrook and others whose policies contained similar exclusions asked a federal district court to order their insurers to pay. They contended that their losses were due to the negligent design, construction, and maintenance of the levees. They argued that the policies did not clearly exclude coverage for an inundation of water induced by negligence. On what does a decision in this case hinge? What reasoning supports a ruling in the plaintiffs' favor? In the defendants' favor? [*In re Katrina Canal Breaches Litigation,* 495 F.3d 191 (5th Cir. 2007)] (See *The Insurance Contract.*)

**30–5. Duty to Cooperate.** James Bubenik, a dentist, had two patients die while under sedation within six months. Bubenik had medical malpractice insurance with Medical Protective Co. (MPC). The families of both patients sued Bubenik for malpractice. A clause in Bubenik's policy stated that the "Insured shall at all times fully cooperate with the Company in any claim hereunder and shall attend and assist in the preparation and trial of any such claim." During the litigation, however, Bubenik refused to submit to depositions, answer interrogatories, or testify at trial, invoking the privilege against self-incrimination. He also refused to communicate with MPC and instead agreed to assist the patients in obtaining payment. MPC filed suit. Under these circumstances, did MPC have a legal or ethical duty to defend against the claim? Could MPC refuse to pay it? Explain. [*Medical Protective Co. v. Bubenik,* 594 F.3d 1047 (8th Cir. 2010)] (See *The Insurance Contract.*)

**30–6. Bad Faith Actions.** Leo and Mary Deters owned Deters Tower Service, Inc., in Iowa. Deters Tower serviced television and radio towers and antennas in a multistate area. The firm obtained a commercial general liability policy issued by USF Insurance Co. to provide coverage for its officers, including Leo. One afternoon, Leo and two Deters Tower employees were working on a TV tower in Council Bluffs when they fell from the tower to their deaths. The workers' families filed a negligence suit against Leo's estate. USF refused to defend the Deters estate against the suit and pay any resulting claim but did not provide a reason for its refusal. Is USF liable to the Deters estate for this refusal? If so, on what basis might the Deters estate recover, and how much? [*Deters v. USF Insurance Co.,* 797 N.W.2d 621 (Iowa App. 2011)] (See *The Insurance Contract.*)

**30–7. Business Case Problem with Sample Answer— Insurance Provisions and Clauses.** Darling's Rent-a-Car  carried property insurance on its cars under a policy issued by Philadelphia Indemnity Insurance Co. The policy listed Darling's as the "insured." Darling's rented a car to Joshuah Farrington. In the rental contract, Farrington agreed to be responsible for any damage to the car and declined the optional insurance. Later, Farrington collided with a moose. Philadelphia paid Darling's for the damage to the car and sought to collect this amount from Farrington. Farrington argued that he was an "insured" under Darling's policy. How should "insured" be interpreted in this case? Why? [*Philadelphia Indemnity Insurance Co. v. Farrington,* 37 A.3d 305 (Me. 2012)] (See *The Insurance Contract.*)

- For a sample answer to Problem 30–7, go to Appendix C at the end of this text.

**30–8. Types of Insurance.** American National Property and Casualty Co. issued an insurance policy to Robert Houston, insuring certain residential property and its contents against fire and other hazards. Twenty months later, Houston issued a quitclaim deed to the property to John and Judy Sykes, reserving a life estate for himself. The American policy was renewed continuously by John, even after Houston died. When a fire substantially damaged the property, John filed a claim with the insurer on behalf of Houston, whom John said was out of town and unavailable. On learning that Houston had died, American refused to pay, claiming that it had no liability. Who will suffer the loss under these circumstances? Why? How might this loss have been avoided? Explain. [*American National Property and Casualty Co. v. Sykes,* __ F.Supp.3d __, 2016 WL 390069 (S.D.Miss., E.Div. 2016)] (See *Types of Insurance.*)

### 30–9. A Question of Ethics—Insurance Coverage.

*Paul and Julie Leonard's two-story home in Pascagoula, Mississippi, is only twelve feet above sea level and fewer than two hundred yards from the Gulf of Mexico. In 1989, the Leonards bought a homeowners' insurance policy from Jay Fletcher, an agent for Nationwide Mutual Insurance Co. The policy covered any damage caused by wind. It excluded all damage caused by water, including flooding. With each annual renewal, Nationwide reminded the Leonards that their policy did not cover flood damage, but that such coverage was available. The policy also contained an anti-concurrent-causation (ACC) clause that excluded coverage for damage caused by the synergistic action of a covered peril such as wind and an excluded peril such as water. In August 2005, Hurricane Katrina battered Pascagoula with torrential rain and sustained winds in excess of one hundred miles per hour. Wind damage to the Leonards' home was modest, but the storm drove ashore a seventeen-foot storm surge that flooded the ground floor. When Nationwide refused to pay for the damage to the ground floor, the Leonards filed a suit in a federal district court against the insurer. [Leonard v. Nationwide Mutual Insurance Co., 499 F.3d 419 (5th Cir. 2007)]* (See *The Insurance Contract.*)

**(a)** Nationwide argued that the storm surge was a concurrently caused peril—a wall of water pushed ashore by hurricane winds. Thus, according to Nationwide, its damage was excluded under the ACC clause. How would you rule on this point? Should a court "enlarge" an insurer's policy obligations? Why or why not?

**(b)** When the Leonards bought their policy in 1989, Fletcher told them that all hurricane damage was covered. Ten years later, Fletcher told Paul Leonard that they did not need additional flood coverage. Did these statements materially misrepresent or alter the policy? Were they unethical? Discuss.

## Legal Reasoning Group Activity

**30–10. Insurance Coverage.** PAJ, Inc., a jewelry company, had a commercial general liability (CGL) policy from Hanover Insurance Co. The policy required PAJ to notify Hanover of any claim or suit against PAJ "as soon as practicable." Yurman Designs sued PAJ for copyright infringement because of the design of a particular jewelry line. Because PAJ did not realize that the CGL policy had a clause that covered infringement claims, it did not notify Hanover of the suit until four to six months after litigation began. Hanover contended that the policy did not apply to this incident because the late notification had violated its terms. PAJ sued Hanover, seeking a declaration that it was obligated to defend and indemnify PAJ. (See *The Insurance Contract.*)

**(a)** The first group will decide whether Hanover had an obligation to provide PAJ with legal assistance.

**(b)** The second group will determine the effect that PAJ's late notice to the insurance company had on its ability to provide assistance and mount a defense. Should the court require the insurance company to indemnify PAJ in this situation? Why or why not?

## CHAPTER 31

# Wills and Trusts

As the adage says, "You can't take it with you." After you die, all of the real and personal property that you own will be transferred to others. A person can direct the passage of his or her property after death by *will,* subject to certain limitations imposed by the state.

Alternatively, a person can transfer property through a *trust.* When a trust is created, the owner (who may be called the *grantor* or the *settlor*) of the property transfers legal title to a trustee. The trustee has a duty imposed by law to hold the property for the use or benefit of another (the beneficiary).

Wills and trusts are two basic devices used in the process of **estate planning**—determining in advance how one's property and obligations should be transferred on death. Estate planning may also involve transferring property through life insurance and joint-tenancy arrangements, as well as executing powers of attorney and living wills.

## 31–1 Wills

A **will** is the final declaration of how a person desires to have her or his property disposed of after death. It is a formal instrument that must follow exactly the requirements of state law to be effective.

A will can serve other purposes besides the distribution of property. It can appoint a guardian for minor children or incapacitated adults. It can also appoint a personal representative to settle the affairs of the deceased.

Exhibit 31–1 presents excerpts from the will of Michael Jackson, the "King of Pop," who died from cardiac arrest at the age of fifty. Jackson held a substantial amount of tangible and intangible property, including the publishing rights to most of The Beatles' music catalogue. Jackson's will also appointed his mother, Katherine Jackson, as the guardian of his three minor children.

### 31–1a Terminology of Wills

A person who makes a will is known as a **testator** (from the Latin *testari,* "to make a will"). A will is referred to as a *testamentary disposition* of property, and one who dies after having made a valid will is said to have died **testate.** The court responsible for administering any legal problems surrounding a will is called a *probate court.* When a person dies, a personal representative administers the estate and settles all of the decedent's (deceased person's) affairs.

An **executor** is a personal representative named in a will, whereas an **administrator** is a personal representative appointed by the court for a decedent who dies without a will. The court will also appoint a representative if the will does not name an executor or if the named person lacks the capacity to serve as an executor.

A person who dies without having created a valid will is said to have died **intestate.** In this situation, state **intestacy laws** (sometimes referred to as *laws of descent*) prescribe the distribution of the property among heirs or next of kin. If no heirs or kin can be found, the property will **escheat**[1] (title will be transferred to the state).

A gift of real estate by will is generally called a **devise,** and a gift of personal property by will is called a **bequest,** or **legacy.** The recipient of a gift by will is a **devisee** or a **legatee,** depending on whether the gift was a devise or a legacy.

### 31–1b Laws Governing Wills

To **probate** a will means to establish its validity and to carry the administration of the estate through a court process. Probate laws vary from state to state. The National

---

1. Pronounced is-*cheet.*

**EXHIBIT 31–1  Excerpts from Michael Jackson's Will**

I, MICHAEL JOSEPH JACKSON, a resident of the State of California, declare this to be my last Will, and do hereby revoke all former wills and codicils made by me.

I. I declare that I am not married. My marriage to DEBORAH JEAN ROWE JACKSON has been dissolved. I have three children now living, PRINCE MICHAEL JACKSON, JR., PARIS MICHAEL KATHERINE JACKSON and PRINCE MICHAEL JOSEPH JACKSON, II. I have no other children, living or deceased.

II. It is my intention by this Will to dispose of all property which I am entitled to dispose of by will. I specifically refrain from exercising all powers of appointment that I may possess at the time of my death.

III. I give my entire estate to the Trustee or Trustees then acting under that certain Amended and Restated Declaration of Trust executed on March 22, 2002 by me as Trustee and Trustor which is called the MICHAEL JACKSON FAMILY TRUST, giving effect to any amendments thereto made prior to my death. All such assets shall be held, managed and distributed as a part of said Trust according to its terms and not as a separate testamentary trust.

If for any reason this gift is not operative or is invalid, or if the aforesaid Trust fails or has been revoked, I give my residuary estate to the Trustee or Trustees named to act in the MICHAEL JACKSON FAMILY TRUST, as Amended and Restated on March 22, 2002, and I direct said Trustee or Trustees to divide, administer, hold and distribute the trust estate pursuant to the provisions of said Trust * * * .
* * * *

IV. I direct that all federal estate taxes and state inheritance or succession taxes payable upon or resulting from or by reason of my death (herein "Death Taxes") attributable to property which is part of the trust estate of the MICHAEL JACKSON FAMILY TRUST, including property which passes to said trust

from my probate estate shall be paid by the Trustee of said trust in accordance with its terms. Death Taxes attributable to property passing outside this Will, other than property constituting the trust estate of the trust mentioned in the preceding sentence, shall be charged against the taker of said property.

V. I appoint JOHN BRANCA, JOHN McCLAIN and BARRY SIEGEL as co-Executors of this Will. In the event of any of their deaths, resignations, inability, failure or refusal to serve or continue to serve as a co-Executor, the other shall serve and no replacement need be named. The co-Executors serving at any time after my death may name one or more replacements to serve in the event that none of the three named individuals is willing or able to serve at any time.

The term "my executors" as used in this Will shall include any duly acting personal representative or representatives of my estate. No individual acting as such need post a bond.

I hereby give to my Executors, full power and authority at any time or times to sell, lease, mortgage, pledge, exchange or otherwise dispose of the property, whether real or personal comprising my estate, upon such terms as my Executors shall deem best, to continue any business enterprises, to purchase assets from my estate, to continue in force and pay any insurance policy * * * .

VI. Except as otherwise provided in this Will or in the Trust referred to in Article III hereof, I have intentionally omitted to provide for my heirs. I have intentionally omitted to provide for my former wife, DEBORAH JEAN ROWE JACKSON.
* * * *

VIII. If any of my children are minors at the time of my death, I nominate my mother, KATHERINE JACKSON as guardian of the persons and estates of such minor children. If KATHERINE JACKSON fails to survive me, or is unable or unwilling to act as guardian, I nominate DIANA ROSS as guardian of the persons and estates of such minor children.
* * * *

Conference of Commissioners on Uniform State Laws issued the Uniform Probate Code (UPC) to promote more uniformity among the states. The UPC codifies general principles and procedures for the resolution of conflicts in settling estates. The UPC also relaxes some of the requirements for a valid will contained in earlier state laws.

Almost half of the states have enacted some part of the UPC and incorporated it into their own probate codes. Nonetheless, succession and inheritance laws still vary widely among the states, and one should always check the particular laws of the state involved.[2]

## 31–1c Types of Gifts

Gifts by will can be specific, general, or residuary. If a decedent's assets are not sufficient to cover all the gifts identified in the will, an abatement is necessary.

---

2. For example, California law differs substantially from the UPC.

**Specific and General Devises or Bequests** A *specific* devise or bequest (legacy) describes particular property (such as "Eastwood Estate" or "my gold pocket watch") that can be distinguished from all the rest of the testator's property.

A *general* devise or bequest (legacy) does not single out any particular item of property to be transferred by will. For instance, "I devise all my lands" is a general devise. A general bequest may specify the property's value in monetary terms (such as "two diamonds worth $10,000") or simply state a dollar amount (such as "$30,000 to my nephew, Carleton").

**Residuary Clause** Sometimes, a will provides that any assets remaining after the estate's debts have been paid and specific gifts have been made are to be distributed in a specific way through a *residuary clause.* Residuary clauses are often used when the exact amount to be distributed cannot be determined until all of the other gifts and payouts have been made. If the testator has not indicated what party or parties should receive the residuary of the estate, the residuary passes according to state laws of intestacy.

■ **CASE IN POINT 31.1** Katherine Hagan executed a will in 1994 that left the residuary of her estate to various organizations, such as the Humane Society. In 2001, Hagan inherited $830,000 from a relative. At this time, Hagan did not have the mental capacity to revise or modify her will. When she died in 2005, her residuary estate was worth $1.48 million.

Hagan's relatives, including Janice Benjamin, tried to invalidate the will's provisions regarding the residuary estate so that the funds would pass to them by intestacy laws. The court, however, found that Hagan's intent controlled. She had not intended to give any portion of her estate to her relatives. Because the will specifically stated that the residuary estate should be distributed to the charities, the court enforced these provisions (and Hagan's relatives received nothing).[3] ■

**Abatement** If the assets of an estate are insufficient to pay in full all general bequests provided for in the will, an *abatement* takes place. An abatement means that the legatees receive reduced benefits. ■ **EXAMPLE 31.2** Julie's will leaves $15,000 to each of her children, Tamara and Lynn. On Julie's death, only $10,000 is available to honor these bequests. By abatement, each child will receive $5,000. ■ If bequests are more complicated, abatement may be

more complex. The testator's intent, as expressed in the will, controls.

**Lapsed Legacies** If a legatee dies before the death of the testator or before the legacy is payable, a *lapsed legacy* results. At common law, the legacy failed. Today, the legacy may not lapse if the legatee is in a certain blood relationship to the testator (such as a child, grandchild, brother, or sister) and has left a child or other surviving descendant.

## 31–1d Requirements for a Valid Will

A will must comply with statutory formalities designed to ensure that the testator understood his or her actions at the time the will was made. These formalities are intended to help prevent fraud. Unless they are followed, the will is declared void, and the decedent's property is distributed according to the laws of intestacy of that state.

Although the required formalities vary among jurisdictions, most states have certain basic requirements for executing a will. Most states require proof of (1) the testator's capacity, (2) testamentary intent, (3) a written document, (4) the testator's signature, and (5) the signatures of persons who witnessed the testator's signing of the will.

**Testamentary Capacity and Intent** For a will to be valid, the testator must have testamentary capacity—that is, the testator must be of legal age and sound mind *at the time the will is made.* The minimum legal age for executing a will in most states and under the UPC is eighteen years [UPC 2–501]. Thus, the will of a twenty-one-year-old decedent written when the person was sixteen is invalid if, under state law, the legal age for executing a will is eighteen.

The concept of "being of sound mind" refers to the testator's ability to formulate and to comprehend a personal plan for the disposition of property. Persons who have been declared incompetent in a legal proceeding do not meet the sound mind requirement.

■ **CASE IN POINT 31.3** Marjorie Sirgo, a Louisiana resident, executed a will in which she left her estate equally to her children, Susie and Rene. Soon after, Marjorie—suffering from Parkinson's disease—began living at a nursing home. She stayed there until August 2005, when she was evacuated due to Hurricane Katrina. Three months later, while Marjorie was a resident of Poplar Springs Nursing Center, Susie took her to execute another will. This will left Marjorie's entire estate to Susie. Marjorie died, and Susie filed a petition in a

---

3. *Benjamin v. JPMorgan Chase Bank, N.A.*, 305 S.W.3d 446 (Ky.App. 2010).

Louisiana state court to probate her mother's second will. Rene objected, claiming their mother had lacked testamentary capacity when she had executed the second will. The court declared the second will void and ordered the probate of Marjorie's first will. Susie appealed.

A state intermediate appellate court affirmed the order of the lower court. Nurses' notes in Marjorie's medical records at Poplar Springs indicated that she suffered from cognitive impairment and lacked the ability to make even small decisions. In the same month in which she executed the second will, it was noted that Marjorie suffered from "short-term and long-term memory problems." For instance, she was unable to recall the current season or the location of her room.[4] ■

Related to the requirement of capacity is the concept of intent. A valid will is one that represents the maker's intention to transfer and distribute her or his property. Generally, a testator must:

1. Know the nature of the act (intend to make a will).
2. Comprehend and remember the people to whom the testator would naturally leave his or her estate (such as family members and friends).
3. Know the nature and extent of her or his property.
4. Understand the distribution of assets called for by the will.

**Undue Influence.** When it can be shown that the decedent's plan of distribution was the result of fraud or undue influence, the will is declared invalid. A court may sometimes infer undue influence when the named beneficiary was in a position to influence the making of the will. A presumption of undue influence might arise, for instance, if the testator ignored blood relatives and named as a beneficiary a nonrelative who was in constant close contact with the testator.

■ **CASE IN POINT 31.4** Belton Johnson, whose family owned the famous King Ranch in Texas, was married three times. He had three children from his first marriage and eight grandchildren. While married to his second wife, he executed a will that provided for her during her lifetime and left the remainder of his estate in a trust for his children and grandchildren. When his second wife died, he changed the will to give $1 million to each grandchild and the remainder to five charities. His children were provided for in a separate trust. While married to his third wife, Laura, he executed a will that left $1 million to each grandchild and the rest to Laura. Later, another will left his entire estate in trust to Laura for her life and then to a foundation that she controlled.

After Johnson's death, a dispute arose over the validity of the latest will.

The court concluded that Johnson's last will was invalid due to Laura's undue influence. Johnson was an admitted alcoholic with permanent cognitive defects and memory problems that would have caused him to be more susceptible to undue influence. Evidence suggested that Laura had exerted substantial control over many aspects of Johnson's life. Other evidence established that Johnson wanted to provide for his descendants, as well as for the charities named in the earlier will.[5] ■

**Disinheritance.** Although a testator must be able to remember the persons who would naturally be heirs to the estate, there is no requirement that testators give their estates to the natural heirs. A testator may decide to disinherit, or leave nothing to, an individual for various reasons. Most states have laws that attempt to prevent accidental disinheritance, however. There are also laws that protect minor children from the loss of the family residence. Therefore, the testator's intent to disinherit needs to be clear.

■ **CASE IN POINT 31.5** In 1975, William Melton executed a will that, among other things, stated that his daughter, Vicki Palm, was to receive nothing. In 1979, he added a handwritten note to the will, saying that his friend, Alberta Kelleher, was to receive a small portion of his estate.

In 1995, Melton sent a signed, handwritten letter to Kelleher. The letter said that Melton wanted to put "something in writing" leaving Kelleher his "entire estate." Melton also said, "I *do not* want my brother Larry J. Melton or Vicki Palm or any of my other relatives to have one penny of my estate."

When Melton died in 2008, Kelleher had already passed away, and Melton's daughter, Vicki Palm, was his only natural heir. The state of Nevada argued that it should receive everything because Palm had been disinherited. Nevertheless, the trial court applied the state's intestacy laws and distributed the entire estate to Palm. The state appealed. The Nevada Supreme Court reversed the judgment of the lower court. It held that the disinheritance clause was clear and enforceable and that Melton's estate should therefore go to the state of Nevada.[6] ■

**Writing Requirements** Generally, a will must be in writing. The writing itself can be informal as long as it substantially complies with the statutory requirements. In some states, a will can be handwritten in crayon or ink.

---

4. *In re Succession of Sirgo*, 164 So.3d 832 (La. 2014).

5. *In re Estate of Johnson*, 340 S.W.3d 769 (Tex.App.—San Antonio 2011).
6. *In re Estate of Melton*, 272 P.3d 668 (Nev.Sup.Ct. 2012).

It can be written on a sheet or scrap of paper, on a paper bag, or on a piece of cloth. A will that is completely in the handwriting of the testator is called a **holographic will** (sometimes referred to as an *olographic will*).

A **nuncupative will** is an oral will made before witnesses. Oral wills are not permitted in most states. Where authorized by statute, such wills are generally valid only if made during the last illness of the testator and are therefore sometimes referred to as *deathbed wills*. Normally, only personal property can be transferred by a nuncupative will. Statutes may also permit members of the military to make nuncupative wills when on active duty.

**Signature Requirements** A fundamental requirement is that the testator's signature must appear on the will, generally at the end. Each jurisdiction dictates by statute and court decision what constitutes a signature. Initials, an X or other mark, and words such as "Mom" have all been upheld as valid when it was shown that the testators *intended* them to be signatures.

**Witness Requirements** A will usually must be *attested* (sworn to) by two, and sometimes three, witnesses. The number of witnesses, their qualifications, and the manner in which the witnessing must be done are generally set out in a statute. A witness may be required to be disinterested—that is, not a beneficiary under the will. The UPC, however, allows even interested witnesses to attest to a will [UPC 2–505]. There are no age requirements for witnesses, but they must be mentally competent.

The purpose of the witnesses is to verify that the testator actually executed (signed) the will and had the requisite intent and capacity at the time. A witness need not read the contents of the will. Usually, the testator and all witnesses sign in the sight or the presence of one another. The UPC does not require all parties to sign in one another's presence, however, and deems it sufficient if the testator acknowledges her or his signature to the witnesses [UPC 2–502].

### 31–1e Revocation of Wills

The testator can revoke a will at any time during her or his life, either by a physical act, such as tearing up the will, or by a subsequent writing. Wills can also be revoked by operation of law. Revocation can be partial or complete, and it must follow certain strict formalities.

**Revocation by a Physical Act** A testator can revoke a will by *intentionally* burning, tearing, canceling, obliterating, or otherwise destroying it.[7] A testator can also revoke a will by intentionally having someone else destroy it in the testator's presence and at the testator's direction. Note that when a state statute prescribes the specific methods for revoking a will by a physical act, only those methods can be used to revoke the will.

In some states, a testator can partially revoke a will by the physical act of crossing out some provisions in the will. The portions that are crossed out are dropped, and the remaining portions are valid. In no circumstances, however, can a provision be crossed out and an additional or substitute provision written in its place. Such altered provisions require that the will be reexecuted (signed again) and reattested (rewitnessed).

In the following case, the court had to decide whether the testator had intended to revoke part or all of her will by making certain changes to it after it was executed.

---

7. The destruction cannot be inadvertent. The testator must have intent to revoke the will.

---

**Case Analysis 31.1**

# Peterson v. Harrell

Supreme Court of Georgia, 690 S.E.2d 151 (2010).

### In the Language of the Court

*THOMPSON, Justice.*

Testator Marion E. Peterson died in 2008. She was survived by her two siblings [brother and sister], Arvin Peterson and Carolyn Peterson Basner (caveators[a]).

---

a. In the context of wills, a *caveator* is one who files a *caveat* attacking the validity of an alleged will.

After testator's death, Vasta Lucas, testator's longtime companion and executor of testator's estate, filed a petition to probate testator's will in solemn form. Lucas died during the pendency of this appeal [while the appeal was pending], and appellee Richard Harrell was appointed as successor executor and trustee for the estate. Caveators filed a caveat to the petition to probate, alleging the will was not properly executed or had been revoked due to obliterations. The trial court admitted the will to probate and caveators appealed.

OCGA [the Official Code of Georgia Annotated] Section 53-4-20(b) of the

**Case 31.1 Continued**

Revised Probate Code of 1998 provides that "a will shall be attested and subscribed in the presence of the testator by two or more competent witnesses." The record evidence in this case establishes that testator executed a will on June 9, 1976. The will was witnessed by two subscribing witnesses, only one of whom was living at the time of trial. Having been provided a copy of testator's will, the surviving witness testified to its due execution by deposition testimony presented at trial and via written interrogatories filed with the court. Caveators presented no evidence challenging either the validity of the signatures on the will or testator's capacity at the time the will was executed. Accordingly, the evidence supports the trial court's finding that the will was duly executed.

The will contained a bequest to Lucas in the form of a trust and provided that upon Lucas's death the trustee shall distribute any remaining assets to four beneficiaries, including caveators. Some time after the will was executed, testator struck through with an ink pen the names of all successor beneficiaries of the trust estate, as well as language in the will nominating Richard Harrell as

successor executor and trustee. None of the strike-throughs were witnessed or attested to. Near the end of the will, testator wrote, "My executrix is Julie Peterson." Caveators contend these alterations constitute material cancellations that effect a revocation of the will.

To effect a revocation of a will by obliteration, caveators must show that testator made material obliterations to her will or directed another to do so and that testator intended for this act to revoke the will. *Joint operation of act and intention is necessary to revoke a will. The intent to revoke the will in its entirety shall be presumed from the obliteration or cancellation of a material portion of the will, but such presumption may be overcome by a preponderance of the evidence.* [Emphasis added.]

Even assuming, arguendo [for the sake of argument], that the alterations to testator's will constituted a material cancellation within the meaning of OCGA Section 53-4-44, we find no error in the trial court's conclusion that testator did not intend to revoke her entire will. The record supports the trial court's findings that caveators had no knowledge of the circumstances surrounding what they

allege to be the revocation of the will, that testator never discussed revoking her will with caveators, and that caveators were not present when testator made the alterations to the will. Caveators presented no evidence of testator's intent other than the alterations themselves, and they satisfied their initial burden only by proving that testator made alterations to the will.

The record also shows, however, that the will was found in good condition on testator's desk among her personal papers. It bore the signatures of both testator and her subscribing witnesses and set out a primary bequest to Lucas which remained intact. Handwritten alterations crossing out the names of the successor beneficiaries with a single line were initialed by testator and she added language to the will indicating her desire to substitute Julie Peterson as her executrix. As found by the trial court, this evidence clearly indicates testator's intent to cancel only certain provisions of the will, not an intent to revoke the will in its entirety as required for revocation under OCGA Section 53-4-44.

\* \* \* \*

Judgment affirmed.

## Legal Reasoning Questions

**1.** Why would the caveators argue that the entire will should be revoked? How would the will's revocation benefit them?

**2.** What could the testator have done differently to clarify her intentions in her will?

**3.** How might the availability of a secure online repository for a person's will affect a challenge to the will?

---

**Revocation by a Subsequent Writing** A will may also be wholly or partially revoked by a **codicil,** a written instrument separate from the will that amends or revokes provisions in the will. A codicil eliminates the necessity of redrafting an entire will merely to add to it or amend it. A codicil can also be used to revoke an entire will. The codicil must be executed with the same formalities required for a will, and it must refer expressly to the will. In effect, it updates a will because the will is "incorporated by reference" into the codicil.

A new will (second will) can be executed that may or may not revoke the first or a prior will, depending on

the language used. To revoke a prior will, the second will must use language specifically revoking other wills, such as, "This will hereby revokes all prior wills." If the second will is otherwise valid and properly executed, it will revoke all prior wills. If the express *declaration of revocation* is missing, then both wills are read together. If there are any discrepancies between the wills, the second will controls.

**Revocation by Operation of Law** Revocation by operation of law occurs when marriage, divorce, annulment, or the birth of a child takes place after a will has been executed.

**Marriage and Divorce.** In most states, when a testator marries after executing a will and the will does not provide for the new spouse, the new spouse can still receive a share of the testator's estate. On the testator's death, the surviving spouse can receive the amount he or she would have taken had the testator died intestate (intestacy laws will be discussed shortly). The rest of the estate passes under the will [UPC 2–301, 2–508].

If, however, the new spouse is otherwise provided for in the will (or by transfer of property outside the will), he or she will not be given an intestate amount. Also, if the parties had a valid *prenuptial agreement*, its provisions dictate what the surviving spouse receives.

Divorce does not necessarily revoke the entire will. Rather, a divorce or an annulment occurring after a will has been executed revokes those dispositions of property made under the will to the former spouse [UPC 2–508].

**Children.** If a child is born after a will has been executed, that child may be entitled to a portion of the estate. Most state laws allow a child of the deceased to receive some portion of a parent's estate even if no provision is made in the parent's will. This is true *unless it is clear from the will's terms that the testator intended to disinherit the child* (see *Case in Point 31.5,* presented earlier). Under the UPC, the rule is the same.

## 31–1f Rights under a Will

The law imposes certain limitations on the way a person can dispose of property in a will. For instance, a married person who makes a will generally cannot avoid leaving a certain portion of the estate to the surviving spouse unless there is a valid prenuptial agreement. In most states, this is called an *elective share* or a *forced share,* and it is often one-third of the estate or an amount equal to a spouse's share under intestacy laws.

Beneficiaries under a will have rights as well. A beneficiary can renounce (disclaim) his or her share of the property given under a will. Further, a surviving spouse can renounce the amount given under a will and elect to take the forced share when the forced share is larger than the amount of the gift. State statutes provide the methods by which a surviving spouse accomplishes renunciation. The purpose of these statutes is to allow the spouse to obtain whichever distribution would be more advantageous. The UPC gives the surviving spouse an elective right to take a percentage of the total estate determined by the length of time that the spouse and the decedent were married to each other [UPC 2–201].

## 31–1g Probate Procedures

Recall that probate is the court process by which a will is proved valid or invalid. As mentioned, probate laws vary from state to state. Typically, the procedures used to probate a will depend on the size of the decedent's estate.

**Informal Probate** For smaller estates, most state statutes provide for the distribution of assets without formal probate proceedings. Faster and less expensive methods are then used. Property can be transferred by *affidavit* (a written statement taken in the presence of a person who has authority to affirm it). Problems or questions can be handled during an administrative hearing. Some states allow title to cars, savings and checking accounts, and certain other property to be transferred simply by filling out forms.

A majority of states also provide for *family settlement agreements,* which are private agreements among the beneficiaries. Once a will is admitted to probate, the family members can agree among themselves on how to distribute the decedent's assets. Although a family settlement agreement speeds the settlement process, a court order is still needed to protect the estate from future creditors and to clear title to the assets involved.

**Formal Probate** For larger estates, formal probate proceedings normally are undertaken, and the probate court supervises every aspect of the process. Additionally, in some situations—such as when a guardian for minor children must be appointed—more formal probate procedures cannot be avoided.

Formal probate proceedings may take several months or several years to complete, depending on the size and complexity of the estate and whether the will is contested. When the will is contested, or someone objects to the actions of the personal representative, the duration of probate is extended. As a result, a sizable portion of the decedent's assets (as much as 10 percent) may go to pay the fees charged by attorneys and personal representatives, as well as court costs.

## 31–1h Property Transfers outside the Probate Process

Often, people can avoid the cost of probate by employing various **will substitutes.** Examples include *living trusts* (discussed later in this chapter), life insurance policies, and individual retirement accounts (IRAs) with named beneficiaries.

One way to transfer property outside the probate process is to make gifts to one's children or others while one is still living. Another way is to own property in a joint tenancy. As previously discussed, in a joint tenancy, when one joint tenant dies, the other joint tenant or tenants automatically inherit the deceased tenant's share of the property. This is true even if the deceased tenant has provided otherwise in her or his will. Not all alternatives to formal probate administration are suitable to every estate, however.

See Concept Summary 31.1 for a review of basic information about wills.

---

## Concept Summary 31.1

### Wills

**Terminology**

- *Intestate*—Describes one who dies without a valid will.
- *Testator*—A person who makes a will.
- *Personal representative*—A person appointed in a will or by a court to settle the affairs of a decedent. A personal representative named in the will is an *executor*. A personal representative appointed by the court for an intestate decedent is an *administrator*.
- *Devise*—A gift of real estate by will, whether general or specific. The recipient of a devise is a *devisee*.
- *Bequest or legacy*—A gift of personal property by will, which can be general or specific. The recipient of a bequest (legacy) is a *legatee*.

**Requirements for a Valid Will**

- The testator must have *testamentary capacity*—that is, be of legal age and sound mind at the time the will is made.
- A will must be in writing (except for nuncupative wills).
- A will must be signed by the testator, and usually several people must witness the signing, depending on the state statute.

**Revocation of Wills**

- *By a physical act*—Intentionally tearing up, canceling, obliterating, or deliberately destroying part or all of a will revokes it.
- *By subsequent writing*—
  1. Codicil—A formal, separate document that amends or revokes an existing will.
  2. Second will or new will—A new, properly executed will expressly revoking the existing will.
- *By operation of law*—
  1. Marriage—Generally revokes a will written before the marriage to the extent of providing for the spouse.
  2. Divorce or annulment—Revokes dispositions of property made to the former spouse under a will made before the divorce or annulment.
  3. Subsequently born child—It is inferred that the child is entitled to receive the portion of the estate granted under intestacy distribution laws.

**Probate Procedures**

- To *probate* a will means to establish its validity and to carry out the administration of the estate through a court process. Probate laws vary from state to state. Probate procedures may be informal or formal, depending on the size of the estate and other factors, such as whether a guardian for minor children must be appointed.

# 31–2 Intestacy Laws

Each state regulates by statute how property will be distributed when a person dies intestate (without a valid will). Intestacy laws attempt to carry out the likely intent and wishes of the decedent.

These laws assume that deceased persons would have intended that their natural heirs (spouses, children, grandchildren, or other family members) inherit their property. Therefore, intestacy statutes set out rules and priorities under which these heirs inherit the property. If no heirs exist, the state will assume ownership of the property.

The rules of descent vary widely from state to state. It is thus important to refer to the exact language of the applicable state statutes when addressing any problem of intestacy distribution.

## 31–2a Surviving Spouse and Children

Usually, state statutes provide that first the debts of the decedent must be satisfied out of the estate. Then the remaining assets pass to the surviving spouse and to the children. A surviving spouse usually receives only a share of the estate—typically, one-half if there is also a surviving child and one-third if there are two or more children.[8] Only if no children or grandchildren survive the decedent will a surviving spouse receive the entire estate.

■ **EXAMPLE 31.6** Adrian dies intestate and is survived by his wife, Betty, and his children, Duane and Tara. Allen's property passes according to intestacy laws. After his outstanding debts are paid, Betty will receive the family home (either in fee simple or as a life estate) and ordinarily a one-third to one-half interest in all other property. The remaining real and personal property will pass to Duane and Tara in equal portions. ■

Under most state intestacy laws and under the UPC, in-laws do not share in an estate. Thus, if a child dies before his or her parents, the child's spouse will not receive an inheritance on the parents' death. In *Example 31.6,* if Duane died before his father (Adrian), Duane's widow would not inherit his share of Adrian's estate.

## 31–2b When There Is No Surviving Spouse or Child

When there is no surviving spouse or child, the order of inheritance is generally grandchildren, then parents

of the decedent. These relatives usually are called *lineal* relatives.

If there are no lineal heirs, then *collateral heirs*—brothers and sisters, nieces and nephews, and aunts and uncles of the decedent—are the next groups that share. If there are no survivors in any of these groups, most statutes provide for the property to be distributed among the next of kin of the collateral heirs.

## 31–2c Stepchildren, Adopted Children, and Illegitimate Children

Under intestacy laws, stepchildren are not considered kin. Legally adopted children, however, are recognized as lawful heirs of their adoptive parents. (This is also true of children who are in the process of being adopted at the time of a prospective parent's death.)

Statutes vary from state to state in regard to the inheritance rights of illegitimate children (children born out of wedlock). Although illegitimate children have inheritance rights in most states, their rights are not necessarily identical to those of legitimate children.

In some states, an illegitimate child has the right to inherit only from the mother and her relatives, unless the father's paternity has been established by a legal proceeding. In the majority of states, however, a child born of any union that has the characteristics of a formal marriage relationship (such as unmarried parents who cohabit) is considered to be legitimate.

Under the revised UPC, a child is generally considered the child of the natural (biological) parents, regardless of their marital status. The child cannot inherit from a natural parent, however, unless that natural parent has openly treated the child as his (or hers) and has not refused to support the child [UPC 2–114].

## 31–2d Grandchildren

Usually, a decedent's will provides for how the estate will be distributed to descendants of deceased children (grandchildren whose parents have died). If a will does not include such a provision—or if a person dies intestate—the question arises as to what share the grandchildren of the decedent will receive. Each state uses one of two methods of distributing the assets of intestate decedents—*per stirpes* or *per capita.*

**Per Stirpes Distribution** Under the *per stirpes*[9] method, within a class or group of distributees (such as

---

8. UPC 2–102(2) provides a formula for computing a surviving spouse's share that is contingent on the number of surviving children and parents. For instance, if the decedent has no surviving children and one surviving parent, the surviving spouse takes the first $200,000, plus three-fourths of any balance of the intestate estate.

9. *Per stirpes* is a Latin term meaning "by the roots" or "by stock." When used in estate law, it means proportionally divided between beneficiaries according to each beneficiary's deceased ancestor's share.

grandchildren), the children of a descendant take the share that their deceased parent *would have been* entitled to inherit. Thus, a grandchild with no siblings inherits all of his or her parent's share, while grandchildren with siblings divide their parent's share.

■ **EXAMPLE 31.7** Michael, a widower, has two children, Scott and Jillian. Scott has two children (Becky and Holly), and Jillian has one child (Paul). Scott and Jillian die before their father. When Michael dies, if his estate is distributed *per stirpes,* Becky and Holly each receive one-fourth of the estate (dividing Scott's one-half share). Paul receives one-half of the estate (taking Jillian's one-half share). Exhibit 31–2 illustrates the *per stirpes* method of distribution. ■

**Per Capita Distribution** An estate may also be distributed on a ***per capita***[10] basis, which means that each person in a class or group takes an equal share of the estate. ■ **EXAMPLE 31.8** If Michael's estate is distributed *per capita,* Becky, Holly, and Paul will each receive a one-third share. Exhibit 31–3 illustrates the *per capita* method of distribution. ■

# 31-3 Trusts

A **trust** is any arrangement by which property is transferred from one person to a trustee to be administered for the transferor's or another party's benefit. It can also

---

10. *Per capita* is a Latin term meaning "per person" or "for each head." When used in estate law, it means divided equally among beneficiaries within a class.

be defined as a right of property (real or personal) held by one party for the benefit of another. A trust can be created to become effective during a person's lifetime or after a person's death. Trusts may be established for any purpose that is not illegal or against public policy, and they may be express or implied.

The essential elements of a trust are as follows:

1. A designated beneficiary (except in charitable trusts, discussed shortly).
2. A designated trustee.
3. A fund sufficiently identified to enable title to pass to the trustee.
4. Actual delivery by the *settlor* or *grantor* (the person creating the trust) to the trustee with the intention of passing title.

## 31-3a Express Trusts

An express trust is created or declared in explicit terms, usually in writing. There are numerous types of express trusts, each with its own special characteristics.

**Living Trusts** A **living trust**—or *inter vivos* trust (*inter vivos* is Latin for "between or among the living")—is a trust created by a grantor during her or his lifetime. Living trusts have become a popular estate-planning option because at the grantor's death, assets held in a living trust can pass to the heirs without going through probate.

Note, however, that living trusts do not necessarily shelter assets from estate taxes. The grantor may also have to pay income taxes on trust earnings, depending on whether the trust is revocable or irrevocable.

**EXHIBIT 31–2** *Per Stirpes* **Distribution**

Under this method of distribution, an heir takes the share that his or her deceased parent would have been entitled to inherit had the parent lived. This may mean that a class of distributees—the grandchildren in this example—will not inherit in equal portions. Note that Becky and Holly receive only one-fourth of Michael's estate while Paul inherits one-half.

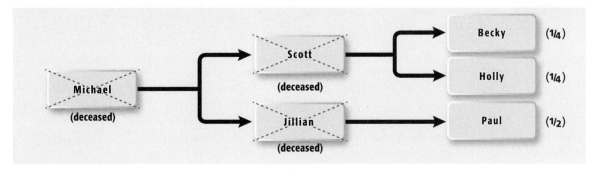

## EXHIBIT 31–3 *Per Capita* Distribution

Under this method of distribution, all heirs in a certain class—in this example, the grandchildren—inherit equally. Note that Becky and Holly in this situation each inherit one-third, as does Paul.

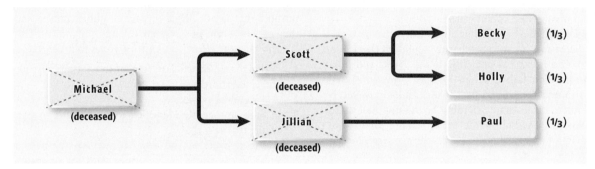

**Revocable Living Trusts.** In a revocable living trust, which is the most common type, the grantor retains control over the trust property during her or his lifetime. The grantor deeds the property to the trustee but retains the power to amend, alter, or revoke the trust during her or his lifetime.

The grantor may also serve as a trustee or co-trustee and can arrange to receive income earned by the trust assets during her or his lifetime. Because the grantor is in control of the funds, she or he is required to pay income taxes on the trust earnings. Unless the trust is revoked, the principal of the trust is transferred to the trust beneficiary on the grantor's death.

■ **EXAMPLE 31.9** James Cortez owns and operates a large farm. After his wife dies, James contacts his attorney to create a living trust for the benefit of his three children, Alicia, Emma, and Jacob. His attorney prepares the documents creating the trust. James executes a deed conveying the farm to the trust and transfers the farm's bank accounts into the name of the trust.

The trust designates James as the trustee and names his son Jacob as the *successor trustee,* who will take over the management of the trust when James dies or becomes incapacitated. Each of the children and James (as *income beneficiaries*) will receive an income from the trust while James is alive. When James dies, the farm will pass to them without having to go through probate. By holding the property in a revocable living trust, James retains control over the farm during his life (and can make changes to the trust at any time). This trust arrangement is illustrated in Exhibit 31–4. ■

The following case involved a revocable living trust that included the phrase "death of each." The resolution of the dispute turned on whether, in the context, "each" meant "either" or "both."

## EXHIBIT 31–4 A Revocable Living Trust Arrangement

# Dowdy v. Dowdy

District Court of Appeal of Florida, Second District, 41 Fla. L. Weekly D85, 182 So.3d 807 (2016).

**Background and Facts**  Betty and Dennis Dowdy created the Dowdy Family Trust. The property of the trust comprised of two parcels of real estate. The trust document identified Betty and Dennis as the settlors, the initial trustees, and the initial beneficiaries. The trust document provided for the revocation or amendment of the trust and for distributions to the settlors. It also appointed one of each settlor's children as co-successor trustees and, following the settlors' deaths, provided for liquidation and distribution to all of their children.

Dennis had three children, and Betty had two—they did not have any children in common. After Dennis died, Betty amended the trust to remove Dennis's children as successor trustees and as beneficiaries. Previously, Betty and Dennis had instructed the trust to sell one of the properties. Now, Betty sold the remaining trust property.

Dennis's son Michael, who was named as a co-successor trustee in the trust document, learned of the sale and filed a petition in a Florida state court against Betty. Michael maintained that Betty's amendment was invalid because it had been executed after Dennis's death. He argued that when Dennis died, the trust became irrevocable and he succeeded Dennis as co-trustee. The court ordered Betty to deposit the proceeds of the sale with the court pending its construction of the trust. Betty appealed.

## In the Language of the Court

*NORTHCUTT,* Judge.

* * * *

* * * Article IV of the original trust document provided as follows:

> During the Settlors' lifetime, the Trustees, in the Trustees' sole discretion, may pay, invade, or apply the income or corpus [trust property], or so much as they may choose, to or for the benefit, support and maintenance of the initial primary beneficiaries * * * .

Thus, if Betty was the only trustee following the death of her husband, she had sole and unfettered authority to sell the trust property for her own benefit.

Michael claims to be a successor co-trustee under article III of the original trust:

> * * * In the event of the death of each of the Initial Trustees, * * * the Settlors nominate and appoint Settlors' son and stepson, Michael R. Dowdy * * * , and Settlors' daughter and stepdaughter, Deborah Ann Andrews [Betty's daughter], as Co-Successor Trustees.

In Michael's view, the phrase "death of each" meant the death of *either* initial trustee. Therefore, he asserts that he became a co-trustee with Betty upon his father's death.

* * * Our view [is] that the succession of trustees occurred only upon the death of *both* initial trustees. This view is confirmed by the use of the same phraseology elsewhere in the original trust document. Article V provides:

> After the death of each of the Settlors, the Co-Successor Trustees are directed to liquidate the Trust Estate and immediately pay and distribute the Trust Estate to the children and stepchildren of the Settlors * * * .

*Clearly, in this instance the phrase "death of each" must mean the death of both. Otherwise, the article's direction to liquidate the trust estate and immediately distribute it to the settlors' children would nullify article IV's grant of authority to invade the income or corpus of the trust for the benefit of the initial primary beneficiaries "or the survivor."* Indeed, upon the death of one settlor it would altogether nullify the survivor's status as beneficiary. This, of course, would be an absurd interpretation in complete contravention [contradiction] of a central purpose of the trust. [Emphasis added.]

There is nothing in the original trust document to suggest that the phrase "death of each" has a different meaning in article III. To the contrary, that article is otherwise consistent with this interpretation. We conclude, then, that Michael did not succeed Dennis as a trustee when Dennis died.

Case 31.2 Continues

Case 31.2 Continued **Decision and Remedy** *The state intermediate appellate court reversed the order of the lower court. Under the appellate court's interpretation of the terms of the trust, "at all times . . . , Betty has been the sole trustee and beneficiary of the trust . . . . As such, she had sole authority and discretion to sell the remaining trust property for her own benefit." The court concluded that Michael's petition had no likelihood of success.*

**Critical Thinking**

- **Legal Environment** *According to Michael's view of the phrase "death of each," how many co-trustees would have succeeded Dennis on his death? Explain.*
- **What If the Facts Were Different?** *Suppose that the Dowdy Family Trust had provided for a specific child to become co-trustee on the death of his or her parent—Deborah to succeed Betty, for example. How would the result have been different?*

---

**Irrevocable Living Trusts.** In an irrevocable living trust, the grantor permanently gives up control over the property to the trustee. The grantor executes a trust deed, and legal title to the trust property passes to the named trustee. The trustee has a duty to administer the property as directed by the grantor for the benefit and in the interest of the beneficiaries.

The trustee must preserve the trust property and make it productive. If required by the terms of the trust agreement, the trustee must pay income to the beneficiaries in accordance with the terms of the trust. Because the grantor has, in effect, given over the property for the benefit of the beneficiaries, he or she is no longer responsible for paying income taxes on the trust earnings.

**Testamentary Trusts** A **testamentary trust** is created by will and comes into existence on the grantor's death. Although a testamentary trust has a trustee who maintains legal title to the trust property, the trustee's actions are subject to judicial approval. The trustee can be named in the will or appointed by the court (if not named in the will). The legal responsibilities of the trustee are the same as in a living trust.

If a court finds that the will setting up a testamentary trust is invalid, then the trust will also be invalid. The property that was to be in the trust will then pass according to intestacy laws, not according to the terms of the trust.

If the court finds that a condition of the trust is invalid because it is illegal or against public policy, the court will invalidate that condition only and enforce the trust without it. ■ **EXAMPLE 31.10** Linzy Herman's will creates a testamentary trust. A condition of Herman's trust states, "to my son, if he never gets married." Because the condition is against public policy, the court will read the terms of the trust as not including the invalid restraint on marriage. ■

**Charitable Trusts** A **charitable trust** is an express trust designed for the benefit of a segment of the public or the public in general. It differs from other types of trusts in that the identities of the beneficiaries are uncertain and it can be established to last indefinitely. Usually, to be deemed a charitable trust, a trust must be created for charitable, educational, religious, or scientific purposes.

**Spendthrift Trusts** A **spendthrift trust** is created to provide for the maintenance of a beneficiary by preventing him or her from being careless with the bestowed funds. Unlike the beneficiaries of other trusts, the beneficiary in a spendthrift trust is not permitted to transfer or assign his or her rights to the trust's principal or future payments from the trust.

Essentially, the beneficiary can draw only a certain portion of the total amount to which he or she is entitled at any one time. The majority of states allow spendthrift trust provisions that prohibit creditors from attaching such trusts, with a few exceptions, such as for payment of a beneficiary's domestic-support obligations.

**Totten Trusts** A **Totten trust**[11] is created when a grantor deposits funds into an account in her or his own name with instructions that in the event of the grantor's death, whatever is in that account should go to a specific beneficiary. This type of trust is revocable at will until the depositor dies or completes the gift in her or his lifetime (by delivering the funds to the intended beneficiary, for instance). The beneficiary has no access to the funds until the depositor's death, when the beneficiary obtains property rights to the balance on hand.

---

11. This type of trust derives its unusual name from *In the Matter of Totten,* 179 N.Y. 112, 71 N.E. 748 (1904).

## 31-3b Implied Trusts

Sometimes, a trust will be imposed (implied) by law, even in the absence of an express trust. Implied trusts include constructive trusts and resulting trusts.

**Constructive Trusts** A **constructive trust** is imposed by a court in the interests of fairness and justice. In a constructive trust, the owner of the property is declared to be a trustee for the parties who are, in equity, actually entitled to the benefits that flow from the trust.

Courts often impose constructive trusts when someone who is in a confidential or fiduciary relationship with another person, such as a guardian to a ward, has breached a duty to that person. A court may also impose a constructive trust when someone wrongfully holds legal title to property. This may occur when the property was obtained through fraud or in breach of a legal duty, for instance.

■ **CASE IN POINT 31.11** Stella Jankowski added her niece Genevieve Viarengo as a joint owner on bank accounts and other financial assets valued at $500,000. Jankowski also executed a will that divided her estate equally among her ten nieces, nephews, and cousins. The will named Viarengo and Richard Golebiewski as coexecutors. She did not tell the attorney who drafted the will about the jointly held accounts.

When Jankowski died, Viarengo emptied Jankowski's safe and removed her financial records. Viarengo also claimed that the funds in the accounts were hers. Jankowski's other relatives filed a suit and asked the court to impose a constructive trust. The court found that Viarengo had committed fraud in obtaining the assets that she had held jointly with Jankowski and would be unjustly enriched if she were allowed to retain them. Therefore, the court imposed a constructive trust.[12] ■

**Resulting Trusts** A **resulting trust** arises from the conduct of the parties. Here, the trust results, or is created, when circumstances raise an inference that the party holding legal title to the property does so for the benefit of another. The trust will result unless the inference is refuted.

■ **EXAMPLE 31.12** Gabriela Fuentes wants to put one acre of land she owns on the market for sale. Because she is going out of the country for two years and will not be available to deed the property to a buyer during that period, she conveys the property to her good friend Raul Cruz. Cruz can then attempt to sell the property while Fuentes is gone.

The transaction in which Fuentes conveys the property to Cruz is intended to be neither a sale nor a gift. Consequently, Cruz will hold the property in a resulting trust for the benefit of Fuentes. When Fuentes returns, Cruz will be required either to deed the property back to her or, if the property has been sold, to turn over the proceeds (held in trust) to her. ■

Concept Summary 31.2 provides a synopsis of basic information about trusts.

## 31-3c The Trustee

The trustee is the person holding the trust property. Anyone legally capable of holding title to, and dealing in, property can be a trustee. If a trust fails to name a trustee, or if a named trustee cannot or will not serve, the trust does not fail. An appropriate court can appoint a trustee.

**Trustee's Duties** A trustee must act with honesty, good faith, and prudence in administering the trust and must exercise a high degree of loyalty toward the trust beneficiary. The general standard of care is the degree of care a prudent person would exercise in his or her own personal affairs.[13] The duty of loyalty requires that the trustee act in the exclusive interest of the beneficiary.

A trustee's specific duties include the following:

1. Maintain clear and accurate accounts of the trust's administration.
2. Furnish complete and correct information to the beneficiary.
3. Keep trust assets separate from her or his own assets.
4. Pay to an income beneficiary the net income of the trust assets at reasonable intervals.
5. Limit the risk of loss from investments by reasonable diversification and dispose of assets that do not represent prudent investments. (Prudent investment choices might include federal, state, or municipal bonds and some corporate bonds and stocks.)

**Trustee's Powers** When a grantor creates a trust, he or she may set forth the trustee's powers and performance. State law governs in the absence of specific terms in the trust, and the states often restrict the trustee's investment of trust funds.

Typically, statutes confine trustees to investments in conservative debt securities such as government, utility, and railroad bonds and certain real estate loans.

---

12. *Garrigus v. Viarengo,* 112 Conn.App. 655, 963 A.2d 1065 (2009).

13. Revised Uniform Principal and Income Act, Section 2(a)(3); and *Restatement (Third) of Trusts (Prudent Investor Rule),* Section 227. This rule is in force in a majority of the states by statute and a small number of states under common law.

## Concept Summary 31.2

### Trusts

| | |
|---|---|
| **Definition and Essential Elements** | • A *trust* is any arrangement by which property is transferred from one person to a trustee to be administered for another's benefit.<br>• The essential elements of a trust are a designated beneficiary, a designated trustee, a fund sufficiently identified to enable title to pass to the trustee, and actual delivery to the trustee with the intention of passing title. |
| **Types of Trusts** | • *Living* (inter vivos) *trust*—A trust executed by a grantor during his or her lifetime. A living trust may be revocable or irrevocable.<br>• *Testamentary trust*—A trust created by will and coming into existence on the death of the grantor.<br>• *Charitable trust*—A trust designed for the benefit of a segment of the public or the public in general.<br>• *Spendthrift trust*—A trust created to provide for the maintenance of a beneficiary by allowing her or him to receive only a certain portion of the total amount at any one time.<br>• *Totten trust*—A trust created when one person deposits funds in his or her own name with instructions that the funds should go to a beneficiary on the depositor's death. |
| **Implied Trusts** | • *Implied trusts*, which are imposed by law in the interests of fairness and justice, include the following:<br>   **1.** *Constructive trust*—Arises by operation of law when a transaction occurs in which the person who takes title to property is, in equity, not entitled to enjoy the benefits from it.<br>   **2.** *Resulting trust*—Arises from the conduct of the parties when an *apparent intention* to create a trust is present. |

Frequently, though, a grantor gives a trustee discretionary investment power. In that circumstance, any statute may be considered only advisory, with the trustee's decisions subject in most states to the prudent person rule.

Of course, a trustee is responsible for carrying out the purposes of the trust. If the trustee fails to comply with the terms of the trust or the controlling statute, he or she is personally liable for any loss.

### Allocations between Principal and Income

Often, a grantor will provide one beneficiary with a life estate and another beneficiary with the remainder interest in the trust. A farmer, for instance, may create a testamentary trust providing that the farm's income be paid to the surviving spouse and that, on the surviving spouse's death, the farm be given to their children. In this situation, the surviving spouse has a *life estate* in the farm's income, and the children have a *remainder interest* in the farm (the principal).

When a trust is set up in this manner, questions may arise as to how the receipts and expenses for the farm's management and the trust's administration should be allocated between income and principal. When a trust instrument does not provide instructions, a trustee must refer to applicable state law.

The general rule is that ordinary receipts and expenses are chargeable to the income beneficiary, whereas extraordinary receipts and expenses are allocated to the principal beneficiaries.[14] The receipt of rent from trust realty would be ordinary, as would the expense of paying the property's taxes. The cost of long-term improvements and proceeds from the property's sale, however, would be extraordinary.

### 31–3d Trust Termination

The terms of a trust should expressly state the event on which the grantor wishes it to terminate—for instance, the beneficiary's or the trustee's death. If the trust instrument does not provide for termination on the beneficiary's death, the beneficiary's death will not end the trust. Similarly, without an express provision, a trust will not terminate on the trustee's death.

Typically, a trust instrument specifies a termination date. For instance, a trust created to educate the grantor's child may provide that the trust ends when the beneficiary reaches the age of twenty-five. If the trust's purpose is fulfilled before that date, a court may order the trust's termination. If no date is specified, a trust will terminate when its purpose has been fulfilled. Of course, if a trust's purpose becomes impossible or illegal, the trust will terminate.

# 31–4 Other Estate-Planning Issues

Estate planning involves making difficult decisions about the future, such as who will inherit the family home and other assets and who will take care of minor children. Estate planning also involves preparing in advance for other contingencies, such as illness and incapacity. For instance, what happens if you become incapacitated and cannot make your own decisions? Who will take care of your finances and other affairs? Do you want to be kept alive by artificial means, and whom do you trust to make decisions about your health care in the event that you cannot? Powers of attorney and living wills are frequently executed in conjunction with a will or trust to help resolve these matters.

### 31–4a Power of Attorney

A power of attorney is often used in business situations to give a person (an agent) authority to act on another's behalf. The powers usually are limited to a specific context, such as negotiating a deal with a buyer or entering into various contracts necessary to achieve a particular

objective. Powers of attorney are also commonly used in estate planning.

**Durable Power of Attorney** One method of providing for future disability is to use a durable power of attorney. A **durable power of attorney** authorizes an individual to act on behalf of another when he or she becomes incapacitated. It can be drafted to take effect immediately or only after a physician certifies that the person is incapacitated. The person to whom the power is given can then write checks, collect insurance proceeds, and otherwise manage the incapacitated person's affairs, including health care.

Adult children may seek a durable power of attorney from their aging parents, particularly if the parents are becoming mentally incapacitated by Alzheimer's disease or some other condition. A husband and wife may give each other a power of attorney to make decisions in the event that one of them is hospitalized and unable to express her or his wishes. A person who is undergoing an operation may sign a durable power of attorney to a loved one who can take over his or her affairs in the event of incapacity.

If you become incapacitated without having executed a durable power of attorney, a court may need to appoint a conservator to handle your financial affairs. Although a spouse may have the ability to write checks on joint accounts, her or his power is often significantly limited. In most situations, it is better to have named a person you wish to handle your affairs in the event that you cannot.

**Health-Care Power of Attorney** A **health-care power of attorney** designates a person who will have the power to choose what type of and how much medical treatment a person who is unable to make such decisions will receive. The importance of appointing a person to make health-care decisions has grown as medical technology enables physicians and hospitals to keep people alive for ever-increasing periods of time.

■ **EXAMPLE 31.13** Terri Schiavo, a Florida woman, was kept alive in a vegetative state from 1990 to 2005. It took more than twenty court hearings for her husband to convince the court that he had a right to ask physicians to remove her feeding tube and let her die. If Schiavo had given her husband a health-care power of attorney, he would have had the right to make the decision to remove the feeding tube without going to court. ■

### 31–4b Living Will

A living will is not a will in the usual sense—that is, it does not appoint an estate representative, dispose of property, or establish a trust. Rather, a **living will** is an

---

14. Revised Uniform Principal and Income Act, Sections 3, 6, 8, and 13; and *Restatement (Third) of Trusts, (Prudent Investor Rule)*, Section 233.

advance health directive that allows a person to control what medical treatment may be used after a serious accident or illness. Through a living will, a person can indicate whether he or she wants certain lifesaving procedures to be undertaken in situations in which the treatment will not result in a reasonable quality of life.

Most states have enacted statutes permitting living wills, and it is important that the requirements of state law be followed exactly in creating such wills. Typically, state statutes require physicians to abide by the terms of living wills, and living wills are often included with a patient's medical records.

## Reviewing: Wills and Trusts

In June 2016, Bernard Ramish set up a $48,000 trust fund through West Plains Credit Union to provide tuition for his nephew, Nathan Covacek, to attend Tri-State Polytechnic Institute. The trust was established under Ramish's control and went into effect that August. In December, Ramish suffered a brain aneurysm that caused frequent, severe headaches with no other symptoms. Shortly thereafter, Ramish met with an attorney to formalize in writing that he wanted no artificial life-support systems to be used should he suffer a serious illness. He also designated his cousin, Lizzie Johansen, to make decisions on his behalf should he become incapacitated.

In August 2017, Ramish developed heatstroke on the golf course at La Prima Country Club. After recuperating at the clubhouse, Ramish quickly wrote his will on the back of a wine list. It stated, "My last will and testament: Upon my death, I give all of my personal property to my friend Steve Eshom and my home to Lizzie Johansen." He signed the will at the bottom in the presence of five men in the La Prima clubhouse, and all five men signed as witnesses.

A week later, Ramish suffered a second aneurysm and died in his sleep. He was survived by his mother (Dorris Ramish), his nephew (Nathan Covacek), his son-in-law (Bruce Lupin), and his granddaughter (Tori Lupin). Using the information presented in the chapter, answer the following questions.

1. What type of trust did Ramish create for the benefit of Covacek? Was it revocable or irrevocable?
2. Does Ramish's testament on the back of the wine list meet the requirements for a valid will? Why or why not?
3. What would the order of inheritance have been if Ramish had died intestate?
4. Was Johansen granted a durable power of attorney or a health-care power of attorney for Ramish? Had Ramish created a living will? Explain.

**Debate This** . . .    *Any changes to existing, fully witnessed wills should also have to be witnessed.*

## Terms and Concepts

| | | |
|---|---|---|
| administrator 602 | health-care power of attorney 617 | probate 602 |
| bequest 602 | holographic will 606 | resulting trust 615 |
| charitable trust 614 | intestacy laws 602 | spendthrift trust 614 |
| codicil 607 | intestate 602 | testamentary trust 614 |
| constructive trust 615 | legacy 602 | testate 602 |
| devise 602 | legatee 602 | testator 602 |
| devisee 602 | living trust 611 | Totten trust 614 |
| durable power of attorney 617 | living will 617 | trust 611 |
| escheat 602 | nuncupative will 606 | will 602 |
| estate planning 602 | *per capita* 611 | will substitutes 608 |
| executor 602 | *per stirpes* 610 | |

## Issue Spotters

**1.** Sheila makes a will leaving her property in equal thirds to Toby and Umeko, her children, and Velda, her niece. Two years later, Sheila is adjudged mentally incompetent, and that same year, she dies. Can Toby and Umeko have Sheila's will revoked on the ground that she did not have the capacity to make a will? Why or why not? (See *Wills*.)

**2.** Rafael dies without having made a will. He is survived by many relatives—a spouse, biological children, adopted children, sisters, brothers, uncles, aunts, cousins, nephews, and nieces. What determines who inherits what? (See *Intestacy Laws*.)

• **Check your answers to the Issue Spotters against the answers provided in Appendix B at the end of this text.**

## Business Scenarios

**31–1. Wills and Intestacy Laws.** Benjamin is a widower who has two married children, Edward and Patricia. Patricia has two children, Perry and Paul. Edward has no children. Benjamin dies, and his typewritten will leaves all of his property equally to his children, Edward and Patricia, and provides that should a child predecease him, the grandchildren are to take *per stirpes*. The will was witnessed by Patricia and by Benjamin's lawyer, and it was signed by Benjamin in their presence. Patricia has predeceased Benjamin. Edward claims the will is invalid. (See *Intestacy Laws*.)

**(a)** Discuss whether the will is valid.

**(b)** Discuss the distribution of Benjamin's estate if the will is invalid.

**(c)** Discuss the distribution of Benjamin's estate if the will is valid.

**31–2. Specific Bequests.** Gary Mendel drew up a will in which he left his favorite car, a 1966 red Ferrari, to his daughter, Roberta. A year prior to his death, Mendel sold the 1966 Ferrari and purchased a 1969 Ferrari. Discuss whether Roberta will inherit the 1969 Ferrari under the terms of her father's will. (See *Wills*.)

**31–3. Revocation of Wills.** While single, James made out a will naming his mother, Carol, as sole beneficiary. Later, James married Lisa. (See *Wills*.)

**(a)** If James died while married to Lisa without changing his will, would the estate go to his mother, Carol? Explain.

**(b)** Assume that James made out a new will on his marriage to Lisa, leaving his entire estate to Lisa. Later, he divorced Lisa and married Mandis, but he did not change his will. Discuss the rights of Lisa and Mandis to James's estate after his death.

**(c)** Assume that James divorced Lisa, married Mandis, and changed his will, leaving his estate to Mandis. Later, a daughter, Claire, was born. James died without having included Claire in his will. Discuss fully whether Claire has any rights in the estate.

## Business Case Problems

**31–4. Intestacy Laws.** A Florida statute provides that the right of election of a surviving spouse can be waived by written agreement: "A waiver of 'all rights,' or equivalent language, in the property or estate of a present or prospective spouse . . . is a waiver of all rights to elective share." The day before Mary Ann Taylor married Louis Taylor in Florida, they entered into a prenuptial agreement. The agreement stated that all property belonging to each spouse would "forever remain his or her personal estate, . . . forever free of claim by the other." The parties would retain "full rights and authority" over their property as they would have "if not married." After Louis died without a will, his only child, Joshua Taylor, filed a petition in a Florida state court for a determination of the beneficiaries of Louis's estate. How much of the estate can Mary Ann elect to receive? Explain. [*Taylor v. Taylor,* 1 So.3d 348 (Fla.App. 1 Dist. 2009)] (See *Intestacy Laws*.)

**31–5. Wills.** Elnora Maxey became the guardian of Sean Hall after his parents died. In 1996, Maxey died, and her will left the two houses in her estate to Hall. Julia Jordan became Hall's new guardian, and when she died, her husband, John Jordan, became Hall's guardian. In 1998, when Hall was eighteen years old, he died intestate, and Jordan was appointed as the administrator of Hall's estate. The two houses had remained in Maxey's estate, but Jordan paid the mortgage and tax payments on the houses for Hall's estate because Hall had inherited the houses. Anthony Cooper, a relative of Maxey, petitioned the probate court to be appointed executor of Maxey's estate, stating that there was now no heir. The court granted the request. Jordan was not aware of the proceedings. Cooper then sold both houses for the incredibly low price of $20,000 each to Quan Smith, without informing Jordan. The houses were then resold to JSD Properties, LLC, for a total of $190,000. Learning of the sale, Jordan sued, contending that Cooper had breached his fiduciary duty and had lied to the court, as Maxey's will had clearly left the houses to Hall. Does Jordan have the right to demand that JSD return the property? What factors would be considered in making this decision? [*Witcher v. JSD Properties, LLC,* 286 Ga. 717, 690 S.E.2d 855 (2010)] (See *Wills*.)

**31–6. Business Case Problem with Sample Answer—Undue Influence.** Susie Walker executed a will that left her

entire estate to her grandson. When her grandson died, Susie executed a new will that named her great-grandson as her sole beneficiary and specifically disinherited her son, Tommy. At the time, Tommy's ex-wife was living with Susie. After Susie died, Tommy filed a suit, claiming that her will was the product of undue influence on the part of his ex-wife. Several witnesses testified that Susie had been mentally competent when she executed her will. Does undue influence appear likely based on these facts? Why or why not? [*In re Estate of Walker*, 80 A.D.3d 865, 164 L.Ed.2d 480 (3 Dept. 2011)] (See *Wills*.)

• For a sample answer to Problem 31–6, go to Appendix C at the end of this text.

**31–7. Requirements of a Will.** Sherman Hemsley was a well-known actor from the 1970s. Most notably, he played George Jefferson on the television shows *All in the Family* and *The Jeffersons*. He was born to Arsena Chisolm and William Thornton. Thornton was married to another woman, and Hemsley never had a relationship with his father or his father's side of the family. Hemsley never married and had no children. He lived with Flora Bernal, his business manager. Diagnosed with cancer, Hemsley executed a will naming Bernal the sole beneficiary of his estate. At the signing, Hemsley indicated that he knew he was executing his will and that he had deliberately chosen Bernal, but he did not discuss his relatives or the nature of his property with his attorney or the witnesses. After his death, the Thorntons challenged the will. Was Hemsley of sound mind? Discuss. [*In re Estate of Hemsley*, 460 S.W.3d 629 (Tex.App.—El Paso 2014)] (See *Wills*.)

**31–8. Wills.** Andrew Walker executed a will giving a certain parcel of real estate in fee simple to his three children from a previous marriage, Mark Walker, Michelle Peters, and Andrea Knox. The will granted a "life use" in the property to Walker's current spouse, Nora Walker. A year later, Andrew, who suffered from asbestosis, was discharged from a hospital to spend his last days at home. He told Nora that he wished to execute a new will to change the disposition of the property to devise half of it to her. Nora recorded his wish and took her notes to the office of attorney Frederick Meagher to have the document drafted. Meagher did not see Nora's notes and did not talk to Walker..When Walker signed the document, he did not declare that it was his will, as required by state law, and no one from Meagher's office was present at the signing. Is the document a valid will? Explain. [*In re Estate of Walker*, 124 A.D.3d 970, 2 N.Y.S.3d 628 (3 Dept. 2015)] (See *Wills*.)

**31–9. A Question of Ethics—Wills.** *Vickie Lynn Smith, an*

*actress and model also known as Anna Nicole Smith, met J. Howard Marshall II in 1991. During their courtship, J. Howard lavished gifts and large sums of money on Anna Nicole, and they married on June 27, 1994. J. Howard died on August 4, 1995. According to Anna Nicole, J. Howard had intended to provide for her financial security through a trust. Under the terms of his will, however, all of his assets were transferred to a trust for the benefit of E. Pierce Marshall, one of J. Howard's sons. While J. Howard's estate was subject to probate proceedings in a Texas state court, Anna Nicole filed for bankruptcy in a federal bankruptcy court. Pierce filed a claim in the bankruptcy proceeding, alleging that Anna Nicole had defamed him when her lawyers told the media that Pierce had engaged in forgery and fraud to gain control of his father's assets. Anna Nicole filed a counterclaim, alleging that Pierce had prevented the transfer of his father's assets to a trust for her. She claimed that, among other things, Pierce had imprisoned J. Howard against his wishes, surrounded him with security guards to prevent contact with her, and transferred property against his wishes. [Marshall v. Marshall, 547 U.S. 293, 126 S.Ct. 1735, 164 L.Ed.2d 480 (2006)] (See Wills.)*

**(a)** What is the purpose underlying the requirements for a valid will? Which of these requirements might be at issue in this case? How should it apply here? Why?

**(b)** State courts generally have jurisdiction over the probate of a will and the administration of an estate. Does the Texas state court thus have the sole authority to adjudicate all of the claims in this case? Why or why not?

**(c)** How should Pierce's claim against Anna Nicole and her counterclaim be resolved?

**(d)** Anna Nicole executed her will in 2001. The beneficiary—Daniel, her son, who was not J. Howard's child—died in 2006, shortly after Anna Nicole gave birth to a daughter, Dannielynn. In 2007, before executing a new will, Anna Nicole died. What happens if a will's beneficiary dies before the testator? What happens if a child is born after a will is executed?

# Legal Reasoning Group Activity

**31–10. Intestacy Laws.** Three and a half years after Lauren and Warren Woodward were married, they were informed that Warren had leukemia. At the time, the couple had no children, and physicians told the Woodwards that the leukemia treatment might leave Warren sterile. The couple arranged for Warren's sperm to be collected and placed in a sperm bank for later use.

Two years after Warren died, Lauren gave birth to twin girls who had been conceived through artificial insemination using his sperm. The following year, Lauren applied for Social Security survivor benefits for the two children. Her application was rejected on the ground that she had not established that the twins were the husband's children within the meaning of the Social Security Act. Woodward then filed a paternity action in Massachusetts, and the probate court determined that Warren Woodward was the twins' father. She then filed an action in court to determine the inheritance rights of the twins. (See *Intestacy Laws.*)

**(a)** The first group will outline how a court should decide the inheritance rights of children conceived from the sperm of a deceased individual and his surviving spouse.

**(b)** The second group will decide if children conceived after a parent's death (by means of artificial insemination or *in*

*vitro* fertilization) still inherit under intestate succession laws, and will explain why or why not.

**(c)** The third group will consider the inheritance rights of a child who was conceived by means of artificial insemination, *in vitro* fertilization, or a surrogate. Should they be different from the rights of a child conceived in the traditional manner? Assuming the biological parent is not part of the child's life, should the child still be able to inherit from the biological parent? Why or why not?

# Business Planning for Divorce

Larry starts Auto Masters, an auto repair service. Through Larry's efforts, Auto Masters becomes successful. At the same time, however, Larry's marriage to Rachel falls apart. Unfortunately, Larry has not taken steps to make sure that his business will not break up along with his marriage.

The court orders a settlement that takes into consideration the value of all of the couple's assets, including the business. To pay the settlement, Larry is forced to sell Auto Masters for cash at a lower price than would otherwise have been possible.

As this example illustrates, planning for divorce is an important part of a business plan for the owners of the business.

## Separate and Marital Property

A divorce formally dissolves a legal marriage. Following a divorce, if the spouses have not otherwise divided their property between them, a court can do it. For this purpose, there are two different types of property—separate and marital.

**Separate Property** Any property that only one spouse owns is *separate property*. This includes property owned by only one spouse before the marriage, as well as inheritances and gifts received by only one spouse during the marriage. Separate property commingled with marital assets may lose its separate status. In addition, in many states, *an increase in value* in separate property during a marriage may be considered a marital asset.[15]

**Marital Property** Any other property that the spouses acquired individually or jointly during the marriage is *marital property*. This can include professional licenses, such as an attorney's license, as well as shares of stock, interests in limited partnerships, and closely held businesses.

**Dividing the Property** In a few states—community property jurisdictions—spouses are held to be equal owners of the marital property.[16] Those assets are allocated in equal shares.

Most states provide instead for an equitable division of assets. An *equitable division* is an allocation consistent with fairness and justice, which may not call for equal shares. A court will consider a number of factors, including at least the following:

- The parties' respective contributions to the accumulation of marital property.
- The parties' respective liabilities.
- Whether only one spouse will receive income-producing property.
- The parties' respective earning capacity and employability.
- The value of each party's separate property.
- The tax consequences.[17]

---

**15.** See, for example, *St. Marie v. Roy*, 29 So.3d 708 (La.App. 3d Cir. 2010).

**16.** There are nine community property states—Arizona, California, Idaho, Louisiana, Nevada, New Mexico, Texas, Washington, and Wisconsin.

**17.** The Uniform Marriage and Divorce Act (UMDA), which has been adopted in eight states, lists these and other factors, including "the age, health, station, occupation, . . . and needs of each of the parties" [UMDA Section 307].

## Is a Business Separate or Marital Property?

A business begun during marriage with joint funds is marital property. A business started before marriage or financed with separate funds during marriage is most likely separate property.

A business may be considered entirely or partially marital property, depending on the spouses' respective contributions to the business during the marriage. The contributions may be financial or operational.

Suppose, for instance, that Rita starts App Solutions, a software coding and development firm, with her own funds before marrying Hector. During the marriage, Hector markets the firm's services and contributes joint funds to its operation. The business grows and appreciates in value. If the spouses divorce, normally the business will be considered marital property.

## Determining Value

To sell a business or to buy out one spouse's interest requires determining the value of the business and of each spouse's interest in it. This calculation usually requires the services of an accredited or certified professional business appraiser. The appraiser reviews the business's financial statements, tax returns, and other relevant data, and determines the value according to the appropriate method.[1]

## Protecting Assets

A business owner can protect business assets from the claims of a spouse without concealing those assets or otherwise committing fraud. One way to obtain this protection is to avoid involving the spouse (or prospective spouse) in the business. If he or she does not contribute to the business, it is not likely to be construed as marital property. Other steps include prenuptial agreements, postnuptial agreements, and an agreement among the owners of the business to adhere to certain conditions.

**Prenuptial Agreements** As defined earlier, a *prenuptial agreement* is an agreement made before marriage that defines each party's ownership rights in the other's property. A court will normally enforce a prenuptial agreement in the following circumstances.

- Each future spouse was represented by an attorney.
- The agreement is in writing.
- Each party signed the agreement voluntarily.
- The assets covered by the agreement were fully disclosed.

If a business is subject to both parties' interests, the agreement should provide a projected split of the assets and a process or a method for determining the value. It should also identify how and when payment is to be made.

---

1. These methods include the *market approach*, which bases value on the price of a similar, recently sold business; the *income approach*, which converts expected profit or cash flow into current value; and the *asset approach*, which bases value on assets and liabilities.

Continues

**Postnuptial Agreements** A *postnuptial agreement* is an agreement made *after* marriage that defines each spouse's rights in the other spouse's property. Like a prenuptial agreement, a postnuptial agreement must involve each party's attorney, be in writing, be signed voluntarily, and be preceded by full disclosure. Unlike prenuptial agreements, postnuptial agreements are not recognized in all states. Even in states where these agreements are recognized, they may be more difficult to enforce than prenuptial agreements.[2]

**Business Agreements** For some types of businesses that could be subject to a spousal claim, an agreement among the owners can protect the owners' interests. This can be true whether the owners are partners, corporate shareholders, or members of limited liability companies.

Such an agreement can require an unmarried owner to provide the firm with a prenuptial agreement before marriage, including a waiver by the owner's prospective spouse of any future interest in the business. The agreement can also restrict the transfer of an owner's interest without the consent of the other owners. The other owners can be given the right to buy the interest to keep control of the enterprise. The method of valuation and means of payment should be included as well.

If both spouses are part of the firm, the agreement should provide that only persons actively involved in the business are entitled to own an interest in it. The agreement should add that if either spouse leaves the firm, his or her interest must be sold to the spouse who is still active. And it should be stipulated that in the event of a divorce, one spouse must quit (and agree not to compete, according to certain reasonable terms).

## Ethical Connection

There is room for debate over the ethics of executing a plan to protect assets that might otherwise be considered the property of another. This is particularly true in the context of a marriage and a divorce.

Of course, everyone who creates a corporation, a partnership, or a limited liability company is taking a step to protect the business's assets from creditors and others. Most do not consider such actions unethical. Similarly, there is nothing unethical about asking a business's co-owner or a future spouse to consent to the terms of the agreements suggested here.

But it is not ethical to form a business organization to keep property out of the hands of an owner's spouse who might deserve better treatment. Perhaps it is the timing and the purpose of a plan that finally determine whether it should be considered ethical.

**Ethics Question** *With respect to the division of property on divorce, should the conduct of the spouses during the marriage be a factor? Why or why not?*

**Critical Thinking** *How might a spouse or ex-spouse overcome the business asset protection devices and techniques discussed in this feature? Explain.*

---

**2.** See, for example, *Bedrick v. Bedrick*, 17 A.3d 17, 300 Conn. 691 (2011).

# APPENDIX A

# How to Analyze Legal Disputes

## Analyzing Case Problems

To fully understand the law with respect to business, students should be able to analyze the facts of a dispute and understand how courts arrive at their decisions. Part of the study of business law and the legal environment usually involves analyzing case problems, such as those included in this text at the end of each chapter.

For each case problem in this book, we provide the relevant background and facts of the lawsuit and the issue before the court. When you are assigned one of these problems, your job will be to determine how the court should decide the issue, and why. In other words, you will need to engage in legal analysis and reasoning. Here, we offer some suggestions on how to make this task less daunting. We begin by presenting a SAMPLE PROBLEM:

> While Janet Lawson, a famous pianist, was shopping in Quality Market, she slipped and fell on a wet floor in one of the aisles. The floor had recently been mopped by one of the store's employees, but there were no signs warning customers that the floor in that area was wet. As a result of the fall, Lawson injured her right arm and was unable to perform piano concerts for the next six months. Had she been able to perform the scheduled concerts, she would have earned approximately $60,000 over that period of time. Lawson sued Quality Market for this amount, plus another $10,000 in medical expenses. She claimed that the store's failure to warn customers of the wet floor constituted negligence and therefore the market was liable for her injuries. Will the court agree with Lawson? Discuss.

## Understand the Facts

This may sound obvious, but before you can analyze or apply the relevant law to a specific set of facts, you must clearly understand those facts. In other words, you should read through the case problem carefully—more than once, if necessary—to make sure you understand the identity of the plaintiff(s) and defendant(s) in the case and the progression of events that led to the lawsuit.

In the sample case problem just given, the identity of the parties is fairly obvious. Janet Lawson is the one bringing the suit; therefore, she is the plaintiff. Quality Market, against whom she is bringing the suit, is the defendant. Some of the case problems you may work on have multiple plaintiffs or defendants. Often,

it is helpful to use abbreviations for the parties. To indicate a reference to a plaintiff, for example, the *pi* symbol—π—is often used, and a defendant is denoted by a *delta*—Δ—a triangle.

The events leading to the lawsuit are also fairly straightforward. Lawson slipped and fell on a wet floor, and she contends that Quality Market should be liable for her injuries because it was negligent in not posting a sign warning customers of the wet floor.

When you are working on case problems, realize that the facts should be accepted as they are given. For example, in our sample problem, it should be accepted that the floor was wet and that there was no sign. In other words, avoid making conjectures, such as "Maybe the floor wasn't too wet," or "Maybe an employee was getting a sign to put up," or "Maybe someone stole the sign." Questioning the facts as they are presented only adds confusion to your analysis.

## Legal Analysis and Reasoning

Once you understand the facts given in the case problem, you can begin to analyze the case. The IRAC method is a helpful tool to use in the legal analysis and reasoning process. IRAC is an acronym for Issue, Rule, Application, Conclusion. Applying this method to our sample problem would involve the following steps:

1. First, you need to decide what legal **issue** is involved in the case. In our sample case, the basic issue is whether Quality Market's failure to warn customers of the wet floor constituted negligence. As discussed in the text, negligence is a *tort*—a civil wrong. In a tort lawsuit, the plaintiff seeks to be compensated for another's wrongful act. A defendant will be deemed negligent if he or she breached a duty of care owed to the plaintiff and the breach of that duty caused the plaintiff to suffer harm.

2. Once you have identified the issue, the next step is to determine what **rule of law** applies to the issue. To make this determination, you will want to review carefully the text of the chapter in which the relevant rule of law for the problem appears. Our sample case problem involves the tort of negligence. The applicable rule of law is the tort law principle that business owners owe a duty to exercise reasonable care to protect their customers ("business invitees"). Reasonable care, in this context, includes either removing—or warning customers of—*foreseeable* risks about which the owner *knew* or *should have known*. Business owners need not warn

customers of "open and obvious" risks, however. If a business owner breaches this duty of care (fails to exercise the appropriate degree of care toward customers), and the breach of duty causes a customer to be injured, the business owner will be liable to the customer for the customer's injuries.

3. The next—and usually the most difficult—step in analyzing case problems is the **application** of the relevant rule of law to the specific facts of the case you are studying. In the sample problem, applying the tort law principle just discussed presents few difficulties. An employee of the store had mopped the floor in the aisle where Lawson slipped and fell, but no sign was present indicating that the floor was wet. That a customer might fall on a wet floor is clearly a foreseeable risk. Therefore, the failure to warn customers about the wet floor was a breach of the duty of care owed by the business owner to the store's customers.

4. Once you have completed Step 3 in the IRAC method, you should be ready to draw your **conclusion.** In our sample problem,

Quality Market is liable to Lawson for her injuries, because the market's breach of its duty of care caused Lawson's injuries.

The fact patterns in the business scenarios and case problems presented in this text are not always as simple as those presented in our sample problem. Often, for example, a case has more than one plaintiff or defendant. A case may also involve more than one issue and have more than one applicable rule of law. Furthermore, in some case problems the facts may indicate that the general rule of law should not apply. For example, suppose that a store employee advised Lawson not to walk on the floor in the aisle because it was wet, but Lawson decided to walk on it anyway. This fact could alter the outcome of the case because the store could then raise the defense of assumption of risk. Nonetheless, a careful review of the chapter text should always provide you with the knowledge you need to analyze the problem thoroughly and arrive at accurate conclusions.

# APPENDIX B
# Answers to the *Issue Spotters*

## CHAPTER 1

**1. *Does this raise an ethical conflict between Acme's employees? Between Acme and its employees? Between Acme and its shareholders? Explain your answers.*** When a corporation decides to respond to what it sees as a moral obligation to correct for past discrimination by adjusting pay differences among its employees, an ethical conflict is raised between the firm and its employees and between the firm and its shareholders. This dilemma arises directly out of the effect such a decision has on the firm's profits. If satisfying this obligation increases profitability, then the dilemma is easily resolved in favor of "doing the right thing."

**2. *Does Delta have an ethical duty to remove this product from the market, even if the injuries result only from misuse? Why or why not?*** Maybe. On the one hand, it is not the company's "fault" when a product is misused. Also, keeping the product on the market is not a violation of the law, and stopping sales would hurt profits. On the other hand, suspending sales could reduce suffering and could stop potential negative publicity.

## CHAPTER 2

**1. *Would a sole proprietorship be an appropriate form for Frank's business? Why or why not?*** Yes. When a business is relatively small and is not diversified, employs relatively few people, has modest profits, and is not likely to expand significantly or require extensive financing in the immediate future, the most appropriate form for doing business may be a sole proprietorship.

**2. *Does this constitute "cause" for termination? Why or why not?*** Yes. Failing to meet a specified sales quota can constitute a breach of a franchise agreement. If the franchisor is acting in good faith, "cause" may also include the death or disability of the franchisee, the insolvency of the franchisee, and a breach of another term of the franchise agreement.

## CHAPTER 3

**1. *When Darnell dies, his widow claims that as Darnell's heir, she is entitled to take his place as Eliana's partner or to receive a share of the firm's assets. Is she right? Why or why not?*** No. A widow (or widower) has no right to take a dead partner's place. A partner's death causes dissociation, after which the partnership must purchase the dissociated partner's partnership interest. Therefore, the surviving partners must pay the decedent's estate (for his widow) the value of the deceased partner's interest in the partnership.

**2. *Because the vehicles would otherwise be sitting idle in a parking lot, can Finian keep the income that results from leasing the delivery vehicles? Explain your answer.*** No. Under the partners' fiduciary duty, a partner must account to the partnership for any personal profits or benefits derived without the consent of all the partners in connection with the use of any partnership property. Here, the leasing partner may not keep the money.

## CHAPTER 4

**1. *What are their options with respect to the management of their firm?*** The members of a limited liability company (LLC) may designate a group to run their firm, in which situation the firm would be considered a manager-managed LLC. The group may include only members, only nonmembers, or members and nonmembers. If, instead, all members participate in management, the firm would be a member-managed LLC. In fact, unless the members agree otherwise, all members are considered to participate in the management of the firm.

**2. *What do these forms of business organization have in common?*** Although there are differences, all of these forms of business organizations resemble corporations. A joint stock company, for example, features ownership by shares of stock, is managed by directors and officers, and has perpetual existence. A business trust, like a corporation, distributes profits to persons who are not personally responsible for the debts of the organization. Management of a business trust is in the hands of trustees, just as the management of a corporation is in the hands of directors and officers. An incorporated cooperative, which is subject to state laws covering nonprofit corporations, distributes profits to its owners.

## CHAPTER 5

**1. *Is there a way for Northwest Brands to avoid this double taxation? Explain your answer.*** Yes. Small businesses that meet certain requirements can qualify as S corporations, created specifically to permit small businesses to avoid double taxation. The six requirements of an S corporation are (1) the firm must be a domestic corporation, (2) the firm must not be a member of an affiliated group of corporations, (3) the firm must have less than a certain number of shareholders, (4) the shareholders must be individuals, estates, or qualified trusts (or corporations in some cases), (5) there can be only one class of stock, and (6) no shareholder can be a nonresident alien.

**2. *Can they grant this authority to their firm? If so, how? If not, why not?*** Broad authority to conduct business can be granted in a corporation's articles of incorporation. For example, the term "any lawful purpose" is often used. This can be important because acts of a corporation that are beyond the authority given to it in its articles or charter (or state statutes) are considered illegal, *ultra vires* acts.

## CHAPTER 6

**1.** *Yvon, a Wonder shareholder, learns of the purchase and wants to sue the directors on Wonder's behalf. Can she do it? Explain.* Yes. A shareholder can bring a derivative suit on behalf of a corporation, if some wrong is done to the corporation. Normally, any damages recovered go into the corporate treasury.

**2.** *Discuss whether Nico owes a duty to Omega or the minority shareholders in selling his shares.* Yes. A single shareholder—or a few shareholders acting together—who owns enough stock to exercise *de facto* control over a corporation owes the corporation and minority shareholders a fiduciary duty when transferring those shares.

## CHAPTER 7

**1.** *What sort of information would an investor consider material?* The average investor is not concerned with minor inaccuracies but with facts that if disclosed would tend to deter him or her from buying the securities. This would include facts that have an important bearing on the condition of the issuer and its business—liabilities, loans to officers and directors, customer delinquencies, and pending lawsuits.

**2.** *Can Lee take advantage of this information to buy and sell Magma stock? Why or why not?* No. The Securities Exchange Act of 1934 extends liability to officers and directors in their personal transactions for taking advantage of inside information when they know it is unavailable to the persons with whom they are dealing.

## CHAPTER 8

**1.** *Can Lou recover from Jana? Why or why not?* Probably. To recover on the basis of negligence, the injured party as a plaintiff must show that the truck's owner owed the plaintiff a duty of care, that the owner breached that duty, that the plaintiff was injured, and that the breach caused the injury.

In this situation, the owner's actions breached the duty of reasonable care. The billboard falling on the plaintiff was the direct cause of the injury, not the plaintiff's own negligence. Thus, liability turns on whether the plaintiff can connect the breach of duty to the injury. This involves the test of proximate cause—the question of foreseeability. The consequences to the injured party must have been a foreseeable result of the owner's carelessness.

**2.** *What might the firm successfully claim in defense?* The company might defend against this electrician's claim by asserting that the electrician should have known of the risk and, therefore, the company had no duty to warn. According to the problem, the danger is common knowledge in the electrician's field and should have been apparent to this electrician, given his years of training and experience. In other words, the company most likely had no need to warn the electrician of the risk.

The firm could also raise comparative negligence. Both parties' negligence, if any, could be weighed and the liability distributed proportionately. The defendant could also assert assumption of risk, claiming that the electrician voluntarily entered into a dangerous situation, knowing the risk involved.

## CHAPTER 9

**1.** *Was Winona an independent contractor?* Yes. An independent contractor is a person who contracts with another—the principal—to do something but who is neither controlled by the other nor subject to the other's right to control with respect to the performance. Independent contractors are not employees, because those who hire them have no control over the details of their performance.

**2.** *When Nadine learns of this, she wants to buy the land and sell it to Dimka herself. Can she do this? Discuss.* No. Nadine, as an agent, is prohibited from taking advantage of the agency relationship to obtain property that the principal (Dimka Corporation) wants to purchase. This is the duty of loyalty that arises with every agency relationship.

## CHAPTER 10

**1.** *Can Davis hold Estee liable for whatever damages he has to pay? Why or why not?* Yes. A principal has a duty to indemnify an agent for liabilities incurred because of authorized and lawful acts and transactions and for losses suffered because of the principal's failure to perform his or her duties.

**2.** *In what circumstance is Vivian liable on the note?* When a person enters into a contract on another's behalf without the authority to do so, the other may be liable on the contract if he or she approves or affirms that contract. In other words, the employer-principal would be liable for the note in this problem on ratifying it. Whether the employer-principal ratifies the note or not, the unauthorized agent is most likely also liable for it.

## CHAPTER 11

**1.** *For Erin to obtain workers' compensation, must her injury have been caused by Fine Print's negligence? Does it matter whether the action causing the injury was intentional? Explain.* Workers' compensation laws establish a procedure for compensating workers who are injured on the job. Instead of suing to collect benefits, an injured worker notifies the employer of an injury and files a claim with the appropriate state agency.

The right to recover is normally determined without regard to negligence or fault, but intentionally inflicted injuries are not covered. Unlike the potential for recovery in a lawsuit based on negligence or fault, recovery under a workers' compensation statute is limited to the specific amount designated in the statute for the employee's injury.

**2.** *Are these conditions legal? Why or why not?* No. A closed shop (a company that requires union membership as a condition of employment) is illegal. A union shop (a company that does not require union membership as a condition of employment but requires workers to join the union after a certain time on the job) is illegal in a state with a right-to-work law, which makes it illegal to require union membership for continued employment.

## CHAPTER 12

1. *Is this sexual harassment? Why or why not?* Yes. One type of sexual harassment occurs when a request for sexual favors is a condition of employment, and the person making the request is a supervisor or acts with the authority of the employer. A tangible employment action, such as continued employment, may also lead to the employer's liability for the supervisor's conduct. That the injured employee is a male and the supervisor a female, instead of the other way around, would not affect the outcome. Same-gender harassment is also actionable.

2. *Could Koko succeed in a suit against Lively for discrimination? Explain.* Yes, if she can show that Lively failed to hire her solely because of her disability. The other elements for a discrimination suit based on a disability are that the plaintiff (1) has a disability and (2) is otherwise qualified for the job. Both of these elements appear to be satisfied in this problem.

## CHAPTER 13

1. *Is this an acceptance of the offer or a counteroffer? If it is an acceptance, is it a breach of the contract? Why or why not? What if Fav-O-Rite told E-Design it was sending the printer stands as "an accommodation"?* A shipment of nonconforming goods constitutes an acceptance of the offer and a breach, unless the seller seasonably notifies the buyer that the nonconforming shipment does not constitute an acceptance and is offered only as an accommodation. Thus, since there was no notification here, the shipment was both an acceptance and a breach. If, however, Fav-O-Rite had notified E-Design that it was sending the printer stands as an accommodation, the shipment would not constitute an acceptance, and Fav-O-Rite would not be in breach.

2. *Is there an enforceable contract between them? Why or why not?* Yes. In a transaction between merchants, the requirement of a writing is satisfied if one of them sends to the other a signed written confirmation that indicates the terms of the agreement, and the merchant receiving it has reason to know of its contents. If the merchant who receives the confirmation does not object in writing within ten days after receipt, the writing will be enforceable against him or her even though he or she has not signed anything.

## CHAPTER 14

1. *Does Country have the right to reject the shipment? Explain.* Yes. A seller is obligated to deliver goods in conformity with a contract in every detail. This is the perfect tender rule. The exception of the seller's right to cure does not apply here, because the seller delivered too little too late to take advantage of this exception.

2. *Can Poster Planet sue Brite without waiting until May 1? Why or why not?* Yes. When anticipatory repudiation occurs, a buyer (or lessee) can resort to any remedy for breach even if the buyer tells the seller (the repudiating party in this problem) that the buyer will wait for the seller's performance.

## CHAPTER 15

1. *Which of these phrases would prevent the instrument's negotiability?* A statement that "I.O.U." money (or anything else) or an instruction to a bank stating, "I wish you would pay," would render any instrument nonnegotiable. To be negotiable, an instrument must contain an express promise to pay. An I.O.U. is only an acknowledgment of indebtedness. An order stating, "I wish you would pay," is not sufficiently precise.

2. *Is Marit's note a demand note? Explain.* Yes. Instruments that are payable on demand may state "Payable on demand." The nature of an instrument may indicate that it is payable on demand. If no time for payment is specified, then the instrument is also payable on demand. Here, the note required installments but did not state a date for their payment. That Donald did not make a demand for payment did not affect this characteristic of the note.

## CHAPTER 16

1. *What type of indorsement is this? What effect does this indorsement have on whether the check is considered an order instrument or a bearer instrument? Explain.* This is a special indorsement, which names the indorsee (Kurt). No special words are needed. A special indorsement makes an instrument order paper. Thus, further negotiation requires Kurt's indorsement.

2. *Can Carl become an HDC? Why or why not?* No. One of the requirements for HDC status is that the holder must have performed the promise for which the instrument was issued. A holder takes the instrument for value only to the extent that the promise has been performed. Because Ben did not perform his promise to repair Amy's roof, he is not an HDC. Thus, Carl—who took the instrument from Ben—cannot trace his title back to an HDC, so he is not be protected as an HDC under the shelter principle.

## CHAPTER 17

1. *Does Suchin have any recourse against the bank for the payment? Why or why not?* No. When a drawer's employee provides the drawer with the name of a fictitious payee (a payee whom the drawer does not actually intend to have any interest in an instrument), a forgery of the payee's name is effective to pass good title to subsequent transferees.

2. *Was the bookstore a holder in due course on Skye's check?* Yes. One of the requirements for HDC status is a lack of notice that an instrument is defective. A party will not attain this status if he or she knows, or has reason to know, that an incomplete instrument was later completed in an unauthorized manner. Notice of a defective instrument is given when a holder has reason to know that a defect exists, given all of the facts known at the time. Here, the bookstore did not have notice that Skye's check was incomplete when it was issued. The bookstore saw only a properly completed instrument.

## CHAPTER 18

**1.** ***Is Lyn liable to Nan? Could Lyn be subject to criminal prosecution? Why or why not?*** Yes, to both questions. In a civil suit, a drawer (Lyn) is liable to a payee (Nan) or to a holder of a check that is not honored. If intent to defraud can be proved, the drawer (Lyn) can also be subject to criminal prosecution for writing a bad check.

**2.** ***Can the bank refuse to recredit Kay's account? If not, can the bank recover the amount paid to Will? Why or why not?*** The general rule is that the bank must recredit a customer's account when it pays on a forged signature. The bank has no right to recover from a holder who, without knowledge, cashes a check bearing a forged drawer's signature. Thus, the bank in this problem can collect from neither its customer nor the party who cashed the check. The bank's recourse is to look for the thief.

## CHAPTER 19

**1.** ***What can Larry and Midwest do?*** Each of the parties can place a mechanic's lien on the debtor's property. If the debtor does not pay what is owed, the property can be sold to satisfy the debt. The only requirements are that the lien be filed within a specific time from the time of the work, depending on the state statute, and that notice of the foreclosure and sale be given to the debtor in advance.

**2.** ***If the employer complies with the order and Alyssa stays on the job, is one order enough to garnish all of Alyssa's wages for each pay period until the debt is paid? Explain.*** No. In some states, a creditor must go back to court for a separate order of garnishment for each pay period. Also, federal and state laws limit the amount of money that can be garnished from a debtor's pay.

## CHAPTER 20

**1.** ***How can Olivia let other creditors know of her interest in the computer?*** A creditor can put other creditors on notice by perfecting its interest: by filing a financing statement in the appropriate public office, or by taking possession of the collateral until the debtor repays the loan.

**2.** ***Liberty could repossess and keep the car, but the bank does not want it. What are the alternatives?*** When collateral is consumer goods with a PMSI, and the debtor has paid less than 60 percent of the debt or the purchase price, the creditor can dispose of the collateral in a commercially reasonable manner, which generally requires notice to the debtor of the place, time, and manner of sale. A debtor can waive the right to notice, but only after default. Before the disposal, a debtor can redeem the collateral by tendering performance of all of the obligations secured by it and by paying the creditor's reasonable expenses in retaking and maintaining it.

## CHAPTER 21

**1.** ***Are these debts dischargeable in bankruptcy? Explain.*** No. Besides the claims listed in this problem, the debts that cannot be discharged in bankruptcy include amounts borrowed to pay back taxes, goods obtained by fraud, debts that were not listed in the petition, domestic support obligations, certain cash advances, and others.

**2.** ***Can Quentin recover the $10,000 paid to Ogden on June 1? Why or why not?*** Yes. A debtor's payment to a creditor made for a preexisting debt, within ninety days (one year in the case of an insider or fraud) of a bankruptcy filing, can be recovered if it gives a creditor more than he or she would have received in the bankruptcy proceedings. A trustee can recover this preference using his or her specific avoidance powers.

## CHAPTER 22

**1.** ***Can the bank successfully sue Dave? Why or why not?*** Yes. In these circumstances, when the accountant knows that the bank will use the statement, the bank is a foreseeable user. A foreseeable user is a third party within the class of parties to whom an accountant may be liable for negligence.

**2.** ***Can Nora be held liable to Pat? Explain.*** No. In the circumstances described, the accountant will not be held liable to a purchaser of the securities. Although an accountant may be liable under securities laws for including untrue statements or omitting material facts from financial statements, due diligence is a defense to liability.

Due diligence requires an accountant to conduct a reasonable investigation and have reason to believe that the financial statements were true at the time. The facts say that the misstatement of material fact in Omega's financial statement was not attributable to any fraud or negligence on Nora's part. Therefore, Nora can show that she used due diligence and will not be held liable to Pat.

## CHAPTER 23

**1.** ***What safeguards promote the ALJ's fairness?*** Under the Administrative Procedure Act (APA), the administrative law judge (ALJ) must be separate from the agency's investigative and prosecutorial staff. *Ex parte* communications between the ALJ and a party to a proceeding are prohibited. Under the APA, an ALJ is exempt from agency discipline except on a showing of good cause.

**2.** ***Does the firm have any opportunity to express its opinion about the pending rule? Explain.*** Yes. Administrative rulemaking starts with the publication of a notice of the rulemaking in the *Federal Register.* A public hearing is held at which proponents and opponents can offer evidence and question witnesses. After the hearing, the agency considers what was presented at the hearing and drafts the final rule.

## CHAPTER 24

**1.** ***To market the drug, what must United prove to the U.S. Food and Drug Administration?*** Under an extensive set of procedures established by the U.S. Food and Drug Administration, which administers the federal Food, Drug, and Cosmetic Act, drugs must be shown to be effective as well as safe before they may be marketed to the public. In general, manufacturers are responsible for ensuring that the drugs they offer for sale are free of any substances that could injure consumers.

**2. What can Gert do?** Under the Truth-in-Lending Act, a buyer who wishes to withhold payment for a faulty product purchased with a credit card must follow specific procedures to settle the dispute. The credit card issuer then must intervene and attempt to settle the dispute.

## CHAPTER 25

**1. Are there any reasons that the court might refuse to issue an injunction against Resource's operation? Explain.** Yes. On the ground that the hardships that would be imposed on the polluter and on the community are greater than the hardships suffered by the residents, the court might deny an injunction. If the plant is the core of the local economy, for instance, the residents may be awarded only damages.

**2. If the Environmental Protection Agency cleans up the site, from whom can it recover the cost?** The Comprehensive Environmental Response, Compensation, and Liability Act of 1980 regulates the clean-up of hazardous waste disposal sites. Any potentially responsible party can be charged with the entire cost of cleaning up a site. Potentially responsible parties include the person that generated the waste (ChemCorp) the person that transported the waste to the site (Disposal), the person that owned or operated the site at the time of the disposal (Eliminators), and the current owner or operator of the site (Fluid). A party held responsible for the entire cost may be able to recoup some of it in a lawsuit against other potentially responsible parties.

## CHAPTER 26

**1. Under what circumstances would Pop's Market, a small store in a small, isolated town, be considered a monopolist? If Pop's is a monopolist, is it in violation of Section 2 of the Sherman Act? Why or why not?** Size alone does not determine whether a firm is a monopoly—size in relation to the market is what matters. A small store in a small, isolated town is a monopolist if it is the only store serving that market. Monopoly involves the power to affect prices and output. If a firm has sufficient market power to control prices and exclude competition, that firm has monopoly power. Monopoly power in itself is not a violation of Section 2 of the Sherman Act. The offense also requires that the defendant intended to acquire or maintain that power through anticompetitive means.

**2. What factors would a court consider to decide whether this arrangement violates the Clayton Act?** This agreement is a tying arrangement. The legality of a tying arrangement depends on the purpose of the agreement, the agreement's likely effect on competition in the relevant markets (the market for the tying product and the market for the tied product), and other factors. Tying arrangements for commodities are subject to Section 3 of the Clayton Act. Tying arrangements for services can be

agreements in restraint of trade in violation of Section 1 of the Sherman Act.

## CHAPTER 27

**1. Does Speedy have a right to recover from the third party for the loss of the documents? Why or why not?** Yes. A bailee's right of possession, even though temporary, permits the bailee to recover damages from any third persons for damage or loss to the property.

**2. Who suffers the loss? Explain your answer.** Rosa de la Mar Corporation, the shipper, suffers the loss. A common carrier is liable for damage caused by the willful acts of third persons or by an accident. Other losses must be borne by the shipper (or the recipient, depending on the terms of their contract). This shipment was lost due to an act of God.

## CHAPTER 28

**1. Delmira wants to have Consuela evicted from the property. What can Consuela do?** This is a breach of the warranty deed's covenant of quiet enjoyment. The buyer can sue the seller and recover the purchase price of the house, plus any damages.

**2. Can Haven transfer possession for even less time to Idyll Company? Explain.** Yes. An owner of a fee simple has the most rights possible—he or she can give the property away, sell it, transfer it by will, use it for almost any purpose, possess it to the exclusion of all the world, or as in this case, transfer possession for any period of time. The party to whom possession is transferred can also transfer his or her interest (usually only with the owner's permission) for any lesser period of time.

## CHAPTER 29

**1. Has Roslyn violated any of the intellectual property rights discussed in this chapter? Explain.** Yes, Roslyn has committed theft of trade secrets. Lists of suppliers and customers cannot be patented, copyrighted, or trademarked, but the information they contain is protected against appropriation by others as trade secrets. And most likely, Roslyn signed a contract agreeing not to use this information outside her employment by Organic. But even without this contract, Organic could make a convincing case against its ex-employee for a theft of trade secrets.

**2. Is this patent infringement? If so, how might Global save the cost of suing World for infringement and at the same time profit from World's sales?** This is patent infringement. A software maker in this situation might best protect its product, save litigation costs, and profit from its patent by the use of a license. In the context of this problem, a license would grant permission to sell a patented item. (A license can be limited to certain purposes and to the licensee only.)

## CHAPTER 30

**1. Can the insurer refuse payment? Why or why not?** No. An incorrect statement as to the age of an insured is a misrepresentation. Under an incontestability clause, however, after a policy has been in force for a certain time (usually two or three years), the insurer cannot cancel the policy or avoid a claim on the basis of statements made in the application.

**2. *Can Al obtain payment for these events? Explain your answers.*** No. To obtain insurance, one must have a sufficiently substantial interest in whatever is to be insured. One has an insurable interest in property if one would suffer a pecuniary loss from its destruction. This interest must exist *when the loss occurs.*

To obtain insurance on another's life, one must have a reasonable expectation of benefit from the continued life of the other. The benefit may be founded on a relationship, but "ex-spouse" alone is not such a relationship. An interest in someone's life must exist *when the policy is obtained.*

## CHAPTER 31

**1. *Can Toby and Umeko have Sheila's will revoked on the ground that she did not have the capacity to make a will? Why or why not?*** No. To have testamentary capacity, a testator must be of legal age and sound mind *at the time the will is made.* Generally, the testator must (1) know the nature of the act, (2) comprehend and remember the "natural objects of his or her bounty," (3) know the nature and extent of her or his property, and (4) understand the distribution of assets called for by the will. In this situation, Sheila had testamentary capacity at the time she made the will. The fact that she was ruled mentally incompetent two years after making the will does not provide sufficient grounds to revoke it.

**2. *What determines who inherits what?*** The estate will pass according to the state's intestacy laws. Intestacy laws set out how property is distributed when a person dies without a will. Their purpose is to carry out the likely intent of the decedent. The laws determine which of the deceased's natural heirs (including the surviving spouse, lineal descendants, parents, and collateral heirs) inherit his or her property.

# APPENDIX C

# Sample Answers for *Business Case Problems* with *Sample Answer*

**Problem 1–3.** *Online Privacy.* Facebook created a program that makes decisions for users. Using duty-based ethics, many believe that privacy is an extremely important right that should be fiercely protected. Accordingly, any program that has a default of giving out information is unethical. Facebook should create the program as an opt-in program. In addition, under the Kantian categorical imperative, if every company created opt-out programs that disclosed potentially personal information, the concept of privacy may be reduced to a theoretical concept only. One could argue that this reduction or elimination of privacy would not make the world a better place. From a utilitarian or outcome-based approach, the benefits of an opt-out program might be in ease of creation and start up, as well as ease of recruiting partner programs. The detriment is the elimination of choice on the part of users to disclose information about themselves. An opt-in program maintains that user control but may be harder to start, as it requires more marketing up front in order to convince users to opt in.

**Problem 2–6.** *Franchise Termination.* Oshana and GTO have stated a claim for wrongful termination of their franchise. A franchisor must act in good faith when terminating a franchise agreement. If the termination is arbitrary or unfair, a franchisee may have a claim for wrongful termination. In this case, Oshana and GTO have alleged that Buchanan acted in bad faith. Their failure to pay rent would ordinarily be a valid basis for termination, but not if it was entirely precipitated by Buchanan. Thus, Oshana and GTO may recover if they can prove that their allegations are true.

**Problem 3–6.** *Partnerships.* Yes, Sacco is entitled to 50 percent of the profits of Pierce Paxton Collections. The requirements for establishing a partnership are (1) a sharing of profits and losses, (2) a joint ownership of the business, and (3) an equal right to be involved in the management of the business.

The effort and time that Sacco expended in the business constituted a sharing of losses, and his proprietary interest in the assets of the partnership consisted of his share of the profits, which he had expressly left in the business to "grow the company" and "build sweat equity" for the future. He was involved in every aspect of the business. Although he was not paid a salary, he was reimbursed for business expenses charged to his personal credit card, which Paxton also used. These facts arguably meet the requirements for establishing a partnership.

In the actual case on which this problem is based, Sacco filed a suit in a Louisiana state court against Paxton, and the court awarded Sacco 50 percent of the profits. A state intermediate appellate court affirmed, based generally on the reasoning stated above.

**Problem 4–6.** *LLC Operation.* Part of the attractiveness of an LLC as a form of business enterprise is its flexibility. The members can decide how to operate the business through an operating agreement. For example, the agreement can set forth procedures for choosing or removing members or managers.

Here, the Bluewater operating agreement provided for a "super majority" vote to remove a member under circumstances that would jeopardize the firm's contractor status. Thus, one Bluewater member could not unilaterally "fire" another member without providing a reason. In fact, a majority of the members could not terminate the other's interest in the firm without providing a reason. Moreover, the only acceptable reason would be a circumstance that undercut the firm's status as a contractor.

The flexibility of the LLC business form relates to its framework, not to its members' capacity to violate its operating agreement. In the actual case on which this problem is based, Smith attempted to "fire" Williford without providing a reason. In Williford's suit, the court issued a judgment in his favor.

**Problem 5–7.** *Piercing the Corporate Veil.* Yes, there are sufficient grounds in the facts of this problem to support piercing the corporate veil and holding Kappeler personally liable to Snapp. First, in a case in which a plaintiff seeks to pierce a corporate veil, there must be a fraud or other injustice to be remedied. In that situation, the factors that a court will consider in determining whether to pierce the corporate veil include (1) a party is tricked or misled into dealing with the corporation rather than the individual, (2) the corporation has insufficient capital to meet its prospective debts or other potential liabilities, (3) corporate formalities, such as holding required corporate meetings, are not followed, and (4) personal and corporate interests are commingled.

In this problem, the amount that Snapp ultimately paid the builder exceeded the original estimate by nearly $1 million—and the project was still unfinished. Kappeler could not provide an accounting for the Snapp project—he could not explain double and triple charges nor whether the amount that Snapp paid had actually been spent on the project. These facts support a conclusion of fraud. And they also indicate that Kappeler may have tricked or misled Snapp into dealing with the corporation rather than with Kappeler as an individual. Castlebrook had issued no shares of stock, which indicates insufficient capitalization. The minutes of the corporate meetings "all looked exactly the same," indicating that in fact the required corporate meetings had not been held. And Kappeler had commingled personal and corporate funds.

In the actual case on which this problem is based, in Snapp's suit against the builder, the court pierced the corporate veil and held Kappeler personally liable. A state intermediate appellate court affirmed.

**Problem 6–4.** *Rights of Shareholders.* Yes. Woods has a right to inspect Biolustré's books and records. Every shareholder is entitled to examine corporate records. A shareholder can inspect the books in person or through an agent such as an attorney, accountant, or other authorized assistant.

The right of inspection is limited to the inspection and copying of corporate books and records for a proper purpose. This is because the power of inspection is fraught with potential for abuse—for example, it can involve the disclosure of trade secrets and other confidential information. Thus, a corporation is allowed to protect itself. Here, Woods, through Hair Ventures, has the right to inspect Biolustré's books and records. She has a proper purpose for the inspection—to obtain information about Biolustré's financial situation. She, along with other shareholders, had not received notice of shareholders' meetings or corporate financial reports for years, or notice of Biolustré's plan to issue additional stock. Hair Ventures had a substantial investment in the company. In the actual case on which this problem is based, the court ordered Biolustré to produce its books and records for Hair Ventures' inspection.

**Problem 7–4.** *Violations of the 1934 Act.* An omission or misrepresentation of a material fact in connection with the purchase or sale of a security may violate Section 10(b) of the Securities Exchange Act of 1934 and SEC Rule 10b-5. The key question is whether the omitted or misrepresented information is material. A fact, by itself, is not automatically material. A fact will be regarded as material only if it is significant enough that it would likely affect an investor's decision as to whether to buy or sell the company's securities. For example, a company's potential liability in a product liability suit and the financial consequences to the firm are material facts that must be disclosed because they are significant enough to affect an investor's decision as to whether to buy stock in the company.

In this case, the plaintiffs' claim should not be dismissed. To prevail on their claim that the defendants made material omissions in violation of Section 10(b) and SEC Rule 10b-5, the plaintiffs must prove that the omission was material. Their complaint alleged the omission of information linking Zicam and anosmia (a loss of the sense of smell) and plausibly suggested that reasonable investors would have viewed this information as material. Zicam products account for 70 percent of Matrixx's sales. Matrixx received reports of consumers who suffered anosmia after using Zicam Cold Remedy.

In public statements discussing revenues and product safety, Matrixx did not disclose this information. But the information was significant enough to likely affect a consumer's decision to use the product, and this would affect revenue and ultimately the commercial viability of the product. The information was therefore significant enough to likely affect an investor's decision whether to buy or sell Matrixx's stock, and this would affect the stock price. Thus, the plaintiffs' allegations were sufficient. Contrary to the defendants' assertion, statistical sampling is not required to show materiality—reasonable investors could view reports of adverse events as material even if the reports did not provide statistically significant evidence.

**Problem 8–5.** *Negligence.* Negligence requires proof that (1) the defendant owed a duty of care to the plaintiff, (2) the defendant breached that duty, (3) the defendant's breach caused the plaintiff's injury, and (4) the plaintiff suffered a legally recognizable injury. With respect to the duty of care, a business owner has a duty to use reasonable care to protect business invitees. This duty includes an obligation to discover and correct or warn of unreasonably dangerous conditions that the owner of the premises should reasonably foresee might endanger an invitee. Some risks are so obvious that an owner need not warn of them. But even if a risk is obvious, a business owner may not be excused from the duty to protect its customers from foreseeable harm.

Because Lucario was the Weatherford's business invitee, the hotel owed her a duty of reasonable care to make its premises safe for her use. The balcony ran nearly the entire width of the window in Lucario's room. She could have reasonably believed that the window was a means of access to the balcony. The window/balcony configuration was dangerous, however, because the window opened wide enough for an adult to climb out, but the twelve-inch gap between one side of the window and the balcony was unprotected. This unprotected gap opened to a drop of more than three stories to a concrete surface below.

Should the hotel have anticipated the potential harm to a guest who opened the window in Room 59 and attempted to access the balcony? The hotel encouraged guests to "step out onto the balcony" to smoke. The dangerous condition of the window/balcony configuration could have been remedied at a minimal cost. These circumstances could be perceived as creating an "unreasonably dangerous" condition. And it could be concluded that the hotel created or knew of the condition and failed to take reasonable steps to warn of it or correct it. Of course, the Weatherford might argue that the window/ balcony configuration was so obvious that the hotel was not liable for Lucario's fall.

In the actual case on which this problem is based, the court concluded that the Weatherford did not breach its duty of care to Lucario. On McMurtry's appeal, a state intermediate appellate court held that this conclusion was in error, vacated the lower court's judgment in favor of the hotel on this issue, and remanded the case.

**Problem 9–7.** *Determining Employee Status.* No, Cox is not liable to Cayer for any injuries or damage that she sustained in the accident with Ovalles. Generally, an employer is not liable for physical harm caused to a third person by the negligent act of an independent contractor in the performance of a contract. This is be cause the employer does not have the right to control the details of the performance. In determining whether a worker has the status of an independent contractor, how much control the employer can exercise over the details of the work is the most important factor weighed by the courts.

In this problem, Ovalles worked as a cable installer for Cox under an agreement with M&M. The agreement disavowed any employer-employee relationship between Cox and M&M's installers. Ovalles was required to designate his affiliation with Cox on his van, clothing, and an ID badge. But Cox had minimal contact with Ovalles and limited power to control the manner in which he performed his work. Cox supplied cable wire and other equipment, but these items were delivered to M&M, not Ovalles. These facts indicate that Ovalles was an independent contractor, not an employee. Thus, Cox was not liable to Cayer for the harm caused to her by Ovalles when his van rear-ended Cayer's car.

In the actual case on which this problem is based, the court issued a judgment in Cox's favor. The Rhode Island Supreme Court affirmed, applying the principles stated above to arrive at the same conclusion.

## Problem 10–6. *Agent's Authority.*

No, Rainbow cannot recoup the unpaid amounts from Basic. Express authority is authority declared in clear, direct, and definite terms. Express authority can be given orally or in writing. In most states, if the contract being executed is or must be in writing, then the agent's authority must also be in writing. Otherwise, the contract may be avoided (or ratified) by the principal. If it is ratified, the ratification must be in writing. An agent has the implied authority to do what is reasonably necessary to carry out express authority. For example, authority to manage a business implies authority to do what is reasonably required to operate the business. But an agent's implied authority cannot contradict his or her express authority. Thus, if a principal has limited an agent's express authority, then the fact that the agent customarily would have such authority is irrelevant.

In this problem, Basic Research advertised its products on television networks owned by Rainbow Media Holdings through an ad agency, Icebox Advertising. Basic paid Icebox for the ads, but Icebox did not make all of the payments to Rainbow. Icebox filed for bankruptcy. Rainbow cannot recover what it was owed from Basic. As Basic's agent, Icebox had the express authority to buy ads from Rainbow on Basic's behalf, but that authority was limited to purchasing ads with cash in advance. Thus, Icebox did not have the authority—express or implied—to buy ads on Basic's credit. And Basic did not ratify the contracts that represented purchases on credit.

In the actual case on which this problem is based, on Basic's appeal from a judgment in Rainbow's favor, the U.S. Court of Appeals for the Tenth Circuit reversed that judgment and ruled in Basic's favor.

## Problem 11–6. *Unemployment Compensation.*

Yes, Ramirez qualifies for unemployment compensation. Generally, to be eligible for unemployment compensation, a worker must be willing and able to work. Workers who have been fired for misconduct or who have voluntarily left their jobs are not eligible for benefits. In the facts of this problem, the applicable state statute disqualifies an employee from receiving benefits if he or she voluntarily leaves work without "good cause."

The issue is whether Ramirez left her job for "good cause." When her father in the Dominican Republic had a stroke, she asked her employer for time off to be with him. Her employer refused the request. But Ramirez left to be with her father and called to inform her employer. It seems likely that this family emergency would constitute "good cause," and Ramirez's call and return to work after her father's death indicated that she did not disregard her employer's interests.

In the actual case on which this problem is based, the state of Florida denied Ramirez unemployment compensation. On Ramirez's appeal, a state intermediate appellate court reversed, on the reasoning stated above.

## Problem 12–5. *Age Discrimination.*

No, sanofi-aventis U.S. LLC (S-A) does not appear to have engaged in age discrimination. The Age Discrimination in Employment Act (ADEA) prohibits employment discrimination on the basis of age against individuals forty years of age or older. For the act to apply, an employer must have twenty or more employees, and the employer's business activities must affect interstate commerce. To establish a *prima facie* case, a plaintiff must show that he or she was (1) a member of the protected age group, (2) qualified for the position from which he or she was discharged, and (3) discharged because of age discrimination. If the employer offers a legitimate reason for its action, the plaintiff must show that the stated reason is only a pretext.

In this problem, Rangel was over forty years old. But he also had negative sales performance reviews for more than two years before he was terminated as part of S-A's nationwide reduction in force of all sales professionals who had not met the "Expectations" guidelines, including younger workers. The facts do not indicate that a person younger than Rangel replaced him or that S-A intended to discriminate against him on the basis of age. Based on these facts, Rangel could not establish a *prima facie* case of age discrimination on the part of S-A.

In the actual case on which this problem is based, in Rangel's suit against S-A alleging age discrimination, a federal district court issued a judgment in S-A's favor. On Rangel's appeal, the U.S. Court of Appeals for the Tenth Circuit affirmed, according to the reasoning stated above.

## Problem 13–4. *Additional Terms.*

No. Under the common law, variations in terms between the offer and the offeree's acceptance violate the mirror image rule, which requires that the terms of an acceptance exactly mirror the terms of the offer. The UCC dispenses with this rule. Under the UCC, a contract is formed if the offeree makes a definite expression of acceptance even though the terms of the acceptance modify or add to the terms of the offer. When both parties to the contract are merchants, the additional terms become part of their contract unless (1) the original offer expressly required acceptance of its terms, (2) the new or changed terms materially alter the contract, or (3) the offeror rejects the new or changed terms within a reasonable time.

In this problem, the UCC applies because the transactions involve sales of goods. The original offer stated, "By signing below, you agree to the terms." This statement could be construed to expressly require acceptance of the terms to make the offer a binding contract (Exception 1 above). The contract stated that JMAM was to receive credit for any rejected merchandise. Nothing indicated that the merchandise would be returned to BSI. Baracsi, BSI's owner (the offeree), signed JMAM's (the offeror's) letter in the appropriate location. This indicated BSI's agreement to the terms. Thus, BSI made a definite expression of acceptance. The practice of the parties—for six years rejected items were not returned—further supports the conclusion that their contract did not contemplate the return of those items. The "PS" could be interpreted as materially altering the contract (Exception 2 above).

In the actual case on which this problem is based, the court dismissed BSI's complaint.

## Problem 14–5. *Nonconforming Goods.*
Padma notified Universal Exports about its breach, so Padma has two ways to recover even though it accepted the goods. Padma's first option is to argue that it revoked its acceptance, giving it the right to reject the goods. To revoke acceptance, Padma would have to show that (1) the nonconformity substantially impaired the value of the shipment, (2) it predicated its acceptance on a reasonable assumption that Universal Exports would cure the nonconformity, and (3) Universal Exports did not cure the nonconformity within a reasonable time. Padma's second option is to keep the goods and recover for the damages caused by Universal Exports' breach. Under this option, Padma could recover at least the difference between the value of the goods as promised and their value as accepted.

## Problem 15–6. *Payable on Demand or at a Definite Time.*
No. Novel is not correct. The instrument is a note, and Novel is bound to pay it. For an instrument to be negotiable under UCC 3–104, it must meet the following requirements: (1) be in writing, (2) be signed by the maker or the drawer, (3) be an unconditional promise or order to pay, (4) state a fixed amount of money, (5) be payable on demand or at a definite time, and (6) be payable to order or to bearer unless it is a check. When no time for payment is stated on an instrument, the instrument is payable on demand.

Applying these principles to the facts in this problem, all of the requirements to establish the instrument as negotiable are met: (1) the instrument is in writing; (2) it is signed by Novel; (3) there are no conditions or promises other than the unconditional promise to pay; (4) the instrument states a fixed amount—$10,000; (5) the instrument does not include a definite repayment date, which means that it is payable on demand; and (6) the instrument is payable to Gallwitz. In the actual case on which this problem is based, the court ruled in favor of Gallwitz for payment of the note.

## Problem 16–5. *Negotiation.*
A negotiable instrument can be transferred by assignment or by negotiation. An assignment is a transfer of rights by contract. A transfer by assignment to an assignee gives the assignee only those rights that the assignor possessed. Any defenses that can be raised against the assignor can be raised against the assignee. When an instrument is transferred by negotiation, the transferee becomes a holder. A holder receives at least the rights of the previous possessor. Unlike an assignment, a transfer by negotiation can make it possible for the holder to receive more rights in the instrument than the prior possessor had. A holder who receives greater rights is a holder in due course (HDC) and takes the instrument free of any claims to it and defenses against its payment. Negotiating order instruments requires delivery and indorsement. If a party to whom a negotiable note is made payable signs it and delivers it to a bank, the transfer is a negotiation, and the bank becomes a holder. If the party does not sign the note, however, the transfer is treated as an assignment, and the bank becomes an assignee instead of a holder.

In this problem, Argent was the payee of the note and its holder. Argent transferred the note to Wells Fargo without an indorsement. Thus, the transfer was not a negotiation but an assignment. Wells Fargo did not then become a holder of the note but an assignee. As an assignee, the bank acquired only those rights that the lender possessed before the assignment. And any defenses—including fraud in connection with the note— that Ford could assert against the lender could also be asserted by the borrower against the bank. If Argent indorsed the note to Wells Fargo after the defendant's response to the complaint, the bank could become a holder of the note, but it could not become an HDC. One of the requirements for HDC status is that a holder must take an instrument without notice of defenses against payment. The bank could not do this, because it would now be aware of the borrower's defenses.

In the actual case on which this problem is based, the court issued a judgment in Wells Fargo's favor, and Ford appealed. A state intermediate appellate court reversed the judgment and remanded the case for trial, finding that the bank had failed to prove that it was a holder, an assignee, or even a transferee of the note.

## Problem 17–4. *Defenses.*
When an instrument is transferred by negotiation, the transferee becomes a holder. A holder can become an HDC if the holder takes the instrument for value, in good faith, and without notice of any defects. An HDC takes an instrument free of most defenses against payment that could be asserted against the transferor. Defenses against payment fall into two categories. Universal defenses are good against all holders, including HDCs. Personal defenses are used to avoid payment to an ordinary holder, but not an HDC. Personal defenses include breach of contract, ordinary fraud, and any other defenses that can be asserted to avoid payment on a contract. Between the maker and the payee, a promissory note is a contract to pay money. Defenses that may be asserted by the maker against payment on a note include the personal defenses.

In this problem, Klutz does not qualify as an HDC. Thorbecke signed a note as the maker for most of the price for the purchase of the restaurant. Klutz may have taken Thorbecke's note for value—at least to the extent that he performed the part of the contract for the sale of the restaurant—but he did not take it in good faith or without notice. He misrepresented his authority to sell the franchise. In other words, under the facts as presented, Klutz appears to have committed fraud in the inducement and to have breached the contract of sale. Thorbecke appears to have reasonably relied on the misrepresentation and to be entitled to damages as a result. Thorbecke may also be justified in asserting these defenses against payment on the note.

In the actual case on which this problem is based, the court issued a decision in Thorbecke's favor to allow the suit to go to trial to determine whether Klutz misrepresented his authority to transfer the franchise, whether Thorbecke reasonably relied on the misrepresentation, the extent of any damages, and the amount due on the note.

**Problem 18–5.  *Honoring Checks.*** A bank that pays a customer's check bearing a forged indorsement must recredit the customer's account or be liable to the customer-drawer for breach of contract. The bank must recredit the account because it failed to carry out the drawer's order to pay to the order of the named party. Eventually, the loss falls on the first party to take the instrument bearing the forged indorsement because a forged indorsement does not transfer title. Thus, whoever takes an instrument with a forged indorsement cannot become a holder.

Under these rules, Wells Fargo is liable to W Financial for the amount of the check. The bank had an obligation to ensure that the check was properly indorsed. The bank did not pay the check to the order of Lateef, the named payee, but accepted the check for deposit into the account of CA Houston without Lateef's indorsement. The bank did not obtain title to the instrument and could not become a holder, nor was it entitled to enforce the instrument on behalf of any other party who was entitled to enforce it. In the actual case on which this problem is based, the court held the bank liable to pay the amount of the check to W Financial.

**Problem 19–5.  *Liens.*** Among the liens discussed in this chapter, a mechanic's lien would likely be most effective to Jirak in its attempt to collect the unpaid cost of its work for the Balks. A creditor can place a mechanic's lien on the real property of a debtor who has contracted for improvements to the property and has not paid the price. When a creditor obtains a mechanic's lien, the debtor's real estate becomes security for the debt. If the debtor does not pay, the creditor can foreclose on the property and sell it to collect the amount due.

In this problem, the Balks contracted with Jirak for the remodel of their farmhouse. Due to the Balks' changes to the project during the course of the work, the costs exceeded the amount of Jirak's original estimate. Although Jirak regularly advised the Balks about the increasing costs and provided an itemized breakdown at their request, they refused to pay the price. The use of a mechanic's lien is likely the best way for Jirak to collect the unpaid amount.

In the actual case on which this problem is based, Jirak filed a suit in an Iowa state court against the Balks to foreclose on their property by way of a mechanic's lien and collect the unpaid amount. The court entered a judgment in Jirak's favor and enforced the lien. A state intermediate appellate court affirmed the judgment.

**Problem 20–7.  *Perfecting a Security Interest.*** Yes, these financing statements were sufficient to perfect the bank's security interests in Tille's equipment. In most situations, perfection is accomplished by filing a financing statement with the appropriate official. To effectively perfect a security interest, a financing statement must contain (1) the debtor's signature, (2) the debtor's and creditor's addresses, and (3) a description of the collateral by type or item.

In this case, all of Union's financing statements were sufficient to perfect security interests. Each of them provided the name and address of the debtor (Tille), the name and address of the secured party (Union Bank), and a description of the collateral covered by the financing statement—for one loan, all of Tille's equipment, including after-acquired property; for another, the truck crane; and for the third, a Bobcat mini-excavator. These descriptions were clearly sufficient to put a prospective creditor on notice that the collateral was the subject of a security interest.

In the actual case on which this problem is based, the court concluded that all of the statements created perfected security interests.

**Problem 21–5.  *Discharge in Bankruptcy.*** No, ECMC cannot now resume its effort to collect on Hann's loans. After the debtor has completed all payments, the court grants a discharge of all debts provided for by the repayment plan. All debts generally are dischargeable, especially those for which the court either declared that there was no obligation or disallowed on the ground that the underlying debt was satisfied.

In this problem, Hann financed her education partially through loans. When she filed a Chapter 13 petition, Educational Credit Management Corp. (ECMC) filed an unsecured proof of claim based on the loans. Hann believed that she had repaid the loans in full and objected. The court held a hearing at which ECMC failed to appear, and Hann submitted correspondence from the lender indicating the loans had been paid. The court then entered an order sustaining Hann's objection to ECMC's claim, in effect declaring that there was no obligation and the underlying debt was satisfied. By later attempting to renew efforts to collect on the loans, ECMC would violate the court's order.

In the actual case on which this problem is based, ECMC resumed collection efforts after the bankruptcy. Hann reopened her case and filed a complaint against ECMC, alleging that it had violated the order sustaining her objection. The court ruled in Hann's favor and sanctioned ECMC for attempting to collect on the debt. On ECMC's appeal, the U.S. Court of Appeals for the First Circuit affirmed.

**Problem 22–7.** *Potential Liability to Third Parties.* KPMG is potentially liable to the hedge funds' partners under the *Restatement (Second) of Torts.* Under Section 552 of the *Restatement,* an auditor owes a duty to "persons for whose benefit and guidance the accountant intends to supply . . . information." In this case, KPMG prepared annual reports on the hedge funds and addressed them to the funds' "Partners." Additionally, KPMG knew who the partners were because it prepared individual tax forms for them each year. Thus, KPMG's annual reports were for the partners' benefit and guidance. The partners relied on the reports, including their representations that they complied with generally accepted accounting principles. As a result, they lost millions of dollars, which exposes KPMG to possible liability under Section 552.

**Problem 23–4.** *Agency Powers.* The United States Supreme Court held that greenhouse gases fit within the Clean Air Act's (CAA's) definition of "air pollutant." Thus, the Environmental Protection Agency (EPA) has the authority under that statute to regulate the emission of such gases from new motor vehicles. According to the Court, the definition, which includes "any" air pollutant, embraces all airborne compounds "of whatever stripe." The EPA's focus on Congress's 1990 amendments (or their lack) indicates nothing about the original intent behind the statute (and its amendments before 1990). Nothing in the statute suggests that Congress meant to curtail the agency's power to treat greenhouse gases as air pollutants. In other words, the agency has a preexisting mandate to regulate "any air pollutant" that may endanger the public welfare.

The EPA also argued that, even if it had the authority to regulate greenhouse gases, the agency would not exercise that authority because any regulation would conflict with other administration priorities. The Court acknowledged that the CAA conditions EPA action on the agency's formation of a "judgment," but explained that judgment must relate to whether a pollutant "cause[s], or contribute[s] to, air pollution which may reasonably be anticipated to endanger public health or welfare." Thus, the EPA can avoid issuing regulations only if the agency determines that greenhouse gases do not contribute to climate change (or if the agency reasonably explains why it cannot or will not determine whether they do). The EPA's refusal to regulate was thus "arbitrary, capricious, or otherwise not in accordance with law," The Court remanded the case for the EPA to "ground its reasons for action or inaction in the statute."

**Problem 24–5.** *Fair Debt-Collection Practices.* Engler may recover under the Fair Debt Collection Practices Act (FDCPA). Atlantic is subject to the FDCPA because it is a debt-collection agency and was attempting to collect a debt on behalf of Bank of America. Atlantic used offensive tactics to collect from Engler. After all, Atlantic gave Engler's employer the false impression that Engler was a criminal, had a pending case, and was about to be arrested. Finally, Engler suffered harm because he experienced discomfort, embarrassment, and distress as a result of Atlantic's abusive conduct. Engler may recover actual damages, statutory damages, and attorneys' fees from Atlantic.

**Problem 25–5.** *Environmental Impact Statements.* Yes, an environmental impact statement (EIS) is required before the U.S. Forest Service (USFS) implements its proposed travel management plan (TMP). An EIS must be prepared for every major federal action that significantly affects the quality of the environment. An action is "major" if it involves a substantial commitment of resources. An action is "federal" if a federal agency has the power to control it. An EIS must analyze (1) the impact on the environment that the action will have, (2) any adverse effects on the environment and alternative actions that might be taken, and (3) irreversible effects that the action might generate.

Here, the resources committed to the implementation of the USFS's TMP could include the resources within the wilderness and the time and effort dedicated by the agency. The wilderness resources would include the soil, the vegetation, the wildlife, the wildlife habitat, any threatened or endangered species, and other natural assets impacted by the TMP. The agency's resources would include its funds and its staff—to design, map, maintain, and enforce the TMP. These resources seem substantial. Of course, the implementation of the TMP is federal because the USFS has the power to control it.

As for the aspects of the environment that the agency might consider in preparing the EIS, some of the important factors are listed above—the soil, vegetation, wildlife, wildlife habitat, and threatened or endangered species. Other aspects of the environment impacted by the TMP might include cultural resources, historical resources, wilderness suitability, and other authorized uses of the wilderness. There is a potential for impact by every route that is designed to be part of the system, as well as the "dispersed vehicle camping" to be permitted on the terrain.

In the actual case on which this problem is based, the USFS considered all of the factors listed above. The agency then issued an EIS and a decision implementing the TMP. On a challenge to the EIS, a federal district court issued a judgment in the USFS's favor. The U.S. Court of Appeals for the Ninth Circuit affirmed. "The Forest Service took the requisite hard look at the environmental impacts."

**Problem 26–5.** *Price Discrimination.* Spa Steel satisfies most of the requirements for a price discrimination claim under Section 2 of the Clayton Act. Dayton Superior is engaged in interstate commerce, and it sells goods of like grade and quality to at least three purchasers. Moreover, Spa Steel can show that, because it sells Dayton Superior's products at a higher price, it lost business and thus suffered an injury. To recover, however, Spa Steel will also need to prove that Dayton Superior charged Spa Steel's competitors a lower price for the same product. Spa Steel cannot recover if its prices were higher for reasons related to its own business, such as having higher overhead expenses or seeking a larger profit.

**Problem 27–4.** *Bailment Obligation.* Moreland should be awarded damages, and Gray should take nothing. The bailee must exercise reasonable care in preserving the bailed property. What constitutes reasonable care in a bailment situation normally depends on the nature and specific circumstances of the bailment. If the bailed property has been lost or is returned damaged, a court will presume that the bailee was negligent.

In the circumstances of this problem, when the bailor (Moreland, the owner of the aircraft) entrusted the plane to the bailee's (Gray's) repair shop for painting, the work was not properly performed. This violated the bailee's duty to exercise reasonable care and breached the bailment contract. Because the plane was returned damaged, this may also constitute negligence. In the event of a breach, the bailor may sue for damages. The measure of damages is the difference between the value of the bailed property in its present condition and what it would have been worth if the work had been properly performed.

Thus, Gray is liable to Moreland for failing to properly paint the plane. In the actual case on which this problem is based, the court upheld a jury award to Moreland of damages and attorneys' fees.

### Problem 28–4. *Adverse Possession.* The McKeags satisfied the first three requirements for adverse possession:

1. Their possession was actual and exclusive because they used the beach and prevented others from doing so, including the Finleys.
2. Their possession was open, visible, and notorious because they made improvements to the beach and regularly kept their belongings there.
3. Their possession was continuous and peaceable for the required ten years. They possessed the property for more than four decades, and they even kept a large float there during the winter months.

Nevertheless, the McKeags' possession was *not* hostile and adverse, which is the fourth requirement. The Finleys had substantial evidence that they gave the McKeags permission to use the beach. Rather than reject the Finleys' permission as unnecessary, the McKeags sometimes said nothing and other times seemingly affirmed that the property belonged to the Finleys. Thus, because the McKeags did not satisfy all four requirements, they cannot establish adverse possession.

### Problem 29–6. *Patents.* One ground on which the denial of the patent application in this problem could be reversed on appeal is that the design of Raymond Gianelli's "Rowing Machine" is *not obvious* in light of the design of the "Chest Press Apparatus for Exercising Regions of the Upper Body."

To obtain a patent, an applicant must demonstrate to the satisfaction of the U.S. Patent and Trademark Office (PTO) that the invention, discovery, process, or design is novel, useful, and not obvious in light of current technology. In this problem, the PTO denied Gianelli's application for a patent for his "Rowing Machine"—an exercise machine on which a user *pulls* on handles to perform a rowing motion against a selected resistance to strengthen the back muscles. The PTO considered the device obvious in light of a patented "Chest Press Apparatus for Exercising Regions of the Upper Body"—a chest press

exercise machine on which a user *pushes* on handles to overcome a selected resistance. But it can be easily argued that it is *not* obvious to modify a machine with handles designed to be *pushed* into one with handles designed to be *pulled*. In fact, anyone who has used exercise machines knows that a way to cause injury is to use a machine in a manner not intended by the manufacturer.

In the actual case on which this problem is based, the U.S. Court of Appeals for the Federal Circuit reversed the PTO's denial of Gianelli's application for a patent, based on the reasoning stated above.

### Problem 30–7. *Insurance Provisions and Clauses.* Farrington should not be included as an insured within the meaning of the property insurance policy between Darling's and Philadelphia. The existence of an insurable interest is a primary concern when determining liability under an insurance policy. In the case of personal property, an insurable interest exists when the insured derives a pecuniary benefit from the preservation and continued existence of the property. One has an insurable interest in property when one would sustain a financial loss from its destruction. As for an insurance policy's language, courts interpret the words according to their ordinary meanings and in light of the nature of the coverage involved.

Darling's is entitled to recover the value of the loss to covered vehicles by virtue of its ownership of those vehicles and the fact that it is the owner that suffers the loss when one of its vehicles is damaged. In other words, under the Philadelphia policy, Darling's had an insurable interest in the car when Farrington smashed into the moose. Farrington might have had an insurable interest as well when he agreed to be responsible for any damage to the car, but he declined the insurance coverage offered in the rental contract.

In the actual case on which this problem is based, in Philadelphia's suit against Farrington, the court entered a judgment in the insurer's favor.

### Problem 31–6. *Undue Influence.* No, undue influence does not appear to have occurred in this problem. To invalidate a will on the basis of undue influence, a plaintiff must show that the decedent's plan of distribution was the result of improper pressure brought by another person. Undue influence may be inferred if the testator ignores blood relatives and names as a beneficiary a nonrelative who is in constant close contact and in a position to influence the making of the will.

In this problem, although Tommy's ex-wife lived with Susie and was thus in a position to influence Susie's will, she was not a beneficiary under it, so there is no inference of undue influence. Moreover, neither of the wills that Walker executed left any property to her son, so there was no indication that she had been influenced to change her mind regarding the distribution of her estate. Additionally, she expressly disinherited her son, and several witnesses testified that she was mentally competent at the time she made the will.

In the actual case on which this problem is based, the court presumed that the will was valid.

# Glossary

## A

**abandoned property** Property that has been discarded by the owner, who has no intention of reclaiming it.

**acceleration clause** (1) A clause in an installment contract that provides for all future payments to become due immediately on the failure to tender timely payments or on the occurrence of a specified event. (2) A clause in a mortgage loan contract that makes the entire loan balance become due if the borrower misses or is late making monthly mortgage payments.

**acceptance** (1) In contract law, the offeree's notification to the offeror that the offeree agrees to be bound by the terms of the offeror's proposal. (2) In negotiable instruments law, the drawee's signed agreement to pay a draft when presented.

**acceptor** The person (the drawee) who accepts a draft and who agrees to be primarily responsible for its payment.

**accession** The addition of value to personal property by the use of labor or materials.

**accommodation party** A person who signs an instrument for the purpose of lending his or her name as credit to another party on the instrument.

**accredited investor** In the context of securities offerings, sophisticated investors, such as banks, insurance companies, investment companies, the issuer's executive officers and directors, and persons whose income or net worth exceeds certain limits.

**actionable** Capable of serving as the basis of a lawsuit.

**actual malice** A condition that exists when a person makes a statement with either knowledge of its falsity or reckless disregard for the truth. In a defamation suit, a statement made about a public figure normally must be made with actual malice for liability to be incurred.

**adequate protection doctrine** In bankruptcy law, a doctrine that protects secured creditors from losing their security as a result of an automatic stay. In certain circumstances, the bankruptcy court may provide adequate protection by requiring the debtor or trustee to pay the creditor or provide additional guaranties to protect the creditor against the losses suffered by the creditor as a result of the stay.

**adjudication** The process of resolving a dispute by presenting evidence and arguments before a neutral third party decision maker in a court or an administrative law proceeding.

**administrative agency** A federal or state government agency created by the legislature to perform a specific function, such as to make and enforce rules pertaining to the environment.

**administrative law judge (ALJ)** One who presides over an administrative agency hearing and has the power to administer oaths, take testimony, rule on questions of evidence, and make determinations of fact.

**administrative process** The procedure used by administrative agencies in fulfilling their three basic functions: rulemaking, enforcement, and adjudication.

**administrator** One who is appointed by a court to administer an estate if the decedent died without a valid will or if the executor named in the will cannot serve.

**adverse possession** The acquisition of title to real property through open occupation, without the consent of the owner, for a period of time specified by a state statute. The occupation must be actual, exclusive, open, continuous, and in opposition to all others, including the owner.

**affirmative action** Job-hiring policies that give special consideration to members of protected classes in an effort to overcome present effects of past discrimination.

**after-acquired property** Property of the debtor that is acquired after the execution of a security agreement.

**agency** A relationship between two parties in which one party (the agent) agrees to represent or act for the other (the principal).

**agency coupled with an interest** An agency, created for the benefit of the agent, in which the agent has some legal right (interest) in the property that is the subject of the agency.

**agent** A person who agrees to represent or act for another, called the principal.

**alien corporation** A corporation formed in another country but doing business in the United States.

**antecedent claim** A preexisting claim. In negotiable instruments law, taking an instrument in satisfaction of an antecedent claim is taking the instrument for value.

**antilapse provision** A clause in an insurance contract that gives the insured a grace period (usually thirty days) within which to pay an overdue premium.

**antitrust law** Laws protecting commerce from unlawful restraints and anticompetitive practices.

**apparent authority** Authority that is only apparent, not real. An agent's apparent authority arises when the principal causes a third party to believe that the agent has authority, even though she or he does not.

**articles of incorporation** The document that is filed with the appropriate state official, usually the secretary of state, when a business is incorporated and that contains basic information about the corporation.

**articles of merger** A document, filed with the secretary of state, that sets forth the terms and conditions of a merger.

**articles of organization** The document filed with a designated state official by which a limited liability company is formed.

**articles of partnership** A written agreement that sets forth each partner's rights and obligations with respect to the partnership.

**artisan's lien** A possessory lien given to a person who has made improvements and added value to another person's personal property as security for payment for services performed.

**assault** Any word or action intended to make another person fearful of immediate physical harm; a reasonably believable threat.

**assumption of risk** A defense against negligence that can be used when the plaintiff was aware of a danger and voluntarily assumed the risk of injury from that danger.

**attachment** (1) In the context of secured transactions, the process by which a security interest in the property of another becomes enforceable. (2) In the context of judicial liens, a court-ordered seizure and taking into custody of property prior to the securing of a judgment for a past-due debt.

**attempted monopolization** An action by a firm that involves anticompetitive conduct, the intent to gain monopoly power, and a "dangerous probability" of success in achieving monopoly power.

**auditor** An accountant qualified to perform audits (systematic inspections) of a business's financial records.

**authenticate** To sign or, on an electronic record, to adopt any symbol that verifies the intent to adopt or accept the record.

**authorization card** A card signed by an employee that gives a union permission to act on his or her behalf in negotiations with management.

**automatic stay** In bankruptcy proceedings, the suspension of almost all litigation and other action by creditors against the debtor or the debtor's property. The stay is effective the moment the debtor files a petition in bankruptcy.

## B

**bailee** One to whom goods are entrusted by a bailor.

**bailee's lien** A possessory (artisan's) lien that a bailee entitled to compensation can place on the bailed property to ensure that he or she will be paid for the services provided.

**bailment** A situation in which the personal property of one person (a bailor) is entrusted to another (a bailee), who is obligated to return the bailed property to the bailor or dispose of it as directed.

**bailor** One who entrusts goods to a bailee.

**bait-and-switch advertising** Advertising a product at an attractive price and then telling the consumer that the advertised product is not available or is of poor quality and encouraging her or him to purchase a more expensive item.

**banker's acceptance** A banker's acceptance is a promised future payment, or time draft, which is accepted and guaranteed by a bank and drawn on a deposit at the bank. The banker's acceptance specifies the amount of money, the date, and the person to which the payment is due, and is commonly used in international trade.

**bankruptcy trustee** A person appointed by the court to manage the debtor's funds in a bankruptcy proceeding.

**battery** The unprivileged, intentional touching of another.

**bearer** A person in the possession of an instrument payable to bearer or indorsed in blank.

**bearer instrument** Any instrument that is not payable to a specific person, including instruments payable to the bearer or to "cash."

**benefit corporation** A type of for-profit corporation, available by statute in a number of states, that seeks to have a material positive impact on society and the environment.

**bequest** A gift of personal property by will (from the verb *to bequeath*).

**binder** A written, temporary insurance policy.

**binding authority** Any source of law that a court must follow when deciding a case.

**blank indorsement** An indorsement that specifies no particular indorsee and can consist of a mere signature. An order instrument that is indorsed in blank becomes a bearer instrument.

**blue sky laws** State laws that regulate the offer and sale of securities.

**bona fide occupational qualification (BFOQ)** An identifiable characteristic reasonably necessary to the normal operation of a particular business. Such characteristics can include gender, national origin, and religion, but not race.

**bond** A security that evidences a corporate (or government) debt.

**bureaucracy** A large organization that is structured hierarchically to carry out specific functions.

**business ethics** Ethics in a business context; a consensus of what constitutes right or wrong behavior in the world of business and the application of moral principles to situations that arise in a business setting.

**business invitees** Those people, such as customers or clients, who are invited onto business premises by the owner of those premises for business purposes.

**business judgment rule** A rule under which courts will not hold corporate officers and directors liable for honest mistakes of judgment and bad business decisions that were made in good faith.

**business necessity** A defense to an allegation of employment discrimination in which the employer demonstrates that an employment practice that discriminates against members of a protected class is related to job performance.

**business trust** A form of business organization, created by a written trust agreement, that resembles a corporation. Legal ownership and management of the trust's property stay with the trustees, and the profits are distributed to the beneficiaries, who have limited liability.

**buyout price** The amount payable to a partner on his or her dissociation from a partnership, based on the amount distributable to that partner if the firm were wound up on that date, and offset by any damages for wrongful dissociation.

**buy-sell agreement** In the context of partnerships, an express agreement made at the time of partnership formation for one or more of the partners to buy out the other or others should the situation warrant.

**bylaws** The internal rules of management adopted by a corporation at its first organizational meeting.

## C

**cashier's check** A check drawn by a bank on itself.

**cash surrender value** The amount that the insurer has agreed to pay to the insured if a life insurance policy is canceled before the insured's death.

**categorical imperative** A concept developed by the philosopher Immanuel Kant as an ethical guideline for behavior. In deciding whether an action is right or wrong, or desirable or undesirable, a person should evaluate the action in terms of what would happen if everybody else in the same situation, or category, acted the same way.

**causation in fact** An act or omission without ("but for") which an event would not have occurred.

**cease-and-desist order** An administrative or judicial order prohibiting a person or business firm from conducting activities that an agency or court has deemed illegal.

**certificate of deposit (CD)** A note of a bank in which the bank acknowledges a receipt of money from a party and promises to repay the money, with interest, to the party on a specified date.

**certificate of limited partnership** The document that must be filed with a designated state official to form a limited partnership.

**certification mark** A mark used by one or more persons, other than the owner, to certify the region, materials, mode of manufacture, quality, or accuracy of the owner's goods or services. Examples of certification marks include the "Good Housekeeping Seal of Approval" and "UL Tested."

**certified check** A check that has been accepted by the bank on which it is drawn. Essentially, the bank, by certifying (accepting) the check, promises to pay the check at the time the check is presented.

**charging order** In partnership law, an order granted by a court to a judgment creditor that entitles the creditor to attach a partner's interest in the partnership.

**charitable trust** A trust in which the property held by the trustee must be used for a charitable purpose, such as the advancement of health, education, or religion.

**chattel** Personal property.

**check** A draft drawn by a drawer ordering the drawee bank or financial institution to pay a certain amount of money to the holder on demand.

**check** A special type of draft that is drawn on a bank, ordering the bank to pay a fixed amount of money on demand.

**choice-of-language clause** A clause in a contract designating the official language by which the contract will be interpreted in the event of a future disagreement over the contract's terms.

**choice-of-law clause** A clause in a contract designating the law (such as the law of a particular state or nation) that will govern the contract.

**clearinghouse** A system or place where banks exchange checks and drafts drawn on each other and settle daily balances.

**close corporation** A corporation whose shareholders are limited to a small group of persons, often family members.

**closed shop** A firm that requires union membership on the part of its workers as a condition of employment.

**closing argument** An argument made at a trial after the plaintiff and defendant have rested their cases. Closing arguments are made prior to the jury charges.

**codicil** A written supplement or modification to a will. A codicil must be executed with the same formalities as a will.

**coinsurance clause** A clause in an insurance contract that encourages property owners to insure their property for an amount as close to full value as possible. If the owner insures the property up to a specified percentage—usually 80 percent—of its value, she or he will recover any loss up to the face amount of the policy.

**collateral promise** A secondary promise that is ancillary (subsidiary) to a principal transaction or primary contractual relationship, such as a promise made by one person to pay the debts of another if the latter fails to perform. A collateral promise normally must be in writing to be enforceable.

**collecting bank** Any bank handling an item for collection, except the payor bank.

**collective bargaining** The process by which labor and management negotiate the terms and conditions of employment, including working hours and workplace conditions.

**collective mark** A mark used by members of a cooperative, association, or other organization to certify the region, materials, mode of manufacture, quality, or accuracy of the specific goods or services. Examples of collective marks include the labor union marks found on tags of certain products and the credits of movies, which indicate the various associations and organizations that participated in the making of the movies.

**commercial use** Use of land for business activities only; sometimes called *business use.*

**commingle** To put funds or goods together into one mass so that they are mixed to such a degree that they no longer have separate identities.

**common stock** A security that evidences ownership in a corporation. A share of common stock gives the owner a proportionate interest in the corporation with regard to control, earnings, and net assets. Common stock is lowest in priority with respect to payment of dividends and distribution of the corporation's assets on dissolution.

**community property** A form of concurrent property ownership in which each spouse owns an undivided one-half interest in property acquired during the marriage.

**comparative negligence** A theory in tort law under which the liability for injuries resulting from negligent acts is shared by all parties who were negligent (including the injured party) on the basis of each person's proportionate negligence.

**compensatory damages** A money award equivalent to the actual value of injuries or damages sustained by the aggrieved party.

**concentrated industry** An industry in which a single firm or a small number of firms control a large percentage of market sales.

**concurrent ownership** Joint ownership.

**condemnation** The judicial procedure by which the government exercises its power of eminent domain. It generally involves two phases: a taking and a determination of fair value.

**conforming goods** Goods that conform to contract specifications.

**confusion** The mixing together of goods belonging to two or more owners to such an extent that the separately owned goods cannot be identified.

**constructive delivery** A symbolic delivery of property that cannot be physically delivered.

**constructive discharge** A termination of employment brought about by making the employee's working conditions so intolerable that the employee reasonably feels compelled to leave.

**constructive eviction** A form of eviction that occurs when a landlord fails to perform adequately any of the duties required by the lease, thereby making the tenant's further use and enjoyment of the property exceedingly difficult or impossible.

**constructive fraud** Conduct that is treated as fraud under the law even when there is no proof of intent to defraud, usually because of the existence of a special relationship or fiduciary duty.

**constructive trust** An equitable trust that is imposed in the interests of fairness and justice when someone wrongfully holds legal title to property.

**consumer-debtor** One whose debts result primarily from the purchase of goods for personal, family, or household use.

**consumer law** The body of statutes, agency rules, and judicial decisions protecting consumers of goods and services from dangerous manufacturing techniques, mislabeling, unfair credit practices, deceptive advertising, and other such practices.

**continuation statement** A statement that, if filed within six months prior to the expiration date of the original financing statement, continues the perfection of the original security interest for another five years. The perfection of a security interest can be continued in the same manner indefinitely.

**contributory negligence** A theory in tort law under which a complaining party's own negligence contributed to or caused his or her injuries. Contributory negligence is an absolute bar to recovery in a minority of jurisdictions.

**conversion** The wrongful taking, using, or retaining possession of personal property that belongs to another.

**conveyance** The transfer of title to real property from one person to another by deed or other document.

**"cooling-off" laws** Laws that allow buyers of goods sold in certain transactions to cancel their contracts within three business days.

**cooperative** An association, which may or may not be incorporated, that is organized to provide an economic service to its members. Unincorporated cooperatives are often treated like partnerships for tax and other legal purposes.

**copyright** The exclusive right of authors to publish, print, or sell an intellectual production for a statutory period of time. A copyright has the same monopolistic nature as a patent or trademark, but it differs in that it applies exclusively to works of art, literature, and other works of authorship, including computer programs.

**corporate governance** A set of policies specifying the rights and responsibilities of the various participants in a corporation and spelling out the rules and procedures for making corporate decisions.

**corporate social responsibility** The concept that corporations can and should act ethically, and be accountable to society for their actions.

**cost-benefit analysis** A decision-making technique that involves weighing the costs of a given action against the benefits of the action.

**co-surety** A joint surety; one who assumes liability jointly with another surety for the payment of an obligation.

**counteradvertising** New advertising that is undertaken to correct earlier false claims that were made about a product.

**course of dealing** Prior conduct between parties to a contract that establishes a common basis for their understanding.

**course of performance** The conduct that occurs under the terms of a particular agreement. Such conduct indicates what the parties to an agreement intended it to mean.

**cover** A buyer's or lessee's purchase on the open market of goods to substitute for those promised but never delivered by the seller or lessor. Under the Uniform Commercial Code, if the cost of cover exceeds the cost of the contract goods, the buyer or lessee can recover the difference, plus incidental and consequential damages.

**cram-down provision** A provision of the Bankruptcy Code that allows a court to confirm a debtor's Chapter 11 reorganization plan even though only one class of creditors has accepted it.

**creditors' composition agreement** An agreement formed between a debtor and his or her creditors in which the creditors agree to accept a lesser sum than that owed by the debtor in full satisfaction of the debt.

**cross-collateralization** The use of an asset that is not the subject of a loan to collateralize that loan.

**crowdfunding** A cooperative activity in which people network and pool funds and other resources via the Internet to assist a cause (such as disaster relief) or invest in a business venture (such as a startup).

**cure** Under the Uniform Commercial Code, the right of a party who tenders nonconforming performance to correct his or her performance within the contract period.

## D

**damages** A monetary award sought as a remedy for a breach of contract or a tortious act.

**debtor** Under Article 9 of the Uniform Commercial Code, any party who owes payment or performance of a secured obligation, whether or not the party actually owns or has rights in the collateral.

**debtor in possession (DIP)** In Chapter 11 bankruptcy proceedings, a debtor who is allowed to continue in possession of the estate in property (the business) and to continue business operations.

**deceptive advertising** Advertising that misleads consumers, either by making unjustified claims about a product's performance or by omitting a material fact concerning the product's composition or performance.

**deed** A document by which title to real property is passed.

**defalcation** Embezzlement or misappropriation of funds.

**defamation** Any published or publicly spoken false statement that causes injury to another's good name, reputation, or character.

**default** Failure to pay a debt when it is due.

**deficiency judgment** A judgment against a debtor for the amount of a debt remaining unpaid after collateral has been repossessed and sold.

**delegatee** One to whom contract duties are delegated by another, called the delegator.

**delegation doctrine**  A doctrine based on Article I, Section 8, of the U.S. Constitution, which has been construed to allow Congress to delegate some of its power to make and implement laws to administrative agencies. The delegation is considered to be proper as long as Congress sets standards outlining the scope of the agency's authority.

**depositary bank**  The first bank to receive a check for payment.

**devise**  A gift of real property by will, or the act of giving real property by will.

**devisee**  One designated in a will to receive a gift of real property.

**digital cash**  Funds contained on computer software, in the form of secure programs stored on microchips and other computer devices.

**dilution**  With respect to trademarks, a doctrine under which distinctive or famous trademarks are protected from certain unauthorized uses of the marks regardless of a showing of competition or a likelihood of confusion. Congress created a federal cause of action for dilution in 1995 with the passage of the Federal Trademark Dilution Act.

**discharge**  (1) The termination of an obligation, such as occurs when the parties to a contract have fully performed their contractual obligations. (2) The termination of a bankruptcy debtor's obligation to pay debts.

**disclosed principal**  A principal whose identity is known to a third party at the time the agent makes a contract with the third party.

**dishonor**  To refuse to accept or pay a draft or a promissory note when it is properly presented. An instrument is dishonored when presentment is properly made and acceptance or payment is refused or cannot be obtained within the prescribed time.

**disparagement of property**  An economically injurious false statement made about another's product or property. A general term for torts that are more specifically referred to as *slander of quality* or *slander of title*.

**disparate-impact discrimination**  Discrimination that results from certain employer practices or procedures that, although not discriminatory on their face, have a discriminatory effect.

**disparate-treatment discrimination**  A form of employment discrimination that results when an employer intentionally discriminates against employees who are members of protected classes.

**dissociation**  The severance of the relationship between a partner and a partnership.

**dissolution**  The formal disbanding of a partnership, corporation, or other business entity. For instance, partnerships can be dissolved by acts of the partners, by operation of law, or by judicial decree.

**divestiture**  A company's sale of one or more of its divisions' operating functions under court order as part of the enforcement of the antitrust laws.

**dividend**  A distribution of corporate profits to the corporation's shareholders in proportion to the number of shares held.

**document of title**  A writing exchanged in the regular course of business that evidences the right to possession of goods (for example, a bill of lading or a warehouse receipt).

**domestic corporation**  In a given state, a corporation that is organized under the law of that state.

**dominion**  Ownership rights in property, including the right to possess and control the property.

**down payment**  The part of the purchase price of real property that is paid in cash up front, reducing the amount of the loan or mortgage.

**draft**  Any instrument (such as a check) drawn on a drawee (such as a bank) that orders the drawee to pay a certain sum of money, usually to a third party (the payee), on demand or at a definite future time.

**dram shop act**  A state statute that imposes liability on the owners of bars and taverns, as well as those who serve alcoholic drinks to the public, for injuries resulting from accidents caused by intoxicated persons when the sellers or servers of alcoholic drinks contributed to the intoxication.

**drawee**  The party that is ordered to pay a draft or check. With a check, a financial institution is always the drawee.

**drawer**  The party that initiates a draft (writes a check, for example), thereby ordering the drawee to pay.

**due diligence**  A required standard of care that certain professionals, such as accountants, must meet to avoid liability for securities violations.

**durable power of attorney**  A document that authorizes a person to act on behalf of another person—write checks, collect insurance proceeds, and otherwise manage the disabled person's affairs, including health care—when that person becomes incapacitated.

**duty-based ethics**  An ethical philosophy rooted in the idea that every person has certain duties to others, including both humans and the planet. Those duties may be derived from religious principles or from other philosophical reasoning.

**duty of care**  The duty of all persons, as established by tort law, to exercise a reasonable amount of care in their dealings with others. Failure to exercise due care, which is normally determined by the "reasonable person standard," constitutes the tort of negligence.

## E

**e-agent**  A semiautonomous computer program that is capable of executing specific tasks.

**easement**  A nonpossessory right, established by express or implied agreement, to make limited use of another's property without removing anything from the property.

**electronic fund transfer (EFT)**  A transfer of funds through the use of an electronic terminal, a telephone, a computer, or magnetic tape.

**eminent domain**  The power of a government to take land from private citizens for public use on the payment of just compensation.

**e-money**  Prepaid funds recorded on a computer or a card (such as a *smart card*).

**employment at will**  A common law doctrine under which either party may terminate an employment relationship at any time for any reason, unless a contract specifies otherwise.

**employment discrimination**  Unequal treatment of employees or job applicants on the basis of race, color, national origin, religion, gender, age, or disability; prohibited by federal statutes.

**enabling legislation**  A statute enacted by Congress that authorizes the creation of an administrative agency and specifies the name, composition, purpose, and powers of the agency being created.

**endowment insurance**  A type of life insurance in which the policyholder pays fixed premiums for a definite term, after which a fixed amount is paid to the policyholder or, if the policyholder has died, to a beneficiary.

**entrepreneur**  One who initiates and assumes the financial risk of a new business enterprise and undertakes to provide or control its management.

**environmental impact statement (EIS)**  A formal analysis required for any major federal action that will significantly affect the quality of the environment to determine the action's impact and explore alternatives.

**equal dignity rule**  A rule requiring that an agent's authority be in writing if the contract to be made on behalf of the principal must be in writing.

**equitable right of redemption**  The right of a defaulting borrower to redeem property before a foreclosure sale by paying the full amount of the debt, plus any interest and costs that have accrued.

**escheat**  The transfer of property to the state when the owner of the property dies without heirs.

**escrow account**  An account generally held in the name of the depositor and escrow agent. The funds in the account are paid to a third person on fulfillment of the escrow condition.

**estate planning**  Planning in advance how one's property and obligations should be transferred on one's death. Wills and trusts are two basic devices used in estate planning.

**estray statute**  A statute defining finders' rights in property when the true owners are unknown.

**ethical reasoning**  A reasoning process in which an individual links his or her moral convictions or ethical standards to the particular situation at hand.

**ethics**  Moral principles and values applied to social behavior.

**eviction**  A landlord's act of depriving a tenant of possession of the leased premises.

**exclusive agency**  An agency in which a principal grants an agent an exclusive territory and does not allow another agent to compete in that territory.

**exclusive-dealing contract**  An agreement under which a seller forbids a buyer to purchase products from the seller's competitors.

**execution**  An action to carry into effect the directions in a court decree or judgment.

**executor**  A person appointed by a testator in a will to administer the testator's estate.

**exhaustion doctrine**  In administrative law, the principle that a complaining party normally must have exhausted all available administrative remedies before seeking judicial review.

**express authority**  Authority expressly given by one party to another. In agency law, an agent has express authority to act for a principal if both parties agree, orally or in writing, that an agency relationship exists in which the agent has the power (authority) to act in the place of, and on behalf of, the principal.

**extension clause**  A clause in a time instrument that allows the instrument's date of maturity to be extended into the future.

**F**

**family limited liability partnership (FLLP)**  A limited liability partnership (LLP) in which the majority of the partners are members of a family.

**Federal Reserve System**  A network of twelve central banks, located throughout the United States and headed by the Federal Reserve Board of Governors. Most banks in the United States have Federal Reserve accounts.

**fee simple absolute**  An ownership interest in land in which the owner has the greatest possible aggregation of rights, privileges, and power. The owner can use, possess, or dispose of the property as he or she chooses during his or her lifetime. On death, the interest in the property passes to the owner's heirs.

**fictitious payee**  A payee on a negotiable instrument whom the maker or drawer does not intend to have an interest in the instrument. Indorsements by fictitious payees are not treated as unauthorized under Article 3 of the Uniform Commercial Code.

**fiduciary**  As a noun, a person having a duty created by his or her undertaking to act primarily for another's benefit in matters connected with the undertaking; as an adjective, a relationship founded on trust and confidence.

**final order**  The final decision of an administrative agency on an issue. If no appeal is taken, or if the case is not reviewed or considered anew by the agency commission, the administrative law judge's initial order becomes the final order of the agency.

**financing statement**  A document prepared by a secured creditor and filed with the appropriate government official to give notice to the public that the creditor claims an interest in collateral belonging to the debtor named in the statement. The financing statement must contain the names and addresses of both the debtor and the creditor, and describe the collateral by type or item.

**firm offer**  An offer (by a merchant) that is irrevocable without consideration for a period of time (not longer than three months). A firm offer by a merchant must be in writing and must be signed by the offeror.

**fixed-term tenancy**  A type of tenancy under which property is leased for a specified period of time, such as a month, a year, or a period of years; also called a *tenancy for years.*

**fixture**  An item of personal property that has become so closely associated with real property that it is legally regarded as part of that real property.

**floating lien**  A security interest in proceeds, after-acquired property, or property purchased under a line of credit (or all three); a security interest in collateral that is retained even when the collateral changes in character, classification, or location.

**forbearance**  The act of refraining from exercising a legal right; an agreement between a lender and a borrower in which the lender agrees to temporarily cease requiring mortgage payments, to delay foreclosure, or to accept smaller payments than previously scheduled.

***force majeure*** (pronounced mah-*zhure*) **clause**  A provision in a contract stipulating that certain unforeseen events—such as war, political upheavals, acts of God, and the like—will excuse a party from liability for nonperformance of contractual obligations.

**foreclosure** A proceeding in which a mortgagee either takes title to or forces the sale of the mortgagor's property in satisfaction of a debt.

**foreign corporation** In a given state, a corporation that does business in that state but is not incorporated there.

**forum-selection clause** A provision in a contract designating the court, jurisdiction, or tribunal that will decide any disputes arising under the contract.

**franchise** Any arrangement in which the owner of a trademark, trade name, or copyright licenses another to use that trademark, trade name, or copyright in the selling of goods or services.

**franchisee** One receiving a license to use another's (the franchisor's) trademark, trade name, or copyright in the sale of goods and services.

**franchisor** One licensing another (the franchisee) to use the owner's trademark, trade name, or copyright in the selling of goods or services.

**fraudulent misrepresentation (fraud)** Any misrepresentation, either by misstatement or omission of a material fact, knowingly made with the intention of deceiving another and on which a reasonable person would and does rely to his or her detriment.

**free-writing prospectus** A written, electronic, or graphic communication associated with the offer to sell a security and used during the waiting period to supplement other information about the security.

**fully integrated contract** A contract that completely sets forth all the terms and conditions agreed to by the parties and is intended as a final statement of their agreement.

## G

**garnishment** A legal process used by a creditor to collect a debt by seizing property of the debtor (such as wages) that is being held by a third party (such as the debtor's employer).

**general damages** In a tort case, an amount awarded to compensate individuals for the nonmonetary aspects of the harm suffered, such as pain and suffering; not available to companies.

**generally accepted accounting principles (GAAP)** The conventions, rules, and procedures developed by the Financial Accounting Standards Board to define accepted accounting practices at a particular time.

**generally accepted auditing standards (GAAS)** Standards established by the American Institute of Certified Public Accountants to define the professional qualities and judgment that should be exercised by an auditor in performing an audit.

**general partner** In a limited partnership, a partner who assumes responsibility for the management of the partnership and has full liability for all partnership debts.

**gift** A voluntary transfer of property made without consideration, past or present.

**gift *causa mortis*** A gift made in contemplation of imminent death. The gift is revoked if the donor does not die as contemplated.

**gift *inter vivos*** A gift made during one's lifetime and not in contemplation of imminent death, in contrast to a gift *causa mortis*.

**Good Samaritan statute** A state statute that provides that persons who rescue or provide emergency services to others in peril—unless they do so recklessly, thus causing further harm—cannot be sued for negligence.

**goodwill** In the business context, the valuable reputation of a business viewed as an intangible asset.

**grant deed** A deed that simply states that property is being conveyed from the grantor to another. Under statute, a grant deed may impliedly warrant that the grantor has at least not conveyed the property's title to someone else.

**group boycott** An agreement by two or more sellers to refuse to deal with a particular person or firm.

**guarantor** A person who agrees to satisfy the debt of another (the debtor) only after the principal debtor defaults. A guarantor's liability is thus secondary.

## H

**health-care power of attorney** A document that designates a person who will have the power to choose what type of and how much medical treatment a person who is unable to make such a choice will receive.

**holder** Any person in the possession of an instrument drawn, issued, or indorsed to him or her, to his or her order, to bearer, or in blank.

**holder in due course (HDC)** A holder who acquires a negotiable instrument for value; in good faith; and without notice that the instrument is overdue, that it has been dishonored, that any person has a defense against it or a claim to it, or that the instrument contains unauthorized signatures, alterations, or is so irregular or incomplete as to call into question its authenticity.

**holding company** A company whose business activity is holding shares in another company.

**holographic will** A will written entirely in the testator's handwriting.

**homeowner's insurance** A form of property insurance that protects the home of the insured person and its contents against losses.

**homestead exemption** A law permitting a debtor to retain the family home, either in its entirety or up to a specified dollar amount, free from the claims of unsecured creditors or trustees in bankruptcy.

**horizontal merger** A merger between two firms that are competing in the same market.

**horizontal restraint** Any agreement that restrains competition between rival firms competing in the same market.

**hot-cargo agreement** An illegal agreement in which employers voluntarily agree with unions not to handle, use, or deal in the non-union-produced goods of other employers.

## I

**I-9 verification** The process of verifying the employment eligibility and identity of a new immigrant worker. It must be completed within three days after the worker commences employment.

**I-551 Alien Registration Receipt** A document known as a "green card" that shows that a foreign-born individual can legally work in the United States.

**implication** A way of creating an easement or profit in real property when it is reasonable to imply its existence from the circumstances surrounding the division of the property.

**implied authority** Authority that is created not by an explicit oral or written agreement but by implication. In agency law, implied authority (of the agent) can be conferred by custom, inferred from the position the agent occupies, or implied by virtue of being reasonably necessary to carry out express authority.

**implied warranty of habitability** An implied promise by a seller of a new house that the house is fit for human habitation. Also, the implied promise by a landlord that rented residential premises are habitable.

**imposter** One who, by use of the mail, telephone, or personal appearance, induces a maker or drawer to issue an instrument in the name of an impersonated payee. Indorsements by imposters are not treated as unauthorized under Article 3 of the Uniform Commercial Code.

**incontestability clause** A clause in a policy for life or health insurance stating that after the policy has been in force for a specified length of time (usually two or three years), the insurer cannot contest statements made in the policyholder's application.

**independent contractor** One who works for, and receives payment from, an employer but whose working conditions and methods are not controlled by the employer. An independent contractor is not an employee but may be an agent.

**indorsee** A person to whom a negotiable instrument is transferred by indorsement.

**indorsement** A signature placed on an instrument for the purpose of transferring ownership rights in the instrument.

**indorser** A person who transfers an instrument by signing (indorsing) it and delivering it to another person.

**industrial use** Land use for light or heavy manufacturing, shipping, or heavy transportation.

**information return** A tax return submitted by a partnership that reports the business's income and losses. The partnership itself does not pay taxes on the income, but each partner's share of the profit (whether distributed or not) is taxed as individual income to that partner.

**initial order** In the context of administrative law, an agency's disposition in a matter other than a rulemaking. An administrative law judge's initial order becomes final unless it is appealed.

**inside director** A person on a corporation's board of directors who is also an officer of the corporation.

**insider** (1) A corporate director or officer, or other employee or agent, with access to confidential information and a duty not to disclose that information in violation of insider-trading laws. (2) In bankruptcy proceedings, an individual, partner, partnership, corporation, or officer or director of a corporation (or a relative of one of these) who has a close relationship with the debtor.

**insider trading** The purchase or sale of securities on the basis of information that has not been made available to the public.

**installment contract** Under the Uniform Commercial Code, a contract that requires or authorizes delivery in two or more separate lots to be accepted and paid for separately.

**insurable interest** (1) A property interest in goods being sold or leased that is sufficiently substantial to permit a party to insure against damage to the goods. (2) An interest either in a person's life or well-being that is sufficiently substantial that insuring against injury to (or the death of) the person does not amount to a mere wagering (betting) contract.

**insurance** A contract by which the insurer promises to reimburse the insured or a beneficiary in the event that the insured is injured, dies, or sustains damage to property as a result of particular, stated contingencies.

**intangible property** Property that is incapable of being apprehended by the senses (such as by sight or touch). Intellectual property is an example of intangible property.

**intellectual property** Property resulting from intellectual, creative processes. Patents, trademarks, and copyrights are examples of intellectual property.

**intentional tort** A wrongful act knowingly committed.

**intermediary bank** Any bank to which an item is transferred in the course of collection, except the depositary or payor bank.

**International Financial Reporting Standards (IFRS)** A set of global accounting standards that are being phased in by companies in the United States.

**interpretive rule** A nonbinding rule or policy statement issued by an administrative agency that explains how it interprets and intends to apply the statutes it enforces.

**intestacy laws** State statutes that specify how property will be distributed when a person dies intestate (without a valid will).

**intestate** As a noun, one who has died without having created a valid will. As an adjective, the state of having died without a will.

**inverse condemnation** The taking of private property by the government without payment of just compensation as required by the U.S. Constitution. The owner must sue the government to recover just compensation.

**investment company** A company that acts on the behalf of many smaller shareholders-owners by buying a large portfolio of securities and professionally managing that portfolio.

**investment contract** In securities law, a transaction in which a person invests in a common enterprise reasonably expecting profits that are derived primarily from the efforts of others.

**issue** In negotiable instruments law, the first transfer, or delivery, of an instrument to a holder.

## J

**joint and several liability** In partnership law, a doctrine under which a plaintiff may sue, and collect a judgment from, all of the partners together (jointly) or one or more of the partners separately (severally, or individually). A partner can be held liable even if she or he did not participate in, ratify, or know about the conduct that gave rise to the lawsuit.

**joint liability** In partnership law, the partners' shared liability for partnership obligations and debts. A third party must sue all of the partners as a group, but each partner can be held liable for the full amount.

**joint stock company** A hybrid form of business organization that combines characteristics of a corporation and a partnership.

Usually, a joint stock company is regarded as a partnership for tax and other legal purposes.

**joint tenancy** Joint ownership of property by two or more co-owners in which each co-owner owns an undivided portion of the property. On the death of one of the joint tenants, his or her interest automatically passes to the surviving joint tenant(s).

**joint venture** A joint undertaking by two or more persons or business entities to combine their efforts or their property for a single transaction or project, or for a related series of transactions or projects. A joint venture is generally treated like a partnership for tax and other legal purposes.

**junior lienholder** A person or business that holds a lien that is subordinate to one or more other liens on the same property.

# L

**lease** Under Article 2A of the UCC, a transfer of the right to possess and use goods for a period of time in exchange for payment. In the context of real property, an agreement by which a property owner (landlord) agrees to give another party (the tenant) the exclusive right to possess the property for a limited time.

**lease agreement** In regard to the lease of goods, an agreement in which one person (the lessor) agrees to transfer the right to the possession and use of property to another person (the lessee) in exchange for rental payments.

**leasehold estate** An interest in real property that gives a tenant a qualified right to possess and/or use the property for a limited time under a lease.

**legacy** A gift of personal property under a will.

**legatee** One designated in a will to receive a gift of personal property.

**legislative rule** An administrative agency rule that carries the same weight as a congressionally enacted statute.

**lessee** A person who pays for the use or possession of another's property.

**lessor** A property owner who allows others to use his or her property in exchange for the payment of rent.

**letter of credit** A written instrument, usually issued by a bank on behalf of a customer or other party, in which the issuer promises to honor drafts or other demands for payment by third parties in accordance with the terms of the instrument.

**levy** The obtaining of money by legal process through the seizure and sale of property, usually done after a writ of execution has been issued.

**libel** Defamation in writing or in some other form (such as in a digital recording) having the quality of permanence.

**license** In the context of intellectual property, a contract permitting the use of a trademark, copyright, patent, or trade secret of certain purposes. In the context of real property, a revocable right or privilege of a person to come on another person's land.

**licensee** One who receives a license to use, or enter onto, another's property.

**lien** (pronounced *leen*) A claim against specific property to satisfy a debt.

**life estate** An interest in land that exists only for the duration of the life of a specified individual, usually the holder of the estate.

**limited liability company (LLC)** A hybrid form of business enterprise that offers the limited liability of a corporation and the tax advantages of a partnership.

**limited liability limited partnership (LLLP)** A type of limited partnership in which the liability of the general partner is the same as the liability of the limited partners—that is, the liability of all partners is limited to the amount of their investments in the firm.

**limited liability partnership (LLP)** A hybrid form of business organization that is used mainly by professionals who normally do business in a partnership. An LLP is a pass-through entity for tax purposes, but a partner's personal liability for the malpractice of other partners is limited.

**limited partner** In a limited partnership, a partner who contributes capital to the partnership but has no right to participate in its management and has no liability for partnership debts beyond the amount of her or his investment.

**limited partnership (LP)** A partnership consisting of one or more general partners and one or more limited partners.

**limited-payment life** A type of life insurance for which premiums are payable for a definite period, after which the policy is fully paid.

**liquidation** The sale of the nonexempt assets of a debtor and the distribution of the funds received to creditors.

**living trust** A trust created by the grantor (settlor) and effective during his or her lifetime.

**living will** A document that allows a person to control the methods of medical treatment that may be used after a serious accident or illness.

**lockout** An action in which an employer shuts down to prevent employees from working, typically because it cannot reach a collective bargaining agreement with the employees' union.

**lost property** Property that the owner has involuntarily parted with and then cannot find or recover.

# M

**maker** One who promises to pay a certain sum to the holder of a promissory note or certificate of deposit (CD).

**malpractice** Professional misconduct or the failure to exercise the requisite degree of skill as a professional. Negligence—the failure to exercise due care—on the part of a professional, such as a physician or an attorney, is commonly referred to as malpractice.

**marketable title** Title to real estate that is reasonably free from encumbrances, defects in the chain of title, and other matters that affect title, such as adverse possession.

**market concentration** The degree to which a small number of firms control a large percentage of a relevant market.

**market power** The power of a firm to control the market price of its product. A monopoly has the greatest degree of market power.

**mechanic's lien** A statutory lien on the real property of another, created to ensure payment for work performed and materials furnished in the repair or improvement of real property, such as a building.

**member** A person who has an ownership interest in a limited liability company.

**merchant** A person who is engaged in the purchase and sale of goods. Under the Uniform Commercial Code, a person who deals in goods of the kind involved in the sales contract; for further definitions, see UCC 2–104.

**metes and bounds** A way of describing the boundary lines of land according to the distance between two points, often using physical features of the local geography.

**minimum wage** The lowest wage, either by government regulation or by union contract, that an employer may pay an hourly worker.

**mislaid property** Property that the owner has voluntarily parted with and then has inadvertently forgotten.

**monopolization** The possession of monopoly power in the relevant market and the willful acquisition or maintenance of that power, as distinguished from growth or development as a consequence of a superior product, business acumen, or historic accident.

**monopoly** A market in which there is a single seller or a very limited number of sellers.

**monopoly power** The ability of a monopoly to dictate what takes place in a given market.

**moral minimum** The minimum degree of ethical behavior expected of a business firm, which is usually defined as compliance with the law.

**mortgage** A written instrument that gives a creditor (the mortgagee) an interest in, or lien on, the debtor's (mortgagor's) real property as security for a debt. If the debt is not paid, the property can be sold by the creditor and the proceeds used to pay the debt.

**mortgage insurance** Insurance that compensates a lender for losses due to a borrower's default on a mortgage loan.

**multiple product order** An order requiring a firm that has engaged in deceptive advertising to cease and desist from false advertising in regard to all the firm's products.

**mutual fund** A specific type of investment company that continually buys or sells to investors shares of ownership in a portfolio.

## N

**necessity** In criminal law, a defense against liability. Under Section 3.02 of the Model Penal Code, this defense is justifiable if "the harm or evil sought to be avoided" by a given action "is greater than that sought to be prevented by the law defining the offense charged." In real property law, a way of creating an easement when one party must have the easement in order to have access to his or her property.

**negligence** The failure to exercise the standard of care that a reasonable person would exercise in similar circumstances.

**negotiable instrument** A signed writing that contains an unconditional promise or order to pay an exact sum of money, on demand or at an exact future time, to a specific person or order, or to bearer.

**negotiation** In regard to dispute settlement, a process in which parties attempt to settle their dispute without going to court, with or without attorneys to represent them. In regard to negotiable instruments, the transfer of an instrument in such a way that the transferee (the person to whom the instrument is transferred) becomes a holder.

**nonpossessory interest** In the context of real property, an interest that involves the right to use land but not the right to possess it.

**notary public** A public official authorized to attest to the authenticity of signatures.

**notice-and-comment rulemaking** An administrative rulemaking procedure that involves the publication of a notice of a proposed rulemaking in the *Federal Register,* a comment period for interested parties to express their views on the proposed rule, and the publication of the agency's final rule in the *Federal Register.*

**nuisance** A common law doctrine under which persons may be held liable for using their property in a manner that unreasonably interferes with others' rights to use or enjoy their own property.

**nuncupative will** An oral will (often called a *deathbed will*) made before witnesses. Usually, such wills are limited to transfers of personal property.

## O

**omnibus clause** A provision in an automobile insurance policy that protects the vehicle owner who has taken out the policy and anyone who drives the vehicle with the owner's permission.

**operating agreement** An agreement in which the members of a limited liability company set forth the details of how the business will be managed and operated.

**order for relief** A court's grant of assistance to a complainant. In bankruptcy proceedings, the order relieves the debtor of the immediate obligation to pay the debts listed in the bankruptcy petition.

**order instrument** A negotiable instrument that is payable "to the order of an identified person" or "to an identified person or order."

**outcome-based ethics** An ethical philosophy that focuses on the impacts of a decision on society or on key stakeholders.

**output contract** An agreement in which a seller agrees to sell and a buyer agrees to buy all or up to a stated amount of what the seller produces.

**outside director** A person on a corporation's board of directors who does not hold a management position at the corporation.

**overdraft** A check written on a checking account in which there are insufficient funds to cover the amount of the check.

## P

**partially disclosed principal** A principal whose identity is unknown by a third party, but the third party knows that the agent is or may be acting for a principal at the time the agent and the third party form a contract.

**partnership** An agreement by two or more persons to carry on, as co-owners, a business for profit.

**partnership by estoppel** A partnership imposed by a court when nonpartners have held themselves out to be partners, or have allowed themselves to be held out as partners, and others have detrimentally relied on their misrepresentations.

**pass-through entity** A business entity that has no tax liability. The entity's income is passed through to the owners, and they pay taxes on the income.

**patent** A government grant that gives an inventor the exclusive right or privilege to make, use, or sell his or her invention for a limited time period.

**payee** A person to whom an instrument is made payable.

**payor bank** The bank on which a check is drawn (the drawee bank).

*per capita* A method of distributing an intestate's estate so that each heir in a certain class (such as grandchildren) receives an equal share.

**perfection** The legal process by which secured parties protect themselves against the claims of third parties who may wish to have their debts satisfied out of the same collateral; usually accomplished by the filing of a financing statement with the appropriate government official.

**perfect tender rule** A common law rule under which a seller was required to deliver to the buyer goods that conformed perfectly to the requirements stipulated in the sales contract. A tender of nonconforming goods would automatically constitute a breach of contract. Under the Uniform Commercial Code, the rule has been greatly modified.

**periodic tenancy** A lease interest in land for an indefinite period involving payment of rent at fixed intervals, such as week to week, month to month, or year to year.

*per se* **violation** A restraint of trade that is so anticompetitive that it is deemed inherently *(per se)* illegal.

**personal defense** A defense that can be used to avoid payment to an ordinary holder of a negotiable instrument but not a holder in due course (HDC) or a holder with the rights of an HDC. Personal defenses are also called *limited defenses.*

**personal property** Property that is movable; any property that is not real property.

*per stirpes* A method of distributing an intestate's estate so that each heir in a certain class (such as grandchildren) takes the share to which her or his deceased ancestor (such as a mother or father) would have been entitled.

**petition in bankruptcy** The document that is filed with a bankruptcy court to initiate bankruptcy proceedings.

**piercing the corporate veil** The action of a court to disregard the corporate entity and hold the shareholders personally liable for corporate debts and obligations.

**policy** In insurance law, the contract between the insurer and the insured.

**potentially responsible party (PRP)** A party liable for the costs of cleaning up a hazardous waste disposal site under the Comprehensive Environmental Response, Compensation, and Liability Act.

**power of attorney** Authorization for another to act as one's agent or attorney either in specified circumstances (special) or in all situations (general).

**precedent** A court decision that furnishes an example or authority for deciding subsequent cases involving identical or similar facts.

**predatory pricing** The pricing of a product below cost with the intent to drive competitors out of the market.

**predominant-factor test** A test courts use to determine whether a contract is primarily for the sale of goods or for the sale of services.

**preemptive rights** The right of a shareholder in a corporation to have the first opportunity to purchase a new issue of that corporation's stock in proportion to the amount of stock already owned by the shareholder.

**preference** In bankruptcy proceedings, a property transfer or payment made by the debtor that favors one creditor over others.

**preferred creditor** In the context of bankruptcy, a creditor who has received a preferential transfer from a debtor.

**preferred stock** A security that entitles the holder to payment of fixed dividends and that has priority over common stock in the distribution of assets on the corporation's dissolution.

**premium** In insurance law, the price paid by the insured for insurance protection for a specified period of time.

**prenuptial agreement** An agreement made before marriage that defines each partner's ownership rights in the other partner's property. Prenuptial agreements must be in writing to be enforceable.

**prepayment penalty clause** A provision in a mortgage loan contract that requires the borrower to pay a penalty if the mortgage is repaid in full within a certain period.

**prescription** A way of creating an easement or profit in real property by openly using the property, without the owner's consent, for the required period of time (similar to adverse possession).

**presentment** The act of presenting an instrument to the party liable on the instrument to collect payment; the act of presenting an instrument to a drawee for acceptance.

**presentment warranty** Implied warranty made by any person who presents an instrument for payment or acceptance that (1) he or she is entitled to enforce the instrument or authorized to obtain payment or acceptance on behalf of a person who is entitled, (2) the instrument has not been altered, and (3) he or she has no knowledge that the signature of the drawer is unauthorized.

**price discrimination** A seller's act of charging competing buyers different prices for identical products or services.

**price-fixing agreement** An agreement between competitors to fix the prices of products or services at a certain level.

*prima facie* **case** A case in which the plaintiff has produced sufficient evidence of his or her claim that the case will be decided for the plaintiff unless the defendant produces evidence to rebut it.

**principal** In agency law, a person who agrees to have another, called the agent, act on his or her behalf.

**principle of rights** The principle that human beings have certain fundamental rights (to life, freedom, and the pursuit of happiness, for example). A key factor in determining whether a business decision is ethical under this theory is how that decision affects the rights of others, such as employees, consumers, suppliers, and the community.

**private equity** Capital funds invested by a private equity firm in an existing corporation, usually to purchase and reorganize it.

**privilege** In tort law, the ability to act contrary to another person's right without that person's having legal redress for such acts. Privilege may be raised as a defense to defamation.

**probate** The process of proving and validating a will, and settling all matters pertaining to an estate.

**proceeds** Under Article 9 of the Uniform Commercial Code, whatever is received when collateral is sold or otherwise disposed of.

**profit** In the context of real property, the right to enter onto another's property and remove something of value from that property.

**promissory note** A written promise made by one person (the maker) to pay a fixed sum of money to another person (the payee or a subsequent holder) on demand or on a specified date.

**property** Legally protected rights and interests in anything with an ascertainable value that is subject to ownership.

**prospectus** A written document required by securities laws when a security is being sold. The prospectus describes the security, the financial operations of the issuing corporation, and the risk attaching to the security.

**protected class** A group of persons protected by specific laws because of the group's defining characteristics, including race, color, religion, national origin, gender, age, and disability.

**proximate cause** Legal cause; exists when the connection between an act and an injury is strong enough to justify imposing liability.

**proxy** Authorization to represent a corporate shareholder to serve as his or her agent and vote his or her shares in a certain manner.

**public corporation** A corporation owned by a federal, state, or municipal government—not to be confused with a publicly held corporation.

**public figure** An individual in the public limelight. Public figures include government officials and politicians, movie stars, well-known businesspersons, and generally anybody who becomes known to the public because of his or her position or activities.

**publicly held corporation** A corporation whose shares are publicly traded in securities markets, such as the New York Stock Exchange or the NASDAQ.

**puffery** A salesperson's exaggerated claims concerning the quality of goods offered for sale. Such claims involve opinions rather than facts and are not considered to be legally binding promises or warranties.

**punitive damages** Money damages that may be awarded to a plaintiff to punish the defendant and deter future similar conduct.

**purchase-money security interest (PMSI)** A security interest that arises when a seller or lender extends credit for part or all of the purchase price of goods purchased by a buyer.

**qualified indorsement** An indorsement on a negotiable instrument in which the indorser disclaims any contract liability on the instrument; the notation "without recourse" is commonly used to create a qualified indorsement.

# Q

**quitclaim deed** A deed that conveys only whatever interest the grantor had in the property and therefore offers the least amount of protection against defects of title.

**quorum** The number of members of a decision-making body that must be present before business may be transacted.

# R

**ratification** The act of accepting and giving legal force to an obligation that previously was not enforceable. reaffirmation agreement An agreement between a debtor and a creditor in which the debtor voluntarily agrees to pay a debt dischargeable in bankruptcy.

**real property** Land and everything attached to it, such as trees and buildings.

**reasonable person standard** The standard of behavior expected of a hypothetical "reasonable person." The standard against which negligence is measured and that must be observed to avoid liability for negligence.

**recording statute** A statute that allow deeds, mortgages, and other real property transactions to be recorded so as to provide notice to future purchasers or creditors of an existing claim on the property.

**Regulation E** A set of rules issued by the Federal Reserve System's Board of Governors under the authority of the Electronic Fund Transfer Act to protect users of electronic fund transfer systems.

**Regulation Z** A set of rules issued by the Federal Reserve Board of Governors to implement the provisions of the Truth-in-Lending Act.

**replevin** (pronounced rih-*pleh*-vin) An action to recover specific goods in the hands of a party who is wrongfully withholding them from the other party.

**requirements contract** An agreement in which a buyer agrees to purchase and the seller agrees to sell all or up to a stated amount of what the buyer needs or requires.

**resale price maintenance agreement** An agreement between a manufacturer and a retailer in which the manufacturer specifies what the retail prices of its products must be.

**residential use** Use of land for construction of buildings for human habitation only.

*respondeat superior* A doctrine under which a principal-employer is liable for any harm caused to a third party by an agent-employee in the course or scope of employment.

**restraint of trade** Any contract or combination that tends to eliminate or reduce competition, effect a monopoly, artificially maintain prices, or otherwise hamper the course of trade and commerce as it would be carried on if left to the control of natural economic forces.

**restrictive covenant** A private restriction on the use of land. If its benefit or obligation passes with the land's ownership, it is said to "run with the land."

**restrictive indorsement** Any indorsement on a negotiable instrument that requires the indorsee to comply with certain instructions regarding the funds involved. A restrictive indorsement does not prohibit the further negotiation of the instrument.

**resulting trust** An implied trust that arises when one party holds the legal title to another's property only for that other's benefit.

**retained earnings** The portion of a corporation's profits that has not been paid out as dividends to shareholders.

**right of contribution** The right of a co-surety who pays more than his or her proportionate share on a debtor's default to recover the excess paid from other co-sureties.

**right of reimbursement** The legal right of a person to be restored, repaid, or indemnified for costs, expenses, or losses incurred or expended on behalf of another.

**right of subrogation** The right of a person to stand in the place of (be substituted for) another, giving the substituted party the same legal rights that the original party had.

**right-to-work law** A state law providing that employees may not be required to join a union as a condition of retaining employment.

**risk** A prediction concerning potential loss based on known and unknown factors.

**risk management** In the context of insurance, the transfer of certain risks from the insured to the insurance company by contractual agreement.

**rulemaking** The process by which an administrative agency formally adopts a new regulation or amends an old one.

**rule of reason** A test used to determine whether an anticompetitive agreement constitutes a reasonable restraint on trade. Courts consider such factors as the purpose of the agreement, its effect on competition, and whether less restrictive means could have been used.

## S

**S corporation** A close business corporation that has most of the attributes of a corporation, including limited liability, but qualifies under the Internal Revenue Code to be taxed as a partnership.

**sales contract** A contract for the sale of goods under which the ownership of goods is transferred from a seller to a buyer for a price.

**seasonably** Within a specified time period. If no period is specified, within a reasonable time.

**secondary boycott** A union's refusal to work for, purchase from, or handle the products of a secondary employer, with whom the union has no dispute, for the purpose of forcing that employer to stop doing business with the primary employer, with whom the union has a labor dispute.

**SEC Rule 10b-5** A rule of the Securities and Exchange Commission that prohibits the commission of fraud in connection with the purchase or sale of any security.

**secured party** A lender, seller, or any other person in whose favor there is a security interest, including a person to whom accounts or chattel paper has been sold.

**secured transaction** Any transaction in which the payment of a debt is guaranteed, or secured, by personal property owned by the debtor or in which the debtor has a legal interest.

**securities** Generally, stocks, bonds, or other items that represent an ownership interest in a corporation or a promise of repayment of debt by a corporation.

**security agreement** An agreement that creates or provides for a security interest between the debtor and a secured party.

**security interest** Any interest "in personal property or fixtures which secures payment or performance of an obligation" [UCC 1–201(37)].

**seniority system** A system in which those who have worked longest for an employer are first in line for promotions, salary increases, and other benefits, and are last to be laid off if the workforce must be reduced.

**service mark** A mark used in the sale or the advertising of services, such as to distinguish the services of one person from the services of others. Titles, character names, and other distinctive features of radio and television programs may be registered as service marks.

**sexual harassment** The demanding of sexual favors in return for job promotions or other benefits, or language or conduct that is so sexually offensive that it creates a hostile working environment.

**shareholder agreement** An agreement between shareholders that restricts the transferability of shares, often entered into for the purpose of maintaining proportionate control of a close corporation.

**shareholder's derivative suit** A suit brought by a shareholder to enforce a corporate cause of action against a third person.

**shelter principle** The principle that the holder of a negotiable instrument who cannot qualify as a holder in due course (HDC), but who derives his or her title through an HDC, acquires the rights of an HDC.

**short sale** A sale of real property for an amount that is less than the balance owed on the mortgage loan, usually due to financial hardship.

**short-swing profits** Profits earned by a purchase and sale, or sale and purchase, of the same security within a six-month period.

**signature** Under the Uniform Commercial Code, "any symbol executed or adopted by a party with a present intention to authenticate a writing."

**slander** Defamation in oral form.

**slander of quality** The publication of false information about another's product, alleging that it is not what its seller claims.

**slander of title** The publication of a statement that denies or casts doubt on another's legal ownership of any property causing financial loss to that property's owner; also called *trade libel.*

**smart card** Prepaid funds recorded on a microprocessor chip embedded on a card; one type of *e-money.*

**sole proprietorship** The simplest form of business organization, in which the owner is the business. The owner reports business income on his or her personal income tax return and is legally responsible for all debts and obligations incurred by the business.

**special damages** In a tort case, an amount awarded to compensate the plaintiff for quantifiable monetary losses, such as medical expenses, property damage, and lost wages and benefits (now and in the future).

**special indorsement** An indorsement on an instrument that indicates the specific person to whom the indorser intends to make the instrument payable—that is, it names the indorsee.

**special-use permit** A permit granted by local zoning authorities that allows for a specific exemption to zoning regulations for a particular piece of land.

**special warranty deed** A deed that warrants only that the grantor held good title during his or her ownership of the property and does not warrant that there were no defects of title when the property was held by previous owners.

**spendthrift trust** A trust created to protect the beneficiary from spending all the funds to which she or he is entitled. Only a certain portion of the total amount is given to the beneficiary at any one time, and most states prohibit creditors from attaching assets of the trust.

**stakeholders** Groups, other than the company's shareholders, that are affected by corporate decisions. Stakeholders include employees, customers, creditors, suppliers, and the community in which the corporation operates.

**stale check** A check, other than a certified check, that is presented for payment more than six months after its date.

**stock** An ownership (equity) interest in a corporation, measured in units of shares.

**stock certificate** A certificate issued by a corporation evidencing the ownership of a specified number of shares in the corporation.

**stock option** A right to buy a given number of shares of stock at a set price, usually within a specified time period.

**stock warrant** A certificate that grants the owner the option to buy a given number of shares of stock, usually within a set time period.

**stop-payment order** An order by a bank customer to his or her bank not to pay or certify a certain check.

**strike** An action undertaken by unionized workers when collective bargaining fails. The workers leave their jobs, refuse to work, and (typically) picket the employer's workplace.

**sublease** A tenant's transfer of all or part of the leased premises to a third person for a period shorter than the lease term.

**substitute check** A negotiable instrument that is a paper reproduction of the front and back of an original check and contains all of the same information required on checks for automated processing.

**superseding cause** An intervening force or event that breaks the connection between a wrongful act and an injury to another; in negligence law, a defense to liability.

**surety** A person, such as a cosigner on a note, who agrees to be primarily responsible for the debt of another.

**suretyship** An express contract in which a third party to a debtor-creditor relationship (the surety) promises to be primarily responsible for the debtor's obligation.

**syndicate** A group of individuals or firms that join together to finance a project; also called an *investment group.*

# T

**taking** The government's taking of private property for public use through the power of eminent domain.

**tangible employment action** A significant change in employment status or benefits, such as occurs when an employee is fired, refused a promotion, or reassigned to a lesser position.

**tangible property** Property that has physical existence and can be distinguished by the senses of touch, sight, and so on. A car is tangible property.

**tenancy at sufferance** A tenancy that arises when a tenant wrongfully continues to occupy leased property after the lease has terminated.

**tenancy at will** A type of tenancy that either the landlord or the tenant can terminate without notice.

**tenancy by the entirety** Joint ownership of property by a married couple in which neither spouse can transfer his or her interest in the property without the consent of the other.

**tenancy in common** Joint ownership of property in which each party owns an undivided interest that passes to his or her heirs at death.

**tender of delivery** Under the Uniform Commercial Code, a seller's or lessor's act of placing conforming goods at the disposal of the buyer or lessee and giving the buyer or lessee whatever notification is reasonably necessary to enable the buyer or lessee to take delivery.

**term insurance** A type of life insurance policy for which premiums are paid for a specified term and payment is made by the insurer only if the insured dies within the term period.

**testamentary trust** A trust that is created by will and therefore does not take effect until the death of the testator.

**testate** Having left a will at death.

**testator** One who makes and executes a will.

**tippee** A person who receives inside information.

**title insurance** Insurance commonly purchased by a purchaser of real property to protect against loss in the event that the title to the property is not free from liens or superior ownership claims.

**tort** A civil wrong not arising from a breach of contract. A breach of a legal duty that proximately causes harm or injury to another.

**tortfeasor** One who commits a tort.

**Totten trust** A trust created when a person deposits funds in his or her own name for a specific beneficiary, who will receive the funds on the depositor's death. The trust is revocable at will until the depositor dies or completes the gift.

**toxic tort** A civil wrong arising from exposure to a toxic substance, such as asbestos, radiation, or hazardous waste.

**trade acceptance** A draft that is drawn by a seller of goods ordering the buyer to pay a specified sum of money to the seller, usually at a stated time in the future. The buyer accepts the draft by signing the face of the draft, thus creating an enforceable obligation to pay the draft when it comes due. On a trade acceptance, the seller is both the drawer and the payee.

**trade dress** The image and overall appearance of a product—for example, the distinctive decor, menu, layout, and style of service of a particular restaurant. Basically, trade dress is subject to the same protection as trademarks.

**trade fixture** The personal property of a commercial tenant that has been installed or affixed to real property for a business purpose. When the lease ends, the tenant can remove the fixture but must repair any damage to the real property caused by the fixture's removal.

**trade libel** The publication of false information about another's product, alleging that it is not what its seller claims; also referred to as *slander of quality.*

**trademark** A distinctive mark, motto, device, or implement that a manufacturer stamps, prints, or otherwise affixes to the goods it produces so that they may be identified on the market and their origins made known. Once a trademark is established (under the common law or through registration), the owner is entitled to its exclusive use.

**trade name** A term that is used to indicate part or all of a business's name and that is directly related to the business's reputation and goodwill. Trade names are protected under the common law (and under trademark law, if the name is the same as the firm's trademark).

**trade secret** Information or a process that gives a business an advantage over competitors who do not know the information or process.

**transferred intent** A legal principle under which a person who intends to harm one individual, but unintentionally harms a different individual, can be liable to the second victim for an intentional tort.

**transfer warranty** Implied warranty made by any person who transfers an instrument for consideration to subsequent transferees and holders who take the instrument in good faith that (1) the transferor is entitled to enforce the instrument, (2) all signatures are authentic and authorized, (3) the instrument has not been altered, (4) the instrument is not subject to a defense or claim of any party that can be asserted against the transferor, and (5) the transferor has no knowledge of any insolvency proceedings against the maker, the acceptor, or the drawer of the instrument.

**traveler's check** A check that is payable on demand, drawn on or payable through a bank, and designated as a traveler's check.

**treble damages** Damages that, by statute, are three times the amount of actual damages suffered.

**trespass to land** The entry onto, above, or below the surface of land owned by another without the owner's permission or legal authorization.

**trespass to personal property** The unlawful taking or harming of another's personal property; interference with another's right to the exclusive possession of his or her personal property.

**triple bottom line** The idea that investors and others should consider not only corporate profits, but also the corporation's impact on people and on the planet in assessing the firm. (The bottom line is people, planet, and profits.)

**trust** An arrangement in which title to property is held by one person (a trustee) for the benefit of another (a beneficiary).

**trust indorsement** An indorsement for the benefit of the indorser or a third person; also known as an *agency indorsement.* The indorsement results in legal title vesting in the original indorsee.

**tying arrangement** A seller's act of conditioning the sale of a product or service on the buyer's agreement to purchase another product or service from the seller.

# U

*ultra vires* **acts** Acts of a corporation that are beyond its express and implied powers to undertake (the Latin phrase means "beyond the powers").

**underwriter** In insurance law, the insurer, or the one assuming a risk in return for the payment of a premium.

**undisclosed principal** A principal whose identity is unknown by a third party, and that person has no knowledge that the agent is acting for a principal at the time the agent and the third party form a contract.

**union shop** A firm that requires all workers, once employed, to become union members within a specified period of time as a condition of their continued employment.

**universal defense** A defense that is valid against all holders of a negotiable instrument, including holders in due course (HDCs) and holders with the rights of HDCs. Universal defenses are also called *real defenses.*

**universal life** A type of insurance that combines some aspects of term insurance with some aspects of whole life insurance.

**usage of trade** Any practice or method of dealing having such regularity of observance in a place, vocation, or trade as to justify

an expectation that it will be observed with respect to the transaction in question.

**U.S. trustee** A government official who performs certain administrative tasks that a bankruptcy judge would otherwise have to perform.

**utilitarianism** An approach to ethical reasoning in which ethically correct behavior is related to an evaluation of the consequences of a given action on those who will be affected by it. In utilitarian reasoning, a "good" decision is one that results in the greatest good for the greatest number of people affected by the decision.

# V

**validation notice** An initial notice to a debtor from a collection agency informing the debtor that he or she has thirty days to challenge the debt and request verification.

**variance** An exception from zoning rules granted to a property owner by local zoning authorities.

**venture capital** Financing provided by professional, outside investors—that is, *venture capitalists,* usually groups of wealthy investors and securities firms—to new business ventures.

**vertically integrated firm** A firm that carries out two or more functional phases (manufacturing, distribution, and retailing, for example) of the chain of production.

**vertical merger** The acquisition by a company at one stage of production of a company at a higher or lower stage of production (as when a company merges with one of its suppliers or retailers).

**vertical restraint** A restraint of trade created by an agreement between firms at different levels in the manufacturing and distribution process.

**vesting** The creation of an absolute or unconditional right or power.

**vicarious liability** Indirect liability imposed on a supervisory party (such as an employer) for the actions of a subordinate (such as an employee) because of the relationship between the two parties.

**voting trust** An agreement (trust contract) under which legal title to shares of corporate stock is transferred to a trustee who is authorized by the shareholders to vote the shares on their behalf.

# W

**warranty deed** A deed in which the grantor promises that she or he has title to the property conveyed in the deed, that there are no undisclosed encumbrances on the property, and that the grantee will enjoy quiet possession of the property; provides the greatest amount of protection for the grantee.

**waste** The use of real property in a manner that damages or destroys its value.

**watered stock** Shares of stock issued by a corporation for which the corporation receives, as payment, less than the fair market value of the shares.

**wetlands** Areas of land designated by government agencies as protected areas that support wildlife and that therefore cannot be filled in or dredged by private parties.

**whistleblowing** An employee's disclosure to government authorities, upper-level managers, or the media that the employer is engaged in unsafe or illegal activities.

**whole life**  A type of life insurance in which the insured pays a level premium for his or her entire life and in which there is a constantly accumulating cash value that can be withdrawn or borrowed against by the borrower; sometimes referred to as *straight life insurance.*

**will**  An instrument made by a testator directing what is to be done with her or his property after death.

**will substitutes**  Various instruments, such as living trusts and life insurance plans, that may be used to avoid the formal probate process.

**winding up**  The second of two stages in the termination of a partnership or corporation, in which the firm's assets are collected, liquidated, and distributed, and liabilities are discharged.

**workers' compensation law**  A state statute establishing an administrative procedure for compensating workers for injuries that arise out of, or in the course of, their employment, regardless of fault. Instead of suing the employer, an injured worker files a claim with the state agency or board that administers local workers' compensation claims.

**working papers**  The documents used and developed by an accountant during an audit, such as notes, computations, and memoranda.

**workout**  See *workout agreement.*

**workout agreement**  In bankruptcy proceedings, a formal contract between a debtor and his or her creditors in which the parties agree to negotiate a payment plan for the amount due on the loan instead of proceeding to foreclosure. Sometimes referred to as a *workout.*

**writ of attachment**  A court's order, prior to a trial to collect a debt, directing the sheriff or other officer to seize nonexempt property of the debtor. If the creditor prevails at trial, the seized property can be sold to satisfy the judgment.

**writ of execution**  A court's order, after a judgment has been entered against the debtor, directing the sheriff to seize (levy) and sell any of the debtor's nonexempt real or personal property. The proceeds of the sale are used to pay off the judgment, accrued interest, and costs of the sale. Any surplus is paid to the debtor.

**wrongful discharge**  An employer's termination of an employee's employment in violation of the law or an employment contract.

## Z

**zoning laws**  Rules and regulations that collectively manage the development and use of land.

# Table of Cases

Following is a list of all the cases mentioned in this text, including those within the footnotes, features, and case problems. Any case that was an excerpted case for a chapter is given special emphasis by having its title **boldfaced.**

# Index